CIVIL PROCEDURE

ASPEN TREATISE SERIES

CIVIL PROCEDURE

Fifth Edition

RICHARD D. FREER

**Charles Howard Candler Professor of Law
Emory University**

Wolters Kluwer
Attn: Order Department
PO Box 990
Frederick, MD 21705

Cover image: iStock.com/uschools

Printed in the United States of America.

1 2 3 4 5 6 7 8 9 0

ISBN 978-1-5438-3900-5

Library of Congress Cataloging-in-Publication Data
Names: Freer, Richard D., 1953- author.
Title: Civil procedure / Richard D. Freer, Charles Howard Candler Professor of Law, Emory University.
Description: Fifth Edition. | New York : Wolters Kluwer, 2022. | Series: Aspen treatise series | Includes bibliographical references and index. | Summary: "This is a student treatise for students taking a civil procedure course in law school"—Provided by publisher.
Identifiers: LCCN 2021048153 (print) | LCCN 2021048154 (ebook) | ISBN 9781543839005 (paperback) | ISBN 9781543839012 (ebook)
Classification: LCC KF8839 .F745 2022 (print) | LCC KF8839 (ebook) | DDC 347.73/5—dc23/eng/20211006
LC record available at https://lccn.loc.gov/2021048153
LC ebook record available at https://lccn.loc.gov/2021048154

MIX
From responsible sources
FSC® C099992

About Wolters Kluwer Legal & Regulatory U.S.

Wolters Kluwer Legal & Regulatory U.S. delivers expert content and solutions in the areas of law, corporate compliance, health compliance, reimbursement, and legal education. Its practical solutions help customers successfully navigate the demands of a changing environment to drive their daily activities, enhance decision quality, and inspire confident outcomes.

Serving customers worldwide, its legal and regulatory portfolio includes products under the Aspen Publishers, CCH Incorporated, Kluwer Law International, ftwilliam.com, and MediRegs names. They are regarded as exceptional and trusted resources for general legal and practice-specific knowledge, compliance and risk management, dynamic workflow solutions, and expert commentary.

This book is intended for two audiences. First, for law students, this book is intended to make sense of matters that are likely foreign to your pre-law school experience. Second, for lawyers, this book is intended to be a resource for whatever civil litigation issue you may be facing.

Dedicated to Louise, Courtney, and Collin

Summary of Contents

Contents

Contents

Contents

Contents

Contents

Contents

Contents

Contents

Contents

Preface, Acknowledgments, and Conventions

Unlike most subjects in the first year of law school, Civil Procedure is foreign to our experience. Before law school, everyone has some exposure to contracts, torts, and property. But very few people spend life before law school pondering the jurisdiction of the federal courts, the appealability of interlocutory orders, or supplemental jurisdiction over impleader claims against nondiverse third-party defendants. Though foreign to pre-law school experience, for a great many lawyers, Civil Procedure addresses the most significant set of doctrines and principles in their practice.

I hope this book is of use not only to law students but also to lawyers. We want to de-mystify Civil Procedure, which we will do in several ways. First, the tone is conversational, informal and (hopefully) occasionally funny.

Second, we break complex doctrines into constituent parts. So, for example, instead of trying to approach the entire constitutional test for personal jurisdiction as one whole, we break it into smaller, easily understood components. And instead of memorizing Rule 12 of the Federal Rules of Civil Procedure to determine when various defenses can be raised, we break it into three easily remembered rules that cover every permutation for a case.

Third, we emphasize how doctrines fit together. Throughout the book, you will see cross-references and footnotes emphasizing how various topics interrelate. For example, we emphasize that many of the most important elements of a Civil Procedure course—personal jurisdiction, service of process, subject matter jurisdiction, and venue—all relate to a single idea: that of choosing a place where litigation will take place. And we discuss in detail why that choice of "forum" is so important that litigants may spend a great deal of money and time arguing over where the litigation will proceed.

Fourth, throughout this book, there are examples and hypotheticals to test your application of the principles discussed. These are not imponderable hypotheticals, but hypos with answers provided and discussed. We need not only to know the doctrines, but to be able to apply them to a fact pattern, either on an exam or in a case.

Fifth, at various points, we pull together complex topics into analytical frameworks. So, for instance, after you study Chapter 2 on personal jurisdiction, we have a section pointing out how to use the tools acquired from the case law to address an examination question. This section walks step by step through how we might analyze any exam question in that area, using each of the relevant factors identified by the Supreme Court.

Finally, though our focus is largely on legal doctrine, we convey an appreciation of the richness and depth of the subject, to put topics in context with each other and with the larger goal of access to justice.

There are 14 chapters in the book. They are arranged largely in chronological order, addressing the various issues that are confronted in bringing, defending, and litigating a case. We should realize, however, that there is no single "right" order in which to cover Civil Procedure. Each chapter is self-contained. At the same time, each, as noted, will identify how the material relates to other material throughout the course. So the order in which you approach the topics is irrelevant. (That said, I do think it a good idea to read Chapter 1 before delving into any particular area. It gives you an overview of the course and discusses some background topics that will be relevant at various points along the journey.)

****

I have been blessed with generous colleagues and friends who have contributed greatly to my work. At Emory, Tom Arthur, Peter Hay, Colleen Murphy, Jonathan Nash, Robert Schapiro, and George Shepherd have given me indispensable guidance for many years. They are model colleagues and friends.

My work has also been enriched by Civil Procedure colleagues at other schools. James Duane has been especially generous with his comments and suggestions on several editions of this book. I hope this edition responds adequately to his much-appreciated analysis and commentary. In addition, Mike Vitiello and Marjorie Silver have made suggestions far beyond the call of friendship.

I owe great thanks as well to Alexi Lahav, Cynthia Ho, Bill Jansen, Hillel Levin, Ben Madison, Rocky Rhodes, Adam Steinman, Steve Subrin, and Margaret Tarkington, all of whom have helped me as a student of procedure.

I give a special note of thanks to Scott Fingerhut, who took time from a very busy schedule to comment on the manuscript for this book, and to Debra Cohen, who has patiently contributed comments on this work as it has evolved. I am proud to say that Scott and Debra are former students, colleagues in the legal academy, and friends for many years.

I owe a special debt to my coauthors of our casebook (now in its eighth edition), Robin Effron and Wendy Perdue. Working with Wendy through the years enabled me to meet Sherman Cohn, who has been a wonderful mentor, to whom Wendy and I dedicated the eighth edition of the casebook.

Dylan Storey, Emory class of 2023, has done superb research and editing work on this entire volume, for which I am grateful. In addition, Michelle Tomkovicz, Emory class of 2021, and Danielle Kerker, Emory class of 2022, stepped forward despite heavy schedules to provide exceptional targeted research assistance in the early phases of this edition, which I also appreciate greatly.

I would be nowhere without my wife, Louise, and our children, Collin and Courtney. When I started the original edition of this book, our children were in grade school. Now they are professionals, pursuing their careers with passion and excellence. I wish for them the joy and fulfillment I continue to find in my life and my profession.

****

Throughout the book, I cite the two standard multivolume works—Moore's Federal Practice and Wright & Miller's Federal Practice and Procedure—in abbreviated form, without noting the authors on specific volumes. Thus, they are cited as specific volumes of "Moore's Federal Practice" and "Wright & Miller," respectively. I am honored to be a contributor to both of those works. The citations to them are through the 2021 supplements. In addition, citations to Charles Alan Wright & Mary Kay Kane, The Law of Federal Courts (8th ed. 2016) are indicated "Wright & Kane, Federal Courts."

Richard D. Freer
Atlanta

CIVIL PROCEDURE

Chapter *1*

The Study of Civil Procedure

§1.1   Civil Litigation and the Adversary System

We start by recognizing three things about our topic. First, Civil Procedure is foreign to one's pre-law-school experience. Every person starting law school has had some exposure to Property, Contracts, Torts, and (perhaps) Criminal Law. For example, anyone who has rented an apartment or bought a cellphone plan has entered into a contract. Everyone knows that if we drive a vehicle negligently and harm someone, we may be subject to liability. But before studying in law school, very few people have encountered problems relating to *in personam* jurisdiction or the subject matter jurisdiction of the federal courts or the right to a jury trial. Civil Procedure addresses topics most people have not seen before entering law school.

Second, Civil Procedure presents a remarkable mix of material. Some of the topics (including pleadings and discovery) are intensely mechanical, and demand memorization of some fairly wooden rules. In contrast, some topics (like personal jurisdiction and the *Erie* doctrine) are amorphous. You should use the different types of material to your advantage. With the mechanical topics, applying the mechanical rules will usually yield a clear right answer. But in the amorphous topics, realize that there is rarely a single right answer. In these areas, reasonable people might disagree as to the outcome. The goal in the amorphous areas (especially personal jurisdiction) is not to get the "right" answer but to come to a conclusion that is within the realm of reasonable answers. What is important in these areas is to have an *analytical approach* that will force you to address all relevant factors. In this book, we set forth such analytical approaches to each of these amorphous topics.

Third, our overall topic is of enormous significance. The American procedural system reflects important normative values. Our litigation is a public, transparent process overseen by a neutral judge. It is rooted in the rule of law. Indeed, the process itself generates the common law that governs much of our lives. The court's judgment is a public document, as is the judge's reasoned application of law to the facts of the case. The judgment can be enforced by the police power of the government (federal or state). Civil Procedure concerns nothing less than our society's vision for the administration of justice.

Litigation

Civil Procedure is about *litigation*, which is the basic model by which disputes are resolved in our society. Suppose someone does something that harms you—maybe by negligently driving a car, or breaching a contract, or stealing your property. How do you resolve your grievance against that person? One possibility is to engage in "self-help," by which you redress the wrong personally; for example, you might want to enter the other person's property to seize what was stolen from you. This is usually a disastrous choice, because you simply compound the wrong by perpetrating one yourself. Another possibility is to contact the person who harmed you and demand some compensation or other remedy. This often works; indeed, people usually resolve their differences informally. If such efforts fail, however, what do you do? The classic choice for dispute resolution is *litigation*, in which you sue the wrongdoer. You invoke the process of litigation and engage the judicial system to resolve the dispute. In our society, litigation is a socially acceptable method for finding a solution to our disputes.

Indeed, litigation is *publicly funded* dispute resolution. The taxpayers provide the courtroom, the judge, and the bureaucratic instrumentalities by which the dispute (now usually called a *case* or *lawsuit*) is resolved. Again, most disagreements in our lives are worked out informally, without the need to file a case. There are also alternative dispute resolution (ADR) mechanisms by which parties can reach a resolution without going through the court litigation process; we discuss the major ADR mechanisms (such as arbitration and mediation) in §1.3. We will see that they have become so mainstream that the adjective "alternative" is used less frequently than in the past. Still, these methods of resolution exist "in the shadow" of litigation. This does not mean that *most* disputes are resolved by litigation. It simply means that litigation is the societally endorsed, publicly funded mechanism against which other dispute-resolution mechanisms are usually measured.

Civil Litigation and the Private Enforcement of the Law

Our course is about civil litigation. "Civil" is juxtaposed with "criminal." For present purposes, it is helpful to think of litigation as falling into one or the other category. In a criminal case, a government (whether federal, state, or local) commences litigation against a defendant who has allegedly violated a law intended to keep the public peace. The goal of criminal litigation (called a *prosecution*) is to vindicate that public interest. If the criminal defendant is found guilty in the criminal litigation, the result can be some form of punishment, such as perhaps a fine or incarceration. Civil Procedure does not deal with criminal prosecutions.

Instead, we address litigation aimed at vindicating *private* rights. Civil litigation is not brought by the government to punish someone for doing something against the public peace. Instead, it is brought by one who believes she has been wronged by another.[1] The person who files suit is the *plaintiff* and the person she sues is the *defendant*. In the civil suit, the plaintiff seeks private remedies from the defendant for the harm done. Often this will be money[2] to compensate for damage done to the plaintiff or her property. Thus, in Civil Procedure, we do not use the word *guilty*. That is a criminal law concept. Instead, we talk about a defendant's being *liable* to the plaintiff for some civil remedy, such as money to compensate for the wrong inflicted by the defendant.

Sometimes, the same act or omission by the defendant will constitute both a crime and a civil wrong. The different goals of criminal and civil litigation can be demonstrated by a simple example.

   ○ ***Example #1.*** *D* breaks into your house and steals your television; *D* then sells it to a third party. *D* has committed a burglary, and the government (probably the state) may prosecute *D* for that crime. If the state

---

[1]A government can be a party to civil litigation. For example, if the government concludes that one of its suppliers of goods has breached the contract between them, it can sue. The case would not be a criminal prosecution, but a civil case, by which the government seeks to vindicate its private rights.

[2]Money to compensate the plaintiff for harm done by the defendant is usually called *damages*. It is a common form of relief sought by plaintiffs but is not the only one. In §1.2.3 we discuss damages and other commonly sought remedies.

wins in that *criminal prosecution, D* will be found guilty of burglary and will be punished, perhaps by a jail term.

The criminal litigation vindicates the public's interest by imposing consequences on someone who violates basic rules by which we live in a decent society. But it does nothing *for you personally.* Putting *D* in jail does not compensate you for the loss of your television and damage to your house. To recover for those losses, you may file a *civil* case, seeking to recover money from *D* to permit you to replace the stolen property and fix the damage to your house.[3] This is a civil case because it vindicates your personal rights against another. You would be the plaintiff and *D* would be the defendant.

The Adversary System: Roles of the Parties, Lawyers, Jury, and the Judge

It is not enough for a government simply to provide a system for resolving disputes. The system must be perceived as legitimate. The government could decree that disputes between citizens be resolved by a coin toss by some government official, with the result enforced by government officers. This would certainly resolve disputes quickly, but it would not comport with any sense of justice. The civil justice system must strive to achieve the *fair* resolution of disputes.[4] To be legitimate, we insist that our system provide a fair method to determine the "truth" of what "really happened" and to apply the rule of law to those facts. We can imagine different systems for determining the facts and the truth. For example, the government could investigate and determine when someone's rights have been breached by another and demand that the transgressor compensate the victim. Anglo-American civil justice has never embraced such a pervasive role for the government. Rather, we adopt the *adversary system* of litigation.

The adversary system is based upon self-interest. If an aggrieved person wishes to vindicate her civil claim by suing the person(s) who harmed her, she must take the initiative and sue. The government will not do it for her. Once the parties are in the litigation process, the adversary system calls for each party to present her case and to attack

---

[3]In many instances, your insurance company will have given you money representing the value of the stolen items (less whatever deductible you may have to pay under your insurance policy). Because of something called *subrogation,* the insurance company will then have the right to sue *D* to recover from *D* for the stolen items. Subrogation is discussed at §12.2.

[4]Rule 1 of the Federal Rules of Civil Procedure provides that all the Rules "should be construed, administered, and employed by the court and the parties to secure the just, speedy, and inexpensive determination of every action and proceeding."

the other's with partisan vigor. The adversary system is founded on the notion that the truth is best determined in the crucible of competition between adversaries. From this battle of self-interested combatants, an independent fact-finder (often a jury, but sometimes the judge) determines what actually happened. In other words, the system relies on partisan presentation by self-interested persons (not governmental investigation) to hone the evidence for presentation to a disinterested fact-finder.

The adversary system is not unbridled combat. There are strict rules for this competition, including important norms of professional responsibility for the lawyers. Lying, destruction of evidence, and other forms of cheating are not permitted. Lawyers who violate the norms can be sanctioned by the court and punished by the bar (including disbarment). Parties who violate the norms can be sanctioned by the court. Within the rules, however, parties are expected to be self-interested, and their lawyers are required to represent them zealously. Within the rules, they may use every ploy, device, and creative effort to secure the best outcome for their client. Litigation is competition. And it is usually a "zero-sum game," which means that one side wins and one side loses.

In this adversary system, the judge's role (at least in theory) is rather limited. Classically, the judge is expected to be a passive umpire. She reacts to requests (called *motions*) by the parties for a variety of court orders. At trial, she oversees the presentation of evidence in accordance with the rules for admissibility (studied in Evidence). Generally, however, the judge is not inquisitorial.[5] Again, our adversary system relies on the parties and their lawyers to determine what evidence to present and how to present it.

The adversarial ideal is not absolute. Not all parties (and not all lawyers) have equal skills or equal resources. Occasionally, a judge may inject herself into the questioning of a witness at trial to correct a mistake made by a lawyer. For example, if a lawyer failed to ask a witness about a particular issue that is relevant to the outcome, the judge might ask the question. After all, the goal is justice. The judge's limited intervention in such circumstances is probably a good thing. On the other hand, the judge must remain impartial, and cannot allow herself to become so involved as to lose the appearance of impartiality. Most judges are extremely good at drawing an appropriate line between avoiding undue involvement (on the one hand) and avoiding an unjust outcome based upon a technicality (on the other).

---

[5]Judges in most continental European countries, in contrast, are inquisitorial, and take an active role in formulating the presentation of evidence at trial.

The role of judge as passive or reactive has eroded significantly in the last 50 years, largely in response to rising caseloads and increasingly complex litigation. The late twentieth century featured what many called a "litigation explosion." The increased number of cases was driven by various developments, including the Supreme Court's invigoration of civil rights in the 1960s, Congress's expansion of private rights, the development of modern tort theories such as strict product liability, the emergence of the modern form of the class action, and the elimination of bans on lawyer advertising.[6] Though caseloads increased dramatically in the federal courts, Congress did not appreciably increase the number of federal judges. State courts (which in the aggregate handle far more cases than the federal courts) face the same problems.

In addition, as addressed in Chapters 12 and 13, civil litigation can become quite complex, with multiple claims and parties packaged into a single case. In some instances (especially in a class action, which we study in §13.3) the judge must play a fiduciary role to ensure adequate representation of the interests of persons who, while not technically parties, will be affected by the outcome of the litigation.

In reaction to the increased caseload and to more complex litigation, courts have taken an increasingly active role in overseeing the progress of cases. The Administrative Office of the federal courts requires each federal judge to report periodically on the number of cases pending and resolved. Without question, this requirement has imposed pressure on judges to drive cases to resolution. Increasingly, resolution has meant settlement.[7] As we discuss in detail in §§8.5 and 8.6, litigation today features far more "managerial judging" than in earlier times. This managerial role includes the judge's cajoling the parties to keep the case moving, often with the goal of having the parties settle their dispute.

---

[6]There is considerable debate about the level of frivolous litigation filed in this country, and concern with abusive litigation has spurred some procedural innovations requiring greater oversight by judges. We see such provisions throughout the book. Moreover, there is evidence that on a per capita basis there are fewer cases filed today than there were in the nineteenth century. Marc Galanter, *Real World Torts: An Antidote to Anecdote*, 55 Md. L. Rev. 1093, 1103 (1996) ("[I]t should be noted that *per capita* litigation rates were higher at some points in nineteenth and twentieth century America—and higher still, from the few studies we have, in colonial America."). *See also* Alexandra D. Lahav, *The Roles of Litigation in American Democracy*, 65 Emory L.J. 1657, 1699 (2016) (rates of litigation); Stephen C. Yeazell, *Unspoken Truths and Misaligned Interests: Political Parties and the Two Cultures of Civil Litigation*, 60 UCLA L. Rev. 1752, 1765-1766 (2013) (collective litigation is constitutionally protected activity).

[7]*See* Judith Resnik, *The Privatization of Process: Requiem for and Celebration of the Federal Rules of Civil Procedure at 75*, 162 U. Pa. L. Rev. 1793, 1803-1806 (2014) (discussing move toward focus on settlement).

Litigation Can Be a Lengthy Process and Usually Will Not Result in Trial

Based on television shows and movies, the public perception of litigation is the trial itself. Media routinely present dramatic moments in the courtroom, with the judge presiding, the jury listening and watching attentively, and a witness testifying on the stand in response to questions by razor-sharp lawyers. Of course, there are such moments in the real world, but not in most cases. In fact, very few civil cases will ever go to trial. (In some studies of the federal courts, fewer than 2 percent of cases go to trial.[8]) Why? Litigation is not an event. It is a process, and that process consists of far more than the trial. During the litigation process, the court may terminate the case without trial through motions to dismiss, motions for summary judgment, or other pretrial procedures. During the process, in the vast majority of cases, the parties will reach a settlement that resolves the dispute.

Those few cases that do go to trial will not do so next week. In federal court, the average time from the date of filing through resolution by trial is more than two years.[9] Remember, litigation is a process, the tip of the iceberg of which is trial. The vast majority of the litigation process is "pretrial litigation."

Indeed, the plaintiff and her lawyer have a great deal of work to do even before filing the case. For one, they must decide *where* to sue. As we will see, parties often spend a great deal of time and money litigating over *forum selection*: whether the case is in a proper court. The decision implicates a variety of important doctrines, including personal jurisdiction, subject matter jurisdiction, and venue. In addition, there are questions of tactics and strategy: Which court would be most convenient for the plaintiff (and perhaps not ideal for the defendant)? Which court system (federal or state) might be most advantageous to the plaintiff (perhaps in terms of her lawyer's familiarity with the judges or the geographic area from which a jury will be drawn)? In which court is the litigation likely to proceed most quickly?

Further, before filing suit, the plaintiff and her lawyer must determine what to put in the complaint. Specifically, what *claims* (or *causes of action*) will the plaintiff assert, and what remedies will she seek? These are important questions, the answers to which are informed by the *substantive law*. Some substantive law is created

---

[8]Reflecting this fact, there is a robust literature on the "vanishing civil trial." *See, e.g.*, Stephen Burbank & Stephen Subrin, *Litigation and Democracy: Restoring a Realistic Prospect of Trial*, 46 Harv. C.R.-C.L. L. Rev. 399, 402 (2011).

[9]https://www.uscourts.gov/sites/default/files/data_tables/fcms_na_distprofile1231.2020.pdf (median time from filing to resolution through trial is 27.5 months).

by the legislative branch of government, for example when Congress permits plaintiffs to sue to recover for deprivations of federal civil rights under 42 U.S.C. §1983 or when state legislatures create claims to vindicate consumers' rights. But many claims are created by *common law*—that is, by court decision. Indeed, most of the claims that arise in daily life—based in contract, torts, or property—are the product of the common law.

Civil Procedure does not define these claims or prescribe the elements that must be proved to prevail on any of these claims. That is the task of the substantive law, studied in courses such as Contracts, Torts, and Property. Civil Procedure provides the mechanism, the process (litigation), by which a plaintiff seeks to vindicate substantive claims. Civil Procedure is thus intended to be "trans-substantive," which means that it provides a content-neutral mechanism for resolving disagreements; in theory, the process works the same way no matter what substantive claim is being asserted.

Once the plaintiff files the case (invoking what we will call the "litigation stream"), the law of Civil Procedure prescribes the rules by which the plaintiff and the defendant proceed. The case must progress through various stages (such as pleadings, motions, discovery, possible pretrial adjudication, conferences, and meetings) before getting anywhere near trial. That takes time. Section 1.4 presents an overview of the litigation process, focusing on how the various subjects of Civil Procedure fit together.

Litigation Expenses and Attorney's Fees

We said above that litigation is publicly funded dispute resolution. That means that the public pays for the courthouse, the judge, and the bureaucracy necessary to support the system. But the public does not pay the costs and attorney's fees incurred in the litigation. Each party bears her own costs and attorney's fees, at least initially.

It is important to distinguish between these two categories of litigation expense. "Costs" are the general expenses of litigation *other than* attorney's fees. These include fees charged to file a case, fees incurred in notifying the defendant of the litigation, expenses of discovery, witness fees, and the like. Attorney's fees are the sums charged by the lawyer to represent the party in the litigation. Generally, the defendant's attorneys bill for their services by the hour. They keep detailed records of the time spent on each matter, and often bill monthly. The plaintiff's lawyer may bill by the hour. More likely, though, plaintiff's counsel will take the case on "contingent fee," which means the lawyer is compensated only if the plaintiff recovers from the defendant. A contingent fee is set as a percentage of the recovery and is agreed to in advance. The requirement that each party bear her own costs and attorney's fees affects the bottom line in litigation.

> ○ ***Example #2.*** *P* sues *D* for breach of contract. Let's assume that *D*'s breach of contract caused *P* $300,000 worth of harm. The case proceeds through the various stages of litigation and, after two years, goes to trial. After hearing all the evidence, the jury agrees with *P*'s version of the facts and returns a verdict of $300,000 for *P*. The court enters judgment in *P*'s favor for $300,000.

From all appearances, *P* has prevailed completely, and should be made whole for the loss she suffered. But is she? She must pay her lawyer, who, let's say, took the case on a one-third contingent fee. Hence the lawyer gets $100,000 (one-third of *P*'s recovery). In addition, *P* has had to pay various costs, including filing fees, witness fees, and discovery expenses of, say, $25,000. In this example, the law provided that *P* is entitled to recover $300,000. But in fact, after paying attorney's fees and costs, *P* will actually recover only $175,000.[10] Now consider matters from a defendant's viewpoint.

> ○ ***Example #3.*** Suppose *D* is convinced that she did not do what *P* alleged in her complaint. *D* litigates the case through trial and the jury returns a verdict in *D*'s favor. The court enters judgment for *D*. The judgment provides that *D* owes nothing to *P*.

From all appearances, *D* has prevailed completely. She owes nothing to *P*. But she has been writing checks to her lawyer all along. She may have paid $150,000 in attorney's fees and $20,000 in costs. Based on the result of the litigation, *D* did nothing wrong. Yet she is out of pocket (in our hypothetical) $170,000.[11]

In both examples, whether *P* won or *D* won, we have a nagging sense that the result is not fair. When *P* won, she was supposed to get $300,000 but really only recovered $175,000. When *D* won, she was faultless, but ended up owing $170,000. Some commentators have argued that the law should permit "shifting" of costs and attorney's fees. The argument is that the loser should be required to pay the winner's costs and attorney's fees. This "loser pays" system is followed in

---

[10]Not only that, but it took a long time to vindicate the claim. The harm of $300,000 was caused, say, two years before *P* wins her case. If she had had that $300,000 over the two years, she would have been earning interest on the money. One might expect the law to require *D* to pay interest on the claim. Generally, however, interest begins to accrue only when the judgment is entered. So *P* has lost two years' worth of interest on that money.

[11]Not to mention the trauma of being sued and the lost opportunity costs of spending untold hours dealing with the litigation.

many other countries. The American system has adopted something of a middle course (known, not surprisingly, as the "American Rule").

In the United States, each party pays her own costs as the case progresses. Once the case is resolved, however, there is a presumption that the winner is entitled to recover her "costs" from the loser.[12] In federal court, this presumption is found in Rule 54(d)(1), which provides that costs "should be allowed to the prevailing party." It is important to understand, however, that the winner recovers not all costs incurred, but only "taxable" costs. That term has nothing to do with paying tax to the government. Rather, it refers to costs that are recoverable by law. In federal court, taxable costs are set by 28 U.S.C. §1920, which is remarkably narrow. It permits recovery of various specific disbursements, including clerk's fees, witness fees, and printing expenses. Most expenses relating to the discovery phase of litigation are not recoverable as costs. Thus, taxable costs will be only a fraction of the out-of-pocket expenses actually incurred by the litigant.

More important, "costs" *does not include attorney's fees*. The American Rule embodies a presumption that each side bears her own attorney's fees, which usually are by far the most significant expense incurred in litigation. Persons are free to contract around the American Rule, so parties to a contract may provide that, in the event of litigation, the prevailing party will recover her attorney's fees from the loser. (In fact, you are probably a party to such a contract; check your contracts with credit card and insurance companies.)

Occasionally, courts recognize a common law exception to the American Rule and order a party to pay the other party's attorney's fees. For example, in *Chambers v. NASCO, Inc.*,[13] the Supreme Court upheld a general power to make such an order against a party who engages in bad faith, vexatious behavior in litigation. Such an award must be limited, however, to attorney's fees incurred because of the misconduct.[14] For the most part, though, courts are reluctant to create exceptions to the general rule. This attitude reflects a sense that fee-shifting provisions should come from the legislative branch.[15] Congress has passed many statutes addressing the award of attorney's fees,

---

[12]This presumption is subject to some exceptions. One of these will be discussed in §4.5.3, which addresses 28 U.S.C. §1332(b). That statute permits the court to force a prevailing plaintiff to pay her own costs and the defendant's costs if the plaintiff recovered less than a certain amount.

[13]501 U.S. 32, 43-51 (1991).

[14]Goodyear Tire & Rubber Co. v. Haeger, 137 S. Ct. 1178, 1186-1187 (2017) (aggrieved party may recover only that portion of her attorney's fees that would not have been incurred but for the misconduct).

[15]*See, e.g.*, Alyeska Pipeline Serv. Co. v. Wilderness Society, 421 U.S. 240, 263 (1975) (rejecting the notion that the judiciary can "jettison the traditional rule against non-statutory allowances to the prevailing party").

some of which permit the prevailing party to recover her fees from the losing party. The broadest fee-shifting provisions permit recovery by successful parties claiming discrimination in violation of various federal laws.[16] State legislatures have passed similar statutes allowing fee shifting in state court litigation.

Outside such piecemeal efforts, however, federal and state legislatures have continued to embrace the American Rule. While there is a facial appeal to the "loser pays" system, as seen above, proponents of the American Rule fear that broad shifting of attorney's fees would make plaintiffs too timid to attempt to vindicate their rights. A plaintiff, particularly one of limited means, might decide not to sue if losing meant that she would be required to pay the defendant's attorney's fees. To avoid "chilling" the right of an aggrieved citizen to pursue justice, the American Rule remains in force. The result is that litigation, even for the winner, can be an expensive proposition.

§1.2 Background and Recurring Themes

§1.2.1 Federalism

Each person in the United States is subject to the authority of at least two governments: the federal government and that of a state.[17] The federal government (or national government) is one of limited powers. The Constitution of the United States *creates* the federal government. Without the Constitution, there would be no national government. There would instead be 50 separate sovereigns. After the War of Independence there were 13 separate former colonies. The leaders of that generation understood that certain functions would best be performed centrally. For example, it made no sense to have each entity coin separate money or impose barriers to travel or trade among the former colonies, or for each to raise its own army.

Our first experiment at centralization, the Articles of Confederation, did not work well. Finally, the Framers met in Philadelphia to work out the Constitution, forging a national

---

[16]*See, e.g.,* 42 U.S.C. §1973l(e) (Voting Rights Act); 42 U.S.C. §3613(c)(2) (Fair Housing Act).

[17]Some people in the United States don't live in states, but in federal enclaves such as the District of Columbia or territories such as Guam or the Commonwealth of Puerto Rico. For such persons, the federal government plays two roles: that of the national sovereign and also that of the local sovereign. For instance, Congress (in its role as legislature for the federal government) passes laws of national application and also passes local laws to govern the District of Columbia.

government to perform certain tasks and leaving independent state governments in charge of the rest. Thus, in the Constitution, the independent states forming the United States surrender power to form the new national government. The federal government is therefore one of limited powers. As the Tenth Amendment makes clear, powers not ceded to the federal government in the Constitution remain vested in the states or in the people. The federal government exists solely because the states and the people centralized certain functions in a national power.

The Constitution spells out the powers of each of the three branches of the federal government. Article I concerns the legislative branch, and establishes that all federal legislative power is vested in the Senate and House of Representatives. It also establishes rules for when those bodies shall meet, how membership is allocated, and age and residency requirements for members. It expressly lists the powers to be exercised by the national legislature and restricts the states from various acts, including imposing duties and entering treaties. Article II addresses the executive branch and provides that the national executive power is vested in the President of the United States. It details the requirements for office and the powers of the presidency, including the authority to appoint (with the advice and consent of the Senate) various federal officers, among whom are federal judges.

We focus on Article III of the Constitution, which establishes the judicial branch of the federal government. It requires the existence of only one federal court (the Supreme Court of the United States). It permits (but does not require) Congress to establish lower federal courts, as discussed in §4.3. Consistent with the limited nature of federal power, the Constitution establishes that the federal judicial power extends only to certain types of cases (listed in Article III, §2, paragraph 1). This is an extremely important point in Civil Procedure: Federal courts *can only hear certain kinds of disputes*. If a case does not fall within this federal "subject matter jurisdiction," it cannot be heard in a federal court. It can be litigated only in a state court.

Thus, there are two completely separate sets of courts in this country: federal courts and state courts. As noted, state courts, generally, can decide *any* type of dispute, whereas federal courts can only hear a limited range of cases. We discuss these points in detail in Chapter 4. For now, it is enough to note two of the types of cases that can be heard in federal courts: those between citizens of different states (called *diversity of citizenship* cases) and those arising under federal law (called *federal question* cases).

○ ***Example #4.*** *P*, a citizen of New York, enters into a contract with *D*, a citizen of California. *D* breaches the contract by failing to perform as required by the agreement. *P* may sue *D* in a federal court, because the dispute is between citizens of different states.[18] The Founders thought it important to permit the federal courts to entertain such interstate disputes, as we see in §4.5.2.[19]

○ ***Example #5.*** *P* claims that *D* terminated her employment in violation of federal law prohibiting discrimination on the basis of national origin. *P* may sue *D* in federal court, because her claim arises under federal law. The Founders thought it important to permit the federal courts to entertain disputes involving federal law, as we see in §4.6.1.[20]

Let's not get distracted by detail. For now, focus on the big picture: The federal judicial system has limited subject matter jurisdiction. Courts in that system can decide only cases falling within the judicial power of Article III, §2, paragraph 1 of the Constitution; the two main examples are cases between citizens of different states and cases arising under federal law.

In addition, Article III, §1 provides extraordinary protection to federal judges. They are appointed by the President, with approval required by the Senate. Federal judges appointed under Article III never face an election, cannot be removed by the voters, and have lifetime tenure, during which their pay cannot be reduced. They can be removed only by impeachment (which has happened only a handful of times in our nation's history). In §4.4, we discuss this remarkable job security accorded federal judges. The point is simple: The Founders thought it important to give federal judges freedom to make decisions without fear of reprisal. A federal judge can rule against local interests without fear of being voted out of office. Likewise, she can rule against Congress without fear that that body will reduce her salary. Many state court judges, in contrast, do not have these protections; they face an electorate at some point to obtain or to keep their jobs.

In addition to forming the national government and vesting its three branches with power, the Constitution also guarantees various individual rights and liberties. Thus, for instance, neither the federal nor state government may abridge an individual's freedom of speech,[21]

---

[18]By statute, the amount in controversy in a diversity of citizenship case must exceed $75,000. We discuss this in §4.5.3.

[19]Interestingly, *P* is not *required* to file this case in federal court. If she prefers, she can litigate in state court.

[20]Here, too, *P* generally is not *required* to file the case in federal court. If she prefers, she can litigate the federal claim in state court. There are some (very few) federal question claims that must go only to federal court—over which federal courts have "exclusive federal question" jurisdiction. See §4.6.1.

[21]The First Amendment to the Constitution provides that the federal legislature may not abridge freedom of speech. As you will study in Constitutional Law, the Fourteenth Amendment is interpreted as incorporating several of the protections of the Bill of Rights—including free speech—and providing that they are also not subject to encroachment by *state* governments.

13

or impose cruel and unusual punishment on anyone, or deprive someone of life, liberty, or property without due process of law. It is helpful
to think of such rights this way: By joining the Union, the states sur-
rendered absolute power. By becoming a member of the United States,
each state agreed that it would not abridge free speech, would not
impose cruel and unusual punishment, and would not deprive persons of life, liberty, or property without due process. (There are, of
course, other individual liberties; we mention these three for simplicity.) One of the major topics in Civil Procedure, personal jurisdiction,
concerns one of these federal constitutional limitations on state power.
Specifically, due process requires that a state cannot enter a binding
judicial order against someone unless that person has sufficient contacts with the state. We study this in detail in Chapter 2.

For our purposes, at this stage we focus on three things. First, the
relationship between the federal and state governments is complex
and evolving and will be studied in Constitutional Law and Civil
Procedure (and other courses in the upper division of law school).
Second, federal courts have authority to adjudicate only certain types
of cases, while state courts can entertain virtually any type of dispute.
Third, the Constitution imposes limits on the power of states (including the state courts). One of these is that a state court cannot enter a
valid judicial order without affording the defendant due process. We
now turn to the structure of judicial systems. One of the important
issues we consider is the interaction of the federal and state court
systems.

§1.2.2 Roles of Trial and Appellate Courts (and the Interaction Between the State and Federal Courts)

The federal government and each state has a judicial *system* — a
group of courts that serve different functions in the resolution of disputes. These systems can differ markedly from state to state, but some
characteristics are common to all. An important common characteristic is the bifurcation between *trial* courts and *appellate* courts. Each
system must have a trial court. Indeed, most of our course on Civil
Procedure addresses activities in the trial court. The basic litigation
stream discussed in §1.1, involving pleadings, discovery, motions, and
adjudication, including trial, takes place in the trial court. The full
trial court process may take a year or two (or, in complex cases, even
longer) or it may be over very quickly, as when the defendant defaults
or the court dismisses the case early in the proceedings.

In the trial court, a single judge presides over the case at a time. (A single trial judge will have many cases on her docket at the same time.) In most systems (including the federal system), the same judge oversees the case at every stage of the trial court litigation. In some states, different judges may rule on different aspects of the case; for example, one judge might rule on motions and another may oversee the trial. But even in such a system, only one judge is involved in making determinations at a time. (If the case goes to trial, a jury might be empaneled to decide the facts, but the judge presides over the trial.) The trial court is called a court of *original* jurisdiction, which signifies that the case is instituted there and the outcome of the dispute is determined there.

The trial court provides the mechanisms for processing the case, including discovery, and for determining the facts, applying the law to the facts, and thus determining who wins. Unless the parties settle the case, the trial court eventually enters a judgment, declaring who wins and what (if any) remedy is to be awarded.

In appellate courts, there is no jury, there are no witnesses, there is no presentation of evidence. Instead, lawyers for each party present oral argument (often 30 minutes per side) to a panel, usually of three judges. The appellate court does not determine what happened; that is the role of the trial court. The appellate court determines whether the trial court did its job properly. If so, the appellate court can affirm the judgment of the trial court. If not, the appellate court can reverse or vacate the judgment and remand to the trial court for further proceedings.

The party instituting the appeal is the *appellant*. The other party is the *appellee*. There is no federal constitutional right to appeal the result in a civil case. Instead, the right to appeal from the federal district court to the United States Court of Appeals is created only by statute; it is a matter of legislative grace. The same is true in many, but not all, state courts. In general, one may appeal only from a final judgment, which is the trial court's ultimate decision on the merits of the entire dispute. The numerous interlocutory (or nonfinal) decisions of the trial court generally cannot be appealed as they are made but may be raised on appeal from the final judgment.

   ◦ ***Example #6.*** *P* sues *D*. *D* moves to dismiss for lack of personal jurisdiction. The court denies the motion. *D* is convinced that the court was wrong, and that applicable law makes it clear that there is no personal jurisdiction. *D* cannot appeal now. Why? The court's ruling is not a final judgment; it does not conclude the litigation on the merits. The court has simply refused to dismiss the case, which means that the litigation will proceed. Unless *D* can satisfy an exception to the final judgment rule, she cannot seek appellate review now. She must litigate the case at the trial court. If she loses, she may raise lack of personal jurisdiction on appeal, along with any other grounds of appeal she may then have.

On appeal, the appellate court does not second-guess everything the trial judge did. Generally, it reviews only those things to which a party made a timely objection at the trial court and which that party then raised on appeal. Because the appellate court does not entertain the presentation of evidence (and thus does not see witnesses testify) it is not in a position to second-guess the trial court's determination of the facts. It defers to the trial court on such issues and will reverse only if the trial court's findings are "clearly erroneous." The appellate court makes this determination by reviewing the trial court record, which means the appellate judges read the transcript of the trial, review the documents and other evidence adduced at trial, etc.

On questions of law, however, the appellate court does not defer to the trial court. Rather, it determines the law *de novo* — afresh, on its own. So if the trial court made an error of law (for example, by putting the burden of proof on the wrong party, or misstating the law, or allowing the introduction of improper evidence) the appellate court may reverse the judgment and remand for further proceedings, including, if necessary, a new trial. We discuss standards of appellate review in detail in §14.7.

Not every trial court error will result in reversal. The error must be "prejudicial," as opposed to "harmless." That is, sometimes a trial judge will make a mistake, but the mistake did not likely affect the outcome of the case. Such an error is harmless and will not result in a reversal. But some errors do affect, or at least taint, the outcome. Such errors are prejudicial and will result in reversal.

From this brief discussion, it is clear that our system of justice values *finality*. There is one trial court and, generally, one chance to litigate issues. If a party does not like the outcome, she can appeal, but the appellate court will reverse only if there was a clearly erroneous factual finding or a prejudicial error of law. But, unless the judgment is set aside or a new trial ordered, or unless it is reversed on appeal, the disgruntled party does not get another chance to litigate the issues. Thus, if one does not like the result of her case at trial court, there is no opportunity for a "do over" or to take a Mulligan.[22] Indeed, in Chapter 11, we study doctrines that limit the party's ability to relitigate issues *even in a different case.*

---

[22]*Mulligan* is a golf term. When you hit a poor shot, taking a Mulligan means you hit a new shot and do not count the poor one.

In most judicial systems, including the federal system, there are two levels of appellate courts. The first, known in many states (and the federal system[23]) as the court of appeals,[24] performs the function we just discussed. It is there to ensure that the trial court reached plausible factual findings, applied the right law, and applied it correctly. It is an "intermediate" court, because it is perched above the trial court but below the jurisdiction's supreme court. That supreme court is also an appellate court.

Not all judicial systems have an intermediate court. In Virginia, for instance, there is a Court of Appeals, but it has very limited jurisdiction, and does not hear appeals in general civil cases. Where the intermediate court does exist, appeal to that court is usually "of right." That means that a party who loses at the trial court has a right to have the appellate court review the case (assuming, of course, that the party taking the appeal satisfies the procedural requirements for doing so). Again, in the federal system, this right is not secured by the Constitution, but is granted by statute.

Generally, there is no right to appeal, however, to the jurisdiction's supreme court.[25] In most civil cases, review by the supreme court is discretionary. Thus, the court is not required to hear any particular civil case,[26] and does so only if convinced by the party seeking review that the case is sufficiently important to warrant its attention. Though the supreme court is an appellate court, and serves the appellate function described above, it does so in a very selective way. Because it hears such a small number of cases, it looks for disputes in which a pronouncement by the ultimate court is needed to bring clarity and certainty to the law. For example, the Supreme Court of the United States may agree to hear a case that raises an issue on which the various federal courts of appeals have reached different conclusions. Thus, supreme courts generally act only when a case raises an important issue on which there is some uncertainty or other need for definitive guidance. Supreme courts rarely agree to review a case simply to

---

[23]In the federal system, the court of appeals is divided geographically into circuits, most of which have a numerical name. For instance, the United States Court of Appeals for the Eleventh Circuit (which lawyers simply call "the Eleventh Circuit") hears appeals from federal trial courts in Florida, Georgia, and Alabama. Congress sets the geographic boundaries by statute. In addition, Congress sets the geographic boundaries of the federal trial courts—the United States District Courts.

[24]Not all states follow suit. In California, this court is known as the Court of Appeal (singular). In New York, it is called the Appellate Division.

[25]Again, there are some exceptions. In Nevada, there is a right to appeal trial results to the Nevada Supreme Court. Such appeal of right of a civil case to the supreme court is rare.

[26]Remember, we deal in this course with civil cases. In many states, the supreme court is required to review criminal convictions in which the death sentence is imposed.

correct some mistake on an established matter; that is the task of an intermediate court of appeals.[27]

The chart below shows the typical tripartite court system, with the trial court at the bottom, the intermediate appellate court in the middle, and the supreme court at the apex. On the left side are the names of those courts in the federal system. The trial court is the United States District Court, which is always followed with a geographic description. For example, in California there are four federal trial districts: The Southern District sits in San Diego, the Central District in Los Angeles, the Northern District in San Francisco, and the Eastern District in Sacramento. In some states, there is only one district, such as the United States District Court for New Jersey. As noted above, the intermediate court in the federal system is the United States Court of Appeals (for whatever circuit is involved). The federal supreme court is the Supreme Court of the United States, which, as you know, consists of nine Justices and sits in Washington, D.C.

On the right side of the chart is the model for most state judicial systems. Trial courts have various names in the different states[28] (and sometimes even within a state). Remember that in some states there is no intermediate court of appeals. The high court in most states is known simply as the supreme court.[29] That court is often called the *court of last resort* because it is the highest court in that judicial system. Courts below it are sometimes called *inferior courts*. This is not a pejorative statement; it does not mean that such courts are not as competent as others. It simply means they are below another court in the judicial system. Thus, a trial court is inferior to an intermediate appellate court. The trial court and intermediate appellate court are both inferior to the supreme court.

Federal System		*State System*
U.S. Supreme Court	HIGH COURT	State Supreme Court
U.S. Court of Appeals	INTERMEDIATE	Court of Appeals (typically)
U.S. District Court	TRIAL COURT	Various names, e.g., District, Circuit, Superior

[27]Nevada has an interesting system. Though there is a court of appeals, appellants do not file appeals in that court. Rather, they file in the Nevada Supreme Court, which then may decide the case itself or deflect it for hearing by the intermediate court of appeals. *See* In re Amendment of the Nev. Rules of Appellate Procedure, ADKT 0501, 2016 Nev. LEXIS 689 (Nev. S. Ct. 2016).

[28]In New York, the trial court is called the supreme court.

[29]Here, too, there is some state variation. In New York, the high court is the Court of Appeals. In Massachusetts, it is the Supreme Judicial Court.

It is important to understand that the supreme court of each state is the final arbiter on the meaning of state law. No federal court, not even the Supreme Court of the United States, has any authority to tell the Iowa Supreme Court what Iowa law is (or should be). We occasionally hear someone say, "I'm going to fight this to the highest court in the land." Well, fine. Just realize that the highest court in the land on matters of state law is not the Supreme Court in Washington, D.C. The highest court in the land on issues of Arizona law is in Phoenix. The highest court in the land on issues of New York law is in Albany.

It is also important to understand that a case filed on one side or the other, either in the federal trial court or a state trial court, must be appealed *through that system*. In other words, a case filed in the state trial court in California is appealed to the California Court of Appeal and ultimately to the California Supreme Court (if that court agrees to hear the case). A case cannot be appealed from a state trial court to a federal appellate court; neither can a case filed in a federal trial court be appealed to a state appellate court.

For our purposes, there is one important exception to the model we just laid out: The Supreme Court of the United States may exercise appellate review over state court decisions, *but only if two things are true*. First, the case must have been appealed all the way through the state system. That means that review at the United States Supreme Court is precluded until a party has sought review by the highest court of the state system that could hear the case (usually, that is the state supreme court).

- ○ ***Example #7.*** *P* sues *D*. The case is fully litigated and the trial court enters judgment for *P*. *D* appeals to the intermediate court of appeals, which affirms the judgment. *D* cannot seek review by the United States Supreme Court because the intermediate court of appeals is not the state's highest court. *D* must seek review at the state supreme court. If that court agrees to hear the case, the party who loses there can seek review by the United States Supreme Court.

- ○ ***Example #8.*** What if the state supreme court refuses to hear the case? After all, the state supreme court's review is usually discretionary. The party who lost at the intermediate court of appeals can seek review by the United States Supreme Court if review was first sought at the highest state court. The requirement, then, is not that the state's highest court actually render a decision. Rather, a party must have "exhausted" all options in the state system before seeking review at the United States Supreme Court.[30]

[30]*See* Costarelli v. Massachusetts, 421 U.S. 193, 197 (1975).

Second, the United States Supreme Court can review *only* matters of federal law.[31]

- ○ ***Example #9.*** The Iowa Supreme Court holds that the state law on abortion prohibits abortions in the third trimester of pregnancy. The United States Supreme Court has no authority to review this holding, because it concerns state law, on which the state supreme court is the authoritative body.
- ○ ***Example #10.*** The Iowa Supreme Court holds that the state law on abortion does (or does not) violate federal constitutional principles concerning personal privacy. The United States Supreme Court may review this issue, because it is one of federal law: the meaning of the federal Constitution.

Accordingly, the Supreme Court of the United States exercises its appellate jurisdiction in two types of cases. First, it has discretion to review decisions of the United States Courts of Appeals.[32] These are cases that have been litigated through the federal system (from the United States District Court to the United States Court of Appeals and, now, to the court of last resort in the federal system). Second, it has discretion to review rulings from state courts if (1) a litigant has sought review at the highest state court that could entertain the matter and (2) the issue presented is one of federal law.

As seen above, Supreme Court review in either instance—over judgments by the United States Court of Appeals or over judgments from the highest state court on matters of federal law—is discretionary. A party seeking review by the Supreme Court files a petition for writ of *certiorari*. The writ will be granted, and the case reviewed by the Supreme Court, only if at least four of the nine Justices agree that the case should be heard. Such action is extremely rare. In an average year, litigants will seek *certiorari* in approximately 8,000 cases. In recent years, the Supreme Court has issued "signed" decisions (that is, cases in which Justices write opinions by name) in only about 70 cases. Obviously, then, the odds of getting the Court review of any case are exceptionally long. If the Court agrees to hear the case, the party who sought review is called the *petitioner* and the other party is called the *respondent*.[33]

Again, note that lower federal courts (the United States District Court and the United States Court of Appeals) do not have appellate jurisdiction over cases decided in the state courts. Many people seem

---

[31]This is the upshot of 28 U.S.C. §1257.

[32]This is established in 28 U.S.C. §1254(1).

[33]Thus, in a Supreme Court opinion, the party whose name is listed first was not necessarily the plaintiff (who filed the case in trial court). Rather, it is the party who lost in the court immediately below, and who (successfully) sought Supreme Court review.

20

to have the idea that federal courts are somehow superior to state courts, and thus that a federal court can review what a state court does. As we have just seen, though, federal appellate review of state judgments is quite rare: It can be done only by the Supreme Court, only over matters of federal law, and only in the extraordinary situation in which the Supreme Court grants a writ of *certiorari*.[34]

Finally, we need to understand the doctrine of *precedent*, or *stare decisis*. The Latin phrase means "to stand by things decided." When an appellate court makes a holding on a question of law, that holding is *precedential*. That means that it binds all lower courts within that judicial system on that question of law; no inferior court in that judicial system can take a different approach on that question of law. Of course, precedent can be overturned—either by the appellate court that set the precedent or by a higher court.

- *Example #11.* Suppose the Georgia Court of Appeals (an intermediate appellate court in that state's judicial system) holds that state law recognizes a particular claim—that it allows someone who has suffered a particular harm to sue the perpetrator of the harm. Lower courts in that judicial system (trial courts in Georgia) must follow that rule on that question of law. The holding of the Court of Appeals establishes precedent for the trial courts in Georgia.

- *Example #12.* Suppose the Georgia Supreme Court decides to review the question and concludes that state law does *not* recognize that claim. The state supreme court's holding on this question overturns the Georgia Court of Appeals' holding.[35] All courts in the Georgia judicial system (trial courts and the intermediate appellate court) must follow the precedent set by the state supreme court.

Obviously, decisions by the United States Supreme Court bind all courts in the United States, federal and state, *on matters of federal law*. Thus, the Supreme Court is the ultimate arbiter on the meaning of federal statutes, regulations, and the Constitution. As suggested

---

[34]The United States Supreme Court has *original* (as opposed to appellate) jurisdiction in certain limited situations. Original jurisdiction, as we saw above, means that it sits as a trial court. Under Article III, §2, paragraph 2 of the Constitution, the Supreme Court has trial jurisdiction in cases affecting ambassadors and other public ministers and consuls, and in cases in which a state is a party. Such cases are rare, and usually not discussed in Civil Procedure.

[35]If the supreme court were reviewing the same case in which the court of appeals had made its pronouncement, we would say that the supreme court reversed the lower court's judgment. The term *reverse* connotes that a higher court disagreed with a lower court in the context of the same case. The term *overrule,* in contrast, refers to a subsequent ruling *in a different case* that rejects the holding of an earlier case. Examples of such "overturning" of precedent are given in the next paragraph of the text with *Brown* and *Erie*.

above, *stare decisis* is not immutable. A court may determine that relevant changes in law and society lead to the conclusion that precedent be overturned. In 1896, the Supreme Court held that separate but equal facilities for different races did not violate constitutional norms.[36] In 1954, in the landmark decision of *Brown v. Board of Education*,[37] the Court overturned the 1896 holding. In 1842, the Supreme Court held that federal courts could fashion their own common law for the resolution of disputes between citizens of different states.[38] In 1938, in the famous decision of *Erie Railroad Co. v. Tompkins*,[39] addressed in Chapter 10, the Court overturned the 1842 holding as having usurped state power in violation of the Tenth Amendment to the Constitution. The circumstances that justify a departure from the doctrine of precedent are subject to debate and can be the source of considerable controversy.

§1.2.3   The English Influence, Bifurcation of Law and Equity, and an Overview of Remedies

The United States evolved, of course, from British colonies. Not surprisingly, then, the roots of much of our procedure and much of our law are found in England. One pivotal event in English history was the Norman Conquest, which was ensured when William the Conqueror defeated the Britons in the Battle of Hastings in 1066. William revolutionized many things in Britain, including the administration of justice. Before William, the justice system consisted of local courts run by feudal lords and barons. The local control of these courts reflected the scattered, feudal nature of life in England at the time. William did much to pull the feudal fiefdoms into a more unified whole that mirrored a single country.

As we will see below, the historical tour on which we now embark is relevant to twenty-first-century American lawyers. William established three sets of royal courts which did not replace the feudal courts but existed alongside them. The courts were the King's Bench, the Court of the Exchequer, and the Court of Common Pleas. Each court entertained only certain types of disputes, each of which was denominated by a particular *writ*. For instance, to sue for an intentional tort, the plaintiff would seek a "writ of trespass *vi et armis*," while to sue for negligence the plaintiff would seek a writ of "trespass

---

[36]Plessy v. Ferguson, 163 U.S. 537 (1896).
[37]349 U.S. 294 (1954).
[38]Swift v. Tyson, 41 U.S. 1 (1848).
[39]304 U.S. 64 (1938).

on the case.[40] Over time, the royal courts expanded the types of cases they could hear by expanding the number of writs they would grant. The local barons were not happy about this, because the expansion of the royal courts' jurisdiction resulted in a contraction of the jurisdiction of the local feudal courts. Ultimately, though, there was little they could do about it, and over time the feudal courts waned in importance.

While expanding their jurisdiction, the royal courts, over the centuries, did two other things, both of which made them less desirable as tribunals of justice. First, they became increasingly rigid. They emphasized form over substance. Many plaintiffs with legitimate claims and solid proof lost because of some arcane procedural slip-up.[41] Second, the royal courts were not creative in awarding relief to those plaintiffs who managed to win. The royal courts recognized one remedy: *damages*, which is a monetary payment to the plaintiff from the defendant. In many, perhaps most, cases today, the plaintiff will be suing for damages. There are many cases, however, in which an award of damages will not make the plaintiff whole.

- ○ ***Example #13.*** *D* trespasses across *P*'s real property[42] every day. *P* sues and wins. The royal courts would permit *P* to recover money to compensate her for the damage caused by *D*'s trespass. Note how this remedy, damages, is aimed only at past behavior—it makes *D* pay for the trespassing she has already done. It does nothing, however, to prevent future trespassing. If *D* wants to keep trespassing, she may do so, and the only sanction will be payment of damages. In all likelihood, the damages will not be prohibitive, and *D* may find it worth her while simply to pay to trespass daily. Because damages are limited to compensating for past harm, *D* can essentially force *P* to grant her a license to travel across *P*'s land.

---

[40]The word *trespass* is widely used in common parlance to mean the unlawful entry onto another's land. As used here, the word has a broader meaning: a wrong committed against another's property or her person. The English common law courts recognized a dizzying array of writs for various forms of trespass. For example, if someone stole your personal property, you would sue in trespass *de bonis asportatis*.

[41]As we see in §7.2, the common law rules of pleading a case were quite unforgiving. If the plaintiff chose the wrong writ (which she had to choose at the outset of the case, when she might not have been clear on the facts), she would lose, even if at trial she showed that she had a right to recover on a different writ.

[42]Real property, or "realty," is land. Many students equate the word *real* with *tangible*, and thus conclude that a car is real property, because they can touch it, so it is in some sense real. If you own something that is not land, it is personal property, often called *chattels*. Personal property can be tangible (like a car) or intangible (like an ownership interest in a corporation, perhaps represented by a stock certificate).

What *P* wants is a court order telling *D* that she cannot trespass, punishable by holding *D* in contempt of court (which may result in a fine or imprisonment of *D*). In other words, *P* wants a *prohibitory injunction*: an order prohibiting *D* from taking some action in the future. The problem was that the royal courts simply did not grant injunctions.

> ○ ***Example #14.*** *D* steals a diamond ring from *P*. *P* sues and wins. The royal courts would require *D* to pay *P* money sufficient to purchase a new diamond ring of comparable value. But *P* doesn't want a new ring. She wants the one that was stolen, because it had great sentimental value. She wants *specific relief*, that is, a remedy that relates to this particular piece of property.

Here, that specific relief would be a *mandatory injunction*: an order requiring *D* to take a specific act (return the ring). The royal courts, however, would not grant such relief. It was basically damages or nothing.

These two factors (the elevation of form over substance and the limited remedy available) led plaintiffs to seek relief outside the royal courts. Specifically, they started going to the King's Council, which was a group of officers serving the King. These plaintiffs would ask the King's Council to intervene and to "do justice" in their case. Gradually, the Chancellor, who was a member of the King's Council, began to issue orders on behalf of the King's Council. These orders were aimed at achieving "equity." By the middle of the fourteenth century, this practice had developed into a separate court, called Chancery (named after the Chancellor).

Thus, nearly seven centuries ago in England, there were two completely separate sets of courts: the law courts (which consisted of the royal courts) and the equity (or Chancery) courts. Over the centuries, equity practice expanded, and the equity courts developed a series of useful remedies that were not available in the law courts.[43]

Law and equity courts also adopted different procedures and terminology. Law courts employed a jury to determine the facts of a case, while

---

[43]In addition to the remedies discussed in the text, equity also upheld the assignment of claims (which law courts would not do) and enforced trusts (which law courts also would not do). The equity court became so brazen that it would issue an order forbidding the enforcement of a judgment from a royal court if the judgment were obtained through fraud. Such an order seemed so invasive of royal court jurisdiction that King James I commissioned a group, headed by Francis Bacon, to resolve the debate. The commission concluded that the equity court indeed had the power to issue an injunction to stop a party from enforcing a fraudulent judgment issued by a law court. Importantly, because the injunction was issued against the party (and not against the court or judge) it was not an impermissible encroachment of the royal courts' power.

equity courts did not. Trials in law courts featured live testimony by witnesses, while equity courts favored presentation of evidence through sworn written statements, or *affidavits*. At law, a case was known as a "legal action," while equity adjudicated a "suit at equity." At law, the court's adjudication resulted in a "judgment," while at equity the court entered a "decree." At law, the judicial officer was the "judge," while at equity the judicial officer was the "chancellor." Law courts enforced their judgments *in rem*, which (as we discuss in Chapter 2) means "against the property." Equity courts, in contrast, enforced decrees *in personam*, or "against the person."

○ ***Example #15: Judgment at law enforced* in rem.** A law court enters a judgment against *D* for $50,000. If *D* does not pay the money to *P*, the court will enforce the judgment by issuing an order to the sheriff to seize *D*'s property (her house, her car, her bank account, whatever the sheriff can seize) and have it sold at a public auction. The first $50,000 raised at the auction would go to *P* (with the rest going to *D*). If the auction failed to fetch $50,000, *P* is only entitled to the sum received. Remember, a judgment at law is enforced against the property. In other words, if the property is insufficient to cover the judgment, *P* is out of luck.

○ ***Example #16: Decree at equity enforced* in personam.** An equity court enters a decree requiring *D* to return a stolen diamond ring to *P*. *D* refuses to do so. The sheriff can arrest *D* and put her in jail until she agrees to return the ring. The equity decree is enforced against the person, so the court can coerce *D* to do as she was ordered.

For at least two reasons, modern American lawyers must know the difference between legal and equitable remedies. First, as a general matter, a plaintiff cannot obtain an equitable remedy if the legal remedy (of damages) is adequate to make her whole. If the harm done to the plaintiff can be vindicated by an award of damages, she must sue at law, and cannot invoke "equity jurisdiction." Thus, the first order of business for a plaintiff in equity is to allege that her legal remedy of damages is inadequate. In Example #14 above, the plaintiff wanted to recover a diamond ring that had sentimental value. In Example #13 above, the plaintiff did not want the defendant continually trespassing across her property. In neither case would damages make the plaintiff whole.

Second, in federal court, the Seventh Amendment preserves the right of jury trial only in civil cases "at law" and not in suits at equity.[44] Thus, determining whether a litigant has a right to jury trial involves the historic lines of demarcation between legal and equitable

---

[44]The Seventh Amendment does not apply to state courts, but most states have granted the right to a jury trial in civil cases along the same law/equity lines followed in federal court. *See* §9.2.2.

remedies. We will discuss the matter in detail in §9.2.2, but for now, assume that if the plaintiff is suing for legal relief (damages), there will be a right to jury trial. If, however, she is suing for equitable relief, there is no right to a jury.

As noted, the principal legal remedy is *damages*. There are different types of damages. *Compensatory damages* compensate the plaintiff for the harm occasioned by the defendant's act. *Punitive damages* are aimed at punishing a defendant for egregious behavior. Do not assume, however, that all awards of money constitute damages. For instance, *restitution* of unjust enrichment is not damages and historically was pursued in equity, not at law.

> o *Example #17.* D performs services for P, for which the bill is $120. P gives D a $100 bill and a $50 bill, mistakenly thinking that the latter was a $20 bill. D has been unjustly enriched by $30. P's claim is not for damages, but for restitution, to disgorge the amount overpaid. Restitution is an equitable remedy.

What are other equitable remedies? We have already seen the *injunction*, which is an order commanding that the defendant either do or refrain from doing something. Another is *specific performance*, which commands a party to perform in accordance with its agreement in a contract. Equity also can order *reformation*, with which the court essentially redrafts a document to accord with the parties' true intentions. Another classic remedy available at equity but not law is rescission, which "undoes" a document.

> o *Example #18.* P signs a deed that purports to transfer her real property to D. P claims that she signed the deed only because of undue influence by D. In a law court, P would be limited to recovery of damages. In equity, however, P can ask the court to rescind the deed.

Equity also developed the "cleanup" doctrine, which allowed the equity court to award damages, so long as they were incidental to the principal equitable relief sought. To this degree, then, an equity court could award a remedy (damages) usually available only at law. The converse was not true, however. Law courts could not grant equitable relief.

> o *Example #19.* P, the owner of real property, sues in equity for a decree ordering D to move out of the premises after D's lease had expired. The equity court can grant the injunction ordering D to move and, as incidental to the decree, order D to pay damages to cover the lost rent for the period during which she overstayed.

This dual set of courts, law and equity, with their different procedures, terminology, methods of enforcement, and remedies, were imported to the American colonies. Throughout most of its history as an independent nation, the United States followed the practice of maintaining separate courts of law and equity. In 1938, though, Congress abolished separate law and equity dockets in the federal courts. It provided instead for a single type of civil case, known as a "civil action." Under the Federal Rules of Civil Procedure, which became effective in that year, there is uniform procedure in all cases in the federal courts, regardless of whether they would have been law or equity in bygone days. Most states did the same, and abolished separate law and equity courts. But not all have done so. Every state is free to do as it pleases. In Delaware, for example, there are still separate law and equity courts.[45]

Remember, the fact that the federal system and those of most states have merged law and equity into a single trial court does not mean that the distinction between law and equity is not important. It is. *To this day*, every American jurisdiction differentiates between legal and equitable remedies and, generally, a plaintiff cannot obtain an equitable remedy without demonstrating that her legal remedy is inadequate. Moreover, the right to a jury trial in civil cases depends upon whether the case is an "action at law," which requires us to know the distinction between legal and equitable remedies.

§1.3 Alternatives to Litigation, Artificial Intelligence, Online Courts, and Implications for Access to Justice

Court litigation is the basic model for dispute resolution in our society. As noted, court litigation can be an expensive and time-consuming process. Some critics note not only the expense and delay, but also question the underlying premise of the adversary system; some feel that the polarizing effects of that system may obscure rather than reveal the truth. They criticize the fact that litigation generally is a zero-sum game: One side wins and the other side loses. Many disputes, they argue, are sufficiently subtle that there should be some "give" on both sides of the case. Moreover, litigation forces the parties to focus on the past, rather than on

---

[45]In Virginia, until 2006, the main trial court (the Circuit Court) was divided into law and equity sides, in which the historical terminological and remedial differences persisted. In that year, Virginia finally abolished the distinctions and now uses a unified procedure in all cases.

building a harmonious future relationship.[46] For these and other reasons, recent decades have seen increasing interest in alternatives to litigation.

American society has long embraced alternative dispute resolution (ADR) in specific settings. For instance, in the workplace, the litigation model was supplanted generations ago by "workers' compensation" statutes. These statutes provide that a worker injured on the job cannot sue her employer. Instead, the employer is required to pay a certain benefit, set by statute or regulation, for specific types of injuries. Under workers' compensation programs, then, workers waive their right to sue their employers in return for an absolute right to recover a specific dollar sum immediately. The award is made without need of showing that the employer was at fault.

Most disputes are settled, often before either side feels the need to file suit. Of those cases that are filed, the vast majority will settle before the court makes a formal adjudication on the merits. Settlement is a form of *negotiation*: The parties may structure the outcome in a way that makes most sense for them. They can avoid the "winner takes all" mentality of litigation and structure an outcome in which each side gives and each side receives. In a dispute between businesses that foresee an ongoing relationship, perhaps the settlement will involve future conduct toward each other. Law schools routinely offer courses on negotiation.

Often, serious settlement negotiations do not commence until after a case is filed and the parties have engaged in some stages of litigation. In the discovery phase of the case, for instance, each side may get a "reality check" about what the evidence actually shows. Maybe an event that seemed clear-cut at the time has more nuance when witnesses give testimony. Also, as each side spends increasing amounts in lawyers' fees, the incentive to negotiate a settlement often increases.

When most people invoke the phrase "ADR," they are referring to two dispute-resolution mechanisms: arbitration and mediation. These have become so common in the last generation that many people believe the term "alternative" should be deleted; both arbitration and mediation have become "mainstream." Indeed, it is increasingly common to speak of dispute resolution generically, inclusive of court litigation and of procedures historically seen as ADR.

Arbitration is in some ways similar to court litigation. The parties submit their dispute to a decision by a third party. The third party,

---

[46]Many disputes are between people who would prefer never to deal with each other again, such as in the typical automobile crash case. But other disputes are between people who envision an ongoing relationship, such as businesses or family members. In such situations, the parties may wish to resolve the dispute as quickly as possible, to allow for an agreeable relationship going forward.

however, is not a judge paid by the taxpayers. She is a civilian, usually chosen and paid by the parties; in some cases, there is a panel of multiple (usually three) arbitrators. The arbitrator is not necessarily a lawyer. Indeed, one advantage of arbitration is said to be the possibility of hiring someone with expertise relevant to the dispute (such as an engineer or architect in construction disputes). And the hearing does not take place in a courthouse built with taxpayer funds. It takes place in somebody's office. JAMS (Judicial Arbitration and Mediations Services), Inc. is the largest provider of "neutrals" to act as arbitrators and mediators. It has offices nationwide (including facilities for holding hearings). The American Arbitration Association (AAA), another private entity, does the same.

An arbitration hearing looks like a trial, at which each side presents evidence. But the hearing is less formal than a trial. The rules governing admissibility of evidence at trial do not apply, and the arbitrator(s) often allow the introduction of hearsay. Evidence is frequently proffered in written form instead of oral testimony. In arbitration, there is no formal discovery, but the arbitrator often facilitates the parties' exchange of relevant information. Like litigation, arbitration usually results in a winner and a loser; it is generally a zero-sum game.

Mediation is quite different from litigation. Here, the parties ask a third party to help them reach a settlement. The mediator is less interested in who is "right" than in getting the parties to find common ground. The mediator is often creative in suggesting ways for the parties to get the dispute behind them and get on with their lives. Often, mediators realize that parties desire a chance to tell their story, and structure hearings to allow each side to do so. In addition to being cheaper and less time-consuming than formal litigation, mediation usually avoids the zero-sum game: The object is to reach accord, rather than to declare a winner and a loser.

Feminist scholars have debated whether the mediation model, with its emphasis on cooperation and communication, is more hospitable to women than the adversary system of litigation.[47] In addition, some

---

[47]*See, e.g.,* Trina Grillo, *The Mediation Alternative: Process Dangers for Women,* 100 Yale L.J. 1545, 1607 (1991) ("To the extent that women are more likely than men to believe in communication as a mode of conflict resolution and to appreciate the importance of an adversary's interests, [the adversary system of litigation] does not always suit their needs"). Professor Grillo concludes, however, that mediation often does not serve women well. *See also* Filat J. Bachar & Deborah R. Hensler, *Does Alternative Dispute Resolution Facilitate Prejudice and Bias? We Still Don't* Know, 70 S.M.U. L. Rev. 817, 836 (2017) ("[W]e have insufficient evidence to conclude whether ADR favors or disfavors women (or men) or minority (or majority) disputants or is unaffected by disputants' identity characteristics."); Kenneth F. Dunham, *I Hate You, But We Can Work It Out: Dealing with Anger Issues in Meditation,* 12 Appalachian J.L. 191, 191-192 (2013) ("Some parties, especially women who have been living in less

commentators criticize ADR as forcing compromise upon persons who have a legal right to vindication and remedy.[48]

Historically, arbitration and mediation were voluntary, meaning that the parties would agree to submit their dispute to a third party for arbitration or mediation. Today, parties will often have a contractual relationship that includes a requirement that any dispute arising from the contract will be submitted to ADR. Occasionally, people who have no contractual relationship but who have a dispute will decide to waive the right to sue and, instead, submit to ADR. Either way, the parties hire a third party to act as arbitrator or mediator. It is common for arbitration clauses in contracts to specify the third party and rules of procedure.

In the past two generations, there has been an increase in "court-annexed" ADR. That means the court will order the parties to arbitrate or mediate before a third party, usually some judicial official.[49] The hope is that the "alternative" method will resolve the dispute. If either party is unhappy with the nonbinding ruling, the parties may return to the litigation stream, though the findings of the arbitrator or mediator might be admitted into evidence if the case goes to trial.

For now, let us focus on contractual arbitration, which has become an increasingly important topic for the Supreme Court. As noted, parties to a contract may include an arbitration clause. Historically, courts refused to enforce these clauses on the ground that they improperly "ousted" courts of their jurisdiction. In 1925, Congress passed the Federal Arbitration Act (FAA)[50] specifically to overcome this judicial hostility. The central goal of the FAA was to establish a national policy embracing arbitration clauses. Thus, the FAA allows a party to an arbitration clause to petition a court for an order compelling the parties to arbitrate[51] and suspending litigation until completion of the

---

than desirable relationships, may have significant concerns that the mediation process will not be fair to them due to power imbalances"); Negar Katirai, *Retraumatized in Court*, 62 Ariz. L. Rev. 81, 97 (2020) ("Most of the mediation study participants in the Michigan study indicated that they would avoid going back to family court, and some indicated that they would not even tell anyone else about the abuse because of the mediator's reactions.").

[48]*See, e.g.*, Owen Fiss, *Against Settlement,* 93 Yale L.J. 1073 (1984); Stephen B. Burbank, Sean Farhang & Herbert M. Kritzer, *Private Enforcement*, 17 Lewis & Clark L. Rev. 637, 649 (2013) ("Owen Fiss has argued that in such situations the settlement of civil cases may resemble plea bargaining in criminal cases and reflect not mutual accord but capitulation to economic necessity").

[49]*See, e.g.*, Fla. R. Civ. P. 1.700 et seq. (presiding judge may order parties to refer contested civil matters to mediation or arbitration).

[50]9 U.S.C. §1 et seq.

[51]9 U.S.C. §2. As a general matter, the Act applies only if the agreement is related to interstate commerce.

arbitration. The parties then submit their case to an arbitrator or arbitration panel chosen in accordance with the arbitration clause. After the arbitration hearing, the arbitrator makes the "award," which is her ruling in the case. If the claimant wins, the arbitrator's award will indicate the remedy she finds appropriate. The FAA provides that a court may then enforce the arbitration award, as it would a judgment. The court is permitted to review the arbitration award only on very limited grounds.[52]

Notice, then, that parties to contractual arbitration waive significant rights. They opt out of court litigation into privatized dispute resolution. In arbitration, there is no jury and there is very little judicial review of the arbitrator's decision. Even the arbitrator's clear mistake is not necessarily a basis for setting aside an arbitration award.[53] Moreover, arbitration is a private proceeding. The public and media have no access to the hearings or records, and the parties generally are forbidden from disclosing details of the dispute or proceeding. Thus, arbitration does not inform the public of potentially important information about defective products or other wrongdoings.

Until the late years of the twentieth century, arbitration clauses were found only in commercial contracts between businesses. Because the businesses were generally of comparable bargaining power and sophistication, courts could be confident that the parties knew what they were waiving by entering the arbitration agreement. Indeed, the FAA was passed specifically to allow businesses (which may have ongoing relationships) to avoid the expense of litigation and provide for privatized dispute resolution.

   o ***Example #20.*** Corporation enters into a contract with Widget, agreeing to buy a certain number of widgets at specified prices. The contract includes an arbitration clause, which provides that disputes arising under the contract will be submitted to arbitration. After delivery of some of the widgets, Corporation concludes that they do not comply with the contract. Corporation files suit against Widget. Widget may go to court for an order staying that case and requiring Corporation to submit

---

[52]*See* 9 U.S.C. §10 (court may vacate arbitration award if (1) it was procured by corruption or fraud, (2) was the result of evident partiality or corruption of the arbitrator, (3) the arbitrator was guilty of misbehavior that prejudiced a party's rights, or (4) the arbitrator exceeded her powers). Section 11 sets forth limited bases for modifying an arbitration award.

[53]*See, e.g.,* Stolt-Nielsen S.A. v. Animal-Feeds Int'l Corp., 559 U.S. 662, 671 (2010) ("It is not enough. . . to show that the [arbitrator] committed an error—or even a serious error"). The theory is that the parties agreed to arbitration and must live with the results except in extreme cases, as listed in the preceding footnote.

to arbitration. The arbitration is conducted in private, and the result is not announced to the public. The arbitration award may be enforced by the court.

In the past three decades, the Supreme Court has changed the landscape of contractual arbitration profoundly. It has done so by vastly expanding the number of cases that are subject to arbitration and therefore are ineligible for court litigation. We focus on two ways in which the Court has done this. First, it has held that the FAA may apply to "contracts of adhesion." These are agreements between parties of significantly different bargaining power, offered on a "take-it-or-leave-it" basis with no negotiation. Each of us is party to many such contracts. Virtually all consumer contracts (with a cellphone service provider, internet provider, health care provider, credit card company, investment advisor, Amazon, Netflix, and a thousand others) are contracts of adhesion. That fact alone does not make them bad. In fact, because there is no individual negotiation, it is likely that adhesion contracts allow consumers to obtain products and services more cheaply than otherwise would be the case.

Almost without exception, these contracts contain arbitration clauses. Unlike clauses in the business context, these are not individually negotiated; indeed, the consumer is likely unaware of the clause. For this reason, courts in several states refused to enforce arbitration provisions in consumer contracts. They were nervous that the consumer did not realize that she was waiving all the rights we detailed two paragraphs before Example #20. The Supreme Court, however, has concluded that such state laws (because they thwart arbitration) are pre-empted by the FAA.[54]

Second, the Court has concluded that various federal rights may be enforced through arbitration and do not require a judicial forum. On this score, the Court changed its mind. In its 1953 decision in *Wilko v. Swan*,[55] the Court held that claims under federal securities laws could not be arbitrated. Congress created those claims to protect investors from fraudulent behavior in the purchase or sale of stocks and other securities. Protection of the investors required a judicial forum. Arbitration, the Court warned, would permit someone without legal training to enter an award "without explanation of reasons and without a complete record of proceedings."[56] The Court overturned

---

[54]*See* Doctor's Assocs., Inc. v. Casarotto, 517 U.S. 618, 686-687 (1996) (courts may not invalidate arbitration agreements under state law that is applicable only to arbitration provisions).

[55]346 U.S. 427, 435-436 (1953).

[56]*Id.* at 436.

Wilko v. Swan in 1989.[57] Thus, Congress's creation of a federal right does not necessarily carry with it a right to litigate in a federal court.

    ○ ***Example #21.*** Individual enters into a contract with Investment Business (IB) under which IB will manage Individual's retirement account. The form contract includes a requirement that any dispute under the agreement will be submitted to arbitration. In managing Individual's account, IB engages in fraudulent behavior that violates federal securities laws. Individual has a claim, created by federal law and invoking the subject matter jurisdiction of the federal courts. Individual sues IB asserting that claim and demanding jury trial. IB petitions the court to order arbitration of the claim. After the abrogation of *Wilko v. Swan*, the court will order the parties to arbitrate the case. Thus, the plaintiff consumer is entitled to no jury, no judge, no public access, no discovery, and virtually no judicial review.

Many criticize the Court's fulsome embrace of the FAA. They argue that what was intended to permit businesses to opt out of the judicial system for commercial disputes is now used to force individuals out of court and into privatized resolution without a knowing waiver of their rights.[58] What was intended to allow privatized decision-making in commercial cases is now used to resolve claims of significant personal importance to consumers, investors, and employees.

These observations force us to consider a very basic question: What is the goal of providing a public means of dispute resolution? Is it simply to resolve disputes peacefully? If so, litigation and arbitration may be fungible. But the American system of court litigation reflects certain normative values.[59] Litigation is public and informs people about

---

[57]Rodriguez de Quijas v. Shearson/Am. Express, Inc., 490 U.S. 477, 486-487 (1989).

[58]*See, e.g.,* Myriam Gilles, *The Day Doctrine Died: Private Arbitration and the End of Law,* 2016 U. Ill. L. Rev. 371. *See also* F. Paul Bland, Myriam Gilles & Taunja Gupta, *From the Frontlines of the Modern Movement to End Forced Arbitration and Restore Jury Rights,* 95 Chi.-Kent L. Rev. 585 (2020); Judith Resnik, *Diffusing Disputes: The Public in the Private of Arbitration, the Private in Courts, and the Erasure of Rights,* 124 Yale L.J. 2804 (2015); Judith Resnik, *The Contingency of Openness in Courts: Changing the Experiences and Logics of the Public's Role in Court-Based ADR,* 15 Nev. L.J. 1631 (2015); Judith Resnik, Stephanie Garlock & Annie J. Wang, *Collective Preclusion and Inaccessible Arbitration: Data, Non-Disclosure, and Public Knowledge,* 24 Lewis & Clark L. Rev. 611 (2020); Judith Resnik, *Lawyers' Ethics Beyond the Vanishing Trial: Unrepresented Claimants, De Facto Aggregations, Arbitration Mandates, and Privatized Processes,* 85 Fordham L. Rev. 1899 (2017).

[59]Professor Bone has written extensively about normative values and policies underlying American procedure, particularly as they should inform the rulemaking process. Robert G. Bone, *Making Effective Rules: The Need for Procedural Theory,* 61 Okla. L. Rev. 319, 321 (2008); Robert G. Bone, *Securing the Normative Foundations of Litigation Reform,* 86 B.U. L. Rev. 1155 (2006); Robert G. Bone, *The Process of Making Process: Court Rulemaking, Democratic Legitimacy, and Procedure Efficacy,* 87 Geo.

events that may affect their lives.[60] It is adversarial and participatory, featuring testimony under oath and subject to cross-examination and engaging the community in jury service. Litigation is overseen by a neutral, generalist trial judge, who is required to apply the rule of law. Her reasoning is set out in an opinion, and her decisions are subject to review on appeal. Court litigation allows individuals to challenge powerful interests; it is an important component in holding persons and institutions accountable, an important part of our democratic system.[61]

At this point you may not have (indeed, perhaps you should not have) an overarching view of the role of litigation in our society. But it is worth remembering something we said in §1.1: Court litigation embodies our country's vision of the proper administration of justice. When legal developments such as the Court's embrace of the FAA force citizens into privatized dispute resolution, we should at least raise the question of whether it constitutes a troublesome denial of access to justice.[62] We will consider a related issue at §13.3.10.

One looming issue is the effect of artificial intelligence on the provision of legal and judicial services. Increasingly, studies consider whether computer programs might replicate lawyer advice and even judicial decision-making. A move in this direction will reduce customization and foster standardized legal services—a topic that will bear more discussion in the near future. Moreover, artificial intelligence may be used to assist negotiation of settlements—for example, by using information concerning other disputes to suggest an outcome on which the parties might agree.

The COVID-19 pandemic forced a great deal of rethinking of how courts operate. Parties have long been able to conduct discovery depositions remotely; that practice has increased during the pandemic. More interestingly, courts came to permit remote trials, at least in the non-jury context. Jury trials, in contrast, require the lawyers to see the jurors' facial expressions and the jurors to see witnesses' expressions. Thus, courts were reluctant to hold jury trials either remotely or, when in person, while participants wore face masks.

L.J. 887 (1999). *See also* Stephen N. Subrin & Thomas O. Main, *The Fourth Era of American Civil Procedure,* 162 U. Pa. L. Rev. 1839, 1856 (2014) (criticizing rulemaking not grounded in normative values).

[60]Professor Lahav speaks of the "information forcing" role of litigation. Alexandra D. Lahav, *The Political Justification for Group Litigation*, 81 Fordham L. Rev. 3193, 3199 (2013). *See also* Alexandra D. Lahav. *The Roles of Litigation in American Democracy*, note 6 above, 65 Emory L.J. at 1661-1662.

[61]For a compelling defense of the court litigation system and its normative bases, see Alexandra D. Lahav, In Praise of Litigation (2017).

[62]The articles cited in note 58 above raise the question.

One possible innovation is to set up online courts. In England and Wales, the Online Solutions Court was established in 2016 to resolve disputes of under 25,000 GBP. It is worth remembering that those countries do not embrace the jury trial in civil matters, so it is easier to move to a non-traditional form of dispute resolution. Even here, though, some online platforms offer online dispute resolution, which is a move toward litigating without lawyers.[63] Still, in this country, the adversarial court litigation model is the norm, and American lawyers must understand it not only to function in the profession, but also to appreciate and evaluate potential changes to it.

§1.4 An Overview of Civil Procedure

One common question is how the various topics in Civil Procedure relate to one another. What might seem disparate individual topics in fact fit into a cohesive whole. This section describes that whole and provides a framework for Civil Procedure. It does so in a largely chronological way, by reflecting how litigation unfolds in the usual case. It is imperative to understand, however, that there is no single right order in which to cover the topics in this course. Your professor may cover them in a different order from the way they are addressed in this book. There is nothing wrong with that. No matter what order, however, it will facilitate understanding to see how the pieces fit together.

Most Civil Procedure professors spend considerable time on topics concerning the selection of the forum in which litigation will proceed. For reasons we discuss in the various chapters, litigants and lawyers care a great deal about where litigation takes place. For now, it is enough to say that we will see cases in which parties paid millions of dollars in attorney's fees and expenses to vindicate their choice of forum. It is a very important issue.

Four topics in the course relate directly to forum selection. First (here, but not necessarily in your course) is *personal jurisdiction*, which governs the geographic question of whether the plaintiff may sue the defendant in a particular *state*. As we see in Chapter 2, this is a far more complex question than may meet the eye and it is affected both by state statutes and the Due Process Clauses of the U.S. Constitution. The statutory and constitutional analyses are aimed at determining whether a particular state has sufficient "power" over the defendant to enable it to enter a judgment that will bind the defendant.

---

[63]There is an exceptional book offering an encyclopedic consideration of these issues in England and Wales: Christopher Hodges, Delivering Dispute Resolution: A Holistic Review of Models in England and Wales (2019).

Second, and closely related, is the topic of *notice*. It is not enough simply to show that a state has personal jurisdiction over the defendant. In addition, due process requires that the defendant be given notice of the proceedings against her and an opportunity to defend. We address these topics in Chapter 3. Thus, together, personal jurisdiction and notice ensure that the plaintiff can sue the defendant *in a particular state*.

The next question is which court *in that state* hears the case. This question raises the third topic: *subject matter jurisdiction*, treated in Chapter 4.[64] Specifically, the choice is between litigating in the state court system or the federal court system. As noted in §1.2.1, the federal courts have limited subject matter jurisdiction, which means that they can entertain only specific types of disputes. The topic raises constitutional and statutory considerations as to the allocation of judicial business between the federal and state governments. Keen awareness of the requirements for invoking federal subject matter jurisdiction, and an understanding of the policy reasons for the various forms of federal subject matter jurisdiction, is part of the arsenal of any litigation lawyer.

The last topic addressing forum selection is *venue*, addressed in Chapter 5. Venue is concerned with the geographic question of *where* the litigation will proceed *within the chosen judicial system*. Subject matter jurisdiction informs us that a particular case can go to a federal district court, but it does not tell us *which* federal district court. The nation is divided into federal districts, and federal statutes prescribe proper venues for various types of cases in the federal system. So, if the plaintiff wants to sue in federal court in California, the venue question would determine where the case goes; i.e., to the Southern District of California (in San Diego), the Central District of California (in Los Angeles), the Northern District of California (in San Francisco), or the Eastern District of California (in Sacramento).

In Chapter 6, we study the avenues available to the defendant for challenging the plaintiff's choice of forum. The timing and method for raising an objection may vary depending on whether the objection is to personal jurisdiction, notice, subject matter jurisdiction, or venue. The rules here are fairly mechanical and can be harsh. Failure to

---

[64]Many professors start with subject matter jurisdiction before addressing personal jurisdiction. Again, there is no single right way to approach these topics. In my view, personal jurisdiction goes first because it is the broader question. It asks whether the plaintiff can sue the defendant in Texas (or any other particular state). If the answer is yes, the next task (it seems to me) is to determine the proper court in Texas (or whatever state). But there is certainly nothing wrong with starting with subject matter jurisdiction.

abide by them may result in waiver of an otherwise valid defense. So, in sum, Chapters 2 through 6 all deal broadly with the topic of forum selection.

From there, we assume that the case is in a proper forum and walk through the litigation in a typical case. Chapter 7 discusses pleadings, which are documents (principally the complaint and the answer) in which parties set forth their claims and defenses. The pleading stage is the gatekeeper of the litigation system: If the plaintiff cannot state a claim that the law would recognize, there is no point in letting the case go forward to other phases, such as discovery. Chapter 8 addresses discovery, which grants very broad rights of access to information held by other parties. This intrusive (and often expensive) process is engaged, however, only if the plaintiff can state her claim in the pleading process.

Thus, together, pleadings and discovery constitute an education process in which each party finds out about the other side's position and evidence. In a fundamental way, the judicial system's desire for free exchange of information and evidence seems at odds with the adversary system discussed in §1.1. After all, if the point is to win, why should a party have to cough up information that hurts her case? Yes, the goal of each party is to win. But the goal of the process is to do justice—to achieve the just and fair resolution of the dispute. So litigation is not unfettered warfare. The search for the truth is fostered by disclosure within the rules. Sometimes the discovery process demonstrates that there is no claim there, and leads to dismissal. Sometimes it convinces the defendant that she really did do something wrong and caused harm to the plaintiff, which may lead to settlement.

In Chapter 9, we address actual adjudication of the dispute. Many cases disappear before getting to this point—perhaps because the court dismissed the case, perhaps because the defendant defaulted, perhaps because the parties settled. Cases that do survive to this stage will not necessarily be tried. It may be that there is no dispute on a material issue of fact, in which case the dispute is simply over the interpretation of a legal issue. In such a case, the court can rule through a procedure known as summary judgment. If, on the other hand, the parties dispute material issues of fact, the case will be tried. Here, we consider the important and sometimes vexing issue of whether the parties are entitled to a jury trial. And in cases involving a jury, it is important to allocate authority between the jury and the judge. One way or another, whether by summary judgment or trial, the dispute is adjudicated and the case ended with the court's entry of judgment. As noted in §1.3, the COVID-19 pandemic affected trial practice profoundly. While courts generally permitted non-jury cases to be tried by remote teleconferencing means, jury trials are a different matter. Generally, jury trials must be held in person.

At this point, the losing party may seek appellate review, which we address in Chapter 14. Before going there, however, the intervening chapters address other topics. One is the *Erie* doctrine, which many people consider the most difficult topic in Civil Procedure. *Erie* is a subject of surpassing importance, because it goes to the heart of the relationship between the state and federal governments. It is important to note, though, that *Erie* raises its troubling specter in rather limited circumstances. It is only an issue when the case is in federal (not state) court. And, even there, it generally arises only when the federal court is exercising diversity of citizenship jurisdiction—that is, the case is in federal court because of the citizenship of the parties. The question addressed by *Erie* is whether the federal judge in such a case must apply state law (or, on the other hand, is free to ignore state law and fashion her own approach). *Erie* is something of a freestanding issue. It can be raised almost anytime in the course.

Remember that Chapter 9 ended with the court's entering a judgment in the case. In Chapter 11, we assess whether that judgment precludes anyone from litigating anything in a different case. The preclusion doctrines of claim and issue preclusion (also known as res judicata and collateral estoppel) emphasize the importance of finality. In general, our system is committed to the notion that a litigant has one opportunity to litigate a matter. She does not get to litigate the same claim or the same issues serially in different cases. So the preclusion doctrines demonstrate how broadly a judgment operates. They may prohibit a plaintiff from asserting the same claim again. They may prohibit someone from litigating a particular issue again.

In Chapters 12 and 13 we complicate the litigation. Through Chapter 9, with its entry of judgment, we presumed a fairly simple case—the typical case of one plaintiff suing one defendant. In real life, there are many such cases. But many cases, on the other hand, involve multiple claims and multiple parties. The rules of joinder, addressed in Chapter 12, define the scope of a single civil case. Specifically, they define how many claims and how many parties may be packed into a single case. In this area, we dip back into topics covered in Chapter 4, about the subject matter jurisdiction of the federal courts. Why? Because each claim asserted in federal court—not just the original claim by the plaintiff against the defendant—must be supported by a basis of federal subject matter jurisdiction. Thus, this area is a rich one for professors. They can test the mechanical joinder provisions of the Federal Rules of Civil Procedure and topics of federal subject matter jurisdiction in a single fact pattern.

Chapter 13 continues themes established in Chapter 12, by addressing special multiparty litigation. Specifically, we discuss interpleader and the class action. Interpleader is a very specific type of litigation in which claimants are vying for ownership of money or some tangible property. In the class action, a representative sues on behalf of a group. Because the result of the litigation binds the class members, we encounter important issues of due process. Beyond this, the class action is controversial because it creates potentially devastating liability for a defendant by aggregating potentially thousands of claims in a single case. The device has always been at the center of a tug-of-war between the plaintiff's bar and business interests.

In 2005, business interests lobbied Congress to pass the Class Action Fairness Act, which funnels many class actions from state to federal court. This funneling is, at least in theory, substance-neutral, which means that it does not affect the substantive law to be applied in the case. On the other hand, there is a general sense that federal courts are less hospitable to class actions than many state courts. Thus, critics charge, the Class Action Fairness Act is actually a version of tort reform[65] sold to the public as a "mere" procedural provision.

---

[65]*See* note 6 above.

Chapter *2*

Personal Jurisdiction

§2.1   Defining the Issue

The concept of personal jurisdiction is foreign to your life before law school. The difficulty in grasping the basic idea of personal jurisdiction is compounded by the fact that most professors study the topic historically. It can be frustrating to take so long to get to an understanding of what the law of personal jurisdiction is *today*. But the historical approach is a good thing. Indeed, in my opinion, it is the only way to "get it." Many professors start with a difficult but wonderful case decided in 1878, the very name of which still resonates with lawyers years after graduating from law school: *Pennoyer v. Neff*. From there most courses launch into a series of cases tracing the development of personal jurisdiction doctrine through the intervening generations.

It is important to study the historical development with one thing in mind: The goal is to develop an analytical framework for addressing personal jurisdiction problems that might arise *today*. That framework will pull together various threads we see in the historical tour. Moreover, the historical tour drives home an important point: The law evolves. The principles distilled at the end of the tour might be thrown into question by a Supreme Court decision the next day. By going through the historical development and seeing how things build and fit together, however, we are equipped to adjust to future changes.[1] So the study of personal jurisdiction requires patience.

Now, what is personal jurisdiction all about? As we said in Chapter 1, this course concerns *litigation*, which is the process by which parties submit their disputes to a court (the judicial branch of the government, state or federal) for resolution. The court (state or federal) is an arm of the government (state or federal). During any case, the court makes orders commanding the parties to do various things. For starters, it issues a *summons*, which commands the defendant to appear and to defend against the plaintiff's accusations.[2] If the defendant fails to do so within the prescribed time, the court may enter a default judgment against her.[3] If the defendant does respond and the parties litigate the dispute, at some point the court enters an order, called a *judgment*, declaring the relative rights and liabilities of the parties. In other words, it decides who wins (and what, if anything, the winner recovers). In so doing, it decides the "merits" of the case.

The government (state or federal) cannot command anyone to do anything (and cannot decide the merits of the dispute) unless it has some basis of authority over the persons affected. For lack of a better term at this stage, let's refer to this authority as *power*.[4] The government (state or federal) must have some power over the litigants to enter valid orders affecting them and their rights. If the government does not have this power over the litigants, the orders made by its courts, including the final judgment, are void. There are two related

---

[1]This chapter is designed to walk through the historical development of personal jurisdiction doctrine and, in §2.7, to suggest an analytical framework for addressing personal jurisdiction problems.

[2]The summons is discussed in detail at §3.3.1.

[3]Default judgments are discussed in detail at §7.5.3.

[4]Some professors do not like using the word *power* in this context. Some feel that using it gives too much weight to early cases, particularly *Pennoyer*, in which the Court spoke in terms of power. I think the term is a helpful shorthand for describing the authority a court must have over the parties to the litigation. Just be sensitive to the fact that your professor might not use this shorthand.

and very important points in this notion: (1) personal jurisdiction is exercised by the (state or federal) government (through its courts) over the *parties* to the litigation;[5] and (2) if the government does not have personal jurisdiction over the litigants, the orders entered by its court are void.

Why would such orders be void? Because (as we see throughout this chapter), the Due Process Clauses of the Constitution require that a defendant be sued in an appropriate forum. They provide the defendant *with protection from litigation in a forum with which she has no relevant contact.* Stated another way, constitutional principles of due process limit the ability of a government (through its courts) to impose binding orders on a litigant. A government may do so only if it has appropriate power over the litigant. Interestingly, this constitutional protection can be relinquished, either by choice or by failing to raise an appropriate objection. Thus, the defendant can waive a personal jurisdiction objection. We discuss this possibility in detail in §6.2. For now, we assume that the defendant does not waive her due process protection against being sued in an inappropriate forum.

One very good question is whether the standards for asserting personal jurisdiction are (or should be) different in federal court than in state court. (Remember the introduction to the difference between federal and state courts in §1.2.1.) We address the question in detail in §2.6. There, we see that the general rule, subject to very few exceptions, is that the standards are the same in federal as in state court. Those exceptions need not concern us now. For our purposes now, we take it as a given that whether a *federal* court would have personal jurisdiction involves the same analysis as whether a *state* court would have personal jurisdiction.

Any court will *always* have personal jurisdiction over the plaintiff. Why? Because she *chose to sue in this court* and thereby agreed that the court could enter binding orders as to her. By suing, she voluntarily submitted to the jurisdiction of the court. The big question is whether the court has sufficient power—has personal jurisdiction—*over the defendant.* The forum court[6] can have power, in the sense of personal jurisdiction, over either of two things: the defendant's *person* or her *property.* Stated another way, the court might have one of two "jurisdictional predicates"—it may exercise power either (1) over the defendant herself or (2) over her property.

---

[5]This kind of power is contrasted with subject matter jurisdiction, which, as we see in Chapter 4, is exercised not over the parties but over the case—over the dispute itself.

[6]For now, the forum simply means the state in which *P* sues *D*. Remember, it does not matter whether *P* sues in a federal court or a state court for these purposes.

To illustrate these principles, we address a hypothetical with several permutations. These fact patterns show the types of problems encountered in personal jurisdiction. Don't worry at this point about what the right answer is. For now, let's just get a sense of what the issues are and why the question of forum selection—choosing which court will resolve the dispute on the merits—is important.

- ○ ***Example #1.*** *D* is a citizen of West Virginia. She was born and raised there and has traveled to various states on the East Coast. At age 20, she and a friend went on vacation to Hawaii. It is the first time *D* has been west of West Virginia. While in Hawaii, *D* gets into a dispute with *P*, who is vacationing in Hawaii from Utah. After *D* returns home, *P* sues *D*, claiming that *D* punched *P* in the nose in Hawaii. The underlying facts and law—about whether *D* actually punched *P* in the nose, whether such an act was excused (as, for example, self-defense), and what damages, if any, were suffered—are the "merits" of the dispute.[7] We do not care about those yet. At this stage, we consider *only* what court will decide the merits of the dispute. (Indeed, throughout Civil Procedure, we are not concerned with the content of the substantive rules of law that govern the dispute, but with the processes by which the merits are decided in court.)
- ○ ***Question 1.*** Can *P* sue *D* in Utah? Think about why *P* would like to do so. First, she would not have to travel; she would litigate in her home state and could employ a lawyer she might already know. Second, she might think that a local jury and judge would view her more sympathetically than they would view the "out-of-stater" *D*. The jurors are drawn from the local community and the judge may well be running for re-election in the local community sometime soon,[8] so it is not unreasonable to think they might favor the local litigant.

The serious question is whether Utah has power *over D*. *D* has never been to Utah. She did not send anything to Utah. She became involved (in Hawaii) in a dispute with a Utah citizen. Does that give Utah power over *D*? After reviewing the cases, we will answer this question by saying no. Even reacting by instinct, there is something that suggests that it would not be fair to *D* to force her to litigate in Utah.

---

[7]The merits of the dispute are determined by applying substantive rules of law, such as those studied in courses on torts, contracts, and property.

[8]As noted in §1.2.1, judges in some states are elected. Federal judges, as we see in §4.4, are not; they are appointed for life and never face an electorate. This difference leads some to conclude that state judges may be more politically motivated to rule in favor of the local litigant against an out-of-state litigant. After all, the job security of a Utah state judge is in the hands of Utah voters, not West Virginians.

- ○ ***Quick change of facts.*** Suppose, however, before *P* sues *D* anywhere, that *D* goes on a skiing trip to Utah. While *D* is in Utah, *P* files suit against *D* in Utah and has a proper person serve the appropriate papers for the suit on *D* in Utah. Now, does Utah have power over *D*? Does it matter that *D*'s presence in Utah had nothing to do with the altercation in Hawaii? After review of the cases, we will probably decide that Utah would have personal jurisdiction over *D* in this scenario.

- ○ ***Question 2.*** Back to the facts in Example #1. Can *P* sue *D* in West Virginia? *P* certainly will not *want* to do this, because it means she will be litigating on *D*'s home turf. And *P* will be required to hire a lawyer in a state in which she probably knows no one. On the other hand, there is no doubt that West Virginia courts would have power over *D*. After all, *D* is a citizen of West Virginia. Does it matter that the dispute occurred in Hawaii? Ultimately, we will see that West Virginia has personal jurisdiction over *D* even for a suit involving an altercation in Hawaii.

- ○ ***Question 3.*** Can *P* sue *D* in Hawaii? Again, this is not ideal for *P*, because it means litigating in unfamiliar surroundings and hiring a lawyer in a state in which she probably knows no one. For *D*, then, this may be better than going to Utah. On the other hand, Hawaii is not *D*'s home turf, and litigating there will impose significant burdens on *D*, too.

But notice another aspect of this situation: Though neither party has much contact with Hawaii (each has vacationed there, that's all), the underlying dispute arose in Hawaii. Litigation is publicly funded dispute resolution. Doesn't Hawaii have an interest in determining who was at fault—*P* or *D*—for a breach of its public peace? Is this interest relevant to whether Hawaii has power over *D*? Ultimately, we will probably conclude that this factor has some bearing on personal jurisdiction, and that Hawaii would have personal jurisdiction over *D* for this case.

- ○ ***Question 4.*** Can *P* sue *D* in California? Neither *P* nor *D* has any connection with California. Moreover, unlike Hawaii, California itself has no interest in the matter. The dispute involves the public peace of Hawaii, not California. Why should the California taxpayers pay their judges and court personnel, and burden their jurors, with a dispute that does not have any connection with the state?

- ○ ***Quick change of facts.*** But suppose, before *P* sues *D* anywhere, that *D* goes on vacation to California to learn to surf. Knowing this, *P* sues *D* in California and has a proper person serve the proper papers on *D* in California. What is different about this hypothetical and the preceding one? Here, *D* has some connection with California (having gone there to learn to surf), though her contact is unrelated to the dispute with *P*. Does this connection give California power over *D*? Ultimately, we may conclude that California does have personal jurisdiction over *D*.

> ○ ***One more change of facts.*** Suppose *P* finds out that *D* has
> money on deposit with a bank in Illinois. Can *P* sue *D* in Illinois?
> Here, the power would not be over *D* herself, but over *D*'s *prop-*
> *erty*. As discussed in §2.2, Illinois's power over this property
> might give Illinois a specialized type of personal jurisdiction,
> called *quasi-in-rem*.

Now let's start acquiring the tools to address problems like these.
Begin with these background principles in mind:

> ○ The forum (the court resolving the merits of the case) must have power
> over *D* or her property before it can issue binding orders to *D*.
> ○ If the court does not have such power over *D* or her property, any order
> entered by the court is void.
> ○ The analysis of whether the forum has power in this sense is the same
> whether the forum is a federal court or a state court.
> ○ A court always has personal jurisdiction over the plaintiff, because the
> plaintiff has invoked its jurisdiction, and thus has waived any objection
> as to whether the court lacked power over her.
> ○ A defendant may waive an objection to a court's lack of power over her,
> and permit a court otherwise lacking personal jurisdiction to enter valid
> orders to her.[9]

One last prefatory point. You may read that due process imposes
two distinct requirements: personal jurisdiction and notice. This is
true. Each is such a large topic, however, that they are treated in separate chapters. This very long chapter addresses only personal jurisdiction. Chapter 3 addresses the due process requirement that the
defendant be given notice of the claims against her and an opportunity to respond.[10]

§2.2 The Types of Personal Jurisdiction (*In Personam*, *In Rem*, and *Quasi-in-Rem*) and the Concept of Full Faith and Credit

In §2.1, we noted that a court might gain personal jurisdiction by
exercising power over either the defendant herself or her property. In

---

[9]In Chapter 6, we discuss in detail how a defendant may assert the objection that
the forum lacks personal jurisdiction. Some professors cover this material along with
the personal jurisdiction cases, so you may need to address some of that material (particularly in §6.2) while studying the personal jurisdiction cases.

[10]For an interesting treatment of the development of the law of personal jurisdiction
and notice, *see* Robin J. Effron, *The Lost Story of Notice and Personal Jurisdiction,* 74
N.Y.U. Ann. Surv. Am. Law 23 (2018).

other words, the jurisdictional predicate might be the person or her property. There are three kinds of personal jurisdiction, the names of which invoke Latin phrases that reflect the jurisdictional predicate used: *in personam, in rem*, and *quasi-in-rem*.

In Personam *Jurisdiction (and the Effect of an* In Personam *Judgment)*

With *in personam* jurisdiction, the court's power is exercised over the defendant herself, because she has some appropriate connection with the forum. This fact is reflected by the word *personam*, which clearly refers to "the person." We cover the kind of connection required for the exercise of *in personam* jurisdiction in great detail. By way of examples, perhaps the defendant is domiciled in the forum, or perhaps she has committed an act there, or has done something that caused an impact there (like sending a defective widget into the forum, which exploded and injured someone). Historically, this form of jurisdiction involved literal physical power over the person. At common law, for instance, the sheriff for the local court arrested the defendant, even in a civil case, to ensure her attendance in the case. The sheriff did this with a writ of *capias ad respondendum*. It was a stark reminder that the jurisdiction was being exercised *in personam*, because it actually resulted in taking the defendant into the custody of the government.

Today, we no longer arrest the defendant in civil cases. But there must be some symbolic "seizure" of the defendant to show that the government is exercising power over her. Today, that symbolic seizure is performed by the service of "process" on the defendant. We discuss service of process in detail in §3.3. For now, we note only that process (the documents that are delivered to the defendant to inform her that she has been sued) consists of a copy of the plaintiff's complaint and a document called a *summons*. The court issues the summons; thus, that document emanates from the government and is the *symbol* of the government's power over the defendant.

A valid judgment *in personam* against a defendant creates a personal obligation (a debt) that the plaintiff is entitled to recover from the defendant. Suppose, for example, that the court determines through adjudication that the plaintiff is entitled to recover $100,000 from the defendant. It will enter a final judgment reflecting this determination. That judgment creates a legal debt for the defendant to pay to the plaintiff $100,000. The defendant might discharge this debt by writing a check to the plaintiff for the judgment amount.

If the defendant does not (or cannot) pay the judgment amount to the plaintiff, the plaintiff will want to enforce the judgment. The plaintiff can "execute" on that judgment by asking the court to seize the defendant's property in that locality and sell it at a public auction. The goal of the auction is to raise money to pay the judgment. We discuss this auction process in addressing the case of *Pennoyer v. Neff* in §2.4.1. For now, it is enough to understand that this legal procedure is available for the enforcement of an *in personam* judgment. Through it, the defendant's property can be seized and sold to satisfy the debt created by the *in personam* judgment.[11]

Full Faith and Credit

A valid *in personam* judgment against the defendant not only creates a personal obligation for her but is also entitled to full faith and credit. This concept is discussed in detail in §11.6. In short, the Constitution, at Article IV, §1, provides that the valid judgments of the courts of one state are entitled to enforcement in the courts of the other states. Full faith and credit is an important statement of the interdependence of the American states—a valid judgment entered by a court in Kansas is entitled to recognition by the courts of Florida. This fact is particularly important for the plaintiff trying to collect her judgment. Let's say the plaintiff's valid judgment against the defendant (for $100,000) was entered by a state court in Kansas. Suppose the defendant refuses to pay the plaintiff. The plaintiff then executes on the judgment by having the court seize the defendant's property in Kansas and sell it at auction. But let's say the auction only fetches $60,000. (That is, the sale of the defendant's Kansas property only raised $60,000 at auction.) The judgment has been satisfied to that extent, but there is still a *personal obligation* of the defendant to pay to the plaintiff the remaining $40,000.

Now let's say the plaintiff discovers that the defendant has a vacation house (or a bank account, a race car, or any other property) in Florida. Because of full faith and credit, the plaintiff can institute an action in Florida and ask a Florida court to enforce the Kansas judgment. Once the Florida court is satisfied that the judgment is entitled to full faith and credit (because the Kansas court had valid *in personam* jurisdiction over the defendant), it will recognize the Kansas judgment. That means that the plaintiff can then have the Florida court "domesticate" the Kansas judgment and enforce it (for the remaining $40,000) by seizing the defendant's property in Florida and selling it at public auction to raise the remaining amount due. If the sale fetches only $25,000, the plaintiff can go to another state in

---

[11]The valid *in personam* judgment creates a "lien" on the defendant's land in the locality. That lien is a right held by the plaintiff against that property to have her debt repaid by the sale of the property at public auction.

which the defendant has property (if there is one) and repeat the process until the entire $100,000 judgment is satisfied.

In Rem *and* Quasi-in-Rem *Jurisdiction (and the Effect of Such Judgments)*

In rem and *quasi-in-rem* jurisdiction are different from *in personam* jurisdiction in a fundamental way: In each, the jurisdictional predicate is not the defendant herself, but her property. The difference is clear from the presence of the word *rem* in their titles. The Latin word *res* means "thing." *Rem*, then, refers to the fact that a thing (property) is the jurisdictional predicate. As you will learn in other courses, property comes in many forms. There is tangible property, such as a book or a yacht or a building—something you can touch. There is also intangible property. For instance, if you borrowed money to pay your tuition, you owe the lender the money in return (plus interest). The lender thus owns intangible property, sometimes called a *chose in action*,[12] which is the right to collect the money from you. And, of course, there is real property, which is land.[13]

The plaintiff will prefer to proceed *in personam*. Why? Because, as we just saw, a valid *in personam* judgment against the defendant creates a *personal obligation*, which can be enforced by having the defendant's property seized and sold at public auction. But sometimes the plaintiff simply cannot proceed *in personam*.[14] In such cases, occasionally, the defendant might nonetheless have some property in the forum. With *in rem* and *quasi-in-rem* jurisdiction, the defendant's property in the forum might give a court in the forum jurisdiction to adjudicate matters that affect the defendant.

Suppose the plaintiff wanted to sue the defendant in Kansas but that, for whatever reason, Kansas would not obtain *in personam* jurisdiction over the defendant. Now suppose the defendant had property in Kansas. Say, for instance, that the defendant's parents lived in Kansas and they created a college fund for the defendant, which they put in a Kansas bank. The plaintiff, unable to get *in personam* jurisdiction, may be able to have the court establish *in rem* or *quasi-in-rem* jurisdiction

---

[12]This is a "law French" term, essentially referring to a type of intangible property such as the right to sue someone.

[13]We saw this at §1.2.3 and it bears repeating. "Real" in this context does not mean tangible. Real property (or realty) is land. It is also tangible, because you can touch it. So all real property is tangible, but not all tangible property is real.

[14]For example, perhaps the state's statutory grants of *in personam* jurisdiction do not apply, even in a case in which such jurisdiction would be constitutional. See §§2.3, 2.5.

over the defendant by seizing the defendant's bank account to use *as the jurisdictional predicate* for a suit *in rem* or *quasi-in-rem*.

Do not confuse this type of seizure of property (as a jurisdictional predicate) with the seizure we talked about five paragraphs above (to enforce an *in personam* judgment). In the latter (to enforce an *in personam* judgment), the court had *in personam* jurisdiction and entered a valid judgment. The seizure of the property in that instance was simply a means to get the defendant to pay what she owed to the plaintiff. That seizure of property routinely takes place after entry of judgment and after the defendant has refused or simply failed to pay the judgment amount to the plaintiff.

Here, we are talking about something fundamentally different. Here, there is no *in personam* jurisdiction, so there is no *in personam* judgment to enforce. The plaintiff is trying the next best thing: *in rem* or *quasi-in-rem* jurisdiction. To do that, the court must have power over the defendant's *property*. And, as seen in our discussion of *Pennoyer v. Neff* in §2.4.1, the Supreme Court has long held that such seizure must take place at the outset of the litigation. Why? To ensure that there is something over which the court actually has power, and that it will not be transferred or destroyed during the litigation. Just as in common law times the court arrested the defendant to ensure that he would be before the court, so the court in *in rem* and *quasi-in-rem* cases must seize the defendant's property at the outset of the litigation (or *ab initio*, which means "at the beginning").

Now we know that *in rem* and *quasi-in-rem* jurisdiction are similar in that each employs the defendant's property as the jurisdictional predicate. But how do they differ? True *in rem* cases involve a dispute over *ownership* of the property that is the jurisdictional predicate, and (believe it or not) determine the ownership interest in that thing *as to every person in the world*. The best example is a case brought by a government for delinquent real property taxes; there are many such cases filed each year. Another example is a government's case to condemn real property under the power of eminent domain, which allows the government to convert the property to some other use. Yet another example is a proceeding in admiralty, to determine the ownership of a ship. The court in these *in rem* proceedings seizes the land or the ship[15] and determines who owns it. In theory, this judgment binds everyone in the world.

---

[15]That sounds strange, I know. We can imagine a court's seizing a fund of money or a diamond ring, simply by ordering the sheriff (or like officer) to go out, get it, and bring it into the courthouse, where it can be kept by the clerk pending litigation (or *pendente lite*, as courts occasionally say). But how does a court seize a ship or, for that matter, land? The court orders the sheriff to post signs on the property announcing that it is subject to the authority of the court. In addition, in the case of real property, the court will ensure that notice is filed in the registry of deeds, to indicate to anyone checking the title records that the property is in the "possession" of the court, so no one can transfer it in the meantime.

What about *quasi-in-rem*? There are two types of this form of jurisdiction, known by number: *quasi-in-rem* "of the first type" (which we will abbreviate QIR-1) and *quasi-in-rem* "of the second type" (which we will call QIR-2). QIR-1 cases adjudicate the *ownership* of the property that is used as the jurisdictional predicate, and purport to determine that ownership as between and among the parties to the case. Thus, QIR-1 is quite similar to true *in rem* — it is litigation about who *owns* the property. The difference from true *in rem* is that a QIR-1 judgment does not purport to bind the whole world. This is not a big deal. As noted, very few types of disputes qualify as true *in rem* cases. The key is to emphasize the similarity between true *in rem* and QIR-1: Both are about *ownership* of the very property being used as the jurisdictional predicate.

- ○ ***Example #2.*** *P* claims that she owns certain real property in Montana because she has established a right to it by adverse possession. (Under that doctrine, one who has occupied real property openly for a statutory period may cut off the ownership rights of another, even one who holds the deed to the property.) *D* holds the deed to the property and believes that *P* has not satisfied the requirements for adverse possession.

We have no idea who should win this case. The merits of the suit will be determined much later. Right now, we're just trying to figure out *which court* will address the merits.

- ○ Let's say *P* resides in Montana, which is where the disputed real property is located. *D* resides in Maine and, aside from claiming to own the real property, has no other contact with Montana.
  - ○ *P* sues *D* in Montana and asks the court to declare the respective rights to the land. Assuming *P* cannot proceed *in personam* against *D*, she can proceed by QIR-1. To do so, she should have the court attach the property at the outset of the case to establish its power over the property. The court would have the authority, under QIR-1, to determine who — between *P* and *D* — owns the property. If the attachment was proper and other requirements met, the QIR-1 judgment would be valid as to the question of ownership.

Why? Because a judgment is valid to the extent that the court had jurisdiction. That is why we said that an *in personam* judgment creates a personal obligation on the defendant. The court had jurisdiction (power) over the defendant herself and thus could create that personal obligation. In a QIR-1 case, however, the court had jurisdiction only over the property, and thus its judgment is valid only to affect that property itself, and not to impose a personal obligation on *D*.

That brings us to QIR-2. Such a case is similar to *in rem* and QIR-1 in that the court's jurisdiction is over property, and not over the person of the defendant. But here, unlike with *in rem* and QIR-1, there is no dispute about who owns the property. Everyone knows that the defendant owns it. The dispute between the parties is one that *would be* in personam *if we could get* in personam. The property is relevant as a jurisdictional predicate only because the plaintiff cannot obtain *in personam* jurisdiction over the defendant. The underlying dispute between the parties is unrelated to ownership of the property; it might be about anything at all.

- *__Example #3.__* P is a lawyer who performed legal services for *D*. *D* failed to pay *P* for the legal services. *D* resides in another state, however, and would not be subject to *in personam* jurisdiction. *D* does, however, own land in the forum state. *P* may proceed against *D* through QIR-2, by using *D*'s land as the jurisdictional predicate. (This is the underlying fact pattern in the famous case of *Pennoyer v. Neff*, discussed in §2.4.1.)

P would prefer to proceed *in personam*, because such a judgment would create a personal obligation that *P* could enforce by seizing other property of *D*'s and having it sold at auction. In a QIR-2 case, the court cannot create such a personal obligation, because it does not have power over the person of *D*. The QIR-2 judgment, however, will be valid to the extent the court has power—which is, of course, to the extent of the value of the property.

- Suppose *P* proceeds QIR-2 and *D* defaults. The court enters a default judgment against *D*, holding that *D* owes *P* $15,000. Because *D* defaulted (and thus will probably not give *P* the $15,000 voluntarily), *P* asks the court to have *D*'s property—the property used as the jurisdictional predicate—sold at auction. Suppose the sale at the auction fetches $10,000. The QIR-2 judgment is valid, but only to that extent, meaning only to the tune of $10,000. *P* cannot take the judgment to a court in another state under full faith and credit to seek enforcement for the other $5,000.

Remember, *P* could do that if the judgment had been *in personam*. Because it was QIR-2, however, the court only had power to the extent of the value of the property, which is set by the auction, and therefore is $10,000.[16] *P* has a $5,000 unsatisfied claim against *D* and can sue *D* to get it. But *P* cannot use this QIR-2 judgment any further—the court's power was over the property, and that has been exhausted.

---

[16]The fair market value of the property is irrelevant. The property is worth only what someone is willing to pay for it at auction. That is the amount of money that goes into the registry of the court and is available for satisfying the claim.

Recap

In sum, then, *in personam* jurisdiction operates on the person of the defendant. The plaintiff seeking money undoubtedly prefers *in personam* because a valid *in personam* judgment against the defendant creates a personal obligation (a debt) for that person to pay the plaintiff. The plaintiff can enforce that judgment by having the defendant's property seized and sold to raise money for the judgment. The judgment is entitled to enforcement in other states under the principles of full faith and credit. *In rem* and both versions of *quasi-in-rem* exercise jurisdiction not over the defendant, but over the defendant's property. *In rem* and QIR-1 are similar in that the dispute between *P* and *D* is over who owns that very property. With QIR-2, in contrast, the dispute is something unrelated to the ownership of the property. In *in rem* and both versions of *quasi-in-rem*, the court's judgment may be valid, but not to create a personal obligation; rather, it is valid only to the extent of the property that served as the jurisdictional predicate.

Jurisdiction by Necessity

We end this subsection with a brief reference to "jurisdiction by necessity." This is a theory, espoused by different commentators over time, that a court may exercise personal jurisdiction when there is no other forum in the world in which justice may be had. The Supreme Court has mentioned the theoretical possibility of such a basis of jurisdiction but has never embraced it.[17] In one case, plaintiffs sued non-U.S. defendants in Texas. After the Court rejected personal jurisdiction under traditional analyses, the Court also rejected the plaintiffs' invitation to adopt the concept of jurisdiction by necessity. It characterized the theory as "a potentially far-reaching modification of existing law" and refused to address it in the absence of a well-developed factual record.[18] Specifically, it noted that the plaintiffs failed to show that they could not pursue their claims against the defendants "in a single proceeding in Colombia or Peru."[19]

It is not clear that the Court was seriously suggesting that the absence of a *single* foreign forum in which to sue *all* defendants in a single case would justify jurisdiction in the United States, notwithstanding the defendants' lack of relevant contacts with this country.

---

[17]In *Shaffer v. Heitner*, 433 U.S. 186, 211 n.37 (1977), the Court mentioned the possibility of jurisdiction when "no other forum is available to the plaintiff." On the facts of this case, however, the plaintiff could pursue litigation in various U.S. courts, so the Court did not have to take a position on jurisdiction by necessity.

[18]Helicópteros Nacionales de Colombia, S.A. v. Hall, 466 U.S. 408, 419 n.13 (1984).

[19]*Id.*

Such a suggestion would indeed be radical, since it would still be probable that the plaintiffs could proceed against the foreign defendants
in individual litigation in foreign countries. Surely Colombian defendants can be sued in Colombia and Peruvian defendants in Peru. The
existence of fora in which the defendants could be sued, even separately, would seem to obviate any need for an American court to take
the case on the basis of jurisdiction by necessity. Moreover, it seems
unlikely that courts in the United States want to be put in the position of declaring that a foreign tribunal, if available, would be so inadequate as to justify personal jurisdiction in the United States. Thus,
jurisdiction by necessity remains at best a theoretical possibility.[20]

§2.3 The Statutory and Constitutional Dimensions of Personal Jurisdiction

The major focus of law school studies on personal jurisdiction is
whether the exercise of jurisdiction comports with the requirements
of due process. This is a *constitutional* inquiry. It is not, however, the
only relevant inquiry in determining whether a court has personal
jurisdiction. There is also a *statutory* inquiry. In this section, we introduce why there are two such levels of assessment, then address each
in detail in §§2.4 and 2.5.

There are two due process provisions in the Constitution (or, technically, in amendments to the Constitution). The Fifth Amendment
provides (among other things) that the federal government may not
deprive anyone of "life, liberty, or property, without due process of
law." This provision is part of the Bill of Rights, ratified in 1791. The
Fourteenth Amendment (among other things) makes a similar provision about *state* governments—no state may deprive one of "life,
liberty, or property without due process of law." This provision was

---

[20]Some commentators have considered *Mullane v. Central Hanover Bank & Trust
Co.*, 339 U.S. 306 (1950), as a case involving jurisdiction by necessity. *See, e.g.*, George
B. Fraser, *Jurisdiction by Necessity—An Analysis of the* Mullane *Case*, 100 U. Pa.
L. Rev. 305 (1951). *Mullane*, discussed at §3.2, establishes the constitutional requirement for notice to be given to one whose rights may be affected by litigation. It involved
claims relating to a pooled trust fund having thousands of beneficiaries—some known
and some not, some residing in the forum state and some not. Having a single court
oversee the administration of the trust, as upheld in *Mullane*, is a commonsense pragmatic reaction to the reality that people from many states may invest in another state.
Though the courts of many states could be involved, it would be a nightmare. So if
Mullane involves jurisdiction by necessity, it is of a different type than the one discussed in this text, in which the motivation is not convenience and common sense, but
the lack of another forum.

adopted after the Civil War, as part of Reconstruction, and became effective in 1868.

These clauses set the outer boundary for the exercise of personal jurisdiction.[21] In other words, due process defines the absolute limit to which a court can exercise power over a person or her property. It is helpful to think of the due process limit as a large circle. Judgments entered in cases that fall within the circle are valid, and thus are entitled to full faith and credit (as discussed in §2.2). Judgments entered in cases falling outside the circle, however, are void, and thus are *not* entitled to full faith and credit. As we will see, defining the constitutional limit on personal jurisdiction is occasionally difficult, and the line can be blurry.

The mere fact that a case falls within the "due process circle," however, does not mean that a court has personal jurisdiction. Why not? Because the power to exercise jurisdiction under the Constitution is not self-executing. Courts do not automatically have the power to exercise personal jurisdiction. That power must be given to them by statute (which, of course, is an act of the legislative branch of the government). In other words, the constitutional power (to the full extent of the due process circle) is available to a court, but only if the legislative branch of the government gives it to the court. The state legislature is not required to grant to its courts the full extent of the constitutional power to exercise personal jurisdiction. A state legislature may declare that the courts of the state exercise only a portion of the authority permitted by due process. (We discuss why a legislature might do this in §2.5.) A state court, then, cannot exercise personal jurisdiction (even over a case that clearly, without question, falls within the due process circle) unless the state legislature has enacted a statute permitting the court to do so.

States generally have a series of statutes granting personal jurisdiction to their courts. Some such statutes are ubiquitous. For example, each state appears to grant its courts *in personam* jurisdiction over defendants who are served with process while present in the state, and over persons who reside in the state, and over businesses incorporated in the state. In addition, each state has a statute (or series of statutes) permitting its courts to exercise *in personam* jurisdiction over non-residents in various circumstances. Such statutes, generically called *long-arm* statutes, can vary considerably from state to state. And each state also has attachment statutes permitting the attachment of property for the exercise of *in rem* and *quasi-in-rem* jurisdiction.

---

[21]In §2.5, we discuss whether the due process limits are different under the Fifth Amendment and the Fourteenth Amendment. For now, we refer simply to due process limits on the power of a court to exercise personal jurisdiction and assume (for now) that they are the same for federal and state courts.

Analytically, then, the statutory question always comes first. Unless there is a statute granting personal jurisdiction in the case, the fact that the case falls within the due process circle is irrelevant. Thus, the lawyer's first task is to determine whether the facts of the case fall within a statutory grant of personal jurisdiction. If so, then the focus shifts to the constitutional analysis of whether jurisdiction on the facts of the case comports with due process.

For our purposes, though, we address these two levels in reverse order. We discuss the constitutional analysis first (in §2.4) and then look at the statutory issues (in §2.5). We do this for two reasons. First, most courses spend substantially more time on the constitutional analysis, so it is clearly more important for exam purposes. Second, once we have discussed the constitutional issues, the statutory analysis is simply easier. After these discussions of both the constitutional and statutory analyses, §2.7 presents an analytical framework to apply for any personal jurisdiction question, tying together both levels of analysis.

§2.4   Constitutional Analysis

§2.4.1   The Traditional Approach: *Pennoyer v. Neff*

The most famous personal jurisdiction case is *Pennoyer v. Neff*.[22] It is the starting point for understanding personal jurisdiction law but cannot be appreciated without an understanding of the (fairly complicated) facts. The iconic opinion, issued in 1878, is the culmination of two cases. Here is the fascinating story behind the cases.

The Facts

John Mitchell was a lawyer in Multnomah County (Portland), Oregon. He claimed to have performed legal work (worth about $300[23]) for Marcus Neff, for which Neff allegedly did not pay. Mitchell sued Neff in a Multnomah County state court to recover that sum. Neff, however, was living in California at the time Mitchell sued him. Because Neff could not be found in Oregon, Mitchell could not proceed *in personam*. (At the time, *in personam* jurisdiction could only be exercised by having the defendant served with process within the forum state.) Accordingly, Mitchell tried to proceed *quasi-in-rem* of the

---

[22]95 U.S. 714 (1878).

[23]Actually, it was $253.14. With the addition of costs and any interest on the claim accruing after entry of the judgment, we will say $300.

second type (QIR-2). (If these terms are unfamiliar, review §2.2.) That case was *Mitchell v. Neff*. It never resulted in a published opinion in the Oregon court system, but the validity of the judgment entered in *Mitchell v. Neff* is at the basis of *Pennoyer*.

QIR-2 requires that the court have power over some *property* that belongs to the defendant, but the dispute is not about ownership of that property. (Again, see §2.2.) Neff owned land in Multnomah County, which Mitchell wanted to use as the jurisdictional predicate for his case against Neff. Mitchell filed suit and had notice published in a newspaper, as required by Oregon law. The problem (it will turn out) was that neither Mitchell nor the Oregon court saw any need for the court to seize Neff's land at the outset of the case. There is no question that Neff owned the land. He got it from the federal government under the Oregon Donation Law, by which the federal government urged people to settle in the then-new state.[24]

Because Neff was in California and had no access to the publication notice in the Oregon newspaper, he knew nothing about Mitchell's case against him and failed to respond to the suit within the time required by law. Accordingly, the Oregon court entered default judgment in *Mitchell v. Neff*, in favor of Mitchell. That gave Mitchell a piece of paper—a judgment—from the court in Oregon, which said, in effect, that Neff owed Mitchell about $300. Obviously, Neff did not write Mitchell a check for the money. What happens when a defendant fails for whatever reason to pay the judgment that has been entered against him? To this day, as we saw in §2.2, the answer is the same: A court will seize some property of the defendant's and have it sold at public auction to satisfy (pay off) the judgment. That is what happened here. The Multnomah County court had Neff's land in Multnomah County seized and sold at public auction. Who showed up to bid for it at the auction? Mitchell, and nobody else. Mitchell apparently bid the amount of the judgment and was the winner of the auction. Thus, the land was delivered to Mitchell via a sheriff's deed, pursuant to the order that the land be sold to satisfy the judgment.

Before continuing, we need to understand how the public auction works. The topic was introduced in §2.2. In theory, anyone could have shown up at the auction and bid on the land. Because the auction is intended to raise money to satisfy the judgment, it is hoped that the auction price will at least equal the amount of the judgment. If it does not, the proceeds are used to satisfy the judgment partially. If it does,

---

[24]This method of getting land from the federal government is sometimes referred to (as it is in the *Pennoyer* opinion) as having received a "patent" for the land. Do not confuse this with getting a patent on an invention. A land patent is a conveyance of land from the government.

the proceeds satisfy the judgment fully. If there is excess, the government keeps the excess funds in an account for the defendant.

○ ***Example #4.*** *P* obtains a judgment against *D* for $50,000. (The judgment might have been entered after *P* and *D* went all the way through a trial or by default or any other way in which judgments are entered.) *P* wants her $50,000. *D* refuses to pay (for whatever reason). *P* seeks an order (writ) from the court to seize some property of *D*'s for sale at auction to raise the $50,000. The court issues a "writ of execution" to the sheriff, commanding her to seize the property. It might be land, or an automobile, or a bank account, or any other kind of property. Then the sheriff oversees the sale of the property at public auction.

○ Suppose at the auction, *X* is the high bidder, at $70,000. *X* pays $70,000 to the court and gets ownership of the property. If the property was land, the sheriff would transfer it to *X* by executing a sheriff's deed, which is then recorded in the register of deeds as a public record that *X* owns the land. What happens to the money? The court pays $50,000 to *P* (to satisfy her judgment) and the remaining $20,000 is kept in an account for *D*. She can get it whenever she wants. If she is absent, it will sit in the account, earning interest at a rate set by law.

○ Suppose at the auction, *X* is the highest bidder, at $40,000. *X* pays $40,000 to the court and gets ownership of the property. The court pays *P* the $40,000, and the judgment against *D* is satisfied to that amount. That means that *P* still has a claim of $10,000 against *D*. If the judgment were valid and *in personam*, the judgment would be unsatisfied to the tune of $10,000, and *P* might be able to enforce it against other property belonging to D in the forum or even in another state under full faith and credit (discussed at §2.2).

Now back to our story. See how Mitchell played two roles at the auction: *P* (the plaintiff) and *X* (the buyer at the auction). There is nothing wrong with that. We just need to keep the two roles separate. As bidder, he offered the judgment amount (about $300). He paid that to the court and got a sheriff's deed to the land. As plaintiff, Mitchell was entitled to the $300, so the court paid him that money. By playing both the role of the bidder and the plaintiff, Mitchell came out of the deal with a deed to Neff's land and without being out of pocket any money. Again, there is nothing wrong with playing both roles. (Though, as we will see, Mitchell was a crook.)

Just days after receiving the sheriff's deed, Mitchell sold the land (at a huge profit; the land was apparently worth about $15,000) to a new player in the controversy, Sylvester Pennoyer. In return for the payment, Mitchell gave Pennoyer a deed to the land. Pennoyer moved onto the land and everything was fine until a few years later when Neff came back from California. Neff was surprised to find Pennoyer living on "his" land. Neff sued Pennoyer in federal court to recover the land.[25] Neff claimed that he got the land originally from the federal grant under the Oregon Donation Law, and that the sheriff's deed purporting to transfer it to Mitchell was void. (If the deed to Mitchell was void, Mitchell's deed to Pennoyer was also void.) The entire case thus depended on whether the sheriff's deed to Mitchell was valid; if so, it cut off Neff's ownership of the land. That issue, in turn, depended on whether the underlying judgment in the case by Mitchell against Neff was valid.

The federal trial court[26] ruled in favor of Neff. According to that court, the judgment in *Mitchell v. Neff* was void, so the sheriff's deed to Mitchell was void. That court based its decision, however, on very narrow grounds. It determined that the publication notice given in the newspaper violated Oregon law because Mitchell's sworn statement (affidavit), which he was required to give as a prerequisite to giving publication notice, was inadequate. On "writ of error," the U.S. Supreme Court affirmed the judgment[27] (in other words, agreed that Neff should win) but did so on different, and far broader, grounds. It is that opinion by the Supreme Court that has graced casebooks in American law schools for nearly a century and a half.

The Holding

In *Pennoyer*, the Court held that the judgment in *Mitchell v. Neff* was void because the Oregon state court that rendered the judgment did not have personal jurisdiction. Today we would say, more precisely, that the Oregon court lacked valid QIR-2 jurisdiction. Why? Because Neff's property had not been attached *at the outset of the case*. Instead, Mitchell had it attached only *after* the court had entered its default judgment against Neff. At that point, Mitchell had the property attached in an effort to satisfy his judgment against Neff.

---

[25]In §1.2.1, we saw that federal courts can only entertain certain types of cases. Among these are cases between citizens of different states. The case by Neff against Pennoyer qualified, because Neff was a citizen of California and Pennoyer was a citizen of Oregon. This form of subject matter jurisdiction is discussed in detail in §4.5.

[26]At that time, federal trial courts were known as circuit courts for the particular district in which they sat. The court deciding Neff's case against Pennoyer was the circuit court for the district of Oregon. Today, the federal trial court is known as the district court, and intermediate court of appeals in the federal system is known informally as the circuit court.

[27]When *Pennoyer* was decided, there was no intermediate court of appeals between the federal trial court and the U.S. Supreme Court. Today, a decision by the federal trial court in Oregon would be appealed to the U.S. Court of Appeals for the Ninth Circuit, which hears appeals from federal trial courts in several western states, including Oregon. In the days of *Pennoyer*, as today, the Supreme Court was not required to hear an appeal taken to it. Rather, it has discretion as to which cases to decide, as discussed in §§1.2.1 and 1.2.2.

The Court's holding, then, concerns only QIR-2 jurisdiction, and requires that the jurisdictional predicate in such a case (which is, of course, property belonging to the defendant) be seized by the court *at the outset* of the litigation. Without such seizure, there is nothing over which the court can exercise power. As the Court explained:

> [T]he jurisdiction of the court to inquire into and determine [the defendant's] obligations at all is only incidental to its jurisdiction over the property. Its jurisdiction in that respect cannot be made to depend upon facts to be ascertained after it has tried the cause and rendered the judgment. If the judgment be previously void, it will not become valid by the subsequent discovery of property of the defendant, or by his subsequent acquisition of it. The judgment, if void when rendered, will always remain void: it cannot occupy the doubtful position of being valid if property be found, and void if there be none .... [T]he validity of every judgment depends upon the jurisdiction of the court before it is rendered, not upon what may occur subsequently.[28]

Though the trial court based its decision on a perceived problem with Mitchell's affidavit under Oregon law, the Supreme Court did not address that issue. Rather, it held that the failure of the Oregon state court to seize the jurisdictional predicate (Neff's property) at the outset of the case violated *federal constitutional and statutory provisions concerning full faith and credit*. As we discussed in §2.2, full faith and credit provides that a valid judgment is entitled to enforcement in other states. Consequently, the Court explained in *Pennoyer*, a void judgment (such as that in *Mitchell v. Neff*) is not entitled to enforcement in other states. The concept of full faith and credit thus provides a limit on state-court power: If Oregon entered a judgment in a case in which it lacked jurisdiction, California is not required to recognize it.

Did full faith and credit apply? *Mitchell v. Neff* was decided by an Oregon state court. *Neff v. Pennoyer* was in federal court *in the same state*, not in a different state. Even though both cases were in Oregon, however, they were in the courts of different sovereigns. Under the concept of full faith and credit, because the Oregon state court judgment in *Mitchell v. Neff* was void, it was not entitled to respect in the subsequent case in federal court in *Neff v. Pennoyer*.[29]

But that left a gap (though not one presented by the facts of the case): If an Oregon state court entered a void judgment, could the judgment

---

[28]95 U.S. at 728.

[29]"Whilst [federal courts] are not foreign tribunals in their relations to the State courts, they are tribunals of a different sovereignty, exercising a distinct and independent jurisdiction, and are bound to give to the judgments of the State courts only the same faith and credit which the courts of another State are bound to give them." 95 U.S. at 732-733.

be enforced in *the same court*? Full faith and credit would not apply here, because it applies only when one seeks to enforce a judgment from the courts of State *A* in the courts of a different sovereign (a state court in State *B* or a federal court). To fill that gap, the Court turned to the Due Process Clause of the Fourteenth Amendment. As noted in §2.3, that Amendment, among other things, prohibits *states* from depriving citizens of property without "due process of law." Before the adoption of the Fourteenth Amendment, the Fifth Amendment prohibited (and still prohibits) the *federal* government from denying citizens due process, but the Constitution was silent regarding such actions by *state* governments. The Fourteenth Amendment was ratified in 1868, which was after entry of the judgment in *Mitchell v. Neff*. Thus, the Fourteenth Amendment did not apply in *Pennoyer* because it did not become effective in time to affect the judgment in *Mitchell v. Neff*.

Nonetheless, the *Pennoyer* Court made clear that enforcing a state-court judgment rendered without a proper jurisdictional predicate (such as the judgment in *Mitchell v. Neff*) would constitute a denial of due process (and thus a violation of the Fourteenth Amendment). As the Court said, "proceedings in a court of justice to determine the personal rights and obligations of parties over whom that court has no jurisdiction do not constitute due process of law."[30] Thus, a judgment entered without jurisdiction is constitutionally void. It cannot be enforced in other courts (because of full faith and credit) and cannot be enforced even in the court that rendered the judgment (because of due process).

Pennoyer injected due process into the personal jurisdiction analysis as a vehicle for asserting that a court lacked personal jurisdiction over the defendant.[31] The defendant need not wait until entry

---

[30]95 U.S. at 733.

[31]Over time, as we will see, the Court has come to see due process as a source of substantive limitations on personal jurisdiction. Significant scholarship questions that conclusion. Several scholars conclude that the Court in *Pennoyer* considered due process solely as a procedural vehicle for raising a direct challenge to the exercise of personal jurisdiction, and not as a source of the substantive criteria for determining whether jurisdiction was valid. Those criteria, instead, are derived either from general law or from state law. *See* Patrick J. Borchers, *The Death of the Constitutional Law of Personal Jurisdiction: From* Pennoyer *to* Burnham *and Back Again,* 24 U.C. Davis L. Rev. 19 (1990) (source of substantive law of personal jurisdiction is state law); Patrick J. Borchers & John N. Drobak, *The Federalism Theme in Personal Jurisdiction,* 68 Iowa L. Rev. 1015, 1029-1031 (1983) (*Pennoyer* did not necessarily establish territorial principles of personal jurisdiction as part of due process); Wendy Collins Perdue, *What's "Sovereignty" Got to Do with It? Due Process, Personal Jurisdiction, and the Supreme Court,* 63 S.C. L. Rev. 729 (2012); Stephen E. Sachs, Pennoyer *Was Right,* 95 Tex. L. Rev. 1249 (2017) (source of substantive law of personal jurisdiction is general law); Roger Trangsrud, *The Federal Common Law of Personal Jurisdiction,* 57 Geo. Wash. L. Rev. 849, 876 (1989) (*Pennoyer* Court "did not contend . . . that the Due

of judgment against her to raise the issue. She can make a "direct attack" on whether the court in which she is sued has personal jurisdiction. That attack is based upon due process: that to exercise personal jurisdiction over her in the pending case would deprive her of due process of law.

Though the precise holding in *Pennoyer* concerned QIR-2 (because the attempted jurisdictional basis in *Mitchell v. Neff* was Neff's property in Oregon), the opinion discussed other bases of personal jurisdiction. For *all* assertions of personal jurisdiction, Justice Field[32] invoked two "principles of public law," which emanated from international law. First,

> every State possesses exclusive jurisdiction and sovereignty over persons and property within its territory. As a consequence, every State has the power to determine for itself the civil status and capacities of its inhabitants; to prescribe the subjects upon which they may contract, the forms and solemnities with which their contracts shall be executed, the rights and obligations arising from them, and the mode in which their validity shall be determined and their obligations enforced; and also to regulate the manner and conditions upon which property situated within such territory, both personal and real, may be acquired, enjoyed, and transferred.[33]

The second principle, which is really a corollary to the first, is:

> that no State can exercise direct jurisdiction and authority over persons or property without [which means "outside"] its territory. The several States are of equal dignity and authority, and the independence of one implies the exclusion of power from all others. And so it is laid down by jurists, as an elementary principle, that the laws of one State have no operation outside of its territory, except so far as is allowed by comity; and that no tribunal established by it can extend its process beyond that territory so as to subject either persons or property to its decisions.[34]

Process Clause was the source of the territorial rules of jurisdiction [it] articulated."); Michael Vitiello, *Due Process and the Myth of Sovereignty,* 50 U. Pac. L. Rev. 513 (2019) (*Pennoyer* Court, "in an elaborate dicta," found support for its holding in the due process clause of the Fourteenth Amendment).

[32]Justice Stephen Field was a younger brother of David Dudley Field, who was an important law reformer in the United States in the nineteenth century. We will meet him in §7.2.

[33]95 U.S. at 722.

[34]*Id.*

The Court focused on the sovereignty of states and equated them to nations in the international sphere.[35] A state has power—physical power—over people and things inside its boundaries. Such power is demonstrated by the fact that the courts of the state can seize people and property found within the state. Thus, California has power over people and things inside California, and Oregon cannot exercise authority over such people or things. More precisely, Oregon cannot exercise *direct* authority over people or things in California. The Court in *Pennoyer* did recognize, however, that a valid judgment by an Oregon court might have an *indirect* effect in California.

○ ***Example #5.*** *X* owns land in California. There is a dispute about whether *X* agreed to transfer that land to *A*. An Oregon court with *in personam* jurisdiction over *X* litigates the dispute and determines that *X* did agree to convey the property to *A*. The Oregon court can enter an *in personam* judgment ordering *X* to execute a deed transferring the property to *A*. Though this Oregon judgment has an effect in California (because it results in transfer of property in California from *X* to *A*), the effect is *indirect* and therefore permissible. That is, the effect in California is ancillary to Oregon's exercise of *in personam* jurisdiction over *X*. Because Oregon had *in personam* jurisdiction over *X*, it had the power to command *X* to do something (even something that has an effect in California).

○ ***Example #6.*** Neff owns land in Oregon but lives in California. Mitchell contends that Neff owes him money for legal services rendered. Mitchell sues Neff using QIR-2 in Oregon and uses Neff's Oregon land as the jurisdictional predicate. Neff defaults, so Mitchell wins. If done properly, the default judgment in this case would dispose of Neff's land in Oregon at a judicial sale to the highest bidder. Though this Oregon judgment has an effect in California (by affecting the Oregon holdings of a California resident), the effect is *indirect* and therefore permissible. If Oregon had QIR-2 jurisdiction over Neff's land, it would have the power to dispose of the property, notwithstanding the incidental effect on a Californian.

If all this is true—if states have all this power—why didn't Oregon have authority to make the order it made in *Mitchell v. Neff*? The two *Pennoyer* principles quoted above must be tempered slightly, because a state in the United States does not have absolute power over people and property within its boundaries. Why? Because of the Constitution

---

[35]*See* Perdue, note 31 above, 63 S.C. L. Rev. at 730 (Justice Field "formulated his jurisdictional inquiry by asking what power a state has over people inside and outside its boundaries, rather than asking when defendants are subject to personal jurisdiction").

of the United States. That document does several things. For present purposes, it creates the federal government by vesting in that government powers otherwise belonging to the people and the states. States ceded some of their powers to create the federal government. Thus, Justice Field said in *Pennoyer*, "[t]he several States of the Union are not, it is true, in every respect independent, many of the rights and powers which originally belonged to them being now vested in the government created by the Constitution."[36] The states of the United States possess authority of independent (international) states "except as restrained and limited" by the Constitution.

Thus, states of the United States do not have *unfettered* power over persons and things inside their boundaries. The Constitution limits their power. One such limitation (emanating from the principles of full faith and credit, enforceable through a direct challenge made on the basis of due process) is that a state may not enter a judgment unless it has a proper jurisdictional predicate. According to *Pennoyer*, a state can exercise QIR-2 jurisdiction only if it seizes the property serving as the jurisdictional predicate at the *outset* of the case. Because this was not done, the judgment in *Mitchell v. Neff* was unconstitutional and thus void. Accordingly, the sheriff's deed to Mitchell was void, which means that Mitchell's deed to Pennoyer was void. Neff won.[37]

What the Opinion Said About In Personam *Jurisdiction*

The opinion in *Pennoyer* is famous and influential for more than its narrow holding about the constitutional need to seize property at the outset in QIR-2 cases. Concerning *in personam* cases—"where the entire object of the action is to determine the personal rights and

---

[36] 95 U.S. at 722.

[37] Notice what this means in the human drama. Mitchell bought the property for about $300. He sold it to Pennoyer for many times that amount (about $15,000). Because of the holding by the Supreme Court, however, Pennoyer lost the land for which he spent so much money. Who was to blame? Not Neff, an illiterate homesteader who, by all accounts, was an honorable man. Not Pennoyer, who was a beloved figure in Oregon history, and went on to serve as governor of the state. Mitchell is the bad guy. He was a Pennsylvania lawyer who abandoned his wife and left the East Coast with a good deal of his clients' money (and with his mistress) and went to Oregon. There, he married his mistress without divorcing his first wife. He became a successful land lawyer in Oregon but also a scandalous member of the community. A local paper published the love letters he wrote to his second wife's younger sister. Interestingly, his personal life did not keep him from serving as a United States Senator from Oregon. He was convicted of land fraud (unrelated to the *Pennoyer* case) and sentenced to jail; he died while the case was on appeal. For a fascinating and entertaining account of the characters involved in this great case, *see* Wendy Collins Perdue, *Sin, Scandal, and Substantive Due Process: Personal Jurisdiction and* Pennoyer *Reconsidered*, 62 Wash. L. Rev. 479 (1987).

obligations of the defendants"[38]—*Pennoyer* set forth what are still considered the "traditional bases" of jurisdiction. Early in the opinion, when discussing the relevant Oregon statute, the Court mentioned three such bases.

First, a defendant can be subject to *in personam* jurisdiction if she "appear[s] in the court."[39] This basis is generally known as *consent*. As we noted in §2.1, a defendant may waive the constitutional protection from being sued in a forum that does not have personal jurisdiction. Accordingly, she can consent to jurisdiction in any state. As we see in §6.2, sometimes such consent is voluntary, and sometimes it is the result of waiver—that is, failing to object appropriately to an attempted exercise of jurisdiction. There is no question to this day that a defendant can consent to personal jurisdiction in any state.

Second, *Pennoyer* recognized that a state may exercise *in personam* jurisdiction over "a resident thereof."[40] After all, if someone resides in the forum, that person is within the boundaries of the state and thus subject to the power of the state's courts. Again, there is no doubt to this day that states have *in personam* jurisdiction over those who have this sort of ongoing association with the forum. It is likely that Justice Field intended to connote not simple residence but the concept of "domicile." In a later case (*Milliken v. Meyer*, decided in 1940 and discussed in §2.4.2), the Court spoke of jurisdiction based on "domicile" rather than "residence." We define and discuss domicile in detail in §4.5.3, regarding a different issue. In short, a person has only one domicile, and cannot have more than one. It is established by presence there plus forming the subjective intent to make that her home for the foreseeable future. It remains the person's domicile until she establishes a new one elsewhere. Residence generally is a more fleeting concept, and a person can have more than one residence. For instance, suppose you are domiciled in State A and attend law school in State B, with which you previously had no contact. You intend, after law school, to return to State A. Though you may now reside in State B, you are probably still domiciled in State A. In all likelihood, in *Pennoyer*, the Court meant that one is subject to jurisdiction where she is domiciled.

Third, a state has *in personam* jurisdiction over a defendant "found within the State."[41] Generally, this is referred to as "presence" as the basis of jurisdiction. There is nothing wrong with using that shorthand expression if we understand that it does not envision jurisdiction

---

[38]95 U.S. at 727. See also §2.2.
[39]95 U.S. at 720.
[40]*Id.*
[41]95 U.S. at 720.

based simply on the fact that the defendant was present in the forum once upon a time. Rather, she must be *served with process while present* in the forum. This is sometimes called "tag"[42] or "transient" jurisdiction.

In addition, later in the opinion, the Court noted another basis for *in personam* jurisdiction. The Court confirmed that a state may "require a nonresident entering into a partnership or association within its limits, or making contracts enforceable there, to appoint an agent or representative in the State to receive service of process" for cases involving that business.[43] This may actually be seen as an amalgam of two bases already seen: consent and presence. A state may require an individual or business, in exchange for the privilege of conducting business in the forum, to appoint someone to receive service of process in that state. A defendant who does so may be consenting to jurisdiction or the case may involve the "constructive" presence of the defendant in the state. By and large, a person can have an agent perform various functions for her. Thus, appointing an agent for service of process in another state may be seen as the defendant's being present in that state through an agent. These notions are developed further in §2.4.2.

The Need for a Jurisdictional Predicate and for Notice to the Defendant

In *Pennoyer*, the Court made clear that the Constitution (due process and full faith and credit) requires not only a jurisdictional predicate, but also that the defendant be given notice and an opportunity to defend herself in the forum. We will discuss the constitutional requirement of notice in §3.2. For now, it is enough to understand that the Constitution requires both personal jurisdiction and appropriate notice. We will see in §3.4 that notice problems arise in a variety of situations. For now, it is enough to focus on the classic method for giving notice to a defendant that she has been sued: service of *process*.[44] As we saw in §2.1 (and will see in greater detail in §3.3), process consists

---

[42]Professor Silberman coined the term "tag" jurisdiction for one served with process in the forum. Linda J. Silberman, Shaffer v. Heitner: *The End of an Era*, 53 N.Y.U. L. Rev. 33, 75 (1978).

[43]95 U.S. at 735.

[44]Service of process remains the classic method by which a defendant is notified that she has been sued. It is not clear that due process requires service of process to perform that function; that is, a less formal method of imparting notice might suffice constitutionally. But old habits die hard and today the applicable rules continue to require formal service of process to serve the function of providing the initial notice to a defendant of the suit against her. *See* Robin J. Effron, note 10 above, 74 N.Y.U. Ann. Surv. Am. Law at 23 (2018).

of a copy of the complaint and a summons, which is the document symbolizing the court's exercise of power over the defendant.

The *Pennoyer* Court drew a sharp distinction between two general types of service of process: personal service and "constructive" service. The former is exactly what it sounds like: The defendant is given (personally) the requisite papers. Constructive service refers to something short of personal service. One example of constructive service is by publication, in which notice is published in a newspaper of general circulation in the forum. Mitchell arranged for such constructive notice in *Mitchell v. Neff*.

According to *Pennoyer*, personal service is absolutely required for *in personam* cases. Moreover, because the Court stressed that a court cannot have a direct effect outside the state boundary, "[p]rocess from the tribunals of one State cannot run into another State, and summon parties there domiciled to leave its territory and respond to proceedings against them."[45] Under *Pennoyer*, then, the only proper form of *notice* for an *in personam* case is personal service of process on the defendant (or her agent) in the forum state.

Oddly, when we think about it, this form of notice subsumes the various jurisdictional predicates for *in personam* jurisdiction. Remember that the Court recognized consent and residence as predicates for jurisdiction, in addition to service of process on the defendant (or her agent) in the forum. If, however, the only notice that can be used is service of process in the forum, the predicates of consent and residence seem superfluous.

> ○ ***Example #7.*** Suppose *P* wants to sue *D* in Oregon, and that *D* is domiciled in Oregon. We know that her domicile in Oregon gives Oregon a jurisdictional predicate for *in personam* jurisdiction over *D*. But the only way to give notice, at least according to *Pennoyer*, is to serve process on *D* in Oregon. Thus, why not just use that basis (presence when served) as the jurisdictional predicate?

We will see in succeeding sections that the Supreme Court will relent on the requirement that process be served in the forum state. The day will come when process from one state can reach into another.

As we saw above, the jurisdictional predicate for QIR-2 (and, by implication, for QIR-1 and true *in rem* cases) is the attachment of the property by the court in the forum at the outset of the proceedings. The notice requirement may then be satisfied by constructive notice, such as publication in a newspaper. Even here, there is some overlap of functions. The Court indicated that the seizure of the property itself will also give notice. As Justice Field said, "The law assumes

---

[45] 95 U.S. at 727.

that property is always in the possession of its owner, in person or by agent; and it proceeds upon the theory that its seizure will inform him . . . that he must look to . . . proceedings authorized by law . . . ."[46] Such "notice" is pretty fictive. So it must, according to the Court, be augmented by publication notice. *Pennoyer* made it clear, however, that publication notice would not suffice in an *in personam* case.

Cases Involving Status

Relatively late in the opinion, the Court in *Pennoyer* affirms that a state may "authorize proceedings to determine the status of one of its citizens toward a nonresident, which would be binding within the State, though made without service of process or personal notice to the nonresident."[47] It then discusses the best example of such a status case: divorce proceedings. A suit for divorce is not a proceeding *in personam*. Rather, it is litigation to determine the interests of persons (the spouses) in the "thing" of marriage. Thus, it is in the nature of an *in rem* or QIR-1 case. The fact that one spouse resides in the forum permits that person to maintain the divorce proceeding without having to serve process on the other party in the state. Publication notice will suffice—again, because this is not an *in personam* proceeding.

This result is dictated by practical reality. If divorce were an *in personam* proceeding, one spouse could prevent the other from getting a divorce simply by moving to another state. It is in everyone's interest to allow the resident spouse to maintain the case in the forum. Note, however, that only the status issue can be determined in this way. If one spouse sought recovery of money from the other (e.g., alimony or child support), the court would have to be able to exercise *in personam* jurisdiction.[48]

Some Hypotheticals

Let's apply the law according to *Pennoyer* to some fact patterns.

     ○ ***Example #8.*** *P* sues *D* in Oregon. *D* is served with process in Oregon but refuses to participate in the litigation. The Oregon court enters a default judgment in favor of *P* for $10,000. Is the judgment valid?[49]

---

[46]*Id.*

[47]*Id.* at 734.

[48]Or QIR-2 over some property in the forum owned by the nonresident spouse.

[49]Yes. The Oregon court had the jurisdictional predicate of presence in the forum when service was effected. Notice consisted of service of process in the forum.

○ ***Example #9.*** *P* sues *D* in Oregon. *D* is served with process while in California, just over the boundary from Oregon. *D* refuses to participate in the litigation. The Oregon court enters a default judgment in favor of *P* for $10,000. Is the judgment valid?[50]

○ ***Example #10.*** *P* sues *D* in Oregon. *P* has an officer go to serve process on *D* in Oregon. As the officer approaches *D*, however, *D* steps over the boundary from Oregon into California. The officer goes to the California side of the boundary and punches *D* in the nose, rendering *D* unconscious. The officer then drags *D* across the border into Oregon. When *D* regains consciousness, the officer serves process on *D*. Does Oregon have *in personam* jurisdiction over *D*?

We are tempted to say no, because we are outraged by the officer's behavior. But does *Pennoyer* say anything at all about *how* a defendant becomes present in the forum? No. Does it say anything at all about whether the exercise of jurisdiction is "fair"? No. It talks about power over people and things within the state. *D* was present in the forum when served with process. Obviously, *D* can sue the officer for committing a tort.[51] Moreover, the officer committed a crime by punching *D*, so the state could prosecute the officer for the crime.[52] Is there anything in *Pennoyer*, however, that indicates that these facts should matter when it comes to the question of whether Oregon has jurisdiction over *D*?

It is probable, under the *Pennoyer* power principle, that Oregon *would* have *in personam* jurisdiction over *D*. After all, *D* was served within the forum, and that's all the Supreme Court required. On the other hand, there is nothing that *requires* Oregon courts to exercise such jurisdiction.

In cases such as these, courts routinely invoked what came to be called the "force and fraud exception" to jurisdiction. This exception recognized that the state could constitutionally exercise personal jurisdiction, but that, under the circumstances, it would be unseemly to do so. Thus, the court refuses to countenance the bad behavior by the officer. Think about the theoretical difference between saying (1) there is no jurisdiction and (2) there is jurisdiction but the court refuses to exercise it. Because nothing in *Pennoyer* says anything about fairness, it seems the second option is the more accurate reflection of the "force and fraud exception."

---

[50]No. Service was not effected in the forum. *Pennoyer* requires that the defendant be served with process in an *in personam* case inside the forum state. The Oregon court has no power in California.

[51]By the way, where would *D* sue the officer, California or Oregon?

[52]By the way, which state would prosecute? Did the officer commit a crime in California? In Oregon? In both?

   o **_Example #11._** *H* and *W* are married, living in Pennsylvania. *H* abandons *W* and moves to Oregon. *W* sues *H* for divorce in Pennsylvania. *H* cannot be served with process personally in Pennsylvania. Notice is given only by publication. The Pennsylvania court enters a judgment declaring the couple divorced. Is the judgment valid?

Yes. This is not an *in personam* case. Rather, it is one to determine the status of persons in a thing: the marriage. The opinion in *Pennoyer* makes it plain that states must have the authority to render such binding judgments based on the residence of one of the parties to the marriage in the state.

   o **_Example #12._** Same case, and in addition to a decree of divorce, *W* seeks an order that *H* pay her $500 per month in alimony and child support. Can the Pennsylvania court validly enter such an order based on publication notice?[53]

   o **_Example #13._** *P* sues *D* for damages of $10,000 in Oregon. *D* is not present in Oregon. *P* has the court attach property belonging to *D*, and present in Oregon. The attachment is made at the outset of the suit. Notice is given by publication. *D* defaults. The court enters judgment in favor of *P* for $10,000. Is the judgment valid?

Yes, but only to the extent of the value of the property attached. This is a QIR-2 case. The jurisdictional predicate of attaching the property at the outset of the case is satisfied, as is the requirement of publication notice. The value of the property will be established at the public auction.

§2.4.2 Stretching *Pennoyer*: *Harris v. Balk*, *Hess v. Pawloski*, and Others

The Supreme Court decided *Pennoyer* in 1878, during the horse-and-buggy era. In the ensuing decades, the horse and buggy gave way to the automobile and the airplane. It became easier to go into a state, have an impact there (maybe by committing a tort or breaching a contract), and to get out before being served with process there. Yet, under *Pennoyer*, one could only get *in personam* jurisdiction in limited ways: residence, consent, presence in the forum when served with process, or presence of an agent in the forum for service of process.

---

[53]No. The requested relief, requiring *H* to pay money, goes beyond a determination of status. *W* is seeking to impose a personal obligation on *H*. But *W* cannot sue *H* *in personam* in Pennsylvania without serving process on *H* in Pennsylvania, which is impossible on these facts.

Thus, if one wanted to sue a nonresident of the forum—and if the nonresident did not have an agent in the forum and would not consent to jurisdiction—one had to be able to serve process on the nonresident in the forum. The wily defendant could easily avoid jurisdiction by getting out and staying out of the forum.

Something had to give. The Supreme Court had to expand the availability of personal jurisdiction to adapt to modern realities. Eventually, as seen in §2.4.3, in the mid-twentieth century, the Court recast the basic personal jurisdiction inquiry. Before that, however, in the early part of that century, the Court expanded the availability of personal jurisdiction by stretching the principles established in *Pennoyer*. There are three principal areas in which the Court stretched *Pennoyer*: (1) QIR-2, (2) *in personam* involving businesses, and (3) *in personam* involving individuals.

QIR-2 Expansion: Harris v. Balk

In cases in which *in personam* jurisdiction was impossible because the defendant could not be served with process in the forum, *Pennoyer* permitted QIR-2. As long as the defendant had property in the forum, it was attached at the outset of the case, and the defendant was given at least publication notice, a QIR-2 judgment would be valid. The only example we have seen (*Mitchell v. Neff*) involved attachment of the defendant's land in the forum.[54] Nothing in *Pennoyer*, however, limited QIR-2 to jurisdiction over land, or even over *tangible* property.

The Supreme Court expanded the availability of QIR-2 jurisdiction in 1905 in *Harris v. Balk*.[55] In that case, Balk owed money to Epstein. Epstein wanted to sue Balk to recover the money, but he wanted to sue in Baltimore (Epstein's home), rather than going to North Carolina, where Balk lived. Epstein could only proceed *in personam* against Balk in Maryland, though, if he could serve process on Balk there. Balk did not go anywhere near Maryland, so *in personam* was out of the question. What about QIR-2? Balk seemed safe from suit in Maryland on that score as well, because he did not own any property in that state. But here's where Balk was in for a surprise. A man named Harris happened to owe money to Balk. When someone owes money to you, you have a property right (the debt). You can try to enforce that property right by suing on the debt. That right to sue to enforce the debt is

---

[54]Remember, however, that the attachment was defective because it was not undertaken at the outset of the case. This was the reason the judgment in *Mitchell v. Neff* was struck down in *Pennoyer v. Neff*. See §2.4.1.

[55]198 U.S. 215 (1905).

"property" of yours, but it is intangible property. You cannot touch it or see it, but it is there.

Harris went to Maryland. Epstein somehow heard about this and brought suit against Balk (QIR-2) to recover the money Balk owed him. But he needed to attach some property of Balk's. Epstein had Harris served with process in Baltimore and asked the Maryland court to make Harris place the property (the money he owed Balk) in the registry of the court. Harris did so. Epstein then had it attached at the outset of the case and proceeded QIR-2 against Balk. The Supreme Court upheld QIR-2 jurisdiction.

The upshot of *Harris v. Balk* is that QIR-2 jurisdiction can be exercised even over *intangible* property. When Harris went to Maryland, the debt he owed to Balk (which was intangible property belonging to Balk) also "went" to Maryland. Thus, property of Balk's was in Maryland. Epstein attached it by suing Balk under QIR-2 and having Harris served with process for the sole purpose of making Harris surrender the money he owed to Balk.[56] Once Harris did that, that money (which belonged to Balk) was attached as the jurisdictional predicate for the QIR-2 proceeding against Balk. It's brilliant, and it's completely consistent with *Pennoyer*.

Notice how the holding in *Harris* makes it more difficult for someone to avoid being sued in another state. Before *Harris*, someone in Balk's position could avoid jurisdiction in another state simply by (1) refusing to go to the state and (2) making sure she did not own property in that state. After *Harris*, however, one can be sued under QIR-2 wherever her debtor happens to go.

The Supreme Court did not address QIR-2 jurisdiction again for 72 years, when it decided *Shaffer v. Heitner*.[57] In that case, discussed in §2.4.4, the Court overruled *Harris v. Balk*. But let's not get ahead of ourselves. The point now is to understand how the Court in the early twentieth century expanded personal jurisdiction by stretching concepts from *Pennoyer*.

---

[56]The court holds what is often called a proceeding *in garnishment* to seize Balk's property, which happens to be in the hands of Harris. (We discuss garnishment in §3.5.) Harris could have contended that he owed Balk nothing and litigated that issue. As it turns out, he admitted his debt to Balk and deposited the money in the court in Maryland. Because the Maryland court's QIR-2 judgment against Balk was valid, Balk was precluded from suing Harris to recover the debt. Harris had already paid the debt by surrendering it to the court in Maryland.

[57]433 U.S. 186 (1977). *See* Linda J. Silberman, Shaffer v. Heitner: *The End of an Era*, 53 N.Y.U. L. Rev. 33, 75 (1978).

In Personam *Expansion Regarding Businesses*

In the nineteenth century, it was clear that a corporation could be sued in the state in which it was incorporated.[58] Thus, if a corporation was formed ("chartered") in Pennsylvania, there was no question that it was subject to *in personam* jurisdiction in Pennsylvania. There was some doubt, however, about whether the corporation could be sued in another state. For a long time, this uncertainty did not impose great hardship, because corporations usually were engaged only in local, intrastate business. In the late nineteenth century, however, this began to change. Increased industrialization and concentration of wealth in corporate hands, along with increased opportunities to travel, vastly increased the interstate transaction of business by corporations and other forms of business. As it became more likely that a Pennsylvania corporation might do business in Virginia, the desire to sue the Pennsylvania business in Virginia also increased.

In *Pennoyer*, the Court suggested that states could essentially coerce *in personam* jurisdiction from businesses formed in another state by requiring them to appoint agents for service of process. The appointment of a local agent was a *quid pro quo*—that is, it was made in exchange for being allowed to do business in the state. Then, at least in cases arising from the transaction of that business, a plaintiff could have process served upon the agent and force the out-of-state business to defend in the forum. The result is consistent with *Pennoyer*: The jurisdictional predicate is consent and notice is given by serving process on the defendant's agent within the forum state.

But what gives a state the authority to coerce the appointment of an agent for service of process? In the case of the corporation, the answer has long been clear: One state can deny a corporation formed in another state to enter. Thus, Virginia can simply exclude a Pennsylvania corporation from entering into business deals in Virginia. Why? Because the Privileges and Immunities Clause of the Constitution (Article IV, §2) does not apply to corporations.[59] That clause, which provides that the citizens of one state "shall be entitled to all privileges and immunities of citizens in the several states," means (roughly)[60] that

---

[58]A corporation is a business form that is seen as an entity—separate from the people who own it and those who run it. The entity comes into existence only upon the satisfaction of the formation requirements, which each state is free to prescribe. A corporation is usually formed in a single state, and then seeks permission to do business in other states. Not all business is transacted by corporations. There are other business structures, including the partnership. Historically, the partnership was not seen as an entity unto itself, but as an amalgam of its partners.

[59]Paul v. Virginia, 75 U.S. 168, 177 (1869).

[60]This aspect of privileges and immunities is studied in the course on Constitutional Law.

Virginia must accord to Pennsylvanians the privileges and immunities it accords its own citizens. But, again, the clause does not apply to corporations. That is why Virginia could bar a Pennsylvania corporation from doing business in Virginia. And if it can exclude the corporation altogether, it has the lesser power of permitting the corporation to enter, *conditioned upon* its appointment of an agent for service of process and its consenting to *in personam* jurisdiction.[61]

But states encountered a problem in this regard in the early twentieth century. Then, though the Privileges and Immunities Clause does not apply to corporations, the Supreme Court concluded that a different part of the Constitution, the Commerce Clause, prohibited a state from excluding a corporation that was engaged in "interstate commerce" within its boundaries.[62] In other words, if a Pennsylvania corporation's activities in Virginia were part of interstate commerce (as opposed to local activity), Virginia could not exclude the corporation. If Virginia could not exclude the Pennsylvania corporation, how could Virginia condition its activities on the appointment of an agent for service of process and on its consenting to *in personam* jurisdiction?

The answer came by an ingenious shifting of emphasis from consent to another basis of *in personam* jurisdiction under *Pennoyer*. In *International Harvester Co. v. Kentucky*,[63] the defendant corporation (formed outside of Kentucky) set up business in Kentucky very deliberately, in an effort to qualify as the transaction of interstate business. The corporation contended that Kentucky thus had no authority to exclude it and, accordingly, no authority to coerce its consent to jurisdiction. The Supreme Court upheld jurisdiction over the corporation in Kentucky. True, jurisdiction could not be based on consent. But, the Court held, the corporation was *present* in Kentucky, and jurisdiction could be upheld on that *Pennoyer* basis. Thus, when consent as a basis for jurisdiction was made unavailable, presence stepped in to fill the void.

The Supreme Court then embarked on a series of decisions in which it discussed how much activity was required to find an out-of-state corporation to be "present" in a particular state.[64] Over time, courts got sloppy and started talking about whether an out-of-state corporation was "doing business" in the forum. If it was, they concluded, the corporation was subject to *in personam* jurisdiction. Why was this

---

[61]*See* Lafayette Ins. Co. v. French, 59 U.S. 404, 407 (1855) ("A corporation created by Indiana can transact business in Ohio only with the consent, express or implied, of the latter state. This consent may be accompanied by such conditions as Ohio may think fit to impose").

[62]International Textbook Co. v. Prigg, 217 U.S. 91 (1910).

[63]234 U.S. 579 (1914).

[64]*See, e.g.*, People's Tobacco Co. v. American Tobacco Co., 246 U.S. 79, 87 (1918).

sloppy? Because *Pennoyer* did not say that "doing business" was a basis for *in personam* jurisdiction. Rather, as we saw in §2.4.1, it gave four traditional bases for such jurisdiction: presence, consent, residence, or presence of an agent. But the phrase took hold, and in thousands of opinions courts wrestled with what constitutes "doing business." We see this point again in our discussion of the *International Shoe* case in §2.4.3.

In Personam *Expansion Regarding Individuals:* Hess v. Pawloski

We have just seen that a state may, at least in some instances, coerce a corporation to consent to jurisdiction. Again, this authority flows from the fact that the Privileges and Immunities Clause does not apply to corporations. There is no question, however, that the Privileges and Immunities Clause does apply to individuals, so a state does not have the blanket authority to exclude a human from entering it. But this fact did not stop states from attempting to base *in personam* jurisdiction on notions of implied consent. The Supreme Court upheld such an effort in 1927 in the famous case of *Hess v. Pawloski*.[65]

In that case, Hess, a citizen of Pennsylvania, drove his car in Massachusetts, where he was involved in an auto wreck with Pawloski, a citizen of Massachusetts. Pawloski sued Hess in an *in personam* action in Massachusetts, seeking damages for harm suffered in the wreck. He did not sue, however, until after Hess had returned to Pennsylvania. Thus, Hess could not be served with process in Massachusetts. But Massachusetts had a statute that allowed its courts to exercise *in personam* jurisdiction over nonresidents involved in a motor vehicle collision in Massachusetts. The statute provided that by operating a motor vehicle in Massachusetts, the nonresident consented to jurisdiction and to the appointment of a Massachusetts state official (the registrar of motor vehicles) as her agent for service of process. It also provided that the plaintiff must serve process on the state official and that a copy of the process be sent to the nonresident at his residence. Pawloski followed the statute diligently, served process on the state officer, and ensured that a copy of process was mailed to Hess in Pennsylvania.

Such nonresident motorist statutes are ubiquitous today. Before discussing the constitutionality of *in personam* jurisdiction over Hess in Massachusetts, we should note that such statutes provide for what we will call "specific jurisdiction" (or "case-linked" jurisdiction). That means that jurisdiction is created only for a claim that arises out of

[65]274 U.S. 352 (1927).

or related to some activity within the forum; it created *in personam* jurisdiction over Hess, but *only* for the motor vehicle crash. This specific jurisdiction is to be contrasted with "*general* jurisdiction," under which a defendant can be sued in the forum for a claim that arose anywhere in the world. We revisit this theme in §2.4.5. *Hess* simply provides our first example of specific jurisdiction. *Pennoyer* did not make any such distinction between specific and general jurisdiction.

In *Hess*, the Court upheld *in personam* jurisdiction in Massachusetts (and, in so doing, paved the way (so to speak) for all states to pass such nonresident motorist statutes). Citing *Pennoyer*, the Court said that "process of a court in one State cannot run into another."[66] But notice how nicely crafted the Massachusetts statute was: It did not permit service of process in Pennsylvania. Rather, the process was served in Massachusetts, on Hess's *agent* (the registrar of motor vehicles). Of course, service on the defendant's agent was allowed by *Pennoyer*. Moreover, the jurisdictional predicate was Hess's consent, which also is recognized by *Pennoyer*.

But how did Hess consent to jurisdiction in Massachusetts? By operating his motor vehicle there. And how does a state have the right to coerce such consent? Interestingly, the Court held, though the Privileges and Immunities Clause means that a state cannot exclude an individual from entering a state, *it can exclude her from entering in a motor vehicle*. In *Kane v. New Jersey*,[67] Justice Oliver Wendell Holmes, writing for the Court, concluded that the state interest in highway safety justified a state's excluding a motorist who refused to appoint a local officer as agent for service of process for actions arising from the operation of the motor vehicle. Accordingly, the Court in *Hess* concluded, the state may simply allow the motorist to enter on condition that she thereby impliedly consents to *in personam* jurisdiction and to the appointment of a local agent for service of process.

Hess is brilliant. Notice how it is consistent with *Pennoyer*: The jurisdictional predicate is consent and the notice consists of service of process *within the forum* on the defendant's agent. In *Hess* and similar cases, the Court adapted *Pennoyer* to the more mobile world. It pushed the idea of consent to include implied consent. And it seized upon the idea of service of process upon the defendant's agent in the forum to include an agent appointed by operation of law.[68]

---

[66]*Id.* at 355.

[67]242 U.S. 160, 167 (1916).

[68]Among other things, the Court in *Hess* justified the result by noting that its holding tended to put nonresident motorists on the same footing with residents. By this it meant that a Massachusetts resident, involved in a motor vehicle wreck in Massachusetts, could be sued in that state based on her residence there. Remember, residence is a basis of *in personam* jurisdiction under *Pennoyer*.

Though we are about to embark on a tour of the modern era of personal jurisdiction, we should note that nonresident motorist statutes operate in every state every day. Every time you have driven across a state line, you have, by operation of law, consented to being sued in that state concerning a motor vehicle crash and you have appointed a state officer as your agent for service of process in such a case.

In 1940, the Court decided a case that serves as a bridge from *Pennoyer* to the modern era. In *Milliken v. Meyer*,[69] the Court upheld *in personam* jurisdiction based upon the defendant's domicile in the forum. As was suggested in discussing *Pennoyer* above and we will see in detail in §4.5.3, a person has only one domicile at a time; it is the state in which she has been present and that she intends to make her permanent home. A person retains her domicile until she acquires another one. Domicile in this sense is probably what the *Pennoyer* Court had in mind when it spoke of a state having *in personam* jurisdiction over its "residents." As the Court made clear in *Milliken*, there is a *quid pro quo*: When someone takes up domicile in a state, she gets certain privileges and benefits from the state. It is only fair, in return, that the domiciliary be amenable to jurisdiction in the state's courts.[70]

Significantly, *Milliken* upheld *in personam* jurisdiction over a domiciliary *even though the defendant was not personally served with process in the forum*. The case involved a domiciliary of the forum who was absent from the state.[71] The Court required only a "reasonable method" for apprising the defendant of the action, which was satisfied by service of process on the defendant outside the forum state. Thus, we see an important weakening of the seemingly inflexible requirement in *Pennoyer* that notice of an *in personam* case consists only of service of process in the forum state. *Milliken* opens the door for *in personam* jurisdiction based upon service of process where the defendant is found at the time, even though that is not in the forum state. In other words, process can cross state lines. We turn now to the modern era, which started about eight decades ago.

---

[69]311 U.S. 457 (1940).

[70]On the other hand, it is certainly conceivable that one could establish a sufficient tie with a state of residence (even if not her domicile) to justify the exercise of *in personam* jurisdiction. For instance, a student or member of the military might reside for several years in a state that she does not consider her domicile.

[71]This can happen easily. Remember, a person has only one domicile at a time. For example, suppose a domiciliary of Illinois moves to California for four years to attend college, but has no desire to make California her permanent home. She is still a domiciliary of Illinois, even though she is absent from Illinois for years.

§2.4.3   Dawn of the Modern Era: *International Shoe*

In 1945, the Supreme Court decided *International Shoe Co. v. Washington*,[72] which ushered in the modern era in personal jurisdiction jurisprudence. Judges, lawyers, professors, and students have spent the ensuing decades trying to figure out (1) what *International Shoe* means and (2) whether it was intended to replace *Pennoyer* or to exist alongside *Pennoyer*.

The International Shoe Company (Shoe) manufactured shoes in St. Louis. The question in the case was whether the company was amenable to *in personam* jurisdiction in Washington for a proceeding brought by the state to force the company to pay unemployment tax there.[73] Lawyers for Shoe had structured the company's activities in Washington very carefully, in an effort to avoid *in personam* jurisdiction there. For instance, Shoe did not own land in Washington, but would occasionally rent rooms in which to display shoe samples. It permitted salesmen to show only one shoe of a pair; the argument was that by failing to ship an entire pair, Shoe was not really doing business in Washington. In addition, though Shoe employed salesmen who resided in the state and were paid on commission, the salesmen had no authority to accept offers. Rather, they forwarded the offers to St. Louis, where all decisions were made. Moreover, the shoes were shipped "f.o.b." from St. Louis. This means "free on board," which requires the buyer to pay the freight charges to get the shoes from St. Louis to the buyer's home. Thus, Shoe argued, it did not ship anything into Washington and should not be held amenable to jurisdiction there.

At the end of §2.4.2, we saw that courts had strayed a bit from the *Pennoyer* bases of jurisdiction when addressing *in personam* jurisdiction over businesses. Instead of adhering to the bases provided by *Pennoyer*, they had come to base jurisdiction on whether the corporation was "doing business" in the forum. Through the years, the courts had found that a corporation that had engaged in soliciting business in the forum "plus some additional activities" there would be deemed to be doing business and thus would be amenable to *in personam* jurisdiction there. In *International Shoe*, the Supreme Court of Washington held that Shoe had engaged in "solicitation plus other activities" and

---

[72]326 U.S. 310 (1945).

[73]Each state has an unemployment compensation system, which is funded by a tax on businesses in the state. Shoe contended that it did not have to pay the tax because it was not doing business in Washington. The state sued Shoe to collect the tax. The question of whether Washington had personal jurisdiction over Shoe is the same for this action as it would have been for any *in personam* case against Shoe.

thus could be sued there under this theory. The Supreme Court of the United States upheld jurisdiction in Washington, but recast the jurisdictional inquiry in very famous terms.

The Court cited *Pennoyer* in noting that "historically," *in personam* jurisdiction was "grounded on [a court's] de facto power over the defendant's person. Hence his presence within the territorial jurisdiction of a court was prerequisite to its rendition of a judgment personally binding him."[74] Now, however, that we no longer are required to arrest the civil defendant,

> due process requires only that . . . to subject a defendant to a judgment *in personam*, if he be not present within the territory of the forum, he have certain minimum contacts with it such that the maintenance of the suit does not offend traditional notions of fair play and substantial justice.[75]

This is the famous *International Shoe* (or, as many people call it, "minimum contacts") test for whether the exercise of personal jurisdiction is constitutional. Although about eight decades have come and gone, we are still trying to interpret that phrase. As we undertake this journey, it is helpful to keep four points in mind:

(1) Now here in this passage or elsewhere did the Court purport to overrule *Pennoyer*. Thus, the question arises: Is the *International Shoe* formulation merely an alternative to *Pennoyer*, or does it replace *Pennoyer*?

(2) Notice that the Court sets out the "minimum contacts" language only *after* referring to the case in which the defendant "be not present within the territory of the forum." This seems to imply that "presence within the territory of the forum" remains a viable basis for the exercise of *in personam* jurisdiction. If so, perhaps the minimum contacts test was intended as an *alternative* to the defendant's presence in the forum as a basis for jurisdiction.

---

[74]326 U.S. at 316.

[75]*Id.* (internal quotation omitted). The Court quoted *Milliken v. Meyer*, discussed in §2.4.2, for the language "traditional notions of fair play and substantial justice." *Milliken* upheld *in personam* jurisdiction over a domiciliary of the forum even without personal service in the forum.

Note the clear statement that "due process requires" at the beginning of the quotation. This signals a shift in the role of the Due Process Clause. In *Pennoyer*, it was seen as a vehicle for challenging a court's illegitimate assertion of authority, and not as the source of standards for determining legitimacy. Those standards derived from full faith and credit and the nature of the state as sovereign. Now, due process is seen as the source of substantive rules for assessing jurisdiction. Perdue, note 31 above, 63 S.C. L. Rev. at 733-734 (discussing "the transformation of due process from a mechanism to allow a direct challenge of jurisdiction to the source of substantive standards by which to assess such a challenge. . .").

As we see in §2.4.4, the Supreme Court finally addressed this issue in 1990 (and failed to resolve it definitively).

(3) The phrase seems to consist of two parts: one about "contacts" and the other about "fair play." We will see that the Court did come to consider the formulation as embodying two prongs of analysis: one about contact and the other about fairness (sometimes called reasonableness).

(4) There is not a single term in the famous phrase that anyone can define. What are "minimum contacts?" What are "traditional notions?" What is "fair play and substantial justice?" The majority opinion itself admits that the inquiry "cannot be simply mechanical or quantitative," but must be more nuanced.

Let's be honest: The quoted words are weasel phrases; they can mean almost anything to anyone. Justice Black's concurring opinion in *International Shoe* makes this point. He concurred with the result in the case because he thought Washington clearly had *in personam* jurisdiction over Shoe. He decried the Court's use of "vague Constitutional criteria" and "uncertain elements" as confusing a simple case. On this score, Justice Black was right: *International Shoe* introduces open-ended, imprecise language for determining whether the exercise of *in personam* jurisdiction is constitutional. This uncertainty is shown in subsequent cases discussed in §2.4.4. The Court's embrace of amorphous words created uncertainty and unpredictability.[76]

After laying out its famous test,[77] the *International Shoe* Court then discussed jurisdiction over a corporation by addressing when a corporation is "present" in the forum state. It put the word in quotations because a corporation is present anywhere only because of the activities of people working on its behalf. It then indicated that an "estimate of the inconveniences" imposed upon the defendant by jurisdiction in the forum was a relevant consideration and constructed a four-part model for when jurisdiction is appropriate. The model assessed two variables: (1) the level of activity of the defendant in the forum and (2) whether the claim asserted against the defendant is related to the defendant's activities in the forum. The *Pennoyer* regime did not deal

---

[76]Justice Black was worried that the weasel words would be used to limit state court *in personam* jurisdiction. This is why he discussed the Tenth Amendment, which retains for the states all powers not ceded to the federal government. He was concerned that the states' power to determine their jurisdiction could be usurped by the federal bench. In fact, however, *International Shoe* led to an expansion of jurisdiction, at least for some decades. Based upon cases decided in 2011 and after, the argument that the Court has unduly limited state jurisdiction is gaining a following.

[77]Though we may refer to the *International Shoe* test by the shorthand of "minimum contacts," remember that there are two components to it: contact *and* fairness. The relevant factors for each will become clearer through considering subsequent cases.

with such nuances: Either there was jurisdiction or there was not. Here, in contrast, we are to assess "the quality and nature of the [defendant's] activity in relation to the fair and orderly administration of the laws."[78]

We can plot the two variables on a chart. On the horizontal axis is the defendant's activity in the forum. The Court indicates that it might range from "casual" to "continuous and systematic." On the vertical axis is the relatedness of the claim asserted to the defendant's activity in the forum. The Court indicates that it might be "related" or "unrelated." The result is a chart with four boxes.

Box 1 is where the defendant has continuous and systematic activities in the forum and the claim arises from those activities. As the Court says, jurisdiction "has never been doubted" in such circumstances. An example would be a suit against Ford Motor Company in Michigan (where it has its world headquarters and manufactures many of its vehicles) on a claim arising from the manufacture of a vehicle in Michigan—for example, for an alleged defect in a car manufactured in Detroit. Thus, Box 1 is labeled "yes," because the forum will have *in personam* jurisdiction in such cases.

Box 2 is where the defendant has limited contact with the forum and the claim does not arise from that activity in the forum. As the Court says, it is "generally recognized" that such casual contacts with the forum "are not enough to subject [the defendant] to suit on causes of action unconnected with the activities there."[79] For instance, a defendant domiciliary of West Virginia, who has been to Hawaii once on vacation, could not be sued in Hawaii for a claim arising from her actions in West Virginia. Thus, Box 2 is labeled "no."

Box 3 involves a defendant with continuous and systematic activities in the forum, but who is sued on a claim unrelated to those activities.

	Casual → Continuous and Systematic
Box 2 NO	Box 3 MAYBE
Box 4 MAYBE	Box 1 YES

Relatedness (Related → Unrelated)

Casual → Continuous and Systematic
Level of Activity

The Court indicates that cases go both ways in this area. Sometimes the activity is not so substantial as to permit suit on an unrelated

[78]326 U.S. at 319.
[79]*Id.* at 317.

claim. On the other hand, "there have been instances in which the continuous corporate operations within a state were thought so substantial and of such a nature as to justify suit against it on causes of action arising from dealings entirely distinct from those activities."[80] This is a recognition of "general jurisdiction" (or "all-purpose" jurisdiction). The idea is that a defendant's contacts with the forum can be so substantial that the defendant can be sued there for a claim that arose anywhere in the world. An example might be a claim asserted against Ford Motor Company in Michigan for an alleged defect in a car built in Mexico. Another example is a suit against a West Virginia domiciliary in West Virginia involving a tort committed by her in Hawaii. (We will see in §2.4.5 that we are in a "new era" of general jurisdiction (which started in 2011), in which the Court has significantly narrowed the scope of general jurisdiction.) Box 3 is labeled "maybe" because sometimes there is jurisdiction in these circumstances and sometimes there is not.

Box 4 involves a defendant with casual contact with the forum, being sued there on a claim that arises from that contact. The Court says that this, like Box 3, is a "maybe" category. Some cases uphold jurisdiction and others do not. An example might be a suit in Hawaii against a West Virginia domiciliary for a tort allegedly committed in Hawaii. Again, because this is a "maybe" category, the difficulty is in determining what factors might cause a case to be on the "yes" side of "maybe" and what factors might cause a case to be on the "no" side of "maybe."

After going through these permutations, the Court in *International Shoe* finally addressed the facts of the case and concluded easily that Shoe was subject to *in personam* jurisdiction in Washington. The Court saw the case as falling into Box 1. It concluded that Shoe's contacts with the forum "were neither irregular nor casual . . . [but] were systematic and continuous."[81] In addition, the claim (liability for unemployment compensation tax) clearly arose directly from the company's activities in the forum. The Court also concluded that jurisdiction was fair on a *quid pro quo* basis: Shoe "received the benefits and protection of the laws of [Washington], including the right to resort to the courts for the enforcement of its rights."[82]

In sum, *International Shoe* was an easy case, and the Court could have addressed it in familiar terms. Instead, the Court went out of

[80]*Id.* at 318.

[81]*Id.* at 320. The Court gave no hint as to why this was true. Is it measured by an objective scale—say, for example, the generation of a certain number of dollars of revenue in a year? Or is it measured by a relative scale—say, for example, a certain percentage of the defendant's overall business activity? We still don't know for sure, as we see in §2.4.5.

[82]326 U.S. at 319-320. Won't this factor always be met? Everyone has the right of access to the courts to assert a claim.

its way to inject new (and uncertain) terms into the assessment of personal jurisdiction. Why? Perhaps the Justices felt it was time to recast the jurisdictional inquiry. It is always a good idea to look at the date of opinions you read, and to try to place the decision in a historical context. *International Shoe* was decided in 1945, toward the end of World War II. At that time, Americans were likely thinking of themselves more as Americans and less as Texans or Californians. After all, the country had just pulled together in an unprecedented effort. Moreover, interstate travel and interstate business were vastly increased. In sum, state lines probably meant less than they had in the past. The Court already had recognized that service of process can cross state lines and here it seems to want to expand the availability of personal jurisdiction. Rather than the rigid *Pennoyer* bases for *in personam* jurisdiction, the Court in *International Shoe* provides a grab-bag of flexible variables, to be assessed on the facts of each case.

It must have seemed quite clear, even in 1945, that the outcome of the jurisdictional inquiry had just become more difficult to predict. Think of your job as a lawyer after the Court decided *International Shoe*. Suppose a client asked you how she can avoid being amenable to *in personam* jurisdiction in a particular state. Under *Pennoyer*, you could give fairly concrete advice: "Do not go to the state and do not appoint an agent for service of process there." After *International Shoe*, what can you tell your client? Something like this: "Do not establish such minimum contacts with that state so that the exercise of jurisdiction would not offend traditional notions of fair play and substantial justice." We now address the Court's efforts to bring meaning to that famous phrase.

§2.4.4 Specific Jurisdiction from *International Shoe* Through 2014

In this section, we review major *specific* jurisdiction cases in which the Supreme Court has applied *International Shoe* through 2014. Remember, specific jurisdiction applies when the plaintiff's claim is related to the defendant's activities in the forum. At that point, in §2.4.5, we take a detour to see how the Court restricted *general* jurisdiction between 2011 and 2017. Remember, general jurisdiction applies when the plaintiff's claim does not relate to the defendant's activities in the forum. Then, in §2.4.6, we will return to two major specific jurisdiction cases decided in 2017 and 2021. These latter specific jurisdiction cases cannot be understood without studying the changes made in general jurisdiction between 2011 and 2017.

As we go through the cases, it is helpful to think of each decision as giving some hint, some relevant factor, for applying *International Shoe*. It is also helpful to remember that the law evolves. As we will see, for example, the Court started interpreting *International Shoe* by applying various factors *ad hoc* and moved to a very rigid two-step approach that by 2021 apparently became a three-step approach.

Decisions in the 1950s

After deciding *International Shoe* in 1945, the Court stayed out of personal jurisdiction jurisprudence for over a decade. Perhaps it wanted to let the state and lower federal courts try their hands at applying the new test. The Court's first important new pronouncement came in 1957, with *McGee v. International Life Insurance Co.*[83] There, a Californian (Insured) purchased a life insurance contract from an Arizona company. The Arizona company was acquired by a Texas company, which was required by law to honor the insurance contract held by Insured. It mailed a certificate of "reinsurance" to Insured, who continued to pay his premiums by mail from California to Texas. Thereafter, Insured died, and his mother (the beneficiary under the policy) made a demand for the insurance money. The insurance company refused to pay the claim; it argued that Insured had committed suicide, which voided the policy. The beneficiary sued the Texas insurance company in California to recover on the policy.

The Supreme Court held that California had *in personam* jurisdiction over the Texas insurance company, even though the defendant's only contact with California was this single insurance policy. The defendant never solicited or accepted any other business from California. Thus, jurisdiction can be based on a single contact with the forum. The Court applied what can be called a "mélange" approach, in which all relevant factors are thrown into the mix, with no single factor taking precedence.[84]

It emphasized three such factors. First, "the suit was based on a contract which had substantial connection with [the forum]." In discussing *International Shoe*, we referred to this as "relatedness" between that one contact and the claim; though the Texas corporation had only one contract in California, the suit involved an alleged breach of that very contract.[85] Second, "California has a manifest interest in providing effective means of redress for its residents." This was shown by California's having passed statutes aimed at regulating the insurance

---

[83]355 U.S. 220 (1957).

[84]The Court had adopted this approach in the first specific jurisdiction case to apply *International Shoe,* which was *Travelers Health Ass'n v. Virginia,* 339 U.S. 643 (1950).

[85]This case falls within Box 4 in the *International Shoe* chart on page 81, because it involves casual contact with the forum, but a claim that arises from that contact. We labeled that box "maybe" for jurisdiction. On the facts of this case, though, *McGee* falls on the "yes" side of "maybe."

industry. Third, the balance of inconveniences favored allowing the plaintiff to sue in California; it would be far more difficult for the beneficiary (a widow whose son has died) to go to Texas to sue than it would be for the Texas corporation to defend in California.[86]

The following year, in *Hanson v. Denckla*,[87] the Court, without explanation, adopted a different approach and tone. In *Hanson*, we see no concern for the state's interest or the relative convenience of the parties. The Court did not consider the relationship among the parties and the forum.[88] Instead, it focused narrowly on whether the defendant itself created sufficient contact with the forum—on whether, in the Court's language, the defendant "purposefully availed" itself of the privilege of acting in the forum. The difference in focus is stark. In *McGee*, the Court emphasized the state: California is where events underlying the dispute took place and had an interest in providing justice for its citizens. The interest of the defendant appeared to be secondary and, at any rate, presented no problem because California was a convenient place for the litigation. In *Hanson*, the focus shifted to the defendant and whether the defendant had voluntarily forged some connection with the forum.[89]

In *Hanson*, a wealthy Pennsylvania widow, Mrs. Donner, set up a trust in Delaware with a Delaware bank.[90] Under the trust, Mrs. Donner received periodic payments of the interest and reserved the right to designate the persons who would receive the property placed in trust.[91]

[86]Interestingly, Justice Black wrote the opinion in *McGee*. Recall that he concurred in *International Shoe* and criticized the open-ended terminology of that case. Now, given a chance to influence how *International Shoe* would be applied, notice his focus on the state. All three of the factors discussed in text concerned the forum state. Starting with the next case discussed in text, however, the Court would part company with Justice Black and start to focus far more on the defendant than on the interest of the sovereign. *See* Perdue, note 31 above, 63 S.C. L. Rev. at 735-737.

[87]357 U.S. 235 (1958).

[88]Not surprisingly, Justice Black, who had pioneered the mélange approach in *McGee,* dissented.

[89]In the work cited in note 31 above, Dean Perdue made this point in broader jurisprudential terms: In *McGee*, the Court emphasized sovereignty, while in *Hanson* it emphasized a defendant's right to be sued only in a state with which she had voluntarily forged ties. For compelling criticism of this shift in focus, *see* Michael Vitiello, Animating Civil Procedure 28-32 (2018).

[90]A trust permits someone with assets to provide for herself or others without having to shoulder the burden of actively managing the assets. The owner, known as the *settlor,* transfers legal title of the assets (usually money or stock) to the *trustee,* who is then under a legal duty to invest and care for the assets for the benefit of the *beneficiaries.* The settlor can be one of the beneficiaries.

[91]This is called the *corpus* of the trust. Remember from the preceding footnote that the settlor (Mrs. Donner) placed the corpus of the trust into the trust and received only the interest during her life. That left the entire corpus to be distributed when Mrs. Donner died.

She moved to Florida and continued to receive the periodic interest payments there and issued occasional orders to the Delaware bank. Mrs. Donner died in Florida. Her will designated (among other things) who should receive the trust assets.

Mrs. Donner's estate was probated in Florida. Her children disagreed over the distribution of assets; sibling sued sibling in Florida. The question was whether the trustee (the Delaware bank) was subject to *in personam* jurisdiction in Florida. The Supreme Court held that it was not, because it lacked a relevant contact with Florida. Under the *International Shoe* test, the defendant must have "purposefully avail[ed] itself of the privilege of conducting activities within the forum State, thus invoking the benefits and protections of its laws."[92] Any tie between the Delaware bank and Florida were caused by Mrs. Donner's moving there. This "unilateral activity of those who claim some relationship with a nonresident defendant cannot satisfy the requirement of contact with the forum State."[93] Thus, Florida lacked jurisdiction over the Delaware bank because that bank lacked a relevant contact with Florida.

The Court contrasted the case with *McGee*. Though Mrs. Donner carried on trust administration from Florida, the Delaware bank had done nothing to reach out to Florida in the way the Texas insurance company reached into California in *McGee*. There, the Texas corporation solicited the contract of insurance from California (recall that it was required by law to honor the contract, which had been entered by a corporation it acquired). Not everyone is convinced that the Court was right in *Hanson*. After all, the Delaware bank did send periodic interest payments to Mrs. Donner in Florida. This seems stronger than *McGee*, in which the periodic payments on the policy went the other way—from the forum to Texas. On a larger point, *Hanson* shifted gears from a "mélange" approach that balanced several factors concerning contact and fairness to one that emphasizes defendant's voluntary affiliation with the forum.[94] State and lower federal courts struggled with which approach to apply. The Court did not decide another major *in personam* case for 22 years, at which point it embraced *Hanson* and rejected *McGee*.

---

[92]357 U.S. at 253.

[93]*Id.*

[94]Some people feel that the Court strained to hold that there was no jurisdiction in *Hanson* because a contrary holding would have benefitted family members who struck the Court as greedy. *See id.* at 240 ("Residuary legatees Denckla and Stewart, already the recipients of over $500,000 each, urge that the power of appointment over the $400,000 appointed to sister Elizabeth's children was not 'effectively exercised' and that the property should accordingly pass to them").

Return to Quasi-in-Rem: Shaffer v. Heitner

The next major case after *Hanson* was *Shaffer v. Heitner*,[95] which addressed *quasi-in-rem* type 2 (QIR-2) jurisdiction. The Court had only addressed QIR-2 twice previously: in *Pennoyer* in 1878 and *Harris v. Balk* in 1905 (discussed in §2.4.2). The upshot of those cases was that QIR-2 jurisdiction was constitutional if the property that served as the jurisdictional predicate was attached at the outset of the case and proper notice (such as publication) was given. With *Shaffer*, the Court reassessed these principles in light of *International Shoe* and its progeny.

In this case, a shareholder of Greyhound Corporation brought a "derivative suit" against directors of the corporation.[96] The claim was that the directors breached fiduciary duties to the corporation by permitting the company to engage in an antitrust violation that resulted in the corporation's losing a judgment of $12,000,000. The plaintiff sought recovery of that sum from the directors of the corporation. Plaintiff sued in a state court in Delaware and attempted to exercise QIR-2 jurisdiction over the defendant directors by asking the court to attach (Delaware law uses the word *sequester*) the shares of stock that the defendants held in Greyhound Corp. (Shares of stock represent an ownership interest in a corporation. Though ownership of stock is usually represented by a stock certificate, the interest itself is intangible property. Directors of corporations are not required to own stock in the company, but often do, and the relevant defendants in *Shaffer* were stockholders in addition to being directors.) A Delaware statute provided that the ownership interest represented by stock in a Delaware corporation (such as Greyhound was at the time) was "present" in Delaware. The Delaware Supreme Court upheld QIR-2 jurisdiction over the defendants. The case seems indistinguishable from *Harris v. Balk*, in which the Court permitted the seizure of intangible property to serve as the jurisdictional predicate for QIR-2 jurisdiction.

In *Shaffer*, the Supreme Court reversed the Delaware decision, and rejected the use of QIR-2 jurisdiction. The opinion had some very broad pronouncements, but also had language that seems to limit the reach of those pronouncements, at least in some circumstances. The

[95]433 U.S. 186 (1977).

[96]In a derivative suit, a shareholder sues to vindicate a claim that belongs to the corporation (not to the shareholder personally). The corporation is an entity in the eyes of the law and is managed by the board of directors. The directors owe fiduciary duties (e.g., a duty of care and a duty of loyalty) to the corporation. Most derivative suits are brought against directors and allege that they breached a fiduciary duty owed to the corporation. Do not let the procedural stance distract you: This is essentially a case against the people who ran Greyhound, asserting that they did not do their jobs well enough, and that their mistakes cost the corporation a lot of money.

ultimate impact of *Shaffer* is still debated. One enormously important question (which the Court addressed in a 1990 case, *Burnham v. Superior Court,* discussed below) is whether the Court in *Shaffer* determined that *International Shoe* replaced *Pennoyer* or, on the other hand, whether it indicated that the two approaches coexist.

In Part II of the majority opinion in *Shaffer*, the Court reviewed the evolution of *in personam* doctrine from *Pennoyer* to *International Shoe.* It concluded that "the relationship among the defendant, the forum, and the litigation, rather than the mutually exclusive sovereignty of the States on which the rules of *Pennoyer* rest, became the central concern of the inquiry into personal jurisdiction."[97] It then noted that "[n]o equally dramatic change has occurred in the law governing jurisdiction *in rem*." But, the Court said, there have been "intimations that the collapse of the *in personam* wing of *Pennoyer* has not left that decision unweakened as a foundation for *in rem* jurisdiction."[98]

Wait a minute. When and where did the "*in personam* wing of *Pennoyer*" collapse? True, *International Shoe* and later cases have looked at different factors than *Pennoyer.* But the Court never expressly *overruled Pennoyer*. Indeed, in *International Shoe*, the Court laid out the minimum contacts test *for cases in which the defendant is not present in the forum when served with process.* The clear implication of that, as addressed in §2.4.3, is that presence of the defendant in the forum (when served with process), in itself, would continue to support *in personam* jurisdiction.

At any rate, the Court in *Shaffer* was facing QIR-2. In the last sentence of Part III of the opinion, the Court makes a sweeping statement: "We therefore conclude that all assertions of state-court jurisdiction must be evaluated according to the standards set forth in *International Shoe* and its progeny."[99] This seems to mean that in *in rem* and *quasi-in-rem* cases, the relevant inquiry is not simply whether the property serving as the jurisdictional predicate is attached at the outset, but, instead, whether the defendant has such minimum contacts with the forum that the exercise of jurisdiction would not offend traditional notions of fair play and substantial justice.[100]

Part III of the opinion deserves a careful read, however. It may be that the sweeping conclusory statement in Part II is not as broad as it seems. In the second paragraph of Part III, the Court is careful to say

---

[97] 433 U.S. at 204.

[98] *Id.* at 205.

[99] *Id.* at 212.

[100] Some people argue that the statement means that *all* cases, including *in personam* cases in which the defendant is served with process in the forum, must be assessed under *International Shoe.* The Court addressed that issue in *Burnham,* which we see below.

that "the presence of property in a State may bear on the existence of jurisdiction by providing contacts among the forum State, the defendant, and the litigation."[101] It discusses three examples. First, "when claims to the property itself are the source of the underlying controversy, it would be unusual for the State where the property is located not to have jurisdiction."[102] In footnote 24 of the opinion, it makes clear that this sentence refers to *in rem* and QIR-1 cases. In such disputes, the Court says, the defendant's claim to the property would indicate that she expected to benefit from the state's protection of the interest. Thus, the state would have a strong interest in assuring that the property is marketable and that the dispute is resolved peacefully. In addition, the relevant evidence and witnesses will be present in the forum. Accordingly, in *in rem* and QIR-1 cases, the presence of the property in the forum probably satisfies the requirement that the defendant meet the *International Shoe* test.

Second, in the same paragraph, the Court indicates that the "presence of property may also favor jurisdiction in cases ... where the defendant's ownership of the property is conceded but the cause of action is otherwise related to rights and duties growing out of that ownership."[103] This language refers to QIR-2 cases in which the property that is the jurisdictional predicate *caused* the injury to the plaintiff. The main example here, as the Court notes, is an injury on land owned by an absentee.

> ○ ***Example #14.*** *D*, a citizen of New York, owns rental property in Florida. *P*, a citizen of Michigan, rents the property. While there, ceiling tiles in the rental property fall on *P*'s head, injuring her. Assuming there is no *in personam* jurisdiction, *P* may proceed with QIR-2 by having the rental property attached at the outset. The facts that *D* owns the property, and that the property itself caused the injury, seem to satisfy the requirement that *D*'s contacts with Florida satisfy the *International Shoe* test.

Third, in footnote 30 of its opinion, the Court says that other jurisdictional doctrines, such as that regarding adjudication of status, may also be consistent with *International Shoe*. Remember from §2.4.2 that *Pennoyer* treated questions of status, such as marriage and divorce, as not being *in personam*. Thus, it was not necessary to get *in personam* jurisdiction over the defendant. Surely, the state interest in determining such status questions is great. And it seems clear from this footnote that *Shaffer* has no effect on the jurisdictional rules concerning such cases.

---

[101]433 U.S. at 207.
[102]*Id.*
[103]*Id.* at 208.

In light of these examples, the Court concluded in *Shaffer* that "jurisdiction over many types of actions which now are or might be brought *in rem* would not be affected by a holding that any assertion of State-court jurisdiction must satisfy the *International Shoe* standard."[104]

In one area, however, *Shaffer* clearly changed the law. This is in cases in which the property seized "is completely unrelated to the plaintiff's cause of action"—in other words, in QIR-2 cases. Here, the Court concluded that seizure of the property is a substitute for jurisdiction over the person. So if jurisdiction over the person would require satisfaction of *International Shoe*, so should QIR-2. Thus, in *Shaffer*, Delaware could not have jurisdiction simply by seizing property owned by the defendants in Delaware. There must be a showing that the defendants' contacts with Delaware satisfy the *International Shoe* standard.

In Part IV of the opinion, the Court concluded that the defendants did not have sufficient contacts with Delaware to uphold jurisdiction. The Court recognized that Delaware might well have an interest in policing whether directors of Delaware corporations perform their fiduciary duties in accordance with state law. But Delaware had never based jurisdiction on the fiduciary capacity of these people. Instead, jurisdiction was based on ownership of stock, which has no necessary correlation with being a director. Thus, the defendants lacked a relevant contact with Delaware.

Justice Powell concurred in the holding that *International Shoe* should govern on the facts in *Shaffer*, but would not have reached the question of "whether the ownership of some forms of property whose situs is indisputably and permanently located within a State may, without more, provide the contacts necessary to subject a defendant to jurisdiction within the State to the extent of the value of the property."[105] As to real property, he would have retained the traditional rule that seizure at the outset of the case is sufficient, at least in *in rem* and QIR-1 cases. Again, the majority seems to have admitted as much; Justice Powell probably wrote in an abundance of caution.

Overall, then, what are we to make of *Shaffer*? No doubt it overrules *Harris v. Balk* and that part of *Pennoyer* that would uphold QIR-2 jurisdiction simply on the basis of seizure of the property at the outset of the case. Clearly, in cases such as *Harris v. Balk* and *Mitchell v. Neff*, today the plaintiff must demonstrate that the defendant's contacts with the forum satisfy *International Shoe*. But the Court went out of its way to say that the presence of the property, by itself, will

---

[104]*Id.*
[105]*Id.* at 217 (Powell, J., concurring).

generally satisfy that standard in *in rem* and QIR-1 cases, in QIR-2 cases in which the property caused the injury suffered by the plaintiff, and in cases involving status. Thus, at the end of the day, the sweeping language—that all assertions of jurisdiction must be assessed under *International Shoe*—may really change only the way the world works in QIR-2 cases in which the property did not cause the injury.

Very shortly after the decision in *Shaffer*, the Delaware legislature passed a statute providing that every nonresident director of a Delaware corporation "shall be deemed" to have consented to the appointment of an agent for service of process and thus to *in personam* jurisdiction in Delaware.[106] Unless the notion of implied consent embraced in *Hess v. Pawloski* is no longer valid, this statute should grant *in personam* jurisdiction. On the other hand, the Court in *Shaffer* did say that "all assertions" of state court jurisdiction must satisfy *International Shoe*. Does that mean that traditional bases, such as residence, consent, and presence in the forum when being served with process, are swept aside in favor of the *International Shoe* equation? The Court will address that issue in *Burnham* in 1990. Before that, we must review significant cases decided in the 1980s.

The 1980s: Adoption of a Rigid Two-Step Approach

The Court's next major *in personam* jurisdiction case[107] was *World-Wide Volkswagen v. Woodson*,[108] decided in 1980. With it and *Burger King* in 1985, the Court brought a mechanical quality to the *International Shoe* methodology. The facts of *World-Wide Volkswagen* are tragic. The Robinson family decided to move permanently from Massena, New York to Tucson. To make the trip, they bought a new Audi from Seaway Volkswagen in Massena. While driving through Tulsa, the Audi was rear-ended by a vehicle driven by an uninsured drunk driver. The Audi burst into flames. Only the heroic efforts of

---

[106]10 Del. Code §3114. The Delaware Supreme Court held that the statute is valid in *Armstrong v. Pomerance*, 423 A.2d 174 (Del. 1980).

[107]*Kulko v. Superior Court*, 436 U.S. 84 (1978), was an *in personam* case, but not a blockbuster. We discuss it in the treatment of *World-Wide Volkswagen*.

[108]444 U.S. 286 (1980). The name "Woodson" in the case name refers to the state court trial judge who held that Oklahoma did have personal jurisdiction. As discussed in Chapter 6, the defendants then had a choice—they could proceed to trial or seek "extraordinary relief" from an appellate court in the Oklahoma system. They attempted the latter, seeking a "writ of prohibition" from the Oklahoma Supreme Court. This is an original proceeding in the appellate court, and in Oklahoma practice, the trial court judge is named as the respondent. (In other states, only the court (not the individual judge) is named.) That does not mean that they sued Judge Woodson as a defendant. Judges are absolutely immune from damages claims for acts taken in their judicial capacity. Rather, Woodson was just named as the respondent in the proceeding by which the defendants sought review by a higher court. See §6.3.

a Good Samaritan saved the two family members who were in the Audi (the others were in another vehicle). Those two, particularly Mrs. Robinson, suffered horrible personal injuries in the fire.

The injured persons sued in an Oklahoma state court. Their theory was that the gas tank of the car was positioned unsafely, in a way that led to the explosion when the car was hit from the rear. The plaintiffs sued four defendants: (1) the manufacturer of the car (Audi, a German corporation); (2) the North American importer (Volkswagen of North America); (3) the regional distributor (World-Wide Volkswagen), which distributed Audis in New York, Connecticut, and New Jersey; and (4) the dealer that sold the car (Seaway), which did business only in Massena. By the time the matter got to the Supreme Court, the only issue was whether the third and fourth defendants (World-Wide and Seaway) were subject to *in personam* jurisdiction in Oklahoma. The other two defendants either did not contest jurisdiction or abandoned that defense by that time.

The Supreme Court held that World-Wide and Seaway were not subject to jurisdiction in Oklahoma.[109] The reason was the same as in *Hanson*: The defendants had no relevant contact with Oklahoma because they did not purposefully avail themselves of any benefit in Oklahoma. Along the way, however, the Court shed more light on the purpose of the *International Shoe* test.

According to the majority opinion, written by Justice White[110] and adopted by five other Justices, the minimum contacts test serves two purposes. First, it protects defendants from litigation in an unduly burdensome forum (this is the defendant's "liberty interest") and, second, it ensures that states (through their courts) do not impinge upon the sovereignty of other states by overreaching their own jurisdictional power (this is the "interstate federalism" interest). He then explained that the minimum contacts test consists of two parts: contact and fairness. And the two parts serve the respective purposes of the overall test. That is, the insistence on "contact" between the defendant and

---

[109]The Court thus reversed the decision of the Oklahoma Supreme Court, which had upheld jurisdiction over these two defendants. Remember from §1.2.2 that the Supreme Court can review decisions by the highest state court only on matters of federal law. Obviously, the question of whether jurisdiction in Oklahoma comports with the Constitution is a question of federal law.

[110]Justice Byron White was a famous college football and basketball star at the University of Colorado before attending Yale Law School. He finished second in the balloting for the Heisman Trophy (college football's highest individual honor) and was at one point the highest paid player in the National Football League. His remarkable life is chronicled by a University of Chicago law professor who served as his law clerk at the Supreme Court. Dennis Hutchinson, The Man Who Once Was Whizzer White: A Portrait of Justice Byron R. White (1998).

the forum protects against the usurpation of power by one state from another. And the insistence on "fair play and substantial justice" protects the defendant from litigation in an inappropriate forum.

Now comes an odd detour. Two years after *World-Wide Volkswagen*, the Court changed its mind as to the theoretical bases of the two prongs of the test. In *Insurance Corp. of Ireland v. Companie des Bauxites*,[111] the Court concluded that the minimum contacts test serves only one goal: "a function of the individual liberty interest preserved by the Due Process Clause."[112] Thus, the part about restraining states from overreaching is not a due process goal in itself, but merely part of the larger concern of protecting the defendant from litigation in an inappropriate forum. Strangely, though, the Court reinvigorated the "interstate federalism" justification of *International Shoe* in the twenty-first century, so both justifications are alive and well today.[113] And, at any rate, the Court's change of theoretical underpinning for *International Shoe* never changed its prescription of the factors to be assessed.

The Fairness Factors. In *World-Wide Volkswagen*, the Court listed five factors as relevant to assessing the "fairness" part of the jurisdictional inquiry (which is sometimes called "reasonableness"). The Court has consistently listed them ever since. They are:

1. the burden on the defendant, which the Court calls "a primary concern";
2. the forum state's interest in adjudicating the dispute, for which the Court properly cites *McGee*;
3. the plaintiff's interest in obtaining convenient and effective relief;
4. "the interstate judicial system's interest in obtaining the most efficient resolution of controversies"; and
5. "the shared interest of the several States in furthering fundamental substantive social policies."

For the third and fifth factors, the Court cited *Kulko v. Superior Court*.[114] In that case, a New York couple obtained a divorce in that state. The ex-husband had custody of their two children and remained in New York. The ex-wife moved to California. Later, the children wanted to live with their mother. The father agreed and purchased a

---

[111]456 U.S. 694 (1982).

[112]*Id.* at 702-703 & n.10.

[113]*See* Ford Motor Co. v. Montana Eighth Judicial District Court, 141 S. Ct. 1017, 1025 (2021) ("These rules derive from and reflect two sets of values—treating defendants fairly and protecting 'interstate federalism.'" (quoting *World-Wide Volkswagen*)). We discuss *Ford Motor* in §2.4.6.

[114]436 U.S. 84 (1978).

one-way ticket for one of the children to go to California. (The mother bought the ticket for the other child.) The mother then sued the father in California for child support. The Supreme Court held that the father was not subject to *in personam* jurisdiction in California, because sending the child to that state did not constitute a sufficient contact to support jurisdiction, even for a claim for child support. The father had not "purposefully availed" himself of the benefits and protections of California.

On the "substantive social policies" point, the Court concluded that permitting suit against the father in California would discourage parents from accommodating the interest of family harmony. Specifically, if the father knew that sending his children to California would subject him to personal jurisdiction there, he might not have acquiesced in their desire to be with their mother. This is not persuasive. Imagine the case from the other viewpoint: If a mother who agrees to take on the responsibility for raising the children in California is required to go to New York to sue for child support, how likely is it that she will accept the responsibility? Moreover, why does California not have a great interest in allowing the mother to sue in California? After all, if the children are not cared for, they will become a drain on the California welfare system. The Court did not address these points.

The Absolute Prerequisite: Contact. After listing the relevant factors for assessing the fairness side of the *International Shoe* test, the Court in *World-Wide Volkswagen* made clear that fairness considerations were only relevant *after* the court found a relevant contact. No matter how overwhelming the showing of fairness in the forum might be, there can be no jurisdiction without an initial finding that the defendant has a relevant contact with the forum. Oklahoma lacked personal jurisdiction over World-Wide and Seaway because the Court found "a total absence of those affiliating circumstances that are a necessary predicate to any exercise of state-court jurisdiction."[115] The Court's holding that Oklahoma lacked jurisdiction was based entirely on the lack of relevant contact, not on any assessment of whether jurisdiction in Oklahoma would have been fair.

The defendants did not sell or service cars in Oklahoma. They did not solicit business there or have salespeople there. Nor did they regularly sell cars to Oklahoma residents or seek to serve the Oklahoma market. There was only one tie between the defendants and Oklahoma: One car they sold in New York exploded when rear-ended in Oklahoma. (Remember throughout this discussion that the only defendants relevant here are World-Wide Volkswagen, which distributed vehicles in New York, Connecticut, and New Jersey; and Seaway, which sold

---

[115]444 U.S. at 295.

vehicles only in Massena, New York.) This tie was not sufficient. Like the contact between the Delaware bank and Florida in *Hanson,* the connection between the defendants and Oklahoma resulted from the "unilateral activities" of the plaintiffs (not the defendants). The plaintiffs drove the car to Oklahoma; the defendants did nothing to reach out to Oklahoma. *World-Wide Volkswagen* marked the victory of the *Hanson* purposeful availment approach over the *McGee* mélange approach to applying *International Shoe.*

A focus on the state and its sovereignty would recognize the connections between Oklahoma and the dispute: The alleged product malfunction occurred there, the harm was suffered there, the plaintiffs were hospitalized there, and an Oklahoman had intervened to save the lives of the people in the car. In addition, Oklahoma had a legitimate interest in the safety of vehicles driven on its roads. Such state-focused facts were influential in *McGee.* In *World-Wide Volkswagen,* they are of no importance; the first inquiry is whether the defendant has forged purposeful ties with the forum.[116]

The Court also addressed "foreseeability." The plaintiffs argued that it was foreseeable that a vehicle sold in Massena, New York would be involved in an accident in Oklahoma. The Court agreed that it might be foreseeable that the automobile would get to Oklahoma. But if that sort of foreseeability were sufficient for personal jurisdiction, there would have been jurisdiction in *Hanson* and in *Kulko.* After all, the Court noted, it was foreseeable that Mrs. Donner would move to Florida and that Mr. Kulko might send his daughter to California. That sort of foreseeability is irrelevant. Rather, the Court held, it must be foreseeable "that the defendant's conduct and connection with the forum State are such that he should reasonably anticipate being haled into court there."[117] This reasoning seems circular. If it is foreseeable that a product will get to State *X,* is it not foreseeable that if the product malfunctions, there will be a lawsuit there?

Justice Brennan wrote a lengthy dissent. He argued that the majority insisted too much on a contact as a prerequisite to jurisdiction and he suggested a sliding scale. If the showing of fairness were overwhelming, he suggests, there ought to be jurisdiction on a lesser showing of contact. He also made much of the interstate system of highways and that the defendants benefitted from Oklahoma highways by selling the car in New York. Justice Marshall, in his dissent, elaborated and argued that the defendants sold more cars in New York because

---

[116]Dean Borchers, Dean Perdue, and Professor Sachs address the shift from a focus on the state to a focus on the defendant in the articles cited in note 31 above. *See also* Patrick J. Borchers, Jones v. Flowers: *An Essay on a Unified Theory of Procedural Due Process,* 40 Creighton L. Rev. 343 (2007).

[117]444 U.S. at 297.

the cars can be driven to places such as Oklahoma. Thus, they argued, there was relevant contact between the two New York defendants and Oklahoma.

World-Wide Volkswagen gives a clear methodology. First, the *International Shoe* test does consist of two parts: contact and fairness. Second, a relevant contact is absolutely necessary before fairness is assessed. All the fairness in the world will not give a court personal jurisdiction if there is no relevant contact between the defendant and the forum. Third, in assessing contact, there must be purposeful availment and foreseeability. Purposeful availment, as we saw in *Hanson*, consists of the defendant's doing something to avail herself of the benefits of the forum in some way. Foreseeability means that it must be foreseeable that the defendant would get sued in the forum. Finally, the Court set out (albeit in *dictum*) five factors to be addressed in assessing whether the exercise of jurisdiction in the forum would be fair. On the other hand, the focus on defendant-initiated contact (the "defendant-centric" focus of *World-Wide Volkswagen*) seems to give short shrift to commonsense considerations of whether a particular forum is fair or reasonable on the facts of a given case.

"Effects" Jurisdiction: Keeton, Calder, *and* Walden

In 1984, the Court decided two companion cases upholding personal jurisdiction for defamation claims. In one, *Keeton v. Hustler Magazine*,[118] the plaintiff, a New York citizen, sued the publisher of a magazine in New Hampshire, seeking to recover for damage to her reputation caused by an article published by the magazine. She sued in New Hampshire because it had a longer statute of limitations than any other state and the case would not be barred there. The Court upheld jurisdiction not only for a claim of damage caused by the publication in New Hampshire, but also for injury suffered in any other state as a result of the distribution of the magazine. The case, like *Kulko v. Superior Court* (see footnote 114 and accompanying text above), gave the Court a chance to comment on the "shared interests" of states in substantive policies that might support the fairness of exercising jurisdiction. According to the Court, New Hampshire had a "substantial interest in cooperating with other States . . . to provide a forum for efficiently litigating all issues and damages claims arising out of a libel in a unitary proceeding."[119]

---

[118]465 U.S. 770 (1984).

[119]*Id.* at 777. The case involved the "single publication rule." It stands for the proposition that a single publication of a defamatory utterance gives rise to only one claim, in which all damages suffered in all jurisdictions can be recovered. When a magazine defames someone, the single publication rule impels the plaintiff to bring one case,

In *Calder v. Jones*,[120] the Court upheld jurisdiction in California over the writer and editor of a story that allegedly defamed the actress Shirley Jones.[121] The article was published in the *National Enquirer* and there was no question about personal jurisdiction over the magazine. The question was whether the writer and editor of the story, both of whom worked only in Florida, could be sued in California. The Court emphasized that these defendants "directed" their tortious conduct at California, which is where Jones lived and would suffer the greatest harm.[122]

Calder is significant because it makes obvious that the relevant contact between the defendant and the forum can be established not only by the defendant's going to the forum and doing something there, but by her intentionally causing an effect there. The contacts consist of the defendant's causing "effects" in the forum. (Hence, the "*Calder* effects" test.)

> ○ ***Example #15.*** D mails a package containing a bomb from New York to P in California. P opens the package in California, the bomb explodes, and P is injured. P sues in California for damages caused by the bomb. It seems obvious that D is subject to *in personam* jurisdiction in California. She directed a package there, intending that it have the injurious effect that it did. The case seems as strong for jurisdiction as *Calder*. Perhaps a better phrase for "purposeful availment" in the context of intentional torts would be "purposeful contact."[123]

But in *Kulko*, didn't Mr. Kulko "aim" his daughter at California when he sent her there? Didn't doing so clearly have the effect of imposing upon the California parent the expenses of raising and supporting the child? Yet in *Kulko* the Supreme Court held that Mr. Kulko was not subject to *in personam* jurisdiction for a child support case in California. Why should directing a bomb or a defamatory story at the

---

seeking to recover for all the damage caused everywhere. The plaintiff cannot sue 50 times, once in each state, for the harm caused in that state. The rule is an example of cooperation among the states, as New Hampshire allows the plaintiff to recover for harm caused, say, in Florida, without having to burden the Florida courts with a suit. The Court elaborated that the single publication rule "reduces the potential serious drain of libel cases on judicial resources. It also serves to protect defendants from harassment resulting from multiple suits." *Id.*

[120]465 U.S. 783 (1984).

[121]Shirley Jones won the Academy Award for Best Supporting Actress in 1960.

[122]465 U.S. at 789-790.

[123]In *J. McIntyre Machinery Ltd. v. Nicastro*, 564 U.S. 873, 879-880 (2011), a plurality of four Justices suggested that a purposeful availment analysis might not fit intentional tort cases. Instead, the defendant in such cases "might well fall within the State's authority by reason of his attempt to obstruct its laws." *Id.* We discuss the case later in this subsection.

forum support jurisdiction, while sending a child does not? Perhaps the difference is that sending a bomb or harmful statement is tortious, while sending a child to a state does not necessarily result in a claim. On the other hand, the child must be fed and housed and clothed, the costs of which are imposed by sending the child to live with the other parent.

Lower courts have had difficulty applying the *"Calder* effects" test,[124] which may have prompted the Court to revisit the doctrine in 2014 in *Walden v. Fiore*.[125] The plaintiffs in that case were professional gamblers who lived in Nevada. On the way back to Nevada from a poker tournament in Puerto Rico, they had a stopover in the Atlanta airport. There, police assisting the Drug Enforcement Agency (DEA) found $97,000 in cash in their luggage. Tests of the luggage showed no sign of drug residue, nor were the two arrested for illegal drug activity. Nonetheless, an officer seized the money and turned it over to the DEA. Allegedly, the officer then drafted an affidavit of probable cause regarding illegal drug activity that, plaintiffs alleged, contained falsehoods and excluded exculpatory facts. Upon investigation, the United States Attorney's office in Atlanta determined that the money was not related to illegal activity and returned it to the plaintiffs.

The plaintiffs sued the police officer in Nevada and asserted that the officer's preparation of the allegedly false affidavit in Atlanta caused effects in Nevada by depriving them of their funds. Thus, the plaintiffs argued that jurisdiction was proper under *Calder*. The Court unanimously rejected the argument. Nevada did not have jurisdiction over the police officer, even though his actions caused the plaintiffs to "suffer[] foreseeable harm" in Nevada.[126]

The Court distinguished *Calder* by focusing on the nature of the harm suffered by the plaintiffs in the two cases. In *Walden*, the plaintiffs' harm was the deprivation of the use of their money. This harm was felt in Nevada only because the plaintiffs chose to live there, and not because the defendant had directed activity toward that state. The harm would have been felt "in California, Mississippi, or wherever else [the plaintiffs] might have traveled and found themselves wanting more money than they had."[127] Consider this analogy: Suppose the police officer had assaulted the plaintiffs in the Atlanta airport and that the plaintiffs returned to Nevada after receiving first aid for

---

[124]*See* Cassandra Burke Robertson, *The Inextricable Merits Problem in Personal Jurisdiction*, 45 U.C. Davis L. Rev. 1301, 1310 (2012) (decisions "often conflicting and contradictory, and the effort to smooth the inconsistent doctrine have been largely ineffective").

[125]571 U.S. 277 (2014).

[126]*Id.* at 289.

[127]*Id.* at 290.

their injuries. Their injuries caused ongoing pain and required further medical attention in Nevada. It seems clear that Nevada would not have personal jurisdiction over the police officer for the assault claim, despite the foreseeability that the plaintiffs would return to Nevada.

Defamation claims, such as that in *Calder*, are different. There, the harm is inflicted *where* the offending remarks are circulated, so directing such remarks to residents of that state constitutes a contact between the defendant and the forum. In *Calder*, the defendants placed phone calls to sources in California, wrote about the California activities of the plaintiff, and caused reputational harm in California by publishing alleged falsehoods about her ability to perform her profession in California.

In sum, "[t]he proper question is not where the plaintiff experienced a particular injury or effect but whether the defendant's conduct connects him to the forum in a meaningful way."[128] Because the defendant in *Walden* did nothing to connect himself to Nevada, there was no jurisdiction. Stated another way, the analysis "looks to the defendant's contacts with the forum State itself, not the defendant's contacts with persons who reside there."[129] As in *World-Wide Volkswagen*, the Court focused on the defendant's efforts to cause some effect in the forum. (The notion of "effects" jurisdiction begs the question of whether and when personal jurisdiction may be based upon Internet contacts.[130] The Court has yet to take a case involving the issue, which we will consider in §2.4.7.)

A Contract Case: Burger King

Burger King Corp. v. Rudzewicz[131] is interesting for several reasons. First, it involved a contract dispute, while the other cases in the *International Shoe* line involved torts. This fact should make no difference, however, in delineating the constitutional test for personal jurisdiction. Second, it upheld jurisdiction, after a series of cases (*Hanson, Kulko*, and *World-Wide Volkswagen*) had rejected jurisdiction. Third, because the elements of contact were overwhelming, the Court had a relatively rare opportunity to address the fairness component

---

[128]*Id.* at 290.

[129]*Id.* at 285.

[130]Professors Rhodes and Robertson conclude that *Walden* may be an influential case because of the frequency with which plaintiffs try to invoke "effects" jurisdiction. They find that there are about twice as many "effects" cases than stream-of-commerce cases, probably because of the growth of the Internet. Charles W. "Rocky" Rhodes & Cassandra Burke Robertson, *Toward a New Equilibrium in Personal Jurisdiction,* 48 U.C. Davis L. Rev. 207, 227-228 (2014).

[131]471 U.S. 462 (1985).

of personal jurisdiction jurisprudence. And fourth, Justice Brennan wrote the majority opinion,[132] while Justice White dissented. This is the opposite of *World-Wide Volkswagen*, in which White spoke for the majority and Brennan dissented.

In *Burger King*, two men in Michigan, Rudzewicz and MacShara, entered into a franchise agreement with Burger King Corporation (BK).[133] The restaurant apparently never flourished, and BK sued Rudzewicz and MacShara in federal court in Miami concerning their alleged breach of the deal.[134] The question was whether there was personal jurisdiction over the two franchisees in Florida. One cannot help but see the relative equities here: A huge multinational corporation wants to litigate at home and to drag two "little guys" from Michigan to litigate in BK's hometown. Nonetheless, the Supreme Court upheld jurisdiction in Florida.

Justice Brennan's opinion for the majority adopted the strict two-step approach set out in *World-Wide Volkswagen*.[135] The starting point, then, consistent with *World-Wide Volkswagen*, is whether there is a relevant contact between the defendant and the forum. The tie must result from the defendant's purposeful availment and render it foreseeable that the defendant could be sued there. Then, "[o]nce it has been decided that a defendant purposefully established minimum contacts within the forum State," the contacts are to be considered in light of other factors to determine whether the exercise of jurisdiction is consistent with "fair play and substantial justice." He listed the same five fairness factors laid out in *World-Wide Volkswagen*.

Here, however, Justice Brennan slipped in an interesting idea (one he floated in his dissent in *World-Wide Volkswagen*): that an especially

---

[132]Justice Brennan wrote more separate opinions about personal jurisdiction than any other Justice. This marked the only time that he wrote for a majority.

[133]Rudzewicz and MacShara are the franchisees. BK is the franchisor. Most fast-food restaurants are not owned by the company whose name appears on the neon signs. Rather, separate persons or businesses (franchisees) own the business and enter into a contract by which they are given permission to operate the store within carefully prescribed standards.

[134]As mentioned in §2.1, however, and discussed in detail in §2.5, the fact that the case was brought in federal court is irrelevant to the personal jurisdiction inquiry. A federal court has the same personal jurisdiction power that a state court does. So personal jurisdiction was proper in *Burger King* in a federal court in Florida *because* it would have been proper in a state court in Florida. In terms of subject matter jurisdiction, the case was properly brought in federal court because of diversity of citizenship jurisdiction, discussed in detail in §4.5.

[135]In this case, Justice Brennan finally gave up after decades of advocating the return to the mélange approach of *McGee*. By acquiescing in the two-step methodology, Brennan was able to write the majority opinion. As we see below, he used the opportunity to inject a sliding-scale device in an attempt to moderate the strictness of the two-step method.

strong showing of fairness might justify jurisdiction on a lesser showing of contact. This would seem in most cases to require that courts at least look at fairness considerations before dismissing for insufficient contact. The Court has never again mentioned this sliding-scale approach, so Brennan's idea has come to nothing.

In Part I-B of the opinion, the Court applies the law to the facts of the case. The conclusion that Rudzewicz and MacShara have relevant contacts with Florida was easy. The Court looked at all the factors in the negotiation of the franchise agreement. Though Rudzewicz never set foot in Florida,[136] he reached out to Florida to negotiate a 20-year, million-dollar contract with a Florida entity. The defendants (who would rather be sued in Michigan) argued that their operation was overseen by the midwest regional authority for BK in Michigan, but the Court pointed out that the corporate headquarters in Miami called all the shots and approved the deal. Moreover, the contract expressly provided that disputes would be governed by Florida law, which is another example of the defendants' availing themselves of Florida. Indeed, "it reinforced [the] deliberate affiliation with the forum State and the reasonable foreseeability of possible litigation there."[137]

The more interesting discussion in *Burger King* concerns fairness. The Court made several things clear. First, the burden is on the defendant to demonstrate the *unfairness* of the forum. Second, mere inconvenience is not enough. The defendant must show that the forum is *unconstitutional*. Due process does not guarantee the *best* forum or even a reasonably good forum. Rather, it protects the defendant against having to litigate in an unconstitutionally bad forum. The defendant must show that litigation in the forum is "so gravely difficult and inconvenient that a party unfairly is at a severe disadvantage in comparison to his opponent."[138] Though the defendants argued that it would be difficult for them to get Michigan witnesses to go to Miami to testify for them, the Court found no support in the record that the inconvenience was of constitutional magnitude. And third, in assessing whether the burden of litigating in Florida was unduly great, the relative wealth of the parties is irrelevant. "Absent compelling considerations, a defendant who has purposefully derived

---

[136]MacShara attended training in Florida, at Burger King University. After the trial court held for Burger King, MacShara did not appeal. Thus, only Rudzewicz took the case to the Supreme Court.

[137]471 U.S. at 482. Though there was this law selection clause, the contract did not contain a forum selection clause, by which the parties would have consented to personal jurisdiction in a particular location.

[138]*Id.* at 478 (internal quotations omitted), *quoting* The Bremen v. Zapata Off-Shore Co., 407 U.S. 1, 18 (1972).

commercial benefit from his affiliations in a forum may not defeat jurisdiction there simply because of his adversary's greater wealth."[139]

A *Traditional Basis:* Burnham

An important question has been lurking in the background: Does *International Shoe* replace the traditional bases of personal jurisdiction recognized by *Pennoyer*, or does it exist alongside them? The Court elided the issue until 1990, when it decided *Burnham v. Superior Court*.[140] Dennis Burnham lived in New Jersey. His wife, Francie, lived in California with the couple's two children. The couple had separated and apparently agreed that Francie would file for divorce in California. But Dennis filed for divorce in New Jersey. Dennis went on a business trip to California and then went to visit his children in that state. When he returned to Francie's house after an outing with one child, he was served with process in a California action for divorce and monetary support.[141] Dennis claimed that California lacked *in personam* jurisdiction over him for that case.

The issue was set up perfectly: Does service of process within the forum ("tag" or "transient" jurisdiction, which was a traditional basis of *in personam* jurisdiction under *Pennoyer*) suffice, or must jurisdiction always be assessed under *International Shoe*? On the facts of *Burnham*, everyone agreed that the claim was unrelated to Dennis's presence in California. The claim arose in New Jersey. Because of this, the case required that California be able to assert "general jurisdiction," which we discuss in §2.4.5.

In *Burnham*, all nine Justices agreed that Dennis was subject to general *in personam* jurisdiction in California. They differed, however, as to why. And on the key issue, they split four-to-four, with the ninth Justice refusing to break the tie.

Justice Scalia, in an opinion joined by three others, concluded that jurisdiction can be based on presence in the forum when the defendant was served with process, without assessment of the *International Shoe* standard. The conclusion is based in some measure on historical pedigree: that service of process on the defendant in the forum

---

[139]471 U.S. at 484 n.25 (citation omitted). The majority also rejected the court of appeals's conclusion that the franchise contract was one of "adhesion," in which BK had taken advantage of the franchisees. Justice Brennan made short work of this point, emphasizing that the trial judge had found no misrepresentations or duress, and that the record supported those findings. The dissent in the case was based almost entirely on the contract of adhesion point.

[140]495 U.S. 604 (1990).

[141]If the case were simply for divorce, the Court could have discussed civil (including marital) status as a basis for *quasi-in-rem* jurisdiction. Instead, because the case involved a claim for monetary recovery (child support), it was a proceeding *in personam*.

was recognized by Roman law and at English common law. More importantly, courts in this country accepted the notion at the time the Fourteenth Amendment was ratified. Not until 1978, in the wake of the broad language of *Shaffer* (that "all assertions" of personal jurisdiction must be assessed under *International Shoe*) did a single U.S. court ever suggest that service in the forum was not sufficient to establish general jurisdiction. Since then, the overwhelming majority of courts continue to apply jurisdiction based on service in the forum.

To this group of four Justices, then, *International Shoe* permitted exercises of jurisdiction that would not have been permitted under *Pennoyer*, but does not displace the *Pennoyer* bases, including in-forum service on the defendant. To them, service in-state is not *necessary* to the exercise of *in personam* jurisdiction, but certainly remains *sufficient* for the exercise of personal jurisdiction. This conclusion is consistent with language in *International Shoe*, noted in §2.4.2, in which the Court set forth its minimum contacts test as applicable if "the defendant be not present in the forum." So *International Shoe* suggested that presence when served is itself sufficient to establish general personal jurisdiction. Finally, these Justices asked, how can a basis of jurisdiction that has been part of the legal landscape for centuries be antithetical to "traditional notions of fair play and substantial justice"? Three of the four Justices opined in Parts II-D and III of Justice Scalia's opinion that *Shaffer*'s broad pronouncement (that "all assertions of state court jurisdiction" be assessed under *International Shoe*) applied only to *in rem* and *quasi-in-rem* cases.

On the other hand, Justice Brennan, in an opinion joined by three others, concluded that the historical pedigree of jurisdiction based on service in the forum is not enough *by itself* to justify it. To them, *Shaffer* meant that *all* assertions of personal jurisdiction, even those set forth in *Pennoyer*, must be assessed by the *International Shoe* test. In other words, *International Shoe* replaced *Pennoyer* and does not exist alongside it. It is important to remember, however, that these Justices also agreed, based on the application of *International Shoe*, that Dennis Burnham was subject to general jurisdiction in California. In other words, to these four, Dennis Burnham's spending a few days in California was sufficient purposeful availment to subject him to general jurisdiction there.[142]

How did he reach this conclusion? Justice Brennan says that any transient defendant avails herself of "significant benefits provided by the State." He mentions three: (1) the health and safety of the transient are protected by the state's police and other services; (2) the transient

---

[142]Part III of Justice Scalia's opinion responds point by point to what Justice Brennan says on this score.

is free to travel in the state; and (3) the transient "likely enjoys the fruits" of the state's economy as well. Moreover, because of privileges and immunities, the state cannot deny her privileges it accords its own citizens, including access to the courts. On the other hand, there are only slight burdens on the transient. Modern transportation and communications make it easier for her to defend in a distant state. Indeed, says Justice Brennan, the defendant, Dennis Burnham, had already journeyed to the forum at least once, so he could hardly complain about the burden. Accordingly, "as a rule the exercise of personal jurisdiction over a defendant based on his voluntary presence in the forum will satisfy the requirements of due process."[143]

Justice Brennan's reasoning would seem to justify the exercise of general *in personam* jurisdiction in California over *anyone* who had spent a couple of days in that state. He seems to conclude that the benefits gained simply by being there outweigh the burden of having to defend in the forum. Indeed, as Justice Scalia pointed out in Part III of his opinion, Justice Brennan seems to say that California can exercise general jurisdiction based on these contacts, regardless of whether the defendant was served with process there. As we will see in §2.4.5, the idea that Dennis Burnham's contacts would render him amenable to general jurisdiction in California today (in light of recent restrictions on the doctrine) is risible. Such are the lengths to which Justice Brennan went to avoid attaching importance to the traditional basis of service of process on the defendant in the forum state.

Whatever one thinks of Justice Brennan's reasoning in applying the *International Shoe* test, the bigger point is clear: The Justices split four-to-four on whether that case replaced the traditional *Pennoyer* bases of personal jurisdiction. Justice Stevens did not take sides on that issue. Because four Justices do not constitute a majority of the Court, there is no definitive ruling on this important point.[144]

In most instances, as in *Burnham* itself, the Scalia approach and the Brennan approach reach the same result. The choice of theory could become important, however, depending on the facts.[145]

---

[143]495 U.S. at 639.

[144]The plurality opinion in *McIntyre* seems to adopt the Scalia approach. 564 U.S. at 880 (2011) ("A person may submit to a State's authority in a number of ways. There is, of course, explicit consent. Presence within a State at the time suit commences through service of process is another example," *citing Burnham*).

[145]Professor Stempel argues that courts have misinterpreted *Burnham* as adopting the traditional basis of "tag" (or, as he calls it, "slap") jurisdiction. Jeffrey W. Stempel, *The Irrepressible Myth of* Burnham *and Its Increasing Indefensibility After* Goodyear *and* Daimler, 15 Nev. L.J. 1203 (2015).

○ ***Example #16.*** *D* is a citizen of Georgia. She plans a vacation in California and decides to drive from Atlanta to San Diego. On the way, she drives through Texas. She stays a night in a hotel in Dallas. *P* serves *D* with process in Dallas for a suit in Texas, concerning a claim that arose in Hawaii.

  ○ Under the Scalia approach, Texas would have jurisdiction because the defendant was served with process in the forum. Moreover, this traditional basis has always supported general jurisdiction, so the fact that the claim arose in Hawaii is irrelevant.

  ○ Under the Brennan approach, Texas would appear to have jurisdiction. Like Dennis Burnham in California, *D* here intended to go to Texas and gained some benefit from being there. It is not clear from Justice Brennan's opinion whether the defendant must be present in the state at a given time to avail herself of enough benefits to justify the exercise of general jurisdiction. Here, *D* was only in Texas for a day or so, but she stayed in a hotel there and thus seems to have availed herself of the fruits of the economy of the state. And because it takes a long time to drive through Texas, she will undoubtedly purchase gasoline and food elsewhere in the state.

○ ***Example #17.*** Same facts, but instead of driving, *D* flies from Atlanta to San Diego. She has to change planes in Dallas and is served with process in the airport in Dallas for the case in Texas (concerning the claim that arose in Hawaii).

  ○ Under the Scalia approach, Texas has jurisdiction, because *D* was served with process while in the forum.

  ○ Under the Brennan approach, perhaps Texas has jurisdiction. After all, *D* intentionally went to Texas. On the other hand, she was not there very long. Is a couple of hours in the Dallas airport sufficient availment to justify jurisdiction? Who knows?

○ ***Example #18.*** Same facts, but *D* books a nonstop flight from Atlanta to San Diego. The plane develops engine trouble over Texas and lands in Dallas to get mechanical attention. *D* is served with process while in the airport in Dallas for the action in Texas (concerning the claim that arose in Hawaii).

  ○ Under the Scalia approach, Texas probably has jurisdiction, because *D* was served with process in the forum. While she did not intend to go there, she was not forced or tricked into the forum.

  ○ Under the Brennan approach, this may be a tough case. Unlike the previous questions, here *D* did not intend to go to Texas. She did not direct her actions toward that state. On the other hand, she may be in Texas longer than she would have been under the preceding hypothetical. (After all, it may take longer to fix the plane than to change planes.) While in the Dallas airport, is *D* availing herself of protections of Texas? Is she partaking of the fruits of the economy of Texas?

Stream of Commerce: Asahi *and* McIntyre

One fact pattern has long vexed the courts under *International Shoe*: the "stream of commerce." The classic stream of commerce scenario is this:

○ ***Example #19.*** Defendant manufactures components in State *A* and sells them to Widget Corp. in State *B*. Widget Corp. incorporates the components into its finished product, which it markets in State *C*. Plaintiff buys the finished product in State *C*. The component malfunctions there and injures Plaintiff there. Has Defendant—which manufactured only in State *A* and sent its product only to State *B*—established a relevant contact for personal jurisdiction in State *C*?

On the one hand, we might say no, because Defendant did not reach out to State *C*. Its component got to State *C* only because of the unilateral act of a third party (Widget Corp., which marketed the finished product in State *C*). Under *Hanson* and *World-Wide Volkswagen*, then, there might be no purposeful availment by Defendant of State *C*.

On the other hand, we might say yes, because Defendant undoubtedly makes money from the resale by Widget Corp. into State *C*. In other words, if Widget Corp. in State *B* did not market its finished product in State *C*, Defendant would not sell as many components. So, arguably, Defendant, at least indirectly, availed itself of the market in State *C*.

One influential early opinion was by the Illinois Supreme Court in 1961.[146] In this case, *Gray v. American Radiator & Standard Sanitary Corp.*,[147] the defendant manufactured valves in Ohio and sold them to a water heater manufacturer in Pennsylvania. The Pennsylvania company then put those valves into its water heaters and sold the heaters nationwide. The plaintiff bought a heater in Illinois. The valve malfunctioned, causing an explosion that injured the plaintiff in Illinois. The court held that Illinois courts had *in personam* jurisdiction over the Ohio valve manufacturer. The court speculated that there must have been many of the Ohio corporation's valves in Illinois (despite the lack of any evidence of this in the record). The court also concluded that the Ohio company's sale of valves to the company in Pennsylvania was "in contemplation of use" in Illinois.

The Supreme Court may have undercut the reasoning in *Gray* with *World-Wide Volkswagen*. Though that case did not involve the stream of commerce, the Court said that foreseeability of a product's getting to the forum is not sufficient; rather, the nature of the defendant's contact with the forum must render it foreseeable that the defendant could get sued there. On the other hand, the majority opinion in *World-Wide Volkswagen* cited *Gray* with apparent approval.[148]

---

[146]The case was not reviewed by the Supreme Court of the United States.
[147]176 N.E.2d 761 (Ill. 1961).
[148]444 U.S. at 298.

Asahi. The Supreme Court finally tried to tackle stream of commerce in 1987, in *Asahi Metal Industry Co. v. Superior Court.*[149] The case followed the classic fact pattern, but in an international context. Zurcher was injured when his motorcycle crashed in California. He alleged that the wreck was caused by a problem with the rear tire. The tube for that tire was manufactured by Cheng Shin, a Taiwanese corporation. Zurcher sued Cheng Shin in California. Cheng Shin admitted that it was subject to personal jurisdiction in California. Cheng Shin filed an "impleader" claim in the case to bring in Asahi,[150] a Japanese corporation that allegedly manufactured the valve installed in the tube. Cheng Shin claimed that the wreck was caused by the valve, and that Asahi was required to indemnify it if it lost to Zurcher. Asahi claimed that California did not have personal jurisdiction over it. Zurcher's claim against Cheng Shin was settled, so the only issue left in the case was the indemnity claim by Cheng Shin against Asahi. And the question was whether Asahi had purposefully availed itself of California so as to establish minimum contacts under *International Shoe.*

Asahi was a major disappointment. The Justices failed to provide definitive guidance on how to assess purposeful availment and contact in a stream of commerce case. Justices O'Connor and Brennan espoused separate theories on the matter. Each commanded four votes and thus failed to garner a majority. On the other hand, eight Justices agreed, in Part II-B of the opinion, that personal jurisdiction in California would not be fair under the unusual circumstances of the case. Accordingly, the holding that California lacked personal jurisdiction over Asahi was based upon fairness (not contact) grounds.

Justice O'Connor's theory, joined by three others, is set out in Part II-A of the Court's opinion. She asserted that merely putting a product into the stream of commerce, even with the knowledge that it will get to the forum, is not enough. To her, purposeful availment requires "additional conduct" that indicates "an intent or purpose to serve the market in the forum State."[151] Examples, according to Justice O'Connor, include designing the product for the forum state market, advertising in the forum, establishing channels for giving advice to customers in the forum, or marketing through a distributor who agrees to serve as the sales agent in the forum. Because Asahi had no such additional conduct in California, the O'Connor group concluded, there was no relevant contact between Asahi and California.

---

[149]480 U.S. 102 (1987).

[150]We study impleader in §12.6.2. Though *impleader* is the term used for this claim by federal courts and most state courts, in California the claim is a *cross-complaint.*

[151]480 U.S. at 112.

The Brennan theory, joined by three others, is set forth at the beginning of Justice Brennan's separate opinion. To Justice Brennan, so long as the defendant placed a product in the stream of commerce and was "aware that the final product is being marketed in the forum State, the possibility of a lawsuit there cannot come as a surprise."[152] Nor, he continued, would the litigation impose a burden for which there was no benefit. The defendant benefitted economically from the retail sale of the final product in the forum. (That is, Asahi sold more valves (and made more money) because Cheng Shin was able to sell its inner tubes in California. If Cheng Shin did not sell tubes in California, Asahi would have sold fewer valves to Cheng Shin.) Brennan would not require any additional factors. On the facts of the case, the Brennan group found that there was a sufficient contact between Asahi and California.

As noted, however, eight Justices[153] concluded in Part II-B of Justice O'Connor's opinion that the assertion of jurisdiction in California would not be fair. This is the only case in which the Supreme Court has rejected personal jurisdiction on the basis of unfairness. (Earlier cases, remember, based the finding of no jurisdiction on the lack of a relevant contact with the forum.)

The problem is that the case for dismissing *Asahi* on fairness grounds was too easy. The dispute was between a Taiwanese corporation and a Japanese corporation, in which California had no discernible interest. The Court set out the same five fairness factors we saw in *World-Wide Volkswagen* and *Burger King*. Litigation in California, thousands of miles from "home," imposed severe hardship on Asahi. As the case stood when it got to the Supreme Court, the only issue was whether Asahi owed Cheng Shin indemnity. This issue had nothing to do with road safety in California and would be determined not by reference to California law, but to the contracts between the two corporations. Moreover, Cheng Shin was not a California resident, making the state's interest even more attenuated. Finally, addressing the fourth and fifth fairness factors (the interests of the states in efficiency and in shared substantive policies), the Court found an interest in trying to keep American courts from determining a dispute between foreign corporations. Thus, dismissal was warranted.

Justice Stevens could have broken the tie between the O'Connor and Brennan theories. In his concurring opinion, however, he refused to take sides. He would not agree with O'Connor because he thought the issue not necessary to a decision. In view of the holding on fairness

---

[152]444 U.S. at 315 (Brennan, J., dissenting).

[153]Justice Scalia did not join this part of the opinion. For him, apparently, the conclusion that there was no contact rendered assessment of the fairness factors superfluous.

grounds, he did not think it necessary to address contact. He was concerned about the sparse record in the case and did not want to make a decision without evidence on the volume of sales of Asahi valves into California and the dangerousness of the product.

McIntyre. The Court did not return to stream of commerce until 2011, when it decided *J. McIntyre Machinery Ltd. v. Nicastro*[154] and *Goodyear Dunlop Tires Operations, S.A. v. Brown.*[155] The latter case raised stream of commerce in the context of general personal jurisdiction, which we discuss in §2.4.5. Here, we focus on *McIntyre.* Surprisingly, the Court managed to split more badly in this case than it had in *Asahi.* Six Justices rejected jurisdiction. They did so, however, in two opinions, neither of which commanded a majority. Justice Kennedy wrote the plurality opinion, joined by three others. Justice Breyer wrote a concurrence, joined by one other. Justice Ginsburg dissented, joined by two others.[156] So while *Asahi* resulted in a four-to-four-to-one split, *McIntyre* was even more disjointed, at four-to-two-to-three.[157]

In *McIntyre,* the defendant manufactured metal-shearing machines in Great Britain. The machines are large and heavy and are used in processing scrap metal. McIntyre sold the machines to an independent company in Ohio, which then sold and distributed the machines throughout North America. In addition, McIntyre attended trade shows throughout the United States to introduce its products to the scrap metal industry. It clearly desired to sell as many machines as possible in any of the states of the United States. The machines cost about $25,000 apiece, so there is not a great volume of sales. At least one of the machines was sold to a scrap metal company in New Jersey (the president of which had seen the machine displayed at a trade show in Las Vegas). Mr. Nicastro worked for that company and suffered a serious physical injury while using the machine at work in New Jersey. He sued the British company in New Jersey.[158] The state courts upheld jurisdiction based upon a stream of commerce theory. The Supreme Court reversed.

---

[154]564 U.S. 873 (2011).

[155]564 U.S. 915 (2011).

[156]This marked the first time in which all dissenters in a Supreme Court case were women, as Justices Sotomayor and Kagan joined Justice Ginsburg.

[157]*See* Patrick J. Borchers, *The Twilight of the Minimum Contacts Test,* 11 Seton Hall Cir. Rev. 1 (2014); Adam N. Steinman, *The Lay of the Land: Examining the Three Opinions in* J. McIntyre Machinery, Ltd. v. Nicastro, 63 S.C. L. Rev. 481 (2012). Dean Citron has analyzed how Justice Stevens, who retired before the Court considered *McIntyre,* would have approached the case. Rodger D. Citron, *The Case of the Retired Justice: How Would Justice John Paul Stevens Have Voted in* J. McIntyre Machinery, Ltd. v. Nicastro?, 63 S.C. L. Rev. 643 (2012).

[158]The Ohio distributor had gone bankrupt.

Justice Kennedy's plurality opinion is consistent with Justice O'Connor's view in *Asahi* and rejects Justice Brennan's opinion from that case. To Kennedy, placing goods in the stream of commerce itself is not a sufficient contact with a particular state. Jurisdiction is possible "only where the defendant can be said to have targeted the forum," and "it is not enough that the defendant might have predicted that its goods will reach the forum State."[159] Because the British manufacturer had not targeted New Jersey, it did not have a relevant contact with that state to support jurisdiction under *International Shoe*.

At a more basic level, Kennedy's opinion adopts a view consistent with the position that due process limitations function to enforce interstate federalism. Improper exercise of jurisdiction by one state "would upset the federal balance, which posits that each State has a sovereignty that is not subject to unlawful intrusion by other States."[160] Recall that in *Insurance Corp. of Ireland* (footnote 111 above) the Court rejected the idea that due process is rooted at limiting state power vis-à-vis other states. Rather, it is intended to protect the defendant's liberty interest, the right to be free from the imposition of authority by a state with which the defendant has not established sufficient ties.[161] Kennedy's discussion of interstate federalism struck some as anachronistic. But, as noted, the Court has since agreed that limits on personal jurisdiction indeed embody interstate federalism as well as the defendant's liberty interest.[162]

---

[159]564 U.S. at 882.

[160]*Id.* at 884.

[161]Professor Brilmayer refers to a person's "rights to be left alone." Lea Brilmayer, *Rights, Fairness, and Choice of Law,* 98 Yale L.J. 1277, 1296 (1989). Though she was discussing choice-of-law doctrine, personal jurisdiction is analogous. *Id.* at 1296. *See also* Lea Brilmayer, *How Contacts Count: Due Process Limitations on State Court Jurisdiction,* 1980 Sup. Ct. Rev. 77. Other thoughtful discussions of political legitimacy and personal jurisdiction are found in Lea Brilmayer & Matthew Smith, *The (Theoretical) Future of Personal Jurisdiction: Issues Left Open by* Goodyear Dunlop Tires v. Brown *and* J. McIntyre Machinery v. Nicastro, 63 S.C. L. Rev. 617, 620-635 (2012); Daniel Klerman, *Personal Jurisdiction and Product Liability,* 85 S. Cal. L. Rev. 1551, 1554 (2012); Wendy Collins Perdue, *Personal Jurisdiction and the Beetle in the Box,* 32 B.C. L. Rev. 529, 534-546 (1991); Todd David Peterson, *The Timing of Minimum Contacts,* 79 Geo. Wash. L. Rev. 101, 101-102 (2010); Charles W. "Rocky" Rhodes, *Liberty, Substantive Due Process, and Personal Jurisdiction,* 82 Tul. L. Rev. 567, 639 (2007); Stephen E. Sachs, note 31 above, 95 Tex. L. Rev. 1249; Allan R. Stein, *Personal Jurisdiction and the Internet: Seeing Due Process Through the Lens of Regulatory Precision,* 98 Nw. U. L. Rev. 411, 412-414 (2004); Allan R. Stein, *Styles of Argument and Interstate Federalism in the Law of Personal Jurisdiction,* 65 Tex. L. Rev. 689, 690-692 (1987); Roger H. Trangsrud, *The Federal Common Law of Personal Jurisdiction,* 57 Geo. Wash. L. Rev. 849, 850 (1989).

[162]Ford Motor Co. v. Montana Eighth Judicial District Court, 141 S. Ct. 1017, 1025 (2021) ("These rules derive from and reflect two sets of values—treating defendants fairly and protecting 'interstate federalism.'" (quoting *World-Wide Volkswagen*)).

Kennedy's opinion also addressed political legitimacy, saying that the lawfulness of a judgment "depends on whether the sovereign has authority to render it."[163] This authority, to Kennedy, is the "central concept" of personal jurisdiction doctrine, and depends upon *submission* by the defendant to the authority of the state. The Court has long adopted a social-contract notion that if one gets a benefit from availing of the forum, one may have to "pay" for that benefit by submitting to jurisdiction there. This focus on "submission," however, seemed to signal a new degree of intentionality.[164] If so, it reflects a limited theory of what creates legitimate government authority. It would seem that a state may have a legitimate right to regulate the affairs of nonresidents short of their voluntarily "submitting" to jurisdiction.[165] Stated another way, the Kennedy opinion goes a long way toward giving defendants near-complete control over where they can be sued.

Justice Breyer wrote a separate concurrence, joined by Justice Alito. He concluded, like Kennedy, that there was no relevant contact between the British manufacturer and New Jersey. But Breyer's opinion is far narrower than Kennedy's. He rejects the plurality's effort to discuss personal jurisdiction in broad terms because, he says, the facts of the case would not even satisfy the Brennan stream-of-commerce test from *Asahi*. This is because there was no regular flow of products from the defendant into New Jersey. The record seemed to indicate that the machine that injured Mr. Nicastro was the only McIntyre product ever to make it to that state. Breyer opined that "[n]one of our precedents finds that a single isolated sale, even if accompanied by the kind of sales effort indicated here, is sufficient."[166]

Note three things about Breyer's opinion. First, he ignored *McGee,* in which the Court upheld jurisdiction in California over a Texas corporation based upon one contract of insurance. Though the contact involved some back-and-forth between the parties, it was a single contact. In addition, the Court has upheld jurisdiction in tort cases based upon a single contact in *Hess, Calder*, and arguably in *Keeton.*

Second, if Breyer's quantitative approach is right, and there is no stream of commerce contact until the defendant markets a flow of

---

[163]564 U.S. at 884 (2011).

[164]Kennedy did not try to fit intentional torts in his "submission" theory of contact. Instead, in intentional tort cases, "the defendant might well fall within the State's authority by reason of his attempt to obstruct its laws." *Id.* at 880.

[165]Interestingly, as Professor Rhodes points out, the Court has never used any form of the word *submit* for assessing personal jurisdiction under *International Shoe.* Instead, it has limited use of the term to jurisdiction by consent. Charles W. "Rocky" Rhodes, *Nineteenth Century Personal Jurisdiction Doctrine in a Twenty-First Century World,* 64 U. Fla. L. Rev. 387 (2012).

[166]564 U.S. at 888 (Breyer, J., concurring in the judgment).

products, defendants seem to have a couple of free shots. If the first few machines it sells in the forum malfunction and hurt people, there is no jurisdiction because there is not yet a stream.[167]

Third, when two opinions combine to create a majority on the Court (as Kennedy's and Breyer's do here), the holding is considered to be the narrower of the two opinions. Thus, the Breyer opinion should be taken as precedential. It is so narrow, purporting only to apply extant case law and unwilling to engage in general discussion, as to be of little guidance.[168]

Justices Kennedy and Breyer set forth hypotheticals worthy of the classroom.[169] For example, Kennedy worried that a finding of contact in *McIntyre* would mean that a small Florida farmer, selling crops through a national distributor, could be sued in Alaska.[170] This approach is too stark, because it rules out jurisdiction in states closer to the farmer. If the Florida farmer (because selling through a distributor) has no contact with Alaska, presumably, he does not have a contact with other states, such as Alabama. And yet jurisdiction in Alabama might be perfectly appropriate. Kennedy and Breyer err by not letting the fairness factors do any of the heavy lifting. The appropriate answer to this hypothetical, it seems, is to conclude that the

---

[167]Instead of a "stream," such cases present merely an "eddy." *Id.* (Breyer, J., concurring in the judgment). Professor Peterson has made this point convincingly. Todd David Peterson, *The Timing of Minimum Contacts After* Goodyear *and* McIntyre, 80 Geo. Wash. L. Rev. Arguendo 1, 20 (2011).

[168]In *Ainsworth v. Moffett Engineering, Ltd.,* 716 F.2d 174 (5th Cir. 2013), the plaintiff's husband was killed by an allegedly defective forklift. The defendant, an Irish company, manufactured forklifts in Ireland and sold them to a separate company, which marketed them in the United States. One forklift was sold to the decedent's employer, which allegedly caused the decedent's death on the job. The Fifth Circuit, relying on the Breyer opinion, upheld jurisdiction on a Brennan-type theory, because the Irish company could reasonably anticipate being sued in Mississippi. It distinguished *J. McIntyre* because over a ten-year period, the defendant had manufactured 203 forklifts that were sold into the forum state (Mississippi). "Thus, even though [the defendant] did not have specific knowledge of sales by [the separate company] in Mississippi, it reasonably could have expected the such sales would be made . . . ." *Id.* at 179.

[169]Neither Kennedy nor Breyer mentions the sliding scale the Court ostensibly adopted in *Burger King.* That approach, set forth by Justice Brennan, would say that a strong showing of fairness can make up for a small amount of contact. Accordingly, upon finding even slight contact between the defendant and the forum, the court should assess fairness. Neither Kennedy nor Breyer does so. For each, all the eggs are in the contact basket, and each goes to remarkable lengths to say that the British manufacturer had no contact with New Jersey.

[170]564 U.S. at 883-885 (Breyer, J., concurring in the judgment). Similarly, Breyer worried that an Appalachian potter who sells to a distributor who then resells a single coffee mug to someone in Hawaii could be sued there. Or that a small Kenyan coffee distributor or Egyptian shirt maker may be sued in the United States based upon the sale of a single item. *Id.* at 890-891 (Breyer, J., concurring in the judgment).

Florida farmer, marketing through a distributor, has contacts with Alaska and other states in which his goods are sold. Then a court would move on to determine whether, on the facts of the case, jurisdiction in Alaska (or Alabama) would be fair. It may be, given the distance and the smallness of the claim, that courts should reject jurisdiction in Alaska, but permit it in Alabama. Kennedy and Breyer, however, seem determined to find no contact, and thus to avoid any assessment of fairness.

Justice Ginsburg wrote a stinging dissent, in which she concluded that the British manufacturer had availed itself of New Jersey (and apparently every state in the United States). It had targeted the entire United States and should be subject to jurisdiction in states in which its product allegedly causes harm. She rejected Kennedy's emphasis on submission to jurisdiction.[171]

Overall, Ginsburg's approach seems consistent with the Brennan theory in *Asahi*. In one way, however, it may differ from Brennan's approach. In contrasting *Asahi,* Ginsburg noted that McIntyre sold only finished products, and not components. Accordingly, it has significant control over where the machines end up. The component maker, in contrast, has little control over where the product ends up. Thus, said Ginsburg, the holding in *Asahi* did not apply to the facts of *McIntyre.*[172]

Ginsburg concluded that the fairness factors supported jurisdiction in New Jersey. Otherwise, the injured plaintiff might be required to sue in England, and a company that targeted the United States would escape suit in any of the individual states of this country. While Ginsburg discussed the traditional fairness factors, she did not do so in the rigid two-step process prescribed by *World-Wide Volkswagen* and *Burger King*. Rather, she appeared to mix contact and fairness considerations in a mélange reminiscent of *McGee*.[173]

At the end of the day, *McIntyre* left considerable uncertainty. On the issue of whether marketing through the stream of commerce constitutes purposeful availment, we had a four-to-four split in *Asahi*: The O'Connor theory and the Brennan theory each garnered four votes. In *McIntyre*, the four Justices of the plurality clearly reject Brennan and adopt O'Connor's theory. The three dissenters adopt a position that seems consistent with (but possibly divergent from) Brennan's. The two Justices in the concurrence do not take a position. To them, the facts of the case failed to fit either O'Connor's or Brennan's test. That

[171]She characterizes this focus as a "return to older practice." 564 U.S. at 901 n.5894 (Ginsburg, J., dissenting).

[172]*Id*. at 908 (to hold that *Asahi* controls "would, to put it bluntly, be dead wrong") (Ginsburg, J., dissenting).

[173]*Id*. at 893 (Ginsburg, J., dissenting).

seems to mean that both the O'Connor and Brennan theories remain viable, because neither has been espoused (or rejected) by a majority of the Court.

The Court has decided two more important specific jurisdiction cases: one in 2017 and one in 2021. To understand them, however, we need to appreciate the surprising change that the Court made between 2011 and 2017 in the law of general jurisdiction.

§2.4.5 General Jurisdiction: The Old Era (*Perkins* and *Helicópteros*) and the New Era (*Goodyear, Daimler,* and *BNSF*)

We first saw the concept of general personal jurisdiction in the wake of *International Shoe* in §2.4.3. That case set out two variables: the defendant's level of activity in the forum and whether the plaintiff's claim is related to the defendant's activity in the forum. We placed those variables on a chart on page 81, which created four scenarios, which we labeled as Boxes 1, 2, 3, and 4. Box 3 addressed situations in which the defendant's activity in the forum is "continuous and systematic," but in which the claim is unrelated to that contact. That box was labeled "maybe," indicating that there are cases in which the defendant's contacts with the forum may be so substantial that she can be sued there even on a claim that arose elsewhere.

Before *International Shoe* called our attention to this possibility, we had largely assumed that a forum would have general (or "all-purpose") *in personam* jurisdiction. *Pennoyer* laid out the traditional bases of personal jurisdiction, without expressing concern about whether the claim arose from the defendant's contact with the forum. It was not until *Hess v. Pawloski* and its treatment of a nonresident motorist statute, discussed in §2.4.2, that we started talking about *specific* (or "case-linked") jurisdiction — that is, jurisdiction for a claim arising from or related to the defendant's contacts with the forum. That limitation was imposed by the Massachusetts nonresident motorist statute.

The Old Era

In the first four decades of the *International Shoe* era, the Supreme Court decided only two general personal jurisdiction cases: *Perkins v. Benguet Consolidated Mining Co.*[174] in 1952 and *Helicópteros*

---

[174]342 U.S. 437 (1952).

Nacionales de Colombia, S.A. v. Hall[175] in 1984. Those cases comprise the "old era." The Court avoided the topic for over two decades before returning with a flurry. From 2011 to 2017, the Court decided three general personal jurisdiction cases: *Goodyear Dunlop Tires Operations, S.A. v. Brown*[176] in 2011, *Daimler AG v. Bauman*[177] in 2014, and *BNSF Railway Co. v. Tyrrell*[178] in 2017.[179] These constitute the "new era" of general jurisdiction. The old era cases focused on the "continuous and systematic" language from *International Shoe*. The new era cases, all authored by Justice Ginsburg, mark an abrupt departure.

In *Perkins,* the defendant was a corporation formed under Philippine law. Though the company was forced to suspend its gold mining operations in the Philippines during the Japanese occupation of that nation during World War II, the corporation continued to exist. Its president, general manager, and main shareholder set up an office and bank accounts in Ohio, from which the corporation paid salaries to office personnel and paid other company expenses. The Court upheld *in personam* jurisdiction over the corporation in Ohio on a claim arising in the Philippines. It noted that the corporation conducted a "continuous and systematic, but limited, part of its general business" in Ohio.[180]

In *Helicópteros*, the Court rejected general jurisdiction. There, representatives of four people killed in a helicopter crash in Peru sued a Colombian corporation in Texas. The parties stipulated that the claim did not arise from the defendant's activities in Texas,[181] which required

---

[175]466 U.S. 408 (1984).

[176]564 U.S. 915 (2011).

[177]571 U.S. 117 (2014).

[178]137 S. Ct. 1549 (2017).

[179]The Court made a mini-foray into general jurisdiction in *Burnham,* which we discussed in §2.4.4. There, four Justices, led by Justice Brennan, concluded that the defendant's presence in the state for a few days constituted sufficient availment and contact to justify general jurisdiction. Nowhere did Justice Brennan explain how a few days' presence could possibly constitute "continuous and systematic" contact with the forum. The conclusion is particularly untenable in light of recent restrictions on general jurisdiction, discussed in the text below. Four other Justices, led by Justice Scalia, concluded that general jurisdiction was proper because of the traditional basis of service of process on the defendant in the forum.

[180]342 U.S. at 438. In *Perkins,* the president of the defendant corporation was served with process in Ohio while acting in his corporate capacity. The Court did not make much of this traditional basis of *in personam* jurisdiction (service of process in the forum on the defendant's agent), and it is difficult to know if the fact of in-state service influenced the Court's decision.

[181]Justice Brennan questioned this stipulation and noted that the claims may have been at least "related to" the defendant's contacts with the forum of Texas. *See* 466 U.S. at 425 n.3 (Brennan, J., dissenting). He urged that courts should look not to whether a claim "arose out of" defendant's contact with the forum, but more broadly to consider whether the claim was "related to" such contact. In *Bristol-Myers Squibb,* 137 S. Ct. at 1780, the Court failed to make that distinction.

the courts to consider the case as one involving general *in personam* jurisdiction. The defendant had these contacts with Texas: (1) its chief executive officer visited Texas to negotiate the contract for the defendant to provide transportation services (the fatal crash occurred during provision of those services); (2) the defendant received more than $5 million in payments for the services, through a Texas bank; and (3) the defendant bought more than $4 million worth of helicopters from a Texas company, with which it provided its transportation services. The Court concluded that these simply did not constitute "continuous and systematic" contacts with Texas.

One important distinction in the cases is the type of contact each defendant had with the forum. In *Perkins*, the actual *operation* of the corporation was centered in Ohio, while in *Helicópteros*, the defendant engaged mainly in purchasing products in Texas. In *Helicópteros*, the majority relied upon the 1923 case of *Rosenberg Bros. v. Curtis Brown Co.*[182] In *Rosenberg*, a company that operated a clothing store in Oklahoma was sued on a general jurisdiction theory in New York. Its contacts with New York included purchases of "a large part of the merchandise" it sold in Oklahoma. The Court in *Rosenberg* rejected general jurisdiction based upon purchases in the forum, even though the company's officers made regular visits to the forum to buy the goods.[183]

In his dissenting opinion in *Helicópteros*, Justice Brennan criticized the majority's uncritical acceptance of *Rosenberg*. He pointed out that that case was decided two decades before *International Shoe* and thus should not necessarily be binding. (As we will see shortly, however, the Court in 2011 *expanded* the influence of *Rosenberg*.)

After *Perkins* and *Helicópteros*, courts and lawyers argued about how much contact constituted "continuous and systematic" activities in the forum. Though there were always problems at the margin, a rough understanding took hold, and most people came to understand the concept when they saw it. There did not appear to be a crisis about what the phrase meant. Nonetheless, the Court has made major changes.

The New Era

The new approach was launched in *Goodyear* in 2011. In that case, two teenagers, citizens of North Carolina, were killed in Paris when

---

[182]260 U.S. 516 (1923).

[183]*Id.* at 518. The Court did not base its holding on whether the contacts were continuous and systematic, because that term was effectively injected into the lexicon in 1945 with *International Shoe*. Instead, it concluded that such contacts with New York did not render the Oklahoma company "present" there.

the van in which they were riding flipped over. The wreck was alleg-edly caused by defective tires. The tires were manufactured by subsid-iaries of Goodyear in Turkey, France, and Luxembourg. The parents of the boys sued for wrongful death in North Carolina and named as defendants Goodyear USA (which did not contest personal jurisdic-tion) and the three European subsidiaries. The record showed that these foreign manufacturers' tires were sold in some appreciable and consistent measure in North Carolina. Relying upon this fact, and noting that the foreign companies had made no effort to keep their products out of North Carolina, a state appellate court upheld general jurisdiction over them.

The Supreme Court reversed unanimously and held that general jurisdiction cannot be based upon a stream-of-commerce theory.[184] That was easy. Until the North Carolina decision, it is not clear that anyone, court or academic commentator, had ever opined that the stream of commerce could be a basis for *general* jurisdiction (it's tough enough to invoke for *specific* jurisdiction, as we saw in *Asahi* and *McIntyre*).

The important part of *Goodyear* is its change of focus for the gen-eral jurisdiction inquiry. No longer is it enough that the defendant has "substantial" or "continuous and systematic" contact with the forum. The contact must be *so continuous and systematic as to render the defendant "at home"* (or, as the Court sometimes says, "essentially at home"—we will just say "at home" for brevity) *in the forum*.[185] The Court did not define "at home," but gave some "paradigms": A human is "at home" where she is domiciled and a corporation is "at home" (1) where it is incorporated and (2) where it has its principal place of business.[186]

And *Goodyear* does more. Above, we saw that in *Helicópteros* the Court relied in part on the 1923 decision in *Rosenberg*. That early case rejected general jurisdiction based upon extensive purchases in the forum (and related trips by officers to arrange the purchases). *Goodyear* extends the holding in *Rosenberg* to cover sales into a forum.[187] Thus, apparently, general jurisdiction cannot be based upon a company's buying or selling in the forum state.

---

[184]564 U.S. 915, 924-930 (2011).

[185]*Id.* at 919.

[186]*Id.* at 924-927. The Court analogized these places to an individual's domicile.

[187]564 U.S. at 928-929. The Court did not refer to *Rosenberg* but quoted from a part of *Helicópteros* that discussed *Rosenberg*. The Court concluded: "We see no reason to differentiate from the ties to Texas held insufficient in *Helicópteros*, the sales of peti-tioners' tires sporadically made in North Carolina through intermediaries." *Id.* at 929.

Goodyear left a lot of people in a quandary. First, the Court did not explain why it appeared to be changing the rules for general jurisdiction. Second, courts had not used any variation of the term "at home" as the test for general jurisdiction; Justice Ginsburg got the term, and apparently the idea, from a law review article.[188] And third, the "at home" test seemed narrower than "continuous and systematic" and, if so, would upset common understandings.[189]

> ○ ***Example #20.*** In *Goodyear*, a suit brought in North Carolina, the discussion was about personal jurisdiction over the European *subsidiaries* of Goodyear USA. Goodyear USA was also a defendant. Goodyear USA is an Ohio corporation with its principal place of business in Ohio. But it operated three manufacturing plants in North Carolina, in which it employed hundreds of people. That level of activity was so obviously "continuous and systematic" that Goodyear USA did not contest general jurisdiction over it. Everyone assumed that Goodyear USA could be sued in North Carolina for a claim that arose in France.

Under the "at home" standard and paradigms stated in *Goodyear*, however, it appears that Goodyear USA would not be subject to general jurisdiction in North Carolina. It is not incorporated there and does not maintain its principal place of business there.

Three years later, in *Daimler*, the Court made clear that it meant what it said in *Goodyear*. In effect, though not expressly, it converted the paradigms from *Goodyear* into rules. Thus, a corporation is subject to general jurisdiction (1) where it is incorporated and (2) where it has its principal place of business.[190] Further, "principal place of business" appears to be the "nerve center"—the place where managers of the business make

---

[188]Lea Brilmayer, *A General Look at General Jurisdiction,* 66 Texas L. Rev. 721, 728 (1988).

[189]In addition, some argue that the Court mischaracterized *International Shoe*'s discussion of general jurisdiction and cases cited in *International Shoe*. Thomas C. Arthur & Richard D. Freer, *Be Careful What You Wish For:* Goodyear, Daimler, *and the Evisceration of General Jurisdiction,* 64 Emory L.J. Online 2001, 2008 (2014) ("If anything, then, *International Shoe* and *Perkins* both suggest that general jurisdiction is *not* limited to a corporation's 'home,' but may be had in any state where it maintains an office") (emphasis original).

[190]The plaintiffs were citizens of Argentina, Chile, and China. They sued Daimler, a German corporation with its principal place of business in Germany, in a federal court in California. They claimed that Daimler's Argentine subsidiary had collaborated with the Argentine police force to torture political dissidents (decades earlier), including the plaintiffs or their relatives. They argued that California had general jurisdiction based upon the California contacts of Daimler's American subsidiary (MBUSA). The Court held that even if all of MBUSA's contacts could be attributed to Daimler, Daimler would not be subject to general personal jurisdiction in California.

management decisions, and (apparently) not a place where the corporation engages in a substantial amount of business activity.[191]

The Court seemed unaware of the profound change it made. In the old era, general jurisdiction was based upon a corporation's *business activities* in the forum: Did it engage in "continuous and systematic" business activities there? Now it is assessed by looking at two things (where the company is incorporated and where its managers call the shots) that have no necessary correlation to where the company conducts any business.[192]

Can a court *ever* exercise general jurisdiction based upon a corporation's *activities* in the forum? In *Daimler,* the Court said yes, but then limited the concept to meaninglessness. First, there can be only one such state. This is because the defendant's contacts with the forum are assessed holistically, in the context of its overall business. It is not enough that the company engages in a level of activity in state that is comparable to that of local businesses.[193] Second, basing general jurisdiction on activities is proper only in an "exceptional case" such as *Perkins*.[194] There, according to Justice Ginsburg in *Daimler*, "[a]ll[195] of [the company's] activities were directed by the company's president from within Ohio."[196] Justice Sotomayor concurred in the result in *Daimler*, but sharply parted company with the majority's reasoning, and particularly with the conclusion that activities-based general jurisdiction cannot be found in more than one state.[197]

---

[191]This conclusion flows the Court's citation to *Hertz Corp. v. Friend*, 559 U.S. 77 (2010), which adopted this "nerve center" definition of "principal place of business" for purposes of federal subject matter jurisdiction (which we will see in §4.5.3). 571 U.S. at 137.

[192]Nothing requires a corporation to do business in the state in which it incorporates. Many national corporations are incorporated in Delaware but do very little, if any, business there. Likewise, there is no requirement that the managers meet and make business decisions in a place where the company carries on business. The corporate headquarters might be in Manhattan, but the company may employ people to manufacture widgets in its plant in South Carolina.

[193]571 U.S. at 139 n.20.

[194]*Id*. at n.19.

[195]As a factual matter, the majority opinion may have been wrong. Nothing in the *Perkins* opinion indicated that "all" business activities were directed from Ohio. Justice Sotomayor noted that when *Perkins* was filed, the corporation had resumed mining in the Philippines and had a significant business presence in California. 571 U.S. at 152 n.8 (Sotomayor, J., concurring).

[196]571 U.S. at 152 n.8. Though the Court points to *Perkins* as an example of general jurisdiction based upon corporate activities, the quoted sentence is consistent with the conclusion that the corporation's principal place of business (defined as where decisions are made) was in Ohio.

[197]571 U.S. at 154 (Sotomayor, J., concurring) ("[T]here is nothing unpredictable about a rule that instructs multinational corporations that if they engage in continuous and substantial contacts with more than one State, they will be subject to general jurisdiction in each one").

○ ***Example #21.*** *P,* who resides in California, goes on vacation to Alaska. While there, she goes shopping at a local Wal-Mart. She slips and falls in the store and is injured. She wants to sue Wal-Mart in her home state. Before *Goodyear,* there would have been a strong argument that California had general jurisdiction over Wal-Mart because it has continuous and systematic ties with that state (hundreds of stores and thousands of employees and probably some regional management office).

Today, however, California does not have general jurisdiction, because Wal-Mart is not "at home" in California. It is not incorporated there, nor does it have its principal place of business there. Moreover, even though Wal-Mart probably has more business activity in California than many California businesses, there cannot be general jurisdiction because nowhere near "all" of its business is conducted in California. As the Court said: "A corporation that operates in many places can scarcely be deemed at home in all of them."[198]

Consider what this means for *P* in Example #21. She can sue Wal-Mart in Alaska. Because the claim arose there, from the activities of Wal-Mart there, Alaska courts would have specific jurisdiction. She can sue under general jurisdiction in Delaware (that is where Wal-Mart is incorporated) and in Arkansas (where Wal-Mart has its principal place of business). But she cannot sue in her home state, notwithstanding the level of business Wal-Mart does in California and notwithstanding that litigating in California would not seem unfairly burdensome to Wal-Mart.

Daimler contains another surprise: The fairness factors (listed in *World-Wide Volkswagen* and subsequent cases, discussed in §2.4.4) *are irrelevant* in general jurisdiction cases. Once a court determines that the defendant is "at home" in the forum, that's the end of it. The court is not to consider whether jurisdiction in the forum would be fair or reasonable under the circumstances. This conclusion was tucked into a footnote in Justice Ginsburg's opinion,[199] and is surprising because the parties did not raise the issue. The rationale, apparently, is that no defendant can argue that litigating "at home" would be unfair.[200] Justice Sotomayor, though concurring in the result, criticized this part

---

Moreover, as a practical matter, most corporations that do "all" business in one state will either be incorporated there or have their principal place of business there. As to such localized businesses, then, activities-based general jurisdiction adds nothing to the "paradigms."

[198]571 U.S. at 139 n.20.

[199]*Id.*

[200]Consider, however, the case of someone who is domiciled in State *A* but resides in State *B* (this is often true for military personnel and students). *Goodyear* and *Daimler* indicate that a human is subject to general jurisdiction in the state of her domicile. In such a case, though, when the person is not currently living there, litigation there might be quite inconvenient.

of the opinion by noting, *inter alia*, that every court of appeals that had addressed the question concluded that a fairness analysis should be required in general jurisdiction cases.[201]

Some state and lower federal courts pushed back against the Court's restriction of general jurisdiction. One example is *BNSF Railway Co. v. Tyrell*,[202] in which the Montana Supreme Court upheld general jurisdiction over a railroad company for claims that did not arise in Montana. The claims were asserted under the Federal Employers Liability Act (FELA), which permits railway workers injured on the job to sue their employers. The state court upheld general jurisdiction by concluding that the new approach to general jurisdiction did not apply to an FELA against a railroad defendant.[203] The Supreme Court reversed. Justice Ginsburg, for the eight-Justice majority, applied *Daimler* and rejected general jurisdiction. The defendant was not incorporated in Montana and did not have its principal place of business there. Though it had more than 2,000 miles of track and employed 2,100 people in Montana, it had similar levels of activity in other states, so the level of activity in Montana did not approach that in *Perkins*. Again, if a corporation operates in several states, it "can scarcely be deemed at home in all of them."[204]

Justice Sotomayor dissented in part, reiterating the grounds she espoused in *Daimler*. She decried the fact that now "it is virtually inconceivable that [interstate] corporations will ever be subject to general jurisdiction in any location other than their principal places of business or incorporation."[205]

The Court's new direction in general jurisdiction has led to considerable commentary, most of it critical.[206] Though the new era is now

---

[201]571 U.S. at 144 n.1 (Sotomayor, J., concurring).

[202]137 S. Ct. 1549 (2017).

[203]In the alternative, the state court concluded that one provision of FELA, 45 U.S.C. §56, conferred general jurisdiction by providing that an FELA case "may be brought" where "the defendant shall be doing business at the time of commencing the action." This part of the Montana decision was easily rejected, because §56 is a venue provision and has nothing whatever to do with personal jurisdiction. 137 S. Ct. at 1555-1557. Venue, which we study in Chapter 5, determines where (within a given judicial system) a case ought to be litigated.

[204]137 S. Ct. at 1559, *quoting Daimler,* 571 U.S. at 139 n.20.

[205]137 S. Ct. at 1560 (Sotomayor, J., concurring and dissenting). Justice Sotomayor agreed with the Court regarding 45 U.S.C. §56, discussed in the preceding footnote. She dissented as to the application of *Goodyear/Daimler*. She asserted that the Court should have remanded for the Montana Supreme Court to apply the "at home" test in the first instance. It had elided the issue by holding that the new approach did not apply to FELA cases.

[206]*See, e.g.*, Patrick J. Borchers, *The Muddy-Booted, Disingenuous Revolution in Personal Jurisdiction,* 70 Fla. L. Rev. 21 (2018); Judy M. Cornett & Michael H. Hoffheimer, *Good-Bye Significant Contacts: General Personal Jurisdiction After* Daimler AG v. Bauman, 76

well established, questions remain. For one, though the Court gave paradigms for where a corporation is "at home," it said nothing about unincorporated businesses. Lower courts are wrestling with that issue among a variety of unincorporated associations.[207]

For another, when the Court stated in *dictum* in *Goodyear* and *Daimler* that a human is "at home" and therefore subject to general jurisdiction where domiciled, it confirmed one of the traditional bases espoused in *Pennoyer*.[208] Did the Court mean that the place of domicile

---

Ohio St. L.J. 101 (2014); Robin J. Effron, note 10 above, 74 N.Y.U. Ann. Surv. Am. L. at 100 ("Limiting the general jurisdiction of domestic defendants to just one or two states drastically changed the presumed access to courts that plaintiffs previously enjoyed against large companies with a hefty business presence in many or even all states."); Richard D. Freer, *Some Specific Concerns with the New General Jurisdiction*, 15 Nev. L.J. 1161 (2015); Bernadette Bollas Genetin, *The Supreme Court's New Approach to Personal Jurisdiction*, 68 SMU L. Rev. 107 (2015); Michael H. Hoffheimer, *The Stealth Revolution in Personal Jurisdiction,* 70 Fla. L Rev. 499 (2018); Zoe Niesel, Daimler *and the Jurisdictional Triskelion,* 82 Tenn. L. Rev. 833 (2015); Zoe Niesel, #PersonalJurisdiction: A New Era of Internet Contacts, 94 Ind. L. 103 (2019); Todd David Peterson, *Categorical Confusion in Personal Jurisdiction Law,* 76 Wash. & Lee L. Rev. 655 (2019); Allan R. Stein, *The Meaning of "Essentially at Home" in* Goodyear Dunlop, 63 S.C. L. Rev. 527 (2012). *But see* Carol Andrews, *Another Look at General Personal Jurisdiction,* 47 Wake Forest L. Rev. 999, 1081 (2012); W. Grayson Lambert, *The Necessary Narrowing of General Personal Jurisdiction,* 100 Marq. L. Rev. 375, 414-423 (2016) (finding the restriction clear and logically coherent).

[207]*See, e.g.,* Waldman v. Palestine Liberation Org., 835 F.3d 317, 332-333 (2d. Cir. 2016) (PLO, a non-sovereign governmental entity, is "at home" in Palestine, where it governs); In re Packaged Seafood Products Antitrust Litigation, 338 F.Supp.3d 1118, 1140 (S.D. Cal. 2018) ("The overwhelming conclusion is that Lion Capital can fairly be regarded at home in the United Kingdom. Lion Capital's principal place of business is the United Kingdom because its primary office is located in London, its employees are located in the U.K., and the majority of Lion Capital's designated members and members are domiciled in the U.K."); Dallas Texans Soccer Club v. Major League Soccer Players Union, 2017 WL 1165662 at *3 (N.D. Tex. 2017) (union that has similar levels of activity in several states is not "essentially at home" in Texas); Finn v. Great Plains Lending, LLC, 2016 WL 705242 at *3 n. 3 (E.D. Pa. 2016) ("While Great Plains is an LLC and not a corporation, the reasoning of *Daimler* applies with equal force.").

It is worth noting some differences between corporations and unincorporated associations. Corporations must be chartered by a particular state, so there is never a question about where the business is formed. This is true with some unincorporated associations (such as the limited liability company) but not with others. A partnership is formed by conduct of the parties, and it may be unclear exactly where the partnership was formed. A corporation's principal place of business is usually the headquarters, which is where managers meet and make decisions for the business. Many unincorporated associations feature less centralized control, and there may be a significant question about where the business's nerve center is located.

[208]For this point, see the paragraph accompanying note 40 above. As discussed there, the Court expressly upheld domicile as a basis for general jurisdiction in *Milliken v. Meyer* in 1940. In *Goodyear/Daimler*, however, the Court did not refer to domicile as a traditional basis of personal jurisdiction. Instead, it based the rule on a contacts analysis under *International Shoe*. This fact reflects the disagreement among the Justices in *Burnham* about whether the traditional bases exist independently of contacts-based jurisdiction under *International Shoe*.

is the *only* forum that would have general jurisdiction? It certainly did not say so. Thus, it seems likely that an individual's being served with process while voluntarily in the forum continues, generally, to support general jurisdiction. (The Court addressed that point in *Burnham,* which we discussed in §2.4.4.)

We have no idea why the Court has restricted general jurisdiction. Indeed, we are not even sure why we have general jurisdiction in the first place.[209] All exercises of personal jurisdiction raise questions of political legitimacy. With specific jurisdiction, the forum determines liability concerning acts that occurred (or had an effect) within it. The legitimacy of such jurisdiction seems obvious. With general jurisdiction, though, the forum is exercising adjudicatory power over a defendant whose conduct took place elsewhere. What gives the state the authority to regulate a defendant in this way? How far should this authority reach? The Court failed to engage such questions. It simply decreed that "at home" is the proxy for the task.

The curious restriction of general jurisdiction leads to cases in which the defendant has continuous and systematic contact with the forum but in which there is no general jurisdiction. Can specific jurisdiction fill the resulting gap? We turn to that question now.

§2.4.6   Specific Jurisdiction in the Era of Restricted General Jurisdiction: The Emerging Focus on Relatedness 2017-2021

In most of the cases in which the Court rejected specific jurisdiction (discussed in §2.4.4), the problem was the lack of a sufficient *contact* between the defendant and the forum. That was the problem, for example, in *Hanson, World-Wide Volkswagen, Asahi, McIntyre,* and *Walden.* Now we turn to cases in which the defendant has plenty of contact with the forum. Indeed, the defendant has so much contact with the forum that, before 2011, the forum would have had general jurisdiction. Now that general jurisdiction is not available based upon continuous and systematic contacts, however, these cases must be handled, if at all, by specific jurisdiction. And the question becomes whether the plaintiff's claims *are sufficiently related to the defendant's contacts* to support specific jurisdiction. The Court has decided two major cases on this point, one in 2017 and one in 2021.

---

[209]*See* Patrick J. Borchers, *The Problem With General Jurisdiction,* 2001 U. Chi. Legal Forum 119, 139 ("[G]eneral jurisdiction exists as an imperfect safety valve that sometimes allows plaintiffs access to a reasonable forum in cases when specific jurisdiction would deny it"); Stanley E. Cox, *The Missing "Why" of General Jurisdiction,* 76 U. Pitt. L. Rev. 153 (2014).

Bristol-Myers Squibb. In *Bristol-Myers Squibb v. Superior Court,*[210] decided in 2017, 678 plaintiffs filed suit in a California state court against pharmaceutical giant Bristol-Myers Squibb (BMS). They sought damages for personal injuries allegedly caused by BMS's drug Plavix (a blood thinner). Though BMS was incorporated in Delaware, had its headquarters in New York, and employed over half its employees in New York and New Jersey, it had substantial ties with California: It maintained five research and lab facilities, 160 employees, 250 sales representatives, and a lobbying office in that state. It also sold hundreds of millions of Plavix pills in California, which generated $900,000,000 over seven years. Obviously, there was no problem establishing contact between BMS and California.

The problem was that 592 of the plaintiffs were not residents of California. They lived in 33 other states. The Plavix they ingested was not manufactured, packaged, labeled, or sold in California, and was not sold under a marketing strategy developed in California. These 592 plaintiffs could not connect their *claims* to BMS's California *contacts*. They did not get Plavix through California doctors, did not ingest Plavix in California, and were neither injured nor treated in California. On the other hand, the California court did have specific jurisdiction over BMS for the claims by the 86 plaintiffs who were residents of California. Their claims did arise from BMS's marketing and selling in the forum; they did ingest the drug, suffer harm, and receive medical treatment in California. The jurisdictional "relatedness" problem was encountered only for the non-California plaintiffs.

The California Supreme Court upheld *specific* jurisdiction over the claims by the non-California plaintiffs by employing a "sliding scale" approach.[211] According to this view, when a defendant has a great deal of contact with the forum, it is easier to show that a plaintiff's claim has some connection to those activities. Because BMS had extensive ties with California, all that was required for relatedness was that the non-California plaintiffs' claims were substantively and factually similar to the claims asserted by the California residents. The California court found that the claims were similar because they involved the identical drug, Plavix, as was sold in California to the California plaintiffs.

---

[210]137 S. Ct. 1773 (2017). *See generally* Matthew P. Demartini, Comment, *Stepping Back to Move Forward: Expanding Personal Jurisdiction by Reviving Old Practices,* 67 Emory L.J. 809 (2018).

[211]This is different from the sliding scale suggested by Justice Brennan in *Burger King* concerning the respective showings of contact and fairness. See page 95. Here, the sliding scale concerns "how related" a claim must be to contacts to support specific jurisdiction.

The Supreme Court rejected this approach in *Bristol-Myers Squibb.* There is no sliding scale:[212] Either the plaintiff's claim "arises out of or relates to" the defendant's forum activities or it does not. The quoted phrase had appeared in several cases, including *Helicópteros.* In *Helicópteros,* Justice Brennan argued that the phrase should be split, with "arise out of" meaning something different from "relate to." Specifically, he argued, "relate to" was broader than "arise out of."[213] In *Bristol-Myers Squibb,* however, the Court refused to parse the phrase.

The Court held that the claims of the non-California plaintiffs were not sufficiently connected to California. Again, the non-Californians were prescribed Plavix, took Plavix, and suffered harm outside California. "When there is no such connection, specific jurisdiction is lacking regardless of the extent of a defendant's unconnected activities in the State."[214] Accordingly, California did not have specific personal jurisdiction over BMS for the claims by the non-California residents.[215]

Bristol-Myers Squibb appears to establish that identical behavior in the forum does not satisfy the relatedness requirement. As the Court said: "[t]he mere fact that other plaintiffs were prescribed, obtained, and ingested Plavix in California—and allegedly sustained the same injuries as did the nonresidents—does not allow the State to assert specific jurisdiction over the nonresidents' claims."[216]

Justice Alito wrote the majority opinion in *Bristol-Myers Squibb* for eight Justices.[217] Justice Sotomayor dissented. She lamented the Court's recent constriction of general jurisdiction and characterized the majority opinion as the Court's "first step toward a similar

[212]The Court characterized the California sliding scale approach as a "loose and spurious form of general jurisdiction." 137 S. Ct. at 1781.

[213]*Helicópteros,* 444 U.S. at 425 (Brennan, J., dissenting). Justice Brennan made this argument in asserting that Texas had specific jurisdiction in *Helicópteros.* The majority of the Court in that case did not address the issue, however, because the parties had stipulated that the case depended entirely on general jurisdiction.

[214]*Id.* The Court contrasted *Keeton,* note 118 above. There, the plaintiff and readers suffered harm in New Hampshire because of the circulation of the allegedly defamatory article in that state. In *Bristol-Myers Squibb,* the non-California plaintiffs suffered no harm in California. 137 S. Ct. at 1782.

[215]It also did not matter that BMS engaged a California company to distribute Plavix nationwide because there was no allegation that BMS engaged in acts with that company in California. *Id.* at 1783.

[216]*Id.* at 1781.

[217]This fact is notable because the opinion contained language we might have expected Justices Ginsburg and Kagan to find objectionable, at least based upon their dissent in *McIntyre.* Specifically, Justice Alito spoke of defendants' "submitting" to jurisdiction and of the limits on personal jurisdiction as protecting state sovereignty as well as a defendant's liberty interest in being protected from litigation in a grossly inconvenient forum. *Id.* at 1780-1781.

contraction of specific jurisdiction . . . ."[218] Specifically, she worried that the holding would make it difficult to put together multistate class actions or other aggregate litigation, which we address in §13.3. One response to this, made by Justice Alito, is that nationwide class action, aggregating the claims of persons from every state, may be pursued in those states in which the defendant is subject to general jurisdiction. This fact will not help, however, in cases involving multiple defendants who are not "at home" in the same state.

Note three things about *Bristol-Myers Squibb.*

- First, specific jurisdiction has shifted from a two-step inquiry under *World-Wide Volkswagen* ((1) contact followed by (2) an assessment of fairness) to a three-step analysis: (1) contact followed by (2) relatedness followed by (3) an assessment of fairness.
- Second, the focus on relatedness forces the court to consider not simply the defendant's ties with the forum but the *plaintiff's* ties (or at least the plaintiff's claim's ties) with the forum.
- Third, in defining the relatedness requirement, *Bristol-Myers Squibb* gives us a series of rather hollow phrases. There must be "an affiliation between the forum and the underlying controversy," which means an "activity or an occurrence that takes place in the forum State and is therefore subject to the State's regulation."[219] Stated another way, "specific jurisdiction is confined to adjudication of issues deriving from, or connected with, the very controversy that establishes jurisdiction."[220]

Do these phrases help us resolve the following?

- o *__Example #22.__* D operates a hotel in Hawaii. It advertises in Indiana. *P,* an Indiana citizen, sees the advertising in Indiana and takes a vacation to the hotel. While there, she falls and suffers personal injuries. She sues *D* in Indiana. Does the Indiana court have specific jurisdiction over *D*?

State and lower federal courts have reached different results in cases such as this. Some apply a "but for" analysis, and uphold jurisdiction because without *D*'s advertising in Indiana, *P* would never have gone to *D*'s hotel.[221] Other courts focus on the fact that none of the acts that caused injury to the plaintiff occurred in Indiana; any negligence in running the hotel took place in Hawaii. These courts deny jurisdiction because the claim did not sufficiently relate to the

---

[218]*Id.* at 1784 (Sotomayor, J., dissenting).

[219]137 S. Ct. at 1780 (quoting Goodyear Dunlop Tires Operations, S.A. v. Brown, 564 U.S. 915, 919 (2011).

[220]*Id.*

[221]*See, e.g.,* Shute v. Carnival Cruise Lines, 897 F.2d 377 (9th Cir. 1990), *rev'd on other grounds,* 498 U.S. 807 (1990).

Indiana contacts.[222] The Court in *Bristol-Myers Squibb* gave no guidance on which, if either, approach is to be followed.[223]

> *Example #23.* Let's reconsider *World-Wide Volkswagen*. Assume that Audi (the manufacturer) sells many cars into Oklahoma. Thus, Audi has established continuous purposeful ties with Oklahoma. The Robinsons buy their Audi in New York and drive it to Oklahoma, where it allegedly malfunctions and injures the Robinsons. Under *Bristol-Myers Squibb*, would Oklahoma have specific jurisdiction *over Audi* for this case?[224] (This was not the issue addressed in *World-Wide Volkswagen*; remember, the question there was jurisdiction over two New York defendants that, according to the Court, had no contact with Oklahoma. Here the question is jurisdiction over the manufacturer, which had significant contact with Oklahoma.)

Here, as in *Bristol-Myers Squibb*, the specific product that harmed the plaintiffs was not manufactured in or marketed to Oklahoma. Unlike that case, though, here the alleged malfunction and the injury did occur in the forum. But the malfunction and injury did not arise from Audi's availment of Oklahoma—this was a car marketed and sold in New York, not Oklahoma. Yes, the defendant's product got into Oklahoma, but the defendant had nothing to do with its getting there. Is there specific jurisdiction? The next case may help.

Ford Motor. *Ford Motor Company v. Montana Eighth Judicial District* involved consolidated cases, one from Montana and one from Minnesota.[225] The facts of the two cases are substantially similar, so we will focus on the facts of the Minnesota case. There, the plaintiff, a resident of Minnesota, was injured in a crash of a 1994 Ford Crown Victoria on a Minnesota road. He sued Ford Motor Company (Ford) in Minnesota, claiming that the vehicle was defective. Ford's contacts with Minnesota were extensive: It maintained 84 independent dealerships in the state, which sold new Fords and offered service and Ford parts for new and used vehicles, it advertised through multiple media in the state, it sold thousands of new vehicles there, including the same year and model that was involved in the plaintiff's wreck, and it provided parts to stores throughout the state.

---

[222]*See, e.g.*, Moki Mac River Expeditions, Inc. v. Drugg, 221 S.W.3d 569, 584 (Tex. 2007) (discussing various tests for relatedness).

[223]Allan Erbsen, *Personal Jurisdiction Based on the Local Effects of Intentional Misconduct*, 57 Wm. & Mary L. Rev. 385 (2015); *see* Charles W. "Rocky" Rhodes, Cassandra Burke Robertson & Linda Sandstrom Simard, Ford's *Jurisdictional Crossroads*, 109 Geo. L.J. Online 102 (2020).

[224]Before the decision in *Bristol-Myers Squibb*, there was support for specific jurisdiction on such facts. *See, e.g.*, Mary Twitchell, *The Myth of General Jurisdiction,* 101 Harv. L. Rev. 610, 661-662 (1988).

[225]141 S. Ct. 1017 (2021).

Ford's contacts with Minnesota were so "continuous and systematic" that under the "old era" of general jurisdiction law, discussed in §2.4.5, it would have been subject to general jurisdiction in that state. Because this was so clear, from 1945 (when *International Shoe* was decided) until 2011, Ford did not make a constitutional challenge to personal jurisdiction in a single American case with similar facts.[226] (And, as you can imagine, there were many such cases.) Now, though, in the "new era" of general jurisdiction, Ford is not subject to general jurisdiction in Minnesota. Why? Because it is not "at home" in Minnesota; it is incorporated in Delaware and has its principal place of business in Michigan.

Jurisdictionally, then, the case had to sink or swim on specific jurisdiction. The issue, as in *Bristol-Myers Squibb,* was not contact but relatedness: Did the plaintiff's claim "arise out of or relate to" Ford's extensive contacts with the forum? Here, the accident took place on Minnesota roads and the plaintiff was a Minnesota resident. But, as in Example #23, the car in which the plaintiff was injured did not get into Minnesota through any act by Ford. Ford did not design or manufacture the car in Minnesota. It did not sell the car initially into Minnesota (it sold the specific car to a dealership in North Dakota). The car got into Minnesota through a series of private sales, eventually being owned by the Minnesota resident who drove it with the plaintiff as a passenger when the plaintiff was injured.[227]

Ford did not argue that it lacked contact with Minnesota. Similarly, Ford did not argue that the exercise of jurisdiction in Minnesota would be unfair to it. Its entire argument was based upon relatedness: The plaintiff's claim did not "arise out of or relate to" Ford's contacts with the forum. It argued that the relatedness requirement can be satisfied only by a "causal" relationship—specifically, that the *very car* in which the plaintiff was injured was either (1) designed or (2) manufactured or (3) sold directly by Ford into the forum.

---

[226]Charles W. "Rocky" Rhodes, *The Roberts Court's Jurisdictional Revolution within Ford's Frame,* 51 Stetson L. Rev. ___ (2021) (Westlaw search shows that Ford made no such challenge in any domestic case during those years).

[227]The basic facts, as noted, were the same in the companion Montana case. There, a Montana resident was killed in the crash of a 1996 Ford Explorer. Ford engaged in the same activities in Montana as in Minnesota, with the exception that it maintained 36 dealerships. The wreck occurred on a Montana highway, and though Ford sold the same model in Montana, the very car involved was manufactured in Canada and initially sold into Washington. It got into Montana through a series of private transactions.

The Court unanimously rejected this argument and upheld specific jurisdiction.[228] The majority opinion by Justice Kagan did what the majority in *Bristol-Myers Squibb* refused to do: It separated the phrase "arise out of" from the phrase "relate to." The former, it concluded, requires causation: that the defendant's contact with the forum *caused* the harm suffered by the plaintiff. But—and this is a major point—a causal relationship is not required for all cases. In some cases, all that is required is that the defendant's contact with the forum "relate to"—have some factual connection with—the plaintiff's claim. In other words, as Justice Brennan suggested long ago in *Helicópteros*, "relate to" is broader than "arise out of."

How does a court decide which test ("arise out of" or "related to") to use? Here the Court also appears to do something else it refused to do in *Bristol-Myers Squibb*: recognize (though not in so many words) a sliding scale. If the defendant has a great deal of contact with the forum, such as Ford's contacts with Minnesota, the plaintiff need only satisfy the "relate to" test to support specific jurisdiction. On the other hand, if the defendant has relatively less contact with the forum, the plaintiff must show a causal relationship between the defendant's contact and her claim. But the Court failed to explain how much of a causal relationship is required for a claim to "arise out of" forum contacts: but-for causation? Proximate causation? Some other type of causation?

More broadly, drawing the line between "arise out of" and "relate to" seems to engage an assessment like the old "continuous and systematic" test for general jurisdiction. Indeed, it is remarkable how much of the majority opinion sounds like "old era" general jurisdiction cases: The Court noted Ford's "substantial business in the state," that Ford "systematically served" the state market, that it "regularly conduct[ed]" business in the state, and, in discussing *World-Wide Volkswagen,* the defendant's "systematic contacts" with the forum.[229] Of course, here such extensive ties with the forum do not support *general* jurisdiction. But these ties do permit *specific* jurisdiction over the defendant for a claim that merely "relates to" those ties. The Court cautions that the "relates to" test does not mean "anything goes" but,

---

[228]Though the decision was unanimous, there were three opinions: Justice Kagan for the majority of five, Justice Alito in concurrence, and Justice Gorsuch concurring in the judgment, in which Justice Thomas joined. Justice Barrett did not participate in the case. Thus, only eight Justices participated in the case.

[229]141 S. Ct. at 1022, 1028, 1028, 1029. Similarly, Justice Alito's concurring opinion referred to Ford's "heavy presence" in Minnesota. 141 S. Ct. at 1032 (Alito, J., concurring). The majority contrasted such continuous ties with "isolated or sporadic" contact. 141 S. Ct. at 1028 n.4.

instead, imposes "real limits" to protect the defendant from litigation in an inappropriate place.[230]

On the facts of the case, *Ford Motor* was easy. Ford's extensive activities in Minnesota were aimed at creating a market for Fords there: By advertising, providing parts, and maintaining dealerships that repair used vehicles, the company encouraged Minnesotans to become Ford owners, even if they bought their car out of state in a second-hand transaction. Ford cultivated ongoing relationships with Minnesota residents. The Court was willing to assume that the plaintiffs "might never have bought" the used car "except for Ford's contacts with their home States."[231] The plaintiff's claim "relate[ed] to" these contacts even though the very car in which the plaintiff was injured got into the forum through the acts of third parties.

Ford Motor is not much help to us in Example #22. First, we do not know the level of the defendant's activity in Hawaii and thus cannot tell which test ("arise out of" or "relate to") to use. Second, if we are to apply the "arise out of" test, we do not know what type or level of causation must be shown.

In *Ford Motor*, the Court emphasized that its holding was presaged by its discussion, in *dictum,* about jurisdiction over the manufacturer of the vehicle involved in *World-Wide Volkswagen.* There, in rejecting jurisdiction over two New York defendants for lack of contact with Oklahoma, the Court said that the forum certainly had personal jurisdiction over the German manufacturer.[232] The Court failed, however, to notice one distinction between the cases: In *World-Wide Volkswagen* (and in Example #23), the plaintiff was not a resident of the forum. The Court's statement in *Ford Motor* makes clear that this difference will not affect jurisdiction. Thus, the answer to Example #23 is plain: There is jurisdiction, at least if the defendant has substantial ties with the forum (such as Ford and Audi do, presumably with every state).

The Court in *Ford Motor* rejected the defendant's reliance on *Bristol-Myers Squibb.* Here, unlike in that case, the plaintiff was a resident of the forum and was injured in the forum. In *Bristol-Myers Squibb*, neither was true.[233] The Court also rejected Ford's reliance on *Walden.* That case, the majority explained, was based entirely upon lack of contact between the defendant and the forum and had nothing to do with relatedness.[234]

[230]141 S. Ct. at 1026.
[231]141 S. Ct. at 1029.
[232]141 S. Ct. at 1027-1028. Moreover, in *Daimler,* the Court said, "we used the Audi/Volkswagen scenario as a paradigm case of specific jurisdiction." *Id.*
[233]141 S. Ct. at 1026.
[234]141 S. Ct. at 1031.

Ford Motor is important but frustrating. The bifurcation of "arise out of" and "relate to" is significant, but, again, the Court does not define either phrase with precision; at what point does a defendant's contact become sufficient to invoke the "relates to" test? Moreover, the holding is narrow. It was important to the Court that Ford had marketed the model of vehicle in which the plaintiff was injured, that the plaintiff was a resident of the forum, and that the injuries were suffered on forum roads. The Court did not tell us what would happen, though, if a Minnesota resident in the plaintiff's position had been injured while driving on the roads of another state or if Ford had never marketed in Minnesota the model in which the plaintiff was injured.[235]

More frustrating, perhaps, is the majority's lack of attention to methodology. We suggested above that specific jurisdiction consists of three steps: (1) contact followed by (2) relatedness followed by (3) an assessment of the fairness factors. It is clear from *Ford Motor* that the starting point is indeed contact, which was obvious on the facts. The majority opinion defines contact as "purposeful availment" but does not mention foreseeability, which had been established as relevant in *World-Wide Volkswagen*. Still, the concept seems implicit in the *Ford Motor* conclusion that Ford's level of contact in the forum gave it "fair warning" that it might be subjected to jurisdiction there.[236]

What is less clear is how one assesses the fairness of specific jurisdiction. The Court long ago (in *World-Wide Volkswagen*) laid out five fairness factors and even Justice Ginsburg came to embrace the consideration of fairness as separate from that of contact.[237] In *Ford Motor,* the majority never addressed the reasonableness of jurisdiction (the fairness factors) expressly. Still, the fairness considerations are present, but they are mixed in with the discussion of relatedness. For instance, concern with burden on the defendant is addressed by the Court's conclusion that there is nothing unfair in making Ford defend where it does such substantial business (and reaps such substantial rewards). And the forum state's interest is present in the Court's embrace of "interstate federalism"—Minnesota has an interest, the Court insists, that other states not intrude on its ability to provide a remedy for its residents. It also has an interest in enforcing its motor vehicle safety laws. The plaintiff's interest in suing at home is clearly facilitated by upholding jurisdiction. Finally, the interest in efficient

---

[235]141 S. Ct. at 1028 ("Contrast a case, which we do not address, in which Ford marketed the models in only a different State or region.").

[236]141 S. Ct. at 1025. This conclusion is consistent with the *World-Wide Volkswagen* requirement of foreseeability that the defendant might be sued in the particular forum.

[237]She did so in *dictum* in *Daimler*. 571 U.S. at 139 n.20.

litigation is fostered by suit in Minnesota because the witnesses and relevant evidence will likely be there and (though the Court does not mention this) the forum state's law will govern on the merits.[238]

Obviously, then, the Court did not jettison considerations of fairness in specific jurisdiction, but it is a fair question whether they are to be considered as a separate third step of analysis or as part of the consideration of relatedness.

Justice Alito concurred in *Ford Motor* and decried the parsing of "arise out of or relate to" into two parts. (Perhaps he was defending turf since his opinion in *Bristol-Myers Squibb* refused to make such a distinction.) To him, a causal connection is always required, but was easily satisfied on the facts of the case.[239] Justice Gorsuch, joined by Justice Thomas, concurred in the judgment in an opinion that will command a good bit of attention. He discussed traditional approaches to personal jurisdiction and expressly discussed *Pennoyer*. Though some will see this as an appeal to restrictive jurisdictional doctrine, the opposite appears to be the case. Justice Gorsuch was particularly concerned that though individuals can be subject to "tag" jurisdiction, corporate defendants have not been,[240] so a return to *Pennoyer* (under which all jurisdiction was general jurisdiction) may signal a desire to expand jurisdiction over businesses.

Ford Motor is a rare personal jurisdiction victory at the Supreme Court for plaintiffs. Notwithstanding the fact that it will govern in a great many cases involving corporate giants like Ford, it leaves many open questions.

> ○ ***Example #24.*** Let's reconsider *McIntyre*. Recall that the British manufacturer of the metal-shearing machines sold the machines to a company in Ohio. The Ohio company then sold the precise machine that injured Mr. Nicastro to his employer in New Jersey. The Court rejected specific jurisdiction over the British company in New Jersey for lack of sufficient contact. Now suppose Mr. Nicastro sued the British company in Ohio. Under *Bristol-Myers Squibb*, would there be specific jurisdiction in Ohio?

---

[238]Not only that, but, as Dean Borchers has noted, the plaintiff's suit against the driver of the vehicle (who was a Minnesota resident) would proceed in that state. Forcing the plaintiff to sue Ford in a different state would be wildly inefficient. *See* Linda Sandstrom Simard, Cassandra Burke Robertson & Charles W. "Rocky" Rhodes, *Ford's Hidden Fairness Defect*, 106 Cornell L. Rev. Online 45 (2020) (noting that Ford's argument for causal relatedness relied upon traditional fairness factors).

[239]141 S. Ct. at 1033 ("[H]ere, there is a sufficient link [for causation].") (Alito, J., concurring).

[240]141 S. Ct. at 1036 (Gorsuch, J., concurring in the judgment).

The British company availed itself of Ohio (it sold and delivered machines to that state and made money doing so), so the purposeful contact prong is satisfied. Does the claim by Mr. Nicastro "arise out of" or "relate to" that activity? To determine which test to use, we need to know whether the defendant's activity in Ohio is substantial, though we have little guidance for how to make that assessment. If we decide that the claim must "arise out of" the defendant's contacts with Ohio, is it satisfied? Maybe. After all, the defendant sold the very machine that hurt the plaintiff into Ohio. Perhaps this is enough, even though the plaintiff was injured in New Jersey.

> ○ ***Example #25.*** Here is a hypothetical the Court raised in *Ford Motor.* A retired man in Maine carves duck decoys out of wood. He sells some of them over the Internet to people in distant states. One, let's say sold to a person in Colorado, injures the plaintiff there. The plaintiff sues in Colorado. Does that state have specific jurisdiction?

The majority opinion dodged the question by noting that the defendant's contacts with a state like Colorado were "isolated or sporadic" and therefore would require some causal connection between the contact and the injury.[241] In his concurrence, Justice Gorsuch criticized the majority for its leaving open "a virtually infinite number of 'affiliations' waiting to be explored" in litigation.[242] And, again, even if we can draw the line between cases invoking "arise out of" and those invoking "relate to," we have precious little guidance on how either test is applied. Perhaps the most noteworthy point (as was true in *McIntyre*) is how little the Justices seem willing to rely on fairness factors. Even if the defendant in Example #25 has a relevant contact with Colorado and relatedness is satisfied, the distance of the forum and size of the claim may dictate that jurisdiction there would not comport with "fair play and substantial justice."

§2.4.7 Minimum Contacts and the Internet

In the late twentieth century, the Court called the Internet "a unique and wholly new medium of worldwide human communication."[243] Justices have noted that the Internet could raise interesting jurisdictional issues,[244] but the Court still has not addressed personal

---

[241]141 S. Ct. at 1028 n.4.

[242]141 S. Ct. at 1035 (Gorsuch, J., concurring in the judgment).

[243]Reno v. ACLU, 521 U.S. 844, 850 (1997).

[244]*See, e.g.,* Ford Motor Co. v. Montana Eighth Judicial District Court, 141 S. Ct. 1017, 1028 n.4 (2021) ("And we do not here consider internet transactions, which may

jurisdiction in the Internet context. Accordingly, state and lower federal courts struggle to assess personal jurisdiction in cases involving contact through e-commerce, social media, and other Internet platforms. The Internet is everywhere (because anyone, anywhere, with a computer can gain access to it) and yet it is nowhere (because it is in cyberspace, not in a discrete physical location). How does a court determine where contacts occur through the Internet? How does it avoid finding universal personal jurisdiction?

Some commentators opined early that the Internet may require rethinking personal jurisdiction doctrine.[245] Others disagreed, and concluded that the new technology would not require modification of long-established jurisdictional principles.[246] Under *International Shoe*, there must still be some contact, caused by purposeful availment, by the defendant with the forum; and the exercise of specific jurisdiction must comport with the fairness factors espoused in the case law.[247] There are some easy cases.

> ○ ***Example #26.*** *D*, in Florida, sends an e-mail to *P*, in California. The e-mail contains outrageous statements intended to cause *P* to suffer emotional distress. As a result of reading the e-mail, *P* suffers emotional distress. There is no reason to treat this case differently from one in which *D* had sent the message by regular mail or had used the telephone to convey the tortious message.[248]

This fact pattern, involving an intentional tort committed from out of state, fits nicely within "effects" jurisdiction permitted by *Keeton* and *Calder*. It is distinguishable from *Walden v. Fiore* because *D* clearly targeted the forum.[249] Thus, jurisdiction in California is clear.

A more difficult question is posed by the claims arising from the maintenance of a blog or other website. The Internet is a global network of thousands of computer networks to which billions of people have access. Businesses, organizations, and individuals can post

---

raise doctrinal questions of their own."; Walden v. Fiore, 571 U.S. 277, 290 n.9 (2014) (" . . . very different questions whether and how a defendant's virtual 'presence' and conduct translate into 'contacts' with a particular state.").

[245]*See, e.g.*, Martin H. Redish, *Of New Wine and Old Bottles: Personal Jurisdiction, the Internet, and the Nature of Constitutional Evolution*, 38 Jurimetrics J. 575 (1998).

[246]*See, e.g.*, Stein, note 161, above, 98 Nw. U. L. Rev. 411.

[247]Remember that the Court said in *Daimler* that there is no assessment of fairness or reasonableness in cases of general jurisdiction.

[248]*See* EDIAS Software Int'l v. Basis Int'l Ltd., 947 F. Supp. 413, 419 (D. Ariz. 1996) ("E-mail does not differ substantially from other recognizable forms of communication . . . where one person has an address or phone number to reach another person").

[249]See the discussion of "effects" jurisdiction in §2.4.4 above.

websites on the Internet, to which these millions of users around the world can gain access. The Internet thus has made it possible to do business anywhere in the world from a computer anywhere else in the world.

Zippo Manufacturing Co. v. Zippo Dot Com, Inc.[250] was an influential early case that is waning in importance. The court in that case opined that there are three types of websites and envisioned a "sliding scale" for assessing contacts based on website activity. According to the court, "the likelihood that personal jurisdiction can be constitutionally exercised is directly proportionate to the nature and quality of commercial activity that an entity conducts over the Internet."[251]

- At one end of the spectrum is the "active" website, on which the defendant engages in activities such as transmitting files to the forum state over the Internet or entering contracts with residents of the forum. Generally, maintaining such a website in State *A* can establish a relevant contact with State *B*, at least if there is interaction with persons in State *B*.
- At the other end of the spectrum is the "passive" website, on which the defendant merely posts information. Even though people in other states may gain access to it, the passive site "that does little more than make information available to those who are interested in it is not grounds for the exercise [of] personal jurisdiction."[252]
  - ***Example #27.*** A nightclub in Missouri established a website in that state to provide information concerning events at the club. The site was not interactive, and people desiring tickets for any of the club's shows were instructed to phone the club in Missouri or to buy tickets at the door. A New York nightclub sued the Missouri club in New York, asserting personal jurisdiction based on the website and alleging that the site infringed its trademark. The Missouri company did not reach out to New York to establish and maintain ties with New York customers and thus was not amenable to *in personam* jurisdiction in New York.[253]
- In the middle, and presenting the most difficult cases, is the "interactive" website from which the defendant can send or receive information. Here, the court is to consider factors such as "the level of interactivity" and "the commercial nature of the exchange of information."[254]

There is some older authority for the questionable conclusion that maintaining a website accessible by persons in any state can constitute a relevant contact in any state. Because the communication can

---

[250]952 F. Supp. 1119 (W.D. Pa. 1997).

[251]*Id.* at 1124. *See also* Mink v. AAAA Dev. LLC, 190 F.3d 333 (5th Cir. 1999) (adopting the sliding scale approach).

[252]952 F. Supp. at 1124.

[253]Bensusan Restaurant Corp. v. King, 126 F.3d 25 (2d Cir. 1997).

[254]*Zippo,* 952 F. Supp. at 1124.

reach anyone, goes the reasoning, the defendant has purposefully availed herself of any state in which a plaintiff gains access to the site, and can be sued by one whose claim arises from accessing the information in State *Z*.[255] This reasoning renders state lines irrelevant, which is impossible to square with the notion that a state needs some legitimate basis for regulating the defendant's conduct.

Accordingly, most courts conclude that simply "creating a site, like placing a product into the stream of commerce, may be felt nationwide—or even worldwide—but, without more, . . . is not an act purposefully directed toward the forum state."[256] Only when the defendant has done something more to serve or exploit the forum, such as creating or maintaining the site in the forum, or encouraging persons in the forum to use the site, should jurisdiction be proper.

Though some courts still cite *Zippo*, it is anachronistic.[257] The Seventh Circuit explains: "If the defendant merely operates a website, even a 'highly interactive' website, that is accessible from, but does not target, the forum state, then the defendant may not be haled into court in that state . . . ."[258] Instead of interactivity, courts now focus on whether the defendant "targeted" the forum. In *Tamburo v. Dworkin,* the plaintiff, which operated a software business online, alleged that various defendants "engaged in a concerted campaign of blast emails and postings on their websites" accusing him of wrongdoing and urging

---

[255]*See, e.g.*, Inset Systems, Inc. v. Instruction Set, Inc., 937 F. Supp. 161, 162 (D. Conn. 1996) (jurisdiction in Connecticut over Massachusetts defendant concerning dispute over website domain name). The court in *Zippo* concluded that *Inset Systems* represented the "outer limits" of the constitutional exercise of personal jurisdiction. *Zippo,* 952 F. Supp. at 1125.

[256]*Bensusan Restaurant Corp.,* note 253 above, 126 F.3d at 29. An interesting case offering the flip side from the typical case (such as *Zippo*) involving personal jurisdiction over the operator of a website is CompuServe, Inc. v. Patterson, 89 F.3d 1257 (6th Cir. 1996). There, a Texas citizen entered into an agreement with an Ohio computer network service under which the service would market his software. After the Texan asserted that the network service had violated his trademark, the Ohio corporation sued in Ohio, seeking a declaratory judgment that it had not acted inappropriately. The court upheld personal jurisdiction over the Texan, concluding that he had availed himself of Ohio by entering the agreement by which the Ohio company would market his software. Further, jurisdiction in Ohio was fair because the Texan was an entrepreneur who anticipated a long-term relationship with an Ohio corporation; moreover, Ohio law governed the parties' agreement.

[257]*See, e.g.*, Stein, note 161 above, 98 Nw. U. L. Rev. at 430-432 (criticizing *Zippo* as creating odd incentives to limit website functionality); Joshua Beldner, Comment, *How Technologically Savvy Do You Have to Be to Apply* Zippo?: *An Approach to Internet Personal Jurisdiction After* Fancaster *and* Edvisors, 17 B.U. J. Sci. & Tech. L. 318, 324-326 (2011).

[258]be2 LLC v. Ivanov, 642 F.3d 555, 559 (7th Cir. 2011).

a boycott of his business.[259] The court upheld jurisdiction in Illinois over those defendants who "aimed their tortious conduct at Tamburo and his business in Illinois with the knowledge that he lived, worked, and would suffer the 'brunt of the injury' there . . . even though their alleged . . . tortious statements were circulated more diffusely across the Internet."[260] This conclusion is bolstered by *Walden*, in which the Court emphasized that the defendant must target the forum, and not simply people who happen to live in the forum.

Each case depends upon its facts, but there are strong arguments for finding purposeful availment to support specific jurisdiction based upon such things as income derived from residents of the forum through Internet activity, knowledge that Internet activity may harm people in that state, statements on a website targeting people in that state, and the presence of the Internet service provider in the forum. Similarly, there is authority for declining specific jurisdiction when the defendant makes clear that the website is intended for a geographically limited audience or that the website is merely informational or when the website is set up so it will not interact with persons in a given state.[261] Even if the court finds sufficient contact and relatedness to support specific jurisdiction, it must then assess whether the exercise of jurisdiction is fair or reasonable under the circumstances.

What about general jurisdiction? In cases predating the "new era," courts suggested that "continuous and systematic" Internet activities could support general jurisdiction.[262] That conclusion is untenable today. Today, general jurisdiction is limited in almost every case, at least regarding a corporate defendant, to the state in which the business incorporated and the state of its principal place of business. Moreover, the Court appears to have held that general personal jurisdiction cannot be based upon sales or purchases within a forum. (We discussed all of this in §2.4.5.) As a result, purposeful availment and contacts via the Internet appear limited to cases involving specific jurisdiction.

The Internet has given rise to the phenomenon of "cybersquatting." This occurs when someone registers a domain name that infringes on the trademark of an established business for the purpose of selling

---

[259]601 F.3d 693, 697 (7th Cir. 2010).

[260]*Id.* at 707.

[261]For discussion of these and other factors, including cases addressing them, *see* 4A Wright & Miller §1073.

[262]An interesting example was *Gator.com Corp. v. L.L. Bean, Inc.,* 341 F.3d 1072, 1079 (9th Cir. 2003), in which a panel of the Ninth Circuit held L.L. Bean subject to general jurisdiction in California, based upon contacts such as a virtual store online. The decision was vacated, however, 366 F.3d 789 (9th Cir. 2004), and the case ultimately dismissed after the parties settled the dispute. 398 F.3d 1125 (9th Cir. 2005).

the name at an inflated price. Any well-known business wants domain names that bear, or at least resemble, the company name, their name, or any others so closely related to their name that customers might associate the site with it. Thus, the car manufacturer Porsche would want to hold the domain name *www.porsche.com* as well as *www.porsch.com*. In fact, the company registered the first name but found that some enterprising persons had already registered the misspelled domain name *www.porsch.com* and scores of others closely related to Porsche's name or the name of a Porsche product. Porsche sued under the Trademark Dilution Act and sought *in rem* jurisdiction over the domains themselves (instead of *in personam* jurisdiction over those who registered the domain names). The district court rejected the claim, holding that the Trademark Dilution Act did not permit *in rem* proceedings.[263]

Around the same time, Congress passed the Anticybersquatting Consumer Protection Act (ACPA), which allows *in rem* proceedings against domain names created by a cybersquatter with the bad faith intent to gain monetary advantage. The Act has significant restrictions to ensure that the case proceeds *in rem* only if the persons responsible cannot be sued *in personam*.[264]

Though the Internet has introduced the new evil of cybersquatting and has changed the way in which defendants avail themselves of different fora, the case law is remarkable for its tendency to treat the brave new world of the Internet within extant Supreme Court precedent. In fact, some cases seem to reflect the split between Justice O'Connor and Justice Brennan in *Asahi*, and the later split in *McIntyre*, discussed in §2.4.4. Maybe this should not surprise us. People release things onto the Internet in much the way they send products through the stream of commerce. The stream may pass through many places and may be acted upon by persons in some of those places. In the big scheme of things, then, perhaps the Internet has not pointed out a need for a new jurisdictional doctrine. Rather, perhaps it shows the adaptability of the minimum contacts analysis. Given the uncertainties in that analysis, it is not surprising that case law is not uniform in approach.

---

[263]Porsche Cars North America, Inc. v. Porsche.com, 51 F. Supp. 2d 707 (E.D. Va. 1999), *vacated* and *remanded*, 215 F.3d 1320 (4th Cir. 2000).

[264]In the *Porsche* case, after plaintiffs asserted an *in rem* claim under the ACPA, some defendants submitted to *in personam* jurisdiction and argued that the ACPA thus did not apply. The Fourth Circuit rejected this argument, holding that the case was *in rem* when filed, and that the defendants could not manipulate jurisdiction by thereafter submitting to *in personam* jurisdiction. Porsche Cars North America, Inc. v. Porsche.net, 302 F.3d 248, 255-260.

§2.4.8   Can One's Contacts Be Attributed to Another?

Plaintiffs sometimes attempt to support a finding of jurisdiction over a defendant by attributing to that defendant contacts that a different person or entity has with the forum. The effort usually involves related businesses. For example, in *Daimler*, the plaintiffs argued that a German company was subject to general jurisdiction in California based upon the contacts of its American subsidiary, MBUSA. The Ninth Circuit upheld attribution under an "agency" theory: that because Daimler had the right to oversee and control MBUSA's activities, the subsidiary's contacts could be attributed to Daimler. That court found attribution appropriate because the tasks performed by MBUSA were "important" to Daimler. This, according to the Ninth Circuit, was shown by the fact that Daimler would have stepped in to perform the tasks if MBUSA failed to get them done.

The Supreme Court rejected this form of the agency theory as too broad.[265] Thus, it is not enough that the parent corporation oversees and controls "important" functions performed by the subsidiary. The Court recognized that in some circumstances a stricter form of "agency" may justify attribution of contacts, at least for specific jurisdiction.[266] It did not describe what such a relationship would look like. State and lower federal courts have addressed the issue and have engaged a confusing set of labels — including "alter ego," "successors-in-interest," and "piercing the corporate veil" — to justify their conclusions. Suffice to say that the cases are heavily fact-dependent and that attribution of contacts is the exception, not the rule.[267]

§2.5   Statutory Analysis

The Need for a Statutory Basis

The fact that personal jurisdiction would be constitutional in a given case is not sufficient to permit a court to exercise personal jurisdiction. As noted in §2.3, the constitutional authority to exercise personal jurisdiction is not self-executing. Thus, *before addressing whether the exercise of jurisdiction would be constitutional*, one must find statutory authority for personal jurisdiction. Each state is free to determine how much or how little of the constitutional power of personal

---

[265]*Daimler*, 571 U.S. 117, 135-136 (2014).

[266]*Id.* at 135 n.13. The Court held that even if MBUSA's contacts were attributable to the German company, the forum would lack general jurisdiction over it.

[267]For detailed discussion, *see* 4A Wright & Miller §1069.4.

jurisdiction to grant to its courts. This is a political decision, made by the state legislature. It bears repeating, however, that even the clearest case of the constitutional exercise of personal jurisdiction cannot be made unless the forum state has passed a statute permitting it.

> ○ ***Example #28.*** P sues D in State X. D is a domiciliary of State X. D was born in State X and has never been outside State X. The claim by P against D arose in State X. There is no question that State X can, constitutionally, exercise personal jurisdiction over D. But unless State X has passed a statute that grants personal jurisdiction in this sort of case, State X cannot exercise jurisdiction.

Statutes Relating to **In Personam** *Jurisdiction*

Each state has legislation granting *in personam* jurisdiction to its courts. Some of these statutes may be ubiquitous. For example, most states appear to have a statute permitting *in personam* jurisdiction over persons who are domiciled or who reside in the state. In addition, each state has authority for exercising such jurisdiction over persons served with process in the state. (As we saw in discussing *Burnham* in §2.4, the question of whether personal jurisdiction in such a case is constitutional may depend on the facts, but the statutory basis is clear: There is statutory power if the defendant is served while in the state.) Similarly, each state has a statute granting *in personam* jurisdiction over corporations that are formed in the state.

Beyond these typical statutes, each state authorizes its courts to exercise personal jurisdiction in some circumstances over nonresidents—that is, defendants who are not domiciled or residing in the forum and who are not served with process in the forum. Generally, states have two such statutes. First is the nonresident motorist statute. These tend to be similar to what we studied in *Hess v. Pawloski* in §2.4.2. These are usually based on implied consent and allow only specific jurisdiction. Thus, the statute grants jurisdiction only for assertion of the claim arising from the motor vehicle crash within its borders. The statutes usually permit personal jurisdiction over the operator and the owner of the vehicle that was involved in the crash.

The second type of statute permitting *in personam* jurisdiction over nonresidents is generically called a *"long-arm"* statute, precisely because it permits the state to exercise its power outside the state lines. These statutes are similar to nonresident motorist statutes. Generally, they grant specific jurisdiction, meaning that the claim asserted against the nonresident must arise from something the defendant did in (or having an effect in) the forum. But they are broader than nonresident motorist statutes because they cover more than the motor vehicle crash case. Historically, states passed nonresident motorist statutes in the 1920s and 1930s, validated by *Hess v. Pawloski*. The more general long-arm statutes came along in the 1940s and 1950s, in the wake of *International Shoe*.

Though long-arm statutes can differ substantially from state to state, most seem to be modeled on one of two general approaches. One is typified by the statute in California, which simply provides that the courts of the state can exercise jurisdiction over a nonresident to the full extent of the Constitution.[268] In such a state, the statutory analysis of personal jurisdiction is coextensive with the constitutional assessment. The second type of long-arm statute, which we can call a "laundry-list" statute, contains a list of activities that subject a nonresident to *in personam* jurisdiction.

Laundry-list long-arm statutes usually provide for *in personam* jurisdiction over nonresidents for claims arising from the nonresident's doing something, such as transacting business or committing a tort, in the forum. There are two things to watch for in applying such statutes. First, study the language very carefully. There is a big difference between a statute that permits jurisdiction over a nonresident who "transacts *substantial* business" in the state and one who "transacts *any* business" in the state.[269] Second, remember that courts may interpret the same language differently.

One example of the latter point concerns language routinely found in long-arm statutes: that the courts have *in personam* jurisdiction over a nonresident "who commits a tortious act or omission" in the forum.[270] Note the careful drafting of including "act or omission." Without the reference to "omission," it would be arguable that the statute should apply only to intentional torts and not to torts based on omissions, such as some forms of negligence. Beyond that, however, would the statute apply in the following hypothetical?

---

[268]Cal. Code Civ. Proc. §410.10 ("A court of this state may exercise jurisdiction on any basis not inconsistent with the Constitution of this state or of the United States").

[269]In some laundry-list states, the courts interpret the statute as granting personal jurisdiction to the full extent of the Constitution. *See, e.g.,* Fields v. Volkswagen of America, Inc., 555 P.2d 48, 52 (Okla. 1976) ("the intention in Oklahoma is to extend the jurisdiction of the Oklahoma courts over nonresidents to the outer limits permitted [by due process]"). If the legislature really intended that result, though, why did it not simply pass a California-style statute?

[270]Some states except the tort of defamation from their long-arm statutes. *See, e.g.,* Code of Ga. Ann. §9-10-91. Thus, in defamation, the plaintiff may have to sue in the state where the defendant resides, unless some other basis for *in personam* jurisdiction can be found. Such legislative restriction does not seem required by the Constitution, in light of the Supreme Court upholding jurisdiction in defamation cases such as *Keeton* and *Calder*, discussed in §2.4.4.

○ ***Example #29.*** D manufactures widgets in State A. P orders a widget directly from D. D ships the widget to P in State Z. While P is using the widget in State Z, it explodes and injures P. P wants to sue D in State Z. The State Z long-arm statute grants *in personam* jurisdiction over nonresidents who "commit a tortious act or omission in State Z."[271] Does that statute grant jurisdiction over D? The answer depends on how the court construes whether there was tortious behavior *in State Z.* And, as you may have studied in class, courts can disagree on this point.

One interpretation is that the statute is *not* satisfied because the tortious act or omission, if any, occurred in State A. After all, that is where D manufactured the widget. So if D was negligent, that negligence took place in State A. The New York Court of Appeals reached this conclusion on similar language and facts in *Feathers v. McLucas.*[272]

The other conclusion is that the statute is satisfied because P was injured in State Z. The idea is that in whatever way D might have been negligent, it did not become tortious until it hurt somebody. And this widget did not hurt anyone until it blew up, which happened in State Z. The Illinois Supreme Court reached this conclusion on the same language in *Gray v. American Radiator & Standard Sanitary Corp.*[273]

Each interpretation is defensible, and each emphasizes a different portion of the statutory language. The New York interpretation emphasizes the language *act or omission* and insists that the defendant's behavior (not the effect or result of the behavior) must take place in the forum state. On the other hand, the Illinois interpretation emphasizes the word *tortious,* and emphasizes the effect of the defendant's behavior. The Illinois court reasoned that no behavior is tortious until someone is hurt. So if the injury takes place in the forum, the statute is satisfied. After the New York Court of Appeals decided *Feathers v. McLucas,* the New York legislature amended the long-arm statute by adding a provision to cover cases in which the tortious act or omission took place *outside* New York but the injury was suffered *in* New York. The legislature added a requirement in such cases, however, making jurisdiction proper *only* if the defendant engaged in a "persistent course of conduct" in New York or "derived substantial

---

[271]There is something incongruous about this inquiry at this stage. It is not known whether the defendant is liable for a tort until the case is decided on the merits, which might be years after this jurisdictional assessment is made. Obviously, the court must avoid a mini-trial on the merits at this stage. Just as obviously, the conclusion that the court has jurisdiction does not predetermine the merits.

[272]209 N.E.2d 68 (N.Y. 1965).

[273]176 N.E.2d 761 (Ill. 1961). The Florida Supreme Court has held that a tortious e-mail sent from outside the state into Florida constitutes the commission of a tortious act in Florida. Wendt v. Horowitz, 822 So. 2d 1252 (Fla. 2002).

revenue" from activities in New York. Several states have adopted this language from the New York statute.

Thus, in several states, there are two long-arm provisions dealing with a nonresident's tortious act or omission. One provides for jurisdiction in the state if the nonresident committed the tortious act or omission *in* the state. The other provides for jurisdiction if the nonresident committed the tortious act or omission *outside* the state, but which injured the plaintiff in the state. This latter provision is satisfied, however, only if the plaintiff can make an additional showing: either that the defendant engaged in some persistent course of conduct in the forum or derived substantial revenue from activities in the forum.

When we think about it, in a state adopting such statutes, the legislature has in essence told its courts *not* to adopt the Illinois interpretation of the language "commits a tortious act or omission" in the forum. After all, if the Illinois interpretation is adopted, the tortious act or omission out of state is considered to be a tortious act or omission in the state (because the plaintiff was injured in the forum). Such an interpretation would render wholly superfluous the legislation addressing the case of the out-of-state tort harming the plaintiff instate. Yet the Georgia Supreme Court adopted the Illinois interpretation of the basic provision, at least for torts involving personal injury.[274] The same court rejected the Illinois interpretation, however, in a case involving fraud.[275] The inconsistency is strange, since the statute purports to make no distinction between torts involving personal injury and torts involving fraud. The interpretation also seems antithetical to the interests of Georgia plaintiffs, since their state supreme court has concluded that it does not want them suing nonresident frauds in Georgia. The Georgia Supreme Court later attempted to remedy the situation,[276] but the main point is clear: Each state's legislature passes the statutes it thinks best, and the interpretation of the statute is up to the state's courts. If the courts misinterpret the statutes, in theory the legislature should amend the statute. Legislatures are rarely so assiduous.

Given the divergent interpretations regarding statutes addressing tortious acts or omissions by nonresidents, let's do another hypothetical and think of how many things can arise *just on this statutory issue.*

- o ***Example #30.*** Defendant is a nonresident who has not engaged in a persistent course of conduct in the forum and has not derived substantial

---

[274]*See* Coe & Payne Co. v. Wood-Mosaic Corp., 195 S.E.2d 399 (Ga. 1973).

[275]*See* Gust v. Flint, 356 S.E.2d 513 (Ga. 1987).

[276]Clinical & Consulting Servs., LLC v. First Nat'l Bank of Ames, 620 S.E.2d 352 (Ga. 2005).

revenue from the forum. Thus that portion of the long-arm statute allowing jurisdiction over a nonresident who commits a tortious act or omission out of state that causes an injury in the forum does not apply. Defendant commits a tortious act out of state that causes an injury in the forum.

The most likely interpretation is that the statute is not satisfied. After all, the legislature dealt specially with defendants who committed a tortious act or omission out of state in that part of the statute requiring a showing of persistent course of conduct or deriving substantial revenue in the forum. Accordingly, the Illinois interpretation of the basic provision ("commits a tortious act or omission in" the forum) seems incorrect.

On the other hand, courts of each state are free to interpret their state's long-arm statutes as they see fit, and it is possible that a court would adopt the Illinois interpretation and find jurisdiction under the provision allowing jurisdiction over a nonresident who "commits a tortious act or omission" in the forum.

In several states with laundry-list long-arm statutes, the courts have concluded that the legislature intended to extend personal jurisdiction to the full limits of the Constitution. This conclusion seems odd in the face of a detailed laundry-list statute. If the legislature intended to grant jurisdiction to the limit of due process, it could have passed a California-type statute in one sentence. But, again, it's up to the courts to interpret what the statute means.

  o In *World-Wide Volkswagen*, the Supreme Court determined that Oklahoma did not have jurisdiction over two defendants. It noted the very detailed Oklahoma long-arm statute and also noted that the Oklahoma Supreme Court had held that the statute reached the constitutional limit. Could the United States Supreme Court have avoided the constitutional issue by holding that the Oklahoma *statute* did not extend to the facts of the case?

No. Remember from §1.2.3 that the U.S. Supreme Court can review state supreme court decisions only on matters of *federal* law. The Supreme Court has no business telling the sovereign state of Oklahoma what the Oklahoma statute means. It can only assess whether jurisdiction was appropriate under the (*federal*) Constitution.

Why would a state choose to give its courts less than the constitutional maximum power to exercise personal jurisdiction over nonresidents? It would seem that each state would want to allow its citizens the full constitutional reach of personal jurisdiction. Failing to do so may mean that the citizen will have to travel to a distant state to sue the defendant. Some have suggested that states may decide that exercise of the full constitutional power takes the courts too close to unfair assertions of jurisdiction. Remember, the Constitution does not require a convenient forum; it only prohibits a grossly inconvenient forum. As one scholar put it, "To say that a law does not violate the due process clause is to say the least possible good about it."[277]

The fact that courts may interpret their state's long-arm statute *not* to apply to a given fact pattern opens another important possibility: the exercise of QIR-2 jurisdiction. Too many people assume that QIR-2 is dead after *Shaffer v. Heitner* (discussed in §2.4.4). True, after that case, the exercise of jurisdiction in QIR-2 cases must satisfy *International Shoe*. But that does not mean that QIR-2 jurisdiction has been subsumed by *in personam* jurisdiction. Suppose the nonresident defendant has sufficient contacts with the forum to satisfy *International Shoe* but that the state courts interpret the long-arm statute so narrowly that the statute does not apply in the case. If the defendant has any property in the forum, which can be seized at the outset as a jurisdictional predicate, there is no reason for the plaintiff not to try to establish QIR-2 jurisdiction. For such cases, the long-arm statute is irrelevant. It grants *in personam* jurisdiction. The proper statute, as we will see now, is an attachment statute.

Statutes Relating to In Rem and Quasi-in-Rem Jurisdiction

The statutory analysis for *in rem* and *quasi-in-rem* cases is usually simple. Each state has an "attachment" statute, which permits attachment of property found in the forum state that a nonresident "owns or claims to own." In *in rem* and QIR-1 cases, of course, the nonresident claims to own the property. In QIR-2 cases, the nonresident clearly owns the property. The statute requires that the property be seized at the outset of the case and provides methods for giving notice to the defendant.

Again, do not overlook QIR-2 jurisdiction in a case in which *in personam* jurisdiction is impossible because the courts have interpreted the long-arm statute narrowly. If the long-arm statute does not apply, and thus *in personam* jurisdiction is not possible, but the defendant nonetheless has sufficient contacts with the forum to satisfy *International Shoe* (and has property in the forum that can be attached at the outset of the case as the jurisdictional predicate), the plaintiff should try QIR-2 jurisdiction.

---

[277]Elliott Cheatham, *Conflict of Laws: Some Developments and Some Questions*, 25 Ark. L. Rev. 9, 25 (1971-1972).

Registration Statutes and Consent as a Basis for In Personam *Jurisdiction*

The tenor of Supreme Court cases on personal jurisdiction since 2011 has been restrictive. *Goodyear, Daimler*, and *BNSF* rejected general jurisdiction. *McIntyre* and *Bristol-Myers Squibb* rejected specific jurisdiction. Discouraged by these precedents, some plaintiffs are attempting to get personal jurisdiction over businesses not on the basis of contacts but because of consent.[278] All states have "registration" statutes that require out-of-state businesses that wish to operate in the state to "register," appoint an agent in state (often found in a "registered office" in state), and to pay fees. The theory is that by adhering to the requirements of the registration statute, the company has consented to jurisdiction.[279]

The first issue is whether a particular state's statute provides that registration constitutes consent to jurisdiction. Statutes vary considerably.[280] Even if the statute envisions consent to jurisdiction, the next question is whether the consent is to specific jurisdiction or to general jurisdiction. Pennsylvania appears to have the only statute that expressly provides that registration establishes general jurisdiction.[281] Other statutes envision only specific jurisdiction, and many are simply not clear on this score.

The most interesting issue, however, is whether a registration statute providing for general jurisdiction based upon consent is constitutional. The Court upheld the validity of such a statute over a century ago.[282] But today, in the "new era" of general jurisdiction, is this still true? Specifically, do *Goodyear, Daimler,* and *BNSF*—permitting

---

[278]We discussed this issue in §2.4.2, in the subsection entitled "*In Personam* Expansion Regarding Businesses." Recall that *Pennoyer* suggested that states, in exchange for permitting businesses to operate within their borders, can require the business to appoint an agent for service of process in the state. In general, courts have not been receptive to upholding jurisdiction over corporations based only upon service of process on a corporate official present in the forum. *See generally* Cody James Jacobs, *If Corporations Are People, Why Can't They Play Tag?*, 46 N.M. L. Rev. 1 (2015).

[279]For discussion of the history of consent to jurisdiction through corporate registration, *see* Charles W. "Rocky" Rhodes, *Nineteenth Century Personal Jurisdiction Doctrine in a Twenty-First Century World,* 64 Fla. L. Rev. 387, 436-441 (2012).

[280]*Compare* Rykoff-Sexton, Inc. v. American Appraisal Assocs., Inc., 469 N.W.2d 88, 90-91 (Minn. 1991) (Minnesota statute envisions consent to personal jurisdiction) *with* DeLeon v. BNSF Rw. Co., 426 P.3d 1, 4 (Mont. 2018) (Montana statute does not envision consent to jurisdiction).

[281]42 Pa. Cons. State. §5301 ("general personal jurisdiction"). *See* Charles W. "Rocky" Rhodes, *The Roberts Court's Jurisdictional Revolution within* Ford's *Frame,* 51 Stetson L. Rev. ___ (2021).

[282]Pennsylvania Fire Ins. Co. of Philadelphia v. Gold Issue Mining & Milling, 243 U.S. 93, 95-96 (1917).

general jurisdiction only where the defendant is "at home"—rule out general jurisdiction in other states based upon consent? The Court has not addressed the question, but the tension is obvious: If a corporation is deemed to consent "to general jurisdiction in every state in which it registered, . . . *Daimler*'s ruling would be robbed of meaning by a back-door thief."[283] This possibility has influenced some courts to interpret registration statutes narrowly, to permit only specific jurisdiction.[284] In fact, the Delaware Supreme Court overturned its older holdings that registration granted general jurisdiction.[285] The issue is of increasing importance as the profession adjusts to the current limited scope of general jurisdiction. There is a strong argument that states ought to be able to provide that registration constitutes consent to jurisdiction only with regard to claims within their sovereign prerogatives, and not to coerce general jurisdiction as a cost of registering to do business.[286]

§2.6 Personal Jurisdiction in Federal Court

§2.6.1 Statutory Analysis (and Why Federal Courts Usually Apply State Personal Jurisdiction Statutes)

In §1.2.1, we noted that federal courts (as opposed to state courts) can hear only certain types of cases (principally "diversity of citizenship" cases and "federal question" cases). We discuss this limited federal subject matter jurisdiction in Chapter 4. State courts, as we see in §4.2, however, have general subject matter jurisdiction; with few exceptions, state courts can hear any kind of case, whether it arises under the law of that state, the law of another state or country, or under federal law.

---

[283]Brown v. Lockheed Martin Corp., 814 F.3d 619, 640 (2d Cir. 2016).

[284]*See, e.g.,* Lanham v. BNSF Ry. Co., 939 N.W.2d 363, 368-371 (Neb. 2020) (consent to general jurisdiction would violate *Daimler*).

[285]Genuine Parts Co. v. Cepac, 137 A.3d 123, 126-128 (Del. 2016) (registration does not subject business to general jurisdiction).

[286]Professor Rhodes made this argument in the article cited in 279 above. He and Professor Robertson have proposed a model act along these lines. Charles W. "Rocky" Rhodes & Cassandra Burke Robertson, *A New State Registration Act: Legislating a Longer Arm for Personal Jurisdiction,* 57 Harv. J. on Legis. 377, 409-410 (2020). Professor Rensberger has made similar arguments against full-scale general jurisdiction in the registration context. Jeffrey L. Rensberger, *Consent to Jurisdiction Based on Registering to Do Business: A Limited Role for General Jurisdiction,* 58 San Diego L. Rev. 309 (2021).

What about personal jurisdiction? The first step in state court, as we just saw in §2.5, is to assess whether there is a state statute that permits the exercise of personal jurisdiction. What about in federal court? In the vast majority of cases, the federal court will use the same state law. This conclusion is compelled by Federal Rule 4(k)(1)(A), which requires the federal court essentially to act, for personal jurisdiction purposes, like a state court in the state in which it sits.[287]

It is not obvious why this should be so. In fact, it seems wrong. After all, in state court, the state is exercising authority, so state law is appropriate. But in federal court, the United States is exercising authority. So one would expect federal law to govern. And it does: Rule 4(k)(1)(A) is federal. But that provision directs the federal court to use state law. Use of state personal jurisdiction statutes makes some sense in federal court if the case invokes diversity of citizenship jurisdiction. There, the claim being asserted is governed by state law (as we see in Chapter 10). In matters of state law, it may be appropriate for the federal court's personal jurisdiction power to be congruent with that of state courts.

- ○ ***Example #31.*** *P*, a citizen of Missouri, sues *D*, a citizen of Kentucky, in a federal court in Missouri. The case invokes diversity of citizenship jurisdiction. To determine whether the federal court in Missouri has personal jurisdiction over *D*, the federal judge will apply the Missouri statutes on personal jurisdiction. If one of those Missouri provisions is satisfied, the judge will then assess whether personal jurisdiction in Missouri is constitutional.

But what about cases that are in federal court under federal question jurisdiction? In these cases, as we discuss in §4.6, the underlying substantive claims must arise under *federal* law. It makes less sense to fetter the personal jurisdiction reach of a federal court when it is enforcing federal law. Sensible or not, however, Rule 4(k)(1)(A) makes no distinction between diversity and federal question cases.

- ○ ***Example #32.*** *P* sues *D* in federal court in Missouri, alleging that *D* violated *P*'s rights under federal anti-discrimination law. The case invokes federal question jurisdiction. To determine whether the federal court in

---

[287]The Rule permits jurisdiction over one "who could be subjected to the jurisdiction of a court of general jurisdiction in the state in which the [federal] district court is located . . . ." Fed. R. Civ. P. 4(k)(1)(A). The reference here to "general jurisdiction" is not general personal jurisdiction. Rather, it is to general *subject matter* jurisdiction. As discussed in §4.2, state courts can generally hear any kind of case and thus have general subject matter jurisdiction.

Missouri has personal jurisdiction over *D*, the federal judge will apply the Missouri statutes on personal jurisdiction. If one of those provisions is satisfied, the judge will then assess whether personal jurisdiction in Missouri is constitutional.

Rule 4(k)(1)(A) is best understood as reflecting a policy of comity. The federal government is not required to limit its courts' reach to the reach of state courts. But it has agreed as a general matter to do so. Accordingly, statutorily and constitutionally, the personal jurisdiction power of federal courts is co-extensive with that of state courts of the state in which the federal court sits.

But Rule 4(k)(1)(A) does not govern in every case. There are three situations in which that Rule does not apply: (1) under Rule 4(k)(1)(C), when Congress has provided a statutory basis for personal jurisdiction, (2) under Rule 4(k)(1)(B), called the "bulge rule," which allows special jurisdictional reach to join parties to litigation in very limited circumstances (which do *not* include the exercise of personal jurisdiction over the original defendant in the case), and (3) under Rule 4(k)(2), in very narrow circumstances involving federal question cases. These scenarios are discussed in detail in §3.3.4.[288]

§2.6.2 Constitutional Analysis (Fifth Amendment or Fourteenth Amendment?)

Assuming there is a statutory grant of personal jurisdiction, the next question is whether the exercise of jurisdiction is constitutional under due process. As discussed in §2.3, however, there are two due process clauses: that in the Fifth Amendment (which limits the federal government), and that in the Fourteenth Amendment (which limits state governments). Which one does a federal court apply? The answer to this question matters because the Fifth Amendment is likely broader than the Fourteenth.

When the case is covered by Rule 4(k)(1)(A), and the federal court finds that the forum state's statutory grant of personal jurisdiction is met, the court will the apply the Fourteenth Amendment to assess whether jurisdiction is constitutionally permissible. Thus, it will look

---

[288]*See* Patrick J. Borchers, *Extending Federal Rule of Civil Procedure 4(k)(2): A Way to (Partially) Clean Up the Personal Jurisdiction Mess*, 67 Am. U. L. Rev, 413 (2017); Stephen E. Sachs, *How Congress Should Fix Personal Jurisdiction*, 108 Nw. U. L. Rev. 1301 (2014); A. Benjamin Spencer, *The Territorial Reach of Federal Courts*, 71 Fla L. Rev. 979 (2019); Patrick Wooley, *Rediscovering the Limited Role of the Federal Rules in Regulating Personal Jurisdiction*, 56 Hous. L. Rev. 565 (2019).

to the defendant's contacts with the forum state. This result is dictated by Rule 4(k)(1)(A), which equates the federal court's personal jurisdiction power with that of a state court. The result is the same in diversity[289] and in federal question cases.[290] To be clear, the Fourteenth Amendment does not apply *directly* to the federal courts. It restrains only the power of state governments. The Fourteenth Amendment applies to federal court cases *indirectly* by virtue of Rule 4(k)(1)(A).

When Rule 4(k)(1)(A) does not apply, however, the constitutional inquiry in federal court is rooted in the Fifth Amendment. In the last paragraph of §2.6.1 (three paragraphs above where we are), we saw three situations in which Rule 4(k)(1)(A) does not govern. The most significant is Rule 4(k)(1)(C), which applies when Congress has provided a statutory basis for personal jurisdiction. The typical statute of this type provides for "nationwide" (sometimes even "worldwide") service of process, often by permitting jurisdiction wherever the defendant "may be found." Most of these statutes apply to claims arising under specific federal laws.[291] A few, however, extend nationwide service of process to cases involving state-law claims.[292] In such cases, the constitutional propriety of personal jurisdiction is assessed under the Fifth Amendment, not the Fourteenth Amendment.

The Court has never explained how the personal jurisdiction analysis might differ under the Fifth and Fourteenth Amendments.[293] One widely accepted contention is that the Fifth Amendment inquiry focuses on contacts between the defendant and the United States as a whole (as opposed to the defendant's contacts with a single state).[294]

---

[289]*See, e.g., Burger King*, 471 U.S. at 464 (applying Fourteenth Amendment in case invoking diversity of citizenship jurisdiction).

[290]*See, e.g., Walden v. Fiore,* 571 U.S. 277, 283 (2014) (applying Fourteenth Amendment in case arising under federal law).

[291]*See, e.g.,* 15 U.S.C. §22 (permitting service wherever the defendant may be found in certain federal antitrust cases).

[292]*See, e.g.,* 28 U.S.C. §1697 (nationwide service of process in certain aggregate-claim cases); 28 U.S.C. §1335 (nationwide service in interpleader cases). We discuss this provision in §13.2.2.

[293]The Court has implied that the Fifth Amendment may be broader than the Fourteenth. *See Bristol-Myers Squibb,* 137 S. Ct. at 1783-1784 ("Since our decision concerns the due process limits on the exercise of specific jurisdiction by a State, we leave open the question whether the Fifth Amendment imposes the same restrictions on the exercise of personal jurisdiction by a federal court").

[294]Two Justices espoused this position in *Stafford v. Briggs,* 444 U.S. 527, 554 (1980) (Stewart, J., and Brennan, J., dissenting). No other Justice in the case commented upon the suggestion, and the Court has not subsequently taken a position on it. *Compare* Douglass v. Nippon Yusen Kabushiki Kaisha, 996 F. 3d 289, 296 (5th Cir. 2021) ("We find unpersuasive the D.C. Circuit's conclusion that Fifth Amendment due process standards must track those imposed by the Fourteenth Amendment. In part, the D.C. Circuit relies on its finding that 'the Supreme Court [has] applied Fourteenth

This "national contacts" approach is appealing, because there is no reason, as a matter of constitutional *power*, that the federal courts should be limited by state lines.

Some courts have adopted a "pure national contacts" approach, under which jurisdiction is proper under the Fifth Amendment if the defendant's contacts with the United States would support jurisdiction under the *International Shoe* test.[295] These courts stop the inquiry there and do not assess the fairness or reasonableness of jurisdiction. This approach emphasizes the sovereignty aspect of personal jurisdiction law at the expense of the concern about fairness to the defendant.

The majority of courts today appear not to apply the "pure national contacts" approach, but to replicate the methodology from *World-Wide Volkswagen* and *Burger King*. The difference, again, is that the contacts prong addresses contacts with the entire country, and not with a single state. First, the plaintiff must show sufficient contacts with the United States to justify jurisdiction. Second, the burden shifts to the defendant to defeat jurisdiction by demonstrating that the forum is so inconvenient that it is at a severe disadvantage in the litigation.

> ○ ***Example #33.*** *P* sues *D* in federal court in Florida. *D* is an American company that has no contacts with Florida but has significant contacts with other states along the Atlantic coast. The claim against *D* arises from those activities. A federal statute provides for nationwide service of process. Does the federal court in Florida have specific personal jurisdiction under the Fifth Amendment?

This fact pattern is adapted from the influential decision in *Republic of Panama v. BCCI Holdings*.[296] There, the Eleventh Circuit renounced its earlier adoption of the "pure national contacts" view and adopted the two-step approach common under progeny of *International Shoe*. It upheld specific jurisdiction in the federal court in Florida. The lack of contacts between the defendant and Florida was irrelevant. The defendant's contact with the United States (as a whole) demonstrated ample purposeful availment and that it was foreseeable the defendant

---

Amendment personal-jurisdiction standards in Fifth Amendment cases . . . .' This is not the case.") *with* Livnat v. Palestinian Authority, 851 F.3d 45 (D.C. Cir. 2017). ("No court has ever held that the Fifth Amendment permits personal jurisdiction without the same 'minimum contacts' with the United States as the Fourteenth Amendment requires with respect to states").

[295]Peter Hay, Patrick J. Borchers & Symeon Symeonides, Conflict of Laws 481-482 (6th ed. 2018).

[296]119 F.3d 935 (11th Cir. 1997). *See also* Reynolds v. Behrman Capital IC L.P., 988 F.3d 1314, 1325 (11th Cir. 2021) ("The court must 'examine a defendant's aggregate contacts with the nation as a whole rather than [its] contacts with the forum state in conducting the Fifth Amendment analysis.'").

could be sued in the United States. And the defendant failed to demonstrate that litigation in Florida was unconstitutionally burdensome or unreasonable.

Does the "new era" in general personal jurisdiction (discussed in §2.4.5) affect the Fifth Amendment? Recall that general jurisdiction permits a court to exercise jurisdiction over a defendant for claims that did not arise in the forum. The Court now holds that general jurisdiction is permissible only where the defendant is "at home." Moreover, in such cases, the "fairness factors" (listed initially in *World-Wide Volkswagen*) are irrelevant. The sole question, then, is whether the defendant is "at home" in the forum. But the cases that ushered in the "new era" in general jurisdiction applied the Fourteenth Amendment, and not the Fifth Amendment.

Applying *Daimler* under the Fifth Amendment could thwart significant policies of the United States. Consider the Anti-Terrorism Act (ATA), which creates a civil right of action for citizens of the United States injured or killed by acts of international terrorism.[297] In a series of cases, American citizens sued the Palestine Liberation Organization (PLO) and Palestinian Authority (PA) for wrongful death and personal injury suffered in terrorist attacks in Israel. The plaintiffs asserted vicarious liability claims against the PLO and PA, arising from their alleged support of the attacks. In each case, specific personal jurisdiction was out of the question because nothing related to the attacks took place in the United States. Because the federal law creating the claim provided for personal jurisdiction, the Fifth Amendment governed the constitutional question.

At the time these cases were filed, general jurisdiction was proper based upon a defendant's "continuous and systematic" ties to the forum. Under the "national contacts" view, the question was whether the PLO and PA engaged in continuous and systematic activity in the United States. Some courts concluded that the answer was yes, based upon the groups' lobbying, fundraising, and other activities in this country.[298] One such case went to jury trial, and the plaintiffs won a judgment of over $655,000,000. After the decision in *Daimler*, however, the Second Circuit held that the judgment must be set aside and the case dismissed with prejudice because, under the "new era" cases on general jurisdiction, neither defendant was "at home" in the United States. It applied the Fourteenth Amendment standard set out in *Daimler* to a Fifth Amendment case.[299]

---

[297]18 U.S.C. §2331-2339.

[298]*See, e.g.,* Estate of Klieman v. Palestinian Authority, 82 F. Supp. 3d 237, 239 (D.D.C. 2015).

[299]*Waldman,* 835 F.3d at 329-330. The judgment was entered after a lengthy jury trial. Under the ATA, damages are trebled. The jury found actual damages of over

The case raises two issues. First, even if *Daimler* governs, where are organizations such as the PLO and PA "at home?" *Daimler* discussed only general jurisdiction over humans and over corporations. It suggested no proxy for where unincorporated associations, including non-sovereign governing bodies, are "at home."

Second, and more importantly, if *Daimler* applies, the fairness factors are irrelevant, which means they cannot be used to *support* jurisdiction. For example, consideration of the plaintiff's interest and the substantive policy of the forum are meaningless. In these cases, unlike *Daimler*, the plaintiffs are United States citizens, seeking recovery under a federal law expressly intended to provide a remedy for American victims of terrorist attacks on foreign soil. And, also unlike *Daimler*, Congress has clearly stated its policy choice that an American forum be available for American plaintiffs.[300]

Some point to cases such as this to argue that the Fifth Amendment should be read more broadly and applied more flexibly than the Fourteenth Amendment.[301] Particularly in litigation by American plaintiffs against foreign defendants, the interests of each (and of the United States) should be part of the equation.[302] Equating the Fifth and Fourteenth Amendments thwarts a congressional policy of providing American plaintiffs access to American courts. Granted, Congress cannot confer a right that would violate the Constitution, but, again, the context calls for an interpretation of the Fifth Amendment that is not congruent with the reach of the Fourteenth.

Dean Perdue has been particularly persuasive in making these points.[303] She argues that "[t]here is no reason to assume that the scope of legitimate judicial authority of the United States as it operates in the international community is essentially parallel to the scope of authority of each of our individual states," and concludes that it is constitutional under the Fifth Amendment for a federal court to assert personal jurisdiction solely on the basis of effects caused in the United

---

$200,000,000, which, trebled and augmented by interest from the date of judgment, made the judgment worth more than $655,000,000.

[300]For detailed discussion of the matter, *see* Ariel Winawer, Comment, *Too Far From Home: Why* Daimler's *"At Home" Standard Does Not Apply to Personal Jurisdiction Challenges in Anti-Terrorism Act Cases,* 66 Emory L.J. 161, 185-188 (2016).

[301]*Id.* at 171-174.

[302]4A Wright & Miller §1068.1.

[303]Wendy Collins Perdue, *Aliens, the Internet, and "Purposeful Availment": A Reassessment of Fifth Amendment Limits on Personal Jurisdiction,* 98 Nw. U. L. Rev. 455 (2004). *But see* Maryellen Fullerton, *Constitutional Limits on Nationwide Personal Jurisdiction in the Federal Courts,* 79 Nw. U. L. Rev. 1, 15 (1984) (arguing for similar treatment of the two Amendments). *See also* Jonathan Remy Nash, *National Personal Jurisdiction,* 68 Emory L.J. 509 (2019).

States, without consideration of "purposeful availment."[304] So far, the Court has not addressed the topic in a meaningful way.

§2.7 Putting It All Together: A Suggested Analytical Framework

We engaged in a lengthy discussion of the principles of the law of personal jurisdiction. Your job as a lawyer will be to apply these principles to a fact pattern given to you by a client to ascertain whether a court will have personal jurisdiction. Your job as a law student is to do the same with a fact pattern provided by your professor. Thus, you need to be armed with an analytical framework with which to address a personal jurisdiction question. This section provides such a framework. It is not sacrosanct. You may discern a better or more helpful framework on your own. This is simply my effort to synthesize the material.

First: Statutory Bases for Personal Jurisdiction

The first analytical step is to determine whether a *statute* permits the exercise of personal jurisdiction. Even in federal court, this will almost always be a *state* statute.[305] If you are dealing with *in personam* jurisdiction, the statute might be one addressed to the traditional bases of jurisdiction, such as those that grant *in personam* jurisdiction over persons who are served with process in the state or who are domiciled there. More likely, the fact pattern will involve purported jurisdiction over a nonresident, in which either a nonresident motorist act or a long-arm statute may apply.

In applying any statute (especially a long-arm statute), study the language carefully. Among other things, look to see whether the statute expressly provides only for specific jurisdiction (which is likely)—that is, jurisdiction over the defendant only for some act done or effect caused in the forum state. Beyond this, look to whether the statute requires that the defendant transact "substantial" business in the forum as opposed to transacting "any" business in the forum. Similarly, there may be a difference between a defendant's committing a "tortious act" in the forum versus a "tortious act or omission" in the forum.

---

[304]Perdue, previous footnote, 98 Nw. U. L. Rev. at 461, 470 (2004).

[305]Except in those rare situations, noted in the last paragraph of §2.6.1, in which the federal courts have been given broader personal jurisdiction power than that of the state courts of the state in which they sit.

Always be aware that the same language may be interpreted differently. As discussed in §2.5, the classic example is the provision for jurisdiction over a nonresident who "commits a tortious act or omission" in the forum. As we saw there, some courts interpret this to require that the tort itself take place in the forum, while others require only that the injury occur in the forum. Many students have thrown away many points on many exams by failing to assess such differing interpretations of statutory bases for personal jurisdiction.[306]

If the case involves *in rem* or *quasi-in-rem* jurisdiction, you will need an attachment statute. These statutes do not vary much from state to state, and generally apply to permit attachment at the outset of the proceedings of property that the defendant "owns or claims to own." Usually, the statutory assessment in such a case is straightforward. And, as we emphasized in §2.5, be prepared to suggest that the plaintiff use QIR-2 jurisdiction if *in personam* is problematic because of a narrow interpretation of a long-arm statute. Of course, the defendant must have property in the forum that can be attached at the outset of litigation as the jurisdictional predicate for QIR-2.

Second: Constitutional Analysis

If you find that there is a statutory basis for the exercise of personal jurisdiction—be it *in personam, in rem*, or *quasi-in-rem*—or even that there likely is a statutory basis, the second part of the analysis is to assess whether the exercise of jurisdiction on the facts would be constitutional. We will detail here an analytical framework for applying the Fourteenth Amendment.[307]

I suggest that you first identify whether the case is *in personam, in rem*, or *quasi-in-rem*. (Remember that it might be more than one, as when the plaintiff seeks *in personam* jurisdiction under a long-arm statute and, in the alternative, QIR-2 under an attachment statute.)

If it is an *in personam* case, you should then identify whether the case involves one of the traditional *Pennoyer* bases of jurisdiction: service of process on the defendant (or her agent) in the forum, consent, or residence (usually meaning domicile) in the forum. As to such bases, it is wise to identify it as a traditional basis and to note that under *Pennoyer* that basis would suffice. Then, however, you should recognize that *International Shoe* may have affected the traditional bases. True, nothing in *International Shoe* purported to overrule *Pennoyer*,

---

[306]Obviously, you must take all of these suggestions with a grain of salt, depending on what your professor covered.

[307]As we saw in §2.6.2, there is less certainty about how to analyze personal jurisdiction under the Fifth Amendment.

but there is that broad language in *Shaffer v. Heitner* that "all assertions of state-court jurisdiction" must be assessed by *International Shoe*. As to the most traditional of bases (service of process on the defendant in the forum), the Justices split four-to-four in *Burnham* as to whether *Pennoyer* applied or whether *International Shoe* applied.

We have no obvious similar split regarding the other traditional bases of jurisdiction. Still, it may be argued, based upon *Shaffer,* that the court must undertake an *International Shoe* assessment as to those as well. For instance, we know that *Hess v. Pawloski* upheld a nonresident motorist statute on the basis of implied consent (and service of process on an agent in the forum). The Court has never overruled *Hess*. But if *Shaffer* really meant that *all* cases must be assessed under *International Shoe*, a nonresident motorist case might not be justified solely on consent but must be analyzed under minimum contacts, too.[308]

You must apply *International Shoe* to assess the constitutionality of personal jurisdiction in cases involving nonresidents or others not falling within a traditional basis. Accordingly, the defendant must have "such minimum contacts" with the forum that the exercise of jurisdiction does not offend "traditional notions of fair play and substantial justice." As noted when we discussed *Ford Motor* in §2.4.6, the Court has not been assiduous in recent cases about the methodology to be employed in applying *International Shoe*.

Still, the Court has never expressly rejected the process set out in *World-Wide Volkswagen* that approached specific jurisdiction in two steps: contact followed by fairness. *Bristol-Myers Squibb* and *Ford Motor* show that there is an intermediary step: After establishing that there is purposeful contact, the next issue is relatedness. That issue will determine whether the case is one of specific or of general jurisdiction. If it is specific, then we proceed to the analysis of whether jurisdiction is fair or reasonable on the facts. It makes little sense to address relatedness until *after* contact is established. Why? Because the relatedness inquiry assumes that there is contact. After all, the relatedness question is whether the plaintiff's claim "arises out of or relates to" *the defendant's contact with the forum*. You cannot assess relatedness until you know whether there is a relevant contact.

---

[308]You should get a sense of what your professor thinks on this score—whether, for example, domicile is a basis for personal jurisdiction in itself (as *Milliken v. Meyer* held) or whether *Shaffer* means that even domicile cases must be assessed under *International Shoe*. Similarly, *Goodyear* and *Daimler* indicated that a human is subject to general jurisdiction where she is domiciled. They did so, apparently, on the basis of *International Shoe* contacts rather than on a traditional basis.

Contact. The court first assesses whether there is "contact" between the defendant and the forum. Indeed, the cases make clear that such contact is an absolute prerequisite to jurisdiction. Even if the forum were undeniably fair and reasonable, there can be no jurisdiction without contact. This requirement proves that state lines are not irrelevant. If anything, *Ford Motor* confirmed the importance of "territoriality" by embracing an "interstate federalism" basis of *International Shoe*.

It has been clear since *Hanson v. Denckla* that a contact must result from the defendant's *purposeful availment* of the forum. The contact between the defendant and the forum must not be fortuitous or accidental. It must relate in some way to the defendant's volition. This does not require that the defendant actually entered the forum. It can be satisfied by her intended *effects* in the forum, as we saw in *Calder*. Purposeful availment does not necessarily require a desire for financial gain (though it often does consist of that). For instance, a desire to use the forum's roads for a vacation can constitute purposeful availment. Perhaps "purposeful contact" is a better phrase. Consider the case of an intentional tort. One who mails a bomb to the recipient in the forum state is not really "availing" of much, but certainly is forging a purposeful contact that will support jurisdiction.

Remember that there is especial uncertainty concerning purposeful contact in stream-of-commerce cases. In *Asahi* and *McIntyre,* the Court failed to generate a majority view on what constitutes a contact. In the process of failing, it gave us arguable approaches to the issue (which we discussed in §2.4.5). Lawyers and courts have been left to struggle with those competing approaches.

In *World-Wide Volkswagen,* the Court said there was a second aspect to contact: foreseeability. Specifically, it is not enough that it is foreseeable that the defendant's product will get into the forum. Rather, it must be foreseeable that the defendant could get sued in the forum. We emphasized the circularity of this point, however, since a defendant who knows that her product is being used in the forum and knows that the product could hurt someone if it malfunctioned could foresee being sued there. Oddly, the Court has not mentioned foreseeability as part of the contact analysis since *World-Wide Volkswagen*. Nonetheless, more recent cases are consistent with what that case said. Both the plurality and concurring opinions in *McIntyre* seem to concede that it was foreseeable that the machine would get to New Jersey, yet neither finds a relevant contact. And in *Ford Motor,* the Court upheld jurisdiction in part because Ford's significant contacts with the forum gave it "fair warning" that it could be sued in the forum. Accordingly, foreseeability still seems to get considered, but not labeled as such.

The consideration of whether there is contact is relevant in every case—whether specific or general jurisdiction. In most cases of general jurisdiction, the contact is obvious. For example, a human defendant who is domiciled in the forum has clearly availed herself of the forum by establishing her home there. Or she is voluntarily in the forum when served with process.

Relatedness. Assuming there is purposeful contact (or if it's arguable that there is), the next issue is relatedness. Here we ask this: Does the plaintiff's claim "arise out of or relate to" the defendant's contact with the forum? *Bristol-Myers Squibb* gave some guidance here, but not much. It rejected jurisdiction over claims by non-forum residents for claims arising completely outside the forum. The fact that similarly situated plaintiffs who resided in the forum were hurt by an identical product was irrelevant.

Ford Motor establishes that "arise out of or relate to" is not a unitary standard. If a defendant has the sort of broad, continuous purposeful contact with the forum that Ford has with nearly every state, the plaintiff's claim need only "relate to" those contacts. If the defendant has lesser contact with the forum (a line the Court does not tell us how to draw), the plaintiff's claim must "arise out of" that contact. The Court tells us this latter test requires some form of causation: The defendant's contact must have caused the harm suffered by the plaintiff. But the Court does not tell us much about what level of causation is required: simple "but for" causation or proximate causation?

If the answer to the relatedness question is yes, then we have a case of specific jurisdiction, and proceed to assess whether jurisdiction is fair or reasonable under the fairness factors below. At least, that is the lock-step approach established in *World-Wide Volkswagen* and discussed through many cases. On the other hand, *Ford Motor* appeared to conflate the fairness factors into the discussion of relatedness. While there is thus some doubt about whether the fairness assessment is a separate step in the analysis, there is no doubt what factors are to be analyzed in determining whether jurisdiction is fair or reasonable. We discuss those factors below.

If the answer to the relatedness question is no, then we have a case of general jurisdiction. In the "new era" (established by *Goodyear*, *Daimler*, and *BNSF*) general jurisdiction is proper if the defendant is "at home" in the forum. For a human, that is where she is domiciled. For a corporation, it is where (1) it is incorporated and (2) it has its principal place of business (meaning, apparently, its "nerve center," where managers direct corporate activities). In addition, the Court has suggested there might be general jurisdiction in a state in which "all" the corporate activities take place. It is not clear this latter point means much since a corporation doing "all" its business in one state will likely be incorporated there or maintain its principal place of business there.

The "new era" is uncertain in at least two particulars. First, we do not know where other defendants — for example, unincorporated associations—are "at home." State and lower federal courts are wrestling with that issue. Second, serving process on a defendant who is voluntarily present in the forum ("tag" or "transient" jurisdiction) has traditionally supported general jurisdiction. In the recent general jurisdiction cases, the Court did not mention that traditional understanding. Given the pedigree of tag jurisdiction, however, it is doubtful that the Court intended to jettison it. (And though tag jurisdiction historically has worked to give general jurisdiction over individuals, the same has not been true for businesses; as Justice Gorsuch lamented in his concurrence in *Ford Motor,* service on a business agent in the forum generally has not given general jurisdiction over the business.)

An emerging area of importance is whether a business that satisfies a registration statute (allowing it to do business in a state in which it is not incorporated) might be subject to jurisdiction (even, depending on the terms of the statute, general jurisdiction) on the basis of consent. Courts increasingly are rejecting general jurisdiction on this basis as inconsistent with the "new era" of general jurisdiction cases.

In general jurisdiction cases, the Court in *Daimler* established that a fairness assessment was irrelevant. Accordingly, if there is general jurisdiction, we assume that the forum is fair. The fairness assessment is relevant, therefore, only in cases of specific jurisdiction.

Fairness (or Reasonableness). Once we have contact and relatedness, the question becomes whether the exercise of specific jurisdiction is fair or reasonable under the circumstances. In *International Shoe* terms, we must determine whether the exercise of jurisdiction comports with "traditional notions of fair play and substantial justice." Starting with *World-Wide Volkswagen,* the Court cited five factors as relevant to this inquiry. As noted, *Ford Motor* may suggest that these factors are part of the relatedness inquiry as opposed to a separate step, but the factors are clear.

First is the burden on the defendant. The defendant will usually complain that the forum is inconvenient, perhaps because it is far from her home or because it will be difficult to get her witnesses or her evidence to the forum. On this score, *Burger King* established that the defendant has a very high burden. She must establish not that the forum is inconvenient, but that it is *unconstitutionally unfair.* The standard is difficult: She must show that the forum is so "gravely inconvenient" that it puts her at a "severe disadvantage" in the litigation. And remember, in determining whether this is true, the relative wealth of the opposing party is not a significant factor. Thus, in *Burger King,* Justice Brennan's opinion concluded that two "little guy" franchisees in Michigan could be forced to litigate in Florida, in the backyard of the huge multinational corporate plaintiff.

159

The second fairness factor is the forum state's interest in adjudicating the dispute. In *McGee*, the Court noted that the forum state had an interest in providing a courtroom for its citizen in her case against a nonresident insurance company. The Court has never told us exactly how such an interest must be manifested. In *McGee*, California had passed statutes regulating the insurance industry and providing for jurisdiction in claims against it. In *Ford Motor*, the forum had an interest in the enforcement of its traffic safety laws. At some level, it seems that every state has an interest in providing justice for its citizens. This does not mean that the plaintiff must always be a citizen of the forum, but that fact may help support jurisdiction.

The third fairness factor is the plaintiff's interest in obtaining convenient and effective relief. It is not clear how much weight this factor is accorded, though it is clearly less important than the burden on the defendant.

The fourth and fifth fairness factors are, respectively, "the interstate judicial system's interest in obtaining the most efficient resolution of controversies" and "the shared interest of the several States in furthering fundamental substantive social policies." Very few cases discuss these factors. *Kulko* spoke of the shared interest in family harmony and purported to further it by denying jurisdiction over a father who had acquiesced in his children's desire to live with their mother. In addition, in *Keeton*, the Court found a shared interstate interest in New Hampshire's exercising jurisdiction concerning the harm caused to the plaintiff in other states by an alleged defamation.

In rem/QIR. If the case involves *in rem* or *quasi-in-rem* jurisdiction, the constitutional assessment must start with *Shaffer v. Heitner*. At the very least, that case means that the *Pennoyer* requirement that attachment of the property at the outset is not enough. *Shaffer* requires that *in rem* and *quasi-in-rem* jurisdiction cases be assessed under *International Shoe*. Specifically, that means that the defendant's contacts with the forum must satisfy *International Shoe*.

It is important to remember, however, that the Court in *Shaffer* recognized that in several instances the presence of the property in the forum (attached at the outset) may satisfy this test. Specifically, in *in rem* and QIR-1 cases, the fact that the defendant claims to own the property in the forum almost always means that the defendant has minimum contacts with the forum. Similarly, in QIR-2 cases in which the property attached caused the injury of which the plaintiff complains, the presence of the property likely satisfies the requirement that the defendant's contacts with the forum satisfy *International Shoe*. Thus, when the dust settles, it seems that *Shaffer* really has its biggest effect in QIR-2 cases in which the property seized as the jurisdictional predicate does not cause the injuries to the plaintiff.

Final Point. Go back and reread §2.1. There is a series of questions there, with suggested answers. Now that you have studied the cases, those hypos, which may have seemed so daunting when we started, should be as comfortable as your favorite old sweatshirt.

Chapter *3*

Notice and Opportunity to Be Heard

§3.1 Defining the Issue

In Chapter 2, we saw that a judgment is valid only if the court entering it had personal jurisdiction over the defendant. This is required by due process.[1] In this chapter, we see that due process also requires that the defendant be given notice and an opportunity to be heard before a judgment can be entered against her. Each jurisdiction prescribes rules by which the defendant is to be given such notice. So, as with personal jurisdiction, this topic entails a two-step inquiry. First, a rule or statute must provide a method for giving notice, which we discuss in §3.3. Second, we must assess whether that rule or statute, as applied in a specific case, comports with the requirements of due process, as we see in §3.2.

---

[1]The Fifth Amendment applies to the federal government, and the Fourteenth Amendment applies to the states. Both provide that one can be deprived of property only with due process of law. This due process includes a court that has personal jurisdiction over the defendant. See §2.6.2.

In most suits, notice to the defendant consists of "process," which includes a formal notification from the court that the defendant has been sued and that she must take certain steps to avoid the imposition of liability. Proper service of process satisfies not only the requirement of notice, but also provides an opportunity to be heard, because it instructs the defendant as to when and how she must respond. Problems with the opportunity to be heard are relatively rare today, but can be encountered, for instance, in some commercial situations when a seller seeks to seize goods without providing a court hearing for the buyer who allegedly has failed to pay for them. We discuss such situations in §3.4. In §3.5 we address temporary (or "provisional") remedies, including pretrial seizure of assets and injunctive relief.

The requirements of notice and opportunity to be heard are separate from, and additional to, personal jurisdiction. Service of process alone, without a basis of personal jurisdiction, is not sufficient. Likewise, personal jurisdiction alone, without appropriate notice and opportunity to be heard, is not sufficient. Again, the classic method for giving notice of a suit is service of process. It is helpful to think of it as the method by which a court *perfects* its personal jurisdiction over the defendant.

§3.2   The Constitutional Standard for Notice

The Due Process Clauses of the Constitution provide, among other things, that the government may not deprive someone of her property without "due process of law." Here, these words mean "that individuals whose property interests are at stake are entitled to 'notice and an opportunity to be heard.'"[2]

The leading case is *Mullane v. Central Hanover Bank & Trust Co.*[3] It involved a New York statute that allowed banks acting as trustees to pool relatively small trusts into one large account, to take advantage of economies of scale.[4] The statute required the trustee/bank to make

---

[2]Dusenbery v. United States, 534 U.S. 161, 167 (2002), *quoting* United States v. James Daniel Good Real Property, 510 U.S. 43, 48 (1993).

[3]339 U.S. 306 (1950).

[4]We encountered the trust in *Hanson v. Denckla*, §2.4.4. It is a device by which a person with money or other property (the settlor) transfers legal title of the property to a third party (the trustee), who is responsible for investing the property for the benefit of the beneficiaries specified by the settlor. Often, the trustee is a bank or other financial institution. The trustee is paid for its services. Some trusts may be so small that individual administration is not feasible, because the expenses are greater than investment potential. The New York statute in *Mullane* addressed exactly that situation and allowed the trustee to administer many small trusts together, as a single large trust, which is more economical. As the Court explained, under such pooling statutes, "income, capital gains, losses and expenses of the collective trust are shared by the

periodic accountings to a court, demonstrating how it had invested the assets and what kind of return the investments had generated. If the court approved the accounting, it entered an order that (1) provided the trustee/bank with its fee (from trust assets) and (2) extinguished the beneficiaries' right to sue the trustee/bank for negligence or misfeasance in discharging its responsibilities. Beneficiaries were entitled to appear at the hearing on the accounting and to object to the trustee/bank's fee or to the way in which it did its job.

Obviously, beneficiaries could attend the hearing only if they knew about it. The New York statute allowed the trustee/bank to give notice to the beneficiaries by publication. That is what the trustee/bank did in *Mullane*, publishing in a local newspaper its name and address, the name and date of the establishment of the pooled fund, and a list of the participating individual trusts. Representatives, appointed to protect the interests of the beneficiaries, objected that this form of notice did not provide due process to the beneficiaries. The New York courts disagreed and upheld the accountings. The Supreme Court reversed, but, importantly, only with regard to some beneficiaries. The Court characterized the words of the Due Process Clauses as "cryptic and abstract,"[5] but proceeded to set forth the classic statement of the constitutional requirement of notice:

> An elementary and fundamental requirement of due process in any proceeding which is to be accorded finality is notice reasonably calculated, under all the circumstances, to apprise interested parties of the pendency of the action and afford them an opportunity to present their objections. The notice must be of such nature as reasonably to convey the required information, and it must afford a reasonable time for those interested to make their appearance. . . .
>
> [W]hen notice is a person's due, process which is a mere gesture is not due process. The means employed must be such as one desirous of actually informing the absentee might reasonably adopt to accomplish it.[6]

This latter sentence, coupled with a reference in the opinion to providing the "best notice practicable,"[7] might seem to require individual notice to all interested persons in every case. But there is no such blanket requirement. Reasonableness of notice in a given case is to be assessed, as the Court said, "under all the circumstances."

---

constituent trusts in proportion to their contribution. . . [and] diversification of risk and economy of management can be extended to those whose capital standing alone would not obtain such advantage." *Mullane*, 339 U.S. at 308.

[5] *Id.* at 313-314.
[6] *Id.* at 314-315.
[7] *Id.* at 317.

Circumstances can differ from case to case, as shown in *Mullane* itself. The beneficiaries in *Mullane* fell into three groups:

- One was those "whose interests or whereabouts could not with due diligence be ascertained."[8] These beneficiaries simply could not be identified. As to them, notice by publication was constitutionally permissible, and the Court upheld the New York judgment. Although there was a great possibility that the publication notice would never be seen by these beneficiaries, it is "not much more likely to fail than any of the choices open to legislators endeavoring to prescribe the best notice practicable."[9] Publication was not, in other words, a mere gesture to give notice to these beneficiaries. The beneficiaries in this group were bound by the judgment in the accounting proceeding, even though they were not given individual notice.

- The second group was beneficiaries whose whereabouts were not known in the ordinary course of business, but which "could be discovered upon investigation." With some effort (and at some expense) these beneficiaries could be identified and contacted. Here, too, the Court upheld the New York judgment and permitted notice by publication. The Court noted "the practical difficulties and costs that would be attendant on frequent investigations into the status of great numbers of beneficiaries, many of whose interests in the common fund are so remote as to be ephemeral."[10] Publication notice was reasonable as to this group *under the circumstances*. So this group also was bound by the judgment in the accounting proceeding, despite lack of individual notice.

- The third group was "present beneficiaries of known place of residence." As to them, notice by publication simply was not "reasonably calculated to reach them." Unlike the other two groups, here there was no excuse for failing to give individual notice. The Court reversed the New York Court of Appeals' judgment as to this group of beneficiaries.

Even as to this latter group, however, due process did not require individual notice to *every* identifiable beneficiary. Because this group consisted of thousands of similarly situated people, all with small monetary interests, notice to some would suffice to protect all. Thus, the Court concluded, due process required only "notice reasonably certain to reach *most* of those interested in objecting."[11] Had the circumstances been different—if, for example, beneficiaries had unique and sizeable monetary interests in the fund—due process might require individual notice before extinguishing their right to challenge

---

[8]For example, suppose a trust provided for income to be given to grandchildren of the settlor who attain the age of 21 or who survive a particular beneficiary. It may be impossible to identify all such contingent beneficiaries at a given time.

[9]*Mullane*, 339 U.S. at 317.

[10]*Id.* at 317.

[11]*Id.* at 319 (emphasis added). The notice to be given was not formal service of process; rather, notice by regular mail sufficed.

the accounting.[12] It is also worth noting that the individual notice required in *Mullane* did not have to be delivered in any special way; regular mail sufficed.

Under *Mullane*, then, we cannot say that publication notice is never appropriate. After all, that case upheld publication notice to two groups of beneficiaries. In the usual *in personam* case, however, publication notice is a last resort. It will rarely be upheld unless nothing else is reasonably practicable.[13]

The constitutional requirement of appropriate notice serves not just the functional goal of informing the parties of proceedings but fulfills an important ceremonial function as well. Giving notice ensures that the termination of one's rights cannot be done in secret.[14] It is important to remember that notice is given by the court, which is a branch of the government. And it is important that the government play by the rules.[15] Thus, even if the trustee/bank could have shown that every known beneficiary in *Mullane* had actually read the notice published in the newspapers, the scheme would still have been unconstitutional.[16] As the Court explained, the publication notice to known beneficiaries was "inadequate, not because in fact it fail[ed] to reach everyone, but because under the circumstances it [was] not reasonably calculated to reach those who could easily be informed by other means at hand."[17] Accordingly, as a general matter, the fact that the defendant has actual independent knowledge of the pendency of suit generally will not suffice in the absence of proper notice from the court.[18]

---

[12]Sometimes, a rule or statute might be stricter than the due process requirement. For instance, the Federal Rule permitting class action suits requires, at least in some situations, that individual notice be given to each member of the class who is reasonably identifiable. *See* Fed. R. Civ. P. 23(c)(2)(B) (requiring such notice in a class action certified under Rule 23(b)(3)). Such notice is routinely given by mail. *See* §13.3.6.

[13]In *Gaeth v. Deacon*, 964 A.2d 621, 628 (Me. 2009), the Maine Supreme Court noted that increasing reliance upon electronic media means that publication in a print newspaper is less likely today than in yesteryear to give actual notice. Accordingly, "it is also less likely to meet the requirements of due process." The court vacated an *in personam* default judgment because notice by publication in a newspaper deprived the defendant of due process. The federal court in Maine cited *Gaeth* in stating, "the Maine Supreme Judicial Court has described service by publication as a 'last resort.'" Douglas v. Lalumiere, 2021 WL 1240625 at * 2 (D. Me. 2021).

[14]*See* Restatement (Second) of Judgments §27, comment g.

[15]In §3.3.1, we will see that in most cases the required notice is actually served on the defendant by a civilian, and not by an officer of the government. Nonetheless, the civilian does so on behalf of the court system, and thereby exercises a governmental function.

[16]*See* Grand Entertainment Group Ltd. v. Star Media Sales, Inc., 988 F.2d 476, 492 (3d Cir. 1993) ("notice cannot by itself validate an otherwise defective service").

[17]*Mullane*, 339 U.S. at 319. The "other means at hand" was mail.

[18]*See, e.g.*, Ayika v. Sutton, 378 Fed. Appx. 432, 434 (5th Cir. 2010); Way v. Mueller Brass Co., 840 F.2d 303, 306 (5th Cir. 1988) ("defendant's actual notice of the litigation. . . is insufficient to satisfy Rule 4's requirements").

On the other hand, actual knowledge based upon notice given by the court may suffice, even in the absence of proper service undertaken by the plaintiff. In *United Student Aid Funds, Inc. v. Espinoza,*[19] a debtor filed suit in bankruptcy court, seeking an order requiring him to repay only the principal on his student loan, and forgiving ("discharging") his responsibility to pay interest on that loan. Under applicable procedural rules, the debtor was supposed to serve a summons and copy of the complaint on the loan company; he failed to do so. Nonetheless, as required by applicable rules, the court itself mailed notice and a copy of the debtor's plan to the loan company, including a warning that its rights may be affected by the proceeding. The bankruptcy court entered a final judgment discharging the interest payment. The loan company sought to set aside that judgment as void because the debtor failed to have it served with summons and a copy of the complaint. The Supreme Court upheld the judgment. Though the debtor failed to do what the rules required him to do, the court itself had given notice to the loan company as required by Bankruptcy Rules. This actual receipt of proper notice from the court "more than satisfied [the loan company's] due process rights."[20]

While actual receipt of proper notice sent from the court will satisfy due process, it is important to understand that the Constitution does not *require* that the defendant actually receive notice. This point was made in *Dusenbery v. United States.*[21] Mr. Dusenbery was convicted of federal drug charges. In executing a valid search warrant on his home, the FBI seized various property, including an automobile and $21,939 in cash. After Dusenbery was convicted and incarcerated, the FBI started administrative proceedings to have the automobile and cash forfeited to the government. Pursuant to applicable federal law, the FBI sent written notice by certified mail to Dusenbery at the federal penitentiary, informing him of the pending forfeiture proceeding and indicating how he could oppose the forfeiture. Dusenbery never responded to the notice, and his property was forfeited.

Five years later, Dusenbery sought judicial relief and claimed that he had never received the notice of forfeiture. The Court confirmed that *Mullane* governs "questions regarding the adequacy of the method used to give notice."[22] Thus, the question was whether the method of

---

[19]559 U.S. 260, 264 (2010).

[20]*Id.* at 261.

[21]534 U.S. 161, 163 (2002).

[22]*Id.* at 168. *See* Patrick J. Borchers, Jones v. Flowers: *An Essay on a Unified Theory of Procedural Due Process,* 40 Creighton L. Rev. 343 (2007).

notice employed by the FBI[23] was, in the words of *Mullane,* "reasonably calculated, under all the circumstances, to apprise interested parties of the pendency of the action and afford them an opportunity to present their objections." The Court concluded that it was, even though Dusenbery never actually received it. The Court explained that due process does not require that the government "*must provide* actual notice"; rather, it requires "that it *must attempt to provide* actual notice."[24]

For decades, states allowed notice to a tenant in eviction cases to be given by posting the process conspicuously on the premises from which the tenant was to be evicted. In *Greene v. Lindsay,*[25] the Court refused to enforce a judgment when service was made in this manner. Applying *Mullane,* the Court held that such notice was not reasonable under the circumstances because the papers could have been torn down by other people before the defendant saw them. In response to this and a subsequent suggestion by the Supreme Court, many states now permit such notice by posting only if it is followed by service on the defendant by mail.[26]

In *Jones v. Flowers,*[27] the Supreme Court demonstrated again the importance of considering the specific facts of the case. There, the state sent a certified letter to a homeowner to inform him that he was delinquent in paying real property taxes and that failure to pay would result in public sale of his land. The letter was returned to the state agency as "unclaimed," after which the state took no additional steps to notify the owner. This inactivity in the face of knowledge that the

---

[23]This consisted of certified mail to Dusenbery at the penitentiary, where the Bureau of Prisons had a procedure for picking up mail each day, signing for all certified mail at the post office, transporting it to the prison, logging it in at the mailroom, and assigning a staff member to deliver it.

[24]*Id.* at 170 (emphases original). Could the government have done more to ensure that Dusenbery actually received the document? Yes. Indeed, after the events giving rise to the case, the Bureau of Prisons imposed a requirement that prisoners acknowledge receipt of certified letters by signing a logbook. But this fact did not, to the majority in *Dusenbery,* make the practice followed in that case unconstitutional. *Id.* at 171-173. Due process does not require *the best* effort at notice—just one reasonably calculated under the circumstances to apprise the defendant of the proceedings. This is consistent with what we saw in discussing the *Burger King* case concerning personal jurisdiction; due process does not entitle the defendant to *the most convenient* forum—just one that is not egregiously inconvenient. *See* §2.4.4.

[25]456 U.S. 444, 450-451 (1982).

[26]*See* Mennonite Board of Missions v. Adams, 462 U.S. 791, 802 (1983) (suggesting that the additional step of mailing could render posting notice constitutional). For an example of a "nail and mail" statute. *See* Va. Code Ann. §8.01-296(2).

[27]547 U.S. 220, 234-239 (2006).

owner had not received the letter violated due process. In other words, although sending a certified letter is usually reasonable and comports with due process, things change when the state knows that the notice was not received. In these circumstances, due process requires that some additional step be taken to give notice.[28]

The flexibility of the *Mullane* standard allows the courts to adapt to technological advances. In upholding the constitutionality of serving process by e-mail, for instance, the Ninth Circuit explained that the "broad constitutional principle" of *Mullane* "unshackles the federal courts from anachronistic methods of service and permits them entry into the technological renaissance."[29] Even though e-mail does not permit confirmation of receipt, the court held such service valid in view of all the circumstances.[30]

Other courts have upheld the constitutionality of service of process via e-mail and even social media platforms. Most of these cases, however, involve service of process outside the United States.[31] Domestically, some courts have rejected electronic service of process because there was no provision for it in the Federal Rules or in

---

[28]"What steps are reasonable in response to new information depends upon what the information reveals. The return of the certified letter marked 'unclaimed' meant either that Jones still lived at 717 North Bryan Street, but was not home when the postman called and did not retrieve the letter at the post office, or that Jones no longer resided at that address. One reasonable step primarily addressed to the former possibility would be for the State to resend the notice by regular mail, so that a signature was not required. . . . Following up with regular mail might also increase the chances of actual notice to Jones if, as it turned out, he had moved. Even occupants who ignored certified mail notice slips addressed to the owner (if any had been left) might scrawl the owner's new address on the notice packet and leave it for the postman to retrieve, or notify Jones directly." *Id.* at 235.

[29]Rio Properties, Inc. v. Rio Int'l Interlink, 284 F.3d 1007, 1017 (9th Cir. 2002). On the facts of the case, e-mail appeared to be the only way to get notice to the defendant, which did not have an office or representative in the United States. *Id.* at 1018 ("[The defendant] had neither an office nor a door; it had only a computer terminal. If any method of communication is reasonably calculated to provide[it] with notice, surely it is e-mail—the method which [it] utilizes and prefers"). *See also* Federal Trade Commission v. Cottelli, 2021 WL 1202463 at *1 (9th Cir. 2021) (". . . we hold that service of process by email here, as pre-approved by the district court pursuant to Federal Rule of Civil Procedure 4(f) was 'reasonably calculated. . . to apprise [the defendant] of the pendency of the action and afford[ed him] an opportunity to present [his] objections.").

[30]*Rio Properties,* 284 F.3d at 1018. This case is discussed in §3.3.5 below.

[31]*Rio Properties* is such a case. It and other cases, cited in §3.3.5, involve service of process under Rule 4(f)(3), which applies only to service of process outside the United States; it is not available for service within the United States. As discussed in §3.3.5 below, Rule 4(f)(3) does not specifically refer to service by electronic means, but rather permits the court to permit service by any means not prohibited by international agreement.

170

applicable state laws.[32] Where a state provision allows for such service, however, some courts have upheld it as constitutional.[33]

Although the Supreme Court's *ad hoc* approach under *Mullane* leads to uncertainty at the margin, relatively few cases raise constitutional problems of notice. In most litigation, it is clear that service of process on a defendant in accordance with Federal Rule 4 or a state counterpart is constitutional. In practice, then, the big question usually is not whether the rule for giving notice is constitutional, but whether the rule was satisfied on the facts of the case. In general, neither the Federal Rules nor state provisions regarding service of process have "pushed the envelope" of permissible service. Despite authority upholding the constitutionality of e-mail service, for example, there is no general provision in the Federal Rules for serving process in that way.[34] We now turn to the rules prescribing methods of serving process.

§3.3 Service of Process

§3.3.1 Definition, Who Can Serve Process, Timing, and Proof of Service

In the typical civil case, notice is given by the formal "service of process" on a defendant against whom a plaintiff asserts a claim.[35]

---

[32]*See, e.g.*, Joe Hand Promotions, Inc. v. Shepard, 2013 WL 4058745 at *2 (E.D. Mo. 2013) (neither Rule 4 nor Missouri law allowed electronic service of process on a defendant in the United States). On the other hand, some courts have permitted service via social media. *See also* Ferrarese v. Shaw, 164 F.Supp.3d 361, 367 (E.D.N.Y. 2016) ("However, petitioner's proposed method of service by email and Facebook alone are not reasonably calculated to provide notice of the action to defendant").

[33]*See, e.g.*, Maharishi Foundation USA, Inc. v. Love, 2016 WL 11606685 at *2 (S.D. Iowa 2016) ("The Court finds plaintiff also has established that service by means of social media accounts associated with defendant reasonably could be expected to provide her with notice of the lawsuit against her. Plaintiff has established that defendant frequently and regularly uses one or all of the social media platforms by which plaintiff proposes to accomplish service."); Baidoo v. Blood-Dzraku, 48 Misc.3d 309, 311-317 (Sup. Ct., New York County, 2015) (permitted service in divorce case by private message to defendant's Facebook account); Matter of Support Proceeding, 2014 N.Y. Misc. LEXIS 4708 at *1-5 (Fam. Ct., Richmond County, N.Y., 2014).

[34]We will see in §3.3.6 that subsequent documents in the case may be sent by electronic transmission in some circumstances. But the basic provision of notice of suit and opportunity to be heard—that is, service of process—cannot.

[35]As seen in *Mullane*, however, notice can be important in other contexts too, such as the notice by mail to beneficiaries in that case of their right to object to the trustee's accounting. *See* §3.2. Though service of process remains the classic method by which a defendant is notified that she has been sued, it is not clear that due process requires service of process to perform that function. A less formal method of imparting notice

"Service" refers to the methods for delivering process to the defendant. "Process," as generally used,[36] consists of two documents: a copy of the complaint and a summons. The complaint is drafted by the plaintiff's lawyer and sets forth the plaintiff's claims asserted against the defendant. See §7.3.1.

The summons stands on a different footing. It is an official document *from the court itself*, signed and sealed by the clerk of the court. It is a symbol of the court's (and therefore the government's) power over the defendant.[37] Federal Rule 4(a)(1) is typical of provisions concerning the summons and requires that this document inform the defendant of various things, including that (1) she has been sued, (2) she has a set time in which to respond, and (3) failure to make a timely response may lead to entry of default judgment against her.

Form summonses are available online on the court's website. These forms contain all the required information except the names of the parties and counsel and the docket number. When filing a case, the plaintiff's lawyer drafts the complaint, fills in names of the parties on the summons, and files suit (almost always online; in the federal courts, the filing system is called PACER). Upon filing, the clerk of the court assigns a docket number to the case, signs the summons, and affixes the court seal to it. The plaintiff then has this document and a copy of the complaint served on the defendant. (Federal Rule 4(b) sets out these steps for the issuance of the summons.) If there are multiple defendants, each can be named on the summons, but a separate summons is issued for each. Defendants not properly served are not brought before the jurisdiction of the court and thus cannot validly be subjected to a judgment.

Under Federal Rule 3, an action is commenced when the complaint is filed.[38] Federal Rule 4(m) then gives the plaintiff 90 days after filing

---

might suffice constitutionally. But old habits die hard and today the applicable rules continue to require formal service of process to serve the function providing the initial notice to a defendant of the suit against her. *See* Robin J. Effron, *The Lost Story of Notice and Personal Jurisdiction*, 74 N.Y.U. Ann. Surv. Am. Law 23 (2018).

[36]In federal court and in most states, process consists of the two documents discussed. In some states, the defendant is served only with the summons, and can gain access to the complaint at the courthouse or through the court's website because, once filed, the complaint is a public document.

[37]The summons is the modern counterpart of the common law *capias ad respondendum*, which empowered the sheriff to arrest a civil defendant and incarcerate her pending trial. Today we do not feel the need to be so physical in demonstrating that the law is reaching out to the defendant, so the summons does not carry with it physical arrest.

[38]This is the rule in many states as well. In some states, however, actions are commenced when process is served on the defendant, even if this precedes filing of the complaint. The provision that an action is commenced when filed is superior, because it focuses on a clear, public event from which to compute various events, including the time in which to serve process.

in which to have process served on the defendant. If service is not made (or "effected") within that period, the court must dismiss the case without prejudice (as to that defendant) or order that service be made within a specific time. The plaintiff will undoubtedly try to show "good cause" for failing to serve process within the 90 days. If she makes such a showing, "the court must extend the time for service for an appropriate period."[39] This provision effectively means that service within 90 days after filing constitutes due diligence. Some state rules are not so liberal.[40]

In earlier times, the United States Marshal's Service usually served process in civil cases in federal court.[41] Today, marshals are rarely involved.[42] Instead, Federal Rule 4(c)(2) provides that service may be effected by "any person who is at least 18 years old and not a party."[43] A civilian serving process need not be appointed by a court.[44] This, too, is more liberal than the practice in some states, in which officers

---

[39]Fed. R. Civ. P. 4(m). Courts have great discretion in determining what constitutes good cause. Most courts insist on a showing of diligence. A showing of repeated but futile attempts to locate the defendant or to determine her address might constitute a showing of good cause and justify the court's granting additional time in which to serve process. *See, e.g.*, DeFrancis v. Bush, 859 F. Supp. 1022, 1023-1024 (E.D. Tex. 1994) (difficulty in locating defendant exacerbated by defendant's frequent moves). *See also* United States v. Rodrigue, 645 F. Supp. 2d 1310, 1323 (Ct. Int'l Trade 2009) (defendant's actual notice of suit does not constitute good cause for failing to effect service within time prescribed by Rule 4(m)).

[40]For example, in Georgia, process is to be served within five days after the process server receives the summons and complaint. Ga. Code Ann. §9-11-4(c)(5). Beyond that, service may be upheld, but only if the plaintiff shows due diligence. Bennett v. Matt Gay Chevrolet, 408 S.E.2d 111, 113 (Ga. App. 1991).

[41]Whenever a marshal serves process, it is incumbent on the plaintiff to give instructions on where to find the defendant. For an amusing opinion, *see Mayo v. Satan and His Staff*, 54 F.R.D. 282, 283 (W.D. Pa. 1971), in which the plaintiff sued the devil himself. The court dismissed the case when the plaintiff failed to tell the marshal how to serve process.

[42]*See* Fed. R. Civ. P. 4(c)(3) (marshals may serve process when plaintiff requests it and must do so in cases in which the plaintiff sues under 28 U.S.C. §1915 (as a pauper) or §1916 (as a seaman suing for wages or salvage or to enforce laws regarding mariners' health and safety)). Taking marshals out of the business of serving process in regular lawsuits reflected (1) funding cutbacks for the Marshal's Service and (2) a sense that the task did not require professional law enforcement personnel. In contrast, however, the Marshal's Service is involved in serving some other types of court documents, such as writs of execution. *See* Fed. R. Civ. P. 4.1(a). A writ of execution directs seizure of the defendant's property so it may be sold at public auction to raise money to satisfy the plaintiff's judgment against the defendant.

[43]*See* Constien v. United States, 628 F.3d 1207, 1213-1214 (10th Cir. 2010) (service by mail on United States ineffective because plaintiff herself mailed it).

[44]*See* Benny v. Pipes, 799 F.2d 489, 494 (9th Cir. 1986) (upholding service of process on prison guards by a prisoner who was not a party).

(typically the sheriff or a deputy) routinely serve process and civilians may do so only if appointed by a judge.[45]

The process server is supposed to file in court a "proof of service" (sometimes called a *return*), which explains what was done to effect service. Federal Rule 4(*l*)(1) is typical of such provisions. Under that Rule, a civilian process server must make proof of service by affidavit, which is a statement under oath. Officers, however, need not make their proofs under oath.

Failure to file a proof of service does not affect the validity of service, so a properly served defendant cannot have a case dismissed for this mere technical failure. On the other hand, if the defendant contests service, failure to file the proof of service means the plaintiff will have the burden of showing that service was in fact made. In contrast, filing the proof of service constitutes *prima facie* evidence that the events stated occurred; this evidence can be overcome only by the defendant's strong showing that service was not properly made.[46] If the defendant presents such evidence, the court will then resolve the factual dispute about whether process was served.

We now turn to the question of *how* process is served.

§3.3.2   Methods for Serving Process on a Human Defendant

Federal Rule 4(e)(2) provides three methods of service of process on an individual in the typical federal civil case:[47] personal service, substituted service, and service upon an agent. We will call these the *basic methods* for service. (In addition, however, Rule 4(e)(1) allows a federal court to incorporate *state* law methods for service, and Rule 4(d) permits the defendant to waive service of process.) At the outset,

---

[45]*See* Rule 4(c), Alaska R. Civ. P. (allowing service by a "person specially appointed by the Commissioner of Public Safety"); Ga. Code Ann. §9-11-4(c) (permitting service by a civilian only if she is "specially appointed by the court for that purpose" or "has been appointed as a permanent process server by the court in which the action is brought").

[46]*See, e.g.,* Howard Johnson Int'l, Inc. v. Wang, 7 F. Supp. 2d 336, 339 (S.D.N.Y. 1998); FROF, Inc. v. Harris, 695 F. Supp. 827, 829 (E.D. Pa. 1988).

[47]We focus in the text on Rule 4(e), which governs the methods of service of process on individuals generally. Other provisions address service on specific defendants. For example, Federal Rule 4(g) governs service upon minors and incompetents, while Rule 4(i) governs service upon the federal government or an agency or officer thereof. Rule 4(j) concerns service upon other governments, including foreign and state governments. Again, due process likely could be satisfied other than by serving process on the defendant. But formal service of process along the lines we discuss remains the choice of rulemakers in federal and state courts for imparting notice of the typical civil case.

it is important to note that Rule 4(e)(2) does *not* prescribe a hierarchy. There is no preferred method for serving process; any of the three basic methods is permissible. In contrast, the practice in some states prescribes a "descending order" rule, in which a second method of service is proper only if the preferred method is not available on the facts of the case.[48]

Personal Service

The first method, found in Rule 4(e)(2)(A) and permitted in every jurisdiction, is service on "the individual personally." Usually referred to as "personal service," this is effected when the process server delivers the process directly to the defendant. There is no question that personal service of process comports with due process. Indeed, it is the archetypal method for giving notice.

Rule 4(e)(2)(A) does not require that personal service be made at any particular place, such as the defendant's home or office. It can be made *anywhere* within the forum state—at the ballpark, at the opera, or wherever the server happens to find the defendant. For example, one process server obtained a ticket to dance on a television special featuring singer Donny Osmond, who was the defendant in the action. The server danced up to Donny and served him with process on live television.[49]

Sometimes, the defendant will try to evade the process server. In such instances, service is usually upheld if the server makes her best effort under the circumstances, even if the defendant does not take the documents into her hands. In one case, the defendant ducked into an automobile and locked the doors. The process server, having already announced his intentions, left the process under the windshield wipers of the automobile. Service was upheld.[50]

In some circumstances, the defendant may be immune from service of process. In §2.4.1, we discussed one such basis for immunity, recognized in federal and many state courts: when the defendant was forced or tricked into the forum. In addition, federal courts and some states recognize immunity for persons who enter the state to participate in

[48]*See, e.g.*, Calif. Code Civ. Proc. §415.20(b) (permitting substituted service only if process "cannot with reasonable diligence be personally delivered"); Va. Code Ann. §8.01-296 (permitting substituted service only if personal service cannot be made with reasonable diligence).

[49]*See* Martin Grayson & Bart Schwartz, *Adventures in Serving Process*, 11 Litigation 11, 12 (1985) (a very amusing article).

[50]Trujillo v. Trujillo, 71 Cal. App. 2d 257, 260 (1945). Another well-known case is *Errion v. Connell*, 236 F.2d 447, 457 (9th Cir. 1956), in which the defendant moved away from the door after determining a process server was knocking. The server slid the papers through a hole in the door. Service was upheld.

another case as a litigant, witness, or lawyer.[51] Recognizing immunity for such persons encourages their appearance in that other proceeding and thus supports the administration of justice.[52] There is a good deal of variety among the states concerning when it is proper to recognize immunity from service. A few jurisdictions, for instance, recognize immunity from service of process on Sunday.[53] Whether a federal court recognizes immunity presents a question of federal law, on which state law is not binding.

Substituted Service

The second method for service of process on an individual, found at Rule 4(e)(2)(B), is service "at the individual's dwelling or usual place of abode with someone of suitable age and discretion who resides there." This method is often called *substituted service*, since it is made not on the defendant but on a substitute. The idea is that a person of suitable age and discretion residing in the defendant's dwelling can be trusted to pass the documents along to the defendant. This rule reposes a good bit of faith in the suitable person. In essence, it appoints such a person as the defendant's agent for service of process. What if she does not bring the documents to the defendant's attention? In all likelihood, the answer is "tough luck": The plaintiff had process served properly under the applicable Rule. Nothing in Rule 4(e)(2)(B) requires that the defendant actually receive it. As we saw in §3.2, the Constitution does not necessarily require actual notice.

There are three potential problems in trying to effect substituted service. First, what is the defendant's "dwelling or usual place of abode"? For most people, there is little uncertainty on this score; they have a house or apartment and live there year-round. But what about a student who resides in a dorm room in Madison, Wisconsin during the school year but at home with her parents in Maryland during the summer? Although Rule 4(e)(2)(B) does not expressly say so, courts generally conclude that one's "dwelling or usual place of abode" is the place where she is living at *present* (when service is made). For our student, then, during the school year, this would be her dorm; in the summer, it would be her parents' house. (The concept is more flexible than the idea of "residence" for venue purposes, which we study at

---

[51]Stewart v. Ramsay, 242 U.S. 128, 130 (1916).

[52]"[I]mmunity should not be granted for the convenience of the person seeking it; rather, it is for the convenience of the court and should be made available only to further the administration of justice." 4A Wright & Miller §1076.

[53]*See, e.g.*, Fla. Stat. §48.20; D.C. Code Ann. §13-303; Md. Cts. & Jud. Proc. Code Ann. §6-304; N.Y. Gen. Bus. Law §11.

§5.4.1. For venue purposes, the student resides in the federal district of her domicile, which is probably Maryland.)

Clearly, a place that was once the defendant's dwelling but that has been abandoned will not work. For example, where the defendant had graduated from high school and lived aboard a ship, his parents' house was no longer his dwelling or usual abode.[54] On the other hand, a person can have more than one dwelling or usual abode. Often, such people live the lifestyles of the rich and famous (because they are rich and famous). For instance, billionaire Adnan Khashoggi's New York condominium, one of his 12 residences worldwide, had enough indicia of ownership to constitute an appropriate abode even though he resided there only one month of the year.[55] In that case, the court noted that the defendant was in New York when service was made on his housekeeper at the New York condo. There is some authority for upholding substituted service even when the defendant is temporarily away from her abode.[56]

The second difficulty comes from the requirement that the person on whom substituted service is made under Rule 4(e)(2)(B) be of "suitable age and discretion." The Rule does not prescribe a specific age (as the provisions in some states do[57]). The Rule also does not require that the person on whom substituted service is made be a member of the defendant's family (as the provisions of some states do[58]). Thus, service on a doorman who controls access to an apartment building where the defendant resides may be proper under Rule 4(e)(2)(B).[59] Whether the person served is of suitable age and discretion is for the court to decide on a case-by-case basis. Many cases involve service on the defendant's spouse or on a child in mid-to-late teen years.[60]

The third source of trouble with substituted service is the requirement that the person on whom substituted service is made *reside* at the place where service is made. Some state provisions adopt the same

[54]Cox v. Quigley, 141 F.R.D. 222, 225 (D. Me. 1992).

[55]National Development Co. v. Triad Holding Corp., 930 F.2d 253, 258 (2d Cir. 1991). Indicia of ownership included multimillion dollar remodeling and continuous employment of servants at the condo.

[56]*See, e.g.*, Polygram Merchandising, Inc. v. New York Wholesale Co., 2000 WL 23287 at *3 (S.D.N.Y. 2000) (one of defendant's multiple residences had sufficient indicia of permanence to be usual place of abode even if she was absent when service made); Jaffe & Asher v. Van Brunt, 158 F.R.D. 278, 280 (S.D.N.Y. 1994) (upholding service at abode in New York when defendant was temporarily in California).

[57]*See, e.g.*, Fla. Stat. §48.031 (age 15 or older); Va. Code Ann. §8.01-296 (age 16 or older).

[58]*See, e.g.*, Va. Code Ann. §8.01-296 (service on a member of defendant's family).

[59]*See, e.g.*, Hartford Fire Ins. Co. v. Perinovic, 152 F.R.D. 128, 130 (N.D. Ill. 1993).

[60]*See, e.g.*, Resolution Trust Corp. v. Polmar Realty, Inc., 780 F. Supp. 177, 180 (S.D.N.Y. 1991) (spouse); Azuma N.V. v. Sinks, 646 F. Supp. 122, 124 (S.D.N.Y. 1986) (18-year-old son).

language, and some have equally unhelpful terms; for instance, the Virginia provision requires that this person is not "a guest or temporary sojourner."[61] The idea is clear enough: The person served should be someone with enough connection to the defendant's dwelling that we are reasonably certain she will give the papers to the defendant. In practice, the issue is to be determined by the court on a case-by-case basis, and it is sometimes difficult to draw a definitive line. Someone who is a guest for the weekend should not suffice. On the other hand, those in-laws who find a way to stick around for a few months may qualify. In one case, the Tenth Circuit upheld substituted service of process made on the defendant's cook even though it appeared that the cook did not reside full-time at the defendant's house; the facts were somewhat unclear and the defendant failed to assert the issue properly, so the court upheld service.[62]

Service Upon an Agent

The third method of service on an individual, found in Rule 4(e)(2)(C), is service on "an agent authorized by appointment or by law to receive service of process." Each of us routinely delegates tasks to an agent. For instance, we engage a travel agent to book our vacation. Similarly, we can appoint someone to serve as our agent for service of process; service upon the agent constitutes service upon us. Such appointment can be express.[63] Or, as we saw in §2.4.2, a defendant may appoint an agent for service of process by operation of law, as with a nonresident motorist statute. Such statutes permit service of process, for example, on a state official and require that official to notify the defendant promptly, usually by registered mail.[64]

State Law Regarding Methods of Service

We have just seen the three basic methods for serving process on an individual under Federal Rule 4(e)(2). Federal Rule 4(e)(1) augments those methods by incorporating *state* provisions concerning service

---

[61]Va. Code Ann. §8.01-296.

[62]Home-Stake Prod. Co. v. Talon Petroleum, 907 F.2d 1012, 1016-1017 (10th Cir. 1990).

[63]The leading case is *National Equipment Rental, Ltd. v. Szukhent*, 375 U.S. 311, 318 (1964), in which parties to a contract appointed an individual as agent for service in New York. That person in fact gave prompt notice to the defendants after service. The Court upheld the service even though the contract did not require the agent to give notice.

[64]Remember *Hess v. Pawloski*, discussed in §2.4.2. *See also* Illinois C.G.R. Co. v. Hampton, 117 F.R.D. 588, 590-591 (S.D. Miss. 1987) (Mississippi nonresident motorist statute).

of process. Indeed, it incorporates the law of *two* states: the state in which the action is pending and the state in which service is effected.

> ○ ***Example #1.*** A civil case is filed in federal court for the Western District of New York. The defendant is in Pennsylvania but is subject to personal jurisdiction in New York and may, under applicable law, be served with process in Pennsylvania. What *methods* of service may be used to serve that defendant? There are three sets of rules that can be used: (1) any methods for service prescribed by the Federal Rules (the major ones of which we have just seen); (2) any methods for service prescribed by the law of New York; and (3) any methods for service prescribed by the law of Pennsylvania.

This incorporation of state laws helps to explain why Federal Rule 4(e)(2) has such a limited menu of basic methods for service of process and why it does *not* have a provision permitting service of process by mail. Rule 4(e)(1) makes up for the parsimony of Rule 4(e)(2) by allowing use of state laws. Thus, in situations in which the relevant state law allows service of process by mail (e.g., with a long-arm statute), the federal court can use that method. As a general matter, state provisions concerning methods of service of process are more detailed than Federal Rule 4(e)(2). They may include, for example, posted notice (accompanied by mail notice) in actions seeking to dispossess a defendant of real property. They may also include publication notice (hopefully in accord with the constitutional requirements of *Mullane*, discussed in §3.2), service on agents under nonresident motorist acts, and, often, out-of-state service by certified mail under a long-arm statute. When it comes to methods of service in a civil case in federal court, then, the Federal Rules are only the starting point.

Rule 4(d): Waiver of Formal Service of Process

We have seen the three basic methods for serving process under Federal Rule 4(e)(2) and the incorporation in federal court of state law methods for serving process under Federal Rule 4(e)(1). These provisions are augmented still further by Federal Rule 4(d), which permits the defendant to waive formal service of process by mail. Technically, this provision does not allow *service* of process by mail. Rather, it permits the defendant to *waive* formal service of process on her. Why would a defendant ever make the plaintiff's life easier by waiving formal service? There are at least three reasons.

First, as Rule 4(d)(5) makes clear, the defendant preserves any objections to venue or personal or subject matter jurisdiction; waiving formal service of process, then, does not waive these potential defenses. Second, the defendant who waives service gets extra time to answer the complaint. Under Rule 4(d)(3), she may answer up to 60 days after the plaintiff sends her the waiver form, instead of the 21 days permitted if process is served upon her.[65] Third, and most important, Rule 4(d)(1) imposes upon the defendant "a duty to avoid unnecessary expenses of serving the summons." Then, Rule 4(d)(2) provides that if a defendant fails, without good cause, to sign and return the waiver, "the court must impose on the defendant" the expenses incurred by the plaintiff in undertaking formal service and the costs and attorneys' fees of any motion the plaintiff brings to collect those expenses.

How does this waiver work? The plaintiff sends to the defendant "by first-class mail or other reliable means" (Rule 4(d)(1)(G)) a form notifying the defendant of suit (Rule 4(d)(1)(D)), a copy of the complaint, two copies of a waiver form, and a "prepaid means for returning the [waiver] form" (Rule 4(d)(1)(C)).[66] Under Rule 4(d)(1)(F), the notice must give the defendant a "reasonable time of at least 30 days after the request [for waiver] was sent" in which to return it. The usual "prepaid means" for returning the waiver form is a self-addressed stamped envelope, by which the defendant returns the executed waiver, usually to the plaintiff's lawyer. The plaintiff then files the waiver form with the court and, under Rule 4(d)(4), the case proceeds "as if a summons and complaint had been served at the time of filing the waiver." Again, as seen in the preceding paragraph, if the defendant fails to return the waiver form, the plaintiff will take steps to have her served formally, and the defendant will be required to pay the expenses of such service.

---

[65]One part of Rule 4(d)(3) is curious. It provides that a defendant who returns the waiver in a timely way "need not serve an answer to the complaint until 60 days after the request was sent. . . ." As seen in Chapter 8, a defendant generally responds to being sued (1) by answer, or (2) by motion. Literally, Rule 4(d)(3) makes the 60-day provision applicable only to the former, not the latter. In other words, it gives her 60 days in which to answer, but not in which to bring a motion. Nonetheless, courts reach the sensible conclusion that the defendant has 60 days in which to answer or make a proper motion under Rule 12. *See, e.g.*, IBA Molecular, North America, Inc. v. Neo-Pet LLC, 2015 WL 1138024 at *1 (E.D. Va. 2015) (defendant "was required to file and serve an answer or a motion under Rule 12 within 60 days from the date the request [for waiver of service of process] was sent").

[66]Other requirements are set forth throughout rule 4(d)(1). Rule 4 itself sets out a form for requesting waiver of service, as well as the waiver form to be signed by the defendant and a statement of the defendant's duty to avoid unnecessary expenses of formal service of process.

180

§3.3.3 Methods for Serving Process on Corporations and Associations

Business associations such as corporations and partnerships do not have a physical existence; they exist through the people who run them and work for them. The question here, then, is how one may serve process on a business. More specifically, who is deemed to be an agent of the business for purposes of receiving service of process? The key provision is Rule 4(h)(1)(B), which allows service of process on a business[67] to be made upon "an officer, a managing or general agent, or any other agent authorized by appointment or by law to receive service of process."

Usually, there is little confusion about who is an "officer." State corporation laws commonly require the appointment of a president, a secretary, and a treasurer (although one person can usually serve in all three capacities). Corporations are required to file information, including the identity of officers, with the state, so it is usually relatively easy to identify an appropriate officer for receiving service under Rule 4(h)(1)(B). The Rule does not permit service on an "owner" of the corporation. Of course, an owner may also be an officer (or general or managing agent), in which case service would be proper because of the latter status.[68]

There can be significant uncertainty, however, as to who is a "managing or general agent" of a business. In addressing a case, the guiding principle should be the purpose of the Rule. The whole point is to find someone who can be said to *represent* the corporation or association, who understands the importance of the papers, and who is likely responsible enough to ensure that they are transmitted to those who can act upon them. Thus, courts look not to labels, but to the level of responsibility and authority exercised by the person receiving process.[69] It is an *ad hoc* assessment.

---

[67]The Rule applies to corporations as well as to partnerships and other nonincorporated associations. This covers all business associations. In §4.5.3, concerning diversity of citizenship jurisdiction, we will see that all businesses are either corporations or nonincorporated associations (which includes partnerships and limited liability companies).

[68]An interesting case is *Fonar Corp. v. Tariq Contracting, Inc.*, 885 F. Supp. 56, 61 (E.D.N.Y. 1995), in which service was made on a nonofficer whom the corporation held out to be an officer. The court upheld service, noting that this person regularly exercised discretion on the corporation's behalf. Thus, the person was deemed to be a managing or general agent. Service would also seem proper because the corporation, by holding the person out as an officer, should be estopped from denying that the person was an officer.

[69]*See, e.g.*, United States v. Ayer, 857 F.2d 881, 888 (1st Cir. 1988) ("Frederick Ayer could supportably be found to have been a leading man in the corporate troupe. . ."); Intra-Lock Int'l, Inc. v. Choukroun, 2014 WL 12479195 at *5 (S.D. Fla. 2014) (upholding

○ ***Example #2.*** Process Server (PS) goes to the principal office of a business with the goal of serving process on an appropriate agent of the business. The only person at the office is the receptionist, who tells PS that the business officers are not in the office that day. PS serves process on the receptionist. In most businesses, one would expect that a receptionist would lack that degree of responsibility and discretion to be a "managing or general agent."[70] But it all depends on the facts; in some businesses, a receptionist might play such a significant role as to uphold service of process.[71]

As Rule 4(h)(1) expressly recognizes, a business (like an individual) may have an agent for service of process whom it appoints expressly or who is appointed by operation of law. As we saw in §2.4.5, each state requires out-of-state businesses to "register" and appoint an agent for service of process before they can transact business in-state. And, as with service of process on individuals, the methods discussed are supplemented by provisions from state law of the state in which the federal court sits and in which service is made. *See* Rule 4(h)(1)(A).

Moreover, the provision in Federal Rule 4(d) for waiver of formal service of process that we saw with regard to individual defendants applies in suits against corporations or associations. This is made clear in the first phrase of Rule 4(h), which provides that the methods prescribed do not apply if "the defendant's waiver has been filed."

§3.3.4 Geographic Restrictions on Service of Process in the United States

There has never been any doubt that a court with personal jurisdiction over a defendant may have process served on the defendant anywhere in that state. This conclusion flows from the fact that personal jurisdiction is exercised by the state itself. So a state court in El Paso may permit service of process on a defendant in Houston, even though those cities are nearly 700 miles apart. The same principle applies

---

service on person who owned majority interest in the defendant business, who held himself out on social media as scientific director of that business, and who was present in the forum to provide a seminar on the system that was the subject of the litigation).

[70]*See, e.g.,* Estate of Baratt v. Phoenix Mut. Life Ins. Co., 787 F. Supp. 333, 334-335 (W.D.N.Y. 1992) (rejecting service on part-time receptionist whose duties including greeting, typing, opening and sorting mail, and answering telephone).

[71]*See, e.g.,* Direct Mail Specialists, Inc. v. Eclat Computerized Techs., Inc., 840 F.2d 685, 688-689 (9th Cir. 1988) ("The company was a rather small one. . . . Presumably, the role played by the receptionist was commensurately large in the structure of the company. She appears to have been the only employee in the office when the process server arrived, demonstrating that more than minimal responsibility was assigned to her." In this case, the receptionist claimed not to be an employee of the corporate defendant).

in federal court. The federal district in El Paso (the Western District of Texas) will recognize service of process on a defendant found in Houston (in the Eastern District of Texas). Lawyers and judges often capture this notion by saying that "process runs throughout the forum state."[72]

What happens, though, if the plaintiff wants to have process served on someone outside the forum state? For starters, this will be proper only if the state from which process issues has personal jurisdiction over the defendant. This means, as we know from Chapter 2, that (1) the forum state has a statute that permits the exercise of personal jurisdiction on the facts of the case (such as a long-arm or nonresident motorist statute) and (2) the exercise of personal jurisdiction satisfies the constitutional requirements of due process. Next, we must have some method for serving process on the defendant outside the forum state. The state statute providing the basis for personal jurisdiction will provide such a method. The typical long-arm statute, as discussed in §2.5, not only grants personal jurisdiction, but allows service of process outside the forum in various ways, such as personal service or service by registered mail. Thus, a state court in El Paso may permit service of process on a defendant in a town in New Mexico (say, La Union, about 20 miles from El Paso) *only* if a Texas long-arm statute (1) applies, (2) is constitutional on the facts of the case, and (3) if service is effected in a manner prescribed by the Texas statute.

How is service outside the forum state handled in federal court? The situation is more complicated than it needs to be. At the outset, remember that the due process restrictions on personal jurisdiction that we studied in §2.4 are limitations on a *state's* power to exercise jurisdiction over the defendant. As a constitutional matter, a *federal* court, being an arm of the federal (not state) government, is not restricted by state boundaries. As long as the defendant has sufficient ties with the United States (as opposed to ties with a single state), a federal court should have the power, constitutionally, to serve process on her, even if she is in Hawaii and the action is pending in federal court in Maine.

As we saw in §2.6.1, however, the federal courts have limited their personal jurisdiction in most civil cases. This limitation is found in Federal Rule 4(k)(1)(A), which provides that a federal court can serve process to establish personal jurisdiction *only if* the defendant would be subject to personal jurisdiction in a state court[73] in the state in

---

[72]This principle is embodied in Federal Rule 4(k)(1)(A), which provides that service of process establishes personal jurisdiction in a federal district over a defendant who could be subjected to jurisdiction of a state court in the state in which the federal court sits.

[73]Rule 4(k)(1)(A) says a "court of general jurisdiction in the state where the district court is located." This reference to "general jurisdiction" is *not* general *personal*

which the federal court is located. In other words, this Rule says that a federal court can exercise personal jurisdiction and permit service of process outside the state in which it sits *only* if a state court in that state could do so. Though it may seem odd (as we argued in §2.6.1), this restriction applies regardless of the basis for federal subject matter jurisdiction. Thus, it applies not only in cases invoking diversity of citizenship jurisdiction (which are governed by state law) but even in cases in which the claim asserted arises under federal law.

> ○ ***Example #3.*** The case is pending in the federal district court for the Western District of Texas, in El Paso. The plaintiff wishes to have that court exercise personal jurisdiction over (and recognize service of process upon) a defendant who can be found in La Union, New Mexico, 20 miles from El Paso. Under Rule 4(k)(1)(A), the federal court in Texas can do so *only* if a state court in Texas could do so. Thus, the assessment of whether the New Mexico defendant is subject to personal jurisdiction in the federal court in El Paso is exactly the same as whether she would be subject to personal jurisdiction in a state court in El Paso; the issue will be determined by the Texas personal jurisdiction statutes and constitutional limits of due process.[74] If personal jurisdiction is proper, service may be effected in New Mexico pursuant to the terms of the Texas long-arm provision for out-of-state service.

That is the general rule. But it is subject to three exceptions (also discussed in §2.6.1). First, there are federal statutory exceptions. Rule 4(k)(1)(C) provides that a federal court can serve process outside the state in which it sits, regardless of state law, "when authorized by a federal statute." Such statutes are relatively rare and represent a congressional assessment that the federal courts ought to be empowered to serve process nationwide in particular kinds of cases.[75]

---

jurisdiction, which we discussed in §2.4.5. Rather, it is a reference to general *subject matter jurisdiction*. This rule is saying that the federal court can serve process if the state court that handles regular, run-of-the-mill civil cases (as opposed to specialized cases such as probate) could do so.

[74]This means, of course, that the New Mexico defendant must have such contacts with Texas as to render exercise of jurisdiction by Texas constitutional. Again, federal courts, constitutionally, could be empowered to exercise personal jurisdiction over any defendant having sufficient contacts with the United States, and to have nationwide service of process. Rule 4(k)(1)(A), however, stands for the proposition that the federal courts have, as a general rule, refused to exercise such power. They have chosen, instead, to limit themselves to the same jurisdictional power (and corresponding power to serve process out of state) as the state courts.

[75]One example is the Federal Interpleader Act, which we study in §13.2. Nationwide service of process means, for instance, that a defendant who has never set foot outside Hawaii can be served with process in Hawaii for a proceeding in federal court in Maine. State courts, limited by the Fourteenth Amendment, could never be empowered to do so.

The second exception—allowing service of process in a federal action outside the forum state regardless of state law—is commonly called the "bulge rule," found at Rule 4(k)(1)(B). The bulge rule is extremely narrow. First, it does not permit nationwide service of process. Rather, it allows service out of state only if it is made within 100 miles of the federal courthouse in which the action is pending.[76] Second, and more important, the bulge rule has absolutely nothing to do with serving process on the typical defendant. Rather, it is for serving process on persons not originally parties to the suit but who are brought into the case later, under Rule 14 (impleader) or Rule 19 (necessary parties).[77] So for the basic task we are addressing—service of process on the *original defendant*—the bulge rule is irrelevant.

- *Example #4.* Same facts as above, in which the case is pending in the federal district court in El Paso. The plaintiff wants to have the court exercise personal jurisdiction over a defendant found in La Union, New Mexico, 20 miles from El Paso, and to permit service of process on her there. Assume that no provision of Texas law would permit personal jurisdiction over, or service of process on, this defendant. Can the defendant be served under Rule 4(k)(1)(B)? No. That Rule does not permit service of process on original defendants. It works only to allow service over persons joined later in the proceedings, under Rule 14 or 19.
- *Example #5.* The case is pending in the federal district court in El Paso; one defendant can be found and served with process in Van Horn, Texas, which is 105 miles from El Paso. Can the federal court in El Paso allow service of process on the defendant? Yes. Why? Because the defendant is in the forum state in which the federal court sits, and service of process runs throughout the forum state. The mileage is irrelevant in such a situation.

The final exception allowing a federal court to serve process outside the state in which it sits (regardless of state law) is found in Rule 4(k)(2). It applies only to claims that invoke federal question jurisdiction (discussed at §4.6) and thus is of no use in diversity of citizenship cases. Rule 4(k)(2) provides that serving process (or filing a waiver of service) establishes personal jurisdiction over a defendant in a federal question case if two things are true. First, there is no state in which the defendant is subject to personal jurisdiction. Second, exercise of personal jurisdiction over the defendant in the United States would be

---

[76]If a long-arm statute in the state in which the federal court sits would permit personal jurisdiction over this person, and the exercise of personal jurisdiction would be constitutional, you would not need the bulge rule. That rule is needed only when forum state law does not permit the exercise of personal jurisdiction over the out-of-stater.

[77]We discuss these methods for joining new parties at §§12.6.1 and 12.6.2.

constitutional.[78] These requirements can be met only when the defendant's contacts with a particular state are not sufficient to support personal jurisdiction in that state, but her contacts with the United States as a whole support personal jurisdiction.

Such cases will be rare. Under modern doctrine, discussed in §2.4.5, a defendant is subject to general jurisdiction where "at home." A corporate defendant is at home where it is incorporated and where it maintains its principal place of business. If either of those is in a state of the United States, the company will be subject to jurisdiction there for any case, meaning that Rule 4(k)(2) cannot apply. On the other hand, if the company is incorporated and maintains its principal place of business abroad, the modern doctrine will likely not permit general jurisdiction in a state in the United States, because that doctrine no longer permits general jurisdiction based upon "continuous and systematic" contacts with the forum.[79]

Thus, Rule 4(k)(2) seems destined to apply to cases involving specific jurisdiction; that is, cases in which the plaintiff's claim relates to the defendant's contacts with the United States. If Rule 4(k)(2) does apply, it permits service of process on the defendant anywhere in the United States. As one court said, the Rule "provides for what amounts to a federal long-arm statute in a narrow band of cases in which the United States serves as the relevant forum for a minimum contacts analysis."[80]

Rule 4(k)(2) does not apply, however, if there is *any* state in the United States in which the defendant would be subject to personal jurisdiction for the present case.[81] This fact raises a potentially difficult question regarding burden of proof on the "negation requirement"; that is, the requirement that the defendant is not subject to personal jurisdiction in any state. There is some support for the position that

---

[78]The constitutional analysis would be pursuant to the Fifth Amendment (not the Fourteenth Amendment) because a federal court (not a state court) is asserting personal jurisdiction. In §2.6.2, we saw that the better view under the Fifth Amendment is that the defendant must have minimum contacts with the United States as a whole, and not with any particular state.

[79]Conceivably, the Supreme Court could conclude that general jurisdiction under the Fifth Amendment (as opposed to the Fourteenth Amendment) could be based upon the defendant's level of activities and not on whether the defendant is "at home" in the forum. At present, however, this is merely an academic argument, unsupported by case law. *See* §2.6.2.

[80]Glencore Grain Rotterdam B.V. v. Shivnath Rai Harnarain Co., 284 F.3d 1114, 1126 (9th Cir. 2002).

[81]In *Saudi v. Northrop Grumman Corp.*, 221 F.R.D. 452, 457-458 (E.D. Va. 2004), the plaintiff's efforts to demonstrate that the defendant had sufficient contacts with the United States as a whole backfired, because it demonstrated that the defendant was subject to personal jurisdiction of at least two states. Accordingly, Rule 4(k)(2) did not apply.

the plaintiff must show that the defendant is not subject to personal jurisdiction in each of the 50 states.[82] But this approach is awkward, because it requires the plaintiff not only to prove a negative (which is hard to do), but to do so 50 times.

Accordingly, the overwhelming majority view employs a burden-shifting approach. First, the plaintiff must make out a *prima facie* case for applying Rule 4(k)(2).[83] Second, the burden shifts to the defendant to demonstrate that it is subject to personal jurisdiction in another state.[84] If the defendant fails to do this, the court is justified in using Rule 4(k)(2).[85]

§3.3.5 International Service of Process

In recent decades, we have seen a "substantial increase in the number of international transactions and events that are the subject of litigation in federal courts."[86] Accordingly, Federal Rule 4(f), which

---

[82]*See, e.g.,* Saudi v. Northrop Grumman Corp., 221 F.R.D. 452, 457 (E.D. Va. 2004) ("The Plaintiff bears the burden of proving that [the defendant] is not subject to the general jurisdiction of any state by a preponderance of the evidence").

[83]*See, e.g.*, Nagravision SA v. Gotech International Technology Limited, 882 F.3d 494, 499 (5th Cir. 2018) (detailing burden-shifting process for Rule 4(k)(2)); Merial Ltd. v. Cipla Ltd., 681 F.3d 1283, 1294 (Fed. Cir. 2012) ("We have therefore adopted a burden-shifting mechanism."); ISI Intern., Inc. v. Borden Ladner Gervais LLP, 256 F.3d 548, 552 (7th Cir. 2001) ("Constitutional analysis for each of the 50 states is eminently avoidable by allocating burdens sensibly."); Lelchook v. Islamic Republic of Iran, 224 F.Supp.3d 108, 115-116 (D. Mass. 2016) (plaintiff failed to establish *prima facie* case for application of Rule 4(k)(2) by failing to certify that defendant was not subject to suit in any state).

[84]Alternatively, the defendant could show that its overall contacts with the United States fail to establish personal jurisdiction under the Fifth Amendment.

[85]Merial Ltd. v. Cipia Ltd, 681 F.3d 1283, 1294 (Fed. Cir. 2012) (referring to this as a "burden-shifting mechanism"); Oldfield v. Pueblo de Bahia Lora, S.A., 558 F.3d 1210, 1219 n.22 (11th Cir. 2009); Holland Am. Line Inc. v. Wartsila N. Am., Inc., 485 F.3d 450, 461 (9th Cir. 2007); Mwani v. bin Laden, 417 F.3d 1, 11 (D.C. Cir. 2005); Adam v. Unione Mediterranea di Sicurta, 364 F.3d 646, 651 (5th Cir. 2004); IST Int'l, Inc. v. Borden Ladner Gervais LLP, 256 F.3d 548, 552 (7th Cir. 2001); United States v. Swiss American Bank, Ltd., 191 F.3d 30, 41 (1st Cir. 1999); Syngenta Crop Protection, LLC v. Willowood, LLC, 139 F. Supp. 3d 722, 731 (M.D.N.C. 2015); Ogden v. GlobalSantaFe Offshore Servs., 31 F. Supp. 3d 832, 840 (E.D. La. 2014).

One interesting issue is whether a defendant may avoid the application of Rule 4(k)(2) by consenting to personal jurisdiction in another forum. The court rejected the effort in *Sunrise Techs., Inc. v. SELC Ireland, Ltd.*, 2016 WL 3360418 at *5 (D. Mass. 2016) ("This court finds that SELC's voluntary consent to jurisdiction in North Carolina is insufficient to defeat Rule 4(k)(2) because the defendant has failed to establish an independent basis for jurisdiction in that forum. Since the defendant is not subject to personal jurisdiction in any other state, this case may proceed in Massachusetts.").

[86]1993 Advisory Committee Notes to Fed. R. Civ. P. 4(f).

grants authority to serve process outside the United States, has become increasingly important.[87]

Rule 4(f)(1) permits "any internationally agreed means of service that is reasonably calculated to give notice." The most important such means are provided by the Hague Convention on the Service Abroad of Judicial and Extrajudicial Documents, to which the Rule expressly refers.[88] That Convention applies only if the country in which service is sought is a signatory. In addition to the United States, more than 70 countries have signed the Convention, including Argentina, Australia, Canada, China, France, Germany, India, Israel, Italy, Japan, Mexico, Spain, and the United Kingdom.

The Hague Convention embraces various methods of serving process. Most important is the requirement that each signatory nation designate a "Central Authority" to which requests for service from other signatory nations are sent. If the documents are proper, the Central Authority serves the process or arranges to have it served by an appropriate agency. The Central Authority also provides a certificate showing either that service was completed or stating why it could not be effected.

Because the Central Authority in many countries works very slowly, Article 10 of the Hague Convention provides for alternative methods of service. Under Article 15, if the Central Authority fails to respond to the request for service within six months, the plaintiff may use alternative methods to serve process. Importantly, each signatory country may object to these alternative methods. The most useful alternative is Article 10(a), which allows the plaintiff "to send judicial documents, by postal channels, directly to persons abroad." Interestingly, this part of Article 10 refers to a right to "send" documents (and not to a right to "serve" documents[89]). This language raised a question as to whether the provision permits mailing only of documents *other than* service of process. Lower federal courts and state courts disagreed on the issue, which led to considerable uncertainty. The Supreme Court resolved

---

[87]The fact that it permits service outside the United States is reflected by its provision for service "at a place not within any judicial district of the United States." It is also worth noting that Rule 4(h)(2) addresses service of process on a corporation or association outside the United States. It expressly embraces the methods of international service in Rule 4(f), except one subdivision of that Rule (Rule 4(f)(2)(C)(i)) that applies only to individual defendants. With that one exception, the permissibility of service on a corporation or association overseas is coextensive with that on an individual.

[88]The United States is party to other such conventions, but the Hague Convention is the most widely used.

[89]The other alternatives under Article 10 include "service" (as opposed to "send[ing]") by someone authorized to serve process in the place where the litigation or in the country where service is sought. Hague Convention, Article 10(b)&(c).

the matter in *Water Splash, Inc. v. Menon.*[90] It held that Article 10(a) does not prohibit service of process by mail. Thus, such service of process by mail is proper if (1) the country in which process is served has not objected to service by mail, and (2) the forum in which the case is filed permits service of process by mail.[91]

If the Hague Convention applies, a plaintiff seeking to serve process in a foreign country must comply with it.[92] In other words, the Convention is mandatory regarding service.[93] Service that is valid under the Hague Convention is deemed to satisfy Rule 4, even if the method does not conform with other provisions of Rule 4.

If there is no internationally-agreed-upon method for serving process in another country (for example, if service is to be made in a country that has not signed the Hague Convention), Rule 4(f)(2) permits service abroad in several ways. First, Rule 4(f)(2)(A) allows service in any manner permitted by the country in which service is made. Second, Rule 4(f)(2)(B) permits the plaintiff to ask the foreign country for instructions on how to serve process. Such a request traditionally has been called a *letter rogatory* but today is also called a *letter of request*. Third, Rule 4(f)(2)(C) provides that unless the foreign law prohibits it, service may be made (1) personally in the foreign country, or (2) by any form of mail that requires a signed receipt, sent by the clerk of the court to the defendant in the foreign country.

Finally, as an alternative to Rule 4(f)(2), Rule 4(f)(3) allows service "by other means not prohibited by international agreement, as the court orders." Thus, a federal judge may order service by any method that does not violate a treaty or other international compact, *even if* that method would violate the law of the country in which service is made.[94] The Advisory Committee notes, while recognizing this

[90]137 S. Ct. 1504 (2017).

[91]*Id.* at 1512-1513.

[92]Societe Nationale Industrielle Aerospatiale v. United States District Court, 482 U.S. 522, 534 n.15 (1987) (contrasting mandatory language of Hague Convention on service with permissive language in Hague Convention relating to discovery).

[93]The Hague Convention on service applies only if service is to take place in a signatory foreign country. It does not apply if service may be made in the United States. Thus, in *Volkswagenwerk Aktiengesellschaft v. Schlunk*, 486 U.S. 694, 706-708 (1988), the Court upheld personal jurisdiction in Illinois over a German corporation by serving process on its subsidiary in Illinois. Illinois law authorized service on the German corporation by making substituted service on its subsidiary without sending documents to Germany. Because that law was satisfied, and the exercise of jurisdiction over the German corporation was constitutional, the Court upheld jurisdiction despite the failure to satisfy the Hague Convention. *See also* John F. Coyle, Robin Effron & Maggie Gardner, *Contracting Around the Hague Service Convention,* 53 U.C. Davis L. Rev. Online 52 (2019).

[94]*See* Mayoral-Amy v. BHI Corp., 180 F.R.D. 456, 459 n.4 (S.D. Fla. 1998). This provision is far broader than that in Rule 4(f)(2)(C), which does not permit use of methods that are prohibited "by the law of the foreign country" in which service is effected.

breadth, counsel courts to be wary of violating foreign law. (And, of course, any method ordered by the court under Rule 4(f)(3) must satisfy the constitutional standard for notice under *Mullane*.)

It bears emphasis that Rule 4(f)(3) is an alternative to the methods permitted by Rule 4(f)(2). One interesting case is *Rio Properties, Inc. v. Rio International Interlink*,[95] in which the operator of a Nevada casino sued a Costa Rican Internet gambling operation for trademark infringement. Unable to find an agent for service of process in the United States or in Costa Rica, the plaintiff sought a court order under Rule 4(f)(3) to permit service of process by e-mail to the defendant's e-mail address. In upholding the service, the Ninth Circuit rejected the argument that Rule 4(f) provides a hierarchy in which some other methods of service (such as letters of request), must be exhausted before a court can order service under Rule 4(f)(3). The plaintiff "need not have attempted every permissible means of service of process before petitioning the court for alternative relief. Instead, [it] needed only to demonstrate that the facts and circumstances of the present case necessitated the district court's intervention."[96]

The Ninth Circuit upheld the constitutionality of e-mail service of process in *Rio Properties*. While recognizing that it "tread upon untrodden ground," since it was aware of no case in which an appellate court had upheld e-mail service, the court found that e-mail satisfied the *Mullane* standard, discussed in §3.2. Not only was e-mail reasonably calculated under all the circumstances to apprise the defendant of the pendency of the case; on the facts of the case (which involved the defendant's attempts to evade service), "it was the method of service most likely to reach [the defendant]."[97] The court was concerned that e-mail does not permit confirmation of receipt and thus presents problems with whether service can be proved. But that was simply one factor to be considered in determining, based upon all the facts

---

[95]284 F.3d 1007, 1012-1013 (9th Cir. 2002). The opinion was written by Judge Stephen Trott, who, before attending law school, was a member of a folk music band in the 1960s that had a number-one hit record with its rendition of "Michael Row the Boat Ashore."

[96]*Id.* at 1016 ("We expressly agree with the district court's handling of this case and its use of Rule 4(f)(3) to ensure the smooth functioning of our courts of law").

[97]*Id.* at 1017. The court relied on an earlier case that upheld service of process by telex on Iranian defendants. In that case, the court explained: "No longer do we live in a world where communications are conducted solely by mail carried by fast sailing clipper... ships. Electronic communication via satellite can and does provide instantaneous transmission of notice and information. No longer must process be mailed to a defendant's door when he can receive complete notice at an electronic terminal inside his very office, even when the door is steel and bolted shut." New England Merchants Nat'l Bank v. Iran Power Generation & Transmission Co., 495 F. Supp. 73, 81 (S.D.N.Y. 1980).

of a given case, whether notice satisfied due process.[98] In the wake of *Rio Properties*, some courts have upheld service under Rule 4(f)(3) via social media portals.[99]

In §3.3.2, we saw that Rule 4(d) permits the defendant to waive formal service of process. Rule 4(d) operates in the international context the same as it does domestically, with two minor adjustments as to timing. First, under Rule 4(d)(1)(F), the defendant must be given at least 60 days (instead of 30 days) to return the waiver form. And second, under Rule 4(d)(3), the international defendant who waives formal service has 90 days (instead of 60 days) from the sending of the waiver form to her in which to respond to the complaint.

§3.3.6 Service of Subsequent Documents

The foregoing discussion, in §3.3.1 through §3.3.5, deals with service of *process*. Process includes the summons, which is an order from the judicial branch, commanding the defendant to appear. It is the symbol of the government's power over the defendant. The law insists on the exacting requirements we have seen to ensure that there is no abuse of that governmental power. Such a show of power, however, need be made only once as to each defendant.

Thereafter, service of other documents in the case (and there may be many, including additional pleadings, motions, and discovery requests and responses) is not as formal. First, no summons is needed. Second, Rule 5(b)(2) permits service of such subsequent documents by

---

[98]*Rio Properties,* 284 F.3d at 1018. The issue arose only because Rule 4(f), discussed in §3.3.5, permits a judge to order a method for serving process (such as by e-mail). That Rule applies, however, only in international cases, and is not available for service within the United States. *See generally* David Stewart & Anna Conley, *E-Mail Service on Foreign Defendants: Time for an International Approach,* 38 Geo. J. Int'l L. 755 (2007).

[99]*See* K.A. v. J.L., 450 N.J.Super. 247, 255 (Del.Ch. 2016) ("[S]ervice by Facebook in this case is permitted. The court is satisfied that after diligent efforts, personal service could not be accomplished. Next, service by publication would be efficient given the nature of the relief sought, an injunction"); Lexmark Int'l, Inc. v. Ink Tech. Printer Supplies, LLC, 295 F.R.D. 259, 261-262 (S.D. Ohio 2013) (upholding constitutionality of e-mail service of process on Chinese and Polish entities); F.T.C. v. PCCare247 Inc., 2013 WL 841037 at *4-6 (S.D.N.Y. 2013) (upholding constitutionality of service of process by e-mail and by Facebook message with relevant documents attached); Fraserside IP LLC v. Letyagin, 280 F.R.D. 630, 630 (N.D. Iowa 2013) (upholding e-mail service on "international intellectual property scofflaws"). *But see* Doe v. Hyassat, 337 F.R.D. 12, 16 (S.D.N.Y. 2020) ("Plaintiff has not demonstrated that service through the Facebook account at issue is 'reasonably calculated. . . to apprise [defendant] of the pendency of the action.' . . . Accordingly, Plaintiff's application to effect service exclusively via Facebook message is denied").

personal delivery, or by leaving them at the party's office, or by regular mail. Moreover, Rule 5(b)(2)(E) permits service of these subsequent documents by "electronic transmission," but only if a party consents in writing to permit it.

In most cases today, parties take advantage of Rule 5 to serve subsequent documents by mail or e-mail. If mail is used, Rule 5(b)(2)(C) provides that the service is complete upon mailing. Similarly, under Rule 5(b)(2)(E), e-mail service is complete upon transmission (unless the party serving later learns that it did not go through). Finally, if a document served by mail is one to which a response is required (such as discovery requests), Rule 6(d) gives the receiving party three extra days in which to respond.[100]

§3.4   Problems with Opportunity to Be Heard

In addition to notice, due process guarantees a defendant a meaningful opportunity to be heard.[101] In most cases, this requirement poses no serious problem. Under Federal Rule 12(a), a defendant has at least 21 days after service of process in which to respond, either by answering or bringing a motion. The practice is comparable in state courts.[102] Allowing this much time, especially following the clear notice provided by the summons, is sufficient to permit the defendant to protect her interests and avoid entry of default judgment. If the defendant needs more time, she may move under Federal Rule 6(b) for an extension (some state counterparts to the rule call it "enlargement") of time in which to respond. The typical case, then, does not present a problem concerning opportunity to be heard.

When do such problems arise? Often, it's when the plaintiff seeks to have the defendant's property seized before the underlying dispute is resolved on the merits. Such pretrial judgment seizure is sometimes called *pendente lite,* which is Latin for "pending litigation." In a series of opinions, the Supreme Court addressed such procedures and offered guidance on the conditions under which a plaintiff might do this.

---

[100]Until 2016, Rule 6(d) applied not only to documents that were mailed, but to documents that were served electronically. The 2016 amendment recognized that electronic transmission is immediate and therefore does not justify the three-day extension allowed by Rule 6(d).

[101]*Mullane*, 339 U.S. at 314 ("right to be heard has little reality or worth unless one is informed that the matter is pending and can choose for himself whether to appear or default, acquiesce or contest"). We discussed *Mullane* at §3.2.

[102]Indeed, some states, including California and Georgia, allow the defendant 30 days from service of process in which to respond. Cal. Code Civ. Proc. §412.20(a)(3); Ga. Code Ann. §9-11-12.

○ ***Example #6.*** Retail Co. sells a stereo system to Buyer on an installment plan, by which Buyer is to pay a given amount each month. Buyer
fails to make payments, and Retail Co. sues. Before that case goes to
trial, pending litigation, Retail Co. wants possession of the property, to
ensure, for instance, that it is not damaged or stolen. But Buyer has a
right to present defenses: to explain why she has not paid for the stereo
(maybe it was defective). Or perhaps Buyer has paid in full for the stereo
and Retail Co. is mistaken. In light of these concerns, who should have
possession of the property before the merits are litigated? The Supreme
Court has attempted to balance the legitimate concerns of both sides.

Before looking at the cases, it is helpful to review some terminology.
Garnishment refers to seizure of a defendant's property that is in the
hands of a third party. A good example is a bank account: The holder
of the account "owns" the property, but it is held by the bank. Creditors
might want to garnish the bank account or the wages of a debtor to
ensure that they get paid. *Replevin* is a procedure by which a seller of
goods seeks to recover the goods or the cash equivalent of the goods.
Sequestration is a process that removes property from the person in
possession pending the outcome of litigation concerning it ownership.

The modern law in this area developed from a series of Supreme
Court cases in the 1960s and 1970s. The first important case was
Sniadach v. Family Finance Corporation.[103] There, the Court held
unconstitutional a Wisconsin law that allowed a creditor to garnish a
debtor's wages before any hearing on the merits of the creditor's claim.
Without some protection for the debtor, such a seizure would "drive a
wage-earning family to the wall"[104] and would violate the debtor's due
process rights.

But what sorts of protections could be built into such statutes to
render them constitutional? The Court gave some guidance in *Fuentes
v. Shevin,*[105] which invalidated replevin statutes in Pennsylvania and
Florida. Those statutes permitted a seller to seize property before the
court held a hearing on the merits of the dispute. They provided the
buyer with some protection by allowing her to reclaim the property
before trial by posting a bond. According to the Court, however, this
protection was insufficient.

The Court was more forthcoming in *Mitchell v. W.T. Grant
Company,*[106] in which it upheld a Louisiana practice that permitted
prehearing sequestration of property when the plaintiff feared the
defendant might remove or damage the property in the interim. The

[103]395 U.S. 337 (1969).
[104]*Id.* at 341-342.
[105]407 U.S. 67, 96 (1972).
[106]416 U.S. 600, 601, 619-620 (1974).

Louisiana statute, unlike those addressed in *Fuentes*, required that the writ (order) allowing seizure of the property be issued by a judicial officer rather than by the sheriff. It also required the plaintiff to set forth reasons for sequestration under oath and in detail, rather than by simple conclusory statements. Moreover, the Louisiana law permitted the buyer to reclaim possession, pending litigation, without delay. Further, the plaintiff had a lien on the property.[107] These factors distinguished the case from *Fuentes* and satisfied due process.

In *North Georgia Finishing, Inc. v. DiChem, Inc.*,[108] the Court struck down a Georgia statute by which a creditor had garnished the defendant's bank accounts. Under that statute, such seizure was permitted based upon conclusory sworn statements by the plaintiff and the plaintiff's posting a bond of twice the amount claimed from the defendant. The writ allowing seizure was issued by a court clerk, not a judicial officer. Although the defendant could repossess the property by posting her own bond, there was no provision for an expedited hearing on the merits. These were insufficient protections for the defendant, and the statute violated due process.

Connecticut v. Doehr,[109] decided in 1991, involved a plaintiff's seizure of the defendant's real property before judgment for the purpose of ensuring sufficient assets to satisfy a judgment on an underlying battery claim. The Court held the Connecticut statute unconstitutional because it permitted seizure based upon the plaintiff's conclusory sworn statement that "there is probable cause to sustain the validity of the plaintiff's claims." Unlike the statute in *Mitchell*, the Connecticut law did not require the plaintiff to post a bond. Also, unlike *Mitchell*, the plaintiff did not have a lien on the property. Thus, the plaintiff had no interest in the real property except the general interest all plaintiffs have in ensuring that the defendant has enough assets to pay a judgment. There was no evidence that the defendant was going to transfer the land or otherwise diminish his assets to avoid having to pay a judgment.

From these cases, we are left with a series of potential protections for the defendant in a pretrial seizure situation, including: (1) involvement of a judicial officer in the determination of whether the seizure should be made; (2) notice to the defendant of the plaintiff's effort to make a prehearing seizure; (3) a requirement that the plaintiff post

---

[107]A lien is a claim on the property. Remember from §2.2 that a valid *in personam* judgment creates a lien against the defendant's real property, which means that the property can be sold at public auction to raise the money to pay off the lien. In *Mitchell*, the plaintiff had a vendor's lien, which is a right against the property to collect for goods sold.

[108]419 U.S. 601, 608 (1975).

[109]501 U.S. 1, 27 (1991).

a bond; (4) a requirement that the plaintiff state under oath specific, particularized reasons for the seizure; and (5) a procedure by which the defendant may get the property back (perhaps by posting a bond) pending the trial on the merits. In addition, it seems clear that the plaintiff is on a better footing if she has a lien on the property to be seized.

But the ultimate question of how many of these safeguards must be present, and in what combination, is not clear. *Mitchell* is the only one of the cases in which the challenged statute was upheld,[110] so one is tempted to say that the factors present in that case would constitute the due process minimum. This conclusion is difficult to reach, however, because each case varies at least slightly on its facts. Perhaps the best we can say is that a court must balance factors such as those listed, and the relative rights of the parties, in a flexible, case-by-case assessment to ensure appropriate protection to the defendant.

§3.5 Provisional Remedies, Including Preliminary Injunctions and TROs

Though the detailed study of remedies is beyond our scope, it is important to have a basic understanding of the field. In §1.2.3, we discussed various classic remedies. Some of these (principally damages to compensate for harm inflicted) developed at law and others (including the injunction, rescission, and reformation) developed at equity. We will see in §7.3.2 that the plaintiff makes a demand for relief in her complaint, in which she informs the court of the remedies she wishes to recover if she wins the case.

But we will not know who wins the case until we get through the adjudication phase, which will routinely take months or years to complete. In the interim, while the litigation is proceeding, one party may want the court to enter temporary relief—a "provisional" remedy. The goal is to protect the parties' interests while the case wends its way

---

[110]In *D.H. Overmyer Co. v. Frick Co.,* 405 U.S. 174, 200 (1972), the Court upheld the use of a *cognovit* provision in a contract. Such a clause authorizes a creditor to sue the debtor and automatically have "judgment by confession" entered against the defendant without notice. The Court emphasized that the provision was the result of good faith bargaining between parties of equal bargaining power, that the plaintiff had given good consideration for this right, and that relevant state law protected the defendant by permitting it to set aside the judgment if it had a valid defense. *Overmyer,* thus, is nothing more than a recognition that one can waive her due process right to an opportunity to be heard. Such waivers are not recognized, however, if the parties are of unequal bargaining power and are imposed upon the weaker party. Moreover, they are especially questionable if used against a debtor of limited financial means. *See* Swarb v. Lennox, 405 U.S. 191, 198 (1972).

through the litigation process. Under Federal Rule 64, the availability of provisional remedies generally is governed by the law of the state in which the federal court sits. (On the other hand, the same Rule makes clear that federal statutes will govern in cases in which they apply. There are a few such federal statutes. For example, 28 U.S.C. §2405 permits garnishment by the United States in a suit against a corporation seeking recovery of money.)

Though states may use different terminology, we should be familiar with two additional generic terms:

- *Garnishment* is the court's seizure of the defendant's property that is in the possession of a third party. It serves the same purpose as attachment.
- *Replevin* is an order allowing repossession of personal property pending the outcome of a dispute about who owns that particular property.

Provisional Asset Seizure

Sometimes, as we saw in Example #6, the goal is to seize specific property. Other times, however, the goal will be to ensure that there will be sufficient assets from which the plaintiff can recover if she ultimately wins a monetary judgment.

- ○ ***Example #7.*** *P* sues *D* in federal court in Georgia, seeking damages of $100,000. While the case is in early stages, *P* learns that *D* is planning to move permanently from Georgia to Australia. *D* has listed his house in Georgia for sale. *P* is worried that by the time she wins a judgment, *D* will have no assets in Georgia from which *D* can pay the judgment. *P* asks the court to order the provisional remedy of "attachment."

If *P* meets the requirements for pre-judgment attachment, the court can enter an order placing a lien on *D*'s property in favor of *P*. This lien creates a charge against *D*'s real property in Georgia in favor of *P*. This lien is a public record, so even if *D* sells the house in the meantime, the sales proceeds are "impressed" with *P*'s interest. That means that $100,000 of the sales funds cannot be transferred out of the state. The money will be there to satisfy *P*'s judgment if she ultimately wins. If *P* loses the judgment, any seized asset is returned to the defendant and the defendant can recover for her losses from the bond posted by the plaintiff.

- ○ ***Example #8.*** Assume we have the same facts as Example #7 except that *D*'s assets consist of money in a bank, which *D* was about to remove to take to Australia. Here, because *D*'s assets are in the possession of a third party (the bank), *P* would seek *garnishment*—that the court seize an appropriate portion of the assets that are in the hands of the bank to hold during litigation so it will be available to satisfy *P*'s judgment.

Let us return to a variation on Example #6.

○ ***Example #9.*** Buyer buys an entertainment system from Retail Co. The agreement requires Buyer to pay $200 per month for 24 months. Buyer makes payments for the first three months but then stops paying. Retail Co. sues Buyer to recover the property. It will take months for the case to come to trial. In the meantime, Retail Co. would like to have possession of the entertainment system, perhaps to ensure that Buyer does not damage it or abscond with it.

Recall from §3.4 that the Court dealt with constitutional problems raised by such provisional remedies. Today, state laws are far more protective of consumers than they were then. For instance, most replevin provisions would require Retail Co. to make a preliminary showing of Buyer's default and of its right to the property. They would require a hearing at which Buyer may present evidence. After all, Buyer may have made payment which Retail Co. misplaced or did not credit, or perhaps the property is defective, which might permit Buyer to withhold payment. Sometimes, a judge will issue a provisional remedy only if the party seeking it posts a bond. That bond is money deposited with the court, from which the other party may be compensated for harm inflicted if it turns out that the seizure of the property was improper. Provisional remedies for asset seizure are not routinely granted. They are ordered only if the party seeking them satisfies the increasingly rigorous requirements of the applicable law.

It bears repeating that we are talking about remedies entered before judgment in the case. Some of them, principally attachment, are also available after judgment is entered, to permit the appropriate authority to seize property belonging to the defendant so that it can be sold to satisfy the judgment entered in favor of the plaintiff. Here, we are dealing with the pre-judgment phase. Courts are properly nervous about entering remedies at this stage, because we do not know (and will not know until judgment is entered) which side in the litigation will prevail.

Provisional Injunctive Relief

We turn now to provisional *injunctive* relief. An injunction is a court order commanding someone either to do something (a mandatory injunction) or to refrain from doing something (a prohibitory injunction). Sometimes, the point of the plaintiff's suit itself will be to get an injunction that will enjoin the defendant for a given time or in perpetuity. This is called a "permanent" injunction because it is issued after final adjudication on the merits. For example, after final adjudication, the court may enjoin the defendant from using a trademark that is confusingly similar to the plaintiff's trademark.

Here, we are not talking about final injunctive relief, but about *preliminary* injunctive relief. This is an injunction against the defendant that remains in place until there is final adjudication on the merits of the underlying dispute. The goal is to maintain the status quo pending the ultimate resolution of the merits. Doing so will minimize the risk that the plaintiff may suffer some irreparable harm while the parties litigate the underlying case on the merits (which, again, may take considerable time).

○ ***Example #10.*** *D* is employed by Company. The employment contract contains a covenant not to compete, which says that for one year after *D* leaves Company's employment, *D* cannot go into competition with Company in the same geographic area. In the course of employment, *D* learns the secret formula by which Company makes its signature product ("trade secret"). *D* quits her job at Company and, one month later, sets up her own business, which competes with Company in making the product. Company sues *D*, alleging that *D* is wrongfully usurping Company's trade secret and is violating the covenant not to compete. *D* asserts (1) the covenant not to compete is void under applicable law, (2) she is not using Company's formula, and (3) even if she is using Company's formula, she has a right to do so because Company waived any trade secret protection it might have had.

We will not know who wins until the litigation runs its course. In the meantime, Company may move for a preliminary injunction: an order stopping *D* from operating her new business (or permitting the business to proceed but without using Company's secret formula). Without such provisional relief, Company argues, *D* will inflict enormous harm on it by using Company's formula. *D* opposes such an order; she claims to have done nothing wrong and that she has a right to pursue her business in the meantime.

The court is nervous about entering the requested order because it has no idea at this stage which party is correct on the merits. On the one hand, if *D* is right, a preliminary injunction will rob her of her livelihood for months or years, until the case is adjudicated. On the other hand, failing to protect Company from what might be unfair competition may subject Company to irreparable harm: It may be driven out of business by the time the merits are decided.

The preliminary injunction is an extraordinary remedy, one that is never awarded as of right. Rule 65(a)(1) requires the party seeking a preliminary injunction (Company in Example #10) to give notice to the other party. The court will hold a hearing on whether to grant the preliminary injunction. The burden is on the party seeking the injunction, and it is a strict burden. As generally stated, the moving party must demonstrate:

1. That she is likely to suffer "irreparable harm" if the injunction is not issued.[111] This is part of the traditional requirement that one seeking an equitable remedy must show that her remedy at law (damages) will not make her whole. Here, Company might show that *D*'s competition will so damage Company that the harm cannot be fixed by a later recovery of damages. Maybe the lost market share simply will not be recoverable.

2. That she is likely to win on the merits. In this case, Company must show that when the case is actually adjudicated, it is likely to prevail.

3. That the balance of hardship favors the party seeking the injunction. The court must weigh who would be worse off: Company if the preliminary injunction is denied or *D* if the injunction is granted.

4. That the injunction is in the public interest. Here, for example, *D* will argue in favor of a public interest supporting competition. Company will argue that public policy demands fair competition.

The burden is on the moving party.[112] Whether to issue the injunction is vested in the sound discretion of the trial court. If it issues a preliminary injunction, Rule 65(d) requires the order to state why it

---

[111]It is not sufficient that the moving party show that irreparable harm is merely possible; such harm must be likely. Winter v. Natural Res. Defense Council, 555 U.S. 7, 20-21 (2008).

[112]Some courts employ a sliding scale, under which an injunction might be proper despite a relatively weaker showing on element 2 if element 3 weighs strongly in favor of the relief. *See, e.g.,* Citigroup Global Mkts., Inc. v. VCG Special Opportunities Master Fund Ltd., 598 F.3d 30, 35 (2d Cir. 2010) (applicant must show (1) irreparable harm, (2) either (a) likelihood of success on the merits or (b) sufficiently serious questions going to the merits to make them a fair ground for litigation, and (3) balance of hardships tipping clearly in favor of applicant); Hoosier Energy Rural Elec. Co-Op, Inc. v. John Hancock Life Ins. Co., 582 F.3d 721, 725 (7th Cir. 2009); Mi Familia Vota v. Abbott, 497 F.Supp.3d 195, 212 (W.D. Tex. 2020) ("[T]his Court must consider the elements jointly, and a strong showing of one element may compensate for a weaker showing of another."). On the other hand, some courts conclude that the *Winter* case, cited in the preceding footnote, invalidated a sliding scale approach. *See, e.g.,* Mountain Valley Pipeline, LLC v. Western Pocahontas Properties Limited Partnership, 918 F.3d 353, 366 (4th Cir. 2019) ("Each of these four requirements must be satisfied."); Real Truth About Obama, Inc. v. Fed. Election Comm'n, 575 F.3d 342, 347 (4th Cir. 2009) ("flexible interplay" among elements no longer valid).

was entered, to lay out the terms with specificity, and to detail what acts are restrained. It may also require the party seeking the injunction to post a bond. Again, that means the party must deposit money with the court. That money is there to protect the other party if it turns out that the injunction should not have been entered.

Trial judges have considerable discretion in ruling on motions for preliminary injunction as well as on the terms of any injunction. The issue is of such importance that federal statutes provide for a right to appeal from an order relating to a preliminary injunction (as we will see in §14.5.2).

A preliminary injunction protects the plaintiff from irreparable injury while the litigation is ongoing. In Example #10, it would tell *D*, for instance, that she cannot use Company's formula in making her product. It will stay in effect until the case is adjudicated on the merits and judgment is entered. At that point, if Company wins, the injunction may become permanent (if so, it will be embodied in the judgment). If *D* wins, the preliminary injunction is "dissolved." In this instance, *D* will be entitled to recover money from any bond the court required Company to post (to compensate *D* for what turns out to have been an improper injunction).

But there is a gap. We know that the party seeking a preliminary injunction will make a motion, give notice to the other side, and that the court will hold a hearing. That will take a few days at least. In the meantime, the moving party will want to be protected — will want an order restraining the other party during the time it takes for the court to rule on the motion for preliminary injunction.

Here, the moving party will seek a "temporary restraining order" (TRO). The TRO requires the defendant to do something (or to refrain from doing something) from the time it is issued until the time the court decides whether to issue a preliminary injunction. As the preliminary injunction maintains the status quo pending the ultimate adjudication of the case, so the TRO maintains the status quo to allow the parties to brief (and the court to decide) whether to issue the preliminary injunction. In Example #10, a TRO would stop *D* from using Company's secret formula immediately. TROs often present exigent circumstances.

     ○ ***Example #11.*** Borrower borrows money from Creditor. As part of the loan deal, to secure repayment, Creditor has a lien on Borrower's main asset, which is a commercial fishing vessel. Repayment of the loan is due in two days. Creditor finds out that Borrower is about to sail the vessel out of the jurisdiction to engage in commercial fishing off Peru for six months. Creditor wants a TRO to stop the boat from sailing before some other arrangement can be made to secure repayment of the loan.

Suppose the boat is set to sail at 6:00 this evening. Obviously, Creditor must act fast. It will make a motion for TRO as quickly as possible, before the vessel sails. Though courts act in contemplative ways, sometimes they need to move very quickly. Because of the need for expedition, a TRO might be issued *ex parte,* which means without notice to the other party. This can be done only under the strict requirements of Rule 65(b)(1). Courts prefer not to act *ex parte* if possible and will make an effort to have all parties participate in the hearing, even if simply by telephone. Often, the court and parties are able to work something out. In Example #11, for instance, all may agree that Borrower may sail the vessel after posting some other security for repayment of the loan.

The party seeking the TRO bears the burden, based upon the same equitable factors discussed above with regard to the preliminary injunction. If the court issues the TRO, it may require the plaintiff to post a bond. A TRO may not be in place for more than 14 days (although a TRO can be extended once for up to 14 additional days). Usually a TRO is not "on the books" that long; in most cases the court will provide that the TRO is effective until the ruling on preliminary injunction, for which it will set the hearing a few days hence. Orders relating to TROs are not appealable as of right. Usually, the short duration and quick timing on TRO litigation would not provide a meaningful opportunity for appellate review.

In recent years, there has been considerable concern about the "nationwide" or "national" injunction. Suppose the executive branch of the federal government issues an order that affects environmental regulations or the immigration system. A group of plaintiffs seeks a preliminary injunction against the enforcement of that order. A federal district court grants the injunction. Does that injunction (1) stop the government from enforcing the order only against those specific plaintiffs or (2) stop the government from enforcing the order anywhere in the country?

If the former, the order may be difficult to enforce, because the government will be required to treat similarly situated persons differently.[113] If the latter, we will be allowing a single trial judge in a single district to decide the nationwide enforceability of an executive order. Doing so will lead to forum shopping and, in essence, convert a case brought by a particular group of plaintiffs into a nationwide

---

[113]That is, the government cannot enforce the order against the plaintiffs who brought the instant case but can enforce it against people who were not joined in this case. *See* Amanda Frost, *In Defense of Nationwide Injunctions,* 93 N.Y.U. L. Rev. 1065, 1069 (2018).

class action on behalf of everyone affected by the regulation.[114] Moreover, a nationwide injunction by one court robs other courts of the opportunity to address the legality of the executive order.[115] In view of these policy concerns, the debate over nationwide injunctions remains robust.

---

[114]*See* Michael T. Morley, *De Facto Class Actions: Plaintiff- and Defendant-Oriented Injunctions in Voting Rights, Election Law, and Other Constitutional Cases*, 39 Harv. J. L. & Publ. Pol'y 487, 556 (2016).

[115]*See* Samuel L. Bray, *Multiple Chancellors, Reforming the National Injunction*, 131 Harv. L. Rev. 417, 421-422 (2017) (national injunction "giv[es] up deliberate decisionmaking for accelerated resolution.").

Chapter *4*

Subject Matter Jurisdiction

§4.1 Defining the Issue

It is important to distinguish between personal jurisdiction and subject matter jurisdiction. Personal jurisdiction is a geographic question: It addresses whether the plaintiff may sue a defendant in a particular state (or states). As we studied in Chapter 2, a defendant may be sued in any state with which she has sufficient contacts to satisfy the statutory and constitutional tests for personal jurisdiction. The assessment of subject matter jurisdiction has nothing to do with geography. Instead, it concerns what court (in a state having personal jurisdiction) will hear the case. Recall from §1.2 that in each state there are two types of courts: those of the state court system and at least one (a trial court) of the federal court system. The subject matter jurisdiction question asks whether a case will be heard in a state court or in a federal court.

Stated another way, personal jurisdiction deals with the court's power over the *parties*. Subject matter jurisdiction deals with the court's power over the *case and the claims asserted in it*. To enter a valid judgment, a court must have both personal and subject matter jurisdiction.

Federal courts have *limited subject matter jurisdiction*, which means that they can hear only limited types of cases. As we will see below, this fact is mandated by the Constitution. We are concerned with *original jurisdiction*, which, as we discussed at §1.2.2, refers to cases filed and decided by trial courts (as opposed to *appellate jurisdiction*, which concerns review of trial courts by "higher" courts). There is a small subset of cases invoking federal jurisdiction in which federal courts have *exclusive subject matter jurisdiction*, which means that no other court may entertain such cases.[1] State court systems, in contrast to the federal courts, have *general subject matter jurisdiction*, which means that they can hear any cognizable claim at all (except those over which the federal courts have exclusive subject matter jurisdiction). Many times, a case can be heard either by a federal or a state court. In such cases, the federal and state courts have *concurrent subject matter jurisdiction*.

§4.2 The General Subject Matter Jurisdiction of State Court Systems

As we just said, each state's judicial system has general subject matter jurisdiction; it can hear any claim (except those rare cases that invoke exclusive federal court jurisdiction). Each state is free to divide subject

---

[1]Examples include admiralty (§1333), bankruptcy (§1334(a)), patent and copyright infringement and plant variety protection cases (§1338(a)), some antitrust (15 U.S.C. §§15-26), and some securities cases (15 U.S.C. §78a et seq.).

matter jurisdiction among whatever courts the state wishes to establish. There is considerable variety in the names that states use for their trial courts. Common names include superior court, municipal court, circuit court, and district court. Some states have more than one trial court. In some states, for instance, there are tribunals specialized by subject matter—for example, to address questions of probate law or family law. In most states, subject matter jurisdiction is divided along monetary lines; for example, one court may hear claims involving $25,000 or less and another court may hear claims involving a greater amount.

The important points are simple. First, the allocation of cases within the state court system is purely a matter of state law. The state may, by constitution or statute, determine what state courts will exist and what types of cases they will hear. Second, every state judicial system—in the aggregate—has general subject matter jurisdiction. Thus, while not every court in a given state will be able to hear every case, a plaintiff will be able to find some court in any state in which to pursue her case. Get used to thinking about the fact that state courts are "always there." If a case cannot invoke federal subject matter jurisdiction, it can always be taken to a state court (again, assuming the case does not involve one of those rare claims invoking exclusive federal jurisdiction).

§4.3 The Limited Subject Matter Jurisdiction of the Federal Courts

In the Constitution, the states ceded powers to the central, or federal, government. The entire federal government is one of limited powers, bestowed on the national government by the people and by the states. We are concerned with Article III of the Constitution. Article III, §2 provides nine categories (or "heads") of jurisdiction—that is, nine types of cases that the federal court system may hear. The federal courts have no power to adjudicate cases that do not fall within these bases of jurisdiction. In reviewing the nine heads of federal jurisdiction, observe that some are based upon the substantive law to be applied to the dispute[2] while others are given a federal forum because of the character of the parties.[3]

---

[2]The first one listed in Article III, §2, is cases arising under federal law; others include cases involving bankruptcies. The Framers apparently thought that federal courts would possess or develop especial expertise in these areas of federal law, or that they might be especially sensitive to the federal policies underlying such substantive laws.

[3]For example, cases involving ambassadors and consuls, disputes between states, and, most important for us, cases involving citizens of different states. With these, the Framers apparently concluded that the involvement of a particular type of litigant commanded the attention (or protection) of the federal courts.

The jurisdiction listed in Article III, §2, is not automatically bestowed on the federal courts. It is incumbent on Congress to determine how much of the constitutional jurisdiction the federal courts are to exercise.[4] Indeed, as Article III, §1, of the Constitution makes clear, the Founders left it up to Congress to decide whether the country would have lower federal courts at all.[5] From the beginning, Congress has provided for such lower federal courts.[6] In setting their jurisdiction, Congress is not required to grant a particular constitutional head of jurisdiction to the full extent that it could. For example, Congress can impose an amount in controversy restriction to limit the number of cases of a particular type that might be filed in federal court. In general, as we will see, the statutory grants of federal subject matter jurisdiction are narrower than the Constitution would permit. The key issue in determining whether a federal court has jurisdiction, then, usually is whether a *statute* has granted it.[7]

Because federal courts may hear only limited kinds of cases, litigants whose dispute does not meet one of the bases of federal subject matter jurisdiction cannot consent to the jurisdiction of a federal court. There is a presumption *against* federal jurisdiction. Accordingly, a party initiating litigation in federal court bears the burden of establishing federal jurisdiction.[8] She must plead it and, if challenged, demonstrate facts showing subject matter jurisdiction.

We see in §6.2 that defendants must assert some defenses early in litigation, or else waive the right to raise that defense. This is not true, however, with lack of subject matter jurisdiction. A defect in subject matter jurisdiction cannot be waived by the parties or the court. The court is under an obligation to dismiss whenever it determines that a

---

[4]There are exceptions to this principle, as Article III makes clear. Section 2, clause 2, provides that in cases affecting ambassadors and similar officers, and in which a state is a party, the Supreme Court has "original" (trial) jurisdiction. Congress has no power to abolish federal subject matter jurisdiction in these. But as to the other heads of jurisdiction, Congress has the authority to decide whether the federal courts should have jurisdiction.

[5]Article III, §1, requires the existence of only one federal court: the Supreme Court. Establishment of lower federal courts was a politically contentious issue, and the Founders decided to leave the decision to the Congress.

[6]The trial courts in the federal system are United States District Courts and the intermediate appellate courts are United States Courts of Appeals for the various circuits. See §1.2.2.

[7]Occasionally, Congress has passed a jurisdictional statute that exceeded the power of federal courts under Article III. Such grants are unconstitutional. For example, in *Hodgson v. Bowerbank*, 9 U.S. 303, 304 (1809), Congress granted jurisdiction over cases in which a foreign citizen was a party. To the extent that this permitted jurisdiction over a case by an alien against an alien, it exceeded Article III. See §4.5.5.

[8]*See* Fed. R. Civ. P. 8(a)(1) (requiring complaint to contain "a short and plain statement of the grounds for the court's jurisdiction").

case before it lacks federal subject matter jurisdiction.[9] This rule may result in enormous waste of federal judicial resources, as when a case is litigated for years before the court determines that it did not belong in federal court.[10]

The two major grants of federal subject matter jurisdiction, which are staples of the daily work of the federal district courts,[11] are diversity of citizenship jurisdiction under §1332(a)(1)[12] and federal question jurisdiction under §1332. One of these grants (diversity of citizenship) is based upon characteristics of the litigants, while the other (federal question) is based upon the substantive law to be applied to determine the outcome of the dispute. Before looking at them in detail, it is important to recognize why it may matter that a case can go to a federal, as opposed to a state court.

§4.4 The Political Insulation of Federal Judges

Article III, §1, of the Constitution provides remarkable job security for federal judges, security not enjoyed by state court judges. First, a federal judge's pay cannot be reduced. Second, a federal judge serves during "good Behaviour," which means she serves for life and can never be forced to retire. Unless a federal judge dies or resigns, she can be removed only by impeachment (and only eight federal judges have been removed by impeachment in our nation's history). Third, under the Appointments Clause, federal judges are appointed by the President, but must be confirmed by vote of the Senate.[13] Thus, federal judges never face an electorate and do not stand for reappointment to specified terms.

---

[9]*See* Fed. R. Civ. P. 12(h)(3) (lack of subject matter jurisdiction may be raised anytime).

[10]*See, e.g.,* Depex Reina 9 Partnership v. Texas Int'l Petroleum Corp., 897 F.2d 461, 462, 465 (10th Cir. 1990) (case dismissed for lack of subject matter jurisdiction after full trial, appeal, remand by the appellate court, and further proceedings in district court).

[11]We are concerned with the jurisdiction of the federal district courts, which are the main trial courts of the federal system. Appeals from these courts go to the United States Court of Appeals. From there, review can be had by the Supreme Court of the United States (if it agrees to hear the case). See §1.2.2. There are other, specialized, federal courts, such as the Court of Federal Claims and the Court of International Trade, the jurisdiction of which is quite specific. Such courts are beyond the scope of this work. Note that when a party erroneously files in the wrong federal court, the case may be transferred to the appropriate court (one with subject matter jurisdiction) under 28 U.S.C. §1631.

[12]Some courses address the related jurisdictional basis of alienage, §1332(a)(2). We address alienage at §4.5.5.

[13]U.S. Constitution, Article II, §2.

These protections are intended to insulate federal judges from political pressure. These "Article III" judges need not worry about offending Congress by interpreting or even striking down legislation as unconstitutional, since Congress cannot reduce their pay. The judges need not worry about offending the public by making unpopular rulings, since the public does not get to vote them out of office. Accordingly, the judges need not worry about ruling against a locally powerful figure or business, since that power broker cannot affect the judge's employment.

State judges are not so lucky. State judges have no federal constitutional guaranty that their salaries cannot be reduced. Their appointment, terms of service, and retention are all dictated by state law, which can vary in important ways. Many state judges, even at the supreme court level, must face the electorate. Either they are elected to their posts originally, or they must get voter approval for a new term, or both. Thus, state court judges who rule against popular opinion may find themselves without a job. In a dramatic example of this principle, Iowa voters removed three justices from the state supreme court in 2010 after an intense campaign criticized a particular decision. After retiring from the Supreme Court, Justice Sandra Day O'Connor (who served as an Arizona appellate judge before President Reagan appointed her to the Supreme Court) has led a national effort to abolish judicial elections and to replace them with merit selection and retention.

§4.5 Diversity of Citizenship and Alienage Jurisdiction

§4.5.1 Introduction

Article III, §2, of the Constitution permits the federal courts to entertain cases "between citizens of different states."[14] Congress has enacted statutes granting this "diversity jurisdiction" to the federal courts since the first Judiciary Act of 1789. These statutes have always included an amount in controversy requirement. Today, diversity jurisdiction is granted in §1332(a)(1), which mirrors the constitutional language by giving courts the power to hear cases "between citizens of different states," but adds the requirement that the amount

---

[14]This is the seventh of the nine categories of jurisdiction listed in Article III, §2. Do not confuse it with the two that precede it: "between two or more States" and "between a State and citizens of another State." Each of these bases involves litigation in which a State is actually a litigant. The latter basis was abrogated by the Eleventh Amendment.

in controversy in the case exceed $75,000. Thus, there are two require-ments for a diversity case: (1) It must involve "citizens of different States" and (2) the amount in controversy must exceed $75,000.

Closely related to diversity of citizenship jurisdiction is "alienage jurisdiction." The last "head" of jurisdiction listed in Article III, §2, is for cases "between a State, or Citizens thereof, and foreign States, Citizens, or Subjects." From this, *alienage,* as lawyers and judges use the term, includes disputes between a citizen of a state of the United States, on one side, and an "alien,"[15] which is the term used to refer to a citi-zen or subject of a country other than the United States, on the other. Congress has always provided for this form of jurisdiction in federal courts. Today, it is found in §1332(a)(2),[16] which mirrors the constitu-tional language but also adds the same dollar requirement applicable in diversity cases: The amount in controversy must exceed $75,000.

As we discuss in the next section, diversity of citizenship juris-diction has always been rather controversial. Despite this, it has in recent years accounted for an increasing percentage of the federal civil docket; recently, about one-third of federal civil cases invoke diversity jurisdiction.[17] Alienage jurisdiction has never been controversial and has never accounted for an appreciable percentage of the federal civil docket. We discuss alienage in §4.5.5. Now we turn to the policy debate concerning diversity of citizenship cases.

§4.5.2 The Debate Over Diversity of Citizenship Jurisdiction

Though the Founders provided for diversity of citizenship juris-diction in the Constitution and the first Congress enacted it in the

---

[15]In contemporary political discourse, the word "alien" bothers some people. In the context we are addressing, however, no one — certainly not Congress or the courts — has taken umbrage at its use. The term simply refers to a non-U.S. citizen.

[16]Because the grant of alienage jurisdiction is found in the same statute as that for diversity of citizenship jurisdiction, some lawyers and judges refer to it as a type or species of diversity jurisdiction. This is fine, but we will be more precise. So we refer to §1332(a)(1) as the grant of diversity jurisdiction and §1332(a)(2) as the grant of alien-age jurisdiction.

[17]For the fiscal year 2020, 470,581 civil cases were commenced in the federal district courts. Of these, 284,603 (60.4 percent) invoked diversity of citizenship jurisdiction. *See* uscourts.gov, Statistics, Table C-2. Both numbers are aberrational; the number of cases filed increased a stunning 58 percent from the previous year, which is attribut-able almost entirely to more than 200,000 product liability cases concerning earplugs. More typical are the numbers from 2019: 286,289 cases were filed, of which 94,206 (32.9 percent) invoked diversity jurisdiction. These numbers are higher than the his-torical average. For instance, in 2001, only 19.5 percent of civil cases filed in federal court were based upon diversity jurisdiction.

original Judiciary Act of 1789, it has always had its critics. Why? These cases go to federal court *not* because federal law applies, but because the litigants happen to be citizens of different states. These cases are governed by state substantive law.[18] Many people (including many law professors) see this as a misallocation of federal judicial resources. In an era of crowded federal court dockets, they argue, the federal courts should not be forced to spend valuable time interpreting and applying state law.

When engaging in this debate, however, it is important to remember that state courts routinely must hear cases arising under federal law. Except in those rare instances in which federal jurisdiction is exclusive, plaintiffs are free to take their federal-law cases to state court. But there are two differences. First, under the Supremacy Clause of the Constitution, the state courts are required to apply governing federal law.[19] Second, when state courts interpret federal law, the cases may, at least in theory, be reviewed by the Supreme Court of the United States.[20] So if the state courts make a mistake concerning the content of federal law, the ultimate federal court might be able to correct it. On the other hand, if a federal court in a diversity case makes a mistake in interpreting state law, there is no way a state court can fix it, because there is no review of federal judgments by state courts.[21]

Why did the Founders provide for diversity of citizenship cases in federal court? The historic justification is that diversity jurisdiction provides a neutral forum for a litigant who might suffer from bias in the local courts of another state (or who might at least *fear* that she could suffer from local bias). Put more simply, the out-of-state litigant fears that she may get "hometowned" in a local court. Remember that many state court judges are elected, and thus must answer to the members of the community. If a state court judge rules against the local litigant (and in favor of the out-of-state litigant), she may risk losing her job.

---

[18]This is the upshot of the *Erie* doctrine, addressed in Chapter 10.

[19]U.S. Constitution, Article VI, §2. *See* Testa v. Katt, 330 U.S. 386, 394 (1947) (Rhode Island must enforce Federal Emergency Price Control Act).

[20]Recall from §1.2.2 that the Supreme Court can hear appeals from a state's highest court, but only on matters of federal law. In fact, however, this might not be a great source of protection, because the Supreme Court can hear so few cases in a given year. Nonetheless, the system does provide this potential protection.

[21]Occasionally, federal courts certainly do misinterpret state law in diversity cases. While the ruling binds the parties in that case, it does not establish precedent in the state court system. The state court system, in subsequent cases, is free to ignore the federal court's interpretation of state law (and even to point out the error of the federal court's ways). To avoid misapplication of state law, over half the states have "certification" statutes, which allow the federal court to ask the state supreme court for guidance on thorny issues of state law. We discuss such statutes at §10.8.

Before ratification of the Constitution, several states had enacted debtor-relief statutes that prevented creditors from collecting on their loans and other contracts. Thus, several scholars, including Felix Frankfurter,[22] suggest that the Founders' principal interest in providing for diversity jurisdiction was to assuage the apprehensions of the commercial class (some members of which sat in the Constitutional Convention, after all).[23] The prospect of a neutral forum, politically insulated from the state power structure, could encourage investment by out-of-state commercial interests. It seems to have worked. William Howard Taft concluded that diversity jurisdiction "was the single most important element in securing capital for the development of the southern and western United States."[24]

The question today is whether diversity jurisdiction has outlived its usefulness. Some believe that it has. They assert that modern travel and mass communication have so homogenized American culture that local and regional biases are no longer prevalent. Moreover, they point out, because federal courts in diversity cases must apply state substantive law, the existence of diversity jurisdiction does not result in a change of law. Anti-diversity commentators assert that the limited federal judicial resources ought to be spent on cases involving questions of federal law.[25] They occasionally urge Congress to abolish diversity jurisdiction.[26]

Others contend, however, that regional bias is not dead, and that the need for diversity jurisdiction continues today. They argue that even if bias against out-of-state litigants cannot be proved, the litigants' *apprehension* of local bias is not irrational. In this regard, consider the following statement from a former justice of the West Virginia Supreme Court:

> As long as I am allowed to redistribute wealth from out-of-state companies to injured in-state plaintiffs, I shall continue to do so. Not only is my

[22]Frankfurter was a Harvard law professor whom President Franklin Roosevelt appointed to the Supreme Court. He served as a Justice from 1939 to 1962.

[23]Felix Frankfurter & James Landis, The Business of the Supreme Court 8-9 (1928).

[24]William Howard Taft, *Possible and Needed Reforms in Administration of Justice in Federal Courts*, 8 A.B.A. J. 601, 604 (1922). Taft is the only person to have been President (1909-1913) and to have served on the Supreme Court (Chief Justice, 1921-1930).

[25]*See, e.g.*, Larry Kramer, *Diversity Jurisdiction*, 1990 B.Y.U. L. Rev. 97; Report of Federal Courts Study Committee 38-43 (1990).

[26]The efforts to abolish diversity jurisdiction are aimed at §1332(a)(1). No one seems to want to abolish statutory interpleader jurisdiction under §1335, which is based upon diversity of citizenship but involves very specialized litigation (a dispute over ownership of property), discussed at §13.2.

sleep enhanced when I give someone else's money away, but so is my job security, because the in-state plaintiffs, their families and their friends will re-elect me.[27]

Again, in theory, the out-of-state litigant has no such fears in federal court, since federal judges never face an electorate; they have lifetime tenure. See §4.4. Moreover, federal courts tend to sit in major cities, not in the rural settings, and to draw their juries from a large region of the state, not simply from a single county. For all these reasons, a modern out-of-state litigant might still prefer to litigate against a local citizen in federal, not state, court. Further, abolition of diversity jurisdiction would simply funnel these cases back to already burdened state court systems. Though our course focuses on the federal courts, we should understand that the vast majority of civil litigation in this country takes place in state courts, not in federal courts.[28]

In terms of practical political reality, Congress is unlikely to abolish diversity jurisdiction, for the simple reason that the practicing bar supports it and is a very strong lobbying force. Congress may, however, cut back on the number of diversity cases from time to time by increasing the amount in controversy requirement or by making narrow changes to §1332(a)(1). For example, even proponents of diversity jurisdiction recognize that its underlying rationale is not implicated when the plaintiff is a citizen of the forum state.[29] Such a plaintiff does not need the protection of the federal court, yet, under the current statute, is able to invoke diversity jurisdiction in a suit against a citizen of another state. In recent years, some members of Congress have suggested changing the diversity statute to remove jurisdiction in such an "instate plaintiff" situation, but Congress has yet to do so.[30]

[27]Richard Neely, The Product Liability Mess: How Business Can Be Rescued from the Politics of State Courts 4 (1988).

[28]There are fewer than 1,000 Article III federal judges: about 670 district judges, 180 court of appeals judges, and nine Supreme Court Justices. In contrast, there are more than 30,000 state court judges. In a typical year, perhaps 450,000 cases (civil and criminal) are filed in federal district courts, compared to an estimated 30,000,000 in state courts. *Federal vs. State Courts–Key Differences*, FindLaw (June 20, 2016), https://www.findlaw.com/litigation/legal-system/federal-vs-state-courts-key-differences.html.

[29]*See* 15 Moore's Federal Practice §102.12.

[30]As we see in §4.8, however, the defendant may well be able to "remove" such a case from state to federal court on the basis of diversity jurisdiction. Thus, prohibiting an instate plaintiff from invoking diversity may not, in the long run, keep many cases out of federal court. It would, however, put the onus on the defendant (in such a case, the one needing the protection of federal court) to get the case into that court.

§4.5.3 Assessing Whether a Case Invokes Diversity of Citizenship Jurisdiction

The Complete Diversity Rule

The most significant and well-known case involving diversity of citizenship jurisdiction is *Strawbridge v. Curtiss*,[31] which the Supreme Court decided in 1806. Chief Justice John Marshall's opinion is startlingly short, both in length and on reasoning. In *Strawbridge*, plaintiffs (called *complainants* in the syllabus of the opinion) were alleged to be citizens of Massachusetts; there were multiple defendants, most of whom were citizens of Massachusetts and one of whom was a citizen of Vermont. The Supreme Court held that the case did not invoke diversity jurisdiction, even though one of the plaintiffs was of diverse citizenship from one of the defendants. In the Court's view, "each distinct interest should be represented by persons, all of whom are entitled to sue, or be sued, in the federal courts."[32] In other words, each plaintiff must be of diverse citizenship from each defendant. This is the famous "complete diversity rule," which persists to this day.

Nothing in the language of the Constitution or the diversity statute compels this rule. A case by a citizen of Massachusetts against a citizen of Vermont and a citizen of Massachusetts would seem to be a case "between citizens of different states." Moreover, Marshall did not give any hint why the Court concluded that complete diversity was necessary. The Supreme Court suggests that because the Vermont citizen has a codefendant who is a citizen of the same state as the plaintiff, she has no need to fear local bias.[33] On the other hand, the Vermont citizen, being the *only* "foreigner" in the case, would seem to have especial fear of being "hometowned" in a Massachusetts state court.

Despite the lack of a convincing rationale for it, the complete diversity rule of *Strawbridge* is good law to this day. Though the rule is difficult to justify (except as a docket control device to reduce the number of cases in the federal courts), it is easy to apply. It is extremely mechanical: Every *plaintiff* must be of diverse citizenship from every *defendant*. Parties on the same side of the dispute, however, can be co-citizens.

[31]7 U.S. 267 (1806).
[32]*Strawbridge,* 7 U.S. at 267.
[33]"The presence of parties from the same State on both sides of a case dispels this concern [about fear of local bias], eliminating a principal reason for conferring §1332 jurisdiction over any of the claims in the action." Exxon Mobil Corp. v. Allapattah Servs., 545 U.S. 546, 554 (2005). *See also* David Currie, *The Federal Courts and the American Law Institute*, 36 U. Chi. L. Rev. 1, 18 (1968) ("the assumption apparently underlying *Strawbridge* is that the presence of Massachusetts people on both sides of a case will neutralize any possibility of bias affecting litigants from other states").

○ ***Example #1.*** Two plaintiffs, each a citizen of California, sue ten defendants, each of whom is a citizen of Arizona. This case satisfies the complete diversity rule. Even though there are co-citizens in the case (the plaintiffs are co-citizens with each other and the defendants are co-citizens with each other), every plaintiff is diverse from every defendant.

The complete diversity rule is a *statutory*, and not a *constitutional*, requirement.[34] It applies to cases brought under §1332(a)(1).[35] The constitutional provision for diversity jurisdiction, in Article III, §2, requires only that there be "minimal" diversity: that at least one plaintiff be of diverse citizenship from one defendant. Accordingly, the facts of *Strawbridge* itself (Massachusetts plaintiff; Vermont and Massachusetts defendants) fall within the federal courts' *constitutional* power over diversity cases but not within the statutory grant of diversity jurisdiction under §1332(a)(1).

Two important consequences flow from the fact that the complete diversity rule is not constitutionally mandated. First, Congress could amend §1332(a)(1) to overrule *Strawbridge* and permit jurisdiction based upon minimal diversity. In view of the burgeoning dockets of the federal courts and the debate about whether diversity of citizenship jurisdiction ought to be retained (see §4.5.2), such a move is politically unthinkable.

Second, even if it does not change §1332(a)(1), Congress can grant jurisdiction under *other statutes,* which base jurisdiction upon *minimal* diversity. It has done so three times. First is statutory interpleader under §1335. Interpleader is a very specialized kind of litigation, which we discuss at §13.2. Permitting its invocation on the basis of minimal diversity makes it more readily available but (because it is so specialized) without a risk of inundating the federal courts. Second

---

[34]This point was established in *State Farm Fire & Casualty Co. v. Tashire*, 386 U.S. 523, 530-531 (1967), which upheld the constitutionality of jurisdiction in "statutory interpleader" cases (discussed in §13.2) based upon "minimal," as opposed to complete, diversity: "Article III poses no obstacle to the legislative extension of federal jurisdiction, founded on diversity, so long as any two adverse parties are not co-citizens." Most observers thought this conclusion was clear from *Strawbridge* itself, in which Marshall never mentioned the constitutional grant of diversity, but spoke only of "[t]he words of the act of Congress." *Strawbridge*, 7 U.S. at 267. But the Court did not expressly so hold until it decided *Tashire*.

[35]The complete diversity rule is not expressed in §1332(a)(1). It is a product of the Supreme Court's interpretation of the predecessor to §1332(a)(1) in *Strawbridge*. If Congress had disagreed with this interpretation, it could have amended the statute to reject the judicial "gloss." After *Strawbridge*, Congress has reenacted the general diversity statute on several occasions, without rejecting the Court's interpretation in that case. When that happens, we assume that Congress adopted the judicial interpretation. Hence, the complete diversity rule, though originally injected by the Court, is now seen as a statutory limitation.

is the Multiparty, Multiforum Trial Jurisdiction Act, which expands jurisdiction for any case "that arises from a single accident, where at least 75 natural persons have died in the accident at a discrete location."[36] We will summarize it at §13.3.9. As with interpleader, there is little risk of docket overload from such cases, and the use of minimal diversity permits a federal court to resolve in one proceeding a dispute that might otherwise involve several state and federal courts. Third is the Class Action Fairness Act (CAFA), which permits jurisdiction based upon minimal diversity to facilitate access to federal courts for some complex litigation. CAFA is controversial and raises significant issues concerning the roles of federal and state courts. We discuss it at §13.3.9.

As a matter of policy, it makes sense to have a constitutional grant of jurisdiction be broader than the statutory grant. It is far easier to change a statute than to amend the Constitution. Thus, a broader constitutional provision gives Congress leeway in determining whether to impose the complete diversity restriction. What is odd, though, is that the operative language of the constitutional provision and the statutory provision in §1332(a)(1) is identical. Each speaks of a case "between citizens of different states." Thus, the same words mean different things in different contexts. (We will see this again in federal question jurisdiction, §4.6.2.)

The Supreme Court drove home the importance of the complete diversity rule in *Exxon Mobil Corp. v. Allapattah Services, Inc.*[37] There, it held that diversity jurisdiction cannot attach at all in a case in which there are co-citizens on both sides of the case.[38] At first glance, this appears to change the historic practice. Historically, the court could use Federal Rule 21 to drop the nondiverse parties from the case[39] and thereby maintain diversity jurisdiction. Under *Allapattah*, however, it seems that the court must dismiss the case. The plaintiff would then be free to refile in federal court without the nondiverse parties, or to file a case joining all parties in state court.

In practice, however, courts appear to use Rule 21 to drop "jurisdictional spoilers" and maintain jurisdiction. They do so under "the fiction that Rule 21 relates back to the date of the complaint. This

---

[36]28 U.S.C. §1369.

[37]545 U.S. 546 (2005).

[38]*Id.*, 545 U.S. at 562. The Court spoke of this as the "contamination theory"—that is, the presence of nondiverse parties on both sides of a lawsuit "contaminates" the case because it "eliminates the justification for providing a federal forum."

[39]*See* Fed. R. Civ. P. 21. *See* Newman-Green, Inc. v. Alfonzo-Larrain, 490 U.S. 826, 832 (1989) (though Rule 21 does not apply in court of appeals (because the Federal Rules of Civil Procedure apply in district courts), appellate court can drop nondiverse parties to preserve diversity, even after entry of judgment).

way, the court may proceed as if the nondiverse parties were never part of the case. With those parties effectively scrubbed from the complaint, they are not present to contaminate the other claims."[40] This is permitted, however, only if the party dropped is not "indispensable" under Federal Rule 19. (We discuss that concept in Chapter 12.)

> ○ ***Example #2.*** Plaintiffs are citizens of Oklahoma, Nebraska, and Texas. There are 28 defendants. Twenty-seven of them are citizens of California and one is a citizen of Nebraska. The case fails to invoke diversity of citizenship under §1332(a)(1) because it does not meet the complete diversity rule. (That rule is met only if *all* plaintiffs are citizens of different states from *all* defendants. Here, there are Nebraska citizens on each side of the case.) Rule 21 permits the plaintiffs to drop the Nebraska defendant (or the Nebraska plaintiff) (assuming the parties dropped would not be indispensable under Rule 19) and keep the case in federal court under diversity jurisdiction.

Determining the Citizenship of Various Litigants

To invoke diversity of citizenship jurisdiction, the case must satisfy the complete diversity rule. But to apply the complete diversity rule, we must understand how to determine each litigant's citizenship. There are different types of litigants, including humans, corporations, other business associations (such as partnerships and limited liability companies), and fiduciaries suing to represent other persons. The tests for determining their citizenship differ. Terminology is extremely important. We are speaking here of diversity of *citizenship*—not "residence" or where a party is "from." Though some courts (and, unfortunately, some professors) are sloppy about terminology, precision is a good lawyerly trait. *Citizenship* is a term of art; it is a specific, technical term and must be used if we want to invoke diversity jurisdiction. If you filed a complaint in federal court, alleging the "residence" of the litigants (and not their "citizenship"), the case should be dismissed for lack of subject matter jurisdiction. There must be diversity of *citizenship*.

Now, how do we determine the citizenship of various litigants?

Natural Persons (Humans). In the eyes of the law, there are different kinds of persons. While humans obviously are persons, so are some entities, such as corporations, at least for some purposes. So it is

---

[40]In re Lorazepam & Clorazepate Antitrust Litig., 631 F.3d 537, 542 (D.C. Cir. 2011) (citation omitted). *See also* Barratt v. Prison Health Servs., Inc., 647 F. Supp. 2d 314, 322 (D. Vt. 2009).

necessary to distinguish: Humans are "natural persons," as opposed to "artificial persons," such as corporations.

For diversity of citizenship jurisdiction, Congress has never generally defined the citizenship of natural persons.[41] It has left the issue to the courts. According to the Supreme Court, to be a citizen of a state (meaning, a state of the United States) for diversity purposes, a human must be (1) a citizen of the United States[42] and (2) domiciled in that state.[43] In most instances, the first part of this requirement will be clear. But the second part can give rise to interesting problems.

A person has only *one* domicile at a time. It is impossible to have more than one domicile at any given point. For diversity purposes, then, a human can only be a citizen of one state at a time. (We see shortly that this is not true of other kinds of litigants.) Minors are usually ascribed the domicile of their parents. At the age of majority, or at emancipation, they are able to establish their own domicile.

In addition, a human *always* has a domicile.[44] You cannot lose your domicile. You retain the domicile ascribed at birth until you affirmatively change it. And you retain that new domicile until you affirmatively change it. In the eyes of the law, there is no such thing as a human without a domicile, and she only has one domicile at a time.

Now, what is a person's domicile? Courts have used different phrases, but one classic definition is that domicile is that place where a person "has [her] true, fixed, and permanent home and principal establishment, and to which [she] has the intention of returning whenever [she] is absent therefrom."[45] Changing one's domicile requires the two concurrent factors: (1) establishing physical presence in the new state with (2) the subjective intent to make that state her home for the foreseeable (or indefinite) future. There are no papers to fill out. There is no official decree. It is a matter of establishing these two elements, one physical and one mental, concurrently. One element alone does not suffice. All the intent in the world to change one's domicile doesn't effect a change until coupled with physical presence in the new state. Similarly, residence in the new state, even for an extended

---

[41]For 21 years, §1332(a) did define the state citizenship of aliens admitted to the United States for permanent residence. This part of the statute was repealed in 2012, as we see at the end of this section.

[42]We deal with cases involving citizens of other countries below. Throughout the materials, however, unless the facts indicate that a party is a citizen of another country, assume that she is a citizen of the United States. This requirement will not be stated in each hypothetical.

[43]Sun Printing & Publ'g Ass'n v. Edwards, 194 U.S. 377, 383 (1904); Brown v. Keene, 33 U.S. 112, 115 (1834).

[44]Katz v. Goodyear Tire & Rubber Co., 737 F.2d 238, 243 (2d Cir. 1984).

[45]Wright & Kane, Federal Courts 163 (paraphrasing Justice Story's famous definition in Story, Conflict of Laws, §41 (8th ed. 1883)).

period, does not constitute a change of domicile unless the intent also is present. Thus, one's residence is not necessarily one's domicile.[46]

An often-cited case on this point is *Mas v. Perry*,[47] in which a married couple sued their landlord, alleging that he invaded their privacy by installing two-way mirrors that allowed him to spy on them in their bedroom and bathroom. The defendant was a citizen of Louisiana. One key question was whether the wife was also a citizen of Louisiana.[48] If so, there would be no diversity jurisdiction. She had been born and raised in Mississippi, and thus started as a citizen of that state. She lived in Louisiana for several years to attend graduate school and to work as a graduate assistant. She and her husband moved to Illinois and intended to return to Louisiana for more schooling. She was undecided about where she would live after that. The court held that the wife had never changed her domicile from Mississippi. Although present in Louisiana for years, she had never formed the subjective intent to make that her home. Thus, she was of diverse citizenship from the defendant.

> ○ ***Example #3.*** Ms. Robinson is a citizen of New York. She forms the intent to change her domicile to Arizona. She packs her belongings in her car and leaves New York, driving toward Arizona. On the way, however, she is involved in an auto wreck with *D* in Oklahoma. Ms. Robinson is still a citizen of New York. Even though she has satisfied the subjective intent requirement to establish an Arizona domicile, she has not satisfied the physical component, since she did not get to Arizona. Even though she has left New York, with no intent to return, she is still a domiciliary (and, therefore a citizen) of New York.

> ○ ***Example #4.*** Now suppose Ms. Robinson, while in New York, forms the clear intent to make Arizona her permanent home. She packs her belongings in her car and drives to Arizona without incident. As soon as she drives across the state line into Arizona, arguably she should be considered a domiciliary (and therefore a citizen) of that state. Her intent

---

[46]Do not fall into the habit of talking about residence when addressing diversity jurisdiction. Residence is relevant to venue, as we see in Chapter 5. It is irrelevant to subject matter jurisdiction. Here, we speak of *citizenship*, not of *residence*.

[47]489 F.2d 1396, 1398 (5th Cir. 1974).

[48]*Mas* discusses a host of important topics. Mr. Mas was a citizen of France, so his claim against the defendant invoked alienage jurisdiction. See §4.5.5. The case also demonstrates that the amount actually recovered by the plaintiff is irrelevant to whether the amount in controversy requirement for §1332 is met. See §4.5.3. It also shows that the requirements for subject matter jurisdiction are assessed at the time the case is commenced. Finally, it rejects the sexist rule that ascribed to a married woman the domicile of her husband. This "derivative domicile" notion "has never been definitively struck down" by the Supreme Court. "In fact, there is some evidence that the derivative domicile rule frequently still functions in a gendered way, even today." Kerry Abrams, *Citizen Spouse,* 101 Cal. L. Rev. 407, 424, 426 (2013).

was especially well established and she is now present in Arizona. There is probably no need to rent an apartment or buy a house before she is considered a domiciliary of Arizona (though she probably would have done so). In most cases, however, the expression of one's intent is not as clear as it was for Ms. Robinson.

o ***Example #5.*** Joe was born and raised in Texas. At age 18, he leaves Texas to attend college in Michigan. He knows he does not want to return to Texas but is not sure where he wants to settle. After two years in Michigan, Joe transfers to a college in Oregon. After two more years, he graduates and attends medical school in Maryland. After four years there, he graduates and moves to Hawaii for a one-year internship. During his travels, he has never formed an intent to make any of these places his domicile, but he is certain that he does not want to go back to Texas. What is his citizenship for diversity purposes? Texas. Although Joe now lives in Hawaii, and has resided in other states, he never formed the intent to make any of them his domicile.

The question of whether someone has formed the subjective intent to establish a new domicile can be difficult. Obviously, most of us do not jump up one day and exclaim: "I have formed the intent to make this state my fixed home!" The issue is often litigated, and no single factor is determinative. Although the intent being tested is subjective, courts often must look to objective facts to determine it. They view all relevant information, including things such as voter registration, qualifying to pay instate tuition, automobile registration, payment of real and personal property taxes, location of bank accounts[49]—as one court explained, a "grab-bag of indicia having to do with everyday life"[50]—that might indicate the intent to establish domicile. The litigant's statement of subjective intent is relevant, but not determinative. Again, the court will look to all relevant factors.

One's reason for changing domicile is irrelevant. What if someone changes her domicile expressly to create diversity jurisdiction? As long as the two-part test for changing domicile is met, she can invoke diversity jurisdiction.[51] This result is consistent with the general rule, to be discussed at §4.5.3, that subject matter jurisdiction is assessed at the time the case is filed, not at the time the claim arose.

Three other issues deserve attention. First, several American political subdivisions, such as the District of Columbia, Puerto Rico, Guam, and the Virgin Islands, are not states. Nonetheless, §1332(e) provides

---

[49]*See, e.g.,* Lew v. Moss, 797 F.2d 747, 750 (9th Cir. 1986).

[50]Simmons v. Skyway of Ocala, 592 F. Supp. 356, 366 (S.D. Ga. 1984).

[51]Williamson v. Osenton, 232 U.S. 619, 625 (1914) (Holmes, J.) ("plaintiff had a right to select her domicil[e] for any reason that seemed good to her"). In §4.5.4, we discuss "collusive joinder" and see that changing one's citizenship for the purpose of creating diversity jurisdiction is not "collusive."

that citizens of such places shall be treated as citizens of states for diversity purposes. Can Congress simply decree that a person who is not a citizen of a state be considered a citizen of a state? The statute is contrary to an 1804 Supreme Court holding that a domiciliary of the District of Columbia is not a citizen of a state for diversity purposes.[52] Nonetheless, in 1949, the Supreme Court upheld §1332(e).[53] So the bottom line is simple enough: Treat the listed subdivisions as states, even though they are not.

Second, a U.S. citizen can establish her domicile in a foreign country. Doing so does not make her a citizen of that country, so she remains a citizen of the U.S and is not an alien. However, though she is still a U.S. citizen, she is not a citizen of a U.S. state—because she is not domiciled in a U.S. state. Accordingly, a U.S. citizen domiciled in another country cannot sue or be sued under diversity jurisdiction. Such people fall through a "hole" in the diversity and alienage statutes.[54]

> o ***Example #6.*** *P*, a U.S. citizen, establishes her domicile in the United Kingdom. She wishes to sue *D*, who is a citizen of New York. Her case will not invoke alienage jurisdiction. Why? Because *P* is not an alien, so the case would not be between an alien, on the one hand, and a citizen of a U.S. state, on the other. Her case also will not invoke diversity jurisdiction. Why? Because *P* is not a citizen of a U.S. state, so the case is not between citizens of different U.S. states.

Does that mean *P* is denied access to justice? No. It means she cannot sue or be sued in federal court under alienage or diversity of citizenship. She can sue or be sued in state court and she can sue or be sued in federal court on some other basis of federal subject matter jurisdiction (such as federal question jurisdiction, see §4.6).

Third, there is the question of how to treat aliens who are admitted to the United States for permanent residence.[55] For 21 years, a sentence in §1332(a) provided that such a person was to be considered a citizen of the state (of the United States) in which she was domiciled. Congress repealed that provision in 2012. As a result, permanent

---

[52]Hepburn & Dundas v. Ellzey, 6 U.S. 445, 453 (1805).

[53]National Mut. Ins. Co. v. Tidewater Transfer Co., 337 U.S. 582, 600 (1949). The opinion is quite unusual, since there is no majority rationale. Five Justices held the statute constitutional, but they did so for two mutually exclusive reasons, neither of which commanded a majority! The provision was codified as §1332(d) until 2005, when it was changed to §1332(e).

[54]This problem is seen again when we discuss alienage in §4.5.5.

[55]In common parlance, permanent resident aliens are called *green card* aliens (although the card issued to them to confirm their status is no longer green). They are to be contrasted with aliens who are legally present in the United States on temporary or student visas and with illegal aliens.

resident aliens are treated as aliens and not as citizens of a state of the United States. We will discuss this issue in detail, including a legislative addition to §1332(a)(2), when we address alienage in §4.5.5.

Corporations. Various types of businesses and entities litigate in federal court. To assess whether they can sue or be sued under diversity jurisdiction, we must be able to determine their citizenship. The law bifurcates business associations: A business is either (1) a corporation or (2) not a corporation. Historically, for a variety of purposes (including taxation of income), the corporation has been seen as an entity, as a distinct "artificial person."[56] But other forms of business and other associations (we will call them the "unincorporated" associations) traditionally were seen not as entities, but as *aggregations* of the persons who run them.

This bifurcation affects the way courts determine citizenship. Congress has defined the citizenship of a corporation, and that definition (as we see in a moment) treats the corporation as a thing, separate from the people who run it. On the other hand, Congress has never defined the citizenship of unincorporated groups. Consistent with the law's general treatment of such businesses as aggregations rather than as entities, courts have assessed their citizenship by looking to the citizenships of the individual members of the group.

A corporation can be formed (lawyers often say "incorporated" or "chartered") *only* by satisfying the formation requirements established by state law. Each state has a corporation law prescribing these requirements. Though the particulars vary from state to state, in every jurisdiction those forming a corporation must file appropriate documents with a state agency, usually the secretary of state. When that agency accepts those documents as proper, the corporation is formed. The corporation is a creature of the state in which it is formed but can "qualify" to do business in other states without having to incorporate in those other states. The federal courts struggled for generations to determine the citizenship of corporations for diversity purposes.

In 1958, Congress stepped in and defined corporate citizenship, in what is now §1332(c)(1). That statute provides that a corporation is a citizen of "every State" (that is plural[57]) in which it is incorporated *and* of "the State" (that is singular) in which it has its "principal place of

---

[56]As opposed to a "natural person," who is a human.

[57]From 1958 until 2012, this part of the statute referred to "any state" in which the corporation was incorporated. Courts interpreted this as plural. The change to "every" makes this more obvious. As we see below, however, the issue is of limited importance today. See note 59 below.

business."[58] As to the former, it is possible for a corporation to incorporate in more than one state. If it does, it is a citizen of each such state.
As a practical matter, though, today it is almost impossible to find a
corporation incorporated in more than one state.[59] A corporation is not
a corporation of states in which it has simply qualified to do business
but not incorporated.

But remember that a corporation is *also* a citizen of the one state
in which it has its "principal place of business." Thus, a corporation,
unlike a human, can be a citizen of more than one state at a time. If
a corporation is incorporated in Delaware and has its principal place
of business in California, it is a citizen of Delaware *and* California.[60]
But not all corporations are citizens of two states. Indeed, most corporations have their principal place of business in the same state in

---

[58]In this section, we will assume that the corporation is incorporated and has its
principal place of business in states in the United States. For treatment of corporations that are formed or have their principal place of business in foreign countries, see
§4.5.5, where we address alienage jurisdiction.

Section 1332(c)(1) also deals with "direct action" cases, which are rarely addressed in
Civil Procedure courses. Suppose *P* is injured by Driver, who has insurance with Insco.
In some states, *P* can sue Insco directly to recover for her injuries from the accident.
In such a "direct action," if Driver (the insured) is not joined as a party, §1332(c)(1)
provides that Insco will be considered a citizen of the state where it is incorporated
and the state where it has its principal place of business as well as of the state of which
Driver is a citizen. The idea is to avoid having *P* get into federal court for a routine car
wreck case by making it more difficult for *P* to invoke diversity.

[59]To the extent there are dual incorporations today, they tend to be bridge or turn-
pike authorities that operate thoroughfares between two states. For political reasons,
they may incorporate in each state. Thus, the authority that operates bridges between
Pennsylvania and New Jersey is incorporated in each state. *See* Yancoskie v. Del. River
Port Auth., 528 F.2d 722, 726-727 (3d Cir. 1975). Dual incorporation used to be common
because states required corporations to charter there if they were going to own land
in the state. Modern corporation law does not require this and permits corporations to
form in one state and qualify to do business in other states.

When multistate incorporation was common, the Supreme Court applied the "forum
doctrine," which held that a corporation incorporated in State *X* and State *Y* would be
deemed a citizen *only* of one of those states when it was involved in litigation in one
such state. So if this corporation were litigating in State *X*, it would be deemed only a
citizen of State *X*, and not of State *Y*. Chicago & N.W. Ry. Co. v. Whitten's Adm'r, 80 U.S.
270, 283 (1871). The doctrine was aimed at increasing access to diversity jurisdiction
for railroads (which then (but not now) were incorporated in more than one state).
Though a stray case or two from decades ago found that the forum doctrine survived
the passage of §1332(c)(1), *see* Hudak v. Port Authority Trans-Hudson Corp., 238
F. Supp. 790, 792 (S.D.N.Y. 1965), "the universal view over recent years" is that the
statute's reference to citizenship in "any" state where incorporated has abrogated the
forum doctrine. 15 Moore's Federal Practice §102.53 (3d ed. 2011). *See* Oslick v. Port
Auth. of N.Y. and N.J., 83 F.R.D. 494, 495 (S.D.N.Y. 1979) (rejecting the holding of
Hudak).

[60]Do not say Delaware *or* California. It is a citizen of *both* states, as §1332(c)(1)
makes clear.

which they are incorporated. Such a corporation is a citizen of only that one state. The fact that a corporation might have more than one citizenship, however, may make it more difficult to invoke diversity jurisdiction.

> ○ ***Example #7.*** Big Co., incorporated in Delaware with its principal place of business in New York, sues XYZ Corporation, which is incorporated in New York with its principal place of business in California. Big Co. is a citizen of *both* Delaware and New York. XYZ Corporation is a citizen of *both* New York and California. There is no diversity jurisdiction because the plaintiff and the defendant are both citizens of New York. The case violates the complete diversity rule.

Remember that there is only *one* principal place of business. It is legally impossible for a corporation to have more than one principal place of business under §1332(c)(1).[61] Even if the corporation has a billion-dollar manufacturing plant in each of the 50 states, it is *not* a citizen of all 50 states. So, assuming the corporation is not incorporated in more than one state (and that is a safe assumption, as we noted above), a corporation will be a citizen of at most two states—the state of incorporation and the state where it has its principal place of business.

> ○ ***Example #8.*** P Corporation is incorporated in Delaware, has its principal place of business in Illinois, and is qualified to do business in California, New York, Ohio, Michigan, and Virginia. Of what states is P Corporation a citizen? Delaware (where incorporated) and Illinois (where it has its principal place of business). That's all. It is not a citizen of other states in which it has merely qualified to do business.

How do we determine a corporation's principal place of business? Neither §1332(c)(1) nor any other statute defines the term, so the courts have had to figure it out. Two possibilities seem obvious. One is the *physical* aspect of the corporation's business. Under this view, the principal place of business would be where the corporation does more of whatever it does (manufacturing widgets, providing services, etc.) than anywhere else.[62] This emphasis was sometimes called the

---

[61]This is because, as we saw in text above, the statute speaks of "the" principal place of business, which means that there is only one. By the way, do not make the mistake of saying that a corporation is a citizen of all states in which it does business. Although some people have proposed such a rule as a way of reducing the number of diversity cases, it is not and never has been the law. We see in §5.4.1 that, for venue purposes, a corporation might *reside* in several states. But *citizenship*, not residence, is the relevant inquiry here.

[62]A leading example was *Kelly v. United States Steel Corp.*, 284 F.2d 850, 853-854 (3d Cir. 1960).

muscle center test. The second possibility is to look to where the business decisions are made, which is called the *nerve center* test.[63] Through the decades, the lower federal courts were not consistent in which of these tests—or some combination of them—should apply to determine the principal place of business.

Fortunately, the Supreme Court brought clarity in *Hertz Corp. v. Friend*.[64] Emphasizing the need for clarity in jurisdictional rules, the Court adopted the nerve center test. It explained:

> We conclude that "principal place of business" is best read as referring to the place where a corporation's officers direct, control, and coordinate the corporation's activities. It is the place that Courts of Appeals have called the corporation's "nerve center." And in practice it should normally be the place where the corporation maintains its headquarters—provided that the headquarters is the actual center of direction, control, and coordination, i.e., the "nerve center," and not simply an office where the corporation holds its board meetings (for example, attended by directors and officers who have traveled there for the occasion).[65]

> o *Example #9.* Plaintiff, a California corporation with its principal place of business in Darien, Connecticut, sues Widget Corp. Widget is incorporated in Delaware, has its headquarters and executive decision makers in Scranton, Pennsylvania, and has manufacturing plants in California (which is the biggest plant, making 30 percent of the company's widgets), Georgia (which makes 25 percent of the widgets), Illinois (which makes 25 percent of the widgets), and Connecticut (which makes 20 percent of the widgets). Obviously, Plaintiff is a citizen of California and Connecticut. What about Widget?

Widget is a citizen of Delaware because it is incorporated there. What is its principal place of business? Under *Hertz,* it is Pennsylvania, because that is where its nerve center is located. Specifically, it is where the corporate managers make their decisions and direct corporate activity. That constitutes the corporation's principal place of

---

[63]The leading example was *Scot Typewriter Co. v. Underwood Corp.*, 170 F. Supp. 862, 865 (S.D.N.Y. 1959).

[64]559 U.S. 77 (2010). The decision was unanimous.

[65]*Id.* at 80-81. The Court criticized the Ninth Circuit, among other things, for concluding that the principal place of business could be a *state* in which a corporation undertook more business activity than any other. The statute refers to a "place" of business, not a "state" in which business takes place. Accordingly, the Court concluded, a principal place of business is *within* a state, but is not the state itself. A corporation's headquarters constitutes such a place. *Id.* at 93.

business.[66] All the facts about how much business is transacted in other states are irrelevant to citizenship.[67]

Unincorporated Associations. Now, what about the citizenship of various associations (including business associations) that are not incorporated? Because they are not corporations, §1332(c)(1) is irrelevant. The job of defining citizenship here has been left to the courts. Happily, they have reached a consistent rule: Such associations take on the citizenship of each of their members. This rule is consistent with the historical view that such associations are not entities but are, instead, aggregations of their members.[68]

The classic unincorporated business is the partnership. It is an association of two or more persons to conduct a business for profit. Forming a partnership (unlike forming a corporation) does not require filing documents with a state agency. The partnership is formed by conduct—operating a business for profit as co-owners. Most partnerships are "general" partnerships, in which each partner has equal authority to run the business and to share in the profits, as well as equal liability for partnership losses.[69] In assessing the citizenship of a partnership for diversity purposes, courts have always looked to the citizenship of all the partners.

- ***Example #10.*** Law Firm, formed as a general partnership under the law of New York, has partners who are citizens of New York, New Jersey,

---

[66]Lawyers should be careful to allege both the state of incorporation and the corporation's "principal place of business." That is what the statute prescribes. The fact that the Court equates "principal place of business" with "nerve center" does not mean that one should allege "nerve center." Use the statutory language. For a harrowing example of a lawyer who did not do so, see *Randazzo v. Eagle-Picher Industries, Inc.*, 117 F.R.D. 557, 558 (E.D. Pa. 1987). There, the plaintiff's lawyer alleged the place of a corporation's registered office and other irrelevant points. The court dismissed the case with prejudice and criticized "counsel whose familiarity with . . . §1332 could be no more than a friendly wave from a distance visible only through a powerful telescope." If *Randazzo* is not in your casebook, you might look it up; it is short and extremely amusing (unless you were the plaintiff's attorney).

[67]In *Hertz,* the Court recognized that adoption of the nerve center test will occasionally yield anomalous results. For example, if the bulk of the company's activities visible to the public take place in State *A*, but the corporate decisions are made in State *B*, the policy underlying diversity of citizenship jurisdiction—avoiding the fear of local bias—would support finding the corporation to be a citizen of State *A*. After all, that is where it is visible to, and interacts with, the community. Nonetheless, the nerve center, and therefore the principal place of business, is in State *B*. Such "counterintuitive results" must occasionally be accepted, said the Court, "in view of the necessity of having a clearer rule." 559 U.S. at 96.

[68]This is occasionally referred to as the "Chapman rule," from Chapman v. Barney, 129 U.S. 677, 682 (1889).

[69]All these things can be modified by agreement, but such an agreement would not affect the citizenship of the partnership for diversity of citizenship purposes.

Pennsylvania, and Florida. Its principal place of business is New York. Law Firm is a citizen of New York, New Jersey, Pennsylvania, *and* Florida. The fact that it was formed under New York law is irrelevant. The fact that its principal place of business is in New York is irrelevant. We only care about the citizenship of the partners.

What about a limited partnership? In such an arrangement, only the "general" partner(s) have any right to run the business. Limited partners invest in the business but have no voice in management and no liability for partnership losses. In *Carden v. Arkoma Associates*,[70] the Supreme Court held that a court must look to the citizenship of all the partners (general *and* limited) in assessing the citizenship of the business.

> ○ ***Example #11.*** Limited Partnership's general partners are citizens of New York and New Jersey; its limited partners are citizens of Connecticut, Pennsylvania, and Ohio. Limited Partnership is deemed to be a citizen of New York, New Jersey, Connecticut, Pennsylvania, and Ohio. Under the complete diversity rule, if an opposing litigant is a citizen of *any* of those states, there can be no diversity of citizenship jurisdiction.

There are many other unincorporated associations. Labor unions are not incorporated; they are associations created and operated by employees. A union's citizenship is the citizenship of all its members.[71] Many insurance companies are not incorporated, but are associations of subscribing members; their citizenship is that of all its members.[72] A real estate investment trust, because it is not incorporated, also takes on the citizenship of all its members.[73] The fact that members of these associations may be citizens of a large number of states means that it may be difficult for the association to sue or be sued under diversity jurisdiction.

---

[70]494 U.S. 185, 192 (1990). A "master limited partnership" is an unincorporated association, the ownership units of which are publicly traded. These businesses may have thousands of "unitholders," who are similar to limited partners. Because these associations are not corporations, they are deemed to be citizens of every state in which its unitholders are citizens. *See, e.g.*, Grynberg v. Kinder Morgan Energy Partners, LP, 805 F.3d 901, 905-907 (10th Cir. 2015) (master limited partnership was citizen of all 50 states because it had unitholders who were citizens of each state).

[71]Steelworkers v. R.H. Bouligny, Inc., 382 U.S. 145, 149-153 (1965) (unincorporated labor union is citizen of all states in which its members are citizens; change to that rule must come from Congress).

[72]*See, e.g.*, United Servs. Auto. Ass'n v. Omega Flex, Inc., 2011 WL 1740192 at *2 (D. Neb. 2011) ("All evidence before the Court indicates that USAA is an unincorporated association with members in all fifty states. . .").

[73]Americold Realty Trust v. Conagra Foods, 136 S. Ct. 1012, 1016-1017 (2016).

o **_Example #12._** National Labor Union (NLU) has members who are citizens of all 50 states. What is (or are) NLU's citizenship(s)? It is a citizen of all 50 states, which means that a suit by it or against it will not invoke diversity of citizenship jurisdiction.[74]

One of the most significant developments in business law over the past generation is the emergence of the limited liability company (LLC). It shares some characteristics of the traditional corporation (such as formation by filing certain documents with a state agency) with some of the characteristics of unincorporated associations (such as the manner in which income taxation is handled). Because of its hybrid nature, there was some initial confusion about how the LLC should be treated for purposes of assessing its citizenship. Despite strong arguments that it should be treated as a corporation under §1332(c)(1),[75] the courts have concluded that the LLC should be treated as other unincorporated associations.[76] Thus, the court looks to the citizenship of all members of the LLC.

As a bottom line, then, we have a clear, mechanical, bright-line rule. Courts look to one thing—whether the business is deemed to be a "corporation" under the law of the state in which it was formed. If it is, §1332(c)(1) applies; if it is not (even if it acts in many ways like a corporation), §1332(c)(1) does not apply and the court looks to the citizenship of all members.[77] Thus, the court applied §1332(c)(1) to an

---

[74]Don't panic over this fact, though. Such an association can sue or be sued in state court. Moreover, if the case arises under federal law (as may often be the case with a labor union, since there is pervasive federal legislation in the labor area), it can go to federal court under federal question jurisdiction. See §4.6.

[75]The leading proponent of this approach is Professor Debra Cohen. *See* Debra R. Cohen, *Citizenship of Limited Liability Companies for Diversity Jurisdiction*, 6 J. of Small & Emerging Bus. Law 435 (2002). I am proud to say that Professor Cohen was a student (and is a friend) of mine.

[76]*See, e.g.*, Vorhees v. Tolia, 761 Fed. Appx. 88, 92 (3d Cir. 2019); CostCommand, LLC v. WH Administrators, Inc., 820 F.3d 19, 21 (D.C. Cir. 2016); Alphonse v. Arch Bay Holdings, LLC, 618 Fed. Appx. 765, 767-768 (5th Cir. 2015); Siloam Springs Hotel LLC v. Century Surety Co, 781 F.3d 1233, 1236-1239 (10th Cir. 2015); Bayerische Landesbank, N.Y. Branch v. Aladdin Capital Mgt., LLC, 692 F.3d 42, 49 (2d Cir. 2012); D.B. Zwirn Special Opportunities Fund LP v. Mehrotra, 661 F.3d 124, 125 (1st Cir. 2011); V&M Star, LP v. Centimark Corp., 596 F.3d 354, 356 (6th Cir. 2010); Ferrell v. Express Check Advance of S.C., LLC, 591 F.3d 698, 700 (4th Cir. 2010); Johnson v. Columbia Props. Anchorage, LP, 437 F.3d 894, 899 (9th Cir. 2006); Rolling Hills MHP, LP v. Comcast SCH Holdings, LLC, 374 F.3d 1020, 1022 (11th Cir. 2004); GMAC Commercial Credit LLC v. Dillard Dep't Stores, Inc., 357 F.3d 827, 828-829 (8th Cir. 2004); Belleville Catering Co. v. Champaign Market Place LLC, 350 F.3d 691, 692 (7th Cir. 2003).

[77]There is one very minor exception: The Puerto Rican "sociedad en comandita," though not incorporated, is treated as a corporation under §1332(c)(1). Why? Because under civil law (as opposed to common law) applicable in Puerto Rico, the sociedad is considered a juridical entity, separate from its members. Puerto Rico v. Russell & Co., Sucesores, S. En C., 288 U.S. 476, 481 (1933).

electrical cooperative, despite the fact that it lacked some classic attributes of a corporation, when the applicable state law referred to it as a corporation.[78] And another court applied §1332(c)(1) to a "professional corporation"—again, despite the fact that it lacked some attributes normally associated with general business corporations—because the relevant state law labeled it a corporation.[79]

It is possible for a corporation to serve as a partner in a partnership. When that happens, be careful to apply the rules we have seen.

> ○ ***Example #13.*** Plaintiff, an LLC with members who are citizens of Arizona, New Mexico, and California, sues Defendant, a limited partnership. The general partner of Defendant is a citizen of New York, and the limited partner is a corporation, incorporated in Delaware with its principal place of business in California. There is no diversity jurisdiction. Why?

For starters, note that both Plaintiff and Defendant are unincorporated associations (an LLC and a limited partnership), so each will be deemed a citizen of each state of which its members are citizens. For Plaintiff, the members are citizens of Arizona, New Mexico, and California; those are Plaintiff's citizenships. For Defendant, under *Carden*, we look to the citizenship of both the general and the limited partners. The facts make it clear that the general partner is a citizen of New York. The limited partner is a corporation, for which §1332 (c)(1) defines citizenship. Because it is incorporated in Delaware and has its principal place of business in California, it is a citizen of both. Thus, Defendant is a citizen of New York, Delaware, and California. Because both Plaintiff and Defendant are citizens of California, there is no diversity of citizenship jurisdiction.

Litigation Through Representatives. Not all persons with litigable interests have the capacity to sue or be sued. For example, minors and persons suffering a mental disability generally cannot represent their own interests in litigation. The minor lacks legal capacity and the person under a mental disability lacks mental (and therefore legal) capacity to litigate. Cases by or against such persons usually are brought by or against a fiduciary who represents the minor or incompetent. Typically, the representative is a guardian, a guardian *ad litem*, or a *committee*.[80] Such a representative owes a duty of utmost loyalty to the person represented. Similarly, when a person dies, there

---

[78]Kuntz v. Lamar Corp., 385 F.3d 1177, 1182-1183 (9th Cir. 2004).

[79]Hoagland v. Sandberg, 385 F.3d 737, 740 (7th Cir. 2004).

[80]A general guardian is one who has daily, general control of the person lacking legal capacity. A guardian *ad litem* does not have general control, but represents the ward only "for the litigation." A *committee* (pronounced comb-ee-TAY) is one who essentially stands in the shoes of the litigant. The decision of which type of representative is chosen generally is made under the law of the state in which the federal court sits.

may be claims by or against her estate. A fiduciary, usually called an executor (if the decedent had a will) or administrator (if the decedent died without a will), represents the interests of the decedent's estate and is the proper party for litigation concerning the estate.

When a representative of a decedent, minor, or incompetent sues (or is sued) on behalf of the person she represents, does the court look to the citizenship of the representative or of the person being represented? Section 1332(c)(2) answers the question: The representative of a decedent, an incompetent, or "an infant" (which means a minor) "shall be deemed to be a citizen only of the same State as the decedent [minor or incompetent]." Accordingly, the court ignores the citizenship of the representative and uses the state of citizenship of the person *being represented* in the litigation. This is a nice mechanical rule that usually results in clear jurisdictional rulings.

> o **_Example #14._** Decedent, who was a citizen of Wyoming, dies in a Wyoming hospital. Her family members want the estate to sue the hospital, alleging that its medical malpractice resulted in Decedent's wrongful death. Decedent's executor is a citizen of Colorado. She, on behalf of Decedent's estate, sues the Wyoming hospital. Under §1332(c)(2), the court looks to Decedent's citizenship, not that of her representative. Thus, the executor's citizenship is irrelevant. The case is seen as by a Wyoming citizen against a Wyoming citizen, so it does not invoke diversity of citizenship jurisdiction.

It does not matter whether the decedent, minor, or incompetent would be the plaintiff or the defendant; the definition is the same in either situation.

Alignment and Realignment

The alignment of parties set forth in the complaint is not sacrosanct. The court has a duty to assess whether the true interests of any of the litigants lie with the other side of the litigation. If so, the court may realign a party to the other side of the litigation. This process may defeat diversity and result in dismissal for lack of subject matter jurisdiction.[81] In *City of Indianapolis v. Chase National Bank*, the Supreme Court indicated that the trial court must determine whether there is an "actual, substantial controversy" or a "collision of interests" between citizens of different states.[82]

---

[81]*See, e.g.*, United States Fidelity & Guar. Co. v. Algernon-Blair, Inc., 705 F. Supp. 1507, 1511 (M.D. Ala. 1988).

[82]314 U.S. 63, 69 (1941).

While the court will make this determination initially on the face of the pleadings, information discovered during the litigation may lead the court to conclude that it should realign the parties.[83] The inquiry is not whether a litigant has changed her citizenship after the case is commenced; as we see below, the existence of jurisdiction is assessed only at the time the case is commenced. Rather, the question is whether the plaintiff's initial alignment of the parties reflected the true dispute.

> ○ ***Example #15.*** *P* knows that *V* plans to sue her for tort damages. *P* believes that the tort to be alleged is covered by her insurance with Insco, and that if *V* wins, Insco should pay the damages (and defend *P* in the suit). *P* sues first, naming as defendants *V* and Insco, and seeking a declaratory judgment[84] that Insco must defend *P* and pay any damages. The court may realign *V* to the plaintiff's side of the litigation, since *V* and *P* have the same interest in having the court hold that insurance would cover the claim.[85]

There is considerable uncertainty in how parties should be aligned in cases involving overlapping interests.[86] The important point is to recognize that the court is the ultimate decision maker of whose interests lie on what side of the case, and that this assessment may affect diversity jurisdiction. That said, such realignment is rather rare.

The Amount in Controversy Requirement

Satisfaction of the complete diversity requirement is only half the battle in invoking diversity of citizenship jurisdiction. The case must also meet the amount in controversy requirement. Let's divide the various rules into two groups. First, the basic rules are not difficult but simply must be kept in mind. Second, the aggregation rules are more difficult conceptually and deserve separate treatment.

The Basic Rules. Nothing in the constitutional grant of diversity or alienage jurisdiction contains an amount in controversy provision. Congress has always included one, however, and has increased it periodically. The amount in controversy requirement is a docket-control device. By mandating that only cases of a certain value invoke jurisdiction, Congress avoids inundating the federal courts. The requirement

[83]*See* American Motorists Ins. Co. v. Trane Co., 657 F.2d 146, 151 (7th Cir. 1981) (subsequent events in litigation may show that original alignment was wrong).
[84]A plaintiff seeking declaratory judgment is seeking a court order describing the relative rights of the parties, as opposed to some form of "coercive" relief, such as damages or an injunction. For more detailed discussion, see §4.6.4.
[85]*See* Wright & Kane, Federal Courts 180.
[86]*See* 16 Moore's Federal Practice §102.20[3]-[5].

also attempts to ensure that federal courts not become small claims courts. Moreover, it may be that the fear of local bias that underlies diversity jurisdiction is greater in cases involving relatively large claims.

The amount in controversy under §1332(a) must exceed $75,000. Congress set it at that level in 1997, having set it at an amount in excess of $50,000 in 1987. Many people argue that the dollar figure should be increased substantially to reduce the number of diversity cases. We saw in footnote 17 that the percentage of diversity cases has increased from 19.5 percent of the civil docket in 2001 to over 30 percent recently; this fact may reflect the effect of inflation. Some therefore argue that the amount should be increased automatically, by tying it to inflation indices. Some assert that various types of damages, such as punitive damages, ought to be excluded from the equation. Currently, however, there is no such provision. We now turn to the basic rules about amount in controversy.

First, that amount must *exceed* $75,000. The plaintiff need not set out an exact figure for damages in her complaint but must allege that the amount *exceeds* $75,000. Exactly $75,000 does not suffice. A stark reminder is *Freeland v. Liberty Mutual Fire Insurance Co.*,[87] which involved a dispute about insurance coverage. One side said the insurance company was on the hook for $100,000. The other said it was on the hook for $25,000. The amount in controversy is the difference between the two, which is *exactly* $75,000. Though neither the parties nor the district court saw the problem, and despite the fact that the district court entered judgment after lengthy litigation, the Sixth Circuit reversed with instructions to dismiss. The case failed by one cent to invoke diversity of citizenship jurisdiction.[88] All the time and effort spent litigating the case in federal court was thrown away, an absolute nullity.

Second, §1332(a) provides that the amount requirement is "exclusive of interest and costs." Thus, the starting point is that neither interest on the claim nor costs of litigation can be included in the amount claimed. The "interest" referred to is that which accrues because of delay in payment. (Most jurisdictions provide that a plaintiff recovers interest at the legal rate on her judgment, which starts accruing at

---

[87]632 F.3d 250 (6th Cir. 2011).

[88]"The penny is easily the most neglected piece of U.S. currency. Pennies tend to sit at the bottom of change jars or vanish into the cracks between couch cushions. Vending machines and parking meters will not accept them. Many people refuse to bend down to pick up a penny off the ground, deeming the reward not worth the effort . . . . In this case, however, the penny gets a rare moment in the spotlight. The amount in controversy in this declaratory judgment action is exactly one penny short of the jurisdictional minimum of the federal courts." *Id.* at 252.

the date of the judgment. That interest is not included as part of the amount in controversy.) (In contrast, if the interest claimed "is itself the basis of the suit" (such as a claim to recover for coupons on a bond), it is included in the amount in controversy.)

"Costs" is a term of art and should be distinguished from attorney's fees. The general rule is that the prevailing party in litigation recovers her costs from the loser.[89] But, under the American Rule, both sides bear their own attorney's fees. Costs refer to the expenses of litigation other than attorney's fees—things like filing fees, fees to compel the attendance of witnesses, mileage fees for witnesses, fees for expert witnesses, some discovery costs, photocopying expenses, and the like. Though these can add up to a healthy sum, costs generated in a case are usually nowhere near as great as attorney's fees. While costs cannot be included in the amount in controversy equation under §1332(a), attorney's fees, if recoverable under an exception to the American Rule, can be.[90]

Third, the plaintiff's ultimate recovery in the case is irrelevant.

> o ***Example #16.*** Plaintiff sues for $100,000 and wins a judgment of $7,000. Defendant argues that the court lacked subject matter jurisdiction because the amount in controversy, as it turns out, did not exceed $75,000.

The argument will fail for the commonsense reason that the judicial system cannot allow cases to be in jurisdictional limbo. To accept the defendant's argument here would mean that no one would know whether there was subject matter jurisdiction until after the judgment was rendered, which may be years after the case was filed. Such uncertainty is untenable. *Mas v. Perry*[91] demonstrates this point. The case was decided when the amount had to exceed $10,000. Both the wife and the husband in that case claimed a proper amount, but the husband's recovery was only $5,000. That fact was irrelevant to jurisdiction; the court properly upheld diversity jurisdiction.

Fourth, if a plaintiff ultimately recovers less than $75,000, §1332(b) provides that the court may order that the plaintiff pay her own costs

---

[89]*See* Fed. R. Civ. P. 54(d).

[90]For example, attorney's fees may be recoverable by contract or a statute may provide that the prevailing party shall recover attorney's fees. If so, a reasonable claim for such fees may be included in the amount in controversy. *See, e.g.,* In re Abbott Laboratories, 51 F.3d 524, 526-527 (5th Cir. 1995) (including statutory attorney's fees in class action representative's claim). Plaintiff must allege that an exception to the American Rule applies. Department of Recreation v. World Boxing Ass'n, 942 F.2d 84, 89 (1st Cir. 1991).

[91]489 F.2d 1396, 1400 (5th Cir. 1974). We saw other aspects of this case when discussing citizenship. See §4.5.3.

(and not recover them from the defendant). Indeed, it says, the plaintiff may have to pay the defendant's costs. The provision deals only with costs, not attorney's fees. And it does not *require* an assessment of costs against such a plaintiff. If the plaintiff claimed the original amount in good faith, courts usually allow her to recover costs from the defendant, even if the ultimate recovery was less than the statutory amount in controversy.[92]

Fifth, the plaintiff's good faith allegation that the jurisdictional amount is satisfied controls *unless* it "appear[s] to be a legal certainty that the claim is really for less than the jurisdictional amount."[93] After the plaintiff alleges that the case involves the requisite amount, the defendant may challenge the allegation.[94] At that point, the plaintiff bears the burden of showing that it is *not* "clear to a legal certainty" that the jurisdictional amount is not involved.[95]

It is rather rare for a court to dismiss for failure to satisfy the amount in controversy requirement. One example is when the plaintiff seeks damages that are not allowed as a matter of law.

> o ***Example #17.*** *P* sues for $50,000 breach of contract and $100,000 punitive damages. Relevant law provides that punitive damages cannot be recovered in contract cases.

As a matter of law, *P* has claimed only $50,000 and thus has failed to invoke diversity jurisdiction.[96] Occasionally (but not often), a court will dismiss because it concludes that the harm alleged, while not precluded by law, simply is not serious enough to meet the amount in controversy requirement. For example, one court considered a plaintiff's claim that a flight attendant had treated him so brusquely as to cause embarrassment as too trivial to meet the amount requirement.[97]

---

[92]*See* Dr. Franklin Perkins School v. Freeman, 741 F.2d 1503, 1523 (7th Cir. 1984) (costs imposed upon plaintiff only if plaintiff acted in bad faith). Regarding costs, see §9.3.

[93]St. Paul Mercury Indem. Co. v. Red Cab Co., 303 U.S. 283, 288 (1938).

[94]Courts rarely raise *sua sponte* the issue of whether the amount in controversy is met. *See* In re A.H. Robins Co., 880 F.2d 709, 724 (4th Cir. 1989) (no affirmative duty to inquire absent "apparent reason" to do so).

[95]Gibbs v. Buck, 307 U.S. 66, 72 (1939).

[96]Similarly, if a statute, for example one relating to liability of hotels for property damage, limits recovery to an amount not exceeding the amount in controversy, it is clear to a legal certainty that the claim does not involve the requisite amount. *See, e.g.*, Pachinger v. MGM Grand Hotel-Las Vegas, Inc., 802 F.2d 362, 364 (9th Cir. 1986).

[97]Diefenthal v. Civil Aeronautics Bd., 681 F.2d 1039, 1052-1053 (5th Cir. 1982). This is an area in which lawyers speak of the "straight-face" test. No one could argue with a straight face that the harm alleged was serious enough to meet the requirement.

In *Ortega v. Star-Kist Foods, Inc.*[98] the plaintiff asserted damages on behalf of a minor who had cut her finger while opening a can of tuna. The plaintiff alleged damages in excess of $75,000, noting that the child had suffered severed tendons, and had to undergo multiple surgeries. The district court, applying Puerto Rico law (the case was brought in the District of Puerto Rico), dismissed for failure to meet the amount in controversy requirement. The Third Circuit reversed. Though the district court had relied on decisions of the Puerto Rico Supreme Court concerning damages, it failed to take into account the fact that in federal court the case would be tried to a jury, while in the Puerto Rico court system there would be no right to a jury trial. Noting that jury awards are usually larger than those awarded in "bench" trials (trials in which there is no jury), and noting the seriousness of the alleged injuries, the Third Circuit held that it was not "clear to a legal certainty" that the damages could not exceed $75,000.[99] It upheld jurisdiction.

Remedies Other than Damages. To this point, we have dealt with claims for damages. What is the amount in controversy, however, when the plaintiff seeks equitable relief, such as an injunction or declaratory judgment?[100]

> ○ **Example #18.** *D* erects a building that encroaches on *P*'s property. *P* sues to have the building moved or modified to remove the encroachment. The "value" of this injunction may differ depending upon whose viewpoint is assumed. If we look at this dispute from *P*'s viewpoint, the damage caused by *D*'s building may be small. It would depend upon how large the encroachment is and how much it interferes with *P*'s enjoyment of her land. If we take *D*'s viewpoint, however, the requested injunction would clearly be substantial, since it would require her to move a building (or part of it).

Cases reflect these contrasting viewpoints. Some courts adopt the "plaintiff's viewpoint" test, and hold that the amount is met only if the defendant's act harms the plaintiff by the requisite amount.[101] Other

---

[98]370 F.3d 124, 128 (3d Cir. 2004). Though the Supreme Court reversed the decision in *Ortega*, it did so on grounds unrelated to the valuation of the plaintiff's individual claim. *See* Exxon Mobil Corp. v. Allapattah Servs., Inc., 545 U.S. 546 (2005).

[99]370 F.3d at 128-129.

[100]We discussed the distinction between law and equity at §1.2.3. Damages are the classic remedy at law. Equity developed separate remedies, such as the injunction. The distinction is important in determining the right to a jury trial in federal civil cases. See §9.2.2.

[101]*See, e.g.,* Ericsson GE Mobile Communications v. Motorola Communications & Electronics, 120 F.3d 216, 218-220 (11th Cir. 1996); K2 Holdings, LLC v. New Cingular Wireless, PCS, LLC, 2017 WL 1134398 at *4 (E.D. Ky. 2017) (though Sixth Circuit has not resolved which approach governs, court viewed the issue from the perspective of the plaintiff). *See* 15 Moore's Federal Practice §102.109 (characterizing this as the majority view, followed by the Second, Third, Eighth, and Eleventh Circuits). *See also* Brittain Shaw, *The $75,000.01 Question: What Is the Value of Injunctive Relief?*, 6 Geo. Mason L. Rev. 1013 (1998).

courts, however, will uphold jurisdiction if the amount in controversy would be satisfied under either the plaintiff's or the defendant's viewpoint.[102] There is some suggestion that courts may look to the viewpoint of the party invoking diversity jurisdiction—the plaintiff's in cases filed originally in federal court and the defendant's in cases removed from state court.[103]

The Aggregation Problem(s). Aggregation is the adding of two or more claims for purposes of the amount in controversy requirement. For example, suppose *P* has two claims against *D*. One is a tort claim for $50,000 and the other is an unrelated contract claim for $30,000. Neither claim alone satisfies the amount in controversy requirement. The only way to meet the requirement is to *aggregate* (add) the two claims. The rules governing aggregation are court-made. They have the advantage of being mechanical, and the disadvantage of being hard to justify.

The basic rule is that if the case involves the claims of a single plaintiff against a single defendant, the plaintiff can aggregate as many claims as she has to satisfy the amount requirement. Thus, in the hypothetical in the previous paragraph, the plaintiff can aggregate the claims and the amount in controversy is $80,000. The claims can be aggregated even though completely unrelated legally and transactionally. And the plaintiff can aggregate as many claims as she has, so long as she is the sole plaintiff and there is only one defendant.

- ○ ***Example #19.*** *P* sues *D* and asserts 100 separate, totally unrelated claims, each worth $800. The amount in controversy is $80,000, because, with one plaintiff against one defendant, the plaintiff is permitted to add all claims she has against the defendant in determining the amount in controversy. The rule seems silly because it can inundate the federal courts with unrelated small claims, but the rule is clearly established.[104]
- ○ ***Example #20.*** Consider the same facts except that *P*'s first claim exceeds $75,000, and thus would satisfy the amount requirement by itself. Her second claim is for $100. These two claims are aggregated, the same as

---

[102]*See, e.g.,* Witte v. General Nutrition Corp., 104 F. Supp. 3d 1, 4-5 (D.D.C. 2015) ("The D.C. Circuit appears to have adopted the 'either-viewpoint' rule"). *See also* 15 Moore's Federal Practice §101.109 (indicating that this approach is followed by the Fourth, Seventh, Tenth, and District of Columbia Circuits).

[103]*See* McCarty v. Amoco Pipeline Co., 595 F.2d 389, 395 (7th Cir. 1979) (refusing to follow plaintiff viewpoint test in diversity case removed from state court; "[w]e believe that the interests of equity and fairness, as well as the purposes behind the removal statute, would here be well served by allowing the plaintiff's claim to be evaluated for jurisdictional purposes by applying the either viewpoint rule").

[104]*See, e.g.,* Jones v. Teledyne, Inc., 690 F. Supp. 310, 317 (D. Del. 1988) (aggregating 54 separate, relatively insignificant, claims). *See generally* 16 Moore's Federal Practice §102.108[1].

in Example #19. In other words, aggregation applies even if one of the claims alone would satisfy the amount in controversy requirement.

The corollary to this rule is this: Claims by or against multiple parties cannot be aggregated. This corollary is said to be subject to an exception, which is that the courts permit aggregation of claims by or against multiple parties if the claims are "joint" or "common and undivided."[105] Thus we focus on whether the liability of multiple defendants, or the rights of multiple plaintiffs, are "joint," as opposed to "several." You study the concepts of joint and several liability in Torts. Though the terms *joint* and *several* are not self-explanatory, common sense goes a long way. (In addition, frankly, so does looking for the word *joint*, which usually is a giveaway that the claim involved is joint.)

- ○ ***Example #21.*** *P-1* and *P-2* are injured in a car wreck with *D*. *P-1*'s personal injury claim is $50,000. *P-2*'s personal injury claim is $30,000. Can these two claims against *D* be aggregated? No. Because these are claims by multiple plaintiffs, the basic aggregation rule does not apply. Moreover, personal injury claims are distinct and separate, not joint, even when they arise from the same transaction or occurrence. This makes sense, because each person's interest in her bodily sanctity is separate from everyone else's. Because the claims cannot be aggregated, the case fails to meet the amount in controversy requirement.

- ○ ***Example #22.*** *P* sues *D-1* and *D-2*, alleging that *D-1* owes *P* $50,000 under a contract to haul goods and that *D-2* owes him $30,000 under a separate contract to haul goods. Can these two claims by *P* be aggregated? No. Because these are claims against multiple defendants, the basic aggregation rule does not apply. Moreover, the claims arise under separate contracts and thus cannot be joint. Because the claims cannot be aggregated, the case fails to meet the amount in controversy requirement.

- ○ ***Example #23.*** *P* sues *D-1* and *D-2* as joint tortfeasors, alleging that they attacked and beat him physically. *P* claims damages of $76,000. Is the amount in controversy satisfied? Yes! True, there are claims against two defendants, but this is a joint claim. With a joint claim, the court looks to the total value of the claim. Here, that claim is $76,000, which exceeds $75,000, and thus meets the statutory requirement.

Because the theory of liability in the preceding hypothetical is *joint* liability, any tortfeasor may be held liable for the full amount of the claim. Thus, *D-1* could be sued and held liable for the full $76,000 *or D-2* could be sued and held liable for the full $76,000. It is not as

---

[105]Zahn v. International Paper Co., 414 U.S. 291, 294 (1973). An older case often cited for this proposition is *Pinel v. Pinel*, 240 U.S. 594, 596 (1916).

though *P* has a $38,000 claim against *D-1* and a different $38,000 claim against *D-2*. There is only one claim—it is against both *D-1* and *D-2* jointly, and it exceeds $75,000.

Viewed this way, we can see that joint claims do not really involve aggregation at all. To aggregate, one needs multiple claims. Here, however, there is only one claim (albeit against two persons), and it meets the amount in controversy requirement. The same reasoning works with the assertion of a jointly held right by more than one plaintiff:

- o ***Example #24.*** *P-1* and *P-2* claim joint ownership of a parcel of real property that *D* also claims to own. *P-1* and *P-2* sue *D* to quiet title to the property. The property is worth $76,000. Does this case satisfy the amount requirement? Yes. The two plaintiffs are asserting a joint claim, so there is only one claim, and both *P-1* and *P-2* "own" it. Because it is one claim and it exceeds $75,000, the requirement is met. Again, it is not as though *P-1* has a $38,000 claim and *P-2* has a different $38,000 claim. Once we see the interest is joint, each plaintiff owns the $76,000 claim.

There are two minor points to complete our discussion of amount in controversy. First, one Supreme Court opinion may provide authority for the proposition that the value of a defendant's counterclaim against the plaintiff can be included in determining whether the *plaintiff's* claim meets the jurisdictional amount requirement.[106] Courts have not read the case expansively, however, and most observers feel that it was based on a peculiarity of Texas law.[107] Thus, today almost everyone agrees: A defendant's counterclaim is irrelevant to determining whether the plaintiff's case meets the amount in controversy. Second, there are special considerations for determining the amount in controversy for a class action invoking diversity jurisdiction. We address that issue at §13.3.8.

Timing the Assessment of Whether There Is Jurisdiction. As a general rule, the requirements of federal subject matter jurisdiction are assessed as of the time the plaintiff "commences" the case,[108] which, under Federal Rule 3, is when she files her complaint.[109] If the requirements of diversity of citizenship jurisdiction are satisfied at that point, jurisdiction attaches and remains intact throughout the case. It is irrelevant that there may not have been diversity when the

---

[106]Horton v. Liberty Mut. Ins. Co., 367 U.S. 348, 358-359 (1961). A counterclaim is a claim asserted by the defendant against the plaintiff in the pending suit. See §12.5.1.

[107]*See* Wright & Kane, Federal Courts 220-222. Under Texas law, a suit by a workers' compensation insurer to set aside part of an award opened the entire compensation award. Arguably, that makes the entire potential award the amount in controversy.

[108]Newman-Green, Inc. v. Alfonzo-Larrain, 490 U.S. 826, 830 (1989); Navarro Sav. Ass'n v. Lee, 446 U.S. 458, 459 (1980).

[109]Fed. R. Civ. P. 3 (action "commenced" when complaint is filed).

claim arose or that a party changes her citizenship to destroy diversity after the case is filed.[110] This rule is consistent with the principle, discussed above, that the amount ultimately recovered in a diversity case is irrelevant to whether the amount-in-controversy requirement is satisfied.

   ○ ***Example #25.*** *P*, a citizen of Minnesota, and *D*, also a citizen of Minnesota, are involved in an automobile wreck. *P* is injured in an amount over $75,000. After the wreck, but before suit is filed, *P* becomes a citizen of Wisconsin. *P* then files suit. Although there was no diversity when the claim arose, there was diversity when the case was filed. The case invokes diversity of citizenship jurisdiction.

   ○ ***Example #26.*** *P*, a citizen of Washington, files a diversity of citizenship case against *D*, a citizen of Oregon, claiming damages in excess of $75,000. After filing, but before any appreciable litigation in the case, *P* becomes a citizen of Oregon. Although there is now no diversity, there was diversity when the case was filed. The case invoked diversity of citizenship jurisdiction and will proceed in federal court.[111]

The converse of this principle is also true: If the parties were not of diverse citizenship when the case was commenced, the defect cannot be cured. The Supreme Court demonstrated this principle in *Grupo Dataflux v. Atlas Global Group, LP*.[112] There, a limited partnership sued a Mexican defendant. It attempted to invoke alienage jurisdiction by alleging that the plaintiff was a citizen of Texas and the defendant was a citizen of Mexico.[113] The case proceeded for years, all the way through trial, before it was discovered that when the case was filed the limited partnership had had a partner who was a citizen of Mexico. As we discussed above, the citizenship of a limited partnership is determined by looking to the citizenship of all its partners. Thus, at the time the case was filed, because of the Mexican limited partner, the plaintiff was a citizen of Mexico. That meant that there was no alienage jurisdiction at that point, because both the plaintiff and the defendant were citizens of Mexico.

During the litigation, however, and before entry of final judgment in the trial court, the Mexican limited partners had withdrawn from the partnership. So, at the time the judgment was entered, there *was* alienage, because the plaintiff was then solely a citizen of Texas.

---

[110]Faysound Ltd. v. United Coconut Chemicals, Inc., 878 F.2d 290, 296 (9th Cir. 1989); Field v. Volkswagenwerk AG, 626 F.2d 293, 304 (3d Cir. 1980).

[111]If *Mas v. Perry* is in your casebook, check footnote 2 of that case—it makes exactly this point.

[112]541 U.S. 567, 570-572 (2004).

[113]An alienage case must be between a citizen of a state of the United States and a foreign citizen, and the amount in controversy must exceed $75,000. See §4.5.5.

Notwithstanding that change, the Court held that there was no jurisdiction, and the case was dismissed. *At the time the case was commenced*, there was no alienage, and a subsequent change in citizenship
of one of the parties could not cure that defect.

This scenario—in which the citizenship of a party changed during litigation—is distinguished from that in which a party might
be dropped from the case to save jurisdiction. In *Caterpillar, Inc.
v. Lewis*,[114] there was not complete diversity when a case was commenced in federal court, but the parties and the court failed to notice
that fact. When the defect was discovered, the court dismissed the
diversity-destroying party. The case then proceeded to judgment
with the other parties. The Supreme Court upheld the judgment and
embraced this post-filing dismissal as a way to cure the jurisdictional
defect. This principle is embodied in the second sentence of Rule 21,
which permits the court to drop parties at any stage of litigation "on
terms that are just." Indeed, the Court has held that such jurisdiction-
curing dropping of parties can even be done on appeal.[115] Whether it
is the trial court or the appellate court that cures the jurisdictional
defect, however, it is important that the party dropped be *dispensable*.
This term refers to an assessment under Federal Rule 19 (discussed at
§12.6.1). Under that Rule, some parties are indispensable to the litigation; they cannot be dropped to preserve jurisdiction. Only a party
who is not indispensable—who is "dispensable"—may be dropped to
cure a litigation defect.

It is important to see the difference between *Grupo Dataflux* and
Caterpillar. In the former, there was no jurisdiction when the case was
commenced, but one of the parties to the case—and who remained a
party throughout the case—*changed its citizenship* during the litigation. This will not cure the jurisdictional defect. In the latter, there was
no jurisdiction when the case was commenced, but the *jurisdiction-
destroying party was dropped from the case* to cure that defect. This is
permitted. The Court in *Grupo Dataflux* explained:

> The purported cure arose not from a change in the parties to the action,
> but from a change in the citizenship of a continuing party. Withdrawal
> of the Mexican partners from [the plaintiff limited partnership] did not
> change the fact that [the limited partnership], the single artificial entity
> created under Texas law, remained a party to the action. Thus, the com-
> position of the partnership, and consequently its citizenship, changed.

---

[114]519 U.S. 61, 68-69 (1996). In a case removed from state to federal court, the general rule is that federal subject matter jurisdiction must exist not only when the case
is filed in state court, but when it is removed as well. We discuss this point at §4.8.

[115]*Newman-Green, Inc.*, 490 U.S. at 832 (1989). This should be done, however, only if
it will cause no prejudice to any party. *Id.* at 838.

But allowing a citizenship change to cure the jurisdictional defect that existed at the time of filing would contravene the principle [of the time-of-commencement rule].[116]

In sum, then, the general rule is that the court assesses subject matter jurisdiction at the time the case is commenced. A change in the citizenship of a party who remains in the case does not affect jurisdiction, either to create it or destroy it.

§4.5.4   Exceptions to Diversity of Citizenship Jurisdiction: Collusive Joinder, Domestic Relations, and Probate Cases

There are three substantive areas in which federal courts will not exercise jurisdiction even if the requirements for diversity of citizenship or alienage jurisdiction are met.

Collusive Joinder

Under §1359, the federal court has no jurisdiction in cases "in which any party, by assignment or otherwise, has been improperly or collusively made or joined to invoke the jurisdiction of such court."[117] For many years, courts took inconsistent positions on whether this statute applied to appointments of representatives, such as guardians, to create diversity. That issue is now moot, since, as we saw in §4.5.3, §1332(c)(2) provides that courts look to the citizenship of the person being represented in the litigation.

Today, §1359 is aimed mostly at efforts to create diversity by assignment of claims. Suppose *P* and *D* are citizens of the same state, but that *P* wants to sue *D* in federal court for $100,000. *P* assigns her claim to *T*, who is of diverse citizenship from *D*. *T* then sues *D* under diversity jurisdiction. In *Kramer v. Caribbean Mills, Inc.*,[118] *T* (the assignee) agreed to remit to *P* (the assignor) 95 percent of any recovery. The Court concluded that this fact, coupled with *T*'s previous lack of connection with the dispute, compelled the application of §1359. *T* was essentially a collection agent for *P*. *Kramer* instructs courts to look to all relevant circumstances in assessing the application of §1359.[119] Some of these include whether there is an actual business purpose for the assignment, the character of any interest retained by the assignor,

---

[116]*Grupo Dataflux,* 541 U.S. at 575.
[117]28 U.S.C. §1359.
[118]394 U.S. 823 (1969).
[119]*Id.* at 827-828.

and the subjective intent of the parties, although courts have reached varying conclusions on the importance of the latter.[120]

The application of §1359 does not invalidate the assignment. Whether the assignment is valid is governed by the law (usually state law) under which it was made. Instead, application of §1359 merely requires the court to ignore the assignment in assessing whether there is subject matter jurisdiction. In a case like *Kramer*, then, the statute counsels the court to look to *P*'s, not *T*'s, citizenship. Section 1359 is not implicated when a litigant changes her citizenship expressly to create diversity jurisdiction. Such an act is unilateral, not collusive. If someone wants to go to all the trouble of changing her citizenship simply so she can invoke diversity jurisdiction, §1359 will not stand in her way. In other words, the motive for changing citizenship is irrelevant.[121]

Domestic Relations

Federal courts do not hear domestic relations cases. "Domestic relations" for this purpose is defined narrowly; the exception does not apply simply because a case might be between or among family members. Rather, it applies only to cases "involving the issuance of a divorce, alimony, or child custody decree."[122] Outside that narrow area, federal courts can exercise diversity of citizenship jurisdiction to hear any intrafamily dispute.

This rule is rooted in history as well as policy. In the original Judiciary Act, Congress granted jurisdiction over cases "at common law or in equity" that were between citizens of different states. Historically, domestic relations cases were heard neither at law or at equity, but by ecclesiastical (church) courts. Accordingly, the statutory grant of diversity jurisdiction did not include domestic relations cases.[123] The fact that more recent versions of the diversity statute, including today's §1332(a)(1), speak not of "law" and "equity," but of "civil actions," does not change this result.[124] In terms of policy, the

---

[120]*See generally* 15 Moore's Federal Practice §102.19[4][a].

[121]Morris v. Gilmer, 129 U.S. 315, 328-329 (1889). Of course, the other party may argue that the one attempting to change citizenship by changing domicile fails to satisfy the subjective intent requirement that she intends to make the new state her home for the foreseeable future. See §4.5.3.

[122]Ankenbrandt v. Richards, 504 U.S. 689, 704 (1992). This opinion is the leading modern discussion of the domestic relations exception, though the discussion was dictum. The Court held that the exception did not apply on the facts of the case, which involved an alleged intrafamily tort.

[123]This rationale was first discussed in a dissent in *Barber v. Barber*, 62 U.S. 582, 603-605 (1859) (Daniel, J., dissenting).

[124]*Ankenbrandt*, 504 U.S. at 700. The Court noted that Congress could change the rule.

Supreme Court has noted that state courts have developed expertise in domestic relations cases and that there is an especial local interest in handling issues related to recognition of marriage and child custody issues.

Probate

When someone dies, the law must provide some mechanism for winding up her affairs, paying her taxes and other debts, and distributing her assets to those she specified in her will (or, if she had no will, in accordance with intestacy statutes). This process is called *probate*. Federal courts do not probate wills or oversee the administration of a decedent's estate. The ultimate contours of this exception for "probate cases" are not clear.[125] For example, a federal court, sitting in diversity, can decide a case against an executor to assert a claim against an estate, but only if the federal court does not take general control over the estate or interfere with state probate proceedings.[126] This principle, created by the courts and not by statute, fosters finality by ensuring that any question about the validity of a will be resolved with the probate proceedings in state court. It also is based upon the recognition that state courts have special expertise in these matters and that the federal courts should avoid interfering unnecessarily with state courts on issues of local concern.

Thinking back to Chapter 2, we can consider a probate proceeding (and a marriage, for that matter) as a "thing" over which the state court has *in rem* jurisdiction; the federal courts will not interfere with that jurisdiction. There is a commonsense general rule that no court will interfere with the power of a court that has taken jurisdiction over property.

The Supreme Court's most famous effort in this area involved a case brought by celebrity Anna Nicole Smith. She was married to a wealthy man named Marshall, who died before she did. She sued the son of her late husband, alleging that the son had thwarted his father's efforts to execute documents necessary to provide a trust for Anna Nicole. She made the claim in a federal bankruptcy case and won a judgment of $449 million in compensatory and $25 million in punitive damages. The son claimed that there was no federal subject matter jurisdiction because of the probate exception. The Court disagreed and emphasized the narrowness of the probate exception. The exception

---

[125]Judge Posner refers to this as "one of the most mysterious and esoteric branches of the law of federal jurisdiction." Dragan v. Miller, 679 F.2d 712, 713 (7th Cir. 1982). For more detailed discussion, *see* 15 Moore's Federal Practice §102.92[3].

[126]*See* Markham v. Allen, 326 U.S. 490, 494 (1946).

does not remove federal jurisdiction over cases involving alleged misconduct of those who administer estates. Anna Nicole's claim was a well-recognized tort and did not require the federal court to interfere with the state court's administration of the husband's estate.[127] Thus, it did not fall within the probate exception.[128]

§4.5.5 Alienage Jurisdiction

As we discussed above, §1332(a)(1), which addresses cases "between citizens of different States," is the grant of diversity of citizenship jurisdiction. Section 1332(a)(2), in contrast, provides for jurisdiction over cases "between a citizen of a State and citizens or subjects of a foreign state."[129] This is known as *alienage* jurisdiction. Though diversity jurisdiction has many critics, alienage jurisdiction is widely embraced. The Founders felt that two strong policies supported alienage, and observers agree that both remain vital today. First, aliens, at least as much as out-of-state citizens, might fear local bias when litigating in a state court. Second, the grant of alienage jurisdiction was a statement to foreign countries that litigation involving their nationals was so important to the United States that it belonged in the national courts, and not the state courts. The Supreme Court has explained:

> Both during and after the Revolution, state courts were notoriously frosty to British creditors trying to collect debts from American citizens . . . . This penchant for state courts to disrupt international relations and discourage foreign investment led directly to the alienage jurisdiction provided by Article III of the Constitution.[130]

---

[127]Marshall v. Marshall, 547 U.S. 293, 299 (2006).

[128]The dispute went back to the Supreme Court five years later. This time, the Court concluded that the bankruptcy court had lacked judicial power under Article III to hear Anna Nicole's claim. Stern v. Marshall, 564 U.S. 462, 487-90. Though the opinion in *Marshall v. Marshall* remains good law concerning the probate exception, because the federal bankruptcy court could not hear the claim, the judgment in Anna Nicole's favor was vacated. That left in effect a Texas probate decision, in which Anna Nicole lost. Thus, after years of litigation and two trips to the Supreme Court, her estate (she had died in the meantime) recovered nothing from the estate of her husband.

[129]When capitalized, as in §1332(a)(1) and (a)(2), the word *states* generally refers to states of the United States. When not capitalized, as in §1332(a)(2), the word refers to foreign countries. This conclusion is clear from context. Note the care with which §1332(a)(2) addresses alienage: It is a case between a citizen of a "State" and a citizen or subject of a "state," which is not only not capitalized, but which is preceded by "foreign."

[130]JPMorgan Chase Bank v. Traffic Stream (BVI) Infrastructure, Ltd., 536 U.S. 88, 94 (2002).

An "alien" is a "citizen or subject" of a foreign country. This language reflects that persons with allegiance to a foreign country may have different relationships to that country. In *JPMorgan Chase v. Traffic Stream (BVI) Infrastructure, Ltd.*,[131] a corporation chartered in the British Virgin Islands claimed that it was not a "citizen" of the United Kingdom because, as a resident of a territory of that Kingdom, it had fewer rights than a citizen. The Supreme Court upheld alienage jurisdiction and emphasized the breadth of the phrase "citizen or subject." While it was true that the corporation was not a citizen of the United Kingdom, it certainly was a subject of that nation and thus was an alien for purposes of alienage jurisdiction. So "it is immaterial for our purposes that the law of the United Kingdom may provide different rights of abode for individuals in the territories."[132] The thrust of the inquiry is whether the litigant is a foreign national.

We note several things about §1332(a)(2). First, alienage requires the same amount in controversy as a diversity jurisdiction case. Thus, all the rules discussed in §4.5.3 concerning amount in controversy apply in alienage.

Second, to invoke alienage jurisdiction, the case must be between a citizen of a state (of the United States) and an alien (a non-U.S. citizen). Thus, §1332(a)(2) does *not* permit jurisdiction simply because an alien is a party to a case. Indeed, such a statutory provision would be unconstitutional, because Article III does not permit jurisdiction over such a case.[133]

> ○ ***Example #27.*** *P*, a citizen of Spain, sues *D*, a citizen of Canada, in federal court. The case cannot invoke alienage jurisdiction because it is not between a citizen of a state of the United States and an alien.

Third, it does not matter whether the alien is plaintiff or defendant — just so the litigant on the other side is a citizen of a state of the United States. In *Mas v. Perry*[134] (which we discussed concerning diversity jurisdiction, §4.5.3), recall that one plaintiff, the husband, was a citizen of France. His claim against a citizen of Louisiana thus invoked alienage, since it was between an alien and a citizen of a state.

Fourth, it is not enough for the non-alien litigant to be a citizen of the United States. She must be a citizen of *a state of the United States.*

---

[131]536 U.S. at 88.

[132]*Id.* at 99.

[133]A statute providing for federal subject matter jurisdiction whenever an alien was a party was held unconstitutional for this reason in *Hodgson v. Bowerbank*, 9 U.S. 303, 304 (1809). The operative language in Article III is found in its last head of jurisdiction. It extends the judicial power of the United States to cases "between a State, or the Citizens thereof, and foreign States, Citizens, or Subjects."

[134]489 F.2d 1396, 1398 (5th Cir. 1974).

○ ***Example #28.*** *P*, a U.S. citizen domiciled in the United Kingdom,[135] sues *D*, a citizen of Morocco, on a state law claim exceeding $75,000. Although *P* is a citizen of the United States and *D* is an alien, there is no alienage jurisdiction. Why? Because *P* is not a citizen of a state of the United States. Recall from §4.5.3 that to be a citizen of a state of the United States, a U.S. citizen must be domiciled in a U.S. state. *P* is not.

Fifth, how do we handle aliens who are admitted to the United States for permanent resident status?[136] From 1990 until 2012, a sentence in §1332(a) provided that such a person was to be considered a citizen of the state (of the United States) in which she was domiciled. This provision was always problematic, because the Supreme Court had long held that one can be a citizen of a state (of the United States) only if she were a *citizen of the United States* and domiciled in the state.[137] Moreover, courts disagreed on the scope of the statute. Fortunately, these problems are a thing of the past, because Congress repealed this part of §1332(a) in 2012.[138] In its place, that legislation added a phrase to §1332(a)(2): There is no jurisdiction over a case between a citizen of a state (of the United States) and an alien who is "lawfully admitted for permanent residence in the United States and who [is] domiciled in the same State."

○ ***Example #29.*** Plaintiff, a citizen of Spain admitted for permanent U.S. residence and domiciled in New York, sues Defendant, a citizen of Peru admitted for permanent U.S. residence and domiciled in California. The claim exceeds $75,000. Before the amendment in 2012, this case arguably invoked diversity, because §1332(a) at that time provided that such aliens were deemed citizens of the states in which domiciled. So this could have been seen as a case by a citizen of New York against a citizen of California. That conclusion is no longer arguable. The statute no longer ascribes state citizenship to an alien. This is a case by an alien against an alien. There is no alienage. There is no diversity.

○ ***Example #30.*** Plaintiff, a citizen of California, sues Defendant, a citizen of Peru admitted for permanent resident status and domiciled in Arizona. The claim exceeds $75,000. This case invokes alienage jurisdiction. It is between a citizen of a state of the United States and an alien. It does not invoke diversity jurisdiction, because Defendant is not a citizen of a state of the United States.

[135]The fact that a U.S. citizen is domiciled in a foreign country does not make that person a citizen of that country. Only the foreign country can bestow citizenship on someone. Thus, *P* is not a citizen (or, as the United Kingdom would say, a subject) of the United Kingdom and therefore is not an alien.

[136]See note 55 above.

[137]See note 43 and accompanying text above.

[138]The legislation was part of the Jurisdiction and Venue Clarification Act of 2011. Despite the name of the Act, it went into effect in January 2012.

○ ***Example #31.*** Plaintiff, a citizen of California, sues Defendant, who is a citizen of Peru admitted for permanent U.S. residence and domiciled in California. The claim exceeds $75,000.

Because of the 2012 legislation, it is clear that there is no jurisdiction in Example #31. Although this case meets the requirements for alienage, the addition to §1332(a)(2) precludes jurisdiction because the dispute is between a citizen of a state (of the United States) and a permanent resident alien domiciled in the same state.

Sixth, recall from §4.5.3 that §1332(c)(1) defines a corporation's citizenship as its state(s) of incorporation and the one state in which it has its principal place of business. For decades, the statute failed, however, to address a corporation that is either formed under the law of a foreign country or has its principal place of business in a foreign country. Courts struggled with the citizenship of such corporations.[139] Congress ended that uncertainty by amending §1332(c)(1) in 2012. It clearly states that a corporation is deemed a citizen of every state (of the United States) and *foreign country* in which it is incorporated, as well as of the state (of the United States) and *foreign country* in which it has its principal place of business. The legislative history of the Act suggests that this change is intended to constrict federal jurisdiction.

○ ***Example #32.*** Plaintiff, a citizen of Ohio, sues Corporation, which is incorporated in Brazil and has its principal place of business in Ohio. There is no alienage or diversity here. Because Corporation is a citizen of both Brazil and Ohio, there is an Ohio citizen on both sides of the case.
○ ***Example #33.*** Plaintiff, a citizen of Sweden, sues Corporation, which is incorporated in West Virginia and has its principal place of business in Italy. There is no alienage or diversity here. Because Corporation is a citizen of both West Virginia and Italy, there is an alien on both sides of the case.

Finally, recall that §1332(c)(2) deals with persons suing on behalf of decedents, minors, and incompetents. It provides that the representative is deemed to be a citizen "of the same State" as the person represented. In the jurisdictional statutes generally, when the word *State* is capitalized (as in §1332(a)(1)), it is interpreted to refer to a state of the United States (and not to a foreign country). When the word state is not capitalized (as in §1332(a)(2)), it refers to a foreign country.

---

[139]Courts tended to treat a corporation formed in another country but with its principal place of business in a state of the United States to be a citizen of that state in the United States. And they tended to treat an American corporation with its principal place of business overseas as a citizen of the state in the United States in which it was incorporated. *See* 13B Wright & Miller §3628.

246

What if a person being represented (the decedent, minor, or incompetent) is not a citizen of a state of the United States? For instance, suppose the decedent was an alien (say, a citizen of Costa Rica), and the executor is a citizen of California. Because §1332(c)(2) speaks of "State," it would seem that §1332(c)(2) would not apply, because the decedent was not a citizen of a "State" (of the United States). Though this argument is cogent, courts have rejected it. Accordingly, they apply §1332(c)(2) even when a decedent, minor, or incompetent is an alien. Under this case law, the court will ascribe alien status to the representative of such a person,[140] which may open the door to invoking alienage jurisdiction.

§4.6 Federal Question Jurisdiction

§4.6.1 Introduction

The first basis of jurisdiction provided for in Article III, §2, is cases "arising under the Constitution, laws, or treaties of the United States." Section 1331 grants jurisdiction to the federal district courts using the same operative language of "arising under." The reference to the Constitution, laws, or treaties of the United States is a reference to federal law. Thus, pursuant to §1331, cases "arising under" a federal law may be filed in federal court. This branch of federal subject matter jurisdiction is usually called *federal question jurisdiction,* though some call it *arising under* jurisdiction.

To be precise, §1331 is the *general* federal question statute. It grants jurisdiction over a case that arises under *any* federal law. There are other specialized federal question statutes that grant jurisdiction over claims arising under specific federal laws, such as some federal antitrust (§1337), civil rights (§1343), and patent laws (§1338). While some of the specialized federal question statutes grant *exclusive federal question jurisdiction,*[141] meaning that a claim arising under them must be asserted only in federal court, §1331 does not. Any claim invoking §1331 may, at the plaintiff's option, be asserted in state court instead.

---

[140]*See, e.g.,* Jungil Lee v. ANC Car Rental Corp., 220 Fed. Appx. 493, 493 (9th Cir. 2007); Rick v. Women's & Children's Hosp., 2010 U.S. Dist. LEXIS 58021 at * 9-10 (W.D. La. May 10, 2010); Velazquez v. Broesche, 2006 U.S. Dist. LEXIS 59400 at *5 (W.D. Tex. June 13, 2006); Kato v. Cnty of Westchester, 927 F. Supp. 714, 716 (S.D.N.Y. 1996); Geler v. National Westminster Bank U.S.A., 763 F. Supp. 722, 726 (S.D.N.Y. 1991). The courts reason that it would make no sense to adopt the decedent's, minor's, or incompetent's citizenship if she were an American but ignore it if she were an alien.

[141]We saw examples at note 1 above.

Unlike diversity of citizenship cases, federal question cases go to federal court not because of any characteristics of the parties, but because of the substantive nature of the claim asserted. In determining whether a case invokes federal question jurisdiction, citizenship is irrelevant, and there is no amount in controversy requirement. For many years §1331 included an amount in controversy requirement, but that was abolished in 1980.[142]

> ○ ***Example #34.*** Plaintiff, a citizen of Colorado, sues Defendant, a citizen of Colorado, seeking to recover one penny as damages for violation of Plaintiff's federal rights.

This case may be heard by a federal court under §1331. The citizenship of the parties is irrelevant. The amount in controversy is irrelevant. As long as Plaintiff's claim "arises under" federal law, the case invokes federal question jurisdiction.

The policy justifications for federal question jurisdiction are clear and are not controversial. Federal judges may be expected to develop special expertise in matters of federal law and might also be more sympathetic than state court judges to the policies underlying federal law. Interestingly, however, from our earliest days as a nation, the state courts have been expected to decide cases arising under federal law.[143] This is shown by the fact that §1331 does not grant exclusive federal jurisdiction. It is also shown by the fact that (aside from a one-year exception[144]) there was no version of a general federal question statute until 1875. Until then a great many federal question cases could *only* go to state trial courts.

While it is usually quite clear when a federal law (e.g., the Constitution, federal statutes) is involved in a case, the tough issue will be to determine when a case "arises under" that federal law. As we will see, the constitutional grant is interpreted more broadly than the statutory grant, despite the fact that they use the same operative language.[145]

---

[142]For this reason, pre-1980 federal question cases you may read discuss amount in controversy. The fact that there is no amount in controversy requirement under §1331 does not mean that there is never a jurisdictional amount in federal question cases. Some specialized grants of federal question jurisdiction still carry an amount in controversy requirement. *See, e.g.*, 15 U.S.C. §2310(d) (claims under Moss-Magnuson Consumer Product Warranties Act must exceed $50,000).

[143]See §4.5.2 (discussion of federal courts deciding state law cases and vice versa).

[144]In 1801, the famous Midnight Judges Act included a general grant of federal question jurisdiction. It was repealed, however, in 1802.

[145]We saw the same thing in §4.5.3 regarding diversity of citizenship jurisdiction, in which the interpretation of the Constitution's use of the phrase "between citizens of different states" is broader than the statutory use of the same phrase.

§4.6.2 The Constitutional Limit of Federal Question Jurisdiction

To arise under federal law, must *every aspect* of the case involve federal law? In *Osborn v. Bank of the United States*,[146] the Supreme Court gave a startlingly broad interpretation to the *constitutional* grant of federal question jurisdiction. Chief Justice John Marshall's opinion held that a case falls within Article III if federal law might "form an ingredient" in the overall case. Even if the federal issue is but a tiny part of a dispute dominated by state law issues, Article III would permit a federal court to decide the entire case. Indeed, Marshall went much further, saying that it does not matter whether the federal issue actually does arise in the litigation; the mere *possibility* that a federal issue might be injected in the litigation is enough to conclude that the case arises under federal law for Article III purposes.

In *Osborn*, the Bank of the United States sued to stop a state official in Ohio from collecting taxes under an Ohio law that taxed non-Ohio banks. The bank contended that the Supremacy Clause of the Constitution, Article VI, §2, prohibited a state from imposing a tax upon it, since it was a federal instrumentality. The mere presence of this federal issue meant that the case arose under federal law for Article III purposes. For example, Marshall continued, if the bank sued on a simple contract, one question that could be raised would be whether federal legislation forming the bank gave it capacity to bring suit.[147] Even if the capacity issue had been resolved definitively, it could at least potentially lurk in every contract case in which the bank was involved. That phantom presence of any federal issue satisfied Article III. Thus, for example, any private state law dispute over ownership of land, in which the title could be traced back to the United States, would satisfy the Article III requirement for federal question jurisdiction.

It makes no sense to have the federal courts inundated with these and similar cases in which some federal issue might conceivably be relevant. Thus, Congress, in passing the statutory grant of federal question jurisdiction, might be expected to narrow this broad constitutional power. But §1331 appears to contain no such limitation, because it mirrors the language of the constitutional grant. Nonetheless, as they did with diversity jurisdiction, the federal courts have long *interpreted* the language in the statute as narrower than the same language in the Constitution. We consider these interpretations next.

---

[146]22 U.S. 738, 823 (1824).

[147]Marshall was actually speaking of a companion case, *Bank of the U.S. v. Planters' Bank of Ga.*, 22 U.S. 904 (1824).

§4.6.3   The Statutory Limits on Federal Question Jurisdiction: Overview and "Substantiality"

Though the constitutional grant of federal question jurisdiction would permit jurisdiction if *any* federal issue *might potentially* be raised in the case, §1331 is not nearly so broad. Again, relative narrowness of the statute does not appear on its face; as noted, the operative language of §1331 is the same as the constitutional grant of federal question jurisdiction. But in applying the statutory language, the courts impose three limitations: (1) the "substantiality" requirement, (2) the "well-pleaded complaint" rule, and (3) the requirement that federal law be sufficiently "central" to the plaintiff's claim. Congress has never acted to undo these court-imposed limitations, so they retain vitality, and we speak of them as "statutory" limitations. Most Civil Procedure courses focus on the "well-pleaded complaint" rule and do very little with the other two.

The first statutory limitation is that the federal issue in the case be "substantial." In other words, an insubstantial or frivolous federal claim will not invoke jurisdiction. This rule has always been vexing, because it is possible that a claim is sufficiently substantial to confer jurisdiction but is a loser on the merits.[148] Often it is not clear where one is to draw the line between dismissal for lack of jurisdiction and dismissal for failure to state a claim on which relief can be granted.[149] Suffice to say that federal claims should be dismissed for lack of subject matter jurisdiction only if they are "so insubstantial, implausible, . . . or otherwise completely devoid of merit as not to involve a federal controversy."[150] Such cases should be as rare as they are obvious.[151]

§4.6.4   The Major Statutory Limitation: The Well-Pleaded Complaint Rule

How It Works. To invoke jurisdiction under §1331, federal law must be part of the plaintiff's "well-pleaded" complaint. There are two

---

[148]*See* 13D Wright & Miller §3564 (discussing this confusion).

[149]Failure to state a claim is grounds for dismissal under Federal Rule 12(b)(6). See §7.3.

[150]Steel Co. v. Citizens for a Better Environment, 523 U.S. 83, 98 (1998).

[151]*See, e.g.*, Avila v. Pappas, 591 F.3d 552, 553 (7th Cir. 2010) ("It is not enough to utter the word 'Constitution' and then present a claim that rests on state law. If it were, every claim that a state employee committed a tort, or broke a contract, could be litigated in federal court").

important points to this rule. First, the court looks only to the plaintiff's complaint—not to the defendant's asserted defenses[152] or to the defendant's filing of counterclaims against the plaintiff[153]—to determine whether there is federal question jurisdiction. Second, in looking at the plaintiff's complaint, the court considers only the "well-pleaded" parts thereof. This is a terrible phrase. It sounds as though the court is judging sentence structure and syntax. In fact, "well-pleaded" refers to that part of the complaint supporting only the plaintiff's *claim*. In other words, the court ignores any extraneous material the plaintiff may have put in her complaint—material that does not relate to her *claim*.

For example, if the plaintiff's complaint anticipates that the defendant might raise a particular defense and attempts to rebut it in advance, such allegations are ignored in assessing federal question jurisdiction. Why? Because they do not relate to the plaintiff's claim itself. Only if the plaintiff's *claim* (not plaintiff's discussion of things beyond her claim) arises under federal law will the case satisfy §1331.

The most famous example of the well-pleaded complaint rule is *Louisville & Nashville Railroad Co. v. Mottley*.[154] The Mottleys (a married couple) were injured in 1871, many years before the case was filed, in an accident on the Louisville & Nashville Railroad (L&N). In settlement of their claim against the L&N, the Mottleys accepted a pass that entitled them to free lifetime passage on the L&N.[155] They enjoyed this pass for many years, until Congress enacted a law forbidding railroads from honoring such passes.[156] Because of this statute, the L&N refused to allow the Mottleys their customary free passage, and the Mottleys sued the railroad in federal court.

In essence, the Mottleys' complaint said: (1) we have a contract with the L&N, pursuant to which we are to get free passage; (2) the L&N refuses to honor the pass, despite our full compliance with everything

---

[152]*See* Gully v. First Nat'l Bank, 299 U.S. 109, 113 (1936).

[153]*See* Holmes Group, Inc. v. Vornado Air Circulation Sys., Inc., 535 U.S. 826, 831 (2002) (counterclaim is part of defendant's answer and therefore cannot be part of a well-pleaded complaint; "we decline to transform the longstanding well-pleaded complaint rule into the 'well-pleaded-complaint-or-counterclaim rule' urged by respondent"). The case involved jurisdiction under §1338(a), concerning patent claims, but its holding concerning the well-pleaded complaint rule applies to general federal question cases under §1331.

[154]211 U.S. 149, 150 (1908).

[155]This fact makes you wonder a bit about the Mottleys. They wanted unlimited free rides on a railroad on which they had been injured.

[156]Interestingly, this statute was an early form of campaign finance reform, since members of Congress had routinely accepted such free passes to go home to see their constituents. The law was an effort to show that members of Congress could not be bribed by railroads giving them free travel.

we were supposed to do; (3) we think the L&N is going to argue that this new federal statute precludes it from continuing to honor our pass; but (4) we think the statute does not apply to us; and (5) even if the statute does apply to us, it violates our constitutional rights by depriving us of property without just compensation.

In the trial court, issues (1) and (2) were not contested. After all, the railroad had a deal with the Mottleys and was breaching the deal. The only contested issues were whether the L&N's defense (issue (3)) would prevail or whether the Mottleys were right that the federal law should not apply to them (issues (4) and (5)). In other words, the only issues to be contested at trial were issues relating to the application of the federal law. The trial court addressed those issues and ruled in favor of the Mottleys.

The Supreme Court agreed to hear the case.[157] The only questions the L&N raised were issues (4) and (5). The Supreme Court refused to address them, however, because the case did not fall within §1331.[158] The federal trial court had no federal question jurisdiction over the case and, thus, the judgment entered by that court was void. The case failed to invoke federal question jurisdiction, because of the well-pleaded complaint rule. The Mottleys' well-pleaded complaint—one that set forth only their claim, not extraneous material—would involve only issues (1) and (2). And neither of those issues implicated federal law in any way. Their claim was simply one for breach of contract, which implicates only state law; there was nothing federal about it. The only way federal law was injected into the case was by the railroad's *defense* that the federal statute forbade it from honoring the pass. The Mottleys anticipated (correctly) that the railroad would raise the federal defense, *but an anticipated defense is not part of a well-pleaded complaint*. Thus, it must be disregarded in assessing whether the case arises under federal law.[159] The Supreme Court remanded to the lower court with instructions to dismiss the case.

Accordingly, the fact that a plaintiff alleges something about federal law in her complaint does not mean that the case arises under federal law under §1331. The *claim itself* must be based upon federal law. One way to force yourself to apply the well-pleaded complaint

---

[157]At the time, there was no intermediate appellate court in the federal system.

[158]Actually, the general federal question statute was then known by a different number and had an amount in controversy requirement. But the operative "arising under" language interpreted in the Supreme Court opinion is the same as in §1331. Remember that it is incumbent on a federal court to dismiss *sua sponte* whenever it determines that there is no basis for subject matter jurisdiction. See §4.3.

[159]There is nothing ethically or professionally wrong with anticipating a defense in one's complaint. The well-pleaded complaint rule simply stands for the proposition that any such anticipated defense cannot be a basis for federal question jurisdiction.

rule is to apply this shorthand test. Ask yourself this: Is the plaintiff attempting to vindicate some right given by federal law?

- o ***Example #35.*** Ask this question about the facts of *Mottley*. Were the Mottleys trying to vindicate a federal right? No. The federal law referred to did not give the Mottleys any rights. Indeed, the federal law *took away* their rights to a free pass on the railroad. Notice that the Mottleys' sole allegations about the federal statute (issues (3), (4), and (5)) were that it *did not apply to them*. So, clearly, they were not trying to vindicate any right given to them by that (or any other) federal law.

The well-pleaded complaint rule has its critics.[160] The most obvious criticism is that the rule clearly channels cases out of federal court in which the central issues to be resolved are purely federal. *Mottley* is an excellent example; the case cannot be filed in federal court even though only issues (4) and (5)—purely issues of federal law—were contested. The result is that such litigation goes to state court, and the state courts determine these issues of federal law. Only in the rare case in which the Supreme Court grants review of the case (and in which the parties pay to fight to the Supreme Court) does a federal court ever address the issues.[161] Indeed, this happened with the Mottleys. After the Supreme Court ordered dismissal of their case, the Mottleys filed anew in state court. The case was appealed through the state court system and the Supreme Court ultimately agreed to review the case *on exactly the same federal issues they attempted to raise in federal court in the first place!* Three years after issuance of the *Mottley* opinion discussed above, the Supreme Court determined the federal issues (the Mottleys lost).[162]

The well-pleaded complaint rule creates these problems. On the other hand, the rule has the advantage of allowing an early decision on whether a federal court has subject matter jurisdiction. The court need only look to the complaint, without awaiting the defendant's response. If the Court had held differently in *Mottley*—if jurisdiction could be based upon defenses—the court would be in limbo until

---

[160]*See, e.g.,* Donald Doernberg, *There's No Reason for It; It's Just Our Policy: Why the Well-Pleaded Complaint Rule Sabotages the Purposes of Federal Question Jurisdiction,* 38 Hastings L.J. 597 (1987).

[161]Remember that only the Supreme Court can review state decisions, and then only decisions of the highest state court, and only as to issues of federal law. See §1.2.3.

[162]219 U.S. 467, 485-486 (1911). The fact that the Supreme Court decided these issues proves that §1331 is narrower than the constitutional grant of federal question jurisdiction. The Supreme Court could only address the issues if they fell within Article III, because Article III limits the jurisdiction of all federal courts, including the Supreme Court. But, as the original *Mottley* opinion held, the issues did not satisfy §1331. Thus, §1331 is narrower than Article III.

the defendant actually raised the federal issue as a defense. Allowing jurisdiction based upon the plaintiff's anticipation of a defense is even more problematic, because there is no guarantee that the defendant will in fact raise the issue. In that situation, the case would be in federal court even though no federal issue is injected. Thus, despite the criticism of the well-pleaded complaint rule, it remains vital: "This bright-line rule prevents the disruption, to both the system and the litigants, of shifting a case between state and federal fora in the middle of an action as federal issues arise or fall out."[163]

In §12.5.1, we see that a defendant might assert a claim—called a counterclaim—against the plaintiff in the pending case. A counterclaim is asserted in the defendant's answer and is not part of the plaintiff's well-pleaded complaint. Thus, in *Holmes Group v. Vornado Air Circulation*,[164] the Court held that a counterclaim is irrelevant to whether a case can be brought in federal court. In that case, the plaintiff's claim did not arise under federal law and did not invoke diversity jurisdiction. The defendant's counterclaim, however, did arise under federal patent law. But federal jurisdiction must be based upon what is in the complaint (not the answer). The counterclaim was irrelevant for determining federal question jurisdiction.[165]

How the Rule Works in Declaratory Judgment Cases. The well-pleaded complaint rule runs into special problems in cases brought for declaratory judgment. We think of most plaintiffs as seeking what

---

[163]Arthur Miller, *Artful Pleading: A Doctrine in Search of Definition*, 76 Tex. L. Rev. 1781, 1783 (1998).

[164]*Holmes Group,* 535 U.S. at 831 (counterclaim appears in defendant's answer, not in the complaint, and thus cannot invoke federal question jurisdiction; "we decline to transform the longstanding well-pleaded-complaint rule into the 'well-pleaded-complaint-or-counterclaim rule'"). Though *Holmes Group* was decided under §1338 (dealing with patent infringement) and not §1331, the "arising under" language in both statutes is interpreted identically. There can be no doubt that the reasoning of *Holmes Group* applies to §1331.

[165]In 2012, as part of a revision of the federal patent laws, Congress amended §1338 to overturn the result of *Holmes Group*. That amendment applies, however, only to patent cases arising under §1338. It does not affect the well-pleaded complaint rule under the general federal question statute, §1331. So, under §1331, a counterclaim is irrelevant for determining whether the case arises under federal law. *See, e.g.,* Capital One Bank (USA), N.A. v. Clark, 2017 WL 1425588 at *2 (D. Ore. 2017) (counterclaim "may not serve as the basis for federal question jurisdiction").

In the non-patent context, *Holmes Group* apparently overturns the result of *Great Lakes Rubber Corp. v. Herbert Cooper Co.*, 286 F.2d 631 (3d Cir. 1961). In *Great Lakes*, *P* purported to assert a federal question against *D*. (The two were citizens of the same state, so there was no diversity jurisdiction.) *D* asserted a counterclaim against *P* that clearly did arise under federal law. The court concluded that *P*'s claim did not arise under federal law, but held that the case was properly in federal court based upon *D*'s counterclaim. This practice appears to be rejected by *Holmes Group*, which permits the court to look only to *P*'s complaint in assessing subject matter jurisdiction.

is usually called *coercive relief*—an order that the defendant pay her money (damages) or that she do something or desist from doing something (injunction). With declaratory judgment, however, the plaintiff seeks a court order defining the relative rights among the parties. Because Article III, §2, provides that federal courts can only hear "cases" or "controversies," those courts cannot issue advisory opinions. To ensure that the declaratory judgment procedure does not permit the issuance of advisory opinions, Congress requires that a request for declaratory judgment be made only "in cases of actual controversy."[166]

The availability of declaratory judgment can result in switching the expected alignment of parties to litigation. Usually, we expect a victim to sue the person who hurt her. We expect the victim to be the plaintiff and the person who hurt her to be the defendant. But with declaratory judgment, the person allegedly responsible for the harm may sue. For example, suppose you think your neighbor is trespassing on your property. Before you sue her, she sues you, seeking a declaration that what she is doing does not constitute trespass.

How does this affect application of the well-pleaded complaint rule? The late Professor Charles Alan Wright synthesized the cases by saying that "the declaratory action may be entertained in federal court only if the coercive action that would have been necessary, absent declaratory judgment procedure, might have been so brought."[167] In other words, a declaratory judgment claim will arise under federal law if *either* party to the case could have brought a coercive action.

- ○ ***Example #36.*** *P* holds a patent (such a person is called a "patentee"). A patent is a *federally* granted right to exclude others from making, using, selling, or offering to sell the patented item. *P* sues for a declaration that her patent is valid and that the defendant is infringing it. Her claim invokes federal question jurisdiction, because she could just as easily have brought a claim for damages or other coercive relief.
- ○ ***Example #37.*** Railroad sues the Mottleys for a declaration that the federal statute under which it refused to honor the Mottleys' passes was valid. This case would not invoke federal question jurisdiction, because neither the Railroad's claim for declaratory judgment nor the Mottleys' claim for coercive relief would have arisen under federal law.[168]

---

[166]Federal Declaratory Judgment Act, 28 U.S.C. §§2201, 2202. The Act provides only a remedy and not a basis of subject matter jurisdiction. Skelly Oil Co. v. Phillips Petroleum Co., 339 U.S. 667, 671-672 (1950).

[167]Wright & Kane, Federal Courts 113.

[168]Railroad has no claim for relief based upon the federal statute. And, under the well-pleaded complaint rule, as discussed above, neither do the Mottleys.

Whatever the merits of the well-pleaded complaint rule, it remains a significant limitation on the ability to invoke federal question jurisdiction. It is not the only one, however.

§4.6.5   Another Statutory Limitation: The Centrality of the Federal Issue

Courts have imposed another limitation on federal question jurisdiction under §1331. This one is more difficult to conceptualize than the well-pleaded complaint rule, and many professors do not cover it in the basic Civil Procedure course. It concerns what may be called the *centrality* of the federal law to the claim being asserted. This is a relatively amorphous inquiry, which requires us to review some Supreme Court decisions that are difficult to reconcile. As we will see, the problem arises because some claims are mixtures of state and federal law. More specifically, sometimes state law creates a right of action (a claim) that is measured by federal standards, and sometimes the converse is true.

The starting point is *American Well Works Co. v. Layne & Bowler Co.*,[169] in which Justice Holmes wrote the majority opinion. There, Company *A* manufactured a pump. Company *B* held a patent on a pump. Company *B* apparently contended that Company *A*'s pump infringed its patent but did not sue (though it was thinking of doing so). Instead, Company *A* sued Company *B*, alleging that Company *B* had wrongfully claimed that Company *A*'s pump violated Company *B*'s patent. Further, it alleged that Company *B* had driven away customers by threatening to sue anyone who bought a Company *A* pump. Company *A* based its claim on *state* trade libel law. Though state law created the claim being asserted, the litigation would focus on a federal issue: whether Company *A*'s pump violated Company *B*'s (federal) patent. The Court held that the case did *not* invoke federal question jurisdiction[170] and adopted a mechanical test: "A suit arises under the law that creates the cause of action."[171] Because the claim was created by state law, the case did not arise under federal law. This approach is sometimes called the "Holmes test" (for Justice Holmes) or the "creation test" (because it looks at what law created the claim).[172]

---

[169]241 U.S. 257 (1916).

[170]The case involved a precursor to §1338, concerning patent cases, and not of §1331, the general federal question statute. Nonetheless, it is clear that the interpretation of "arising under" is the same in both.

[171]*American Well Works*, 241 U.S. at 260.

[172]*See* Ann Woolhandler & Michael Collins, *Federal Question Jurisdiction and Justice Holmes,* 84 Notre Dame L. Rev. 2151 (2009).

Though the Holmes test is easy to apply, the Court seemed to forget about it just five years later. In *Smith v. Kansas City Title & Trust Co.*,[173] the plaintiff was a shareholder in a corporation, and sued to stop that corporation from investing in bonds issued under a federal statute (the Federal Farm Loan Act). He argued that the federal statute was unconstitutional and, therefore, that the corporation's investment would violate Missouri law (which forbade corporations from investing in unlawfully issued investments). The case seems indistinguishable from *Well Works*—state law created the claim, but the litigation would focus on federal law (the constitutionality of a federal statute). Surprisingly, though, the Court upheld federal question jurisdiction. According to the majority opinion, "where it appears from the [complaint] . . . that the right to relief depends upon the construction or application of the Constitution or laws of the United States, and that such federal claim . . . rests upon a reasonable foundation, the District Court has jurisdiction."[174] The entire analysis seems antithetical to *Smith,* since the Court was willing to assess what might be called "litigation reality"—that is, what issues would actually arise if the case went to trial. Not surprisingly, Justice Holmes dissented.

The Court confused things even more 13 years later with *Moore v. Chesapeake & Ohio Railway.*[175] There, the plaintiff sued his employer under a state employer's liability law. Under that law, the employer could not claim that the plaintiff was guilty of contributory negligence if the employer had violated a statute "enacted for the safety of employees." The plaintiff claimed that his employer had violated the Federal Safety Appliance Act. Like *Well Works* and *Smith*, then, *Moore* involved a state-created claim in a case to be decided by the construction of federal law. In *Moore*, the Court held that there was no federal question jurisdiction.

Two years later, the Court decided *Gully v. First National Bank in Meridian.*[176] There, a national bank transferred its rights and liabilities to another (successor) bank. By contract, the successor bank was liable for state taxes, which were assessed on the stock of the national bank. When it failed to pay them, a state officer sued the bank in state court. The successor bank removed the case to federal court. The lower courts upheld federal question jurisdiction. While recognizing that the claim was created by state contract law, the lower courts were impressed by the fact that the power to tax a national bank was based in a federal statute. The Supreme Court reversed and rejected federal question jurisdiction. The analysis was similar to that in *Smith,* since

[173]255 U.S. 180, 195 (1921).
[174]*Id.* at 199.
[175]291 U.S. 205, 214-217 (1934).
[176]299 U.S. 109, 116-118 (1936).

the Court looked to litigation reality and concluded that the federal issue was merely "lurking" in the background and probably would not arise. In sum, then, *Gully* was pretty easy. It involved a state law claim in which litigation would center on issues of state contract law. Clearly, there was no need for a federal forum.

The Court then left the area for 50 years, when it decided the vexing case of *Merrell Dow Pharmaceuticals, Inc. v. Thompson.*[177] That case involved claims for damages allegedly caused by the plaintiffs' mothers' ingestion of a drug (Bendectin) while the mothers were pregnant. The plaintiffs asserted a variety of state law claims, including negligence per se. They alleged that the defendant drug manufacturer was guilty of negligence per se because it allegedly violated the Federal Food, Drug, and Cosmetic Act (FDCA) by "misbranding" Bendectin. So once again, the Court faced a case in which state law created the claim, but in which the litigation would focus on interpretation of federal law.[178] The Court held that there was no federal question jurisdiction. Review these four cases in the following chart. It would seem impossible for the Court to decide *Merrell Dow* without deciding whether the one aberrant case—*Smith*—is still good law.

Case	Law Creating Claim	Law to Be Interpreted	§1331 Jurisdiction?
Well Works	State	Federal	No
Smith	State	Federal	Yes
Moore	State	Federal	No
Gully	State	State	No
Merrell Dow	State	Federal	No

We need some background before looking at *Merrell Dow* in detail. Sometimes Congress passes a statute proscribing certain behavior but fails to create a claim to allow those harmed by such behavior to sue. In the vernacular, Congress fails to create "a private right of action." Instead, such statutes often permit administrative agencies of the federal government to undertake enforcement actions, or they permit the attorney general to bring suits for injunctions or even criminal prosecutions against those violating the statutes. Occasionally, federal courts hold that Congress *did* create a private right of action even though the legislation failed to say so. These "implied rights of

---

[177]478 U.S. 804 (1986).

[178]Plaintiffs filed the case in state court. It was the defendant who tried to invoke federal jurisdiction; it did so by "removing" the case to federal court. We discuss removal at §4.8.

action" are controversial because they ascribe to Congress an intent that Congress did not express. When courts find such implied rights of action, however, there is clearly a federally created claim. In such a case, the Holmes test would uphold the invocation of federal question jurisdiction (because federal law creates the claim).

In *Merrell Dow*, the parties stipulated that the FDCA *did not* create a private right of action (express or implied) to sue for violations of its provisions. For this reason, *Merrell Dow* involved a state-created claim (for negligence per se). But, as noted, deciding whether the defendant's behavior constituted negligence per se would require application of a standard set out in federal law (the FDCA). Would the Court adopt *Smith* or would it adopt *Moore*? The majority (five Justices, in an opinion by Justice Stevens) spoke of the lack of "importance" of the federal law involved and emphasized the fact that Congress had not created a federal right of action. The majority concluded that once Congress determined there was no federal remedy, the Court was "not free to 'supplement' that decision in a way that makes [that decision] 'meaningless.'"[179]

There are at least two problems with this conclusion. First, it is a *non sequitur*. There is nothing inconsistent with Congress's decision not to create a right of action and a decision to permit a case arising under the law to invoke federal question jurisdiction. As one commentator explains, "[t]o provide federal *jurisdiction* for a state-created cause of action . . . does not itself 'supplement' the federal remedy; the *state* remedy itself has already done that."[180] Second, the Court's conclusion would seem to dictate that *Smith* be overruled, because the holding in that case clearly is inconsistent with what the Court says. Oddly, however, the majority opinion did not overrule *Smith*. Instead, it tried to reconcile *Smith* and *Moore* by saying that the "nature of the federal interest" in *Smith* was more important than that in *Moore*.[181]

The dissent by Justice Brennan (found compelling by most commentators)[182] concludes that *Smith* and *Moore* are irreconcilable, and that *Moore* (which has never generated much of a following) ought to be overruled.[183] In its view, the majority's reliance on the "importance" of the federal interest is so malleable as to be unworkable. Indeed, in

[179]*Merrell Dow*, 478 U.S. at 812, n.10.

[180]15 Moore's Federal Practice §103.31[4] (emphases original).

[181]*Merrell Dow*, 478 U.S. at 814, n.12. The entire debate over the continued vitality of *Smith* is set forth in footnotes.

[182]*See, e.g.*, 15 Moore's Federal Practice §103.31[4]; Patti Alleva, *Prerogative Lost: The Trouble with Statutory Federal Question Doctrine After* Merrell Dow, 52 Ohio St. L.J. 1477 (1991); Martin Redish, *Reassessing the Allocation of Judicial Business Between State and Federal Courts: Federal Jurisdiction and "The Martian Chronicles,"* 78 Va. L. Rev. 1769 (1992).

[183]*Merrell Dow*, 478 U.S. at 821, n.1 (Brennan, J., dissenting).

the wake of *Merrell Dow,* lower courts were unclear as to whether the requirement of an important federal issue required a federal constitutional issue to be raised, rather than a federal statutory issue.

At a more fundamental level, the majority and dissenting opinions in *Merrell Dow* reflect different views of the role of federal question jurisdiction. The majority clearly sees the purpose of §1331 as providing a federal forum for the vindication of *federally created* remedies. If one adopts this view, the fact that Congress created no right of action means that a lower federal forum is not necessary—there is no federal right to vindicate. On the other hand, Justice Brennan embraced a broader view. To him, §1331 has a role in ensuring uniformity of federal law. In this view, there should be lower federal court jurisdiction whenever, as in *Merrell Dow,* the outcome of the case depends upon an *interpretation* of federal law.[184] (For that matter, under this view, there should be federal question jurisdiction in cases such as *Mottley.* See §4.6.4. Yet even Justice Brennan would refuse to undo the venerable well-pleaded complaint rule established in that case.[185])

Fortunately, *Merrell Dow* is not the last word. The Supreme Court gave some much-needed guidance in *Grable & Sons Metal Products v. Darue.*[186] In that case, the Internal Revenue Service (IRS) seized *P*'s land for nonpayment of taxes. After *P* failed to redeem the property, it was sold at public auction to *D.* Thereafter, *P* sued *D* in state court, on a state law claim for quiet title. *P*'s claim was that *D* did not receive valid title from the IRS because the IRS had failed to follow proper procedure for giving notice to *P* that it was in default on its taxes. *D* removed the case to federal court and a unanimous Supreme Court upheld federal question jurisdiction. In doing so, the Court revived *Smith* and rejected any notion that federal question jurisdiction required a federally created claim. Rather, a state law claim can satisfy the centrality requirement by implicating sufficiently a federal law. Thus, federal question jurisdiction exists at least in part to provide lower federal courts for the interpretation of federal law. And that federal law need not be constitutional—federal statutory issues can suffice.

Moreover, the Court set forth three factors for determining whether a state law claim should be seen to arise under federal law. Specifically, if (1) the case necessarily raises a federal issue, (2) the federal issue is actually disputed and substantial, and (3) federal jurisdiction will not disturb "any congressionally approved balance of federal and state

---

[184]Such lower court jurisdiction under §1331 would be necessary because the Supreme Court's discretionary review of cases decided by state courts can only be invoked rarely.

[185]Franchise Tax Bd. v. Construction Laborers Vacation Trust, 463 U.S. 1, 12 (1983).

[186]545 U.S. 308 (2005).

judicial responsibilities,"[187] the centrality requirement is satisfied. The test is wonderfully pragmatic. It permits a court to look at litigation reality—to assess whether the federal issue will actually be litigated if the case proceeds to trial. The third factor acts as a "veto" that can keep cases out of the federal courts if recognizing federal question jurisdiction would swamp those courts.

On the facts in *Grable*, all three factors supported federal question jurisdiction. First, the case necessarily raised the federal issue of what constitutes proper notice for an IRS proceeding. Second, that federal issue was actually disputed and was substantial. Indeed, as a matter of litigation reality, whether the IRS had satisfied the notice requirement of federal law was the *only* disputed issue. It was substantial because it implicated the federal government's interest in prompt collection of taxes. Third, the exercise of federal jurisdiction would not affect the allocation of cases between state and federal courts. Why? Because very few state law cases involving title to realty will raise a serious federal issue. Thus, exercising federal jurisdiction will not swamp the federal courts. In contrast, the Court said, recognizing federal question jurisdiction in *Merrell Dow* would have shifted an enormous number of tort cases from state to federal court.

This latter point can be seen in another way as well. By refusing to take cases that would swamp the federal courts, the *Grable* test also leaves to state courts the job of interpreting and developing state law. For instance, in *Merrell Dow,* the plaintiffs had asserted several cutting-edge common law tort theories under state law. Had the federal courts recognized federal question jurisdiction, many of those cases would have gone to federal court, which would have robbed the state courts to a degree of the ability to shape the development of state law.

The Court has applied the *Grable* holding twice, both times to reject federal question jurisdiction. First, in *Empire Healthchoice Assurance, Inc. v. McVeigh*,[188] an insurance company sued under state contract law to be reimbursed for benefits it had paid to an insured under a federal law. By contract, the insured was required to refund payments received from another source to the insurance company. The suit did not invoke federal question jurisdiction in part because it failed to satisfy the first *Grable* factor: As a matter of litigation reality, it was not clear that adjudication of the dispute required application of any federal law.

Second, *Gunn v. Minton*[189] is more important because it suggests that the three-factor *Grable* test (laid out four paragraphs above) is

---

[187]545 U.S. at 313-314.
[188]547 U.S. 677, 690-693 (2006).
[189]568 U.S. 251 (2013).

actually a four-factor test. Specifically, it splits what is listed as the second factor into two factors. So now *Grable* requires that: (1) the case necessarily raise a federal issue, (2) the federal issue actually be disputed, (3) the federal issue be substantial or significant, and (4) recognizing federal jurisdiction will not skew the proper allocation of cases between federal and state courts.[190] *Gunn* required the separate explication of what are now factors (2) and (3) because, on its facts, (2) was satisfied and (3) was not.

In *Gunn*, *P* held a patent on a computer program. He sued a third party for patent infringement. He lost that case, which resulted in a judgment holding his patent invalid. Now, *P* sued the lawyers who had represented him in the patent suit, alleging malpractice in handling his patent case. His claim for malpractice arose under state law. To prove malpractice, though, *P* would be required to demonstrate that had the lawyers raised a particular issue of federal patent law, he would have won the earlier case (and thus that his patent would have been held valid). Accordingly, (1) the case necessarily raised a federal issue and (2) that issue was actually in dispute (indeed, the outcome of the malpractice case hinged on it). But, the Court concluded, the issue was not sufficiently substantial or significant to justify federal jurisdiction. The Court emphasized that this inquiry (what is now the third factor in a *Grable* analysis) looks not to whether the question is important in the pending litigation (that will always be true). Rather, it "looks . . . to the importance of the issue to the federal system as a whole."[191] The question—whether *P* would have won the infringement suit had his lawyers raised a particular issue—did not implicate an important federal issue, in part because one way or the other *P*'s patent would remain invalid.[192] Thus, what is now the third factor under *Grable* is that the federal issue actually disputed in the case "is significant to the federal system as a whole."[193]

Grable, as refined in *Gunn*, is a welcome addition to the jurisprudence of the centrality requirement for federal question jurisdiction. The Holmes test will remain the first word on assessing centrality. Its hard-and-fast test will be determinative in most cases. But Holmes

---

[190]*See, e.g.*, Ranck v. Mt. Hood Cable Regulatory Comm'n., 2017 WL 1752954 at *2 (D. Ore. 2017) (interpreting *Grable* as setting out a four-factor test).

[191]568 U.S. at 258.

[192]Even if *P* won the malpractice case, the earlier judgment declaring his patent invalid would still stand. The Court distinguished *Smith*, where decision of the federal issue could affect the validity of securities issued by the federal government. 568 U.S. at 261.

[193]*Id.* at 263-264. For clarity, this factor might be called "significance" rather than "substantiality." Using the latter term confuses this point with the substantiality requirement discussed in §4.6.3.

is not always the last word. In appropriate cases, *Grable / Gunn* supplants its rule with a set of pragmatic standards.

§4.7 Supplemental Jurisdiction

§4.7.1 When You Need It and When You Don't Need It

Many people have trouble with supplemental jurisdiction. The trouble usually is caused by failing to understand what supplemental jurisdiction does. To this point, the plaintiff has filed a claim that invokes a basis of federal subject matter jurisdiction—she has filed a claim that meets the requirements of diversity of citizenship, alienage, or federal question jurisdiction.[194] We can say that this claim satisfies an "independent" basis of subject matter jurisdiction—it gets into federal court by itself. Because of this, the *case* is now in federal court. But (and this is crucial) there may be "additional" claims asserted in that case. The plaintiff herself may have additional claims in her original complaint (or may add some later by amendment). The defendant may assert claims in the pending case (maybe back against the plaintiff, maybe against a codefendant, maybe even against someone who has not yet been joined in the case). Indeed, an absentee (a nonparty) may intervene into the case and assert a claim or have a claim asserted against her. And here is the key: Every single claim asserted in a case in federal court (not just plaintiff's original claim that got the case into federal court) must satisfy a basis of federal subject matter jurisdiction.

We need to distinguish, then, between the original jurisdiction-invoking claim—the one that got the case into federal court—and these "additional" claims. We can refer to these simply as the "original" or "jurisdiction-invoking" claim, on the one hand, and "additional" claims, on the other. All of them must have a basis of subject matter jurisdiction, or they simply cannot be asserted in federal court. If an additional claim satisfies an independent basis of subject matter jurisdiction—such as diversity of citizenship, alienage, or federal question—it can be asserted in the pending case in federal court.

But what if one of these additional claims does *not* satisfy an independent basis of subject matter jurisdiction? Then, it is still possible that the claim can be heard in federal court under *supplemental jurisdiction.*

---

[194]Remember that there are other bases of federal subject matter jurisdiction, such as cases involving the United States as a party or disputes between an individual and a state. Civil Procedure courses rarely address such bases. The focus, as above in this chapter, is on diversity, alienage, and federal question.

Supplemental jurisdiction allows a federal court to hear *claims* that could not get into federal court by themselves—claims that do not invoke diversity, alienage, or federal question.[195] But two points are critical here. First, supplemental jurisdiction does not get the original *case* itself into federal court; it is only available for additional claims asserted in a case that is already properly in federal court. The plaintiff *absolutely must* assert at least one claim that meets diversity, alienage, or federal question (or some other basis of original federal subject matter jurisdiction) to get the *case* into federal court. After that happens, supplemental jurisdiction might be available to get *additional claims* into federal court. Second, supplemental jurisdiction is not needed if there is a standard independent basis of subject matter jurisdiction over the claim. In other words, supplemental jurisdiction is only relevant if there is no diversity, alienage, or federal question jurisdiction over the claim.

- ○ ***Example #38.*** *P*, a citizen of Minnesota, asserts a state law claim against *D*, also a Minnesota citizen. This case cannot go to federal court. There is no diversity of citizenship jurisdiction, and there is no federal question jurisdiction (because *P* is asserting a state law claim). Supplemental jurisdiction cannot apply here; it is not available until a case is properly in federal court.

- ○ ***Example #39.*** *P*, a citizen of Minnesota, sues *D*, a citizen of Wisconsin, alleging (1) that *D* violated *P*'s rights under the federal securities law and (2) that *D* also violated *P*'s rights under state securities law. *P* claims damages of $400,000. Here, claim (1) invokes federal question jurisdiction, so the case gets into federal court. Claim (2) invokes diversity of citizenship jurisdiction. So claim (2) has an independent basis of federal jurisdiction. It "belongs" in federal court by itself. Thus, supplemental jurisdiction is irrelevant.

- ○ ***Example #40.*** *P*, a citizen of Minnesota, sues *D*, also a citizen of Minnesota, alleging (1) that *D* violated *P*'s rights under the federal securities law and (2) that *D* also violated *P*'s rights under state securities law. *P* claims damages of $400,000. Here, claim (1) invokes federal question jurisdiction, so the case gets into federal court. Claim (2), however, does not satisfy diversity of citizenship jurisdiction (because there is no diversity at all). Claim (2) also does not invoke federal question jurisdiction (because *P* is asserting a state law claim).

Supplemental jurisdiction may apply to get claim (2) into federal court. First, the case itself is already in federal court (because claim (1) invoked federal question jurisdiction), so we are talking here about jurisdiction over an additional claim. Second, this additional claim cannot invoke one of the basic, independent bases of subject matter jurisdiction. The only way a federal court can hear claim (2) is if the court exercises supplemental jurisdiction over it.

[195]Or any other basis of original federal subject matter jurisdiction.

§4.7.2 The Constitutionality of Supplemental Jurisdiction: The *Gibbs* Test

Supplemental jurisdiction gets nonfederal, nondiversity additional claims into federal court. How can this be constitutional? After all, the federal courts have limited subject matter jurisdiction (basically, for our purposes, hearing diversity of citizenship, alienage, and federal question cases). How can it be constitutional for a federal court to entertain claims that do not satisfy one of the limited bases of federal subject matter jurisdiction?

The answer: When the plaintiff files an original claim that invokes federal subject matter jurisdiction (e.g., a diversity, alienage, or federal question claim), the federal court takes jurisdiction over the entire "case" or "controversy" of which that claim is part. Article III grants subject matter jurisdiction over "cases" or "controversies" involving the various heads of federal jurisdiction.[196] Thus, the Supreme Court has long recognized that a federal court may take jurisdiction over claims that do not, by themselves, satisfy an independent basis of federal subject matter jurisdiction *if and only if* the claims are so closely related to the claim that invoked the federal court's jurisdiction as to be considered part of the same case or controversy as that claim. In other words, if the additional claim is so closely related to the plaintiff's original claim (which invoked diversity, alienage, or federal question) as to be part of the same overall dispute, the federal court can hear the additional claim. It does so through supplemental jurisdiction.

Although the Supreme Court first recognized the concept of supplemental jurisdiction in 1861,[197] and had addressed the topic sporadically through the years,[198] the most important case is *United Mine Workers v. Gibbs*,[199] decided in 1966. In that case, both the plaintiff and the defendant were citizens of Tennessee,[200] so there was no possibility of diversity jurisdiction. Simplifying a bit, the plaintiff asserted two

---

[196]In listing federal subject matter jurisdiction, Article III, §2, refers to "cases" involving some heads of jurisdiction and "controversies" involving others. There is no difference in the scope of a case and a controversy. Similarly, the statutory grants of diversity, alienage, and federal question jurisdiction extend jurisdiction to the entire "civil action," and not simply to the individual claim that gets the case into federal court.

[197]Freeman v. Howe, 65 U.S. 450, 460-461 (1861).

[198]*See, e.g.*, Hurn v. Oursler, 289 U.S. 238, 245-246 (1933).

[199]383 U.S. 715 (1966).

[200]The plaintiff was human. Why was he a citizen of Tennessee? The defendant was an unincorporated association. Why was it a citizen of Tennessee? Constantly test these points, so they become second nature to you. (The answers: Citizens of the United States are deemed citizens for diversity purposes of the state in which they are domiciled; unincorporated associations are deemed citizens of all states of which their members are citizens.) See §4.5.3.

claims: (1) that defendant had violated his rights under federal labor laws and (2) that the same behavior by the defendant also violated the plaintiff's rights under state law. Obviously, claim (1) invoked federal question jurisdiction (because the claim arose under federal law). Just as obviously, claim (2) failed to invoke either diversity or federal question jurisdiction (the parties are co-citizens and the claim arose under state, not federal, law). Stated another way, claim (2), by itself, could not get into federal court; it did not have an independent basis of subject matter jurisdiction.

The Court held that the federal courts had supplemental (which it called "pendent") jurisdiction[201] over claim (2) because that claim "derive[d] from a common nucleus of operative fact" with the claim that invoked federal subject matter jurisdiction.[202] Claims sharing such a common nucleus of operative fact, then, are part of the same constitutional case or controversy as the claim that invoked federal jurisdiction, and thus may be decided by the federal court. Through the years, courts and commentators agreed that the "common nucleus" test is always satisfied if claims arise from the same "transaction or occurrence" (indeed, we will see below, "common nucleus" is even broader than "transaction or occurrence").[203] This is a nice equation, because many of the joinder rules under the Federal Rules (as we see throughout Chapter 12) use the "transaction or occurrence" label.

Gibbs presented another interesting problem. Before it got to the Supreme Court, the case had been tried, and the jury had returned a verdict for the plaintiff on both claim (1) and claim (2). But the trial

[201]Before the supplemental jurisdiction statute, §1367, was passed in 1990, courts spoke not of "supplemental" but of "pendent" and "ancillary" jurisdiction. (Largely, pendent referred to claims by plaintiffs while ancillary referred to claims by nonplaintiffs.) With §1367, Congress employed a generic rubric—supplemental jurisdiction—for the entire area. So do not let older cases' discussion of pendent or ancillary jurisdiction bother you; today, the entire area is known as supplemental jurisdiction.

[202]Stated more pragmatically, the Court said that supplemental jurisdiction would be proper over claims that one "would ordinarily . . . expect[] to try . . . all in one judicial proceeding." *Gibbs*, 383 U.S. at 726-727. Oddly, the quoted matter is preceded with "But if," as opposed to "And if." Realistically, however, the point quoted will rarely be all that meaningful. Obviously, if claims are transactionally related, one would expect to try them together, since evidence of one set of facts would underlie both claims. Moreover, as we see in §11.2, the doctrine of claim preclusion may require the plaintiff to assert transactionally related claims in a single case or else waive the right to assert them.

[203]This point is made most clearly in §12.5.1, concerning supplemental jurisdiction over permissive counterclaims. These claims do not arise from the same transaction or occurrence as the underlying case, but can, depending on the facts, invoke supplemental jurisdiction. Though the Federal Rules cannot expand the jurisdiction of the federal courts, Fed. R. Civ. P. 82, the Supreme Court in *Gibbs* recognized that the Rules' view of the appropriate joinder was entitled to respect. *Gibbs*, 383 U.S. at 725.

judge threw out the verdict on claim (1) because he held, as a matter of law, that the evidence did not support it.[204] So the *only* claim left in the case for final judgment was one over which there was only supplemental jurisdiction. The jurisdiction-invoking claim was now gone! Can a federal court enter a judgment on a supplemental claim? The Supreme Court answered the question by distinguishing between a federal court's *power* and its *discretionary decision* to use supplemental jurisdiction.

If the nonfederal, nondiversity claim meets the common nucleus test, the federal court has *power* to hear it. Jurisdiction is proper. But, according to the Court, there is a series of discretionary factors under which a court with power to hear the claim might decide not to exercise it. We discuss these factors in detail below. For example, if the jurisdiction-invoking claim is dismissed early in the proceedings, or if the state law issues predominate substantially in the litigation, or if trying the jurisdiction-invoking claim together with the additional claim would confuse the jury, the court may decline to exercise supplemental jurisdiction.[205] In *Gibbs*, the nonfederal, nondiverse claim satisfied the common nucleus test (because the same behavior was alleged to violate federal and state law) and was not dismissed until after trial (in other words, only after the federal court had invested a good deal of time and effort). Thus, there was power and none of the discretionary factors required declining it. The Supreme Court upheld the judgment of the trial court.

Note the practical consequences of supplemental jurisdiction. Suppose the Court had not permitted supplemental jurisdiction over claim (2) in *Gibbs*. One of two things would have ensued, both of them bad. First, because the plaintiff could not bring claim (2) in federal court, she would proceed in federal court only on claim (1) and file a separate action based upon claim (2) in state court. This result is inefficient for the plaintiff, who now must pay for (and prosecute) two separate lawsuits. It is also inefficient for the judicial system, since it requires two cases in two systems to decide a dispute arising from a single set of facts. (Plus, it is conceivable that the two cases would be resolved inconsistently, which might erode public confidence in the judicial system.) Second, the plaintiff can avoid these problems only by filing both claims (1) and (2) in state court. This route is efficient but requires the plaintiff to forego a federal forum for her federal claim. Moreover, if the jurisdiction-invoking claim were within the exclusive

---

[204]When *Gibbs* was decided, this procedure was called judgment notwithstanding the verdict (JNOV). Now it's called a renewed motion for judgment as a matter of law. See §9.5.

[205]*Gibbs*, 383 U.S. at 727.

jurisdiction of the federal courts, she could not do this, and would have to proceed with two cases.

Thus, supplemental jurisdiction fosters efficiency, convenience, and consistency of outcome. It permits a federal court to determine all claims that are factually related to a claim that invokes federal subject matter jurisdiction. But supplemental jurisdiction raises some problems. Notably, if extended to its limits in diversity cases, supplemental jurisdiction would eviscerate the complete diversity rule. For example, suppose *P*, a citizen of Maryland, sues *D-1*, a citizen of Virginia, on a state law claim for $400,000. This claim invokes diversity of citizenship jurisdiction. Now suppose *P* adds a factually related state law claim against *D-2*, a citizen of Maryland. This claim does not invoke either diversity or federal question. But because it arises from the same transaction as the claim against *D-1* (which is properly in federal court), it satisfies the common nucleus test of *Gibbs* and thus can be supported by supplemental jurisdiction. To do so, though, makes a mockery of the complete diversity rule of *Strawbridge* (§4.5.3). In addition, it would risk inundating the federal courts with too many cases. Through the years, the Supreme Court tried to balance the desire for supplemental jurisdiction with the need to protect the complete diversity rule.[206]

From 1861 until 1990, the federal courts made the rules concerning supplemental jurisdiction with no general involvement from Congress.[207] This fact might create a constitutional problem, because the Constitution empowers Congress (not the courts) to prescribe the subject matter jurisdiction of the federal courts. Nonetheless, the Court continually indicated that supplemental jurisdiction was proper as long as the *Gibbs* test was met and as long as Congress had not *prohibited* it. Thus, the Court created a presumption that Congress approved supplemental jurisdiction over claims satisfying *Gibbs* unless Congress acted to reject such jurisdiction.[208] In other words, congressional silence was to be seen as congressional approval of supplemental jurisdiction. This presumption went unquestioned until 1989, when the Supreme Court decided *Finley v. United States*.[209]

---

[206]*See, e.g.*, Owen Equip. & Erection Co. v. Kroger, 437 U.S. 365, 377 (1978), which we refer to as *Kroger* and discuss in detail when we address impleader at §12.6.2.

[207]Except, however, with regard to patent cases. Section 1338(b) permits supplemental jurisdiction over state law claims related to patent infringement actions even in the absence of diversity jurisdiction.

[208]In *Aldinger v. Howard*, 427 U.S. 1, 18-19 (1976), the Court concluded that Congress had precluded supplemental jurisdiction in cases brought under 42 U.S.C. §1983, which permits civil actions against state actors for violation of federal constitutional rights. The Court found a clear congressional mandate to this effect despite the fact that Congress made absolutely no mention of supplemental jurisdiction in that statute or any of its legislative history. *See also Kroger*, 437 U.S. 365 (1978).

[209]490 U.S. 545 (1989).

§4.7.3 The *Finley* Case Leads to the Supplemental Jurisdiction Statute

In *Finley*, the plaintiff's husband and children were killed in the crash of a small airplane. She had two theories of liability. First, the Federal Aviation Administration (FAA) might be liable because of negligence in air traffic control and maintenance of runway lights. Second, the city and a utility company might be liable for maintaining electrical power lines too close to the airfield. The plaintiff sued the FAA,[210] asserting liability under the Federal Tort Claims Act (FTCA), which gives exclusive federal jurisdiction. She also joined a claim against the city and utility for liability under state tort law. The claim against the FAA invoked federal question jurisdiction, but the claim against the city and utility did not invoke federal question or diversity jurisdiction. Thus, the only way to have the latter heard in federal court was through supplemental jurisdiction. Courts at the time spoke of such a case as involving "pendent parties" jurisdiction, because the nonfederal, nondiverse claim involved a different party from the claim that invoked federal subject matter jurisdiction.[211]

Under *Gibbs*, supplemental jurisdiction was clearly constitutional, because the state law claim shared a common nucleus of operative fact with the jurisdiction-invoking FTCA claim; both claims arose from the same crash. But the Supreme Court, in a five-to-four decision, rejected supplemental jurisdiction. Along the way, the Court reversed the presumption in favor of supplemental jurisdiction in the absence of congressional action. Instead of presuming that supplemental jurisdiction applies if the *Gibbs* test is met and Congress has not precluded it, the Court held that there can be no supplemental jurisdiction unless Congress *affirmatively granted* it. Since Congress had never addressed the issue of supplemental jurisdiction under the FTCA, the Court reasoned, it did not exist.

The decision created a nightmare for the plaintiff. Mrs. Finley was forced to continue her case against the FAA in federal court (because federal courts have exclusive jurisdiction over FTCA cases) and to file her claims against the city and the utility in state court. Thus, she (and the taxpayers) had to pay for two suits and run the risk of inconsistent judgments, despite the obvious fact that there had been only one crash. Moreover, the Court's broad language reversing

[210]Actually, because the FAA is a federal agency, the claim was against the United States, which has waived its sovereign immunity under the Federal Tort Claims Act.

[211]In contrast, *Gibbs* involved "pendent claim" jurisdiction because the nonfederal, nondiversity claim involved the same party as the claim that invoked federal subject matter jurisdiction.

the historic presumption (in favor of supplemental jurisdiction in the absence of congressional action) may have threatened all supplemental jurisdiction.

Because of this, Congress responded to *Finley* with a statute that addressed the whole area, rather than simply overrule the result in *Finley*.[212] In short order, Congress passed the supplemental jurisdiction statute, §1367. The stated aims of the statute were to overrule the result in *Finley* and, in other respects, to codify the practice that the courts had developed before *Finley*. This statute now governs all questions of supplemental jurisdiction in general civil cases.

The statute has accomplished some of the stated goals. It clarified the language by creating a generic term—supplemental jurisdiction—for what had previously been called pendent and ancillary jurisdiction. It also ensured that the wasteful result wrought by *Finley* would not befall other plaintiffs. But the statute also created problems that did not previously exist.[213] Rather than codify pre-*Finley* practice, it changed that practice overtly in some ways and inadvertently in others. Nonetheless, it is the law, and we must be able to work with it.

§4.7.4   Applying the Supplemental Jurisdiction Statute: Jurisdictional Aspects

Before looking at the statute in detail, note the overall structure of §1367. Subsection (a) is the grant of supplemental jurisdiction. After *Finley*, Congress felt it necessary to make an affirmative grant of supplemental jurisdiction. Subsection (b) then withdraws supplemental jurisdiction in certain instances. Understanding those instances is critical to successful application of the statute. Subsection (c) is

---

[212]Interestingly, the federal courts addressing the impact of *Finley* had basically limited it to its facts. *See, e.g.*, Alumax Mill Prods., Inc. v. Congress Fin. Corp., 912 F.2d 996, 1005-1007 (8th Cir. 1990). Nonetheless, most observers concluded that a well-crafted universal supplemental jurisdiction statute would be a good idea.

[213]Section 1367 generated a stunning amount of commentary. The first article criticizing the statute was Richard D. Freer, *Compounding Confusion and Hampering Diversity: Life After* Finley *and the Supplemental Jurisdiction Statute*, 40 Emory L.J. 445 (1991). This provoked a response from three professors who were involved in drafting the statute. Thomas D. Rowe, Stephen B. Burbank & Thomas M. Mengler, *Compounding or Creating Confusion About Supplemental Jurisdiction? A Reply to Professor Freer*, 40 Emory L.J. 943 (1991). This, in turn, led to a spirited debate between those professors, defending the statute, and Professor Freer and Professor Thomas Arthur, criticizing the statute. *See* 40 Emory L.J. 943-1014 (1991). This colloquy was followed by an exchange of other commentators at 41 Emory L.J. 31 (1992). Later, there was a symposium concerning possible amendments to §1367 at 74 Ind. L.J. 1 (1998). There are scores of articles in between and after.

Congress's effort to codify the discretionary factors the Court set forth in *Gibbs*, in which the court might decline to exercise supplemental jurisdiction. Subsection (d) is a tolling provision, which stops the running of the statute of limitations in certain instances. Finally, subsection (e) defines "State" to include the District of Columbia and other political subdivisions, just as §1332(d) does.

Subsection (a) grants supplemental jurisdiction in the broadest possible terms. Congress was quite clear that it intended to reach to the full extent of Article III in permitting federal courts to exercise supplemental jurisdiction. There is little doubt that §1367(a) is meant to codify the *Gibbs* common nucleus test.[214] Thus, §1367(a) grants supplemental jurisdiction over all claims asserted in a federal civil action if they share a common nucleus of operative fact with the claim that invoked federal subject matter jurisdiction in the case.[215] The last sentence of that subsection makes it clear that supplemental jurisdiction includes claims involving additional parties, which makes it clear that the statute overrules the result in *Finley*.

As we discussed above, though, such a grant of supplemental jurisdiction would eviscerate the complete diversity rule, unless Congress restrained it in some way. Congress addressed this problem in §1367(b). It is imperative that we understand three things about §1367(b). First, it prohibits supplemental jurisdiction. Accordingly, although subsection (a) gives such jurisdiction, subsection (b) takes it away in certain circumstances. Second, §1367(b) *applies only in cases in which the jurisdiction-invoking claim was asserted solely under §1332*. In other words, §1367(b) is never applicable if the plaintiff's original claim—the one that got the case into federal court in the first place—invoked federal question jurisdiction. It applies only if that original claim was brought solely under diversity jurisdiction.[216]

---

[214]H.R. Rep. 734, 101st Cong., 2d Sess. (1990), *reprinted in* 1990 U.S.C.C.A.N. 6873, 6875 n.15. While everyone agrees that this test includes claims arising from the same transaction or occurrence as a jurisdiction-invoking claim, courts generally conclude that the statute is broader. One representative opinion concludes that the statute requires nothing more than some "loose factual connection" between the claims. *See, e.g.*, Jones v. Ford Motor Credit Co., 358 F.3d 205, 210-215 (2d Cir. 2004) (upholding supplemental jurisdiction over permissive counterclaim). *See also* Global Naps, Inc. v. Verizon New England Inc., 603 F.3d 71, 76 (1st Cir. 2010) (same). The issue is discussed in more detail at §12.5.1.

[215]The statute does not say this expressly. Rather, it speaks of granting supplemental jurisdiction to the extent of Article III. *Gibbs* is universally regarded as defining the Article III reach of supplemental jurisdiction.

[216]Apparently, the restrictions of §1367(b) also apply if original jurisdiction were based upon alienage. This seems clear because §1367(b) refers to cases brought under §1332, not just under §1332(a)(1) (diversity). Some professors who assisted in drafting the legislation have indicated that they did not intend §1367(b) to apply in alienage cases, but the statute, on its face, seems to do so.

Third, §1367(b)'s prohibition of supplemental jurisdiction in diversity cases applies only to claims asserted by plaintiffs or parties subsequently joined on the plaintiff's side of the litigation.[217] Study the language carefully. Although the statute does not delineate these categories specifically, it is handy to break the detailed provisions of §1367(b) into three parts. Doing so makes it clear that the section precludes supplemental jurisdiction over three categories of claims:

(1) "claims *by plaintiffs* against persons made parties under Rule 14, 19, 20, or 24 of the Federal Rules . . .";

(2) "claims by persons proposed to be joined *as plaintiffs* under Rule 19 . . ."; and

(3) claims by persons "seeking to intervene *as plaintiffs* under Rule 24 . . ." (emphasis added).

Note, then, that §1367(b) does not apply to claims asserted by parties other than plaintiffs. Thus, claims satisfying §1367(a) asserted in a diversity case *by a defendant (or a party joined on the defendant's side)* will invoke supplemental jurisdiction.

In Chapter 12, we address these Federal Rules to which the statute refers, and we address the availability of supplemental jurisdiction over each kind of claim at that time. It is more effective to review the availability of supplemental jurisdiction for each type of claim when we study the procedural availability of each type of claim. For now, the important point is to understand that §1367(b) precludes supplemental jurisdiction claims only when (1) asserted in diversity jurisdiction cases (2) by plaintiffs. Even without knowing the intricacies of the various Federal Rules, we can apply the statute in the following fact patterns.

o ***Example #41: The Gibbs Scenario.*** *P*, a citizen of Tennessee, sues *D*, a citizen of Tennessee, asserting (1) violation of federal labor law and (2) violation of state labor law. The two claims are based upon the same alleged actions by *D*. Claim (1) invokes federal question jurisdiction but claim (2) does not satisfy diversity or federal question jurisdiction.[218] Claim (2) invokes supplemental jurisdiction under §1367(a) because it arises from a common nucleus of operative fact as claim (1) (the jurisdiction-invoking claim). Section 1367(b) does not apply at all, because the underlying basis of subject matter jurisdiction in the case (the reason the case is in federal court in the first place) is *not* §1332.

---

[217]As we see in Chapter 12, various joinder rules provide for addition of parties after the case has been filed.

[218]There is no diversity because *P* and *D* are co-citizens. There is no federal question jurisdiction over claim (2) because it is based upon state, not federal, law.

(Rather, it is §1331 (federal question).) So supplemental jurisdiction supports claim (2).

○ ***Example #42: The* Finley *Scenario.*** *P*, a citizen of California, asserts (1) an FTCA claim against the FAA and (2) a state law negligence claim against *D-2*, who is a citizen of California. The claims arise from a single airplane crash. Claim (1) invokes federal question jurisdiction but claim (2) does not satisfy diversity or federal question. Claim (2) invokes supplemental jurisdiction under §1367(a) because it arises from a common nucleus of operative fact as claim (1). Under the last sentence of §1367(a), it is irrelevant that supplemental jurisdiction is sought for a claim against an additional party, as in this hypothetical. Section 1367(b) does not apply, because the underlying basis of subject matter jurisdiction in the case is *not* §1332. (Again, it is §1331.) So supplemental jurisdiction applies to claim (2).

○ ***Example #43.*** *P*, a citizen of Michigan, sues *D*, a citizen of Iowa, on a state law claim for $400,000. *D* asserts a counterclaim (which is a claim against an opposing party) against *P* for $60,000; the counterclaim arises from the same transaction as *P*'s claim. *P*'s claim invokes diversity jurisdiction, but *D*'s counterclaim does not satisfy diversity jurisdiction (because it does not exceed $75,000) and does not satisfy federal question (because it is based upon state law).[219] *D*'s claim satisfies supplemental jurisdiction under §1367(a) because it arises from a common nucleus of operative fact as *P*'s claim (which invoked federal subject matter jurisdiction by invoking diversity jurisdiction). But §1367(b) must be addressed, because the underlying basis of jurisdiction in the case is §1332. Here, however, the prohibition against supplemental jurisdiction does not apply, because this is not a claim by a plaintiff or by one joined on the plaintiff's side of the case. It is by a defendant. Thus, supplemental jurisdiction applies to claim (2).

§4.7.5 Applying the Supplemental Jurisdiction Statute: Discretionary Aspects

We saw above that in *Gibbs*, the Supreme Court distinguished between the *power* to exercise supplemental jurisdiction and the *discretion* to refuse to do so. According to *Gibbs*, supplemental jurisdiction is rooted in "considerations of judicial economy, convenience, and fairness to litigants; if these are not present a federal court should hesitate to exercise jurisdiction over state claims."[220] These have come

---

[219]Remember that we address supplemental jurisdiction only if we need it. If the facts were the same but *D*'s claim against *P* were for $80,000, *D*'s claim would invoke diversity jurisdiction (since it would be by a citizen of Iowa against a citizen of Michigan and would exceed $75,000). In that instance, supplemental jurisdiction would be irrelevant.

[220]*Gibbs*, 383 U.S. at 726.

to be known as the "animating values" of supplemental jurisdiction under *Gibbs*. The Court then gave three examples of when these animating values might lead a court to refuse to exercise supplemental jurisdiction: first, if the federal claims were dismissed early in the proceedings; second, if the state issues "substantially predominate, whether in terms of proof, of the scope of the issues raised, or of the comprehensiveness of the remedy sought"; and third, if considerations of "judicial economy, convenience, and fairness to litigants" counseled such a refusal to exercise supplemental jurisdiction.[221] Specifically, the Court noted that a "likelihood of jury confusion in treating divergent legal theories of relief . . . that would justify separating state and federal claims for trial."[222]

In passing the supplemental jurisdiction statute, Congress embraced the notion that the court has discretion to decline to exercise supplemental jurisdiction. Rather than leave the discretionary factors to case law development, Congress codified them in §1367(c). Despite a stated objective of codifying the law as it existed under *Gibbs,* the statute fails to do so in two ways. First, it does not refer at all to the "animating values" of "judicial economy, convenience, and fairness to litigants." Instead, it sets out examples of when a court might decline supplemental jurisdiction. Second, its list of examples does not track that in *Gibbs*. Section 1367(c) provides that a court "may decline to exercise supplemental jurisdiction over a claim" on the basis of any of these factors: (1) the claim "raises a novel or complex issue of State law"; (2) the claim "substantially predominates" over the claim that invoked federal subject matter jurisdiction; (3) the court "has dismissed all claims over which it has original jurisdiction"; or (4) "in exceptional circumstances, there are other compelling reasons for declining jurisdiction."

The first two statutory factors relate to the *Gibbs* concern that the state law tail should not wag the federal dog. That is, if the major thrust of the case would be state law—either because the claims predominate or involve novel questions (which presumably should be left to state courts to decide)—the court may decline jurisdiction. The third statutory factor relates to the first *Gibbs* factor. These recognize the most obvious basis for declining supplemental jurisdiction—that the claims that got the case into federal court initially have been dismissed. When this happens early in the proceedings (e.g., before the federal court has invested considerable time in the supplemental claim) it makes sense to dismiss and let the parties litigate

---

[221]*Id.* at 726-727.
[222]*Id.* at 727.

the supplemental claim in state court. On the other hand, if the jurisdiction-invoking claims are dismissed late (e.g., after the court has invested time and resources in the litigation of the supplemental claim) it may make sense to keep the supplemental claim for final decision in federal court.[223] The specific example discussed in *Gibbs* of avoiding jury confusion is not reflected in the statute.

In view of Congress's failure to mention the "animating values" and to track the *Gibbs* examples carefully, courts have gone down somewhat different roads. The big question is whether the "animating values" have any significance independent of the terms of §1367(c). The majority view — adopted by the Second, Third, Eighth, Ninth, Tenth, and Eleventh Circuits — is that unless one of the factors of §1367(c) is met, the court *must* exercise supplemental jurisdiction.[224] In other words, the court has no discretion to decline jurisdiction unless one of the four statutory bases is satisfied. Once one of the statutory factors applies, however, the court may look to the full range of *Gibbs's* "animating values" of "judicial economy, convenience, and fairness to litigants" to decide whether to decline jurisdiction.[225]

The second approach — adopted by the Seventh and District of Columbia Circuits — is that §1367(c) does not restrain the common law discretion of *Gibbs*.[226] These courts will not say that a court *must* exercise supplemental jurisdiction whenever a specific provision of §1367(c) does not apply. Indeed, they seem to conclude that the *Gibbs* discretionary factors operate independently of the statute. It is worth noting, however, that neither court seems to have permitted a discretionary decline of jurisdiction in the absence of a statutory factor under §1367(c).[227]

---

[223]Indeed, this is exactly what happened in *Gibbs,* when the federal question claims were dismissed only after trial.

[224]*See, e.g.*, Catzin v. Thank You & Good Luck Corp., 899 F.3d 77, 85-86 (2d Cir. 2018); Shariar v. Smith & Wollensky Rest. Gp., 659 F.3d 234, 239 (2d Cir. 2011); Oliver v. Ralphs Grocery Co., 654 F.3d 903 (9th Cir. 2011); Estate of Amergi ex rel. Amergi v. Palestinian Auth., 611 F.3d 1350, 1366 (11th Cir. 2010); Nielander v. Board of Cnty. Commrs., 582 F.3d 1155, 1172 (10th Cir. 2009); McLaurin v. Prater, 30 F.3d 982, 983 (8th Cir. 1994); Growth Horizons, Inc. v. Del. Cnty., Pa., 983 F.2d 1277, 1283 (3d Cir. 1993).

[225]*See, e.g., Shahriar*, 659 F.3d at 250 n.9 ("[E]ven if one of the four statutory bases were applicable, it would still be error to decline supplemental jurisdiction where exercising it would promote the values of economy, convenience, fairness and comity identified in [*Gibbs*]"); *Catzin*, 899 F.3d at 86.

[226]LaShawn A. v. Barry, 87 F.3d 1389, 1393 (D.C. Cir. 1996); Timm v. Mead Corp., 32 F.3d 273, 276-277 (7th Cir. 1994).

[227]Indeed, the Seventh Circuit may subsequently require citation to a statutory factor. Montano v. City of Chicago, 375 F.3d 593, 602 (7th Cir. 2004) (reversing rejection of supplemental jurisdiction, noting district court's failure to cite statutory basis for its decision).

The Fifth Circuit has adopted a third approach. It concluded that courts must balance what it calls the *Gibbs* "animating factors" *with* the statutory provisions of §1367(c).[228] A spirited dissent in that Fifth Circuit case argued that "[o]n its face, §1367(c) is a list of situations in which it may be permissible for a district court to remand pendent state law claims, and not a set of factors to be balanced."[229]

The split of approach means that the ultimate scope of discretion under §1367(c) is not entirely clear. For example, can a court decline supplemental jurisdiction (as it could under *Gibbs*) because it is likely that the jury will be confused if both the original jurisdiction-invoking claim and the supplemental claim are tried together? No factor in §1367(c) expressly addresses the issue. Perhaps, at least for some courts, such a case would fall within the discretion accorded under §1367(c)(4), as an exceptional circumstance.

When a court exercises its discretion under §1367(c) and declines supplemental jurisdiction, it dismisses only the supplemental claim. It does not dismiss the original claim that properly invoked federal subject matter jurisdiction.[230]

> o *Example #44.* P asserts two claims against *D*: (1) for violation of federal antitrust laws and (2) for violation of state antitrust laws. The two claims arise from a common nucleus of operative fact. *P* and *D* are co-citizens, so there is no diversity of citizenship jurisdiction. Claim (1) invokes federal question jurisdiction. Claim (2) does not (because it arises under state law), and also does not invoke diversity of citizenship jurisdiction, as we just saw.

Claim (2) invokes supplemental jurisdiction because it shares a common nucleus of operative fact with claim (1). Suppose the court makes the discretionary determination that it will decline supplemental jurisdiction because, for instance, claim (2) would predominate substantially and involves novel questions of law. The court will dismiss only claim (2). Claim (1) will continue through litigation in federal court.

§4.7.6 The Tolling Provision of the Supplemental Jurisdiction Statute: §1367(d)

When the court dismisses the state-law claim under §1367(c), it does so without prejudice, so the plaintiff can assert the claim in state

---

[228]Enochs v. Lampasas Cnty., 641 F.3d 155, 159-161 (5th Cir. 2011). The court also considered comity as one of the *Gibbs* animating factors. *Id.* at 159.
[229]*Id.* at 164 (Prado, J., dissenting).
[230]*See, e.g.,* Borough of West Mifflin v. Lancaster, 45 F.3d 780, 787 (3d Cir. 1995).

court.[231] The plaintiff might worry, however, about whether the statute of limitations has run on her claim. Section 1367(d) allays her fears (at least to a degree) by providing that the plaintiff may file her case in state court within 30 days after the federal court dismissal under §1367(c). Courts disagreed, however, on whether this provision operates to toll the state statute of limitations or, instead, merely provides a 30-day grace period (after dismissal of the state-law claim) in which to assert the state claim.

> ○ ***Example #45.*** *P* files in federal court, asserting a federal question claim and a state-law claim that invokes supplemental jurisdiction. She files this case 50 days before the statute of limitations would have run on her state-law claim. A year later, the federal court dismisses the federal question claim and dismisses the state-law claim under §1367(c)(3). Everyone agrees that *P* now has 30 days in which to file her state law claim in state court. But what if she does not file, say, until 40 days after the federal court dismissed under §1367(c)? Is she barred because §1367(d) merely gives the 30-day grace period and does not operate to stop the state statute of limitations from continuing to run during pendency of the federal suit? Or is she protected because she files in state court within 50 days after the federal dismissal?

The Supreme Court resolved the debate in 2018: §1367(d) is a true tolling provision, which means that the state statute of limitations is held in abeyance during the pendency of the federal suit.[232] (We discuss tolling in §7.6.3.) In Example #45, then, *P*'s claim is asserted in a timely fashion. Why? Because she filed the federal suit (including the state-law claim) 50 days before the statute ran; tolling means that the statute does not advance while the case is pending, so she now gets those 50 days after the federal dismissal of the state-law claim in which to file in state court.

It is clear that the tolling provision of §1367(d) applies when a claim is dismissed under §1367(c). By the better view, §1367(d) applies *only*

---

[231]*See, e.g.,* Gold v. Local 7 United Food & Commercial Workers Union, 159 F.3d 1307, 1311 (10th Cir. 1998).

[232]Artis v. District of Columbia, 138 S. Ct. 594, 600-606 (2018). The lower court had held, incorrectly it turns out, that §1367(d) provides only a grace period and does not otherwise toll a state statute of limitations. On the other hand, the Court held that §1367(d) does not toll the statute of limitations on a claim dismissed under the Eleventh Amendment. Raygor v. Regents of Univ. of Minn., 534 U.S. 533, 542 (2002). The Eleventh Amendment removes jurisdiction of *federal* courts to entertain cases brought against a state (or an "arm" of a state). It does not prohibit suits against states in *state* court. Thus, the fact that the claim in *Raygor* could not be asserted in federal court did not mean that the plaintiff could not sue in state court. But, the Court held, the statute of limitations on the claim dismissed under the Eleventh Amendment was not tolled under §1367(d).

to such dismissals. Suppose instead the court dismisses a state law claim because it does not satisfy the requirements for supplemental jurisdiction. Section 1367(d) should not apply to this dismissed claim. Why? Because it provides for tolling for a "claim asserted under subsection (a)." A claim that did not properly invoke supplemental jurisdiction is not a "claim asserted under [§1367](a)."

§4.8 Removal Jurisdiction

§4.8.1 The Concepts of Removal and Remand

To this point, the decision to proceed in federal court has been made by the plaintiff. Removal is a remarkable procedure that gives the *defendant* sued in state court the authority to "remove" the case to federal court. This allows the defendant to override the plaintiff's choice of forum. (As discussed in detail below, this is only possible in a case that satisfies a basis of federal subject matter jurisdiction.) Removal is not mentioned in the Constitution and is wholly the product of statutory law. Today, most provisions for removal jurisdiction and procedure in general civil cases[233] are found in §§1441, 1446, and 1447.

Removal, then, is a mechanism to transfer a case, at the defendant's behest, from a *state* trial court to a *federal* trial court.[234] Although removal effects a transfer of the case, we do not call it *transfer. Transfer* is a term of art to lawyers and judges and, as we see in §5.5, refers to changing venue from one *federal* trial court to another *federal* trial court (or from one state trial court to another state trial court in the same state). What we deal with here—going from a state trial court to a federal trial court—is referred to with the term of art *removal.* Remember that removal is a one-way street. A case can be removed *only* from state court to federal court. If a case is removed to federal court improperly (either because the defendant made a procedural mistake or because there is no federal subject matter jurisdiction), the federal court can *remand* the case to state court.

---

[233]There are several specialized statutes allowing removal of particular kinds of cases. These are beyond the scope of the Civil Procedure class, in which we deal with the general removal provisions.

[234]Removal is not an appeal. Remember from §1.2.2 that one cannot appeal a general civil case from a state trial court to a federal court.

§4.8.2 Procedural Issues

Who Can Remove? Section 1441(a) grants the right to remove to "the defendant or the defendants." There are two important consequences of this language. First, plaintiffs have no right to remove to federal court. This is true even if a claim is asserted against them in the case.[235] After all, the plaintiff had the original choice of forum; if she wanted to be in federal court (and the case invokes federal subject matter jurisdiction), she should have filed in federal court at the outset.

> o *Example #46.* P sues D in state court. Now D files a counterclaim against P in that case. (We study counterclaims in §12.5.1.) Assume that the counterclaim would invoke federal subject matter jurisdiction. Can P now remove the case?

The answer is no. Even though in this example a claim has been asserted against the plaintiff, she is not a "defendant" under the removal statutes.

Second, courts have long concluded that *all* defendants must agree to remove a case.[236] This "rule of unanimity" means that if there are multiple defendants, and any of them refuses to join the notice of removal, the case cannot be removed.[237] However, in applying this "rule of unanimity," courts look only to defendants who have been named in the complaint *and served with process.* Thus, §1446(b)(2)(A) requires that removal be joined by *all* defendants "who have been properly joined and served."

> o *Example #47.* Plaintiff files a case in state court against three defendants, *D-1, D-2,* and *D-3,* stating a claim that is removable. Plaintiff has process served only on *D-1* and *D-2. D-1* and *D-2* remove the case to federal court. Removal is effective, even though *D-3* did not join in the removal, because *D-3* had not yet been served with process.

To What District? Cases removed from state court have their own venue provision, separate from cases filed initially by the plaintiff in federal court. Under §1441(a), a case can be removed only to the federal district "embracing the place where [the] action is pending." Thus,

---

[235]Shamrock Oil & Gas Corp. v. Sheets, 313 U.S. 100, 108 (1941). *See also* Home Depot U.S.A. v. Jackson, 139 S. Ct. 1743, 1747-51 (2019) (defendant added on counterclaim cannot remove).

[236]Chicago, R.I. & P. Ry. Co. v. Martin, 178 U.S. 245, 248 (1900); Brown v. Demco, Inc., 792 F.2d 478, 481 (5th Cir. 1986).

[237]There is a very narrow exception to this rule under §1441(c), which we will see at the end of this chapter. Moreover, Congress has made exceptions to the rule of unanimity in specific statutes, such as the Class Action Fairness Act, allowing removal by one of multiple defendants.

the *only* federal district court to which a case can be removed is the one that "embraces"—that means geographically—the state court in which the case is pending. The general venue provisions that govern which federal districts are appropriate in cases filed by the plaintiff directly in federal court (28 U.S.C. §1391, addressed in §5.4) do not apply to cases removed from state court. For example, a case filed in state court in Buffalo can be removed only to the United States District Court for the Western District of New York, since that is the district "embracing" Buffalo. This is true regardless of whether venue would have been proper there under the general venue statutes.

Timing of Removal (and Problems with Multiple Defendants). Section 1446(b)(1) requires that the notice of removal be filed in federal court within 30 days after "receipt by the defendant, through service or otherwise" of the complaint in the case she wishes to remove.[238] For now, let's assume that the case as originally filed is removable. (We will see below that a case might not be originally removable but can become removable later.) What does "receipt . . . through service or otherwise" mean?

> ○ ***Example #48.*** Plaintiff files a removable case in state court and e-mails a copy of the complaint to Defendant on July 1. Plaintiff does not, however, effect service of process. The two discuss possible settlement but reach no agreement. Plaintiff then has process served on Defendant on July 20. Did Defendant's 30 days to remove start to run on July 1 or on July 20?

In *Murphy Brothers, Inc. v. Michetti Pipe Stringing, Inc.*,[239] the Supreme Court held that the 30 days runs from *service of process*, and not from the informal sending of a copy of the complaint. In Example #48, then, Defendant would have 30 days after the service of process on July 20 in which to remove. This raises an interesting problem, however, if there are multiple defendants served with process at different times.

> ○ ***Example #49.*** Plaintiff sues two defendants, *D-1* and *D-2*. Plaintiff has process served on *D-1* on March 1. *D-1* does not remove the case to federal court within 30 days. Then Plaintiff has process served on *D-2* on May 1. Does *D-2* have until May 31 to remove? Or did *D-1*'s failure to remove waive *D-2*'s right to remove?

---

[238]In some states, the plaintiff files the complaint in court and then is required only to serve a summons (and not a copy of the complaint). This is what the remainder of §1446(b) is addressing, when it grants 30 days "after the service of summons." Either way, the point will be that it is *service* (of process, in most states, or of the summons, in those states allowing filing without service of the complaint).

[239]526 U.S. 344, 353-354 (1999).

The answer is found in §1446(b)(2)(B) & (C):[240] The 30 days begins to run afresh once process is served on *D-2*. That means that *D-1*'s failure to remove within 30 days of service on her does not bind *D-2*. Moreover, *D-1*'s failure to remove when she had the chance does not estop her from joining *D-2*'s removal. The rule of unanimity still applies, so *D-2* must get *D-1* to join in the removal.

No Court Permission Is Required. The defendant does not need permission to remove the case. She simply removes by following the statutory process. First, she files a "notice of removal" in the federal court. (The required contents of the notice are set forth in §1446(a).) Second, after filing the notice in federal court, under §1446(d) the defendant "promptly" gives written notice of the removal to "all adverse parties." And third, also under §1446(d), she files a copy of the notice in the state court. That filing in the state court "shall effect the removal and the State court shall proceed no further unless and until the case is remanded." In other words, that act divests the state court of jurisdiction over the case.

A defendant can waive the right to remove by taking some action in the state court that she is not required to take.[241] The idea is that by engaging in such non-essential litigation in state court, the defendant has shown a desire to forego access to federal court. For example, filing a permissive counterclaim (as opposed to a compulsory counterclaim) in state court probably waives the right to remove.[242] Generally, however, filing an answer in state court that raises a conclusive defense does not result in such waiver.[243] In addition, by removing a case to federal court, the defendant does not waive the defense of lack of personal jurisdiction.[244]

Timing of Defensive Response. Once the case is removed, the Federal Rules govern the timing and procedure in federal court. The federal court takes the case as it is removed, so if the defendant had already answered before removing, she is not required to refile her answer. On the other hand, if the defendant had not answered in state court, Rule 81(c)(2) governs the timing of her defensive response in

---

[240]Specifically, §1446(b)(2)(B) provides that "each defendant" has 30 days from service upon her in which to seek removal, and §1446(b)(2)(C) makes clear that an earlier-served defendant's failure to remove does not estop her from joining the later-served defendant's removal.

[241]*See* 16 Moore's Federal Practice §107.18[3][a].

[242]*See, e.g.,* Isaacs v. Group Health, Inc., 668 F. Supp. 306, 308-309 (S.D.N.Y. 1987). Counterclaims are asserted by the defendant against the plaintiff. A permissive counterclaim is not transactionally related to the plaintiff's claim and does not have to be asserted in the pending case. A compulsory counterclaim is transactionally related to the plaintiff's claim and generally must be asserted in the pending case. See §12.5.1.

[243]*See, e.g.,* Miami Herald Publ'g Co. v. Ferre, 606 F. Supp. 122, 124 (S.D. Fla. 1984).

[244]Lambert Run Coal Co. v. Baltimore & Ohio R.R. Co., 258 U.S. 377, 382 (1922).

federal court. It provides that the defendant must respond by motion or answer within 21 days after service of process or seven days after the notice of removal is filed, whichever is longer. Thus, the defendant will never have fewer than seven days after removal in which to make her defensive response.

Motion to Remand. If removal is improper for some reason *other than* lack of subject matter jurisdiction—for example, if the defendant failed to include in the notice of removal all the information required by §1446(a) or if fewer than all defendants joined in the notice of removal—the plaintiff must move to remand within 30 days after the removal. §1447(c). If she does not, the procedural defect is waived, and the case will not be remanded. On the other hand, if there is no federal subject matter jurisdiction, there is no time limit for the plaintiff's moving to remand the case to state court. Indeed, as §1447(c) also makes clear, the court must remand *sua sponte* whenever it determines that subject matter jurisdiction is lacking.

§4.8.3   Issues of Jurisdiction

A defendant can remove a case only if it is one "of which the district courts of the United States have original jurisdiction." §1441(a). That means that the case must satisfy a basis of federal subject matter jurisdiction. The rules for invoking federal subject matter jurisdiction addressed above (including, for example, the complete diversity rule and amount in controversy requirement in diversity cases and the well-pleaded complaint rule in federal question cases) apply in cases in which the defendant seeks to remove. As we see below, however, the statutes impose two important restrictions on removing diversity of citizenship cases.

If the case does not satisfy a basis of federal subject matter jurisdiction, the federal court *must* remand to state court. Usually, the lack of jurisdiction will be clear immediately. Occasionally, however, a federal court will not appreciate that it lacks subject matter jurisdiction until long after removal. Even if the court has invested a great deal of time and resources in the case, it must be remanded *whenever* it is discovered that there is no subject matter jurisdiction. §1447(c). We saw this principle in §4.3, where we said that a case filed originally in federal court must be dismissed whenever it is determined that it does not invoke federal subject matter jurisdiction. But note the difference in the operation of this principle in the removal context. If the case in which jurisdiction is lacking was filed originally in federal court, the case is dismissed. If the case in which jurisdiction is lacking was filed originally in state court and removed to federal court, the federal court does *not* dismiss, but remands the case to the state court.

In removed cases, the *defendant* is invoking the federal court's jurisdiction, and has the burden of establishing federal subject matter jurisdiction. She must do so, however, on the basis of the plaintiff's complaint, not through her answer or counterclaim. It is the *plaintiff's* case that must invoke federal subject matter jurisdiction. It might do so, of course, because the plaintiff asserted a claim arising under federal law; a defendant removing on the basis of federal question jurisdiction will allege that plaintiff's claim invokes federal question jurisdiction under §1331.

○ ***Example #50.*** Mottley, a citizen of Kentucky, sues Railroad, also a citizen of Kentucky, in state court for $80,000, alleging that Railroad has breached a contract by which it agreed to furnish her with a lifetime pass. Mottley also alleges that a federal statute prohibiting such passes does not apply to her and, if it does, that it is unconstitutional. Railroad removes the case to federal court and plaintiff moves to remand for lack of subject matter jurisdiction. How does the court rule? The court will grant the motion and remand to state court. First, there is no diversity, since the plaintiff and defendant are co-citizens. Second, the case also fails to invoke federal subject matter jurisdiction. Why? Under the well-pleaded complaint rule, see §4.6.4, this claim does not arise under federal law; the federal provision mentioned is raised as an anticipated defense, and does not constitute part of her claim.

○ ***Example #51.*** Same facts, same claim, except here Mottley is a citizen of Illinois, Railroad is a citizen of Kentucky, and the claimed value of the railroad pass is $80,000. Railroad removes the case to federal court and plaintiff moves to remand for lack of subject matter jurisdiction. How does the court rule? The court will deny the motion to remand. This case is removable because it satisfies the requirements for diversity of citizenship jurisdiction.

○ ***Example #52.*** State sues Indian Tribe in state court, asserting that the Tribe owes various state taxes. The Tribe asserts the defense that federal law makes it immune to claims for state taxes. The Tribe removes the case to federal court and the plaintiff moves to remand for lack of subject matter jurisdiction. How does the court rule? The court will grant the motion and remand to state court. Even though the Tribe has raised a serious federal issue, it cannot remove because this case does not invoke federal question jurisdiction. The federal issue is being injected by way of defense, which violates the well-pleaded complaint rule. Only if the federal law is part of the plaintiff's well-pleaded complaint is there federal question jurisdiction. Because that is not the case here, the Tribe cannot remove.[245]

---

[245]Oklahoma Tax Comm'n v. Graham, 489 U.S. 838, 840-841 (1989). Although the Court recognized that it might make sense to jettison the well-pleaded complaint rule for removal, it concluded that only Congress could do so.

On the other hand, if the jurisdictional defect is cured before entry of judgment in federal court, removal might be upheld. The Supreme Court addressed such a situation in *Caterpillar, Inc. v. Lewis*.[246] There, when the defendant removed the case, there was no basis for federal subject matter jurisdiction, but the federal court did not appreciate that fact. The case was litigated, during which the claim against the defendant who destroyed diversity jurisdiction was dismissed before judgment was entered. In this circumstance—although the case should not have been removed, but the defect was cured before entry of judgment—the Supreme Court upheld the judgment.[247]

Removal on the basis of diversity may be difficult because state pleading rules do not require the plaintiff to plead citizenship of the parties and often do not require allegation of amount in controversy. That means that the defendant's notice of removal must allege the citizenship of the parties and the amount in controversy. The general rule is that removal is permitted on the basis of diversity jurisdiction only if the requirements for diversity are met *both* at the time the case was filed in state court *and* at the time the defendant removes the case.[248] Historically, the reason for this rule was to prevent the state court defendant from changing her citizenship after being sued and then removing on the basis of diversity.[249]

That rule—invented to prevent manipulation of federal jurisdiction by the defendant—should not apply, however, where no such gamesmanship is possible. Accordingly, over time, the federal courts came to uphold removal if a case that was originally not removable *became removable by voluntary act of the plaintiff.*

○ ***Example #53.*** Plaintiff, a citizen of California, sues *D-1*, a citizen of Arizona, and *D-2*, a citizen of California, in a state court in Nevada[250] on a state law claim for $500,000. There is no federal question jurisdiction

---

[246]519 U.S. at 61. We discussed the case earlier. *See* notes 114-115 and accompanying text above.

[247]*See also* Barbara v. New York Stock Exch., Inc., 99 F.3d 49 (2d Cir. 1996) (federal judgment permitted although case lacked subject matter jurisdiction when removed; plaintiff amended complaint to set forth federal question claim). This situation is to be contrasted with that in *Grupo Dataflux v. Atlas Global LP*, notes 116-120 and accompanying text above, in which the Court held that a jurisdictional defect at the date of invoking federal jurisdiction cannot be cured by the change of citizenship of a party during litigation. In *Caterpillar*, in contrast, the cure came from dropping a nondiverse party during litigation. (We discussed this distinction at §4.5.3.)

[248]Pullman Co. v. Jenkins, 305 U.S. 534, 537 (1939).

[249]*See* Wright & Kane, Federal Courts 233.

[250]Do not let this fact throw you. Whether *P* can sue these defendants in Nevada (state or federal court) is a question of personal jurisdiction. Maybe the defendants have sufficient contacts to justify personal jurisdiction in Nevada. If the defendants do not object, the defense of personal jurisdiction is waived.

(because the claim arises under state law). Also, there is no diversity jurisdiction (because Plaintiff is a co-citizen with *D-2*). So, as it stands initially, then, the defendants cannot remove the case. After a few months, suppose the claim against *D-2* is dismissed. *Now there is diversity of citizenship jurisdiction*, because the claim involving the nondiverse defendant has been taken out of the case. Can *D-1* remove now?

If the claim against *D-2* was dismissed by the plaintiff voluntarily,[251] yes, the case has become removable. Under §1446(b)(3), *D-1* may remove within 30 days.[252] If, however, the claim against *D-2* was dismissed involuntarily (e.g., the court held there is no personal jurisdiction over *D-2*), generally, *D-1* cannot remove the case.[253] The theory is that an involuntary dismissal may be overturned on appeal, in which case the claim may be reinstated and diversity destroyed. If the dismissal is voluntary, however, the plaintiff cannot appeal it, and it cannot be overturned.

One interesting issue concerning removal is the amount in controversy for diversity cases. As noted, in some states, plaintiffs are not required to state the amount they are claiming.[254] Or suppose the plaintiff sues for $75,000 or less. Such a claim, the plaintiff will contend, cannot be removed because it does not meet the amount in controversy requirement for diversity jurisdiction. We are tempted to say that the plaintiff has defeated removal, because she has limited herself to recovering less than the jurisdictional amount for a diversity case. But there is a problem. In most states, the plaintiff's demand for judgment in her complaint does not limit the amount she can recover if the case is adjudicated. So a plaintiff who demands $75,000 or less in her complaint might actually recover far more than that. Can a

---

[251]Fed. R. Civ. P. 41(a).

[252]Section 1446(b)(3), which was added in 2012, addresses cases that were not originally removable but became removable later (like the hypo we are doing). It allows removal within 30 days of any "paper" from which "it may first be ascertained" that the case has become removable. The paper here would be Plaintiff's voluntary dismissal of the claim against *D-2*.

[253]*See* Poulos v. Naas Foods, Inc., 959 F.2d 69, 72 (7th Cir. 1992); Insinga v. LaBella, 845 F.2d 249, 254 (11th Cir. 1988) (stating that the voluntary-involuntary rule does not apply to a dismissal based on jurisdictional grounds, rather than the merits of the case). *But see* Hoyt v. Lane Constr. Corp., 927 F.3d 287, 297 (5th Cir. 2019) ("When a state court order creates diversity jurisdiction and that order cannot be reversed on appeal, our precedent treats the voluntary-involuntary rule as inapplicable."); Wade v. Johnson & Johnson, 54 F. Supp. 3d 1247, 1251 (W.D. Okla. 2014) (holding that the voluntary-involuntary rule did not defeat removal because the state court order resulted in the dismissal of a nondiverse *plaintiff*, rather than a nondiverse defendant, and was not on the merits).

[254]In California, for example, a plaintiff suing for personal injuries or wrongful death is forbidden to state a damages claim.

defendant (assuming the complete diversity rule is met) do anything to effect removal in such a case?

Congress addressed this issue for the first time in 2012, when it amended §1446 in salutary ways. First, it added §1446(c)(2), which provides as a starting point that the plaintiff's dollar demand in her complaint is deemed to be the amount in controversy. There are exceptions, however, if the plaintiff (a) sues for nonmonetary relief (such as an injunction), or (b) sues for monetary relief without stating an amount, or (c) sues for monetary relief of $75,000 or less in a state in which the claim does not cap what she can recover. In any of these situations, the defendant may allege the amount in controversy in her notice of removal.[255]

Second, the defendant merely needs to allege that the amount in controversy requirement is satisfied; she is not required in the notice of removal to present evidence supporting her contention on this point.[256] If the plaintiff contests the issue by asserting that the amount in controversy is not satisfied, §1446(c)(2)(B) requires the court to hold a hearing, at which evidence is presented. The court will retain the case if it finds "by a preponderance of the evidence" that the amount in controversy is satisfied. The burden in this regard is on the defendant, who, after all, is the party attempting to invoke federal subject matter jurisdiction.

Federal jurisdiction is measured at the time the case is removed and cannot be based upon subsequent events. Thus, if the case involves more than $75,000 when removed, the plaintiff cannot then force remand to state court by stipulating to a recovery of a lesser amount.[257] On the other hand, if the plaintiff stipulates *before*

---

[255]The statute provides that the sum demanded by the plaintiff "shall be deemed to be the amount in controversy, except that the notice of removal may assert the amount in controversy" in the circumstances discussed in text. §1446(c)(2)(A).

[256]Dart Cherokee Basin Operating Co., LLC. v. Owens, 574 U.S. 81, 89 (2014) ("[A]s specified in §1446(a), a defendant's notice of removal need include only a plausible allegation that the amount in controversy exceeds the jurisdictional threshold. Evidence establishing the amount is required by §1446(c)(2)(B) only when the plaintiff contests, or the court questions, the defendant's allegation"). The court noted that §1446(a) tracks operative language from Federal Rule 8(a) in requiring a "short and plain statement."

Dart Cherokee was a class action removed under the Class Action Fairness Act, which requires that the class claims, in the aggregate, exceed $5,000,000. Because the opinion interprets the removal provision of §1446(c), however, its holding will apply to the removal of diversity cases under §1332(a).

[257]In re Brand Name Prescription Drugs Antitrust Litig., 248 F.3d 668, 670-671 (7th Cir. 2001) ("If the plaintiffs' original claim was worth more than [$75,000], removal was proper, the case was within federal jurisdiction, and the plaintiffs could not defeat that jurisdiction by scaling back their claim").

removal that she will not *recover* more than $75,000, removal should be unsuccessful.[258]

After a case is removed on the basis of diversity, what happens if the plaintiff seeks to join additional defendants who destroy diversity? Under §1447(e), "the court may deny joinder, or permit joinder and remand the action to the State court."

Recall from §4.2 that state courts, at least in the aggregate, have general subject matter jurisdiction. Thus, almost every case removed from state to federal court will be one over which there is *concurrent subject matter jurisdiction*, which means that both the state and federal court systems can properly entertain the claim. This is not always the case, however, since there are some rare situations in which state courts lack subject matter jurisdiction because there is exclusive federal question jurisdiction.[259] Suppose the plaintiff files such a case—one falling within the exclusive jurisdiction of the federal courts—in state court. As the law stood for many years, the defendant could not remove the case to federal court. Removal was then thought to be "derivative," so it was proper only if the state court had subject matter jurisdiction. Congress abolished this notion, however, in §1441(f). That provision rejects the notion that removal jurisdiction is "derivative" of state court jurisdiction and makes clear that removal is proper regardless of whether the state court had subject matter jurisdiction over the case.

Suppose a plaintiff wants to litigate only in state court. Can she plead her state court case in such a way as to thwart removal? As a general rule, the plaintiff is "master of her complaint," so if she pleads a case that cannot be removed, there is not much the defendant can do about it. But this "master of her complaint" notion is not absolute. We saw above that the defendant might be able to remove on the basis of diversity jurisdiction even when the plaintiff pleads a claim of $75,000 or less. Moreover, the defendant might successfully remove when the plaintiff joined a nondiverse defendant in

---

[258]In *Standard Fire Insurance Co. v. Knowles*, 568 U.S. 588 (2013), defendants removed a class action case on the basis of the Class Action Fairness Act, which requires an aggregated amount in controversy in excess of $5,000,000. The class representative attached an affidavit to his complaint expressly limiting the amount in controversy to under $5,000,000. The obvious intent was to defeat removal. Defendant removed and the district court held a hearing on the actual amount in controversy. Defendant showed that the class claims added to more than $5,000,000. The Supreme Court upheld the removal because at this point in the litigation (because the class had not been "certified"), the representative had no authority to bind class members to the lower figure. In §13.3.5, we will see that a class representative cannot make decisions that bind class members until the class is "certified."

[259]We saw examples at note 1 above.

state court in an effort to thwart removal.[260] The defendant in such a case must convince the federal court that joinder of the jurisdiction-defeating party was "fraudulent." In this context, *fraudulent* is a term of art and does not impugn the integrity of the plaintiff or her lawyer. Rather, it means that there is no bona fide claim by or against that party.[261]

Many real-world events give rise to a state law claim and a federal law claim. What happens if a plaintiff chooses to sue in state court and to assert only the state law claim? Can she thwart removal by eschewing the federal claim?[262] Generally, the answer is yes. No one can be forced to assert a federal claim. Moreover, the defendant cannot convert a state law claim into a federal question by asserting a federal defense, because the federal question must be presented in a well-pleaded complaint, as we studied in §4.6.3.

On the other hand, there is a narrow exception to this rule — though it is an exception rarely covered in Civil Procedure courses. If a substantive area has been "completely" preempted by federal law, there is no basis for a state law claim. In such a situation, a plaintiff cannot avoid removal by purporting to assert a state law claim.[263] Such areas of complete preemption are very rare, and include the Labor Management Relations Act and ERISA. For some claims in such areas, because federal law has completely supplanted state law, *any* claim is, by definition, a federal claim and invokes federal question jurisdiction. The courts thus permit removal in such cases even though the plaintiff's complaint does not mention a federal claim.[264]

---

[260]Or she might join a defendant who is a citizen of the forum state, which would defeat removal on the basis of diversity even if the other requirements of diversity jurisdiction were met. We discuss this point below, in the next subpart of this section.

[261]Pete Rose sued the Commissioner of Major League Baseball (to challenge his banishment from baseball) in state court in his hometown of Cincinnati. He joined as a defendant the Cincinnati Reds, whose presence defeated diversity and precluded removal. The court found, however, that Rose had no real claim against the Reds, and permitted removal. Rose v. Giamatti, 721 F. Supp. 906, 919 (S.D. Ohio 1989).

[262]We are assuming here that there is no basis for diversity of citizenship jurisdiction.

[263]*See, e.g.*, Pilot Life Ins. Co. v. Dedeaux, 481 U.S. 41, 47-48 (1987) (ERISA preempts common law action by employee against insurer). For an excellent discussion of the doctrine, *see* Margaret C. Tarkington, *Rejecting the Touchstone: Complete Preemption and Congressional Intent After* Beneficial National Bank v. Anderson, 59 S.C.L.Rev. 225 (2008).

[264]Trying to avoid removal by stating only state-law claims in such cases is referred to as "artful pleading." *See* 16 Moore's Federal Practice §107.14[3][b]. The ultimate contours of the doctrine are not clear. *See* Arthur Miller, *Artful Pleading: A Doctrine in Search of Definition*, 76 Tex. L. Rev. 1781 (1998).

§4.8.4 Two Important Restrictions on Removal of Diversity of Citizenship Cases

As we noted above, removal is permitted only if the case invokes federal subject matter jurisdiction. There are two important restrictions on this rule, each of which applies only in diversity of citizenship cases.

The Instate Defendant Rule. Under §1441(b)(2), removal of a diversity case is improper if any defendant who has been "properly joined and served [with process]" is a citizen of the forum.[265] This "instate defendant" rule is consistent with the traditional rationale for diversity of citizenship; if one of the defendants is a citizen of the forum, she has no need for the protection of the federal court. See §4.5.2.

- ***Example #54.*** Plaintiff, a citizen of Florida, sues *D-1,* a citizen of New York, and *D-2,* a citizen of Alabama, in an Alabama state court. The case does not arise under federal law and the amount in controversy exceeds $75,000. Even though this case could have been filed initially in federal court (because it meets all the requirements for diversity jurisdiction), removal is not proper. Why? Because *D-2* is a citizen of the forum, Alabama. Accordingly, the theory goes, the defendants need not fear any local bias in the state courts of Alabama.
- ***Example #55.*** If the same case were brought in state court in Alabama but Plaintiff asserted a federal claim, the defendants could remove the case. Remember, the instate defendant rule applies only to cases removed under §1332 (diversity), and not those removed under §1331 (federal question).

The instate defendant rule applies, as noted above, only if one of the defendants who has been joined *and served with process* is a citizen of the state in which the case is pending. Return to Example #54 and let's assume that D-1 and D-2 have been named as co-defendants but have not yet been served with process. They learn about the case through the state court's online judicial portal and file notice of removal in federal court. Literally, the instate defendant rule does not apply. After all, D-2 is an instate defendant, but she was not served with process. This actually happens. In fact, it is happening so much that it has a name: "snap" removal. The Third Circuit has held that removal in such a case is permitted and that the case should not be remanded to state court.[266]

---

[265]That section addresses joinder under §1332(a) and forbids removal "if any of the parties in interest properly joined and served as defendants is a citizen of the State in which such action is brought."

[266]Texas Brine Co. v. Am. Arbitration Ass'n, 955 F.3d 482, 487 (5th Cir. 2020); Gibbons v. Bristol-Myers Squibb Co., 919 F.3d 699, 704-707 (2d Cir. 2019); Encompass Ins. Co. v. Stone Mansion Restaurant Inc., 902 F.3d 147, 153 (3d Cir. 2018). *See generally* Arthur

The One-Year Rule. Section 1446(c)(1) provides that a case invoking §1332 is not properly removed "more than 1 year after commencement of the action." Be careful with this provision. It does *not* say that the defendant has a year in which to remove a diversity case. Defendants have only 30 days in which to remove any case. But it is 30 days from when the case becomes removable. Most cases will be removable, if at all, when they are filed and the defendant is served with process, so this one-year limit usually will be irrelevant. This provision applies only in cases that were not removable when filed but which became removable later.

The case in Example #53 could not be removed because of a lack of complete diversity. Later, however, the plaintiff voluntarily dismissed the claim against the nondiverse defendant. The case then became removable. Under §1446(b)(3), the remaining defendant must remove within 30 days of receipt of "an amended pleading, motion, order or other paper from which it may first be ascertained that the case is one which is or has become removable."

This is where the one-year limitation may become relevant. If the case did not become removable until more than one year after it was commenced in state court, generally it cannot be removed. This limitation is clearly susceptible to manipulation. A plaintiff desiring to keep her case in state court could simply join a nondiverse defendant (or an instate defendant), wait a year and a day, and then dismiss her claim against the jurisdiction-defeating defendant.

In an effort to curb this gamesmanship, Congress amended §1446 (c)(1) to provide that a diversity case may be removed more than a year after commencement in state court if "the district court finds that the plaintiff has acted in bad faith . . . to prevent a defendant from removing the action." Thus, if the federal court found that the plaintiff initially joined the nondiverse defendant for the purpose of defeating removal, and that this constituted bad faith by the plaintiff, it may permit the remaining defendant to remove even beyond one year.[267]

Hellman et al., *Neutralizing the Stratagem of "Snap Removal": A Proposed Amendment to the Judicial Code*, 9 The Fed. Courts L. Rev. 103 (2016) (discussing divergent judicial approaches to "snap" removal and proposing legislation to address the conflict).

[267]Some courts adopt a two-stage analysis to determine whether there is "bad faith" under this statute. First, the court assesses whether the plaintiff actively litigated in state court against the party whose joinder defeated removal. If so, there is a rebuttable presumption that the plaintiff acted in good faith. Second, however, the defendant may rebut that presumption with evidence showing that the plaintiff would not have named the removal-spoiling party but for plaintiff's desire to keep the case in state court. The leading case establishing this approach is Aguayo v. AMCO Ins. Co., 59 F. Supp. 3d 1225, 1262-1263 (D.N.M. 2014). Some courts, however, have chosen not to apply the test in *Aguayo*. *See* Hopkins v. Nationwide Agribusiness Ins. Co., 2018 WL 3428610 at *4 (N.D. Ala. 2018) (bad faith exception requires "a showing that the

Sometimes it will not become apparent that a state court case involves more than $75,000 (and thus that it is removable, assuming the complete diversity rule is also met) until the litigation proceeds for a while. For example, discovery might make it clear that the plaintiff could recover more than $75,000. Under §1446(c)(3)(A), any "information" that is "in the record of the State proceeding, or in responses to discovery," constitutes a "paper" under §1446(b)(3) that will support removal.

Defendants must be careful, however, about the one-year limitation. If the information showing that the plaintiff's claim actually exceeds $75,000 is discovered after the case has been pending for more than one year, the limitation will prevent removal—unless the defendant can show, under §1441(c)(1), that the plaintiff acted in bad faith. Section 1446(c)(3)(B) provides that the plaintiff's deliberate failure to disclose the actual amount in controversy is deemed to be such bad faith.

Raising the Issue. Remember that defendants need not get permission to remove a case. They simply remove it. If they do so in a case that does not invoke federal subject matter jurisdiction, the case must be remanded to state court—and there is no time limit on the order of remand. Remember, too, however, that if the problem with removal was not a problem with subject matter jurisdiction—for example, if defendants removed a case in violation of the instate defendant rule or the one-year limitation—the plaintiff must move to remand within 30 days of when the defendants the filed notice of removal. Return to Example #54. The case invokes diversity jurisdiction, but removal would violate the instate defendant rule. Because there was subject matter jurisdiction, however, the plaintiff must move to remand to state court within 30 days. If she fails to do so, she waives the issue and the case can remain in federal court.

Section 1441(c)

For many years, §1441(c) provided that if the plaintiff joined a "separate and independent" federal question claim "with one or more otherwise nonremovable claims," the defendants could remove the *entire case*, including the otherwise nonremovable matters. The provision was the source of enormous confusion, and, happily, Congress rewrote

---

plaintiff intentionally engaged in misconduct to prevent removal before the one-year time limit expired."); McAdam Props, LLC v. Dunkin' Donuts Franchising, LLC, 290 F. Supp.3d 1279, 1291 (N.D. Ala. 2018) (exception requires intentional misconduct, not merely fraudulent joinder); Dutchmaid Logistics, Inc. v. Navistar, Inc., 2017 WL 1324610, at *3 (S.D. Ohio 2017) (noting that Sixth Circuit had not adopted *Aguayo*).

it entirely in 2012. Now, §1441(c) applies only when a state court case asserts a claim arising under federal law, to which the plaintiff joins a state law claim that does not invoke diversity and does not invoke supplemental jurisdiction. The entire case may be removed to federal court, but the federal court *must* then sever the state law claims and remand them to state court. The usual rule of unanimity is not required here, since removal can be effected by the defendant against whom the federal question is asserted.

Chapter 5

Venue

§5.1   Defining the Issue

It is helpful to think of venue as the third of three hurdles to be crossed in selecting a forum. First, *personal jurisdiction* determines whether the plaintiff can sue the defendant in a particular state. Second, *subject matter jurisdiction* determines whether the plaintiff can sue in state court or federal court in that state. Third, *venue* determines where (geographically) the case will be filed *within the chosen court system*. For example, suppose the plaintiff sues in state court in California. Where does she file: San Diego? San Francisco? Los Angeles? Calexico? That is the venue consideration. Subject matter jurisdiction places the case within a judicial *system* (federal or state). Venue determines where—in a geographic sense—the case is filed *within that system*.[1]

---

[1]Section 1390(a) defines venue as "the geographic specification of the proper court or courts for the litigation of a civil action that is within the subject matter jurisdiction of the district courts in general, and does not refer to any grant or restriction of subject matter jurisdiction."

In state court systems, as we see in §5.3, venue is laid in political subdivisions, such as counties. In the federal system, as we discuss in §5.4, venue is laid in federal districts. Venue statutes, whether state or federal, give the plaintiff choices of where to bring suit. Generally, these choices reflect a legislative assessment of where litigation would be convenient. The commonest choices permitted by venue statutes are (1) where the defendant resides and (2) where the claim arose. These choices recognize, as a general matter, that litigation is convenient for defendants where they reside, and that the place where the claim arose is convenient because relevant witnesses and evidence likely will be found there and because both the plaintiff and the defendant have at least some connection with that locale. Only occasionally do statutes permit venue where the *plaintiff* resides.

There is no federal constitutional right to have a case brought in a particular place.[2] Thus, the venue hurdle in federal court involves a statutory inquiry. As we will see in §5.2, there may be a common law issue as well. For more than two centuries, federal venue implicated the common law "local action" doctrine. Congress abolished this doctrine in federal court in 2012, but there is some question about whether the doctrine survives.[3] And because the defense of improper venue does not involve the court's subject matter jurisdiction, a court generally will not raise a venue problem on its own. Rather, the defendant must assert the defense of improper venue in a timely fashion, or it will be waived, as we see in §6.2.[4] In most state court systems, the venue inquiry is statutory, though some states have constitutional venue provisions.[5]

All judicial systems (federal and state) provide for transfer of venue from one place to another *within that system*. Such transfers may be permitted to move a case from an improper venue to a proper one. Or transfer may be permitted from one proper venue to another, perhaps because the latter is far more convenient for the parties and witnesses or more desirable from the standpoint of judicial resources. See §5.5. Transfer is possible, however, only from one court to another *in that same judicial system*. Thus, transfer is impossible if the more convenient and appropriate forum is in a different judicial system. In such a case, though the court cannot order transfer, it may dismiss or stay[6]

---

[2]Neirbo Co. v. Bethlehem Shipbuilding Corp., 308 U.S. 165 (1939).

[3]The courts that believe the doctrine survives consider the local action rule as one of subject matter jurisdiction, not venue. See §5.2.

[4]*See* Fed. R. Civ. P. 12(h)(1).

[5]*See, e.g.*, Ga. Const. Art. VI, §II, para. III through VI (prescribing venue in specific cases).

[6]To "stay" a case means to suspend it. The case remains on the docket, but nothing happens—there are no proceedings. We'll see why a court might do this in §5.6.

the case under *forum non conveniens*, which allows the plaintiff to pursue the case in the more convenient forum. See §5.6.

Finally, regardless of venue statutes, the parties generally are free to agree where a case between them is to be filed. Such an agreement may be made after the claim arises. More often, however, it is made before litigation, in a "forum selection clause" that is part of a contract between the parties. Federal law, and the law of most states, presumes that such clauses are enforceable. Such clauses are common in commercial contracts, including consumer contracts and may affect a court's analysis of motions to transfer (see §5.5.2) and motions based upon *forum non conveniens* (see §5.6).

§5.2 Local Actions and Transitory Actions

Under the venue schemes of most states, the first question is whether the case is a *local action*. This is a term of art, the definition of which varies from state to state. But, in general, a local action is one directly involving title, possession, or injury to land.[7] Specifically, local actions include (1) *in rem* or *quasi-in-rem* cases in which the land is used as a basis for jurisdiction; (2) cases claiming a remedy in real property, such as a claim to foreclose on a mortgage or to quiet title or eject a tenant; and, in some states, (3) cases involving damage to realty, including harm caused by trespass. All cases that are not local actions are, for venue purposes, called *transitory actions*.

Though the definition of local action can vary, the rule concerning where venue is proper in such cases is universal: Venue may be laid *only* where the relevant real property is found. So the plaintiff must sue in the county (or other relevant political subdivision) in which the land is located. If the realty lies in more than one county, venue is proper in a county in which any part of the land lies.

In federal court, the local action doctrine was recognized not by statute but by common law,[8] tracing to the celebrated case of *Livingston v. Jefferson*.[9] There, the plaintiff sued Thomas Jefferson *in personam*, seeking damages for trespass to the plaintiff's land in Louisiana.[10]

---

[7]Land is usually referred to as "real property" or "realty." Do not confuse "real" property with "tangible" property, which is any property that has a corporeal existence. A wristwatch is tangible property but is not real property.

[8]The general venue statute, §1391, has never referred to "local actions." The sole statutory reference to the concept in federal venue statutes was in §1392, which addressed cases involving realty located in more than one federal district. Congress repealed §1392 in 2012.

[9]15 Fed. Cas. 660 (C.D. Va. 1811).

[10]The plaintiff did not contend that Jefferson trespassed personally. Rather, the claim was that Jefferson instructed United States marshals to eject the plaintiff from

The plaintiff sued in Virginia because (in those days, long before *International Shoe*) he could not establish personal jurisdiction over the former president in Louisiana. Jefferson objected that Virginia was not a proper venue. A decision that the case was a local action (in which venue could only be laid in Louisiana) would be tantamount to telling the plaintiff that he had a right without a remedy. That is exactly what happened: The court held that trespass to land was a local action, and that venue must be placed where the land was located.[11] Although the court was inclined to limit local actions to *in rem* and *quasi-in-rem* cases, it felt obliged by English precedent to include trespass claims as well.

Effective in 2012, Congress abolished the local action doctrine in federal court.[12] Thus, §1391(a)(2) now provides that venue "shall be determined without regard to whether the action is local or transitory in nature."

But this is where things get complicated. There was always a debate about whether the common-law local action doctrine in federal court was a rule about venue or a rule about subject matter jurisdiction.[13] If it is a matter of subject matter jurisdiction,[14] the 2012 statutory amendment to §1391, aimed only at venue, would not affect it

---

his land abutting the Mississippi River in New Orleans. Jefferson thought, incorrectly, that the land belonged to the federal government.

[11]The judge deciding the case was John Marshall, who was Chief Justice of the United States. In those days, the Justices were required to "ride circuit," which meant that they served as judges in federal trial courts in the circuit for which they were responsible. (The Chief Justice has always been the Circuit Justice for the Fourth Circuit, since its headquarters, Richmond, is relatively close to Washington, D.C.) On a personal level, it must have rankled Marshall to rule as he did, since he and Jefferson, though cousins, were political rivals. *See* Ronan Degnan, *Livingston v. Jefferson — A Freestanding Footnote*, 75 Cal. L. Rev. 115 (1987).

[12]It did so in the Jurisdiction and Venue Clarification Act of 2011, which, despite its title, did not go into effect until 2012.

[13]*See, e.g.*, Trust Co. Bank v. United States Gypsum Co., 950 F.2d 1144, 1149 n.7 (5th Cir. 1992) (noting split of authority and not taking position); Hayes v. Gulf Oil Corp., 821 F.2d 285, 287 (5th Cir. 1987) (local action rule jurisdictional). Indeed, as one court noted, "there is a divergence of authority on nearly every aspect of the [local action] doctrine." Fisher v. Virginia Elec. & Power Co., 243 F. Supp. 2d 538, 540 (E.D. Va. 2003).

[14]The view that the local action doctrine implicates subject matter jurisdiction is anachronistic, rooted in mystical notions of real property. It seems to ignore the fact that a court with *in personam* jurisdiction over a defendant can compel her to execute a deed conveying property in another state (or even another country). In *Penn v. Lord Baltimore*, 27 Eng. Rep. 1132 (1750), the English Court of Chancery ordered Lord Baltimore (over whom it had *in personam* jurisdiction) to abide by an agreement conveying land in the American Colonies to William Penn. Because the court had *in personam* jurisdiction over Lord Baltimore, it could enforce its decree by contempt citation if necessary.

(because §1391 deals with venue and the local action rule deals with subject matter jurisdiction).

The Ninth Circuit reached this conclusion in *Eldee-K Rental Properties LLC v. DIRECTV, Inc.*[15] There, the plaintiff sued in federal court in California, asserting a claim that a satellite television provider trespassed on its land by placing equipment on its buildings without permission. The court concluded that the claim was a local action and that the local action doctrine implicated subject matter jurisdiction.[16] Because the land on which the trespass allegedly occurred was in Connecticut, the Ninth Circuit held, the federal court in California lacked subject matter jurisdiction over the case.[17] The Fifth Circuit has adopted this approach.[18]

Accordingly, in federal court today, all agree that the local action doctrine is abolished *as a matter of venue law.* But in those courts that consider the local action doctrine to implicate subject matter jurisdiction, such as the Fifth and Ninth Circuits, the doctrine is unaffected by §1391(a)(2).[19]

Meanwhile, the local action rule, as a matter of venue law, is alive and well in state courts. In most states, it is statutory.[20] Laying venue where the subject realty lies makes especial sense in *in rem* and *quasi-in-rem* cases. There, as discussed in §2.2, the property is the very basis of jurisdiction; it can be attached only in the venue where it is found.[21]

---

[15]748 F.3d 943 (9th Cir. 2014). Technically, §1391(a)(2) did not apply in *Eldee-K*, because the case was filed before the statute was amended in 2012. In *dictum*, the court concluded that §1391(a)(2), as a venue statute, did not affect subject matter jurisdiction. 748 F.3d at 949.

[16]*Id.* at 948-949.

[17]*Id.* at 953 ("Because the real property at issue is in Connecticut, the district court here lacked subject matter jurisdiction to adjudicate Eldee-K's action"). *See also* Kakalia v. Hawaii, 808 Fed. Appx. 582, 583 (9th Cir. 2020) (affirming dismissal for lack of subject matter jurisdiction in a case brought in California concerning real property in Hawaii).

[18]Boaz v. Legacy, L.P. v. Roberts, 628 Fed. Appx. 318, 319 (5th Cir. 2016) ("Even where the requirements of diversity jurisdiction are met, the subject matter jurisdiction of the federal courts is limited by the local action doctrine.").

[19]*See, e.g.*, Aldridge Electric, Inc. v. American Muni. Power, 2017 WL 986682 at *6 (W.D. Ky. 2017) ("The Sixth Circuit has not yet addressed whether the local action doctrine affect jurisdiction or venue. This is significant, as 'Congress abolished the local action doctrine in federal courts' as it relates to venue in the 2011 amendments to the venue statute").

[20]*See, e.g.*, Md. Ann. Code §6-202(b). In some states, it is constitutional. *See, e.g.*, Ga. Const. Art. VI, §II, para. IV ("Cases respecting title to land shall be tried in the county where the land lies, except where a single tract is divided by a county line, in which case the superior court of either county shall have jurisdiction").

[21]Remember also that with *in rem* and *quasi-in-rem* jurisdiction, the property that serves as the jurisdictional predicate does not have to be land; it can be any property. The local action rule for venue, in contrast, deals only with real property.

In most jurisdictions, as noted above, the definition of local action also includes *in personam* cases involving trespass to real property.[22] One court stated the justification as follows:

> The distinction between local and transitory actions is not fanciful or technical. It is founded on a keen sense of justice. An action at law involving essential characteristics of land ordinarily can be tried with a stronger likelihood of ascertaining the truth and doing right between the parties in a jurisdiction where the land is situated than in a foreign state. In the vicinity the nature of the land can be understood, the evidence bearing upon its title be conveniently presented, its properties and adaptability for valuable use comprehended, the elements of damage to it ascertained, its essential features recognized, and their accurate worth established in every and in all respects much better than at a distance.[23]

True, litigating in the venue where the land lies permits ready access to the land to determine what damage it sustained. But it is not apparent why the situs of the property (rather than, say, the residence of the defendant or the plaintiff) ought to be the *only* proper venue in an *in personam* trespass case. Accordingly, not all states treat trespass-to-land cases as local actions.[24]

§5.3   Venue for Transitory Actions in State Court

Remember, for purposes of venue, all cases are either local or transitory (see §5.2). Assuming a state-court case is not a local action (see §5.2), the plaintiff must address the state law governing venue in transitory actions. In most states, this law is embodied in a statute (though some states address the topic constitutionally). And almost always, the statute consists of a "laundry list" of choices for laying venue in the appropriate political subdivision. These provisions vary greatly from state to state in terms of complexity and content, so counsel must study the relevant provisions with care. One common statutory model lists particular venues as permissible generally and adds others for specific types of cases. For example, the general Maryland

---

[22]*See, e.g.*, Piven v. Comcast Corp., 916 A.2d 984, 990 (Md. App. 2007) (plaintiffs owning property in separate counties unable to aggregate claims); Reasor-Hill Corp. v. Harrison, 249 S.W.2d 994, 995 (Ark. 1952); Ingram v. Great Lakes Pipe Line Co., 153 S.W.2d 547, 550 (Mo. App. 1941). *See* Annotation, 30 A.L.R.2d 1219.

[23]Arizona Commercial Mining Co. v. Iron Cap Copper Co., 128 N.E. 4, 6 (Mass. 1920).

[24]*See, e.g.*, Cooper v. Chevron U.S.A., Inc., 49 P.3d 61, 70 (N.M. 2002) (Serna, C.J., dissenting) ("New Mexico has departed from the common law's designation of an action for trespass seeking damages for unlawful entry upon land as a local action").

statute provides for venue where the defendant (1) resides, (2) carries on a regular business, (3) is employed, or (4) habitually engages in a vocation.[25] In addition, another provision permits venue in a tort negligence case in the county where the claim arose.[26]

Venue statutes represent the legislature's assessment of where litigation would likely be convenient. The Maryland statute is typical in placing venue generally where the defendant resides or has significant ties, which permits the defendant to litigate "at home." Moreover, laying venue where the claim arose makes sense; it is a place with which both the defendant and plaintiff have some familiarity, and is likely to be a place where witnesses may be found. A few statutes permit venue where the *plaintiff* resides; a common example is cases in which the defendant is a nonresident.[27]

§5.4 Venue for Transitory Actions in Federal Court

§5.4.1 Cases Filed Originally in Federal Court

We saw in §5.2 that the local action rule has been abolished as a matter of venue in federal court. In some courts, however, the doctrine survives as a rule of subject matter jurisdiction. If the case is not a local action, then by definition it is a transitory action. The general venue statute, §1391(b), generally prescribes venue in such cases.[28] Venue in the federal courts is determined *solely* by federal law, no matter what the basis of federal subject matter jurisdiction. State venue law is irrelevant in federal court.

Section 1391(b)[29] gives the plaintiff two basic venue options: one based upon residence of the defendants and one based upon the events underlying the claim.[30] The language of the statute makes

---

[25]Md. Code Ann. §6-201(a).

[26]Md. Code Ann. §6-202(8).

[27]Most long-arm statutes and nonresident motorist statutes lay venue where the claim arose. In those instances, the defendant is a nonresident, so the place where the defendant resides is not an option.

[28]There are dozens of specialized venue statues in the United States Code. *See, e.g.,* 28 U.S.C. §1391(e)(1) (venue in cases against federal agencies, officers, and employees); §1397 (venue in statutory interpleader cases); §1403 (venue in eminent domain cases brought by United States).

[29]For many years, §1391(a) prescribed venue for diversity of citizenship cases and §1391(b) did the same for federal question cases. This made no sense, since the rules had become the same in each. So, in 2011, Congress put the venue provisions for all civil cases (regardless of basis of subject matter jurisdiction) in §1391(b).

[30]Section 1391(b)(2) also provides for venue in a district where "a substantial part of property that is the subject of the action is situated." This provision is particularly relevant in interpleader cases, discussed at §13.2.2.

these alternatives, and neither is favored. In other words, if one choice would permit venue in District *A* and the other would permit venue in District *B*, the plaintiff may choose the one she prefers. She is not required to choose the alternative that is most convenient for the defendant.[31]

Venue in the federal system is tied to federal *districts*. Congress has divided the country into 94 districts and has established a federal district court (with multiple judges) in each district.[32] With one inconsequential exception (involving Yellowstone National Park), districts do not cross state lines. In Arizona, New Jersey, Massachusetts, and several other states, the entire state comprises a single federal district. Other states, however, are subdivided into two, three, or even four federal districts. Only three states (California, New York, and Texas) have four districts. Congress legislates which counties go into each district and names each district. The names are geographical and not creative, for example, the District of Arizona, the Southern District of California, the Middle District of Florida, and so forth.[33]

Venue Based Upon Residence of Defendants ("Residential Venue")

Under §1391(b)(1), the plaintiff may lay venue in any district where "any defendant resides, if all defendants are residents of the State in which the district is located." Here is what the statute means: Venue is proper (1) in any district in which all defendants reside, and (2) if all defendants reside in different districts of the forum state (the state in which suit is filed), venue is proper in any district in which one of the defendants resides.

- ○ ***Example #1.*** *P* sues *D-1*, who resides in the Northern District of New York, and *D-2*, who resides in the Central District of California. Neither of those districts is a proper venue. Although each is one in which "any defendant resides," the two defendants do not reside in the same state, so §1391(b)(1) is not satisfied.
- ○ ***Example #2.*** *P* sues *D-1*, who resides in the Southern District of New York, and *D-2*, who also resides in the Southern District of New York.

---

[31]*See, e.g.*, Susman v. Bank of Israel, 56 F.3d 450, 457 (2d Cir. 1995) (no sanctions can be imposed for selection of an inconvenient forum if it is a proper venue).

[32]There are federal districts in each state. In addition, Congress has established federal districts in U.S. possessions that are not states, including the District of Columbia, Puerto Rico, the Virgin Islands, Guam, and the Northern Mariana Islands.

[33]Congress subdivides some districts into divisions. For example, Minnesota is one district, but consists of six divisions, with at least one district judge sitting in each division. This means that people in more rural areas are not required to litigate in Minneapolis.

Venue is proper in the Southern District of New York, because all defendants reside there. Note, though, that venue would *not* be proper under this provision in the Eastern District of New York or the Northern or Western Districts of New York (because no defendant resides in any of those districts).

- *__Example #3.__* *P* sues *D-1*, who resides in the Northern District of Illinois, and *D-2*, who resides in the Southern District of Illinois. The case against the two defendants may be filed in either of those two districts. Even though neither is a district in which all defendants reside, all defendants reside in different districts of the forum state. In that situation, venue is proper against both defendants in either district.

- *__Example #4.__* *P* sues *D-1*, who resides in the Northern District of Georgia, and *D-2*, a corporation that resides in the Southern District of Georgia and in the District of Delaware (we will see below that businesses may reside in more than one district). Can *P* lay venue against both defendants in the District of Delaware? No, because even though *D-2* resides there, *D-1* does not. Plaintiff can only use a district where one defendant resides if all defendants reside in different districts of that same state. Thus, *P* could lay venue against both defendants in either the Northern or Southern District of Georgia.

- *__Example #5.__* Would the answer to any of the preceding three hypotheticals be different depending upon the basis of subject matter jurisdiction? In other words, does it matter whether the cases invoked diversity of citizenship or federal question jurisdiction? No. Section 1391(b)(1) applies to all cases, regardless of the basis of subject matter jurisdiction.

Section 1391(b)(1) provides for venue based upon where the defendants *reside*. The venue statutes do not refer to citizenship. Though some lawyers, professors, and even judges are occasionally sloppy, we should keep the language of subject matter jurisdiction and venue distinct. In discussing diversity of citizenship jurisdiction, the focus is on the parties' *citizenship* (not residence). The Constitution and statutes grant diversity of *citizenship* jurisdiction, not diversity of *residence* jurisdiction. See §4.5.1. In discussing venue under §1391(b)(1), the focus is the defendants' *residence* (not citizenship). Why? Because that's what the statute says.

__Residence of Natural Persons.__ It was not until 2012 that Congress defined for venue purposes the residence of a human. Before that, courts were required to define the term. Long ago, the Supreme Court suggested that a human U.S. citizen defendant resides in the district in which she is domiciled.[34] This interpretation equates the test for residence (for venue purposes) with that for a human's citizenship (for subject matter jurisdiction) purposes.[35] It also means that a

---

[34]Shaw v. Quincy Mining Co., 145 U.S. 444, 449 (1892).

[35]Recall that a citizen of the United States is deemed to be a citizen (for diversity of citizenship purposes) of the U.S. state in which she is domiciled. As we discussed

human defendant has only one residence at a time (because she can have only one domicile at a time, as we saw in §4.5.3). This approach is now codified at §1391(c)(1). It provides that natural person "shall be deemed to reside in the judicial district in which that person is domiciled."

- ○ ***Example #6.*** Student is domiciled in the District of Arizona. She leaves home to go to college in Florida, where she attends classes during the school year and works during the summer. Under §1391, she "resides" only in the District of Arizona, notwithstanding that Florida presumably would be a convenient forum for her.

What if the defendant is a citizen or subject of a foreign country? For many years, §1391 provided that such a person could be sued in any district. Now, however, §1391(c)(1) (defining residence as the district in which the person is domiciled) expressly applies not only to U.S. citizens but to aliens who are admitted to the U.S. for permanent resident status.[36] Under this provision, a "green card" alien resides in the district in which she is domiciled, and it does not matter that she is not a U.S. citizen.

In addition, §1391(c)(3) provides that any natural person not residing in the U.S. may be sued in any district. So instead of drawing the line between aliens and U.S. citizens, the statute now draws the line between people who reside (legally) in the U.S. and those who do not reside in the U.S. Nonresidents, regardless of whether they are citizens of the U.S., may be sued in any district.

- ○ ***Example #7.*** P sues D, a citizen of the U.S. domiciled in France. P can lay venue in any federal district. The defendant is not domiciled in a federal district and thus does not "reside" in any district.

Residence of Business Associations. For many years, §1391(c) defined the residence of a corporation for venue purposes. According to that provision, a corporation resided in all districts in which it was "subject to personal jurisdiction when the case is commenced." The statute did not undertake to define the residence of unincorporated

---

in §4.5.3, domicile is established by presence plus the intent to make that place one's home for the foreseeable future. Congress evidently intended to permit venue where the defendant was a "citizen" in this sense. Technically speaking, however, humans are citizens of *states*, not of federal districts. Because venue is placed in federal districts, and not states, Congress apparently concluded that it could not use the word "citizen" in the venue statutes. Technically, there is no such thing as a citizen of a *district*; one is a citizen of a *state*. So Congress used the term *resides* instead.

[36]Presumably, aliens residing in the United States unlawfully do not fall within this provision and thus do not reside in any district.

businesses such as partnerships and limited liability companies. Nonetheless, most courts concluded that §1391(c) applied to unincorporated businesses as well. Congress codified this approach in §1391(c)(2), which provides that *all* business associations — corporate and unincorporated — are treated the same way.[37]

Under §1391(c)(2), businesses reside "in any judicial district in which such defendant is subject to the court's personal jurisdiction with respect to the civil action in question."[38] Defining residence by reference to personal jurisdiction incorporates the vagaries of personal jurisdiction law (which we saw in Chapter 2) into venue. But it also brings a benefit: Once the court assesses personal jurisdiction, it has also assessed the defendant's residence; there is no separate test for that issue. The statutory requirement that the defendant be subject to personal jurisdiction "with respect to the civil action in question" includes general and specific personal jurisdiction.[39]

Things are more complicated if the case is filed in a state having more than one federal district. Then, as §1391(d) provides, a business's residence is assessed with respect to each district, and not with regard to the state as a whole. In other words, the fact that the corporate defendant is subject to personal jurisdiction in California does not necessarily mean that it resides in each of the four federal districts in that state. Instead, the court treats each district as a separate state to see if the corporation's contacts with the district would justify personal jurisdiction there. Accordingly, a corporation subject

---

[37]That provision refers to "an entity with the capacity to sue and be sued in its common name under applicable law." This phrase clearly includes corporations and unincorporated businesses such as partnerships and limited liability companies. We discussed such business associations with regard to subject matter jurisdiction at §4.5.3.

[38]The section goes on to define the residence of a business association that sues as a *plaintiff*. This provision is meaningless under §1391(b), because that statute does not allow venue to be laid where the plaintiff resides. The definition of the residence of the plaintiff is relevant, however, to some specialized venue statutes that are beyond our scope.

[39]We saw in §2.4.5 that the Supreme Court has in recent years limited the availability of general personal jurisdiction. This development constricts venue. Before the recent cases, courts upheld general personal jurisdiction wherever the defendant business had continuous and substantial ties. There was a widespread sense that companies like Wal-Mart might thus be subject to personal jurisdiction in several states, because they have many stores and employees in several states. Under this interpretation, such a defendant would "reside" in every district in the United States under §1391(b), because it was subject to personal jurisdiction in every district. The Court's restriction of general jurisdiction in the 2010s changes that result by holding that defendant businesses are subject to general personal jurisdiction only where they are "at home," which is narrower than where they have continuous and substantial contacts. Today, businesses are likely subject to general personal jurisdiction in no more than two states (the state of formation and the state in which it maintains its principal place of business). See §2.4.5.

to personal jurisdiction in California, but which has contacts only in the Northern District of California, resides in the Northern District of California. It does not reside in the Central, Eastern, or Southern Districts of California.[40]

Things are even more complicated, however, if a corporation is subject to personal jurisdiction in a particular state but lacks sufficient contacts to be subject to personal jurisdiction in a specific district in that state. Such cases will arise rarely, if ever.[41] Here, §1391(d) provides that the corporation resides in the district in which it has the "most significant contacts."

> o **_Example #8._** A corporate defendant has enough contacts, in the aggregate, to be subject to personal jurisdiction in California. But it does not have enough contacts with any of the four individual federal districts in California to be subject to personal jurisdiction in any one of them. But of the four districts in California, it has more contacts with the Southern District than any other. Under §1391(c), it would reside *only* in the Southern District of California.

Venue Based Upon Events ("Transactional Venue")

Under §1391(b)(2), the plaintiff may lay venue in any district "in which a substantial part of the events or omissions giving rise to the claim occurred."[42] The theory underlying transactional venue is that

---

[40]Bicicletas Windsor, S.A. v. Bicycle Corp. of America, 783 F. Supp. 781, 785-786 (S.D.N.Y. 1992) (venue requires analysis of personal jurisdiction "confined to" district in which suit is filed).

[41]The statute seems irrelevant for cases involving specific jurisdiction. After all, if the claim arose from the defendant's contact with a particular district, that district (if it were a separate state) would have specific personal jurisdiction, and §1391(d) would not apply. Thus, the statute was probably aimed at cases involving general personal jurisdiction. It was drafted when general personal jurisdiction could be based upon a business's "continuous and systematic" ties with a state. But, as we saw in §2.4.5, today a corporation is subject to general personal jurisdiction only where it is "at home," which is the state of its incorporation and the state of its principal place of business. Accordingly, a fact pattern such as Example #8 seems extremely unlikely today.

One way it might come up is if a corporation incorporates in a multidistrict state in which it conducts no other activities. The incorporation subjects it to general jurisdiction. It is unclear, however, whether incorporation means that the corporation is deemed to reside for venue purposes in each district in the state. Perhaps its contacts are limited to the district in which incorporation was consummated (likely the district in which the state capital is situated). For an insightful discussion of this and related issues, see John P. Lenich, *A Simple Question That Isn't So Simple: Where Do Entities Reside for Venue Purposes?*, 84 Miss. L.J. 253 (2015).

[42]Or, as that section says, in the district where "a substantial part of property that is the subject of the action is situated." Thus, for example, a suit regarding ownership of personal property could be filed in the district where the property (or a substantial

304

the place where a substantial part of the claim arose will be convenient for the litigants, because witnesses to any events are likely to be found there, evidence may be present there, and both plaintiff and defendant have some contacts there.

An earlier version of the venue statute permitted venue in the district "where the claim arose," which implied that there was only a single district that would qualify. That is no longer true. Now, so long as a "substantial part" of the events giving rise to the claim took place in a district, it is a proper venue under §1391(b)(2).

Can more than one district satisfy §1391(b)(2)? Yes. Moreover, there is no requirement that venue be placed in the district in which the most substantial or important events took place.[43] Thus, in tort cases, venue may be proper both where the tortious acts took place and where the harm was felt.[44] In contract cases, venue might be proper where the agreement was negotiated or executed, where it was to be performed, and where it was allegedly breached.[45]

> ○ ***Example #9.*** Creditor sent a letter to Borrower, demanding payment of a bill and making threats. The letter violates federal debt collection laws. Creditor mailed the letter from Pennsylvania to Borrower's home address in New York. But Borrower had moved to Arizona and the new occupant at the New York address forwarded the letter to Borrower in Arizona, where Borrower read it. Borrower sues Creditor under the federal debt collection laws, invoking federal question jurisdiction. Is venue proper in the District of Arizona? Yes, because a substantial part of the events giving rise to the case occurred there.[46]

The Fall-Back Provision

Section 1391(b)(3)—called the "fall-back" venue provision—is *not* an alternative to §1391(b)(1) and §1391(b)(2). The provision applies

---

part of it) is found. This provision is particularly important in interpleader cases, discussed at §13.2.2.

[43]*See, e.g.,* Employers Mut. Cas. Co. v. Bartile Roofs, Inc., 618 F.3d 1153, 1165-1166 (10th Cir. 2010) (statute does not limit venue to the district with the most substantial events or omissions; multiple districts may satisfy transactional venue).

[44]*See, e.g.,* Hawbecker v. Hall, 88 F. Supp. 3d 723, 731 (W.D. Tex. 2015) (in a defamation case, venue was proper where harm felt and likely also where the writing was created).

[45]*See, e.g.,* Reilly v. Meffe, 6 F. Supp. 3d 760, 765-766 (S.D. Ohio 2014) (though contract was negotiated, executed, and breached in another district, venue was proper at the place of performance).

[46]This fact pattern is adapted from *Bates v. C&S Adjusters, Inc.*, 980 F.2d 865, 868 (2d Cir. 1992). Transactional venue would also be proper in Pennsylvania, in the district in which the letter was written.

only when *no district anywhere in the United States* satisfies either of the two venue choices under §1391(b)(1) or (b)(2).[47] Fall-back venue cases are rare. They involve a claim that arose entirely outside the United States. Why? Because if a substantial part of the claim arose anywhere in the United States, there will be a federal district that satisfies §1391(b)(2). Even in a case in which the claim arose entirely outside the United States, §1391(b)(3) does not apply if all defendants reside in the forum state in the United States. If they do, venue will be proper in a district in which any defendant resides under §1391(b)(1).

○ ***Example #10.*** Defendant resides in the District of Oregon. Plaintiff sues Defendant in the District of Nevada, which is not a proper venue under §1391(b)(1) or (b)(2), but which would be proper under §1391(b)(3) because Defendant is subject to personal jurisdiction there. Venue is not proper. Section 1391(b)(3) cannot apply. Why? Because there is another district (the District of Oregon) in which venue would be proper. Section 1391(b)(3) applies only if no district anywhere in the country would satisfy either §1391(b)(1) or (b)(2).

In the rare cases in which the fall-back provision applies, the plaintiff may lay venue in any district "in which any defendant is subject to the court's personal jurisdiction with respect to such action."

§5.4.2   Cases Removed from State Court

The venue provisions discussed in §5.4.1 apply *only* when a plaintiff files suit in a federal district court. Section 1391 simply does not apply to cases filed in state court and removed to federal district court.[48] Rather, in removed cases, as we saw in §4.8, venue is proper under 28 U.S.C. §1441(a) *only* in the federal district embracing the state court in which the case was filed.

○ ***Example #11.*** P sues D in state court in St. Louis. D removes the case to the federal district court for the Eastern District of Missouri (which embraces St. Louis). D does not reside in the Eastern District of Missouri. No part of the claim arose in the Eastern District of Missouri. In other words, the Eastern District of Missouri is not a proper venue under §1391(b)(1) or (2). Nonetheless, the Eastern District of Missouri is a proper venue. Why? Because in removed cases, §1391 is irrelevant; venue is proper only in the federal district embracing the state court

[47]Section 1391(b)(3) provides that it applies only "if there is no district in which an action may otherwise be brought as provided in this section."
[48]Section 1390(c) provides that §1391 "shall not determine the district court to which a civil action pending in a State court may be removed."

in which the case was originally filed—here, the Eastern District of Missouri.

§5.5 Transfer of Venue

§5.5.1 Introduction

All states and the Federal Judicial Code have provisions allowing for transfer of cases. Transfer can be effected only *within* a single judicial system. For example, a state court in Birmingham, Alabama can transfer a case to a state court in Mobile, Alabama, since both courts are in the Alabama court system. But that court in Birmingham *cannot* transfer a case to a state court in Missouri, because those courts are not in the same judicial system. Similarly, outside of removal jurisdiction,[49] there can be no transfer of a case from a state court to a federal court or vice versa. Within the federal system, cases can be transferred from one federal district to another; state lines are irrelevant. Why? Because the transfer, though crossing state lines, is from one court to another within the same (the federal) judicial system. Thus, a *federal* court in Alabama can transfer a case to a *federal* court in Missouri.

An order of transfer overrides the plaintiff's choice of forum. Assuming the plaintiff had sued in a proper venue, transfer should not be ordered lightly. The plaintiff had a right to bring suit in the present forum, so the party seeking transfer has the burden of showing that the case should proceed in another place in the judicial system. The court ordering transfer is the *transferor court*. The one to which the case is transferred is the *transferee court*. The transferor court makes the decision; the transferee court does not have a voice in the matter. Under the general transfer statutes discussed in §5.5.2, an order of transfer puts the entire case in the transferee court for all purposes; once the case is transferred, the transferor court has no jurisdiction over any aspect of the case. The transferee court takes over the case at its present stage; it does not start the litigation over afresh.

The bases on which a party may seek a transfer of venue vary from state to state, but common themes emerge. First, virtually all judicial systems permit transfer when the transferor court is not a proper venue; such a case can be transferred to a proper venue in the same judicial system. In such cases, the plaintiff's initial choice (being an

---

[49]Recall that removal permits the defendant in a state court case to "remove" the case to the federal district embracing the state court. Removal is thus a species of transfer but is so exceptional (in involving more than one court system) that it warrants discussion in the materials on subject matter jurisdiction. See §4.8.

improper venue) is entitled to no deference. Second, when plaintiff filed the case in a proper venue, statutes generally permit transfer based upon an assessment of the relative convenience to the parties and witnesses.[50] For instance, suppose Birmingham was a proper venue under Alabama law, because the defendant corporation did business there. Suppose, though, that the claim arose in Mobile, the relevant witnesses and evidence were in Mobile, and the corporation was headquartered in Mobile. The Birmingham court, in its discretion, might order transfer because the transferee court is the more convenient and logical place for the case to proceed.

Usually, the defendant is the party moving for transfer. Occasionally, however, a plaintiff will do so. This is rare, because, after all, the plaintiff chose the original forum. Nonetheless, it does happen, and there is nothing in the federal transfer statutes to prevent it.[51] Although the basic federal transfer statute, discussed below, does not impose time limits for making a motion to transfer, it behooves the moving party to make the motion relatively early. As a practical matter, courts are less likely to transfer after having invested time and resources in the case. It is also appropriate for courts to order transfer on their own initiative, without a motion from any party. In such a case, the judge should inform the parties of this possibility and hear their objections, if any.[52]

Transfer must also be distinguished from dismissal under the doctrine of *forum non conveniens*. The latter, which we discuss in §5.6, is used when the case *cannot* be transferred. Why could a case *not* be transferred? Because the more convenient forum is in a *different judicial system*. The factors assessed in ordering transfer for convenience of the parties and witnesses are the same as those used to order a *forum non conveniens* dismissal. (Some refer to a transfer of this type as a "*forum non conveniens* transfer.")

§5.5.2 General Transfer Provisions in Federal Court

The Two Statutes

In federal court, there are two general transfer statutes: §1404(a) and §1406(a). Lawyers and judges routinely refer to them by number

---

[50]In addition to these reasons, many states add other specific grounds for seeking transfer; for example, one party cannot receive a fair trial because of pretrial publicity in the original venue. One of the best is a Florida statute that permits transfer when the moving party "is so odious to the inhabitants of the county that he or she could not receive a fair trial" in the original venue. Fla. Stat. Ann. §47.101(1)(b).

[51]*See, e.g.*, Coffey v. Van Dorn Iron Works, 796 F.2d 217, 219 (7th Cir. 1986) (under federal transfer statute §1404(a)).

[52]*See* Fort Knox Music, Inc. v. Baptiste, 139 F. Supp. 2d 505, 512 (S.D.N.Y. 2001).

and speak of a "1404 transfer" or "1406 transfer." The major difference between them is this: §1404(a) applies when the transferor court is a proper venue, while §1406(a) applies when the transferor court is an improper venue. This fact explains why §1406(a) provides for transfer or, in the alternative, dismissal of the case. A case filed in an improper venue is subject to dismissal under Federal Rule 12(b)(3). Section 1404(a), on the other hand, does not permit dismissal, because the court in which the case was filed is a proper venue.

The assessment of which statute applies, then, requires an analysis of whether the original federal district court is a proper venue. If it is, transfer (if ordered) will be under §1404(a). If it is not, transfer (if ordered) will be under §1406(a). The assessment of whether the original federal district court is a proper venue will be made for cases filed initially in federal court by applying §1391(b), which we discussed in §5.4.1.[53] Remember, though, that for cases removed from state court, §1391(b) is irrelevant.

> ○ ***Example #12.*** *P* sues *D* in state court in St. Louis and *D* removes the case to the federal district for the Eastern District of Missouri (which embraces St. Louis). Any transfer from the Eastern District of Missouri will be made under §1404(a), and not under §1406(a). Why? Because venue is proper in the Eastern District of Missouri, regardless of whether it would have been proper under §1391(b). Section 1391(b) does not apply to removed cases. Venue is proper in the district embracing the state court in which the case was originally filed. See §5.4.2.

The issue of which statute applies—§1404(a) or §1406(a)—may determine the application of various transfer principles that come from four important Supreme Court cases, which we address below. First, however, let's look in more detail at the operation of the two statutes.

Applying §1404(a)

Section 1404(a) permits transfer for "the convenience of parties and witnesses, in the interest of justice." A court considering transfer has great discretion, which is reflected by these flexible terms. Because venue is proper in the present court, the plaintiff's choice of forum is entitled to some deference. Transfer is the exception, not the rule.[54]

---

[53]We assume here that the case is not a local action. Though the local action rule is abolished for venue purposes, some courts conclude that it survives as a rule of subject matter jurisdiction. See §5.2.

[54]Professors Clermont and Eisenberg showed that transfer affects outcome rates, which may suggest that plaintiffs whose cases are transferred were engaged in forum shopping. Kevin M. Clermont & Theodore Eisenberg, *Exorcising the Evil of Forum-Shopping,* 80 Cornell L. Rev. 1507 (1994).

The party moving for transfer must convince the judge that the other district is what many lawyers and courts call the "center of gravity" for the case.

In making this determination, the court will look to a series of "public interest factors" and "private interest factors." The public factors include: (1) administrative difficulties of keeping the case, (2) local interest in having localized controversies decided at home, (3) the desire to have a case tried in a forum well versed in the law that will apply, (4) avoiding undue problems with conflict of laws or in the application of different law, and (5) overburdening citizens with jury duty in a case unrelated to the forum.

> ○ ***Example #13.*** Defendant moves to transfer from the District of Arizona to the District of Oregon. It is likely that the dispute will be governed by Oregon law. The case load in the district of Arizona is heavier than that in Oregon, so the case would proceed through litigation more quickly in Oregon than in Arizona. These factors support transfer. Note, however, that no single factor is determinative; the court has great discretion in deciding whether to order transfer.

The private factors focus on issues of convenience, relating to the expeditious and inexpensive resolution of the case. They include: (1) relative ease of access to evidence, (2) ability to compel attendance of witnesses at trial through subpoena, and (3) expense of obtaining attendance of willing witnesses.[55]

> ○ ***Example #14.*** In addition to the facts in Example #13, suppose that most of the witnesses who are expected to testify at trial reside in Oregon. In addition, most of the relevant evidence is present in Oregon. These factors support transfer.

Applying §1406(a)

Because cases involving §1406(a) are pending in an improper venue, the court may dismiss or, if it is "in the interest of justice," transfer. Earlier versions of the statute did not permit transfer. Thus, a court lacking venue was required to dismiss, which put the plaintiff to the burden of filing a new suit in a proper venue. Transfer under §1406(a)

---

[55]The classic statement of these public and private factors is found in *Gulf Oil Corp. v. Gilbert*, 330 U.S. 501, 509-511 (1947). In that case, the Court upheld a *forum non conveniens* dismissal of a claim in federal court in New York when the more appropriate forum was a federal court in Virginia. (We discuss *forum non conveniens* at §5.6.) At the time, the case could not be transferred because there was no applicable transfer statute. Indeed, Congress passed §1404(a) in reaction to *Gulf Oil*.

avoids that inconvenience. Most courts conclude that transfer is superior to dismissal.

Four Important Supreme Court Cases

The Goldlawr **Case.** In *Goldlawr, Inc. v. Heiman,*[56] the Supreme Court upheld a §1406(a) transfer by a court that lacked personal jurisdiction over the defendant. Most courts agree that this rule applies to §1404(a) transfers as well.[57] Some courts disagree, however, and permit a §1404(a) transfer only if the transferor court has personal jurisdiction over the defendant.[58] The majority view is clearly correct. After all, in *Goldlawr* itself, the Supreme Court upheld transfer by a court that had *neither* personal jurisdiction nor venue (since it was a §1406(a) transfer, venue in the original forum was improper). It is difficult to fathom why a court lacking *only* personal jurisdiction over the defendant should not have the same power.

There is another statute, which we mentioned in §4.3, which may have some relevance here. Section 1631 allows transfer from one federal court to another to cure a "want of jurisdiction." Though the statute seems aimed at curing lack of subject matter jurisdiction,[59] there is support for its invocation to cure a lack of personal jurisdiction.[60] It is not clear, however, why §1631 would ever be used in such a way. After all, under *Goldlawr* (which, as noted, should apply in §1404(a) and §1406(a) transfers), even courts lacking personal jurisdiction may transfer to a proper venue. The better view, therefore, is that §1631 applies only to transfers to cure a lack of subject matter jurisdiction.[61]

---

[56]369 U.S. 463, 466 (1962).

[57]*See, e.g.*, Muldoon, 1 F.3d 964, 967 (9th Cir. 1993); Cote v. Wadel, 796 F.2d 981, 984 (7th Cir. 1986).

[58]*See, e.g.*, Ross v. Colorado Outward Bound School, Inc., 822 F.2d 1524, 1526 (10th Cir. 1987).

[59]*See* Carefirst of Md., Inc. v. Carefirst Urgent Care Center, LLC, 305 F.3d 253, 257 n.2 (4th Cir. 2002) (discussing cases); Songbyrd, Inc. v. Estate of Grossman, 206 F.3d 172, 179 n.9 (2d Cir. 2000) (noting in *dictum* "legislative history of §1631 provides some reason to believe that this section authorizes transfers only to cure lack of subject matter jurisdiction").

[60]*See, e.g.*, Jackson v. L&F Martin Landscape, 421 Fed. Appx. 482, 483 n.1 (6th Cir. 2009).

[61]*See* 15 Wright & Miller §3842. Though detailed discussion is beyond our scope, note that some claims must be pursued not in district court but in specialized federal tribunals. Section 1361 may be invoked to transfer a case from district court to such a specialized court. *See, e.g.,* ATK Launch Sys., Inc. v. U.S. E.P.A., 651 F.3d 1194, 1196-1197 (10th Cir. 2011) (under federal environmental law, petition for appellate review was proper only in the District of Columbia Circuit; Tenth Circuit transferred appeal wrongfully filed before it to that court); Orix Public Fin., LLC v. Lake County Hous. & Redev. Auth., 2011 WL 3628958 at *8 (N.D. Tex. 2011) ("The better view is that §1631 applies only to defects in subject matter jurisdiction, not personal jurisdiction.").

The *Hoffman* Case. Section 1404(a) permits transfer to a district where the action "might have been brought." In *Hoffman v. Blaski*,[62] the Supreme Court interpreted this phrase to mean that the transferee court must be a proper venue (see §§5.2, 5.4) and must have personal jurisdiction over the defendant. Although *Hoffman* was a §1404(a) case, the same result follows under §1406(a), because the latter statute permits transfer only to a district where the case "could have been brought."[63] Importantly, though, *Hoffman* held that these two requirements — venue and personal jurisdiction in the transferee court — must be met *independently*, without waiver by the defendant. The Court reasoned that a contrary rule would give the defendant too much power; the defendant could essentially decree that the case be transferred to a particular federal district by waiving objections to venue and personal jurisdiction. The plaintiff's venue choice should not be so readily overturned by the defendant.

> ○ ***Example #15.*** P sues D in the District of Minnesota. D moves to have the case transferred to the District of Hawaii. Venue is not proper in the District of Hawaii, nor would Hawaii have personal jurisdiction over D. But D declares that she will waive both defenses and submit to the venue and personal jurisdiction of the federal court in Hawaii. Under *Hoffman*, the District of Minnesota cannot transfer to the District of Hawaii, because that latter court is not one in which venue and personal jurisdiction were independently proper. Waiver does not count. Again, this is true for transfer under either §1404(a) or §1406(a).

So, under *Goldlawr* and *Hoffman*, transfer under either statute can only be made *to* a district that is a proper venue and has personal jurisdiction. But transfer can be made *from* a court that lacks venue (§1406(a)) and lacks personal jurisdiction over the defendant.

In 2012, Congress made an inroad on the holding in *Hoffman*. It added the final phrase to §1404(a), which permits a court to transfer to "any district" (even one that is not a proper venue or that does not have personal jurisdiction over the defendant) "to which all parties have consented." This inroad may be a limited one, for two reasons. First, it is not clear why the plaintiff would consent to such a transfer. Second, and more important, the "consent prong" of §1404(a) does not permit transfer solely on the basis of the parties' consent. The court must still find cause to transfer the case under the center-of-gravity

---

[62]363 U.S. 335, 343-344 (1960).

[63]*See, e.g.*, Minnette v. Time Warner, 997 F.2d 1023, 1026 (2d Cir. 1993). It is odd that Congress did not use precisely the same language in this regard. In §1404(a), the transferee court is one where the case "might have been brought" and in §1406(a) it is one where the case "could have been brought." No court, to my knowledge, has found that the different language should lead to a different result under the two statutes.

analysis discussed above. Only if that analysis supports transfer will it be ordered, but, unlike under *Hoffman*, the case may now be transferred to any district on which the parties agree, even if that district is not a proper venue or lacks personal jurisdiction over the defendant.

Return to Example #15; if the District of Minnesota determined that the public and private factors supported transfer to the District of Hawaii, and if both parties consented to the District of Hawaii,[64] the court could order transfer to that court.

The* Van Dusen *Case. In *Van Dusen v. Barrack*,[65] the Supreme Court held that a transferee court in a §1404(a) transfer must apply the choice of law rules that the transferor (the original district) would have applied. It reasoned that the change of venue should simply change the courtroom, and not the law to be applied to the merits of the case. In a diversity of citizenship case, as we see in Chapter 10, federal courts must apply state *substantive* (as opposed to procedural) law. Choice of law provisions are considered substantive, so a federal court sitting in diversity must apply state choice of law rules. Thus, a federal court in California must apply California's choice of law rules.

What are choice of law rules? They determine what law governs a particular dispute.

> o ***Example #16.*** A citizen of Massachusetts enters into a contract with a citizen of Arizona. They negotiate the contract in Texas. The contract calls for performance in California and Guam. When a dispute arises between the parties, what law will govern to determine whether a party breached the contract and, if so, the appropriate remedy?

The answer to that question is governed by choice of law doctrine, which is the centerpiece of a course on Conflict of Laws (and is beyond the scope of Civil Procedure). We need to understand, however, that if the case is filed in Texas, the judge will apply Texas choice of law rules to determine whether the dispute will be governed by the substantive contract law of Massachusetts or Arizona or Texas or California or Guam (or some other jurisdiction). If the case is filed in California, the judge will use California choice of law rules to determine whether the dispute will be governed by the contract law of Massachusetts or Arizona or Texas or California or Guam (or some other jurisdiction). And this is true regardless of whether the case is in federal or state

---

[64]It is not clear why *P* would consent to that transfer. *P* filed suit in a proper venue and would not be likely to agree to have the case sent to an improper venue. The "consent prong" of §1404(a) may eventually play its most important role in cases involving forum selection clauses, which we discuss in the text accompanying Example #18 below. When such a provision applies, a court may be able to conclude that "all parties" have consented to transfer to the district designated in the clause.

[65]376 U.S. 612 (1964).

court. The Texas *federal* judge will use Texas choice of law rules and the California *federal* judge will use California choice of law rules.

The point here is relatively simple: When a case is transferred under §1404(a), *Van Dusen* requires the transferee court (the one to which the case is transferred) to apply the choice of law rules that the transferor court (the original federal court) would have used. Thus, *Van Dusen* ensures that the choice of law rules do not change just because the venue has changed.

> ○ ***Example #17.*** Plaintiff files a diversity case in the Northern District of California. That court transfers the case under §1404(a) to the Southern District of Florida. California choice of law rules would dictate that the merits of the dispute should be determined under the law of Singapore. Florida choice of law rules would dictate that the dispute should be decided under the law of Florida. The Florida federal judge must apply California choice of law rules and, thus, the merits will be decided under Singapore law.

In the unfortunate case of *Ferens v. John Deere Co.*,[66] the Supreme Court extended *Van Dusen* to a §1404(a) transfer initiated by the *plaintiff*. In that case, the plaintiff was injured while using an appliance manufactured by the defendant. The accident took place in Pennsylvania, which has a two-year statute of limitations for tort claims. The plaintiff failed to sue within two years. After two years, the plaintiff sued in federal court in Mississippi. Mississippi has a six-year statute of limitations for tort claims, and the plaintiff sued within that time. Shortly after filing, the plaintiff moved to transfer under §1404(a) to a federal court in Pennsylvania. The court granted the motion. Under *Van Dusen,* the Mississippi choice of law rules (which dictated the application of the longer statute of limitations) accompanied the case when it was transferred. Accordingly, the plaintiff ended up in Pennsylvania federal court able to assert a claim that would have been barred by the Pennsylvania statute of limitations had he sued there in the first place. In other words, the plaintiff, by suing in Mississippi, was allowed to "capture" the longer Mississippi statute of limitations (through application of Mississippi's choice of law rules) and use it even after the case was transferred to federal court in Pennsylvania. *Ferens* thus allowed the plaintiff to do indirectly what he could not do directly (i.e., assert a tort claim in Pennsylvania).

Van Dusen was a §1404(a) case. Its holding should *not* apply to a §1406(a) transfer, because in such a case the transferor court is not a proper venue. Applying *Van Dusen* in §1406(a) would allow the plaintiff to capture favorable choice of law rules from an improper venue. Courts

---

[66]494 U.S. 516 (1990).

properly conclude, then, that *Van Dusen* does not apply in a §1406(a) case.[67] In a diversity of citizenship case, the transferee court in a §1406(a) transfer applies the choice of law rules of the state in which it sits.

This is also the proper result in any *Goldlawr* transfer. In such cases, the transferor court lacks personal jurisdiction over the defendant. It would be outrageous to permit a plaintiff to sue a defendant where she is not subject to personal jurisdiction and capture favorable choice of law rules for determining the outcome of the case. Thus, the vast majority of courts properly hold that *Van Dusen* does not apply to *Goldlawr* transfers.[68]

The* Atlantic Marine *Case (and the Effect of a Forum Selection Clause). Many contracts contain a *forum selection clause*, which provides that litigation arising from the contract will be litigated in a particular place. Historically, courts did not enforce these clauses, but today federal common law and the vast majority of states uphold them.[69] Indeed, in the majority view, they are presumed valid, so the party resisting enforcement of the clause has the burden to show that the other party engaged in fraud or overreaching or that the chosen forum is unreasonable.[70] Such clauses may be "mandatory" or "permissive." The former provides that the specified forum is the *only* permitted place for litigation. The latter provides that litigation is proper in the specified forum, but not prohibited elsewhere. We will assume that the clause is valid and mandatory.[71] The presence of a such a clause raises interesting issues for motions to transfer.

> ○ ***Example #18.*** *A* and *B* enter into a contract that contains a valid forum selection clause requiring litigation to be pursued in the Eastern District

---

[67]*See, e.g.,* Davis v. Louisiana State Univ., 876 F.2d 412, 413 (5th Cir. 1989).

[68]*See, e.g.,* Eggleton v. Plasser & Theurer Export Von Bahnbaumaschinen Gesellschaft, MBH, 495 F.3d 582, 588 (8th. Cir, 2007); Muldoon v. Tropitone Furniture Co., 1 F.3d 964, 967 (9th Cir. 1993); Manley v. Engram, 755 F.2d 1463, 1467 n.10 (11th Cir. 1985). At least one court concluded to the contrary, though, and applied *Van Dusen* to a *Goldlawr* transfer. *See* Myelle v. American Cyanamid Co., 57 F.3d 411, 412 (4th Cir. 1995).

[69]The leading federal case is *M/S Bremen v. Zapata,* 407 U.S. 1, 15 (1972) (enforcing negotiated forum selection clause in admiralty). *See also* Carnival Cruise Lines, Inc. v. Shute, 499 U.S. 585, 593-595 (1991) (enforcing a boilerplate forum selection clause, even though it had not been negotiated by the parties).

[70]*See, e.g.,* Huffington v. T.C. Gp., LLC, 637 F.3d 18, 23-26 (1st Cir. 2011) (party resisting clause bears "heavy burden").

[71]Generally, a clause that says litigation "shall" (as opposed to "may") be brought in the chosen forum is mandatory. Another issue of contract interpretation will be whether the clause governs the dispute at hand. For instance, a provision prescribing a forum for claims "arising from this contract" is narrower than one applying to claims "arising from or related to this contract." We assume throughout this discussion that the clause governs the dispute at hand.

of Virginia. Under §1391(b)(1), venue would be proper in that district because *A* and *B* reside there. Under §1391(b)(2), venue would also be proper in the Western District of Texas because a substantial part of the claim arose there. *A* sues *B* in the Western District of Texas. *B* moves to transfer to the Eastern District of Virginia to enforce the forum selection clause. Whether *B* moves under §1404(a) or §1406(a) depends upon whether venue is proper in the Western District of Texas.

As noted, on the facts of the case venue would be proper in the Western District of Texas under §1391(b)(2).[72] But does the forum selection clause render invalid all districts other than the one prescribed by the clause? In *Atlantic Marine Construction Co. v. U.S. District Court*,[73] the Court resolved that question, on which the lower courts had split badly. It held that a forum selection clause does not render venue improper in other districts; whether venue is proper is determined by statute, not by the parties' agreement. Because venue was proper under §1391(b) in the Western District of Texas, transfer, if ordered, would be under §1404(a) and not §1406(a).[74]

Notice that in Example #18 the clause expressly called for litigation in a particular federal district. This fact makes transfer possible because the chosen forum is in the same judicial system as the pending case (both are federal courts). If the clause prescribed a *state* court in Virginia, the Western District of Texas could not transfer, because the state court is in a different judicial system.[75] In that situation, the federal court would enforce the clause by dismissing the case under *forum non conveniens,* which we discuss in §5.6.

---

[72]If venue were not proper in that district, transfer could only be ordered under §1406(a).

[73]571 U.S. 49, 53-55 (2013). Example #18 is based upon the facts of this case. There is an excellent symposium at 66 Hastings L.J. 617 et seq. (2015), featuring articles by Professors Andrew Bradt, Kevin Clermont, Scott Dodson, Robin Effron, Linda Mullenix, Stephen Sachs, Bradley Scott Shannon, and Adam Steinman.

[74]The Court had no occasion to discuss what would happen if the forum selection clause called for litigation in a district that is not a proper venue. If *Hoffman* applies in such cases, the court would lack authority to order transfer under §1404(a). It would likely enforce the clause by dismissing the case under *forum non conveniens,* which is discussed in §5.6. On the other hand, the "consent prong" of §1404(a) (discussed with regard to Example #15 above) permits transfer to any district to which all parties agree. Arguably, the forum selection clause constitutes all parties' consent to transfer to the designated district.

[75]Some clauses are not clear in this regard. Reference to the courts "of" a particular state may be interpreted as prescribing a state court, while reference to the courts "in" a particular state may be interpreted as permitting suit in either state or federal courts there. *See, e.g.,* Doe 1 v. AOL LLC, 552 F.3d 1077, 1081-1082 (9th Cir. 2009) (reference to "courts of Virginia" as opposed to "courts in Virginia" meant parties referred to state court only).

In *Atlantic Marine*, the Court established three rules for enforcing a forum selection clause through §1404(a) transfer. In other words, *Atlantic Marine* modifies the transfer analysis in three ways. First, "the plaintiff's choice of forum merits no weight."[76] Second, the "private interest factors" (discussed in "Applying §1404(a)" above in this section) must be considered to "weigh entirely in favor of the preselected forum."[77] Thus, the court may consider only the "public interest factors," which will rarely defeat enforcement of the forum selection clause.[78] Finally, in §1404(a) transfers of diversity cases to enforce a forum selection clause, *Van Dusen* does not apply. This makes sense. Applying *Van Dusen* would allow a party to violate the forum selection clause (as *B* did in Example #18) and capture favorable choice of law rules by suing in another district. Because *Van Dusen* does not apply, the transferee district will apply the choice of law rules of the state in which it sits.[79]

Under *Atlantic Marine*, then, the court in Example #18 will order transfer under §1404(a) from the Western District of Texas to the Eastern District of Virginia unless public interest factors weighed against the transfer (which will be rare). The district court in Virginia will apply Virginia choice of law rules to determine what law governs the dispute between *A* and *B*.

Let's summarize the various rules applicable to §1404(a) and §1406(a):

Transfer Statute	Transferor District	Transferee District	Hoffman Apply?	Goldlawr Apply?	Van Dusen Apply?
§1404(a)	Proper venue	Proper venue & personal jurisdiction independently	Yes[80]	Yes	Yes[81]
§1406(a)	Improper venue	Proper venue & personal jurisdiction independently	Yes	Yes	No

---

[76]571 U.S. at 63.

[77]*Id.* at 64.

[78]*Id.* ("[T]hose [public interest] factors will rarely defeat a transfer motion").

[79]*Id.* at 65-66.

[80]As noted in the last paragraph of the discussion of *Hoffman*, §1404(a) was amended in 2012 to make a slight inroad on the *Hoffman* rule.

[81]Unless the transferor court lacks personal jurisdiction. In *Goldlawr* transfers (under either §1404(a) or §1406(a)), *Van Dusen* should not apply, as we discuss in the text immediately above the chart. Also, unless the transfer is ordered pursuant to a forum selection clause. Under *Atlantic Marine*, in such a case, *Van Dusen* does not apply.

Multidistrict Litigation

In addition to §1404(a) and §1406(a), the Judicial Code provides for "multidistrict litigation" (MDL) under §1407. Transfers under §§1404(a) and 1406(a), as we have seen, are ordered by the transferor court. Moreover, they are transfer for all purposes, so the entire litigation will thereafter proceed in the transferee court. MDL transfers under §1407 are wholly different. First, they are ordered by a panel of seven federal judges, appointed by the Chief Justice, sitting as the Judicial Panel for Multidistrict Litigation. The Panel seeks to centralize related litigation from federal courts throughout the federal district courts to a single district, for consolidated proceedings. Second, the transfers are for *pretrial* purposes only.

In theory, after the transferee court completes pretrial litigation, each case is transferred back to its original court to complete the case. Section 1407 was intended to allow consolidated discovery in related cases. But MDL transferee courts are not limited to overseeing discovery. They can oversee all pretrial matters, including dispositive motions.[82] They can also oversee pretrial settlement. Recent years have brought a marked increase in the number of cases transferred and coordinated under §1407. Nearly 40 percent of the civil cases in the federal courts (and some 90 percent of tort cases in the federal courts) are being handled by MDL transfer.[83] Increasingly, the MDL transferee judge attempts to get the parties to reach a "global settlement" resolving all (or almost all) of the cases. It is possible (indeed, likely), therefore, that the case will be wrapped up in the transferee court and never be sent back to the original district. MDL is studied in detail in the course on Complex Litigation.

§5.6 *Forum Non Conveniens*

Background

Forum non conveniens is Latin for "the forum is not convenient." Some courts invoke the phrase when speaking of transfer under §1404(a), which, as we saw in §5.5, involves transfer from a proper venue to a more convenient proper venue. More commonly, though, the phrase is used to refer to a doctrine by which a court will dismiss or

---

[82]*See, e.g.*, In re Donald J. Trump Casino Securities Litig., 7 F.3d 357, 367 (3d Cir. 1993) ("Apparently, transferee courts frequently terminate consolidated cases in practice"; upholding dismissal of MDL case under Rule 12(b)(6)).

[83]For interesting analysis of the recent increase in cases subject to MDL transfer, *see* Thomas Metzloff, *The MDL Vortex Revisited,* 99 Judicature 37 (2015).

stay[84] a pending case because a different forum is far more appropriate. But why would a court ever dismiss, as opposed to transfer? It will do so because transfer is legally impossible—that is, when the more convenient court is in a *different judicial system*. Remember that transfers are possible only to another court in the same judicial system.

- ○ ***Example #19.*** Plaintiff files a case in a proper state court in Alabama. The court has personal jurisdiction, subject matter jurisdiction, and is a proper venue under Alabama law. Under the relevant factors, however, litigation in Indiana would make far more sense. The Alabama state court cannot transfer to an Indiana state court, however, because the courts are in different judicial systems. Instead, the Alabama court might dismiss the case under *forum non conveniens.* Assuming Plaintiff wants to pursue her claim, she will file a new suit in Indiana.
- ○ ***Example #20.*** If the case had been filed in a federal court in Alabama (and invoked federal subject matter jurisdiction), that court could transfer to a federal court in Indiana. Transfer between federal courts can cross state lines because both courts are in the same judicial system.
- ○ ***Example #21.*** Let's say a case is filed in federal *or* state court in New York. The court has personal jurisdiction, subject matter jurisdiction, and is a proper venue. Under the relevant factors, however, litigation in Bolivia would make far more sense. Neither a federal nor a state court can transfer a case to Bolivia, because it is a separate sovereign. If the showing is strong enough, the federal or state court might dismiss under the doctrine of *forum non conveniens.* Plaintiff could then pursue litigation in Bolivia.

Example #21 raises an interesting issue: Why should a plaintiff who has a right to sue in a U.S. court be required to pursue her claim in the courts of a foreign land? *Forum non conveniens* may be criticized as an abdication by the U.S. court of an obligation to litigate those cases that invoke its jurisdiction, which drives home two points: (1) *forum non conveniens* is and should be exceptional, not routine, and (2) it should be invoked only when there is some reasonable assurance that the plaintiff (particularly, perhaps, an American plaintiff) will have access to justice in the foreign court. As we consider the content of federal *forum non conveniens* doctrine, assess whether you think it addresses these two concerns sufficiently.

The Federal Doctrine: The Piper *Case*

Each state is free to develop its own rules for applying *forum non conveniens.* Most states have adopted a version very similar to the

---

[84]The option of "staying" a case is discussed in the subsection entitled "Procedural Issues" below.

federal law on the issue. The leading case on the federal doctrine is *Piper Aircraft Co. v. Reyno.*[85] *Piper* involved the crash of a small commercial airplane that killed all six persons aboard. The crash occurred in Scotland. The five passengers and the pilot were Scottish. The company that owned and maintained the plane was Scottish. The company that operated the charter business using the plane was Scottish. The heirs and next of kin of those killed were Scottish. But the airplane involved was manufactured in Pennsylvania by Piper Aircraft Company, and the propellers on the plane were manufactured in Ohio by Hartzell Corporation. The plaintiff asserted that the two manufacturers were liable for the wrongful deaths of the passengers under various tort theories, including negligence and strict product liability.

Gaynell Reyno was a U.S. citizen, domiciled in California. She was not related to any of the parties in the case but was appointed by a state court in Los Angeles to administer the estates of the five passengers. That means that she represented the estates of those decedents in the California court, and was entitled to assert the wrongful death claims on behalf of the passengers' estates. Those estates had already filed wrongful death cases in Scotland but stood to recover far more under the law of almost any U.S. state because American tort law generally permits recovery for anguish. (Scottish law does not; neither does Scotland recognize strict liability in tort.) Reyno filed the case in state court in Los Angeles. She named only Piper and Hartzell as defendants. The Scottish owner and operators of the plane, as well as the estate of the pilot, were not subject to personal jurisdiction anywhere in the United States, so were not included as defendants. Piper and Hartzell removed the case to federal court for the Central District of California (which embraces Los Angeles).

That court granted the defendants' motion to transfer under §1404(a) to the federal district court for the Middle District of Pennsylvania (which is where Piper manufactures its airplanes). (The details involved in the removal and transfer are discussed in the following subsection and provide an interesting story.) The federal judge in Pennsylvania dismissed the case under *forum non conveniens.* Ultimately, the Supreme Court upheld the district court's dismissal and clarified the federal doctrine of *forum non conveniens.*

A court has great discretion in applying the doctrine, and the result always depends on the particular facts of the case.[86] Still, three general observations are possible:

---

[85] 454 U.S. 235 (1981).

[86] The Supreme Court admits that the discretionary nature of the doctrine makes "uniformity and predictability of outcomes almost impossible." American Dredging Co. v. Miller, 510 U.S. 443, 455 (1994). The open-endedness and other problems have led

1. The plaintiff's choice of forum is entitled to some deference, just as it is in cases involving transfer under §1404(a).[87] Indeed, one might expect greater deference here because dismissal is harsher than an order of transfer. Still, the issue depends on the facts of the case, so, for example, courts generally accord less deference to the plaintiff if she is a foreign citizen.[88]

2. The court is to address the same "public interest factors" and "private interest factors" as §1404(a) transfer (footnote 6 of *Piper* lists the factors, which are discussed above at §5.5.2). Because dismissal is harsh, the defendant must make a very strong showing that the alternative forum is *clearly* more appropriate based upon those factors.[89]

3. The alternative forum must be "available" and "adequate."

On the facts in *Piper*, the Court concluded, dismissal was warranted. First, though Reyno was an American citizen, she sued on behalf of foreign nationals, so her choice of forum was not entitled to much deference.

Second, the public and private factors strongly supported dismissal. The alternative forum in Scotland already had jurisdiction over related litigation involving all interested persons, including Piper and Hartzell. Administratively, the case would be very difficult for a Pennsylvania federal court, because (for reasons discussed in the next section) Pennsylvania law applied to the claims against Piper and Scottish law to the claims against Hartzell. This fact would force the court to rely upon experts in Scottish law. It could also confuse the jury and burden the citizens of a community (in Pennsylvania)

---

some to argue that the doctrine as currently understood should be jettisoned. *See, e.g.,* Maggie Gardner, *Retiring Forum Non Conveniens,* 92 N.Y.U. L. Rev. 390 (2017).

[87]We are assuming that the court in which the case is pending has subject matter jurisdiction, personal jurisdiction, and is a proper venue. If any of those are not met, the case can be dismissed on any of those grounds.

[88]As a further reflection of this point, some courts virtually never grant a *forum non conveniens* motion if the plaintiff resides in the forum. A resident plaintiff has an especially strong interest in litigating there. *See* 2 Witkin, California Procedure §377 (2011) (if plaintiff is a resident, forum is presumed convenient and "the state has a strong interest in giving its own residents an adequate forum for the redress of grievances").

[89]Professor Effron cogently criticizes the use of the same factors to assess transfer and *forum non conveniens*. She explains:

> [B]oth §1404(a) and *forum non conveniens* account for convenience, but in notably different ways. Section 1404(a)'s center of gravity inquiry focuses the attention of the court on the relative convenience of the transferee forum, whereas the *forum non conveniens* factors demand closer scrutiny to the inconvenience of the initial forum.

> Robin Effron, Atlantic Marine *and the Future of Forum Non Conveniens,* 66 Hastings L.J. 693, 712 (2015) (emphases original).

far removed from the events underlying the suit (in Scotland). In contrast, Scotland had a substantial stake in the outcome of the case. Because the owner and operator of the plane and the estate of the pilot could not be sued in the United States, permitting the case to go forward in this country fostered inefficient, piecemeal litigation. (Remember, for personal jurisdiction reasons, litigation against the Scottish defendants could only proceed in Scotland.) In sum, then, the factors indicated that a Scottish court was far more appropriate than the federal court in Pennsylvania.

Third, an alternative forum in Scotland was "available" and "adequate." It is here that *Piper* may have its greatest impact. When the alternative forum is in a foreign country, plaintiffs will complain that it is not "adequate" because foreign law generally is not as "pro-plaintiff" as American law. Certainly, most countries have not adopted progressive theories of tort liability and do not permit recovery for things like anguish. In addition, they may not permit trial by jury. In *Piper*, the Court established that such differences in the law are not dispositive. Only "if the remedy provided by the alternative forum is so clearly inadequate or unsatisfactory that it is no remedy at all"[90] should the difference be given substantial weight. On the facts in *Piper*, the Court held, there was no such showing.[91]

The Effect of a Forum Selection Clause: The Atlantic Marine Case (Again)

In §5.5.2, we discussed *Atlantic Marine*, in which the Court modified the transfer analysis under §1404(a) in cases involving a valid mandatory forum selection clause. Transfer in such cases is possible only when the forum selection clause prescribes suit in a federal district court. When the clause calls for litigation in a state court or in a court outside the United States, §1404(a) cannot apply (because the prescribed court is in a different judicial system). In such a case, assuming the clause is valid, mandatory, and covers the dispute at hand,[92] *Atlantic Marine* modifies *forum non conveniens* analysis in two ways.

First, the court gives no deference to the plaintiff's choice of forum.[93] Second, the court presumes that the "private interest factors"

---

[90]*Piper*, 454 U.S. at 254.

[91]Some commentators have criticized the Court's reasoning and application of *forum non conveniens* doctrine in *Piper. See, e.g.*, Kevin M. Clermont, *The Story of* Piper: *Fracturing the Foundation of Forum Non Conveniens*, in Civil Procedure Stories 193-216 (2d ed. 2004).

[92]See note 71 and accompanying text above.

[93]*Atlantic Marine*, 571 U.S. at 63.

all support litigation in the alternative forum.[94] Accordingly, the court will dismiss the case in favor of the forum selection clause unless the public interest factors demand a contrary conclusion (which will rarely be the case).[95]

Procedural Issues

Most motions brought under *forum non conveniens* seek dismissal. In the alternative, the court may "stay" the case. To stay a case means to suspend it. The court keeps the case on the docket but does not permit any activity in that case. This allows the court to ensure that litigation in the other court actually may proceed. If there is some problem (say, with invoking jurisdiction in the other forum), the court may permit the parties to return to the pending litigation.

That said, most cases in which the defendant is successful under *forum non conveniens* seem to result in dismissal. When the litigation is dismissed in favor of proceeding in another country, the results often are not good for plaintiffs. There are not many data, but such dismissals usually mean the plaintiff will recover, at most, a paltry settlement. One old survey of 85 cases dismissed in favor of a foreign court showed that every case was abandoned or settled for very little.[96] As a case in point, after dismissal in *Piper*, no lawyer in Scotland found it worthwhile to proceed with the case there.

Forum non conveniens dismissals are often "conditional." That is, the court will grant the defendant's motion to dismiss *conditioned upon* the defendant's waiving certain defenses or agreeing to certain things. For instance, the defendants in *Piper* stipulated that they would not object to the personal jurisdiction of the Scottish courts. They also agreed to waive any statute of limitations defense in that action. As another example, a defendant agreed to allow the plaintiff to undertake American-style discovery even though such intrusive

---

[94]*See, e.g.*, Barnett v. Dyncorp Int'l, 831 F.3d 296, 309 (5th Cir. 2016) (public interest factors did not weigh against enforcing forum selection clause prescribing litigation in Kuwait).

[95]*Atlantic Marine*, 571 U.S. at 51 ("the court should not consider the parties' private interests aside from those embodied in the forum-selection clause; it may consider only public interests. Because public-interest factors will rarely defeat a transfer motion, the practical result is that forum-selection clauses should control except in unusual cases.").

[96]David W. Robertson, Forum Non Conveniens *in America and England: "A Rather Fantastic Fiction,"* 103 L.Q. Rev. 398, 418-420 (1987). *See also* Jacqueline Duval-Major, *A One-Way Ticket Home: The Federal Doctrine of Forum Non Conveniens and the International Plaintiff*, 77 Cornell L. Rev. 650 (1992).

measures would not be allowed in the foreign tribunal.[97] Of course, defendants are usually happy to make such concessions to avoid litigation in the United States, with its relatively pro-plaintiff tort laws and remedies.[98] So it is routine for defendants to move to dismiss on grounds of *forum non conveniens* while offering to submit to jurisdiction or to waive some defense in the overseas court.

In §6.2.1, we will see that *forum non conveniens* is not included in Federal Rule 12(b), which lists certain defenses that may be raised either by motion or in one's answer. Because it is thus not a Rule 12 motion, the federal courts generally conclude that there is no set time limit for raising it.[99] The matter is in the court's discretion and, whenever that is true, it always behooves a litigant to raise the issue earlier rather than later. Some states, in contrast, set time limits for raising *forum non conveniens*.

In an early *forum non conveniens* case, the Supreme Court had said that the doctrine "can never apply if there is absence of jurisdiction."[100] In reaction, some lower federal courts concluded that they could not dismiss under this doctrine until they had concluded that they had personal jurisdiction over the defendants. The Supreme Court ultimately rejected this approach and held that a court may, "when judicial economy so warrant[s]," bypass questions of personal and subject matter jurisdiction and dispose of a suit under the doctrine of *forum non conveniens*.[101]

"Boomerang" Litigation

A *forum non conveniens* dismissal does not always spell defeat for the plaintiff. Occasionally, a court in a foreign country enters a sizeable award against an American defendant, which then leads to "boomerang" litigation, which consists of three cases. First, a foreign plaintiff sues an

---

[97]This happened in litigation concerning a toxic tort disaster in Bhopal, India. *See* In re Union Carbide Corp. Gas Plant Disaster at Bhopal, India, 809 F.2d 195 (2d Cir. 1987).

[98]"As a moth is drawn to the light, so is a litigant drawn to the United States. If he can only get his case into their courts, he stands to win a fortune." Russell Weintraub, *International Litigation and Forum Non Conveniens*, 29 Tex. Int'l L.J. 321, 322 (1994) (*quoting* Lord Denning). *See also* Kevin M. Clermont & Theodore Eisenberg, *Xenophilia in American Courts,* 109 Harv. L. Rev. 1120 (1996).

[99]*See, e.g.*, American Home Assur. Co. v. TGL Container Lines, Ltd., 347 F. Supp. 2d 749, 765 (C.D. Cal. 2004). A defendant asserting *forum non conveniens* is not contesting jurisdiction or venue. Rather, she is arguing that *even though* the present forum is proper, there is another court in another judicial system in which litigation would make far more sense. *See, e.g.*, Abiola v. Abubakar, 267 F. Supp. 2d 907, 918 (N.D. Ill. 2003).

[100]*Gulf Oil,* 330 U.S. at 505.

[101]Sinochem Int'l Co. Ltd. v. Malaysia Int'l Shipping, 549 U.S. 422, 433 (2007). See also §6.5.

American defendant in a U.S. court concerning an event in the foreign country. The U.S. court dismisses on the basis of *forum non conveniens*. Second, the plaintiff sues the American in the foreign court and wins a judgment. The plaintiff is unable to enforce the judgment in the foreign country because the defendant lacks substantial assets there. Third, the plaintiff sues in the United States, seeking to enforce the foreign judgment.

Hence the boomerang: The litigation that started in the U.S. ends up back in the U.S.—but this time not for litigation on the merits, but to enforce a foreign judgment. Now, frequently, the defendant argues that the foreign judgment should not be enforced by the U.S. court because the procedures in the foreign tribunal were not fair. In other words, the very defendant who moved to dismiss under *forum non conveniens* by arguing that the foreign court would be adequate now claims that that court was inadequate.[102]

The issue of whether a foreign judgment is entitled to enforcement in a U.S. court is beyond the scope of Civil Procedure. Suffice to say that the procedures followed in some cases litigated in foreign courts are so lacking in fundamental fairness as to preclude enforcement in this country. A well-known example is litigation against Chevron for alleged contamination of land in Ecuador. Plaintiffs won a judgment in that country of nearly $18,000,000,000. In 2018, the Permanent Court of Arbitration in The Hague concluded unanimously, however, that the Ecuadorean judgment was fraudulent and corrupt and "should not be recognized or enforced by the courts of other States." Among other things, according to its decision, the plaintiffs blackmailed an Ecuadorean judge and bribed experts.[103]

§5.7 Using *Piper Aircraft Co. v. Reyno* to Review Forum Selection Issues (Why *Piper* Is the Greatest of All Civil Procedure Cases)

The facts of *Piper* involve many elements of forum selection we have already seen in Chapters 2, 4, and this chapter. As we recount

---

[102]*See generally* Alexander F. Moss, Comment, *Bridging the Gap: Addressing the Doctrinal Disparity Between* Forum Non Conveniens *and Judgment Recognition Enforcement in Transnational Litigation,* 106 Geo. L.J. 209 (2017).

[103]Karen Nagarkatti and Gary McWilliams, *International Tribunal Rules in Favor of Chevron in Ecuador Case,* Reuters, Sept. 7, 2018, https://www.reuters.com/article/us-chevron-ecuador-idUSKCN1LN1WS.

See generally Patrick Radden Keefe, *Reversal of Fortune,* The New Yorker, Jan. 12, 2012, https://www.newyorker.com/magazine/2012/01/09/reversal-of-fortune-patrick-radden-keefe. *See* Christopher A. Whytock & Cassandra Burke Robertson, various facts, the text asks questions that force you to apply doctrines we covered in those chapters. The answers to the questions are in the footnotes.

Reyno sued Piper Aircraft Company, which manufactured the airplane involved in the crash giving rise to the suit. Piper is head-quartered and manufactures airplanes in the Middle District of Pennsylvania. At the time the case was decided, Piper was subject to general personal jurisdiction in California because it did substantial and continuous business there. (That is no longer the law, as we studied in §2.4.5, and today Piper would not be subject to general personal jurisdiction in California.) General personal jurisdiction allowed suit against Piper in California even though the claim did not arise there. On the other hand, everyone seemed to agree that Harzell was not subject to personal jurisdiction in California. It manufactures aircraft propellers, including the propellers on the plane involved in the crash in this case. Its headquarters and plant are in Ohio. It sells many of its props to Piper in Pennsylvania.[104] For the rest of this discussion, assume that California had personal jurisdiction over Piper but not over Hartzell. Reyno sued in state court in Los Angeles. She was the executrix of the Scottish citizens killed in the crash. Reyno is a U.S. citizen domiciled in California. Piper is a Pennsylvania citizen; Hartzell is an Ohio citizen. The claims were for millions of dollars. We are assuming that the state court in Los Angeles had personal jurisdiction over Piper but not over Hartzell.

Did the state court in Los Angeles have subject matter jurisdiction over the case?[105] The defendants removed the case to the federal district court for the Central District of California. Did the case invoke federal subject matter jurisdiction?[106] (Be careful with this one.

Forum Non Conveniens and the Enforcement of Foreign Judgments, 111 Colum. L. Rev. 1444 (2011).

[104]Perhaps you can construct a stream-of-commerce argument for jurisdiction over Hartzell in California. See §2.4.4. For the discussion in the text, we will assume that California did not have personal jurisdiction over Hartzell.

[105]Yes. State courts have general subject matter jurisdiction. They can hear any case not falling within exclusive federal question jurisdiction. This is a case for wrongful death, based upon various tort theories. There is no federal question at all, let alone an exclusive federal question. See §4.2.

[106]There is no federal question jurisdiction; the claims are based wholly on state law, and do not implicate federal interests. What about diversity or alienage? Reyno was a citizen of California. The defendants were citizens of Pennsylvania and Ohio. The amount in controversy is clearly met. But Reyno represented Scottish citizens. Is it her citizenship or that of the decedents that controls? If it is hers, the case invokes diversity of citizenship jurisdiction. If it is the decedents', the case invokes alienage jurisdiction. See the next footnote.

Whose citizenship is relevant on the plaintiffs' side?[107]) That federal court transferred the case to the federal district court for the Middle District of Pennsylvania. Why *must* that transfer have been pursuant to §1404(a) and not §1406(a)?[108] In other words, why was the Central District of California a proper venue *even though* it would not have been a proper venue under §1391?[109] (By the way, why would the Central District of California not be a proper venue under §1391(b)?[110] In other words, why did Hartzell not *reside* in the Central District?[111])

The judge in the Central District of California transferred the case to the Middle District of Pennsylvania. Under *Hoffman v. Blaski*, what must be true about that transferee court?[112] In other words, (1) why does

---

[107]In §4.5.3, we saw that 28 U.S.C. §1332(c)(2) provides that in cases involving decedents, minors, or incompetents represented in litigation by a fiduciary, the court looks to the citizenship of the decedent, minor, or incompetent, and not to that of the fiduciary. At first glance, then, that statute would seem to tell us that it is the decedents' citizenship (Scotland) and not the representative's (California) that governs. So the case would invoke alienage rather than diversity. But §1332(c)(2) provides that the representative is deemed to be a citizen of "the same State" as the decedent, minor, or incompetent. In the jurisdictional statutes, the capitalized word *State* generally refers to a state of the United States. Because the decedents were not citizens of any state of the United States, arguably, §1332(c)(2) does not apply on this fact pattern. If that is correct, we look to the citizenship of the representative, which is California, so the case would invoke diversity of citizenship jurisdiction and not alienage. As we saw in §4.5.5, however, the courts have applied §1332(c)(2) to cases involving alien representatives. So the case invokes alienage jurisdiction.

[108]Because §1404(a) applies to transfers *from* a proper venue. The Central District of California was a proper venue. If the reason for this is not clear, see the next footnote.

[109]Section 1391(b) is irrelevant in a case removed from state court. It applies only to cases filed by the plaintiff in federal court. In a removed case, venue is proper only in the federal district embracing the state court in which it was originally filed. 28 U.S.C. §1441(a). See §5.4.2. Los Angeles is in the Central District of California.

[110]The plane was manufactured in Pennsylvania and crashed in Scotland. Thus, no part of the claim arose in the Central District of California and venue was not proper there under §1391(b)(2). Moreover, the Central District is not one in which all defendants reside, so venue was not proper there under §1391(b)(1). One defendant (Piper) resided there (under the law at the time), but not the other (Hartzell). If the reason for this is not clear, see the next footnote.

[111]Under §1391(c)(2), a business resides in all districts in which it is subject to personal jurisdiction for the case. Hartzell was not subject to personal jurisdiction in California. Under the doctrine of general personal jurisdiction as it stood at the time, Piper was subject to personal jurisdiction in California because it did continuous and systematic business in that state. It would not be subject to general jurisdiction in California under the law as it stands today because it is not "at home" in that state. See §2.4.5. Because at the time Piper was subject to personal jurisdiction in California, it resided there for venue purposes, but venue is proper under §1391(b)(1) only if *all* defendants reside in the district or in different districts of the forum state.

[112]Under *Hoffman*, transfer is proper only to a court that has personal jurisdiction over the defendants and is a proper venue under §1391, absent waiver by the defendant. See §5.5.2.

the Middle District of Pennsylvania have personal jurisdiction over the defendants,[113] and (2) why is the Middle District of Pennsylvania a proper venue under §1391?[114] But how could the Central District of California transfer as to Hartzell, when that court lacked personal jurisdiction over Hartzell?[115]

After the case was transferred, why would the Middle District of Pennsylvania be required to apply different choice of law rules to the two defendants?[116] (In other words, why does *Van Dusen* apply to Piper but not to Hartzell?[117]) Thus, when the case got to the federal judge in Pennsylvania, he had to apply the choice of law rules of California as to Piper and the choice of law rules of Pennsylvania as to Hartzell. He concluded that California choice of law rules would dictate that Pennsylvania governed concerning the liability of Piper. He also concluded that Pennsylvania choice of law rules would apply Scottish law to determine the liability of Hartzell.

[113]Piper has its principal place of business in the Middle District of Pennsylvania, and thus was (and still is today) subject to general personal jurisdiction there. Hartzell manufactures its propellers in Ohio but ships a large percentage of them to Piper in Pennsylvania, pursuant to a long-term commercial relationship. Thus, it undoubtedly has minimum contacts with Pennsylvania and is subject to personal jurisdiction there for this case. (By the way, Hartzell's relationship with Pennsylvania is not based upon a stream-of-commerce theory. It ships these goods directly and purposefully to Pennsylvania; they are not carried there by the vagaries of the stream of commerce.) See §2.4.4.

[114]Because all defendants reside there, venue is proper under §1391(b)(1). Again, a business resides in every district in which it is subject to personal jurisdiction for the case. Also, there is a strong argument that a substantial part of the claim arose there, because that is where the plane was manufactured, so venue would be proper under §1391(b)(2).

[115]Because *Goldlawr* permits transfer even by a court lacking personal jurisdiction over the defendant. See §5.5.2.

[116]Because under *Van Dusen*, the choice of law rules of California are transferred along with the case. This is so, however, only as to Piper, not Hartzell. See §5.5.2. Why? See the next footnote.

[117]Because *Van Dusen* does not apply to *Goldlawr* transfers, that is, to a transfer involving a defendant over whom the transferor court lacked personal jurisdiction. See §5.5.2. The Central District of California had personal jurisdiction over Piper under the law as it stood at the time, so *Van Dusen* applied to the transfer of the case against it. The court did not have personal jurisdiction over Hartzell, however, so *Van Dusen* did not apply to the transfer of the claim against it.

Chapter 6

Challenging the Selection of Forum

§6.1   Defining the Issue

We have spent a good deal of time addressing the selection of a proper forum for litigation. The doctrines of personal jurisdiction, subject matter jurisdiction, and venue guide this selection. Here, we address how the defendant might challenge the plaintiff's selection of forum.[1]

The basis for the challenge affects how the challenge might be raised. Limitations on personal jurisdiction (including propriety of service of process) and venue, as we saw in Chapters 2, 3, and 5, give the defendant personal rights, which may be waived. Moreover, because they present a threshold issue of whether the litigation is in the proper court, it seems advisable to determine them as early as possible. It is wasteful to litigate for some lengthy period only to find out that the case is not in a proper court. Thus, procedural rules in all states impose limits on when and how the defendant may

---

[1]In a case removed from state to federal court (see §4.8), it may be the plaintiff who challenges the defendant's selection of a federal forum; for example, through a motion to remand to state court.

challenge personal jurisdiction and venue, to ensure that they are raised early or else waived. In §6.2, we will see different approaches to those challenges. In §6.3, we consider the factors relevant to a defendant's decision of whether to challenge personal jurisdiction directly or in a collateral proceeding.

Subject matter jurisdiction, as we discuss in §6.4, is a different proposition. True, it would be efficient to force the defendant to raise a subject matter jurisdiction objection early or else waive it. But, as we saw in §4.3, subject matter jurisdiction does not implicate a litigant's personal rights. Instead, subject matter jurisdiction involves the proper allocation of litigation between federal and state courts. They are rules about the structure of government.[2] Thus, litigants cannot waive strictures on subject matter jurisdiction. Despite the possible inefficiency, it is clear, at least generally, that a court's lack of subject matter jurisdiction can be raised for the first time almost anytime—even after entry of judgment. There is a significant question, however, as to whether one can attack subject matter jurisdiction in a collateral proceeding.

§6.2   Different Approaches to Challenging Personal Jurisdiction, Venue, and Process Issues (and How Rule 12 Works)

§6.2.1   *In Personam* Jurisdiction: Special Appearance and the Modern Approach Under Rule 12

Development of the Special Appearance

Consider the dilemma facing a defendant who wants to argue that the state in which she has been sued lacks personal jurisdiction. She will want to go to that state and make a motion to dismiss. But by going to that state, or even by sending her lawyer, has the defendant subjected herself to personal jurisdiction there? After all, is she not present in the forum when she raises the challenge? Did she consent to jurisdiction by going there? Understanding this dilemma, courts developed the "special appearance," which allows the defendant to appear in the forum for the sole purpose of arguing that the court lacks personal jurisdiction. The special appearance is to be contrasted with a "general appearance," which constitutes a submission to personal

---

[2]Remember that federal courts can entertain only certain types of cases, because the Constitution says so. U.S. Const. art. III, §2. We discussed this point at §4.3.

jurisdiction. Usually, the vehicle for making a special appearance is to file a "motion to quash service of summons."

The special appearance method of questioning personal jurisdiction is not the majority view today; most states have adopted the modern approach, which we discuss below. It is important to remember, though, that a few states—including such populous states as California, Texas, and Virginia—still employ the special appearance. Though some states are stricter than others, traditionally, the defendant making a special appearance could raise *only* an objection to personal jurisdiction. Asserting another defense or filing an answer *before or even contemporaneously with* the motion to strike service of summons historically constituted a general appearance and thus a waiver of the personal jurisdiction objection.[3] The idea with the general appearance is that the defendant has at some point become so engaged in the proceedings that it is fair to say, essentially, that she has consented to the court's personal jurisdiction.

The special appearance has the advantage of presenting a single, potentially dispositive issue to the court. If the court concludes that it lacks personal jurisdiction, early dismissal avoids meaningless litigation on the merits of the claim. On the other hand, though, it has the obvious disadvantage of forcing the defendant to put all the eggs in one basket, at least initially. Generally, in special appearance jurisdictions, the defendant may raise other possible defenses only after losing on the personal jurisdiction defense.[4]

Another problem is that the special appearance rule can be a trap for the unwary. Again, some states are stricter than others about what can be raised in a special appearance without waiving the personal jurisdiction defense. For example, in most states, a defendant may safely raise a lack of personal jurisdiction in the alternative with a motion to

---

[3]*See generally* Clifford Plunkett, *Waiver and the Special Appearance in Arkansas,* 47 Ark. L. Rev. 883 (1994). California followed this approach until 2003, when it liberalized its practice to a degree by providing that an objection to personal jurisdiction may be brought simultaneously with other defensive responses. Cal. Code Civ. Pro. §418.10(e)(1). Other states, including Virginia, retain the old practice of requiring a motion to quash service of summons to be brought by itself and before any other defensive response. Va. Code Ann. §8.01-277.1.

[4]A good example of this limitation is *Asahi v. Superior Court,* discussed at §2.4.4. There, the valve manufacturer, Asahi, made a special appearance to challenge California's assertion of jurisdiction. After losing that challenge, Asahi succeeded in getting appellate review of the personal jurisdiction issue by the California appellate courts and, ultimately, by the Supreme Court of the United States. During the lengthy delay caused by all the appellate involvement, Asahi's lawyers apparently discovered that it had not even manufactured the valve involved in the accident. But if it presented that fact to the court (e.g., through a motion for summary judgment), it would have been making a general appearance and would waive the personal jurisdiction objection.

dismiss for *forum non conveniens* (which we discussed at §5.6). In especially strict states, however, the combination of the personal jurisdiction issue with the alternative motion can constitute a general appearance.[5] Counsel must be very careful about whether her jurisdiction allows a defendant to raise other defenses with her objection to personal jurisdiction. Interestingly, some strict special appearance states appear to permit the defendant to challenge subject matter jurisdiction along with personal jurisdiction, without waiver.[6]

The Modern (Rule 12) Approach

The modern approach to challenging the selection of a forum is typified by Federal Rule 12. It applies (of course) in federal court, and most states have modeled their rules on the Federal Rules. Rule 12 abolishes the special appearance by allowing the defendant to raise various defenses, including personal jurisdiction, simultaneously. Doing so does not waive a personal jurisdiction objection. In the words of Rule 12(b), "[n]o defense or objection is waived by being joined with one or more other defenses or objections in a responsive pleading or motion."

How does Rule 12 work? For starters, it is important to understand that a defendant has a choice of how to respond to litigation against her: She may respond by *pleading* (called an *answer*) or she may bring a *motion*. (We discuss these options in detail at §7.4.) In the answer, the defendant responds to the plaintiff's complaint and raises affirmative defenses. With a motion, a party requests that the court enter a particular order. In the course of litigation, there may be dozens of motions—for example, motions to amend pleadings, to compel discovery, to extend the time in which to respond, for summary judgment—the list is endless. Some of the most important motions are motions to dismiss because of a problem with the selection of the forum.

Here we focus on the seven defenses found in Federal Rule 12(b). Take a close look at these seven "12(b) defenses" (and be sure to notice that the first five all relate to selection of a forum): (1) lack of subject matter jurisdiction; (2) lack of personal jurisdiction; (3) improper

---

[5]While nervously waiting to make his first oral argument in the practice of law, the author witnessed an oral argument in California Superior Court where exactly that happened. The defendant was deemed to have made a general appearance and thus to have waived its personal jurisdiction objection. Indeed, some courts have been so strict as to say that requesting a continuance (delay) of the hearing on the motion to dismiss for lack of personal jurisdiction constitutes a general appearance. *See, e.g.*, Bumgarner v. Federal Deposit Ins. Corp., 764 P.2d 1367, 1369 (Okla. App. 1988); Pfeiffer v. Ash, 206 P.2d 438, 439 (Cal. App. 1949). On the other hand, removing a case from state to federal court does not waive a challenge to personal jurisdiction. Lambert Run Coal Co. v. Baltimore & Ohio R.R., 258 U.S. 377, 382-384 (1922).

[6]*See, e.g.*, Goodwine v. Superior Court, 407 P.2d 1, 3-4 (Cal. 1965).

venue; (4) insufficient process; (5) insufficient service of process[7]; (6) failure to state a claim on which relief can be granted; and (7) failure to join an absentee under Rule 19. Rule 12(b) provides that all seven of the 12(b) defenses may be raised *either* by motion or in the defendant's answer.[8]

The fact that the defendant has a choice of how to assert the Rule 12(b) defenses raises the possibility of inadvertent waiver. Be careful about Rules 12(g) and (h). They impose timing requirements on raising the Rule 12(b) defenses and contain traps for the unwary. Rule 12(g)(2) requires a defendant who makes a *motion* under Rule 12[9] to join in that motion "a defense or objection that was available to the party but omitted from its earlier motion." If she does not do so, she "must not make another motion under this rule," with exceptions as provided in Rule 12(h)(2) and (h)(3). Thus, Rule 12(g) is concerned with a defendant's asserting two Rule 12 *motions*. If she omits from the first one some Rule 12 defense that is available to her at the time, she cannot make a second Rule 12 motion, unless she falls within the saving grace of Rule 12(h)(2) or (h)(3). In other words, as a general matter, omitting a Rule 12 defense from a Rule 12 motion waives the right to bring a second motion under Rule 12.

Rule 12(h) addresses waiver of all seven of the Rule 12(b) defenses, but clusters them into three groups for purposes of timing. Four of the five defenses relating to selection of a forum (lack of personal jurisdiction, improper venue, insufficient process, and insufficient service of process) are found in Rule 12(h)(1). That subsection provides that such defenses are waived if omitted from a Rule 12 motion *or* if omitted from a responsive pleading (or a pleading amended as a matter of course, which we see at §7.5.1). Notice, then, how (as to these four defenses) Rule 12(h)(1) supplements Rule 12(g) by providing for waiver not only if the defendant tries to bring two Rule 12 motions, but also if the defendant omits one of the defenses from *either* a motion or the answer and then tries to raise it with a subsequent motion or answer.

---

[7]What is the difference between 12(b)(4) and 12(b)(5)? The former is aimed at problems with the process itself—for example, failure to have both summons and a copy of the complaint. See §3.3.1. Such problems are rare. The latter is aimed at problems not with the documents, but with how they were served on the defendant—for example, that substituted service was not made on a person of suitable age and discretion or on a proper corporate agent. See §§3.3.2, 3.3.3. Such problems are more common.

[8]Why, then, would a defendant raise any of these in her answer, rather than by motion? Putting the defense in the answer preserves it, so a defendant who thinks one of the 12(b) defenses *might* be plausible does not have to make a motion on it now, but can preserve it and push the issue later, when she has more factual grounding for it.

[9]A Rule 12 motion might be based upon any of the seven Rule 12(b) defenses, or it might be a Rule 12(e) motion for more definite statement or a Rule 12(f) motion to strike. See §7.4.1.

This gets complicated, but we will make it simpler in a moment. Before we do, though, notice that Rule 12(h)(3) addresses timing of the other forum selection issue (lack of subject matter jurisdiction) and provides, essentially, that it can be raised anytime. And Rule 12(h)(2) addresses the two Rule 12(b) defenses that do not concern forum selection—the motion to dismiss for failure to state a claim and to dismiss for failure to join an absentee under Rule 19.

All of the timing issues in Rule 12(g) and (h) can be summarized in three principles.

Principle Number 1. The defenses in Rule 12(b)(2), (3), (4), and (5) must be included in the first defensive response under Rule 12—whether that is a motion or an answer. If they are not included, they are waived. This rule makes sense, because these four defenses—lack of personal jurisdiction, improper venue, insufficiency of process, and insufficiency of service of process—are threshold issues, which ought to be determined at the outset. They are also waivable defenses, so the rule appropriately puts the burden on the defendant to raise them early or else lose them.

Principle Number 2. The defenses in Rule 12(b)(6) and (7) may be raised as late as "at trial," which means any time before entry of judgment by the trial court. This result is dictated by Rule 12(h)(2), and also makes sense, because these defenses—failure to state a claim on which relief can be granted and failure to join an absentee under Rule 19—may mature later in the litigation.[10] These two defenses need not be put in the defendant's *first* Rule 12 response. They are waived only if they are not raised sometime before judgment is entered by the trial court.

Principle Number 3. The defense in Rule 12(b)(1) may be raised anytime. This result is dictated by Rule 12(h)(3) and also makes sense, because the defense is lack of subject matter jurisdiction. Remember, the limited subject matter jurisdiction of the federal courts is a matter of governmental structure, which litigants cannot waive or change. If a case does not invoke federal subject matter jurisdiction, a federal court must dismiss, even if it has invested years in the case under the incorrect impression that it had subject matter jurisdiction. See §6.4.

These principles will resolve any fact pattern in this area.

○ ***Example #1.*** P sues D. Within the proper time, D makes a motion to dismiss for lack of personal jurisdiction. The court denies the motion.

[10]This is especially so with Rule 12(b)(7), which involves failure to join an absentee under Rule 19, often called a "necessary" party (although the rule calls it a "required" party). Often, the fact that such an absentee exists will not be ascertainable until the case unfolds a bit, perhaps in discovery. See §12.6.1.

Then *D* makes a motion to dismiss for improper venue. She has waived the venue defense under Rule 12(g). Why?[11]

○ ***Example #2.*** *P* sues *D*. Within the proper time, *D* makes a motion to dismiss for lack of personal jurisdiction. The court denies the motion. Then *D* files an answer, in which she asserts the defense of improper service of process. That defense is waived and may be stricken. Why?[12]

○ ***Example #3.*** *P* sues *D*. Within the proper time, *D* serves and files an answer raising the defense of improper venue. Then she makes a motion to dismiss for lack of personal jurisdiction. She has waived the defense. Why?[13] (Your professor may add facts making it overwhelmingly clear that *D* had absolutely no contacts with the forum; still, personal jurisdiction there is proper because *D* waived the personal jurisdiction defense.)

○ ***Example #4.*** *P* sues *D*. Within the proper time, *D* makes a motion to strike *P*'s pleading under Rule 12(f). The court denies the motion. Then *D* serves and files an answer (or makes a motion) raising lack of personal jurisdiction. Again, she has waived the latter defense. Why?[14]

○ ***Example #5.*** *P* sues *D*. Within the proper time, *D* makes a motion to extend the time in which she may respond to the complaint. The court grants the motion, after which *D* files an answer (or makes a motion) raising lack of personal jurisdiction. Has she waived this defense? No! Why not?[15]

○ ***Example #6.*** *P* sues *D*. *D* makes a motion to dismiss under the doctrine of *forum non conveniens* (which we discussed in §5.6). The court denies the motion, after which *D* moves to dismiss for lack of personal jurisdiction. Has she waived this defense? No. Why not?[16]

---

[11]This hypothetical is covered by Principle Number 1. *D* made a Rule 12 motion, followed by another Rule 12 motion raising one of the four "waivable" defenses; the waiver is effected by Rule 12(g).

[12]This example is also covered by Principle Number 1. *D* waived this defense under Rule 12(h)(1)(B)(i). Rule 12(g) does not apply because that subsection addresses only the situation in which the defendant makes a Rule 12 motion followed by another Rule 12 motion. Here she made a motion followed by a pleading, but the timing principle is the same.

[13]Again, this case is governed by Principle Number 1. It is not governed by Rule 12(g) because that applies only when *D* makes a motion followed by a motion. Here, she filed a pleading followed by a motion. The waiver is effected by Rule 12(h)(1)(B)(ii).

[14]Principle Number 1. Her original motion was one permitted under Rule 12(f), so it constitutes a "motion under this rule," as Rule 12(g) says.

[15]Principle Number 1. Under Rules 12(g) and 12(h)(1)(A), *D* must include the "waivable defenses" in a "motion under this rule," which means a motion made under Rule 12. A motion for extension of time is made under Rule 6(b), not Rule 12.

[16]Again, Principle Number 1 covers this situation. Though lack of personal jurisdiction is a waivable defense, that means it must be included in the first response under Rule 12. Most courts conclude that a motion to dismiss under *forum non conveniens* is not a Rule 12 response. The defendant raising the issue is not contesting jurisdiction or venue. Rather, she is arguing that *even though* the present forum is proper, there is another court in another judicial system in which litigation would make far more sense. *See, e.g.*, Abiola v. Abubakar, 267 F. Supp. 2d 907, 918 (N.D. Ill. 2003).

o ***Example #7.*** *P* sues *D*. Within the proper time, *D* serves and files an answer. The case proceeds to trial and the trial court enters judgment for *P*. On appeal, *D* asserts for the first time that the case should have been dismissed for failure to join an absentee under Rule 19. The defense is waived. Why?[17]

o ***Example #8.*** *P* sues *D*. Within the proper time, *D* serves and files an answer. The case proceeds to trial and the trial court enters judgment for *P*. On appeal, *D* asserts for the first time that the case should have been dismissed for lack of federal subject matter jurisdiction. *D* has not waived the defense. Why not?[18]

Finally, it is worth repeating (as stated in footnote 16) that Rule 12(b) fails to mention dismissal for *forum non conveniens* (see §5.6). Because it is thus not a Rule 12 motion, the federal courts generally conclude that there is no set time limit for raising it.[19] The matter is in the court's discretion and, whenever that is true, it always behooves a litigant to raise the issue earlier rather than later. If one waits until the court and parties have invested significant resources in the litigation, the court should not hesitate to deny the motion.[20] The practice in some states is less open-ended; in California, for example, a statute provides that the motion must be made within the time for responding to the complaint.[21]

§6.2.2 *In Rem* and *Quasi-in-Rem* Jurisdiction

What if the defendant wishes to challenge a court's *in rem* or *quasi-in-rem* jurisdiction? Such cases involve seizure of the defendant's

[17]This example is governed by Principle Number 2. Waiver is under Rule 12(h)(2). This defense must be asserted for the first time no later than "at trial," which means no later than entry of judgment at the trial court. Here, *D* did not raise the defense until after judgment.

[18]This case is governed by Principle Number 3. Rule 12(h)(1) makes it clear that the lack of subject matter jurisdiction can be raised "whenever" it becomes apparent. See §6.4.

[19]*See, e.g.*, Grynberg v. Ivanhoe Energy, Inc., 490 Fed. Appx. 86, 93 (10th Cir. 2012) ("Unlike objections to venue or personal jurisdiction, an objection on *forum non conveniens* grounds is not waived by a defendant failing to raise the issue in its first responsive pleading"). The same is true for cases governed by a forum selection clause, which is enforced either through a motion to transfer or a motion to dismiss under *forum non conveniens. See* §5.5.2.

[20]*See, e.g.*, SerVaas Inc. v. Republic of Iraq, 540 Fed. Appx. 38, 41-42 (2d Cir. 2013) (district court did not err in denying motion brought two and one-half years after case was filed, after briefing on motion for summary judgment was nearly complete); Zelinski v. Columbia 300, Inc., 335 F.3d 633, 643 (7th Cir. 2003) (district court did not abuse discretion by denying motion brought one month before trial date).

[21]Cal. Code Civ. Pro. §418.10(a)(2).

property as the jurisdictional predicate. (If this is unclear, see §2.2.) The defendant's dilemma is whether she can go to the forum and challenge jurisdiction without thereby submitting to *in personam* jurisdiction.[22] States have taken different approaches to this issue. Most of the cases addressing the question are old, which reflects the decreasing importance of *in rem* and *quasi-in-rem* jurisdiction in an era of expanded *in personam* jurisdiction.

In some states, the defendant is allowed to appear and litigate the merits of the underlying claim without submitting to *in personam* jurisdiction if she makes a "limited appearance."[23] As with the special appearance, states may impose different technical requirements about how one makes a limited appearance. In fact, some states evidently do not permit a limited appearance.[24]

In federal court, the practice is not entirely clear. Federal Rule 4(n)(2), which addresses service of process, permits a federal court to seize a defendant's property in accordance with the law of the state in which the federal court sits. Neither it nor any other Federal Rule, however, mentions limited appearances. The cases are unclear on two points: (1) whether to permit limited appearances in federal court,[25] and (2) if so, whether the federal court is required to follow state law on the topic.[26] Because the issue simply does not come up much anymore, there will probably never be a Federal Rule on point. If there were, it would govern the practice in federal courts under the rule in *Hanna v. Plumer*, discussed in §10.6.

§6.3   Direct and Collateral Attacks on Personal Jurisdiction

Regardless of whether a jurisdiction employs the special appearance or Federal Rule 12 as its model, the defendant who wishes to

---

[22]Remember, a judgment *in rem* or *quasi-in-rem* is valid only to the value of the property that serves as the jurisdictional predicate. In an *in personam* case, however, a valid judgment creates a personal obligation for the defendant to pay the amount of the judgment to the plaintiff. The plaintiff can enforce a valid *in personam* judgment in any state through full faith and credit.

[23]A classic case is *Cheshire National Bank v. Jaynes*, 112 N.E. 500, 503 (Mass. 1916).

[24]*See, e.g.*, Johnson v. Holt's Adm'r, 31 S.W.2d 895, 897 (Ky. 1930) (act of contesting propriety of seizure converts case to *in personam*).

[25]*See, e.g.*, McQuillan v. Nat'l Cash Register Co., 112 F.2d 877, 882 (4th Cir. 1940) (yes); Campbell v. Murdock, 90 F. Supp. 297, 299 (N.D. Ohio 1950) (no).

[26]*See, e.g.*, Cargill, Inc. v. Sabine Trading & Shipping Co., 756 F.2d 224, 227-228 (2d Cir. 1985); U.S. Industries, Inc. v. Gregg, 58 F.R.D. 469, 474-476 (D. Del. 1973) (state law applied); Dry Clime Lamp Corp. v. Edwards, 389 F.2d 590, 596-598 (5th Cir. 1968) (federal law applied).

challenge personal jurisdiction must decide whether to make a *direct* or a *collateral* attack on that issue. A *direct attack* is when the defendant seeks dismissal of the pending case by making an appropriate motion in that very case.[27] As we just saw in §6.2, such a motion must be made early in the proceedings. The whole idea is to have the issue cleared up at the outset, before the court and parties invest significant time and resources in litigating the merits of the case. If the motion is successful, of course, the case is dismissed and the defendant goes home happy (although the plaintiff may, of course, sue the defendant in the defendant's home state).

But the defendant has another option. She could simply refuse to appear in the case and allow the court to enter default judgment against her.[28] Then she would wait for the plaintiff to seek to enforce that judgment—to collect on it—in the defendant's home state. That judgment is enforceable (and therefore entitled to full faith and credit) only if the first court had personal jurisdiction. Accordingly, the defendant may argue *in this second case* that the first court did not have personal jurisdiction. This is a *collateral attack* on personal jurisdiction, because it takes place in a separate (collateral) suit.

  o   ***Example #9.*** *P* sues *D* in Michigan. *D* is a citizen of Arizona,[29] and thinks that Michigan does not have personal jurisdiction over her. Rather than go to Michigan and make a direct attack there, *D* fails to appear in Michigan and allows the court there to enter a default judgment against her. Now *P* takes that judgment to a court in Arizona (where there clearly is personal jurisdiction over *D*, and where *D* presumably has assets) for enforcement.[30] *D* may appear in the Arizona proceeding and argue that the Michigan judgment is not entitled to full faith and credit because Michigan did not have personal jurisdiction over her.

[27]As noted in §6.2.1, most states employing the special appearance call this a "motion to quash service of process." Under Rule 12, and in most states, it is simply a "motion to dismiss for lack of personal jurisdiction," or, sometimes, a "motion to dismiss for want of personal jurisdiction." All states permit some form of direct attack, although the Supreme Court long ago held that due process does not require the states to provide for such challenges. York v. Texas, 137 U.S. 15 (1890).

[28]We discuss default and default judgments at §7.5.

[29]When you hear these facts about citizenship, you may start thinking about diversity of citizenship jurisdiction. Remember, though, that diversity of citizenship is totally irrelevant to what we are discussing here. Diversity of citizenship is a basis for federal *subject matter jurisdiction*. See §4.5. What we're talking about here (personal jurisdiction) raises the same issues whether the case is in federal or state court. The fact that different states are involved here raises the question of whether a judgment in Michigan (state or federal court) would be enforceable in Arizona (state or federal court).

[30]That means she wants to convert the judgment into money. *P* could do this wherever *D* has assets that can be seized and sold to satisfy the Michigan judgment (if that judgment is valid and therefore entitled to full faith and credit).

This scenario assumes, however, that D does not have any significant property in Michigan. If she does, she may never get a chance to make the collateral attack in Arizona. Why? Because after P gets the default judgment in Michigan, P will execute the judgment against that property in Michigan. If the assets are sufficient to cover the judgment, P will not need to ask the Arizona court to enforce the Michigan judgment. Similarly, suppose D has property in Ohio. After P obtains the default judgment in Michigan, she can execute the judgment against that Ohio property by asking an Ohio court to give the Michigan judgment full faith and credit. D may at this point make a collateral attack in Ohio but will be litigating in Ohio about whether Michigan had personal jurisdiction over her. Thus, the collateral attack route, in which the defendant wants to litigate the personal jurisdiction issue in her home state, will not work if she has significant property in other states.

Assuming that D does not have property in another state, the collateral attack has some advantages over the direct attack. The defendant need not travel from Arizona to Michigan and does not have to find and retain a Michigan lawyer[31] to raise the direct jurisdictional challenge there. Instead, she gets to litigate at home in Arizona with her own lawyer in familiar surroundings. There is, however, one enormous drawback to the collateral attack: In it, the defendant may raise *only* the question of whether the first court had personal jurisdiction. If the Michigan court is held to have had personal jurisdiction, the defendant cannot litigate the underlying merits of the claim in the second action. In other words, by defaulting in Michigan, the defendant has waived any argument concerning the merits of the underlying claim,[32] at least if the Michigan court is held to have had personal jurisdiction.

> ○ ***Example #10.*** P sues D in Michigan on a claim for battery. On the merits of that claim, D admits that she slugged P, but wants to argue that she did so in self-defense, because P had attacked her. If the Arizona court determines that Michigan did have personal jurisdiction over D, the Michigan default judgment is entitled to full faith and credit, and P

---

[31]As you probably know, lawyers are licensed by individual states. In all likelihood, a member of the Arizona bar will not also be a member of the Michigan bar (although she could be). A non-Michigan lawyer cannot appear in Michigan courts unless allowed to practice there for the purpose of a single case (called *pro hac vice* admission). Even then, most bars require that a local lawyer at least be associated on the case. So going to Michigan to litigate will involve the expense and delay of having to find a Michigan lawyer.

[32]The word "merits" refers to the underlying claim itself. If P had sued D for battery, the decision on the merits would be whether D did commit battery and, if so, whether D had any excuse for doing so. It might be that D did punch P, but that she did so in self-defense.

can enforce it in Arizona. *D* will have no opportunity to litigate the self-defense issue.[33]

If *D* relies on a collateral attack, she puts all the eggs in the personal jurisdiction basket. Obviously, then, if *D* has a strong defense to the claim on the merits (such as compelling evidence from witnesses that she acted in self-defense), she will not want to take this route. Rather, she should opt for a direct attack. That avenue will allow *D* to raise the personal jurisdiction issue and then, if she loses on that, to litigate the claim on the merits.

There are some problems, however, with this approach, too. Some of these are obvious: *D* will need to hire a Michigan lawyer and will litigate far from home, presumably on *P*'s home turf. But one problem is less obvious: What happens if the Michigan court rules that it has personal jurisdiction? Can *D* appeal that ruling to the state appellate courts immediately?

In most states, the answer is no. The decision that the court has personal jurisdiction is not a "final judgment," and thus, under the general rule, is not appealable at this point. See §14.4. The issue can be taken to the appellate level only after a decision on the merits of the case. Thus, once the defendant loses on the personal jurisdiction issue, she should be prepared to stick around and litigate the merits of the underlying dispute. In some states, however, the defendant may seek immediate appellate review of the personal jurisdictional issue, either by an express exception to the final judgment rule or by extraordinary writ.[34] These are rarely available, though, so the general rule is that the court's finding that it has personal jurisdiction is not subject to appeal until the merits of the case have been decided.

Notice, then, the range of factors an Arizona lawyer would need to consider in advising *D* whether to make a direct attack in Michigan (again, we are assuming *D* does not have significant property outside Arizona). She would have to assess at least these factors:

1. how direct attacks are made in Michigan;
2. the strength of the personal jurisdiction challenge in Michigan;
3. the strength of *D*'s defense on the merits;

---

[33]Of course, if the Arizona court determines that Michigan did *not* have personal jurisdiction, the Arizona court will not enforce the Michigan judgment; it is not valid, and not entitled to full faith and credit. *P* might then attempt to sue *D* in Arizona, where there clearly is personal jurisdiction over *D*.

[34]We discussed this possibility in *World-Wide Volkswagen* and *Asahi*, §2.4.4. In each of those cases, the defendant was permitted to seek immediate appellate review of the personal jurisdiction issue through extraordinary writ. California is especially liberal in its review of jurisdictional issues by extraordinary writ. *See* Cal. Code Civ. Proc. §418.10(c).

4. whether Michigan permits immediate (interlocutory) review in an appeals court from the personal jurisdiction ruling or, on the other hand, requires a decision on the merits of the claim;
5. if Michigan permits interlocutory review, whether it is automatic or discretionary; and
6. whether the personal jurisdiction issue can be raised on appeal from a decision on the merits.[35]

The lawyer must be careful to explain to *D* that the decision to make a direct attack means that the personal jurisdiction issue will be decided by a Michigan court and appealed in Michigan. In a collateral attack, the question of whether Michigan had personal jurisdiction will be decided by an Arizona court and appealed in Arizona. And, of course, it is critical to explain that making a collateral attack means *D* will not be able to litigate the merits unless the Arizona court determines that Michigan had no jurisdiction.

> ○ ***Example #11.*** Suppose *D*'s defense on the merits is very strong. She has independent witnesses who will testify that *P* attacked *D* without warning, and that *D* slugged *P* in self-defense. Suppose the question of whether Michigan has personal jurisdiction is close. What do you recommend to *D*? This seems to be a strong case for a direct attack. If personal jurisdiction is a toss-up, and since *D* is strong on the merits, there is little sense in putting all the eggs in the jurisdiction basket.
> ○ ***Example #12.*** On the other hand, if jurisdiction is a toss-up and *D* has a weak case on the merits, *D* might as well make a collateral attack. That way, she litigates the jurisdiction issue at home and the waiver of the defense on the merits is not that big a deal, since the defense was weak anyway.

Whichever route the defendant chooses—direct or collateral attack—it is important to follow through with it, and not to mix approaches. Do not make the mistake made by the hapless defendant in *Baldwin v. Iowa State Traveling Men's Association.*[36] There, the plaintiff brought suit in Missouri against an Iowa citizen. The defendant made a direct attack, going to Missouri to argue that that state did not have personal jurisdiction over it. After the parties argued the issue, the Missouri court held that it had personal jurisdiction. The defendant then refused to participate further in the Missouri proceedings. The court in Missouri then had no choice but to enter default

---

[35]As a general rule, the defendant can raise the personal jurisdiction issue on appeal after trial on the merits, so long as she properly preserves her objection on the record. See §14.6. Certainly, that is the rule in federal practice. Toledo Ry. & Light Co. v. Hill, 244 U.S. 49, 51-52 (1917).

[36]283 U.S. 522 (1931).

judgment against the defendant. The plaintiff then sought to enforce the Missouri judgment in Iowa,[37] and the defendant raised a collateral attack there, asserting that the Missouri judgment was no good because Missouri had lacked personal jurisdiction.

The Supreme Court held that the Missouri judgment was entitled to enforcement. Under the doctrine of issue preclusion (or collateral estoppel),[38] a party gets one chance to litigate an issue. Once it has been litigated and determined, the disgruntled party may appeal the decision, but may not relitigate it in another court. In *Baldwin*, the defendant litigated the question of personal jurisdiction in a direct attack in Missouri. Thus, it could not relitigate that issue in a collateral attack in Iowa. It should have appealed the Missouri ruling in Missouri. The defendant in *Baldwin* mixed approaches. Having lost in a direct attack, it tried a collateral attack. The doctrine of issue preclusion prohibits this.[39]

The lesson is clear: Once a defendant chooses to make a direct attack, she must follow through in that state — either with an immediate appeal on the personal jurisdiction issue (if that is allowed) or with a decision on the merits followed by an appeal on the personal jurisdiction issue.[40] This lesson flows from the fact that every court has jurisdiction to determine whether it has jurisdiction. If a litigant does not like the determination made, she must appeal, and not attempt a collateral attack.[41]

---

[37]Actually, the Missouri and Iowa proceedings were in federal court in those states. That fact, however, does not affect the personal jurisdiction issue.

[38]See §11.4. In fact, the Court used the term *res judicata,* but did so as a generic term that includes collateral estoppel. More modern terminology refers to collateral estoppel as issue preclusion.

[39]Instead, a court might conclude that the defendant waived the personal jurisdiction issue. In *City of New York v. Mickalis Pawn Shop, LLC*, 645 F.3d 114, 134-136 (2d Cir. 2011), defendants moved to dismiss for lack of personal jurisdiction. The court denied the motion, after which defendants decided to withdraw from the litigation, despite a warning from the court that it could enter default judgment. The court entered default judgment. On appeal, defendants sought to raise the personal jurisdiction defense. The Second Circuit affirmed the judgment, but not on the preclusion theory employed in *Baldwin*. Instead, it held that the defendants waived the defense by withdrawing from suit. Obviously, then, a defendant who contests personal jurisdiction should decide whether to make a direct attack and, if so, should be prepared to litigate fully in that court.

[40]The defendant in *Baldwin* would have been all right even if it had defaulted on the merits, so long as it had appealed the judgment in Missouri on the basis of the personal jurisdiction issue. The problem was that it submitted the issue for decision in Missouri and then failed to follow through.

[41]An appeal of the decision in the court in which the direct attack is made is not a collateral attack. It is considered part of the direct attack.

§6.4   Challenging Subject Matter Jurisdiction

As with a challenge to personal jurisdiction, a challenge to subject matter jurisdiction can be direct or collateral. A defendant makes a direct attack under Rule 12(b)(1), usually through a motion to dismiss for lack of subject matter jurisdiction. (In cases removed from state court to federal court, it is the *plaintiff*, if anyone, who asserts that the case does not belong in federal court. See §4.8.) Under Rule 12(h)(3), the court must dismiss if it "determines at any time that it lacks subject-matter jurisdiction." See §6.2 (especially *Principle Number 3*). Indeed, that rule also makes it clear that the court has the duty to raise the issue of subject matter jurisdiction *sua sponte*. Even if a party fails to assert a lack of subject matter jurisdiction, the court must dismiss *whenever* it discovers that the case does not invoke such jurisdiction. See §4.3. Accordingly, the defendant can assert a lack of subject matter jurisdiction for the first time after entry of judgment, either at the trial court or on appeal.[42] See §4.3.

These facts have led to this famous catechism: "Subject matter jurisdiction is not waivable; it can be raised for the first time anytime." This assertion is absolutely correct in direct attacks. It may require some amendment, however, when we consider collateral attacks. Before doing that, however, consider how wasteful and inefficient this rule is.

Because subject matter jurisdiction is not a waivable defense, even the party who brought the case in federal court can appeal an adverse judgment after trial by asserting lack of subject matter jurisdiction. In the venerable case of *Capron v. Van Noorden*,[43] the plaintiff sued in federal court, allegedly invoking diversity of citizenship jurisdiction. After losing at trial, however, the plaintiff appealed, asserting that there never had been diversity of citizenship in the case. It turns out that the plaintiff was correct, and the Supreme Court held that the case had to be dismissed, notwithstanding that the judiciary (and parties) had invested considerable resources in trying the case. The result is the same with a defendant who removes a case to federal court. In *American Fire & Casualty Co. v. Finn*,[44] the defendant removed and lost at trial in federal court. It then appealed because, as it turns out, there was no federal subject matter jurisdiction. The Supreme Court again held that the case had to be remanded to state court because there was no federal subject matter jurisdiction.

---

[42]Such a challenge is still a direct attack (as opposed to a collateral attack) because it takes place in the original action. There cannot be a collateral attack without a second (or collateral) litigation. An appeal is not a collateral attack. It is a continuation of the litigation, not a new litigation.

[43]6 U.S. 126 (1804).

[44]341 U.S. 6 (1951).

In addition to wasting resources, this rule opens the door to some outrageous tactics. Suppose the plaintiff alleges that she and the defendant are of diverse citizenship. The defendant knows, however, that the plaintiff is incorrect about her citizenship and that, in fact, there is no diversity. The defendant fails to reveal this fact and litigates the case. If she wins on the merits, the defendant will say nothing about the jurisdictional problem. If she loses, however, the defendant may reveal her true citizenship and appeal because of the lack of subject matter jurisdiction. Though such concealment may create problems under professional ethics rules or under Rule 11 (see §7.7), the judgment will be set aside.[45] So, too, some defendants have waited to assert a lack of subject matter jurisdiction until after the statute of limitations has run. Even in such a case, if in fact the federal court lacked subject matter jurisdiction, it must dismiss the case, and the plaintiff might be left with no remedy in state court.[46]

Reacting to cases such as these, some commentators have argued that litigants should be estopped from raising a lack of subject matter jurisdiction, at least in cases involving bad faith.[47] Such arguments have gone nowhere, however, and the principle that a case must be dismissed "whenever" it appears that there is no subject matter jurisdiction remains vital for direct attacks.[48]

But what about collateral attacks on subject matter jurisdiction? Can a court's purported lack of subject matter jurisdiction provide a basis for attacking a judgment in a separate suit? Here, it is helpful to recognize that such collateral attacks on subject matter jurisdiction might come up in two ways: (1) cases in which the parties litigated the subject matter jurisdiction issue in the first suit and (2) cases in which the issue was not raised in the first case.

As to the former class of cases, the rule is basically the same as it is with challenges to personal jurisdiction. As we saw in §6.3, the Supreme Court held in *Baldwin v. Iowa State Traveling Men's Association*[49] that once the issue of a court's personal jurisdiction had

---

[45]*See, e.g.*, Mennen Co. v. Atlantic Mut. Ins. Co., 147 F.3d 287, 293-294 (3d Cir. 1998); Rubin v. Buckman, 727 F.2d 71, 73 (3d Cir. 1984).

[46]*See, e.g.*, Wojan v. General Motors Corp., 851 F.2d 969, 974-976 (7th Cir. 1988).

[47]*See, e.g.*, Dan Dobbs, *Beyond Bootstrap: Foreclosing the Issue of Subject Matter Jurisdiction Before Final Judgment*, 51 Minn. L. Rev. 491 (1967); Bruce A. Wagman, Comment, *Second Bites at the Jurisdictional Apple: A Proposal for Preventing False Assertions of Diversity of Citizenship*, 41 Hastings L.J. 1417 (1990).

[48]Two cases seemed to demonstrate adoption of such an estoppel approach. *See* DiFrischia v. New York Cent. R.R., 279 F.2d 141, 144 (3d Cir. 1960); Klee v. Pittsburgh & W. Va. Ry. Co., 22 F.R.D. 252, 254-255 (W.D. Pa. 1958). The "trend" amounted to nothing. In fact, the Third Circuit later expressly rejected *DiFrischia*. Rubin v. Buckman, 727 F.2d 71, 72 (3d Cir. 1984).

[49]283 U.S. 522 (1931).

been litigated and determined, it could not be attacked in a collateral proceeding. The reason was the doctrine of issue preclusion—the rule that a litigant has one chance to litigate an issue—either in a direct or collateral attack. Once it is litigated, the party cannot relitigate the question. See §11.4.

The analogous case concerning subject matter jurisdiction is *Durfee v. Duke*,[50] which involved a dispute over the ownership of land along the Missouri River, which forms the state line between Missouri and Nebraska. The dispute focused on whether the land was in Missouri or Nebraska. (The result would depend upon why the river had changed its course.[51]) In the initial case, Durfee sued Duke in state court in Nebraska. That court had subject matter jurisdiction *only* if the disputed land was in Nebraska. The parties litigated the issue and the court determined that the land was in Nebraska. The disgruntled Duke appealed to the Nebraska Supreme Court, which affirmed.

Duke did not, however, seek further review by the United States Supreme Court. Instead, he launched a collateral attack by bringing a second suit (against Durfee) in a Missouri state court. He sought an order of quiet title, arguing that the land was in Missouri. Durfee removed the case to the federal court. This case ultimately went to the United States Supreme Court, which held that Missouri had no authority to redetermine the question of Nebraska's subject matter jurisdiction. The Nebraska judgment was entitled to full faith and credit on those issues "fully and fairly litigated and finally decided in the court which rendered the original judgment."[52] Just as we saw with regard to personal jurisdiction, §6.3, a court has jurisdiction to determine its own jurisdiction. A litigant who does not like the result must appeal the judgment, and not rely on a collateral attack.

The Supreme Court's opinion in *Durfee* recognized, however, that this principle of finality was not inflexible. There can be exceptions when that principle is simply overborne by other considerations.[53] For instance, a state court's determination that it had subject matter jurisdiction was subject to collateral attack in a federal bankruptcy court because Congress had given the federal bankruptcy court exclusive

---

[50]375 U.S. 106 (1963).

[51]This sort of thing happens more frequently than one might guess (especially, it seems, with regard to Nebraska borders). In §12.6.2, we see a dispute about whether a corporation's principal place of business (and therefore its citizenship) was in Nebraska or Iowa. The uncertainty, again, came from the Missouri River's changing course. Owen Equip. & Erection Co. v. Kroger, 437 U.S. 365, 373 n.5 (1978).

[52]*Durfee*, 375 U.S. at 111.

[53]The principle of finality of a judgment (i.e., its *res judicata* or collateral estoppel effect) is always subject to being overridden by other factors. The Court noted this fact in *Durfee*, 375 U.S. at 114. See §11.5.

subject matter jurisdiction.[54] There, permitting the state court to determine the issue plainly violated the exclusive jurisdiction of the federal forum. Absent such a clear violation of an important policy, however, the principle of finality should prevail.

Now to the more difficult situation: What about a collateral attack on subject matter jurisdiction when the issue of subject matter jurisdiction was *not* litigated in the first case?[55] Can a party raise the issue for the first time in a collateral attack? Straightforward principles of issue preclusion would say yes; after all, the issue was not litigated and determined, and therefore cannot be the subject of issue preclusion. See §11.4.2.

But the answer from the Supreme Court seems to be that a party may *not* raise the issue in a collateral attack in such circumstances. In *Chicot County Drainage District v. Baxter State Bank*,[56] a statute purported to establish federal subject matter jurisdiction. No one had any reason to suspect a problem with the statute, so the parties litigated the merits of the dispute in federal court. Later, in a completely unrelated action, that statute was stricken as unconstitutional. The party that lost the first case, understandably, mounted a collateral attack on the judgment. After all, the federal court in that case had exercised subject matter jurisdiction based upon a statute now declared unconstitutional. Surprisingly, however, the Court did not permit the collateral attack. According to the Court, the party should have challenged the constitutionality of the jurisdictional statute in the first case.[57] This result seems quite harsh, since there was no reason to suspect that there was no subject matter jurisdiction in the first case, but the Court has never questioned *Chicot County* since.

There is one final subset of this question. What if the first case ended in a default judgment, in which there was no litigation of

---

[54]Kalb v. Feuerstein, 308 U.S. 433, 438-440 (1940). *Kalb* preceded *Durfee*. The Court in *Durfee* discussed *Kalb* as an exception to the principle of finality on which the holding in that case was based. It should be noted, however, that the subject matter jurisdiction issue in *Kalb* evidently was not litigated in the state court action. *Durfee*, 375 U.S. at 114 n.12.

[55]We know that a party could raise the subject matter jurisdiction issue for the first time on appeal from the first judgment, but that would be part of a direct attack. See §6.3.

[56]308 U.S. 371 (1940). This case was decided the same day as *Kalb v. Feuerstein*, discussed two footnotes above.

[57]Some may suggest that this result is proper because claim preclusion (also known as *res judicata*) precludes relitigation not only of issues actually litigated and determined in the first case, but also of those issues that could have been raised in the first case. This seems wrong, however, because the question here is one implicating issue preclusion (also known as collateral estoppel), not claim preclusion. And issue preclusion is proper only as to questions actually litigated and determined in the first case. See §11.4.2.

anything related to the merits of the claim? It may be one thing to say — as *Chicot County* evidently does — that parties who litigated the merits in the initial case should have raised a problem with subject matter jurisdiction (even if doing so would have required prescience). But is it another thing to say that a defendant who defaults should be precluded from raising a subject matter jurisdiction defense? Such a defendant has litigated *nothing at all*.[58] Such a defendant would be permitted to raise a collateral attack on the issue of personal jurisdiction. Nonetheless, there is little support for a collateral attack on subject matter jurisdiction in this situation.[59]

But why should there be a difference in the treatment of personal and subject matter jurisdiction in default cases? Perhaps the answer lies in the profound difference between those two defenses. Personal jurisdiction protects defendants from litigation in an inappropriate place. It is a waivable defense. If the defendant does not raise it, the court need not address it. In a default case, the defendant has raised nothing, so the issue of personal jurisdiction is simply not before the judge. Subject matter jurisdiction is different. A court is under a continuing obligation to determine whether it has subject matter jurisdiction—regardless of whether any party raises the question. Indeed, it should be the first thing the judge addresses, as soon as the complaint is filed. Perhaps, then, we engage in the supposition that the court has made a determination on this issue—even if the parties do not raise it, and even if the defendant defaults. Put bluntly, a court has no business entering a default judgment unless it has already satisfied itself that it has subject matter jurisdiction. So maybe we are justified in assuming that the issue was, if not actively litigated, at least determined in the first case, and is therefore entitled to finality.

§6.5 Rejection of Hypothetical Jurisdiction

For many years, lower federal courts employed "hypothetical jurisdiction" to avoid difficult questions of subject matter jurisdiction.

---

[58]In *Chicot County*, the claimants did not appear in the first case. *See* 103 F.2d 847 (8th Cir. 1939). Others did, however, and the underlying merits were litigated vigorously. The Supreme Court did not mention the claimants' absence or a default judgment. Nonetheless, Professor (now Judge) Karen Moore regards *Chicot County* as a default judgment case. *See* Karen Moore, *Collateral Attack on Subject Matter Jurisdiction: A Critique of the Restatement (Second) of Judgments*, 66 Cornell L. Rev. 534, 553 (1981).

[59]*See* Restatement (Second) of Judgments §12, comment f (1982). The Restatement (Second) of Judgments §66(2) would permit a collateral attack on a default judgment for lack of subject matter jurisdiction unless doing so "would impair another person's substantial interest of reliance on the judgment."

Under this doctrine, if the decision on the merits would be easy, and would be unfavorable to the party seeking to invoke federal subject matter jurisdiction, the court would bypass the difficult jurisdictional question and decide the case on the merits.[60] After all, if there were no jurisdiction, the same party would win anyway. In 1998, in *Steel Company v. Citizens for a Better Environment,*[61] the Supreme Court disapproved of this practice: "We decline to endorse such an approach because it carries the courts beyond the bounds of authorized judicial action and thus offends fundamental principles of separation of power."[62] In other words, a court of limited subject matter jurisdiction cannot rule on the merits until it is convinced that it has power to speak—that is, until it is convinced that it has jurisdiction.

The following year, however, the Court held that while federal courts must determine jurisdictional questions before proceeding to the merits of the case, they need not necessarily determine subject matter jurisdiction before dismissing for lack of personal jurisdiction. In *Ruhrgas AG v. Marathon Oil Co.,*[63] the question of subject matter jurisdiction was especially difficult. Indeed, it was a question of first impression. The personal jurisdiction issue, in contrast, was relatively straightforward and did not raise a difficult question of state law, because the state long-arm statute reached to the constitutional limit. Under these circumstances, the Court held, it was not an abuse of discretion to determine that the court lacked personal jurisdiction without addressing subject matter jurisdiction.

The Court may have retreated a bit from the strictness of *Steel Company* in *Sinochem International Co. Ltd. v. Malaysia International Shipping.*[64] In an early *forum non conveniens* case, the Supreme Court

---

[60]*See, e.g.*, Isby v. Bayh, 75 F.3d 1191, 1196 (7th Cir. 1996) (because there would be no practical difference in the outcome of the case, court would disregard potentially difficult jurisdictional questions and proceed directly to the merits); Burlington Northern R.R. Co. v. Interstate Commerce Comm'n, 985 F.2d 589, 593 (D.C. Cir. 1993) (when the merits of a case are clearly against the party seeking to invoke subject matter jurisdiction and the jurisdictional question is exceptionally difficult, the court of appeals would rule on the merits without addressing the jurisdictional issue).

[61]523 U.S. 83 (1998).

[62]*Id.* at 93. On the other hand, "where the jurisdictional issue and substantive issues are so intertwined that the question of jurisdiction is dependent on the resolution of factual issues going to the merits, the jurisdictional determination should await a determination of the relevant facts on either a motion going to the merits or at trial." McGraw v. United States, 281 F.3d 997, 1001 (9th Cir. 2002) (*quoting Augustine v. United States,* 704 F.2d 1074, 1077 (9th Cir. 1983), *amended on other grounds,* 298 F.3d 754 (9th Cir. 2002)).

[63]526 U.S. 574 (1999). *See also* Forras v. Rauf, 812 F.3d 1102, 1105 (D.C. Cir. 2016) (district court erred in ruling on complicated subject matter jurisdiction and statute of limitations issues when case should clearly be dismissed for lack of personal jurisdiction).

[64]549 U.S. 422 (2007).

had said that that doctrine "can never apply if there is absence of jurisdiction."[65] In reaction, some lower federal courts concluded that they could not dismiss under *forum non conveniens* until they had concluded that they had personal jurisdiction over the defendants. In *Sinochem,* the Court rejected this approach, and held that a court may, "when judicial economy so warrant[s]," bypass questions of personal and subject matter jurisdiction and dispose of a suit under the doctrine of *forum non conveniens.*[66]

---

[65]Gulf Oil Corp. v. Gilbert, 330 U.S. 501, 505 (1947).
[66]*Sinochem*, 549 U.S. at 433.

Chapter 7

Pleadings, Amended Pleadings, and Judgments Based upon Pleadings

§7.1 Defining the Issue

In modern civil litigation, there are few surprises at trial. Modern procedure has abandoned the notion of "trial by ambush." Instead, our system is geared toward pre-trial disclosure and discovery to ferret out the truth, rather than to reward clever lawyers who can seize upon surprise to their client's advantage. Generally, a case goes to trial only after lengthy pretrial litigation; on average, civil cases that go to trial in federal court take 27.5 months to resolve.[1] Much of that pretrial period is spent in an education process, in which each party learns the contentions that each other party will make if the case goes to trial.

The education process starts with the pleading stage of litigation. Pleadings are documents in which claimants set forth their claims and defending parties respond to the claims and raise defenses. Whereas in earlier times pleadings were expected to perform several functions, as we will see in §7.2, today their principal role is to inform the other parties of each party's positions. Under the Federal Rules, the pleading stage is relatively brief, and gives way to the discovery phase, which we study in Chapter 8. While pleadings set the basic boundaries and tenor of the litigation, in discovery the parties learn the details and find whether the evidence supports the contentions they made in their pleadings.

Pleadings are the gatekeepers of the judicial system. The plaintiff must allege a cognizable claim in her pleading (usually called the *complaint*) to get the case into the litigation stream. If she cannot do this, the case can be dismissed at the pleading stage, without wasting litigant and judicial time in discovery and other aspects of litigation. Much of the historical development of pleading reflects a debate about how high the pleading barrier should be. Generally, older procedure systems raised a very high pleading barrier, sometimes thwarting deserving plaintiffs who sought justice. Modern procedure has lowered that barrier considerably and has made it easier for the plaintiff to get past the pleading stage and into discovery. This policy choice is not without critics. Given the expense of the discovery phase of litigation, some commentators and judges believe that the pleading barrier should be raised to make it more difficult to state a claim and get the case into the litigation stream.

After being sued, the defendant must respond in a timely and proper fashion. She does so either by making a motion or by serving and filing a pleading (usually called the *answer*). Failure to make an appropriate response puts the defendant at risk of losing by default. Factual assertions properly made by the plaintiff in her complaint and denied by the defendant in her answer are said to be "joined," and the case can go forward into the discovery phase on those issues.

---

[1]https://www.uscourts.gov/sites/default/files/data_tables/fcms_na_distprofile1231.2020.pdf.

Undeniably, pleading practice is less important than it was in earlier eras. And undeniably, pleading practice today is more forgiving than it was in earlier eras. This is true not only about the rigor with which one must state a claim, but about the liberality in allowing parties to amend their pleadings as the case evolves. But it is a mistake to conclude that pleading practice is unimportant or that one can be slipshod about it. Pleadings matter, and a lawyer can get her client (and herself) into serious trouble by neglecting the requirements of the pleading rules.

In §7.2, we see that there are two major approaches to pleading in the United States: "code" pleading and the Federal Rules. As always, the Federal Rules govern practice only in the federal courts. States are free to adopt their own rules about all matters of procedure, including pleading, for use in their courts. Though most states have adopted the Federal Rules provisions on pleadings, some have not. Moreover, the Supreme Court decided important pleading cases in 2007 and 2009, which created some uncertainty as to some aspects of practice under the Federal Rules. Some states that otherwise adopt the Federal Rules as to those topics have embraced the Supreme Court opinions, while others have not. As a result, pleading practice can vary from state to state. Throughout this chapter, we focus on the Federal Rules, but also note dominant variations adopted in some states.

§7.2 Evolution of the Role of Pleading

Through the history of Anglo-American civil litigation, there have been three great theories of pleading: (1) common law pleading, (2) "code" pleading, and (3) Federal Rules pleading. Code and Federal Rules pleading are both vital in the United States today. Though no American jurisdiction uses common law pleading today, we need historical exposure to it for two reasons. First, vestiges of common law remain and influence some of what we do today. Second, both code and Federal Rules pleading emerged in reaction to the untoward restrictions imposed by common law pleading.

Common law pleading held sway in England for centuries and dominated in the colonies and the first century of the United States. It was based on the "writ system." A plaintiff wishing to sue was required to select the appropriate substantive writ for her claim. She asked the court to issue that writ for her type of case, and then had to plead the "form of action" for that kind of case. There was a different writ and form of action for assumpsit, trover, trespass—in short, for all the recognized claims. In common law practice, the parties had no plenary right to discovery. That is, there were no formal litigation mechanisms for finding out what relevant information the other party (or third parties) might have.[2]

That meant that the pleadings were the principal vehicle for developing facts and narrowing issues to be tried. With common law pleading, the parties went back and forth through round after round of allegations. This exercise was aimed at framing a single disputed factual issue, which was then tried. What happened, though, if that issue did not fit the writ the plaintiff chose at the outset of the case? This was a common occurrence, since the parties, without discovery, had to make an educated guess at what facts would be established at trial. Moreover, the writs were extremely narrow, so it could be that a plaintiff would prove at trial a right to recovery that was different from the writ she had chosen. The price to pay for this "variance" was steep: The plaintiff lost.

○ ***Example #1.*** The common law writ of "trespass" basically addressed intentional torts. The common law writ of "trespass on the case" basically addressed negligence. Plaintiff was injured when the carriage in which she was riding collided with another carriage. She sued the driver of the vehicle under the writ of trespass on the case; her theory was that the other driver had been negligent and that that negligence caused the collision. At trial, however, the evidence established that the driver had collided with the other vehicle intentionally, in an effort to injure Plaintiff. Though Plaintiff was injured and the other driver was clearly responsible for her injuries, it turns out that she sued under the wrong writ. She should have pursued a writ of trespass, not trespass on the case. The variance was fatal; Plaintiff lost the case.

Common law pleading was an excruciating exercise, better calculated to lead to a decision based upon technicalities than on the merits. Pleading became a goal in itself, more important than the fact-finding to be done by the jury. Common law pleading elevated form over substance and often hindered the administration of justice.

There were many cries for reform both in England and the United States. The most extraordinary reformer in this country was David Dudley Field,[3] a lawyer in Albany, New York. He wrote a codification

---

[2]Modern litigation, in contrast, is characterized by broad discovery rights, as we see in Chapter 8.

[3]The Fields were an interesting family. David Dudley was the principal law reformer in the United States in the nineteenth century. His brother Henry was a world traveler and writer of widely read books on exotic places like Gibraltar. Another brother, Cyrus, played an important role in establishing the trans-Atlantic telegraph cable. And brother Stephen served as an Associate Justice on the United States Supreme Court for 34 years (and wrote the opinion in *Pennoyer v. Neff*, which we studied in detail in §2.4.1). *See* Stephen N. Subrin, *David Dudley Field and the Field Code: A Historical Analysis of an Earlier Procedural Vision*, 6 Law & Hist. Rev. 311 (1988). An iconic historical study of the development of American procedure is Stephen N. Subrin, *How*

of reforms that was adopted in New York in 1848. To this day, the codification is known as the "Field Code," and is the basis for the phrase "code pleading." The starting point of Field's effort was to abolish the common law writs and forms of action. Then, Field limited the number of pleadings; instead of round after round, there would be a complaint by the plaintiff and an answer by the defendant (and sometimes a "reply" by the plaintiff). Most important, Field recognized that pleadings were a poor vehicle for determining what actually had happened in the real world. His reform shifted the role of fact development from the pleading stage to a discovery stage. Pleadings, Field thought, should state facts and should play one central role: putting the other parties on notice of one's contentions.

By the beginning of the twentieth century, code pleading had largely supplanted common law pleading in the United States. But some courts were unable to handle the new system. So steeped in the hypertechnical ways of common law pleading, some judges imported nonsense into code pleading. At worst, they stifled the reform effort by replacing one set of arcane rules with another. We see how they did this in §7.3.2. For now, it is enough to note that problems with implementing Field's vision led to another call for reform.

That call was answered by the Federal Rules in 1938. Federal Rules pleading is not a revolutionary departure from the Field approach. In fact, the Federal Rules largely refine the code-pleading approach. Again, there is a limited number of pleadings, pleadings are limited to the role of putting parties on notice, and fact development is accomplished by the use of discovery tools. The difference between Federal Rules pleading and code pleading is largely confined to the detail with which one is expected to plead. As discussed in §7.3.2, the code states, even today, generally require a statement of the *facts* underlying a claim, which generally entails slightly more detailed allegations than the Federal Rules. The Federal Rules do not require a statement of *facts* but merely a "short and plain statement of the claim, showing that the pleader is entitled to relief."[4] In cases we will discuss in §7.3.2, the Supreme Court sent a discordant message by requiring that a claimant state "facts" supporting a "plausible" claim.

Most states model their pleading provisions on the Federal Rules. A few, however, including California, still use code pleading. The modern approach, whether under the Federal Rules or code pleading, avoids the arcane rules of common law pleading. It adopts a simplified approach to pleading, which goes hand in hand with broad discovery

---

Equity Conquered Common Law: The Federal Rules of Civil Procedure in Historical Perspective, 135 U. Pa. L. Rev. 909 (1987).

[4]Bell Atlantic Corp. v. Twombly, 550 U.S. 544 (2007).

mechanisms. It also embraces liberal amendment rules, which we see in §7.6, to allow the parties to adjust and adapt to the facts as they develop throughout the litigation stream.

§7.3 The Pleadings in Modern Practice

§7.3.1 Matters of Form

Modern pleading rules, both in code states and under the Federal Rules (and, obviously, states that adopt the Federal Rules), limit the number of pleadings each party may file in a case. Federal Rule 7(a) provides for only three pleadings: the complaint (in Rule 7(a)(1)), the answer (which may be filed in response to various claims, as seen in Rule 7(a)(2), (3), (4), and (6)), and the reply (in Rule 7(a)(7)), which will be filed only if the court orders a party to do so.[5] A "motion," by which a party asks the court to enter a particular order, is not a pleading. We revisit this point in §7.3.4.

Federal Rule 10 gives general guidance for the form of all pleadings. Rule 10(b) requires the party to set forth her allegations in "numbered paragraphs" (as opposed to lettered paragraphs), "each limited as far as practicable to a single set of circumstances." In addition, Rules 10(b) and 10(c) expressly allow incorporation by reference of paragraphs. Rule 10(c) also provides that parties may attach a written instrument as an exhibit to a pleading, and that the instrument thus is considered a part of the pleading for all purposes.

These provisions are helpful. If the case involves a dispute over a contract, the plaintiff may simply append a copy of the contract to the complaint. It is thus considered part of the complaint, without the make-work of having to cut and paste the contract into the complaint. In addition, rather than reiterate allegations of a paragraph as needed in different parts of a pleading, the party simply incorporates the previous allegation by reference.

> ○ ***Example #2.*** Plaintiff's complaint sets forth two claims against Defendant. In Paragraph 5 of the complaint, which was part of the first claim, Plaintiff made allegations that are also relevant to her second claim. In stating the second claim, say in Paragraph 10 of

---

[5]The Rule also allows the "third-party complaint," which is a mechanism by which another party may be added to the dispute in limited circumstances, as we see in §12.6.2. Aside from that, Rule 7(a) also talks of answers to various claims, such as the third-party claim and a crossclaim, which we study in §12.5.2. So we say there are three "basic" pleadings (complaint, answer, and reply) because those are the pleadings asserted by the plaintiff and defendant in a typical two-party case.

the complaint, she need not retype Paragraph 5, but may simply allege "Plaintiff here incorporates by reference the allegations of Paragraph 5."

Rule 10(a) concerns the form of all pleadings and requires that each "must have a caption with the court's name, a title, a file number, and a Rule 7(a) designation." When a plaintiff files a civil action, the clerk of the court assigns a file number (or "case number" or "docket number") to the litigation. This number must appear on every document in that case. The file number usually is preceded by the designation "Civ.," showing that it is a civil (not a criminal) case. After that, the first number of the file number is a two-digit indication of the year in which the case was filed. That number is followed by the case's specific number, which is assigned in the order in which cases are filed in that district in that year. The 305th case filed in the district in 2022 would have file number: "Civ. 22-00305." Following this number, the clerk will affix the initials of the district judge to whom the case is assigned. Assignments are made at random among the judges in the district.[6] The caption for the complaint in this fictitious case in the Southern District of New York would look like this:

United States District Court
Southern District of New York

Bee Taylor, Plaintiff,	)))	Civ. 22-00305-JS[7]
vs.	))	COMPLAINT
Enid Markey, Defendant.	))	

---

[6]Most districts have a Local Rule providing that related litigation may be assigned to the district judge to whom the first related case was assigned. If Judge Jane Smith was assigned the first case involving an airplane crash, all other cases in that district involving the same crash would not be assigned at random to other judges but would be assigned to Judge Smith. This process is often called *low-numbering,* because the subsequent cases are sent to the judge to whom the lowest numbered (that is, earliest filed) case was assigned.

[7]These are the judge's initials (Judge Jane Smith in our imaginary case). It is increasingly common for the clerk to assign a magistrate judge to the case as well, whose initials may be shown in parentheses after the judge's initials. We discuss the role of magistrate judges in §8.6.

The body of the complaint would then set forth Taylor's claims in numbered paragraphs. The caption for the defendant's answer would look the same except for indicating "answer" instead of "complaint." It would set forth Markey's responses to the complaint and affirmative defenses in numbered paragraphs.

Rule 11(a) provides, *inter alia*, that "[u]nless a rule or statute specifically states otherwise, a pleading need not be verified or accompanied by an affidavit." A "verified" pleading is one executed under penalty of perjury (as is an affidavit). Thus, this provision of Rule 11(a) means that, generally, parties are not required to plead under oath. Pleadings can be executed on the basis of the best information and belief of the parties. As we see in §7.7, pleadings ordinarily are not even signed by the parties; they are signed by the lawyer. Only if a Rule or statute requires must the party execute a verified pleading. (One of the few instances of verified pleading in federal court is found in Rule 23.1, which concerns a specialized kind of litigation, the shareholder derivative suit.) Now we turn to the requirements of each pleading.

§7.3.2   The Complaint (Including *Twombly* and *Iqbal*)

Under the Federal Rules, and under the law of nearly every state, the principal pleading by the plaintiff—and the initial pleading in any case—is the *complaint*. A few states use different terms for this pleading, such as *petition* or *declaration*. Under Federal Rule 3, the case is commenced when the plaintiff files the complaint. (Recall from §3.3.1 that the plaintiff must then arrange to have a summons and a copy of the complaint (together, called *process*) served on the defendant.) Federal Rule 8(a) sets forth the three requirements of any complaint in federal court: (1) a statement of the grounds of subject matter jurisdiction, (2) a statement of the claim, and (3) a demand for the relief sought. A complaint lacking any of the three requirements is subject to dismissal, although the court usually will permit the plaintiff to file again to correct the problem.[8]

Rule 8(a) is not limited to complaints. Indeed, the word *complaint* does not even appear in Rule 8(a). Rather, that Rule provides

---

[8]A dismissal "without prejudice" results in dismissal of the present case but permits the plaintiff to reinstitute the action by filing a new complaint that fixes the problem that resulted in dismissal. A dismissal "with leave to amend" is an order in which the court threatens to dismiss the case unless the plaintiff files an amended complaint (fixing the problems) within a set time. When the problem with the complaint is one of form or lack of detail, courts will often enter a dismissal with leave to amend. At some point, though, if the court becomes convinced that the deficiency in the complaint cannot be fixed, the court will dismiss without leave to amend.

requirements for any "pleading that states a claim for relief." In other words, it gives the rules for the assertion of *any claim*. The complaint will set forth an original claim, and thus is subject to Rule 8(a). In Chapter 12, we discuss other documents in which a party asserts a claim—including the counterclaim, crossclaim, and third-party claim. Each of these is asserted *after* the plaintiff has commenced the case with the filing of the complaint that invokes the subject matter jurisdiction of the federal court. When you see these claims in Chapter 12, remind yourself that the requirements of Rule 8(a) apply. For convenience, we discuss Rule 8(a) in the context of the complaint. Most challenges to pleadings concern the requirement in Rule 8(a)(2). We will focus on that after discussing the other two requirements briefly.

Rule 8(a)(1): Statement of Grounds of Subject Matter Jurisdiction

The requirement of Rule 8(a)(1) should not cause any trouble to the careful lawyer. The complaint must contain a "short and plain statement of the grounds for the court's jurisdiction . . . ."[9] The reference is to subject matter jurisdiction, not to personal jurisdiction.[10] The requirement makes sense because federal courts are of limited subject matter jurisdiction; plaintiff has the burden of pleading that her claims can be heard by a federal court. (For a case removed from state to federal court, defendant bears this burden, because she is the one seeking to invoke federal subject matter jurisdiction. See §4.8.)

For federal question jurisdiction, it is sufficient to allege that the claim "arises under" federal law, and it is typical (but not necessary) to cite the relevant federal provision. For diversity of citizenship, it is sufficient to allege the citizenship of the plaintiff and of the defendant and to state that the matter in controversy exceeds $75,000.[11] There is no need to allege why a party is a citizen of a particular state or *why* the matter in controversy exceeds $75,000.[12]

[9]The Rule provides an exception when the court already has subject matter jurisdiction. This exception will not apply to the complaint, because it is the pleading that first vests the court with subject matter jurisdiction.

[10]2 Moore's Federal Practice §8.03[1]. Some state rules add a requirement that the plaintiff allege grounds of personal jurisdiction if the defendant is not a resident of the forum.

[11]Until 2016, the Federal Rules included an Appendix of Forms, which set forth acceptable methods for alleging a variety of things, including subject matter jurisdiction and various claims and affirmative defenses. The suggestions in this paragraph are consistent with the Forms. The Rules Advisory Committee (responsible for drafting the Federal Rules) abolished them in 2016.

[12]Remember, under §1332, the amount in controversy must *exceed* $75,000, not including interest and costs. So an allegation for exactly $75,000 will fail to invoke diversity of citizenship jurisdiction. See §4.5.3.

It is important to use the proper terminology in pleading diversity of citizenship jurisdiction. The word *resides* should never appear here. It is the parties' *citizenship* that is relevant to diversity of citizenship; residence is relevant to venue, which need not be alleged under Rule 8(a). In addition, in alleging a corporation's citizenship, one must allege both its state of incorporation *and* (not *or*) the one state in which it has its principal place of business. Do not allege things like "headquarters" or "licensed to do business" or any other irrelevant fact. Section 1332 is absolutely clear on what terms must be alleged. (If this is unclear, review §4.5.3.)

A pointed reminder is found in *Randazzo v. Eagle-Picher Industries, Inc.*[13] In that case, the district court dismissed the case without leave to amend, so the plaintiff could not refile the action in federal court. The opinion, though amusing, is a chilling indictment of a lawyer who brazenly failed to take advantage of an opportunity to plead diversity of citizenship correctly. Criticizing counsel's failure to understand the difference between "and" and "or" in alleging the citizenship of a corporation, the judge concludes that the plaintiff's lawyer's "familiarity with . . . §1332 could be no more than a friendly wave from a distance visible only through a powerful telescope."[14] The court reminds us that proper pleading of subject matter jurisdiction is not an exercise of formalism. Subject matter jurisdiction addresses the constitutional allocation of authority between the federal and state governments.

Rule 8(a)(3): Demand for Relief Sought

Rule 8(a)(3) requires the plaintiff to make her "demand for the relief sought." This demand is often called the *prayer* for relief. When the plaintiff demands a monetary recovery (as opposed to equitable relief such as an injunction), the demand is sometimes called the *ad damnum* clause. By common practice, the plaintiff puts the demand for judgment at the end of the complaint, preceded by the word *Wherefore* or *Therefore*. Thus, a common pleading is: "Therefore, the plaintiff demands judgment against defendant for $[insert dollar figure], plus interest and costs."

---

[13]117 F.R.D. 557 (E.D. Pa. 1987).

[14]*Id.* at 558. In Heinen v. Northrop Grumman Corp., 671 F.3d 669, 670 (7th Cir. 2012), defendant removed a case from state to federal court, ostensibly on the basis of diversity of citizenship jurisdiction. In doing so, however, defendant pleaded the "residence" and not "citizenship" of the parties. "When we raised the issue at oral argument, counsel for both sides were surprised to learn that 'citizenship' for the purpose of 28 U.S.C. §1332 depends on domicile rather than residence . . . . Counsel have wasted the court's time, and their clients' money, by postponing essential inquiries until after the case reached the court of appeals." These issues are discussed at §4.5.3.

Damages usually are pleaded as a lump sum. In some circumstances, however, such as a demand for "special damages," the plaintiff must plead in detail. (We discuss pleading such special matters in §7.3.3.) There is nothing in Rule 8(a) (or anywhere else) that requires the plaintiff to plead a dollar figure for her damages. Some plaintiffs put a dollar figure in the complaint. Others do not, but instead demand "damages in an amount to be shown at trial." Of course, in a diversity of citizenship case, the plaintiff will have alleged in satisfying Rule 8(a)(1) that the amount in controversy exceeds $75,000. There is nothing wrong with doing that and then demanding judgment in an amount to be determined at trial.[15]

Of course, damages are not the only possible remedy. Instead (or perhaps in addition) to damages, the plaintiff may seek equitable relief, such as an injunction, declaratory judgment, rescission, reformation, or specific performance. We discussed equitable remedies in §1.2.3. As we see in §9.2.2, the relief sought will have a significant impact on whether there is a right to jury trial in federal court.

It is interesting, and perhaps surprising, that the plaintiff's recovery is not limited by what she seeks in her demand for judgment. Federal Rule 54(c) makes it clear that the plaintiff is entitled to recover whatever amount and whatever type of relief shown appropriate at trial, regardless of what she asked for in the demand. There is one exception to this rule, however, which is also set forth in Rule 54(c): In cases of default judgment (discussed in §7.5), the plaintiff cannot recover more (or a different kind of relief) than she sought in her demand for judgment.

- ○ ***Example #3.*** *P* files a proper complaint in which she demands recovery of damages from *D* in an amount of $250,000. Based upon the evidence at trial, the jury returns a verdict in favor of *P* for $350,000 and the judge determines, based upon the evidence presented at trial, that *P* is entitled to an injunction too. This relief is appropriate, even though it amounts to more damages and a different type of relief than *P* demanded.
- ○ ***Example #4.*** On the other hand, if *P* won the same case by default judgment, she could recover no more than $250,000 in damages and could not be granted the injunction (because she did not demand an injunction in her complaint).

Rule 8(a)(2): Statement of the Claim

Under Rule 8(a)(2), the plaintiff must set forth "a short and plain statement of the claim showing that the pleader is entitled to relief." In code states, in contrast, a plaintiff must set forth "a statement of the facts

---

[15]Remember that the good-faith claim that the amount in controversy exceeds $75,000 will satisfy that requirement of §1332 unless it is "clear to a legal certainty" that the plaintiff cannot recover that much. Such cases are rare. See §4.5.3.

constituting a cause of action." As we noted in §7.2, the federal provision was a reaction to what some courts in some code states did in applying the code requirement. They created a monster by burdening the code requirement with arcane definitions of "facts" and "causes of action."

In assessing whether the plaintiff has pleaded enough to satisfy Rule 8(a)(2) or the code requirement of facts constituting a cause of action, it is important to understand that the complaint can be attacked for two kinds of insufficiency: It might be insufficient *legally* or *factually*. (The difference between the Federal Rules and code approaches, and the ferment caused by the Supreme Court decisions in *Twombly* and *Iqbal*, discussed below, relates to *factual* sufficiency.)

How does the defendant challenge either legal or factual sufficiency of the complaint? We need a bit of terminology here. In federal court, the defendant will make a motion to dismiss for failure to state a claim under Federal Rule 12(b)(6).[16] In many state courts (certainly those following code pleading), she will file a *demurrer*.[17] One more bit of terminology: A motion to dismiss under Rule 12(b)(6) in federal court is either *granted* or *denied*; in contrast, a demurrer in most state courts is either *sustained* or *overruled*. Again, in federal court, the motion to challenge either factual or legal sufficiency is the motion to dismiss for failure to state a claim under Rule 12(b)(6); there is no such thing as a demurrer in federal court.

Legal Sufficiency. The complaint must state a claim (or, in code states, a "cause of action"). If it does not, the court may dismiss *sua sponte* (which means it may do so on its own, without a motion by a party) or may grant a motion to dismiss under Rule 12(b)(6) (or, in code states, may sustain a demurrer). If the complaint sets forth several purported claims, only one of which is insufficient, the court may dismiss the defective claims. Dismissals of this sort are usually made with leave to amend, which allows the plaintiff another chance to try to state a legally sufficient claim. At some point, however, when it becomes clear that the plaintiff cannot state a legally sufficient claim, the court will dismiss without leave to amend.[18] After all, if the plaintiff does not have a claim that the law recognizes, it is a waste of the defendant's (and the court's) time and resources to have the litigation go further.

---

[16]The defense of failure to state a claim can be raised anytime through trial (*see* Rule 12(h)(2)). Usually, the defendant will bring such a motion at the outset, under Rule 12(b)(6), in lieu of an answer. But she can make the motion after answering, in which case it is brought under Rule 12(c), and is called a *motion for judgment on the pleadings*. See §7.3.4.

[17]Technically, in most code states, if she is challenging *legal* sufficiency, she will file a *general demurrer*; and if she is challenging *factual* sufficiency, she will file a *special demurrer*.

[18]See note 13 and accompanying text above.

In ruling on legal sufficiency of the complaint (or of an individual claim in the complaint), the court looks only to the face of the complaint. It does not look at evidence. (In this regard, testing the legal sufficiency of the complaint is quite different from a motion for summary judgment under Rule 56, which we study in §9.4. With a motion for summary judgment, the court may look at evidence.[19]) When it looks at the face of the complaint, the court asks: "If the plaintiff proved everything she has alleged here, would she win?" In other words, does the law recognize a right to recover on the facts she has alleged?

If the answer is no, as we just noted, there is no point in having the litigation continue. If the answer is yes, the litigation should continue to see whether plaintiff indeed can prove what she has alleged. Thus, if the court determines that the complaint is legally sufficient, it is *not* saying that the plaintiff wins. It is simply allowing the case to go forward to the next stages of the litigation stream. The plaintiff may ultimately fail to demonstrate the facts necessary to win a judgment. Or the defendant may have a valid defense to the claim. Those considerations—the merits of the case—are for another day. Right now, the court is simply determining whether the plaintiff gets "past the pleading stage" and can engage in further litigation. As the Supreme Court has said, "[T]he issue is not whether a plaintiff will ultimately prevail but whether [she] is entitled to offer evidence to support her claims."[20]

○ ***Example #5.*** Suppose relevant law defines *consortium* as "conjugal fellowship and sexual relations between spouses." *P*'s live-in lover is severely injured by the negligence of *D*. *P* sues *D*, seeking damages for loss of consortium. *P* alleges that *D* caused the injuries to the injured person and that the injuries have robbed *P* of conjugal fellowship and sexual relations with the injured person. *P* fails, however, to allege that *P* and the injured person are spouses. The court will grant *D*'s motion to dismiss under Rule 12(b)(6). Why? Because if *P* proved everything she alleged, the law would not allow recovery, because she has not alleged that she and the injured person were spouses. The law allows recovery for lost consortium only between spouses.

○ ***Example #6.*** Suppose the court dismissed the case in Example #5 under Rule 12(b)(6) without prejudice, and that *P* tries again to state a claim. Because *P* and the injured person in fact are not married, she cannot allege that they are spouses. She files an amended complaint, however, alleging what she had alleged in the original complaint and adding the

---

[19]Rule 12(d) provides that if a court does look at matters extraneous to the pleadings in a motion under Rule 12(b)(6), it can convert the motion into one for summary judgment.

[20]Scheuer v. Rhodes, 416 U.S. 232, 236 (1974).

allegation that *P* and the injured person are "live-in lovers." The court will grant *D*'s motion to dismiss under Rule 12(b)(6). Why? Again, if *P* demonstrated everything she has alleged, the law would not allow her to recover, because she and the injured person are not spouses. This time, the court would dismiss with prejudice, and enter final judgment for the defendant.

At that point, *P* is free to appeal the final judgment to the court of appeals.[21] There, she can argue that the law ought to be changed to recognize a claim for loss of consortium between persons who are not spouses. In §1.2.2, we discussed the doctrine of precedent, or *stare decisis*. That doctrine provides that appellate courts' pronouncements on matters of law are binding on lower courts within that jurisdiction. The question of whether consortium should be recognized beyond the marital relationship is a question of law. The trial court is not free to change the law but must apply it as declared by the appellate courts in its jurisdiction. On appeal, however, *P* may certainly attempt to convince the court of appeals to change the law. If so, the appellate court would reverse the judgment and remand the case to the trial court for appropriate proceedings, including trial on the consortium claim. Moreover, from that point on, trial courts in that jurisdiction would have to apply the "new" law.[22] If the appellate court failed to change the law, however, it would affirm the judgment against *P*.

Clearly, counsel for the plaintiff must do her homework on what claims are legally cognizable. She must hit the books—whether statutes or case law—to determine the elements of the claim, and, as we just saw, address the elements in her complaint. On the other hand, the plaintiff is not required in the complaint to cite the law under which she sues. In *Johnson v. City of Shelby*,[23] former police officers sued city aldermen, alleging that they were fired because they had reported the criminal activities of one of the city's bosses. The plaintiffs' claim was based upon 42 U.S.C. §1983, which creates a claim for denial of federal civil rights "under color of state law." The lower court held that the plaintiffs' failure to cite §1983 in their complaint was fatal. The Court summarily reversed and noted that nothing in Rule 8(a) requires citation of legal authority. The Rules "do not countenance

---

[21]In the federal system, appeal is to the court of appeals for the circuit in which the federal district court sits. In state court systems, there may be an intermediate appellate court that can entertain the case. If not, *P* may be able to seek discretionary review by the state supreme court. See §§1.2.2, 14.2.

[22]There are circumstances (beyond our scope) in which an appellate pronouncement on a matter of law might be applied retroactively and thus be binding on cases filed before the appellate pronouncement. You may study that topic in Constitutional Law.

[23]574 U.S. 10 (2014). The Court made clear that *Twombly* and *Iqbal*, which are discussed in detail in the following subsection, dealt only with factual sufficiency and not with legal sufficiency.

dismissal of a complaint for imperfect statement of the legal theory supporting the claim asserted."[24]

Factual Sufficiency. We just saw that the substantive law erects barriers to entering into the litigation stream. Here our focus is different. Assuming the law recognizes a claim, how much detail must the plaintiff allege to support that claim? As a general answer, the code-state requirement that the plaintiff plead "a statement of facts constituting a cause of action" mandates somewhat more detailed pleading than the Federal Rules requirement of "a short and plain statement of the claim showing that the pleader is entitled to relief."

As discussed in §7.2, code pleading developed in the nineteenth century in response to the arcane technicalities that flourished in the earlier common law "writ" system of pleading. It was a liberal advance to have the plaintiff allege simply "a statement of facts constituting a cause of action." The problem was that old habits die hard, and many of the judges weaned on the technicalities of the common law system could not help but import silly subtleties into the new system. Though the code requirement of pleading "facts" seems clear enough, courts refined it to require a statement of the "ultimate facts" (whatever that means). If the plaintiff alleged too generally to suit the judge, she was said to be pleading "conclusions of law" rather than facts, and the court would sustain a demurrer and dismiss the case. On the other hand, if the plaintiff alleged with too much detail to please the judge, she was said to be pleading "evidentiary facts," and the court would sustain a demurrer and dismiss the case. Erecting formalistic barriers depending on the individual judge's conception of what constituted "ultimate facts" thwarted the administration of justice by keeping potentially deserving plaintiffs out of the litigation stream by promoting dismissal at the pleading stage.

There are many examples of this formalism. In one case, the plaintiff, a lineman, suffered serious personal injuries when he fell 30 feet from a power pole when a spike in the pole broke when he stepped on it. The defendant had put the spikes into the pole. The plaintiff alleged that the defendant "negligently caused said step to be driven and placed in said pole not far enough to make it reasonably safe." The trial court overruled the defendant's demurrer, and the case went to trial. The plaintiff won a substantial judgment. On appeal, however, the Missouri Supreme Court held that the trial court should have sustained the demurrer. The plaintiff's allegation, the court concluded, was too conclusory; it constituted a conclusion of law rather than the

---

[24]*Id.* at 11. Somewhat oddly, the Court instructed that upon remand the plaintiffs should be allowed to amend their complaint to cite §1983. *Id.* at 11. It did not explain why the plaintiffs should do something that is not required.

allegation of "facts constituting a cause of action."[25] Thus, the plaintiff was robbed of his victory because the verbal formulation of his claim did not meet the fancy of the reviewing court.

The result is absurd. There was no chance that the defendant had been misled by the allegation. Reading it, the defendant clearly understood what plaintiff was charging. The judicial system and parties had invested great effort and expense litigating the matter. Yet it was all undone because of a petty technicality. The cases (particularly older cases) concerning factually sufficient allegations in code states cannot be reconciled. For almost any situation, there is a plausible argument that the plaintiff is alleging either too generally or with too much specificity.

- ○ ***Example #7.*** *P* sues to eject *D* from real property. Under the applicable law, *P* must plead and prove several issues; one of them is that she has superior title to the disputed property. How does one allege the "ultimate fact" of superior title?
    - ○ An allegation that *P* "has superior title to the property" might be attacked as too general and thus as alleging a legal conclusion rather than facts.[26]
    - ○ Similarly, an allegation that *P* is "entitled to possession of the property" might be attacked on the same ground.[27]
    - ○ Suppose *P* alleges that she "paid for the property pursuant to contract and [that *D*] delivered to her a deed to the property." This allegation might be attacked as too specific—as pleading of evidence, and not of facts.[28]

I do not suggest that all code-state courts would have found (or would today find) fault with these formulations. The courts in code-pleading states are more liberal now than they were in earlier times. I simply give a word of caution: Some code-pleading courts can still require a verbal precision that is very difficult to divine or describe. In particular, some code-state courts still ignore what they see as conclusions of law in determining whether the plaintiff has stated a cause of action. In the 1990s, the Nebraska Supreme Court reminded lawyers that trial courts in that state will consider "the pleaded facts, as distinguished from legal conclusions."[29] (Nebraska has since abandoned code pleading and adopted the Federal Rules approach.)

---

[25]Kramer v. Kansas City Power & Light Co., 279 S.W 43 (Mo. 1925).

[26]Sheridan v. Jackson, 72 N.Y. 170, 173 (1878).

[27]*Id.*

[28]That was the result in *McCaughey v. Shuette*, 117 Cal. 223 (1896), on a very similar allegation.

[29]Gallion v. Woytassek, 504 N.W.2d 76, 79 (Neb. 1993). *See also* Papin Builders, Inc. v. Litz, 734 S.W.2d 853, 858 (Mo. Ct. App. 1987) (code pleading not as liberal as Federal Rules pleading).

The Federal Rules were intended to liberalize pleading requirements. Instead of worrying about what constitute "facts" (let alone
"ultimate facts") that constitute a "cause of action," Rule 8(a)(2)
requires a "short and plain statement of the claim showing that the
pleader is entitled to relief." An indisputable goal of the drafters was
to lower the formal barrier erected by the pleading rules to entering
into the litigation stream. This lowered barrier went hand in hand
with expanded discovery provisions under the Federal Rules (as we
will see in Chapter 8). The idea is that the plaintiff is not in a position
to plead much detail at the outset of litigation, and pleading rules
should not impose an unrealistic barrier to her getting to the discovery phase of litigation.

How much detail is required to satisfy Rule 8(a)(2)? It is not enough
to allege "*D* owes me $1,000,000." But how much more is needed?
One old but famous case is *Dioguardi v. Durning*,[30] a Second Circuit
opinion authored by Judge Charles Clark.[31] Clark was the principal
drafter of the original Federal Rules, which were promulgated in 1938.
This case, decided in 1944, gave Clark a chance to explain the Federal
Rules' theory on the role of pleading and the type of detail required by
Rule 8(a)(2).

Mr. Dioguardi was an Italian immigrant with limited facility in
English. A shipment of "tonics" was sent from Italy to Mr. Dioguardi,
evidently under a consignment agreement; this meant that Mr.
Dioguardi (the "consignee") was to sell the tonics and remit certain
payments to the sender in Italy (the "consignor"). The customs officers in New York seized the tonics because the duty was not paid.
Mr. Dioguardi claimed that the consignor was to have paid the duty.
At any rate, the customs collector, acting under a federal statute,
held the tonics for a year and then sold them at public auction.
Apparently, Mr. Dioguardi bid $110 for the tonics, but someone else
at the auction bid $120, and the sale was made to this other person.
Mr. Dioguardi, appearing *pro se* (without a lawyer), sued the collector of customs. He drafted his own complaint alleging the defendant
had "sold my merchandise to another bidder with my price of $110,
and not of his price of $120." In addition, the complaint alleged that
"three weeks before the sale, two cases, of 19 bottles each case, disappeared."[32]

---

[30]139 F.2d 774 (2d Cir. 1944).

[31]Before he was appointed to the Second Circuit, Clark was dean of the Yale Law
School. Clark's protege at Yale in the 1930s was J.W. Moore, who became a legendary
figure in legal education and was the principal author of an important multivolume
treatise that still bears his name, Moore's Federal Practice.

[32]139 F.2d at 774.

The district court granted a motion to dismiss for failure "to state facts sufficient to constitute a cause of action." On appeal, Judge Clark pointed out that the "new" Federal Rules, which had been in effect for several years before the district court ruled in *Dioguardi*, do not mention the phrase "facts sufficient to constitute a cause of action." He then proceeded to explain why Mr. Dioguardi's complaint satisfied the requirement of Rule 8(a)(2) that he make a "short and plain statement of the claim showing [he was] entitled to relief." In language that has been widely quoted, Judge Clark explained that

> however inartistically they may be stated, the plaintiff has disclosed his claims that the collector has converted or otherwise done away with two of his cases of medicinal tonics and has sold the rest in a manner incompatible with the public auction he had announced . . . . [W]e do not see how the plaintiff may properly be deprived of his day in court to show what he obviously so firmly believes . . . .[33]

Some observers criticized the *Dioguardi* decision by pointing out that the plaintiff lost when the case went to trial. But that fact is irrelevant to the pleading question. The only issue under Rule 8(a)(2) is whether the plaintiff has alleged enough to justify having the case proceed in litigation. Whether the plaintiff wins at trial is a different matter. Despite the criticism, *Dioguardi* long stood the test of time. In fact, the Supreme Court specifically endorsed Judge Clark's approach in *Conley v. Gibson*.[34]

In *Conley,* the Court said Rule 8 requires only that the plaintiff give the defendant "fair notice of what the plaintiff's claim is and the grounds upon which it rests."[35] This phrase gave rise to the shorthand expression that the Federal Rules use "notice pleading": that all the plaintiff must do is put the defendant "on notice" of what the claim is. Details can be fleshed out in discovery.[36] The Federal Rules operate on the assumption that there is nothing intrinsically so important about good pleading that it should cost a plaintiff a potentially meritorious claim for failure to meet the formal niceties. As one opinion explains, the Federal Rules "make a complaint just the starting point. Instead of lavishing attention on the complaint

---

[33]*Id.* at 775.

[34]355 U.S. 41 (1957).

[35]*Id.* at 46.

[36]Judge Clark did not like the term "notice pleading," because he considered it imprecise. Charles Clark, *Pleading Under the Federal Rules*, 12 Wyo. L. Rev. 177, 181 (1958). Nonetheless, it became commonly used as a shorthand statement of the federal pleading standard.

until the plaintiff gets it just right, a district court should keep the case moving . . . ."[37]

Another passage from *Conley* became standard fare for citation by any federal court entertaining a motion under Rule 12(b)(6) for failure to plead with appropriate factual sufficiency:

> In appraising the sufficiency of the complaint we follow, of course, the accepted rule that a complaint should not be dismissed for failure to state a claim unless it appears beyond doubt that the plaintiff can prove no set of facts in support of his claim which would entitle him to relief.[38]

This is pretty liberal, all right. Judge Posner, of the Seventh Circuit, concluded that "[a]lthough the exceedingly forgiving attitude toward pleading deficiencies evidenced that was expressed . . . in *Conley v. Gibson* . . . continues to be quoted with approval, it has never been taken literally."[39]

The Twombly *Case*

Judge Posner was on to something. In 2007, the Supreme Court sent a surprising signal in *Bell Atlantic Corporation v. Twombly.*[40] *Twombly* is a complicated case on the merits, and understanding it requires background concerning the operation of telephone companies. In 1984, American Telephone & Telegraph Co., which had held a virtual monopoly on telephone service in the United States, was required to give up local phone service. Regional businesses, known as Incumbent Local Exchange Carriers (ILECs), were set up to handle local phone service in various regions. They were expressly to be free of competition in their local markets but could not provide long-distance phone service. In 1996, Congress tried to increase competition in the local telephone markets by passing a law that permitted the ILECs to provide long-distance service (which was very lucrative), but *only* if they permitted other ILECs to compete with them for their local phone service.

As expected, ILECs went into the long-distance business. Not as expected, however, ILECs did not attempt to do business in other local markets. They did not compete with one another in the local telephone markets. As a consequence, the prices for local telephone service did not go down (as they would with competition).

---

[37]Bennett v. Schmidt, 153 F.3d 516, 518 (7th Cir. 1998).
[38]*Conley*, 355 U.S. at 45-46.
[39]Sutliff, Inc. v. Donovan Cos., Inc., 727 F.2d 648, 654 (7th Cir. 1984).
[40]550 U.S. 544 (2007).

If the ILECs' failure to compete with each other in local markets was the result of a conspiracy (an agreement among the ILECs), it would violate federal antitrust law. Specifically, §1 of the Sherman Antitrust Act prohibits contracts "in restraint of trade," and there is no question that such an agreement among the ILECs would fall within the heart of that provision. A violation of the Sherman Act could lead to criminal indictment and would certainly lead to private damages cases by local telephone customers. On the other hand, if the ILECs' failure to compete in local markets was *not* the result of an agreement—if, for instance, the ILECs thought *independently* "Gee, I'll stay out of the other guy's market and maybe he'll stay out of mine"—there would be no violation of the antitrust laws.

In *Twombly,* the plaintiffs brought a class action on behalf of local telephone customers, seeking to allege a violation of §1 of the Sherman Act. They tried to allege that the ILECs had conspired not to compete with each other in local phone service. The plaintiffs had no direct proof of such an agreement. For instance, they had no witnesses to a meeting at which the ILECs conspired and no memoranda confirming an understanding among them. Obviously, the plaintiffs would like to get to the discovery phase of the litigation to see if they could find any such "smoking gun" evidence in the ILECs' files or by taking testimony from people who might know of any such deal. But to get to the discovery phase—indeed, to proceed in the litigation stream at all—the plaintiffs must survive a motion to dismiss for failure to state a claim under Rule 12(b)(6).

The plaintiffs attempted to state the existence of a conspiracy by alleging "conscious parallel behavior." That means they alleged that the defendants were aware of what each other was doing (offering long-distance service but not competing outside their own regions in local service) and did the same thing. For example, if Company X is aware that Company Y is not trying to compete for local service in Company X's region, then Company X might let sleeping dogs lie by refusing to compete in Company Y's backyard. Under the substantive antitrust law, however, the plaintiffs must prove at trial that any conscious parallel behavior was the result of an agreement. Under the law, they can do this by showing conscious parallel behavior and some "plus factor" to demonstrate that the behavior was the result of agreement.

The question in *Twombly* was what the plaintiff must *plead* to satisfy Rule 8(a)(2). Remember that *Conley* had said the complaint was sufficient "unless it appears beyond doubt that the plaintiff can prove no set of facts in support of his claim which would entitle him to relief." But the Court held that the plaintiffs failed to state a claim. In the course of its decision, the Court overruled the quoted language from

Conley.[41] The plaintiffs in *Twombly* failed to allege facts that tended to rule out that the ILECs were simply acting independently. They did not set forth "enough factual matter . . . to suggest that an agreement was made."[42] While there was of course a "possibility" that there had been an agreement, the plaintiffs must go beyond possibility and allege "plausibility."

The core of *Twombly* is its statement of what is required to state a claim. According to the majority opinion: "we . . . require . . . only enough facts to state a claim to relief that is plausible on its face. Because the plaintiffs here have not nudged their claims across the line from conceivable to plausible, their complaint must be dismissed."[43] The Court insisted that it was not imposing a "probability requirement at the pleading stage." Instead, the plaintiff must state enough facts to raise "a reasonable expectation that discovery will reveal evidence" supporting the claim.[44]

The most striking thing about this standard is that it finds no grounding in Rule 8(a)(2). Nowhere does that Rule, or any Federal Rule, mention "plausibility." And the focus on "facts" is surprising, given that the Rules were intended specifically to avoid that word and, hopefully, all the baggage that went with it in code-pleading states.

The result of *Twombly* was that the plaintiffs never got to the discovery phase and thus never searched the files of the defendants for proof of conspiracy. The majority recognized this effect of the holding. It said:

> [I]t is no answer to say that a claim just shy of a plausible entitlement to relief can, if groundless, be weeded out early in the discovery process . . . given the common lament that the success of judicial supervision in checking discovery abuse has been on the modest side. And it is self-evident that . . . the threat of discovery expense will push cost-conscious defendants to settle even anemic cases before reaching [trial]. Probably, then it is only by taking care to require allegations that reach the level suggesting conspiracy that we can hope to avoid the potentially enormous expense of discovery in cases with no reasonably founded hope

---

[41]550 U.S. at 556. The Court noted that the language had long been questioned and criticized, as the quotation from Judge Posner above demonstrated. *Conley*'s "no set of facts" phrase had, according to the Court, "earned its retirement" after 50 years of confusing the profession. *Id.* at 563. "The phrase is best forgotten as an incomplete, negative gloss on an accepted pleading standard: Once a claim has been stated, it may be supported by showing any set of facts consistent with the allegations in the complaint." *Id.* Plaintiffs' problem in *Twombly*, according to the Court, is that they failed to state a claim.

[42]*Id.* at 556.

[43]*Id.* at 570.

[44]*Id.* at 556.

that the [discovery] process will reveal relevant evidence to support a §1 claim.[45]

This passage reflects a sentiment expressed by many observers that the liberality of Federal Rules pleading is not entirely good. To the extent that those rules make it very easy to get through the pleadings gate, they make it easy to get into discovery. And discovery can be very expensive and intrusive. Allowing shaky claims to get through the gate and force the defendant to go through discovery can waste judicial resources and put the defendant to unfair expense.[46]

It may be difficult to square *Twombly* with a case decided just two weeks later. In *Erickson v. Pardus,*[47] the Court cited *Conley* with favor. In *Erickson,* a prisoner suffering from illness sued prison officials, and alleged that their deliberate indifference to his medical needs violated his constitutional rights. He alleged that the defendants had diagnosed his condition and put him in treatment, but then removed him from the treatment. The Supreme Court, reversing a dismissal, upheld the complaint, saying that "specific facts are not necessary; the statement need 'only give the defendant fair notice of what the . . . claim is and the grounds upon which it rests.'"[48] It surprises some that the same Court that wrote *Twombly* could make this statement two weeks later.

Twombly unleashed an avalanche of litigation. Within 18 months of the decision, it had been cited in over 6,000 opinions. Presumably, defendants were encouraged to bring on motions to dismiss under Rule 12(b)(6) by what most think is *Twombly's* heightened pleading burden for plaintiffs. Some observers argued that *Twombly* would be limited to antitrust cases. In fact, in his harsh dissent, Justice Stevens accused the majority of "protecting antitrust defendants — who are some of the wealthiest corporations in our economy — from the burdens of pretrial litigation."[49] But other observers assumed the Court would extend its reasoning to all cases. After all, the decision in *Twombly* was an interpretation of Rule 8(a)(2), not of any antitrust law. Moreover, the

---

[45]*Id.* at 544 (quotations and citations omitted).

[46]Another, more hidden, potential cost of liberal pleading rules is that they may allow a plaintiff to proceed through litigation without sufficient focus on the elements she must plead at trial. The elements of a claim are determined by the substantive law. At trial, the plaintiff will have to prove those elements. All we are discussing here is how much detail she must plead with. At trial, there is no question that she has to prove all the elements, even if she could skate a bit in pleading them. Sloppy pleading may lead to sloppy case preparation — preparation that is insufficiently focused on gathering evidence to prove the elements at trial.

[47]551 U.S. 89 (2007).

[48]*Id.* at 93-94, *quoting Conley.*

[49]*Id.* at 596 (Stevens, J., dissenting).

majority opinion strongly rejected the argument that it was imposing a "heightened pleading standard" for any particular substantive
claim.[50]

The Iqbal *Case*

Two years later, in *Ashcroft v. Iqbal*,[51] the Court made clear that
the "plausibility" standard of *Twombly* applies to all cases. The majority opinion clarified the methodology set forth in *Twombly*. First, the
court ruling on a motion to dismiss under Rule 12(b)(6) ignores "legal
conclusions" alleged in the complaint. Second, the court looks to the
factual allegations to see if the claim is plausible. In ruling on this,
the court is to "draw on its judicial experience and common sense."[52]
The former point is susceptible to the criticism that it draws a line
between "facts" and "legal conclusions" reminiscent of such exercises
in code-pleading states. The latter point is susceptible to the criticism
that it makes the standard extremely subjective. A judge with a background as corporate counsel may see things differently from one who
was a public defender.

The plaintiff in *Iqbal* was a Pakistani Muslim. After the terrorist
attacks on September 11, 2001, federal officers arrested and detained
him in conditions that allegedly violated his federal constitutional
rights. Among the defendants were John Ashcroft, who was Attorney
General of the United States, and Robert Mueller, who was Director
of the FBI. The plaintiff alleged that those two high-ranking officials
had adopted policies that led to his designation as a person "of high
interest" and that subjected him to harsh conditions of confinement,
all on the basis of the plaintiff's race, religion, or national origin.

Under relevant law, Ashcroft and Mueller could be liable only if the
rights they allegedly violated were "clearly established" at the time
they acted. If the rights were not "clearly established," Ashcroft and
Mueller were entitled to "qualified immunity" and could not be sued.
The Court, in a contentious five-to-four decision, held that the plaintiff failed to state a claim against Ashcroft and Mueller. The majority
applied the methodology discussed above. First, it ignored legal conclusions, such as the statements that the two defendants "knew of,
condoned, and willfully and maliciously" agreed to subject the plaintiff
to harsh conditions. To the Court, these were nothing but a "formulaic
recitation of the elements" of a claim, and thus were not entitled to a
presumption of truth.

---

[50]*Id.* at 544 ("Here, the Court is not requiring heightened fact pleading of specifics,
but only enough facts to state a claim to relief that is plausible on its face").

[51]556 U.S. 662 (2009).

[52]*Id.* at 679-680.

Second, turning to the factual allegations, the Court found that the complaint did make statements consistent with the defendants' acting on the basis of the plaintiff's race, religion, or national origin. For instance, the allegation that the FBI "arrested and detained thousands of Arab Muslim men" in the wake of the 9/11 attacks could support the claim of improper discrimination. But the Court found that the claim was not plausible, "given more likely explanations" for the actions. It noted that the attacks were perpetrated by 19 Arab Muslim men, so it "should come as no surprise that a legitimate policy of directing law enforcement to arrest and detain individuals because of their suspected link to the attacks would produce a disparate, incidental impact on Arab Muslims, even though the purpose of the policy was to target neither Arabs nor Muslims."[53]

Subsequent Supreme Court Cases and Possible Retrenchment

Twombly and *Iqbal* (together known as *"Twiqbal"*) inspired a stunning amount of academic commentary.[54] Most of it was negative and concluded that the Court had improperly raised the bar for entry to federal litigation, though Professor Redish made a strong argument in 2010 that the plausibility standard of *Twiqbal* was consistent with

---

[53]*Id.* at 682.

[54]"It would probably not be an overstatement to suggest that the combination of lower court confusion and intense scholarly controversy caused by two Supreme Court decisions concerning the Federal Rules over so short a time period is unprecedented." Martin H. Redish, *Pleading, Discovery and the Federal Rules: Exploring the Foundations of Modern Procedure,* 64 Fla. L. Rev. 845, 849 (2012). The initial wave of academic commentary included: Robert Bone, *Plausibility Pleading Revisited and Revised: A Comment on* Ashcroft v. Iqbal, 85 Notre Dame L. Rev. 845 (2010) (lamenting that plaintiffs will more readily lose at the pleading stage, without access to discovery); Scott Dodson, *New Pleading, New Discovery,* 109 Mich. L. Rev. 53 (2010); Allan Ides, Bell Atlantic *and the Principle of Substantive Sufficiency Under Federal Rule of Civil Procedure 8(a)(2): Toward a Structured Approach to Federal Pleading Practice,* 243 F.R.D. 604 (2007); Arthur R. Miller, *From* Conley *to* Twombly *to* Iqbal: *A Double Play on the Federal Rules of Civil Procedure,* 60 Duke L.J. 1 (2010) (broad criticism of the decisions, including usurpation of legislative function); Bradley Scott Shannon, *I Have Federal Pleading All Figured Out,* 61 Case W. Res. L. Rev. 453 (2010); A. Benjamin Spencer, *Plausibility Pleading,* 49 Boston Coll. L. Rev. 431 (2008); Adam N. Steinman, *The Pleading Problem,* 62 Stan. L. Rev. 1293, 1296 (2010); Suja Thomas, *Oddball* Iqbal *and* Twombly *and Employment Discrimination,* 2011 U. Ill. L. Rev. 215 (2011); Suja Thomas, *The New Summary Judgment Motion: The Motion to Dismiss Under* Iqbal *and* Twombly, 14 Lewis & Clark L. Rev. 15 (2010). Professors Clermont and Yeazell foresaw confusion in the wake of *Twiqbal.* Kevin M. Clermont & Stephen C. Yeazell, *Inventing Tests, Destabilizing Systems,* 95 Iowa L. Rev. 821, 840-844 (2010).

traditional notice pleading of federal practice.[55] Most of the academic discussion was general, but some studies focused on ramifications for specific substantive areas[56] and for particular forms of litigation.[57] Despite the argument that *Twombly* and *Iqbal* dealt with unique and therefore limiting facts, it is now clear that the Court intended *Twiqbal* to be trans-substantive—that is, applicable in all cases.

Now, years later, there is a sense that *Twiqbal* may not have been as revolutionary as feared. Certainly, some subsequent Supreme Court cases reassured plaintiffs. In *Skinner v. Switzer*,[58] brought by a prisoner against state officers for alleged violation of his due process rights, the Court reversed a Rule 12(b)(6) dismissal and emphasized, in language reminiscent of *Dioguardi*, that the issue is not whether the plaintiff ultimately will prevail, but whether the case should proceed in litigation. The Court accepted the allegations of the complaint without assessing whether they were "plausible."

In *Matrixx Initiatives, Inc. v. Siracusano*,[59] the Court unanimously agreed that a securities fraud class action should not have been dismissed for failure to state a claim. While noting the "plausibility" requirement, the Court accepted as true the plaintiff's allegations of materiality. As mentioned earlier, the Court confirmed in *Johnson v. City of Shelby* that the plausibility requirement of *Twiqbal* applies only to factual (and not to legal) sufficiency of pleadings.[60] In that case, the Court found that plaintiffs' allegation "that they were fired by the city's board of aldermen, not for deficient performance, but because they brought to light criminal activities of one of the aldermen" was factually sufficient.[61] The Court sounded as though it was speaking of notice pleading when it said that once the plaintiffs "informed the [defendant] of the factual basis for their complaint, they were required to do no more to stave off threshold dismissal for want of an adequate statement of their claim."[62]

---

[55]Redish, *Pleading, Discovery and the Federal Rules,* note 54 above, 64 Fla. L. Rev. at 863-870. Other commentary found merit in *Twiqbal. See, e.g.*, Victor E. Schwartz & Christopher E. Appel, *Rational Pleading in the Modern World of Civil Litigation: The Lessons and Public Policy Benefits of* Twombly *and* Iqbal, 33 Harv. J.L. & Publ. Pol'y, 1107, 1110 (2010).

[56]A particularly good example is William Janssen, Iqbal *"Plausibility" in Pharmaceutical and Medical Device Litigation,* 71 La. L. Rev. 541 (2011).

[57]For example, Professor Effron urged a "plaintiff neutrality" principle regarding allegations of plaintiff conduct in class actions. Robin Effron, *The Future of Complex Litigation in the Era of* Twombly *and* Iqbal, 51 Wm. & Mary L. Rev. 1997 (2010). The issue and her suggestion are addressed in §13.3.5.

[58]562 U.S. 521, 529 (2011).

[59]563 U.S. 27, 38-45 (2011).

[60]574 U.S. 10 (2014). See notes 23 and 24 and accompanying text above.

[61]574 U.S at 10.

[62]*Id.* at 12.

Thus, the ultimate impact of *Twiqbal* is a question of debate.[63] Professor Steinman concluded, as Professor Redish had suggested, that the Court's line of cases "confirms that the framework set out in *Twombly* and *Iqbal* is consistent with a notice-pleading approach."[64] Professor Steinman emphasizes, though, that courts must give appropriate attention to the more recent cases to avoid having the negative narrative (that *Twiqbal* has appreciably raised the fact-pleading barrier) take hold. After the dust has settled, perhaps *Twiqbal* had less of an impact than feared.

One interesting case on the application of *Twiqbal* is *Swanson v. Citibank, N.A.*,[65] decided by the Seventh Circuit in 2010. All three judges on the panel (Diane Wood, Frank Easterbrook, and Richard Posner) were not only respected judges, but had been leading academics at the University of Chicago School of Law. The fact that jurists of this caliber disagreed on the outcome drives home the fact that the application of *Twiqbal* is more art than science. In *Swanson*, the plaintiff, a Black woman appearing without a lawyer, sued Citibank and the appraisers it hired, alleging that she was denied a home equity loan because of her race. She alleged that she applied for the loan, in which she stated that her house was worth $270,000. Citibank gave conditional approval but, after its appraiser concluded the house was worth only $170,000, denied the loan; the conditional approval had been based upon the higher figure. The district court held that Ms. Swanson failed to state a claim for racial discrimination under the Fair Housing Act.

On appeal, the Seventh Circuit reversed.[66] The majority opinion, by Judge Wood, found it plausible, as alleged by the plaintiff, that the

---

[63]*See, e.g.*, Kevin M. Clermont, *Three Myths About* Twombly-Iqbal, 45 Wake Forest L. Rev. 1337 (2010) (*inter alia*, academics should be careful not to overstate likely impact of cases); Robin J. Effron, *Putting the "Notice" Back into Pleading*, 41 Cardozo L. Rev. 981 1002, 1004, 1012 (2020); Kelsey Finn, Comment, *The Harsh Reality of Rule 8(a)(2): Keeping the* Twiqbal *Pleading Standard Plausible, Not Pliable*, 49 Sw. U. L. Rev. 309, 328 (2020); Lonny Hoffman, *Plausible Theory, Implausible Conclusions*, 83 U. Chi. L. Rev. Online 143 (2016); William H.J. Hubbard, *A Fresh Look at Plausibility Pleading*, 83 U. Chi. L. Rev. 693, 756-757 (2016); William H.J. Hubbard, *Testing for Change in Procedural Standards, with Application to* Bell Atlantic v. Twombly, 42 J. Legal Stud. 35 (2013). Interestingly, a study by the Federal Judicial Center in 2011 concluded that there was no increase from 2006 to 2010 in the rate at which cases are terminated by motion to dismiss for failure to state a claim. Joe E. Cecil, et al., *Motions to Dismiss for Failure to State a Claim After* Iqbal, Federal Judicial Center (March 2011). The study discusses other empirical work on the topic, including Kendall Hannon, *Much Ado About* Twombly, 83 Notre Dame L. Rev. 1811 (2008).

[64]Adam N. Steinman, *The Rise and Fall of Plausibility Pleading?*, 69 Vand. L. Rev. 333, 375 (2016).

[65]614 F.3d 400 (7th Cir. 2010).

[66]It did so with regard to the claimed violation of the Fair Housing Act. It affirmed the district court's dismissal of fraud claims. *Id.* at 407.

defendants deliberately lowered the appraised value of the home to provide an excuse to deny a loan to a Black applicant. The question, according to the opinion, is "*could* these things have happened, not *did* they happen."[67] It was sufficient that the complaint identified the type of discrimination the plaintiff thought occurred, by whom it was exercised, and when. Among other things, the majority noted that a subsequent appraisal acquired by the plaintiff valued the property at $240,000.

In dissent, Judge Posner concluded that the claim of racial discrimination was not plausible. He noted various allegations in the complaint, including (1) that the plaintiff had been turned down for a loan by another lender earlier and (2) that the house was appraised for $260,000 in 2004 and, plaintiff alleged, had fallen in value at least 16 percent since then. Based upon these allegations, the plausible cause of the low appraisal, to Judge Posner, was error, not racial discrimination.[68] He concluded that these allegations meant the plaintiff had pleaded herself out of court by stating facts that suggested an error in the appraisal. In contrast, the majority opinion concluded that these extraneous allegations were irrelevant to determining whether the plaintiff had stated a claim.[69] Upon remand, the defendants moved for summary judgment and the case settled.[70] Again, the fact that judges of this caliber disagreed on plausibility underscores the subjectivity of the inquiry.

Twiqbal *in State Courts.* While federal courts must follow the Court's directives in *Twiqbal* and progeny, state courts are free to adopt their own pleading standards. Code states are not affected by the emergence of *Twiqbal*. After all, those cases interpret Federal Rule 8(a)(2), which has no effect on the requirements to state a cause of action under the codes. Most states have adopted the Federal Rules on pleading. The highest courts in some of those states—including Colorado, Massachusetts, Montana, Pennsylvania, South Dakota, and Wisconsin, as well as the high court of the District of Columbia—have embraced the *Twiqbal* gloss on Rule 8(a)(2).[71] But the highest courts of

---

[67]*Id.* at 404 (emphasis original).

[68]*Id.* at 408 (Posner, J., dissenting).

[69]*Id.* at 405-406 (majority opinion).

[70]*See generally* William H.J. Hubbard, Swanson v. Citibank *and the IL Canon,* 87 U. Chi. L. Rev. 2377 (2020).

[71]*See* Briggs v. Southwestern Energy Production Company, 224 A.3d 334, 351 (Pa. 2020); Hallberg v. South Dakota Board of Regents, 937 N.W.2d 568, 577 (S.D. 2019); Warne v. Hall, 373 P.3d 588, 593-594 (Colo. 2016) (noting among other things that adopting *Twiqbal* is convenient for lawyers because the standard is the same in federal and state court); McCall v. D.C. Housing Auth., 126 A.3d 701, 704-705 (D.C. App. 2015); Data Key Partners v. Permira Advisers LLC, 849 N.W.2d 665, 679-680 (Wisc. 2014); Doe v. Board of Regents, 788 N.W.2d 264, 278 (Mont. 2010); Iannacchino v. Ford Motor

more states—including Hawaii, Iowa, Minnesota, Nevada, Tennessee, Washington, West Virginia, Wyoming, and Vermont, as well as the territories of Guam, the Northern Marianas, and the Virgin Islands—have rejected *Twiqbal* in favor of the *Dioguardi* and *Conley* views of Rule 8(a)(2).[72] The courts in many states have not taken sides in the debate. The procedural divergence between federal and state courts in those states that reject *Twiqbal* may well create an incentive for forum shopping.[73]

The Common Counts. Courts have always allowed plaintiffs to assert certain claims in a sort of legal shorthand called the *common counts*. These are basically one-sentence statements of claims that have long been accepted in virtually every court, no matter how

---

Co., 888 N.E.2d 879, 890 (Mass. 2008) ("[W]e take the opportunity to adopt the refinement of that standard that was recently articulated by the United States Supreme Court in [*Twombly*]").

[72]*See* Mountaineer Fire and Rescue Equipment, LLC v. City National Bank of West Virginia, 854 S.E.2d 870, 884 (W. Va. 2020) ("a claim for relief need only give general notice as to the nature of his or her claim"); Oxley v. Sugar Bay Club & Resort Corp., 2018 WL 4002726 at *3 (V.I. 2018) (procedural rules of 2017 reject plausibility pleading); Bank of America, N.A. v. Reyes-Toledo, 428 P.3d 761, 775 (Haw. 2018) ("our well-established notice pleading standard governs in Hawai'i"); Wyoming Guardianship Corporation v. Wyoming State Hospital, 428 P.3d 424, 431 (Wyo. 2018) ("this court has not adopted the federal 'plausibility' standard for determining whether a complaint states a claim for relief"); Ukau v. Wang, 2016 WL 4582244 at *5 (Guam 2016); Walsh v. U.S. Bank, N.A., 851 N.W.2d 598, 603 (Minn. 2014); Landers v. Quality Commc'ns, Inc., 2014 WL 3784254 at *1 (Nev. 2014); Syed v. Mobil Oil Mariana Islands, Inc., 2012 WL 6738436 at *4 (D. N. Mar. I. 2012) ("We are not convinced that the 'plausibility' standard is the proper standard for the Commonwealth at this time"); Hawkeye Foodservice Distribution, Inc. v. Iowa Educators Corp. 812 N.W.2d 600, 607 (Iowa 2012); Webb v. Nashville Area Habitat for Humanity, Inc., 346 S.W.3d 422, 430 (Tenn. 2011) ("We decline to adopt the new plausibility standard and adhere . . . to the notice pleading standard"); McCurry v. Chevy Chase Bank, FSB, 233 P.3d 861, 863 (Wash. 2010) ("The Supreme Court's plausibility standard is predicated on policy determinations specific to the federal trial courts . . . . Neither party has shown these policy determinations hold sufficiently true in the Washington trial courts to warrant such a drastic change in court procedure"); Colby v. Umbrella, Inc., 955 A.2d 1082, 1087 n.1 (Vt. 2008) ("We recently affirmed our minimal notice pleading standard . . . and are unpersuaded by the dissent's argument that we should now abandon it for a heightened standard").

[73]*See* Jill Curry & Matthew Ward, *Are* Twombly *and* Iqbal *Affecting Where Plaintiffs File? A Study Comparing Removal Rates by State*, 45 Tex. Tech L. Rev. 827, 872 (2013) (finding no statistically significant variation in plaintiff forum selection decisions). *But see* Stephen N. Subrin & Thomas O. Main, *The Fourth Era of American Civil Procedure*, 162 U. Pa. L. Rev. 1839, 1848 (2014) ("[I]t is difficult to measure the practical effect of the shift in the Court's pleading jurisprudence because there are many confounding factors . . ."). Professor Dodson notes that the move from notice pleading to more fact-based pleading puts the United States in sync with much of the rest of the world. Scott Dodson, *The Changing Shape of Federal Civil Pretrial Practice: Comparative Convergences in Pleading Standards*, 158 U. Pa. L. Rev. 441 (2010).

demanding or strict those courts might be about stating other claims. The common counts plainly do not satisfy the code-pleading requirement of a "statement of facts constituting a cause of action," yet may satisfy the Federal Rules standards of stating a claim on which relief can be granted. The classic common counts include *quantum meruit* (a claim for the value of labor performed), *quantum valebant* (a claim for the value of goods delivered), and *indebitatus assumpsit* (a claim for money owed). The Federal Rules do not refer to the term common counts, but they are a part of federal practice.[74]

§7.3.3 Special "Heightened" Pleading Requirements

We have seen the level of detail required to state a claim under Rule 8(a)(2). In some substantive areas, the Federal Rules (and sometimes statutes) impose more rigorous pleading requirements, usually referred to as "heightened" pleading requirements.

For example, under Rule 9(b), "[i]n alleging fraud or mistake, a party must state with particularity the circumstances constituting fraud or mistake." Similarly, Rule 9(g) provides that "an item of special damage . . . must be specifically stated." Together, then, these two provisions prescribed detailed pleading about three topics: fraud, mistake, and special damage. Of the three, the great majority of case law concerns allegations of the circumstances constituting fraud,[75] and there are several well-understood reasons for requiring detailed allegations as to that topic. Primarily, the requirement is intended to protect the other party (the party accused of fraud) from the reputational harm caused by imputation of fraudulent behavior. In addition, experience shows that assertions of fraud are often made for nuisance value or to increase the chances of a favorable settlement. Further, fraud comes in a huge variety of fact patterns, meaning that the party accused of it should be given a detailed charge to enable her to respond and defend.

The purpose of a heightened pleading requirement is to make it more difficult for allegations to get past the pleading stage and into the litigation stream. Though fraud is often asserted as a *claim*, Rule 9(b)

---

[74]*See, e.g.*, Clear Connection Corp. v. Comcast Cable Commc'ns. Mgmt., LLC, 149 F. Supp. 3d 1188, 1202-1203 (E.D. Cal. 2015) (common count claim dismissed with leave to amend).

[75]Very few cases deal with failure to plead circumstances of mistake with sufficient detail. In *Bankers Trust Co. v. Old Republic Ins. Co.*, 959 F.2d 677, 683 (7th Cir. 1992), the court indicated that in over 50 years only two reported cases held that a complaint should be dismissed for insufficient allegation of mistake. Moreover, the court concluded that the reason for requiring detailed allegations regarding mistake was "a mystery." *See* 2 Moore's Federal Practice §9.03[2].

applies to all parties who assert fraud or mistake. For example, the defendant in a contract case may raise the affirmative defense of fraud in the inducement or of mistake. She must allege the circumstances of the fraud or mistake with particularity. Similarly, a party may seek to set aside a judgment under Rule 60(b)(1) on the ground of mistake or under Rule 60(b)(3) on the ground of fraud. One making such a motion must plead the circumstances of either fraud or mistake with sufficient detail to satisfy Rule 9(b).

The vexing question, of course, is how much detail is required to satisfy Rule 9(b). In this regard, Rule 9(b) should be read in conjunction with Rule 8(a)(2), which requires only a short and plain statement of the claim, and Rule 8(d)(1), which says that "[e]ach allegation must be simple, concise, and direct." The idea is to balance the need for detail in allegations of fraud and mistake with the desire for a simple pleading regime that facilitates decisions on the merits, rather than on technicalities. Decades of experience have not clarified things greatly. Indeed, the number of cases involving motions concerning pleading under Rule 9(b) has been "quite stunning," and leading commentators have concluded that "the costs of requiring particularized pleading of fraud and mistake outweigh the benefits."[76]

The appropriate path for enforcing Rule 9(b) would seem to be a motion to dismiss for failure to state a claim under Rule 12(b)(6)[77] or a motion to strike under Rule 12(f).[78] Curiously, though, some courts simply refuse to grant either motion, and thus fail to enforce the heightened pleading requirement of Rule 9(b).[79] Other courts have held that insufficiently detailed pleadings of fraud and mistake are subject to a Rule 12(e) motion for a more definite statement. This approach seems problematic, since Rule 12(e) is aimed at pleadings so vague or ambiguous that the defending party cannot form a response. Nonetheless, some courts have granted Rule 12(e) motions aimed at providing more detailed allegations of fraud or mistake, even when the pleading was not so vague or ambiguous as to satisfy Rule 12(e).[80]

[76]5 Wright & Miller 582, 581 (2d ed. Supp. 2005).

[77]*See, e.g.*, Caballero-Rivera v. Chase Manhattan Bank, N.A., 276 F.3d 85, 87 n.3 (1st Cir. 2002). The motion to dismiss will generally be granted without prejudice, to allow the claimant another opportunity to assert the claim sufficiently.

[78]Because Rule 12(b)(6) can be used only to challenge claims (not defenses), the motion to strike is the only appropriate avenue when the insufficiently pleaded allegations of fraud are contained in a defensive pleading. *See, e.g.*, Dynasty Apparel Indus., Inc. v. Rentz, 206 F.R.D. 603, 606 (S.D. Ohio 2002) (motion for summary judgment denied; plaintiff should have moved to strike insufficient allegation of affirmative defense of fraud).

[79]*See* 5 Wright & Miller 667-669 (2d ed. Supp. 2005).

[80]*See, e.g.*, David K. Lindemuth Co. v. Shannon Fin. Corp., 637 F. Supp. 991, 993-994 (N.D. Cal. 1986).

We can draw some general conclusions from the case law. First, the heightened pleading requirement of Rule 9(b) must be raised by the opposing party. Failure to raise the issue in some appropriate way clearly waives the requirement of particularity.[81]

Second, conclusory allegations of fraud are not sufficient. For example, the allegation that the defendant "actively practiced fraud upon the plaintiffs" by failing to tell them about dangers of contamination was insufficient.[82]

Third, an allegation of fraud should generally include the identity of the person making the statement, when and where the misrepresentation was made, how it was communicated, and the resulting injury.[83] As one court said, the plaintiff "must adequately specify the statements [she] claims were false or misleading, give particulars as to the respect in which the plaintiff contends the statements were fraudulent, state when and where the statements were made, and identify those responsible for the statements."[84]

Finally, in some situations, statutes prescribe special pleading requirements. The Private Securities Litigation Reform Act of 1995 (PSLRA) imposes more stringent requirements than Rule 9(b). It applies in particular securities fraud cases and requires, *inter alia*, that the plaintiff "state with particularity facts giving rise to a strong inference that the defendant acted with the required state of mind."[85]

Rule 9(g), as noted above, requires that an "item of special damage" must be "specifically stated." Special damages are to be distinguished from "general damages." General damages are those that naturally flow from an event; they can be foreseen readily as the normal consequence of an act or omission. For example, a person injured in a car wreck could suffer such foreseeable damages as medical expenses, lost wages, and pain and suffering. Because such damages are general, they can be pleaded generally and demanded as a lump sum.

Special damages are those that do not normally flow from an event. In other words, they are "unusual for the type of claim in question."[86] For example, in a claim for false arrest, the plaintiff's demand for "great financial damage" constituted special damage.[87] While one normally expects false arrest to lead to pain, emotional suffering,

[81]*See, e.g.*, Burton v. R.J. Reynolds Tobacco Co., 181 F. Supp. 2d 1256, 1263 n.5 (D. Kan. 2002).

[82]Coffey v. Foamex LP, 2 F.3d 157, 162 (6th Cir. 1993).

[83]2 Moore's Federal Practice §9.03[1][b].

[84]Cosmas v. Hassett, 886 F.2d 8, 11 (2d Cir. 1989).

[85]15 U.S.C. §78u-4(b)(1).

[86]Aviate v. Metro. Club, Inc., 49 F.3d 1219, 1226 (7th Cir. 1995). *See generally* 2 Moore's Federal Practice §9.08[1][a].

[87]Funk v. Cable, 251 F. Supp. 598, 601 (M.D. Pa. 1996).

and even humiliation, a claim that it inflicted financial harm generally does not follow. Similarly, most claims for attorney's fees constitute special damage, because of the American Rule that each party is presumed to bear her own attorney's fees.[88] Though it is difficult to describe exactly how much detail is enough in a given case, the requirement of a detailed pleading of special damages is intended to give the defending party sufficient notice to permit a response.

Some federal courts have imposed heightened pleading requirements in circumstances not covered by Rule 9 or by statute. Faced with burgeoning caseloads, these courts have attempted to weed out cases by requiring the plaintiff to plead in detail in certain classes of cases. The main example is litigation brought under 42 U.S.C. §1983, which permits suit for actions "under color of state law" that result in a deprivation of the plaintiff's federal civil rights. Thousands of such cases are brought each year by state prisoners, and many of the claims lack merit.[89]

A municipality (such as a city or a county) is liable under §1983 only if the deprivation alleged was caused by an official policy, custom, or practice of the municipality.[90] Many lower courts required plaintiffs to allege such a policy, custom, or practice with particularity. The effort was understandable. Most cases of this type fail on the merits, and by imposing a heightened pleading requirement, these courts hoped to dismiss at the pleading stage those in which the plaintiff could not allege a city policy, custom, or practice in detail. The Supreme Court rejected the effort quite bluntly, however, in *Leatherman v. Tarrant County*.[91] The reasoning was quite simple and direct: Because nothing in Rule 9 or in any statute requires detailed pleading in a §1983 case, the courts have no authority to impose a heightened pleading requirement.

The Court had to send the same message to the lower courts nine years later in *Swierkiewicz v. Sorema N.A.*,[92] in which it rejected efforts to require detailed pleading in employment discrimination

[88]*See, e.g.*, National Liberty Corp. v. Wal-Mart Stores, Inc., 120 F.3d 913, 916 (8th Cir. 1997).

[89]One court, acknowledging congressional efforts to reduce the amount of such litigation, noted "the number of frivolous cases filed by imprisoned plaintiffs, who have little to lose and excessive amounts of free time with which to pursue their complaints." Napier v. Priestlike, 314 F.3d 528, 531 (11th Cir. 2002).

[90]Monell v. New York City Dep't of Social Servs., 436 U.S. 658 (1978). In other words, a plaintiff whose civil rights were violated by a city officer may sue that officer for damages but may sue the city for whom the officer worked only if the plaintiff can prove that the officer's acts toward the plaintiff were part of an official city policy, custom, or practice.

[91]507 U.S. 163 (1993).

[92]534 U.S. 506 (2002).

cases. Though the substantive federal law required a plaintiff to establish certain facts at trial to demonstrate a *prima facie* case, nothing in Rule 9 or in federal statute required the plaintiff to *plead* each element in detail. Again, the Court was blunt: Heightened pleading requirements can be imposed by Federal Rule or by statute, but not by judicial fiat. Notwithstanding this clear Supreme Court precedent, some interesting scholarship demonstrates that district courts have de facto continued to require greater specificity in certain types of cases.[93] It is worth remembering that in the *Twombly* decision, discussed in detail at §7.3.2, the Court insisted that it was not imposing a heightened pleading requirement and reiterated the impropriety of doing so in the absence of a Rule or statute.[94]

In addition to heightened pleading requirements, Rule 9 contains other notable provisions about pleading. Rule 9(b) permits malice, intent, knowledge, and other "conditions of a person's mind" to be alleged. This provision reflects the fact that one alleging such topics simply is not in a position to know another party's subjective intent. Thus, she cannot allege such things in detail. Rule 9(c) allows one to "allege generally that all conditions precedent have occurred or have been performed." It also provides that "when denying that a condition precedent has occurred or been performed, a party must do so with particularity." These provisions recognize that a defending party in a contract case may be in the best position to raise which of several conditions precedent might not have been satisfied. The defendant would do so, of course, by asserting an affirmative defense. Similarly, Rule 9(a)(1)(A) provides that a plaintiff need not allege capacity to sue or be sued. This Rule, too, recognizes that a party claiming that a litigant lacks capacity may raise the issue as an affirmative defense.

§7.3.4 Defendant's Response: Answer and Motions

Choices and Timing

In addition to filing her complaint, the plaintiff must arrange to have process served on the defendant under Rule 4 (or the defendant might waive formal service of process under Rule 4(d)). Under the rules of every jurisdiction, the defendant must respond to the complaint in

---

[93]Christopher Fairman, *The Myth of Notice Pleading*, 45 Ariz. L. Rev. 987 (2003); Christopher Fairman, *Heightened Pleading*, 81 Tex. L. Rev. 551 (2002).

[94]"[W]e do not apply any 'heightened' pleading standard, nor do we seek to broaden the scope of Federal Rule . . . 9, which can only be accomplished 'by the process of amending the Federal Rules, and not by judicial interpretation.'" *Twombly*, 550 U.S. at 569 n.14 (2007) (citation omitted).

a prescribed way within a given period, or else risk losing by default (which we address in §7.5).[95] Federal Rule 12(a)(1) imposes the general requirement that the defendant respond within 21 days after being served with process.[96] Though many states provide the same period, some require the defendant to respond in 20 days and some in 30 days.

Under Rule 12, the defendant has a choice of how to respond to the complaint. One choice is to serve and file a pleading called an *answer*, which we discuss in detail below. The other option is to bring a *motion*. These choices are reflected, respectively, in Rule 12(a)(1)(A) and Rule 12(a)(4). A motion is not a pleading. Rather, it is a request that the court order something. During the pendency of a case, there may be dozens of motions. Some of them will be made in writing, such as a motion to dismiss for lack of personal jurisdiction or to transfer for improper venue. Others may be made orally, such as a motion to strike a witness's answer at trial. In this chapter, we focus on the defensive motions that might be brought in lieu of an answer. These are found in Rules 12(b), 12(e), and 12(f).

The question of whether the defendant should respond by motion or by answer is a strategic one. A motion may result in dismissal of the case, thereby obviating the need to draft an answer at all. On the other hand, responding by answer may be more appropriate when the defendant needs more time to develop the facts supporting a particular motion to dismiss. Often, a defendant responds both by motion and answer. For example, upon being sued, the defendant might move[97] to dismiss (say, for lack of personal jurisdiction). If the court grants the motion, the case is over and the defendant need not answer. But suppose the court denies the motion. At that point, the defendant must serve and file an answer. In that instance, then, she will have responded both by motion and by answer. It is imperative, however, that one not run afoul of the important waiver provisions of Rules 12(g) and (h), which we discuss below.

Before discussing the two types of defensive responses in depth, we need to know how to compute the number of days. Specifically, how do we calculate the passage of 21 days from the service of process on the defendant? Rule 6(a) makes clear that the day of the event that

---

[95]Throughout, we refer to the defendant responding to the complaint. Remember, however, that every defending party must respond to a claim against her. Thus, for example, the plaintiff against whom a counterclaim is asserted and the party against whom a crossclaim is asserted must also respond under Rule 12 or risk default on that claim. *See* Rule 12(a)(2).

[96]If the defendant waives formal service of process under Rule 4(d), Rule 12(a)(1)(A)(ii) requires her "to serve an answer" within 60 days after the plaintiff sent the waiver form to the defendant.

[97]*Motion* is *not* a verb. A party *moves* for something or *makes a motion*. No one *motions* the court.

triggers the relevant period (here service of process) is *not* included in that period. The computation of the period includes Saturdays, Sundays, and legal holidays. If the last day falls on a Saturday, Sunday, or a legal holiday, the act may be performed on the next business day.[98]

> ○ ***Example #8.*** *D* is served with process on June 2. She must respond by answer or motion within 21 days of service. June 2 does not count in the calculation of the 21 days. June 3 is Day 1, June 4 is Day 2, June 5 is Day 3, etc. That means June 23 is Day 21 and the last day on which she can respond. Thus, *D* must respond as prescribed by Rule 12 no later than June 23. If June 23 is a Saturday, Sunday, or legal holiday, however, *D* may respond on the next business day.

Under Rule 12(a)(1), the defendant must serve (not file) her "responsive pleading" no later than 21 days after being served with process. Because motions are not pleadings, the phrase "responsive pleading" refers only to the answer, as is made clear in Rule 12(a)(1)(A)(i). What if the defendant wants to respond by motion? Rule 12(a)(4) provides that "serving a motion under this rule" (meaning Rule 12 as a whole) changes the time in which to serve the answer. Specifically, under Rule 12(a)(4)(A), if the court denies the motion (or postpones its disposition), "the responsive pleading must be served within 14 days after notice of the court's action." Thus, within 21 days after being served with process, the defendant must either serve an answer or serve a motion under Rule 12. Either action will (at least for the time being) avoid the risk of default. If the defendant makes a motion and the court denies it (or postpones its disposition), the defendant must serve her answer within 14 days after being informed of the court's ruling on the motion.

> ○ ***Example #9.*** *D* is served with process on June 2. She serves and files a motion to dismiss for lack of personal jurisdiction on June 20. The motion is timely, because it was served no later than 21 days after *D* was served with process. On July 10, the court denies *D*'s motion to dismiss and informs the parties of that fact. So now *D* will have to serve and file an answer. She must do so no later than July 24. Why? Because, under Rule 12(a)(4)(A), she must respond no later than 14 days after being informed of the court's ruling on her motion to dismiss.

---

[98]Rule 6(d) is a general provision allowing three extra days in which to respond when service is made in certain ways other than personal service. The most commonly encountered is when the document is served by mail. It applies not only in pleadings, but other areas of the practice as well, such as discovery. So, for example, while Rule 33(b)(2) requires a response to interrogatories within 30 days of service, if the interrogatories are served by mail, the responding party will have 33 days from the mailing.

It bears noting that the court is free to order a different timetable. In addition, under Rule 6(b), a party may move for an extension of time in which she is required to do something. Moreover, the parties can (and often do) stipulate to extensions. In federal court, such stipulations do not take effect automatically, but are effective only if approved by the court and contained in an order. Thus, if the plaintiff agrees to allow the defendant 45 days from service in which to respond to the complaint, the parties will sign written stipulation and prepare an order to that effect for the judge's signature.

Also, notice the difference a single word can make. A plaintiff might be willing to stipulate to an extension of time in which the defendant may "answer" the complaint, but not in which she may "respond" to the complaint. Why? A stipulation allowing the defendant more time to "answer" allows the defendant only to serve and file an answer. It does not permit her more time in which to bring a *motion*. In contrast, a stipulation allowing the defendant more time in which to "respond" would include the option to answer or bring a motion.

Responding by Motion

Motions Under Rule 12(b). We just saw that the defendant might respond by answer or by a motion under Rule 12. What motions are possible under Rule 12? The major motions are based upon Rule 12(b), which lists seven defenses and provides that the defendant may choose either to raise them in her answer (as affirmative defenses) or by motion. Specifically, the Rule 12(b) defenses are (1) lack of subject matter jurisdiction, (2) lack of personal jurisdiction, (3) improper venue, (4) insufficient process,[99] (5) insufficient service of process,[100] (6) failure to state a claim on which relief can be granted (discussed in §7.3.2), and (7) failure to join an absentee under Rule 19 (traditionally known as an "indispensable party") (which we will see in §12.6.1).

The most important thing to remember about the Rule 12(b) defenses are the waiver provisions of Rules 12(g) and (h). We discussed these in detail (and had some hypotheticals applying them) in §6.2.1. In a nutshell, those provisions require the defendant to assert any of four Rule 12(b) defenses—those relating to personal jurisdiction (12(b)(2)), venue (12(b)(3)), process (12(b)(4)), and service of process (12(b)(5))—

---

[99]This defense is pretty rare. It deals with a defect in the papers served upon the defendant. Recall from §3.3.1 that process consists of a summons and a copy of the complaint. If a copy of the complaint were not served, or if the summons did not comply with Rule 4(a), for example, the defendant would raise the issue under Rule 12(b)(4).

[100]This defense is far more common than that discussed in the previous footnote. Here, the papers constituting process are fine, but there was a problem with how they were served on the defendant.

in her *first response* under Rule 12. Thus, if her first response is a Rule 12 motion, those four defenses must be included in it or else they are waived. If her first response is an answer, likewise, those four defenses must be included in it or else they are waived. On the other hand, the defenses of failure to state a claim (12(b)(6)) and failure to join an absentee under Rule 19 (12(b)(7)) need not be put in the first response. They can be raised anytime through the end of trial. And the defense of lack of subject matter jurisdiction, as we saw both in §6.2.1 and §6.4, may be raised anytime in the case, even for the first time on appeal.

Motion for Judgment on the Pleadings Under Rule 12(c). Rule 12(c) permits a motion for judgment on the pleadings. This is precisely the same as the motion to dismiss for failure to state a claim under Rule 12(b)(6). It is called a motion for judgment on the pleadings if it is brought after the defendant has served her answer. The standards for granting it are the same as we discussed in addressing the Rule 12(b)(6) motion in §7.3.2. Thus, the court will take all allegations of the complaint as true and determine whether they state a legally cognizable claim.

Motion for More Definite Statement Under Rule 12(e). Rule 12(e) permits the defendant to bring a motion for more definite statement, which addresses a complaint that "is so vague or ambiguous that the party cannot reasonably prepare a response." This motion does not address legal or factual insufficiency, as a Rule 12(b)(6) motion does (see §7.3.2). Rather, it is aimed at a complaint that simply cannot be understood. The motion for more definite statement must "point out the defects complained of and the details desired." The defendant must make the Rule 12(e) motion before answering. After all, she is saying that the complaint is so vague or ambiguous that she *cannot* respond. If the court grants the motion, the plaintiff has 14 days in which to plead with more clarity. The defendant must respond to the (hopefully) clarified complaint within 14 days after it is served on her.[101]

Note that a motion for more definite statement can only be used to challenge a pleading to which a "responsive pleading is allowed." Because, generally, no responsive pleading is allowed to an answer, the plaintiff cannot assert a Rule 12(e) motion against an *answer* she finds unintelligible. Rather, she might move to strike the answer under Rule 12(f).

Motion to Strike Under Rule 12(f). Though we consider Rule 12(f) among the motions available to a defendant, the Rule permits any party to move to strike pleadings or portions thereof. Specifically, "the court

---

[101]*See* Rules 12(a)(4)(B) and 12(e). Of course, the court is always free to change the time requirements.

may strike from a pleading an insufficient defense or any redundant, immaterial, impertinent, or scandalous matter." The Rule appears to be strict about the timing of this motion. Rule 12(f)(2) requires that the defendant make a motion to strike before responding to the complaint, and that the plaintiff move to strike within 21 days after being served with the defendant's response. Despite this, however, the Rule also provides that the court can strike "on its own." This phrase has been interpreted to allow the court to grant a party's untimely motion to strike.[102]

The motion to strike is disfavored because it is often used simply to delay proceedings. It is rarely granted. Indeed, even though Rule 12(f) says nothing about prejudice, courts simply will not grant the motion unless the moving party shows that the matter to be stricken will cause her some harm if left in the pleading. One example of such prejudice is when the pleadings may be given to the jury for review during their deliberations. The jury might be unduly swayed by inappropriate or immaterial allegations in a pleading, causing prejudice to a party. There are undoubtedly other examples of prejudice, and the matter is always vested in the discretion of the trial judge. As a practical matter, however, it seems clear that successful motions to strike are especially rare in cases to be tried to the court (without a jury). We have considerable confidence in a judge's ability not to be diverted or swayed by inappropriate allegations in a pleading.

Rule 12(f) specifically allows the court to strike "an insufficient defense." A defense might be insufficient as a matter of law or the defendant may have failed to allege it with sufficient factual detail (though not much detail is required). The court might grant the motion to strike with leave to amend, to allow the defendant to assert the defense appropriately. Rule 12(f) also allows the court to strike "redundant," "immaterial," and "impertinent" matter. Again, however, as a practical matter, the moving party must show prejudice, and it is usually difficult to point to any harm caused by the other party's prolixity. Unnecessary detailed allegations about jurisdiction or irrelevant allegations about venue do not belong in good pleadings, but, unless they cause harm to some party, it is difficult to see why a court would spend time pruning such things from pleadings. It is not clear that "impertinent" adds much to "immaterial."

On the other hand, sometimes a motion to strike can be used to determine an important issue early in the proceedings. For instance, suppose one party in federal court demands trial by jury, and the other

---

[102]*See, e.g.,* Zeelan Indus., Inc. v. De Zeeuw, 706 F. Supp. 702, 704-705 (D. Minn. 1989) ("[E]ven if a party's motion to strike is not made within the time limits established by [Rule] 12(f), a district court has authority to consider the motion because a court may strike material from the pleadings on its own initiative").

party believes that the Seventh Amendment would not accord a jury in the case. She might raise the issue by a motion to strike the jury demand, and have the issue determined well in advance of trial.

The Rule allows the court to strike "scandalous" matter. Parties here have slightly more success in bringing a motion to strike, because scandalous allegations may hold them up to ridicule, either to the jury or to the public (because pleadings are usually considered public records). A party is not entitled to have all distasteful allegations about her stricken. It is not enough that the allegation is unfavorable or even that it offends the party about whom the allegation is made. After all, an allegation of outrageous behavior may be relevant to a claim for an intentional tort or for punitive damages. But unduly derogatory allegations may be stricken. For example, in a case for physical and emotional injuries allegedly suffered by employees at the hands of their employer, the court struck allegations that the defendant attempted to "brainwash" and "torture" the plaintiffs like "Chinese communists in Korea."[103]

Finally, as we saw in §7.3.3, some allegations must be made with particularity or specificity. If the plaintiff fails to plead the required detail on such matters, some courts permit the defendant to respond with a motion to strike the pleading under Rule 12(f).

Responding by Answer

Instead of responding by motion (or if her pre-answer motion was denied), the defendant may respond by answer. An answer is a pleading. (Remember, motions are not pleadings.) In the answer, the defendant must accomplish two primary goals: She must respond to the allegations in the complaint and she must raise affirmative defenses. Responding to the allegations of the complaint is addressed in Federal Rule 8(b). Raising affirmative defenses is addressed in Federal Rule 8(c).

Responding to Allegations in the Complaint. Drafting a good answer takes considerable patience and attention to detail. The job is to respond to each allegation the plaintiff has made in her complaint. Careful lawyers go through the complaint word by word to ensure that they respond carefully. Rule 8(b)(1)(A) and Rule 8(b)(5) (along with common sense) instruct the defendant that there are three possible responses to the plaintiff's allegations. The defendant can (1) admit allegations, (2) deny allegations, or (3) say she lacks sufficient information on which to admit or deny. Rule 8(b)(5) makes clear that the third option (if properly employed) "has the effect of a denial."

---

[103]Alvarado-Morales v. Digital Equip. Corp., 843 F.2d 613, 618 (1st Cir. 1988).

These three options—admit, deny, or claim a lack of sufficient information to admit or deny—must be assessed against the serious consequence provided in Rule 8(b)(6): An allegation (except one regarding the dollar amount of damages) "is admitted if a responsive pleading is required and the allegation is not denied." This is why lawyers are so careful here: The failure to deny an allegation in the complaint is considered an admission of that allegation. (As noted, though, a failure to deny does not constitute an admission of damages.) So Rule 8(b)(6) creates some nervousness.

> ○ ***Example #10.*** *P* alleges in a particular paragraph of her complaint that *D* drove her automobile in a reckless fashion, causing the accident and causing personal injuries to *P*. *D* fails to deny the allegations. *D* has admitted the allegations. There need be no adjudication on these points. They are deemed established for purposes of this case.

We discuss denials in more detail below. Now, we look at the two other possible responses. First, the defendant may simply admit various allegations. This may seem antithetical to the competition of litigation, but there are usually allegations that the defendant simply cannot deny in good faith. As we discuss in §7.7, Rule 11 and other norms of professionalism require that a party (and a lawyer) not make unsupportable assertions. It would be a violation of these norms to deny an allegation that the party (or lawyer) knows is true. Thus, the defendant may admit the plaintiff's allegation that the two parties entered into a contract on a certain date. Admitting such issues establishes these points as facts that need not be adjudicated. Obviously, admitting one fact does not admit another. Thus, the defendant may well admit the existence of the contract and deny the allegation that she breached it.

Second, a defendant must be careful when invoking Rule 8(b)(5) to assert that she "lacks knowledge or information sufficient to form a belief about the truth of an allegation." The requirements of Rule 11 and professional responsibility mean that the defendant cannot use this approach if she is in possession of the relevant information or if the matter alleged is something of public record. Thus, for example, if the plaintiff alleges something as to which the defendant has no precise recollection, but which is contained in her files, she cannot simply respond by saying she is without sufficient information. She must attempt to find the answer and, if appropriate, deny the allegation. If she fails to do so, she will be deemed to have failed to deny the allegation. Under Rule 8(b)(6), this means that she will have admitted the allegation. On the other hand, if the matter alleged by the plaintiff is truly beyond the defendant's knowledge and information, she may say so, and such a statement acts as a denial.

Now, how does the defendant deny allegations contained in the complaint? Rule 8(b)(2) warns the defendant that "[a] denial must fairly respond to the substance of the allegation." This tells the defendant to keep it simple. Do not get argumentative. Do not inject new facts. Just deny.

- ○ ***Example #11.*** In Paragraph 6 of her complaint, *P* alleges that "On November 20, 2022, *D* negligently drove her motor vehicle on Wilshire Boulevard in Los Angeles and struck the plaintiff." *D* should respond in her answer by alleging: "*D* denies the allegations of Paragraph 6 of the complaint." If she did so, the issues alleged by the plaintiff would be "joined," which means they would require adjudication.
- ○ ***Example #12.*** Instead, *D* alleges in her answer: "*D* demands that *P* demonstrate the truth of her allegations by evidence at trial." *D* has just failed to deny the allegation and, under Rule 8(b), has admitted the allegation. If you want to deny an allegation, deny it.
- ○ ***Example #13.*** Instead, *D* alleges in her answer: "On November 20, 2022, *D* was on vacation in Barbados." This is called an "argumentative denial." In code states, it may well be treated as an admission, because it does not directly deny the allegation made by *P*. In federal court, *D* will probably get away with this, but it is sloppy. Again, if you want to deny an allegation, deny it.
- ○ ***Example #14.*** Instead, *D* alleges in her answer: "*D* denies that on November 20, 2022, she negligently drove her motor vehicle on Wilshire Boulevard in Los Angeles and struck the plaintiff." This literal denial is fraught with the possibility of the "negative pregnant." What is that? Some courts treat such allegations as a denial of the precise allegation made, but as an admission of other possibilities. Thus, *D* here has denied something very precisely, but the denial is "pregnant" with the admission that she drove recklessly (instead of negligently) on that date, or that she drove negligently on another date.[104]

The negative pregnant is an example of elevating form over substance. Federal courts are likely to be forgiving on these technicalities, but some courts in code states might not be. But why tempt fate? Why make an easy job hard? Wise counsel will avoid the problem by responding so as to avoid the negative pregnant.

One technique for drafting an answer is to respond in sequence to each paragraph of the complaint. For example, "*D* admits the allegations of Paragraph 1 of the complaint. *D* denies the allegations of Paragraph 2 of the complaint," and so forth. One need not do that,

---

[104]Another example: *P* alleges that the value of the damaged vehicle "exceeded" $80,000, to which the defendant "denies that the value of the vehicle exceeded $80,000." The defendant's response is "pregnant" with an admission that the vehicle was worth exactly $80,000. *See* National Bank v. Northern Illinois Corp., 202 F.2d 601 (7th Cir. 1953).

however. Instead, the defendant might list together those paragraphs she wishes to admit and those she wishes to deny. For example, "*D* admits the allegations of Paragraphs 1 and 6 of the complaint. *D* denies the allegations of each other paragraph of the complaint."

In reality, though, the task is usually more difficult, because each paragraph of the complaint may contain material the defendant wishes to deny *and* material she should admit. The preferred way to respond is to admit expressly what can be admitted and to deny the remainder of the paragraph. The second sentence of Rule 8(b)(3) instructs that when a party intends to deny only part of an allegation, she "must either specifically deny designated allegations or generally deny all except those specifically admitted." And Rule 8(b)(4) says that "[a] party that intends in good faith to deny only part of an allegation must admit the part that is true and deny the rest."

> ○ ***Example #15.*** In Paragraph 4 of her complaint, *P* alleges that "*D* is a corporation formed under the laws of Pennsylvania with its principal place of business in West Virginia." *D* is a Pennsylvania corporation, but its principal place of business is in New Jersey. In its answer, *D* should allege: "In response to Paragraph 4 of the complaint, *D* admits that it is a corporation formed under the laws of Pennsylvania and denies the remainder of the Paragraph."

Finally, there is the "general denial," which is a very short document. In it, the defendant simply alleges something like: "Defendant denies each and every allegation of the complaint." The first sentence of Rule 8(b)(3) recognizes the possibility of the general denial, and code states generally permit them, but one should be careful. In view of Rule 11 and other rules of professional responsibility, it is difficult to imagine a case in which a defendant can properly use a general denial. After all, if there is *anything* in the complaint that should be admitted, the defendant should admit it. It is a rare case in which the defendant can, in good faith, deny every allegation of the complaint.

Raising Affirmative Defenses. In addition to responding to the allegations of the complaint, the defendant will assert affirmative defenses in her answer. As we just saw, the defendant, in responding to the plaintiff's allegations, will not (or at least should not) inject allegations of new facts. Instead, she simply admits or denies what the plaintiff has alleged. With affirmative defenses, however, the defendant does inject a new fact into the dispute. An affirmative defense is something additional to that alleged by the plaintiff, which, if true, entitles the defendant to judgment. The affirmative defense is the modern counterpart to what common law pleading called the "plea of confession and avoidance." That plea permitted a defendant to admit the facts pleaded by the plaintiff but to avoid liability by raising a new fact.

Federal Rule 8(c)(1) lists 19 affirmative defenses but is not an exhaustive list. The Rule says that the defendant "must affirmatively state any avoidance or affirmative defense, including" the 19 that are listed. Review the list of 19. Each is an example of how a defendant may inject into the case a new fact in an effort to avoid liability. The most routinely invoked are probably statute of limitations, statute of frauds, contributory negligence, and assumption of risk. Notice that self-defense is not listed in Rule 8(c), but it certainly constitutes an affirmative defense.

> ○ ***Example #16.*** *P* sues *D* for battery and alleges that *D* punched her in the nose. If *D* denies that she punched *P*, she will simply deny this allegation. On the other hand, if *D* did actually punch *P*, but did so in self-defense, she will admit the allegation, and raise the affirmative defense of self-defense. It is an affirmative defense because it injects a new factual element into the case that, if correct, will result in judgment for *D*.

Failure to assert the affirmative defense in the answer may result in waiver of the defense. As we will see in §7.6.1, if a defendant realizes the omission within 21 days of serving the answer, she will have a right to amend her answer and save the defense. Beyond that, she will need to convince the court that she should be permitted to amend. A prudent lawyer will not put herself in this position; she will be assiduous in asserting affirmative defenses in the answer.[105]

---

[105]The purpose of Rule 8(c) is to inform the plaintiff of the affirmative defense and give her an opportunity to rebut it. Thus, even if the defendant fails to plead an affirmative defense, courts tend to look to whether the plaintiff was put on notice in some other way—for example, through a motion for summary judgment—that the defendant intended to rely on an affirmative defense. Unless the plaintiff was prejudiced by the failure to assert the affirmative defense in her answer, courts may entertain the issue on the merits. *See, e.g.*, Smith v. City of Detroit, 2017 WL 3279170 at *5 (E.D. Mich. 2017) ("Defendants did not waive their affirmative defense because their failure to raise it did not prejudice Plaintiffs' ability to respond.").

In very rare cases, a court may raise an affirmative defense for the defendant. In *Day v. McDonough*, 547 U.S. 198 (2006), a prisoner sued for federal habeas corpus relief. He argued that he was being detained by the state illegally. In its response, the state indicated that its calculation of the timing showed that the plaintiff had sued in a timely fashion. The district court noted, however, that the state had erred. By the court's calculation, the plaintiff's case was filed outside the eligible window permitted by statute. The district court dismissed on its own, and the Supreme Court affirmed. The defense was not jurisdictional, so the court had no obligation to raise it. And the defendant had not deliberately waived the defense. Under the circumstances, the court's raising it was permitted. Obviously, though, a defendant should not expect the court to rescue her from a mistake or miscalculation.

It is helpful to think of the elements of a claim and of affirmative defenses as setting up what Professor Edward Cleary long ago called a series of "conditional imperatives." Suppose, for example, that there are four elements to a claim. That is, the substantive law provides that the plaintiff will recover if A, B, C, and D are established.[106] At trial, the plaintiff attempts to persuade the fact-finder that A, B, C, and D are true. The defendant attempts to persuade the fact-finder that at least one of those elements is not true. But even if the plaintiff persuades the jury that all the elements of her claim are true, the defendant will win if she can establish an affirmative defense. For instance, the defendant might show that she struck the plaintiff in self-defense or that the plaintiff assumed the risk or that the statute of limitations has expired, etc.

Stated as an equation, then, the plaintiff will win *if* A plus B plus C plus D are true *unless* the defendant establishes an affirmative defense. Roughly speaking, the plaintiff has the burden of pleading and proving the *ifs* (i.e., the elements of her claim), and the defendant has the burden of pleading and proving the *unlesses* (i.e., the affirmative defenses).

There are some cases, however, that do not fit this allocation. One is a claim for defamation, which seeks recovery for the publication of an *untrue* statement about the plaintiff that holds the plaintiff up to scorn. A statement is defamatory only if it is untrue. Another way to say the same thing is to invoke the well-known phrase that "truth is a defense." Thus, the question becomes this: Must the plaintiff plead and prove that the statement was false, or must the defendant plead and prove that the statement was true? Usually, the burden of proof at trial follows the burden of pleading, so if a party is required to plead an issue, she is usually required to prove it as well.

The situation of defamation is anomalous, however, because *both* the plaintiff and the defendant must make allegations concerning truth or falsity. The plaintiff must allege that the defendant's statement was false. Instead of merely denying the allegation, however, the defendant must allege the affirmative defense of truth.

○ ***Example #17.*** *D defamed P by stating to a group that P is an embezzler who stole money from P. P sues D for defamation, and alleges, inter alia, that the statement is untrue. D, however, believes that P is indeed an embezzler and thus that her statement about P is true. She alleges the affirmative defense of truth.*

---

[106]The elements for various claims are determined by the relevant substantive law. Many claims are common law, which means that the courts (rather than the legislature) declared what the elements are. Most of the law that governs daily life—the law of contracts, torts, and property—is state-created common law.

As a practical matter, *D* must have the burden of proof on the issue. At common law, when a defamation case went to trial, the burden of proof was on the defendant to prove that the statement she made was true. In part, this was because of a presumption that a person's reputation was good. In part, it reflected a concern with the difficulty of trying to "prove a negative." That is, how can the plaintiff prove that she is not an embezzler? Because the defendant said the plaintiff was an embezzler, the common law put the defendant to her proof by requiring her to demonstrate, for instance, that the plaintiff stole from her. In the United States, First Amendment considerations of freedom of speech have resulted in a change on this score, and today the plaintiff generally is required to prove that the defendant's statement was false. Be that as it may, defamation is one of the few cases in which the burden of proof does not follow the burden of pleading. Both parties must plead regarding the issue of truth, but one will have the burden of proof at trial.

Finally, there is an interesting question about whether the plausibility requirement of *Twiqbal* (discussed in §7.3.2) should apply to pleading affirmative defenses. Some courts, including the Second Circuit, have decided that the answer is yes,[107] but there are strong arguments that the answer should be no. First, Rule 8(c) requires only that a defendant "affirmatively state" an affirmative defense, while Rule 8(a)(2) requires a claimant to plead "a short and plain statement of the claim showing that the pleader is entitled to relief." Second, plausibility pleading is based in large measure on concerns about subjecting the defendant to the expense of discovery. An affirmative defense, in contrast, generally does not subject the plaintiff to any particular additional burden. Finally, the defendant has limited time in which to respond to a complaint and may find it difficult to discover significant support for an affirmative defense. Thus, she should not be required to plead with the detail needed to satisfy *Twiqbal*. In his leading study on the matter, Professor Janssen demonstrates that the clear majority of courts have held that *Twombly* and *Iqbal* do not apply to the pleading of affirmative defenses.[108]

---

[107]GEOMC Co. v. Calmare Therapeutics Inc., 918 F.3d 92, 98 (2d Cir. 2019). *See also* Soos & Associates, Inc. v. Five Guys Enterprises, LLC, 425 F.Supp.3d 1004, 1010 (N.D. Ill. 2019) ("The *Twombly* and *Iqbal* pleading standard applies to affirmative defenses"); 6001 May, LLC v. Stamatis Enterprises, 2015 U.S. Dist. LEXIS 136608 at *3 (W.D. Okla. 2015) (affirmative defenses held insufficient under *Twiqbal* and ordered stricken); Dodson v. Strategic Rests. Acquisition Co., 289 F.R.D. 595, 600-603 (E.D. Cal. 2013).

[108]William M. Janssen, *The Odd State of* Twiqbal *Plausibility in Pleading Affirmative Defenses*, 70 Wash. & Lee L. Rev. 1573, 1606 (2013) ("national majority" . . . "decidedly in the direction of refusing to apply 'plausibility' to [affirmative defenses]"). *See also* Anthony Gambol, *The* Twombly / Iqbal *Plausibility Pleading Standard and Affirmative Defenses: Gooses and Ganders Ten Years Later*, 41 Pace L. Rev. 193, 198 (2020) ("Rather,

§7.3.5   The Reply

A reply is a pleading by the plaintiff made in response to the defendant's answer.[109] As Rule 7(a)(7) makes clear, this pleading is required only "if the court orders one." Courts rarely do so. A reply is not necessary, because other provisions protect the plaintiff from anything raised in the defendant's answer. For instance, the second sentence of Rule 8(b)(6) says that "[i]f a responsive pleading is not required, an allegation is considered denied or avoided." Because no responsive pleading is required to an answer, this means that any allegations by the defendant in her answer are automatically deemed denied by the plaintiff. The only exception is if the court, for some reason, orders the plaintiff to file a reply. This system avoids a further layer of documents that, in all likelihood, simply is not worth the effort.

In some states that do not follow the Federal Rules, a plaintiff must assert a reply if the defendant raises an affirmative defense in her answer that the plaintiff wants to avoid.

> ○ ***Example #18.*** *P* files a proper complaint against *D*. *D* responds with a proper answer in which she asserts the affirmative defense of the Statute of Frauds.[110] *P* feels that the Statute of Frauds defense does not apply in this case, because of partial performance of the contract.[111] In some states, *P* will have to file a "reply" in which she controverts the affirmative defense of the Statute of Frauds. No such filing is required in federal court, however, unless the court orders it.

---

the movement in the district courts over the last decade has been decidedly away from the extension of the plausibility pleading standard to affirmative defenses. Courts selecting not to extend the plausibility pleading standard to affirmative defenses now comprise a sizable majority"). *See, e.g.,* Whetstone Industries, Inc. v. Yowie Group, Ltd., 2019 WL 5102817 at *1 (M.D. Fla. 2019) ("Courts differ on whether the pleading standard for claims applies to affirmative defenses, with courts holding 'no' appearing to be in the majority"); Leviton Mfg. Co. v. Pass & Seymour, Inc., 264 F. Supp. 3d 421, 427 (E.D.N.Y. 2017) ("The overwhelming majority view, to which I subscribe, is that the concept of plausibility has no application to affirmative defenses.").

[109]Until 2007, Rule 7(a) recognized two documents with the name *reply*. One was the reply that survives and is discussed in the text here. The other was the defensive responsive pleading to a counterclaim. In §12.5.1, we see that a counterclaim is an affirmative claim for relief filed by the defendant against the plaintiff. The plaintiff must respond to this claim or risk default. For some reason, the responsive pleading was called a *reply*. This made no sense, and now Rule 7(a)(3) now simply refers to such a responsive pleading as "an answer to a counterclaim." Similarly, Rule 7(a)(4) now calls the responsive pleading to a crossclaim (seen in §12.5.2) "an answer to a crossclaim."

[110]Of course, certain types of agreements must be put in writing under the Statute of Frauds and cannot be enforced if they are simply oral.

[111]This is a widely recognized situation in which a contract that otherwise would have to be in writing under the Statute of Frauds might be enforced even if not in writing.

§7.3.6   Hypothetical and Inconsistent Pleading

Under Rule 8(d)(2), any party "may set out 2 or more statements of a claim or defense alternatively or hypothetically, either in a single count or defense or in separate ones." Further, "[i]f a party makes alternative statements, the pleading is sufficient if any one of them is sufficient." And Rule 8(d)(3) allows a party to "state as many separate claims or defenses as it has, regardless of consistency." Of course, parties must keep in mind that their allegations are subject to Rule 11, which, as we discuss in §7.7, imposes professionalism standards of good faith.

Rules 8(d)(2) and (d)(3) mark a liberal advance over earlier practice under common law and the codes. Those systems generally did not permit pleading of inconsistent facts or theories. They required a party to adopt a theory and guess on a set of facts to be pursued throughout the case. If the facts, as adduced through discovery and at trial, differed from those pleaded, the party was generally out of luck. Even if the facts showed that the plaintiff was entitled to relief, if it was on a different theory or different set of facts from those alleged, she would lose.

The Federal Rules approach is far superior. It recognizes that a party may not be in a position at the outset of the case to know what actually happened or what facts may be established at trial. Alternative pleading permits the parties to plead even inconsistent theories and facts and recognizes that the parties will learn about the facts through discovery. As part of this liberal pleading practice, the Federal Rules recognize that pleadings may have to be amended as the litigation unfolds. We discuss amendment of pleadings in §7.6.

A good example of alternative pleading is provided by an older case decided by the Illinois Court of Appeals under rules that mirror the Federal Rules. In *McCormick v. Kopmann*,[112] Mrs. McCormick sued two sets of defendants in a single case, seeking recovery for the alleged wrongful death of her husband. Mr. McCormick was killed in a motor vehicle collision; he was driving his own vehicle after visiting a tavern. Mrs. McCormick sued Kopmann, who was the driver of the vehicle that collided with Mr. McCormick's car, and also sued the Hulses, who operated the tavern in which Mr. McCormick had been drinking.

The claim against Kopmann (Count I) alleged that Kopmann was negligent in driving his truck, and that the negligence caused the death of Mr. McCormick. As part of this claim, the plaintiff alleged that Mr. McCormick was free from contributory negligence. In the claim against the Hulses (Count IV), the plaintiff alleged a violation of

---

[112]161 N.E.2d 720 (Ill. Ct. App. 1959).

the dram shop law — in other words, that the Hulses had served alcohol to Mr. McCormick even though he was intoxicated. Obviously, the allegation in Count I that Mr. McCormick was free from negligence is inconsistent with the allegation in Count IV that he was drunk when the collision took place. At trial, the jury concluded that Mr. McCormick had not been drunk and that Kopmann was negligent. The court entered judgment in favor of the plaintiff against Kopmann for $15,500.

On appeal, Kopmann renewed an argument he had made at the trial court — that the inconsistency in the plaintiff's pleading required dismissal of the claim against him. The court disagreed and affirmed the judgment against Kopmann. After citing the relevant Illinois provision, which mirrored Rule 8(d)(2), the court reviewed the situation from Mrs. McCormick's standpoint:

> There is nothing in the record before us to indicate that the plaintiff knew in advance of trial, that the averments of Count I, and not Count IV, were true. In fact, at the trial, Kopmann attempted to establish the truth of the allegations of Count IV that McCormick was intoxicated at the time of the collision and that his intoxication caused his death. He can hardly be heard now to say that before the trial, the plaintiff should have known that these were not the facts. Where . . . the injured party is still living and able to recollect the events surrounding the accident, pleading in the alternative may not be justified, but where, as in the case at bar, the key witness is deceased, pleading alternative sets of facts is often the only feasible way to proceed.[113]

Think of Mrs. McCormick's plight if she were not permitted to plead in the alternative. She would have to choose a theory at the outset and proceed against only one defendant at a time. If she sued the Hulses and lost, she would have to bring a second suit against Kopmann. And there is no guarantee that she would win that case. It is conceivable that the jury in the case against the Hulses would conclude that Kopmann was liable, and that the jury in the case against Kopmann would conclude that the Hulses were liable. Alternative pleading allows the claims against both to go forward in a single case and allows that plaintiff to avoid the possibility of being left out in the cold if she has to sue the defendants in separate suits.

Again, however, a lawyer in federal court must sign pleadings under Rule 11. As we discuss in §7.7, the lawyer's signature constitutes a certification, *inter alia*, that she has read the document, has made a reasonable investigation, and has in good faith concluded that the allegations are grounded in fact and law. There may be cases in which

---

[113]*Id.* at 728 (citations omitted).

the state of the party's knowledge will rule out alternative pleading. On the other hand, a party is not required to adopt a single theory if she is in doubt about the factual background or legal theories underlying her claim or defense.

Inconsistent pleading is not limited to plaintiffs. As we discuss in §12.5.1, the defendant may assert a counterclaim against the plaintiff in the pending case, rather than suing on her claim separately. It is not uncommon for a defendant to adopt alternative theories in her defenses, on the one hand, and her counterclaim, on the other. For example, a defendant sued for breach of contract may assert as a defense that the parties never entered into a contract while at the same time asserting a counterclaim seeking recovery from the plaintiff on the contract.[114] Again, the defendant is freed from the burden of having to guess which set of facts will be established at trial, and the judicial system is empowered to determine the overall dispute in a single case.

§7.4 Voluntary and Involuntary Dismissal

Rule 41(a) addresses voluntary dismissal and Rule 41(b) addresses the effect of an involuntary dismissal. Whenever a case is dismissed — voluntarily or involuntarily — the plaintiff will be very concerned with whether the dismissal is "without prejudice." Such a dismissal means that the plaintiff may assert the claim again (assuming the statute of limitations has not run). Another way to say the same thing is that the dismissal is "not on the merits." In contrast, a dismissal "with prejudice" (or "on the merits") means that the plaintiff may not assert the claim again. The claim is extinguished.

§7.4.1 Voluntary Dismissal (Rule 41(a))

Voluntary dismissal is exactly what it says — the plaintiff has filed suit and now wants to dismiss the case. Perhaps the plaintiff has had a change of heart. Or perhaps the parties have settled the case and entered into an agreement that requires the plaintiff to dismiss the proceeding. Whatever the plaintiff's reason, Rule 41(a)(1)(A) limits her ability to take a voluntary dismissal without a court order.

As we will see, the plaintiff can move for a court order of voluntary dismissal. But can the plaintiff get voluntary dismissal without the

---

[114]*See, e.g.,* Olympia Hotels Corp. v. Johnson Wax Dev. Corp., 908 F.2d 1363 (7th Cir. 1990).

court's involvement? Yes, though in only two narrow situations. First, under Rule 41(a)(1)(A)(i), the plaintiff, unilaterally, may file a notice of dismissal. The requirement that the notice be *filed* makes clear that it cannot be an oral notice; it must be in writing. The plaintiff has a right to do this, however, *only* before the adverse party "serves either an answer or a motion for summary judgment." Second, under Rule 41(a)(1)(A)(ii), the plaintiff may dismiss by stipulation of dismissal "signed by all parties who have appeared." This second option does not permit unilateral action by the plaintiff—she must get the signed agreement of all parties who have appeared.

> ○ ***Example #19.*** *P* sues *D*. *D* files and serves her answer. Now *P* wants to take a voluntary dismissal. May she do so unilaterally by filing a notice of dismissal? No. Why? Because under Rule 41(a)(1)(A)(i), she may do that only before *D* served her answer. She may dismiss voluntarily without court order only if she gets a written stipulation that she and *D* sign.
>
> ○ ***Example #20.*** *P* sues *D*. *D* files and serves a motion to dismiss for failure to state a claim under Rule 12(b)(6). Now *P* wants to take a voluntary dismissal. May she do so unilaterally, by filing a notice of dismissal? Yes. Why? Because she has a right to do so any time before *D* "serves either an answer or a motion for summary judgment." *D* in this hypothetical has done neither. A motion to dismiss for failure to state a claim is neither an answer nor a motion for summary judgment.

Under Rule 41(a)(1)(B), dismissal by either method—notice of dismissal or by stipulation of parties—is generally without prejudice. Thus, the plaintiff can file her case. There is one exception, though, found in the second sentence of Rule 41(a)(1)(B): "But if the plaintiff previously dismissed any federal- or state-court action based on or including the same claim, a notice of dismissal operates as an adjudication on the merits." In other words, the first voluntary dismissal is without prejudice. But if the plaintiff refiles the case and then dismisses *by filing a notice of dismissal* (not by stipulation), the second dismissal operates as an adjudication on the merits (which means it is with prejudice). This is true whether the first case was in federal or state court. So long as the second case is in federal court and is dismissed *by filing a notice of dismissal*, that dismissal is with prejudice.

> ○ ***Example #21.*** *P* sues *D* in state (or federal) court. *P* takes a voluntary dismissal of that case. It is without prejudice. *P* then sues *D* in federal court, asserting the same claim (and invoking federal subject matter jurisdiction). Now *P* files notice of dismissal. That dismissal is with prejudice.
>
> ○ ***Example #22.*** *P* sues *D* in state (or federal) court. *P* takes a voluntary dismissal of that case. It is without prejudice. *P* then sues *D* in

federal court, asserting the same claim (and invoking federal subject matter jurisdiction). Now *P* dismisses this second case by stipulation of the parties. This dismissal is *without* prejudice. The language of Rule 41(a)(1)(B) clearly provides that the second dismissal operates on the merits *only* if it is accomplished by notice of dismissal, not by stipulation.[115]

It makes sense to limit the number of times a plaintiff can take a unilateral voluntary dismissal without prejudice. Otherwise, the plaintiff could harass the defendant by repeatedly suing and dismissing the claim. It also makes sense to limit the plaintiff's right to take a unilateral voluntary dismissal to a time early in the litigation. That way, it is unlikely that a case will be dismissed after the defendant or the court have invested substantial resources in it. Because Rule 41(a)(1)(A)(i) permits unilateral voluntary dismissal only before the defendant has served an answer or a motion for summary judgment, it is unlikely that dismissal will have wasted substantial resources. Suppose a plaintiff files a complaint to which the defendant files an answer. Now the plaintiff files an amended complaint. Does the plaintiff now have a new right to file notice of dismissal under Rule 41(a)(1)(A)(i)? No; the answer to the original complaint extinguishes the plaintiff's right to file a notice of dismissal.[116]

On the other hand, there are cases in which the defendant and the court will have invested significant time and resources before the defendant has served an answer or motion for summary judgment. In such cases, should the plaintiff nonetheless have the right to dismiss under Rule 41(a)(1)(A)(i)? The answer appears to be yes. In *American Soccer Co. v. Score First Enterprises*,[117] the parties litigated the difficult issue of whether the plaintiff was entitled to a preliminary injunction for two months after the case was filed. The defendant and the court invested a great deal of time and effort on the matter. On the other hand, however, the defendant had not served an answer or a motion for summary judgment. After two months, the plaintiff filed a notice of dismissal. The court held that the plaintiff had a right to do so, because the terms of Rule 41(a)(1)(A)(i) were satisfied. The wasted effort by the defendant and the court was irrelevant.

Our discussion of voluntary dismissal to this point has not required action by the court. Now we shift to Rule 41(a)(2), which addresses

---

[115]*See* Sutton Place Dev. Co. v. Abacus Mortg. Inv. Co., 826 F.2d 637 (7th Cir. 1987).

[116]Welsh v. Correct Care, L.L.C., 915 F.3d 341, 344 (5th Cir. 2019) ("filing an amended complaint does not revive the plaintiff's absolute right to dismissal under Rule 41(a)(1)(A)(i).").

[117]187 F.3d 1108 (9th Cir. 1999).

voluntary dismissal by court order. It provides that in any situation not covered by Rule 41(a)(1), the court may grant a plaintiff's motion for voluntary dismissal. The court may impose whatever terms and conditions it deems proper.

> ○ ***Example #23.*** *P* sues *D*. *D* files and serves her answer. *P* wants to dismiss voluntarily, but *D* does not agree to the dismissal. *P* cannot act unilaterally under Rule 41(a)(1)(A)(i), because *D* has served an answer. *P* cannot dismiss under Rule 41(a)(1)(A)(ii), because D will not stipulate to the dismissal. *P* can have the case dismissed only if the court orders dismissal under Rule 41(a)(2).

Unless the court says otherwise in the order, a dismissal under Rule 41(a)(2) is presumed to be without prejudice. Under what circumstances would a court grant a motion for voluntary dismissal *with* prejudice? After all, doing so means that plaintiff cannot refile the case. One example is *Grover v. Eli Lilly Co.*,[118] in which the Sixth Circuit held that the district court abused its discretion in entering a dismissal without prejudice. The case invoked diversity of citizenship jurisdiction and involved a claim alleged under Ohio law. Because Ohio law on the question of liability was not clear, the district court certified the question to the Ohio Supreme Court for clarification (we see that procedure in §10.8). That court held, four to three, that the plaintiff did not have a claim. The district court entered an order of dismissal *without* prejudice, reasoning that the Ohio court might change its mind or that the Ohio legislature might provide a remedy for persons such as the plaintiff. The Sixth Circuit reversed and explained that the "primary purpose" of requiring court approval for dismissal under Rule 41(a)(2) "is to protect the nonmoving party [the defendant] from unfair treatment."[119] Such unfair treatment consisted of the "plain legal prejudice" caused by dismissing without prejudice and leaving the defendant open to potential liability based upon a subsequent change in the law. It concluded: "At the point when the law clearly dictates a result for the defendant, it is unfair to subject him to continued exposure to potential liability by dismissing the case without prejudice."[120]

> ○ ***Example #24.*** *P* sued *D* in state court and took a voluntary dismissal. *P* now sues *D* in federal court, invoking federal subject matter jurisdiction. *D* has not responded to this case by answer or motion for summary judgment. Now *P* moves for voluntary dismissal under

---

[118]33 F.3d 716 (6th Cir. 1994).
[119]*Id.* at 718.
[120]*Id.* at 719.

Rule 41(a)(2). *D* insists, however, that *P* may only dismiss by notice of dismissal under Rule 41(a)(1)(A)(i). Why? Because *D* has not answered or moved for summary judgment in this case, that route certainly is available.

Notice what is at stake here. If *P* must dismiss by notice of dismissal, it will be with prejudice and extinguish *P*'s claim. But if *P* may dismiss by court order, the presumption is that the dismissal is without prejudice, so *P* may refile. In *Wellfount, Corp. v. Hennis Care Centre of Bolivar, Inc.*, the Sixth Circuit concluded that *P* was not required to file a notice of appeal and thus that the district court could order voluntary dismissal without prejudice.[121] Nothing in Rule 41(a)(1)(A)(i) *requires* a plaintiff to use notice of dismissal when it is available. Thus, she remains able at any time in the case to seek a court order of voluntary dismissal.[122]

When a dismissal is without prejudice, the plaintiff may refile the case. When she does, Rule 41(d) permits the court in the second case to order the plaintiff to pay all or part of the costs incurred by the defendant in the first case. This provision makes sense, because the defendant was put to expense by the plaintiff's filing a case she later withdrew. This provision applies, however, only when the second case is brought in federal court (though the first case—the one voluntarily dismissed—may have been filed either in state or federal court).[123]

Rule 41(a)(2) addresses dismissal of the case if a counterclaim is pending. (In other words, if the defendant has asserted a claim against the plaintiff in the pending case before the plaintiff moves to dismiss the case.) In such a situation, the court should dismiss against the defendant's objection "only if the counterclaim can remain pending for independent adjudication." Thus, if the counterclaim cannot remain in court,[124] the court should not allow the plaintiff to dismiss her claim.

---

[121]951 F.3d 769, 772-774 (6th Cir. 2020).

[122]*Id.* at 773-774. The court relied in part upon *Cunningham v. Whitener,* 182 Fed. Appx. 966, 969-971 (11th Cir. 2006), in which the Eleventh Circuit reached the same conclusion.

[123]Sargeant v. Hall, 951 F.3d 1280, 1281 (2020) ("The question presented in this appeal—one of first impression in our circuit—is whether Rule 41(d) applies when a plaintiff, after dismissing the first federal action, files a subsequent action in state court. For the reasons which follow, we conclude that Rule 41(d) does not apply in such a scenario.").

[124]An example is if the counterclaim is inextricably linked to the plaintiff's claim. *See, e.g.*, Wentworth v. Hedson, 248 F.R.D. 121, 122 (E.D.N.Y. 2008) (denying voluntary dismissal, *inter alia*, because counterclaims were "wholly dependent upon the same evidence" supporting plaintiff's claim); Bosteve Ltd. v. Marauszwki, 110 F.R.D. 257, 259 (E.D.N.Y. 1986). *See generally* 8 Moore's Federal Practice §41.40[8].

If the counterclaim can remain in court for independent adjudication, the court may allow the plaintiff to dismiss her claim. This rule is intended to ensure that the defendant's claim against the plaintiff remain on the court's docket if the defendant so desires.

§7.4.2 Involuntary Dismissal (Rule 41(b))

Rule 41(b) provides for dismissal in three situations: for failure of the plaintiff (1) to prosecute the case, (2) to comply with the Federal Rules, or (3) to comply with a court order. Three initial points are important. First, Rule 41(b) is not exclusive. We already know that there are several ways in which a case may be dismissed against the plaintiff's wishes. For instance, all the defenses in Rule 12(b)—including lack of personal jurisdiction, lack of subject matter jurisdiction, or improper venue—may result in an involuntary dismissal. In addition, as we see in §7.7, a serious violation of rules of professionalism may also result in dismissal. In §8.4, we see that dismissal is possible as a discovery sanction in extreme cases as well. Accordingly, Rule 41(b) augments other provisions that permit involuntary dismissal. Second, Rule 41(b) permits dismissal "of the action or any claim." There may be circumstances in which dismissal of less than the entire case is appropriate, such as when the plaintiff fails to comply with a court order concerning a particular claim. Third, though Rule 41(b) expressly provides that "a defendant may move to dismiss" for any of the enumerated reasons, the Supreme Court concluded in *Link v. Wabash Railway Co.*[125] that the Rule permits a district court to dismiss *sua sponte*, without a motion by the defendant.

Link is a widely cited case on involuntary dismissal.[126] In that case, the plaintiff filed suit in August 1954. The case was dismissed without having gone to trial in October 1960, which meant that this relatively simple personal injury case lingered on the docket for six years without going to trial. How did that happen? Sixteen months were spent in the plaintiff's securing reversal of the district judge's

---

[125]370 U.S. 626 (1962).

[126]There are others. The Supreme Court seems to issue such an opinion every so often as a reminder to plaintiffs' lawyers that they must play by the rules and prosecute their cases with appropriate diligence. *See, e.g.,* Henderson v. United States, 517 U.S. 654, 662 (1996) ("Rule 41(b) [provides] for dismissal 'for failure of plaintiff to prosecute,' and could be invoked as a check against unreasonable delay"); Roadway Express, Inc. v. Piper, 447 U.S. 752 (1980); National Hockey League v. Metropolitan Hockey Club, Inc., 427 U.S. 639 (1976).

erroneous dismissal of the case. Beyond that, though, the reason for the delay was the plaintiff's lawyer seeking extensions in which to complete discovery. The precipitous event, though, was when the plaintiff's lawyer failed to attend a pretrial conference (something we discuss in §8.5) in October 1960. The lawyer called the judge's chambers on the day of the hearing and reported that he was busy working on a state-court case and could not attend the conference. The district judge's patience was exhausted, and he dismissed the case "for failure of the plaintiff's counsel to appear at the pretrial, for failure to prosecute this action."

The Supreme Court affirmed and held that the district judge did not abuse his discretion by dismissing. Justice Black wrote a spirited dissent and criticized the Court's willingness to punish the plaintiff for the misdeeds of his lawyer. The majority opinion, by Justice Harlan, concluded that the plaintiff had retained the lawyer, and thus had to live with the consequences.[127] By implication, the majority seems to be saying that a reasonable client would figure out that there is a problem when his (relatively simple) case has not gone to trial in six years. Each viewpoint creates problems. Justice Black's view would seem to make it impossible to dismiss, no matter how dilatory a lawyer has been, if the client did not participate in the delay. On the other hand, Justice Harlan's view that the docket may be cleared of such cases may ignore the fact that the dismissal may result in the plaintiff's filing of a malpractice case against the lawyer.

In *Link*, the district judge did not warn the plaintiff or his lawyer that failure to attend the pretrial conference could result in dismissal. Moreover, the court did not provide the lawyer a hearing at which the lawyer could explain why he did not attend. On the record of the case, however, the Supreme Court concluded that it was clear that the lawyer knew how serious the situation was. Still, it is clearly preferable for a court to provide a warning and an opportunity to explain dilatory behavior before entering dismissal. As we discuss in §7.7, Rule 11 now expressly requires notice and an opportunity to be heard before a court may impose sanctions less drastic than dismissal.

---

[127]This theory—that the client has hired the attorney and thus is bound by the mistakes of her "agent"—is a pervasive one. We see it again in §9.7, concerning motions to set aside a judgment. When an attorney's errors have resulted in a default judgment against a defendant, the defendant might move to set aside the judgment under Rule 60(b)(6) for extraordinary circumstances. Though the traditional view has been that the attorney's mistakes do not justify setting aside a judgment, some courts will accord relief if the attorney was guilty of gross negligence.

Federal Rule 83(a) permits each federal district to adopt Local Rules that augment the Federal Rules. It is crucial that you consult the relevant Local Rules; never let any of the provisions in those rules sneak up on you. Local Rules can vary dramatically from district to district. Some districts have a Local Rule providing for involuntary dismissal if the docket sheet shows that there has been no activity in the case for a given period, say, for one year. In such circumstance, the court will issue an Order to Show Cause (an OSC[128]), which requires the plaintiff to demonstrate why the court should not dismiss the case for lack of prosecution.[129] Even in the absence of a Local Rule, the court certainly has the inherent authority to issue an OSC when it thinks the plaintiff has not been diligent in prosecuting the case. In §8.5, we see that the Federal Rules seek to avoid such lulls in the case by imposing several scheduling requirements and conferences to keep the parties' feet to the fire.

The second sentence of Rule 41(b) addresses whether an involuntary dismissal is with prejudice (or "operates as an adjudication on the merits"). The general answer is yes, so an involuntary dismissal is considered to be on the merits, and thus the claim is extinguished. But Rule 41(b) recognizes exceptions to this general rule. First, the court may provide to the contrary in its order of dismissal. Thus, if the court dismisses the case "without prejudice," it does *not* act as an adjudication on the merits. Second, if the dismissal is based upon lack of jurisdiction (personal or subject matter), improper venue, or failure to join a party under Rule 19, the dismissal is not considered to be on the merits. This provision recognizes that such dismissals—essentially for the court's lack of power over the case or parties—do not address the merits in any way and thus should not bar the plaintiff from reasserting the claim.

On the other hand, this provision means that a dismissal for failure to prosecute would (absent court order to the contrary) act as an adjudication on the merits and thus bar refiling. This seems odd. When the court dismisses on this basis, there has been no adjudication on the merits in fact. But Rule 41(b) says that an involuntary dismissal "operates as an adjudication on the merits." We revisit this topic in Chapter 11, when we discuss claim and issue preclusion. It will be

[128]In some states, the OSC is referred to by the ancient term *rule nisi* (pronounced *nigh-sigh*). Courts may issue an OSC (or *rule nisi*) for any number of reasons; for example, it may want a party to explain why the court should not enter sanctions against it. Here we are concerned with an OSC for failure to prosecute the case.

[129]Many states have similar provisions. California has stronger medicine. By statute, the trial court loses jurisdiction over the case if trial has not commenced within five years after the case was filed. Cal. Code Civ. Proc. §583.360.

important there whether a judgment is considered "on the merits." We also see (in §11.2.2) that the Supreme Court has opened the door to limiting the preclusive effect of Rule 41(b). For now, though, the general rule is straightforward: Any involuntary dismissal except one based upon jurisdiction, venue, or indispensable parties is deemed to be with prejudice.

§7.5 Failure to Respond: Default and Default Judgment

§7.5.1 The Difference Between Default and Default Judgment

In §7.4, we saw that a case might be dismissed for the plaintiff's failure to play by the rules—for her failure to prosecute the case, to abide by the Federal Rules, or to obey a court order. In this section, we consider a bad fate that can befall the defendant—specifically, default and default judgment under Federal Rule 55. Rule 55 is not the only provision that can result in entry of default judgment against the defendant. We see in §8.4 that the court may in extreme cases order default judgment against a defendant for failure to abide by the discovery provisions of the Federal Rules. Here, however, we are concerned with default caused by the defendant's failure to respond appropriately to a suit against her. This situation raises conflicting policies. For one, we prefer to decide cases on their merits, rather than on procedural technicalities. On the other hand, though, the plaintiff should not be put to undue delay, and the defendant should be required to play by the rules.

At the outset, we must distinguish a "default" from a "default judgment." A default is a notation made by the court clerk's office on the docket sheet for the case, indicating that the defendant has failed to respond within the time required by Rule 12. The entry of default, however, does not entitle the plaintiff to relief. To recover relief on her claim, the plaintiff must obtain a default *judgment*, which can then be enforced like any other judgment. Under Rule 55, in limited circumstances, the clerk of the court may enter the judgment. In other circumstances, however, the judgment can only be entered by the court itself. The entry of default is an absolute prerequisite to obtaining a default judgment. Thus, the first step when the defendant fails to respond timely under Rule 12 is for the plaintiff to seek entry of the default. When that is done, she can seek entry of default judgment.

§7.5.2   Entry of Default (Rule 55(a))

The default is usually entered by the clerk of the court,[130] and not by the judge.[131] Under Rule 55(a), the clerk has no discretion in the matter. If the plaintiff shows "by affidavit or otherwise" that the defendant[132] has failed "to plead or otherwise defend as provided by these rules," the clerk "shall" enter the defendant's default.[133] On the other hand, Rule 55(a) does not provide for the automatic entry of default once the defendant's time for responding has run. The practice is different in some state courts, in which entry of default is automatic when the time for responding has expired. Rule 55(a), though, clearly requires that the plaintiff do something to have the default entered.

In §7.4.1, we saw that the defendant generally must serve her response under Rule 12 within 21 days after being served with process. The person who served process on the defendant is supposed to make a report to the court indicating when service was effective. (We discussed this requirement in §3.3.) The clerk's office records this information on the docket sheet for the case. Even if the server failed to make the report to the court, the plaintiff can present proof of when service was made. For default, the plaintiff must show the clerk that the defendant has failed to serve a response within the appropriate time.

Though the entry of the default does not entitle the plaintiff to relief (she needs a judgment for that), it does one important thing: It cuts off the defendant's right to file a response to the complaint. What happens if the defendant wants to serve and file her answer more than 21 days after she was served with process? If the plaintiff has had the default entered, the defendant cannot file the answer, and will have to make a motion to set aside the default (which we address in §7.5.4).

---

[130]Do not confuse clerks of the court with law clerks. The former are employees of the court system, who are required to oversee the filing of documents and maintenance of files and other administrative tasks. The latter are usually recent law school graduates hired by a judge (or by the court itself) to provide research and drafting assistance for the judge.

[131]Technically, though Rule 55(a) permits entry of default by the clerk, it does not prohibit the court (judge) from doing so. So the judge certainly has the authority to enter a default, but generally there is no reason to go to anyone but the clerk for entry of default.

[132]Actually, any defending party. Remember, a plaintiff might be sued by the defendant on a counterclaim. The plaintiff is a defending party on the counterclaim and must respond to it under Rule 12. Here we assume that the defaulting party is the defendant.

[133]Despite this mandatory language, occasionally a clerk's office fails to discharge this duty. In such a case, the court may declare that default has been entered. Cohen v. Rosenthal, 2015 WL 7722391 at *2 (D. Conn. 2015).

If the plaintiff has *not* had the default entered, technically the defendant should move for an extension of time in which to respond under Rule 6(b). In practice, however, courts have permitted the defendant simply to respond any time before the clerk enters the default, even without making a motion for extension of time.[134] Thus the plaintiff will want to get the default on the books as soon as possible, because it will preclude the defendant from responding.

- *Example #25.* P files her complaint against D and has process served on June 1. Under Rule 12(a)(1)(A)(i), D must respond no later than June 22. She fails to do so. P demonstrates to the clerk of the court that D has not responded in a timely fashion. The clerk enters the default on the record. D cannot now answer or otherwise respond to the complaint unless she convinces the court to set aside the default.
- *Example #26.* Same facts except here P fails to request entry of default. On June 24, D serves and files an answer in the case. The answer is not timely, because it is not served within 21 days after D was served with process. On the other hand, though, P has not had the clerk enter a default. In all likelihood, the clerk will allow D to answer. The more appropriate course for D would have been to make a motion for extension of time in which to respond under Rule 6(b). But many courts seem willing to let the defendant respond late rather than go to the trouble of making such a motion. After all, P could have cut off D's right to respond by having the default entered as soon as D was late.

§7.5.3 Entry of Default Judgment (Rule 55(b))

Once the plaintiff gets the default, she will want to obtain the default judgment, which she can enforce to recover relief. Entry of default judgment in federal court is governed by Rule 55(b). It provides that the clerk of the court can enter default judgment in very limited circumstances. Outside those circumstances, however, the clerk cannot act and the plaintiff must seek the default judgment from the court itself (meaning from a judge). It is appropriate to limit the situations in which a clerk can enter judgment. After all, a judgment is an order, issued under the authority of the court, that creates a legal obligation from the defendant to the plaintiff. We are reluctant to allow a bureaucratic officer to enter such an order, and thus limit the types of cases in which this can be done.

Under Rule 55(b)(1), the clerk can enter default judgment at the behest of the plaintiff *only* if four things are true. First, the claim must

---

[134]*See, e.g.,* Bach v. Mason, 190 F.R.D. 567, 574 (D. Idaho 1999); DeTore v. Local No. 245, 511 F. Supp. 171 (D.N.J. 1981).

be for a sum certain or for an amount that can be made certain by calculation. This requirement is not satisfied by the plaintiff's general assertion in the complaint of a dollar amount due or by the plaintiff's requesting only a certain dollar recovery when the value of the underlying claim is not readily certain.[135] The requirement can be satisfied, for example, in a suit for liquidated damages or to recover the amount of a promissory note.[136]

Second, the plaintiff must provide an affidavit (which is a sworn statement, executed under penalty of perjury) of the damages due.

Third, the defendant must have failed to appear in the case. We see in Example #28 that it is possible to default after having made an appearance. Default judgment from the clerk is available only if the defendant has failed to appear at all.

Fourth, the defendant cannot be a minor or an incompetent.[137]

If all of these requirements are satisfied, the clerk has no discretion, but "shall enter judgment for [the amount shown in the affidavit] and costs against the defendant." In sum, then, the clerk enters the judgment only in those cases in which there is no need for judicial discretion: The claim is for a sum certain, and the defendant has shown no interest in responding, let alone litigating the merits or the question of damages.

> o ***Example #27.*** *P* sues *D* for $100,000 liquidated damages. *D* is served with process on June 1. *D* failed to respond in any way within the 21 days permitted for response under Rule 12. *P* has the clerk enter the default. *P* can ask the clerk to enter the judgment under Rule 55(b)(1), so long as *D* is neither an infant nor an incompetent, and provided *P* provides an affidavit that the $100,000 is the sum of damage she has suffered. The clerk can enter the default judgment because this case is for a sum certain and *D* has made no response whatsoever.

On the other hand, if any of the four requirements mentioned above are not satisfied, the clerk cannot enter the judgment under Rule 55(b)(1). Then, the plaintiff must seek entry of default judgment from the judge under Rule 55(b)(2). She does so by making what the Rule calls an "application" for default judgment.

---

[135]*See, e.g.,* AGCO Fin., LLC v. Littrell, 320 F.R.D. 45, 49-50 (D. Minn. 2017) (plaintiff's requesting recovery of a specific dollar amount not a sum certain for a claim for unpaid remaining lease payments on a tractor minus the value of the tractor plus repairs and miscellaneous costs).

[136]*See* 10A Wright & Miller §2683.

[137]Though Rule 55(b) speaks only of the defendant being neither an infant or incompetent, provisions of the Soldiers' and Sailors' Civil Relief Act, 50 U.S.C. App. §501 *et seq.*, also impose certain requirements for obtaining a default judgment when a defendant is a member of the Armed Services.

○ ***Example #28.*** Same facts as in the preceding hypothetical, but here *D* responds to the complaint by making a timely motion to dismiss for lack of personal jurisdiction. The court denies the motion. *D* then fails to serve and file an answer within the appropriate time. *P* again asks the clerk to enter default. Here, however, *P* cannot ask the clerk for entry of default judgment. Why? Because here, *D* has made an appearance in the case (the motion to dismiss) and thus the requirements of Rule 55(b)(1) are not all satisfied. *P* can obtain a judgment only from the court.

The court will almost always hold a hearing on the application for default judgment.[138] In these cases, the plaintiff has no *right* to a default judgment under Rule 55(b)(2), even though the defendant is clearly in default.[139] Why? Because, as we have said before, our system of justice prefers to resolve disputes on the merits rather than on technicalities. The matter is in the district judge's discretion, and she may ask for evidence on any relevant matter, including the strength of the plaintiff's claim on the merits and the viability of any defense the defendant might have. Courts generally will determine whether to grant a motion for entry of default judgment based upon (1) whether the defendant's failure to respond is willful, (2) whether the plaintiff has been harmed, and (3) whether the defendant has a meritorious defense to the underlying case.[140]

The judge might refuse to enter judgment when it is clear that the merits are disputed and the potential liability is large.[141] On the other hand, if the defendant's contentions on the merits are weak, or if the delay has harmed the plaintiff, or if the defendant has acted in bad faith, the court would be inclined to enter default judgment.[142] In one case, the court entered judgment even though the defendants had a meritorious defense, because the defendants had been willful in failing to communicate with their lawyers and had simply not taken the suit seriously until after default, and the resulting delay prejudiced the plaintiff by leaving unresolved an important issue of whether the plaintiff's patent on a product was invalid.[143]

---

[138]There are, however, clear cases in which no hearing is required. *See, e.g.,* United States v. Cabrera-Diaz, 106 F. Supp. 2d 234 (D.P.R. 2000).

[139]*See* Ganther v. Ingle, 75 F.3d 207, 209 (5th Cir. 1996).

[140]*See* Jackson v. Beech, 636 F.2d 831, 836 (D.C. Cir. 1980). At this point, according to some courts, it is not necessary that the defendant show that the defense is likely to win. Rather, merely alleging a colorable defense is sufficient. *Id.* at 837.

[141]*See, e.g.,* Pinaud v. County of Suffolk, 52 F.3d 1139 (2d Cir. 1995).

[142]*See, e.g.,* Bambu Sales v. Ozak Trading, 58 F.3d 849 (2d Cir. 1995).

[143]Honda Power Equip. Mfg., Inc. v. Woodhouse, 219 F.R.D. 2, 9-13 (D.D.C. 2003). Mere delay in obtaining relief ordinarily does not constitute the kind of "prejudice" relevant under Rule 55(b). *Id.* at 12-13. In *Honda Power,* however, the delay caused harm to the plaintiff because it left hanging over its head the allegation that a patent it held might be invalid.

Does the defendant get notice of the hearing on the application for a default judgment under Rule 55(b)(2)? The Rule requires written notice to the defendant, served at least seven days before the hearing on the application, but *only* if the defendant has "appeared personally or by a representative" in the case.[144] The most obvious examples of an appearance are the defendant's making a motion or answering in the case. But courts are fairly liberal here in defining what constitutes an appearance. There is even support for finding that a defendant can make an appearance without submitting anything to the court. In one case, the defendant's lawyer did not file anything with the court but wrote a letter to plaintiff's counsel noting the defendant's lack of money and expressing a desire to settle the case and to avoid default.[145]

If the court decides to enter default judgment, how does it determine the relief to be granted to the plaintiff? As we saw above, when the clerk enters the default judgment under Rule 55(b)(1), the judgment is for the sum claimed in the plaintiff's affidavit. Under Rule 55(b)(2), if the plaintiff has sued for a sum certain and the defendant does not contest that sum, the court may enter judgment for that amount without the need for further inquiry. But when the sum is not readily calculable, or if the defendant contests the amount, the court will hold a hearing to determine the appropriate remedy. Though a defaulting defendant has basically conceded her liability, a default generally does not concede the dollar amount of damage.[146] The court essentially holds a trial on the question of damages, at which there may be a right to trial by jury (discussed at §9.2.2).

In this regard, however, Rule 54(c) provides that the judgment can never exceed the dollar amount of damages the plaintiff demanded in the complaint, nor can it include a type of relief that she did not seek in the complaint.[147] These limitations reflect uneasiness about default judgments. The defendant should not be subjected to greater loss than that for which she was given notice.

---

[144]Whether the defendant appeared in the case was also important for another reason. If she appeared, the clerk cannot enter default judgment under Rule 55(b)(1). (Just as if the claim were not for a sum certain or if the case were against an infant or incompetent, the clerk could not enter judgment.)

[145]*See* Key Bank of Maine v. Tablecloth Textile Co., 74 F.3d 349 (1st Cir. 1996).

[146]*See, e.g.*, Gowen, Inc. v. F/V Quality One, 244 F.3d 64 (1st Cir.), *cert. denied*, 534 U.S. 886 (2001) (defendant who did not oppose entry of default judgment entitled to contest damages).

[147]Neither of these limitations applies in nondefault cases. As we see in §9.2.4 (and mentioned in §7.3.2), in nondefault cases, in which the defendant's liability is adjudicated, the plaintiff can recover any and all relief to which the evidence shows she is entitled.

○ ***Example #29.*** P sues D for damages of $100,000 in federal court, properly invoking subject matter jurisdiction and stating a claim. Within 21 days after being served with process, D moves to dismiss for lack of personal jurisdiction. The court denies the motion and orders D to respond to the complaint within 14 days. D fails to do so. P has the clerk enter the default under Rule 55(a) but cannot have the clerk enter the default judgment under Rule 55(b)(1). Why not? Because here, D made an appearance in the case, so the requirement of Rule 55(b)(1) that D have defaulted for failure to appear cannot be met.

That means that P must apply to the court for entry of default judgment. D will get notice of the hearing because she appeared in the case. If, after the hearing, the court enters default judgment, it will do so in an amount shown appropriate at the hearing *except* that it cannot exceed $100,000, because that is the amount claimed in the complaint. P cannot be given a different type of relief than that which she demanded in her complaint. Thus, even if the facts adduced at the hearing demonstrated that she was entitled to an injunction against D, she cannot get the injunction. Judgment by default is limited to the type of relief sought in the complaint. P will, however, recover from D the costs P incurred in the case.[148]

§7.5.4 Motions to "Set Aside" (Rule 55(c) and Rule 60(b))

A defendant who has suffered a default or a default judgment may move to set it aside. It is important, however, to distinguish the two situations. Rule 55(c) provides that the defaulting party may move to set aside a default "for good cause." Regarding a default *judgment*, however, the rule refers to Rule 60(b) as the appropriate vehicle for relief. Rule 60(b) applies to a motion to set aside any judgment, not just default judgments, and we discuss it in §9.7. For present purposes, it is enough to note that courts are usually more willing to set aside a default than a default judgment. This general rule makes sense. A default is merely an interlocutory (nonfinal) ruling in the course of the case. A judgment, in contrast, is the official judicial order that the plaintiff is entitled to recover from the defendant. Thus, "[w]hile a

---

[148]This is consistent with the general rule that the winner in litigation recovers her costs from the loser. Costs, remember, do not include attorney's fees. See §§1.1, 9.3. City of San Antonio, Texas v. Hotels.com, L.P., 141 S. Ct. 1628, 1631 (2021) ("each party, win or lose, generally bears many of its own litigation expenses, including attorneys' fees"); Patrick Henry Estates Homeowners Ass'n, Inc. v. Miller, 758 F.Supp.2d 331, 341 (N.D.W. Va. 2010) ("Attorneys' fees, on the other hand, are generally not taxable as costs").

default judgment may be vacated only by satisfying the stricter standards applied to final, appealable orders under [Rule] 60(b), an entry of default may be set aside for 'good cause shown.'"[149]

A defendant is not entitled to have the default or default judgment set aside merely for the asking. The matter is entrusted to the district court's discretion. In ruling on a motion to set aside, the court must be mindful of two conflicting policies. One, of course, is that the plaintiff's quest for justice should not be delayed unduly by the defendant's failure to play by the rules. The other is that our system of justice prefers to resolve disputes on their merits, and not on technicalities.

Motion to Set Aside a Default. To accommodate these policies, Rule 55(c) requires that the defendant moving to set aside the default show "good cause" for her failure to defend in a timely fashion. Good cause means a reasonable excuse. For example, if default resulted from a misunderstanding between the lawyers for the respective parties,[150] or from an error by the defendant's lawyer (as opposed to the defendant herself),[151] or an inability to communicate with counsel,[152] or illness,[153] or from some honest oversight by the defendant, a court might find that the defendant has shown good cause.

Although Rule 55(c) does not mention timing, courts insist that the motion to set aside the default be made within a "reasonable time." As a practical matter, the longer the defendant waits to bring her motion to set aside the default, the tougher it will be to convince the court that she has "good cause." Each case is decided on its own facts, so the wise defendant, obviously, will make the motion as soon as possible. She will be aided if the court is convinced that she is acting in good faith. The district court has authority to require the defendant to post a bond or other security as a condition of setting aside the default.

But there is an important second requirement. Though Rule 55(c) does not mention it, the court may well insist that the defendant show that she has a viable defense.[154] It makes no sense to set aside

---

[149]Berthelsen v. Kane, 907 F.2d 617, 620 (6th Cir. 1990). When this case was decided, Rule 55(c) spoke of "good cause shown." Now, as restyled in 2007, it speaks of "good cause."

[150]*See, e.g.*, Shepard Claims Serv., Inc. v. William Darrah & Assocs., 796 F.2d 190 (6th Cir. 1986) (misinterpretation of extension of time granted by plaintiff's lawyer).

[151]*See, e.g.*, Augusta Fiberglass Coatings, Inc. v. Fodor Contracting Corp., 843 F.2d 808 (4th Cir. 1988).

[152]*See, e.g.*, Biton v. Palestinian Interim Self Govt. Auth., 233 F. Supp. 2d 31, 33 (D.D.C. 2002) (defendants involved in Palestinian-Israeli conflict unable to communicate with lawyers in the United States).

[153]*See, e.g.*, Leshore v. County of Worcester, 945 F.2d 471 (1st Cir. 1991).

[154]*Berthelsen,* 907 F.2d at 620-621.

a default, and thus to put the case back in the litigation stream, if the defendant has no colorable defense on the merits.[155] Because the issue is addressed to the discretion of the court, there is no uniform approach to how strong a showing the defendant must make. Most courts seem to insist at least that the defendant allege specific facts, as opposed to conclusory allegations, that constitute a defense on the merits. Some courts seem more demanding and insist that the defendant demonstrate not merely the existence of a meritorious defense, but a "fair probability of success on the merits."[156]

It is not easy to reconcile the case law regarding setting aside a default. In some opinions, courts seem unwilling to set aside a default if the defendant was culpable in some way in her failure to respond in a timely fashion, regardless of the presence of a viable defense.[157] In other cases, courts have set aside a default despite the defendant's culpability when there was no showing of prejudice to the plaintiff and when the defendant had a viable defense.[158]

Motion to Set Aside Default Judgment. As we discuss in detail in §9.7, any judgment, including a default judgment, is subject to being vacated by the court that entered it under Rule 60(b). That Rule states several possible grounds for setting aside a judgment, including, in Rule 60(b)(4), that the judgment is void. For example, if the court entering the default judgment lacked personal jurisdiction or subject matter jurisdiction, the judgment can be attacked on that ground.

A more likely possibility in the default judgment situation is Rule 60(b)(1), in which the motion to set aside is based upon "mistake, inadvertence, surprise, or excusable neglect." The defendant moving under this ground must convince the court that she was guilty of a mistake or of excusable neglect that should be forgiven by setting aside the judgment. There is a split of authority as to whether "mistake" under this part of the Rule refers to legal errors committed by the court. Some courts permit relief from judicial mistakes under Rule 60(b)(1), at least under some circumstances,[159] while others do

---

[155]The defense must be on the merits of the case. The mere recitation that European defendants lacked resources to obtain counsel in the United States "[did] not address the merits of [the plaintiff's] claims in a substantive way." Honda Power Equip. Mfg., Inc. v. Woodhouse, 219 F.R.D. 2, 10 (D.D.C. 2003).

[156]*See, e.g,* FSLIC v. Kroenke, 858 F.2d 1067, 1071 (5th Cir. 1988). *See also* Sik Gaek, Inc. v. Yogi's II, Inc., 682 Fed.Appx. 52, 55 (2d. Cir. 2017) ("defendant need not establish his defense conclusively, but he must present evidence of facts that, if proven at trial, would constitute a complete defense").

[157]*See, e.g.,* Alan Neuman Prods., Inc. v. Albright, 862 F.2d 1388, 1391-1392 (9th Cir. 1988).

[158]*See, e.g., Berthelsen,* 907 F.2d at 621.

[159]*See, e.g.,* U.S. v. Fernandez, 797 F.3d 315, 319 (5th Cir. 2015) ("Rule 60(b)(1) allows a court to provide relief in the case of 'mistake, inadvertence, surprise, or excusable

not.[160] Even if the defendant succeeds in establishing good cause under Rule 60(b)(1), however, she must show the existence of a viable defense.[161] The district court has great discretion in determining whether the defendant has made the required showings, and how to weigh factors such as prejudice to the plaintiff and good faith of the defendant. In addition, a court granting a motion to set aside a default judgment may require the defendant to post a bond or other security.

Many opinions make the general assertion that default judgments are not favored because our system of justice prefers to resolve disputes on the merits rather than technicalities.[162] Interestingly, however, in the wake of large caseloads in the federal courts, there may be a trend toward taking a harder line toward defendants. The Seventh Circuit has "moved away from the traditional position" of leniency and is "increasingly reluctant to reverse refusals to set aside [default judgments]." As the court elaborated: "The entry of a default judgment is becoming—without interference from this court—a common sanction for late filings by defendants . . . . At a time of unprecedented caseloads, federal judges are unwilling to allow the processes of the federal courts to be used for purposes of delaying the payment of debts."[163]

§7.6　Amended and Supplemental Pleadings

Modern pleading provisions, as exemplified by the Federal Rules, are liberal in allowing parties to amend their pleadings. This liberality makes sense. Often, as the case goes on, parties will learn things that

---

neglect.' That error can be on the part of the court as well as a party"); United Airlines, Inc. v. Brien, 588 F.3d 158, 175 (2d Cir. 2009) ("Rule 60(b)(1) is 'available for a district court to correct legal errors by the court.'"); Phelps v. McCoy, 189 Fed.Appx. 528, 530 (7th Cir. 2006) ("Rule 60(b)(1) encompasses mistakes by judicial officers as well as others"); Phonometrics, Inc. v. Hospitality Franchise System, Inc., 126 Fed.Appx. 793, 794 (9th Cir. 2005) ("The 'mistakes' of judges may be remedied under this provision, which also encompasses mistakes in the application of the law."). Some courts conclude that a motion made on the basis of judicial error must be made before the time for appeal runs. *See, e.g.,* Daniel v. DTE Energy Co., 592 Fed.Appx. 489, 490 (6th Cir. 2015) ("While Rule 60(b)(1) encompasses judicial mistakes of law, such a motion must be made 'within the normal time for taking an appeal'"); International Controls Corp. v. Vesco, 556 F.2d 665, 669 (2d Cir. 1977) (same).

[160]*See, e.g.,* Parke-Chaptley Constr. Co. v. Cherrington, 865 F.2d 907, 914-915 n.7 (7th Cir. 1989); Page v. Schweiker, 786 F.2d 150, 154-155 (3d Cir. 1986). *See also* Lowry v. McDonnell Douglas Corp., 211 F.3d 457, 460-461 (8th Cir. 2000) ("It remains the law in this Circuit that 'relief under Rule 60(b)(1) for judicial error other than for judicial inadvertence' is not available").

[161]*See* 12 Moore's Federal Practice, §60.24.

[162]*See, e.g.,* Adriana Int'l Corp. v. Thoronen, 913 F.2d 1406, 1412-1413 (9th Cir. 1990).

[163]In re State Exch. Fin. Co., 896 F.2d 1104, 1106 (7th Cir. 1990).

make it necessary or desirable to change what they asserted earlier. Federal Rule 15 governs amendments in federal practice and is broad-ranging. It is helpful to see that each subpart addresses a different factual scenario. It is helpful to divide the discussion or Rule 15 into four subparts, one for each of its subsections, Rule 15(a) through Rule 15(d).

§7.6.1 Amendments of Right and Leave to Amend (Rule 15(a))

Rule 15(a) addresses two kinds of amendments: "as a matter of course" (in Rule 15(a)(1)) and what are usually called "permissive" amendments (in Rule 15(a)(2)). When a party has a right to amend, she need not get court approval. She files and serves the amended pleading. If the other party feels that there was no right to amend, she may file a motion to strike the pleading under Rule 12(f). Permissive amendment applies in all cases in which there is no right to amend. Under permissive amendment, the party may amend only if the opposing party consents in writing or if the court grants "leave" to amend. Granting "leave" to amend is just another way of saying the court allows the party to amend.

Rule 15(a)(1)(A) defines when the defendant has a right to amend; Rule 15(a)(1)(B) defines when the plaintiff has a right to amend. Each has a right to amend only once. A second amendment will be possible only with leave of court.

The plaintiff has a right to amend *once* within 21 days "after service of a responsive pleading" or 21 days "after service of a motion under Rule 12(b), (e), or (f), whichever is earlier."

> ○ ***Example #30.*** *P* files her complaint and has process served on June 15. *D* files and serves her answer (or a motion under Rule 12(b), (e), or (f)) on July 1. *P* now has 21 days from the service of *D*'s answer (or motion under Rule 12(b), (e), or (f)) in which to amend her complaint as of right. She might do so, for example, because *D*'s response pointed out in a Rule 12(b)(6) motion that P had pleaded her claim insufficiently.

Usually, the amended pleading will set forth an additional claim against the same defendant who was named in the original complaint. Sometimes, though, the plaintiff may wish to amend to add new parties to (or drop extant parties from) the case. Some courts conclude that amendment of right does not cover such a situation, and that the plaintiff must make a motion (and thus get court permission) to add or drop parties under Rule 21.[164] Most courts seem to conclude,

---

[164]*See, e.g.*, Moore v. Indiana, 999 F.2d 1125 (7th Cir. 1993).

however, that the right to amend—being able to amend "as a matter of course"—includes the right to add or drop parties without court permission.[165]

Under Rule 15(a)(1)(B), the defendant[166] has a right to amend her answer *once* "within 21 days after serving" her answer. This right to amend the answer can save waivable defenses that the defendant failed to put in her original answer.

> ○ ***Example #31.*** P files her complaint and has process served on *D* the same day. Within the appropriate time, *D* files and serves her answer. Eighteen days after serving her answer, *D* realizes that she failed to assert lack of personal jurisdiction as an affirmative defense in the answer. As we saw in Chapter 6, personal jurisdiction is a waivable defense; failure to assert it in her first Rule 12 response will result in waiver. If she acts within three days (before the end of 21 days from when she served her answer), she has a right to amend and thus can save the personal jurisdiction defense.[167]

Note that the right to amend applies to *pleadings*. Remember that a motion is not a pleading. Thus, if the defendant in Example #31 had first responded with a motion to dismiss (instead of an answer), in which she failed to assert the personal jurisdiction defense, the right to amend would not help her.

What happens if the time in which there is a right to amend (for either party) has expired? Then Rule 15(a)(2) applies. It provides that the party seeking permission to amend must get court permission or

---

[165]*See, e.g.*, United States ex rel. Precision Co. v. Koch Indus., Inc., 31 F.3d 1015 (10th Cir. 1994).

[166]Actually, any defending party. For instance, a defendant may assert a counterclaim against the plaintiff; the plaintiff would be a defending party on that claim and technically would be known as "plaintiff and counter-defendant." She would have to respond to the counterclaim just as the defendant has to respond to the complaint. For present purposes, we simply consider the defendant to be the defending party.

[167]Rule 6(d) provides that "3 days are added" after an act is due when a document is served by mail. See Chapter 3, note 100 and accompanying text. Through 2005, that Rule expressly applied only to parties *responding* to the document that was served by mail. In 2007, the Rule was amended in a way that inadvertently changed that feature. Read literally, the Rule allowed any party an extra three days—even the party *that served* the document. James Joseph Duane, *The Federal Rule of Civil Procedure That Was Changed by Accident: A Lesson in the Perils of Stylistic Revision*, 62 S.C. L. Rev. 41 (2010). Suppose *D* serves her answer on June 1. Under Rule 15(a)(1)(A), she has a right to amend within 21 days thereafter, or no later than June 22. Suppose, though, that she served her answer by mail. Rule 6(d), on its face, permitted her an extra three days (through June 25) in which to amend as of right. In response to Professor Duane's argument, the Advisory Committee amended Rule 6(d) to comport with the historic limitation. Thus, it provides an extra three days only for the party on whom the document is served by mail.

written consent of the adverse party to amend. Amendment under Rule 15(a)(2) does not extinguish one's right to amend under Rule 15(a)(1) (provided, of course, that the time for amendment of right under Rule 15(a)(1) has not expired).[168]

To obtain court permission under Rule 15(a)(2), the party makes a "motion for leave to amend." The liberality of the Federal Rules is suggested by the phrase that "[t]he court should freely give leave when justice so requires." This standard both reposes great discretion in the district judge and indicates a preference for permitting amendment. Consistent with that preference, the Supreme Court made it clear in the leading case of *Foman v. Davis*[169] that the district court must state its reasons for *denying* a motion for leave to amend.

Each case is decided on its own facts, and courts tend to balance the same factors in reaching their decisions. In *Foman v. Davis*, the Court listed the relevant factors and emphasized the need to balance harm to the moving party if she is not permitted to amend against prejudice caused to the other party if leave to amend is granted. It instructed courts to consider other factors as well: whether the moving party has delayed unduly in seeking leave to amend, bad faith or dilatory purpose of the moving party, whether the moving party has failed to fix deficiencies in previous amendments, and whether amendment would be futile. Obviously, if amendment would be futile—for example, if a claim to be added by amendment is not legally cognizable[170]—the court should deny leave to amend. Just as obviously, a court will likely deny leave to amend if the amendment sought would prejudice the other party.[171]

Whenever the plaintiff amends (either of right or by permissive amendment), Rule 15(a)(3) says that the defending party must respond (unless the court orders otherwise) "within the time remaining to respond to the original pleading or within 14 days after service of the amended pleading, whichever is later." The time remaining for response to the original pleading refers to the time set forth in Rule 12 for defensive responses. Ordinarily, as we saw in §7.3.4, this period is 21 days from the date of service. Thus, unless the court orders otherwise, the

---

[168]Ramirez v. City of San Bernardino, 806 F.3d 1002, 1006-1007 (9th Cir. 2015) (amendment by stipulation per Rule 15(a)(2) followed by timely amendment of right).

[169]371 U.S. 178, 182 (1962).

[170]*See, e.g.*, Sinay v. Lamson & Sessions Co., 948 F.2d 1037 (9th Cir. 1991).

[171]*See, e.g.*, McKnight v. Kimberly Clark Corp., 149 F.3d 1125, 1130 (10th Cir. 1998) (if amendment were granted, defense witnesses would have to be deposed again, causing prejudice to the defendant; denial is especially appropriate because of delay by plaintiff in seeking amendment despite being aware of facts underlying the newly asserted claim).

defendant will never have fewer than 14 days after service of the amended complaint in which to respond.

§7.6.2   Amendments During and After Trial: "Variance" (Rule 15(b))

Rule 15(b) becomes relevant, if ever, *only at trial*. More specifically, it comes up only when a party seeks to introduce evidence at trial of a claim or defense *that she did not plead*. Though the Rule does not use the word, you should know that this is a *variance*, which means that somebody is trying to put on evidence of something she did not plead. It may be the plaintiff, seeking to put on evidence of a claim she did not include in her complaint. Or it may be the defendant, seeking to put on evidence of an affirmative defense she did not include in her answer.[172]

At common law and under some codes, variance could be fatal if the other party objected to it. An example is *Wabash Western Railway v. Friedman*,[173] in which the plaintiff sued for personal injuries sustained when the train on which he was a passenger derailed. He had purchased a ticket to travel from Moberly to Ottumwa, and he boarded at Moberly. The train derailed between two intermediate stops on the route, between Kirksville and Glenwood Junction, and there is no question the plaintiff was on the train when it derailed and that he was hurt badly. The jury returned a verdict of $30,000 and the trial court entered judgment for the plaintiff in that amount. On appeal, though, the defendant pointed out that the plaintiff had alleged that he had boarded the train at Kirksville to travel to Glenwood Junction. The Illinois Supreme Court reversed because what the plaintiff alleged (that he boarded at Kirksville, bound for Glenwood Junction) was at variance from what he proved (that he boarded at Moberly, bound for Ottumwa). The result is preposterous. The issue of where the plaintiff boarded the train does not change the fact that he was onboard when it derailed and that he was badly injured. The railroad certainly understood that it was being sued over a derailment between Kirksville and Glenwood Junction. Yet the plaintiff lost his recovery because of the variance on the inconsequential matter of where he boarded the train.

---

[172]Throughout this subsection, we speak of amendments to the complaint or the answer. In fact, it is likely that the operative document to be amended is the pretrial conference order. In §8.5, we see that the pretrial conference order takes the place of the pleadings; it supersedes the pleadings. Because problems of variance, by definition, come up at trial, it is likely that the amendment to conform to the evidence will amend that document.

[173]30 N.E. 353 (Ill. 1892).

Rule 15(b) represents the modern way of treating variance. Even in code states, today it is doubtful that any court would come to the conclusion reached in *Wabash Western*. Today, variance is a basis for objection by the other party *at trial*. In other words, when a party seeks to introduce evidence at trial that goes beyond the scope of her pleadings, the other party may object and ask the court to exclude the evidence, so it will not be part of the trial record the fact-finder considers in reaching a conclusion. But variance should not be a basis for upsetting a trial judgment.

Rule 15(b) addresses two possible variance scenarios: one in Rule 15(b)(1) and the other in Rule 15(b)(2). The scenarios depend upon what the other party does in the face of a variance. The other party may do one of two things: (1) she might agree to allow the variance, or (2) she might object to the variance. In situation (1), the court applies Rule 15(b)(2), and we are concerned with conforming the pleadings to the evidence. In situation (2), the court applies Rule 15(b)(1), and we are concerned with the possibility of amending the pleadings at trial.

First, assume Party A (it does not matter whether she is the plaintiff or the defendant) introduces evidence at trial that goes beyond the scope of her pleadings. As we know, the opposing party (Party B) may object to that evidence on the ground of variance with the pleadings and ask the court to deny its introduction at trial. But Party B might acquiesce and allow the introduction of the evidence either by failing to object to it or by expressly consenting to it. When Party B acquiesces in allowing the evidence, the first sentence of Rule 15(b)(2) provides that the issues addressed in that evidence "must be treated in all respects as if raised in the pleadings." Thus, the variance is ignored, the evidence is admitted at trial, and we treat the pleadings as though they included the issues raised by the evidence.

In addition, the second sentence of Rule 15(b)(2) provides that "[a] party may move—at any time, even after judgment—to amend the pleadings to conform them to the evidence and to raise an unpleaded issue." Failure to do so, the next sentence provides, does not affect the outcome of the trial. In other words, when Party A introduced evidence beyond the scope of the pleadings and Party B either did not object or expressly consented to its admission at trial, the evidence is received into evidence and Party A can move to amend the pleadings to conform to that evidence—to mirror what was actually litigated at trial. Amendment to conform to the evidence is a housekeeping measure. It ensures that the pleadings will mirror what actually was tried and decided.[174]

---

[174]This fact may be helpful to clarify the record on appeal or to determine the pre-clusive effect (*e.g.*, issue preclusion) of the judgment in this case.

- ○ ***Example #32.*** P sues D for breach of contract and alleges only a claim for damages. At trial, however, P introduces evidence not only of damages, but of evidence that would support the grant of equitable relief, such as rescission of the contract. D does not object to introduction of the evidence. That means the evidence is admitted at trial and the court will treat P's complaint as though it asserted the claim for equitable relief. Assume P wins, and the court awards damages as well as rescission. P may make a motion (even after judgment) to amend her complaint to conform to the evidence—to show the equitable claim. Regardless of whether she does so, however, the judgment on the equitable claim will stand.[175]
- ○ ***Example #33.*** P sues D for battery. In her answer, D fails to raise the affirmative defense of self-defense. At trial, however, D introduces evidence that she hit P in self-defense. P does not object to the evidence. That means the evidence is admitted at trial and the court will treat D's answer as though it had raised that affirmative defense. D may move to amend her answer to reflect the affirmative defense.

The second possibility is that a party facing variance will object to it. Here, when Party A introduces evidence beyond the scope of her pleading, Party B objects and asserts that the evidence should be excluded at trial. If the court agrees that one party's proffered evidence goes beyond the scope of the pleadings, it will uphold the other party's objection and bar the introduction of the evidence.

At that point, however, Rule 15(b)(1) permits the party proffering the evidence to move to amend! As the Rule says, when Party B objects to the introduction of evidence by Party A on the ground of variance, "the court may permit the pleadings to be amended." Thus, even though the variance points out a deficiency in Party A's pleading at a very late stage (we are at trial, remember), Party A may still be able to amend her pleading to cover the issues raised by the evidence she is proffering at trial. The standard for being allowed to amend is found in the second sentence of Rule 15(b)(1): "The court should freely permit an amendment when doing so will aid in presenting the merits and the objecting party fails to satisfy the court that the evidence would prejudice that party's action or defense on the merits." This provision demonstrates how liberal the Federal Rules can be about amendment. Even though Party A's pleading is deficient and even though the issue does not come to light until the case is in trial, the burden is *on the other party* to show prejudice. The final sentence in Rule 15(b)(1) furthers the liberal pleading ethos by reminding the court that it can enter a continuance of

---

[175]*See, e.g.,* D. Federico Co. v. New Bedford Redev. Auth., 723 F.2d 122 (1st Cir. 1983).

the trial to allow Party *B* to do what she has to do to respond to the evidence.

Though there is no denying the liberality of Rule 15(b)(1), such amendment at trial is rare. Again, the case is in trial; discovery has been completed. The parties have spent months (probably even years) to get to this point. Especially if there is a jury, a court will be reluctant to stay the trial to allow Party *B* to engage in discovery or do what she must to respond to this new evidence. After all, it is Party *A*'s fault that she did not include the allegation relating to this evidence. In most such instances, then, we would expect the court to deny admission of the evidence and to deny Party *A*'s motion to amend. In rare cases, though, if the proffered evidence truly advances the decision on the merits and there is little if any prejudice, an amendment would be appropriate.

○ ***Example #34.*** *P* sues *D*, alleging only a claim for fraud. At trial, *P* seeks to introduce evidence that would support *D*'s liability on the basis of vicarious liability. Though *P* did not plead vicarious liability, it is essentially just another theory on which *P* might win recovery for the same harm caused by the fraud. Because it is directly related to the fraud claim, and because the defendant had a full opportunity to present evidence to avoid liability, the court might permit amendment at trial.

§7.6.3 Amendments and the Statute of Limitations: "Relation Back" (Rule 15(c))

Rule 15(c) deals with amendment of pleadings after the statute of limitations has run. The problem can come up in two ways. First, the plaintiff may seek leave to amend her complaint to add a claim (or the defendant to raise a defense) after the statute has run. This scenario is addressed in Rule 15(c)(1)(B). Second, the plaintiff may seek leave to amend to join a new defendant after the statute has run. This scenario is addressed in Rule 15(c)(1)(C). In each case, there is an obvious clash of important policies. On the one hand, we favor resolution of disputes on the merits, and thus favor a liberal amendment policy. On the other hand, the statute of limitations protects the defendant from the assertion of stale claims; she should be protected by that policy from an unfair lengthening of the time for which she may remain subject to suit.

The Federal Rules balance these two policies through the doctrine of "relation back." Rule 15(c) provides that an amended pleading — asserted after the statute of limitations has run — "relates back" to a pleading that was filed before the statute of limitations ran. This simply means that the amended pleading is treated as though it was filed when an earlier, timely pleading was filed. Relation back thus avoids the bar of the statute of limitations.[176]

We start with some background on statutes of limitations. For every claim, whether created by statute or by common law, there is a period of limitations, which sets the outer temporal boundary in which the claimant must commence her action. These periods vary from state to state and from claim to claim. Generally, the statute for tort cases is shorter than that for contract cases. A typical statute would allow the plaintiff two years in which to assert a tort claim. That means that the plaintiff would have two years from "accrual" of her claim in which to "commence" her suit. When the claim "accrues,"[177] the statute starts to "run."[178] That means the clock starts ticking on the two years (or whatever other period is prescribed by the statute). If the plaintiff fails to commence suit before the clock expires, her claim will be barred by the statute of limitations.

With this background, we can more readily appreciate the importance of the doctrine of relation back under Rule 15(c).

> o ***Example #35.*** P files her complaint against D on May 10, and has process served on D the same day. The relevant statute of limitations expires on July 30. Thus, P's complaint was timely—she commenced the case before the statute ran. P seeks leave to amend her complaint (maybe to add a claim or to add a defendant) on September 24. The problem is that September 24 would be too late if she were filing her complaint now (because the statute of limitations ran on July 30). But if the amendment satisfies the requirements of Rule 15(c), her September amended complaint, even though filed after the statute ran, will relate back to the original complaint. That means it will be treated as though the amended complaint had been filed when the original was filed. This was May 10, so P avoids the bar of the statute of limitations.

In this fact pattern, the defendant will not be pleased with the application of relation back. To her, it extends the time for which she can be sued and vitiates the protection of the statute of limitations. Because of the seriousness of the issue, Rule 15(c) permits relation

---

[176]Relation back is an example of treating something *nunc pro tunc*. That Latin phrase creeps into lawyerly discussions from time to time and you should be familiar with it. It means "now as then." So with relation back, an amended pleading *now* is treated as though it had been filed when the original pleading was filed—*then*.

[177]This is another term on which jurisdictions may adopt different definitions. The majority rule is that the claim accrues when the defendant breached a duty to the plaintiff.

[178]This should not be confused with "tolling" of the statute, which refers to events that stop the ticking of the statute of limitations clock. For instance, if the plaintiff is a minor, the statute of limitations is tolled until she reaches the age of majority. That means the statute does not start to run until she turns age 18 (or whatever the relevant age of majority is). Tolling is relevant to an issue we discuss in §10.5.

back in three limited circumstances. One, under Rule 15(c)(1)(A), is quite obvious: Relation back applies when "the law that provides the applicable statute of limitations allows relation back." Thus, if the statute providing the period of limitations also expressly allows relation back of amendments, there will be relation back.

Second, under Rule 15(c)(1)(B), deals with amendment *to add a claim* after the statute has expired. It makes no sense for the court to allow such an amendment if the claim to be added is barred by the statute of limitations. The standard under Rule 15(c)(1)(B) is clear: Relation back is permitted if the amended pleading "arose out of the conduct, transaction, or occurrence set out — or attempted to be set out — in the original pleading." The rationale is that if the amended pleading arises from the same real-world events as the original pleading, the defendant was put on notice of her potential liability before the statute expired. This notice — of potential culpability from some conduct, transaction, or occurrence — satisfies the policy of the statute of limitations. Thus, courts routinely permit amendment with relation back when the claim being added simply espouses a different theory of liability arising from the same real-world events alleged in the original complaint. Likewise, if the amendment merely fixed a defective jurisdictional allegation from the original complaint, but concerns the same real-world events as the original, relation back is appropriate. Only if the amendment raises new matter for which the defendant was not fairly put on notice by the original complaint would relation back not be appropriate. For example, in one case, when the amended complaint alleged an injury on a date earlier than that alleged in the original complaint, relation back was inappropriate.[179]

Third, Rule 15(c)(1)(C) addresses a more difficult situation: Amendment after the statute of limitations has expired *to add a new defendant*. Here, we are understandably concerned that the defendant being added is not brought into the case until after the statutory period. Rule 15(c)(1)(C) permits relation back in this context only if three requirements are satisfied: (1) the claim arises from the same conduct, transaction, or occurrence as that stated in the original complaint;[180] (2) within 90 days after *filing* of the original complaint, the new defendant has received such notice of the suit that she will not be prejudiced in defending (Rule 15(c)(1)(C)(i)); and (3) within the same period, the new defendant "knew or should have known that the action would have been brought against it, but for a mistake concerning the proper party's identity" (Rule 15(c)(1)(C)(ii)).

---

[179]O'Loughlin v. National R.R. Passenger Corp., 928 F.2d 24 (1st Cir. 1991).

[180]Of course, we just saw this requirement in Rule 15(c)(1)(B); it is incorporated by reference in Rule 15(c)(1)(C).

There is one generic type of case that satisfies these requirements—one in which the plaintiff sued the "wrong" defendant originally, but the "right" defendant knew about the case and knew that, but for a mistake, she would have been named originally.

> ○ ***Example #36.*** *P* is injured in a slip and fall at Acme Supermarket. On March 1, she filed her original complaint, in which she names "Acme Supermarket" as the defendant. In fact, there is no such legal entity as "Acme Supermarket." The store was operated by Joe, Inc. Joe is the president of Joe, Inc. On March 10, the statute of limitations on *P*'s claim expired. On March 20, *P* had process served on Joe, as agent for the Acme Supermarket. On April 15, *P* seeks leave to amend her complaint to name Joe, Inc., as the defendant.

The amendment would bring Joe, Inc., into the suit after the statute of limitations had run. Nonetheless, Rule 15(c)(1)(C) would permit the amended complaint to relate back to the date of the original. Thus, the case would be treated as though it had been filed against Joe, Inc., on March 1, which is timely. Why does relation back apply here?

First, the amended complaint concerns the same slip and fall as the original complaint. Second, Joe, Inc., was on notice of the suit on March 20 (when Joe was served with process), which is within 90 days of the filing of the original complaint on March 10. Third, Joe, Inc., is charged with notice on March 20 (when Joe was served with process) that "but for a mistake concerning the identity of the proper party," the action would have been brought against it. That is, when Joe received service of process on March 20, he saw that *P* named a defendant that did not exist and understood that *P* should have named Joe, Inc.

One point deserves especial attention in applying Rule 15(c)(1)(C). Note that the second and third requirements—that the proper defendant be on notice of the case and that she know that but for a mistake in identity she would have been sued—must be met "within the period provided by Rule 4(m) for serving the summons and complaint." Rule 4(m) provides that service should be made within 90 days after filing of the complaint. Thus, the only thing that absolutely must occur before the statute of limitations expires is the filing of the complaint. The new defendant need not be put on notice before the statute expired. As long as the new defendant is put on notice within 90 days after the filing of the complaint, the Rule is satisfied.[181]

---

[181]The Rule was amended to make this clear in 1991. That amendment was in reaction to the decision in *Schiavone v. Fortune*, 477 U.S. 21 (1986), in which the Supreme Court held under the earlier version of Rule 15(c) that the new defendant had to be on notice before the statute of limitations expired. The Rule was amended because this holding was considered too harsh.

§7.6.4 Supplemental Pleadings (Rule 15(d))

Supplemental pleadings differ from amended pleadings in a fundamental way: They concern the assertion of things that occurred *after* the pleading was filed. As Rule 15(d) says, a supplemental pleading "set[s] out any transaction, occurrence, or event that happened after the date of the pleading to be supplemented." Amendment, on the other hand, concerns setting forth matters that occurred *before* the pleading was filed, but that were not asserted until after pleading. Supplemental pleadings thus serve to update the parties and the court on the dispute by bringing to their attention facts that had not occurred when the pleading was filed. They may, among other things, add new claims or even new parties.

Though there is a right to *amend* pleadings in certain instances, as we saw in §7.6.1, there is no right to supplement pleadings. The matter must be raised on motion by the party seeking leave to supplement, and the district judge has great discretion in determining whether to grant the motion. Based upon the same policies that underlie the federal courts' liberal approach to amendment, most courts allow supplementation unless it will cause undue delay or prejudice, or if the party seeking leave to supplement is guilty of bad faith. Note, too, that Rule 15(d) permits supplemental pleadings even if the original pleading was defective — for example, if it failed to state a claim. When the plaintiff is permitted to supplement her complaint, it seems likely that the court will allow the defendant to respond.

○ ***Example #37.*** *P* has a contract with Manufacturing Corp. (MC), under which MC is to deliver widgets to *P* each month. MC fails to deliver the widgets for January 2018, and *P* sues MC in February 2018 concerning the failure. In September 2018, while the case is in the discovery phase, MC fails to deliver widgets for that month. If *P* wants to sue MC for the September 2018 failure to deliver, and to assert the claim in the pending case, it will seek leave to supplement its complaint. If the court feels that the pleading can be supplemented by adding this matter without causing undue delay and without prejudicing MC, it will grant the motion.[182]

---

[182]*Twin Disc, Inc. v. Big Bud Tractor, Inc.,* 772 F.2d 1329 (7th Cir. 1985), involved facts along these lines. In this case, however, the plaintiff did not seek leave to supplement its complaint until one week before trial. The court denied the motion to supplement because of the plaintiff's delay and because the defendant could not be expected to prepare for trial on the new facts. It refused to delay the trial to permit inclusion of the new facts. The Court of Appeals affirmed, concluding that the district judge did not abuse his discretion in denying the motion to supplement.

§7.7   Professional Responsibility: Rule 11 and Other Bases for Sanctions

Our profession, and each of us, should be dedicated to the highest ideals of professional responsibility. Our rules must balance zealous advocacy with the need to ensure veracity in pleading and other aspects of litigation practice. Several procedural provisions augment the rules of professional responsibility to attempt to strike that balance.

Federal Rule 11. The history of Rule 11 reflects cycles of concern. The original Rule, promulgated when the Federal Rules were adopted in 1938, simply required that a lawyer have "good grounds to support" her contentions in pleadings. In over 40 years, fewer than one dozen reported cases applied the Rule.

In 1983, the Supreme Court amended the Rule to toughen it dramatically. The amendments were fueled by the perception of a "litigation explosion," caused at least in part by frivolous litigation. The amended Rule 11 applied not only to pleadings but to all documents in the case and imposed a certification requirement. The lawyer's signature on a document constituted a certification of various things, aimed primarily at ensuring that the lawyer had made an investigation and in good faith could support the assertions made. Interestingly, the 1983 version of Rule 11 *required* the imposition of sanctions for violations. The invigorated Rule led to a stunning amount of litigation over sanctions for alleged violations of Rule 11. This, in turn, led to a stunning amount of academic commentary on the Rule, including criticism that the required sanctions chilled the assertion of viable claims and created a debilitating amount of satellite litigation.

Reacting to such criticism, the Supreme Court amended Rule 11 to its present basic form in 1993. The amendment clearly took some of the bite out of Rule 11 in an effort both to reduce the amount of litigation over sanctions and to ensure that the fear of sanctions not inhibit creative lawyering. Rule 11(a) imposes a signature requirement on the attorney of record for a party.[183] It also makes clear that Rule 11 applies to "[e]very pleading, written motion, and other paper." At the same time, Rule 11(d) makes it clear that the Rule does not apply to discovery documents. (As we see in §8.4, there is a similar certification for discovery documents, found in Rule 26(g).) Thus, pleadings, motions, briefs—all documents except discovery documents—are to

---

[183]If there is no attorney of record—that is, if the party is litigating *pro se* (representing herself)—the Rule imposes the signature requirement on the party herself. In most cases, of course, the parties are represented by counsel, which means that in most cases the parties never sign the documents. Their lawyers do.

be signed under Rule 11. The last sentence of Rule 11(a) makes clear that the court "must strike" any document that is unsigned, unless the omission is promptly corrected.

What does the signature represent? Under Rule 11(b), it is a *certification to the court* of several important things. Though it is natural to focus on the four specific numbered items listed in Rule 11(b), there is some important prefatory language. Specifically, the Rule says that by signing, the person "certifies that to the best of the person's knowledge, information, and belief, formed after an inquiry reasonable under the circumstances," the four specific items are true. Thus, the Rule presumes that the lawyer signing the document has made an "inquiry reasonable under the circumstances" and has satisfied herself that the listed things are true. What constitutes a reasonable inquiry depends on the facts of the case. It also depends on timing. For instance, a lawyer consulted the day before the statute of limitations will run simply cannot undertake the kind of detailed investigation that is possible if she is not laboring under such a time constraint. The main point is simple, though: The Rule imposes a duty of reasonable inquiry before signing a document to be filed with the court.

Rule 11(b) imposes a continuing certification. Specifically, the certification under Rule 11(b) is made not just when the lawyer signs the document, but every time she *presents* a document to the court. The first sentence indicates that "presenting" includes "signing, filing, submitting, or later advocating" something asserted in the document. Before 1993, the certification was simply as of the time of signing. The difference is stark.

- **_Example #38._** Lawyer drafts, signs, and files a complaint on behalf of Plaintiff. She satisfies Rule 11(b) in so doing, because she has made a reasonable inquiry and has a good faith belief that the thing stated in the complaint satisfies Rule 11(b). Six months later, she advocates to the court a position set forth in the complaint. At that point—even though it is six months after she signed and filed the complaint—Lawyer is "recertifying" that the certification under Rule 11(b) is still true. If she can no longer make that certification, she violates Rule 11 by presenting the issue to the court.

What are the items certified in Rule 11(b)? In the aggregate, they are aimed at ensuring that there are reasonable bases for the version of the facts and law asserted. First, under Rule 11(b)(1), the signer certifies that the document is not presented for an improper purpose, such as delay or harassment. Second, under Rule 11(b)(2), she certifies that the legal contentions are warranted by law or "by a nonfrivolous argument for extending, modifying, or reversing existing law or for establishing new law." This is intended to protect creative lawyering and the assertion of novel theories of the law; the only limitation is that they not be frivolous. The third and fourth items specified relate to allegations of fact, as opposed to allegations of law. Specifically, under Rule 11(b)(3), the signer certifies that the factual contentions "have evidentiary support or, if specifically identified, will likely have evidentiary support after a reasonable opportunity for further investigation or discovery." This is good language and protects the lawyer who believes that evidence will be found to support a factual assertion. Finally, Rule 11(b)(4) provides in like terms for the *denials* of factual allegations. Obviously, then, Rule 11(b)(3) is aimed at parties asserting a claim and Rule 11(b)(4) is aimed at parties defending against a claim.

Violations of Rule 11 may be raised in two ways. First, the court may raise them on its own. Under Rule 11(c)(3), the court will enter an order to show cause (an OSC) requiring a party, attorney, or law firm to show cause why specified behavior did not violate Rule 11(b). Second, a party may move for sanctions against another party or her attorney or law firm under Rule 11(c)(2). The motion must state specifically what conduct violated Rule 11(b) and must be brought separately from any other motions. It is important to appreciate, however, that Rule 11(c)(2) has a "safe harbor" of 21 days for the party allegedly violating Rule 11.

> ○ ***Example #39.*** Plaintiff believes that Defendant (or her lawyer or law firm) has violated Rule 11. Plaintiff's lawyer drafts a motion for sanctions under Rule 11(c)(2), specifying the alleged violations by Defendant (or her lawyer or law firm). Plaintiff's lawyer serves the motion on Defendant and files it in court.

Plaintiff is wrong. Rule 11(c)(2) expressly forbids a party from *filing* the motion at this point. Instead, she must *serve* the motion on the other party but then allow that party a "safe harbor" of 21 days in which to fix the problem. If she does fix the problem, no sanctions may be sought. If she does not fix the problem, then (after the 21 days) the motion may be filed in court. The purpose of this provision is "to provide litigants the opportunity of avoiding sanctions by withdrawing offending filings or contentions within the 21-day period and thereby reducing the number of sanctions motions brought before the courts."[184]

Regardless of how the matter gets to the court—on the court's initiative or by motion after the safe harbor period—what sanctions are available? First, sanctions are not required, but are to be imposed in

---

[184]Rector v. Approved Fin. Corp., 265 F.3d 248, 251 (4th Cir. 2001).

the discretion of the court. Second, the purpose of sanctions is *not* to punish wrongful behavior, but to deter such behavior in the future. As Rule 11(c)(4) states, "A sanction imposed under this rule must be limited to what suffices to deter repetition of the conduct or comparable conduct by others similarly situated."

Rule 11(c)(4) suggests that nonmonetary sanctions are appropriate. These can include reprimands or warnings or directives that the offender take some act, such as attend continuing legal education courses on professional responsibility. Occasionally a court will order the lawyer to circulate the judicial opinion concerning misconduct to her client and law partners. The Rule also permits an order that the offender "pay a penalty into court."

Also, if imposed on motion and "warranted for effective deterrence," the court may require the offender to pay all or part of the expenses—expressly including attorney's fees—incurred by the moving party as a direct result of the violation of Rule 11. Under Rule 11(c)(5)(A), a party represented by counsel cannot be held liable for a monetary sanction for violating Rule 11(b)(2). This makes sense, because that certification relates to the legal contentions; a party represented by a lawyer cannot be presumed to know the law sufficiently to satisfy that certification item.

Other Provisions. Rule 11 is not the only provision aimed at litigation behavior. Indeed, there are many others, and a full discussion is beyond our scope. One example is Rule 3.1 of the Model Rules of Professional Conduct, which provides that "[a] lawyer shall not bring or defend a proceeding, or assert or controvert an issue therein, unless there is a basis for doing so that is not frivolous." In addition, 28 U.S.C. §1927, which applies only in federal courts, provides that an attorney who "multiplies the proceeding in any case unreasonably and vexatiously may be required . . . to satisfy personally the excess costs, expenses, and attorney's fees reasonably incurred because of such conduct." Thus, §1927 is aimed at a lawyer who causes needless litigation.

Section 1927 is one of many "fee shifting" provisions. As we saw in §1.1 (in the "Litigation Expenses and Attorney's Fees" section), the law distinguishes between "costs" and "attorney's fees." Costs are the expenses of litigation, such as filing fees, fees for serving process, discovery costs, fees paid to witnesses, including expert witnesses, costs of giving notice to class members when required in class action litigation, etc. In short, costs generally consist of litigation expenses *other than* attorney's fees. Federal Rule 54(d)(1) provides that such costs "should be allowed to the prevailing party" unless the court directs otherwise. In other words, generally, the losing party pays the winning party's costs. As we saw in §1.1, the winning party likely will not recover every penny of her out-of-pocket expenses. Rather, she recovers only those that are "taxable," which means those recoverable under the relevant statute. Such costs are "taxed" by the court clerk to the losing party and are included in the judgment. See §9.3.

In contrast, the American Rule is that each party bears her own attorney's fees (which are generally far greater than the litigation costs). In other words, generally, the loser does *not* pay the winner's attorney's fees. Many people have proposed that litigation in the United States be run as it is in Great Britain, where the loser pays the winner's attorney's fees. Despite debate, the American Rule retains its force; it is rooted in the belief that the contrary rule would chill meritorious litigation. That is, a person with a legitimate claim, but who (like most litigants) is not assured of victory, will not take the chance of incurring liability for the defendant's attorney's fees should she lose. Thus, in the United States, each party bears her own attorney's fees *unless* there is an exception, like §1927, that permits "fee shifting." (The discovery rules permit fee shifting in some circumstances. See §8.4.) There are many fee-shifting statutes for particular substantive claims, such as civil rights claims.

Inherent Power. Courts have "inherent power" to enter sanctions against egregious litigation conduct by lawyers or litigants. This authority augments the courts' power under Rules and statutes to sanction bad behavior by requiring one who acts in "bad faith" in litigation to pay the costs and attorney's fees incurred by other parties because of the abusive conduct.

One vivid reminder of this power is *Chambers v. NASCO, Inc.*,[185] in which the Supreme Court upheld a district court order requiring the losing party to pay just under $1,000,000 in attorney's fees to the plaintiff. It was the defendant, and not its attorney, who acted inappropriately in the conduct of the litigation. Some of the sanctioned conduct did not violate Rule 11 or §1927. Nonetheless, the Court upheld the entire award, invoking the inherent authority of courts to punish inappropriate litigation behavior.

In *Goodyear Tire & Rubber Co. v. Haeger*,[186] the Court established that any award of attorney's fees under a court's inherent power must be compensatory, not punitive. This means that the party moving for sanctions must demonstrate a "causal link—between the litigant's misbehavior and legal fees paid by the opposing party." Because the lower courts had not required causation, the Court reversed the judgment awarding $2,700,000 in attorney's fees and remanded the case for application of the "but for" causation test: The moving party may

---

[185]501 U.S. 32 (1991).
[186]137 S. Ct. 1178, 1186 (2017).

recover only that portion of her fees that she would not have paid but for the litigation misconduct.

In another case, lawyers failed to assess appropriately whether there was subject matter jurisdiction over the dispute. The district court also failed to address the issue, and the case went through trial, resulting in a judgment for the plaintiff. On appeal, the Seventh Circuit vacated the judgment, because, as it turned out, there was no subject matter jurisdiction. Despite the lack of subject matter jurisdiction, the appellate court required the lawyers to relitigate the case in state court without charging their clients. The court explained:

> The costs of a doomed foray into federal court should fall on the lawyers who failed to do their homework, not on the hapless clients. Although we lack jurisdiction to resolve the merits, we have ample authority to govern the practice of counsel in the litigation . . . . The best way for counsel to make the litigants whole is to perform, without additional fees, any further services that are necessary to bring this suit to a conclusion in state court, or via settlement. That way the clients will pay just once for the litigation. This is intended not as a sanction, but simply to ensure that clients need not pay for lawyers' time that has been wasted for reasons beyond the clients' control.[187]

---

[187]Belleville Catering Co. v. Champaign Market Place LLC, 350 F.3d 691, 694 (7th Cir. 2003).

Chapter *8*

Discovery and Judicial Management of Litigation

§8.1 Defining the Issue

We saw in §7.3 that modern American litigation does not require great detail in pleadings. Even under the regime of *Twombly* and *Iqbal* in federal court, the parties are not required to plead all the factual details of their claims or defenses. Often, in the early stage of a case, the parties simply do not know all the relevant facts. Modern practice permits them to "discover"—that is, to obtain—relevant information from (and to ask questions of) each other and third parties. "Discovery," then, is a term of art that refers to the rules by which the procedural system permits one party to compel others to respond to their questions and requests for information. Put another way, our system allows one litigant to force others to divulge information, even if that information may be harmful to the responding party's case. Moreover, as a general rule, the responding party must pay the expense of finding and producing this information.[1] Note that there are many informal, non-compulsory mechanisms by which lawyers acquire information about a case. They interview their clients and potential witnesses, scour the Internet, inspect relevant places and things, and hire detectives—all in an effort to help their clients' case.[2] This chapter concerns the formal discovery stage of litigation.

The American civil justice system is unique in two ways. First, consistent with the adversary theory of adjudication (see §1.1), the parties are in charge of running the discovery phase of litigation. The parties decide what information they seek. This system is contrary to discovery practice in civil law countries, including most of western Europe, in which the court (not the parties) determines what discovery will be taken and, in general, asks the questions. In §8.5, we will see that the court's role in American litigation has become more managerial in recent times, but the parties (under the watchful eye of the court) are in charge of discovery. Second, the scope of discovery in American courts is broader and more intrusive than that in other systems. As we see in §8.3, in general, a party can discover any information "relevant to a claim or defense" in the case; discoverable information includes tangible things and electronically stored information (ESI), as well as old-fashioned papers. No other country envisions such broad compelled discovery.[3]

These two characteristics of American discovery practice contribute to criticism that American discovery is too expensive and intrusive.[4]

---

[1]There are provisions for "cost shifting," as we will see in §8.4, but they apply in relatively limited circumstances. Professor Redish makes an intriguing argument that the imposition of costs by one's opponent constitutes a litigation subsidy with "troubling democratic, economic, and constitutional implications." Martin H. Redish & Colleen McNamara, *Back to the Future: Discovery Cost Allocation and Modern Procedural Theory,* 79 Geo. Wash. L. Rev. 773, 778 (2011). *See also* Martin H. Redish, *Discovery Cost Allocation, Due Process, and the Constitution's Role in Civil Litigation,* 71 Vand. L. Rev. 1847 (2018).

[2]In addition, there is increasing interest in "bespoke discovery," by which parties may opt out of the discovery provisions. *See e.g.,* Robin Effron, *Outsed: The New Dynamics of Privatized Procedure and Judicial Discretion,* 98 B. U. L. Rev. 127 (2018); Jessica Erickson, *Bespoke Discovery,* 71 Vand. L. Rev. 1873 (2018). *See also* Seth Katsuya Endo, *Contracting for Confidential Discovery,* 53 U.C. Davis L. Rev. 1249 (2020); Jay Tidmarsh, *Opting Out of Discovery,* 71 Vand. L. Rev. 1801 (2018) (proposing a system in which parties may opt out of discovery and become immune from dispositive motions).

[3]*See* Stephen N. Subrin, *Discovery in Global Perspective: Are We Nuts?,* 52 DePaul L. Rev. 299 (2002).

[4]Indeed, recall from §7.3.2 that the Supreme Court's decisions in *Twombly* and *Iqbal* adopted "plausibility" pleading largely to allow defendants to avoid the expense of discovery when the plaintiff did not already have evidentiary support for a plausible

In part, the expense of discovery is driven by technology. In an era of typewriters and carbon paper, there were relatively few documents to discover. Today, with word processors, photocopiers, cut and paste, e-mail, photos and videos on smartphones, information on fitness trackers, voicemail, texting, social media, etc., the amount of discoverable material has increased exponentially. The drafters have amended the Federal Rules periodically in an effort to curtail overly burdensome discovery.[5] Some commentators have argued that these limiting efforts embodied an anti-plaintiff bias.[6]

American procedure, typified by the Federal Rules, adopts the philosophy that more information is better than less, and that each side should, before going to trial, have the opportunity to discover relevant information that is in the possession of others. This philosophy, in turn, promotes the search for truth and can provide a reality check for the parties, which may foster settlement instead of trial. For example, a party may find through discovery that her position is not as well supported by the evidence as she had thought. Learning this gives the party an incentive to settle, and perhaps a realistic view of what to seek in settlement. And the exchange of information may hone issues for trial, by pointing out questions on which there is no dispute and questions on which the parties truly need adjudication. It avoids "trial by ambush" and ensures that the adjudication phase can be based

---

claim. Along these lines, two judges have proposed abolishing discovery in cases involving less than $500,000. Debra Cassens Weiss, *Judge on Trump's Supreme Court Short List Proposes Discovery Ban for Cases Worth Less than $500K*, A.B.A J. (Dec. 10, 2018, 8:15 AM), http://www.abajournal.com/news/article/judge_on_trumps_supreme_court_shortlist_proposes_discovery_ban_for_cases_wo.

[5]Not every case involves enormous expenditures of effort and money on discovery. Some data suggest that parties use extensive discovery in relatively few cases. *See, e.g.*, Linda Mullenix, *The Pervasive Myth of Pervasive Discovery Abuse and the Consequences for Unfounded Rulemaking*, 46 Stan. L. Rev. 1393 (1994). The ultimate value of the case guides the lawyers in assessing the needs of discovery; clearly, for instance, the lawyers will not undertake $100,000 worth of discovery in a case involving a $10,000 claim. *See generally* Seth Katsuya Endo, *Discovery Hydraulics,* 52 U.C. Davis 1317 (2019).

[6]*See, e.g,* Patricia W. Hatamyar Moore, *The Anti-Plaintiff Pending Amendments to the Federal Rules of Civil Procedure and the Pro-Defendant Composition of the Federal Rulemaking Committees*, 83 U. Cin. L. Rev. 1083, 1108 (2015); Stephen N. Subrin & Thomas O. Main, *The Fourth Era of American Civil Procedure,* 162 U. Pa. L. Rev. 1839 (2014) (discussion of anti-plaintiff developments, including limits on discovery). Professor Lahav notes that defendants in mass tort and environmental cases often have an interest in not funding studies of potential harms caused by their products or actions. Because such studies are usually too expensive for plaintiffs to fund, she proposes a "knowledge remedy" which requires defendants to fund independent studies into risks they create. Alexandra D. Lahav, *The Knowledge Remedy,* 98 Texas L. Rev. 1361 (2020).

upon the presentation of evidence that everyone knows is coming, rather than on the ability of a lawyer to pull a surprise witness or surprise evidence out of the hat.

In §8.2 we survey the tools available for discovery. The Federal Rules permit parties to employ five discovery tools (which are also available in every state court system). These may be used to discover information from other parties (and some tools, as we will see, allow discovery from nonparties). These tools are augmented under the Federal Rules by "required disclosures," which, as the name makes clear, mandate that each party disclose certain information even in the absence of a request.

In §8.3, we discuss the scope of discovery. Knowing what tools can be used, here we determine how broadly each party can inquire. Concepts of "relevance," "privilege," and "proportionality" define the scope of discoverability. Moreover, courts have significant discretion to limit use of discovery. Section 8.4 addresses the court's role in enforcing the discovery rules. The sanction imposed for discovery abuse, if any, depends upon the nature of the transgression, and in all cases the court has effective tools to coerce compliance.

In §§8.5 and 8.6, we consider topics relevant far beyond the discovery phase of the litigation. As we see in §8.5, the judge in modern litigation plays an increasingly bureaucratic role: She is responsible for "keeping the case moving" to resolution. The Federal Rules impose significant case-management duties on the judge. The federal judicial system's caseload is heavy,[7] and judges are under considerable pressure to process cases through the system.[8]

In part because of this pressure, as we saw in §1.1, very few cases (in the federal system, fewer than 2 percent) go to trial. And the few cases that do go to trial will not do so next week. In federal court, the average time from the date of filing through resolution by trial is over two years.[9] Much of that time is spent in discovery, under the supervision of the trial-court judge. In discovery and other phases of litigation, the increasing caseload has led to more use of adjunct judicial personnel in the federal system, including "magistrate judges" and "masters." We discuss these personnel in §8.6. Their service to the judicial system is

---

[7]Congress, which sets the number of federal judges, generally has resisted calls to increase dramatically the number of federal judgeships. Many state court systems face even more daunting caseloads.

[8]Detailed discussion is beyond our scope, but it is worth noting that much of the pressure on federal judges comes from large criminal caseloads. Criminal defendants have a right to a speedy trial, while civil litigants do not. Thus, criminal trials often take precedence over civil trials. State court judges face similar pressures.

[9]https://www.uscourts.gov/data-table-numbers/c-5 (for the year 2020, the median time to disposition in federal district courts was 28.4 months).

not limited to discovery matters. They may be employed to help the judge in a variety of ways.

§8.2   Tools Available for Discovering Information

In federal court, each party has six methods for discovering information from others: the five traditional discovery devices (depositions, interrogatories, requests for production, medical examinations, and requests for admission) and "required disclosures."

§8.2.1   Required Disclosures

Federal Rule 26(a) provides that each party must make various required disclosures, even though nobody asks them to do so. When promulgated in 1993, required disclosures were controversial; they seemed antithetical to the adversary system of litigation: They rob parties, to some extent anyway, of autonomy to determine how and when to engage in discovery.[10] Required disclosures have proved successful, probably because they mandate the production of what good lawyers would have requested anyway. Despite this favorable experience, however, in many states, you will find no counterpart to Rule 26(a).

Rule 26(a) requires that each party produce information at three stages of the case. Each of the three sets of required disclosures must be written and signed and served on the other parties.[11] Only the final set of disclosures, however, must be filed with the court.

Required Initial Disclosures. Rule 26(a)(1)(A) requires parties to provide the following information to each other party:

(1) the name, address, and telephone number of each person "likely to have discoverable information—along with the subjects of that information—that the disclosing party may use to support its claims or defenses, unless the use would be solely for impeachment";

(2) a copy (or a description by category and location) of all documents, electronically stored information, and tangible things in the

---

[10]Indeed, three Justices dissented from promulgation of the required disclosure regime. 507 U.S. 1099-1100 (1993) (dissenting statement of Justice Scalia, joined by Justices Thomas and Souter) ("By placing upon lawyers the obligation to disclose information damaging to their clients—on their own initiative . . .—the new Rule would place intolerable strain upon lawyers' ethical duty to represent their clients and not to assist the opposing side").

[11]They can simply be served by mail (or e-mail, if the party agrees) under Rule 5. See §3.3.6. If they are mailed, Rule 6(d) gives the responding party an additional three days in which to respond. See §7.6, footnote 167.

possession or control of the disclosing party that she may use to support her claims or defenses (again, unless solely for impeachment);

(3) the plaintiff must provide a computation of damages claimed, and evidentiary material on which the computation is based; and

(4) the defendant must identify (and make available for copying) any insurance agreement under which an insurer may be liable to satisfy all or part of the judgment.

The first two categories require identification of persons and things with discoverable information the responding party may use to *support* her case. She is not required to divulge (at least under Rule 26) information (or the identities of persons with information) that will hurt her case. This does not mean that the party may suppress information that is harmful to her case. If the material is otherwise discoverable, it must be produced when requested using the discovery tools. Moreover, material that conclusively disproves a party's contention at some point raises ethical issues for counsel under the rules of professional conduct.

We discuss the timing of required initial disclosures in §8.5. For now, it is sufficient to understand that a party is under an obligation to produce the information listed in Rule 26(a)(1) quite early in the litigation. Gaining access to this information early in the case may jump-start the discovery process and assist the parties in determining how to proceed.

Rule 26(a)(1)(B) exempts certain kinds of cases from the required initial disclosures. The cases listed are quite specialized; most civil cases of the type addressed in the course on Civil Procedure will *not* be exempted. Rule 26(a)(1)(A) permits a court order or stipulation of the parties to vary the timing and scope of the initial disclosures.

Required Disclosures Concerning Expert Witnesses. The second set of required disclosures, under Rule 26(a)(2), concern expert witnesses. These disclosures usually become relevant after discovery through the traditional discovery devices (see §8.2.2) has largely run its course and the parties have focused on whether they will have expert testimony at trial. Ordinarily, the court will direct the parties when to exchange this information concerning expert witnesses. Absent a court order or stipulation to the contrary, Rule 26(a)(2)(C)(i) requires that the information must be produced at least 90 days before the trial date. Failure to produce the required information can result in sanctions, as discussed in §8.4 below. (One possible sanction is an order that one's expert not be allowed to testify at trial.[12]) Unlike

---

[12]*See, e.g.,* Merchant v. Corizon Health, Inc., 993 F.d 733, 737 (9th Cir. 2021); China Resource Prod. v. FAYDA Intl., 856 F. Supp. 856, 866-867 (D. Del. 1994).

the initial disclosure under Rule 26(a)(1), here there is no provision for exempted cases and there is no general provision for avoiding the requirement by court order or stipulation of the parties.

In this context, "witness" refers not simply to someone who observed something in the real world, but to a person who testifies at trial. Most witnesses are "lay witnesses," meaning they have no special expertise, but are testifying about things they observed or otherwise know. Lay witnesses generally are not permitted to offer opinions about events they observed. "Expert witnesses" are different. Under Federal Rule of Evidence 702, they are "qualified . . . by knowledge, skill, experience, training, or education" and may give opinions at trial. Indeed, that is why they are retained — to give a professional opinion. For instance, a psychiatrist, testifying as an expert witness, may give her opinion that a party to the case was suffering from delusions at the time of an accident. In an antitrust case, an economist, testifying as an expert witness, may opine that the defendant's commercial practices caused a restraint of trade in the market.[13]

To avoid surprise by expert testimony at trial, Rule 26(a)(2)(A) requires each party to disclose to each other party the identity of anyone who may be used at trial to present expert testimony. (Note that this Rule applies only to experts who will actually testify at trial. It does not apply to "consulting experts," whose testimony is not offered at trial (see §8.3.3).) Two types of expert witnesses must be identified: those who must also provide a written report (Rule 26(a)(2)(B)) and those who are not required to provide a written report (Rule 26(a)(2)(C)).

The written report requires a great deal of work. The report must be produced along with the party's identification of her expert witnesses. The report is prepared by the expert and must contain the information listed in Rule 26(a)(2)(B)(i) through (vi), which includes a statement of all opinions to be expressed and the basis for them, the information used to form these opinions, the expert's qualifications (including publications for the last ten years), and how much she is

---

[13]An expert is permitted to testify as to her opinion at trial if (1) her specialized knowledge will help the trier of fact understand the evidence or determine a fact in issue, (2) her testimony is based on sufficient data, (3) her testimony is a product of reliable methods, and (4) she has reliably applied the methods to the facts of the case. Fed. R. Evid. 702(a)-(d). The federal judge exercises a gatekeeping function by determining the relevance and reliability of proposed expert testimony. Daubert v. Merrell Dow Pharm., Inc., 509 U.S. 579 (1993). This is true not only of scientific experts but of "other experts [such as engineers] who are not scientists." Kumho Tire Co., Ltd. v. Carmichael, 526 U.S. 137, 141 (1999).

being paid for the case. (Rule 26(b)(4) is also relevant to discovery concerning experts. It is discussed at §8.3.4.)

There are two types of expert witnesses who must provide the written report. Both are described in the first sentence of Rule 26(a)(2)(B). One is the expert retained expressly to provide expert testimony in this case. This is the most common: A party goes out and hires an expert to present opinions in this case. The other is "one whose duties as the party's employee regularly involve giving expert testimony." For example, this might be an engineer who works for the defendant and who routinely testifies as an expert. Both types must be identified under Rule 26(a)(2)(A) and provide the written report under Rule 26(a)(2)(B).

That leaves expert witnesses who will be testifying but who are not required to file the written report. These are addressed in Rule 26(a)(2)(C). Who is included here? It is an expert who was not hired for this case and who is not an employee of a party and who routinely testifies as an expert. For instance, in a case involving personal injuries, the plaintiff's personal physician would fall in this category. She will testify as to her opinion but was not hired for this case. Another example would be an expert (say, a chemist) employed by a party but who does not routinely testify as an expert. These people must be identified in the required disclosures under Rule 26(a)(2)(A) but need not produce the written report. Instead, the party must disclose the subject matter on which they will testify and a summary of their facts and opinions.

Required Pretrial Disclosures. The final set of required disclosures becomes relevant as the case nears trial. Under Rule 26(a)(3)(A), each party must serve on each other party detailed information about evidence she anticipates presenting at trial (except solely for impeachment). At this stage, the parties will have been litigating for months, perhaps years (through pleadings, motions of various types, and discovery) and now have honed the issues remaining to be adjudicated at trial.

The information required under Rule 26(a)(3)(A) includes the name, address, and telephone number of each witness to be called by that party (and those who may be called if the need arises at trial), designation of those witnesses whose testimony will be presented by deposition transcript rather than by live testimony, and the identification of each document or other exhibit to be offered at trial. Under Rule 26(a)(3)(A), the party not only serves the information on other parties, but files it with the court as well. (The pretrial required disclosures are the only required disclosures that must be filed with the court. The court does not get copies of the other required disclosures.)

§8.2.2   The Five Traditional Discovery Devices

The parties may use five discovery tools to request information from other parties. One (the deposition) can be used to get information directly from a nonparty. As discussed below, occasionally a medical exam can be ordered of a nonparty and documents and things can be discovered from a nonparty using a subpoena. We discuss timing of discovery requests and responses in §8.5.[14]

1. *Depositions.* In a deposition, the person being deposed (called the *deponent*) is asked questions, to which she responds orally. Her testimony is recorded[15] and can later be transcribed into hard copy.[16] The deponent may request the opportunity to review the deposition testimony and correct any errors before signing it under penalty of perjury.[17] At the outset, the court reporter administers an oath to the deponent, who thus affirms that the testimony she gives is the truth, under penalty of perjury.[18] In this way, a deposition looks like testimony at trial. The deponent is "sworn in" and then responds to questions "live." In some ways, though, it is not like a trial. Depositions do not take place in a courtroom, and no judge is present. Instead, the parties and their lawyers are entitled to attend; the lawyer for each party has a right to ask questions.[19] The only other person usually present is the court reporter, who administers the oath and records the deposition. There are provisions, such as Rule 30(b)(4), for depositions "taken by telephone or other remote means," which became especially relevant during the COVID-19 pandemic. These allow depositions to

---

[14]Some older cases, including the famous *Hickman v. Taylor*, discussed in §8.3.2, refer to parties' *filing* discovery responses with the court. It was long required that parties file a copy of all discovery requests and responses, including deposition transcripts. This is no longer the rule.

[15]Traditionally, the recording is done by a court reporter on a stenographic machine. Rule 30(b)(3) allows recording by sound or video/sound mechanisms as well. The party taking the deposition must arrange to have a court reporter attend and record the deposition. Each city has court reporting firms that provide these services. *See also* Rule 30(b)(4) (allowing court order or stipulation for depositions by telephone or other remote means).

[16]If a deposition (or any part of it) will be offered for evidence at trial, it (or the portions offered) must be transcribed. Fed. R. Civ. P. 32(c).

[17]Rule 30(e)(1) permits the deponent or a party to request that the deponent have 30 days after being notified by the court reporter that the transcript is available in which to review it. If she makes changes "in form or substance," the deponent must sign a statement reciting the changes and why they were made. The court reporter must note whether any such review was requested and, if so, append any changes to the transcript.

[18]Rule 28(a)(1) requires that depositions be taken before an officer authorized to administer a valid oath. Court reporters are licensed to do so.

[19]A party who is not represented by an attorney, called a *pro se* party, is entitled to attend and ask questions. The nonparty deponent may have her lawyer present.

be taken without having all participants (the deponent, court reporter, and attorneys) in one room. On the other hand, lawyers taking depositions generally prefer to be in the same room with the deponent, to get a better sense of the deponent's physical and emotional reactions to questions.

A party wishing to depose someone must "notice" the deposition, which means she must give written notice to all parties of her desire to take the deposition. Under Rule 30(b)(1), the notice (a very short document) must name the person to be deposed and indicate the date, time, and place of the deposition.[20] Importantly, a party can depose *anyone* who has discoverable information—even nonparties.[21]

A nonparty deponent should be *subpoenaed* to attend the deposition. Otherwise, she is under no obligation to attend.[22] A subpoena, issued under Rule 45, emanates from the court and commands a person to attend an event (such as a deposition or a trial) and give testimony.[23]

To take a deposition of a party to the case, however, no subpoena is required; the properly served notice of deposition suffices to require the party to attend her own deposition. This distinction makes sense. A party has already been brought before the jurisdiction of the court (the plaintiff by suing, the defendant by being served with process), so no further court order is necessary. A nonparty, in contrast, has never been brought before the jurisdiction of the court, so this exercise of "power" is necessary to compel her attendance.[24] A subpoena can require the nonparty not only to attend and be deposed, but to bring documents and things with her; such an order is called a *subpoena duces tecum*.[25]

---

[20]The notice of deposition is served on all parties under Rule 5, which allows service, *inter alia,* by mail or by delivery to a party's attorney. See §3.3.6. Rule 27(a) addresses depositions taken before a case is filed. The purpose of such a deposition is to preserve evidence (or "perpetuate testimony") for the case. For instance, if a key eyewitness was seriously ill, a potential party might want to take a deposition prefiling to perpetuate the witness's testimony. A court order is required for such depositions, upon showing satisfying the standards in Rule 27(a)(1).

[21]Rules 30(a)(1) and 31(a)(1) permit the deposition of "any person, including a party."

[22]If a party notices the deposition of a nonparty and fails to subpoena her, and she does not show up because of the lack of a subpoena, that party is liable for costs and attorney's fees incurred by other parties that showed up for the deposition. Fed. R. Civ. P. 30(g).

[23]Rule 45(a) provides that a subpoena compelling attendance at a deposition issues from the court in the district in which the deposition is to be held. Rule 45(c) protects nonparty deponents from undue burden or expense by limiting where the nonparty can be deposed.

[24]Of course, a nonparty who has not been subpoenaed is free to show up and be deposed if she so chooses. Without a subpoena, though, she cannot be sanctioned for failing to do so.

[25]*Duces tecum* is Latin for (roughly) "bring with you."

The deponent is required to testify based upon her present knowledge and recollection. If she knows that the answer to a particular question would be contained in files in her office, but does not remember what the documents say, she indicates her lack of recollection; she is under no obligation to review all relevant files before being deposed. Because they are "live," and because lawyers can adjust their questioning in response to what the deponent says, depositions can become tense, even dramatic. A deponent (or counsel) may lose her composure. Occasionally, the lawyer for the deponent may object and instruct the deponent not to answer.[26] Rule 30(c)(2) limits the types of objections that are properly raised in depositions. Ultimately, the judge may be required to determine whether the objections are proper.

Depositions can be very useful. But they are expensive. Lawyers prepare for the deposition, studying relevant documents and devising lines of questioning. Under Rule 30(a)(2)(A)(ii), no one can be deposed more than once in a case unless the parties agree or the court orders an additional deposition. Because parties only have one chance at a deposition, then, they must be fully prepared to take advantage of each deposition. If the lawyer is billing by the hour,[27] all this preparation time—as well as time spent in the deposition—is billable.

Lawyers are careful to use the discovery devices in a coordinated way. Rarely will the deposition be used first. Usually, it makes more sense to serve interrogatories (discussed below) first, to get helpful background information, before deciding whom to depose and what lines of questioning to pursue.

Suppose a party wants to depose someone but does not know the person's name. Suppose there is a case in which the design of an automobile's gas tank is relevant. A party may wish to depose the engineer responsible for that design. If the manufacturer for which this person works is a party to the litigation, one way to proceed would be to serve interrogatories on the manufacturer, asking it to identify the engineer. Once the engineer is identified, her deposition can be taken. There is another way to proceed (indeed, this is the only way to proceed if the manufacturer is not a party and thus, as we see below, cannot be served with interrogatories). Rule 30(b)(6) permits the party to name the entity (here the manufacturer) as the deponent and to describe the matters on which discovery is sought. The manufacturer then is

---

[26]For example, counsel might do so to preserve an evidentiary privilege, as we discuss in §8.3.1.

[27]Defense counsel generally bill by the hour. Plaintiff's lawyers often take the case on a contingent fee basis, which requires the plaintiff to pay her counsel a percentage of any recovery she wins (whether by judgment or settlement). Even though a plaintiff is not paying her lawyer as the case proceeds, lawyers are aware of how much time has been sunk into a case and are not likely to invest more time than the case is worth.

445

required to identify and produce the appropriate person for the deposition. As amended in 2020, the Rule requires the serving party and the entity to confer in good faith about the scope of the deposition; if the entity is a nonparty, the subpoena must advise it of its duty to confer and to designate a proper person for the deposition.

The Federal Rules impose presumptive limits on depositions. Unless a court order or stipulation of the parties[28] permits, Rule 30(a)(2)(A)(i) limits each party to no more than ten depositions in the case. Also, unless a court order or stipulation permits, Rule 30(d)(1) limits each deposition to a single day of no more than seven hours.

Finally, most depositions are taken under Rule 30, which allows deposition on oral examination. That means that the questions put to the deponent are asked orally by the lawyers for each party. Rule 31, however, permits a deposition on written questions. These are fairly rare. They work in all ways as an oral deposition, with one exception: The questions are not asked orally by counsel for a party. Instead, they are submitted in advance and are read by the court reporter, who then records the deponent's oral responses. Rule 31 depositions are cheaper than Rule 30 depositions, because the party taking the deposition need not have her attorney attend and ask questions. They suffer a significant and obvious drawback, though, in that the questions are prescripted and cannot be changed to account for responses by the deponent. Most lawyers want to take oral depositions so they can watch the deponent as well as listen to her responses. This enables the lawyer to sense weaknesses in the deponent's position and to home in with appropriate follow-up questions.

2. *Interrogatories.* Interrogatories are governed by Rule 33. They are written questions, to which the responding party must respond in writing within 30 days of being served with the questions.[29] Unlike depositions, then, interrogatories will rarely uncover a "smoking gun." Someone under the pressure of a deposition might "crack under the strain" and blurt out something damaging to her case. But interrogatories rarely lead to such dramatic moments, in part because the party has 30 days in which to respond and in part because a party's lawyer will assist the party in drafting her answers. Answers to

---

[28]Rule 29(b) permits parties to stipulate to various aspects of discovery procedure. The one area on which parties cannot stipulate under that Rule is the time for responding *if* an extension would interfere with the time already set for completing discovery or for hearing a motion or commencing trial. In such a situation, a stipulation will work only if approved by the court. Outside that, the parties have a good deal of leeway in working out the scheduling and scope of discovery. See §8.5.

[29]This timing is found in Rule 33(b)(2). The responses are served on all parties under Rule 5(b). If the interrogatories were served by mail, the responding party is allowed an extra three days from the date on which they were mailed. Fed. R. Civ. P. 6(d). See §3.3.6.

interrogatories are signed by the responding party under oath. The responding party may object to an interrogatory, *inter alia*, because it calls for material that is protected by an evidentiary privilege; if she does, she must expressly invoke the relevant privilege, which we discuss in §8.3.1.

Interrogatories can be invaluable to discover background facts—names and addresses of relevant persons, dates of contracts, the number of contacts between the parties—any objective data relevant to the claims or defenses of any party. They also are helpful to clarify a party's pleadings. Recall that federal court pleadings can be fairly conclusory. A defendant sued for negligence will want to send interrogatories to the plaintiff to force her to detail the allegedly negligent behavior. Usually, parties use answers to interrogatories to prepare for the deposition of the other party. Thus, responses to interrogatories and initial required disclosures usually provide valuable information for deciding whom to depose and what sorts of questions to ask.

Rule 33(a)(2) provides that an interrogatory "is not objectionable merely because it asks for an opinion or contention that relates to fact or the application of law to fact." Thus, parties may serve "contention" interrogatories, which force the other side to take a position or to state facts and evidence supporting assertions in its pleadings. And though "interrogatories" sound as though one must ask a question, they are often drafted as a form of command, such as "state the facts that support your allegation that the defendant breached the contract." Interrogatories "that ask a party what it contends or to state all the facts upon which it bases a contention are perfectly legitimate."[30] They are useful in narrowing and focusing the issues to be adjudicated.[31]

As we just saw, a party may take the deposition of a nonparty. Interrogatories, however, may be sent only to other parties.[32] There

---

[30]In re Rail Freight Fuel Surcharge Antitrust Litigation, 281 F.R.D. 1, 4 (D.D.C. 2011). In this case, the court required the plaintiffs to state whether they contended that persons agreed to surcharges in such a way that constituted a conspiracy in violation of the antitrust laws. Further, if the answer was yes, the plaintiffs were required to state what persons made such an agreement and when. *Id.* Note that contention interrogatories can be objectionable if overly broad. *See, e.g.,* Ritchie Risk-Limited Strategies Trading (Ireland) Ltd. v. Coventry First LLC, 273 F.R.D. 367, 369 (S.D.N.Y. 2010) ("Defendant's requests, insofar as they seek every fact, every piece of evidence, every witness, and every application of law to fact—rather than, for example, certain principal or material facts, pieces of evidence, witnesses and legal applications—supporting the identified allegations, are overly broad and unduly burdensome.").

[31]To avoid requiring a party to take a position on a contention interrogatory prematurely, a court has discretion to defer the parties' answers until after they have had a chance to discover material pertinent to the answers. As Rule 33(a)(2) provides, "the court may order that the [contention] interrogatory need not be answered until designated discovery is complete, or until a pretrial conference or some other time."

[32]Rule 33(a)(1) provides that interrogatories may be served on "any other party."

is no provision for sending interrogatories to nonparties. Another difference concerns the type of information the responding party must assess before responding. Recall that the deponent is required to testify only as to her present knowledge or recollection. In responding to interrogatories, however, the party must give information reasonably available to her. Thus, if an interrogatory asks for information the party does not recall, but that is contained in her files, she must go through the files and find that answer.

In this regard, however, Rule 33(d) provides the "business records option."

> ○ ***Example #1.*** Party *A* sends an interrogatory to Party *B*, the answer to which is contained in Party *B*'s business records (hard copy or electronic). If the burden of finding the answer to the interrogatory would be substantially the same for both parties, Party *B* (instead of finding the answer herself) can simply give Party *A* access to the business records so she can find the answer.

Rule 33(a)(1) imposes a presumptive limit: Each party may serve one set of a maximum of 25 interrogatories (including subparts) on each other party in the case. District courts may not change this limitation by Local Rule. On the other hand, the court may make a case-specific order increasing the number of interrogatories allowed, or the parties may stipulate to a larger number.[33]

3. *Requests for Production (and Subpoena for Information from Nonparties).* The request to produce, found in Rule 34, permits one party to request that another party produce documents, electronically stored information (ESI), or tangible things, or allow entry upon land to permit various acts, such as testing. The materials must be "in the possession, custody, or control" of the party to whom the request is made. The most common use of Rule 34 is to gain access to documents and ESI, which the requesting party may then inspect and copy. The Rule is useful far beyond that, however. For instance, where Plaintiff sues Defendant for infringing Plaintiff's patent on a widget, Rule 34 would permit Plaintiff to gain access to Defendant's widget and to inspect it (or have her consultants inspect it). In a case involving damages to Plaintiff's house, Defendant may gain access to the property to inspect it (or have her consultants inspect it).

Rule 34 specifically mentions ESI.[34] One area of concern has been discovery of e-mails. Often, these exist only on a server and not in

---

[33]Rule 29(b) permits the parties to stipulate to many issues concerning the scheduling and scope of discovery. See note 28 above.

[34]*See generally* Tanya Pierce, *Righting the Ship: What Courts Are Still Getting Wrong About Electronic Discovery*, 72 S.M.U. L. Rev. 785 (2019).

hard-copy format. Nonetheless, they are discoverable. Rule 34(b)(1)(C) permits a party sending a request for production of ESI to specify the form in which ESI is to be produced. For example, a party may ask for hard copies of such information. Under Rule 34(b)(2)(D), the responding party may object to the requested form for producing ESI. She may then indicate what form she intends to use in producing the information. For instance, she may prefer to produce such information in a form that can be searched electronically.

The party requesting information drafts a request under Rule 34(b)(1) and serves it on all parties.[35] The request must set forth the documents or things desired "with reasonable particularity." It can specify documents individually (e.g., "the letter from *A* to *B* dated November 4, 2019") or by categories (e.g., "sales receipts from October 1, 2017, to January 5, 2019"). The responding party must respond in writing within 30 days of service of the request[36] and must either indicate that the inspection will be allowed or assert objections to the inspection. Rule 34(b)(2)(E) provides that "[a] party must produce documents as they are kept in the usual course of business or must organize and label them to correspond to the categories in the request." This requirement is intended to make it difficult for the responding party to bury a key document in a mountain of unimportant material.

Frequently, a party will want to discover documents, ESI, or things from a party whose deposition will be taken. The request to produce can be served along with the notice of deposition; then the party will be required to show up for her deposition with the requested materials. On the other hand, it might be more useful to obtain the documents and review them before taking the other party's deposition. So counsel might prefer to use the requests for production before taking the deposition. In practice, there is a great deal of cooperation between counsel to schedule the exchange of documents and depositions of the parties.[37]

Rules 34(a) and (b) speak only of making requests for production from parties; they do not permit a party to send requests to produce to nonparties. Rule 34(c), however, reminds us that nonparties can be compelled to produce documents or things under Rule 45, with a subpoena. Rule 45(a)(1)(A), in turn, makes clear that a nonparty can be compelled to produce documents, ESI, and tangible things for

---

[35]The requests are served on parties under Rule 5(b), usually by mail. See §3.3.6.

[36]This timing is found in Rule 34(b)(2)(A). The responses are also served on all parties under Rule 5(b). If the requests were served by mail, the responding party is allowed an extra three days from the date on which they were mailed. Fed. R. Civ. P. 6(d).

[37]Rule 29(b) permits the parties to stipulate to many issues concerning the scheduling and scope of discovery. See note 28 above.

inspection or to allow access to property.[38] Accordingly, a party can get discovery from a nonparty as broadly as she can from a party—but through a subpoena rather than a request to produce.[39]

4. *Medical Examinations.* This discovery tool is unique because, as Rule 35(a)(2)(A) makes plain, it is available only if the court grants a party's motion to subject someone to a physical or mental examination (which we will simply call a *medical exam*). The party seeking the order must demonstrate two things. First, under Rule 35(a)(1), she must show that a person's "mental or physical condition, including blood group, is in controversy." Second, under Rule 35(a)(2)(A), she must demonstrate good cause for the examination. Upon such a showing, the court can order someone to undergo a medical exam before a "suitably licensed or certified examiner." The motion (and the court order, if granted) must state the time, place, manner, and scope of the exam, and give the name of the person who will perform it. The requirement of a court order makes sense; without it, this tool could easily be used to harass other parties.[40]

Conclusory allegations are not sufficient to justify an order of a medical exam. Rather, the party seeking the examination must make "an affirmative showing . . . that each condition as to which the examination is sought is really and genuinely in controversy and that good cause exists for ordering each particular examination."[41] Moreover, the ability to obtain the desired information in some less intrusive fashion is relevant to whether the party establishes good cause for the order.

Rule 35(a)(1) permits an order for a medical exam only of "a party," but also permits the court to order a party to "produce for examination a person who is in its custody or control." Courts have interpreted this phrase narrowly. It includes, for example, a child of a party, because a

---

[38]Notice how Rule 45(a)(1)(A)(iii) speaks of commanding a "person" as opposed to a "party." Thus, the target of a subpoena need not be a party to the litigation.

[39]The availability of a subpoena solely to gain the production of documents and things from a nonparty is handy. Before this could be done under Rule 34(c), a party seeking documents from a nonparty was required to notice the nonparty's deposition and serve the nonparty with a *subpoena duces tecum* (which required the nonparty's attendance and required her to bring specified documents or things with her). The nonparty would then be sworn in for the deposition and asked if she brought the requested documents with her. Once she identified the documents, the deposition would end and the parties would inspect the documents. Now, if one wants documents or things (and no deposition) from the nonparty, she need merely serve the nonparty with a subpoena for production of the materials; there is no need to go through the inconvenience of noticing her deposition. The older practice is still followed, however, in some state courts.

[40]On the other hand, Florida has long permitted some medical examinations without court orders, seemingly without substantial abuse. *See* Fla. R. Civ. P. 1.360 (2004).

[41]Schlagenhauf v. Holder, 379 U.S. 104, 118 (1964).

child is (at least in theory) in the custody and control of her parent.[42] It does not include an employee.[43]

- ○ ***Example #2.*** A bus operated by BusCo and driven by Driver collides with another vehicle. Plaintiff, a passenger on the bus, was injured and sues BusCo. Plaintiff believes that Driver's poor eyesight contributed to the wreck and seeks a court order that Driver have her eyesight examined by a suitably licensed professional. Obviously, if Driver were a party, Plaintiff could seek the order. But in this case, Plaintiff sued only BusCo. Plaintiff cannot get the order, because Driver, though an employee of a party (BusCo), is not considered to be "in the legal control or custody" of BusCo.
- ○ ***Example #3.*** That being the case, how could the party get information about Driver's eyesight? For one thing, Plaintiff can take the deposition of Driver. She would have to secure Driver's attendance with a subpoena. At the deposition, Plaintiff can inquire about Driver's eyesight. She can ask Driver about how often she has her eyes checked, whether she wears glasses, etc. Another approach would be to require Driver, through a *subpoena duces tecum* (either before or concurrent with the deposition), to produce her glasses for examination by Plaintiff's experts. Plaintiff can also gain production of any documents relating to Driver's glasses or prescriptions. Moreover, in deposition, Plaintiff could ask Driver to identify her doctor and then depose the doctor about Driver's eyesight.[44]

The medical exam will often be performed by a medical doctor but note that Rule 35 envisions an exam by any suitably licensed or certified person. Many such people do not hold the M.D. degree. The Rule is intended to facilitate examinations by any suitable health care professional. Thus, exams may be performed by chiropractors, podiatrists, physical therapists, and other such professionals. Of course, the professional is compensated for performing the medical exam. The party requesting the exam pays for it, and that expense becomes a "cost" of the litigation. (Remember from §1.1 that, generally, the prevailing party recovers her costs (which do not include attorney's fees) from the loser.)

After the medical exam has been performed, the examining professional sends her report to the party who sought the exam. The person who was examined has a right to receive a copy of the report simply by requesting it from the party who sought the examination. Under Rule 35(b)(1), that party must deliver it to the person making the request. But requesting the report carries a price. Under Rule 35(b)(4),

---

[42]*See, e.g.,* Schempp v. Reniker, 809 F.2d 541, 542-543 (8th Cir. 1987) (parental custody or legal control of minor child).

[43]From time to time, there have been proposals to expand Rule 35 to cover an employee or agent of a party, but all such efforts have failed. *See* 7 Moore's Federal Practice §35.06.

[44]We see in §8.3.1 that confidential communications between Driver and her doctor would be privileged and thus could not be discovered.

by requesting and obtaining the report, the person who was examined "waives any privilege it may have—in that action or any other action involving the same controversy—concerning testimony about all examinations of the same condition." In other words, the person examined waives any privilege in the reports of other professionals concerning the same condition. Indeed, under Rule 35(b)(3), once the person examined receives the report from the court-ordered examination, she must (upon request of the other party) produce reports of her own doctors concerning that medical condition.

5. *Requests for Admission.* Rule 36(a)(1)(A) permits a party to force another party to admit or deny any discoverable matter relating to "facts, the application of law to fact, or opinions about either." And Rule 36(a)(1)(B) permits the same regarding "the genuineness of any described documents." Pursuant to rules of evidence, documents may be admitted for consideration at trial only if they are authenticated—that is, established as genuine. Litigants should cooperate in admitting the genuineness of documents whenever possible to avoid the expense of finding the author of each document and asking her under oath whether she wrote it.

Requests for admission can put a party's feet to the fire and may narrow the scope of issues to be tried. Though Rule 36 does not impose a presumptive limit on the number of requests to be served in a case, Rule 26(b)(2)(A) empowers the court to impose such restrictions by order or by Local Rule.

Requests for admission may be served only on parties.[45] There is no provision for sending them to nonparties. The responding party has 30 days from the service of the requests in which to serve on all parties her written and signed response to the requests.[46] In the responses, she must either admit or specifically deny the matter, or "state in detail" why she is unable to admit or deny. As to the latter, she may not say that she lacks knowledge on the matter unless she states that she has made a reasonable inquiry and that the information obtainable is insufficient to permit her to admit or deny. (Or she may object to any request for admission that asks for improper matter, such as irrelevant or privileged material. See §8.3.1.)

If the responding party fails to deny a request to admit, the other party may wish to have the matter deemed admitted. It does this by proving that it served a proper request and that the other party failed to respond. Under Rule 36(b), a matter admitted under Rule 36

---

[45]Rule 36(a)(1) states that requests for admission may be served on "any other party." Service is usually done by mail under Rule 5. See §3.3.6.

[46]The responses are also served on all parties under Rule 5. If the requests were served by mail, the responding party is allowed an extra three days from the date on which they were mailed. Fed. R. Civ. P. 6(d).

"is conclusively established unless the court, on motion, permits the admission to be withdrawn or amended." And Rule 36(a)(1) makes clear that admissions are binding only in the pending case and thus cannot be used in other litigation.

§8.2.3 Duty to Supplement Responses

The litigation process often takes years to complete. Thus, it is possible that a party's response to discovery, though accurate when made, might not be accurate after further facts are uncovered. Rule 26(e)(1) imposes a duty on the responding party. It is a duty to "supplement or correct" any required disclosure as well as responses to interrogatories, requests for production, and requests for admission. The duty attaches under Rule 26(e)(1)(A) only "if the party learns that in some material respect the disclosure or response is incomplete or incorrect."[47] And even then, the duty applies only "if the additional or corrective information has not otherwise been made known to the other parties during the discovery process or in writing."

These supplemental responses are required even though no party asks for them. Thus, Rule 26(e)(1) requires each party to monitor the situation to ensure that responses previously made have not become misleading or inaccurate as the case unfolds. Thus, it is incumbent on each party (guided by her lawyer) to review the responses to required disclosures to ensure that they are accurate as the case develops.

Rule 26(e)(2) addresses only the very specific case of required disclosures about expert witnesses, which are found in Rule 26(a)(1)(B). It requires a party to supplement or correct not only the information included in the expert's report but also information given during her deposition.

§8.3 Scope of Discovery

§8.3.1 Standard Under Rule 26(b)(1)

Under Rule 26(b)(1), unless the court orders otherwise, parties may discover:

> any nonprivileged matter that is relevant to any party's claim or defense and proportional to the needs of the case, considering the importance of

---

[47]Rule 26(e)(1)(B) requires supplemental responses if the court orders them. The more important self-policing provision in Rule 26(e)(1)(A) is discussed in text.

the issues at stake in the action, the amount in controversy, the parties' relative access to relevant information, the parties' resources, the importance of discovery in resolving the issues, and whether the burden or expense of the proposed discovery outweighs its likely benefit. Information within this scope of discovery need not be admissible in evidence to be discoverable.

Let's dissect this standard.

"Nonprivileged." The information sought must be "nonprivileged." The concept of *privilege,* which is studied in detail in the course on Evidence, refers to a privilege to keep something secret. If something is privileged in this sense, the person holding the privilege cannot be forced to divulge it, either in discovery or at trial. The law recognizes very few evidentiary privileges, and they protect *confidential communications between particular people.* Confidential communications between lawyer and client, between clergy member and parishioner, and between spouses are privileged in federal court. For instance, if the defendant admits in a confidential communication with her lawyer, her pastor, or her spouse that she was speeding at the time of the accident, she cannot be made to divulge that statement.[48] And if she asserts her privilege, her lawyer, priest, or spouse cannot be made to divulge the statement. The privilege is said to be "absolute," meaning that no party can make a showing strong enough to overcome the protection.

To be privileged, the communication must be between persons having one of the specific relationships recognized as raising a privilege. If the woman who was speeding was not married and told her boyfriend, even if in "strictest confidence," that she had been speeding, that communication would not be privileged. There is a spousal privilege. There is not a "significant other" privilege or "family" privilege.

Moreover, privileges attach only to *confidential* communications. If a client tells her lawyer something in a crowded elevator, and others overhear, the communication is not privileged. Also, the confidential communication with a professional, like a lawyer, must have been made in furtherance of providing professional services. Something said in confidence to a lawyer as part of an initial interview to see whether she will retain the lawyer will be privileged, even if she does

---

[48]Assuming, of course, that the relevant law recognizes privileges for confidential communications between these people. Nearly every jurisdiction recognizes the ones listed in the text, though it is worth noting that federal law generally does not recognize a physician-patient privilege. *See, e.g.,* Patterson v. Caterpillar, Inc., 70 F.3d 503, 506 (7th Cir. 1995). In federal court cases involving state law, however, a state physician-patient privilege may apply.

not ultimately hire that lawyer. But something said in confidence to a lawyer on a golf course, without relating to retention of her legal services, will not be privileged. The concept of privilege embodies a policy determination that particular relationships would be harmed if parties to confidential communications were forced to divulge the content of those communications.

All evidentiary privileges (including the constitutional privilege against self-incrimination) inhibit the truth-seeking function. Society abides this hindrance because it values these relationships. If the truth-seeking function of litigation were the only relevant goal, there would be no privileges. But we want people to speak freely to their lawyers, spouses, clergypersons, etc., without fear that the confidential communications will later be divulged.

Even though Rule 26(b)(1) implies that a requesting party should only ask for "nonprivileged" information, the burden is on the party asserting the privilege to raise it. If a discovery request would require the responding party to divulge privileged material, the responding party must, in the words of Rule 26(b)(5)(A), withhold the information and "expressly make the claim" of privilege. Moreover, she must "describe the nature of the documents, communications, or tangible things not produced or disclosed—and do so in a manner that, without revealing information itself privileged or protected, will enable other parties to assess the claim." The responding party will provide this detailed information in a document called a "privilege log."[49] Failure to assert the privilege or work product protection properly, with appropriate detail in the privilege log, can result in waiving it.

One scary possibility is waiver of privilege[50] by inadvertent disclosure. Suppose a lawyer, in reviewing documents to be produced by her client, misses one that is protected by privilege. She produces it, along with other documents. Has the lawyer waived her client's privilege? Some older opinions were surprisingly harsh in finding waiver, which caused sleepless nights for many lawyers. The worry now is largely a thing of the past. Federal Rule of Evidence 502(b) provides that inadvertent disclosure of privileged material does not operate as a waiver, so long as the holder of the privilege took reasonable steps to prevent disclosure and promptly tried to remedy the problem once she found out about it.[51] It specifically refers to Federal Rule of Civil

---

[49]Though the Rules do not use this term, lawyers and judges do. The same procedure is mandated under Rule 26(b)(5)(A) when claiming the work product protection, which we discuss at §8.3.2, even though work product is not a privilege.

[50]Everything in this paragraph also applies to inadvertent production of work product material, which we discuss at §8.3.2.

[51]Moreover, Federal Rule of Evidence 502(a) narrowed the scope of waiver. So even if a party is found to have waived her privilege, the waiver is to that document alone.

Procedure 26(b)(5)(B). That Rule instructs the responding party who made an inadvertent disclosure to notify the requesting party. That party must then "promptly return, sequester, or destroy the specified information." In other words, the party who requested the material may not use the privilege matter in the case (unless the court later finds that there was a waiver, perhaps because the disclosing party had not taken reasonable steps to prevent the disclosure).

"Relevant" to a Claim or Defense. The requested information must be "relevant." Generally, courts consider something relevant if it has "any tendency to make the existence of any fact . . . more probable or less probable than it would be without [it]."[52] And the requested information must be relevant "to a claim or defense." For many years, parties could discover anything "relevant to the subject matter involved in the action," which could include *potential* claims or defenses. Now, discovery must be relevant to a claim or defense presently in the case.

> ○ *Example #4.* P sues D for personal injuries, alleging that she was injured by D's negligence. She seeks compensatory damages of $100,000. P wants discovery concerning D's net worth. Is the requested information discoverable?

The answer is no, because the information is not relevant to a claim or defense in the case. P seeks compensatory damages. Such damages are intended to compensate the plaintiff for harm caused. Whether D has $1 or $1,000,000 in the bank does not affect the calculation of how much money is needed to make P whole.[53]

> ○ *Example #5.* P sues D for personal injuries allegedly caused by D's wanton conduct and for punitive damages, which are permitted under applicable law for wantonly caused harm. She seeks compensatory damages of $100,000 and punitive damages of $1,000,000. P wants to discover information concerning D's net worth. Is the requested information discoverable?

Here the answer should be yes, because D's net worth is relevant to the question of punitive damages. Such damages are intended to punish a defendant for egregious conduct. They simply cannot be assessed

---

Previously, waiver was deemed to extend not just to the document in question, but to all materials dealing with the same subject matter.

[52]Fed. R. Evid. 401.

[53]*See, e.g.,* Henderson v. Zurn, 131 F.R.D. 560, 562 (S.D. Ind. 1990) (because the financial status of defendant is irrelevant to compensatory damages, defendant's tax returns are not relevant). *But see* Baker v. CNA Ins. Co., 123 F.R.D. 322, 329-330 (D. Mont. 1988) (permitting discovery in similar circumstances).

without knowing the defendant's net worth; it would take a far larger punitive damages award to punish a billionaire than it would to punish someone of modest means. Until the court knows the net worth of the defendant, it cannot know how large a punitive damages award will suffice.[54]

Though discovery is thus limited to information that is relevant to a claim or defense, the concept of relevance is broader in discovery than in assessing whether evidence is admissible at trial. Detailed discussion of admissibility is beyond our scope (it is studied in Evidence). For present purposes, it is sufficient to know that there are limits on what evidence may be presented for consideration by the fact-finder at trial. One restriction relates to "hearsay," which is information that the witness (the person testifying at trial) has encountered, but that she did not observe or otherwise perceive firsthand. Suppose, for instance, a friend tells you that she saw your roommate cheat on an exam. If you relate that information to someone, your report is hearsay. It may be true, but you don't know it to be true; you have no independent knowledge on the subject. The general rule is that hearsay evidence is not admissible at trial. (The rule is subject, though, to a startling number of exceptions.)

For decades, Rule 26 provided that material was discoverable if it was "reasonably calculated to lead to the discovery of admissible evidence." This language was deleted from the Rule in 2015. The Sixth Circuit has concluded that this change was intended to limit discovery by emphasizing "proportionality" (discussed in the next subsection).[55] Still, the last sentence of Rule 26(b)(1) provides that information within the scope of discovery "need not be admissible in evidence to be discoverable." Thus, "discoverable" continues to be broader than "admissible."

- o ***Example #6.*** In an automobile collision case, W could testify at trial that she heard brakes screech shortly before hearing the sound of the collision. The evidence is admissible because it is within W's personal perception: She heard it. But W could not testify at trial that her boyfriend told her that he had heard the sound of screeching brakes immediately before the collision. That evidence is hearsay; she is testifying

---

[54]*See, e.g.,* Caruso v. Coleman Co., 157 F.R.D. 344, 348 (E.D. Pa. 1994). Most courts, like the one in *Caruso,* permit discovery even in the absence of a *prima facie* showing that the circumstances exist for the imposition of punitive damages. Though some courts delay discovery until liability for punitive damages has been established, the relevant point is the same: A claim for punitive damages implicates the defendant's net worth.

[55]Helena Agri-Enterprises, LLC v. Great Lakes Grain, LLC, 988 F.3d 260, 273-274 (6th Cir. 2021) (increased emphasis on proportionality was a reaction to expense of discovery).

about something someone told her, and not about something she perceived.

Nonetheless, *W*'s hearsay testimony is likely *discoverable*. Learning
this hearsay will alert the parties to follow up with witnesses who were
in a position to hear the screeching brakes. It would also give them something relevant to ask the parties to the accident. It is relevant to a claim
or defense in the case, so a party can ask *W* (in a deposition, for instance)
about her boyfriend's telling her what he had heard.[56]

> o ***Example #7.*** *P* sues *D*, her supervisor at work, for sexual harassment.
> She seeks discovery of evaluations of *D* as a supervisor at different
> times, when *D* oversaw other employees.

Though this evidence is probably not admissible to show sexual
harassment of *P*, it is likely discoverable.[57]

"Proportional to the Needs of the Case." Finally, discovery is
permissible only if the requested material is proportional to the needs
of the case. Until 2015, the concept of proportionality was not part
of the definition of discoverability in Rule 26(b)(1). Instead, it was a
concept by which the court could step in and limit discovery of relevant, nonprivileged information. With that change, proportionality
moved from being a filter that the court might invoke to limit discovery to a factor the parties must weigh when they seek discovery.[58]
Though many plaintiff's lawyers criticized (and defendant's lawyers
embraced) this change as limiting discovery, in practice, it is not clear
that the change has had much impact on discovery practice.[59]

---

[56]Another example may be the requirement in Rule 26(a)(1)(A)(iv) that a defendant
divulge (in required disclosures) the amount of insurance coverage she has for the
claims asserted against her. The existence of insurance is not admissible at trial but,
obviously, is subject to discovery, even without a showing that it would lead to discovery of admissible evidence.

[57]*See* Jones v. Commander, Kansas Army Ammunitions Plant, 147 F.R.D. 248, 251
(D. Kan. 1993).

[58]There was a widespread sense before 2015 that courts had not used proportionality as an effective filter. *See* Redish & McNamara, note 1 above, at 781 ("has not proven
to be an effective limitation on the scope or costs of discovery"). The 2015 amendment
is based on the presumption that making proportionality a part of the definition of
what may be discovered will force parties to police themselves on this score.

[59]*See, e.g.,* Robert H. Klonoff, *Application of the New "Proportionality" Discovery
Rule in Class Actions: Much Ado About Nothing,* 71 Vand. L. Rev. 1949, 1991 (2018)
("The class action discovery cases do not support the hysteria by the plaintiffs' bar or
the euphoria by the defense bar. At least in the class action context, the proportionality
amendment thus far does not appear to have had a major impact."); Adam N. Steinman,
The End of an Era? Federal Civil Procedure After the 2015 Amendments, 66 Emory L.J.
1, 4 (2016) (nothing in text, structure, or advisory committee notes concerning proportionality suggests restriction of discovery). *See also* Linda Sandstrom Simard, *Seeking*

Remember that the responding party generally must pay to produce the information requested in discovery.[60] The idea of proportionality is simple enough: One does not necessarily have a right to discover *all* relevant, nonprivileged material. Parties are now under an obligation, under Rule 26(b)(1), to limit their requests to what will be proportional to the case. The Rule sets out various factors as relevant in assessing proportionality:

- the importance of the issues at stake in the action,
- the amount in controversy,
- the parties' relative access to relevant information,
- the parties' resources,
- the importance of discovery in resolving the issues, and
- whether the burden or expense of the proposed discovery outweighs its likely benefit.[61]

Clearly, a party should not seek cumulative or duplicative discovery. In a case decided before the 2015 amendments, but which should come out the same way today, when material already produced contained sufficient information to determine whether there was ethnic bias against a group of employees, the court refused to require the defendant employer to review 1,700 personnel files for additional information.[62] And though the Rule no longer says so with regard to proportionality, discovery may be unnecessary if the same information can be obtained from another source (perhaps a governmental source) less expensively or more conveniently.

The factors listed in considering proportionality make clear that the trial judge has considerable discretion in determining the scope of discovery. Of course, the judge would rather not be involved. The hope is that the parties will take the proportionality portion of Rule 26(b)(1) seriously and limit their requests accordingly. But when a court becomes involved, Rule 26(b)(2)(C) becomes relevant and specifically permits the court to "limit the frequency or extent of discovery" if the court finds that the discovery sought is unreasonably cumulative, can

---

Proportional Discovery: The Beginning of the End of Procedural Uniformity, 71 Vand. L. Rev. 1919, 1927 (2018) (2015 proportionality amendment "is a head-scratching solution to an ill-defined problem.").

[60]See note 1 and accompanying text above.

[61]Until 2015, the concept of proportionality required the court to limit discovery for any of three reasons: (1) the requests were cumulative or duplicative, (2) the propounding party had some other opportunity to obtain the information, or (3) the burden or expense would outweigh the likely benefit. The present version retains the latter verbatim and is certainly broad enough to encompass the first two as well. Indeed, should the court become involved, Rule 26(b)(2)(C) permits the court to limit discovery based on such factors.

[62]Aramburu v. Boeing Co., 885 F. Supp. 1434, 1444 (D. Kan. 1995).

be obtained less burdensomely from another source, or, of course, if the proposed discovery does not fall within the scope permitted by Rule 26(b)(1).

§8.3.2   Electronically Stored Information (ESI)

Drafters of the Federal Rules have had to adjust to technological change. The big issue in recent years has been discovery of ESI. The Internet, smartphones, CDs, optical scanners, e-mail, instant messaging, fitness trackers, Snapchat, and other staples of contemporary daily life have been a blessing and a curse in litigation. They are a blessing because digital search capacity obviates the need to go through thousands of documents by hand and to travel to the physical site of the materials. They are a curse, however, because they vastly expand the universe of discoverable material and because they can be ephemeral. Modern technology exacerbates an ever-present clash of policies: the search for the truth versus the potential for abuse and excessive expense. Ultimately, the judge must lead the way in striking the right balance in each case.

The Federal Rules address ESI in several provisions. As we saw in §8.2.2, initial required disclosures under Rule 26(a)(1) require a party to identify ESI (and other materials) containing relevant information. We saw in §8.2.3 that ESI is relevant to various discovery devices. Under Rule 33(d), for instance, a party responding to an interrogatory can refer the requesting party to business records to find the answer; business records include ESI. Rule 34 includes ESI as a form of discovery, and the requesting party, under Rule 34(b)(1)(C), "may specify the form or forms in which electronically stored information is to be produced." At their Rule 26(f) conference (see §8.5), the parties must discuss various topics, including the disclosure and discovery of ESI. Here we address a major issue: the problem of ESI that has been deleted from servers and can be recovered only with great effort or expense; such ESI is referred to as "inaccessible."

The leading case concerning retrieving inaccessible ESI is *Zubulake v. UBS Warburg LLC*.[63] There, an equities trader (who had been making $650,000 a year) sued her erstwhile employer for gender discrimination. She sought discovery of e-mails concerning her employment written by five employees, including her supervisors. The e-mails had been deleted and could be recovered only from backup tapes. Ninety-four tapes had responsive e-mails. As a sample, the court ordered the

---

[63]216 F.R.D. 280 (S.D.N.Y. 2003). This opinion is known as *"Zubulake III"* and was one of several published opinions in this long-running litigation.

defendant to have five of them restored, which produced some 600 discoverable e-mails. The cost of restoring the five tapes was over $19,000. The expense of restoring the remaining 89 tapes was estimated to be $273,000. Ordinarily, as we've seen, the cost of complying with discovery requests is borne by the responding party.[64] Defendant, facing this remarkable expense, sought an order shifting the cost to the plaintiff. The court found that the backup tapes were not reasonably accessible and that the plaintiff had shown good cause to get access to them. It then set out a seven-factor test[65] and concluded that the plaintiff should bear 25 percent of the cost of retrieving the e-mails from the backup files.

The *Zubulake* situation is now addressed by Rule 26(b)(2)(B), which was amended to its present form after that case was decided. The provision is best understood as setting up three steps, with shifting burdens:

- ○ First, the responding party objects to discovery on the basis that the sources she identifies are "not reasonably accessible because of undue burden or cost" (e.g., because the ESI must be retrieved from backup tapes). Unless the responding party establishes that the ESI is not reasonably accessible, she must pay to produce it; there will be no cost shifting to the requesting party.[66]
- ○ Second, the party requesting the information may respond by showing good cause for the discovery notwithstanding the expense or burden. In assessing this step, the advisory committee notes to Rule 26(b)(2)(B) list seven factors that clearly resemble the *Zubulake* factors.[67]
- ○ Third, the court may then order discovery, subject to conditions, including an order of cost shifting: that the responding party must produce the information, but that the expense of doing so be shared between the parties (in a percentage set by the court).

[64]See note 1 above and accompanying text above.

[65]The factors were: (1) the extent to which the request is specifically tailored, (2) the availability of such information from other sources, (3) the total cost of production compared to the amount in controversy, (4) the cost of production compared to the resources available to each party, (5) the relative ability of each party to control costs, (6) the importance of the issues at stake, and (7) the relative benefits to the parties in obtaining the information. *Zubulake,* 216 F.R.D. at 284.

[66]*See, e.g.*, Peskoff v. Faber, 244 F.R.D. 54, 62 (D.D.C. 2007) ("[C]ost-shifting does not even become a possibility unless there is first a showing of inaccessibility").

[67]The advisory committee's (non-exclusive) factors are: (1) the specificity of the discovery request; (2) the quantity of information available from other and more easily accessed sources; (3) the failure to produce relevant information that seems likely to have existed but is no longer available on more easily accessed sources; (4) the likelihood of finding relevant, responsive information that cannot be obtained from other, more easily accessed sources; (5) predictions as to the importance and usefulness of the further information; (6) the importance of the issues at stake in the litigation; and (7) the parties' resources.

In applying the provision, the court is to apply the proportionality factors of Rule 26(b)(1) (discussed in "Proportional to the Needs of the Case" in the preceding section). In addition, in all cases (involving ESI or other material), the court may limit discovery under Rule 26(b)(2)(C) (discussed in the last paragraph of the preceding section). Some courts continue to rely on the *Zubulake* factors in considering whether to order cost shifting.[68]

Rule 26(b)(2)(B), dealing with "inaccessible" ESI, is distinguished from Rule 37(e), which concerns cases in which ESI is truly lost and cannot be retrieved. We discuss that provision in §8.4.3.

§8.3.3   Work Product

In §8.3.1, we saw that the law of privilege protects confidential communications between particular people. The law also affords protection for "work product." We should speak of a work product "protection" and not a work product "privilege." Work product protection is different from privilege in two important ways: (1) it does not necessarily consist of confidential communications, and (2) its protection is often not absolute. The concept of work product in federal court is governed by Rule 26(b)(3), which, interestingly, does not use the term. Instead, it refers to "trial preparation materials."[69] Notwithstanding the language used in the Rule, just about everybody calls it *"work product."*

What is it? Rule 26(b)(3)(A) defines work product as "documents and tangible things that are prepared in anticipation of litigation or for trial." Why should such materials be protected from discovery? The Supreme Court discussed the issue in the famous case of *Hickman v. Taylor*,[70] which established the common law rules concerning work product, before the Federal Rules addressed the topic. The case involved the sinking of a tug boat that was towing a car ferry across the Delaware River near Philadelphia. Five of the nine crew members of the tug drowned. Shortly after the disaster, the owners of the tug (and their insurance company) employed a lawyer named Fortenbaugh to defend them against potential suits for wrongful death and to sue the railroad for which the tug was pulling the car ferry. Fortenbaugh interviewed the surviving crew members and had

[68]*See, e.g.,* Hawa v. Coatesville Area Sch. Dist., 2017 WL 1021026 at *2 (E.D. Pa. 2017). Those factors are set out three footnotes above this one.

[69]This title is misleadingly narrow. The protection covers materials generated in anticipation of *litigation*, not of *trial*. As we see in Chapter 9, very few cases that start in the litigation stream (by filing of the complaint) end up in trial.

[70]329 U.S. 495 (1947).

their statements recorded and signed.[71] In a wrongful death action against the tug owners and the railroad, brought by relatives of one of the crew members who drowned, the plaintiff attempted to discover the witness statements taken by Fortenbaugh.[72]

Everyone agreed that the statements were not protected by the attorney-client privilege, because they were not confidential communications between a lawyer and her client. They were conversations between Fortenbaugh and third parties. Because at the time there was no Federal Rule concerning work product, the plaintiff argued that the materials were not protected and thus were discoverable. The Supreme Court disagreed. While recognizing the Federal Rules' policy of liberal discovery, the Court found a countervailing policy protecting material prepared "with an eye toward . . . anticipated litigation."[73] Such material "falls outside the arena of discovery and contravenes the public policy underlying the orderly prosecution and defense of legal claims. Not even the most liberal of discovery theories can justify unwarranted inquiries into the files and the mental impressions of an attorney."[74] Absent a showing of necessity, or that "denial of such production would unduly prejudice the preparation of [a party's] case or cause him any hardship or injustice," a court should not permit discovery of such material.[75]

Hickman v. Taylor led to the adoption of Rule 26(b)(3), which now governs the topic in federal court. States have adopted work product provisions by statute or rule of court; they can vary from state to state. We focus on Rule 26(b)(3). For starters, work product consists of materials "prepared in anticipation of litigation or for trial." That phrase is important. Work product must be generated, in the words of *Hickman v. Taylor*, "with an eye toward litigation," even if no case has yet been filed. So long as the party-to-be prepares the material *because she anticipates that there will be litigation*, this requirement is met. On the other hand, "materials assembled in the ordinary course of business, or pursuant to public requirements unrelated to litigation, or for other nonlitigation purposes" are not protected.[76] Accordingly, if a

---

[71]These witness statements were informal; they were not depositions.

[72]There was a serious problem with the effort to get *any* information from Fortenbaugh. The plaintiff sought information from him through an interrogatory asking for the content of the witness statements. As we saw in §8.2.2, interrogatories cannot be used to get information from nonparties. Fortenbaugh was not a party and thus could not have been subject to any discovery by interrogatory. The Supreme Court noted this fact, but, under the circumstances, "deem[ed] it unnecessary and unwise to rest [its] decision upon this procedural irregularity." 329 U.S. at 505. Because the issue of work product protection was so important, the Court went on to address it.

[73]329 U.S. at 498.

[74]*Id.* at 510.

[75]*Id.* at 509.

[76]Fed. R. Civ. P. 26(b)(3), advisory committee's note (1970).

manufacturer routinely creates a report about each accident involving one of its products, those reports (at least in some courts) might not be protected as work product.[77]

Rule 26(b)(3)(A) provides that "[o]rdinarily, a party may not discover" work product. The starting point is clear: Once we identify something as work product, it is protected from discovery.[78] This rule avoids a free-rider problem. If Party *A* engages in investigation in anticipation of litigation (like the investigation done by Fortenbaugh in *Hickman v. Taylor*), Party *B* should not be able to gain access to it. To allow Party *B* easy access to the material would reward freeloading. If Party *B* wants the benefit of investigation, she should do her own investigation (or hire someone to investigate).[79] As with privilege, Rule 26(b)(5)(A) places the burden on the party asserting work product protection to raise the claim "expressly" and to describe the material in a way that enables others to assess the claim. She will do this by preparing a "privilege log."[80] Failure to assert work product properly can result in waiving the protection. On the other hand, the liberal provisions for avoiding waiver by inadvertent disclosure,[81] which we saw when discussing privilege, apply here as well.

According to Rule 26(b)(3)(A), work product consists of "documents and tangible things" prepared in anticipation of litigation. Technically, this language would seem to allow Party *B* to send interrogatories to

---

[77]*See, e.g.*, Soeder v. General Dynamics Corp., 90 F.R.D. 253, 255 (D. Nev. 1980). This interpretation seems overly narrow, since accidents lead almost inevitably to litigation. In another case, a consumer complained to a manufacturer that its product was defective. The manufacturer generated internal memoranda discussing the possible defect in the product. Later, the consumer sued the manufacturer. The court permitted discovery of the memoranda and held that they were prepared in an effort to maintain good customer relations and not with an eye toward litigation. Scott Paper Co. v. Ceilcote Co., 103 F.R.D. 591, 596 (D. Me. 1984). Another court drew the distinction between investigating the *accident* (which does not create work product) and investigating a potential *claim* (which does). Spaulding v. Denton, 68 F.R.D. 342, 346 (D. Del. 1975). Such decisions reflect the fact that work product protection (like privileges) thwart the truth-finding function of litigation and thus will be interpreted narrowly.

[78]Noting that work product protection robs the parties of useful information, Professor Thornburg has concluded that this cost outweighs its benefits. Elizabeth Thornburg, *Rethinking Work Product*, 77 Va. L. Rev. 1515 (1991).

[79]While a professor at the University of Chicago (before he became a judge on the Seventh Circuit), Frank Easterbrook questioned whether we ought to encourage independent investigation by all parties. "To say . . . that a restriction of the scope of the attorney-client and work product privileges would reduce the investment in information in litigation may be to praise that result, not to condemn it." Frank Easterbrook, *Insider Trading, Secret Agents, Evidentiary Privileges, and the Production of Information*, 1981 Sup. Ct. Rev. 309, 361.

[80]We discussed this with regard to the assertion of privilege at note 53 and accompanying text above.

[81]See notes 50 and 51 and accompanying text above.

Party *A* in which she asks about the content of interviews with witnesses. After all, the interrogatory does not seek the discovery of the document or tangible thing. Courts have long rejected such an end-run around work product protection. As one court explained shortly after the adoption of Rule 26(b)(3), the "discovery of a detailed description of the contents of documents through interrogatories is equivalent to discovery of the documents themselves" and should not be permitted.[82]

Under Rule 26(b)(3)(A)(ii), the work product protection can be overcome if the party seeking the information (Party *B* in our example) shows two things: (1) "substantial need for the materials to prepare [her] case" and (2) that she "cannot, without undue hardship, obtain their substantial equivalent by other means."[83] In other words, she needs this material and basically cannot get it elsewhere. In such circumstances, the protection is overcome and the material is discoverable (this is known as "conditional work product"). This rule makes sense because, if Party *B* can make that showing, there is no danger of her being a freeloader.

> ○ ***Example #8.*** After an accident, and in anticipation of litigation concerning the accident, *A*'s agent investigates the accident scene and interviews Joe, who was a witness to the accident. *A*'s agent records Joe's statement. Suppose *B* sues *A* concerning the litigation and seeks discovery of Joe's statement.

The statement is work product, because it was prepared in anticipation of litigation, so (assuming *A* asserts the protection) *B* cannot get it. If *B* wants information from Joe, *B* can interview Joe or take his deposition.

> ○ ***Example #9.*** Suppose, though, that Joe is unavailable. He is a citizen of Brazil and has returned home. Now *B* will be able to overcome *A*'s work product protection.

First, *B* has substantial need of Joe's statement, because he was a witness. Second, she is unable without undue hardship (traveling to Brazil and finding Joe) to obtain the information. Thus, the court will likely order *A* to produce the statement for *B*. It is work product, but *B* has overcome the protection ordinarily accorded it by invoking the exception to work product.

---

[82]Peterson v. United States, 52 F.R.D. 317, 320 (S.D. Ill. 1971).

[83]Rule 26(b)(3)(A)(i) simply says that the material sought must be discoverable under Rule 26(b)(1), which means that it is relevant and not privileged, as we saw in §8.3.1.

Some types of work product, however, appear to be absolutely protected. Rule 26(b)(3)(B) provides that the court, in ordering the production of materials as to which the exception to work product has been invoked, "must protect against disclosure" of certain things: "mental impressions, conclusions, opinions, or legal theories." Many lawyers and judges refer to such matter as "opinion work product," which is a fine shorthand as long as we remember that the quoted list covers more than opinions. The directive that the court "must protect against disclosure" of such materials seems absolute, and some courts have concluded that no showing can overcome the protection.[84] On the other hand, other courts will permit discovery of opinion work product, but only on a showing of extraordinary circumstances.[85]

If a single document contains discoverable work product (such as Joe's witness statement) and nondiscoverable work product (such as a conclusion of counsel that Joe seems trustworthy and would be a good witness at trial), the court should order production with the nondiscoverable material redacted. That means the protected material would be blocked out from the copy given to the party seeking discovery.

Importantly, work product under Rule 26(b)(3) is *not* limited to material generated by a lawyer. Many people refer to this topic as "attorney work product,"[86] which is inaccurate.[87] Rule 26(b)(3)(A) protects material generated in anticipation of litigation "by or for [a] party or its representative (including [her] attorney, consultant, surety, indemnitor, insurer, or agent)." This language is quite broad. Work product can be generated by a party's attorney *but need not be.* So long as it is generated in anticipation of litigation—by the party herself, her lawyer, her private investigator, her insurer, or any other agent of hers—it is protected under Rule 26(b)(3)(A). Even "opinion work product," consisting of things like legal theories, need not be generated by a lawyer.

---

[84]*See, e.g.*, In re Grand Jury Investigation, 412 F. Supp. 943, 949 (E.D. Pa. 1976).

[85]*See, e.g.*, Loftis v. Amica Mut. Ins. Co., 175 F.R.D. 5, 11-12 (D. Conn. 1997) (discovery of opinion work product is not favored and is permissible only in extraordinary cases). It seems clear that a party waives opinion work product by putting those opinions directly in issue in the litigation, as by designating the person who made the opinions an expert witness. *See, e.g.*, Minnestoa Specialty Crops, Inc. v. Minnesota Wild Hockey Club, L.P., 210 F.R.D. 673, 677 (D. Minn. 2002); Hager v. Bluefield Reg'l Med. Ctr., Inc., 170 F.R.D. 70, 78 (D.D.C. 1997). Such cases are rare.

[86]They may get this term from *Hickman v. Taylor*, which discussed work product created by a lawyer and thus used the term *attorney work product.*

[87]Rule 26(b)(3), like all Federal Rules, applies only in federal courts. States are free to define work product in any way they like, or, alternatively, not to protect work product at all. *See, e.g.*, Pa. R. Civ. P. 4003.3 (permitting discovery of most materials prepared in anticipation of litigation). States may limit the concept of opinion work product to materials generated by lawyers. In California, for instance, work product must be generated by an attorney or her agent. Cal. Code Civ. Proc. §2018.020.

Rule 26(b)(3)(B) plainly provides protection for opinion work product generated by "the attorney or *other representative*."

There are two items that may, under the facts of a case, seem like work product but are not. First, Rule 26(b)(3)(C) gives anyone (regardless of whether she is a party) a right to obtain her "own previous statement about the action or its subject matter."

> ○ ***Example #10.*** After a car wreck between *A* and *B*, *A* asks *B* if she is hurt and what happened. *A* videorecords *B*'s response on her smartphone. When litigation is filed between them, *B* serves a request to produce on *A* asking for the video. *A* cannot claim that the video is protected as work product. Rule 26(b)(3)(C) gives *B* a right to her previous statement.

Second, until 2015, Rule 26(b)(1) specifically permitted discovery of "the existence, description, nature, custody, condition, and location of any documents and other tangible things and the identity and location of persons who know of any discoverable matter." This phrase was omitted in the 2015 amendment to the Rule. The advisory committee notes make clear, however, that the deletion was not intended to change the practice.[88] Thus, if one party undertakes to learn the identities of witnesses to a relevant event, the other party may discover those identities.

Finally, Rule 26(b)(4) expressly applies work product protection to draft reports by and communications with expert witnesses. These changes are discussed in the next section.

§8.3.4 Consulting Experts and Expert Witnesses

Experts are people with specialized training or knowledge who often bring that expertise to bear in litigation. Experts are used in two ways in litigation. First is the "consulting expert," who is hired to assist the lawyer in preparing and monitoring a case. In a medical malpractice case, for instance, both sides might find it helpful to have a medical expert behind the scenes with whom to consult as the case unfolds. Second is the "expert witness," who will testify at trial on behalf of the party. Expert witnesses, unlike lay witnesses, are entitled to testify as to their opinions. Expert witnesses are hired to give their professional opinions.[89]

---

[88]Fed. R. Civ. Pro. 26(b)(1), advisory committee note (2015) ("Discovery of such matters is so deeply entrenched in practice that it is no longer necessary to clutter the long text of Rule 26 with these examples").

[89]See note 13 and accompanying text above.

Discovery concerning expert witnesses is handled by required disclosure under Rule 26(a)(2). We discussed this in §8.2.1. We saw there that the party must provide information concerning experts retained to testify at trial. In addition, certain expert witnesses (those retained specially for this case or employees of a party who routinely give expert testimony in litigation) must provide a detailed report. But Rule 26(b)(4) *also* applies to expert witnesses. It does four things.

First, Rule 26(b)(4)(A) gives parties a right to take the deposition of any expert witness identified through Rule 26(a)(2) (assuming she has produced the written report (if required)).

Second, Rule 26(b)(4)(E) provides that the party seeking discovery of an expert witness (most commonly, taking her deposition) generally must pay a reasonable fee to the expert for her time spent responding to the discovery request.

Third, Rule 26(b)(4)(D) addresses experts "retained or specially employed . . . in anticipation of litigation or to prepare for trial" but who are *not* expected to testify at trial — in other words, the consulting expert.[90] The Rule states a long-standing general rule that there will be no discovery of "facts known or opinions held"[91] by such a person. This makes sense. Because this expert is not going to testify, and therefore cannot influence the jury, it is not clear why the other party should be concerned with her opinions. On the other hand, the Rule permits discovery in "exceptional circumstances." This is a high burden and courts are reluctant to find that it is satisfied.[92] Among the rare fact patterns that might satisfy it is a case in which a consulting expert

[90]The Rule does not apply to experts who are consulted informally but not "retained or specially employed," even if the informal consultation concerned the litigation at issue. If the expert is informally consulted, there can be no discovery (not even of her identity). Ager v. Jane C. Stormont Hosp. & Training School for Nurses, 622 F.2d 496, 501 (10th Cir. 1980). Courts have looked to various factors to determine whether an expert was retained or merely informally consulted, including the manner in which the consultation was initiated, the extent of information or material provided to the expert, and the duration of the relationship. *Id.*

[91]The Rule speaks of facts and opinions, but does not impose any special requirement for discovery of the consulting expert's *name*. Some courts have permitted the discovery of the consulting expert's identity without any special showing. *See, e.g.,* Roesberg v. Johns-Manville Corp., 85 F.R.D. 292, 303 (E.D. Pa. 1980). But if the identity of consulting experts were freely discoverable, the protection accorded by this Rule would be illusory. A party could simply ask another party to identify any experts consulted but who will not be testifying at trial. Armed with the expert's identity, the discovering party could then simply talk to that expert or take her deposition. Accordingly, the better view is that a showing of "exceptional circumstances" must be made even to gain discovery of the consultant's identity, as well as her facts known and opinions held. *See Ager,* 622 F.2d at 502-504.

[92]Wright & Kane, Federal Courts 586 ("Most cases have refused to find the exceptional circumstances that will justify this discovery").

examined a machine or piece of equipment before it was destroyed or lost or rendered inoperative. The information from the consulting expert's tests might be discoverable because there is no other way other parties can gain access to such information.[93]

Fourth, and most importantly, Rule 26(b)(4)(B) and (C) extend work product protection to two things: (1) drafts of reports and disclosures under Rule 26(a)(2) and (2) communication between a party's lawyer and an expert witness who was required to produce a written report under Rule 26(a)(2)(B).

Before Rule 26(b)(4)(B) and (C) extended work product protection, drafts of an expert witness's Rule 26(a)(2) report and communications between her and the party's lawyer generally were discoverable. Accordingly, the lawyer would be less likely to share facts with the expert witness that might be risky to the party's position. That is where consulting experts came in. Because generally there is no discovery of facts known or opinions held by consulting experts, a lawyer would hire such a person and could talk freely. The lawyer could relate hypotheticals to the consultant and ask for opinions, even on risky scenarios, without fear of discovery. Then, having mapped out the exact contours of her position, the lawyer would retain a separate expert—the expert witness—who would testify at trial. And the lawyer would relate to the expert witness only a narrow, nonrisky, set of facts.

Now, things are different. Because Rule 26(b)(4)(B) and (C) extend work product protection to drafts by expert witnesses and to communications between such witnesses and the party's lawyer, there is no need to hire a separate consulting expert. The lawyer can run through all scenarios with the expert, knowing that their communications and the drafts of the expert's report are protected.

§8.3.5 Protective Orders

As we have seen, the Federal Rules envision broad discovery. If the parties know each others' contentions and the facts, they can, in theory, either resolve their differences without trial or focus on truly disputed facts and streamline the adjudication. On the other hand, discovery imposes burden and expense, and can be very intrusive. That is why the Rules place presumptive limits on the number of depositions and interrogatories (see §8.2.4), impose a certification requirement in Rule 26(g) (see §8.4.3), and require the parties to make only proportional requests (see §8.3.1).

---

[93]*See Ager*, 622 F.2d at 503 n.8 (giving this example).

The Rules also reflect concern about discovery costs by allowing the judge, in the context of each case, to protect parties (or nonparties from whom discovery is sought) from overly expensive and overly intrusive discovery. Rule 26(c)(1) permits the judge to enter a "protective order" to shield the responding party from "annoyance, embarrassment, oppression, or undue burden or expense." The Rule details eight situations in which protective orders might be appropriate. This list is not exhaustive, though, and the court has great discretion in fashioning protective orders.

Rule 26(c) does not permit the judge to exempt parties from discovery or to rewrite the discovery provisions. But it does permit her to protect parties from overzealous discovery efforts. It also provides the responding party with a choice of how to proceed.

> o ***Example #11.*** Party *A* serves upon Party *B* a request to produce, seeking documents covering a period far greater than necessary for discovery of relevant material. Party *B* may move for a protective order under Rule 26(c)(1) because the request is overburdensome. She must certify that she has endeavored in good faith to confer with other parties to resolve the dispute without court involvement. Party *A* may oppose the motion, and the court will decide whether Party *B* must respond and, if so, to how much. It may enter a protective order limiting the time frame for which Party *B* must respond.
>
> o ***Example #12.*** As an alternative, Party *B* may object under Rule 34(b)(2)(B). If Party *A* disagrees with the assertion that the request is overburdensome, she will make a motion to compel the discovery (see §8.4). At the hearing on that motion, the court will determine whether the request was overburdensome and, if so, what materials are appropriately discoverable.

In rare cases, the court might enter a protective order under Rule 26(c)(1)(E) that discovery proceed with only limited persons present. For instance, suppose a party will take the deposition of a child. The court might limit the number of persons in the room in an effort to make the child more comfortable. In other cases, the court may, under Rule 26(c)(1)(D), limit the scope of discovery to ensure that a deponent or party is not badgered or embarrassed. Again, however, the court must weigh the need to protect with the duty to permit discovery as envisioned by the discovery provisions.

In one situation, under Rule 37(d)(2), seeking a protective order is the only recourse available. Specifically, a party who fails completely to respond to a notice of her own deposition, to respond to interrogatories, or to respond to a request to produce cannot assert that the discovery was objectionable unless she moved for a protective order before failing to provide the discovery.

What we have discussed so far is the use of a protective order to avoid or limit discovery. Protective orders may instead be aimed at limiting the *dissemination* of information gleaned in discovery. An example is trade secrets. These include secret formulae, such as those for Coca-Cola™ or the recipe for Kentucky Fried Chicken.™ Businesses do not patent such things, because patents are effective for only a limited period. By retaining them as trade secrets, companies seek to use the secrets forever. If discovery is proper, however, the company may be compelled to produce the information. The court might, under Rule 26(c)(1)(G), order that disclosure be made only for purposes of litigation and in ways that protect competitive advantage.[94]

§8.4 Sanctions for Discovery Abuse

The Federal Rules have always envisioned that parties will cooperate and conduct discovery in good faith. Within the relatively broad confines of the scheduling provisions (discussed in §8.5) and with the exception of required disclosures (discussed in §8.2.1), the parties have considerable leeway to determine what discovery tools to use and when to use them. They also have the responsibility to play by the rules. Rule 37 is the repository of most of the court's tools to ensure that the parties to abide by the discovery rules. In general, as Rule 37(a)(2) makes clear, sanctions against a party are to be sought in the court in which the action is pending, while sanctions against nonparties are sought in the court for the district in which discovery was sought. As to depositions, interrogatories, and requests to produce, problems with discovery will be addressed either by what we will call "one-step" or "two-step" sanctions. (The other discovery tools (medical exams and requests to admit) have specialized sanction rules, discussed in §8.4.2.)

---

[94]On the other hand, there is a First Amendment right of access to judicial proceedings and to court documents. Because the scope of discovery is broader than the scope of admissibility at trial (see §8.3.1), it is possible that discovered material will not be presented at trial. If it is, however, it probably becomes public information. The extent of the First Amendment right in this regard is beyond our scope. *See generally* Seattle Times Co. v. Rhinehart, 467 U.S. 20, 31-36 (1984) (upholding protective order that newspaper not publish information produced in discovery concerning membership and contributions to organization).

§8.4.1   The One-Step Versus Two-Step Approach to Common Discovery Abuses

Rule 37 draws an important distinction between what we will call a *"partial failure"* to comply, on the one hand, and a *"total failure"* to comply, on the other.[95] For partial failures (defined below), the Rule envisions the parties going through two steps before the party failing to play by the rules is subject to significant sanctions. In contrast, a party guilty of a total failure to abide by the basic discovery provisions may be subject to the immediate imposition of serious sanctions.

Partial Failure and the First Step: The Motion to Compel

The partial failures to comply with the basic discovery provisions are listed in Rule 37(a)(3)(B) and consist of: (1) failure to answer a question at a deposition; (2) failure of an entity to designate a proper person for a deposition under Rule 30(b)(6); (3) failure to answer an interrogatory; and (4) failure to state in response to a request for production under Rule 34 that inspection will be permitted or to permit the actual inspection. We call these *partial failures* because the party did comply in part (maybe even for the most part). For instance, she might have answered every question at her deposition except one, or every interrogatory except one. Such situations are contrasted with situations in which the party simply does not respond.

> ○ ***Example #13.*** A party whose deposition is properly noticed shows up at the deposition. She answers some of the questions asked but refuses to answer others. Or a party on whom interrogatories are properly served answers some of the interrogatories, but not others. At most, these are partial failures: The party did respond, but not fully.

It is important to understand, though, that the failure to answer some of the questions might not be a "failure" at all. Sometimes, refusal to answer particular questions is justified. For example, perhaps the question would invade a privilege, calls for protected work product, or seeks other nondiscoverable information. In such situations, the party seeking discovery has no right to it, and the responding party has every right to refuse to answer and to raise the appropriate objection. But we will not know whether the responding party's claim of privilege or of work product (or other excuse) is justified until a court rules on the issue.

---

[95]Neither the Rules nor anyone else uses the terms *partial failure* and *total failure* as we use them here. This is just our shorthand way of distinguishing between different sets of sanctions.

How does the court get involved? Rule 37(a) makes it clear that the *only* sanction available at this stage for the partial failures listed above is a court order compelling the responding party to answer the unanswered questions. Thus, the party seeking discovery will make a motion to compel answers under Rule 37(a)(1). This Rule requires the moving party to certify to the court that she has tried in good faith to get the information without court involvement.[96] In briefing and arguing the motion, the responding party may try to convince the judge that the material is privileged, or not proportional to the needs of the case, or not relevant, or is otherwise protected from discovery. The court will consider the parties' contentions and rule, either granting or denying the motion to compel. The motion to compel discovery, then, is the first step in the two-step trip toward serious sanctions for failure to abide by the discovery provisions.

Along these lines, under Rule 37(a)(4), an evasive answer is treated as a failure to respond. Assume that a party, in her deposition testimony, hems and haws or is otherwise nonresponsive to a question. She has failed to respond to that question. Similarly, an incomplete answer to an interrogatory is treated as a failure to respond to that question. The party seeking discovery might make a motion to compel answers to these questions.

If the court grants the motion to compel, the party making the motion may be able to recover (from the other party) her expenses, including attorney's fees, incurred in making the motion.[97] The party against whom the order is entered is permitted to answer the unanswered questions. If she does so, the matter is resolved and the case moves on. Put another way, the sanction for a partial failure is an order to compel the party to answer the unanswered questions (and, perhaps, to pay the moving party's expenses and attorney's fees incurred in bringing the motion).

Partial Failures and the Second Step: Violation of the Order Compelling Responses

What happens, though, if a party disobeys an order under Rule 37(a) compelling her to answer questions? The answer is found in Rule 37(b)(2)(A), which permits the court to impose what many call "merits

---

[96]This requirement is aimed at forcing the parties to try to work out discovery squabbles before coming to court with them, and thus to cut down on the number of motions to compel discovery.

[97]This matter is controlled by Rule 37(a)(5)(A), which provides, *inter alia*, that the court may deny recovery of such expenses if the moving party failed to attempt to resolve the dispute without going to court or if the responding party's failure to respond to the question(s) was "substantially justified."

sanctions"[98] against the recalcitrant party. That Rule empowers the court to make orders that are "just," and sets forth a list of possibilities in Rule 37(b)(2)(A)(i) through (vii). One of these, found at Rule 37(b)(2)(A)(i), is an *establishment order,* which establishes facts as true for purposes of this litigation.

> ○ ***Example #14.*** Defendant claimed that she was not subject to personal jurisdiction. In interrogatories and in her deposition, Plaintiff asked Defendant about her contacts with the forum. Defendant refused to answer these questions. After the court ordered Defendant to answer, she still refused. As a sanction, the court may enter an order establishing that Defendant is subject to personal jurisdiction.[99]

Another possible merits sanction, under Rule 37(b)(2)(A)(ii), is to refuse to allow the disobedient party to introduce evidence at trial on issues relevant to the discovery. Under Rule 37(b)(2)(A)(iii), the court can strike the disobedient party's pleadings as to matters relating to the discovery. Rule 37(b)(2)(A)(v) and (vi) are the ultimate merits sanctions: dismissal against the plaintiff or default judgment against the defendant. These should be reserved for extreme cases, involving bad faith. We saw such involuntary dismissals at §7.4.2 and default judgment at §7.5.3.

In addition (or in lieu of the foregoing), Rule 37(b)(2)(A)(vii) permits the court to hold the recalcitrant party in contempt. A court has discretion to find a party in contempt anytime she violates a court order, which, of course, is the situation here because the party is violating an order compelling her to respond to discovery.[100] A contempt citation is appealable. See §§14.5.2, 14.6.

The court is not required to enter any of the listed merits sanctions. Under Rule 37(b)(2)(A)(iv), the judge may simply stay proceedings until the recalcitrant party complies with the earlier order compelling responses. The sanctions listed in Rule 37(b)(2)(A) are not exclusive. The matter is left to the judge's discretion. In any event, Rule 37(b)(2)(C) allows the court to require the responding party to pay expenses and attorney's fees of the moving party.

So, in the partial failure situations listed above, we go through two steps before a party can be subject to merits sanctions. First, there must be an order compelling her to answer the specific unanswered

---

[98]Merits sanctions, as opposed to monetary sanctions, are intended to have an impact on the merits of the case.

[99]Insurance Corp. of Ireland, Ltd. v. Compagnie des Bauxites de Guinee, 456 U.S. 694, 707-708 (1982).

[100]As Rule 37(b)(2)(A)(vii) makes clear, there is an exception: A party failing to submit to an ordered medical examination under Rule 35 cannot be held in contempt. We address sanctions regarding medical examinations in §8.4.2.

questions; that order is only appropriate if the responding party's excuse (such as a claim of privilege) is rejected or was not properly asserted. Second, only if the party against whom the order is entered violates the order compelling her to answer is she subject to merits sanctions (and possibly a contempt citation).

Total Failures and Sanctions

The "total failure" situation is addressed in Rule 37(d). Here, instead of simply refusing to answer one or more questions, the party is guilty of one of the misdeeds listed in Rule 37(d)(1)(A): (1) failure to appear for her deposition; (2) failure to serve answers or objections to interrogatories; or (3) failure to serve a written response to a request for production. In these situations, there is no need for the party seeking discovery to move for an order compelling discovery. Instead, she can move immediately for merits sanctions.

Rule 37(d)(3) incorporates by reference the sanctions we already saw at Rule 37(b)(2)(A), with one exception: It does not permit an order of contempt.[101] Why not? Because here, the recalcitrant party has not violated a court order. When we considered contempt as a sanction under Rule 37(b)(2)(A)(vii), it was because a party had violated a court order to respond to discovery.

The permitted sanctions, as we just saw, include the establishment order, refusal to allow the recalcitrant party to introduce evidence at trial, and striking her pleadings. In addition, under Rule 37(d)(3), the party sanctioned "must" be required to pay the expenses, including attorney's fees, that the other party incurred in seeking the sanctions (unless the failure was substantially justified or other circumstances make such an award unjust).

There are two other points to make with Rule 37(d). First, Rule 37(d)(1)(B) provides that if the failure concerned interrogatories or a request for production (not a deposition), the party seeking sanctions must certify that she tried in good faith to obtain the discovery without court intervention. The moving party need not make this certification if the other party did not show up for her deposition.[102]

Second, Rule 37(d)(2) tells us that the party failing to respond cannot escape sanctions by arguing that the discovery request was

---

[101]This is clear by the reference in Rule 37(d)(3) to the sanctions in Rule 37(b)(2)(A)(i) through (vi). This list omits Rule 37(b)(2)(A)(vii), which is the sanction of contempt.

[102]You must read Rule 37(d)(1)(B) carefully to catch this. It requires certification only when the motion for sanctions concerns "failing to answer or respond." This phrase refers to Rule 37(d)(1)(A)(ii), which addresses failure to answer interrogatories or to respond to a request for production. It does not apply to Rule 37(d)(1)(A)(i), which is aimed at failure to "appear" at a deposition.

objectionable. Rather, she must invoke her objection by seeking a protective order under Rule 26(c), which we discussed in §8.3.4. This is quite different from the partial failure situation under Rule 37(b). There, the responding party did respond to the discovery request, but not fully. That procedure is sufficient there because the party has made some response to the discovery request. In the total failure situation, in contrast, because the party from whom discovery is sought was a "no-show," the Rule places the burden on her to seek protection from the discovery request under Rule 26(c)(1).

§8.4.2   Specialized Sanctions

Required Disclosures

In §8.2.1, we discussed the Rule 26(a) required disclosures. Rule 37(a)(3)(A) deals with a party's failure "to make a disclosure required under Rule 26(a)." This provision is aimed at parties who file something as required disclosures, but whose disclosures are not complete. This situation is like the partial failure scenario discussed above. Under Rule 37(a)(3)(A), any other party may make a motion "to compel disclosure and for appropriate sanctions." The party making this motion to compel must certify that she has attempted to confer with the party failing to make the disclosures in an effort to resolve the issue without court involvement. If a party violates an order compelling her to make required disclosures, Rule 37(b)(2)(A) allows the court to enter merits sanctions, including contempt, as discussed in §8.4.1.

In addition, Rule 37(c)(1) addresses a party who "fails to provide information or identify a witness as required by Rule 26(a)." This provision deals with the total failure to provide any of the three required disclosures. The Rule provides that such a party will not be permitted to use at trial any evidence that should have been provided under Rule 26(a), unless the failure was substantially justified or is harmless.

In addition to that sanction, the court may, upon motion and upon affording the party an opportunity to be heard, impose other appropriate sanctions, including attorney's fees caused by the failure and including the merits sanctions listed in Rule 37(b)(2)(A)(i) through (vii). Further, at trial, the jury may be informed of the party's failure to abide by Rule 26(a). The incorporation of the listed sanctions from Rule 37(b)(2)(A) mirrors those for the total failure with regard to the discovery devices, discussed in §8.4.1. Because a party in this position will not have violated a court order at this point, contempt is not an available sanction.

Failure to Supplement

In §8.2.3, we saw that Rule 26(e) imposes a duty on parties, under certain circumstances, to supplement, correct, or amend their responses to various forms of discovery. What sanctions are available if a party fails to discharge this duty? Rule 37(c)(1) applies in this situation, just as it does when a party fails to make required disclosures. The sanctions are thus the same as those we saw in the two paragraphs preceding this one.

Medical Examination

In §8.2.2, we discussed Rule 35, which allows a court, upon proper showing by a party, to order another party or someone in that party's "custody or legal control" to undergo a medical examination. If a party is ordered to undergo an exam and fails to do so, she can incur sanctions under Rule 37(b)(2)(A).[103] That Rule provides for whatever sanctions the court considers just and lists specific merits sanctions from Rule 37(b)(2)(A)(i) through (vi). These, as we have seen, include an establishment order, an order refusing to allow that party to support or defend against claims by prohibiting the production of evidence at trial, and an order striking the disobedient party's pleadings. In addition, under Rule 37(b)(2)(C), the court can order the disobedient party to pay the moving party's expenses, including attorney's fees, that were incurred in seeking sanctions.

Rule 37(b)(2)(B) makes clear that a party who is ordered to produce for examination someone in her "custody or legal control," and who fails to do so, is subject to the same sanctions. She is excused, however, if she can show that she is unable to obey the order. Perhaps, for instance, the person ostensibly under her custody or legal control is out of the jurisdiction.

Because violation of a Rule 35 order involves failure to obey a court order, we would expect to find an order of contempt as an available sanction. On this score, however, Rule 37(b)(2)(A)(vii) expressly provides that contempt is not to be imposed as a sanction for failing to

---

[103]Rule 37(a)(1), which permits the party requesting discovery to move for an order compelling another party to respond, is not relevant in this situation. Under Rule 35, there is already a court order compelling the party to attend her medical exam (or to produce someone in her custody or legal control for a medical exam). Violation of that order invokes Rule 37(b)(2).

comply with an order to submit to a medical examination. And in listing sanctions for failure to produce someone in one's "custody or legal control" for a medical exam, Rule 37(b)(2)(B) does not include the sanction of contempt.[104]

Requests for Admission

In §8.2.2, we discussed Rule 36, which permits a party to require another party to admit discoverable matter. As we saw there, the responding party's failure to deny a request of this sort may be treated as an admission of the fact for purposes of the litigation.

What happens, though, if the responding party denies a request for admission, but the propounding party later establishes at trial that the matter was true? Rule 37(c)(2) provides that the party who propounded the request for admission may move for an order that the recalcitrant party "pay the reasonable expenses, including attorney's fees, incurred" in proving the issue at trial. If the moving party makes this showing, the court "must" make such an order, unless one of the factors listed in Rule 37(c)(2)(A) through (D) is satisfied. For example, such an order would be excused if the court finds that the party failing to admit had a reasonable ground to believe that it would prevail on that issue.

> ○ ***Example #15.*** *P* was injured when involved in a collision with a truck owned by *D*, Inc. The truck was being driven by *X. P* claims that *D*, Inc., is vicariously liable for the tort of *X*, and alleges that *P* was the agent of *D*, Inc., and was acting within the scope of her employment at the time of the collision. *D*, Inc., claims that *X* was not acting within the scope of her employment, but was on a "frolic," and therefore that *D*, Inc., is not vicariously liable for any tort committed by *X. P* sends a request for admission to *D*, Inc., asking it to admit "that *X* was acting in the course of her employment with *D*, Inc., at the time of the collision." *D*, Inc., specifically denies the request. At trial, *P* establishes to the jury's satisfaction that *X* was acting within the scope of her employment at the time of the collision.

Under Rule 37(c)(2), *P* may seek to recover all expenses, including attorney's fees, incurred in proving at trial that this was true. The court may deny that sanction, however, if it finds that *D*, Inc., had reasonable ground to conclude that it would prevail on the issue at trial or other good reason to fail to admit.

---

[104]This fact is shown by its reference to Rule 37(b)(2)(A)(i) through (vi), which does not include contempt (which is found at 37(b)(2)(A)(vii)).

§8.4.3 Certification Under Rule 26(g), "Litigation Holds," and Loss of ESI for Failure to Preserve

Certification. Rule 11, which we discussed at §7.7, requires attorneys (or, if there is no lawyer, by the *pro se* party herself[105]) to certify that various documents are justified in law and fact. They make the certification initially by signing the document. But Rule 11, as we saw, does not apply to discovery documents. Instead, Rule 26(g) applies. It is divided into three parts. First, Rule 26(g)(1) imposes a certification requirement regarding certain required disclosures and other discovery requests and responses. Second, Rule 26(g)(2) says that parties need not respond to an unsigned disclosure, request, response, or objection. Third, Rule 26(g)(3) lists the sanctions for improper certification.

Required disclosures under Rule 26(a)(1) and (a)(3) must be signed by at least one lawyer of record in her individual name (or by a *pro se* party) and must include her address. The Rule does not apply to required disclosures under Rule 26(a)(2). Under Rule 26(g)(1)(A), the signature on disclosures under Rule 26(a)(1) and (a)(3) constitutes a certification that "to the best of the person's knowledge, information, and belief, formed after a reasonable inquiry," the disclosure "is complete and correct as of the time it is made." The first quoted part of this requirement mirrors language from Rule 11 and imposes a duty to make a reasonable inquiry.

As for the traditional discovery devices, Rule 26(g)(2)(B) requires that "[e]very discovery request, response, or objection" must be signed, which constitutes a certification—again, as to the best of the signer's knowledge, information, and belief, formed after a reasonable inquiry—that various things are true. Specifically, the signer certifies that the request, response, or objection is (1) consistent with the Federal Rules and warranted by existing law or a good faith argument for change in the law; (2) not interposed for an improper purpose (such as to harass or delay); and (3) not unreasonably or unduly burdensome. This provision is quite broad. It applies to both parties: the party making the request and the responding party. It also applies to responses and to objections asserted to the discovery requests.[106]

Rule 26(g)(3) provides that a court may impose sanctions for violation of the certification requirement, either on motion of a party or on its own. It applies to violations of the certification requirement

---

[105]*Pro se* means that a party is representing herself in the proceeding, without a lawyer. Occasionally, such a party is said to be acting *in propria persona* (or *in pro per*), which means in her own stead.

[106]Remember that the party herself must sign the substantive answers to interrogatories and her deposition testimony under oath, as we saw in §8.2.2.

concerning required disclosures (in Rule 26(g)(1)(A)) and concerning the traditional discovery devices (in Rule 26(g)(2)(B)). Sanctions are permitted if a party violates the Rule "without substantial justification." The Rule calls for "an appropriate sanction," which may include an assessment of the expenses, including attorney's fees, incurred by another party because of the violation of the Rule. The sanction may be levied against the lawyer making the certification or upon the party on whose behalf the disclosure, request, response, or objection was made.

Litigation Holds and Loss of ESI. Common law imposes a duty to preserve evidence for litigation. It arises even before a case is filed, "when a party reasonably should know that the evidence may be relevant to anticipated litigation."[107] Every litigator must be aware of (and instruct her client about) the duty to preserve evidence. It is a good idea for businesses to have formal "information (or document) retention policies."[108] This is actually a bit of a misnomer, because they are really destruction policies. No business keeps all records for all time, either in hard copy or electronic format. Each has some method for determining what gets shredded or deleted from the computer and when. It is common to have computer systems delete e-mails after a set period.

When litigation is reasonably anticipated, however, parties should go into a "litigation hold," which engages the duty to preserve relevant information. Destruction of material after that, even if pursuant to a well-established policy, can have serious consequences in the litigation. Lawyers must instruct their clients to interrupt programs that would routinely destroy documents or delete ESI that may be relevant to the litigation. Moreover, much ESI, such as Snapchat, is ephemeral and presents serious problems of preservation.[109] Destruction of material that should have been preserved may constitute "spoliation," which is defined as "the intentional destruction, mutilation, alteration, or concealment of evidence."[110] Courts have broad discretion in setting a sanction for spoliation, and usually balance (1) the need to deter future destruction, (2) protection of the other party's interest, and (3) remedying the prejudice caused.[111]

---

[107]Velez v. Marriott PR Mgt., Inc., 590 F. Supp. 2d 235, 258 (D. P.R. 2008).

[108]Historically, lawyers referred to "document retention policies." Increasingly, given the prevalence of ESI, lawyers speak about "information retention policies." Even when the older term is used (which is frequent), it includes ESI as well hard-copy papers.

[109]*See* Agnieszka McPeak, *Disappearing Data,* 2018 Wis. L. Rev. 17 (2018).

[110]Black's Law Dictionary 1690 (11th ed. 2019). In some states, spoliation constitutes a tort. *See, e.g.,* Hazen v. Municipality of Anchorage, 718 P.2d 456, 463 (Alaska 1986); Smith v. Superior Court, 198 Cal. Rptr. 829, 832 (Cal. App. 1984).

[111]*See, e.g.,* West v. Goodyear Tire & Rubber Co., 167 F.3d 776, 780 (2d Cir. 1999). The court quoted the English legal historian Chitty for "that favourite maxim of the

In extreme cases, a court may dismiss the case if plaintiff engages in spoliation (or enter default judgment against a defendant spoliator). One potential lesser sanction for spoliation is an "adverse inference" instruction. This tells the jury that it may (or even must) assume that the missing evidence would have supported the other party.

Rule 37(e) addresses the loss of ESI.[112] It is best considered mechanically. First, the provision applies only when (1) ESI that should have been preserved (in a litigation hold) (2) is lost "because a party failed to take reasonable steps to preserve it," and (3) cannot be recovered. The Rule does not define when the duty to preserve arises, leaving the issue instead largely to common law. Nor does the Rule indicate who has the burden of proof on what constitutes "reasonable steps to preserve" ESI.

Second, if these things are established, the court assesses whether the party seeking discovery is prejudiced by the loss of the ESI. If so, the court "may order measures no greater than necessary to cure the prejudice." Notably, the Rule refers to "measures," as opposed to "sanctions." Nowhere does it suggest what "measures" might be appropriate.

Third, the court can impose a significant sanction—such as an adverse inference instruction, dismissal, or entry of default judgment—only if the court finds that the party who lost the ESI "acted with intent to deprive another party of the information's use in the litigation." This is a difficult burden to satisfy. As a result, adverse inference instructions and other merits sanctions appear more difficult to get in cases involving loss of ESI than those involving other sorts of information.[113] Moreover, courts have not agreed on what constitutes "intent to deprive" under this provision.[114]

---

law, *omnia presumuntur contra spoliatorem*," which means that spoliators should not benefit from their wrongdoing. *Id.* at 779.

[112]This situation is contrasted with ESI that is "inaccessible" because of undue burden or cost, which we discussed in §8.3.2. There, ESI can be retrieved, but it will be expensive. Here, the ESI is lost and cannot be retrieved. Rule 37(e) was completely redrafted, effective in 2015, and has been criticized as excessively protective of parties that destroy ESI. *See, e.g.*, Moore, note 6 above, 83 U. Cin. L. Rev. at 1124 ("Notice how many obstacles a party seeking [ESI] would have to surmount to obtain sanctions for the failure of the responding party to preserve ESI.").

[113]Professor Moore argues, based on the language of Rule 37(e), that the provision might not permit a contempt citation even for intentionally disobeying an order for the preservation of ESI. *Id.*, 83 U. Cin. L. Rev. at 1135.

[114]*See, e.g.*, Jung Won Jun & Rockyoun Ihm, *The Federal Rule of Civil Procedure 37(e) and Achieving Uniformity of Case Law on Sanctions for ESI Spoliation,* 70 Cath. L. Rev. 177 (2021).

§8.5 Managerial Judging: Scheduling and Promotion of Settlement

This section addresses more than the discovery phase of the litigation. There are two important themes to keep in mind throughout this material. First, the Federal Rules, particularly Rules 16 and 26, impose significant burdens on the parties to keep the case moving. In earlier days, the Rules left more of the timing issues to the discretion of the parties. Second, the judge is involved in managing the progress of the case and actively promoting settlement. This is one of the significant developments of the past 50 years: The role of the judge has changed from that of passive umpire, reacting to the parties, to active case manager. The Administrative Office of the federal courts requires each federal judge to report caseloads and the progress of each case every six months. This requirement creates implicit pressure on the judge to keep things rolling along expeditiously. In §8.6, we discuss the concomitant increase in the use of judicial adjuncts to help reduce case backlog.

It is helpful to address Rules 16 and 26 together to see the timeline they impose. The driving point at the early stage is Rule 16(b)(1), which provides, with some exceptions, that the court must enter a scheduling order mapping out the progress of the litigation from that point until trial. As we saw in §1.1, the median time in federal court from filing the complaint through resolution by trial is 27.5 months.[115] Notice how much the parties must do before the court enters that scheduling order, and how little time they have in which to do it. Under Rule 16(b)(2), the scheduling order is to be entered no more than 90 days after the defendant is served with process.

What must be done in those 90 days?[116] In a given case, these requirements and the timing may be altered by court order or stipulation, but we will outline the timeline as modeled in the Rules, assuming no exceptions. First, at least 21 days before the scheduling order, the parties must hold their Rule 26(f) conference. This event, attended by the parties and their lawyers, requires significant preparation. Under Rule 26(f)(2), the parties must confer to consider their claims and defenses and the possibility that the case might be settled or otherwise resolved promptly. In addition, they must arrange for their Rule 26(a)(1) required disclosures and, significantly, "develop a proposed discovery plan."

---

[115]https://www.uscourts.gov/sites/default/files/data_tables/fcms_na_distprofile1231.2020.pdf.

[116]In a given case, it could be fewer than 90 days; Rule 16(b)(2) provides that 90 days is the *longest* time that can elapse between service of process on the defendant and the scheduling order.

This plan is quite detailed, as shown by Rule 26(f)(3), and requires the parties to express their "views and proposals" concerning various issues. Among the issues addressed in the discovery plan are any changes that should be made for required disclosures, the subjects on which discovery may be needed, when discovery should be completed, whether it should be conducted in phases, and, under Rule 26(f)(3)(C), "any issues about disclosure, discovery, or preservation of electronically stored information, including the form or forms in which it should be produced." Second, no later than 14 days after the Rule 26(f) conference, the parties must agree on a proposed discovery plan for the litigation and submit to the court a written report outlining the plan. Thus, there will be a good deal of work after the Rule 26(f) conference, since the parties must agree on a discovery plan and submit a jointly crafted written report laying out the plan.

Third, also no later than 14 days after the Rule 26(f) conference, the parties must make their required disclosures under Rule 26(a)(1), which we discussed in §8.2.1. Obviously, complying with that Rule requires further effort.

In sum, these provisions require a significant investment of time and effort for each party in the first 90 days after the defendant is served with process. The era when a plaintiff could file a case and sit back for a few months is gone, at least in federal court.[117] This intense activity costs the parties a good bit of money. One implicit goal of these requirements is to make the litigants do a reality check on how expensive the case may get and thus to become more amenable to settling the dispute. The time frame for the first phase of a typical suit looks like this:

Day 1	Day 69	Day 83	Day 90
Service of process[118]	Rule 26(f) conference	Written discovery plan to court and Rule 26(a)(1) disclosures made	Rule 16(b) schedule order

Timing of the Use of Discovery Tools. Where do the discovery tools, studied in §8.2.2, fit into this schedule? Under Rule 26(d)(1), a party "may not seek discovery from any source before the parties have conferred as required under Rule 26(a)(1)(B)." This provision precludes seeking discovery not only from parties but "from any source"

---

[117]Some states impose similar responsibilities, though it is worth noting that required disclosures under Rule 26(a) have not been widely adopted in state courts.

[118]Recall from §3.3.1 that process generally must be served within 90 days of filing of the complaint.

before the Rule 26(f) conference, and therefore applies to discovery from nonparties as well as parties.

There is one exception to the timing restriction. Under Rule 26(d)(2)(A), a party may serve upon another party requests to produce under Rule 34 at an earlier time. Specifically, they may serve these requests anytime "[m]ore than 21 days" after the party is served with process. Any such "early Rule 34 requests" are then deemed to have been served at the Rule 26(f) conference (so responses to the requests would be due 30 days after that conference).

Subsequent Progress of the Case. Employing and responding to each discovery tool requires time and effort from each party and her lawyer. As the months go on, and discovery is completed, the case will become ripe for adjudication. If the case involves expert witnesses, as discussed in §8.3.3, the parties will have required disclosures under Rule 26(a)(2) and will take the depositions of the other parties' experts.

Somewhere along the way, most cases are disposed of without trial. Most of these are settled, with the parties agreeing to terms of the settlement and the plaintiff taking a voluntary dismissal of her case under Rule 41(a)(1), as we addressed in §7.3.5. Other cases may be disposed of on motion or by default judgment.

In those cases that go to trial, Rules 16 and 26 impose further tasks on the parties. Rule 16(a) permits *pretrial conferences* in the court's discretion for a variety of purposes, such as expediting disposition of the action and "establishing early and continuing control" of the case.[119] Rule 16(c)(2) lists various topics that can be considered at any such conference. Courts sometimes will call a conference simply to assess where the parties are and why the case seems not to be moving as well as the judge expects; these are often called *status conferences*. Under Rule 16(d), all pretrial conferences result in entry of an order "reciting the action taken." That Rule also provides that this order "controls the course of the action unless the court modifies it." Accordingly, the court's order summarizing the pretrial conference order serves as a roadmap for the litigation. Often, it sets dates for accomplishing various tasks.

Ultimately, if the case continues, there will be a *final pretrial conference* under Rule 16(e).[120] This must be held "as close to the start of trial as is reasonable," and will result in the formulation of a plan for trial. The parties discuss matters in considerable detail here, as the plan for trial will include "a plan to facilitate the admission of evidence" at trial. Their preparation for the conference is guided by

---

[119]Under Rule 16(f), the court has access to a serious panoply of sanctions to punish parties and lawyers who do not participate appropriately in such conferences.

[120]In many cases, this may be the *only* pretrial conference.

the final set of required disclosures, under Rule 26(a)(3). That section requires each party to disclose extremely detailed information about what she plans to produce at trial, including the name and address of each witness to be called (and those who may be called if the need arises at trial[121]) and the identification of each document and exhibit to be introduced at trial.[122] These disclosures require a great deal of work and must be made as directed by the court, but in no event fewer than 30 days before trial.[123]

After the final pretrial conference, the court will enter an order (not surprisingly, the *final pretrial conference order*). This order lists the contentions of the parties, the witnesses and evidence to be proffered by each party, and other information required by Rule 26(a)(3) or by the court. Pursuant to Rule 16(d), this document then controls subsequent events, which means it becomes the roadmap for the trial itself. Essentially, the document supersedes the pleadings.

Thus, a party who raised an issue in pleadings must ensure that it is preserved and presented in the final pretrial conference order, or risk losing the right to present evidence on that point at trial. Similarly, a party who forgets to list a witness may encounter a serious problem when she attempts to call that witness at trial. Rule 16(f) makes it clear that the "court may modify the order issued after a final pretrial conference only to prevent manifest injustice."[124] The party seeking amendment bears the burden of proof, and, generally, a court will allow amendment only if refusing to do so would result in injustice to the party seeking amendment, the party opposing the amendment will not be substantially harmed by the amendment, and the court will not be inconvenienced thereby.[125]

Courts can be rather strict on this score. In *Walker v. Anderson Electric Connectors*,[126] the plaintiff sued for sexual harassment,

---

[121]Perhaps a party has a witness who will testify to counteract testimony from a witness another party may call. Only if that other witness actually testifies will the need arise.

[122]Before the required disclosures were promulgated in 1993, most federal districts required this sort of detailed disclosure by Local Rule. Thus, Rule 26(a)(3) was not all that revolutionary.

[123]Within 14 days after disclosure of the materials required by Rule 26(a)(3), each party must raise various objections to the proposed evidence of other parties, risking waiver of certain evidentiary objections if she fails to do so.

[124]By way of review, suppose a party presents evidence at trial on a matter not reflected in the final pretrial conference order, and the other side does not object. What might happen? Under Rule 15(b)(2), the evidence might be admitted (because there was no objection) and might then form the basis for amending the final pretrial conference order to conform to the evidence. *See, e.g.*, Kirkland v. District of Columbia, 70 F.3d 629, 634 (D.C. Cir. 1995). We discussed this possibility in §7.5.2.

[125]*See, e.g.*, DP Solutions, Inc. v. Rollins, Inc., 353 F.3d 421, 435 (5th Cir. 2003).

[126]944 F.2d 841, 844 (11th Cir. 1991).

seeking damages and equitable relief, including a declaratory judgment that the defendants had engaged in such harassment. At the final pretrial conference, though, the plaintiff abandoned the equitable claims and proceeded to trial seeking only damages. The jury found that the defendants had indeed committed sexual harassment, but also found that the plaintiff had suffered no monetary harm. Plaintiff sought to amend the pretrial order to reinstate her claim for equitable relief, including an order that the defendants had engaged in prohibited conduct. She did this because a "prevailing party" could, under a federal statute, seek recovery of attorney's fees. Without the equitable relief, she could not argue that she was a "prevailing party." The court refused to amend the pretrial conference order and the Eleventh Circuit affirmed, holding that modification would work injustice on the defendants. The plaintiff had chosen her litigation strategy and had to live with the consequences of that choice.

One of the hallmarks of the move toward managerial judging has been the emphasis on settlement. The original Federal Rules, promulgated in 1939, did not refer once to settlement. Now, one sees settlement throughout the Rules. For example, notice that the Rule 26(f) conference is to include prospects of settling the case. To this end, the local rules of many districts require parties to submit to court-annexed mediation to attempt to make the case go away. The goal of settlement is so well ingrained that some judges consider going to trial a systemic failure. That attitude is disappointing to those who believe strongly in the crucible of the American adversarial system of justice.[127] While it is true that most cases have always settled, the percentage of those going to trial in recent years has plummeted.

The urge to manage and cajole settlement is especially acute in complex litigation. In §5.5, we discussed multidistrict (MDL) litigation, in which multiple related federal cases are transferred into a single district for what amounts to more processing than adjudication. (See also §13.3.9.) One trend in MDL cases is "Lone Pine" orders, which require claimants to make *prima facie* showings of injury—long before trial would be held. Failure to abide by the order can result in dismissal. Such additional hurdles, many argue, have the effect of pressuring claimants to settle.[128]

---

[127]*See* Stephen N. Subrin & Thomas O. Main, *The Fourth Era of American Civil Procedure,* 162 U. Pa. L. Rev. 1839 (2014).

[128]For an excellent discussion, *see* Nora Freeman Engstrom, *The Lessons of* Lone Pine, 129 Yale L.J. 2 (2019). The name derives from an unpublished state court order in *Lore v. Lone Pine Corp.,* 1986 WL 637507 (N.J. Super. Ct. Law Div. 1986).

§8.6 Use of Judicial Adjuncts

In the preceding section, we saw that the role of the trial judge (especially, perhaps, the federal trial judge) has become more bureaucratic or administrative in recent decades. The judge is responsible not only for deciding motions and overseeing trials and other traditional "judicial" roles, but, increasingly, for managing the court's caseload. For example, Rule 16(a)(2) expressly envisions the judge's "establishing early and continuing control" of the case. As the tasks have increased, so has a movement toward use of adjuncts to assist the federal district judge.

The principal adjunct officer in the federal court system is the U.S. magistrate judge. Magistrate judges are not Article III judges. Thus, they are not appointed by the President with the advice and consent of the Senate, nor do they enjoy constitutional grants of lifetime tenure and protection against salary reduction.[129] Rather, magistrate judges serve a term of years and are selected by the federal district judges for each district.

Congress first provided for magistrate judges in 1968, in response to a glut of complex cases in federal courts growing out of a huge series of antitrust cases. From the beginning, Congress intended that magistrate judges would assist federal district judges in processing cases. Though magistrates may perform duties regarding criminal cases, our focus is on what they do in civil litigation. The authority of these adjunct judicial officers is defined in 28 U.S.C. §636 and is reflected as well in Rules 72 and 73. Magistrates perform a variety of functions at the behest of the district judge, who "refers" matters to the magistrate by order. It is difficult to imagine how the courts could handle their present caseloads without magistrates. Among other tasks in civil cases, they often oversee the progress of discovery, preside over scheduling and pretrial conferences, and become involved in attempts to settle cases.

The division of labor between district judges, on the one hand, and magistrates, on the other, must be clear. Because magistrate judges are not Article III judges, they cannot rule dispositively in a case unless the parties waive their right to decision by an Article III judge. Under §636(b)(1)(A) and Rule 72(a), a district judge may (without consent of the parties) refer *nondispositive pretrial* matters (such as motions to compel discovery) to be heard by a magistrate judge.[130] The

---

[129]We discussed Article III judges, and the extraordinary protections accorded them by the Constitution, in §4.4. Magistrate judges, in contrast, have rights conferred by statute, not the Constitution.

[130]Section 636(b)(1)(A) does not use the term *nondispositive*. Rather, it permits the district judge to refer "any pretrial matter" to the magistrate and then lists exceptions—including motions for injunctive relief, motions for certification of a class

magistrate's orders on such issues are subject to review by the district judge. Such review is on the record created by the magistrate judge (so the district judge is not required to hold a new hearing). On non-dispositive matters, the magistrate judge's orders are presumptively correct. The district judge will uphold the magistrate judge's orders unless there was "clear error."

Under §636(b)(1)(B) and Rule 72(b), a district judge may (also without consent of the parties) refer to the magistrate judge *dispositive pretrial* matters.[131] For example, she could refer a motion for summary judgment to the magistrate judge. The magistrate enters findings and recommendations on such dispositive matters under §636(b)(1)(C), which are subject to review by the district judge. Because the issue is dispositive, however, the district judge must review the magistrate judge's decision *de novo*. This standard of review (which we address regarding appeals at §14.7) means that the district judge does not defer to what the magistrate decided, but applies the legal standard to the facts on her own.

What about trial? Section 636(c)(1) expressly provides that a magistrate can preside over a civil trial (jury or non-jury) *only* if all parties consent to it. By doing so, they waive the right to have an Article III judge determine their case. In *Roell v. Withrow*,[132] the Supreme Court held that such consent need not be express but can be inferred from the conduct of the parties. There, the magistrate repeatedly told the parties that they could object to trial before her and insist on trial before the district judge. No one objected and the case proceeded. No one objected when the magistrate indicated her belief that all parties had consented to her trying the case. Only after an adverse verdict and judgment did defendants object to trial before the magistrate. In light of their voluntary participation in the entire litigation and failure to voice objection, however, the Court found that the defendants had consented to trial before the magistrate. When the parties consent to trial by the magistrate judge, the final judgment is not reviewed by the district judge; it is appealed directly to the court of appeals. Section 636 ensures that the court will not exert undue pressure on parties in an effort to get them to waive their right to trial by an Article III judge.

Often, magistrate judges preside over pretrial conferences and manage the progress of the case. They may also be important in trying to settle a case. The district judge who will preside over trial is reluctant

---

action, and motions for summary judgment. Lawyers and judges routinely refer to what is left as "nondispositive." Rule 72(a), on the other hand, does speak of referring "nondispositive matters" to the magistrate judge.

[131]Section 636(b)(1)(B) does not use the term dispositive, but Rule 72(b) does.

[132]538 U.S. 580, 586-587 (2003).

to become too closely involved with settlement efforts, because she might become aware of something that would not be admissible at trial and that might jeopardize her impartiality. The magistrate, however, who will probably not preside over the trial, may be more willing and able to cajole the parties into settlement.

Another judicial adjunct is the "master." This person is not employed by the federal judiciary but is appointed by the district judge to perform various tasks under Rule 53.[133] Masters are paid at a rate set by the court and paid by the parties.[134] They may be employed to address pre- or post-trial matters when district judges and magistrates are so overburdened that they cannot address them in a timely way. Though district and magistrate judges are generalists, masters may be experts in a relevant field. Perhaps the most common use for special masters is to perform an accounting or to resolve a difficult computation of damages for the court, as reflected in Rule 53(a)(1)(B). The court may find it helpful, for example, to have an accountant or economist serve as a master to make computations. Masters also are frequently employed to oversee the implementation of complex courts orders.[135]

[133]Historically, there were "general masters" and "special masters." The former were appointed from a standing list of persons available for the task. The latter were appointed on a case-by-case basis. When the post of magistrate judge was created in 1968, there was no longer a need to keep lists of general masters, so all masters are appointed on a case-by-case basis. Thus, Rule 53 refers only to "masters." Because old habits die hard, though, many judges and lawyers continue to refer to "special masters."

[134]Section 636(b)(2) provides that a magistrate judge may serve as a master; in such a case, the magistrate would receive only her salary, and not an additional amount from the parties.

[135]See, e.g., Cordoza v. Pacific States Steel Corp., 320 F.3d 989, 994-995 (9th Cir. 2003) (master employed to oversee conversion of contaminated steel plant into projects that could generate money to fund steelworkers' medical plan).

Chapter 9

Adjudication and Related Motions

§9.1   Defining the Issue

We saw in Chapter 7 that a case enters into the litigation stream when the plaintiff files her complaint. There are many ways the case might leave the litigation stream. It may be dismissed for a variety of reasons, such as failure to state a claim or lack of personal jurisdiction, subject matter jurisdiction, or venue. Or the defendant might fail to respond, after which the court might enter default judgment. Or perhaps the parties engaged in alternative dispute resolution, such as arbitration or mediation, as we saw in §1.3. Most likely, the case will settle. The parties, perhaps after a "reality check" provided by the discovery phase, resolve the dispute, and the plaintiff voluntarily dismisses the case.[1]

---

[1] Litigators must be skilled at contract negotiation and drafting. Settling a case involves having the parties enter into a contract, with the terms well defined. Generally,

491

In this chapter, we study what happens to cases that are not taken from the litigation stream in any of these ways. Such cases are adjudicated. Adjudication means that there will be a judicial resolution of the *merits* of the dispute. The merits involve the underlying dispute, including such questions as these: Did the defendant breach the contract? Did the defendant commit a tort? Was the plaintiff contributorily negligent? How fast was the car going? How serious are the injuries suffered? Who is telling the truth? At some point, these issues are ready to be decided.

In adjudicating the merits, the judicial system must accomplish two tasks. First, it must have a mechanism for determining what the facts are. This is the "fact-finding" function. It may be performed by a jury or by the judge (in a "bench" trial). Second, it must apply the law to those facts to determine who should win the judgment. Stating the relevant law is always a function for the judge.

The typical model for adjudication is the trial, which we address in §9.2. This is the phase of litigation usually depicted in movies and television shows. It is the courtroom drama: witnesses testifying under oath, counsel objecting, the judge rapping her gavel for order in the courtroom. The trial is the ultimate litigation experience. After months (or, more likely, years) of pretrial litigation—through pleadings, motions, discovery, etc.—the parties and their lawyers are ready to present the evidence in the courtroom. Trials take place in "open court," which means, as a general matter, that the public is free to attend.[2]

For present purposes, we focus on several points regarding adjudication by trial. In §9.2.1, we discuss the relative roles of the judge and the jury at trial. In §9.2.2, we see that there is a constitutional right to have a jury make fact determinations in some (but not all) civil disputes in federal court. (Even then, the parties may waive the right to jury trial and have the facts determined by the judge in a "bench" trial.)

---

the plaintiff agrees to accept money from the defendant, in return for which the plaintiff signs a release of all claims and of any right to sue the defendant concerning the same matter. When the money is paid, usually the plaintiff will then take a voluntary dismissal, as we saw in §7.4.1.

[2]Judicial business other than trials, such as hearing oral argument and ruling on various motions, is generally conducted in open court. This is to be contrasted with a court's acting *in camera* (or "in chambers"), which refers to proceedings in the judge's office rather than in the courtroom. During the COVID-19 pandemic, courts, lawyers, and litigants learned to hold virtual trials, at least in non-jury cases. Jury trials, on the other hand, generally need to be held in person. Trial lawyers would find it unnatural and ineffective to have jurors wearing facemasks. Part of what trial lawyers do is "read" the reactions of jurors. Moreover, jurors need to be able to "read" the facial expressions of witnesses testifying at trial.

In cases tried to a jury, the judge serves an important gatekeeping function. A motion for "judgment as a matter of law" permits the judge to circumvent the jury and to determine facts herself, but only if the facts are so clear that they are subject to only one reasonable interpretation. Similarly, in very limited circumstances, the judge may "undo" what the jury decided by granting a "renewed motion for judgment as a matter of law," or by ordering a new trial, or by setting aside the judgment. We address these motions, respectively, in §§9.5, 9.6, and 9.7.

Though the trial is the typical model for adjudication, very few cases go to trial.[3] There are many reasons for the "vanishing trial," including the embrace of managerial judging, one focus of which is to foster settlement. Here, we focus on a trial court's adjudication through summary judgment. A judge may grant summary judgment for precisely the same reason it might not let the case "go to the jury" at trial: There is no dispute as to the material facts. This fact allows the judge to rule in the case as a matter of law. We study summary judgment in §9.4. We start, however, with the centerpiece of American civil dispute resolution, the trial.

§9.2 The Trial

§9.2.1 The Purpose and Conduct of Trial and the Roles of Judge and Jury

We said above that adjudication requires fact-finding and application of the law to the facts as determined. The *only* reason to go to trial is to resolve a dispute of material fact. If there is no genuine dispute of material fact, there is no need for trial (and, as we see in §9.4, the court may enter summary judgment). In this section, we will assume that there is a genuine dispute of fact (or, more likely, several genuine disputed facts).

Remember how such disputed facts arise. The plaintiff alleged things in her complaint, which the defendant either admitted or denied. If she admitted them, they are deemed established and need not be tried. Those issues the defendant denied, however, are "joined," or disputed. During discovery, the parties might be able to narrow the

---

[3]Nora Freeman Engstrom, *The Diminished Trial*, 86 Fordham L. Rev. 2131, 2131 (2018) (in 1938, 20 percent of federal civil cases went to trial; in 1990, the percentage was down to 4.3; by 2000, the percentage was 2.2, and by 2016 fewer than 2 percent of federal civil cases went to trial). Most of the data we have concern federal, not state, courts.

number of disputed facts. The final pretrial conference order lists the disputed factual issues that must be adjudicated at trial. The parties are well aware of what these issues are and have planned carefully about what evidence to introduce at trial to prove their version of the disputed facts. In addition to the facts relating to the elements of the plaintiff's claims and the defendant's affirmative defenses (if any), the trial will resolve, often by implication, the credibility of various witnesses. Specifically, when witnesses have given opposing testimony on a fact, the outcome will hinge in part on which witness the fact-finder believes.

Who resolves these disputed facts? In many cases, the parties will have a choice: Either the judge can do it (in a "bench trial") or the jury[4] can do it. The choice of the jury is not always available for this function. In §9.2.2, we see when the right to jury trial attaches in federal civil cases. When there is no jury, either because there was no right to jury trial or because the parties waived the right, the judge determines the facts. Under Rule 52(a)(1), she must record her findings of fact and, separately stated, her conclusions of law deriving from those facts. The findings and conclusions may be stated on the record or in an opinion or memorandum. Often, judges put the findings of fact and conclusions of law in a single document, labeling each section separately.

In all trials, bench or jury, the judge is responsible for discerning the applicable law. In jury cases, the judge instructs the jury on that law to guide its determination of the facts. We discuss this process in §9.2.4. Also, in all trials, the judge oversees the presentation of the evidence and the behavior of the participants. She must resolve any disagreements about what evidence is admissible. She must ensure that the trial moves along expeditiously, while allowing each party a fair opportunity to present her evidence. In jury trials, she will be especially diligent in policing the admission of evidence and behavior of the parties and lawyers, to ensure that the jurors are not exposed to matters that might prejudice them or make it difficult for them to discharge their task dispassionately.

At the outset of trial (after selection of the jury, if there is one), the lawyers for each party usually will make an "opening statement." This oral statement is intended to acquaint the judge and jury (if there is

---

[4]Throughout our materials, technically we are speaking of a "petit" (pronounced "petty") jury, members of which sit as fact-finders in trials. These jurors are to be contrasted with "grand" jurors, who are also drawn from the citizenry, but whose job is far different. Grand jurors work in secrecy and hear evidence of alleged crimes presented by appropriate law enforcement officials. In the federal system, a lawyer for the U.S. Attorney for the local district presents the evidence. The grand jury is to determine whether there is sufficient evidence for an indictment. If so, it "returns" an indictment.

one) with background of the dispute and with that lawyer's assessment of what the evidence will show. The opening statement is the first chance the jury has to learn any details about the case. Opening statements may be accompanied by visual aids, but not the introduction of evidence. The plaintiff's lawyer gives her opening statement first, followed by the defendant's lawyer.[5] Lawyers understand the importance of the opening statement in educating and hopefully winning the confidence of the fact-finder.

After opening statements, the plaintiff presents her "case-in-chief." She does this by calling witnesses, who are "sworn in" and thus testify under oath before the judge and the jury in open court, so the public may attend. Witnesses testify in response to questions by the lawyers, rather than holding forth with soliloquies. After the plaintiff's lawyer examines a witness, the defendant's lawyer is allowed to cross-examine the witness. In cross-examination, the lawyer often attempts to create doubt about the witness's recollection or to expose inconsistencies between her testimony and that of other witnesses. This process is repeated for each of the plaintiff's witnesses. The plaintiff may present documentary and other evidence in addition to the oral testimony of the witnesses. Generally, a witness will need to establish the authenticity of documentary evidence, and each piece of evidence is marked as an "exhibit." The exhibits are marked sequentially, and may be referred to, for example, as "plaintiff's exhibit A" when asking witnesses about a particular piece of evidence. When she has presented her case, the plaintiff "rests," which closes the presentation of the plaintiff's case-in-chief.

As we see in §9.5, at this point the defendant may make a motion for judgment as a matter of law (JMOL), which, if granted, will obviate the rest of the trial and result in judgment for the defendant.[6] If such a motion is not made or is denied, the defendant then puts on her case-in-chief.[7] She does this just as the plaintiff did—witness by witness, asking questions to elicit testimony under oath. The plaintiff's lawyer may cross-examine each defense witness. The defendant may also introduce documentary and other evidence. When she has

---

[5]Sometimes, the defendant's lawyer may choose to delay her opening until after the plaintiff's presentation of evidence. Usually, however, the defense lawyer wants to make the opening statement immediately after the plaintiff's lawyer, to blunt the impact of the plaintiff's lawyer's statement.

[6]This motion, as we see in §9.5, can only be made after the other side "has been fully heard," which is satisfied after she has had a chance to present evidence.

[7]At common law, the defendant who moved for judgment as a matter of law (then called *directed verdict*) waived the right to present evidence if the motion were denied. That is no longer true, as we see in §9.5.

presented her case, the defendant "rests," which closes the presentation of her case.

At that point, the plaintiff may move for JMOL, which, if granted, would obviate the rest of the trial and result in judgment for the plaintiff. If such a motion is not made or is denied, the plaintiff may then present "rebuttal" evidence. This is done in the same way as the case-in-chief but consists of testimony and other evidence designed to rebut what the defendant presented. The defendant then may also present rebuttal evidence. At some point, the parties will have presented all of their cases-in-chief and rebuttal evidence, and the court will "close all the evidence."

Then, both parties might move for JMOL. If granted, the court will decide the case, dismiss the jury, and enter judgment. If no such motion is made, or if it is denied, the judge will instruct the jury (if there is one) on the law, and the jury will retire to deliberate and determine the facts. The jury is to do so based upon the "record evidence"—that is, what the judge allowed into evidence in the trial. The jurors are to disregard any evidence to which they might have been exposed in the trial but which the court found inadmissible.[8] The jury will announce its result in a "verdict," which the court will embody in its "judgment." Even then, as we see in §§9.5 and 9.6, parties may make motions to avoid or undo the judgment. If there is no jury, of course, the judge will determine the facts, make conclusions of law, and announce her judgment in the case.

§9.2.2   The Right to a Jury Trial

The Seventh Amendment

In federal court, the right to a jury trial in civil cases[9] is embodied in the Seventh Amendment, which provides that "[i]n suits at common law, where the value in controversy shall exceed twenty dollars, the right of trial by jury shall be preserved . . . ." Federal Rule 38(a)(1) echoes the importance of this constitutional guarantee by providing that the right to jury trial under the Seventh Amendment "is preserved to the parties inviolate."

---

[8]This might happen, for example, when a witness testifies that someone told him that X, Y, and Z happened. Upon objection, the court might declare that this statement is inadmissible because it is "hearsay" (which you will study in depth in your course on Evidence). The judge will then instruct the jury to disregard what the witness said about X, Y, and Z, because it is inadmissible. (Of course, as all trial lawyers know, it may be difficult for people to disregard something they have heard.)

[9]The Sixth Amendment, in contrast, addresses the right to jury trial in criminal cases. The Sixth Amendment is beyond our scope.

496

We imported the civil jury from England. Though Great Britain abolished the right to jury trial in most civil cases in 1920, Americans continue to embrace it as one of their most cherished rights. The jury is praised for bringing the wisdom of the common person to bear in the legal system. The jury is the voice of the community, a repository of democratic values and virtue.[10] There are critics, however, who see jury trial as expensive and cumbersome, and who would rather entrust fact-finding to the learned trial judge than to the layperson jury. Whatever the merits of the debate, in the United States, the jury system is here to stay. Repeal of the right to a jury trial in the federal system would require a constitutional amendment.

The Seventh Amendment applies only to civil cases in federal court. It is one of the provisions of the Bill of Rights that has *not* been incorporated to apply to the states through the Fourteenth Amendment. Accordingly, it does not apply in state courts, and states are free to determine for themselves whether and when a jury trial will be provided in civil cases. That said, all states appear to allow jury trials in civil cases, either by state constitution or statute, and most appear to do so in terms quite similar to those in the Seventh Amendment.

Two phrases in the Seventh Amendment require particular attention. First, the Amendment applies only to "[s]uits at common law." Such suits are distinguished from cases "at equity." At §1.2.3, we discussed that England developed separate courts for law and equity; a jury was available in the law courts but not at equity.[11] American jurisdictions, including the federal courts, bifurcated their court systems into courts of law and courts of equity throughout most of our history. In 1938, the federal system did away with that formal bifurcation. Almost all states have done so as well. But the distinction between law and equity remains important for several purposes, including the right to a jury trial. Second, the Seventh Amendment does not "create" or "grant" a right of jury trial. Instead, the right is "preserved." This fact locks the federal courts into a historical test, so determining

---

[10]"There would not have been an acceptable Bill of Rights without a right to trial by jury." Stephen Burbank & Stephen Subrin, *Litigation and Democracy: Restoring a Realistic Prospect of Trial*, 46 Harv. Civ. Rts.-Civil Lib. L. Rev. 399, 402 (2011). *See also* Alexandra D. Lahav, *The Jury and Participatory Democracy*, 55 Wm. & Mary L. Rev. 1029 (2014); Benjamin V. Madison, III, *Trial by Jury or by Military Tribunal for Accused Terrorist Detainees Facing the Death Penalty? An Examination of the Principles That Transcend the U.S. Constitution*, 17 U. Fla. J.L. & Pub. Pol. 347, 391 (2006) ("In the Anglo-American tradition . . . persons of all political stripes have agreed on one thing: the jury system serves justice by allowing average citizens to serve as a check within the broader scheme of governmental checks and balances").

[11]Occasionally, the chancellor at equity would empanel an advisory jury to assist him in deciding a case. There was, however, no general right to a jury trial in equity.

whether one gets a jury trial today entails historical research, as we will now see.

Reflecting these two phrases, the Court has adopted a two-part test for determining the right to a jury trial under the Seventh Amendment. One leading case is *Chauffeurs Local 391 v. Terry*.[12] It instructs the court to look, first, to whether the claim asserted has a relevant historical analog and, second, to the nature of the remedy sought.

First: The Historical Analog Inquiry. The Seventh Amendment became effective in 1791. Because it "preserve[s]" the right to jury, courts first ask whether the case asserted would have been heard by a jury at common law in 1791. To take it a step further, the relevant common law is that of England! Justice Story determined this point in 1812, in a case in which he was sitting as a circuit judge.[13] He concluded:

> Beyond all question, the common law here alluded to is not the common law of any individual state (for it probably differs in all), but it is the common law of England, the grand reservoir of all our jurisprudence. It cannot be necessary for me to expound the grounds of this opinion, because they must be obvious to every person acquainted with the history of the law.[14]

So, bizarre as it seems, to determine whether there is a right to a jury in a twenty-first century civil case in federal court, the judge must assess whether the matter would have been tried in the law (as opposed to equity) courts in 1791 in England. In the real world, most cases are easy on this point,[15] because most cases involve claims that clearly existed in 1791—things like negligence, battery, conversion, fraud, trespass, and breach of contract.

---

[12]494 U.S. 558 (1990). Some people refer to this case as *Terry*. We will call it *Chauffeurs*.

[13]For many years after the formation of the United States, Justices of the Supreme Court were required to "ride circuit." This meant that they sat as trial judges at the circuit courts, in addition to their duties on the Supreme Court. At that time, the circuit court was the trial court in the federal system. Now, of course, the trial court is the district court. The practice of making Supreme Court Justices sit as trial judges was abolished long ago. What survives, however, is the assignment of Justices to serve as Circuit Justices for each circuit of the U.S. Court of Appeals. Some extraordinary matters, such as requests for a stay of execution in a death penalty case, may be addressed to the Circuit Justice.

[14]United States v. Wonson, 28 F. Cas. 745, 750 (No. 16,750) (C.C.D. Mass. 1812).

[15]"[T]he number of cases in which existence of a jury right will be difficult to determine is very small . . . . [T]he vast and controversial literature that has developed about the scope of the jury right is, fortunately, not in proportion to the practical importance of the problem in the actual working of the courts." Wright & Kane, Federal Courts 652.

On the other hand, many modern substantive claims did not exist in 1791. Cutting-edge tort theories such as strict liability, claims for infliction of emotional distress, virtually the entire field of civil rights and labor law, as well as securities fraud and antitrust statutes developed after 1791. This fact does not automatically mean that there is no right to a jury on such claims. Instead, the court must assess whether the case is analogous to a right that would have been litigated at law in 1791 in England. Many federal judges have considered this job better suited to historians than judges. Indeed, Justice Brennan suggested that this historical analog part of the Seventh Amendment inquiry should be jettisoned.[16] Without doubt, this part of the inquiry is less important than the second part (assessing remedy). Sometimes, the Court goes through the motions of the historical analysis and essentially punts.

A good example is *Chauffeurs*, which involved suit by workers against the local chapter of their labor union. The plaintiffs worked for a trucking company that was party to a collective bargaining contract with the local. The plaintiffs were members of the local. The trucking company closed some facilities and terminated the employment of the plaintiffs, who then filed a grievance with their local union. The local refused to refer their charges to the grievance committee (which is the way the grievance was to be adjudicated under the collective bargaining agreement). The plaintiffs then sued the local.[17] The plaintiffs alleged that the union breached a duty of fair representation that it owed to them. They sought reinstatement and compensation for back pay and for lost health care benefits. The plaintiffs sought trial by jury, which the defendant opposed.

The claim against the union for breach of the duty of fair dealing did not exist in 1791. (Indeed, labor unions were illegal in 1791.) Nonetheless, the Court in *Chauffeurs* upheld the right to jury trial. It determined that the claim asserted, though of recent origin, had an eighteenth-century analog in the English common law. Finding such an analog is more art than science. The party wishing to defeat the

---

[16]Justice Brennan concurred but argued that the Court should jettison the first part of the inquiry. Finding a historical analog for a modern claim is inexact and needlessly difficult. Moreover, he argued, judges are not trained in legal history. Though many professors disagree, I certainly think there is much to what Justice Brennan says. Indeed, the malleability of the analogue test is shown by the majority opinion. Essentially, one can argue for almost any outcome in almost any case. The real crux of the matter boils down to how the court characterizes the remedy. Justice Brennan was careful to say that *some* historical analysis is required by the Seventh Amendment. The requirement is met, however, when the court analyzes whether the remedy is essentially legal or equitable.

[17]They also sued the trucking company, but it went bankrupt and was dismissed from the case.

jury claim will posit analogs from *equity* practice of 1791, to show that there should be no jury. The party seeking a jury will posit analogs from *law* practice of 1791. In *Chauffeurs,* the Court roamed around inconclusively through a series of possibilities proffered by the parties. The opinion shows the malleability of this part of the Seventh Amendment test. The claim for breach of the duty of fair representation, said the majority, is similar to an action by a beneficiary against a trustee for breach of fiduciary obligation. In 1791, such a claim would have been heard by an equity court, not a law court. This fact counsels against a jury today. On the other hand, the case was somewhat akin to an attorney malpractice action, which was heard by a law court in 1791. But, the majority waffles, the malpractice analogy is not so good. Ultimately, the majority concludes (sort of) that the trustee analogy is the best, which seems to support the conclusion that there is no right to a jury.

But the Court was not done. It then decided to assess the *issues* to be addressed in the case, rather than the overall claim. (This approach is consistent with *Beacon Theaters,* which we will discuss below.) Here, the Court noted that the plaintiffs must prove two things: (1) that the *trucking company* breached the collective bargaining agreement,[18] and (2) that the union breached the duty of fair representation. Though issue (2) was analogous to a fiduciary claim, which is equitable, issue (1) was more like breach of contract, which is legal. Thus, at the end of Part III(A) of the opinion in *Chauffeurs,* the Justices in the majority basically throw up their hands and say they are left in "equipoise," equally unsure about whether this kind of case would have gone to law or equity in 1791.

Second: Analysis of the Remedy. After determining that the plaintiff is asserting something that has a 1791 English common law analog (or, as in *Chauffeurs,* that that question is in equipoise), the federal court then assesses the remedy sought in the case. Without doubt, this has become the more important part of the analysis, and the Court's efforts here are more important than those on the historical analog prong. The point is to determine whether the remedy plaintiff seeks would have been granted by a law court or by an equity court in 1791 England. This requires background in the development of remedies, for which you might review §1.2.3.

The classic common law (or "legal") remedy is damages, which is a monetary recovery to *compensate* the plaintiff for harm suffered; this is why they are often called "compensatory" damages. For instance,

---

[18]They must show this even though the trucking company was no longer a party to the case. The union could not be liable for breach of its duty of fair representation if the trucking company had not acted in violation of the collective bargaining agreement.

a plaintiff in contract may sue to recover damages representing her "benefit of the bargain": to make her whole because of the other side's breach. In a typical case, if the defendant breaches a contract, the plaintiff is expected to "cover" the breach by obtaining the equivalent from another source. The plaintiff may then recover from the defendant the amount by which this "cover" exceeded the amount she would have paid under the contract. Similarly, in tort, a plaintiff may recover damages to compensate her for lost wages, medical expenses, and pain and suffering inflicted as a result of the defendant's tortious act or omission. Assessment of such damages is a fact issue at the heart of the jury function.[19]

Punitive damages, in contrast, are intended to punish the defendant for egregious behavior. They are sometimes called "exemplary damages," because an award is to make an example of the defendant. Jurisdictions take different approaches to the types of behavior that will justify an award of punitive damages. One common standard is that punitive damages are permitted only if the defendant engaged in malicious, oppressive, or fraudulent behavior to be subject to such an award. The assessment of punitive damages (the decision of how large an award is necessary to punish a defendant) generally is also a jury question.[20]

As we saw in §1.2.3, equity developed a panoply of other remedies. They could be sought only when one's legal remedy (of damages) was inadequate. The classic equitable remedies include (1) the injunction (by which a court orders a party to do something or to refrain from doing something); (2) specific performance (by which the court commands a party to do something she has a duty to do); (3) rescission of a document; and (4) reformation of a document. In 1791, as noted, law courts were separate from equity courts, so the assessment of whether one had a right to a jury was relatively easy. Jury trials could be had in the law courts, but not in the equity courts. Today, however, law and equity are merged in the federal system and in almost all states. Still, it is true to this day in all American court systems (federal and state), that one cannot obtain equitable relief (cannot "invoke equitable jurisdiction") until she has shown that damages are inadequate to remedy her situation.

---

[19]*See generally* Colleen P. Murphy, *Determining Compensation: The Tension Between Legislative Power and Jury Authority,* 74 Texas L. Rev. 345 (1995); Colleen P. Murphy, *Judicial Assessment of Legal Remedies,* 94 Nw. L. Rev. 153 (1999).

[20]Professor Murphy argues persuasively that the assessment of punitive damages should be entrusted to the judge, not the jury. She likens punitive damages to the assessment of civil penalties, which, as we see below, are assessed by the court, not a jury. *See* Colleen P. Murphy, *Integrating the Constitutional Authority of Civil and Criminal Juries,* 61 Geo. Wash. L. Rev. 723, 739-782 (1993).

o ***Example #1.**** A* and *B* enter into a contract under which *B* is to deliver certain products to *A* at set times. *B* fails to deliver goods as required by the contract. *A* sues *B* for specific performance: an order requiring her to deliver the goods pursuant to the agreement. *A* cannot seek this equitable remedy, however, until she establishes that her legal remedy of damages is inadequate. In the ordinary case, for example, the court would expect *A* to go out and "cover" (get the goods from another source), and then to seek damages from *B* for the extra amount she had to pay the third party for the goods. Absent extraordinary circumstances, then, damages are an adequate remedy and *A* would not be able to avail herself of equitable remedies such as specific performance. (Because damages are legal relief, the right to jury trial would attach.)

o ***Example #2.**** P* owns real property. *D* trespasses across the property each day. If *P* sues at common law, her legal remedy will be damages (say *X* dollars per day), calculated to compensate her for the harm done by *D*'s trespassing. *D* may happily pay *P* the damages of *X* dollars per day and continue trespassing. *P* has a strong argument that her legal remedy is inadequate. She does not want *X* dollars per day. She wants *D* to stop trespassing. She wants an injunction—a court order to *D*, telling her to stop trespassing on *P*'s property.

If the court entered an injunction against *D*, and *D* violated the injunction, she would be in contempt of the injunction. The court could fine *D* or could order her incarcerated until she agreed to stop trespassing on *P*'s land. An equitable decree is enforceable through such a contempt citation, which is usually effective.

These cases are pretty easy, because they involve claims either for entirely legal relief or entirely equitable relief. If *P* seeks only equitable relief, there would be no right to a jury trial under the Seventh Amendment. But if *P* seeks only damages, the Seventh Amendment would grant a jury trial on all questions of fact, including the question of how large a recovery of damages would be required to compensate the plaintiff for the harm done her by the defendant. Things get more interesting when a single case involves some legal aspects and some equitable aspects. We turn to these "hybrid" cases now.

Hybrid Cases: Law and Equity

What happens if a single case involves both issues of law and issues of equity? In England, historically, courts were guided by what they considered to be the primary thrust of the case. For instance, if the court considered the case to be *mainly* about an equitable remedy—that is, if the center of gravity of the case, the most important part of the case, was equitable—the entire case would be heard in the equity court. There was no jury. The equity courts in England developed the "cleanup doctrine," which allowed them to provide limited, or "incidental," legal relief. The cleanup doctrine thus avoided the need for two cases, one at law and one at equity. On the other hand, because the case was in equity, there was no jury, *even as to the incidental legal issues decided.* Because of the cleanup doctrine, then, a plaintiff might lose access to a jury trial on a legal remedy. Equity would determine the entire dispute. In contrast, the law courts had no such cleanup power. A law court, in which the plaintiff sought damages, had no authority to grant equitable relief.

> ○ ***Example #3.*** Let's return to Example #2, where *P* sues *D* for an injunction (equitable relief) to stop *D*'s trespassing on *P*'s land. In addition, though, *P* seeks damages (legal relief) to compensate her for past trespasses on the land.

The central thrust of the case, the center of gravity, is equity, because (as we discussed above) *P* is most interested in the injunctive relief. The damages *P* seeks are merely incidental to the injunction: They flow naturally from the fact that there has been trespassing in the past. Historically, the entire case (for injunction and for damages) would be heard at equity. The claim for the injunction would invoke equity jurisdiction and the claim for damages could be heard at equity without a jury under the cleanup doctrine.

This is the way the federal courts did things until the Supreme Court decided *Beacon Theatres, Inc. v. Westover.*[21] *Beacon Theatres* is one of the pivotal cases in the development of the Seventh Amendment and established important new perspectives on the Seventh Amendment. First, according to the Court, the historical test used to determine a right to jury trial is not static. The inquiry is not *entirely* how the case would have been handled in England in 1791. Rather, courts today are to take account of modern procedural reforms, including the Federal Rules of Civil Procedure.[22] Remember that equity acts only when one's legal remedy is inadequate. Modern procedure, including liberal joinder provisions under the Federal Rules, allows the assertion of more claims in a single case than the common law rules did. Accordingly, cases seeking legal relief (to which a jury trial would attach) may be joined with claims for equitable relief.

Second, this reassessment spelled the end of the center-of-gravity theory and the cleanup doctrine. Those practices "must be re-evaluated

---

[21]359 U.S. 500 (1959).

[22]The Court also cited the Declaratory Judgment Act, 28 U.S.C. §§2201, 2202, as such a procedural development. That Act permits a federal court to declare the relative rights of the parties when there is an actual dispute. For example, an insurance company might seek a declaration that a particular event is not covered under a policy with the insured.

in the light of the liberal joinder provisions of the Federal Rules, which allow legal and equitable causes to be brought and resolved in one civil action."[23] After *Beacon Theatres*, then, federal courts do not assess whether the central thrust of the case is equitable or legal and thus whether the case as a whole is tried with a jury. Instead, they are to assess the availability of a jury on an issue-by-issue basis. The mere presence of equitable issues cannot rob a party of the right to a jury on the facts underlying legal issues. The Court established these rules:

- If an issue of fact underlies a claim for legal relief, it must be tried to a jury, without regard to whether the overall thrust of the case is equitable.
- If an issue of fact underlies both a claim for legal relief and equitable relief, it must be tried to a jury.
- Only if an issue of fact underlies a purely equitable matter is it tried to the judge without a jury.
- Unless there are "imperative circumstances, circumstances which in view of the flexible procedures of the Federal Rules we cannot now anticipate" to the contrary, the jury issues shall be tried before the equity issues. This order of trial ensures that the judge will be bound by the jury's determination of the facts, rather than vice versa.

Beacon Theatres vastly expanded the right to jury trial in federal civil cases. Instead of looking to the main thrust of the case, the Seventh Amendment right is seen to attach to factual *issues*, not to *claims*. Return to Example #2, in which *P* sues for an injunction to stop *D* from trespassing on her land and also seeks damages for *D*'s past trespasses. As we saw above, before *Beacon Theatres,* no issue would have been determined by a jury, because the central thrust of the case was equitable and the equity court, under the cleanup doctrine, would be permitted to determine the issues related to legal relief (damages).

Under *Beacon Theatres*, however, the court would consider the jury right issue by issue. The issue of whether *D* has trespassed underlies the claim for damages (legal relief), so a jury would decide that question. The issue of damage caused by the past trespass underlies the legal claim, so a jury would decide that issue as well. Only the question of whether *P* is entitled to an injunction (equitable relief) would be decided by the judge. And on that question, the judge is guided by what the jury found regarding past trespass, which may affect the need for an injunction.

Moreover, the order in which the legal and equitable issues are asserted in the case is irrelevant.

---

[23]*Beacon Theatres*, 359 U.S. at 510.

○ ***Example #4.*** *P* sues *D* regarding a contract between them. *P* claims
that the contract should be rescinded because he was induced to enter
into it by *D*'s fraudulent misrepresentations. *D* claims that the contract
is valid, should not be rescinded, and that *P* has breached the contract
and owes her damages. *P* sues *D* for rescission, which is classic equitable
relief. *D* answers and asserts a counterclaim[24] against *P* for breach of the
contract damages. The counterclaim states a claim for legal relief (damages).

Before *Beacon Theatres*, there would have been no jury in this case.
P's claim for rescission would have invoked equity jurisdiction, and
the equity court, under the cleanup doctrine, could have adjudicated
D's counterclaim and thus would have determined whether *D* was
entitled to damages if the contract were valid.

After *Beacon Theatres*, however, the jury question is assessed issue
by issue, regardless of the order in which the claims are asserted. *D*'s
counterclaim for damages states a claim for legal relief. Obviously,
every issue underlying that claim, including whether the contract was
valid and whether it was breached, would be decided by a jury. Thus,
much of the equitable claim for rescission would be affected by the
jury determination, because its determination of the validity of the
contract would affect the judge's determination of whether rescission
is proper. In other words, if the jury determined that the contract is
valid, it would be very difficult for the judge to order rescission.

In 1962, the Supreme Court reinforced *Beacon Theatres* with *Dairy
Queen, Inc. v. Wood*.[25] In that case, the plaintiff sought an injunction
to stop the defendant from using its trade name and also sought an
"accounting" for the past improper use of the name. The latter claim
was for damages, but by using the phrase "accounting" (which was
historically a proceeding in equity), the plaintiff hoped to defeat any
claim for a jury trial. In the old days, this situation would have been
handled by the cleanup doctrine in equity: Seeking the injunction
invoked equity jurisdiction and the claim for accounting, even if seen
as damages, could be decided by equity as incidental to the injunction. Thus, back in the day, there would have been no jury trial on any
issue. Despite *Beacon Theatres*, the lower courts applied the cleanup
doctrine and struck the defendant's demand for a jury trial.

The Supreme Court used the occasion to drive home what it said
in *Beacon Theatres*. First, it does not matter whether a claim to legal
relief is seen as "incidental." The right to a jury trial on such fact
issues underlying a claim at law cannot be deprived because the case

---

[24]A counterclaim is a claim asserted by the defendant against the plaintiff in the
pending case. See §12.5.1.
[25]369 U.S. 469 (1962).

also contains a claim for equitable relief. Whether the equitable claim is somehow more important is irrelevant. Second, the jury issues are to be tried first, absent exceptional circumstances that the Court could not foresee.

That left the question of whether the claim for accounting was equitable or legal. Again, the Court was willing to consider modern procedural developments in making the assessment. Historically, claims for an accounting were handled in equity precisely so there would be no jury. The theory was that complicated matters of calculation were beyond the capacity of lay jurors, so such claims should be tried at equity and not at law. The Court in *Dairy Queen* noted, however, that Federal Rule 53(b) permits a district court to appoint a master to aid the jury in calculating damages. (We discussed the use of masters in §8.6.) Because of the availability of a master, it was more difficult for the plaintiff to show that her legal remedy of damages was inadequate. Thus, it was more difficult to show that she needed the equitable remedy of an accounting. Only in rare situations, not presented in *Dairy Queen*, will a party be able to show that damages are inadequate.

In the end, then, the defendant was entitled to a jury trial on all issues underlying the plaintiff's claim for damages. Those issues also underlay the plaintiff's claim for an injunction, so the jury would determine all important issues in the case. The judge would determine the propriety of an injunction but would be bound to follow the jury's determination of the facts concerning whether the defendant had used the plaintiff's trade name inappropriately.

Remember, however, that the Seventh Amendment applies only in federal court, so states are not required to follow any of these holdings. In California, though there is a state-law right to a jury at law (and not at equity), courts continue to follow the center-of-gravity and cleanup doctrines. In California state courts, then, if a case is primarily about equitable relief, there is no right to a jury trial on any issue.[26]

Procedures That Developed in Equity

Various procedures for asserting claims—including the class action, the shareholder derivative suit, and interpleader (all of which we see in Chapter 13)—developed in equity courts, not in law courts. Does that mean that there is no jury right in such cases? No. *Ross v. Bernhard*[27] was a shareholders' derivative suit, which permits a stockholder of a corporation to sue on behalf of the corporation against

---

[26]C&K Engineering Contractors v. Amber Steel Co., 587 P.2d 1136, 1141 (Cal. 1978) (claim for damages "does not convert what is essentially an equitable action into a legal one for which a jury trial would be available").

[27]396 U.S. 531 (1970).

officers and directors whose mismanagement harmed the company. Even though that type of claim developed at equity, the Court upheld the right to a jury by looking at the underlying claim. Because the underlying claim for mismanagement sought recovery of damages for harming the corporation, there was a right to jury trial. Thus, "nothing turns now upon . . . the procedural devices by which the parties happen to come before the court."[28] The same is true with declaratory judgment cases. Though declaratory judgment developed largely in equity, the remedy of a declaration of rights is neither equitable nor legal. The court must look to the underlying assertion in the case to see if the jury trial right attaches. In other words, the court looks to see how the dispute would arise if it were asserted as a traditional case for "coercive" relief (such as damages or an injunction).

Problems with Some Monetary Remedies

Not all monetary recoveries constitute damages and, thus, legal relief. For instance, restitution, though monetary, is not necessarily legal relief. While damages compensate for harm, restitution generally seeks the disgorgement of an unjust benefit.[29] Parties often argue about the proper characterization of monetary relief, because the issue affects the availability of a jury trial.

For example, in *Tull v. United States*,[30] the federal government sought civil penalties under the Clean Water Act, alleging that the defendant had violated the Act by dumping material on wetlands. Under the Act, the government sought civil penalties of $10,000 per day, totaling $22,000,000. The Court refused to rely on an "abstruse historical search for the nearest 18th-century analog,"[31] and focused instead on the remedy. Because the penalties were intended to deter and punish (rather than restore the status quo), they were analogous to damages, which traditionally were available at law.

Interestingly, while the Court concluded that the Seventh Amendment thus required a jury determination on the question of the defendant's *liability*, the determination of the civil penalty was

---

[28]*Id.* at 540.

[29]If a toll collector charges you $2.00 instead of $1.50, he has been unjustly enriched by 50 cents. Your claim for return of that sum would be restitution, not damages. The Court suggested in *Chauffeurs* that restitution was entirely equitable. Professor Murphy concludes, however, that most claims for restitution historically would have been tried at law, and therefore to a jury. Colleen P. Murphy, *Misclassifying Monetary Restitution*, 55 S.M.U. L. Rev. 1577, 1598-1607, 1626-1628 (2002).

[30]481 U.S. 412 (1987).

[31]*Id.* at 421. The defendant argued that the claim was akin to an action in debt, which was at law. The government claimed it was more like an action to abate a public nuisance, which would historically have been heard at equity.

not for the jury. According to the Court, the quantification of the civil penalty was largely unconstrained by meaningful standards and thus entrusted to the discretion of the judge; the assessment was simply not a "fundamental element" of jury trial.[32]

On the other hand, *Feltner v. Columbia Pictures Television, Inc.*[33] upheld the right to have a jury determine the dollar amount of statutory damages to be awarded for violation of the Copyright Act. Under that Act, the plaintiff has a choice of showing actual damages or recovering statutory damages of at least $750 and no more than $30,000, "as the court considers just." Though the Act envisioned that the judge would set the amount for statutory damages, the Court concluded that the Seventh Amendment required a jury determination. The Court found "overwhelming evidence that the consistent practice at common law was for juries to award damages."[34] It distinguished *Tull* by noting that there was "no evidence that juries had historically determined the amount of civil penalties to be paid to the Government."[35]

In *Chauffeurs,* which we discussed above regarding the historical analog test, the plaintiffs sought back pay and health care benefits lost when they were fired. The majority concluded that the claims were for compensation and thus constituted damages, which, of course, is legal (not equitable) relief.[36] Accordingly, the plaintiffs were entitled to a jury on all issues in the case.

The lesson from these cases is that one should not assume that a monetary recovery automatically constitutes damages. While an award aimed at compensating the claimant for harm done, or at punishing the defendant for egregious behavior, constitutes classic legal relief, civil penalties and restitution might not.

Can the Seventh Amendment Be Overridden by Practical Concerns or by Congress?

In a cryptic footnote in *Ross v. Bernhard*,[37] the Court suggested (with no citation to authority) that one factor to be addressed in determining the right to a jury is "the practical abilities and limitations of

---

[32]*Id.* at 426 n.9.

[33]523 U.S. 340 (1998).

[34]*Id.* at 353.

[35]*Id.* at 355.

[36]The Court concluded that the monetary recovery sought was to compensate the plaintiffs for harm, and not to force the defendant to return a sum unjustly held. Thus, the claim was not for restitution.

[37]We saw this case at note 27 above in discussing the application of the Seventh Amendment to procedures that developed in equity.

juries."[38] This language raised the possibility of a "complexity exception" to the Seventh Amendment. That is, perhaps there are some cases that are so difficult to understand that the jury simply cannot be expected to do its job meaningfully. In such a case, perhaps the Seventh Amendment does not require a jury trial. Some scholars have concluded that the common law of 1791 recognized such an exception to the right to jury trial.[39]

The lower courts have been reluctant to find such an exception, even in cases that might seem to justify one. In *In re U.S. Financial Securities Litigation*,[40] the district court refused to allow a jury trial, because the case involved complex issues, would tie up the jury for two years, and involved evidence that was "the equivalent of reading the first 90 volumes of the Federal Reporter, Second Series."[41] The Ninth Circuit reversed, and rejected the notion of a complexity exception to the Seventh Amendment. The court noted that the Supreme Court has never embraced the idea expressly. Moreover, there is no reason to believe that a judge has any greater background in complex issues of electronics or economics, for example, than jurors would.

The Third Circuit has embraced a very narrow exception to the right of a jury trial in complex cases. It is not based upon the historical possibility that courts recognized such an exception in 1791, nor is it based upon the footnote from *Ross* as an exception to the Seventh Amendment. Instead, it is rooted in due process. If a case is so complicated that it is "beyond the ability of a jury to decide by rational means with a reasonable understanding of the evidence and applicable legal rules," it would violate due process to submit the matter to a jury.[42] The case raises at least two interesting questions. One, why should due process (which is established in the Fifth Amendment) trump the Seventh Amendment? After all, the latter amended the Constitution of which the former is part. The Third Circuit implicitly found due

---

[38]396 U.S. at 538 n.10. The Court reiterated the point in a footnote in *Chauffeurs*, 494 U.S. at 565 n.4. The quoted language came after the Court listed the two well-established factors discussed above: the historical inquiry and the assessment of remedies. The addition of this third factor in the *Ross* footnote raised a general possibility that the jury trial right is susceptible to a balancing test. But, as Professor Redish concludes, "the footnote is so cursory, conclusory, and devoid of cited authority or reasoned analysis that it is difficult to believe it could have been intended to reject such established historical practice or Supreme Court precedent." Martin H. Redish, *Seventh Amendment Right to Jury Trial: A Study in the Irrationality of Rational Decision Making*, 70 Nw. U. L. Rev. 486, 526 (1975).

[39]*See generally* Roger Kirst, *The Jury's Historic Domain in Complex Cases*, 58 Wash. L. Rev. 1 (1982).

[40]609 F.2d 411 (9th Cir. 1979).

[41]*Id.* at 416 n.13.

[42]In re Japanese Electronic Prods. Antitrust Litig., 631 F.2d 1069, 1088 (3d Cir. 1980).

process to be more important than the Seventh Amendment. Two, why do we assume that a judge is better able than jurors to comprehend complex financial, economic, or scientific evidence?

The Supreme Court raised a few eyebrows concerning jury competence in *Markman v. Westview Instruments, Inc.*[43] There, it held that the judge, rather than a jury, should determine the issue of the scope of a patent. Thus, though there is a right to a jury in patent infringement cases, the issue of how to construe the patent is to be decided by the judge. The Court employed a functional analysis and was impressed by the relative ability of the judge, as opposed to the jury, to determine the question. *Markman* has not supported a movement toward embracing a general "complexity exception." First, the Court did not speak in expansive terms, but expressly limited its holding to the interpretation of "terms of art in patent cases."[44] Second, it did not refer to the *Ross* footnote mentioning the practical abilities of jurors. Third, historic practice was not clear as to whether the issue of the interpretation of the patent was for the judge or jury. So *Markman* is interpreted narrowly.

The Supreme Court does not always uphold a right of jury trial. In Chapter 11, we discuss how a valid judgment entered in one case may have a binding effect on subsequent litigation, through the "preclusion doctrines." In *Parklane Hosiery Co. v. Shore*,[45] which we discuss in §11.4.5, the Court held that these doctrines may deprive a litigant of having a jury determine fact issues. There, the first case was brought in federal court by a federal agency, seeking only injunctive relief, so there was no right to jury trial. The second case was a private civil case in federal court, in which a jury trial would have been proper. Under preclusion law, however, the first case determined issues that were relevant in the second, and those determinations bound the parties in the second case. This was true even though the result was to remove those issues from the jury's purview in the second case.

Moreover, Congress can create claims and provide for their enforcement before administrative tribunals, which are not Article III courts. The general congressional power to do this is beyond our scope. Suffice it to say for present purposes that the Supreme Court generally has recognized Congress's power to do this, at least when the case involves "public rights" (meaning rights between citizens and the government).[46] Indeed, the Court later explained that its reference to the

[43]517 U.S. 370 (1996).
[44]*Id.* at 384 n.9.
[45]439 U.S. 322 (1979).
[46]*See* Atlas Roofing Co. v. Occupational Safety & Health Review Comm'n, 430 U.S. 442, 460 (1977).

"practical abilities and limitations of juries" in the *Ross* footnote was aimed only at such cases.[47]

What about disputes between private citizens? Occasionally, Congress creates a substantive right to be enforced in the federal courts and expresses a preference that the issues be decided by the judge, without a jury. Because provisions of the Constitution are supreme over contrary provisions in legislation, Congress cannot override the Seventh Amendment in this way.[48] As to the converse situation, Congress can grant a jury trial right by statute even as to matters that would not fall within the Seventh Amendment.[49] Thus, if Congress provides for a jury trial, the court need not determine whether the Seventh Amendment applies. The statutory provision is sufficient.

Requirement of Written Demand for Jury

A jury is not automatically empaneled in those cases in which the Seventh Amendment allows a jury trial. Under Rule 38(b)(1), a party must demand a jury trial in writing "no later than 14 days after the last pleading directed to the [jury-triable] issue is served." The demand can be made in a pleading or in a separate document but must be in writing. A party who fails to make such a written demand and serve it on the other parties waives her right to a jury trial and the case is tried to the judge, as Rule 38(d) makes clear. On the other hand, Rule 39(b) provides that the court has discretion to grant a motion for jury trial on proper issues even when a party failed to make a proper demand.

Under Rule 38(d), a party who demands a jury and then changes her mind can withdraw the jury demand only with the consent of all other parties. Moreover, it is worth noting that there is no right *not* to have a jury. If one party does not want a jury but another party does (and makes a timely, proper written demand for it on jury-triable issues), there will be a jury.

---

[47]Granfinanciera, S.A. v. Nordberg, 492 U.S. 33, 42 n.4 (1989) (the quoted language is aimed at "whether Congress has permissibly entrusted the resolution of certain disputes to an administrative agency or specialized court of equity, and whether jury trials would impact the functioning of the legislative scheme").

[48]*Id.* at 52-53 (Congress "lacks the power to strip parties contesting matters of private right of their constitutional right to a trial by jury"); Curtis v. Loether, 415 U.S. 189 (1974) (statutory claim for damages for racial discrimination invoked Seventh Amendment right to jury trial, notwithstanding congressional ambivalence on whether the case should be tried to a jury). *See generally* Mary Kay Kane, *Civil Jury Trial: The Case for Reasoned Iconoclasm*, 28 Hastings L.J. 1, 20-27 (1976).

[49]*See generally* 9 Wright & Miller §2302.2.

§9.2.3   Selecting the Jury

Lawyers take jury selection very seriously. Each trial lawyer has things she looks for in potential jurors and develops a "sixth sense" about potential jurors who will be sympathetic and those who will not. Jury selection has become a cottage industry for consultants, who are often employed by lawyers, at least in high-profile cases, to help select the jury. We focus here on the process by which the jury is selected.

In federal and state judicial systems, court administrators generate a "master roll" of potential jurors from a variety of public sources. Rosters of registered voters, licensed drivers, taxpayers, and welfare recipients are common sources of this list. For much of our history, some racial and societal groups were systematically excluded from the master rolls in various communities. The Supreme Court struck down such exclusions and established that the Constitution requires that the master roll reflect a reasonable cross-section of the local population.[50] The jury is the voice of that community. There is no right to have the jury as ultimately empaneled "composed in whole or in part of persons of [one's] own race," but a litigant "does have the right to be tried by a jury whose members are selected pursuant to nondiscriminatory criteria."[51]

The court administrator summons citizens as needed to report for jury duty. A group of those summoned each day is sent to a courtroom in which a jury is needed. They constitute the *venire* from which the jury itself will be chosen. The members of the *venire*, perhaps a couple dozen persons, then go through the *voir dire* process, which consists of a series of questions. *Voir dire* means "to speak the truth" or "to see what is said." The goal is to empanel a jury of unbiased persons who have no independent knowledge of the transaction in question.[52] Thus, the questions are aimed at determining whether any potential juror has a bias, personal knowledge of the facts, or a relationship with one of the parties or the lawyers. In federal court, Federal Rule 47(a) permits the judge to conduct the *voir dire* questioning, or to allow the parties or their lawyers to do so. The judge has great discretion in running the *voir dire*, and may, for instance, use written questionnaires

---

[50]*See, e.g.*, Taylor v. Louisiana, 419 U.S. 522, 531 (1975) (reversing defendant's conviction because jury excluded women and was not a fair cross-section of the community).

[51]Batson v. Kentucky, 476 U.S. 79, 85 (1986).

[52]The jury's verdict is to be based upon the evidence introduced at trial. A juror who was an eyewitness or who otherwise had independent knowledge of the facts might base her decision on that independent knowledge. Moreover, other jurors might be swayed by the independent knowledge of this one juror. So such persons are weeded out in the *voir dire* process.

in conjunction with oral questioning. Invariably, when the judge conducts the *voir dire*, she will allow the parties and lawyers to suggest lines of questioning. The lawyers for each party watch each potential juror closely, study the responses to the various questions, and try to pick up clues about which way that person might "lean" in the case.

In every judicial system, each side in the litigation has two methods for disqualifying potential jurors from serving on the case. These challenges (also called *strikes*) can be "for cause" (also known as "for favor") or "peremptory." Each judicial system permits unlimited strikes for cause but limits the number of peremptory challenges. In federal civil cases, 28 U.S.C. §1870 provides that each party shall have three peremptory strikes.[53] A strike for cause is based upon the potential juror's bias or relationship with a party or lawyer. For example, the plaintiff's sister could be challenged for cause, as could an employee of the defendant corporation or a potential juror who was an eyewitness to the events that are the subject of the litigation. The court determines whether a party's challenge for cause should be granted.

In contrast to this type of challenge, a peremptory strike historically was exercised without statement of a reason and could not be questioned. Such challenges date to the thirteenth-century English practice (at least in criminal cases). In this country, peremptory strikes have been recognized in civil cases from colonial times. Many lawyers and commentators defend the use of peremptory challenges as permitting the lawyer who suspects bias, but who cannot elicit direct evidence of it in *voir dire*, to remove a potential juror. Some commentators have also argued that the ability to strike potential jurors without stating a reason legitimizes the resulting verdict.[54]

Today, however, if the other party charges discrimination in the use of a peremptory challenge, the party exercising the challenge must proffer a nondiscriminatory reason for the strike. The leading case is *Batson v. Kentucky*.[55] There, the Court held that a prosecutor's use of peremptory strikes on the basis of race violated constitutional principles of equal protection. Because *Batson* was based upon constitutional provisions applicable to the states under the Fourteenth Amendment,

---

[53]It also provides that in cases of multiple plaintiffs or defendants, the court may consider the multiple parties "as a single party" for this purpose. Thus, each side—the plaintiff's side and the defendant's side—would have a total of three peremptory strikes. The same statute goes on, however, to allow the court to permit additional peremptory strikes.

[54]Blackstone made this point by saying that a party "should have a good opinion of his jury, the want of which might totally disconcert him, the law wills not that he should be tried by any one man against whom he has conceived a prejudice, even without being able to assign a reason for such . . . dislike." 4 William Blackstone, Commentaries * 353 (1859).

[55]476 U.S. at 85.

its holding affected practice in state as well as in federal courts. All courts have gained experience in holding "*Batson* hearings" to determine whether the use of peremptory strikes is racially discriminatory.

Batson was a criminal case, in which the prosecutor, who is a government actor, engaged in racially discriminatory conduct. What about civil cases between private parties, in which there is no government actor? The Constitution protects persons from deprivation of equal protection of the laws, but the deprivation must be caused by "state action." Purely private discrimination is not unconstitutional (though it may violate statutes). In the important 1991 case of *Edmonson v. Leesville Concrete Co.*,[56] the Supreme Court extended *Batson* to civil cases between private parties. The majority opinion emphasized that the government (either federal or state) sets up the court system that permits the use of peremptory strikes. The use of those challenges, even in litigation involving nongovernmental parties, constitutes state action.

The Court extended its conclusion in *Edmonson* to gender-based discrimination three years later in *J.E.B. v. Alabama*.[57] In that case, Alabama, acting on behalf of the mother of a minor child, sued a man for paternity and child-support payments. The suit was in state court, and Alabama used nine of its ten peremptory strikes (under state law) to remove potential male jurors. As a result, the jury was entirely female. The defendant objected to the state's use of peremptory strikes based on gender and claimed that it violated his rights of equal protection. The case was much easier than *Edmonson* on the question of state action; it was, after all, a *state* that was using the peremptory challenges. The tougher issue was whether discrimination on the basis of *gender* violated equal protection. The Court concluded that it did, in ways similar to racial discrimination. It also painted with a broad brush in determining whose rights were violated:

> Discrimination in jury selection, whether based on race or on gender, causes harm to the litigants, the community, and the individual jurors who are wrongfully excluded from participation in the judicial process. The litigants are harmed by the risk that the prejudice which motivated the discriminatory selection of the jury will infect the entire proceedings. . . . The community is harmed by the State's participation in the perpetuation of invidious group stereotypes and the inevitable loss of confidence in our judicial system that such state-sanctioned discrimination in the courtroom engenders. When state actors exercise peremptory challenges in reliance on gender stereotypes, they ratify and reinforce prejudicial views of the relative abilities of men and

---

[56]500 U.S. 614, 631 (1991).
[57]511 U.S. 127 (1994).

women. . . . [I]ndividual jurors themselves have a right to nondiscriminatory jury selection procedures. . . . Striking individual jurors on the
assumption that they hold particular views simply because of their
gender . . . denigrates the dignity of the excluded juror. . . .[58]

There is no question that the holding in *J.E.B.* applies in wholly
private litigation as well. *Edmonson* commands that result. And it is
also absolutely clear that both *Edmonson* and *J.E.B.* apply equally in
state and federal courts. The holdings are based upon equal protection
guarantees applicable to the federal government and applicable to the
states through the Fourteenth Amendment.

There are some notable problems in the wake of *Edmonson* and
J.E.B. First, what classes of potential jurors are protected? We can
say with certainty that a litigant may not use her peremptory challenges to strike potential jurors because of their race or their gender.
What about national origin? What about religion? The Supreme Court
has not addressed such questions and lower federal courts and state
courts are having difficulty discerning where to draw the line. One
state appellate court concluded that it is permissible to use a peremptory strike to remove a potential juror on the basis of her religion. It
reasoned that one's religion imparted to her certain beliefs, and that
it has always been permissible to strike jurors because of their beliefs.
In contrast, one's race or gender does not say anything about one's
beliefs.[59]

The second troublesome issue after *Edmonson* and *J.E.B.* is the
procedure the court should use for determining whether a litigant
is using peremptory challenges in an unconstitutional way. As noted
above, though there is no right to a jury composed of one's own
race, there is a right to be tried by a jury selected through nondiscriminatory criteria. In her concurrence in *J.E.B.*, Justice O'Connor
lamented that the Court's "further constitutionalizing jury selection procedures . . . increases the number of cases in which jury
selection—once a sideshow—will become part of the main event."[60]
Though the steps in this "sideshow" are clear, the standards have not
been applied consistently.

A party challenging another party's use of a peremptory strike must
raise the issue promptly—specifically, at the time the peremptory
challenge is asserted. The court has no duty to raise the issue on its
own motion, and a party's failure to object in a timely fashion waives

---

[58]*Id.* at 140-142 (footnotes and citations omitted).
[59]Casarez v. Texas, 913 S.W.2d 468, 495 (Tex. Ct. Crim. App. 1995).
[60]*J.E.B.*, 511 U.S. at 147 (O'Connor, J., concurring).

the objection.[61] The court must then inquire into the matter. In the "*Batson* hearing," the objecting party must make a *prima facie* showing that the would-be juror was a member of a relevant group and was removed *because* of her membership in that group. Courts have had great difficulty determining what constitutes a *prima facie* showing.[62]

If the objector makes a *prima facie* showing of discrimination, the burden shifts to the other party to show a neutral reason for her use of the peremptory challenge to strike this particular juror. The objecting party is then allowed to present rebuttal evidence in an effort to show that the other party's "neutral" reason is actually a pretext for improper discriminatory behavior. The burden of persuading the court lies with the party objecting to the use of the peremptory strike. Because the issue involves subjective matters, the trial court's decision on whether to uphold the peremptory challenge is rarely disturbed on appeal.

In his concurring opinion in *Batson*, Justice Marshall argued that peremptory challenges should be eliminated. He was concerned that any trial lawyer worth her salt would be able to state a "neutral" reason for her exercise of a peremptory strike. For instance, if a lawyer's assertion that a potential juror was "uncommunicative" or "never cracked a smile" constituted a legitimate nondiscriminatory reason for exercising the peremptory strike, "the protection erected by the Court today may be illusory."[63] Some people feel that it is. In addition, it is not clear what a court should do if race or gender is one of multiple reasons for striking a potential juror. The Second Circuit has concluded that "*Batson* challenges may be brought by [parties] who can show that racial discrimination was a *substantial part* of the motivation for a . . . peremptory challenge[]."[64]

The *voir dire* process winnows the *venire* to the jury itself (often called the jury *panel*). Historically, courts empaneled 12 jurors in civil (and criminal) cases and employed "alternate jurors." The alternate jurors (usually two) would sit in the jury box with the other jurors but would play a role only if one of the original jurors was excused during the case. Jurors can always be excused, even during the trial, for "good cause." Such cause includes things such as illness or a family

---

[61]*See, e.g.*, Dawson v. Wal-Mart Stores, Inc., 978 F.2d 205, 210 (5th Cir. 1992) (objection after trial was untimely); Clark v. Newport News Shipbuilding & Dry Dock Co., 937 F.2d 934, 939 (4th Cir. 1991) (court under no obligation to raise *Batson* issue).

[62]*Compare* Byram v. Ozmint, 339 F.3d 203, 207 (4th Cir. 2003) (use of nine of ten peremptory strikes and four additional challenges to exclude white jurors not a *prima facie* showing) *with* Mahaffey v. Page, 162 F.3d 481, 485 (7th Cir. 1998) (use of peremptory strikes to exclude every juror of the defendant's race made a *prima facie* showing).

[63]*Batson*, 476 U.S. at 106 (Marshall, J., concurring).

[64]Howard v. Senkowski, 986 F.2d 24, 30 (2d Cir. 1993) (emphasis added).

emergency.[65] If an original juror is taken off the case for such a reason, an alternate juror takes her place and participates in deliberations and in rendering the verdict. If no original juror is excused, the alternate jurors play no role in the deliberations and verdict.

This is still the system in most state courts. In the federal system, however, things have changed. Though, as noted, tradition supported 12-person juries, some federal districts experimented with smaller juries, mostly as a way to reduce costs. The Supreme Court upheld the use of a six-person jury in a civil case in *Colgrove v. Battin*.[66] Though the Seventh Amendment preserves jury trial as it existed at "common law," that reference is to the *right* that existed at common law, and not to "the various incidents of trial by jury."[67] The size of the jury is simply an "incident" of jury trial, and thus the federal courts today are not locked into the common law practice of using 12 jurors.

The size of the civil jury in federal court is governed by Federal Rule 48, which allows juries of no fewer than six and not more than 12 members. For economic reasons, the use of six jurors is routine. In 1991, Rule 48 was amended to abolish the alternate juror in civil cases in federal court. Thus, in general, every juror empaneled participates in the trial, deliberation, and verdict unless excused under Rule 47(c) for "good cause." Rule 48 requires, unless the parties stipulate to the contrary, that the verdict must be "returned by a jury of at least 6 members." That means that a prudent judge in a case involving a lengthy trial will empanel at least seven jurors. Then, if one is excused for cause (for example, illness), the remaining six can return a verdict.

§9.2.4 Jury Instructions, Deliberation, and Verdict

After all parties have presented their evidence at trial—at the "close of all evidence"—the lawyer for each party makes her "closing statement" (or "summation"). As with the opening statement, the plaintiff goes first. The lawyers summarize the evidence in a light most favorable to their clients and urge the jurors to find the facts in favor of their client. Then the case is ready for submission to the jury.[68]

We noted in §9.2.1 that the jury's job is to determine the *facts*, while the judge determines the *law*. When the case is submitted to the jury, the court instructs the jury on the applicable law through "jury

---

[65]One interesting case is *Bondie v. Bic Corp.*, 947 F.2d 1531, 1535 (6th Cir. 1991), in which the court dismissed the juror for chronic tardiness.

[66]413 U.S. 149 (1973).

[67]*Id.* at 156.

[68]In §9.5, we will see that in rare cases the judge may grant a motion for judgment as a matter of law and refuse to let the jury decide the case.

instructions."[69] Jury instructions are delivered by the judge orally. Under Rule 51(a)(1), each party submits proposed jury instructions to the judge at the close of all evidence at trial (or earlier if the court directs).[70] Under Rule 51(b), before final arguments to the jury, the judge must inform the parties of (1) the instructions she intends to give and (2) those proposed instructions she rejects. She must also permit each party to object on the record (and out of the jury's hearing) to the judge's proposals. Under Federal Rule 51(c)(1), a party objecting to a jury instruction must make her objection "distinctly" and state the grounds for objection before final arguments and the instructions are delivered. This means that objections are to be made early enough to give the judge a chance to correct any errors in her proposed instructions.

The reading of jury instructions ("charging the jury") is rarely a scintillating event. Imagine listening as the judge reads on about the elements of a claim, such as negligence, the definition of proximate cause, the elements of defenses such as assumption of risk, and the like. In addition to stating the law, at least in federal practice, the judge may also comment on the evidence. This authority, which comes from the common law, has been abolished in many state courts. Though she can thus discuss the evidence, the federal judge should make it clear that the ultimate decision of what the facts *are* is for the jury. She must also be careful not to argue a particular point of view to the jury. Outside that, however, the federal judge certainly may "clear away false issues and lead the jury to a proper understanding of the facts."[71]

After the court instructs the jury, the jurors "retire from the bar" to deliberate the case. Jury deliberations are conducted in secret, in the privacy of the jury room. How a jury works is one of the great unknowns in the law. The jury is instructed to select a foreperson, who can communicate with the judge if there is a problem or question during the deliberations, and who will be called upon to announce the jury's verdict. It is up to each jury to determine how to select its own foreperson. And how the jury proceeds from that point is up to the jurors. Sometimes the jury takes a "straw poll" at the outset, to see if there is much disagreement. There is no rule book for how the jury is to discharge its function.

---

[69]Traditionally, jury instructions have been read to the jury immediately before the jury retires to deliberate. In some rare situations, a court might give at least some jury instructions at the outset of the trial, to allow jurors to hear the evidence at trial against the background of the law.

[70]There are collections of "form jury instructions" from which lawyers and the court may pick and choose. The use of such forms probably contributes to the stilted nature of the instructions.

[71]Wright & Kane, Federal Courts 672.

One of the most important things on which the judge instructs the jury is the burden of persuasion. We discussed this burden, along with the burdens of pleading and proof, in §7.3.4. There we said that (as a general rule) the party that must plead a particular issue must also offer evidence on it and must also persuade the trier of fact that it is true. In civil cases, the burden of persuasion is to establish a fact "by a preponderance of the evidence." That means that the party with the burden must persuade the fact-finder that something is "more likely than not." The burden of persuasion is important as a tie-breaker.

For example, suppose the parties present evidence on the existence of Issue *A*. This issue could be anything—whether the parties entered into a contract, whether the defendant owed the plaintiff a duty, or whether a vehicle's brakes were defective. One party introduces evidence to show that *A* is true. The other party introduces evidence to show that *A* is not true. If the jury concludes that the issue is just as likely as not—that is, that neither scenario is more likely than the other—the evidence is said to be in "equipoise." In that instance, the party with the burden of persuading the fact-finder on Issue *A* will lose. If the burden was on the plaintiff, she will lose for failing to persuade the jury that *A* was true. If the burden was on the defendant, she will lose for failing to persuade the jury that *A* was *not* true.

In assessing the facts, the jury determines how much weight to ascribe to various pieces of evidence and whether various witnesses are credible. The jury, in essence, has this chart in mind, by which it weighs the evidence:

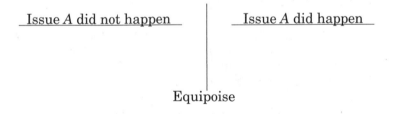

Some cases involve a greater burden of persuasion. In criminal cases, the government must prove the defendant's guilt "beyond a reasonable doubt." Thus, if the government in a criminal case showed that the defendant's guilt was more likely than not (but not that it was true beyond a reasonable doubt), the prosecution would fail. In civil cases, there can occasionally be an intermediate standard for the burden of persuasion. For example, plaintiffs may be required to prove a right to punitive damages by "clear and convincing" evidence. This is a greater showing than "preponderance of the evidence," but less than "beyond a reasonable doubt."

The jury's decision is the *verdict*. The judge determines which of three forms the verdict will take:

- *General verdict.* The simplest form is the "general verdict," in which the jury declares which party wins and, if a claimant won, what the recovery will be. For instance, the jury could say "verdict for the plaintiff for $100,000" or "verdict for the defendant." Such verdicts have the advantage of certainty but reveal nothing about the jury's reasoning.[72]
- *Special verdict.* With the special verdict under Rule 49(a), the jury does not declare a winner, but responds in writing to a series of written questions posed by the judge. Usually, there is one question for each issue of fact presented in the trial. The questions are submitted when the jury commences its deliberations. The judge applies the law to the facts as found by the jury and approves an appropriate judgment. Some commentators criticize the use of the special verdict because it makes the process of fact-finding too precise and scientific, robbing it of the sense of the common person as the general decision maker.[73]
- *General verdict with written questions.* A middle course for verdict forms is provided by Rule 49(b), which has the jury return a general verdict *and* answer specific questions. The questions relate to disputed facts on which the verdict will depend. This process is intended to focus the jury's attention on the important factual questions of the case and thus to ensure that the jury reaches the proper general verdict.

Whatever the form of the verdict, Rule 48 provides, unless the parties stipulate to the contrary, that "the verdict must be unanimous." Generally, then, the jury is required to deliberate on and on until the members are unanimous in the verdict. This is not the case, of course, if the parties have stipulated, for example, that the decision of five jurors will constitute the verdict. If the jury is hopelessly deadlocked, at some point the judge will declare a mistrial and order a new trial before a new jury.

In assessing damages, the jury is not limited by the demand for relief sought in the claimant's pleading, which we studied at §7.3.2. Rule 8(a)(3) requires a claimant to make a demand, but there is no requirement that the demand state a particular dollar figure. Some claimants, however, do make specific dollar demands. In federal court, these demands do not limit the dollar amount of damages a jury may grant.[74] Neither does the demand for judgment limit the type of recovery that may be awarded by the court's judgment.

[72]*See* Skidmore v. Baltimore & O. R. Co., 167 F.2d 54, 60 (2d Cir. 1948) ("The general verdict is as inscrutable and essentially mysterious as the judgment which issued from the ancient oracle of Delphi. Both stand on the same foundation—a presumption of wisdom").

[73]*See, e.g.,* Wright & Kane, Federal Courts 678-679.

[74]An exception to this statement in federal court is the default judgment. As we discussed in §7.5.3, in a default case, the plaintiff cannot recover more than she demanded in her complaint. Moreover, in some states, the demand for judgment does limit the plaintiff's ultimate recovery even in cases that are tried. *See, e.g.,* Va. Code Ann. §8.01-421.

○ ***Example #5.*** *P* sues *D*, and seeks $100,000 in damages, plus costs of litigation.[75] At trial, *P*'s evidence demonstrated that she had suffered damage of $150,000 and that *P* would be entitled to an injunction to stop *D* from acting in a particular way. The jury returns a verdict of $150,000 and the judge enters a judgment for that amount and imposes an injunction on *D*. The judgment is valid. Even though *P* asked only for damages (and only for $100,000), a greater recovery and recovery of a different form of relief is permitted.[76]

§9.3 Entry and Enforcement of Judgment and Award of Costs and (Maybe) Attorney's Fees

Under Rule 54(a), a judgment constitutes "any order from which an appeal lies." We see in §14.4 that an appeal ordinarily lies from a "final judgment," which is the trial court's ultimate conclusion on the merits of the entire case.[77] Thus, the court's grant of a motion to dismiss for failure to state a claim, granted with leave to amend to attempt again to state a claim, will not constitute a judgment. Why? Because the order does not finally adjudicate the case; the plaintiff may replead her complaint.

No matter how a case is adjudicated—whether by jury trial, bench trial, motion for summary judgment, or otherwise—the final outcome will be embodied in a *judgment*. Thus, while not all cases will involve jury verdicts (because, for example, there is no right to a jury trial or a motion of JMOL has been granted), every case that is finally adjudicated in the trial court will result in a judgment. The judgment is a very short document, the operative language of which can often be contained in a single sentence. For instance, it might say "judgment is entered for the plaintiff in the amount of $100,000, plus costs" or "judgment is entered for the defendant, plus costs." Indeed, Federal Rule 54(a) counsels that the document be kept short by saying that the judgment "should not include" extraneous things such as a recital of pleadings or the record of proceedings.

Rule 58(a) mandates that every judgment "must be set out in a separate document."[78] The clerk of the court generally prepares this

---

[75]We have noted before the general rule that the prevailing party recovers her costs from the losing party, and that costs do not include attorney's fees.

[76]The court, not the jury, would determine the equitable relief applicable. See §9.2.2.

[77]There are also situations, studied in §14.5, in which a nonfinal, or interlocutory, order can be appealed. The court's ruling on such an appealable order would also be embodied in a judgment under Rule 54(a).

[78]The Rule also says that a separate document is not required for an order disposing of five specific motions, including orders granting or denying various post-trial motions, including those we see in §§9.5, 9.6, and 9.7. Note that Rule 54(b) permits a court to enter separate judgments for separate claims or regarding different parties

document.[79] The purpose of the separate document requirement is to avoid uncertainty about whether an order or ruling is intended to be a judgment. If the court intends a judgment, it must say so in a separate document. In addition, the clerk of the court is required to note the judgment on the docket sheet promptly.[80]

Together, these two acts — (1) rendition of the judgment on a separate document and (2) notation on the docket sheet — constitute "entry" of the judgment. This is an important event, because it starts the clock for bringing postjudgment motions such as the motion for renewed JMOL, motion for new trial, and motion to set aside the judgment ("for relief from judgment"). In addition, as we see in Chapter 14, it starts the clock running for filing one's notice of appeal.

- ○ ***Example #6.*** After a verdict, the clerk drafts the judgment and stamps it "filed." The judgment has not been entered. Not until the clerk makes the notation of judgment on the docket sheet for the case has the judgment been entered.
- ○ ***Example #7.*** After a verdict, the clerk marks judgment on the docket sheet, but fails to draft a separate document embodying the judgment. The judgment has not been entered. Both rendition of judgment on a separate document and entry on the docket sheet are required to enter the judgment.

The claimant who wins a judgment will want to "execute" (enforce) it.[81] For instance, if the plaintiff wins a judgment for $100,000, she will want to collect her $100,000. The defendant, however, may want

---

in a single case. We discuss this Rule in conjunction with when a party may take an appeal in §14.4.3.

[79]Rule 58(b)(1) details the execution of the judgment by the clerk. In certain instances, such as the return of a general verdict, the clerk of the court prepares, signs, and enters the judgment without any order from the judge. In more complex cases, such as the jury's returning a special verdict, the judge must approve the form of the judgment under Rule 58(b)(2) before the clerk enters it. In exceptional cases, the court might ask counsel to submit a draft judgment for the court's consideration. *See, e.g.*, Gold v. United States, 552 F. Supp. 66, 72-73 (D. Colo. 1982) (because of counsel's familiarity with complex calculations in a tax case, the court asked counsel to draft judgment).

[80]In every case, Rule 79(a) requires the clerk's office to maintain a "civil docket" on which it marks various events briefly and in chronological order. Thus, the docket sheet will indicate the dates on which the complaint was filed, when process was served, when the defendant appeared, the filing and results of motions, etc. One thing the clerk's office must record, as a ministerial duty, is the entry of judgment.

[81]Rule 69(a)(1) permits a district court to issue writ of execution on defendant's property to enforce a money judgment. Rule 70 addresses a district court's authority for enforcing a judgment for a specific act. *See generally* 12 Wright & Miller §§3014 (monetary relief), 3021 (specific relief).

to pursue one of the postjudgment motions discussed in §§9.5, 9.6, and 9.7 or to appeal the judgment. If so, she may claim that the plaintiff is not entitled to any recovery until resolution of such motion or appeal. Rule 62(a) provides that execution of a judgment is automatically stayed for 30 days unless the court orders otherwise. The purpose of this stay is to permit the losing party time to pursue a motion (most of which must be made no more than 28 days after judgment) or to file notice of appeal (which generally must be done no later than 30 days after judgment).

Rule 62(b) permits the losing party to obtain stay of execution beyond the 30 days by posting a bond with the court. Historically, such a bond was called a *supersedeas* bond, but Rule 62 no longer uses that term. We see such a bond on appeal at §14.3, Example #1. The bond suspends the operation of the judgment to allow resolution of the motions or appeal. As a general matter, the victorious claimant is entitled to recover interest on the judgment, paid at the statutory rate, from the date of the judgment.[82]

In §1.1, we noted that each party in litigation pays her own costs and attorney's fees as the case progresses. We also saw the important difference between costs and attorney's fees. Once judgment is entered, and thus once there is a prevailing party, the prevailing party will seek to "shift" her costs (and maybe her attorney's fees) to the other party. Under the "American Rule," embodied in Rule 54(d), the winner generally is entitled to recover her *costs* from the loser.[83] The general rule, though, is that she is not entitled to recover her *attorney's fees* from the other side. Only if some exception applies (some of which we observed in §1.1) will the law permit the shifting of attorney's fees.

Under Rule 58(e), ordinarily, a motion for "taxation" (which just means "recovery") of costs or the award of attorney's fees will not delay the entry of judgment in the case. We see in §14.4 that a losing party has 30 days from entry of judgment in which to file a notice of appeal. That period runs from entry of the judgment, and not 30 days from when the court rules on the motion for taxation of costs or attorney's fees. (We discuss this point at §14.4.2.)

---

[82]The interest rate for federal judgments is based upon Treasury yields as published by the Federal Reserve. 28 U.S.C. §1961. Prejudgment interest is permitted only if allowed by the relevant substantive law.

[83]There are a couple of exceptions to this rule. First, under Rule 68, a defendant may offer to allow judgment to be entered against her on stated terms. If the plaintiff rejects the offer and fails ultimately to recover a more favorable judgment, the plaintiff may be required to pay the defendant's costs incurred after the offer was made. Second, as we saw in §4.5.3, the plaintiff in a diversity of citizenship case who recovers less than $75,000 may be required to pay the defendant's costs.

An award of costs does not necessarily make the prevailing party whole for all out-of-pocket expenditures incurred in the litigation. The taxable costs are listed in §1920 of the Judicial Code, which imposes statutory caps on some allowances. Strangely, the expenses of paying a private process server to serve process on the defendant generally are not taxable, and thus cannot be recovered.[84]

Rule 54(d)(1) imposes no time limit for moving to tax costs. Many districts impose a limit by Local Rule. Without such a provision, the motion must simply be made within a reasonable time. The prevailing party's "bill of costs" must be verified—meaning that it must be executed under oath by the party, her agent, or her attorney. The clerk of the court has the initial responsibility for determining what costs will be recovered. The other party may then object to the clerk's taxation of costs, in which case the district judge reviews the matter *de novo*.

§9.4 No Need for Trial: Summary Judgment (Federal Rule 56)

Background and Standard

In §9.2.1, we noted that adjudication consists of determination of the facts and application of the law to those facts. We also said that the only reason to have adjudication by trial is to resolve genuine disputes of material fact. If the court determines (before trial) that there is no genuine dispute as to any material fact, it may adjudicate without trial by entering summary judgment. In federal court, summary judgment is governed by Rule 56.[85] The summary judgment provisions in most states mirror Rule 56.

Do not confuse a motion for summary judgment with a motion to dismiss for failure to state a claim under Rule 12(b)(6). The latter motion, as we discussed in §7.3.2, is a device to test whether the claimant[86] has alleged enough to have the case remain in the litigation stream. A Rule 12(b)(6) motion does not address evidence; the court does not look beyond the face of the pleadings. In entertaining a Rule

---

[84]*See* 10 Moore's Federal Practice §54.191. Moreover, the court has general equitable authority to limit or deny an award of taxable costs to the prevailing party, though such denial is rare outside the circumstances discussed in the preceding footnote. *Id.* at §54.101[1][b].

[85]An especially useful text on all aspects of federal summary judgment practice is Edward Brunet, John Parry, & Martin H. Redish, Summary Judgment: Federal Law and Practice (4th ed. 2017).

[86]A claimant is anyone asserting a claim. In every case, of course, the plaintiff is a claimant. But other parties may be claimants, as when the defendant asserts a counterclaim against the plaintiff. For simplicity, we refer to the claimant here as the plaintiff.

12(b)(6) motion, the court assumes that the plaintiff's allegations of fact are true and asks whether those allegations plausibly support a claim that the law recognizes.

With summary judgment, the plaintiff has stated a claim, so we are past the Rule 12(b)(6) stage. The case is in the litigation stream. Now, one of the parties asserts that there is no need for a trial. Why? The standard for granting the motion is found in the second sentence of Rule 56(a): "there is no genuine dispute as to any material fact and . . . the movant is entitled to a judgment as a matter of law." The first phrase in that quote is the most important, because it indicates *why* there is no need for a trial. If there is no "genuine dispute as to any material fact," then there is no need for trial. And if that is true, the second part of the quote generally will follow: Because there is no genuine dispute of material fact, all that remains is a question of law, which the judge may decide without trial. Because summary judgment obviates trial and therefore any chance to present one's case to a jury, we are properly nervous about its overzealous application.[87]

In ruling on a motion for summary judgment, the court may go beyond the pleadings and consider evidence. That is, it may view sworn statements and verified evidence that might be proffered if a trial were held. This is why some people say summary judgment "pierces" the pleadings to look to what happened in the real world. Though the parties alleged various disputes in their pleadings, now—looking at evidence, at proof, about what really happened (not the allegations of what the parties thought happened)—it turns out there is no real-world factual dispute.

Consider the old case of *Dyer v. MacDougall*.[88] Plaintiff sued for defamation and alleged that Defendant said derogatory untruths about Plaintiff to various third parties. The allegations stated a claim cognizable by the law. Defendant moved for summary judgment, supported by sworn statements (admissible evidence) from the third parties, in which they said that Defendant had not made any such statements in their presence. Summary judgment in favor of Defendant was appropriate. The *evidence* showed that there was no dispute of fact, and Defendant was entitled to judgment.

---

[87]Professor Thomas asserts, based upon historical study, that summary judgment violates the Seventh Amendment. Suja A. Thomas, *Why Summary Judgment Is Unconstitutional,* 93 Va. L. Rev. 139 (2007). Professor Brunet's historical research leads him to conclude that the practice is constitutional. Edward Brunet, *Summary Judgment Is Constitutional,* 93 Iowa L. Rev. 1625 (2008). *See also* Suja A. Thomas, *Why Summary Judgment is Still Unconstitutional: A Reply to Professors Brunet and Nelson,* 93 Iowa L. Rev. 1667 (2008).

[88]201 F.2d 265 (2d Cir. 1952).

Summary judgment is not a vehicle for trying the facts. Summary judgment is a vehicle for determining *whether the facts are in dispute*. If the materials proffered in a summary judgment motion show that there *is* a genuine dispute on a material fact, the judge cannot choose the version of facts she finds most likely. When the materials show there is a genuine dispute of fact, the court *must* deny summary judgment, and the matter must go to trial.

Any party may move for summary judgment: A claimant may seek summary judgment on her claim or a defendant may seek it on an affirmative defense or because the claimant has no evidence to support her claim. A moving party need not seek summary judgment on the entire case but can move for "partial summary judgment."[89] Rule 56(a) makes this clear by providing that a party can move on a "claim or defense" or on a "part of each claim or defense." Accordingly, the court can determine that specific *issues* need not be tried (because they are not in dispute). In this regard, Rule 56(g) allows the court to treat "any material fact" as established. The case can then proceed to trial on the contested issues of material fact, with the jury instructed that the undisputed facts are taken as established.

- ○ ***Example #8.*** Plaintiff sues Defendant on a claim that has four elements: *A, B, C,* and *D.* Though Defendant's answer denied Plaintiff's allegations on all four issues, as the litigation proceeded it became clear (perhaps in discovery) that there is no question that *A* is true. Plaintiff's motion for partial summary judgment—to establish that *A* is true—can be granted. If it is, the case will then proceed to trial to determine whether *B, C,* and *D* are true (as well as any affirmative defense asserted by Defendant). If that case is tried to a jury, the judge will instruct the jury that *A* is true and that Plaintiff will prevail if she establishes *B, C,* and *D.*

Materials Used in Summary Judgment

How does the court determine whether there is no "genuine dispute of material fact"? Rule 56(c)(1) permits a party to rely upon particular parts of the record, "including depositions, documents, electronically stored information, affidavits or declarations, stipulations (including those made for purposes of the motion only), admissions, interrogatory answers, or other materials."

---

[89]The name, which appears in the title of Rule 56(a), is a bit misleading. As we saw in §9.3, the word *judgment* should be used to refer to an order that disposes of the entire case, not just part of it. Nonetheless, the term "partial summary judgment" is routinely used. In some states, any awkwardness is avoided by referring to "partial summary adjudication" instead of partial summary judgment.

Though the Rule does not require the use of affidavits or declarations, they are quite common in summary judgment motions. An affidavit or declaration is a written statement executed under oath (under penalty of perjury). Rule 56(c)(4) requires that affidavits and declarations be (1) made on personal knowledge, (2) "set out facts that would be admissible in evidence," and (3) show that the "affiant or declarant is competent to testify on the matters stated." These requirements are aimed at ensuring that affidavits and declarations contain the sort of information (under oath, based upon personal knowledge) that would be admissible at trial.[90]

The parties' lawyers usually draft the affidavits or declarations of their client and witnesses who support their client. The documents can be targeted at specific issues and "tailor-made" to support (or oppose) a motion for summary judgment. The lawyer drafts the affidavits and declarations based upon discussions with the persons making them and must be careful to ensure that the document reflects the person's true recollection. Because the affiant signs under oath, the lawyer must tell her of the seriousness of that fact.

Anytime the court considers documentary proof such as a contract or a deed, the document must be "authenticated." This means that the party proffering it must provide admissible evidence from a person with firsthand knowledge sufficient to allow her to have the document admitted into evidence if the case were at trial. Otherwise, the documentary evidence cannot be considered.

- ○ ***Example #9.*** In a wrongful death case, Plaintiff was required to prove that the company leasing a helicopter to her husband was responsible for placing the fuel in the helicopter. She moved for summary judgment based upon fuel invoices showing that the company had purchased the fuel. Because the invoices were unauthenticated, however, they could not be used, and summary judgment was denied.[91]

---

[90]In fact, affidavits themselves might not be admissible as proof at trial, because they constitute hearsay if they would be used to establish the truth of what they assert. The concepts of admissibility and hearsay are beyond our scope. We should realize, though, that Rule 56 allows the court to address evidence proffered in affidavits and declarations that satisfy Rule 56(c)(4) in assessing what the parties or their witnesses will be able to say at trial (if there is one). This is relevant in ruling on the motion for summary judgment. Professor Duane has written extensively about the relationship between Rule 56 and the rules of evidence. *See, e.g.*, James Joseph Duane, *The Four Greatest Myths About Summary Judgment*, 52 Wash. & Lee L. Rev. 1523, 1523-1533 (1996). *See also* DA Realty Holdings, LLC v. Tennessee Land Consultants LLC, 631 Fed. Appx. 817, 822 (11th Cir. 2015) (evidence satisfying exception to hearsay rule would be admissible at trial and may be considered on motion for summary judgment).

[91]Canada v. Blain's Helicopters, Inc., 831 F.2d 920, 925 (9th Cir. 1987). *See also* Hoffman v. Applicators Sales & Services, Inc., 439 F.3d 9, 16 (1st Cir. 2006) (chart purporting to show number of employees and their ages could not be considered because it was based on data that was not authenticated).

The court may look at various discovery materials, including depositions and answers to interrogatories. These documents, like affidavits and declarations, are executed under oath. (See §8.2.2.) To be used in summary judgment, deposition testimony and interrogatory answers must satisfy the requirements listed above for affidavits and declarations—they must be based upon personal knowledge, set forth admissible facts, and demonstrate that the person making the statement is competent to testify to the issues.[92]

On the other hand, pleadings generally are not considered in assessing summary judgment. This makes sense. Remember from §7.7 that pleadings are not executed under oath and therefore do not constitute evidence. Accordingly, courts hold "that pleadings by definition do not constitute factual proof and therefore that a party cannot rely on the pleadings to create an issue of fact for purposes of overcoming a summary judgment motion."[93] Only in rare situations, when parties file "verified pleadings," are pleadings executed under oath.[94] If verified pleadings satisfy the requirements of Rule 56(c)(4) (discussed two paragraphs above Example #9), they may be considered the functional equivalent of affidavits or declarations. Thus, they can constitute proof on a motion for summary judgment.

But remember, too, that summary judgment can be supported by "admissions." This term applies not only to admissions under Rule 36 (which we saw in §8.2.2) but to admissions made at any point during the case (e.g., in pleadings, in open court, in stipulations of the parties, in answers to contention interrogatories, or even in correspondence with the court).[95] One source of admissions may be unverified pleadings. Accordingly, unverified pleadings may be relevant on summary judgment—not because they constitute proof, but because they contain admissions. For example, some courts have refused to allow a party to use affidavits to contradict allegations contained in its pleading.[96] Or a defendant's failure to deny an allegation of fact concerning an essential element of the plaintiff's claim (see §7.4.2) may be taken as an admission on summary judgment.

If admissions permit the court to rule as a matter of law, it may enter summary judgment.

---

[92]*See, e.g.*, Hoover v. Switlik Parachute Co., 663 F.2d 964, 965-967 (9th Cir. 1981) (deposition). *See generally* 11 Moore's Federal Practice §56.14[2][a] & [b].

[93]Brunet, Parry & Redish, note 85 above, at 300.

[94]In federal court, under Rule 23.1, a complaint in a shareholder derivative suit (defined in §13.1) must be verified.

[95]*See* 11 Moore's Federal Practice §56.14[2][d][iii].

[96]*See, e.g.,* Davis v. A.G. Edwards and Sons, Inc., 823 F.2d 105, 108 (5th Cir. 1987) (affirming summary judgment based upon admission in complaint: Plaintiffs were "bound by the admissions in their pleadings, and thus no factual issue can be evoked by comparing their pleadings with [their] affidavits.").

○ ***Example #10.*** Government brought a civil action against Taxpayer to establish Taxpayer's liability for taxes, based upon an allegation that Taxpayer fraudulently transferred property to another person in a sham effort to evade tax. Government sent requests to admit to Taxpayer, asserting that Taxpayer's conveyance of property was a sham, intended as tax evasion. Taxpayer failed to deny the request to admit. On the Government's motion for summary judgment, the "fact" that Taxpayer made a fraudulent conveyance to evade tax liability is established.

Rule 43(c) provides that when a motion relies on facts not in the record, the court may hear the evidence by live testimony. Despite this provision, it is exceptionally rare for a court to order oral testimony in considering a motion for summary judgment.[97] The very purpose of summary judgment is to *avoid* a trial; having witnesses testify in court would turn the hearing on the motion into at least a mini-trial.

When a party moves for summary judgment supported by evidence, the burden shifts to the opposing party to proffer evidence showing that there is a genuine dispute of material fact. She cannot defeat the motion merely by relying on her pleadings. If she could, Rule 56 would have no efficacy.

○ ***Example #11.*** Plaintiff sues Defendant on a promissory note, alleging that Defendant borrowed $100,000, which she agreed to repay with interest by a particular date. Plaintiff alleged that the date has come and gone, and Defendant has failed to pay. Defendant files an unverified answer in which she alleges that she never signed the note. Plaintiff moves for summary judgment, based upon affidavits of two witnesses, who state under oath that they saw Defendant sign the agreement. Defendant opposes the motion by relying on her answer (in which she denied signing the note).

The court may grant summary judgment for Plaintiff here. In ruling on the motion, the court looks to the admissible evidence proffered by the parties—in the form, for example, of affidavits, declarations, deposition testimony, answers to interrogatories—in addition to admissions (including any admissions from the pleadings). It views that evidence in the light most favorable to the nonmoving party.[98] The judge then asks herself this question: Based upon these things, is there a *genuine* dispute of *material* fact? If the answer is no, there is

---

[97]*See, e.g.*, Seamons v. Snow, 206 F.3d 1021, 1025 (10th Cir. 2000) (oral testimony should rarely be used in motion for summary judgment).

[98]Tolan v. Cotton, 572 U.S. 650, 657 (2014) (evidence of the nonmoving party is to be believed, and all justifiable inferences are to be drawn in favor of the nonmoving party). In this case, the Court reversed a grant of summary judgment. The lower court "credited the evidence of the party seeking summary judgment and failed properly to acknowledge key evidence offered by the party opposing that motion." *Id.* at 657-659.

no need for a trial, the court may apply the law to the established facts and enter summary judgment.

And that is the case in Example #11. The only evidence proffered to the court consists of the affidavits in favor of Plaintiff's position. Defendant has attempted to rely on her unverified pleading to rebut evidence. To allow her to do so would contravene the very purpose of summary judgment. If Defendant wants to oppose the motion, she should proffer *evidence* showing that she did not sign the agreement (or, perhaps, that she did, but under duress). If Defendant proffered such evidence, the motion for summary judgment would be denied.

If the party moving for summary judgment fails to demonstrate that there is no genuine dispute of material fact and that she is entitled to judgment as a matter of law, the motion is denied. This is true even if the opposing party presented nothing.[99] The party opposing summary judgment need respond only if the moving party has satisfied the standard set forth in Rule 56(a).

What Constitutes a "Genuine" Dispute as to a "Material" Fact?

Summary judgment is not defeated by a mere dispute as to some facts. Rather, the dispute must be "genuine" and must concern a "material" fact. Materiality is determined by the substantive law creating the claim or defense. A material fact is one that might affect the outcome of the case under the governing law. Thus, "[f]actual disputes that are irrelevant or unnecessary will not be counted."[100] What constitutes a material fact is often obvious. In Example #11, the fact of whether Defendant signed the promissory note was obviously material.

What constitutes a "genuine" dispute on such a material fact? The Supreme Court addressed this issue in *Anderson v. Liberty Lobby*,[101]

---

[99]A famous example is *Adickes v. S.H. Kress & Co.*, 398 U.S. 144 (1970), in which a White woman sued a store for alleged violation of her civil rights. She alleged that the store refused to serve her because she was in the company of Black people. One issue in the case was whether the store employees operated in agreement with the police officer who was present at the time the plaintiff was refused service. (Such involvement of a state officer was required under the substantive law, to show deprivation of civil rights by state action.) The defendant moved for summary judgment based upon the affidavit of its store manager that he had not communicated with the police officer. Plaintiff presented no evidence that would satisfy Rule 56(c)(4). Nonetheless, the Supreme Court held, the defendants' motion for summary judgment must be denied. The defendant failed to present evidence foreclosing the possibility that the police officer and some store employee had reached an agreement that plaintiff not be served.

[100]Anderson v. Liberty Lobby, 477 U.S. 242, 248 (1986).

[101]477 U.S. 242 (1986).

which is one of three cases decided the same day in 1986. In the aggregate, these three cases (known as "the trilogy") sent an unequivocal message to the lower federal courts: Loosen up and grant summary judgment more readily. Obviously, the message was not a license to ignore the requirements of Rule 56. But the Court was saying that lower courts should not invent reasons *not* to grant summary judgment. With these three cases, "summary judgment went from being seen as a motion reluctantly granted only in rare cases to being viewed as a fulcrum for adjudicating the heavy caseload facing federal courts."[102] It is helpful to see each of the trilogy cases as a rejection of a lower court's raising a nontext-based barrier to summary judgment.

The **Anderson** *Case. Anderson* is important for two reasons. First, it made clear that the summary judgment inquiry is functionally similar to that made in ruling on a motion for directed verdict (which is now called a motion for judgment as a matter of law, or JMOL, which we address in §9.5). Second, it clarified the standard for considering evidence from the nonmoving party to create a "genuine" issue of material fact and thus to defeat a motion for summary judgment. *Anderson* requires some background in defamation law.

The Court established in 1964 that a "public figure" can sue for defamation only if she can show that the defendant acted with "actual malice," which means that she acted knowing that the defamatory statement was false (or with reckless disregard for whether the statement was false).[103] In addition, the plaintiff must establish such malice by "clear and convincing evidence." In *Anderson*, public figures sued for defamation over articles that characterized them as racist, anti-Semitic, and neo-Nazi. The defendants moved for summary judgment based largely upon an affidavit by the author of some of the allegedly defamatory articles. The affidavit stated that the author had researched the articles exhaustively, and that he believed the statements made about the plaintiffs to be true. The plaintiffs opposed the motion for summary judgment by asserting that the defendants had failed to verify their information and that an editor of the magazine in which the articles were published characterized them as "ridiculous."

The Court addressed whether this opposition by the plaintiffs had created a "genuine" dispute on a material issue of fact. Some courts had held that summary judgment should be denied if the nonmoving party (the plaintiffs in *Anderson*) produced even a "scintilla" of evidence in support of her position. In *Anderson*, the Court rejected this approach and held that the nonmoving party must produce more than a scintilla; she must produce sufficient evidence from which a

---

[102]11 Moore's Federal Practice §56-26.
[103]New York Times v. Sullivan, 376 U.S. 254, 279-280 (1964).

reasonable jury could find in favor of the nonmoving party. Moreover, the "clear and convincing" requirement is relevant in determining whether the plaintiff could avoid summary judgment. In other words, the plaintiff was required to produce sufficient evidence in opposition to the summary judgment motion from which a reasonable jury could conclude that the plaintiff showed actual malice by clear and convincing evidence. Because the lower courts did not apply this standard, the Court remanded for reconsideration of the motion for summary judgment.

The Celotex Case. The second of the three cases decided in 1986 is *Celotex Corp. v. Catrett*,[104] which involved a wrongful death claim brought against several manufacturers of asbestos. One defendant moved for summary judgment not by producing evidence but by pointing out that the plaintiff lacked evidence showing that the decedent had been exposed to asbestos that it (as opposed to other manufacturers) had manufactured. The moving party used its motion to establish that the plaintiff's responses to interrogatories and other discovery failed to reveal any evidence that the decedent had been exposed to its products. The district court granted the motion, but the court of appeals reversed. According to the appellate court, an earlier Supreme Court case, *Adickes v. S.H. Kress & Co.*,[105] required a party making a motion for summary judgment to support its motion with *evidence*.

The Supreme Court reversed and concluded that nothing in *Adickes* supported the court of appeals' reasoning. Thus, after *Celotex*, a party who does not have the burden of proof at trial may move for summary judgment without producing evidence. Such a party may point out that the record is devoid of evidence supporting the other party's position. This practice is now reflected in Rule 56(c)(1), which permits summary judgment because "a fact cannot be . . . supported."

Once the moving party makes such a showing, the burden shifts to the party with the burden at trial to produce evidence supporting its position. Obviously, *Celotex* is especially helpful to defendants, and allows them to move for summary judgment on the basis of an absence of record evidence supporting an element of the plaintiff's claim. By doing so, the defendant forces the plaintiff to "put her cards on the table" and produce evidence supporting that aspect of her claim. Though finding "mixed signals" in the opinion, Professor Miller concludes that it is "not surprising that *Celotex* has been read as an instruction to the lower courts to increase the disposition of cases

---

[104]477 U.S. 317 (1986).
[105]The case is discussed at note 99 above.

under Rule 56 either to protect defendants or to achieve systemic efficiency."[106]

The **Matsushita Case.** The third of the 1986 cases is *Matsushita Electric Industrial Co. v. Zenith Radio Corp.*,[107] which was a complex antitrust case. Speaking quite generally, antitrust law concerns anticompetitive business behavior. In *Matsushita*, U.S. manufacturers of televisions sued several Japanese manufacturers, and alleged that the Japanese companies had conspired to keep prices of their products sold in the United States artificially low. Such "predatory pricing" could support a claim for violation of the antitrust laws of the United States.

The Supreme Court upheld the defendants' motion for summary judgment. It noted that the plaintiffs' theory of predatory pricing was "implausible" because it would have required the defendants to endure many years of losses to drive the U.S. manufacturers out of business. Because their theory was implausible, the Court held, the plaintiffs were required to come forward with more persuasive evidence than would otherwise be required to defeat summary judgment. Courts routinely say that the party opposing the motion for summary judgment is to receive the benefit of all reasonable doubts as to whether there is a genuine dispute of fact.[108] But the doubts must be reasonable, and courts should "not slip into sheer speculation"[109] when assessing the nonmoving party's position. *Matsushita* indicates that the courts will insist on especially strong evidence when the nonmoving party is the plaintiff and has espoused an implausible theory of liability.

Inspired by *Matsushita*, the defendant in a later case, *Kodak Co. v. Image Technical Services, Inc.*,[110] moved for summary judgment in an antitrust case by arguing that the plaintiff's theory was economically implausible. The Supreme Court rejected the effort because it found the plaintiff's theory plausible. Because a reasonable jury might accept the plaintiff's theory of antitrust violation, *Matsushita* did not apply. It is difficult to know whether *Kodak* speaks more to summary judgment law or to antitrust law. At the very least, however, *Matsushita* demonstrates two things. First, it is worth noting that summary judgment can be appropriate in large complex litigation. Second, a court may properly assess plausibility of a theory in

---

[106]Arthur R. Miller, *The Pretrial Rush to Judgment: Are the "Litigation Explosion," "Liability Crisis," and Efficiency Cliches Eroding Our Day in Court and Jury Trial Commitments?*, 78 N.Y.U. L. Rev. 982 (2003), at 1133 [hereinafter *Pretrial Rush to Judgment*].

[107]475 U.S. 574 (1986).

[108]*See generally* Wright & Kane, Federal Courts 712.

[109]Gibson v. Old Town Trolley Tours, 160 F.3d 177, 181 (4th Cir. 1998).

[110]504 U.S. 451 (1992).

determining how much evidence a nonmoving party must produce to defeat a motion for summary judgment.

An Important Subsequent Case. In *Scott v. Harris,*[111] police officers clocked the plaintiff driving 73 miles per hour in a 55-mile-per-hour zone. The plaintiff led the officers on a high-speed chase, during which the officers attempted to force the motorist's vehicle into a spin. Instead, they caused the car to run off the road, and the plaintiff was severely injured. The plaintiff sued the officers. If the motorist had been driving in a way that endangered human life, the officers' action would have been warranted. The officers moved for summary judgment on this point, supported by the video taken from the police vehicle during the chase. The lower courts denied summary judgment, based upon the plaintiff's version of the facts.

The Court reversed and ordered summary judgment. The lower courts erred in relying on the plaintiff's version of the events, because it was so obviously belied by the video. The Court concluded that "[w]hen opposing parties tell two different stories, one of which is blatantly contradicted by the record, so that no reasonable jury could believe it, the court should not adopt that version of the facts for purposes of ruling on a motion for summary judgment."[112]

Accordingly, it is possible that the record on summary judgment will contain evidence that renders one side's version of events unsupportable. In this era of near ubiquitous security cameras and cellphones with video and photo capacity, it seems likely that there will be more claims that an independent record contradicts the position of a litigant.[113] On motions for summary judgment, the court may ignore evidence that is "blatantly contradicted."[114]

Among others, Professor Arthur Miller laments the movement toward more vigorous use of summary judgment. He asserts that largely unfounded assumptions about a "litigation explosion" and clichés about efficiency have been used to justify what he sees as a dangerous modern trend in favor of summary judgment and concomitant

---

[111]550 U.S. 372 (2007).

[112]*Id.* at 380.

[113]Of course, it is possible that evidence such as video or audio may not contradict the position of the party opposing summary judgment. *See, e.g.,* Coble v. City of White House, 634 F.3d 865, 869-870 (6th Cir. 2011) (police audio did not "blatantly contradict" plaintiff's claim that police officer used excessive force).

[114]Such cases do not always involve video or audio recordings. *See, e.g.,* White v. Georgia, 380 Fed. Appx. 796, 798 (11th Cir. 2010) (court refused to credit plaintiff's testimony that she was shot where medical records demonstrated injuries were not caused by gunshot); Cooper v. City of Rockford, 2010 U.S. Dist. LEXIS 79539 at *2 n.3 (N.D. Ill. 2010) (court refused to credit witness statement that victim was running away when shot where autopsy showed bullet entered victim from front).

erosion of the right to trial.[115] The trend toward resolving cases without trial has accelerated in recent years.[116]

Credibility Issues and the Court's Discretion

If the standard for summary judgment is satisfied, *must* the court enter summary judgment? On the one hand, Rule 56(a) provides that summary judgment "shall" be entered, which appears to be a command to grant the motion.[117] On the other hand, "in situations in which the moving party seems to have discharged its burden of demonstrating that no genuine issue of fact exists, the court retains some discretion to deny a Rule 56 motion."[118] The discretion to deny a proper motion is narrow, and should be limited to cases in which the court has some legitimate concern about ending the case without trial.[119] The purpose of summary judgment (and the message of the 1986 trilogy cases) would be lost if courts could simply deny a proper motion

---

[115]Miller, *Pretrial Rush to Judgment.*

[116]The trilogy cases "signaled to the lower courts that summary judgment can be relied upon more so than in the past to weed out frivolous lawsuits and avoid wasteful trials, and the lower courts have responded accordingly." 10A Wright & Miller 483. Leading scholars have discussed the role summary judgment may play in the fact that civil jury trials are becoming rarer. Stephen B. Burbank, *Vanishing Trials and Summary Judgment in Federal Civil Cases: Drifting Towards Bethlehem or Gomorrah?,* 1 J. Empirical Legal Stud., 591 (2004); Martin H. Redish, *Summary Judgment and the Vanishing Trial: Implications of the Litigation Matrix,* 57 Stan. L. Rev. 1329 (2005).

[117]In 2007, as part of a project by which the Federal Rules were "restyled," the word "shall," which appeared in several provisions, was changed to "must." The purpose of the change was to make clear that the court lacked discretion on the matter. Interestingly, however, the word "shall" in Rule 56 was changed to "should," which supports the inference that the court had discretion to deny a motion even when the standard was satisfied. In 2010, however, the Rule was amended to restore the word "shall" and the Advisory Committee notes expressed the desire to capture pre-2007 practice.

[118]10A Wright & Miller 534-535. Professor Nash notes that denials (as opposed to grants) of motions for summary judgment are rarely appealed and urges courts of appeals to recognize district courts' discretion to deny summary judgment motions in close cases that turn in part on an issue of fact as to which jury trial has been demanded. Jonathan Remy Nash, *Unearthing Summary Judgment's Concealed Standard of Review,* 50 U.C. Davis L. Rev. 87 (2016).

[119]*See, e.g.,* Lind v. United Parcel Serv. Inc., 254, F.3d 1281, 1285-1286 (1st Cir. 2001) (despite lack of dispute as to material fact, court may conclude the case should be tried); Saint John's African Methodist Episcopal Church v. GuideOne Specialty Mut. Ins. Co., 902 F. Supp. 2d 783, 788 (E.D. Va. 2012) ("the court may exercise its discretion to deny a motion for summary judgment 'even when the standard appears to have been met'"). *See generally* Jack H. Friedenthal & Joshua E. Gardner, *Judicial Discretion to Deny Summary Judgment in the Era of Managerial Judging,* 31 Hofstra L. Rev. 91 (2002).

for no reason.[120] Sometimes, the concern is that the party opposing summary judgment has not had time to obtain evidence demonstrating that there is a genuine question of material fact. That problem is addressed by Rule 56(d), which allows that party to demonstrate its inability by affidavit or declaration. The court in these cases should defer ruling on the motion until that party has had time to obtain its proof.[121]

It is completely legitimate to resolve reasonable doubts against entering summary judgment. One source of doubt may be the credibility of a person giving evidence. Answers to interrogatories and affidavits can be crafted with care, with the assistance of counsel, and are given without cross-examination. Deposition testimony, on the other hand, is given "live" and lawyers for each party are entitled to ask questions. These characteristics may make courts less nervous about accepting deposition testimony at face value.

This does not mean that affidavits and answers to interrogatories cannot be taken at face value. It is simply to raise the possibility that doubts about credibility may make summary judgment inappropriate. The 1963 advisory committee notes to Rule 56 specifically warn that "[w]here an issue as to a material fact cannot be resolved without observation of the demeanor of witnesses in order to evaluate their credibility, summary judgment is not appropriate." On the other hand, this cannot mean that the party opposing summary judgment should be able to defeat the motion simply by saying, in essence "the affiant has motivation to lie." Instead, courts generally look for specific facts from which a legitimate question is raised concerning credibility.[122]

A good example is *Thomas v. Great Atlantic & Pacific Tea Co.,*[123] in which the plaintiff, representing a pedestrian killed when hit by a motor vehicle, sued a supermarket under a dram shop theory. The plaintiff alleged that the supermarket had sold beer to the driver of the vehicle, in violation of dram shop provisions because the driver was visibly intoxicated. The supermarket moved for summary judgment, supported in part by the affidavit of the driver of the vehicle, in which she stated that she had not consumed the beer she bought at the supermarket before hitting the pedestrian. The court denied summary judgment, noting that the affiant's credibility could be

---

[120]Given the crowded state of federal dockets, it is unlikely that there are many such cases. Indeed, the concern is with the opposite: a court's granting summary judgment when the standard is not satisfied.

[121]Similarly, Rule 56(e) permits the court to deal with technical problems a party may be encountering in proffering evidence for consideration in the motion.

[122]*See* 10A Wright & Miller 446 ("specific bases for possible impeachment").

[123]233 F.3d 326, 329-330 (5th Cir. 2000).

questioned because any contrary statement in the affidavit would have harmed her position in her pending criminal case.[124]

Other circumstances may counsel a court to deny summary judgment in a given case. For example, though circumstantial evidence is admissible and can provide the basis for a judgment, a court might conclude that trial should be held. Moreover, even though Rule 56 applies to all cases, as a practical matter, summary judgment seems more likely in certain types of litigation than others. There is a widespread sense that summary judgment is more often applied in cases on debts and notes than in negligence cases. Indeed, "particular deference has been accorded the jury in [negligence] cases in light of its supposedly unique competence in applying the reasonable person standard to a given fact situation."[125] In addition, some courts seem reluctant to enter summary judgment in cases involving matters of subjective intent (though *Anderson* may be read as rejecting any blanket rule against summary judgment in such cases).

The court has no discretion, and therefore must deny summary judgment, if the evidence shows a genuine dispute of material fact. As an example, in a case involving a vehicular collision at an intersection, suppose one party produced a proper affidavit from an eyewitness stating that the traffic light was green at the time of the accident. The other party produced a proper affidavit from a different eyewitness stating that the traffic light was red. Neither statement is contradicted by the record (for example, there is no video of the scene). Here, the court must deny a motion for summary judgment because the admissible evidence creates a genuine dispute as to a material issue of fact. That is precisely the situation in which we need a trial to resolve a dispute of fact.

The court should not *decide* credibility—that is, who is lying and who is telling the truth—on a motion for summary judgment. Put another way, credibility of the affiants is a genuine question of fact.[126]

---

[124]In *Arnstein v. Porter,* 154 F.2d 464, 469-471 (2d Cir. 1946), plaintiff sued the legendary songwriter Cole Porter for copyright infringement. Under the relevant law, plaintiff had to show that Porter had had access to plaintiff's music. In his deposition, Porter denied that he had seen or heard the music. Plaintiff admitted that he had no evidence to support his assertion that Porter had had access. The court, in a split decision, rejected summary judgment, on the ground that Porter's credibility was a question of fact that required trial. Judge Charles Clark (who oversaw the drafting of the original Federal Rules) dissented vehemently. Reasonable people can disagree, but many observers today agree with Judge Clark and consider *Arnstein* wrongly decided. Absent some specific basis for questioning credibility, such as in the *Thomas* case in the preceding footnote, summary judgment should not be defeated simply because a jury might find a witness unimpressive at trial.

[125]10A Wright & Miller 533.

[126]This statement is not inconsistent with our discussion immediately preceding. There, we said that a court might deny summary judgment if it has reason to question

The question of which affiant is telling the truth (the one who said the light was red or the one who said it was green) cannot be judged on summary judgment. The fact-finder must decide based upon seeing the two testify at trial. Similarly, the court generally should not grant summary judgment simply because the moving party produces more affidavits than the opposing party. Thus, if the party claiming the light was green had five affidavits to that effect and the party claiming it was red had one, summary judgment would still be denied. The evidence showed a genuine dispute on a material issue of fact, making summary judgment improper. Remember that the denial of a motion for summary judgment does not result in victory for the nonmoving party. It simply results in having the dispute go to trial for resolution.

Timing and Presentation of the Motion

Though in rare cases a court may enter summary judgment on its own motion, ordinarily a party will make a motion for summary judgment. Rule 56(b) provides that the motion may be made "at any time until 30 days after close of all discovery." Local rule or court order can permit different timing. As a practical matter, summary judgment generally becomes an option after the parties have engaged in some discovery and the lack of a genuine dispute on a material fact has become obvious (at least to the moving party). The court has great discretion in setting the timing for hearings and responses to motions for summary judgment and will usually be quite generous with time limits. For example, when appropriate, it may allow the responding party time to conduct discovery on issues subject to the motion.

The motion will include a brief, arguing why summary judgment is appropriate, supported by affidavits or declarations and other documents used to support the motion. The opposing party will also file a brief and should also append affidavits or declarations and other documents in opposition to the motion. It is incumbent on the parties to put the specific relevant evidence in the judge's hands with the motion papers. As one court explained: "District judges are not archaeologists. They need not excavate masses of papers in search of revealing tidbits—not only because the rules of procedure place the burden on the litigants, but also because their time is scarce."[127] To this end, Rule 56(c)(1)(A) requires each party to cite particular materials in the record supporting its position.

---

the credibility of an affiant. Here we are saying that the court should not grant summary judgment based upon its conclusion that one set of affiants is more believable than another.

[127]Postscript Enterprises v. City of Bridgeton, 905 F.2d 223, 226-227 (8th Cir. 1990).

§9.5 Motion for Judgment as a Matter of Law (and the "Renewed" Motion) (Federal Rules 50(a) and 50(b))

Background and Comparison to Motion for Summary Judgment

We saw in the preceding section that a grant of summary judgment averts trial altogether. We also saw that summary judgment is appropriate only when evidence and admissions proffered before trial show that there is no genuine dispute as to a material issue of fact. In such a case, no trial is required, and the court can rule as a matter of law.

In this section, we address motions that are functionally similar to the motion for summary judgment, but which are made at (or even after) trial. Here, the court did not enter summary judgment (perhaps because nobody moved for it), and the case went to jury trial. Now, *at trial*, and based upon evidence adduced at trial, the judge concludes that the jury should not be permitted to determine the facts—that the case should not "go to the jury." Why? Because there is insufficient evidence to justify having the jury consider it. Put another way, the evidence at trial shows, essentially, that there is no dispute on a material issue of fact—reasonable people could conclude only one way. That being the situation, there is no need to have the jury deliberate, and the court can simply enter judgment as a matter of law. Historically, this procedure has been called *directed verdict,* which is a very good name, because the judge indeed directs the outcome of the case, without jury involvement. In the federal system, under Rule 50(a)(1), it has a more cumbersome name: the motion for *judgment as a matter of law* (JMOL).[128] Most state courts still refer to it by its classical name, directed verdict (indeed, many judges and lawyers still call it directed verdict in federal court).

There is another motion that comes up even later. With this second motion, the judge has let the case go to the jury for deliberation, and the jury has reached a conclusion that reasonable people simply could not have reached. Here, the court may be able to take the victory away from the winner (as chosen by the jury) and enter judgment for the other party! Historically, this procedure has been called judgment notwithstanding the verdict, or JNOV, which is an abbreviation of the Latin words for that phrase (judgment *non obstante veredicto*). This is also a very good name, because the court is doing exactly that: entering

---

[128]Rule 50(a) was amended in 1991 to change the name from directed verdict to JMOL. Many lawyers and judges still routinely use the older terminology.

judgment for one side notwithstanding the verdict for the other side. In the federal system, under Rule 50(b), this is called the *renewed motion for judgment as a matter of law* (or RJMOL).[129] Here, too, generally, state courts use the older terminology.

These devices—JMOL and RJMOL—seem intrusive on the jury function. In one, the judge refuses to let the jury play a role. In the other, the judge ignores what the jury has done and enters judgment for the opposing party. Why are these procedures not unconstitutional encroachments on the Seventh Amendment right to jury trial? The answer is that there is no absolute right to a jury trial, even under the Seventh Amendment, in a civil case in federal court. The situation is different in criminal cases in that the *defendant* has an absolute right to have her case go to the jury. Even if she has no defense and even if the evidence of guilt is overwhelming and unassailable, the criminal defendant can force the prosecution to put on evidence and to persuade the jury of her guilt beyond a reasonable doubt. In other words, in a criminal case, there is no equivalent of JMOL in favor of the prosecution.[130]

In a civil case, either party may move for JMOL by asserting that there is not sufficient evidence to warrant submission of the case to the jury. The judge should grant the motion under Rule 50(a)(1) only if "a reasonable jury would not have a legally sufficient evidentiary basis to find for the party on that issue." When the court grants JMOL, it is saying, essentially, that there is no genuine dispute as to a material issue of fact. When that is true, as in summary judgment, all that remains is a question of law as to who should prevail, which the judge can decide by herself.

The difference between JMOL and summary judgment, then, is one of timing. A motion for summary judgment is brought before trial (based mostly on evidence proffered by the parties); granting it obviates the need for trial. A motion for JMOL is brought at trial (based on trial evidence); granting it obviates the need to have the jury deliberate. The Supreme Court emphasized the similarity between the motions in *Anderson v. Liberty Lobby*, discussed above, in which it noted that "the inquiry under each is the same: whether the evidence presents a sufficient disagreement to require submission to a jury or whether it is so one-sided that one party must prevail as a matter of law."[131]

---

[129]Again, many lawyers and judges still call this JNOV.

[130]There is the equivalent of JMOL for the defendant, if the defendant shows that the prosecution has failed at trial to produce evidence sufficient to sustain a conviction. Fed. R. Crim. P. 29(a) (motion for judgment of acquittal).

[131]477 U.S. 242, 251-252 (1986). Professor Miller criticizes this equation of the motions as having permitted entry of summary judgment too readily. He notes that JMOL motions arise at trial and involve better-developed evidence than motions for

Timing of the Motion

Under Rule 50(a)(1), any party may move for JMOL, but only after the other party "has been fully heard on an issue in a jury trial." In determining whether this requirement was met, we must understand the order of trial in a civil case, which we addressed in §9.2.1. The plaintiff puts on her evidence and then rests. This point is the close of the plaintiff's case. At that point, the defendant may move for JMOL, because the plaintiff has been fully heard (she has presented her case-in-chief). The plaintiff may not move for JMOL at this point, because the defendant has not been heard yet (she has cross-examined the plaintiff's witnesses but has not yet presented her own evidence).

At common law, the defendant faced a difficult choice here: If she moved for JMOL, and the motion was denied, she waived the right to put on her evidence. That draconian rule is no longer followed. If the defendant's motion is denied, the case then proceeds to the next phase of trial: presentation of evidence by the defendant. After the defendant has presented her case, and the parties have presented any rebuttal evidence, the court will close all the evidence. At that point, both sides (plaintiff and defendant) may move for JMOL. Why? Because at that point, each side has been "fully heard."

Thus, the defendant might move for JMOL twice — typically, once at the close of the plaintiff's case and again at the close of all the evidence. Or she might simply move at the close of all the evidence. There is no requirement that she move at the close of the plaintiff's case. Generally, the plaintiff will move only at the close of all the evidence, because it is usually at that point that the defendant has been fully heard. There is no requirement that a party move for summary judgment before trial to preserve the right to move for JMOL at trial.

   o ***Example #12.*** Plaintiff sues Defendant on a claim that has four elements. Thus, for Plaintiff to win, she must establish elements *A, B, C,* and *D.* She properly pleads the elements in her complaint, and Defendant properly denies them in her answer. Neither party moves for summary judgment. At trial, Plaintiff puts on her evidence and rests. Defendant believes that Plaintiff presented evidence on elements *A, B,* and *D,* but

---

summary judgment, which are, of course, brought before trial and based largely upon untested evidence. "One would expect that some significant attention would have been devoted to adjusting the trial motion practice to the pretrial motion context. That does not appear to have happened, however; at least there is no evidence of it in judicial opinions." Miller, *Pretrial Rush to Judgment,* note 106 above, at 1062. Professor Mullenix has made similar arguments in advocating a more limited role for summary judgment. Linda Mullenix, *Summary Judgment: Taming the Beast of Burdens,* 10 Am. J. Trial Advoc. 433 (1987).

that Plaintiff presented no evidence on element *C.* Defendant should move for JMOL. On this state of the record, the court should agree that "a reasonable jury would not have a legally sufficient evidentiary basis to find for [Plaintiff] on that issue," and can grant Defendant's motion for JMOL. Defendant thus will win the case.

○ ***Example #13.*** If Defendant failed to move for JMOL at the close of Plaintiff's case (or if her motion was denied) she is *not* estopped from moving again at the close of all the evidence. Again, if there is a "hole" in Plaintiff's case (if she failed to put on evidence of one of the elements of her claim), there is no need for the court to allow the jury to deliberate. On the state of the record, no reasonable jury could find for Plaintiff, and the court may enter judgment for Defendant as a matter of law.

Suppose, however, that the court let this case go to the jury. Some judges are reluctant to grant JMOL, because doing so robs the parties of any jury deliberation.[132] And if the facts are as we just indicated, with Plaintiff lacking evidence to support one of the elements of her claim, the odds are quite good that the jury will get it right and return a verdict for Defendant. But what if the jury returns a verdict for Plaintiff? Here, Defendant may be able to seek RJMOL under Rule 50(b), which, if granted, would do an extraordinary thing. It would take the victory away from Plaintiff and give it to Defendant. The motion for RJMOL must be brought no more than 28 days after entry of the judgment (which we defined in §9.3).

Granting RJMOL is a serious slap in the face to the jury. Worse than not letting the jury hear the case, RJMOL literally undoes what the jury concluded and enters judgment for the other side. What can justify this extraordinary action? The standard is the same as with JMOL—the court must conclude, based on the evidence at trial, that there was no "legally sufficient evidentiary basis to find for [the party who won the jury's verdict]." In other words, the jury reached a conclusion that reasonable people could not have reached. In the facts we've dealt with—where Plaintiff failed to introduce evidence on one of the elements of her claim—that standard clearly would be met. As with summary judgment, however, the fact that the standard for granting RJMOL is met does not compel the court to grant it. It might instead enter an order for the lesser remedy of a new trial, which we discuss in §9.6.

---

[132]For a candid assessment, *see* Konik v. Champlain Valley Physicians Hosp., 733 F.2d 1007, 1013 n.4 (2d Cir. 1984): It is preferable "to refrain from granting a motion for [JMOL] and instead allow the case to be decided, at least in the first instance, by the jury . . . . [I]f the jury reaches what the judge considers to be an irrational verdict, the judge may grant [RJMOL]. If this ruling is reversed on appeal, the jury's verdict may simply be reinstated. If, however, [the trial court granted JMOL], and that ruling is reversed on appeal, an entire new trial must be held."

Under Rule 50(b), the party seeking RJMOL must move for it no later than 28 days after entry of judgment. In addition, there is an important prerequisite: The moving party must have moved for JMOL appropriately at trial.[133]

- ○ ***Example #14.*** *P* puts on all of her evidence at trial and rests. *D* then moves for JMOL under Rule 50(a)(1). The court denies the motion. *D* then puts on her evidence at trial and rests. The evidence is then closed. The jury returns a verdict for *P*, and the court enters judgment for *P* on the basis of that verdict. Now *D* moves for RJMOL.

The RJMOL motion is proper because *D* moved for JMOL at an appropriate time[134] at trial. Specifically, *D* moved for JMOL after *P* had been fully heard, so she has preserved the right to bring the RJMOL motion.

- ○ ***Example #15.*** *P* puts on all of her evidence at trial and rests. *D* does not move for JMOL under Rule 50(a)(1). *D* then puts on her evidence at trial and rests. The evidence is then closed. Again, *D* fails to move for JMOL. The jury returns a verdict for *P*, and the court enters judgment for *P* on the basis of that verdict. Now *D* moves for RJMOL.

Here, *D* should be out of luck. By failing to seek JMOL at trial, she has waived the right to seek RJMOL. To preserve her RJMOL motion, a party must move for JMOL at an appropriate time at trial. Here, *D* never did and thus waived the Rule 50(b) motion.[135] The reason for this rule is that RJMOL is technically a renewal of a JMOL motion. Some courts have found exceptions to the operation of this rule,[136] but, obviously, the careful lawyer will avoid the problem.

---

[133]The reexamination clause of the Seventh Amendment provides that federal courts may not reexamine facts determined by juries "otherwise . . . than according to the rules of the common law." Common law permitted RJMOL (then called judgment notwithstanding the verdict) only if the party seeking it had moved for JMOL (then called directed verdict) at the close of all evidence at trial. Thus, the post-trial RJMOL was seen as an extension of the JMOL motion and therefore did not constitute an improper reexamination of the facts. This requirement was incorporated into Rule 50(b). Until 2006, the Rule required that the motion for JMOL be made at the close of all evidence at trial. Now, it simply requires that the JMOL motion be made at an appropriate time at trial, and not necessarily at the close of all the evidence. This point is made in Example #14 in the text.

[134]By "appropriate time," we mean that the party move, as Rule 50(a)(1) requires, after the other party has been "fully heard" at trial.

[135]*See, e.g.,* Braxton v. Jackson, 782 Fed. Appx. 240, 244-245 (4th Cir. 2019) ("At trial, Defendants failed to move for judgment pursuant to Fed. R. Civ. P. 50. Accordingly, this issue is not preserved.").

[136]*See, e.g.,* Foreman v. Acceptance Indem. Co., 730 Fed. Appx. 191, 195 (5th Cir. 2018) (excusing "technical noncompliance" when the purpose of the Rule (alerting the court and opposing party on the grounds advanced) is satisfied).

As we have seen, RJMOL is strong medicine. It takes victory away from one party and gives victory to the other party. In contrast, the motion for new trial, which we see in §9.6, is less harsh. It results in taking victory away from one party but then in starting over with a new trial; so the same party might ultimately win. A party that waived the right to seek RJMOL (for example, as *D* did in the last hypothetical, by failing to move for JMOL at trial) might seek the lesser remedy of a new trial. And even a party who did preserve her right to seek RJMOL might move for a new trial in the alternative. Then, if the court denies RJMOL, she might still obtain the lesser relief of an order of new trial. We see these alternative motions in §9.6.

Sufficiency of Evidence Required to Avoid JMOL

The examples we've seen so far have been fairly easy. In each, the plaintiff failed to produce evidence as to one of the elements of her claim. There is no doubt in such a case that the standard for JMOL (and RJMOL) would be satisfied because there is no dispute as to the facts and, as a matter of law, the defendant is entitled to judgment. Most JMOL motions involve subtler situations, and many (including most of those in Civil Procedure casebooks) raise the question of how much evidence the plaintiff must set forth to overcome a defense motion for JMOL and, thus, to get the case to the jury.

One older but helpful case is *Lavender v. Kurn*,[137] in which the plaintiff sued under the Federal Employers' Liability Act (FELA). That Act allows recovery for personal injuries to (and wrongful death of) employees of railroads (and others) engaged in interstate commerce, if the injuries result from negligence of the employer. The employee (or her representative) may sue in state or federal court.[138] In *Lavender*, a railroad employee (Mr. Haney) was killed by a blow to the back of the head while working as a switchman in the railroad terminal in Memphis. Haney worked for Illinois Central Railroad. When he was killed, he was throwing a switch to allow a train operated by the St. Louis-San Francisco (Frisco) Railroad to travel on a spur track to the station. There were no eyewitnesses, and no one knew what had struck Haney's head. The parties, of course, had different theories. Haney's personal representative sued both railroad lines, on alternative theories. As to Frisco, he asserted that the train had a mail hook that dangled from the train and, while negotiating a curve, swung out from the car and struck Haney. As to Illinois Central, the theory was

---

[137]327 U.S. 645 (1946).

[138]Congressional policy on some aspects of procedure in such cases is so strong that a state court will have to follow the federal directive. We study this point (often called reverse *Erie*) in §10.8.

that it had failed to provide Haney with a safe working environment; it was dark and he was permitted to work so close to the track that the mail hook could hit him. The railroads argued that they were not liable, because someone murdered Haney.

The suit, filed in state court in Missouri,[139] went to trial. The defendants moved for a directed verdict (now called JMOL in federal court). The trial court denied the motion and let the case go to the jury, which returned a $30,000 verdict against both defendants. The defendants moved for judgment notwithstanding the verdict (now called RJMOL in federal court). On appeal, the Missouri Supreme Court reversed, and held that the case should not have been submitted to the jury, because the plaintiff had failed to produce sufficient evidence to overcome the defendant's motion for directed verdict. The United States Supreme Court reversed; the plaintiff had produced sufficient evidence to get to the jury. Because the plaintiff won at trial, the Court noted that it was required to consider the facts in the light most favorable to him. The evidence showed that it was possible, given Haney's height and the height of the ground near where he was struck — and the height of the mail hook from the car and the distance it could swing out — that the mail hook hit Haney.

As to the defendants' theory that Haney was murdered, this was also possible. But the Court observed that Haney had not been robbed; his watch was on his body, and his wallet was later found nearby (with no cash, but Mrs. Haney testified that her husband never carried much cash). No one will ever know what or who killed Mr. Haney. The jury determined that it was the mail hook, and thus the negligence of the defendants. The question is whether there was sufficient evidence from which a jury could make that finding. If not, the jury engaged in mere speculation, and the judgment should not stand.

The Supreme Court concluded a jury verdict may be set aside on RJMOL "[o]nly when there is a complete absence of probative facts to support the conclusion reached . . . ."[140] Because there was evidence from which a reasonable jury could find that Haney was killed by the mail hook, the jury verdict should be respected. Some people have

---

[139]Always review matters of forum selection. First, Missouri would undoubtedly have personal jurisdiction over two national railroads. Second, by statute, state courts have subject matter jurisdiction to hear FELA cases. Also by statute, the defendants cannot remove a FELA case to federal court. 28 U.S.C. §1445. Third, the vexing issue is venue. Haney was killed in Memphis. The suit was filed in St. Louis. Don't refer to 28 U.S.C. §1391, which we addressed in Chapter 3. That prescribes venue for civil cases in *federal* court. This case was brought in state court. We don't know what the Missouri venue rules are, but it is interesting that Haney's representative did not sue in Memphis, where Haney must have lived and where the railroads would also be subject to personal jurisdiction.

[140]327 U.S. at 653.

read *Lavender* as adopting a "scintilla" test—that is, that JMOL (and RJMOL) must be denied if the nonmoving party has produced a scintilla of evidence supporting her claim. The Court never used the word, but the language just quoted does seem to argue for such an approach. Remember, however, that the Supreme Court rejected the scintilla test in *Anderson v. Liberty Lobby*,[141] which we discussed in §9.4. *Anderson* was a summary judgment case, but the Court emphasized that summary judgment and JMOL should be decided by the same standard. If *Lavender* indeed embraced a scintilla test, it may be limited to FELA cases.[142]

From *Anderson*, we should conclude that one produces sufficient evidence to overcome a motion for JMOL if she shows enough that a reasonable jury could find for her.[143] Courts routinely refer to the need for "substantial evidence" from the nonmoving party.[144] This is said to mean "evidence of such quality and weight that reasonable and fair-minded jurors may reach different conclusions."[145] In other words, a court "should not be satisfied by evidence that establishes only the mere theoretical possibility that the nonmovant could prevail."[146] The Supreme Court has also held that, in ruling on the motion, the court should look to *all* evidence—that supporting the nonmoving party and unfavorable evidence as well.[147] Lower courts routinely say that they will make all "legitimate" inferences from that evidence in favor of the nonmoving party.[148] But what inferences are "legitimate" may be debated on the facts of each case.

Like it or not, there is no precise mathematical formula for ruling on such motions. We must recognize forthrightly that juries are required to speculate to a degree. The question, and the focus for the court, is whether the speculation would be so far-fetched as to result in an unfair, unfounded verdict. Is there enough evidence in the record from which a reasonable juror could infer that the nonmoving party

---

[141]477 U.S. 242 (1986).

[142]*See, e.g.*, Boeing Co. v. Shipman, 411 F.2d 365, 370-373 (1969).

[143]If her claim requires a showing of "clear and convincing" evidence (as opposed to the usual "preponderance of the evidence" test), which is rare, and which we discussed in §9.2.4 above, the burden is greater—she must produce evidence from which a reasonable jury could conclude that she has met that standard. Professor Clermont has written thoughtfully in the area. *See generally* Kevin M. Clermont, *Common Sense on Standards of Proof,* 48 Seton Hall L. Rev. 1057 (2018); Kevin M. Clermont, *Standards of Proof Revisited,* 33 Vt. L. Rev. 469 (2008) (study of different standards of proof and psychological explanations of cognitive processes in applying them); Kevin M. Clermont, *Jurisdictional Fact,* 91 Cornell L. Rev. 973 (2005) (proof of "jurisdictional" facts).

[144]*See, e.g.*, Konkel v. Bob Evans Farms, Inc., 165 F.3d 275, 279 (4th Cir. 1999).

[145]9 Moore's Federal Practice at 50-91.

[146]*Id.* at 50-92.

[147]Reeves v. Sanderson Plumbing Prods., Inc., 530 U.S. 133, 151-152 (2000).

[148]*See* Wright & Kane, Federal Courts 683.

should win? Or is the evidence so lopsided that a reasonable jury could only come out one way? In the final analysis, much is in the eye of the beholder.

> ○ ***Example #16.*** Plaintiff's cow got onto a train track, was hit by a train, and was killed. The train track and right-of-way is fenced, and Railroad is responsible for maintaining the fence. If the cow got onto the track through a hole in the fence, Railroad would be liable. If the cow got onto the track through a gate left open, Railroad is not liable. The cow was struck next to the gate, a mile from a point where there was a hole in the fence. After the plaintiff introduces this evidence, Railroad moves for JMOL. How should the court rule?

As in *Lavender*, nobody knows how the underlying events occurred. The question is whether the jury is left simply to guess or speculate, which is not permissible, or whether there is sufficient evidence to allow the jury to determine how the cow got on the tracks. The federal courts routinely say that the evidence should be viewed in the light most favorable to the nonmoving party and that that party should be given the benefit of legitimate inferences from the facts.[149]

Here, it seems likely that the cow went through the gate. But a reasonable person could, it seems, conclude that the cow went through the hole in the fence and walked a mile before being hit.[150] Some courts would thus deny the motion for JMOL. On the other hand, it is certainly possible that some courts would find the hole-in-the-fence theory so implausible that they would grant the motion.

One important function of the jury is to assess credibility of witnesses at trial. If witness testimony produces enough evidence to get to the jury, the judge should not grant JMOL because she thinks the witness is not trustworthy. The questions of what witnesses are to be believed, and of how much weight to accord the testimony of each, are for the jury. Thus, "credibility of witnesses and weight of the evidence . . . are not the concern of the court on a motion for [JMOL or RJMOL]."[151]

---

[149]*See, e.g.*, Simblest v. Maynard, 427 F.2d 1, 4 (2d Cir. 1970) ("whether the evidence is such that, without weighing the credibility of the witnesses or otherwise considering the weight of the evidence, there can be but one conclusion as to the verdict that reasonable [people] could have reached").

[150]The facts here are taken from an old case, *Reid v. San Pedro, Los Angeles & Salt Lake R.R.*, 118 P. 1009, 1011 (Utah 1911), in which the Utah Supreme Court held that the case should not have been submitted to the jury because the plaintiff had failed to put forth enough evidence from which the jury could conclude that it was more likely than not that the cow went through the hole in the fence.

[151]Wright & Kane, Federal Courts 683.

Though ordinarily a motion for JMOL will be made in writing, Rule 50(a) does not require that, and there is authority for granting an oral motion.[152] Indeed, there is authority for a court's power to enter JMOL on its own, without a motion from a party.[153] On the other hand, RJMOL should not be granted without a motion by a party.[154] In fact, because RJMOL is a renewal of the JMOL motion, a court may not grant RJMOL on grounds not set forth in the motion for JMOL.[155]

§9.6   Motion for New Trial and for "Reconsideration" (Federal Rule 59)

Background and Comparison of New Trial to RJMOL

Though a motion for new trial under Federal Rule 59(a) is made at the same time as a motion for RJMOL (no later than 28 days after entry of the judgment[156] (which we defined in §9.3)) it is a radically different motion. As we just saw, when a court grants RJMOL, the effect is (1) to take the judgment away from the party whom the jury declared the winner and (2) to enter judgment for the other party. In contrast, when a court grants a motion for new trial, the effect is (1) to take the judgment away from the party whom the jury declared the winner, and (2) to start over with a new trial. Clearly, then, an order of new trial is less drastic than the grant of a motion for RJMOL. The party declared the winner by the jury has her victory taken away, but she still has a chance to win, because there will be a new trial.

A motion for new trial must state the grounds for the new trial. Under Rule 59(d), however, the court is free to grant a new trial on any ground, even one not stated in the motion. This salutary provision can rescue a party when the court has difficulty determining the basis on which counsel is seeking a new trial. Indeed, as Rule 59(d) also makes clear, the court can order a new trial on its own, without a motion from a party.

---

[152]*See, e.g.*, Retractable Techs., Inc. v. Becton, Dickinson & Co., 653 F.3d 1296, 1308 (Fed. Cir. 2011) (noting Fifth Circuit law that "oral motions that succinctly state the basis for the motion" are sufficient).

[153]*See, e.g.*, American & Foreign Ins. Co. v. General Elec. Co., 45 F.3d 135, 139 (6th Cir. 1995).

[154]*See, e.g.*, Murphy v. City of Long Beach, 914 F.2d 183, 185-186 (9th Cir. 1990).

[155]*See* 9B, Wright & Miller §2537.

[156]This timing requirement is found in Rule 59(b).

Grounds for Ordering New Trial

Background. Interestingly, Rule 59 does not provide specific grounds on which a new trial can be ordered. Rather, Rule 59(a)(1)(A) provides that a new trial can be ordered in a jury case "for any reason for which a new trial has heretofore been granted in an action at law in federal court." In general, the motion is based upon some error that may have tainted the result of the trial. In ruling on a motion for new trial, as opposed to a RJMOL, the court *may* consider credibility of the witnesses and the weight of the evidence. Moreover, in ruling on the motion for new trial, the court is not required to view the evidence in the light most favorable to the party who won at trial.[157]

Many grounds may support a motion for new trial. For instance, perhaps the judge made some mistake (such as putting the burden of persuasion on the wrong party, giving an erroneous jury instruction, or wrongfully allowing the introduction of improper evidence) that leads her to believe that justice would be served by having the parties retry the case before a new jury. Or maybe there is probative new evidence, which could not have been discovered with due diligence in time to move for a new trial.[158] Or perhaps a party or lawyer engaged in misconduct that justifies a new trial. Whoever made the mistake or acted inappropriately, however, the error or misconduct will not justify an order for new trial unless it was *prejudicial*. If the error or misconduct was harmless, and did not infect the outcome of the case, new trial is inappropriate.[159]

Juror Misconduct. A motion for new trial may be based upon juror misconduct, but there may be significant problems demonstrating the misconduct. At common law, a juror could not be heard to "impeach" the verdict rendered.[160] This rule enhanced the stability of verdicts and the finality of judgments, and also protected jurors from possible harassment by the losing litigant. There is a trend, however, toward permitting impeachment of a jury verdict based upon "extrinsic" (as opposed to "intrinsic") influences on jurors. Extrinsic influences are

[157]Holzapfel v. Town of Newburgh, 950 F. Supp. 1267, 1272 (S.D.N.Y. 1997).

[158]We consider this basis for setting aside a judgment under Rule 60(b) in §9.7. The standard for seeking a new trial on this basis is the same as that under Rule 60(b). *See* 12 Moore's Federal Practice §60-113.

[159]*See, e.g.*, Patrolmen's Benevolent Ass'n of N.Y. v. City of New York, 310 F.3d 43, 54-55 (2d Cir. 2002) (affirming denial of motion for new trial because error in jury instruction was harmless); Crowley v. L.L. Bean, Inc., 303 F.3d 387, 411 (1st Cir. 2002) (affirming denial of motion for new trial because jury's possible error in concluding there was systematic sexual discrimination was harmless).

[160]Technically, the common law rule was one of evidence: a juror's testimony regarding misconduct was not admissible. Because jurors themselves will be the only witnesses to most examples of juror misconduct, however, the rule had the effect of shielding juror activity from review.

things that can be verified objectively.[161] For example, if the jurors based their decision on an independent investigation of the facts outside the courtroom, or upon being bribed by a party, such "extrinsic" factors can be considered in ordering a new trial. Intrinsic factors, on the other hand, are those that are inherent to reaching the verdict, such as the jurors' thought processes.

Federal Rule of Evidence 606(b), applicable in federal court, reflects the bifurcation between extrinsic and intrinsic influences, and is not as liberal as the rule in some state courts.[162] It starts with the rule that a court may not consider evidence from a juror as to "any matter or statement occurring during . . . deliberations." It allows exceptions, though: A juror may testify that (1) "extraneous prejudicial information was improperly brought to the jury's attention," (2) an "outside influence" was brought to bear on a juror, or (3) an error was made in entering the verdict on the verdict form.

The Court has interpreted the exceptions narrowly. In *Tanner v. United States*,[163] the Supreme Court held that evidence that some jurors drank alcohol during lunch breaks and that two jurors ingested cocaine during the trial was not admissible to impeach the verdict. Alcohol and drug use, said the Court, are "internal" matters, like illness or lack of sleep. Jurors bring such things, like their experience and worldview, with them into the jury room. Parties must rely on the *voir dire* process to ferret out such things, and not *post-hoc* investigation of the jurors.

What happens, though, if a juror lies in the *voir dire* process? In *McDonough Power Equipment, Inc. v. Greenwood*,[164] the Court held that a juror's incorrect answer during jury selection can serve as a basis for new trial *only* if the moving party can demonstrate (1) that the juror failed to answer a material question on *voir dire*, and (2) that

---

[161]This approach is generally called the "Iowa Rule." In *Wright v. Illinois & Mo. Tel. Co.*, 20 Iowa 195 (1866), the Iowa Supreme Court held that the affidavits of four jurors should have been considered in ruling on a new trial for juror misconduct. The jurors alleged that the jury had not reasoned to a damages figure as a group, but had merely taken the average of each juror's conclusion about the proper damages figure (this is called a "quotient verdict"). The court concluded that such misconduct was an "independent fact" that could be proved even by juror evidence.

[162]Federal Rule of Evidence 606(b) provides that "a juror may not testify as to any matter or statement occurring during . . . deliberations . . ., except that a juror may testify on the question whether extraneous prejudicial information was improperly brought to the jury's attention or whether any outside influence was improperly brought to bear upon any juror." In *McDonald v. Pless*, 238 U.S. 264, 267-268 (1915), decided before promulgation of Rule 606(b), the Court held that a federal court may not consider juror testimony concerning quotient verdicts. This conclusion was the opposite of that underlying the "Iowa Rule." See text accompanying the preceding footnote.

[163]483 U.S. 107 (1987).

[164]464 U.S. 548 (1984).

a correct response to the question would have provided a valid basis for striking the juror for cause. This is a difficult standard to meet because of the prohibition on juror testimony concerning "intrinsic" matters. In *Warger v. Shauers*,[165] the plaintiff in a vehicle crash case moved for a new trial based upon the affidavit by one juror that another juror concealed at *voir dire* that her daughter had been involved in a crash and that her life would have been ruined if she had been sued. If the juror had admitted this view in *voir dire*, she would have been stricken for cause for her anti-plaintiff disposition. The Court unanimously held that the evidence was inadmissible under Rule 606(b). The evidence concerned an "internal" matter concerning the juror and did not constitute extrinsic evidence on the case at hand.

More recently, however, the Court held that the Sixth Amendment, which guarantees the right to jury trial in *criminal* cases, requires a court to consider juror testimony about another juror's racial bias. In *Pena-Rodriguez v. Colorado*,[166] jurors reported after a criminal conviction that one juror claimed to decide, and to attempt to influence others to decide, based upon racial animus toward the defendant. The general rule that juror testimony should not be considered on internal matters must give way to the constitutional right to a fair trial. Because *Pena-Rodriguez* is based upon the Sixth Amendment, it does not apply in civil cases, though it seems clear that the Seventh Amendment right to a fair trial should command the same answer.

Verdict Against the Weight of the Evidence. Another controversial ground for a new trial motion is that the verdict was against the weight of the evidence adduced at trial. It is controversial because, at least potentially, it seems to invite the judge to substitute her fact-finding for that of the jury. The trial judge should respect the jury's assessment, even if she would have decided the case differently, unless doing so essentially leads to an unjust result. A helpful statement of the standard for granting a new trial on this ground is: "If, having given full respect to the jury's findings, the judge on the entire evidence is left with the definite and firm conviction that a mistake has been committed, it is to be expected that he or she will grant a new trial."[167] Consequently, most courts will say that this ground for new trial is that the verdict is against the "*great* weight" of the evidence.

This ground for a new trial should be kept in mind in cases in which a party entitled to RJMOL has waived the right to bring that motion by failing to seek JMOL at an appropriate time at trial. As discussed in §9.5, RJMOL allows the court to take victory away from one party

---

[165]574 U.S. 40, 43-46 (2014).
[166]137 S. Ct. 855, 857, 869-870 (2017).
[167]Wright & Kane, Federal Courts 677.

and enter judgment in favor of another party. This path is proper, however, only when the jury reached a conclusion that reasonable people could not have reached *and* when the party seeking RJMOL moved for JMOL properly at trial. Let's return to an example we saw above.

  ° ***Example #17.*** Plaintiff sues Defendant on a claim with elements *A, B, C,* and *D*. Plaintiff presents her evidence at trial and presents evidence supporting elements *A, B,* and *D*. She presents nothing to support element *C*. Defendant presents her evidence and the court closes all the evidence. Defendant fails to move for JMOL at trial (though she certainly had grounds to do so[168]). The jury returns a verdict for Plaintiff and the court enters judgment on the basis of that verdict.

   Defendant cannot move for RJMOL. As we saw in §9.5, she waived the right to bring that motion by failing to move for JMOL at an appropriate time at trial. But Defendant certainly can move for a new trial on the basis that the verdict was against the great weight of the evidence. Obviously, Defendant would rather have gotten RJMOL, because that order would result in entry of a judgment in her favor. Having waived that, though, she should be thrilled with an order of new trial. She will escape the judgment in favor of Plaintiff and have a chance to prevail at that new trial.

Excessive or Inadequate Damages. Another troublesome basis for an order of new trial is that the damages awarded in the verdict were excessive or inadequate. Again, the judge cannot simply supplant the jury's decision with her sense of what the damages should be. On the other hand, if the jury's determination of damages is sufficiently off the mark, the judge can order a new trial. How far off the mark must the determination be? Though Rule 59 does not say so, federal courts apply a "shock the conscience" test; the jury's assessment of damages may be the basis for a new trial order if it shocks the judge's conscience. On the other hand, in *Gasperini v. Center for Humanities, Inc.*,[169] the Supreme Court held that a federal court in a diversity of citizenship case may be required to apply a state law standard for assessing whether damages are excessive or inadequate. In *Gasperini*, the New York legislature passed a statute allowing judges to order a new trial when a jury's verdict "deviates materially" from verdicts returned in similar cases. This standard permits a judge to intervene more permissively than the ordinary federal "shocks the conscience" standard.

---

[168]Why? Because *P*'s failure to present evidence on one of the elements of her claim meant, as a matter of law, that *D* should win the case. A reasonable jury could not conclude that *P* should win under these circumstances. See §9.5.

[169]518 U.S. 415 (1996).

Partial and Conditional Orders of New Trial, Remittitur *and* Additur

Suppose the trial judge considers the jury's finding of liability clearly supported by the evidence, but is shocked by the size of the verdict (either high or low). Instead of ordering a new trial on all issues, she might grant a partial new trial—as to damages only. Thus, at the new trial, liability would be deemed established, and the parties would try the damages issue afresh to a new jury.

Or the judge might consider a *conditional* order of new trial. This order would grant a new trial on damages (or on all issues, as appropriate) *only* if a party rejects the condition the court puts on the order. In federal court, this is the method by which the court attempts *remittitur* of an excessive verdict.

- ○ ***Example #18.*** *P* sues *D* for personal injuries. At trial, *P* produces substantial evidence of *D*'s liability but the evidence of damages shows minimal harm. The jury returns a verdict in favor of *P*, and against *D*, for $750,000. The court finds the award shockingly excessive, because the evidence clearly supported only relatively minor damages. *D* moves for a new trial on the ground of excessive damages. The court may grant the motion and order a new trial on damages.
- ○ ***Example #19.*** The court may avoid the new trial by ordering *remittitur* to $40,000. This is saying, in essence, "unless you, plaintiff, agree to accept $40,000 instead of the $750,000 the jury gave you, I'm going to order a new trial on damages (and you might not even get that much)."

This use of the conditional new trial through *remittitur*, obviously, is a way the court might play hardball with the plaintiff. The court tries to pressure the plaintiff to remit what the court believes is excessive damages. *Remittitur* is permitted in most state courts. It is permitted in federal court, but *only* if the court allows the plaintiff the option of accepting either (1) the figure set by the court or (2) the order of new trial. In other words, the Seventh Amendment prohibits a federal court from entering an order for the lesser amount.[170] All the court can do is give the plaintiff the option.

The converse situation, when the jury's damages determination is shockingly low, raises the question of whether *additur* might be appropriate. Here the court would play hardball with the defendant.

- ○ ***Example #20.*** *P* sues *D* for personal injuries and produces substantial evidence of *D*'s liability and of the very serious harm caused by the event. The jury returns a verdict in favor of *P*, and against *D*, but for only

---

[170]Hetzel v. Prince William County, 523 U.S. 208 (1998).

$40,000. The low figure shocks the conscience of the judge. *P* moves for new trial on the ground of the inadequate verdict. The court may grant the motion and order new trial on damages.

- ○ ***Example #21.*** But may the court avoid the new trial by giving the defendant a choice? The choice would be either to pay an augmented amount in damages, say $500,000, or face a new trial. This would be playing hardball with the defendant—saying "either pay this poor plaintiff $500,000 or I'll order a new trial (in which you might get hit for a more substantial verdict)."

This latter course is not permitted in federal court. In *Dimick v. Schiedt,*[171] the Supreme Court held that a conditional new trial based upon *additur* violates the Seventh Amendment. *Dimick* has no friends today, and the Supreme Court hinted a generation ago that the case's days may be numbered.[172] But the Court has not acted, so *Dimick* remains vital, and *additur* is unconstitutional in federal court. Because the Seventh Amendment does not apply to the states, as we saw in §9.2.2, state courts are not bound by *Dimick*. Accordingly, *additur* is permitted in many state courts.

Moving for New Trial and RJMOL in the Alternative

A party often will move for RJMOL and new trial in the alternative (assuming, of course, that the party preserved the right to move for RJMOL by moving for JMOL at an appropriate time at trial, as we saw in §9.5). Rule 50(c)(1) allows a party whose motion for RJMOL is granted to ask the court to rule "conditionally" on the motion for new trial as well. At first this seems silly, because the entry of RJMOL obviates the need for new trial. But asking for the conditional ruling on the new trial motion actually makes great sense. Why? The entry of RJMOL is appealable.[173] If the court of appeals were to vacate the RJMOL as improper, the case would have to be remanded to the district court for a ruling on the new trial motion. To save this step, Rule 50(c)(1) tells the district court to rule on both motions. Under Rule 50(c)(2), the conditional grant of the motion for new trial does not affect finality (and therefore appealability), and if the RJMOL is reversed on appeal, the case is remanded to the trial court for the new trial.

There is some authority that a litigant waives the right to move for new trial if she does not seek a conditional ruling on the alternative

---

[171]293 U.S. 474 (1935).

[172]Gasperini v. Center for Humanities, Inc., 518 U.S. 415, 433 n.16 (1996).

[173]As we see in §14.4.1, this ruling would constitute a final judgment and could be appealed.

motions. In *Arenson v. Southern University Law Center*,[174] the plaintiff won at trial. The defendant moved for RJMOL and new trial in the alternative. The court granted the RJMOL and did not rule on the motion for new trial. The court of appeals reversed the entry of RJMOL and remanded to the district court. The defendant renewed his motion for new trial, which was granted. The defendant won at the second trial. The plaintiff appealed, arguing that the grant of new trial was improper. The Fifth Circuit reversed the order of new trial. It held that Rule 50(c)(1) creates a "use-it-or-lose-it" option. By failing to have the district judge rule conditionally on the original new trial motion, the defendant waived its right to seek new trial on remand. The district court had no authority to grant the new trial after remand from the court of appeals.

To seek a new trial on appeal on the basis of insufficiency of the evidence, a party must be careful to move either for RJMOL or new trial on that basis in the trial court. In *Unitherm Food Systems, Inc. v. Swift-Eckrich, Inc.*,[175] the Court held that failure to do so precludes that party from seeking a new trial on appeal on the basis of insufficiency of the evidence.

Motion for "Reconsideration"

Rule 59(e) permits a party to move to "alter or amend" a judgment. Often, parties bring a motion under this provision to seek reconsideration.[176] The motion is not a proper method of raising arguments that could have been presented to the court earlier, nor is it supposed to be used simply to ask the court to rethink its position or for a party to reargue its case. Rather, reconsideration is proper in rare situations, such as (1) to correct the court's own error, (2) to take account of new evidence that was not available when the judgment was entered, (3) to accommodate an intervening change in the law, or (4) to prevent manifest injustice.[177] Beyond reconsideration, a Rule 59(e) motion may be based upon a wide variety of grounds. In fact, there is significant overlap between Rule 59(e) and the motion to set aside a judgment under Rule 60(b), discussed in the next section. One distinction is timing—while Rule 59(e) motions must be made

---

[174]43 F.3d 194 (5th Cir. 1995).

[175]546 U.S. 394, 405 (2006).

[176]*See* Jones v. Pittsburgh Nat'l Corp., 899 F.2d 1350, 1352 (3d Cir. 1990) ("This court views a motion characterized as a motion for reconsideration as the 'functional equivalent' of a Rule 59(e) motion to alter or amend a judgment").

[177]Leisure Caviar, LLC v. United States Fish & Wildlife Serv., 616 F.3d 612, 615 (6th Cir. 2010).

no later than 28 days after entry of judgment, Rule 60(b) is more open-ended.

§9.7   Motion for Relief from (to "Set Aside") a Judgment or Order (Federal Rule 60)

Rule 60 permits a party to seek relief from a judgment or order. It consists of two parts. First, Rule 60(a) allows a court to correct "a clerical mistake or a mistake arising from oversight or omission" that is found "in a judgment, order, or other part of the record." The court can act on its own or pursuant to a motion of any party. A "clerical mistake" is one that misrepresents what the court actually intended to order. For instance, the judgment might transpose numbers in an award,[178] misname a party,[179] or mistakenly note the dollar amount of attorney's fees awarded.[180] The thrust of Rule 60(a) is to clarify a judgment to ensure that the court's original intent is implemented; it is aimed at errors resulting from inadvertence, not from mistaken judgment.

Second, Rule 60(b) permits the trial court to correct substantive errors that cannot be addressed under Rule 60(a). Many lawyers refer to a motion under Rule 60(b) as one to "set aside" a judgment or order. One court explained the effect of the motion:

> The basic distinction between "clerical mistakes" and mistakes that cannot be corrected pursuant to Rule 60(a) is that the former consist of "blunders in execution" whereas the latter consist of instances where the court *changes its mind*, either because of a legal or factual mistake in making its original determination, or because on second thought it has decided to exercise its discretion in a manner different from the way it was exercised in the original determination.[181]

Rule 60(b) lists six bases on which the court may grant relief from "a final judgment, order or proceeding": (1) mistake, inadvertence, surprise, or excusable neglect; (2) newly discovered evidence; (3) fraud, misrepresentation, or other misconduct of an adverse party; (4) the judgment is void; (5) the judgment has been satisfied, or a prior

---

[178]*See, e.g.*, Esquire Radio & Electronics, Inc. v. Montgomery Ward & Co., 804 F.2d 787, 795-796 (2d Cir. 1986) (changing judgment from $269,000 to $296,000).

[179]*See, e.g.*, McNamara v. City of Chicago, 138 F.3d 1219, 1221 (7th Cir. 1998) (changing "Chicago Police Department" to "Chicago Fire Department" in opinion).

[180]*See, e.g.*, Dura-Wood Treating Co. v. Century Forest Industries, 694 F.2d 112, 114 (5th Cir. 1982).

[181]United States v. Griffin, 782 F.2d 1393, 1397 (7th Cir. 1986) (citation omitted) (emphasis original).

judgment upon which it is based has been reversed or vacated; and (6) "any other reason that justifies relief." The relief sought, almost always, is an order setting aside a judgment. The Rule requires that a party move for relief and provides that it may be granted on terms that are "just."

Under Rule 60(c)(1), a motion under Rule 60(b) must be made "within a reasonable time." Moreover, if the motion is based upon grounds (1), (2), or (3) listed above, the motion cannot be made more than one year after entry of the judgment or order or date of the proceeding. Note that on those three grounds, the moving party does not necessarily have one year in which to make the motion. One year is the *absolute limit*; the court may determine that a period of less than a year violated the requirement that the motion be brought "within a reasonable time."

Except for judgments that are void (addressed by Rule 60(b)(4)), the decision of whether to grant the motion is always vested in the court's discretion. In other words, outside the situation of a void judgment, there is no *right* to have a judgment set aside.[182] Our judicial system ascribes great importance to finality of judgments, so a judgment should not be set aside lightly. In addition, a party who failed to prosecute a timely appeal ordinarily should not be allowed to use a Rule 60(b) motion to raise grounds that could have been raised on appeal. Further, the system of justice favors decisions based upon the merits rather than on technicalities, so default judgments may be more readily set aside than those entered after full litigation.[183] And, unless the judgment is void, the party seeking to set aside a judgment must show that she has a meritorious claim or defense. It makes no sense to set aside a judgment against a party if that party has either no claim to assert or no defense to a claim.

Rule 60(b)(1) is often the basis for a motion to set aside a default judgment (which we saw in §7.5.3). There, the defendant who defaulted will attempt to convince the court that she was guilty of a mistake or of excusable neglect that should be "forgiven" by setting aside the judgment. There is a split of authority as to whether "mistake" under this part of the Rule refers to legal errors committed by the court. Some courts permit relief under Rule 60(b)(1) from judicial mistakes, at least under some circumstances,[184] while others do

---

[182]*See, e.g.,* UMWA 1974 Pension v. Pittston Co., 984 F.2d 469, 476 (D.C. Cir. 1993).

[183]*See* 12 Moore's Federal Practice §60.22[3][a].

[184]*See, e.g.,* Acadian Diagnostic Laboratories, L.L.C. v. Quality Toxicology, L.L.C., 965 F.3d 404, 414 (5th Cir. 2020) ("A 'mistake' under Rule 60(b)(1) includes judicial errors, but such an error must be a 'fundamental misconception of the law,' and not merely an erroneous ruling."); Pearson v. Target Corporation, 893 F.3d 980, 984 (7th Cir. 2018) ("Rule 60(b)(1) applies to 'errors by judicial officers as well as parties.'"); U.S. v. Rohner, 634 Fed.Appx. 495, 506 (6th Cir. 2015); United Airlines, Inc. v. Brien, 588

not.[185] Rule 60(b)(2) expressly limits the use of newly discovered evidence to that which "with reasonable diligence, could not have been discovered in time to move for a new trial under Rule 59(b)." A Rule 59 motion, as we saw in §9.6, must be brought within 28 days of entry of judgment, so the Rule 60(c)(1) timing requirement for bringing a Rule 60(b) motion is considerably more liberal. Courts require essentially the same showing for a motion for new trial and a motion to set aside based upon newly discovered evidence.[186] Although cases discuss various factors, for the most part, the moving party will have to show that the evidence existed at the time of the original adjudication, that it could not have been discovered, even with reasonable diligence, in time for the first adjudication, *and* that the new evidence is so important that it would likely change the outcome of the case.[187] Obviously, this is a difficult standard to satisfy.

Under Rule 60(b)(3), the court may set aside a judgment for fraud or other misconduct by an adverse party. This provision addresses a wide variety of misdeeds. For example, a party's failure to respond to discovery requests, which hindered the moving party's ability to prepare for trial, might be sufficient.[188]

Rule 60(b)(5) permits setting aside a judgment for various reasons, including that the judgment "is based on an earlier judgment that has been reversed or vacated." There has been some uncertainty about what the drafters intended by the word "based." Courts generally interpret this provision to mean that one judgment is so closely related to another that it has a preclusive effect on it.[189] The Rule thus is not implicated when a judgment relies on an earlier judgment as legal precedent and it is reversed or vacated.[190]

F.3d 158, 175 (2d Cir. 2009) ("Rule 60(b)(1) is 'available for a district court to correct legal errors by the court.'"). Some courts conclude that a motion made on the basis of judicial error must be made before the time for appeal runs. *See, e.g.,* Daniel v. DTE Energy Co., 592 Fed.Appx. 489, 490 (6th Cir. 2015) ("While Rule 60(b)(1) encompasses judicial mistakes of law, such a motion must be made 'within the normal time for taking an appeal'"); International Controls Corp. v. Vesco, 556 F.2d 665, 669 (2d Cir. 1977) (same).

[185]*See, e.g.,* Parke-Chaptley Constr. Co. v. Cherrington, 865 F.2d 907, 914-915 n.7 (7th Cir. 1989); Page v. Schweiker, 786 F.2d 150, 154-155 (3d Cir. 1986). *See also* Lowry v. McDonnell Douglas Corp., 211 F.3d 457, 460-461 (8th Cir 2000) ("It remains the law in this Circuit that 'relief under Rule 60(b)(1) for judicial error other than for judicial inadvertence' is not available").

[186]*See generally* 12 Moore's Federal Practice §60.42[2].

[187]*See, e.g.,* Jones v. Aero/Chem Corp., 921 F.2d 875, 878 (9th Cir. 1990).

[188]*See, e.g.,* Schultz v. Butcher, 24 F.3d 626, 630-631 (4th Cir. 1994).

[189]*See, e.g.,* Tomlin v. McDaniel, 865 F.2d 209, 210-211 (9th Cir. 1989). We discuss preclusive effects—claim preclusion and issue preclusion—in Chapter 11.

[190]*See, e.g., Tomlin,* 865 F.2d at 211.

Rule 60(b)(6) is a catchall provision allowing relief for "any other reason that justifies relief." This Rule can be invoked *only* when two things are established. One, the case must not satisfy any of the other bases for relief under Rule 60(b). Thus, Rule 60(b)(6) cannot save a party who failed to move for relief within a reasonable time, or failed to move on the bases in Rule 60(b)(1), (2), or (3) within the absolute one-year limit.[191] Two, the moving party must establish "extraordinary circumstances" for relief.[192] In the words of Judge Richard Posner, "The first five subsections [of Rule 60(b)] seem to cover the waterfront. The only work left for (6) to do is to allow judgments to be set aside, without limitation of time, when the circumstances of its invocation are 'extraordinary.'"[193]

Can misconduct by a party's lawyer justify relief under Rule 60(b)(6)? In cases such as *Link v. Wabash Ry. Co.*,[194] the Supreme Court has indicated that the lawyer is the agent of the client, and the client must suffer the consequences of her lawyer's misdeeds. After all, the reasoning goes, the client hired the lawyer, and thus must pay the price if she hired a poor lawyer. The issue is often presented under Rule 60(b)(6) in a default judgment situation.

○ ***Example #22.*** Defendant's lawyer failed to plead or otherwise defend her client, and the court entered default judgment against Defendant. Now Defendant moves to set aside the judgment under Rule 60(b)(6). Is the lawyer's negligence an "extraordinary" circumstance that justifies relief?

The general rule is no; if the lawyer is guilty of simple malpractice, courts will not set aside the judgment. There is a split of authority, however, when the client can show *gross* negligence by the lawyer. While some courts refuse relief even under these circumstances,[195] others will set aside a judgment on such grounds. An example is *Community Dental Services v. Tani*,[196] in which the defendant's counsel filed an answer (albeit late) but never served it on the plaintiff, despite a court

---

[191]*See* Pioneer Investment Servs. Co. v. Brunswick Assocs. LP, 507 U.S. 380, 393 (1993) ("A party who failed to take timely action due to 'excusable neglect' may not seek relief more than a year after the judgment by resorting to section (6)").

[192]Gonzalez v. Crosby, 545 U.S. 524, 535 (2005). *See* Buck v. Davis, 137 S. Ct. 759, 777-778 (2017) (judgment denying federal habeas corpus relief should be set aside under Rule 60(b)(6) because possibility that race was a factor in criminal sentencing risked undermining public confidence in judicial process).

[193]Lowe v. McGraw-Hill Cos., 361 F.3d 335, 342 (7th Cir. 2004).

[194]370 U.S. 626 (1962) (upholding involuntary dismissal of case based upon counsel's failures to prosecute case and follow court orders). We discussed *Link* at §7.4.2.

[195]*See, e.g.,* Dickerson v. Bd. of Educ., 32 F.3d 1114, 1118 (7th Cir. 1994); Heim v. Commissioner, 872 F.2d 245, 248 (8th Cir. 1989).

[196]282 F.3d 1164 (9th Cir. 2002).

order to do so, and failed to abide by other court orders, all the while telling the defendant that things were proceeding smoothly. Because the lawyer was guilty of "extreme negligence or egregious conduct,"[197] the Ninth Circuit ordered the district court to set aside its default judgment and allow the case to proceed.

As noted above, Rule 60(b)(4) is unique. It provides for relief from a void judgment. Unlike the other bases for relief under Rule 60(b), here the court has no discretion; if the court determines that a judgment is void, it *must* set aside the judgment.[198] Why? Because a void judgment is a nullity; it is beyond the court's power and thus does not exist. Most often, "void" means that the court lacked personal jurisdiction or subject matter jurisdiction.[199] It certainly does not include an erroneous decision by the court.

The Court drove home this point in *United Student Aid Funds v. Espinoza*.[200] There, a bankruptcy court confirmed a plan that forgave a debtor's liability for interest on his student loan. The order was erroneous because the court did not, as required by law, make a finding that repayment of interest would have imposed undue hardship on the debtor. But the error did not support a Rule 60(b)(4) motion. Justice Thomas explained: "a motion under Rule 60(b)(4) is not a substitute for a timely appeal. Instead, Rule 60(b)(4) applies only in the rare instance where a judgment is premised either on a certain type of jurisdictional error or on a violation of due process that deprives a party of notice or the opportunity to be heard."[201] Because the bankruptcy court did not act without jurisdiction (it simply made an error) and because the creditor had been given proper notice, Rule 60(b)(4) did not apply.

Finally, it bears emphasis that the motion for relief under Rule 60, like the motion for RJMOL (discussed in §9.5) and the motion for new trial (discussed in §9.6), is addressed to the trial court that entered the judgment or order from which relief is sought. In other words, no appellate review is sought here. A losing litigant might be able to seek review by an appellate court, as we discuss in Chapter 14.

---

[197]*Id.* at 1168. *See also* William Darrah & Assocs., 796 F.2d 190, 195 (6th Cir. 1986); Boughner v. Secretary of Health, Educ. & Welfare, 572 F.2d 976, 978 (3d Cir. 1978) (granting relief in cases involving grossly negligent attorney).

[198]*See, e.g.*, Bally Export Co. v. Balicar, Ltd., 804 F.2d 398, 400 (7th Cir. 1986).

[199]*See, e.g.*, Farm Credit Bank v. Ferrera-Goitia, 316 F.3d 62, 67 (1st Cir. 2003); Garcia Fin. Group, Inc. v. Virginia Accelerators Corp., 3 Fed. Appx. 86, 88 (4th Cir. 2001).

[200]559 U.S. 260 (2010).

[201]*Id.* at 270-271.

Chapter 10

The Erie *Doctrine(s)*

§10.1   Defining the Issue

Erie Railroad Co. v. Tompkins[1] is widely heralded as one of the most important cases in American history. Many students and professors consider *Erie* the most difficult material in Civil Procedure. Part of the problem is that what we call *Erie* (or "the *Erie* doctrine") is really two doctrines. Before we get to that, though, the initial task is simply to recognize what the material is about. *Erie* problems arise only in federal court and concern the choice between federal and state law. Specifically, when does a federal court apply state law?

---

[1]304 U.S. 64 (1938).

The issue generally arises in diversity of citizenship cases. After all, in a federal question case, the claim arises under federal law and federal law will likely provide the rules for deciding the case. In a diversity case, however, the litigation is in federal court simply because the parties happen to be citizens of different states (and, of course, the amount in controversy requirement is met). Because the claim asserted in a diversity of citizenship case does not arise under federal law, there is room for the application of state law. Indeed, as we will see, the Constitution *requires* the application of state law to some aspects of the case.

Two words of caution are important about *Erie*. First, more than with most topics in Civil Procedure, professors have a variety of views in this area; many disagree on the interpretation and importance of particular cases. What is presented here is simply one professor's vision. This topic is rich and can offer a springboard for discussion of deep jurisprudential themes, as we will see. Second, it is impossible simply to jump into *Erie*. Understanding and applying current doctrine requires background, including historical development through a series of Supreme Court cases. After reviewing that development in §§10.4 through 10.6, I suggest in §10.7 a mode of analysis for addressing any *Erie* problem. Before getting to the cases, however, we discuss why *Erie* raises a "vertical" (as opposed to a "horizontal") choice of law issue.

§10.2   Vertical Choice of Law Versus Horizontal Choice of Law

It may seem strange, but courts routinely apply the laws of other jurisdictions. A California court may apply the law of New York or a Florida court may apply the law of Colorado to determine the outcome of a dispute. The question of which state's law governs raises a *horizontal choice of law* inquiry. That is, the choice of applicable laws is between equal political entities (states). Courts make this determination based upon doctrines of "choice of law," which constitutes a large part of the law school course on Conflict of Laws. For our purposes in Civil Procedure, we need to know only that this body of law exists and that each state is free to adopt its own rules for determining horizontal choice of law questions.

For example, in contract cases, a common (but not universal) horizontal choice of law approach is to apply the law of the state in which the parties entered into the contract. In addition, parties generally are free to provide by contract that the law of a particular state will govern their dispute. Such a provision is called a *law selection clause*,[2]

---

[2]Remember the *Burger King* case from personal jurisdiction (§2.4.4)? There, the Michigan franchisees entered into a contract with Burger King that contained a law

and most states enforce them so long as they are reasonable and not the product of overreaching. In tort cases, one common (but not universal) approach provides that the court should apply the law of the place of the injury.

> ◦ ***Example #1.*** *P*, a citizen of Ohio, and *D*, a citizen of New Mexico, do not know each other. Each is on vacation in Hawaii. *D*, driving a rental car there, negligently hits *P*, who was walking by the side of the road. *P* sues *D* to recover for personal injuries in New Mexico. (For review, why New Mexico?[3]) The court in New Mexico, applying New Mexico's "choice of law" rules, will probably conclude that Hawaii tort law governs, because the injury was suffered in Hawaii. Thus, the New Mexico court will look to Hawaii law to determine the elements of *P*'s claim and of *D*'s defenses.

The *Erie* doctrine addresses a different choice of law issue. Here, the question is not whether the law of State *A* or State *B* will apply, but whether the federal court should apply state law at all. If the court decides that an issue should be determined by state (rather than federal) law, it will *then* undertake the horizontal choice of law inquiry to determine which state's law applies. But this antecedent question—the focus of this chapter—is a *vertical choice of law* inquiry.[4]

§10.3   The Rules of Decision Act and the Regime of *Swift v. Tyson*

The starting point in studying vertical choice of law is the Rules of Decision Act, which has been part of the Judicial Code since 1789.

---

selection clause that provided for the application of Florida law to any dispute under the contract. It was relevant to the question of whether the defendants had purposefully availed themselves of Florida. A forum selection clause, on the other hand, constitutes an agreement of the parties that litigation between will take place in a particular location. See §5.5.2. Many contracts include both law selection and forum selection clauses.

[3]Because she can get personal jurisdiction over *D* in New Mexico. The facts say that *D* is a citizen of that state, which, as we know from §4.5.3, means that she is domiciled there. The *Goodyear* case, discussed in §2.4.5, makes it clear that one is "essentially at home," and therefore subject to general personal jurisdiction, in the state of her domicile. It is doubtful that *P* could sue in Ohio (her home state) unless *D* for some reason had sufficient contacts to be subject to personal jurisdiction there. Of course, *P* might also sue in Hawaii, where there would be personal jurisdiction over *D* because the accident occurred there. For this hypothetical, assume *P* sues in New Mexico.

[4]Professor Bauer suggests that horizontal choice of law doctrine should inform the vertical choice of law inquiry. Joseph Bauer, *Shedding Light on* Shady Grove: *Further Reflections on the* Erie *Doctrine From a Conflicts Perspective,* 86 Notre Dame L. Rev. 939 (2011).

Today it is codified at 28 U.S.C. §1652.[5] Look carefully at the language, which provides in full:

> The laws of the several states, except where the Constitution or treaties of the United States or Acts of Congress otherwise require or provide, shall be regarded as rules of decision in civil actions in the courts of the United States, in cases where they apply.

This is an awkward provision but gets across the message that federal courts must apply state law as the *rules of decision* in civil cases, except where federal law applies. It is important to understand why the statute carves out the exception for cases in which *federal* law requires that state law not apply. Under the Supremacy Clause of the Constitution, federal law is "the supreme law of the land."[6] Thus, for example, when Congress legislates in an area in which the Constitution gives it authority, that legislation becomes supreme and is binding in federal and state courts.[7]

Whatever Congress may have intended in the Rules of Decision Act, the Supreme Court concluded in 1842 that federal courts were not required to apply state law on *all* aspects of a diversity case. The famous decision in which it did so, *Swift v. Tyson*,[8] stood for 96 years, until it was overruled by *Erie* itself. *Erie* cannot be understood without background in *Swift*. In that old case, the question was one of contract law: whether discharge of a debt constituted consideration for a contract. It was an issue on which courts of various states had reached different conclusions. The traditional view was that discharge of a debt did not constitute consideration, but a then-modern trend reached the opposite conclusion.

Swift was a diversity of citizenship case brought in federal court in New York. The New York courts adhered to the traditional rule that discharge of a debt did not constitute valid consideration. The Supreme Court held that the federal courts sitting in diversity need not follow New York precedent on this issue. The Court embraced the then-modern principle that discharge of a debt *was* consideration for a contract. How did the Court justify ignoring state law? It interpreted

[5]The statute was §34 of the original Judiciary Act of 1789. Some of the cases you read—including *Swift v. Tyson* and *Erie* itself—refer to it as "§34." Don't be confused by that; it is the same statute that you have in your statutory supplement as 28 U.S.C. §1652.

[6]U.S. Const. art. VI, cl. 2.

[7]*Erie* is usually an issue in diversity of citizenship jurisdiction cases, not federal question cases, because diversity cases involve assertion of state-created rights. *See* Patrick Borchers, *The Origins of Diversity Jurisdiction, the Rise of Legal Positivism, and a Brave New World for* Erie *and* Klaxon, 72 Tex. L. Rev. 79, 79-81 (1993).

[8]41 U.S. 1 (1842).

the phrase "laws of the several States" in the Rules of Decision Act to include only state *statutes* and state common law of *local concern* (e.g., perhaps, land). As to common law matters of *general* concern (e.g., basic principles of torts and contract, including what constitutes consideration for a contract), the Court concluded, federal courts in diversity cases were free to apply "general" common law.[9] Interpreting "laws of the several states" in the Rules of Decision Act, Justice Story's opinion in *Swift* said:

> In the ordinary use of language, it will hardly be contended that the decisions of courts constitute laws. They are, at most, only evidence of what the laws are; and are not, of themselves, laws. . . . The laws of a state are more usually understood to mean the rules and enactments promulgated by the legislative authority thereof, as long-established customs having the force of laws. . . . It never has been supposed by us, that the [Rules of Decision Act] did apply, or was designed to apply, to questions of a more general nature . . . as, for example, . . . questions of general commercial law.

There are several problems with *Swift*. First, the notion that decisions of courts do not constitute "laws" strikes modern lawyers as odd. We today routinely think of judicial opinions as "law." Remember that *Swift* was decided in the first half of the nineteenth century. It was not until the early twentieth century, with the advent of the "legal realist" school of jurisprudence, that there was widespread acceptance of the notion that judges make "law" just as surely as legislatures make law. Throughout your law school career, you have become comfortable with this notion. For example, in your Torts class, you see the common law development of negligence and strict liability doctrines. We consider those to be "law" even though they were decreed by courts rather than legislatures.

Second, *Swift* was based upon a notion, widespread in the nineteenth century, that there was only one true general common law. It was transcendental, a "brooding omnipresence" that emanated from reason and nature, and not from any particular sovereign. Justice Story expressed this belief with a colorful phrase from Cicero that the law cannot mean one thing in Rome and another in Athens.[10] To Story, and to most legal philosophers of the day, judges would "discover" that one true approach, and someday all courts would come to see the wisdom of it and to embrace it. This notion, like the one that state court decisions are not law, is foreign to us today. We are quite

---

[9]*Id.* at 18-19. Common law, as we discussed in §1.1, consists of judicial opinions. Statutory law, in contrast, is legislation.

[10]41 U.S. at 19.

comfortable nowadays with the idea that common law, like statutory law, can vary from state to state. Again, you have seen examples in your other classes, as when some states embrace certain tort theories that others do not.

Third, under *Swift,* federal judges were able to divine the true general common law. They would set it forth in diversity of citizenship cases in an effort not only to decide those cases but also to educate the state courts on the content of the true general common law. The state judges, so the theory went, would follow the approach taken by their federal counterparts.

But *Swift* did not compel the state courts to adopt federal judicial reasoning on matters of general common law. They could persist in applying a different version of the general common law in their decisions. This fact led to the most devastating shortcoming of the *Swift* doctrine: The general common law to be applied depended upon what court (state or federal) was hearing the case. For example, after *Swift,* the New York courts continued to embrace the traditional rule that discharge of a debt was not consideration for a contract. Federal courts, guided by *Swift,* decreed that discharge of a debt was consideration to support a contract. So where did that leave the citizens of New York? They were subject to two sets of contract law, one applicable in state court and another in federal court. This phenomenon is called "vertical disuniformity"—the law is different *within a single state* depending upon whether the issue is to be decided in federal or state court. The disuniformity caused by *Swift* obviously made it difficult for people in New York (or people dealing with New York citizens) to plan their commercial activities.

In addition, vertical disuniformity creates strong incentives for forum shopping. After all, the only people who can avoid New York law and avail themselves of the federal courts' version of the general common law are those who can invoke diversity of citizenship jurisdiction. A New York citizen in a dispute with another New York citizen will not be able to gain access to federal court (because there is no diversity). When a New York citizen entered into a contract with a citizen of another state, however, a dispute could go either to state or federal court (assuming, of course, that the amount in controversy requirement for a diversity case was satisfied). Thus, when a dispute arose, a litigant could choose the court likely to apply a version of general common law more to her liking. And even if a dispute raised an issue on which the federal courts had not expressed an opinion, a party invoking diversity of citizenship jurisdiction had the opportunity to persuade the federal court to adopt a view of some general common law different from that adopted by the state courts.

An egregious example of forum shopping to exploit vertical disuniformity is *Black & White Taxicab Co. v. Brown & Yellow Taxicab Co.*[11] There, Brown & Yellow, a taxicab operator, entered into an exclusive dealing contract with Railroad. Under the contract, Railroad's passengers at the station in Bowling Green, Kentucky could *only* use taxicabs provided by Brown & Yellow. Obviously, other taxicab companies— including one called Black & White—opposed this contract, because it froze them out of serving Railroad's passengers. The Kentucky courts had held that exclusive dealing contracts such as this were void. Because of that, Black & White continued to serve passengers at the Bowling Green station, secure in the knowledge that the contract purporting to exclude it was void under state common law.

Brown & Yellow, meantime, wanted to sue Black & White in federal court, to argue that general common law would enforce such contracts. The problem was that Brown & Yellow and Black & White were both citizens of Kentucky, so there was no way to invoke diversity of citizenship jurisdiction. The enterprising proprietors of Brown & Yellow then dissolved the corporation and reincorporated in Tennessee, thus making the corporation a citizen of Tennessee.[12] That corporation then sued Black & White (a citizen of Kentucky) in federal court under diversity of citizenship jurisdiction. Brown & Yellow sought an injunction prohibiting Black & White from competing with it at the Bowling Green train station. The federal court held that federal general common law permitted exclusive dealing contracts and entered an injunction that prohibited Black & White from competing with Brown & Yellow. The Supreme Court upheld the injunction.

The result is troubling.[13] It rewarded the proprietors of Brown & Yellow for manufacturing diversity of citizenship jurisdiction by allowing them to exploit the vertical disuniformity made possible by *Swift*. After the Supreme Court opinion in *Black & White Taxicab*, imagine the position of a Kentucky lawyer faced with the question of whether exclusive dealing contracts were enforceable in that state. The lawyer would have to say: "in state court no, but in federal court yes." This

---

[11]276 U.S. 518 (1928).

[12]Recall that under §1332(c)(1), a corporation is a citizen of both the state of incorporation and the state of its principal place of business. See §4.5.3. That statutory definition did not come into existence until 1958. At the time the *Black & White Taxicab* case was decided, a corporation was deemed to be a citizen *only* of the state of its incorporation. Thus the reincorporation created diversity of citizenship. Today, if Brown & Yellow's principal place of business was in Kentucky, it would also be a citizen of Kentucky, and there would be no diversity between it and Black & White. Also, §1359, discussed at §4.5.4, which addresses the collusive creation of diversity of citizenship jurisdiction, was not on the books at the time the case was decided.

[13]Justice Oliver Wendell Holmes wrote a memorable dissent in the case, which the Court quoted extensively when it overruled *Swift* in *Erie*. See §10.4.

put the citizens of Kentucky in an untenable position, subject to irreconcilable laws on the topic depending upon what court they might end up in. The *Black & White Taxicab* case was met with criticism, which reflected dissatisfaction with the regime of *Swift v. Tyson*. No one knew it at the time, but *Swift* would be overruled a decade later.

Before getting to that point, we should flag one other problem created by *Swift*. As noted, the case established a dividing line between common law of "local" concern, as to which a federal court must follow state court pronouncements, and common law of "general" concern, which a federal court may ignore. The federal courts wrestled unsuccessfully throughout the near-century reign of *Swift* to define where that line was. Many matters were obvious, such as basic issues of contract and tort law—things like offer, acceptance, and consideration for a contract and duty and breach for negligence. Those were clearly matters of general common law, as to which *Swift* permitted the federal courts to decree their own interpretation. What constituted local common law was far less clear, but it was usually thought to include interpretation of state statutes and issues relating to land.[14] But the *Erie* case itself involved an issue that was neither plainly local nor general. The parties argued the case at the Supreme Court on that basis but, as we will see, the decision rendered the distinction meaningless.

§10.4   The *Erie* Case Itself

§10.4.1   The Facts

Harry Tompkins, a citizen of Pennsylvania, was walking along a path next to a train track on a dark night near Hughestown, Pennsylvania. A freight train operated by the Erie Railroad (Erie) passed by from behind Mr. Tompkins. Something (perhaps a door) protruded from one of the cars and hit Mr. Tompkins in the head. He suffered serious personal injuries. He sued the railroad in federal court in New York. Erie was a citizen of New York and the claim met the amount in controversy requirement, so the case invoked diversity of citizenship jurisdiction.

The path on which Mr. Tompkins was walking was on the railroad's right-of-way, which is a strip of land astride the tracks. Tompkins contended that the path was openly and commonly used by members of

---

[14]*See, e.g.*, Kuhn v. Fairmont Coal Co., 215 U.S. 349, 369-370 (1910) (following local common law on questions of land, unless state law unsettled). One commentator of the day noted that there were hundreds of cases involving the distinction between local and general common law under *Swift*, but "these rules and their application are notoriously far from clear." Armistead Dobie, Federal Procedure 558 (1928).

the public and that the railroad was aware of this fact. That, argued Tompkins, made him an "invitee" on the property. When one is an invitee, the owner of the property owes him a duty, which is breached by simple negligence. Thus, asserted Tompkins, he could sue the railroad for its negligence in having the object protrude from the train and hit him. On the other side, the railroad contended that Tompkins was not an invitee, but a trespasser. If he were a trespasser, the railroad would not be liable for simple negligence. The only duty owed to a trespasser is not to harm him willfully or wantonly. Tompkins could probably prove that the railroad was negligent, but there was no way he could prove willful or wanton behavior. So, ultimately, if Tompkins was an invitee, the railroad could be held liable to him for simple negligence; if Tompkins was a trespasser, though, the railroad could not be held liable to him for simple negligence.

On this score, state law[15] was clear: Tompkins was a trespasser and, therefore, would lose. That is why Tompkins's lawyer sued in federal court. He wanted the federal court, under *Swift v. Tyson*, to apply general common law and hold that Tompkins was an invitee, who could win by showing mere negligence. The federal district court agreed with Tompkins and applied general common law; based upon a jury verdict, that court entered judgment for Tompkins for $30,000. The Court of Appeals for the Second Circuit affirmed, and the Supreme Court agreed to hear the case.

Why did the Supreme Court agree to hear the case? Ostensibly, the reason was to determine whether Tompkins's status (as invitee or trespasser) was a matter of general or local common law. Under *Swift v. Tyson*, as we saw in the preceding section, the federal court could apply its own view of the common law *only* if this was a general (and not a local) matter. That was the issue on which the parties briefed and argued the case at the Supreme Court. Imagine everyone's shock, then, when the first sentence of Justice Brandeis's opinion in *Erie* announced: "the question for decision is whether the oft-challenged doctrine of *Swift v. Tyson* shall now be disapproved." No one involved in the case had argued that *Swift* should be overruled. The parties, the lower courts, and seemingly the Supreme Court at oral argument all assumed that *Swift* was good law.

---

[15]Though the case was litigated in federal court in New York, the relevant state law was that of Pennsylvania. Why? Remember from §10.2 that the doctrine of horizontal choice of law determines whether the law of State *A* or State *B* shall apply. We see below that horizontal choice of law is an issue on which state (not federal) law will govern. Under the New York choice of law rules, the law of Pennsylvania would govern (because the accident took place there). Don't lose sleep over this fact. Remember, how courts make the horizontal choice of law decision is covered in a different course—that on Conflict of Laws.

§10.4.2　The Opinion and Its Two Themes: Litigant Equality and the Tenth Amendment

The Court's opinion, written by Justice Brandeis, is divided into four parts (of which the third is the real bombshell). In the first section, the Court noted that "more recent research of a competent scholar" suggested that *Swift* was wrongly decided. The research was by Professor Charles Warren, a legendary Harvard Law School professor,[16] who concluded, after reviewing the text of the original Rules of Decision Act, that the drafters intended that federal courts would apply state law—statutory and common law—as rules of decision in matters in which federal law does not apply.[17] Regardless of whether Professor Warren was correct,[18] the Court also noted widespread criticism of the vertical disuniformity caused by *Swift*, particularly after the decision in the *Black & White Taxicab* case,[19] discussed in §10.3.

In the second section of the opinion, the Court recognized forthrightly that the theory of *Swift* (that the federal courts would divine the one true general common law for the states to follow) had failed in practice. State courts had persisted in their own views on matters of general common law and the hoped-for transcendental, universal general common law had not emerged. That fact created the problem of vertical disuniformity and what the Court called the "mischievous" result of *Swift*: "In attempting to promote uniformity of law throughout the United States, the doctrine had prevented uniformity in the administration of the law of the State."[20] Because those with access to federal court had access to a different body of general common law, *Swift*

> introduced grave discrimination by non-citizens against citizens. It made rights enjoyed under the unwritten "general law" vary according to whether enforcement was sought in the state or in the federal court; and the privilege of selecting the court in which the right should be determined was conferred upon the non-citizen. Thus the doctrine *rendered impossible equal protection of the law.*[21]

---

[16]Some people say that Professor Warren was the model for Professor Kingsfield in the movie *The Paper Chase*. If you've never seen that film, you might want to watch it. Despite the 1970s clothes and hairstyles, it's a timeless portrayal of the first year of law school.

[17]Charles Warren, *New Light on the History of the Federal Judiciary Act of 1789*, 37 Harv. L. Rev. 49, 51-52, 81-88, 108 (1923).

[18]Some disagree with Warren's conclusion. *See, e.g.*, Wilfred J. Ritz, *Rewriting the History of the Judiciary Act of 1789*, 148 (1990).

[19]We discussed that case above. See text accompanying notes 12-13.

[20]304 U.S. at 75. The Court is discussing what we have called *vertical disuniformity.*

[21]*Id.* (emphasis added).

By referring to "equal protection of the law," the Court was not speaking of the Equal Protection Clause of the Constitution. Rather, as the context of the statement made clear, the Court was concerned with the sort of unfairness caused by vertical disuniformity—specifically, that those who can invoke diversity of citizenship jurisdiction get access to law (in federal court) that those in state court cannot. I have referred to this concern as one for "litigant equality."[22] It is a basic notion that similarly situated persons ought to be treated alike: If exclusive dealing contracts are void in state court in Kentucky, they should be void in federal court, too; if discharge of a debt is not good consideration for a contract in state court in New York, it should not be good consideration in federal court. *Swift* violated this important tenet.

In the last paragraph of the second part of its opinion in *Erie*, the Court clearly seems to be leading up to overruling *Swift*. To do so, of course, all the Court needed to do was hold that the phrase "laws of the several states" in the Rules of Decision Act includes state decisional law of the general common law type. Such a holding would have rid the justice system of the "injustice and confusion incident to the doctrine of *Swift v. Tyson*."[23] But then the Court took a surprising turn: "If only a question of statutory construction were involved, we should not be prepared to abandon a doctrine so widely applied throughout nearly a century."[24] In other words, the Court would be reluctant to overrule *Swift* simply to fix that case's interpretation of the phrase "laws of the several states" in the Rules of Decision Act.

Then, in the last sentence of the second part of the opinion, the Court says something stunning: "But the *unconstitutionality* of the course pursued has now been made clear and compels us to [overrule *Swift*]."[25] Thus, in a case in which no party argued that *Swift* should be overruled, the Court overruled *Swift*—and not just as a matter of the construction of the Rules of Decision Act, but as a matter of constitutional law. Not only had *Swift* misinterpreted the Rules of Decision Act, but, according to the last sentence of the second part and the entire third part of the opinion, the *Swift* doctrine was unconstitutional!

Part three of the opinion discusses the constitutional basis of the holding, which we address in detail below. Part four of the opinion remanded the case to the Second Circuit for further proceedings. This required the Second Circuit to remand the case to the district court, which would then apply state law on the underlying issue of what

---

[22]Richard D. Freer, *Some Thoughts on the State of* Erie *After* Gasperini, 76 Tex. L. Rev. 1637, 1645 (1998).

[23]304 U.S. at 77.

[24]*Id.*

[25]*Id.* (emphasis added).

duty the railroad owed to Mr. Tompkins. Because the applicable state law provided that Tompkins was a trespasser, he could recover only if he showed that the railroad had acted willfully or wantonly in hurting him. Tompkins could not make such a showing, so the application of state law resulted in his losing the case.[26]

The most important part of the opinion is the third section. Many observers have wondered why the Court based its holding in *Erie* on the Constitution and not simply upon the Rules of Decision Act. After all, the Court could simply have overruled *Swift* by holding that the phrase "laws of the several states" in that statute included general common law decisions by state courts (and not just statutes and local common law decisions). Ordinarily, the Court decides a case on statutory grounds when it can thus avoid a constitutional question. Yet, in *Erie*, the Court seemed to go out of its way to base its holding on the Constitution. Ultimately, then, the Justices felt compelled to hold that the Rules of Decision Act itself was constitutional but that the *Swift application* of that statute was unconstitutional.

The Court's constitutional discussion is curious for this reason: Though making a constitutional holding, the Court never expressly identifies which part of the Constitution was violated by the regime of *Swift v. Tyson*. Despite this omission, most commentators agree that the holding is based upon the Tenth Amendment, which provides that "[t]he powers not delegated to the United States by the Constitution, nor prohibited by it to the States, are reserved to the States respectively, or to the people." The Tenth Amendment embodies the important principle of federalism — the states retain those powers that they did not cede to the federal government in the Constitution.[27]

[26]Mr. Tompkins won a judgment of $30,000 at trial. On appeal, the railroad offered him $7,500 to settle the case. This would have been a significant sum in the 1930s, especially for an unemployed married man with a young child. Apparently, Tompkins leaned toward accepting the settlement, but his lawyer, who wanted to appear in a Supreme Court case, urged him not to do so. The lawyer had Tompkins stay with him at his New York house for two weeks during the appellate process, until the railroad withdrew the settlement offer. As it turns out, the lawyer realized his dream of litigating at the Supreme Court. The result, unfortunately, was that Mr. Tompkins did not recover a penny for his injuries. *See* Irving Younger, *What Happened in* Erie, 56 Tex. L. Rev. 1011, 1021-1022 (1978).

[27]Justice Brandeis's majority opinion in *Erie* relied upon a lengthy quotation from Justice Field's dissent in *Baltimore & Ohio R. Co. v. Baugh*, 149 U.S. 368, 401 (1893), in which he rather clearly asserted that *Swift* violated the Tenth Amendment. He spoke of that part of the Constitution that "recognizes and preserves the autonomy and independence of the States" and of *Swift* as "an invasion of the authority of the State." We have met Justice Field before — he wrote the majority opinion in *Pennoyer v. Neff*, discussed at §2.4.1. See also §1.2.1 concerning creation of the federal government by states' ceding power to it.

Erie is an important statement of federalism. As the Court said in part three of the opinion:

> Except in matters governed by the Federal Constitution or by Acts of Congress, the law to be applied in any case is the law of the State. And whether the law of the State shall be declared by its Legislature in a statute or by its highest court in a decision is not a matter of federal concern. *There is no federal general common law. Congress has no power to declare substantive rules of common law applicable in a State, whether they be local in their nature or "general," be they commercial law or a part of the law of torts. And no clause of the Constitution purports to confer such a power on the federal courts.*[28]

In other words, *Swift* was an unconstitutional grab by the federal courts of power vested in the states. Put powerfully: "It is impossible to overstate the importance of the *Erie* decision. It announces no technical doctrine of procedure or jurisdiction, but goes to the heart of the relations between the federal government and the states and returns to the states a power that had for nearly a century been exercised by the federal government."[29]

The three italicized sentences from the indented quotation above make two significant points. One point (made in the last two sentences) is structural: Nowhere does the Constitution give the federal government—either the legislature or the courts—authority to declare substantive rules of common law. The second point, made in the first italicized sentence, concludes that there is no such thing as "federal general common law." Of course, *Swift* was based upon the search for the one true general common law, which was to be declared by the *federal* courts. Now, 96 years later, it turns out *Swift* sent the federal courts in search of something that does not exist—indeed, cannot exist. Let's look more closely at these two points.

The Constitution creates and limits the federal government. The federal government may exercise only those powers granted to it by the people and the states in the Constitution. So when the Court said that "Congress has no power to declare substantive rules of common law applicable in a State," it was not saying that Congress can *never* pass legislation that displaces state law. It can, but *only* as to matters that the Constitution entrusts to the federal legislature. Could Congress pass a statute declaring the duty to be owed by a railroad to a person walking along the railroad's right-of-way (the core issue in *Erie*)? Yes, but *only* if it had a constitutional basis for using its federal

---

[28]304 U.S. at 78 (emphasis added).
[29]Wright & Kane, Federal Courts 378.

legislative power. No doubt, Congress's power to regulate interstate commerce would give it the power to pass such a statute.

But Congress had not legislated on the topic. Can the federal *courts* jump in and create common law? No. As the Court said in the last sentence of the quoted material above, nothing in the Constitution gives the federal *judiciary* any general power to make common law. Thus, because there was no federal law on point (no act by Congress and no authority for the judiciary to act), the Tenth Amendment (and the Rules of Decision Act) commanded the application of state law.

But why does the federal *judiciary* not have the power to make common law in all areas in which the federal legislature can pass legislation? The answer seems to be this: The federal *judicial* authority is not as broad as the federal *legislative* authority. This fact reflects the concept of separation of powers, which circumscribes the courts' role vis-à-vis the legislature. It also reflects federalism in two ways. First, as provided in the Tenth Amendment, power not expressly given to the federal government is reserved to the states or to the people. Second, while the states' interests are represented in Congress (because the citizens of the states elect members of the House and the Senate[30]), those interests are not necessarily represented by members of the federal judiciary (who are not elected at all).

In addition to the constitutional basis for the *Erie* holding, there is no question that the case represented a different jurisprudential model than that reflected in *Swift*. The opinion quotes from Justice Holmes's famous statement that *Swift* was based upon the assumption that there was one true general common law, "a transcendental body of law outside of any particular State but obligatory within it unless and until changed by statute."[31] By the early twentieth century, judges, lawyers, and scholars, influenced by the legal realists, more readily understood that the common law was whatever the highest court of each state said it was. As Justice Frankfurter later explained:

> In overruling *Swift* . . . *Erie* . . . did not merely overrule a venerable case. It overruled a particular way of looking at law which dominated the judicial process long after its inadequacies had been laid bare. Law was

---

[30]Originally, members of the Senate were elected by the state legislatures. Not until 1913, with the ratification of the Seventeenth Amendment, were members of the Senate elected directly by the people of the state.

[31]304 U.S. at 79, *quoting* Black & White Taxicab Co. v. Brown & Yellow Taxicab Co., 276 U.S. 518 (Holmes, J., dissenting) (we discussed this case in text accompanying notes 12-13 above).

conceived as a "brooding omnipresence" of Reason, of which decisions [by state courts] were merely evidence and not themselves the controlling formulations.[32]

Legal realists such as Holmes and Brandeis embraced the idea that "law" consists not only of statutes but of judicial declarations of the law. In a famous law review article, Holmes said, "[T]he prophecies of what the courts will do in fact, and nothing more pretentious, are what I mean by the law."[33] Another jurisprudential school in the ascendancy at the time of *Erie* was positivism. One tenet of positivism is that law is not some abstract and transcendental truth, but, rather, simply the command of a sovereign. Thus, to a positivist, all law must be either commanded by the federal or by the state government. The two schools together support the conclusions in *Erie* that (1) common law is what judges say it is; and (2) there is no overarching, general federal common law; each state is free to decree its own. From there, the Tenth Amendment makes the commandment quite clear: State common law is to govern in diversity of citizenship cases.

Though *Erie* was startling, its importance escaped the popular press. Felix Frankfurter, then a professor at Harvard Law School, wrote a letter to President Roosevelt, saying, "I certainly didn't expect to live to see the day when the Court would announce, as they did Monday, that it itself has usurped power for nearly a hundred years. And think of not a single New York paper—at least none that I saw—having a nose for the significance of such a decision."[34] Justice Stone was so distraught over the lack of coverage that he wrote a letter to a columnist of the *New York Times*, prodding him to bring the "momentous decision" to the attention of the public.[35]

To recap, then, *Erie* overruled *Swift* and identified two major themes for doing so. The constitutional theme comes from the Tenth Amendment: that state law must govern on matters of general common law. The other theme, which is not based in the Constitution, but in policy, is the notion of litigant equality. This is the idea that similarly situated persons should be treated alike: that the governing law should not differ depending upon whether the case is in federal or state court. In later cases, the Court will sometimes emphasize one of these themes over the other.

---

[32]Guaranty Trust Co. v. York, 326 U.S. 99, 101-102 (1945).

[33]Oliver Wendell Holmes, Jr., *The Path of the Law*, 10 Harv. L. Rev. 457, 461 (1897).

[34]Roosevelt and Frankfurter: Their Correspondence 1928-1945, at 456 (Max Freedman ed., 1967).

[35]Wright & Kane, Federal Courts, at 378 n.13. Interestingly, Chief Justice Stone later referred to the constitutional holding in *Erie* as "unfortunate dicta." *Id.* at 383 n.4.

§10.4.3 Birth of the Dichotomy Between Substance and Procedure

Justice Stanley Reed concurred in the result in *Erie* and wrote an important separate opinion.[36] He agreed that *Swift v. Tyson* should be overruled and he agreed with Justice Brandeis's reasoning *except* as to holding *Swift* unconstitutional. Justice Reed would have based the holding on the Rules of Decision Act alone and would have held that "the laws of the several states," as used in that statute, should include all decisions of the state courts.

Justice Reed suggested that Article III of the Constitution, together with the Necessary and Proper Clause, might empower Congress to pass "rules of substantive law" to be applied in federal court. Certainly, he asserted, *Erie* did not compel the federal courts to comply with every provision of state law. After all, "no one doubts federal power over procedure."[37] Here, Reed addressed an issue the majority did not: whether *Erie* left the federal courts free to ignore state law on any points. His concurring opinion gave rise to labels that are commonly invoked: that in a diversity of citizenship case, the federal court must apply state "substantive" law but may apply federal "procedural" law.[38] At one level, there is nothing wrong with using "substance" as a label for those matters as to which a federal court must follow state law and "procedure" for those as to which the federal court need not follow state law. As we see in subsequent sections, however, the labels should not be used as substitutes for analysis.

An important distinction between substance and procedure seems clear from the Rules of Decision Act itself. That Act requires application of state law (as does *Erie*) *only* as to "rules of decision." Purely procedural matters would not seem to constitute rules of *decision* and thus a federal court in a diversity of citizenship case may be free to ignore state law as to such matters.

We will see in §10.6.1 that Congress passed the Rules Enabling Act (REA), now codified at 28 U.S.C. §2072, in 1934. With that statute, Congress delegated to the Supreme Court the authority to "prescribe general rules of practice and procedure" for the federal

---

[36]Justice Cardozo took no part in the *Erie* decision because he was quite ill at that time. Of the eight Justices participating, Brandeis and four others joined the majority opinion, and Justice Reed concurred. Two Justices—Butler and McReynolds—dissented from overruling *Swift v. Tyson*.

[37]304 U.S. at 92 (Reed, J., concurring).

[38]This analysis was reflected in *Sibbach v. Wilson,* 312 U.S. 1, 10-11 (1941), in which the Court upheld Federal Rule 35, which permits discovery through a court order of a medical exam, even though state law of the forum did not permit such orders.

courts. The Federal Rules of Civil Procedure are promulgated under this authority. Legal thinking in that era seemed to assume that procedure and substance were separate things, hermetically sealed from each other. Rules of procedure, it was thought, could not affect substantive legal rights. Modern thinking is quite different. Today, we recognize that rules of procedure may affect the vindication of legal rights. This fact drives home an important point: that vertical choice of law involves subtle analysis in which a retreat to labels is not helpful.

§10.4.4 The Remarkable Year of 1938

Erie was not the only source of change in 1938. As noted in the immediately preceding paragraph, the Rules Enabling Act permitted the Supreme Court to prescribe uniform rules of procedure for the federal courts. The original Federal Rules of Civil Procedure promulgated under this authority took effect in 1938. Before that, the Conformity Act required federal district courts to apply the procedural law of the state in which the federal court sat. Think of the changes thrust upon the federal courts in diversity of citizenship cases in 1938. Until then, federal judges applied state procedural law and forged their own interpretation of general common law. After that year, in contrast, they applied uniform federal rules of procedure but adhered to state common law.

The events of 1938 must also be seen in the overall political context of the New Deal, which marked a massive expansion of federal power, unquestionably at the expense of state autonomy. The Court, after initial reluctance, ultimately upheld most of these federal assertions of power. *Erie* seems out of step with the tenor of such times, because it embraces the importance of the state pronouncements of law. On the other hand, diversity of citizenship jurisdiction under the regime of *Swift v. Tyson* was widely thought to create a favorable litigation climate in federal courts for large corporate interests, often at the expense of the "little guy."[39] So *Erie*, which stripped the federal court of its power to fashion general common law, may be seen as a decision against corporate interests and thus as more consistent with some thrusts of the New Deal.[40]

---

[39]*See* Edward Purcell, Jr., Litigation and Inequality: Federal Diversity Jurisdiction in Industrial America, 1870-1958 (1992).

[40]Ironically, and unfortunately for Mr. Tompkins, the decision in *Erie* itself favored the corporate defendant.

§10.5 Progeny of *Erie* Until 1965: *Klaxon* Through *Byrd*

After *Erie*, federal courts must apply state law (including general common law) as the rules of decision (or, in shorthand, on law of *substance*) in diversity of citizenship cases. Whatever "substance" means — whatever "rules of decision" are — the bottom-line issue in *Erie* fell within both. The issue in that case was Mr. Tompkins's status as a trespasser or invitee and the resultant duty owed to him. Without doubt, those issues define the very circumstances under which one party is liable to another and thus constitute rules of substance.

In the wake of *Erie*, the Court was forced to address a variety of topics that are not so easy to characterize, such as choice of law, statutes of limitations, when a statute of limitations may be tolled, and the burden of proof at trial. For nearly three decades, in addressing vertical choice of law, the Court seemed to establish different tests for determining when a federal court in diversity must apply state law. Our job in this section is to review those cases and the tests they formulated. Though the Court will make a dramatic discovery in 1965, as we see in §10.6, the cases we study here have never been overruled. Ultimately, we need to decide how they fit into an overall approach to vertical choice of law.

Four years after *Erie*, the Court decided *Klaxon v. Stentor Electric Manufacturing Co.*,[41] in which it held that a federal court in diversity must apply *state* choice of law rules. Stated in a conclusory way, then, choice of law rules are substantive; they constitute rules of decision, as to which state law must govern. We discussed choice of law rules in §10.2. They are the rules for determining "horizontal choice of law" issues — that is, whether the law of State *A* or of State *B* will govern a dispute. *Klaxon* holds that a federal court in diversity must apply the choice of law rules of the state in which that federal court sits. The Court had done this by implication in *Erie* itself. That case was tried in a federal district court in New York. New York choice of law doctrine dictated that the law of Pennsylvania would govern the dispute (because the injury was suffered in Pennsylvania).[42] Though commentators have criticized *Klaxon*, the Court has reaffirmed the holding of the case and it is good law today.[43]

---

[41]313 U.S. 487 (1941).

[42]See note 15 above. This inquiry can get convoluted. In one case, a judge noted, "Our principal task . . . is to determine what New York courts would think California courts would think on an issue about which neither has thought." Nolan v. Transocean Air Lines, 276 F.2d 280, 281 (2d Cir. 1960).

[43]Day & Zimmerman, Inc. v. Challoner, 423 U.S. 3, 4 (1975). We saw an issue regarding this point in discussing transfer of venue in §5.5.2. There, we noted that a case

Guaranty Trust

In 1945, the Court decided *Guaranty Trust Co. v. York*.[44] The plaintiff's claim, asserted in federal court under diversity of citizenship jurisdiction, was barred by the state statute of limitations. But it was an equitable claim. Traditionally, equity courts applied the doctrine of "laches" to determine whether a plaintiff should be barred for having "slumbered on his rights" too long; laches could trump a statute of limitations in a case involving the assertion of an equity claim. In *Guaranty Trust*, the federal district court recognized that the state statute of limitations barred the claim. Nonetheless, as a court of equity, it determined that the plaintiff was not guilty of laches and thus should be able to proceed. The Supreme Court held that the district court was wrong and that *Erie* required it to apply the state statute of limitations. Justice Frankfurter's opinion recognized that courts and commentators talked a great deal about how *Erie* set up a "great divide cutting across the whole domain of law"—a divide between "substance" and "procedure."[45]

The Court refused to apply a labeling test, however, and instead analyzed the problem functionally. Justice Frankfurter's opinion recognized that federal courts should be free to prescribe the way in which substantive rights are enforced.[46] On the other hand, the Court noted "since a federal court adjudicating a State-created right solely because of diversity of citizenship of the parties is for that purpose, in effect, only another court of the State, it cannot afford recovery if the right to recover is made unavailable by the State . . . ."[47] Ultimately, the Court posited: "[T]he outcome of the litigation in the federal court should be substantially the same, so far as legal rules determine the outcome of a litigation, as it would be if tried in a State court."[48] The state law (the statute of limitations) required dismissal of the case. The district court's ignoring that law under the doctrine of laches would permit the case to proceed. Because ignoring state law would thus lead to a different "outcome" than applying state law, it would violate the command of *Erie*.

In §10.4.2, we discussed the two underlying themes of *Erie*. One is the constitutional provision protecting state sovereignty in the Tenth Amendment. The other was the nonconstitutional notion of "litigant equality"—that similarly situated persons should be treated alike.

---

transferred under §1404(a) would carry with it the choice of law rules of the transferor court.

[44]326 U.S. 99 (1945).

[45]*Id.* at 109.

[46]*Id.* at 108.

[47]*Id.* at 108-109.

[48]*Id.* at 109.

Guaranty Trust, as applied, seemed to say that *Erie* requires that the *outcome* of litigation in federal court be the same as it would have been in state court. Nothing in *Erie* said that. Thus, some criticize the case as adopting an overly wooden approach to the litigant equality theme from *Erie*. This criticism is unfair to a degree. Justice Frankfurter's opinion was more subtle than later cases that applied it. As noted above, Justice Frankfurter actually said that the outcome should be the same in federal and in state court "so far as *legal rules* determine the outcome of a litigation."[49]

But later cases, particularly in the lower courts, missed this nuance in *Guaranty Trust*. These cases interpreted *Guaranty Trust* as prescribing an "outcome determinative" test, which indeed requires the federal court to ensure that the *outcome*—who wins and who loses—not differ from the result in state court. This reading is unfortunate, because it led to the view that federal courts in diversity cases were simply clones of the state courts. The federal courts comprise a system of justice separate from that in the states and that system must have the authority to prescribe its own rules except for rules of decision. Every rule, even the most plainly nonsubstantive, at some point becomes "outcome determinative." And reading *Guaranty Trust* woodenly seems to require the federal court to adopt the state rule even on such points.

> ○ ***Example #2.*** Suppose state courts require that pleadings be filed on 14-inch paper. The federal court, however, requires that pleadings be on 11-inch paper. There is nothing even remotely "substantive" about the length of paper on which one drafts her pleadings. There is no chance that the size of the paper on which pleadings are asserted is a "rule of decision." Still, a wooden application of *Guaranty Trust* might proceed this way when a plaintiff files in federal court on 14-inch paper: (1) the 14-inch document would be accepted in state court, so the case could proceed; (2) if the clerk's office in federal court does not accept the 14-inch paper, the case will not proceed; (3) therefore, the rule about 14-inch paper is outcome determinative; and (4) the federal court must follow state law and permit the filing on 14-inch paper.

Such a result would be absurd. Obviously, the federal judicial system must be able to prescribe such rules for itself. As Justice Frankfurter said in *Guaranty Trust*, "the forms and mode of enforcing the right may at times, naturally enough, vary because the two judicial systems are not identic."[50] But the Supreme Court seemed to forget this point in the years following *Guaranty Trust*. It transformed a concern

---

[49]*Id.* (emphasis added).
[50]*Id.* at 108.

with litigant equality into an inflexible rule of "outcome equality." Nowhere was this more obvious than in what are known as the "triple play" cases.

The "Triple Play" Cases

On one day in 1949, the Supreme Court decided three cases that signaled to many observers that *Erie* might eviscerate the Federal Rules of Civil Procedure. All three seemed to require a federal diversity court to apply what clearly seemed to be state "procedural" rules. In *Ragan v. Merchants Transfer & Warehouse Co.*,[51] the question was when an action is "commenced" for purposes of tolling the statute of limitations. Understanding the case requires some background in the application of statutes of limitations. Such statutes allow a claimant no more than a specified period—say two years[52]—in which to commence the action. The period starts to "run" from "accrual" of the claim. That means the clock starts ticking on the plaintiff's two years (or whatever the period is) when her claim accrues. Jurisdictions adopt different standards for when a claim accrues. One typical approach is that accrual occurs on the date the defendant allegedly breached a duty or caused harm, even if the claimant is unaware of the breach or harm. The other major approach is that accrual occurs when a reasonable claimant would have discovered that she had been harmed. At any rate, *commencing* the action before the limitations period expires will "toll" the running of the statute. Tolling means that the ticking of the limitations clock is stopped.[53] The bottom line is this: The claimant must "commence" the action before the limitations period expires.

In *Ragan*, the statute of limitations expired after the plaintiff filed the case but before the defendant was served with process. (Recall from §3.3.1 that Rule 4(m) permits 90 days from the date of filing in which to serve process, so there is often a gap between the two events.) State law provided that the statute was tolled from the date on which the defendant was served with process and *not* from the date on which

---

[51]337 U.S. 530 (1949).

[52]Statutes of limitations can vary substantially from state to state and for various claims within a state. Typically, tort claims have a shorter statute of limitations than contract or property claims. Defamation usually has a short limitations period, often one year from accrual of the claim.

[53]Other things can toll the running of the statute of limitations. For example, lack of mental or legal capacity generally tolls the statute. Suppose *D* commits a tort that injures *P*, who is 14 years old. Let's say the relevant statute of limitations is two years. But *P* lacks legal capacity because she is a minor at the time the claim accrued. The statute is tolled (and therefore does not start to run) until *P* reaches age 18 (the age of majority, when she has legal capacity). Accordingly, the two-year statute would start to run when *P* turned 18. She can sue until she turns age 20.

the complaint was filed. Thus, under state law, the plaintiff would be barred by the statute of limitations. On the other hand, Federal Rule 3 provides that "a civil action is commenced by filing a complaint with the court." The plaintiff in *Ragan* argued that, under Rule 3, the statute of limitations was tolled from the date on which the complaint was filed. The Supreme Court rejected this argument and held that state law governed the question of tolling. Why? Because of "outcome determination." If state law were applied, the case would be dismissed. If state law were ignored, the case would proceed. As in *Guaranty Trust*, the Court felt it inappropriate to have a different "outcome" in federal court than there would have been in state court.

The second case decided that day was *Woods v. Interstate Realty Co.*[54] There, a Mississippi statute provided that corporations formed in other states must register with the state before doing business in Mississippi. Under the statute, failure to do so waives that corporation's right to sue in Mississippi courts. (Such a provision is called a *door-closing statute* because it closes the (state) courthouse door to such a corporation.) A non-Mississippi corporation commenced suit in federal court under diversity of citizenship jurisdiction and the question was whether the state door-closing statute should be followed by the federal court. The Supreme Court held that it should. Again, it invoked outcome determination as the test. If state law were applied, the case would be dismissed. If it were ignored, the case would proceed. This different outcome — like that in *Guaranty Trust* — dictated that the federal court must apply state law and dismiss the case.[55]

The third case was *Cohen v. Beneficial Industrial Loan Corp.*,[56] which involved specialized litigation called a *shareholder derivative suit*. Federal Rule 23.1 enumerates prerequisites for bringing a derivative suit in federal court. (We discuss these suits in §13.1.) It does *not* require the plaintiff in such a case to post a bond with the court. The law of some states, including New York (which was the relevant state in *Cohen*), does require that the plaintiff post a bond as a prerequisite to the derivative suit. The purpose of such a requirement is to deter "strike" or "nuisance" suits. A shareholder who has to post a bond (which is money from which the corporation can recover its litigation expenses if the suit is frivolous) is less likely to bring a bogus

---

[54] 337 U.S. 535 (1949).

[55] *Id.* at 541. This does not mean that federal courts must follow every state door-closing statute. The one involved in *Woods* served a state purpose (requiring out-of-state corporations to register and pay fees) that would be subverted if the federal courts allowed them to sue. A door-closing statute aimed merely at reducing state court caseload would not be violated by entertaining a diversity case. *See* Szantay v. Beech Aircraft Corp., 349 F.2d 60 (4th Cir. 1965).

[56] 337 U.S. 541 (1949).

derivative suit than one who does not have such a financial stake in the case. In _Cohen_, the Supreme Court held that a federal court must apply the state law bond requirement, even though, as noted, Federal Rule 23.1 does not include such a requirement.

Though it was decided earlier (and so is not technically one of the "triple play" cases), _Palmer v. Hoffman_[57] should be mentioned here. The case concerned which party assumes the burden of proof at trial on the issue of the plaintiff's contributory negligence. In some states, the defendant must prove that the plaintiff was negligent; in others, the plaintiff must prove her own lack of negligence. Federal Rule 8(c)(1) lists contributory negligence as an affirmative defense that the defendant must plead. In _Palmer_, the Supreme Court held that notwithstanding Rule 8(c)(1) (which was then simply Rule 8(c)), a federal court sitting in diversity jurisdiction must apply state law concerning burden of proof at trial. That law placed the burden of proof on the plaintiff and thus governed in _Palmer_.

Many observers saw these cases as a serious threat to the authority of the federal courts to apply their own rules even as to clearly procedural aspects of a case. The 1949 decisions got their name as the "triple play" cases from a famous law review article. The author concluded that the cases had worked a triple play on the Federal Rules of Civil Procedure themselves.[58] Charles Clark, who was the principal drafter of the Federal Rules, concluded that few of the Rules could "be considered safe from attack" after the triple play cases.[59]

Was this nervousness justified? Yes. On the face of things, _Ragan_ seemed to eviscerate Rule 3. After all, that Rule clearly provided that a case is commenced when filed, yet the case held that a federal court must apply the state law definition of when a case was commenced. _Palmer_ seemed to make light of Federal Rule 8(c)(1) by requiring the plaintiff to prove her lack of contributory negligence. Similarly, _Cohen_ seemed to eviscerate Rule 23.1 by requiring federal courts to engraft on its list of prerequisites for a derivative suit the state law requirement of a bond. In some ways, however, _Woods_ seems most threatening to the federal judicial system. It held that a _state_ statute could require the _federal_ judicial system to close its doors and to refuse to exercise its validly invoked diversity of citizenship jurisdiction.

Together, these cases show that the pendulum had swung too far toward the "state" side of things and away from the "federal" side.

---

[57]318 U.S. 109 (1943).

[58]Edward Merrigan, Erie _to_ York _to_ Ragan: _A Triple Play on the Federal Rules_, 3 Vand. L. Rev. 711 (1950). _Triple play_ is a baseball reference. In a triple play, three outs are recorded on a single play. The batting team thus loses its at-bat in one fell swoop. It is a bad thing (for the batting team).

[59]Charles Clark, _Book Review_, 36 Cornell L.Q. 181, 183 (1950).

The fixation on outcome equality (itself a perversion of one theme of *Erie)* seemed destined to relegate the federal courts to the status of mere clones of the state judicial systems. It was time for the Supreme Court to reassert that the federal judicial system has legitimate interests that need not be subjugated to state law. It did so nine years after the triple play cases in *Byrd v. Blue Ridge Rural Electrical Cooperative, Inc.*[60]

Byrd v. Blue Ridge

Mr. Byrd was injured while working for a construction company. The construction company was part of the Blue Ridge Rural Electrical Cooperative ("Co-op"), which sold electric power in rural South Carolina. Mr. Byrd could not sue his immediate employer (the construction company) because of workers' compensation laws. Those laws provide that an employee cannot sue her employer for work-related injuries. Rather, the employer is strictly liable and must compensate the employee for injuries according to a statutory schedule. On the one hand, this is a disadvantage to the seriously injured employee, because she cannot sue and recover more than the statutory schedule permits. On the other hand, this is an advantage to the employee, because she does not have to sue at all; she is entitled to the workers' compensation benefits automatically and is not required to litigate.

Lawyers for Mr. Byrd brought a diversity of citizenship case against the Co-op,[61] on the theory that Byrd was not an employee of the Co-op and thus was not limited to workers' compensation recovery. The Co-op argued that Byrd was a "statutory employee," which meant that he would be treated as an employee of the Co-op and thus was limited to workers' compensation benefits from it. Obviously, the question of whether Byrd was a statutory employee of the Co-op was the crucial issue. If he was, he had no right to sue and his case would be dismissed. Just as obviously, the question was one of fact—someone had to determine, based upon the evidence, whether Byrd was a statutory employee of the Co-op. And the fight that went to the Supreme Court was over who was to make that factual decision—the judge or a jury.

Under South Carolina case law, the judge, without a jury, would make the decision. Though the South Carolina Supreme Court had clearly held this to be the law, it had not explained *why* the judge, and not a jury, was to make the decision. Byrd's lawyers argued that the South Carolina law was not binding on the federal court sitting

---

[60]356 U.S. 525 (1958).

[61]Byrd was a citizen of North Carolina, the Co-op was a citizen of South Carolina, and the amount in controversy requirement was satisfied.

in diversity of citizenship jurisdiction; thus, the issue should be determined by a jury.[62]

The Court held that *Erie* did *not* require the federal court to follow state law on this issue.[63] Note, then, *Byrd* is the first case after *Swift v. Tyson* was overruled in which the Court upheld a federal court prerogative in the face of a contrary state law. The Court's interpretation of *Erie* is found in Part II of the opinion, drafted by a young Justice Brennan. That part of the opinion is subdivided into three sections. Before assessing them, another word of caution. I consider *Byrd* to be the Court's finest hour in laying out a test for determining when *Erie* requires federal courts to apply state law. Not all professors agree; indeed, some think *Byrd* is moribund. And even fans of *Byrd* have to admit that the Court has not recognized its influence in subsequent cases.

In the first sentence of the first subsection of Part II, the Court says, "It was decided in [*Erie*] that the federal courts . . . *must* respect the definition of state-created rights and obligations by the state courts."[64] Notice the word *must*—connoting that there is no discretion. This is a command to the federal courts and thus obviously emanates from the Tenth Amendment. Also notice that the *must* attaches to the "definition of state-created rights and obligations." This phrase seems to refer to matters all would agree are purely substantive—the elements of a claim or defense, for example. As to them, *Erie* commands federal courts to respect state law, which makes sense. After all, elements of a claim or defense, without question, constitute rules of decision for a case and, thus, the Rules of Decision Act requires application of state law. We can refer to these issues as raising questions of "pure substance."

The following sentence is equally interesting. "We must, therefore, first examine the rule in [the South Carolina case holding that the judge is to decide the statutory employee issue] to determine whether it is *bound up* with these rights and obligations in such a way that its application in the federal court is required."[65] Notice the phrase

---

[62]Think about why Mr. Byrd wanted a jury and the Co-op did not. Byrd was seriously hurt. A jury would presumably be more sympathetic to him and less sympathetic to the large Co-op's argument that Mr. Byrd should be limited to the (limited) remedies provided by workers' compensation law. As we saw in §9.2.2, parties are willing to spend a great deal of time and money in litigating the issue of who will be the factfinder on a particular issue.

[63]The Court addressed this question after holding, in Part I of the *Byrd* opinion, that the lower courts erred by not permitting Mr. Byrd to present evidence on the statutory employee issue. Because the case had to be remanded for fact-finding on that question, the Court had to determine who (judge or jury) would make that determination.

[64]356 U.S. at 535 (emphasis added).

[65]*Id.* (emphasis added).

"bound up," which the Court fails to define. Clearly, though, it must mean that there are some state rules that are so closely related to matters of pure substance that the Tenth Amendment requires federal courts to respect them; they fall within the Tenth Amendment command.

Unfortunately, the Court has never defined "bound up." It seems, though, that the phrase encompasses things that refine the state's assessment of when someone is entitled to recover from another. We have seen examples. *Klaxon* required a federal diversity court to apply state choice of law rules. Such rules do not define the elements of a claim or defense, but do serve to refine the state law assessment of when a claimant can recover. They instruct the court which state's law to apply and thus seem bound up with "rights and obligations" defined by state law. In addition, *Palmer v. Hoffman* held that a federal diversity court must apply state law on the burden of proof at trial. Again, the burden of proof does not exactly define when a party may recover, but is closely related to it. It seems bound up with the definition of when a claimant can recover because it determines the winner when no proof is introduced on a particular issue.[66]

In *Byrd*, the Court then launches into a lengthy paragraph in which it determines that the South Carolina rule does not define state-created rights and obligations and is not bound up with such rules. Instead, it is "merely a form and mode of enforcing the immunity."[67] What happens with issues of "form and mode"? The Court explains in the second subsection of Part II. The first sentence is long but interesting:

> But cases following *Erie* have evinced a *broader policy* to the effect that the federal courts should conform as near as may be — in the absence of other considerations — to state rules even of form and mode where the state rules may bear substantially on the question whether the litigation would come out one way in the federal court and another way in the state court if the federal court failed to apply a particular local rule.[68]

---

[66]I think statute of limitations would be another example. Such statutes do not define the rights and obligations, but put a temporal limitation on the claimant's ability to assert a right of pure substance. Given the holding in *Guaranty Trust*, however, in which the Court described the statute of limitations as a matter of the "form and mode" of enforcing a right, perhaps such rules are not bound up. In his concurring opinion in *Shady Grove Orthopedic Associates v. Allstate Ins.*, 559 U.S. 393, 419-420 (2010), Justice Stevens noted that state procedural rules may be "so bound up with the state-created right or remedy that it defines the scope of that substantive right or remedy." He cited statutes of limitations as an example. As we will see in §10.6.2, however, Justice Stevens undertook the "bound up" analysis in a different context than the one we address here.

[67]356 U.S. at 536. *Guaranty Trust* had first used the term *form and mode* to describe the statute of limitations.

[68]*Id.* at 536-537 (emphasis added).

This sentence is a gold mine. The term *broader policy* refers to *Erie's* theme about litigant equality. Recall from our discussion in §10.4.2 that *Erie* embodied not only the constitutional basis of the Tenth Amendment but the nonconstitutional policy underpinning of a concern that similarly situated parties be treated alike. *Guaranty Trust*, at least as it came to be applied, had perverted this interest in *litigant* equality into one of *outcome* equality. Here, in *Byrd*, the Court for the first time explains that this policy applies to cases in which the state law issue is not purely substantive or bound up with pure substance. This policy counsels, *but does not compel,* the federal courts to apply state law *in cases in which* failure to apply state law will be outcome determinative. It thus gives a context for the *Guaranty Trust* analysis: As to issues of form and mode, and when failure to apply state law would be outcome determinative, the federal court will apply state law "in the absence of other considerations." The Court opens the door to the possibility that "other considerations" might override outcome determination and permit a federal court to refuse to follow state law.

Indeed, *Byrd* itself is such a case. The Court makes the very important point that the federal courts, as an independent system for the administration of justice, have an interest in keeping "essential characteristic[s]" of that system free from interference by state law. Such an interest constitutes an "affirmative countervailing consideration[]"[69] that justifies a federal court's ignoring state law. In *Byrd*, the federal systemic interest is in the division of labor between judge and jury, which is influenced by the Seventh Amendment.[70] State law—at least state law that is not pure substance or bound up with it— "cannot in every case exact compliance with a state rule . . . which disrupts the federal system of allocating functions between judge and jury."[71] Because the state system had articulated no reason for its rule, while the federal system had a strong interest in allocating fact-finding functions between judge and jury, the federal courts were justified in ignoring the state rule about having the judge decide the issue of whether Byrd was a statutory employee.

In the third subsection of Part II of the opinion, the Court notes that its preceding analysis was based upon the supposition that the question of who decided whether Mr. Byrd was a statutory employee was "outcome determinative" in the *Guaranty Trust* sense. Here, it hints that the issue is probably not outcome determinative. That being the

---

[69]*Id.* at 537.

[70]It is curious that the Court did not simply hold that the issue of whether Mr. Byrd was a statutory employee was one as to which the Seventh Amendment applied to grant a right to jury trial in federal court. Had it done so, the Supremacy Clause would render *Erie* inapplicable.

[71]*Id.* at 538.

case, it is possible that much of what the Court said in the second subpart of Part II is dicta. One hopes, however, that it is not, because that part of the opinion makes so much sense. It told us that on matters of form and mode, as to which the Tenth Amendment does not command the federal court to apply state law, the federal court can nonetheless be conscripted to apply state law. It will do so if failing to do so would be outcome determinative *and* if no federal system interest in the allocation of duties outweighs the state interest. *Byrd* is famous for bringing "balancing" into the *Erie* equation, but it is important to see that it did so only in the limited circumstances summarized in this paragraph.

Byrd thus sets up a helpful linear model, diagrammed below. At one polar extreme are things that all would agree are purely substantive (like the elements of a claim), which the Court characterized as rules "respect[ing] the definition of state-created rights and obligations." At the other polar extreme are things that all would agree are purely procedural (like the length of paper on which pleadings are to be filed). Clearly, the federal court can "do its own thing" on purely procedural matters. Nothing in the Rules of Decision Act or *Erie* requires the federal court to apply state law there. Just as clearly, the Tenth Amendment commands the federal court to apply state law on matters of pure substance. As one moves away from pure substance, however, there are rules that are so bound up with the definition of rights and obligations as to be treated as pure substance under *Erie*. The Tenth Amendment requires the federal diversity court to follow such state rules, such as choice of law and burden of proof rules.

Further removed from pure substance are rules of form and mode (which may be a fancy way of saying "procedure"). Here, *Byrd* establishes, the Tenth Amendment does not apply. But the policy of litigant equality espoused in *Erie* does. If ignoring the state law on this point will be outcome determinative, the federal court will—as a matter of comity, to avoid differing outcomes in the two systems—apply state law. *But* it will not do this if it would violate some interest of the federal courts as a separate judicial system. Here, it will balance the relative interests of the systems. In *Byrd*, the federal systemic interest was great, while the state gave no reason for its rule and thus had little interest in it. The federal interest outweighed the state's and the federal court was justified in ignoring state law.

In sum, *Byrd* is not perfect (it does not define "bound up" and does not tell us how to weigh truly competing federal and state interests), but it is far better than anything we've seen before or since. It permitted the federal courts to avoid the application of state law that would disrupt the operation of the federal system and told us what part of *Erie* is commanded by the Tenth Amendment and what part

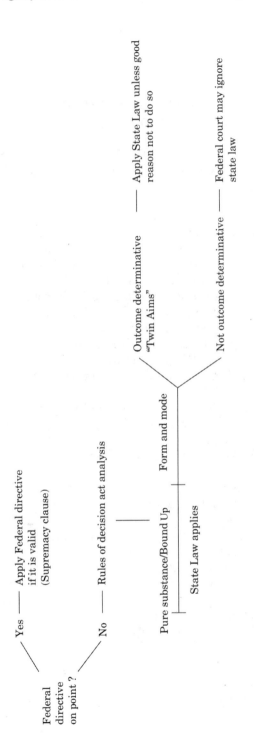

is counseled by policy. It also gave us a context for application of the outcome-determination test of *Guaranty Trust*.

§10.6　The *Erie* Doctrine Splits: *Hanna v. Plumer* and Subsequent Developments

§10.6.1　*Hanna's* Establishment of Two Levels of Vertical Choice of Law: The *Hanna* Prong and the *Erie* Prong

The next case is a giant: *Hanna v. Plumer*,[72] which was decided in 1965. There, the plaintiff brought a diversity case in federal court in Massachusetts. The defendant was the executor of a deceased person. He was served with process under a provision now found in Federal Rule 4(e)(2)(B), which allows for "substituted" service of process by serving someone of suitable age and discretion who resides at the defendant's dwelling or usual abode.[73] Under Massachusetts law, however, service on a representative of a decedent, such as an executor, had to be effected personally; substituted service was not permitted. The question was clear: Did *Erie* require the federal court to apply state law in this instance, or was the federal court free to ignore state law and apply Rule 4?

Based upon what we have seen (especially *Byrd*), we would expect a federal court to look at whether the state rule requiring personal service of process was part of the definition of state-created rights and obligations or was bound up with such a definition. If (as seems likely) it was not (but was merely a rule of form and mode), the court would next look to whether it was outcome determinative under *Guaranty Trust*. It certainly seems so: If state law were applied, the case would be dismissed; if state law were ignored, the case would proceed. Thus, we would expect the court to apply state law unless there was a federal systemic interest that outweighed the state interest in its rule. No such interest seems obvious, so we might expect *Erie*, as we have seen it, to require the application of state law. The lower courts concluded that state law should govern and held that service of process was improper because it was not effected in the way required by state law. At the Supreme Court, the defendant (who had won in the lower

---

[72]380 U.S. 460 (1965). The iconic study of this case is John Hart Ely, *The Irrepressible Myth of* Erie, 87 Harv. L. Rev. 693 (1974).

[73]At the time the case was decided, the "substituted" service of process rule was found in Federal Rule 4(d)(1), so the opinion refers to that. We discussed substituted service at §3.3.2.

courts) argued that the lower courts were right under *Guaranty Trust* because the rule was outcome determinative.

So what did the Court do? It did not purport to approach the case under the *Byrd* scheme. Thus, it did not discuss whether the state law was part of the definition of state-created rights or bound up with such a definition. It did, however, discuss *Guaranty Trust* and outcome determination. Consistent with *Byrd*, it seemed to discuss outcome determination as something that applies only to state rules of form and mode. But *Hanna* proposed a fundamentally different way to look at outcome determination. Chief Justice Warren's opinion noted that "[o]utcome-determination analysis was never intended to serve as a talisman.[74] Indeed, the message of [*Guaranty Trust*] itself is that choices between state and federal law are to be made not by application of any automatic 'litmus paper' criterion, but rather by reference to the policies underlying the *Erie* rule."[75] This is important language because it recognizes that courts had come to apply *Guaranty Trust* woodenly. In fact, the Court noted (as we did in §10.5) that at some point *every* procedural variation between the federal and state courts will be outcome determinative in the sense that the courts had come to apply that test.

***The Twin Aims of* Erie.** The Court then posited that outcome determination, while relevant to a Rules of Decision Act inquiry, should be guided by what it called the *twin aims* of *Erie*: (1) discouragement of forum shopping and (2) avoidance of the inequitable administration of the laws. This is the first time the Court identified these twin aims as such. It traced them not to the Tenth Amendment basis of *Erie*, but to what we have called the litigant equality theme from that case: "a realization that it would be unfair for the character or result of a litigation to differ materially because the suit had been brought in a federal court."[76] According to the Court, *Erie* was based (at least in part) upon a reaction to the forum shopping that was inspired by *Swift v. Tyson*, which we discussed in §10.3. Guided by these principles, the outcome-determination test should focus not at the point in litigation where compliance with the state rule becomes a problem, but at the *outset* of the case. The question should be whether the difference between applying state law and ignoring state law would lead the plaintiff to prefer the federal forum. If so, the federal court should lean toward applying state law.

---

[74]At this point, the Court cited *Byrd*, which was the only time the Supreme Court cited *Byrd* between 1958 and 1996. It failed, however, to discuss *Byrd*.

[75]380 U.S. at 466-467.

[76]*Id.* at 467. In his concurring opinion, which we discuss toward the end of this subsection, Justice Harlan decried the majority's focus on litigant equality. *Erie*, to Justice Harlan, was more about the Tenth Amendment than about forum shopping.

This new outcome-determination analysis from *Hanna* is known as the "modified-outcome-determination" test or the "twin aims" test. It appears to be far more sensitive and consistent with what Justice Frankfurter implied in *Guaranty Trust* than the wooden test that courts evolved from that case. Moreover, it seems consistent with *Byrd* in treating the outcome-determination analysis as part of the policy of litigant equality rather than the Tenth Amendment core of *Erie*.[77]

Some commentators have questioned, however, whether there really are two aims in the twin aims test. Instead, it seems that the Court was worried about only one thing—avoidance of forum shopping. If there is forum shopping, it seems that the "inequitable administration of the laws" follows automatically. Stated another way, if ignoring a state law will cause litigants to flock to federal court, this will automatically result in the inequitable administration of the laws. Why? Because only citizens of another state will be able to gain access to the federal court (because only they can invoke diversity jurisdiction).

> ○ ***Example #3.*** Assume the law of State *A* requires plaintiffs in a medical malpractice suit to file with their complaint an affidavit of a health care professional stating her professional conclusion that malpractice was likely to have occurred. Plaintiffs do not like this requirement because it makes it more expensive and difficult simply to initiate such a suit. Plaintiff, a citizen of State *B*, sues Doctor, a citizen of State *A*, in federal court for medical malpractice. If the federal court does not follow state law, Plaintiff will be able to sue without an affidavit. This undoubtedly would cause forum shopping—every plaintiff who could go to federal court would do so, because she would thus evade the affidavit requirement. Because only citizens of states other than State *A* can go to federal court (because only they can invoke diversity of citizenship against a doctor who is a citizen of State *A*), the federal court's failure to follow state law would automatically create the inequitable administration of the laws.

Whether the test really has one aim or two, it is important to see how the *Hanna* approach differs—in focus and result—from that of *Guaranty Trust*. The issue in *Hanna* (whether service of process was proper) certainly was outcome determinative in the wooden *Guaranty Trust* sense. Why? Because, as we already noted, if state law applied, the case would be dismissed; if state law were ignored, the case would proceed. This is exactly the scenario the Court found to be outcome determinative in *Guaranty Trust*. But the facts of *Hanna* were not outcome determinative in the new twin aims sense. Why? Because no litigant, in assessing where to sue *at the outset of litigation*, would sue

---

[77]It is odd that *Hanna* cites *Byrd* only once and does not discuss *Byrd*'s overall approach to vertical choice of law.

in federal court just to avoid the personal service of process requirement of state law. The plaintiff in *Hanna* probably had every intention
of effecting personal service on the defendant. Not until service was
attempted did the need for substituted service arise.

Thus, the question of how one serves process upon the defendant
is not "outcome determinative" in the new sense of that phrase as
reflected in *Hanna*. Because the issue was not outcome determinative,
state law need not be applied. At this point in the opinion, then, the
Court seems to be modifying the outcome-determination test and to
be on the verge of holding, under *Erie*, that state law did not govern.
Instead of doing so, however, the Court suddenly informs us that its
new twin aims analysis is irrelevant to the issue before it! In fact,
everything we have read so far in *Hanna* is irrelevant. Why? Because
everything we have read so far in the opinion deals with the Rules
of Decision Act, and that statute is irrelevant to the issue before the
Court in *Hanna*. Instead, the Court explains, the vertical choice of
law issue in *Hanna* implicates an entirely different statute: the Rules
Enabling Act.

The Rules Enabling Act and the Supremacy Clause. The
Hanna Court stuns the reader by saying that the defendant's argu-
ment (that the *Guaranty Trust* test should apply) is subject to a "fundamental flaw"—namely, "the incorrect assumption that the rule of
Erie constitutes the appropriate test of the validity and therefore
the applicability of a Federal Rule [of Civil Procedure]."[78] When a
Federal Rule of Civil Procedure applies, *Erie* is irrelevant! In such a
case, the question "is a far cry from the typical, relatively unguided
Erie choice."[79] Instead, the Federal Rule constitutes an instruction by
Congress to apply that provision, so long as the provision is valid. And
to determine whether the Rule is valid, the Court must analyze it
under the Rules Enabling Act.

The Rules Enabling Act (REA), 28 U.S.C. §2072, made possible the
promulgation of the Federal Rules of Civil Procedure.[80] With the REA,
Congress delegated to the Supreme Court the congressional authority to promulgate rules of "practice and procedure" for the federal

---

[78]380 U.S. at 469-470.

[79]*Id.* at 471.

[80]The REA was passed in 1934. The leading historical study of the Act is Stephen
Burbank, *The Rules Enabling Act of 1934,* 130 U. Pa. L. Rev. 1015 (1982). The REA
has been amended, notably in 1988 to make the proceedings before the Advisory
Committee more public and participatory. This "politicization" is a topic of interest-
ing commentary by other prominent academics. *See, e.g.,* Linda Mullenix, *Hope Over
Experience: Mandatory Informal Discovery and the Politics of Rulemaking,* 69 N.C.
L. Rev. 795 (1991); Martin H. Redish & Uma M. Amuluru, *The Supreme Court, the
Rules Enabling Act, and the Politicization of the Federal Rules: Constitutional and
Statutory Implications,* 90 Minn. L. Rev. 1303 (2006).

courts.[81] The Supreme Court does not actually draft the Federal Rules. It delegates that job to an Advisory Committee. That group seeks public comment on proposed changes, and sends its new provisions to a Standing Committee, which acts under the auspices of the Judicial Conference.[82] The Standing Committee then sends the amendments to the Judicial Conference, which approves them for submission to the Supreme Court. If the Supreme Court approves, the proposed rules are sent to Congress. If Congress does not amend or reject any of the proposals within a given period, they become effective. Thus, by the time a Federal Rule goes into effect, it has been reviewed (at least in theory) by the Advisory Committee, the public, Standing Committee, the Judicial Conference, the Supreme Court, and the Congress.

These layers of review are intended to ensure not only that any amendment or new Federal Rule is clearly drafted, but it does not violate the REA. Section 2072(a) requires that a Federal Rule address only procedural matters. Section 2072(b) provides that the Federal Rules "shall not abridge, enlarge, or modify any substantive right." These two parts embody important constitutional concepts of separation of powers and federalism. First, it attempts to limit rulemaking authority to matters of "procedure." If the judicial rulemaking process were to stray into matters of substantive law, it would constitute a usurpation of legislative power. To the extent the federal government wishes to legislate regarding substantive law and policy, it must do so through Congress. Such matters must be passed by the politically accountable branches, and not imposed by the judiciary.[83] Second, it attempts to ensure that the federal government does not use the guise of a rule of procedure to encroach on state substantive law.

Hanna explained that a Federal Rule must be assessed for validity at two levels: the constitutional and the statutory. On both points, the

---

[81]Though our focus is the Federal Rules of Civil Procedure (which we will call the "Federal Rules"), the REA is also the source for authority for promulgation of the Federal Rules of Appellate Procedure, Criminal Procedure, Evidence, and Bankruptcy.

[82]The Judicial Conference is the main policy-making body for the federal judiciary, and is chaired by the Chief Justice. It and the Advisory Committee, then, are lodged in the judicial branch of the federal government.

[83]The politically accountable branches, of course, are the legislature, which passes statutes, and the executive, which has the power to veto them. (They are politically accountable because their members can be voted out of office; federal judges cannot.) Professor Vitiello has urged a more active role for Congress in the rulemaking process. Michael Vitiello, *Revising the Federal Rules of Civil Procedure: Carving Out a More Active Role for Congress,* 35 Notre Dame J.L. Ethics & Pub. Pol'y 147 (2021). Professor Redish has written about the threat to democratic theory posed by federal rulemaking. *See* Martin H. Redish, Wholesale Justice: Constitutional Democracy and the Problem of the Class Action Lawsuit 62-86 (2009); Martin H. Redish & Dennis Murashko, *The Rules Enabling Act and the Procedural-Substantive Tension: A Lesson in Statutory Interpretation,* 93 Minn. L. Rev. 26 (2008).

Court relied on *Sibbach v. Wilson*,[84] a 1941 case that upheld the valid-ity of the discovery provision of Rule 35 permitting medical examina-tions of a party. Under the *Sibbach / Hanna* test, judicial rulemaking is constitutional if the provision is "rationally capable of classification" as procedural.[85] Even the Court recognized that this "arguably proce-dural" test is not rigorous.

Under *Sibbach / Hanna,* the statutory hurdle under the REA is also not rigorous. Indeed, it is redundant of the constitutional test. Thus, a Federal Rule passes muster under the REA if it "really regu-lates procedure—the judicial process for enforcing rights and duties recognized by substantive law and for justly administering remedy and redress . . . ."[86] In *Hanna*, the Court had no trouble concluding that Federal Rule 4 was both constitutional and fell within the REA. Thus, Rule 4 governed and trumped state law for cases in federal court.[87]

In view of the deferential tests for validity under the Constitution and the REA, it is not surprising that the Court has never found a Federal Rule invalid. Indeed, the process by which the Rules are pro-mulgated gives them "presumptive validity under both the consti-tutional and statutory constraints."[88] We will consider this issue in more detail when we discuss the *Shady Grove* decision in §10.6.2. For now, there is a more basic question: Why does a valid federal pro-vision trump state law? Though the Court in *Hanna* did not make the point as clearly as it could have, the answer is dictated by the Supremacy Clause of the Constitution.[89] It provides that federal law is "the supreme law of the land." So once a court determines that a federal directive (such as a Federal Rule of Civil Procedure) (1) applies to the facts of the case and (2) is valid, the Supremacy Clause requires that it be applied.

And that was the holding in *Hanna*. Federal Rule 4 applied to the facts of the case and was valid both under the Constitution and the REA. Thus, Rule 4 trumps state law in federal court. There is no anal-ysis of *Erie* at all: no outcome determination, no twin aims, no *Byrd*. Those are all relevant to analysis under the Rules of Decision Act, but do not apply when there is a valid federal directive on point.

Two Prongs of Analysis. It is difficult to overstate the importance of *Hanna*. The case establishes that what we had thought of as a

---

[84]312 U.S. 1, 14 (1941).

[85]*Hanna*, 380 U.S. at 464.

[86]*Sibbach*, 312 U.S. at 14.

[87]State law still applies in state court, however. The Federal Rules apply only in federal court.

[88]Burlington Northern R.R. Co. v. Woods, 480 U.S. 1, 6 (1987).

[89]U.S. Const., art.VI, cl. 2.

single doctrine (the *Erie* doctrine) is actually two. Before applying the "typical, relatively unguided" *Erie* inquiry, a court must ask whether there is a federal directive on point. If so, the federal directive applies, so long as it is valid. We call this the *Hanna prong* of vertical choice of law doctrine. Though in *Hanna* the federal directive was a Federal Rule of Civil Procedure, remember that the *Hanna* prong applies to any federal provision, including the Constitution and federal statutes, as well as Federal Rules.

So when does *Erie* come up? When there is no federal directive on point. In such situations, the federal government has not prescribed a rule, so the court must apply the *Erie,* or the Rules of Decision Act (RDA), inquiry of vertical choice of law. We call this the *Erie prong* (or RDA prong) of vertical choice of law. We saw in §10.5 that it is a confused analysis. *Hanna* added to the confusion by suggesting its twin aims amendment to the outcome-determination test. Because the Court based its holding in *Hanna* on the REA, however, the twin aims material was dicta. Nonetheless, as we discuss in §10.6.3, subsequent cases have adopted twin aims as part of the *Erie* prong of the analysis.[90]

Justice Harlan's Concurrence. Justice Harlan concurred with the result in *Hanna*. His reasoning, however, was quite different from that of the majority. The Harlan opinion is worth studying. Justice Harlan forthrightly admitted that the Court had not articulated a workable doctrine under *Erie* but worried that the majority opinion in *Hanna* was simplistic. In particular, he decried the majority's focus on the litigant equality theme; to Justice Harlan, *Erie* was far more than a case that expressed worry about forum shopping. It was about the Tenth Amendment, and the majority in *Hanna* gave short shrift to that part of the analysis. To Justice Harlan, the primary question should be whether state law must govern when the issue is one that "would substantially affect those primary decisions respecting human conduct."[91] If it does, state law must govern. If it does not, state law can be ignored. On the facts in *Hanna*, he concluded, no one would structure her real-world human conduct on the method for serving process in a wrongful death case. Therefore, state law would not control.

The Harlan equation—that state law governs those "primary decisions respecting human conduct"—has strong appeal, perhaps especially as a proxy for determining whether a Federal Rule is valid under the REA. We will consider the issue in §10.6.2.

---

[90]*See, e.g.,* Walker v. Armco Steel Corp., 446 U.S. 740, 753 (1980).
[91]*Hanna,* 380 U.S. at 475 (Harlan, J., concurring).

§10.6.2 Post-*Hanna* Cases Applying the *Hanna* Prong

Determining Whether a Federal Directive Is On Point

Under the *Hanna* prong, the first step is to determine whether a federal directive is on point and covers the issue to be decided by the federal judge. According to the Court, *Hanna* was the first time a Federal Rule of Civil Procedure conflicted directly with a state provision. This suggestion seems belied, however, by cases such as *Ragan* and *Cohen*,[92] in which the Court appeared to eviscerate a Federal Rule. The majority opinion in *Hanna* explained, though, that those cases did not hold that a Federal Rule was displaced by state law. Instead (and this is an important point), they held that the Federal Rule *was not sufficiently broad to cover the issue in dispute*. Thus, in *Palmer v. Hoffman*,[93] in which the issue was burden of proof at trial, the Court held that Rule 8(c) required that the defendant assert an affirmative defense. As explained in *Hanna*, though, Rule 8(c) addressed only pleading the affirmative defense; it did not address the issue of which party had the burden of proof at trial. Because there was no federal directive on point, then, the Court was justified in treating the issue of burden of proof under the *Erie* prong of vertical choice of law.

Justice Harlan's concurring opinion in *Hanna* expressed skepticism on this issue. He did not understand how *Ragan*, in which the Court held that a federal diversity court must apply state law concerning tolling of the statute of limitations, could survive *Hanna*. He concluded that Federal Rule 3, which provides that an action is commenced when filed, covers the tolling question and thus must trump state law. The Court returned to this issue in 1980 in *Walker v. Armco Steel Corp.*,[94] the facts of which were indistinguishable from those in *Ragan*. The Court upheld *Ragan* and explained that Federal Rule 3 did not address tolling at all. Rather, it defines the commencement of a suit *only* for purposes of applying the Federal Rules and not for purposes of whether the statute of limitations is tolled. Because there is no federal directive on point, the Court addressed the issue of tolling under the *Erie* prong, and concluded that state law must govern.

Through the years, the Court has stated the initial *Hanna*-prong inquiry in different ways. In *Hanna* it asked whether the federal directive "covers the point in dispute."[95] In two other cases, it asked whether the federal directive was "sufficiently broad to control the issue before the Court."[96] The language is relevant to the important

---

[92]These are two of the "triple play" cases discussed in §10.5.

[93]This case is also discussed in text accompanying notes 57-58 above.

[94]446 U.S. 740 (1980).

[95]380 U.S. at 470.

[96]Burlington Northern R.R. v. Woods, 480 U.S. 1, 5 (1987); *Walker*, 446 U.S. at 750 n.9.

question of whether federal directives are to be read broadly or narrowly. Though most of the cases involve interpretations of Federal Rules of Civil Procedure, remember that the federal directive might be any federal law — the Constitution, a statute, or a Federal Rule.

It seems appropriate that federal courts should read federal directives narrowly in applying the *Hanna* prong. In other words, *Hanna* should be invoked only if the federal directive clearly covers the point in dispute. Doubts should be resolved by refusing to invoke *Hanna*. Why? Because applying *Hanna* means that the federal directive will govern the situation (assuming it is valid). Federal law trumps state law in such circumstances, without any assessment of outcome determination, twin aims of *Erie*, or any balancing of the relative interests of the federal and state judicial systems. *Hanna* is heavy-handed and hard-hearted. Overzealous use of *Hanna* may undermine important state policies.

In at least six cases, the Court has found that a federal directive was not on point, and thus that the *Hanna* prong did not apply.[97] In some of these, it has demonstrated great sensitivity to the possibility that application of a federal directive might have a deleterious effect on state law. In *Walker*, for example, though the Court said it would give Federal Rule 3 its "plain meaning,"[98] it actually seems to have read it narrowly. The Court held that Rule 3 governs "commencement" of an action for purposes *other than* tolling the statute of limitations. Doing so allowed the Court to avoid a conflict between the Federal Rule and state law on the topic. This permitted the Court to find, under the *Erie* prong, that state law should govern.[99]

The Court did something similar in *Semtek*,[100] in which it interpreted Federal Rule 41(b). That Rule, as we saw in §7.4.2, governs involuntary dismissals and provides (with some exceptions) that such dismissals are to operate as adjudications on the merits. That is, they are to be considered dismissals "with prejudice." The Court read Rule

---

[97]The six cases are: *Cohen v. Beneficial Ind. Loan Corp.*, note 56 above; *Palmer v. Hoffman*, note 57 above; *Ragan*, note 51 above; *Walker*, note 94 above; *Semtek Int'l., Inc. v. Lockheed Martin Corp.*, 531 U.S. 497 (2001); and *Gasperini v. Center for Humanities, Inc.*, 518 U.S. 415 (1996).

[98]446 U.S. at 750 n.9.

[99]Oddly, however, the Court found that Rule 3 had a different "plain meaning" in *West v. Conrail*, 481 U.S. 35, 39 (1987). There, in a federal question case, the Court concluded that Rule 3 *did* cover tolling of the statute of limitations. It distinguished *Walker* by noting that the latter was a diversity of citizenship case. Again, however, a narrower reading of the federal directive is most appropriate when it can avoid overriding state law, as in *Walker*.

[100]Semtek Int'l., Inc. v. Lockeheed Martin Corp., 531 U.S. 497 (2001). *See* Stephen Burbank, Semtek, *Forum Shopping, and Federal Common Law,* 77 Notre Dame L. Rev. 1027 (2002).

41(b) narrowly, holding that it meant only that the case could not be refiled in another *federal* court, and that the dismissal did not bar refiling in state court. In his opinion for the Court, Justice Scalia expressed concern that a broader interpretation of Rule 41(b), one that would bar refiling of a claim even in state court, would run afoul of the Rules Enabling Act by modifying a substantive right. He opined that when a federal directive is susceptible of alternative readings, a court should adopt the narrower of the two.

Another example of the Court's demonstrating sensitivity to state interests is *Gasperini v. Center for Humanities, Inc.*[101] There, the defendant admitted liability and the case went to trial solely to determine damages; the jury returned a verdict of $450,000. The defendant moved for new trial under what is now Rule 59(a)(1)(A), which permits such orders "for any reason for which a new trial has heretofore been granted in an action at law in federal court." One of the historic reasons was that the jury's damages figure "shocked the conscience" of the court. A New York statute, however, provided for new trial on more liberal terms: A court would order a new trial if the verdict in the present case "deviates materially" from those in similar cases. The Court concluded that Rule 59 was not on point. Justice Ginsburg's opinion then stated that federal courts "have interpreted the Federal Rules . . . with sensitivity to important state interests and regulatory policies."[102]

The statement is consistent with what the Court did in the cases just discussed. Unfortunately, it is inconsistent with what the Court has done in other cases. In at least six cases, the Court concluded that federal directives were on point, conflicted with state law, and (because valid) trumped state law in federal court.[103] In some of these, the application of the federal directive was obvious and undeniable. For instance, in *Hanna*, there is no question that Rule 4 permitted substituted service of process. In *Sibbach*, there was no question that Rule 35 permitted the federal court to order a party to undergo a medical examination.

In other cases, though, the Court seemed to read federal directives broadly. *Burlington Northern R.R. v. Woods*[104] involved the possible application of Rule 38 of the Federal Rules of Appellate Procedure.[105]

[101]518 U.S. 415 (1996).

[102]*Id.* at 421 n.7.

[103]The six cases are: *Sibbach*, note 38 above; *Mississippi Publ'g Corp. v. Murphree*, 326 U.S. 438 (1946); *Burlington Northern R.R. Co. v. Woods*, 480 U.S. 1 (1987); *Hanna v. Plumer*, 380 U.S. 460 (1965); *Stewart Org., Inc. v. Ricoh Corp.*, 487 U.S. 22 (1988); and *Shady Grove Orthopedic Assoc., P.A. v. Allstate Ins. Co.*, 559 U.S. 393 (2010).

[104]480 U.S. 1 (1987).

[105]This is not one of the Federal Rules of *Civil* Procedure, which govern in federal district courts and on which we spend so much time in Civil Procedure. This was a

That Rule permits (but does not require) a Court of Appeals to impose an award of double costs if it finds that an appeal was frivolous. State law, on the other hand, required that an appellant be fined 10 percent of the judgment if the appellant had obtained a stay of the trial court judgment and lost on appeal. The Court concluded that Rule 38 covered the matter in question by permitting only permissive sanctions and prohibiting mandatory sanctions. This interpretation of Rule 38 seems overly broad, because there is nothing on the face of that Rule indicating an intent to preclude a mandatory penalty in the circumstances covered by the state rule. In other words, Rule 38, with its discretionary sanctions, could have coexisted with state law mandating a sanction in certain circumstances. The Court had recognized such coexistence of state and federal directives in *Cohen*.[106]

Perhaps the most overzealous interpretation of a federal directive was in *Stewart Organization, Inc. v. Ricoh Corp.*[107] This case (unlike the others discussed) involved a federal statute, and not a Federal Rule. In *Stewart*, an Alabama citizen entered into a contract with a New York citizen. The contract contained a forum selection clause that provided that litigation arising from the contract would take place in New York. Alabama law prohibited the enforcement of forum selection clauses, while New York law permitted such clauses.[108] The Alabama citizen sued the New York citizen in state court in Alabama. The defendant removed the case to federal court and sought enforcement of the forum selection clause by transfer to federal court in New York. The Supreme Court held that the venue-transfer statute, 28 U.S.C. §1404(a),[109] was on point and directed federal courts to consider the existence of a forum selection clause as a *factor* in favor of transfer under the statute. The Court considered this "a straightforward exercise in statutory interpretation to determine if the statute covers the point in dispute"[110] and enforced the clause by upholding transfer of the case to federal court in New York.

Notice the problem created by the holding in *Stewart*. After the decision, in Alabama the enforceability of forum selection clauses depends

---

provision of the Federal Rules of *Appellate* Procedure, which govern in federal courts of appeals. They are also adopted under the Rules Enabling Act, in the same fashion as the Federal Rules of Civil Procedure. They are included in your Rules booklet.

[106]See note 56 and accompanying text above. There, the Court held that Federal Rule 23.1, which imposed requirements for shareholder derivative suits, did not preempt application of a state law requirement that plaintiff post a bond.

[107]487 U.S. 22 (1988).

[108]Parties to such a clause agree that litigation concerning a contractual matter will be held in a particular forum. While the modern trend is clearly to enforce such clauses so long as they are not the product of overreaching, some states will not enforce them.

[109]We discussed transfer of venue under this statute at §5.5.2.

[110]487 U.S. at 30.

on whether a case is in state or federal court.[111] In federal courts, such clauses are enforceable through transfer; in state courts, they are not. This is the sort of vertical disuniformity caused by *Swift v. Tyson* and criticized by *Erie*. By holding that the federal directive was on point, the Court may have run roughshod over legitimate state interests. This possibility should counsel courts to "sneak a peek" at state interests when determining whether a federal directive is on point.[112]

Shady Grove Orthopedic Assoc., P.A. v. Allstate Ins. Co.[113] is an important effort in applying the *Hanna* prong. It involved assertion of a statutory claim under New York law for allegedly unpaid interest concerning insurance benefits. Under New York law, the claim could not be asserted as a class action. Under Federal Rule 23, however, the case qualified to proceed as a class action. The Court held that Rule 23 "answers the question in dispute"[114] and therefore, if valid, would apply under *Hanna*. Justice Scalia wrote the plurality opinion, joined by three others. Justice Stevens concurred, thereby creating the majority, which upheld the application and validity of Rule 23. Justice Ginsburg dissented, joined by three others.

Justice Scalia insisted that the question of whether Rule 23 was on point was easy.[115] He was unwilling to sneak a peek at state law to see whether a narrow interpretation of the federal directive might be appropriate. In *Semtek*, Justice Scalia had asserted that courts should interpret ambiguous federal directives narrowly, to avoid different outcomes in federal and state court.[116] Here, he agreed with that view, but concluded that Rule 23 was not ambiguous. Indeed, "there is only one reasonable reading of Rule 23,"[117] and it was met on

---

[111]Moreover, nothing in §1404(a) suggested that Congress had considered that the statute should be a means of enforcing forum selection clauses. At the time the statute was passed, few if any states enforced such clauses, so such embrace would have been unlikely.

[112]*See* Richard D. Freer & Thomas C. Arthur, *The Irrepressible Influence of* Byrd, 44 Creighton L. Rev. 61, 73 (2011) (federal court "may take a quick look to see whether a broad reading of the [federal directive] would have a deleterious effect on state law").

[113]559 U.S. 393 (2010). The case generated three symposia, each featuring several articles. *See* 44 Akron L. Rev. 897 (2011), 44 Creighton L. Rev. 1 (2010), and 86 Notre Dame L. Rev. 987 (2011).

[114]*Id.* at 393.

[115]Professor Koppel concludes that "*Shady Grove* signals a return to the pre-*Gasperini* propensity not to read Federal Rules to avoid a conflict with state law." Glenn S. Koppel, *The Fruits of* Shady Grove: *Seeing the Forest for the Trees,* 44 Akron L. Rev. 999, 1002 (2011).

[116]Scalia opined that a broad interpretation of Rule 41 (one that would allow an involuntary dismissal to preclude filing a case in any court) was to be avoided because it might prescribe a binding effect for involuntary dismissals in state court. 531 U.S. at 503-504 (a reading of Rule 41(b) that extinguished a claim in state court "would seem to violate" §2072(b)).

[117]559 U.S. at 405 n.7.

the facts of the case. Because Justice Stevens concurred in this portion of Justice Scalia's opinion, five Justices agreed on the point.[118] (Scalia and Stevens parted company on how one assesses whether a Federal Rule is valid, as we will see below.)

The dissent concluded that Rule 23 did not apply, and therefore assessed the case under the *Erie* prong, concluding that state law should govern. Its conclusion about Rule 23 is questionable. The dissenters were willing not simply to "sneak a peek" at state law, but to let state law essentially trump a Federal Rule. Justice Stevens's concurrence criticized the dissent on this score, saying "[s]imply because a [federal] rule should be read in light of federalism concerns, it does not follow that courts may rewrite the rule."[119]

The preliminary question of whether a federal directive is on point and conflicts with state law is of critical importance. It determines whether the matter will be assessed under the *Hanna* prong or the *Erie* prong. Though the Court has been inconsistent, in some decisions we see recognition that it is appropriate to interpret federal directives narrowly, to avoid unnecessary friction with state law. Of course, a narrow interpretation is possible only when a federal rule is susceptible to at least two interpretations. *Shady Grove* reminds us that some Federal Rules are not.

Determining Whether the Federal Directive Is Valid

We just saw that assessing the applicability of a federal directive can be difficult. Here, we will assume that such a directive is on point. If it is, it will apply and trump state law (under the Supremacy Clause of the Constitution). If it is not valid, it cannot be applied. The federal directive will not always be a Federal Rule of Civil Procedure. It might be a federal statute (as in *Stewart*) or even a constitutional provision. What are the tests for validity of the various federal directives?

By definition, a constitutional provision is always valid. So if a federal constitutional provision is on point, it applies. Period. An example could have come from the facts in *Byrd*. There, the Court might have concluded that the Seventh Amendment applied and mandated that a jury (not the judge) determine the facts surrounding the question

---

[118]The conclusion seems correct. Rule 23 is not like Rule 59(a), which was considered in *Gasperini*. That Rule allows an order for new trial but gives no specific bases for it. Nor is Rule 23 like Rule 23.1, which was addressed in *Cohen*. That Rule imposes some non-exclusive requirements on shareholder derivative suits, which might coexist with a state requirement for posting a bond. Rule 23 is more like Rule 4 in *Hanna*—either it is met or it is not. On its face, Rule 23 "creates a categorical rule entitling a plaintiff whose suit meets the specified criteria to pursue his claim as a class action." 559 U.S. at 398-399 (Scalia, J.).

[119]*Id.* at 431 (Stevens, J., concurring).

of whether Mr. Byrd was a statutory employee. Had the Court done so, the Seventh Amendment would have trumped state law, and there would have been no *Erie*-prong issue.[120]

What about statutes? Congressional authority to legislate is enumerated in the Constitution. In §10.4.2, we surmised that Congress could pass a valid statute declaring the duty owed by railroads to persons such as Mr. Tompkins in the *Erie* case. The statute would have come within Congress's power to regulate interstate commerce, which is one of the most expansive bases of federal legislative power. The breadth of federal legislative power is beyond our scope; it is the domain of the course on Constitutional Law.

What if the federal directive is a Federal Rule? In §10.6.1, we saw that a Federal Rule must be checked for validity against the Constitution and the Rules Enabling Act (REA). *Hanna,* as we saw, adopted the approach taken by the older case of *Sibbach v. Wilson.*[121] That case essentially conflated the constitutional and statutory tests into one inquiry. Under *Sibbach/Hanna*, a rule promulgated under the REA is constitutionally valid if it is "rationally capable of classification" as procedural. Under the REA, such a rule is valid if it "really regulates procedure—the judicial process for enforcing rights and duties recognized by substantive law and for justly administering remedy and redress . . . ."[122] Thus, so long as the Federal Rule can be characterized as dealing with a procedural matter, it is valid constitutionally and under the REA.

The *Sibbach/Hanna* approach seems skewed. It overlooks that the REA imposes two requirements. One, under §2072(a), the Rule must be a provision dealing with "practice or procedure" in the federal courts. And two, under §2072(b), the Rule "shall not abridge, enlarge or modify any substantive right." The "arguably procedural" test of *Sibbach/Hanna* may be appropriate for assessing validity of a rule under §2072(a), but it ignores §2072(b).[123]

Sibbach was decided in 1941, just three years after the Federal Rules went into effect. Like any decision, it is a product of its time.

---

[120]See note 70 above.

[121]See text accompanying notes 84-85 above.

[122]312 U.S. at 14.

[123]Dean Ely made this argument in 1974. *See* Ely, note 72 above. Professor Redish calls this the "redundancy" construction of the REA, and notes that "[u]nder this approach the second provision [§2072(b)] effectively serves solely to place emphasis on the first [§2072(a)]." Redish & Murashko, note 83 above, at 28. Professor Burbank concludes that the *Sibbach/Hanna* methodology reflects a fundamental misunderstanding of the REA. He finds that the statute was intended to allocate authority between the Supreme Court and Congress, with protection of state law "deemed a probable effect, rather than the primary purpose, of the allocation scheme established by the Act." Burbank, note 80 above, at 1025-1026.

The drafters of the REA understood that Congress could not delegate to the judicial branch the power to prescribe and define substantive rights.[124] They thought they avoided this possibility by delegating only the power to prescribe "procedural" rules. There were two problems with this view. First, the drafters did not have a good sense of where any such line between the two is drawn. Indeed, it seems clear that Congress hoped that the Court would draw the line appropriately when it promulgated the Federal Rules.[125] Second, the view assumes that procedure and substance are different things that can be roped off, perhaps even hermetically sealed, from each other.

But this is simply not so. Choices we make about procedural rules can have a profound impact on one's ability to vindicate a substantive right. For example, requiring a plaintiff to allege facts supporting a "plausible" claim (instead of merely putting the defendant on notice) may make it more difficult to engage the litigation process. The compulsory counterclaim provision of Rule 13(a)(1) requires a defending party to assert a claim in the pending case, on pain of losing the right to sue in another forum. In other words, that "procedural" rule can result in extinguishing a substantive claim. Similarly, expanding the availability of the class action in Rule 23 made possible small-claim consumer cases that would never have been filed had people been required to sue individually. In other words, that "procedural" rule increased the incidence in which substantive rights would be vindicated.

Over the years, the Court has recognized that the Federal Rules can affect substantive rights. In *Burlington Northern*,[126] in upholding a Federal Rule of Appellate Procedure, the Court said: "Rules which incidentally affect litigants' substantive rights do not violate [the REA] if reasonably necessary to maintain the integrity of [the federal] system of rules."[127] In *Business Guides, Inc. v. Chromatic Communications Enterprises, Inc.,* in upholding Federal Rule 11, it explained: "[i]mposing monetary sanctions on parties that violate the Rule may confer a benefit on other litigants, but the [REA] is not violated by such incidental effects on substantive rights."[128]

In these cases, then, the Court recognized that procedure and substance can overlap—that the relationship between them is more nuanced and subtle than *Sibbach* and *Hanna* implied. This realization,

---

[124]See note 83 and accompanying text above.

[125]Burbank, note 80 above, at 1137. *See also See* Kevin M. Clermont, *The Repressible Myth of* Shady Grove, 82 Notre Dame L. Rev. 988 (2011).

[126]We discussed this case above, when discussing how a court determines whether a federal directive is on point. See notes 104-106 and accompanying text above.

[127]480 U.S. at 5.

[128]498 U.S. 533, 553 (1991).

it seems, should invigorate §2072(b). Because a Federal Rule might tread on substantive rights, a court should endeavor to ensure that the rule not (in the words of the §2072(b)) "abridge, enlarge, or modify any substantive right." This, in turn, would require the judge at least to consider the content of the state law to see whether the federal provision abridges, enlarges, or modifies it. If that impact were "incidental," the Rule would be valid. If it were more than "incidental," the Rule would be invalid under the REA. The *Sibbach/Hanna* approach does not do this. All it requires is that the court satisfy itself that the federal provision can be characterized as procedural.

One impediment to an invigorated assessment under the REA is the Court's unfortunate holding in *Hanna*, repeated in *Burlington Northern,* that Federal Rules are *presumptively* valid under the REA. This presumption is based upon the fact that the Rules are reviewed by so many groups: the Advisory Committee, the Standing Committee, the Court, and Congress.[129] There is an enormous problem with this thinking. The ultimate authority for the Rules lies with Congress. It delegated to the Court the power to legislate concerning procedure. In the rulemaking process, Congress does not vote on the proposed rules. Instead, its inaction—its failure to reject or amend the rules—is what constitutes legislative "approval." In the words of Justice Frankfurter: "to draw any inference of tacit approval from non-action by Congress is to appeal to unreality."[130] Moreover, as we saw above, it is likely that Congress assumes the Court engages the serious analysis of whether a proposed rule affects a state substantive right.

All of this came to the fore in *Shady Grove.* There, as we discussed in §10.6.1, the majority consisted of a four-Justice plurality opinion by Justice Scalia and a concurrence by Justice Stevens. All five Justices agreed that Rule 23 was on point. All five agreed that Rule 23 was valid under the REA. They differed, however, on the appropriate test for validity under the REA.

The plurality opinion by Justice Scalia relied entirely upon *Sibbach*, as reaffirmed in *Hanna*. To the plurality, the question was "not whether the rule affects a litigant's substantive rights; most procedural rules do."[131] Instead, the question was merely whether Rule 23 can be characterized as a procedural provision. Because it concerns the aggregation of claims, it "really regulates procedure" and, under *Sibbach*, is valid.

---

[129] A challenge to a Federal Rule can succeed "only if the Advisory Committee, this Court, and Congress erred in their prima facie judgment that the Rule . . . transgresses neither the terms of the Enabling Act nor constitutional restrictions." *Hanna*, 380 U.S. at 471.

[130] *Sibbach*, 312 U.S. at 18 (Frankfurter, J., dissenting).

[131] 559 U.S. at 406-407.

Interestingly, Justice Scalia recognized tension between *Sibbach* and §2072(b). "[I]t is hard to understand how it can be determined whether a Federal Rule 'abridges' or 'modifies' substantive rights without knowing what state-created rights would obtain if the Federal Rule did not exist."[132] But *Sibbach* forbids assessment of the state law. Its focus is purely on the federal provision.[133] If it "really regulates procedure," it displaces state law, no matter how "substantive" the state may consider that law.[134] And, to the plurality, *Sibbach* remains the governing standard.[135]

As a policy matter, the plurality defended *Sibbach* because it ensures that procedure will be uniform in every federal district. If the REA required the federal court to refuse to follow a Federal Rule when it conflicted with a law the state considered "substantive," federal practice would be inconsistent from district courts in one state to district courts in another. On the facts of *Shady Grove*, for instance, finding that Rule 23 would displace a law New York considered "substantive" would mean that Rule 23 would not apply in federal courts in New York (for such claims). But Rule 23 would apply in other districts. To the plurality in *Shady Grove*, Congress intended with the REA to ensure uniform practice among the federal courts.

In his concurrence, Justice Stevens criticized the plurality's singular reliance on *Sibbach*. The *Sibbach* analysis gives credence only to §2072(a), and ignores the concerns of §2072(b). Thus it "ignores the balance that Congress struck between uniform rules of federal procedure and respect for a State's construction of its own rights and remedies."[136] For Stevens, assessment of validity under the REA requires the court to consider the state law itself. In this regard, he undertook a functional analysis reminiscent of that used under the *Erie* prong. His point was to determine whether the New York statute prohibiting class assertion of the claims was integrally related ("bound up")

---

[132]*Id.* at 411-414.

[133]"We have held since *Sibbach*, and reaffirmed repeatedly, that the validity of a Federal Rule depends entirely upon whether *it* regulates procedure. If it does, it is authorized by §2072 and is valid in all jurisdictions with respect to all claims, regardless of its incidental effect upon state-created rights." 559 U.S. at 410 (emphasis added; citations omitted).

[134]"The concurrence is correct that under our disposition any rule that 'really regulates procedure' will pre-empt a conflicting state rule, however 'bound up' the latter is with substantive law." 559 U.S. at 1446 n.13 (citations omitted). *See* Allan Ides, *The Standard for Measuring the Validity of a Federal Rule of Civil Procedure: The* Shady Grove *Debate Between Justices Scalia and Stevens,* 86 Notre Dame L. Rev. 1041 (2011).

[135]The plurality noted that some recent cases had not cited *Sibbach*, but concluded that no case had overruled it. 559 U.S. at 415 n.14 ("Thus, while *Sibbach* itself may appear infrequently in the U.S. Reports, its rule—and its particular focus on the Federal Rule as the proper unity of analysis—is alive and well").

[136]559 U.S. at 423-426 (Stevens, J., concurring).

with the definition of the claim itself.[137] If it were, he would find that the Rule, as applied, violated the REA.[138] Ultimately, Justice Stevens found that the New York law did not implicate substantive interests. Thus, it would be trumped by Rule 23.[139]

Justice Stevens recognized the importance of context. Because *Shady Grove* was a *Hanna*-prong case, there was a federal directive on point. Because the federal government has declared a preference for how the issue should be handled, the burden is on the party opposing application of the Federal Rule, and that burden is "a high one."[140]

So here, too, we are left with uncertainty.[141] The Court did adopt the *Sibbach* test in *Hanna*. But the sole reliance on *Sibbach* in *Shady Grove* garnered the support of only four Justices. While it is true that only Justice Stevens embraced a more searching test in the context of validity under the REA, the tenor of the dissent in *Shady Grove*—which focused strongly on state interest—suggests that the four dissenting Justices might, when focused on the *Hanna* prong, conclude that §2072(b) has some teeth. For the moment, however, the *Sibbach/Hanna* approach, though under attack, survives.

As we noted in §10.6.1, some observers conclude that Justice Harlan's concurring opinion in *Hanna* gave a nice proxy for determining when a provision would affect a substantive right. According to Harlan, state law must govern regarding "primary decisions respecting human conduct."[142] A provision masquerading as a Federal Rule of Civil Procedure but dealing with such primary decisions of human conduct would modify a substantive right and thus violate §2072(b).

---

[137]*Id.* at 417-421 (Stevens, J., concurring).

[138]Justice Stevens would permit an "as applied" attack on Federal Rules under the REA, while Justice Scalia would not. Ides, note 134 above, at 1044-1045.

[139]559 U.S. at 431-436 (Stevens, J., concurring).

[140]559 U.S. at 432 (Stevens, J., concurring). Professor Cox regrets that "*Hanna* improperly made congressionally enacted procedures immune from *Erie* analysis" and that the Court should "always defer to state laws that are substantive for *Erie* purposes." Stanley Cox, *Putting* Hanna *to Rest in* Shady Grove, 44 Creighton L. Rev. 43, 50 (2010). He concludes that Justice Stevens's approach in *Shady Grove* is essentially correct, but would conclude that Rule 23 was invalid. *Id.* at 59.

[141]As one court notes: "So four Justices adopted one formulation. One Justice adopted a different formulation. And four Justices did not address the question. What should we do in the face of such an unresolved 4-1 disagreement? Neither the 4-Justice view nor the 1-Justice view on its own is binding in these unusual circumstances." Abbas v. Foreign Policy Grp., LLC, 783 F.3d 1328, 1336-1337 (D.C. Cir. 2015). The court concluded that *Sibbach* governs until the Supreme Court clearly instructs otherwise. *Id.* at 1337.

[142]*Hanna*, 380 U.S. at 475 (Harlan, J., concurring).

§10.6.3 Post-*Hanna* Cases Applying the *Erie* Prong

If there is no federal directive on point, the federal court must determine whether the Tenth Amendment and the Rules of Decision Act (RDA)—in other words, whether *Erie*—compels it to apply state law to determine the issue before it. This is the *Erie* prong (or the RDA prong) of analysis. In very rough terms, state law must be applied if the issue is one of "substance." Drawing that line has proved difficult, as we saw in tracing the development of cases from *Erie* through *Hanna* in §§10.5 and 10.6.1. There, we saw that the Court gave us different strands for the assessment, including "outcome determination," "balancing the interests," and "twin aims of *Erie*," but never molded those disparate notions into a single test.

Lower federal courts have wrestled with this uncertainty for decades. In particular, it has never been clear whether the "outcome determination" test of *Guaranty Trust* survived the "twin aims" test of *Hanna*. In *Gasperini v. Center for Humanities, Inc.*,[143] the Court said that *Hanna* had "qualified" the outcome-determination test of *Guaranty Trust*. This statement might imply that the wooden test of *Guaranty Trust* should be relegated to the dustbin, but doing so is not so easy. The concept still has currency in a surprising number of lower court opinions, at least as a starting point for the *Erie*-prong analysis.[144]

The Court had a golden opportunity to reconcile *Guaranty Trust*, *Byrd*, and *Hanna* in 1996, with *Gasperini*.[145] Unfortunately, the Court failed to do so.[146] In *Gasperini,* the plaintiff invoked diversity

---

[143]518 U.S. 415, 428 (1996).

[144]*See, e.g.*, Giovanniello v. ALM Media, LLC, 660 F.3d 587, 593 (2d Cir. 2011) ("federal courts adjudicating state causes of action pursuant to diversity jurisdiction must apply outcome-determinative statutes of limitations"); Torres v. Bayer Corp., 616 F.3d 778, 787 (8th Cir. 2010) ("we must determine whether the California Code provision is substantive or procedural, and to do so, we apply the outcome determinative test first articulated in *Guaranty Trust*," which the court then read with reference to the twin aims test); Windy City Metal Fabricators & Supply, Inc. v. CIT Tech. Fin. Servs., 536 F.3d 663, 670 (7th Cir. 2008) ("district courts take as their starting point the 'outcome-determinative' test of *Guaranty Trust*"); Daubert v. City of Lindsay, 37 F. Supp. 3d 1168, 1180 (E.D. Cal. 2014) ("Therefore, we determine if the requested action is procedural or substantive by whether it is outcome determinative") (*citing Guaranty Trust*).

[145]518 U.S. at 415.

[146]Commentators generally did not have good things to say about *Gasperini. See, e.g.*, C. Douglas Floyd, Erie *Awry: A Comment on* Gasperini v. Center for Humanities, Inc., 1997 BYU L. Rev. 267 (1997); Wendy Perdue, *The Sources and Scope of Federal Procedural Common Law: Some Reflections on* Erie *and* Gasperini, 46 U. Kan. L. Rev. 751 (1998). Even the positive comments were less than strongly embracing. *See* Thomas Rowe, *Not Bad for Government Work: Does Anyone Else Think the Supreme Court Is Doing a Halfway Decent Job in Its* Erie-Hanna *Jurisprudence?*, 73 Notre Dame L. Rev. 963 (1998).

of citizenship jurisdiction in a federal court in New York. The defendant admitted liability and the case went to trial solely to determine damages; the jury returned a verdict of $450,000. The defendant moved for new trial under what is now Rule 59(a)(1)(A), which permits such orders "for any reason for which a new trial has heretofore been granted in an action at law in federal court." The Court's *Hanna* assessment, and its decision that Rule 59(a)(1)(A) was not on point, are discussed in §10.6.2. Here we focus on the Court's *Erie*-prong analysis.

The defendant contended that the verdict was excessive, which is a traditional basis for an order of new trial. Rule 59 does not prescribe a standard for determining when a verdict is excessive, but federal courts had determined that a new trial is proper if the verdict "shocks the conscience" of the court.[147] On the other hand, under New York tort reform law, state courts applied a more intrusive test and were to assess whether a verdict "deviates materially from what would be reasonable compensation." In addition, the New York tort reform statute required appellate courts to assess the question of whether a verdict was excessive de novo. In other words, the appellate court would not defer to the trial court assessment, but would apply the "deviates materially" standard independently. The New York legislature was clear in stating its goals. The "deviates materially" standard was intended to invite more careful judicial scrutiny of verdicts. The state concluded that the "shocks the conscience" test was an insufficient protection against excessive verdicts. The state wanted to influence the outcome of litigation by limiting the range of jury awards.

The vertical choice of law issues were clear: Must a federal court sitting in diversity (1) apply the state provision defining when a new trial is to be granted for an excessive verdict, and, if so, (2) must it also apply the state provision providing that the appellate court applies that standard *de novo*? The Supreme Court concluded that the federal court must apply the New York "deviates materially" standard for granting a new trial, but not the provision for *de novo* appellate review. Stated in rough (and not very helpful) conclusory parlance, the "deviates materially" standard was substantive and the allocation of that issue for *de novo* appellate review was not. Most criticism of *Gasperini* is not with these bottom lines, but with the Court's reasoning.

Gasperini is the first Supreme Court case since *Byrd* to discuss *Byrd*. (*Hanna* contained a citation to *Byrd*, without discussion.[148]) Yet,

---

[147]*See, e.g.*, M.D. Mark, Inc. v. Kerr-McGee Corp., 565 F.3d 753, 755 (10th Cir. 2009) ("the jury award is inviolate unless we find it so excessive that it shocks the judicial conscience and raises an irresistible inference that passion, prejudice, corruption, or other improper cause invaded the trial") (internal citations omitted).

[148]In *Shady Grove*, Justice Stevens's concurrence cites *Byrd* and appears to engage in the sort of "bound up" analysis that case prescribed. 559 U.S. at 423-427 (Stevens, J.,

surprisingly, the Court fails to discuss *Byrd* with regard to the issue of whether the federal court must apply the New York standard for new trial. It makes no effort to assess whether the state "deviates materially" standard is part of the state's definition of rights and obligations or is bound up with such a definition. Instead, the Court goes to the twin aims test of *Hanna*, which raised the question of whether a federal court's refusal to apply state law would lead to forum shopping. The answer would seem to be yes—a plaintiff would prefer to avoid the "deviates materially" standard because it permits the judge to meddle with the plaintiff's verdict readily. But after setting up the issue, the Court then fails to apply the twin aims test. Instead, it jumps to a point not debated by the parties (and that seems a *non sequitur*)—that a statutory cap on damages would be "substantive" under *Erie*.

The Court then analogizes the "deviates materially" standard to such a cap, saying that it has the same purpose to limit recoveries. Thus, the Court concludes, the "deviates materially" standard must be substantive. Having concluded this, the Court *then* applies the twin aims test and concludes that ignoring state law would cause plaintiffs to flock to federal court. This is a strange application of twin aims, because it comes *after* determining that the rule is substantive, rather than as *part of* the assessment of whether it is substantive.

The Court concluded that the New York provision requiring appellate application of the "deviates materially" standard was not binding on the federal courts. It is here that the Court discusses *Byrd* for the first time in nearly four decades. According to the Court, *Byrd* established that *Guaranty Trust* had provided insufficient protection for "countervailing" federal interests. In *Byrd*, the countervailing federal interest was the Seventh Amendment right to jury trial for the determination of issues of fact in cases at law. In *Gasperini*, it was another part of the Seventh Amendment: the "reexamination clause." That clause provides that "no fact tried by a jury, shall be otherwise reexamined in any Court of the United States, than according to the rules of the common law."

It is not at all clear, however, whether the Court bases its holding in this regard on *Erie* or on the Seventh Amendment. If it is based upon the Seventh Amendment, if the Seventh Amendment commands that appellate courts may not apply a *de novo* standard, no discussion of *Erie* factors would be relevant. Why? Because a federal directive

---

concurring). Moreover, Justice Ginsburg's dissent engages in the same sort of analysis, without citation to *Byrd*. 559 U.S. at 437-445 (Ginsburg, J., dissenting). The difference is that Stevens undertook the analysis as part of his *Hanna* assessment of whether the Federal Rule was valid under the REA, and Ginsburg undertook it as part of her *Erie*-prong analysis.

would be on point on this issue and, under the Supremacy Clause, would prevail without assessment of state concerns.[149] If it is based upon *Erie*, however, the Court's effort is vexing. When applying *Erie* as to the deviates materially standard, as we just saw, the Court used the twin aims test (sort of). Here, however, the Court fails even to mention twin aims.

The Court's conclusion in *Gasperini* is clearly right: The state law allocation of authority between trial and appellate courts should not affect how that allocation is made in the federal courts. The federal judicial system certainly has a strong interest in deciding for itself how to assign the functions of trial and appellate courts—just as it did in assigning functions between judge and jury in *Byrd*. The Court's path to that conclusion in *Gasperini* is not clear and does not shed much light on how one goes about making the *Erie* assessment.

§10.7 A Suggested Synthesis

Lawyers, judges, and law students have to apply the lines of cases discussed in §§10.4, 10.5, and 10.6, to the facts of a given case and make a determination about whether state law will govern. In this section, I suggest a synthesis for analyzing vertical choice of law problems.[150] Throughout, we assume that state law provides a particular rule. The question is whether a federal court, hearing a diversity of citizenship case, must apply that state rule.

The first question *always* is whether there is a federal directive on point. In other words, is there some federal provision (from the Constitution, federal statutes, Federal Rules—any federal source) that governs the matter addressed by the state law? If the answer is yes, the case is governed by the *Hanna* prong and does not implicate *Erie* or the Rules of Decision Act (RDA). When a federal directive is on point, it applies, so long as it is valid. We discussed the tests for assessing validity of various federal directives in §10.6.3.

Do not give the *Hanna* prong short shrift. Remember that the Court has taken inconsistent approaches to how broadly one should read the federal directives. The most recent effort, *Shady Grove*, recognizes

---

[149]Remember from §9.2.2 that the Seventh Amendment applies only in federal court civil cases. It does not apply to the states.

[150]The approach suggested here is simply my best interpretation of the cases. The difficulty of the topic is suggested by this lament from the Ninth Circuit: "Every year, tens of thousands of first-year law students learn about *Erie R. Co. v. Tompkins*, and, soon after that, they become second-and-third-year law students with poor understanding of the doctrine. Some of these students take the bar exam, fail, and try again or do other things. Others pass and become attorneys who still do not understand *Erie*." Briseno v. Henderson, 998 F.3d 1014, 1029 (9th Cir. 2021).

that courts should employ the narrower of two possible interpretations of a federal directive, but also concludes that Federal Rule 23 was susceptible of only one interpretation. *Gasperini* counsels a narrow interpretation. And though the Court did not say it was applying Federal Rule 3 narrowly in *Walker*, it certainly did so in practice. The problem is that other cases, such as *Burlington Northern* and *Stewart*, are still on the books and adopted very broad readings of the federal provisions. Be prepared to argue the point both ways.

If the federal directive is *not* on point, the *second* step in vertical choice of law is to apply the *Erie* prong (or RDA prong). This analysis is especially difficult, because, as we have seen, the Court has thrown different factors into the equation at different times. Moreover, the case that arguably does the best job of integrating various factors—*Byrd*—has suffered from neglect. Still, the starting point under *Byrd* makes great sense: Is the state law part of that state's definition of rights or obligations? Examples include the elements of a claim or defense. If so, the Tenth Amendment *requires* the federal court to apply the state law in a diversity case. If not, we must ask whether the state rule is bound up with the state's definition of rights or obligations. Such rules are so closely related to matters of pure substance that here, too, the Tenth Amendment *requires* the federal court to follow state law in a diversity case.

Though the Court has never defined "bound up," the phrase seems to apply to matters such as choice of law rules and the burden of proof and may well explain the results of *Klaxon* and *Palmer v. Hoffman.* Justice Stevens's concurrence in *Shady Grove* seems to adopt such an interpretation of those cases but fails to use the term "bound up."

If the state law is neither pure substance nor bound up with it, then, in the parlance of *Byrd*, we face an issue concerning "form and mode." Here, we ask whether ignoring the state law in federal court would be outcome determinative. But we have two outcome-determination tests. The *Guaranty Trust* version is rough-hewn and asks whether the case would come out differently if we ignore the state law than if we apply it. Thus, in *Guaranty Trust* itself, applying state law meant the case must be dismissed, while ignoring state law meant that it could proceed. This was deemed outcome determinative. But we also have the twin aims or "modified outcome-determination" test of *Hanna.* That requires us to ask whether ignoring state law at the outset of litigation would give parties an incentive to flock to federal court. To avoid such forum shopping, the federal court ought to apply state law.

This step opens two large questions. First, which version of outcome determination do we use? Second, how does it fit in with *Byrd*? The Court has never answered either question. As to the first question, it suggested in *Gasperini* that the twin aims test has modified *Guaranty*

Trust. On the other hand, *Gasperini* was not clear in its application of the twin aims test, so we are left to do what prudent lawyers do. A prudent person, faced with two tests, would be prepared to argue for both of them. Though many observers believe that the *Guaranty Trust* version of outcome determination is a dead letter, lower courts still rely upon it occasionally.

As to the second question, the two outcome-determination tests might be incorporated into the *Byrd* analysis. Thus, if ignoring state law will either lead to a different outcome or encourage litigants to shop for federal court, *Byrd* teaches that the federal court is to apply state law *unless* there is a good reason not to do so. Importantly, this conclusion is *not* mandated by the Tenth Amendment, but is counseled in *Erie*'s theme of litigant equality.

What is a good reason not to apply state law? We have two examples. In *Byrd*, it was the federal judicial system's interest in allocating responsibility between judge and jury. In *Gasperini*, it was the federal judicial system's interest in allocating responsibility between trial and appellate courts. In both cases, the federal interest in its systemic integrity outweighed any state interest to the contrary.

We turn to some hypotheticals.

- ○ ***Example #4.*** In a diversity case, Plaintiff seeks to have her case certified as a class action. Under the state class action rule, the case would not be certified. Under Federal Rule 23 (the federal class action rule, which we discuss in §13.3), the case would be certified as a class action. Which provision does the federal court apply?
  - ○ Is there a federal directive on point? Yes. The issue is what standards must be met to qualify as a class action. Federal Rule 23 covers the issue in question. This fact pattern is even clearer than that in *Shady Grove*, where the majority found that Rule 23 was on point for a particular substantive claim for which state law would not permit class treatment. Under *Hanna*, then, Rule 23 applies, so long as it is valid.
  - ○ Is the Rule valid? *Hanna* established that a Rule must be valid both under the Constitution and the Rules Enabling Act (REA). The constitutional test is easy: The Rule is valid if it is rationally characterized as procedural; this requires only that the Rule be "arguably procedural." Because Rule 23 defines the procedural requisites for a class, and is not affected by the substantive law applied, the Rule is plainly procedural.
  - ○ Under the REA, there are two requirements: that the rule regulate procedure (§2072(a)) and that it not modify a substantive right (§2072(b)). In *Shady Grove*, the plurality opinion by Justice Scalia adopted the test from *Sibbach*, which was adopted in *Hanna*. That test seems to ignore §2072(b) and holds that the Rule is valid if arguably procedural. In other words, it seems to duplicate the test of §2072(a). Recall from §10.6.2 that Justice Stevens, concurring in *Shady Grove*,

criticized the application of *Sibbach* and undertook a functional analysis of the state rule, to see whether application of the Federal Rule would harm a state policy. So, as seen above at footnote 141, the statutory standard is not clear, and many courts appear simply to apply *Sibbach*.

○ ***Example #5.*** *P* sues *D* in state court. *D* moves for summary judgment. Applying state law, the state court denies the motion. *D* removes in timely fashion to federal court, invoking diversity of citizenship jurisdiction. *D* moves for summary judgment in federal court. Though the state court standard for summary judgment was not met, the standard under Federal Rule 56 (which governs summary judgment in federal court, and which we addressed in §9.4) would be met. Should the federal court grant the motion for summary judgment under Rule 56?

  ○ Yes. This matter is covered by *Hanna*, as in Example #4. There is a federal directive on point. The case is in federal court now, and valid provisions of the Federal Rules govern.[151]

○ ***Example #6.*** The legislature of State *A* is concerned about rising medical insurance rates, and passes a statute aimed at reducing the verdicts recovered in medical malpractice cases. The statute requires that such cases be heard by an arbitration panel consisting of health care professionals and lawyers. The panel is to render its decision. The plaintiff may accept that decision or continue to jury trial. If she goes to trial, the arbitration panel's decision is admissible in evidence. Plaintiffs do not like the arbitration process, because they believe that panels of doctors and lawyers are less likely to hold for plaintiffs (and less likely to award large damages) than juries. A citizen of State *B* is treated by a doctor who is a citizen of State *A* in State *A*. She claims malpractice and sues the doctor in federal court in State *A*, invoking diversity of citizenship jurisdiction. Is the federal court in State *A* required to apply the arbitration procedure, or can the case simply proceed through discovery to jury trial in federal court?

  ○ First, there is no federal directive on point. There is no provision in the Federal Rules concerning medical malpractice arbitration cases, and no federal statute addresses the issue. So this case does not invoke *Hanna*. It is an *Erie*-prong, or RDA-prong, problem.

  ○ Second, is the state law part of the definition of rights and obligations? It seems not, since the arbitration provision does not say anything about the standard to be applied for finding liability. Is it bound up with such a rule? Perhaps one can make a reasonable argument that the arbitration panel proceeding is closely related to the standards for who wins a medical malpractice action, but that seems unlikely. Thus, the state rule seems a matter of form and mode.

  ○ Would ignoring the state provision in federal court be outcome determinative?

    ○ It is not clear that it is outcome determinative in the *Guaranty Trust* sense. After all, the panel and the jury might reach the same

---

[151]Fairbank v. Wunderman Cato Johnson, 212 F.3d 528, 532-533 (9th Cir. 2000).

conclusion. On the other hand, the panel provision seems calculated to reduce recovery by plaintiffs.

- ○ What about modified outcome determination, or twin aims? Would ignoring the state law in federal court lead litigants to "shop" for federal court? Absolutely. Every plaintiff who could go to federal court would do so, to avoid the arbitration panel.
- ○ Because only noncitizens of State *A* can go to federal court (by invoking diversity of citizenship jurisdiction), failure to apply state law in federal court would lead to the inequitable administration of the laws. State *A* citizens would be stuck with the arbitration panel, while other citizens would not.
- ○ Because this rule of form and mode is outcome determinative, the federal court should apply state law unless there is a good federal systemic reason not to do so.
- ○ The federal courts have an interest in trial by jury. But, unlike the situation in *Byrd*, this state law provision does not vitiate that right. It merely delays it until after the arbitration hearing. Also unlike the situation in *Byrd*, here the state has a compelling interest in its rule. It is attempting to reduce medical malpractice judgments in an effort to reduce medical expenses, which is clearly an important state interest.

A Current Area of Ferment: Anti-SLAPP Statutes

In recent years, many states have passed statutes to curb "strategic lawsuits against public participation" (SLAPP). These are cases brought against someone who has exercised her right of free speech or petitioned the government on a matter of public interest. The suit is brought to quiet that person (and to make others think twice before speaking out on issues of public importance). Under these statutes, the defendant may file an "anti-SLAPP" motion to dismiss (or, in some states, to strike) the suit. If the defendant makes the required showing (usually that she is being sued because she exercised a constitutional right to speak), the burden shifts to the plaintiff. Typically, that burden is to demonstrate, with evidence, the "probability" that she will prevail on the merits of the case.[152] If the plaintiff cannot make the showing, the case is dismissed (or stricken).

As Example #7 demonstrates, courts have had difficulty dealing with whether a federal judge in a diversity case must apply a state anti-SLAPP statute.

---

[152]Anti-SLAPP statutes vary from state to state, which may account for some of the split of authority we will see in Example #7. For example, the Fifth Circuit concluded that the Texas statute did not apply in federal court, Klocke v. Watson, 936 F.3d 240, 245 (5th Cir. 2019), while the Louisiana statute does govern in federal court. Lozovyy v. Kurtz, 813 F.3d 576, 582-583 (5th Cir. 2015).

○ ***Example #7.*** *D* reports to the local health authorities that Grocer is violating various public safety laws concerning cleanliness. The authorities investigate Grocer. Grocer is furious at *D* and sues *D* for defamation. *D* claims that the suit is in retaliation for her exercise of her right to petition the government. *D* makes an anti-SLAPP motion to strike. If the case is in federal court under diversity of citizenship jurisdiction, must the federal judge apply the State *A* law?

　　○ First, the *Hanna* prong: Is there a federal directive on point that clashes with state law? One possibility is Federal Rule 12(b)(6), which permits dismissal for failure to state a claim. (Another is Rule 56, which permits summary judgment if there is no dispute of material fact and one party is entitled to judgment as a matter of law.) Under Rule 12(b)(6), a plaintiff must state a plausible claim, and the court does not consider evidence in ruling on the motion. Under the typical anti-SLAPP law, in contrast, a plaintiff must demonstrate, with evidence, *probable* success on the merits. Is Rule 12(b)(6) on point and does it clash with state law? The most influential decision to date is *Abbas v. Foreign Policy Group*, in which the District of Columbia Circuit, applying D.C. law, answered "yes."[153] Other courts of appeals have found the *Abbas* decision (which was authored by then-Judge Kavanaugh before his appointment to the Supreme Court) persuasive.[154] On the other hand, the First Circuit concluded that Federal Rule 12(b)(6) does not address the same issue as the Maine anti-SLAPP statute, and therefore that the federal directive is not on point.[155]

　　○ If Rule 12(b)(6) or Rule 56 is on point, is it valid constitutionally and under the REA? This assessment is undertaken as in Example #4. Because Rule 12 prescribes the level of detail required to enter the litigation stream, and Rule 56 prescribes the level of level of factual dispute required to avoid summary judgment, courts have concluded that these are valid procedural provisions.[156]

　　○ Second, if no federal provision is on point (as some courts conclude), we move to the *Erie,* or RDA, prong.

　　　　○ Is the state law part of the definition of rights and obligations? Or is it bound up with such a definition? Some courts conclude that

---

[153]738 F.3d 1328, 1336 (D.C. Cir. 2015) ("In short, Federal Rules 12 and 56 answer the same question as the [District of Columbia] Anti-SLAPP Act's special motion to dismiss provision").

[154]*See, e.g.,* La Liberte v. Reid, 966 F.3d 79, 87-89 (2d Cir. 2020) (applying California law); Carbone v. Cable News Network, Inc., 910 F.3d 1345, 1350 (11th Cir. 2018) (applying Georgia law).

[155]Godin v. Schencks, 629 F.3d 79, 88-92 (1st Cir. 2010) (Federal Rules 12(b)(6) and 56 (regarding summary judgment) do not address same issue as Maine anti-SLAPP statute).

[156]*See, e.g., Abbas*, 738 F.3d at 1337 (applying *Sibbach* to uphold the validity of Rules 12(b)(6) and 56, concluding: "A federal court exercising diversity jurisdiction therefore must apply Federal Rules 12 and 56 instead of the D.C. Anti-SLAPP Act's special motion to dismiss provision").

anti-SLAPP statutes implicate substantive rights.[157] They deal with a particular kind of claim: that one is being sued for exercising her constitutional rights. The statute does not apply to other claims. If it defines a right or obligation or is bound up with such things, the federal court must apply the state law.

o If it is not substantive or bound up with substantive law, it is a rule of "form and mode" and we must ask whether the state law is outcome determinative in the *Guaranty Trust* sense. If the law applies, the plaintiff must demonstrate, with evidence, that it is probable that she will win on the merits. We do not know that a given plaintiff cannot meet this standard. On the other hand, it is a difficult standard. Is that enough for *Guaranty Trust*? The point is arguable.

o What about the modified outcome-determination, or twin aims, test? If federal courts do not apply the anti-SLAPP statute, plaintiffs will have a significant incentive to go to federal court— precisely to avoid having to demonstrate probability of success on the merits. Because only citizens of another state can gain access to federal court (by invoking diversity of citizenship jurisdiction), failing to apply the state law will lead to the inequitable administration of the laws.[158]

o Because this rule of form and mode (if it is) is outcome determinative (at least in the twin aims sense), the federal court should apply state law unless there is a federal systemic interest in not doing so. The First Circuit concluded that there was no such federal interest.[159] If that is right, then the federal court should apply the state anti-SLAPP law.[160]

The Ninth Circuit, dealing with the California statute, has addressed the question more than other circuits. Initially, it held that federal courts must apply that statute.[161] Over time, though, that court has cut back on the holding and now concludes that some aspects of the

---

[157]*See, e.g.*, Newsham v. Lockheed Missiles & Space Co., 190 F.3d 963, 973 (9th Cir. 1999) ("California has articulated the important, substantive state interests furthered by the Anti-SLAPP statute").

[158]*See, e.g., Newsham*, 190 F.3d at 973 (9th Cir. 1999) ("Plainly, if the anti-SLAPP provisions are held not to apply in federal court, a litigant interested in bringing meritless SLAPP claims would have a significant incentive to shop for a federal forum").

[159]*Godin*, 629 F.3d at 87 ("the dual purposes of *Erie* are best served by enforcement of [the Maine statute] in federal court"); *see also Newsham*, 190 F.3d at 973 (after noting that defendant failed to identify any federal interest that would be undermined by application of the California anti-SLAPP statute, court said "[o]n the other hand, . . . California has articulated the important, substantive state interests furthered by the Anti-SLAPP statute").

[160]*See generally* 19 Wright & Miller §4509.

[161]This was the holding in *Newsham*, 190 F.3d at 972 (statute was "crafted to serve an interest not directly addressed by the Federal Rules: the protection of the 'constitutional rights of freedom of speech and petition for redress of grievances.'"). The court considered only the statute's provision of a special motion and burden-shifting.

state statute—dealing with timing and providing for an automatic stay of discovery—clash with Federal Rules and therefore do not apply in federal court. On the other hand, the burden-shifting feature of the motion and the provision for an award of attorney's fees do not conflict with a Federal Rule and must be applied in federal court.[162] This approach—considering different parts of a statute individually for a clash with the Federal Rules—seems appropriate.[163]

Finally, we summarize this suggested approach to vertical choice of law with a flowchart, which is set out on page 589.

§10.8   Other Issues: Determining the Content of State Law, Certification Statutes, and "Reverse *Erie*"

In this section, we address two ancillary issues raised by vertical choice of law. One of these issues affects federal courts and one affects state courts. Specifically, how does a federal court determine what state law is? And are state courts ever required to apply federal "procedural" law?

Assume that a federal court has determined that an issue is one on which it must apply state law. Where does the court look to find that law? Obviously, some matters clearly may be governed by state statutory provisions. If not, and the court has to look to common law or to judicial interpretations of statutes, what are the rules? In *Erie*, Justice Brandeis indicated that federal courts must follow state law as determined by the "highest court"[164] of the state. Often, however, there is no state high court pronouncement on an issue. For many years, the federal courts concluded that they were compelled to apply *whatever* appellate authority they found from that state. In one case, the federal court held that it was bound to follow an unpublished opinion by a state intermediate court of appeals—even though the opinion had no precedential value in the state court system![165]

Now, however, it is clear that the federal court is not required to do this. Instead, it should apply the law that *it believes* the state high court would apply. In blunt terms, the federal judge has to make her best "*Erie* guess" at what the state high court would rule on the question. It looks to all available data to make this assessment, including

---

[162]Planned Parenthood Fed'n of Am. v. Center for Progress, 890 F.3d 828, 833-835 (9th Cir. 2018); Metabolife Int'l, Inc. v. Wornick, 264 F.3d 832, 840-846 (9th Cir. 2001).

[163]*See* Sydney Buckley, Comment, *Getting SLAPP Happy: Why the U.S. District Court for the District of Kansas Should Adopt the Ninth Circuit's Approach When Applying the Kansas Anti-SLAPP Law,* 68 U. Kan. L. Rev. 791 (2020).

[164]*Erie*, 304 U.S. at 78.

[165]Gustin v. Sun Life Assurance Co., 154 F.2d 961, 962 (6th Cir. 1946).

trends in the law in other states and the particular state's high court practice in the past of adopting such trends.

Sometimes, a federal court's guessing incorrectly on the content of state law will prod the state courts into expressing their view on the matter. For instance, in *Dick Proctor Imports v. Sumitomo Corp.*,[166] the federal judge held that the Missouri Supreme Court (which had not spoken on the relevant issue in over 80 years) would embrace the modern trend permitting enforcement of forum selection clauses. The following year, the Missouri Court of Appeals made it clear that the state would cling to the old law holding such clauses void.[167] The federal court's guess is binding on the parties to the case before it, but, obviously, cannot bind the state courts.

If a federal district judge is wrong on the assessment of state law, there is not much the parties can do about it.[168] The losing party can appeal but faces a practical problem. The federal district judge is usually a member of the bar of the state in which the court sits and thus might be relatively comfortable in guessing what the state high court would say on a particular matter. Judges of the federal courts of appeals, however, are drawn from throughout the circuit and frequently are not members of the bar of the state whose law is being assessed. Naturally, out-of-state judges on the appellate bench might be deferential to the determination made by a district judge who is a member of the bar of that state. For instance, a court of appeals judge who is a member of the bar of New Mexico, who is reviewing the decision of a Colorado federal district judge, might be inclined to defer to the local judge's guess about what the Colorado Supreme Court would say on a question of law. For many years, such deference was common on the courts of appeals—that court would defer to the decision by a

---

[166]486 F. Supp. 815 (E.D. Mo. 1980). *See generally* Connor Clerkin, Note, *Predicated Predictions: How Federal Judges Predict Changes in State Law,* 54 Colum. J.L. & Soc. Probs. 305 (2021); Connor Shaull, Comment, *An* Erie *Silence:* Erie *Guesses and Their Effects on State Courts, Common Law, and Jurisdictional Federalism,* 104 Minn. L. Rev. 1133 (2019).

[167]619 S.W.2d 928, 930 (Mo. App. 1981).

[168]In *Deweerth v. Baldinger*, 38 F.3d 1266, 1273 (2d Cir. 1994), the plaintiff lost because of the Second Circuit's interpretation of New York statute of limitations law. Later, in an unrelated case, the New York Court of Appeals held that the Second Circuit's interpretation of the state law was wrong. The plaintiff therefore brought a motion to set aside the judgment to bring it into alignment with now-clear New York law. Granting a motion to set aside the judgment was error, however, because "*Erie* simply does not stand for the proposition that a plaintiff is entitled to reopen a federal court case that has been closed for several years . . . to gain the benefit of a newly-announced decision of a state court, a forum in which she specifically declined to litigate her claim." The plaintiff who chooses federal court in a diversity case (and the defendant who declines to remove such a case) is taking the chance that the federal court will misapply state law.

local district judge at the trial court level. The Supreme Court rejected the practice, however, in *Salve Regina College v. Russell*.[169] There, the Court held that the court of appeals must review an *Erie* guess as they would any other question of law, without deferring to the expertise of the local judge.

The vast majority of states have adopted a "certification" procedure by which a federal court can refer questions of state law to the state high court for guidance.[170] This procedure can be useful and avoids making the federal judge guess about what the state court would do. The certification statutes vary significantly from state to state. Some, for instance, do not permit the state court to decide questions that depend on issues of fact.[171] In some states there may be a problem if the question certified asks the state court to render an advisory opinion.[172] And there have been cases in which the federal court cannot decipher the answer given to it by the state high court. Moreover, one scholar has concluded that notwithstanding the popularity of certification statutes, "the certification procedure raises serious questions involving the scope of federal jurisdiction and judicial power."[173]

Of course, the Supremacy Clause requires state courts to follow applicable federal law. For instance, railroad employees injured at work can sue their employers either in federal or state court under the Federal Employees' Liability Act (FELA). If an employee brings a FELA case in state court, federal law creates the claim and governs concerning the railroad's liability. The presumption is that the state court will apply its own rules of procedure. On the other hand, the Supreme Court has held that some procedures are "essential to effectuate" the purposes behind the federal substantive law. Such procedures, which are "part and parcel of the [federal] remedy afforded," must be followed in state court. Accordingly, in *Dice v. Akron, Canton & Youngstown Railroad*,[174] from which these quotations are taken, the Court required state courts to grant a right of jury trial, even when

[169]499 U.S. 225 (1991).

[170]Many of these are based upon a Uniform Certification of Questions of Law Act, which was approved in 1967 and amended in 1995. It requires that the issue certified be "determinative of an issue in the pending litigation."

[171]*See, e.g.*, Exxon Co. v. Banque de Paris et des Pays-bas, 889 F.2d 674, 678-679 (5th Cir. 1989).

[172]Federal courts cannot issue advisory opinions, because Article III of the Constitution only gives the federal judiciary power over "cases" or "controversies." But state law on the propriety of advisory opinions can differ. For instance, the Florida Constitution permits the courts of that state to issue advisory opinions under the certification procedure. Sun Ins. Office, Ltd. v. Clay, 133 So. 2d 735, 739 (1961).

[173]Jonathan Remy Nash, *Examining the Power of Federal Courts to Certify Questions of State Law,* 88 Cornell L. Rev. 1672, 1675 (2003).

[174]342 U.S. 359, 361 (1952).

such a right would not be available under state law. This result is sometimes referred to as "reverse *Erie*," and applies only to such procedural issues that are closely related to the underlying federal claim. Thus, state courts in FELA cases must also follow federal law concerning the sufficiency of evidence to sustain a verdict.[175]

§10.9 Federal Common Law

Erie did not hold that there is no federal common law. It held that there is no *general* federal common law. The same day the Court decided *Erie*, it also decided *Hinderlider v. La Plata River & Cherry Creek Ditch Co.*,[176] in which it concluded that federal common law controlled the issue of whether an interstate stream must be apportioned between two states. The holding makes great sense. After all, the dispute was between two states; we can imagine that the law of State *A* would declare State *A* the winner and the law of State *B* would declare State *B* the winner. Such interstate disputes must be determined by federal law. Because there is no constitutional or statutory provision on point, the only federal law available is federal common law.

Obviously, then, there can be circumstances in which the creation of federal common law is appropriate. Through the years, the Supreme Court has not always been clear in stating the justifications for federal common law or in defining the circumstances in which it is appropriate. Federal common law is justified either to effectuate some congressional policy, in which Congress left gaps in a statutory scheme, or to protect "unique" federal interests. In a concurring opinion, Justice Jackson echoed these considerations in helpful terms:

> The federal courts have no *general* common law, as in a sense they have no general or comprehensive jurisprudence of any kind, because many subjects of private law which bulk large in the traditional common law are ordinarily within the province of the states and not of the federal government. But this is not to say that wherever we have occasion to decide a federal question which cannot be answered from federal statutes alone we may not resort to all of the source materials of the common law, or that when we have fashioned an answer it does not become a part of the federal non-statutory or common law.[177]

---

[175]Brady v. Southern R. Co., 320 U.S. 476, 479-480 (1943). *See* Kevin M. Clermont, *Reverse*-Erie, 82 Notre Dame L. Rev. 1 (2006).

[176]304 U.S. 92 (1938).

[177]D'Oench, Duhme & Co. v. Federal Deposit Ins. Corp., 315 U.S. 447, 469 (1942) (emphasis original).

Detailed consideration of federal common law is featured in the course on Federal Courts. Few Civil Procedure courses deal with the topic in depth. For our purposes, we note some of the general areas in which federal common law has been found appropriate. One, as noted, is when Congress has left "gaps" in statutory schemes. For example, Congress may enact a general regulatory scheme and provide that the federal courts are to develop rules for effectuating it. The best example is §301 of the Labor Management Relations Act, which granted federal subject matter jurisdiction over suits for violation of collective bargaining (labor union) contracts. Congress failed to provide any rules for adjudicating the dispute. In *Textile Workers Union v. Lincoln Mills*, the Supreme Court held that the statute "authorizes federal courts to fashion a body of federal law for the enforcement of these collective bargaining agreements . . . ."[178]

In addition, there are various substantive areas in which the Supreme Court has upheld federal common law even in the absence of a statutory gap. One involves the federal government's acting in a "proprietary" role. The government does this in many ways, such as by entering into contracts, overseeing regulatory programs, issuing commercial paper, etc. Any dispute involving these activities involves an undeniable federal interest. Sometimes the Court finds such interests so "uniquely federal" that federal law (including federal common law) will apply and preempt state law.[179] The best example is *Clearfield Trust Co. v. United States.*[180] There, the United States issued a check that was thereafter stolen and cashed. The Supreme Court concluded that federal common law, and not state law, governed the liability for the funds. The Court emphasized that the federal government's authority to issue the check originated with the Constitution and federal statutes. It then concluded that it was important to have a uniform standard for determining liability on such commercial paper, and that the United States thus not be subject to law that differed from state to state.[181]

---

[178]353 U.S. 448, 451 (1957).

[179]If there is no unique federal interest in the issue at hand, federal common law is not allowed. In *Rodriguez v. F.D.I.C.*, 140 S. Ct. 713, 717-718 (2020), the Court rejected a federal common law rule for allocating tax refunds among related businesses. It explained: "The federal government may have an interest in regulating how it *receives* taxes from corporate groups . . . . But what unique interest could the federal government have in determining how a consolidated corporate tax refund . . . is *distributed* among group members?" (emphasis original).

[180]318 U.S. 363 (1943).

[181]In contrast, in *Empire HealthChoice Assurance, Inc. v. McVeigh*, 547 U.S. 677 (2006), the Court concluded that the Federal Employees Health Benefits Act of 1959, under which the federal government negotiates and regulates health benefits plans for federal employees, did not require the generation of federal common law. The

The Court has sometimes held that federal common law applies, but that the content of the federal common law should mirror state law—in other words, that federal common law should adopt state law as the federal common law. One example is *United States v. Yazell*,[182] in which the Court held that federal common law governed the issue of whether a wife was legally obligated on her husband's Small Business Administration (SBA) loan. Because the SBA loan, unlike the check in *Clearfield Trust*, was not part of a nationwide program, and because Texas had a strong interest in applying its law of domestic relations, the Court held that federal common law adopted Texas law as its own. Another example, discussed in detail on this point in §11.2.2, is *Semtek International, Inc. v. Lockheed Martin Corp.*[183] There, the Court held that the preclusive effect of a judgment entered by a federal court in a diversity of citizenship case is to be determined by federal common law. On the facts of the case, however, that Court held that federal common law would adopt California law.

Another substantive area in which federal common law applies is international relations. Again, the need for federal law is obvious, because it is the federal government that engages in international affairs. The nation must speak in one voice and have one set of laws for determining international relations. Thus, issues involving relations of the United States with foreign countries are determined by federal common law. Admiralty can also raise issues in which a federal standard is desirable. Admiralty is a fascinating topic and addresses all manner of concerns occurring on navigable waters. In some of these areas, application of state laws could be awkward, so the Court has used a balancing test to determine whether federal common law should supersede state law on various admiralty topics. In *Bivens v. Six Unknown Named Agents of Federal Bureau of Narcotics*,[184] the Supreme Court recognized a private right of action against federal officers for damages for alleged violations of the Fourth Amendment prohibition against unreasonable searches and seizures. The Amendment itself is silent on any such right of action, and Congress has never provided one for such deprivations by federal officers.[185] The Court

---

contractual claim for reimbursement in that case did not threaten an identifiable federal interest. *Id.* at 692-693.

[182]382 U.S. 341 (1966). The Court discussed the "prudent course" as being "to adopt the ready-made body of state law as the federal rule of decision until Congress strikes a different accommodation" in *United States v. Kimbell Foods, Inc.*, 440 U.S. 715, 740 (1979).

[183]531 U.S. 497 (2001).

[184]403 U.S. 388 (1971).

[185]Congress has provided an express right of action—42 U.S.C. §1983—for deprivation of federal rights under color of *state* law, for example, by state officers. Federal common law can be used to recognize a defense rather than a cause of action. *See* Boyle

nonetheless concluded that the issue was proper for treatment by federal common law.

Whenever federal common law is allowed, it commands the same deference under the Supremacy Clause as other federal law.[186] Thus, it can displace state law in the particular substantive area. Moreover, claims asserted under federal common law invoke federal question jurisdiction under §1331.[187] Congress can undo federal common law by legislating in the area.[188]

---

v. United Tech. Corp., 487 U.S. 500 (1988) (recognizing a federal "military contractor defense" a to wrongful death claim against the manufacturer of a helicopter in which a servicemember was killed).

[186]Banco Nacional de Cuba v. Sabbatino, 376 U.S. 398, 424-427 (1964).

[187]Illinois v. City of Milwaukee, 406 U.S. 91, 99-100 (1972).

[188]New Jersey v. New York, 283 U.S. 336, 348 (1931).

Chapter 11

The Preclusion Doctrines

§11.1   Defining the Issue

The material covered in this chapter is known by a variety of names. Your casebook may refer to it as the "doctrine of former adjudication" or "*res judicata*" or "claim and issue preclusion" or "effect of judgments" or the "preclusion doctrines." The Supreme Court tends to refer to the individual doctrines as claim preclusion and issue preclusion, and to the general topic as *res judicata*.[1] Whatever the

---

[1] "The preclusive effect of a judgment is defined by claim preclusion and issue preclusion, which are collectively referred to as '*res judicata*.'" Taylor v. Sturgell, 553 U.S.

terminology, however, this material can be raised only when the fact
pattern involves at least two cases. The first case (which we call Case
1) has ended, and a judgment has been entered. Now the question is
whether that judgment from Case 1 precludes anyone from litigating anything in Case 2, which is pending.[2] It might do so through
the operation of either of two doctrines: claim preclusion or issue
preclusion.

Claim preclusion is the modern terminology for *"res judicata"*
(which literally means "the thing has been decided"); it is also sometimes called the *rule against splitting a claim*. The modern terminology is influenced by the Restatement (Second) of Judgments.[3] Both
"claim preclusion" and *"res judicata"* are currently in use and they
are interchangeable. We address claim preclusion in detail in §11.2. It
stands for the proposition that a claimant gets only one opportunity to
assert a claim. If you have one claim, you get one suit to vindicate it.
You get "one bite at the apple." If you sue a second time on the same
claim, the case will be dismissed under claim preclusion. That means
that the claimant must be careful to seek all rights to relief encom-
passed in a single claim in Case 1. If she does not, she cannot seek the
other rights to relief in Case 2. Jurisdictions can define the scope of
one's claim in different ways.

- ○ ***Example #1.*** *P* is involved in an auto collision with *D*. *P* suffers personal
  injuries and her car is damaged. In Case 1, she seeks only damages for
  the personal injuries. After judgment is entered in that case, she brings
  Case 2, seeking to recover for property damage to her car from the same
  collision. If the law defines her "claim" as all rights to relief arising from
  a single transaction (which we explore in §11.2.3), Case 2 will be dismissed under claim preclusion, because she is suing twice on the same
  claim. If, however, the law defines her claims as the individual rights

---

880, 892 (2008). For comprehensive discussion of preclusion law, *see* Robert C. Casad
& Kevin M. Clermont, Res Judicata: A Handbook on Its Theory, Doctrine, and Practice
(2001).

[2]Throughout the chapter, we refer to Case 1 and Case 2. The designations do not
necessarily reflect the order in which the cases were filed. Rather, Case 1 is Case
1 because it has gone to judgment first. Preclusion—either claim or issue preclusion—flows from entry of a final judgment that meets certain criteria. See §§11.2.2,
11.4.1.

[3]Restatements of the law are promulgated by the American Law Institute (ALI), a
prestigious group of lawyers, judges, and academics with about 3,000 members. Though
they do not have the force of binding law, Restatements are highly respected and many
courts have found them influential. Though there are Restatements in many fields, we
are concerned with the Restatements of Judgments. There have been two: the original
Restatement of Judgments promulgated in 1942 and the Restatement (Second) published in 1982.

invaded (also explored in §11.2.3), Case 2 will not be dismissed under claim preclusion, because there she is vindicating a different right (and therefore a different claim) from that vindicated in Case 1.

Issue preclusion is the modern terminology (influenced by the Restatement (Second) of Judgments) for "collateral estoppel" (or, more rarely "direct estoppel"). Both the older and the more modern terminology are used today. We will use the "issue preclusion" and discuss the doctrine in detail in §11.4. In an important way, issue preclusion is narrower than claim preclusion—it precludes relitigation in Case 2 of a particular *issue* that was litigated and determined in Case 1. The focus, then, is not on something relatively broad—the scope of a "claim"—but on something fairly narrow—an *issue* that was litigated and decided in Case 1. If issue preclusion applies, that issue is deemed established in Case 2. It will not be relitigated; the fact-finder in Case 2 will be instructed that that issue is established. Issue preclusion, then, does not necessarily result in dismissal of Case 2. Rather, it may simply narrow the scope of what must be litigated in Case 2.

- *__Example #2.__* In Case 1, P sues D on a claim that requires P to establish four issues: A, B, C, and D. After trial, P wins, and judgment is entered in her favor. Now P sues D in Case 2, asserting a different claim (so there's no claim preclusion). The claim in Case 2 requires P to establish five issues: W, X, Y, Z, and A. If issue preclusion applies, issue A will be deemed established in Case 2. P need not put on evidence on that issue, and D cannot relitigate it. At trial, P will be required only to establish issues W, X, Y, and Z.

When reading cases about preclusion, keep in mind another source of terminological confusion. Some courts (particularly in older cases) use "*res judicata*" in a generic sense to refer to both claim and issue preclusion. Therefore, you may read a case in which the court talks about *res judicata* but is actually applying issue preclusion.[4]

Both claim and issue preclusion are affirmative defenses under Federal Rule 8(c)(1).[5] Thus, it is incumbent on the defendant to raise them or risk waiving them. And once the defendant raises a defense of

---

[4]An example is the famous case of *Cromwell v. County of Sac*, 94 U.S. 351 (1877), which we discuss in §11.4.2.

[5]Rule 8(c)(1) lists both "estoppel" and "*res judicata*" as affirmative defenses. There is no question that these references encompass both claim and issue preclusion. Simi Inv. Co. v. Harris County, Texas, 236 F.3d 240, 252 n.16 (5th Cir. 2000); Mozingo v. Correct Mfg. Corp., 752 F.2d 168, 172 (5th Cir. 1985) (reference to *res judicata* in Rule 8(c) includes issue preclusion). We saw affirmative defenses at §7.3.3.

claim or issue preclusion, she bears the burden of proof on the issue.[6] Reflecting the contemporary concern with crowded judicial dockets, some courts seem willing to raise preclusion on their own motion, at least in some circumstances.[7]

Though the rules of claim and issue preclusion can be treated rather mechanically, it is important to realize that these are not just procedural technicalities. Several closely related and important policies support these doctrines. First, there is a legitimate interest in *finality*. At some point, litigation must be declared finished. It is not productive for the parties or for society to allow serial relitigation of a claim already asserted or an issue already decided by a competent court. Second, at some point a defendant has a right to *repose*—to know that she cannot be sued repeatedly on the same claim. Third, there is an interest in *consistency*. If the same issue were to be relitigated several times, there is a chance that it would be resolved differently in different cases—one jury might find that the defendant was driving her car recklessly while another jury, determining the same issue, might find to the contrary. Such inconsistency may erode the public's confidence in the judicial system by making that system seem more like a lottery than an orderly mechanism for resolving disputes. Fourth, the community has a legitimate interest in *efficiency*. Litigation is publicly funded dispute resolution, and the public has a right to expect that the resources of the judicial system will not be wasted. The use of preclusion reflects confidence in the judicial system: One opportunity to litigate a claim or an issue suffices to ensure each party of her "day in court."[8]

---

[6]Taylor v. Sturgell, 553 U.S. 880, 907 (2008) ("Claim preclusion, like issue preclusion, is an affirmative defense. Ordinarily, it is incumbent on the defendant to plead and prove such a defense").

[7]*See, e.g.*, LaCroix v. Marshall County, 409 Fed. Appx. 794, 798-799 (5th Cir. 2011) (though preclusion defense is usually raised if not asserted by defendant, court may raise it *sua sponte* if both cases were brought in the same court or if demands of justice mandate such judicial invocation); Lerch v. City of Green Bay, 406 Fed. Appx. 46, 47 (7th Cir. 2010) (court of appeals may raise preclusion *sua sponte*); Shurick v. Boeing Company, 623 F.3d 1114, 1116 n.2 (11th Cir. 2010) (court may raise preclusion *sua sponte* in the interest of judicial economy when both cases were brought in the same court). *But see* McKithen v. Brown, 481 F.3d 89, 104 (2d Cir. 2007) (defendant waived defense of claim preclusion by failing to raise it; court under no obligation to consider preclusion); Scherer v. Equitable Life Assur. Soc'y of Am., 347 F.3d 394, 398-399 (2d Cir. 2003) (trial court erred in raising preclusive effect of prior state court; defendant waived preclusion defense by failing to assert it). *See also* Arizona v. California, 530 U.S. 392, 412 (2000) (court may raise preclusion on its own in "special circumstances"—such as when it is on notice that it had previously decided an issue—which were not present in this case).

[8]*See* Kevin M. Clermont, *Res Judicata as Requisite for Justice,* 68 Rutgers L. Rev. 1067 (2016) (discussing policies served by preclusion). Of course, if the trial court errs

These underlying precepts are significant. Thus, the Supreme Court has said that preclusion embodies "public policy and private peace"[9] and serves "vital public interests."[10] Leading commentators have referred to preclusion as a "pillar of modern judicial philosophy."[11] On the other hand, the preclusion doctrines must be flexible. There are occasions on which the use of preclusion would not be fair, or when the policies underlying preclusion should give way to some other policy. We see such exceptions to the operation of preclusion in §11.5. The narrowness of these exceptions again manifests the seriousness with which the judicial system takes the policy of finality.

In addition, there is the occasionally vexing question of what preclusion law to apply when Case 1 and Case 2 are litigated in courts of different jurisdictions. If Case 1 was decided in a Kansas state court and Case 2 is pending in a Massachusetts court, what preclusion law applies—that of Kansas or that of Massachusetts? Each state is free to determine its own preclusion rules, so long as they do not violate due process, and states have adopted different approaches to various issues. This question becomes more complicated when a federal court is involved, particularly if the federal court is exercising diversity of citizenship jurisdiction. These situations implicate constitutional and statutory notions of full faith and credit and related doctrines. We study them in §11.6.

Before addressing claim preclusion and issue preclusion, we should contrast them with similar concepts you may encounter. *Double jeopardy* is the criminal law analogue to claim preclusion; it ensures that no criminal defendant is made to answer twice for the same crime. Because it is a doctrine of criminal law, we do not encounter it in Civil Procedure.

Stare decisis, as we discussed in §1.2.2, is the doctrine of precedent. It requires that courts of a jurisdiction adhere to the legal pronouncements by appellate courts of that jurisdiction. Such pronouncements potentially affect all citizens; *res judicata* and collateral estoppel, in contrast, only bind those who were litigants in Case 1 (or in privity with a litigant in Case 1).

Law of the case establishes that issues decided in a suit will not be relitigated later in the same case. It is different from issue preclusion because the issues are raised in a single case. With issue preclusion, a judgment has been entered in Case 1, and the question is whether that judgment affects one's ability to relitigate issues in Case 2.

---

in its resolution of a case, the proper avenue is not to file a new case to relitigate, but to appeal. See §14.2.

[9]Hart Steel Co. v. Railroad Supply Co., 244 U.S. 294, 299 (1917).

[10]Federated Dep't Stores, Inc. v. Moitie, 452 U.S. 394, 401 (1981).

[11]18 Moore's Federal Practice 131-121.

Finally, *judicial estoppel* prevents a litigant from taking inconsistent positions in different cases. It is a doctrine of equity, for which there are no immutable rules. An example is *New Hampshire v. Maine*,[12] which involved a dispute over the boundary between those two states. The Court noted that New Hampshire had taken a different position regarding the point of the boundary in litigation some three decades earlier, and invoked judicial estoppel to reject the state's different position in the more recent case.

§11.2   Claim Preclusion (*Res Judicata*)

As noted in §11.1, claim preclusion provides that a claimant may sue only once to vindicate a claim. What constitutes a claim is a matter of some debate, as we see in §11.2.3. Suffice it to say now that a single claim might include more than one right to recover. For example, as we showed in §11.1, a single claim arising from an automobile accident may include the right to recover both for personal injuries and for property damage. Because the claimant gets to sue on the claim only once, she must be careful to seek recovery for all rights to relief in that one case. If she does not, her second bite at the apple—her second case—will be dismissed under claim preclusion, which historically has been called *res judicata*. We noted above that both terms are in use currently, though in this book we tend to use the modern terminology. In addition, some courts (generally in states adopting "code" pleading, which we saw in §7.2), refer to the doctrine as prohibiting two cases based on the same *cause of action*, while courts in most states talk about cases based on the same *claim*. For our purposes here, those terms also are interchangeable.

Courts occasionally state the requirements of *res judicata* in different ways. When push comes to shove, however, there are three requirements for the operation of claim preclusion. First, both Case 1 and Case 2 must have been brought by the same claimant against the same defendant. Second, Case 1 must have ended in a valid, final judgment on the merits. And third, both Case 1 and Case 2 must be based upon the same "claim."[13]

One more bit of terminology. Some courts refer to claim preclusion as resulting either in *merger* or *bar*. Do not let these terms give you any trouble. Merger is simply claim preclusion when the claimant *won* Case 1. The claim she attempts to set forth in Case 2 is "merged" with the judgment from Case 1 and thereby precluded. Bar is claim

---

[12]532 U.S. 742, 749-755 (2001).
[13]*See, e.g.*, Kale v. Combined Ins. Co., 924 F.2d 1161, 1165 (1st Cir. 1991).

preclusion when the claimant *lost* Case 1. That claimant is said to be "barred" from proceeding with Case 2. These terms do not mean a great deal, and the requirements for claim preclusion are the same whether the case is one of merger or bar. Now we turn to the individual requirements for claim preclusion.

§11.2.1   Case 1 and Case 2 Were Asserted by the Same Claimant Against the Same Defendant

Claim preclusion applies only if Case 1 and Case 2 are brought by the same claimant against the same defendant.[14] Resist the temptation to say, as some students (and courts) do, that the requirement is simply that both Case 1 and Case 2 "involve the same parties." That statement is not sufficiently precise. Remember, claim preclusion tells *claimants* that they have only one bite at the apple—that they only get to sue on a claim one time. So unless the same party is *asserting a claim* in both cases, claim preclusion simply cannot apply.

> ○ ***Example #3.*** A and Z are involved in an automobile collision, and each is injured. In Case 1, A sues Z. The case is litigated and the court enters judgment. Now, in Case 2, Z sues A. Is Z barred by *res judicata*? No! Z has never been a claimant before, so it is impossible for her to be suing on the same claim twice.

Still, it does not seem right that Z should be able to file a separate case about this accident. What could lead us to conclude that Z should not be able to bring this suit? The compulsory counterclaim rule! Under Federal Rule 13(a)(1), which we discuss at §12.5.1 (and which is adopted in most states), if a defendant has a claim against the plaintiff, and the claim arises from the same transaction or occurrence as the plaintiff's claim, she must assert it in the pending case. Failure to do so waives the claim. But this preclusion of Z's claim comes from the operation of the compulsory counterclaim rule, and not from claim preclusion.

We should also resist the temptation to say that claim preclusion requires that Case 1 and Case 2 be brought by the same "plaintiff" against the same defendant. As we see in the materials in Chapter 12, a defendant can assert claims against the plaintiff in a pending case. If she does so, she could be subject to claim preclusion in a second case.

---

[14]Actually, as we see later in the text of this subsection, it would be sufficient if Case 2 was brought by one who was in privity with the claimant in Case 1 or against one who was in privity with the defendant in Case 1. We discuss these concepts in detail at §§11.4.4 and 11.4.5.

Claim preclusion applies to parties who assert the same claim twice; thus, it applies to "claimants" and not just "plaintiffs."[15]

- ○ ***Example #4.*** *A* and *Z* are involved in a business deal. Independent of their business deal, *A* and *Z*, each driving her own car, collide; each is injured and each car is damaged. In Case 1, *A* sues *Z* for a problem arising from their business deal. *Z* files a permissive counterclaim[16] against *A* in Case 1, seeking recovery for personal injuries from the auto collision. The entire case goes to judgment. Now, in Case 2, *Z* sues *A* to recover for property damage to her car from the collision. If the applicable law adopts a transactional test for claim (discussed at §11.2.3), Case 2 will be dismissed under claim preclusion.
- ○ Why? Because *Z* has sued twice on the same claim (first in Case 1 by the counterclaim and second in Case 2 as plaintiff). She was a claimant in both cases, even though she was only a plaintiff in Case 2. And under a transactional test for claim, both assertions by *Z* involved the same claim (because they involved the same transaction—the car wreck).[17]

The requirement that claim preclusion applies only when Case 1 and Case 2 are brought by the same claimant against the same defendant reflects an important constitutional precept. Due process provides that one may be bound by a judgment only if she was a party to the case in which that judgment was entered. This requirement is satisfied by our definition of claim preclusion, since it may be asserted only *against* one who was a claimant in Case 1. We discuss this point in detail at §11.4.4.

Finally, claim preclusion does not necessarily require that the claimant and defendants be exactly the same persons in Case 1 and Case 2. There is some flexibility, to reflect the fact that some people or entities are so closely related that litigation by one ought to bind the other. In other words, under some circumstances, preclusion might affect someone who was not a party to Case 1. This "nonparty preclusion" is often said to apply when the nonparty is in "privity" with one who was a party to Case 1. Accordingly, claim preclusion will apply if Case 1 and Case 2 are brought by the same claimant (or someone in "privity" with the claimant) against the same defendant (or someone in "privity" with the defendant). Although the leading case on the meaning of

---

[15]All plaintiffs are claimants, but not all claimants are plaintiffs.

[16]Fed. R. Civ. P. 13(b). This Rule allows a defendant to assert any claim she has against the plaintiff in the pending case, even if it has no relation to the plaintiff's claim. We discuss the permissive counterclaim at §12.5.1.

[17]If the applicable law adopted the "primary rights" theory for defining claims (which we see in §11.2.3), however, Case 2 will not be dismissed under claim preclusion.

"privity" arose in the context of claim preclusion,[18] the issue usually arises in cases involving issue preclusion. We discuss it (and that leading case) in detail at §11.4.4.

§11.2.2 Case 1 Ended in a Valid Final Judgment on the Merits

Preclusion (either claim preclusion or issue preclusion) does not attach to every judicial order. Only a particular kind of judicial order is entitled to preclusive effect—one that has three characteristics: (1) it must be valid, (2) it must be a final judgment, and (3) it must be on the merits. Only such an order is worthy of such respect as to preclude parties from subsequent litigation.[19]

Validity

First, the order must be *valid*. This requirement addresses the competence of the court in Case 1. That inquiry typically focuses on whether the court in Case 1 had subject matter jurisdiction over the case and personal jurisdiction over the parties. If it did, the judgment is considered valid.[20] The assessment of whether an order is valid has nothing to do with whether it was right in deciding the merits of the underlying claim. A judgment may be valid even though it is incorrect. If the judgment was wrong on the merits, the losing party should have

---

[18]That case is *Taylor v. Sturgell*, 553 U.S. 880 (2008). See the discussion in §11.4.4, especially with regard to Example #28.

[19]Almost always, the valid final judgment in Case 1 will be entered by a court. It is possible, however, that the litigation in Case 1 took place before an administrative or arbitral tribunal. Their judgments can give rise to claim and issue preclusion in subsequent judicial cases. For detailed discussion of the preclusive effect of nonjudicial determinations, see 18B Wright & Miller §4475.

[20]There is a trend toward recognizing judgments as preclusive even when the court in Case 1 lacked subject matter jurisdiction. *See* 18A Wright & Miller 4 ("Today, it is safe to conclude that most federal-court judgments are res judicata notwithstanding a lack of subject matter jurisdiction. There may be exceptions, however, and matters are more complicated when state courts become involved."). This trend balances the interests in finality and efficiency (recognized in preclusion law) against the concern with jurisdictional limitations on courts (reflected in the requirements of personal and subject matter jurisdiction). Of course, if the defendant in Case 1 raised and litigated the jurisdictional question in Case 1—and lost—she will be bound by issue preclusion on that point (unless the holding on jurisdiction is reversed on appeal). *Id.* at 40-41. We discussed this fact with regard to personal jurisdiction in §6.3. There, we also saw that a defendant who defaults in Case 1 may make a collateral attack on personal jurisdiction when the plaintiff seeks to enforce the default judgment in Case 2. Regarding possible collateral attacks on subject matter jurisdiction, see §6.4.

appealed the judgment in Case 1 to the appropriate appellate court. In the words of the Supreme Court, "[T]he *res judicata* consequences of a final, unappealed judgment on the merits [are not] altered by the fact that the judgment may have been wrong or rested on a legal principle subsequently overruled in another case."[21]

Final Judgment

Second, the order must be a *final judgment*. As we see in §14.4, this is the same requirement most judicial systems impose for determining whether an order can be appealed.[22] A final judgment is one that "ends the litigation on the merits and leaves nothing for the [trial] court to do but execute the judgment."[23] It wraps up the case; it announces who won and, if the claimant won, what relief is appropriate. Every other order in a case is "interlocutory," which just means that it is not final. During litigation, the court may make hundreds of interlocutory rulings before entering the one final judgment. It makes sense that only the final judgment is appealable, and that only the final judgment is entitled to claim preclusive or issue preclusive effect. An interlocutory order may be amended during the course of the litigation. It would be wasteful to allow an appeal from such an order or to give it preclusive effect, because the order might not stand the test of time;[24] it might be changed or abandoned as the litigation develops.[25]

[21]Federated Dep't Stores, Inc. v. Moitie, 452 U.S. 494, 398 (1981). In *Fauntleroy v. Lum*, 210 U.S. 230, 237 (1908), a Missouri court entered judgment upon an arbitration award. The plaintiff sought to enforce the Missouri judgment in Mississippi. The defendant argued that the underlying transaction (based upon gambling) had taken place in Mississippi and was illegal and void in Mississippi. The Court held that the judgment was enforceable in Mississippi. It was possible that the Missouri court had misapplied Mississippi law, but that error could have been remedied on appeal in Missouri. So long as the Missouri court had subject matter jurisdiction and personal jurisdiction, its judgment was valid and enforceable in another state. We discuss interjurisdictional preclusion in §11.6.

[22]The analogy is not perfect, because sometimes "definitions of finality cannot automatically be carried over from appeals cases to preclusion problems," 18A Wright & Miller 55, but the analogy is appropriate for most cases and for our purposes.

[23]Catlin v. United States, 324 U.S. 229, 233 (1945).

[24]Even though interlocutory orders are not entitled to claim preclusive or issue preclusive effect, the court may decide to defer to such rulings under the "law of the case" doctrine, which we mentioned briefly in §11.1.

[25]We see at §14.5 that there are exceptions to the final judgment rule, in which a party is allowed to appeal even though the court has not entered final judgment; these exceptions are relatively rare, though. In addition, we saw in §9.7 that a final judgment may be attacked in the court in which it was entered by a motion to set aside the judgment. The existence of this procedure, however, does not vitiate the preclusive effect of the judgment. Obviously, if the court later sets aside the judgment, it may no longer be worthy of carrying a preclusive effect; until that happens, though, the judgment is entitled to preclusive effect.

What happens, though, if the final judgment in Case 1 is appealed? The appellate process will certainly take months (and perhaps years) to complete. Obviously, if the appellate court reverses or vacates the final judgment of the trial court, that judgment is no longer entitled to preclusive effect—it simply no longer exists in the same form in which it was entered. Just as obviously, if the appellate court affirms the trial court's final judgment, it is entitled to continued preclusive effect.

But what is the status of things during the pendency of the appeal? Before the appellate court has acted, is the final judgment entitled to preclusive effect or is it held in abeyance until the resolution of the appeal? Federal law on the subject says that the judgment is entitled to preclusive effect,[26] and most states agree.[27] In some states, however, the fact that an appeal is pending means that the final trial court judgment does not create preclusion.[28] As a policy matter, the majority rule accords with the reality that most appeals result in affirming the trial court's judgment.

On the Merits

The third characteristic of an order entitled to preclusion is that it be *on the merits*. The term *merits* refers to the underlying dispute: whether the claimant has shown that she is entitled to judgment because, for instance, the defendant breached a contract or committed a tort, and if so, what damage befell the claimant. Thus, for a valid

---

[26]*See, e.g.*, United States v. Five Unlabeled Boxes, 572 F.3d 169, 175 (3d Cir. 2009) ("the pendency of an appeal does not affect the potential for *res judicata* flowing from an otherwise valid judgment"); Smith v. Securities & Exch. Comm'n, 129 F.3d 356, 362 n.7 (6th Cir. 1997) ("The fact that Smith has an appeal of that judgment pending does not deprive the judgment of *res judicata* effect"). *See also* 18A Wright & Miller §4433.

[27]*See, e.g.*, Phelps v. Hamilton, 122 F.3d 1309, 1318 (10th Cir. 1997) ("Kansas courts have adopted the now-majority view regarding the pendency of appeals which provides that the fact that an appeal is pending in a case does not generally vitiate the *res judicata* effect of the judgment"); Campbell v. Lake Hallowell Homeowners Ass'n, 852 A.2d 1029, 1041 (Md. App. 2004) (pendency of appeal does not affect preclusive effect of judgment); Cully v. Lutheran Med. Ctr., 523 N.E.2d 531, 532 (Ohio App. 1987) ("It is well-settled that the pendency of an appeal does not prevent the judgment's effect as *res judicata*"); Jones v. American Family Mut. Ins. Co., 489 N.E.2d 160, 166 (Ind. App. 1986) ("an appeal from the judgment of the trial court does not have the effect of vacating the judgment of the trial court").

[28]*See, e.g.*, Pitts v. City of Sacramento, 138 Cal. App. 4th 853, 857 (Cal. App. 2006) ("As the prior judgment was still pending on appeal, the doctrine of claim preclusion was not available"); Faison v. Hudson, 417 S.E.2d 302, 305 (Va. 1992) ("[T]he better rule . . . is that a judgment is not final for the purposes of *res judicata* or collateral estoppel when it is being appealed or when the limits fixed for perfecting the appeal have not expired").

final judgment to be entitled to preclusive effect, it must have been based on the underlying dispute, on the question of who did what. In contrast, a judgment based upon something unrelated to the underlying dispute—say, for example, on some procedural or jurisdictional basis—should not carry a preclusive effect.

But, as we will see, many judgments are accorded preclusive effect even though there has been no true assessment of the merits of the case. For this reason, some commentators have argued that the phrase "on the merits" should be jettisoned.[29] Courts continue to use the phrase, however, and it is important that we review what it means as applied. For starters, it is helpful to recognize that preclusion does not require that the judgment in Case 1 be determined *literally* on the merits. Rather, it is more accurate to think of the requirement as one that the court had the *opportunity* to get to the merits of the case, even if it did not actually do so. A review of the relevant situations will demonstrate the point.

Let's start with the easiest situation. If Case 1 went to trial, the resultant valid final judgment is undoubtedly on the merits. This paradigm, in fact, is the archetype of what it means for a judgment to be on the merits. But "on the merits" does not require that there be a trial. For instance, suppose a valid final judgment is entered on summary judgment (which we discussed at §9.4). Recall that summary judgment allows a court to rule as a matter of law without trial, because there is no dispute on a material issue of fact. Such a judgment is entitled to preclusive effect. It is on the merits for these purposes. It is an adjudication that a party is entitled to prevail as a matter of law.[30]

Obviously, then, "on the merits" is not tantamount to "litigated at trial." But how far can we push this concept? Suppose the plaintiff wins on default judgment (discussed at §7.4.3). With default, the defendant has failed to respond within the prescribed time. Can a default judgment be on the merits for preclusion purposes? The general answer is yes,[31] because default does establish (albeit by defendant's failure to respond) that the plaintiff's claim is substantively valid.

But what about dismissals that seem to have nothing to do with the underlying substantive claim? For example, with a voluntary dismissal (discussed at §7.4.1), the plaintiff simply pulls the plug on the case. Is that dismissal on the merits for preclusion purposes? Federal

---

[29]The Restatement (Second) of Judgments does not use the phrase. *See* Restatement (Second) of Judgments §§24, 25, and 26.

[30]*See, e.g.*, Campanelli v. Allstate Ins. Co., 119 F. Supp. 2d 1073, 1076 (C.D. Cal. 2000) ("Summary judgment constitutes a final adjudication on the merits" and is entitled to claim preclusive effect).

[31]*See, e.g.*, Morris v. Jones, 329 U.S. 545, 550-551 (1947) (Missouri default judgment *res judicata* against Illinois insurance company).

Rule 41(a) provides that such a dismissal is "without prejudice," which means that it is not deemed on the merits, unless the notice or stipulation or order of dismissal provides otherwise.[32]

That brings us to *involuntary* dismissals, which can be entered for an almost infinite number of reasons. Are they on the merits for preclusion purposes? Here the starting point is Rule 41(b), which bears careful scrutiny and envisions three scenarios. First, if the involuntary dismissal is based upon lack of jurisdiction (meaning either personal or subject matter[33]), improper venue, or failure to join a party under Rule 19 (the indispensable party issue, discussed at §12.6.1), the Rule provides that the dismissal does *not* "operate[] as an adjudication on the merits." That means, of course, that such a dismissal is not entitled to preclusive effect. This rule makes sense: A judgment based upon any of these three defenses truly does not involve an investigation of the underlying merits of the case.

Second, for "failure of the plaintiff to prosecute or to comply with these rules or any order of court," a dismissal "operates as an adjudication on the merits" unless the court says otherwise in its dismissal order. Note how broadly this provision can sweep. The reference to failure to prosecute is fairly precise,[34] as is the failure to comply with a court order. Beyond that, though, dismissals for failure to comply "with these rules" means dismissals for failure to comply with *any* of the Federal Rules. For instance, a court might dismiss the plaintiff's case as a penalty for abusing the discovery provision. Unless the court indicates otherwise in its order of dismissal, such a dismissal "operates as an adjudication on the merits" and bars a second action on the same claim.[35] This rule also makes sense, because a plaintiff who is guilty of failing to prosecute the action or of failing to comply with the Federal Rules has had an *opportunity* to present her case for consideration of the merits, but has failed to do so properly. The legal system has given her a chance and has an interest in enforcing its own rules for how cases are to proceed. Thus, unless the court provides otherwise in its order of dismissal, Rule 41(b) treats such a judgment as on the merits for purposes of claim and issue preclusion.

Third, under Rule 41(b), unless the court orders otherwise, "any dismissal not under this rule . . . operates as an adjudication on the merits." Literally, this provision requires that every involuntary dismissal (other than those based upon jurisdiction, venue, or Rule 19) is to be

[32]Or, you will recall, unless it is a second voluntary dismissal and is by notice. See §7.4.3.
[33]*See* American Nat'l Bank v. FDIC, 710 F.2d 1528, 1535-1536 (11th Cir. 1983). *See generally* 18A Wright & Miller 149.
[34]We discussed dismissals for failure to prosecute at §7.4.2.
[35]*See, e.g.*, In re Reed, 861 F.2d 1381, 1382 (5th Cir. 1988).

637

treated as on the merits. But the Supreme Court decision in *Semtek International, Inc. v. Lockheed Martin Corp.*,[36] makes it clear that the Rule is not always to be read literally in this regard. In *Semtek*, the plaintiff filed Case 1 in a California state court and the defendant removed it to federal court on the basis of diversity of citizenship jurisdiction. The federal court dismissed the case as barred under California's two-year statute of limitations.[37] The order of dismissal stated expressly that the dismissal was "on the merits and with prejudice."[38] The plaintiff filed Case 2, on the same claim, in state court in Maryland, a state where the statute of limitations (three years) would not bar the claim.[39] Was Case 2 barred by claim preclusion? More specifically, was the judgment in Case 1 on the merits for purposes of preclusion? Again, the court in Case 1 expressly said that its judgment was on the merits. And even without that statement, Rule 41(b) declares that such a dismissal will operate as an adjudication on the merits (because it was a "dismissal not provided for in this rule").

Nonetheless, the Supreme Court held (unanimously) that the California federal judgment was not entitled to a claim-preclusive effect. Accordingly, the plaintiff could proceed with suit in Maryland. Why? First, the Court concluded, Rule 41(b) is not aimed at claim preclusion at all. Its provision that a dismissal "operates as an adjudication on the merits" means only that the plaintiff cannot refile the same claim *in the same federal court that entered the judgment of dismissal*. According to the Court, the Rule does not purport to establish federal law on claim preclusion. As the opinion explained, it would be "highly peculiar" to find a rule on claim preclusion "ensconced in rules governing the internal procedures of the rendering court itself."[40]

Second, because the Federal Rule was not on point, the Court then addressed whether a federal court was required to apply state law on the issue. It concluded that the issue should be governed by federal common law.[41] Surprisingly, however, the federal common law in

---

[36]531 U.S. 497 (2001).

[37]Recall that under the *Erie* doctrine a federal court sitting in diversity applies state statute of limitations law. See §10.5.

[38]531 U.S. at 499-500.

[39]Defendant removed that case to federal court in Maryland, which remanded to the state court. Though the requirements of diversity of citizenship jurisdiction were satisfied, the case could not be removed because the defendant was a citizen of the forum. (We saw this limitation on removal jurisdiction at §4.8.) So the litigation proceeded in state court in Maryland. *Id.*

[40]*Semtek*, 531 U.S. at 503. Indeed, if Rule 41(b) *did* prescribe the requirements for claim preclusion, the Court indicated, the rule might run afoul of the Rules Enabling Act by prescribing a substantive rule. See §10.6.2.

[41]In §10.9, we saw that there are narrow areas in which federal common law operates to provide the rule of decision. The *Erie* doctrine established that there is no *general* federal common law but did not rule out the possibility of federal common law in

this instance—where Case 1 was in federal court under diversity of citizenship jurisdiction—would adopt the law of the state in which that federal court sat.[42] The Court then decided that California law would not have ascribed claim preclusion to a dismissal based upon the statute of limitations. That is, a California state court would have dismissed the plaintiff's case but would not have objected to the plaintiff's suing in Maryland to take advantage of Maryland's longer statute of limitations.

Semtek makes it clear that the language of Rule 41(b)—that an involuntary dismissal other than under that rule (and other than one based upon jurisdiction, venue, or Rule 19) "operates as an adjudication on the merits"—does not state a universal truth for purposes of preclusion. True, the rule stops the plaintiff from refiling in the same federal court that dismissed the action. But whether the first court's dismissal is on the merits for claim preclusion and issue preclusion in other courts requires an analysis of federal common law, which, in turn, in a diversity case usually will look to the law of the state in which the federal court deciding Case 1 sat. So ultimately, the question of whether the California federal judgment should result in claim preclusion in a Maryland court will depend upon whether a California state court would have treated it as on the merits for preclusion purposes.

§11.2.3 Case 1 and Case 2 Were Based on the Same Claim

Even if Cases 1 and 2 are brought by the same claimant against the same defendant and Case 1 ended in a valid final judgment on the merits, claim preclusion applies only if the two cases are based upon the same claim. The essence of claim preclusion is that a claimant gets one chance—meaning one suit—to vindicate her claim. Unfortunately, *claim* is not a self-defining word. It might mean different things in different contexts.[43] More important for present purposes, even in the

---

specialized areas. *Semtek* involves one such area—the question of the preclusive effect of a federal court judgment. The Court reiterated the point in *Taylor v. Sturgell*, 553 U.S. 880, 891 (2008) ("The preclusive effect of a federal-court judgment is determined by federal common law").

[42] *Semtek*, 531 U.S. at 507-508. See §11.6.4.

[43] For example, what constitutes a "claim" for pleading purposes under Federal Rule 12(b)(6) might not be the same as what constitutes a claim (or "cause of action") for claim preclusion purposes. In the words of Justice Cardozo:

A "cause of action" may mean one thing for one purpose and something different for another. It may mean one thing when the question is whether it is good upon demurrer, and something different when there is a question of the amendment of claim preclusion context, the word can mean different things in different jurisdictions. The differing definitions reflect policy choices each state is free to weigh for itself. It is likely that your casebook contains cases applying different definitions of claim.

While there is thus some variation in approach among jurisdictions, the undeniable trend has been toward a broader definition of claim. This broader definition has not been created in a vacuum. Rather, it reflects developments in related areas of the law. In earlier procedural regimes, pleading and joinder rules imposed severe restrictions on the plaintiff's ability to assert rights of action and join parties in a single case. Consequently, the law of claim preclusion defined the scope of the claim narrowly, reflecting the fact that the plaintiff might need Case 2, in which to seek something that was unavailable under the joinder rules in Case 1. The generally broader definition of claim today reflects the more liberal rules of pleading and joinder. Because those rules permit the plaintiff to package a great deal into Case 1, there is less need for the legal system to provide the plaintiff with an opportunity to bring Case 2.

Two Major Themes: Focus on Transaction or on Primary Rights Invaded

Federal law and the law of most states today adopt a transactional test for defining one's claim.[44] This transactional focus has been stated in different ways, including whether the two cases involve the same "operative facts,"[45] "transaction or occurrence,"[46] "basic factual situation,"[47] "defendant's wrongdoing,"[48] or "a single core of operative facts."[49] The most influential articulation comes from the Restatement

---

a pleading or of the application of the principle of *res judicata* . . . . At times and in certain contexts, it is identified with the infringement of a right or the violation of a duty. At other times and in other contexts, it is a concept of the law of remedies . . . . Another aspect reveals it as . . . the group of operative facts out of which a grievance has developed.

United States v. Memphis Cotton Oil Co., 288 U.S. 62, 67-68 (1933).

[44]*See, e.g.*, Mitchell v. City of Moore, 218 F.3d 1190, 1202 (10th Cir. 2000) ("We employ the transactional approach of the Restatement (Second) of Judgments"); River Park, Inc. v. City of Highland Park, 703 N.E.2d 883, 893 (Ill. 1998); O'Brien v. City of Syracuse, 429 N.E.2d 1158, 1159 (N.Y. 1981); Rush v. City of Maple Heights, 147 N.E.2d 599, 607 (Ohio 1958); Adape v. Akins, 668 P.2d 130, 134-135 (Idaho App. 1983).

[45]*See, e.g.*, Landscape Properties, Inc. v. Whisenhunt, 127 F.3d 678, 683 (8th Cir. 1997).

[46]*See, e.g.*, Great Lakes Trucking Co. v. Black, 477 N.W.2d 65, 68 (Wis. App. 1991).

[47]Gasbarra v. Park-Ohio Indus., 655 F.2d 119, 121 (7th Cir. 1981).

[48]Plotner v. AT&T, 224 F.3d 1161, 1170 (10th Cir. 2000).

[49]Mandarino v. Pollard, 718 F.2d 845, 849 (7th Cir. 1983).

(Second) of Judgments, which provides that a claim encompasses all rights to relief "with respect to all or any part of the transaction, or series of connected transactions, out of which the action arose."[50]

But not all jurisdictions have adopted a transactional test for defining the scope of a claim. Another school of thought focuses on the rights allegedly invaded by the defendant's behavior. Under this approach—often called the *primary rights* theory—the claimant has a separate claim (and therefore can file a separate case) for each right violated by the defendant.

There are other approaches to the question as well, some of which are mentioned below. Most jurisdictions seem, however, to adopt some form of one of these two approaches—one focusing on the underlying *transaction* and the other on the *rights* invaded. The difference in scope between these two is aptly demonstrated using a fact pattern we saw in §11.1.

- o ***Example #5.*** *P* is involved in an auto collision with *D*. *P* suffers personal injuries and property damage to her car. In Case 1, she seeks only damages for the personal injuries. After judgment is entered in that case, she brings Case 2, seeking to recover for property damage from the same collision.
  - o Is Case 2 barred by claim preclusion? The answer depends entirely on the definition of claim adopted by the jurisdiction. If the law defines her "claim" transactionally—as all rights to relief arising from a transaction—Case 2 will be dismissed under claim preclusion. Why? Because *P* is suing twice about the same transaction; thus, she is suing twice on the same claim. On the other hand, if the law defines her claims as the individual rights invaded, Case 2 will not be dismissed under claim preclusion, because there she is vindicating a different right from that vindicated in Case 1.

Policy and Efficiency Considerations

A transactional definition of claim is clearly more efficient than a focus on the rights invaded. It coerces the plaintiff to join her personal injury and property damage rights in a single case. If she fails to do so, her second case will be dismissed under claim preclusion. Thus, the judicial system deals with only one suit for what is, defined in transactional terms, one event. Moreover, the transactional test comports broadly with tests for joinder and for supplemental jurisdiction. In Chapter 12 we discuss various joinder devices—including the compulsory counterclaim, crossclaim, and various claims under Federal Rule 14(a)—that adopt the "same transaction or occurrence" test.

---

[50]Restatement (Second) of Judgments §24(1).

In §4.7, we saw how supplemental jurisdiction also adopts a largely transactional test for determining when claims failing to satisfy an independent basis of subject matter jurisdiction may nonetheless be asserted in federal court. The transactional test for claim reflects and complements these developments in other areas of the law.[51]

Of course, the system can only allow its claim preclusion doctrine to demand a claimant to assert all transactionally related claims in a single suit if the procedural rules for joinder allow the claimant to do so in Case 1. Because Federal Rules are liberal (especially regarding claim joinder, as we see in §12.3), and permit a claimant to assert all claims — even those not transactionally related — in a single suit, it is fair to impose a claim preclusion rule requiring her to assert all trans- actionally related claims in Case 1.

In contrast, the primary rights approach seems potentially wasteful of judicial resources. It allows the plaintiff in Example #5 to bring two suits over what the parties probably view as one real-world event.[52] Witnesses can be required to testify at two trials. The defendant can be made to go through the trauma of being sued twice. And, of course, the judicial system can be made to accommodate two cases. Given con- temporary concern with crowded judicial dockets, it is no surprise to see an increasing number of jurisdictions adopting the broader trans- actional test for claim.

One federal district court, applying Illinois law, expressed frustra- tion that Illinois had not yet embraced a transactional test:

> Because of crowded dockets, it is difficult for courts to give litigants the one day in court they deserve. The Plaintiff in this case insists on hav- ing three. Thus, we press on in the hope that Illinois courts will eventu- ally see fit to follow the current trend among state courts to follow the approach of the Restatement.[53]

Perhaps reflecting such criticism, the primary rights theory has only a handful of adherents today (though one of them is the most populous state in the country). California has never repudiated its

---

[51]For a discussion of how the rules of joinder, preclusion, and supplemental juris- diction can operate together to facilitate efficient packaging of litigation, see Richard D. Freer, *Avoiding Duplicative Litigation: Rethinking Plaintiff Autonomy and the Court's Role in Defining the Litigative Unit,* 50 U. Pitt. L. Rev. 809, 813-837 (1989).

[52]Just because a claimant *can* bring two separate cases does not mean that she will. In Example #5, *P* could join the personal injury and property damage assertions in Case 1. But the primary rights theory, unlike a transactional theory, does not *require* her to do so.

[53]Salaymeh v. St. Vincent Memorial Hosp. Corp., 706 F. Supp. 643, 646-647 (C.D. Ill. 1989).

embrace of that standard.[54] In Georgia, the primary rights theory is prescribed by statute in motor vehicle crash cases.[55] The experience in Virginia is interesting. In 1949, in the well-known case of *Carter v. Hinkle*,[56] the Virginia Supreme Court expressly rejected a transactional test and embraced primary rights in a case involving facts similar to Example #5. In *Carter*, Case 1 was for property damage and Case 2 for personal injuries from a single collision. After reviewing the arguments in favor of both approaches, the court adopted the primary rights theory, which it described as the "less practical but . . . more logical path."[57] The court thus recognized that a transactional test was more efficient but concluded that primary rights was more consistent with other aspects of the law. For instance, as pointed out, the statutes of limitations are different for personal injury and property damage causes; a property damage claim can be assigned and does not abate at the plaintiff's death, while one for personal injuries cannot be assigned and does abate at death.

In 2006, the Virginia Supreme Court promulgated a Rule of Court adopting the transactional test for defining a claim.[58] Interestingly, though, the rule contains an express exception for cases in which

---

[54]Grisham v. Philip Morris USA, Inc., 40 Cal. 4th 623, 643 (2007) (claim that addiction to tobacco caused economic harm was a separate claim from personal injuries caused by smoking, noting, *inter alia*, different statutes of limitations); Fujifilm Corp. v. Yang, 223 Cal. App.4th 326, 333 (Ct. App. 2014) ("Appellant urges that we apply the 'transaction' doctrine of federal law, instead of California's primary rights theory, to find Fuji wrongfully split its cause of action. We need not linger on appellant's request, however, because she does not cite any California authority applying the transaction doctrine to define a cause of action."). The California primary rights definition of claim is criticized in Walter Heiser, *California's Unpredictable Res Judicata (Claim Preclusion) Doctrine*, 35 San Diego L. Rev. 559, 584 (1998). *See also* Boeken v. Philip Morris USA, Inc., 48 Cal. 4th 788, 806 (2010) (Moreno, J., dissenting) ("no generally approved and adequately defined system of classification of primary rights exists . . . .").

[55]Off. Ga. Code Ann. §51-1-32. There is a special argument in favor of the primary rights theory in such cases. Suppose an insured driver is involved in an auto crash and suffers personal injury and property damage. Her insurance company may pay her for the property damage and then (as "subrogee"—which means as someone to whom the claim is assigned by operation of law) sue the other driver. If the insured has already sued that other driver for personal injuries, there is a risk in a transactional state that the insured driver and the insurance company (which stands in her shoes as subrogee) have split the claim. *See* Smith v. Hutchins, 566 P.2d 1136, 1137 (Nev. 1977).

[56]52 S.E.2d 135 (Va. 1949).

[57]*Id.* at 138.

[58]Va. Sup. Ct. R. 1.6(a) provides: "A party whose claim for relief arising from identified conduct, a transaction, or an occurrence, is decided on the merits by a final judgment, shall be forever barred from prosecuting any second or subsequent civil action against the same opposing party or parties on any claim or cause of action that arises from the same conduct, transaction or occurrence . . . ."

one event causes both personal injuries and property damage.[59] Accordingly, despite this Rule of Court in Virginia, a case like *Carter* would be decided as it was in 1949.

Still, that leaves only about three primary rights jurisdictions, depending on the type of case. Experience in these states suggests that the primary rights theory might not be as inefficient as we might think. Though the theory would allow the plaintiff in *Carter* to bring Case 2 to recover for personal injuries, it does not require her to do so. She is free to package both claims in a single case. Indeed, many claimants undoubtedly do so, simply to avoid having to sue twice.

Moreover, even if the claimant does bring two cases, the litigation in Case 2 will likely be rendered simpler by the use of *issue* preclusion. For instance, if the court in Case 1 found that the defendant was not negligent, Case 2 will be decided against the plaintiff on summary judgment. Why? Because *issue* preclusion will establish for Case 2 the issue that the defendant was not negligent in causing the wreck. If the court in Case 1 found for the plaintiff, including a finding that the defendant was negligent, Case 2 is streamlined because issue preclusion results in the establishment of the defendant's negligence for that case.

In addition, the findings from Case 1 may influence the parties to settle Case 2, in which situation Case 2 does not impose a significant burden on the court system. One court explained the effect of issue preclusion, even in a primary-rights claim preclusion jurisdiction, this way:

> The total judicial time consumed, even if both parts are actually tried, may not be significantly greater than trying them together. In fact, it is likely that both will not be tried. If the decision in the property damage case is against the plaintiff, there can be no second trial. If it is in favor of the plaintiff, the parties may well settle the damages claim.[60]

Applications

The examples above were relatively easy—personal injury and property damage clearly flowed from a single transaction. Not all cases are so easy.

---

[59]Va. Sup. Ct. R. 1.6(c) provides: "The provisions of this Rule shall not bar a party or a party's insurer from prosecuting separate personal injury and property damage suits arising out of the same conduct, transaction or occurrence . . . ."

[60]Andrews v. Christenson, 692 P.2d 687, 690 n.1 (Or. App. 1984). Oregon subsequently adopted the transactional test for defining a claim. Peterson v. Temple, 918 P.2d 413 (Or. 1996) (rule that personal and property damage arising from a single accident constitute one claim to be applied prospectively).

○ ***Example #6.*** *P* and *D*, each driving her own automobile, collide, and each suffers personal injuries and property damage. Immediately after the collision, *D* jumps from her car, runs to *P*'s car, reaches through the window and punches *P* in the face. *D* then screams obscenities at *P*, threatens to kill *P*, and defames *P* by shouting to the crowd of onlookers various libelous falsehoods about *P*.

How many claims are involved here? Under a primary rights approach, *P* would seem to have these separate claims: (1) property damage to her automobile; (2) personal injuries from the accident and the punching;[61] (3) emotional injuries from the threats and obscenities; and (4) slander for the libelous falsehoods. Why? Because it seems that four rights have been invaded: (1) right to have her property free from injury; (2) right to have her person free from injury; (3) right to have her psyche free from injury; and (4) right to have her reputation free from injury.

What about under a transactional test? How many transactions were there here? Did one transaction end at the collision and another one start when *D* got out of her car, approached *P*, and struck her? Did another transaction occur with the obscenities and threats, and yet another with the defamation? It is hard to say.[62] But remember, as we saw above, that the Restatement (Second) also instructs us to look at transactions or a "series of connected transactions."[63] The Restatement (Second) adds to this definition an instruction to adopt a pragmatic approach, with a focus on whether facts are connected closely "in time, space, origin, or motivation [and] whether, taken together, they form a convenient unit for trial purposes," as well as whether treating them as a single claim will be consistent with the expectations of parties and businesses.[64] Thus, the inquiry becomes a practical one, guided by experience with particular kinds of cases, sensitive to the relevant policies.

On the facts of Example #6, it is at least arguable that everything was the result of a series of connected transactions. Considered

---

[61]Could these injuries be subdivided into two claims—one for personal injuries from the wreck and another for personal injuries from the punching? The primary rights test focuses on the harm caused, so perhaps not. *But see* Wood v. Allison Apparel Marketing, Inc., 398 S.E.2d 110, 111 (Va. App. 1990) (administrative holding that plaintiff failed to show that carpal tunnel syndrome was caused by industrial accident did not bar subsequent workers' compensation claim that the same injury was caused by an industrial disease).

[62]We encounter similar problems under the "single wrongful act" test. Was the collision the result of one wrongful act, the battery the result of another, and the defamation of yet a third? The Restatement (Second) approach counsels us to address the situation in commonsense, real-world terms.

[63]Restatement (Second) of Judgments §24(1).

[64]Restatement (Second) of Judgments §24, cmt. b.

pragmatically, should the judicial system countenance separate suits in this hypothetical? Should the defendant have to defend more than one action? Should the plaintiff be expected to package all of these claims into a single case? Arguably, based on such considerations, the fact pattern seems to present a single claim. The participants might well consider all the events as a single episode. Everything occurred in a relatively small area and within a relatively short time. Thus, the witnesses to one aspect of the episode—say, for example, the collision—were probably witnesses to the punching and the oral tirade as well. Having more than one case could burden the witnesses to testify more than once,[65] and having redundant testimony in multiple cases would waste judicial resources.

The point, of course, is that determining whether Case 1 and Case 2 involve the same claim is more art than science. It is imperative, though, that counsel be aware of whether the jurisdiction adopts a transactional or a rights-based approach to the issue. In her research, counsel may be surprised to find multiple tests adopted by a single state.[66] The lawyer who is aware of these cases may be equipped with multiple arguments in favor of a particular result. (And the law student who is aware of the various tests covered in her course materials will be able to demonstrate their application on the exam.)

New Factual Developments

Suppose we are in a jurisdiction that adopts a transactional test in defining the scope of a claim. It is possible that facts arising after the entry of a judgment will create a new claim and justify a new suit. For instance:

○ ***Example #7.*** Imagine a group of prisoners who claim that they are being forced to drink contaminated water. These prisoners file suit against the facility where they are incarcerated. If at first their suit is dismissed because a court does not believe that the harm would be severe enough to be unconstitutional, it would make no sense to prevent the same prisoners from bringing a later suit if time and experience

---

[65]And we should not forget that if all assertions were packaged in a single case, the trial court has the discretion to order separate trials of various issues to avoid confusion or embarrassment. See §12.4.

[66]For example, in Virginia, before adoption of the Rule of Court cited and discussed at note 58 above, that state's supreme court had embraced at least three definitions of claim. *See* Flora, Flora & Montague, Inc. v. Saunders, 367 S.E.2d 493, 495-496 (Va. 1988) (sameness of evidence); Brown v. Haley, 355 S.E.2d 563, 568-569 (Va. 1987) (transactional test); Carter v. Hinkle, 52 S.E.2d 135, 138-139 (Va. 1949) (primary rights).

eventually showed that prisoners were dying from contaminated water.[67]

Other Formulations of "Claim"

Courts can employ other formulations for defining the scope of a claim, but they are just variations on the two major approaches we have seen. Under one, a claim consists of all rights to relief arising from the defendant's "single wrongful act." This test obviously engages a transactional inquiry but is narrower than the Restatement (Second) approach, which includes in the claim related transactions. Some commentators conclude that the single-wrong phrase should be discarded "because it may lead to unsound results by inviting abstract speculation about the number of rights that can dance on the head of a single transaction."[68]

Some courts espouse a "sameness of the evidence" test, under which claims are the same if "the evidence needed to sustain the second action would have sustained the first."[69] This is meaningless, as we see if we apply it to the facts in *Carter*, in which plaintiff sued in Case 1 for property damage and in Case 2 for personal injuries, both caused in the same wreck. If the sameness of the evidence test means all the evidence in the entire action, Case 2 should be allowed to proceed. Why? Because in Case 2, the plaintiff must produce evidence of personal injuries that was not required in Case 1. But if by sameness of the evidence this test refers only to the evidence necessary to establish liability, Case 2 should be dismissed. Why? Because the showing required to establish that the defendant was liable for the wreck is exactly the same in Case 1 as in Case 2 — her negligence is not affected by the type of damage claimed. Most courts seem to apply the test in this latter fashion.[70] As such, in focusing on liability, this test seems to add nothing to a transactional test, which focuses on the transaction that gives rise to defendant's liability.

A particularly antiquated approach provides that a claimant has different claims for "different legal theories," even if they arise from a single transaction. This approach was a product of the narrow pleading rules imposed by the common law. Under common law pleading,

---

[67]The Court set out this fact pattern in *Whole Woman's Health v. Hellerstedt*, 136 S. Ct. 2292, 2305 (2016). It cited Restatement (Second) §24, cmt. f (facts operating after judgment may comprise a different transaction and therefore a different claim).

[68]18 Wright & Miller 167.

[69]*See, e.g.*, Agriserve, Inc. v. Belden, 643 N.E.2d 1193, 1195 (Ill. App. 1994).

[70]*See, e.g.*, Sure-Snap Corp. v. State Street Bank & Trust Co., 948 F.2d 869, 874-875 (2d Cir. 1991); Kent County Bd. of Educ. v. Billbrough, 525 A.2d 232, 236-237 (Md. 1987).

a claimant could pursue only one legal theory in a case. Accordingly, preclusion law could not "punish" her for failing to assert more than one theory in the first case. Because such common law restrictions on pleading are now relegated to the history books, the "different legal theories" should be similarly interred.

- ○ ***Example #8.*** Plaintiff sues her employer in Case 1 for damages from alleged discrimination under state law and contract principles. After judgment is entered, she brings Case 2 against the employer, alleging that the same acts described in Case 1 also violated federal antidiscrimination law. Under a "different legal theories" test, Case 2 involves a different claim and would proceed. Today, however, it is likely that Case 2 would be dismissed under claim preclusion, because it involves the same transaction—and therefore the same claim—as Case 1.[71]
- ○ ***Example #9.*** Similarly, an offer to produce different evidence in Case 2 should not defeat claim preclusion.[72] The point of claim preclusion is that the claimant gets one shot at a claim, and thus cannot blame anyone but herself for leaving out some element of recovery or for failing to marshal facts in an effective way.

Claim as Personal to Holder

A claim—no matter how defined—is personal to its holder. Suppose Louise and Patti are passengers on a bus that is involved in a wreck. Both Louise and Patti suffer personal injuries and property damage (to their luggage). Suppose further that the jurisdiction adopts a transactional test for claim. That test will coerce Louise to sue the bus company for personal injuries and property damage in a single case. (Both personal injuries and property damage are elements of a single claim, because both were caused in a single transaction.) Similarly, the transactional test will coerce Patti to sue for personal injuries and property damage in a single case. *But the definition of claim does not coerce Louise and Patti to join together as coplaintiffs in a single case.* Louise's claim is hers and Patti's is hers. Claim preclusion does not force every person injured in a single case to join together in one suit. It simply forces each claimant to join the various elements of damage and legal theories arising from a claim into a single case.[73]

---

[71]*See, e.g.*, Boateng v. InterAmerican Univ., 210 F.3d 56, 62 (1st Cir. 2000) (Case 1 based upon Puerto Rico and contract law; Case 2 based upon Title VII of the Americans with Disabilities Act).

[72]*See, e.g.*, New York Life Ins. Co. v. Gillespie, 203 F.3d 384, 387-388 (5th Cir. 2000).

[73]In §12.4, we discuss how two plaintiffs *may* join together as coplaintiffs in a single proceeding. Whether they do so, however, is a choice given by the joinder rules, and has nothing to do with claim preclusion.

Contract Cases

There are some well-established general rules governing the scope of a claim in contract and similar cases. First, a claim, at least with regard to a single contract, is usually deemed to consist of all breaches that have occurred to the time of filing Case 1.

- ○ ***Example #10.*** *D* leases a farm, including farm implements, from *P*. The lease provides that *D* will pay monthly rent and, upon failure to pay rent, will return the farm implements to *P*. *D* fails to pay rent and fails to return the equipment. *P* sues *D* in Case 1 for conversion of property (the farm implements). A valid final judgment is entered. Now *P* brings Case 2, seeking to recover the unpaid rent. Case 2 is barred by claim preclusion, because both rights to recover—the right to recover the property and the right to recover the rent—existed at the time Case 1 was filed, so they both constituted part of the same claim.
- ○ ***Example #11.*** *P* and *D* enter an installment contract, under which *D* is to make monthly payments to *P*. *D* makes the payments for January and February, but fails to pay for March, April, and May. If *P* sues at that point, the claim consists of the failure to pay for those three months. If she sues only for the payment due for March, she would be prohibited by claim preclusion from ever seeking the payments for April and May.

Second, these hypotheticals assume that there is only one contract. If there are separate contracts, they generally are treated as separate claims. Thus, if *D* breached Contract 1 and Contract 2 in similar ways, *P* would probably have two claims—one for each contract. This rule is usually applied even if Contract 2 is identical in every way to Contract 1.[74]

Effect of Claim Preclusion

Remember that the effect of claim preclusion generally is to "rob" a claimant of getting into court for some right to relief. Unless some exception to claim preclusion applies (see §11.5), a claimant in a jurisdiction adopting a transactional definition of claim makes an enormous mistake if she sues only for property damage, and not personal injuries (or vice versa), in Case 1. If she commits this mistake, Case 2 will be dismissed and she never gets her day in court for personal injuries. But it's her own fault (or her lawyer's). The judicial system has given her one opportunity to vindicate her claim. It is up to her (or her lawyer) to know what that "claim" includes.

---

[74]*See* Gonzales v. Lopez, 52 P.3d 418, 424 (N.M. App. 2002).

§11.3 Defense Preclusion

In *Lucky Brand Dungarees v. Marcel Fashions Group,*[75] the Supreme Court for the first time discussed a doctrine called "defense preclusion." It is the defense analogue to claim preclusion. As we studied in §11.2, claim preclusion compels a claimant to seek, in Case 1, all rights to relief arising from a single claim. The claimant is precluded in Case 2 from seeking relief she could have sought (but did not) against the same defendant on the same claim asserted in Case 1. Defense preclusion compels a defendant to assert, in Case 1, all defenses to a claim. The defendant is precluded from asserting a defense in Case 2 that it could have asserted (but did not) in Case 1. Defense preclusion is a very narrow doctrine.

Lucky Brand involved three protracted and complicated trademark infringement actions between competing clothing manufacturers. In Case 1, Marcel (M) sued Lucky Brand (LB). The case resulted in a consent judgment that did two things: (1) barred LB from using the phrase "Get Lucky" on its clothing and (2) released any claims M might have against LB regarding LB's use of its own (LB's) trademarks, including the phrase "Lucky Brand."

In Case 2, M sued LB (via a counterclaim), and asserted (1) that LB was still using "Get Lucky" in violation of the judgment in Case 1 and (2) that LB's use of its own mark (including "Lucky Brand") was confusingly similar to M's trademarks, *but only insofar* as LB did so in connection with the phrase "Get Lucky." The case went to trial and resulted in a judgment for M and a permanent injunction against LB's use of its own trademarks (including "Lucky Brand") in connection with the phrase "Get Lucky."[76]

In Case 3, M sued LB, finally alleging that LB's use of LB's own trademarks—even without the phrase "Get Lucky"—violated LB's trademark. LB asserted that M had released such claims in the judgment in Case 1. The Second Circuit held that LB was precluded from raising that defense in Case 3. According to the court, LB should have

---

[75]140 S. Ct. 1589, 1595 (2020). The Court defined the issue as "when, if ever, claim preclusion applies to defenses raised in a later suit." 140 S. Ct. at 1594.

[76]The record is confusing. The jury's findings of fact arguably were broader than the injunction entered. It appears, for example, that the jury determined that LB's use of any mark with the word "Lucky" constituted a violation of M's trademark. But the injunction entered by the court applied only to LB's use of its marks *in connection with* the phrase "Get Lucky." For more detailed discussion of *Lucky Brand*, see Richard Freer, *"Defense Preclusion": Exploring a Narrow Gap in Preclusion Law,* 40 Rev. Litig. 101, 111 (2021).

pursued that defense in Case 2.[77] Failure to do so ran afoul of "defense preclusion."[78]

The Supreme Court reversed and established a rule: Defense preclusion *cannot* apply if the case involves the claimant's assertion of a different claim from the earlier case. In other words, if the claimant in Case 1 and Case 2 (or, in the circumstance of *Lucky Brand,* Case 2 and Case 3) is asserting a different claim in the two cases, defense preclusion cannot apply. In *Lucky Brand,* M's claim in Case 2 and its claim in Case 3 were different: "the two suits here were grounded on different conduct, involving different marks, occurring at different times."[79] Accordingly the Second Circuit was wrong to apply defense preclusion.

The Court was not required to decide, however, when defense preclusion *is* permitted. There is very little case law in the area[80] and it is worth emphasizing that the doctrine is extremely narrow. By definition, defense preclusion can arise only when the claimant in Case 1 and Case 2 asserts different claims. But the two cases must involve the same potential defense, which means that the two cases must involve the same real-world event, arising from the same transaction or occurrence. (If the cases were based on different events, a potential defense in Case 1 would seem not to constitute a defense in Case 2.)

When can two cases assert different claims yet arise from the same transaction or occurrence? One possibility, as we saw in §11.2.3, is when the applicable law embraces the primary rights definition of claim, which would allow a claimant to sue twice regarding the same real-world event; for example, once for personal injuries and separately for property damage. Recall, however, that only two or three states adopt this view. Even in such cases, there is debate about how broadly defense preclusion should be recognized.

> ○ ***Example #12.*** In Case 1, P sues D for personal injuries suffered in an automobile crash between the two. D defends by asserting that P was

---

[77]Again, the record is confusing. In Case 2, LB initially raised the release as a defense. But apparently it did not pursue the matter, leading the Second Circuit to conclude that LB had not asserted it in Case 2. It is arguable on the state of the record, however, that the issue was actually litigated in Case 2 and therefore should have been subject to issue preclusion in Case 3. *See id.* at 112-113. On the other hand, no court held that the issue had been litigated.

[78]LB could not be guilty of claim preclusion because it had not been a claimant in consecutive cases. It could not be bound by issue preclusion because (evidently) the question of whether M had released these claims had not been litigated and determined in an earlier case. *See id.* at 113.

[79]140 S. Ct. at 1595. "[I]dentity of claims" in the two cases, the Court explained, is a "necessary predicate" of defense preclusion. *Id.*

[80]There are excellent discussions of defense preclusion in Clermont, note 8 above, and 18 Wright & Miller §4414 (referring to "defendant preclusion").

negligent per se because she was driving over the speed limit. The jury returned a verdict for *P*, on which the court entered judgment. In Case 2, *P* sued *D* for property damage suffered in the same crash. Under the primary rights theory, Case 2 will not be dismissed for claim preclusion. In Case 2, *D* raises the defense that *P* caused the wreck because she was distracted by the actions of her passenger. Assuming *D* could have raised that defense in Case 1, should she be precluded from asserting the defense in Case 2?

Some people argue that the interests of repose and consistency support precluding *D* in Case 2. By permitting *D* to raise the new defense in Case 2, we run the risk that the result in that case will be different from the result in Case 1. Different outcomes make the judicial system look inconsistent. To avoid that possibility, the argument goes, we should invoke defense preclusion in Example #12.

On the other hand, the jurisdiction invited such inconsistent results (and duplicative litigation) when it adopted the primary rights definition of claim and permitted two suits about a single real-world event. Accordingly, some people argue that defense preclusion should apply only narrowly—for instance, when assertion of the defense in Case 2 may "nullify the initial judgment or would impair rights established in the initial action."[81] On the facts of Example #12, this standard is not satisfied. True, the outcomes may be different in the two cases, but judgment in favor of *D* in Case 2 does not impair *P*'s rights to collect on the judgment from Case 1.[82]

The ultimate reach of defense preclusion is unclear. Reasonable people can disagree, but it seems appropriate, in sculpting the doctrine, to consider the different positions of claimants and defendants. Claimants have unlimited time (cabined only by the statute of limitations) in which to plan their case—to decide which claims and remedies to pursue. Defendants, in contrast, must respond to a complaint within a very limited time (21 days in federal court). It seems unfair to require a defendant to raise not only defenses to the present case but to foresee defenses that might be relevant in a potential future case. Unless the defendant's defense in Case 2 threatens the integrity of a

[81]The quoted language is found in §22(b) of the Restatement (Second) of Judgments, which suggested something that has been called the "common-law compulsory counterclaim." *See* Kevin M. Clermont, *Common-Law Compulsory Counterclaim Rule: Creating Effective and Elegant Res Judicata Doctrine,* 79 Notre Dame L. Rev. 1745 (2004).

Despite preclusion law, occasionally cases do reach inconsistent results. The traditional view is that the latter judgment (assuming the requirements of preclusion are met) should take precedence over the earlier one. But that rule is subject to exceptions. *See* Kevin M. Clermont, *Limiting the Last-in-Time Rule for Judgments,* 36 Rev. Lit. 1 (2017).

[82]The doctrine may also be encountered in cases involving installment obligations under contracts. *See* 18 Wright & Miller §4414; Freer, note 76 above, at 117-120.

prior judgment, the defendant should be allowed to pick and choose defenses as she sees fit.

§11.4 Issue Preclusion (Collateral or Direct Estoppel)

Issue preclusion is the modern terminology for the doctrine historically known as collateral estoppel (or, more rarely, direct estoppel), which occurs in the unusual situation when Case 1 and Case 2 assert the same claim. Both "collateral estoppel" (or "direct estoppel") and "issue preclusion" are in use today. Whatever we call it, the focus of issue preclusion is narrower than that of claim preclusion. As we saw immediately above, the application of claim preclusion usually prohibits the claimant from asserting a right to relief that she *could* have raised in Case 1 but failed to; it results in the dismissal of Case 2. Issue preclusion, in contrast, applies only to preclude *relitigation* of an issue that the parties *actually did litigate and the court determined* in Case 1; it generally does not in itself cause dismissal of Case 2. Rather, issue preclusion streamlines the number of issues to be litigated in Case 2, as noted in §11.1.[83]

On the other hand, in a way, issue preclusion is broader than claim preclusion, because its operation is not tied to transactional relatedness. That is, an issue determined in Case 1 may be deemed established in Case 2 even though the cases involve radically different real-world events. For example, a determination in Case 1 that a drug causes a particular side effect may be used to establish that issue in other cases involving different persons, hurt at different times in different places.

The standard definition of issue preclusion contains five requisites. First, as with claim preclusion, Case 1 must have ended in a valid final judgment on the merits. Second, the same issue presented in Case 2 must have been litigated and determined in Case 1. Third, that issue must have been essential to the judgment in Case 1. Fourth, as a matter of due process, issue preclusion can only be asserted against one who was a party to Case 1 (or in "privity" with a party to Case 1). And fifth, the court in Case 2 must assess "mutuality," which concerns the question of who may assert issue preclusion. As we will see, the modern trend is to reject the traditional view that only parties to Case

---

[83]In some circumstances, however, the establishment of a single issue in Case 2 through issue preclusion may be determinative. Suppose, for instance, that the jurisdiction recognizes the doctrine of contributory negligence. Suppose also that in Case 1, a litigant, Z, was found negligent. Now Z brings Case 2 as plaintiff, concerning the same event. If issue preclusion is used to establish in Case 2 that Z was negligent, it would result, ultimately, in dismissal of Case 2.

1 may assert issue preclusion in Case 2. Now we turn to these individual requirements.

§11.4.1   Case 1 Ended in a Valid Final Judgment on the Merits

Preclusion—either claim preclusion or issue preclusion—flows from entry of a valid final judgment on the merits. The requirements discussed on this point for claim preclusion in §11.2.2 apply with equal force to issue preclusion.

§11.4.2   The Same Issue Was Litigated and Decided in Case 1

Issue preclusion allows a judicial system to avoid the burden—and the concomitant risk of inconsistent results—caused by relitigating an issue that has already been decided. Innumerable cases discuss this point.[84] The classic is *Cromwell v. County of Sac.*[85]

In *Cromwell*, the plaintiff sued to recover on bonds issued by a county. (Bonds are IOUs. People lend money to the county (in *Cromwell* they did so to build a new courthouse) and the county issues a bond—a piece of paper saying that the county will pay back the loan amount within a set period with specified interest.) The bond issuance in *Cromwell*, however, was fraudulent. It was set up by crooks who absconded with the money. Under the law of negotiable instruments, the county would not have to pay on the bonds if the bond issuance was fraudulent, with one exception: If the bond is in the hands of a "holder in due course" (HDC), the county must pay on the bond even though the issuance was fraudulent. An HDC is somebody who paid value for the bond and was unaware of the fraudulent issuance. (In some other contexts, the concept is referred to as being a "bona fide purchaser.")

In Case 1, Cromwell sued the county to recover on certain claims for interest on particular bonds.[86] The county proved that the bond

---

[84]There are a few opinions in which a court has permitted issue preclusion on an issue not actually litigated in Case 1. *See, e.g.*, Sutphin v. Speik, 15 Cal. 2d 195, 203-204 (1940). Such cases are aberrational; the overwhelming majority of courts hold that an issue cannot be the subject of issue preclusion unless it was litigated and determined in Case 1.

[85]94 U.S. 351 (1877). This classic opinion, included in many casebooks, was written by Justice Stephen Field, who wrote the majority opinion in *Pennoyer v. Neff.*

[86]Actually, Case 1 was brought by someone named Smith and Case 2 was brought by Cromwell. The opinion makes clear, however, that Smith was acting as an agent

issuance was fraudulent. Cromwell did not attempt to show that he was an HDC. In Case 2, Cromwell sued the county to recover on different claims for interest on the bonds. The county was entitled to issue preclusion on the issue that the bond issuance was fraudulent, so in Case 2 it was deemed established that the bond issuance was fraudulent. (Why?[87]) But Cromwell then wanted to put on evidence in Case 2 that he was an HDC. The Supreme Court held that he was entitled to do so. The fact that Cromwell *could have* asserted the HDC issue in Case 1 was irrelevant. The HDC issue had not been litigated and determined in Case 1, and thus was not subject to issue preclusion.[88]

Though stated as a single requirement of issue preclusion—that the same issue must have been litigated and determined in Case 1—this phrase actually contains three requisites. First, the issue must have been "litigated" in Case 1. Second, even though litigated, the issue must also have been "determined" in Case 1. And third, of course, we must be speaking of the "same issue" in both cases.

Determining Whether the Issue Was Litigated in Case 1

The situation is easy if Case 1 went to trial and evidence was presented on the particular issue. Then, clearly, the issue was litigated for purposes of issue preclusion. Even if the evidence presented was not sufficient to meet a party's burden at trial, the issue was litigated in

---

for Cromwell and thus was in "privity" with him. Thus, we treat the two cases as having been brought by Cromwell. We will see this concept in §11.4.4. *See also* Nestorio v. Assocs. Commercial Corp., 250 B.R. 50, 55 (D. Md. 2000). As you will study in an upper-level course on Business Associations, an agent is someone who acts for someone else (called the principal). The agent's acts, at least if done within the scope of the agency, will bind the principal. That is why Smith's litigation in Case 1 bound Cromwell in Case 2.

[87]Because that issue was litigated and determined in Case 1 and the other requirements of issue preclusion were met as well.

[88]The case was decided long before the terms *claim preclusion* and *issue preclusion* were coined. In *Cromwell*, the Court never actually says "collateral estoppel." This is a case in which the Court uses "*res judicata*" in a generic sense—to discuss both claim and issue preclusion. In reading the opinion, pay special attention to two paragraphs. One, a lengthy one, starts "In considering the operation of this judgment, it should be borne in mind, as stated by counsel, that there is a difference . . . ." That sentence goes on to draw the distinction between what we would call claim preclusion and issue preclusion. The following paragraph (which starts "But where the second action . . .") is about issue preclusion and makes the point that the issue must be litigated and determined in Case 1.

Case 1.[89] Indeed, there is even support for the position that an issue framed by the pleadings, but as to which no evidence was presented at trial, was litigated.[90]

But what if Case 1 was decided without trial, or without a hearing on the particular issue? For example, as we saw in §11.2.2, a voluntary dismissal with prejudice will have a *claim* preclusive effect; because no issue was litigated in such a dismissal, however, it will not have an *issue* preclusive effect.[91] Similarly, though a default judgment can have a claim preclusive effect, it will probably not carry issue preclusion consequences, because no issue was actually litigated in the default.[92] So, too, facts that are admitted in pleadings or an admission for failure to respond to a request under Federal Rule 36 are not litigated and should not support issue preclusion in a subsequent case.[93]

On the other hand, a judgment based upon summary judgment can carry issue preclusive effect. Recall (as we saw in §9.4) that summary judgment entails a judicial determination that there is no dispute on a material issue of fact and that the moving party is entitled to judgment as a matter of law. The determination that there is no material factual dispute is an adjudication on what facts exist and constitutes "litigation."[94]

---

[89]*See, e.g.*, Peck v. Commissioner, 904 F.2d 525, 530 (9th Cir. 1990) (failure to satisfy burden of persuasion in Case 1 establishes the nonexistence of a fact for issue preclusion purposes).

[90]*See* 18 Wright & Miller 500-503.

[91]St. Vincent's Hosp. v. Div. of Human Rights, 553 F. Supp. 375, 379 (S.D.N.Y. 1982).

[92]The Court made this point in *Cromwell*, 94 U.S. at 356-357 ("It could hardly be pretended that a judgment by default . . . would make the several statements evidence in any other proceeding"). *See also* In re Biselow, 271 B.R. 178, 185 (B.A.P. 9th Cir. 2001) (applying Washington law); Baron v. Bryant, 556 F. Supp. 531, 538 (D. Haw. 1983) (adopting "the preponderant view that a default judgment should not be given conclusive effect under the doctrine of collateral estoppel"). Some courts have held to the contrary, though, seeing the default judgment as a confession of the material allegations and justifying issue preclusion on those allegations. *See, e.g.*, In re Calvert, 105 F.3d 315, 318 (3d Cir. 1997) (applying California law and finding that "a party who permits a default to be entered confesses the truth of all the material allegations in the complaint. A default judgment is as conclusive upon the issues tendered by the complaint as if rendered after an answer is filed and a trial is held"). Also, as we saw in §7.5.3, some issues, such as damages, may actually be litigated in a default judgment case; such litigated issues should be subject to issue preclusion.

[93]*See* United States v. Young, 804 F.2d 116, 118 (8th Cir. 1986). Rule 36 expressly provides that admissions thereunder are limited to the pending case only.

[94]*See* Roskam Baking Co. v. Lanham Machinery Co., 288 F.3d 895, 905 (6th Cir. 2002) ("Michigan law permits preclusion of issues decided by a judge as part of summary disposition"); Matosantos Commercial Corp. v. Applebee's Int'l, Inc., 245 F.3d 1203, 1211 (10th Cir. 2001); Exhibitors Poster Exch., Inc. v. Nat'l Screen Serv. Corp., 421 F.2d 1313, 1319 (5th Cir. 1970).

Determining Whether the Issue Was Determined in Case 1

Not every issue litigated in a case will be determined. For instance, a claimant may present alternative theories of recovery at trial. The fact-finder may base its decision on one of the alternatives and ignore the other. Similarly, a defendant may present alternative defenses. Once the fact-finder determines that one such theory is established, it may ignore the others. Or the parties may present evidence on an issue and then withdraw the issue before submission to the fact-finder. Because issue preclusion applies only to issues that are litigated *and* determined in Case 1, it will not apply to such issues.

In most cases, the issues that have been determined will be clear. In nonjury trials, the judge will enter findings of fact and conclusions of law, which ought to make clear what issues were actually determined. In jury trials, the jury can be pinned down on specific determinations through the use of special verdicts or interrogatories to the jury. See §9.2.4. In some cases, however, the issues actually litigated and determined will not be clear. Bench trials occasionally result in less-than-full findings and conclusions. More frequently, the problem will arise in a jury trial in which neither special verdicts nor jury interrogatories were used. If it is not clear what issues were litigated and determined in Case 1, how should the court in Case 2 proceed? The party asserting issue preclusion bears the burden of establishing that the requirements are met; this burden includes presenting to the court in Case 2 an adequate record from Case 1 to support the assertion.[95] The court in Case 2 may have to review the trial record (including the transcript) from Case 1, to determine what issues were actually litigated, and whether any of those issues are presented in Case 2.

An example of the difficulty is *O'Connor v. G&R Packing Co.*,[96] in which a teenaged boy was injured while trespassing on railroad property. Defendants won Case 1, with the judge finding that the boy "disobeyed . . . statutes which were enacted for the benefit of the public" and "deliberately and needlessly exposed himself to a known danger." In Case 2, a different defendant sought to establish issue preclusion on the boy's contributory negligence. The New York Court of Appeals reviewed the transcript of the trial judge's ruling in Case 1. Though the quoted language is consistent with a finding of contributory negligence, in the context of the entire transcript, that court concluded, the trial judge in Case 1 had not ruled on contributory negligence at all.[97]

---

[95]*See, e.g.*, Matter of King, 103 F.3d 17, 19 (5th Cir. 1997) (party failed to satisfy burden of proving requisites for issue preclusion).

[96]423 N.E.2d 397 (N.Y. 1981).

[97]*Id.* at 399 ("litigation [in Case 2] of the contributory negligence issue is not precluded by such a nonspecific nonfactual determination").

The following hypotheticals show how the form of a verdict can affect the assessment of what issues were determined in Case 1. Assume in each case that the applicable law recognizes contributory negligence as a bar to recovery in a negligence case. To win a case for negligence, then, (1) the claimant must have been free from negligence and (2) the defendant must have been negligent. We also assume that both of these issues were raised and litigated—that the parties put on evidence at trial concerning the possible negligence of each other. The question in these examples is what issue(s) were determined in the case.

- ○ ***Example #13.*** *A* sues *Z* for negligence. The case is tried to a jury.[98] The jury returns a *general verdict* in favor of *A*. Do we know what issues were determined in this case? Yes. A general verdict in favor of the claimant is never ambiguous. The only way *A* could win is if the jury found (1) *A* was not negligent *and* (2) *Z* was negligent. (In other words, if either of those things was not true, *Z* would have won the verdict.) So in a second case, there can be issue preclusion on either issue, since both issues actually were determined by the jury in Case 1.

- ○ ***Example #14.*** *A* sues *Z* for negligence. The case is tried to a jury. The jury returns a general verdict in favor of *Z*. Can we know what issues were determined in this case? No. A general verdict in favor of the *defendant* is ambiguous. Why? Because it might be that the jury found (1) that *A* was negligent, *or* (2) that *Z* was not negligent, *or* (3) both of the above. But we do not know. So in a second case, there cannot be issue preclusion because we do not know what issue(s) actually were determined by the jury in Case 1.

- ○ ***Example #15.*** *A* sues *Z* for negligence. The case is tried to a jury. The jury returns a *special verdict* finding that *A* was negligent. The court, accordingly, enters judgment for *Z*. Can we know what issue was determined in this case? Yes. The jury told us exactly what issue it decided: the negligence of *A*. In a second case, the negligence of *A* could be established by issue preclusion. What about the negligence (or freedom from negligence) of *Z*? No. There is no issue preclusion on it because the jury made no findings concerning the negligence of *Z* in Case 1.

- ○ ***Example #16.*** *A* sues *Z* for negligence. The case is tried to a jury. The jury returns a special verdict finding (1) that *Z* was negligent and (2) that *A* was not negligent. The court enters judgment, accordingly, in favor of *A*. Do we know what issues were determined here? Certainly. There is no doubt here. (This case is just like Example #13, but here the two facts that justify judgment in favor of the claimant are stated expressly, rather than embodied in a general verdict.) So in a second case, there could be issue preclusion on either of the issues.

---

[98]Or the case could have been a bench trial in which the judge made findings of fact, either because no right to jury trial existed or because the parties waived their right to jury trial. See §9.2.2.

Determining Whether the Cases Involve the Same Issue

Of course, issue preclusion is appropriate only when the same issue is presented in both Case 1 and Case 2. The entire thrust of issue preclusion is to ensure that we not *relitigate* something that has already been determined by a competent court. Sometimes, a party will try to justify relitigating an issue in Case 2 by asserting that she has new evidence supporting an assertion that was rejected in Case 1. While discovery of new evidence may justify setting aside a judgment under Federal Rule 60(b)(2) (but only in limited circumstances (see §9.7)), it does not avoid the operation of issue preclusion.[99] The party had her chance to litigate that issue; she does not get another.

Serious problems can arise concerning the characterization in Case 2 of just what "issue" was litigated and determined in Case 1. For example, if the claimant in Case 1 pursued a particular theory of negligence, is she precluded from raising a different theory of negligence in Case 2? If the defendant in Case 1 raised a defense that was rejected, is she precluded from raising a different defense in Case 2? The assessment of the scope of the issue determined in Case 1 may differ depending upon the party against whom preclusion is asserted.

> o ***Example #17.*** *P* and *D*, each driving her own car, collide at an intersection. *P* suffers personal injuries and property damage to her car. In Case 1, *P* sues *D* for damages for the personal injuries, alleging that *D* was negligent because *D* was speeding into the intersection where the collision took place. After trial, judgment is entered for *D*, with a specific finding that *D* had not been speeding. In Case 2, *P* sues *D* for property damage arising from the same crash. Assume that the litigation is in a primary rights jurisdiction, so *D* cannot have the case dismissed under claim preclusion.[100] Clearly *P* cannot reassert that *D* was speeding. But can *P* assert that *D* was negligent in another way? For instance, can *P* claim that *D* failed to keep a proper lookout, or that *D* ran a red light to come into the intersection?

The answer to these questions depends upon how the court in Case 2 characterizes the issue decided in Case 1. If it sees the issue narrowly—as the factual issue of whether *D* was speeding—Case 2 does not present the same issue, and issue preclusion will be rejected. On the other hand, if the court sees the issue broadly—as the legal conclusion about whether *D* was negligent—Case 2 does present the same issue, and issue preclusion will be allowed. There are problems with either of these two approaches. First, the narrow reading of

---

[99]*See, e.g.*, Heim v. United States, 50 Fed. Cl. 225, 233-234 (2001); Harline v. Barker, 912 P.2d 433, 443 (Utah 1996).

[100]If this does not ring a bell, review §11.2.3.

the issue permits *P* to vex *D* with a theory of negligence that could have been asserted in Case 1; it also creates the risk of inconsistent results in Case 1 and Case 2, which reflects ill on the system of justice. Second, the broad reading of the issue precludes *P* from litigating specific questions that truly have never been before a court; this result seems to violate the requirement that issue preclusion apply only to questions actually litigated and determined.

So what does a court do? The Restatement (Second) of Judgments urges a pragmatic course. Specifically, it instructs the court to look at such things as the degree of overlap between the evidence or arguments made in Case 1 and Case 2; whether new evidence or argument in Case 2 involves the same rule of law as that in Case 1; whether pretrial preparation (including discovery) in Case 1 could reasonably have embraced the new evidence or argument in Case 2; and whether there is a close relationship between the claims asserted in Case 1 and Case 2.[101]

On the facts of Example #17, the Restatement (Second) of Judgments counsels a finding of issue preclusion in Case 2.[102] First, there is substantial overlap between the evidence in Case 1 and the new evidence of liability in Case 2; both deal directly with how *D*'s car got into the intersection and, presumably, will entail testimony from the same eyewitnesses. Second, the evidence of liability in Case 1 and in Case 2 seems to implicate the same rules of negligence law. Third, it seems likely that pretrial preparation of Case 1 would have uncovered any issue of *D*'s failure to keep proper lookout or running a red light. Finally, the claims asserted in Case 1 and Case 2 are quite closely related. Indeed, for claim preclusion purposes, most jurisdictions would have concluded that both cases assert the very same claim. Let's try a hypothetical about defenses.

○ ***Example #18.*** *P* and *D* enter a contract that requires *D* to make periodic payments for goods sold. In Case 1, *P* sues *D*, alleging that *D* has defaulted on three periodic payments. *D* defends by claiming that the contract violated the statute of frauds. The parties litigate in Case 1 and *P* wins, with the court expressly rejecting the statute of frauds defense. *D* subsequently fails to make other payments under the same contract. *P* brings Case 2 to recover these later defaults in payment. (Because these defaults came after Case 1 was filed, they are not part of the same claim as Case 1, so there can be no claim preclusion.)[103] Clearly, *D* cannot raise the defense of statute of frauds. But can *D* raise a different defense

[101]Restatement (Second) of Judgments §27, cmt. c.
[102]Restatement (Second) of Judgments §27, cmt. c, illustration 4 is similar to the facts of Example #17.
[103]If this does not ring a bell, review §11.2.3.

to the contract? Can he claim, for instance, that the contract violated fundamental public policy, or usury laws, or antitrust laws, etc.?

Using the pragmatic factors listed above, the Restatement (Second) here suggests that *D* should be able to raise the new defense.[104] Stated another way, it views the "issue" determined in Case 1 narrowly, as statute of frauds. In Example #17, the Restatement (Second) viewed the "issue" litigated in Case 1 broadly, as negligence. The lesson is clear: The drafters of the Restatement (Second) deem it appropriate to expect a *claimant* to assert every possible basis for recovery in Case 1 but tend to allow a *defendant* to pick and choose among potential defenses, retaining others for another day. It is not clear why the issue preclusion rules ought to be more solicitous of defendants than of claimants on this score.

Of course, the application of the factors suggested by the Restatement (Second) will not always lead to a clear answer. As we saw with defining a claim in claim preclusion, this is an area of more art than science. We are well counseled, however, by these words:

> In the end, it may prove best to find that identical issues are involved only on a strong showing that relitigation would present matters that clearly bore on ultimate issues that were raised in the first action or that would jeopardize significant interests of justifiable reliance or repose. As with claim . . . preclusion, such showings must be tailored to the distinctive considerations that arise from litigating and living under different rules of substantive law.[105]

Almost always, a party will seek to invoke issue preclusion as to a question of fact that was litigated and determined in Case 1. But does issue preclusion apply to rulings of law from Case 1? The general answer (assuming the other requirements for issue preclusion are satisfied) is yes. For instance, a court's determination that a claim for wrongful discharge of employment was preempted by federal law—clearly a question of law as applied to a given set of facts—was entitled to issue preclusive effect.[106] The Supreme Court has indicated that issue preclusion might not be available, however, for "unmixed" or "pure" questions of law that arise in successive cases "involving unrelated subject matter."[107] The scope and even the purpose of this exception are not terribly clear.[108]

---

[104]Restatement (Second) of Judgments §27, cmt. c, illustration 6 is similar to the facts of Example #18.

[105]18 Wright & Miller 432.

[106]Jarvis v. Nobel/Sysco Food Servs. Co., 985 F.2d 1419, 1424-1425 (10th Cir. 1993).

[107]United States v. Stauffer Chem. Co., 464 U.S. 165, 169-170 (1984).

[108]For a helpful discussion of this and the related exception for "separable facts," *see* 18 Moore's Federal Practice §132.02[5].

§11.4.3 That Issue Was Essential to the Judgment in Case 1

The Concept of Essentiality

As we just saw, the issue on which someone wants issue preclusion must have been litigated and determined in Case 1. But that is not enough. The issue must also have been *essential* to the outcome of Case 1. The assessment of essentiality forces us to focus on the difference between the *issue* decided and the *judgment* entered in the case. The issue, of course, is relatively narrow—for example, whether *D* was driving her car too fast. The judgment is broader—it focuses on who won the case, not on why she won. The requirement of essentiality is illustrated by *Rios v. Davis*,[109] which is found in some Civil Procedure casebooks. We simplify the facts slightly in demonstrating the point.

- ○ ***Example #19.*** Rios and Davis, each driving a vehicle, collide. Each vehicle is damaged. In Case 1, Davis sues Rios to recover for damage to his vehicle. The case is litigated and the jury expressly finds that *both* Davis and Rios were negligent in causing the collision. Thus, two issues were litigated and determined—Davis was negligent and Rios was negligent. Under the doctrine of contributory negligence, as you know from Torts, a claimant loses if she is shown to have been negligent. Applying that doctrine, the court entered judgment for Rios (because Davis, the plaintiff, was negligent).
  - ○ In Case 2, Rios sues Davis to recover for his injuries from the same collision. (There can be no claim preclusion. Why?[110]) Davis seeks to have issue preclusion applied concerning the finding in Case 1 that Rios was negligent. Indeed, that issue had been litigated and determined in Case 1. But issue preclusion should not apply to that issue because it was not *essential* to the judgment in Case 1.[111] Why not?

To determine essentiality, we ask this: If the finding on this issue had come out the other way, would the judgment be the same? If so, the finding is not essential to the judgment, because the judgment does not rest on the finding on that issue. Let's try that test regarding

---

[109]373 S.W.2d 386, (Tex. Ct. Civ. App. 1963).

[110]Claim preclusion requires, among other things, that Case 1 and Case 2 be asserted by the same claimant against the same defendant (see §11.2.1). Rios was not a claimant in Case 1. He has never asserted a claim before, and thus cannot be guilty of trying to assert the same claim twice.

[111]*See* Kloth v. Microsoft Corp., 355 F.3d 322, 328 (4th Cir. 2004) (issue preclusion does not apply to findings that "support" a judgment; rather, they must be "critical and necessary" to the judgment).

the two findings in *Rios*—one that Davis was negligent and one that Rios was negligent.

- If the finding (in Case 1) that Rios was negligent had been instead that he was *not* negligent, would the judgment in Case 1 have been the same? Yes. Because of contributory negligence, once Davis (the claimant) was found negligent, the judgment could only come out one way—it must be in favor of the defendant (Rios). Rios's behavior—whether he was negligent or not negligent—is irrelevant to the judgment. Because changing the finding on this issue would not change the judgment, the finding is not essential to the judgment.
- If the finding (in Case 1) that Davis was negligent had been instead that he was *not* negligent, would the judgment in Case 1 have been the same? No! If Davis were not negligent, he would have won the judgment in Case 1. Why? Because then there would be findings (1) that the claimant was not negligent and (2) that the defendant was negligent. In such a case, the judgment would have been in favor of the claimant. Because changing the finding on this issue would change the judgment, the finding is essential to the judgment.

There are two policy reasons for refusing to accord issue preclusive effect to the finding in Case 1 that Rios was negligent. First, because Rios won the judgment in that case, he would not have been able to appeal the finding that he was negligent.[112] The right to appeal is from the *judgment*, not from an individual finding. The party losing the *judgment* has a right to appeal. Because Rios would have had no opportunity to have the finding of his negligence reviewed on appeal, that finding was not subject to full judicial scrutiny and thus is not worthy of issue preclusion. Second, because the finding on Rios's negligence was irrelevant to the outcome (Rios had to win once Davis was found contributorily negligent), there is a sense that the jury may not have devoted sufficient attention on the issue.[113] For these two reasons, courts conclude that they should accord issue preclusive effect only to those findings that mattered in the ultimate judgment.

- ***Example #20.*** Suppose in Case 1 *P* in a negligence case wins a general jury verdict. In Case 2, what issues were essential to the judgment in Case 1? We know from §11.4.2 that a general verdict in favor of *P* in a negligence case is not ambiguous. Such a verdict is possible in a contributory negligence state only if two things are true: (1) *D* is negligent and (2) *P* is not negligent. Thus, we know those two issues were litigated and

---

[112]*Rios*, 373 S.W.2d at 387-388 ("the finding . . . that Rios was negligent proximately causing the accident would, if it had been controlling, have led to a different result").

[113]*See* Northgate Motors, Inc. v. General Motors Corp., 111 F. Supp. 2d 1071, 1078 (D. Wis. 2000) (fact-finder "may have devoted less care to determining an issue that did not affect the result").

determined in Case 1. But which (if either) was *essential* to the judgment in favor of *P*?

- Both are essential, and thus entitled to issue preclusive effect in subsequent litigation. Why? Because if either issue were decided differently, the judgment would be different.
- First, if the finding that *D* was negligent were different, the judgment could not be in favor of *P*. If the finding were that *D* was not negligent, the judgment would have to be for *D*.
- Second, if the finding that *P* was not negligent were different, the judgment could not be in favor of *P*. If the finding were that *P* was negligent, the judgment would have to be for *D*.

The Problem of Alternative Determinations

What happens if the court enters findings on more than one issue, each of which is consistent with the judgment? This possibility raises the problem of "alternative" determinations—that is, findings on issues, any one of which would be sufficient to compel the judgment that was entered.

- ***Example #21.*** *A* sues *Z* for negligence. The case is tried to a jury. The jury returns a special verdict finding (1) that *Z* is not negligent and (2) that *A* is negligent. The court enters judgment, accordingly, in favor of *Z*.

These are alternative findings because *either* one of the two—alone—would result in judgment for *Z*. If you take away either one of the two findings, the judgment in favor of *Z* would still stand. For instance, if all the jury in Case 1 did was decide that *Z* was not negligent, *Z* would win regardless of whether *A* was negligent. Likewise, if all the jury in Case 1 did was decide that *A* was negligent, *Z* would win (because of the finding that *A* was contributorily negligent). Alternative findings, then, offer two reasons for the same conclusion.

Courts have not agreed on whether to consider alternative findings essential for issue preclusion purposes. The traditional approach to the problem, reflected in the first Restatement of Judgments, holds that *both* of the alternative findings are essential.[114] Thus, both the finding that *Z* was not negligent and that *A* was negligent would be entitled to issue preclusion in Case 2.[115] This view has been criticized,

---

[114]Restatement of Judgments §68, cmt. n (1942).

[115]Case 2 here might be brought by *Z* against *A* concerning the wreck (assuming the jurisdiction did not have a compulsory counterclaim rule that required her to assert this claim in Case 1; see §12.3.1). Or perhaps a third party injured in the same wreck (maybe a passenger in one of the vehicles) brings Case 2 and seeks to assert nonmutual issue preclusion, which we address in §11.4.5. Or perhaps we are in a primary rights jurisdiction and *A* will sue *Z* again, this time for property damage as opposed to personal injuries, see §11.2.3.

however, and when the American Law Institute reconsidered the question in the Restatement (Second) of Judgments, it took a different approach. Under the Restatement (Second), alternative determinations are deemed *not* to be essential to the judgment in Case 1 and thus neither one is entitled to issue preclusion in Case 2.[116] There is an exception, however, that provides for issue preclusion on one or both of the alternative determinations if they are upheld expressly on appeal.[117]

The Restatement (Second) approach is odd. It seems to punish a litigant for doing too well. That is, if *Z* had proved simply that she was not negligent, that finding would be entitled to issue preclusion; by proving not only that she was not negligent but that *A* was negligent, however, she loses an issue preclusive effect for either finding. Why did the Restatement (Second) take this approach? There were two main reasons. First, because the alternative determination is not necessary to the decision, it might not have been considered as fully by the fact-finder. In other words, once the fact-finder determined that *A* was negligent, it might not have paid all that much attention to the determination of whether *Z* was negligent, because the ruling on that issue would not affect the outcome. Second, the losing litigant, faced with two negative findings, might be dissuaded from seeking appellate review. On appeal, she would still lose even if the appellate court affirmed on just one of the two issues. Forcing her to appeal to avoid the effect of issue preclusion would increase the burdens on courts and litigants. To avoid that burden, the drafters decided to free the losing litigant from the effects of issue preclusion altogether (unless there is an appeal that results in affirming either or both of the issues).[118]

These reasons for the Restatement (Second) approach to alternative findings are not persuasive. The concerns could be accommodated, it seems, by careful attention to the requirement that the issue must be litigated and determined in Case 1 (which we saw in §11.4.2). For instance, in Example #21, suppose the court in Case 2 looked at the record and determined that the fact-finder in Case 1 really did focus on one of the two issues, so that the second issue was basically an afterthought. Rather than deny preclusive effect to both findings, the court in Case 2 should hold that the first issue is entitled to preclusive effect and the second is not. But not because of essentiality. The second issue would not be subject to preclusion because it was not actually litigated and decided in Case 1. Some courts have adopted this flexible approach to the problem.[119]

---

[116]Restatement (Second) of Judgments §27, cmt. i.

[117]Restatement (Second) of Judgments §27, cmt. o.

[118]Restatement (Second) of Judgments §27, cmt. i.

[119]*Cf.* Malloy v. Trombley, 405 N.E.2d 213, 216 (N.Y. 1980) (though fact-finder in Case 1 said that a finding on contributory negligence was not necessary to the decision, the

It is important to be able to recognize alternative determinations in a fact pattern. It is also important to remember that courts disagree on how to treat them.[120]

Moreover, be careful not to confuse alternative determinations—in which *either* of two findings would dictate the same judgment—with the situation in which *both* findings are necessary to a result. For example, let's return to the facts of Example #16:

> ○ ***Example #22.*** A sues Z for negligence. The case is tried to a jury. The jury returns a special verdict finding (1) that Z was negligent and (2) that A was not negligent. The court enters judgment, accordingly, in favor of A.

These two findings are *not* alternative determinations. With alternative determinations, remember, *either* finding would dictate the judgment. That is not the case here. If all the court in Case 1 determined was that Z was negligent, that finding alone would not justify the judgment in favor of A. Why not? Because in a contributory negligence state, the claimant can win only if two things are established: that the defendant was negligent and that the claimant was free from negligence. In this fact pattern, *both* of the findings are necessary to get a judgment for A. Stated another way, if you took away either of the findings, the judgment in favor of A could not stand. So here, both issues are essential to the judgment and both are entitled to issue preclusive effect in Case 2.

§11.4.4   Due Process: Against Whom Is Preclusion Asserted?

Distinguishing Between Due Process and Mutuality

In addition to the requirements already discussed, issue preclusion requires that we address two other issues: due process and mutuality. The due process inquiry concerns the question of *against whom* preclusion may be asserted; it is the topic of this subsection. The mutuality

---

court in Case 2 gave the finding issue preclusive effect because it was convinced that the alternative determination was the product of "thorough and careful deliberation").

[120]Here's some advice for law school examinations. Whenever your class has covered an area on which courts disagree, be prepared to discuss the approaches taken by the courts. I cannot tell you how many exams I have read in which the student recognizes the problem of alternative determinations and then applies only one of the approaches—either the original Restatement or the Restatement (Second). The professor puts topics such as this on an exam precisely so you can demonstrate that you know the different approaches.

inquiry concerns the question of *by whom* preclusion may be asserted; it is addressed in §11.4.5.

Due process ensures that one can be bound by a judgment from Case 1 only if she had a full and fair opportunity to litigate in Case 1.[121] So preclusion can be asserted only against someone who had a full and fair opportunity to litigate in Case 1.[122] Because this precept is commanded by constitutional principles, it must apply in all cases, in whatever court system—federal or state. And though we discuss it here, in a section concerning issue preclusion, it also applies in claim preclusion.[123]

The Starting Point: Parties to Case 1 Can Be Bound

Preclusion, as just discussed, can be asserted only against one who had a full and fair opportunity to litigate in Case 1. Although the concept of a full and fair opportunity to be heard is flexible, it certainly includes someone who was properly joined as a *party* to Case 1.[124] Conversely, a *nonparty* to Case 1 generally will not be bound by the judgment in Case 1.

- *Example #23.* In Case 1, *P-1* sues Airline, alleging that she was injured in a crash of a plane operated by Airline, and that Airline's negligence caused the crash. The case goes to trial and Airline wins because the jury makes an express determination that Airline was not negligent. In Case 2, *P-2* (who was not a party to Case 1) sues Airline to recover for her injuries suffered in the same crash. Clearly, Airline cannot invoke claim preclusion against *P-2*. (Why?[125]) But can Airline assert issue preclusion on the finding that it was not negligent? (It's the same issue; it was litigated and determined in Case 1, and Case 1 ended in a valid final judgment on the merits.)

---

[121]Allen v. McCurry, 449 U.S. 90, 95 (1980) ("the concept of collateral estoppel cannot apply when the party against whom the earlier decision is asserted did not have a 'full and fair opportunity' to litigate that issue in the earlier case"); Blonder-Tongue Laboratories, Inc. v. University of Ill. Found., 402 U.S. 313, 317-320 (1971).

[122]Though this section deals with issue preclusion, this rule holds true in claim preclusion as well. Recall from §11.2.1 that one requirement of claim preclusion was that Case 1 and Case 2 be brought by the same claimant against the same defendant. We refine this point a bit, as we will with issue preclusion, below.

[123]We discussed this in §11.2.1. Accordingly, claim preclusion can only be asserted against one who had a full and fair opportunity to litigate in Case 1.

[124]*See generally* 18 Moore's Federal Practice §132.04[1][a]. This assumes that any defending party is properly brought before the personal jurisdiction of the court by appropriate service of process.

[125]Because claim preclusion applies only if Case 1 and Case 2 were brought by the same claimant against the same defendant. See §11.2.1. Here, Case 1 was brought by *P-1* and Case 2 was brought by *P-2*.

○ Based upon what we have seen so far, the answer is clear: Airline cannot use issue preclusion. *P-2*, the party in Case 2 against whom preclusion is sought, was not a party to Case 1 and thus cannot be said to have had a full and fair opportunity to litigate in Case 1. Many commentators and courts would say that *P-2* has never had her "day in court" and cannot be bound by issue preclusion.

Note, by the way, how difficult due process makes things for Airline. Suppose 100 persons were injured in the crash, and that they bring 100 separate suits against Airline. Even if Airline wins 50 cases in a row, with each case resulting in an express finding that Airline was not negligent, Airline cannot assert issue preclusion against the next plaintiff because no plaintiff was a party to a preceding case.

Nonparty Preclusion: Expanding "Privity"

It is clear, then, that the judgment from Case 1 binds parties to Case 1. But can it ever bind litigants in Case 2 who were *not* technically joined as parties to Case 1? The answer is yes, though the circumstances in which this is true are not always clear. The judgment in Case 1 binds not only parties, but persons deemed to be in "privity" with parties to Case 1.[126] *Privity* is a slippery word, encrusted with historical baggage. Originally, it was limited to arcane notions of property rights, and no opinion dealing with privity seemed complete without citation to Lord Coke's discussion of the classes of privies at common law.[127]

Over time, courts expanded the circumstances in which nonparties to Case 1 can be bound by the judgment in that case. Though those circumstances no longer are limited to common law privity, many courts continue to use the word. Today, *privity* is simply a label that expresses "the conclusion that nonparty preclusion is appropriate. . . ."[128] It refers to a *relationship* between a nonparty to Case 1 and a party to Case 1. The idea is that the nonparty may be so closely aligned with a party to Case 1 that the nonparty has, in effect, had her "day in court." In the important case of *Taylor v. Sturgell*, the Supreme Court catalogued the circumstances in which this "nonparty preclusion" may be appropriate.[129] They are:

---

[126]Parklane Hosiery Co. v. Shore, 439 U.S. 322, 327 n.7 (1979) ("It is a violation of due process for a judgment to be binding on a litigant who was not a party nor a privy and therefore has never had an opportunity to be heard").

[127]*See, e.g.*, Stacy v. Thrasher, 47 U.S. 44, 59 (1849). Incidentally, you will encounter the great Lord Coke in many classes. Please be aware that it is pronounced "Cook," and not like the author's favorite soft drink.

[128]Taylor v. Sturgell, 553 U.S. 880, 894 n.8 (2008). The Court in this case said that it would eschew use of the word *privity* in an effort "[t]o ward off confusion." *Id.*

[129]*Id.* at 893-895.

1. *Nonparty agrees to be bound.* Sometimes, someone who is not a party to a case will agree to be bound by the outcome of a case. The classic way to do this is with the "test case."

- ○ ***Example #24.*** Six sets of cases are pending, brought by six groups of plaintiffs against the same defendant, seeking tort damages for an allegedly defective product. All of the parties to the six cases agree that one of the six cases will proceed to trial first, and that the result of that trial will bind all others—win or lose—on the issue of defendant's liability.

2. *Nonparty is bound by a pre-existing substantive legal relationship with a party.* The classic situation here is successive holders of an interest in real property. For instance, a nonparty to Case 1 may be bound by the judgment in that case if she succeeds to a property interest held by someone who was a party in Case 1. The relationship of successor-in-interest closely approximates the common law definition of privity. The succession might be effected in any way—including sale or inheritance—and the property may be real or personal. Recognizing that the successor-in-interest is bound by the judgment involving her predecessor protects the other party from repetitive litigation and thus also avoids potentially inconsistent results.

- ○ ***Example #25.*** In Case 1, *P* sues *D-1*, who owns the lot and house next door to *P*'s, concerning a boundary dispute. The court enters a valid final judgment on the merits, based upon its finding that the boundary runs over a particular course. *D-1* sells his property to *D-2*, who now claims that that boundary is incorrect. In Case 2, *P* sues *D-2* to enforce the boundary as determined in Case 1. Though *D-2* was not a party to Case 1, she is bound by the judgment. She is a successor-in-interest to the property and is thus bound.[130]
- ○ ***Example #26.*** In Case 1, *P-1* sues *D*, asserting that she (and not *D*) owns certain securities. The court enters a valid final judgment on the merits in favor of *D*. *P-1* dies and *P-2* inherits everything that *P-1* owned. In Case 2, *P-2* sues *D* for a declaratory judgment that she owns the same securities. *P-2* is bound by the judgment in Case 1.

In a 1974 case, the Supreme Court may have expanded this notion of binding a successor-in-interest. In that case, Corporation 1 was held to have violated federal labor law by firing Employee. Corporation 2 bought

---

[130]In Oklahoma v. Texas, 256 U.S. 70 (1921), Case 1 was between the United States and Texas and set the boundary between Texas and federal land. After judgment, the United States transferred the property to the new state of Oklahoma. In Case 2, Oklahoma sued Texas concerning the boundary. Oklahoma, as successor-in-interest to the property, and Texas, as litigant in Case 1, were held bound to the judgment in Case 1.

669

Corporation 1. The Supreme Court held that Corporation 2 was bound by the judgment that Employee's labor law rights had been violated and thus that Corporation 2 could be ordered to reinstate the worker. Allowing Corporation 2 to escape the judgment could create repetitive litigation and threaten labor law policy.[131] Even if this case can be seen as expanding the concept of binding a successor-in-interest, this particular theory of binding a nonparty is fairly narrow.

3. *Nonparty is bound because she was adequately represented by one who was a party in Case 1.* Such representation can arise in a variety of ways.[132] The clearest instance is the class action. As we see in §13.3, in a class action a representative sues expressly on behalf of class members.[133] Though the class members thus are not technically parties, they will be bound by the judgment in a case certified to proceed as a class action.[134] Indeed, the very utility of the class action is that it can bind the numerous class members.

In a certain type of class action, members of the class are permitted to "opt out" of the proceeding; those who do so will not be bound by the judgment.[135] Generally speaking, though, those who do not opt out of such a class, and members of other types of class actions, are bound by the judgment. As the Supreme Court explained: "There is . . . no dispute that under elementary principles of prior adjudication a judgment in a properly entertained class action is binding on class members in any subsequent litigation."[136]

Another clear instance of binding representation involves litigation by or against fiduciaries. Some people cannot litigate in their own names because they lack legal capacity (this group includes minors and people under a mental disability). Litigation by or against such people can be conducted by a fiduciary, such as a guardian, guardian *ad litem*, conservator, or committee, whose express function is to represent the interest of the person lacking legal capacity. So long as

---

[131]Golden State Bottling Co. v. Nat'l Labor Rel. Bd., 414 U.S. 168 (1973).

[132]We deal with the major examples of binding through representation. There are several that we do not address here, such as whether litigation by a trade association or labor union binds its members and whether litigation by a governmental entity or agency binds other parts of the government or individuals. For detailed discussion of such points, see 18A Wright & Miller §§4456, 4458, and 4458.1.

[133]As we see in §13.3.5, there can be defendant classes, in which the representative is sued on behalf of a group of defendant class members.

[134]A case can be certified as a class action in federal court only if the court finds that the requirements set forth in Federal Rule 23(a) are satisfied. These requirements are aimed expressly at ensuring that the representative will represent the class members adequately. See §13.3.4.

[135]*See, e.g.,* Robinson v. Sheriff of Cook County, 167 F.3d 1155, 1157 (7th Cir. 1999); In re Corrugated Container Antitrust Litigation, 756 F.2d 411, 418-419 (5th Cir. 1985).

[136]Cooper v. Federal Reserve Bank of Richmond, 467 U.S. 867, 874 (1984).

the fiduciary is validly appointed, acts within the scope of the appointment, and is not guilty of prejudicial misconduct or conflict of interest, a judgment will bind the person represented.[137] Similarly, when a trustee litigates on behalf of beneficiaries to the trust, or an executor litigates on behalf of beneficiaries of the estate,[138] those beneficiaries will be bound by the result, even though they are not parties to the case.[139]

4. *Nonparty controlled the litigation in Case 1.* The best-known instance of this form of nonparty preclusion is *Montana v. United States*,[140] which grew out of a federal dam project in Montana. The United States hired a contractor to build the dam. The state of Montana imposed a tax on the contractor's gross receipts. The contractor and the federal government felt that this tax discriminated unconstitutionally against contractors dealing with the federal government. In Case 1, the contractor sued Montana. Though the United States was not a party to that case, it controlled almost every detail of the litigation for the contractor. It urged the contractor to file the case, reviewed the pleadings, paid the attorney's fees and litigation costs, directed that the contractor appeal an adverse judgment in the Montana court system, and submitted an *amicus curiae*[141] brief on the appeal.

The contractor lost Case 1, with the final judgment coming from the Montana Supreme Court. Thereafter, the United States filed Case 2, in which it raised the same challenge to the state tax. The Supreme Court held that the federal government was bound by the judgment in Case 1. While recognizing that the relationship between the United States and the contractor was not technically privity, two factors led the Court to conclude that the government should be bound. First, as a practical matter, the United States had run the show in Case 1; it "plainly had a sufficient 'laboring oar' in the conduct of the state-court litigation to actuate principles of estoppel."[142] Second, the United States also had "a direct financial or proprietary interest" in the litigation.[143]

---

[137]*See generally* 18A Wright & Miller §4454.

[138]*See* Restatement (Second) §41(1)(a), (c).

[139]Sea-Land Services v. Gaudet, 414 U.S. 573, 593-594 (1974) (beneficiaries "are bound by the judgment with respect to the interest which was the subject of the fiduciary relationship").

[140]440 U.S. 147 (1979).

[141]Amicus curiae is Latin for "friend of the court." Sometimes, nonparties to litigation—such as a governmental entity, interest group, organization, or interested citizen—will want to brief issues of import to assist the court (often the Supreme Court) in assessing an issue. Generally, one must receive permission of the court to file such a brief.

[142]*Montana*, 440 U.S. at 155, *citing* Drummond v. United States, 324 U.S. 316, 318 (1945).

[143]*Montana*, 440 U.S. at 155. *See also* 18 Moore's Federal Practice §132.04[1][b].

While courts often mention both factors in addressing whether to bind a nonparty to a judgment, clearly the first factor is the most important. Indeed, as a practical matter, it seems extremely unlikely that any nonparty would take control of litigation if it had no interest in the case. Thus, commentators urge that the "direct financial or proprietary interest" requirement be jettisoned.[144] Perhaps it has been; although the discussion was dicta, the Supreme Court's catalogue of nonparty preclusion in *Taylor v. Sturgell* did not mention any requirement beyond controlling the litigation.[145]

In assessing control, courts have not read *Montana* expansively. They tend to require some combination or aggregate of factors such as those in *Montana* itself. No single factor by itself—such as paying for counsel or financing the litigation or filing an amicus curiae brief—will suffice. The inquiry always depends on the specific facts of the case. The court in Case 2 must be satisfied that the nonparty, as a practical matter, controlled the litigation and the opportunity for review to such an extent that it ought to be treated as having been a party in Case 1. At the end of the day, this fact pattern applies in a narrow range of cases.

5. *Nonparty litigates through a proxy.* It is clear that one cannot avoid the preclusive effect of a judgment by litigating through an agent or proxy. We saw this in *Cromwell v. County of Sac*, which is discussed in §11.4.2. There, Case 1 was brought by Smith, who was litigating as an agent for Cromwell. Case 2 was brought by Cromwell. To the extent that Case 1 was entitled to preclusive effect, Cromwell was bound by its judgment. Though he was not a party to Case 1, he was bound by the acts of his agent. Similarly, if a party litigates and loses in Case 1, she cannot try to escape the binding effect of that judgment by having someone else sue in a separate case on her behalf.

6. *Nonparty may be bound by litigation under special statutory schemes.* This form of nonparty preclusion is very narrow. Occasionally, legislatures pass statutory schemes under which successive litigation is not permitted. Generally, a single case can be brought on behalf of the public at large, and the world must live with the result, without the opportunity to litigate afresh. For instance, federal bankruptcy proceedings are unitary events that foreclose separate litigation. State probate proceedings are another example.

[144]18A Wright & Miller 384. The Restatement (Second) §39, cmt. a, also concluded that any interest requirement be dropped.
[145]553 U.S. at 895.

Taylor v. Sturgell *Rejects "Virtual Representation"*

After cataloguing that a nonparty can be bound to a judgment in any of these six ways, the Court in *Taylor v. Sturgell* rejected the efforts of some lower courts to expand nonparty preclusion through what they called "virtual representation." The lower courts never agreed on a universal definition of virtual representation.[146] The general idea, though, was that a nonparty to Case 1 should be bound if she asserted a legal position in Case 2 that had been asserted by a party in Case 1. At its extreme, virtual representation would justify preclusion based upon identical legal theory; a court would say, in essence: "This point has been litigated before, and there is no good reason to relitigate it, even with a different party." The nonparty is bound because the party litigating that position in Case 1 "virtually" represented her.

The emergence of virtual representation was understandable in an era of crowded courts and mass torts. Judges were understandably frustrated at having to relitigate the same issues over and over; virtual representation was a manifestation of this frustration. Ultimately, though, the theory was an unseemly attempt to deal with contemporary litigation reality and threatens due process protection. Let's return to a hypothetical we saw in Example #23.

> o ***Example #27.*** In Case 1, *P-1* sues Airline, alleging that she was injured in a crash of a plane operated by Airline, and that Airline's negligence caused the crash. The case goes to trial and Airline wins because the jury makes an express determination that Airline was not negligent. In Case 2, *P-2* (who was not a party to Case 1) sues Airline to recover for her injuries suffered in the same crash.

We discussed before that Airline cannot invoke issue preclusion against *P-2* because *P-2* was not a party to Case 1. We also mentioned the frustration for Airline if there had been 100 injured passengers on the flight. If Airline litigated and won the first 50 cases against it, it would still have to litigate the next 50 cases. Due process gives each successive plaintiff her day in court. Now consider the added frustration of the judicial system. Judges have to preside over all of these cases, each rehashing the same issue. Over and over the system runs its wheels over the same ground.

One way to avoid the repetitive litigation in this scenario, of course, would be to have a class action on behalf of the 100 passengers. For

---

[146]Indeed, in *Taylor*, the Court noted that several lower court cases purporting to invoke virtual representation in fact merely applied one of the six permissible types of nonparty preclusion discussed above. "Some Circuits use the label but define 'virtual representation' so that it is no broader than the recognized exception for adequate representation." 553 U.S. at 896.

any of several reasons, however, a plaintiff might choose not to pursue a class action. (One reason is litigant autonomy—why litigate as part of a class of 100 if you can get more personal focus by suing individually?) Virtual representation was an effort to gain the efficiency of the class action by providing that once litigated, an issue cannot be relitigated by similarly situated nonparties. The problem, of course, is that the class action procedure contains safeguards to protect due process rights of class members; virtual representation does not.

The Fifth Circuit was the birthplace of the virtual representation theory. It got the ball rolling with *Aerojet-General Corp. v. Askew.*[147] In that case, Corporation entered a deal with two state agencies (Agencies) that owned land in Dade County, Florida. The deal gave Corporation a ten-year lease on the land and an option to buy the land at any time during the lease. Four years into the lease, before Corporation exercised the option to buy the land, Florida passed a statute providing that no state agency could sell land to anyone without first offering to sell it to the county in which it was situated. After that law went into effect, Corporation exercised its option to buy the land. But Dade County also wanted to buy the land and asserted that it had a right to do so under the new statute.

In Case 1, Corporation sued the Agencies, seeking specific performance of the contract. Strangely, the defendants did not rely on the defense that the statute required them to offer the land to Dade County; they never mentioned the statute at all. In addition, Dade County was not joined as a party. Corporation won on summary judgment, and the court ordered the defendants to transfer the land to Corporation. At this point, Dade County went to the Florida Supreme Court to seek an extraordinary writ of mandamus that the Agencies convey the land to it. (We discuss such writs at §14.6.) The claim was based entirely on the new statute. The defendants here did not contest such an order, and the Florida Supreme Court granted the writ.

Corporation then filed Case 2 against the Agencies and Dade County. It sought an order to stop interference with its judgment from Case 1 and to stop further prosecution of the writ of mandamus from the Florida Supreme Court. The case was appealed to the Fifth Circuit, where Corporation won on alternative grounds. First, the court held that the statute could not be applied retroactively to the contract entered by Corporation. (Indeed, if the statute were deemed to apply to this contract, it would violate the Contract Clause of the Constitution.[148]) Second, in the influential part of the opinion, the court held that Dade County was bound by the judgment from Case 1.

---

[147]511 F.2d 710 (5th Cir. 1975).
[148]*Id.* at 722-723.

Though the county had not been a party to Case 1, the Agencies were its "virtual representatives" in that litigation. In famous language, the court said, "[A] person may be bound by a judgment even though not a party if one of the parties to the suit is so closely aligned with his interests as to be his virtual representative";[149] Dade County and the Agencies were sufficiently closely related for the latter to bind the former.

The facts of *Aerojet-General* should have ensured that the holding had limited impact. First, the county and the Agencies are related as political entities in ways that private litigants rarely are. It is often the case that Agencies are deemed to represent counties and other political entities in litigation.[150] Second, there was some sense that the Agencies had been playing games by not contesting Dade County's request for a writ of mandamus; the court wondered whether the Agencies weren't trying to undo the judgment in Case 1.[151] Third, of course, there was an alternative basis for the conclusion—that the statute did not apply at all to the contract. Indeed, one judge concurred in the judgment in the case only because of this statutory issue.[152]

Thereafter, the Fifth Circuit moderated its approach to virtual representation. In the well-known case of *Hardy v. Johns-Manville Sales Corp.*,[153] plaintiffs asserted that their personal injuries were caused by exposure to asbestos.[154] In Case 1 (*Borel v. Fibreboard Paper Products Corp.*[155]), plaintiffs sued six manufacturers of asbestos (Manufacturers 1-6) for personal injuries allegedly caused by exposure to asbestos. Plaintiffs won, and the court in Case 1 made a series

---

[149]*Id.* at 719 (citations omitted).

[150]And, if there are enough defendants, they might be represented in a defendant class action. See note 133 above.

[151]*Aerojet-General*, 511 F.2d at 721.

[152]*Id.* at 723 (Roney, J., concurring) (agreeing on statutory issue "makes my difference as to the *res judicata* effect of the first lawsuit of no consequence").

[153]681 F.2d 334 (5th Cir. 1982). Another example of moderation was *Pollard v. Cockrell*, 578 F.2d 1002, 1008 (5th Cir. 1978). There, Case 1 was brought by a group of massage parlor owners, challenging a local ordinance. After they lost, Case 2 was brought by a different group of massage parlor owners, challenging the same ordinance. Though the two groups of plaintiffs employed the same lawyers and had nearly identical pleadings, the court refused to apply virtual representation. Thus, the second group was not bound by the judgment in Case 1.

[154]Asbestos is a fireproof building material used in innumerable structures over several decades. In the 1970s it became apparent that breathing asbestos fibers could cause potentially deadly lung diseases, including mesothelioma. Plaintiffs brought thousands of cases for personal injuries. In addition, there were thousands of cases regarding the expenses incurred in satisfying a federal mandate to remove asbestos from structures. There were also thousands of cases involving insurance coverage. Managing these asbestos-related cases was a judicial nightmare.

[155]493 F.2d 1076 (5th Cir. 1973).

of specific findings, including a finding that the defendants had failed to warn workers of the dangers of asbestos. In Case 2 (*Hardy*), different plaintiffs sued Manufacturers 1-6 and a second group of manufacturers (Manufacturers 7-14).

The trial court allowed the plaintiffs to use issue preclusion against all 14 manufacturers. There was no question from a due process standpoint that the court in Case 2 can invoke issue preclusion against Manufacturers 1-6. After all, they were parties to Case 1 and are clearly bound by the judgment in that case. But how did the trial court justify use of issue preclusion against Manufacturers 7-14, who were not parties to Case 1? It did so through virtual representation. According to the trial court, all 14 manufacturers shared an "identity of interests," which constituted privity. They all manufactured the same product. They raised the same legal issues as Manufacturers 1-6 had in Case 1.

The Fifth Circuit reversed. It held that Manufacturers 7-14 could not be bound by the judgment in Case 1 and chastised the trial court for stretching the notion of privity "beyond meaningful limits."[156] The fact that all 14 manufacturers are engaged in the manufacture of the same product does not create privity. The fact that all defendants assert similar defenses does not create privity. As in *Pollard*, the defendants in Case 1 (Manufacturers 1-6) were not accountable to the nonparties (Manufacturers 7-14). They had no right or responsibility to represent them. The court even minimized its holding in *Aerojet-General* by characterizing that case as involving one governmental entity litigating on behalf of another, which "appears to be an unexceptional [situation of nonparty preclusion]."[157]

Other courts, however, expanded the notion of virtual representation. For instance, in *Tyus v. Schoemehl*,[158] the Eighth Circuit held that a group of plaintiffs who had dropped out of Case 1 were bound by the judgment in that case because they had been "virtually represented" by the plaintiff who remained. The court set forth a seven-factor test that counseled when the relationship between the party and nonparty was sufficiently close to justify preclusion. Other courts followed suit, with equally flexible and unpredictable multifactor balancing tests.

The Supreme Court put an end to virtual representation in *Taylor v. Sturgell*. There, Plaintiff, an antique aircraft enthusiast, used the

---

[156]*Hardy*, 681 F.2d at 339.

[157]*Id.* at 340 ("two government entities were so closely aligned that a prior judgment against one entity bound the other"). The court cited Restatement (Second) §41(1) for this proposition; that section contains classic examples of nonparty preclusion, including the case of an "agency invested by law with authority to represent" another person's interest.

[158]93 F.3d 449 (8th Cir. 1996).

Freedom of Information Act to attempt to gain access to documents concerning a vintage airplane. He wanted the information to help him restore his airplane to its original condition. The Federal Aviation Administration (FAA) rejected the request on the basis that the materials were exempt from disclosure because they were trade secrets. Plaintiff sued the FAA in federal court. The case was litigated, and Plaintiff lost. Thereafter, a friend of Plaintiff made a similar request for the same information. When the FAA refused to release, this second plaintiff sued the FAA. The question was whether this second plaintiff should be bound by the judgment in Plaintiff's case. The District of Columbia Circuit applied virtual representation to hold the second plaintiff bound.[159] The Supreme Court reversed and ended the experimentation into virtual representation. Outside the six paradigms discussed above, the Court concluded, nonparties cannot be bound.

Taylor manifests that due process is deeply rooted in our sense of justice. It is simply unfair to bind someone who has not had an opportunity to litigate either in person or through an appropriate representative. The question is what constitutes an appropriate representative. The fact that the Court will not permit virtual representation—in view of the tremendous cost of relitigation—demonstrates just how important the concept is. If we are willing to allow similarly situated litigants to raise the same issues in the same pleadings, using the same lawyers over and over, we must be protecting something very important.

§11.4.5   Mutuality: By Whom Is Preclusion Asserted?

Distinguishing Again Between Due Process and Mutuality

In the preceding subsection, we saw that preclusion may be asserted only *against* one who was a party (or in privity with a party) to Case 1. In this subsection, we deal with a completely separate question: *By* (not against) whom can preclusion be asserted? This question involves the concept of *mutuality*. Because mutuality is not rooted in due process (or any other constitutional principle), courts are not compelled to apply it. Thus, jurisdictions may take different approaches to mutuality: They may embrace it, modify it, or reject it.

---

[159]*Taylor* was a claim preclusion case. That is, the lower court concluded that because the plaintiff in Case 2 was virtually represented by the plaintiff in Case 1, the second plaintiff could not assert his claim to the documents. The question at hand—whether a stranger to Case 1 may be bound by the judgment in Case 1—arises in both claim and issue preclusion. See §11.2.1.

The Starting Point: Mutuality of Estoppel and Exceptions to It

Mutuality of estoppel is a very simple idea: The only people who can *use* preclusion in Case 2 are people who would be *bound* by the judgment in Case 1. The rule is based upon some basic sense of fairness—one should not be able to take advantage of the judgment from Case 1 if she would not be burdened by that judgment. Thus, under the traditional mutuality approach, the only people who can assert preclusion in Case 2 are those who were parties (or in "privity" with a party[160]) to Case 1.

But fairness can cut the other way. Why should one who has already litigated and lost in Case 1 get to relitigate the same issue against a different party in Case 2? True, the "new" litigant in Case 2 has not yet been burdened with litigation, so there is no harm to the interest of repose. But systemic interests are relevant. Relitigation burdens the courts by forcing them to repeat a task. Moreover, relitigation creates the possibility of inconsistent outcomes. Thus, mutuality has always had critics. Indeed, almost two centuries ago, Jeremy Bentham criticized mutuality for creating the "aura of the gaming table" precisely because it allowed someone to try again and again to seek a different outcome from Case 1.[161]

Because mutuality of estoppel is not rooted in any constitutional provision, courts are free to jettison it. The most important development in preclusion law over the past two generations has been the move to permit "nonmutual" assertion of issue preclusion. "Nonmutual" means that issue preclusion is being used by someone who was not a party to Case 1. This process of permitting nonmutual issue preclusion began not with outright rejection of the mutuality, but with recognition of *exceptions* to its operation.

The common law developed these exceptions long ago. They apply, however, only in cases involving an indemnification relationship. A good illustration is vicarious liability, under which one party is held liable for the tort of another because of a relationship between the two. For instance, assume that Driver borrows Owner's car, with Owner's permission. Driver is negligent in driving the car, and her negligence injures *P*. Of course, *P* can sue Driver, who is *primarily* liable (because she caused the wreck that harmed *P*). But *P* can also sue Owner, who is *vicariously* (or *secondarily*) liable for what Driver does.

Though the law imposes this vicarious liability on Owner, it also provides Owner with a right to be indemnified by Driver. In other words, the ultimate loss should be borne by the primarily liable person

---

[160]We discussed privity at §11.4.4.
[161]3 Jeremy Bentham, Rationale of Judicial Evidence 579 (1827).

(Driver). If *P* sues Owner and wins, Owner will be required to pay the judgment to *P*. But Owner then has the right to sue Driver for indemnification. If Owner wins this indemnification claim, Driver must make Owner whole for the judgment she lost to *P*. In this roundabout way, then, Driver ends up reimbursing Owner for her vicarious liability. This result is appropriate, because Driver is the one who caused the harm to begin with.[162] Driver is the *indemnitor* and Owner is the *indemnitee.*

- **_Example #28._** In Case 1, *P* sues Driver. The parties litigate and Driver wins a valid final judgment on the merits, because the fact-finder expressly finds that Driver was *not* negligent. In Case 2, *P* sues Owner, asserting that Owner is vicariously liable for Driver's negligence. Traditionally, courts would conclude that Owner cannot have Case 2 dismissed under *claim* preclusion. (Why?[163]) But wait a minute! *P* is saying that Owner is vicariously liable for Driver's negligence, but in Case 1 Driver was found *not* negligent! Can Owner assert issue preclusion against *P* on the issue of Driver's not being negligent? Let's see:
  - All the basic requirements for issue preclusion are satisfied: (1) Case 1 ended in a valid final judgment on the merits; (2) in Case 1, the issue of Driver's negligence was litigated and determined; and (3) the finding on that issue was essential to the judgment in Case 1. So far, so good.
  - In addition, the invocation of issue preclusion would not violate due process. Owner is asserting issue preclusion against *P*, and *P* was a party to Case 1, so due process is satisfied.
  - The problem is mutuality. Issue preclusion here is being asserted *by* Owner, who was not a party to Case 1. Under the mutuality doctrine, Owner cannot use issue preclusion, so Case 2 would go forward. Let's run with this a bit further and assume that Case 2 proceeds.

---

[162]Of course, *P* could avoid this merry-go-round by suing both Driver and Owner as defendants in a single case. But, as we see in §12.4, the joinder rules do not require *P* to do so. Here we will proceed on the assumption that *P* sues only one defendant in Case 1.

[163]Because one requirement for claim preclusion is that Case 1 and Case 2 be brought by the same claimant against the same defendant. See §11.2.1. On the other hand, if Driver and Owner were considered to be in privity, claim preclusion would apply. Why? Because then Case 1 and Case 2 would be treated as though they were brought against the same defendant. Historically, courts have not deemed indemnitors and indemnitees (like Driver and Owner) to be in privity. For this reason, claim preclusion did not apply and the courts endeavored to find an exception to mutuality to allow Owner at least to assert issue preclusion. Professor Koppel has demonstrated, however, that there is a significant trend toward expanding the notion of privity to include the relationship of indemnitor and indemnitee (including employee and employer). Thus, as he convincingly argues, cases such as the one in this Example should be decided on the basis of claim preclusion as opposed to issue preclusion. Glenn S. Koppel, *The Case for Nonmutual Privity in Vicarious Liability Relationships: Pushing the Frontiers of the Law of Claim Preclusion,* 39 Campbell L. Rev. 1 (2017).

- There are two possible outcomes of Case 2. For one, Owner might win, by convincing the fact-finder that Driver was not negligent. If this happens, the system will have accommodated two suits about the same issue, but the results of Case 1 and Case 2 would be consistent.
- But the other possibility is that Owner loses, because the fact-finder in Case 2 finds that Driver was negligent and that Owner is vicariously liable for it. Now what happens? Nothing good. Presumably, Owner pays the judgment to P and then sues Driver to get indemnified for the loss. If she wins, Driver ends up paying for damage in an accident that, according to Case 1, she did not cause. If she loses, however, Owner ends up paying for a judgment the law says is not her primary responsibility.

This latter scenario is a disaster. Failing to allow Owner to use issue preclusion in Case 2 can lead only to two undesirable outcomes: either (1) Driver's victory in Case 1 is rendered meaningless, or (2) Owner's right to indemnification is rendered meaningless. To avoid these bad outcomes, common law courts felt compelled to recognize what is usually called the *narrow exception* to the mutuality rule. The narrow exception is truly narrow. *It applies only in a vicarious liability situation in which the primarily liable party is found not negligent*[164] *in Case 1*. Only in that instance does Case 2 lead to the two undesirable outcomes that may be avoided by allowing Owner to use issue preclusion in Case 2. Today, while there are states that have not outrightly *rejected* the mutuality doctrine, apparently every state will allow nonmutual issue preclusion in this situation.

Common law courts developed another exception to mutuality, also applicable only in vicarious liability cases. It involves a variation on the fact pattern above.

- ***Example #29.*** In Case 1, P sues Owner, the vicariously liable party. After litigation, Owner wins a valid final judgment on the merits, because the fact-finder expressly finds that Driver was not negligent and thus that Owner cannot be vicariously liable. In Case 2, P sues Driver, asserting that Driver's negligence injured her. As in Example #28, the traditional view is that Driver cannot assert claim preclusion.[165] What about issue preclusion? After all, the issue of her negligence was litigated and determined in Case 1 and satisfies all the requirements for issue preclusion. In addition, because P was a party to Case 1, issue preclusion would not violate due process. The problem, as above, is mutuality. Under the mutuality doctrine, Driver could not assert issue preclusion, because she was not a party to Case 1.

---

[164]Or the plaintiff is found contributorily negligent.
[165]See note 163 above.

Recognizing an exception to mutuality in this fact pattern is not as compelling as it was in Example #28. There, failing to allow issue preclusion led to additional litigation concerning Owner's right to indemnification from Driver. Here, failing to allow issue preclusion will not create such additional litigation. If Driver is not allowed to assert issue preclusion, she may lose Case 2 at trial and be held liable. But that will be the end of the matter. Driver will not be able to sue Owner, because Owner does not owe indemnification to Driver. Accordingly, the policy that compelled the narrow exception does not apply here. Nonetheless, some courts have recognized what is usually called the *broad exception* to mutuality, by which they permit Driver to assert issue preclusion in Case 2. Such courts thus will reject mutuality in vicarious liability cases, even if Case 1 was against the vicariously liable party and that party won.

It is important to remember two things about the narrow and broad exceptions to mutuality. First, they are just that—*exceptions* to the general rule that mutuality is required. Second, they apply only in cases involving indemnification rights. Thus, they do not touch the majority of cases. In the mid-twentieth century, some courts took the next step. Instead of searching for an exception to mutuality, they would simply reject the requirement, at least in certain circumstances.

Rejection of Mutuality for Defendants (Nonmutual Defensive Issue Preclusion)

The California Supreme Court led the way in the rejection of mutuality with the landmark opinion by Justice Roger Traynor in *Bernhard v. Bank of America*.[166] The case involved the estate of an elderly woman. For some time before her death, the woman lived with a married couple named Cook. She gave Mr. Cook authority to write checks on her behalf from one of her accounts. Mr. Cook wrote a large check to himself (and his wife) from the account and put the money in his personal account. After the woman died, Mr. Cook became the executor of the woman's estate. In Case 1, the woman's relatives sued to challenge his accounting of the estate, insisting that he return the money he had taken from her account. After litigation, the court expressly found that Mr. Cook had had the woman's permission to take the money as a gift. It entered judgment in his favor.

Later, Mr. Cook resigned as executor and one of the woman's daughters was appointed executrix of the estate. In Case 2, she sued the bank that had handled the woman's checking account. She asserted that her mother had never authorized Mr. Cook's taking money from the account,

---

[166]122 P.2d 892 (Cal. 1942).

and thus that the bank was liable to the estate for that amount. The question was whether the bank could assert issue preclusion on the finding that the woman had given the money to the Cooks as a gift. Under the mutuality doctrine, of course, issue preclusion could not be invoked, because it was being asserted by the bank, which was not a party to Case 1. Issue preclusion was likewise impossible under the exceptions we just saw, because those apply only in vicarious liability cases.

Nonetheless, the California Supreme Court let the bank assert issue preclusion. Justice Traynor said, "No satisfactory rationalization has been advanced for the requirement of mutuality. Just why a party who was not bound by a previous action should be precluded from asserting it as *res judicata*[167] against a party who was bound by it is difficult to comprehend."[168] Again, the court did not try to find an exception to mutuality; it just rejected it. Thus, nonmutual preclusion was available beyond the vicarious liability cases.

But is issue preclusion *always* available to someone in Case 2, regardless of whether she was a party (or in privity with a party) in Case 1? No. For starters, remember that every state is free to determine its own preclusion rules, so long as those rules do not violate constitutional guarantees. Beyond this caveat, courts have emphasized that preclusion of any sort, including nonmutual preclusion, requires that the person against whom it is asserted had a full and fair opportunity to litigate in Case 1. See §11.4.4.

The Supreme Court embraced *Bernhard* in its explication of federal law of issue preclusion in *Blonder-Tongue Laboratories, Inc. v. University of Illinois Foundation*.[169] *Blonder-Tongue* involved the alleged infringement of a patent (which is a federally granted monopoly to use one's invention). In Case 1, the plaintiff sued one defendant (*D-1*), alleging that *D-1* infringed the plaintiff's patent. After litigation, the court entered a valid final judgment on the merits in favor of *D-1*, based upon its express finding that the plaintiff's patent was invalid. In Case 2, the plaintiff sued a different defendant (*D-2*), alleging that it had infringed the same patent. Obviously, *D-2* wanted to assert issue preclusion on the finding in Case 1 that the patent was invalid. Just as obviously, though the basic requirements for issue preclusion were met, the mutuality rule would not permit *D-2* to use it. *D-2* had not been a party to Case 1. Moreover, the exceptions to mutuality would not apply, because the case did not involve vicarious liability.

---

[167]Remember that courts often use "*res judicata*" in a generic sense to refer to preclusion. See §11.1.

[168]*Bernhard*, 122 P.2d at 895.

[169]402 U.S. 313 (1971). In addition to each state having its own preclusion law, there is a federal common law of preclusion. For discussion of when it applies, see §§11.6.1, 11.6.4, and 11.6.5.

The Supreme Court permitted *D-2* to use issue preclusion. The opinion relied in considerable part on *Bernhard* and rejected mutuality while employing an express safeguard. The Court recognized that relitigation imposes a burden on the judicial system and raised the possibility that avoiding that burden might justify jettisoning the mutuality rule.[170] Importantly, however, the Court then noted, "it is clear that more than crowded dockets is involved."[171]

> The broader question is whether it is any longer tenable to afford a litigant more than one full and fair opportunity for judicial resolution of the same issue . . . . Permitting repeated litigation of the same issue as long as the supply of unrelated defendants holds out reflects either the aura of the gaming table or "a lack of discipline and of disinterestedness on the part of the lower courts, hardly a worthy or wise basis for fashioning rules of procedure." Though neither judges, the parties, nor the adversary system performs perfectly in all cases, the requirement of determining whether the party against whom an estoppel is asserted had a full and fair opportunity to litigate [in Case 1] is a most significant safeguard.[172]

Thus, the Court concluded that the system of justice affords a litigant one full and fair opportunity to litigate an issue. Once that protection has been afforded, the litigant may be bound by the finding on that issue in subsequent litigation, even by persons who were not parties (or in privity with a party) to Case 1. Though some observers suggested that the holding in *Blonder-Tongue* should be limited to patent cases, lower courts have not limited the holding in that way.[173]

Bernhard and *Blonder-Tongue* involved "nonmutual defensive issue preclusion." "Nonmutual" means that issue preclusion is being used by one who was not a party to Case 1. "Defensive" means that the person using issue preclusion in Case 2 is the defendant. (Some refer to it as using nonmutual issue preclusion "as a shield," because it is being used by a defendant.) Federal law (through *Blonder-Tongue*) and the law of most (but apparently not all) states allows nonmutual defensive issue preclusion, as long as the party against whom it is used in Case 2 was afforded a full and fair opportunity to litigate in Case 1.

But neither the *Bernhard* nor the *Blonder-Tongue* opinion expressly limited its holding to the nonmutual defensive situation. They thus

---

[170]Later in the opinion, the Court seemed to conclude that any saving to the judicial system was "an incidental matter" and merely "de minimis." *Blonder-Tongue*, 402 U.S. at 348, 349.

[171]*Id.* at 328-329.

[172]*Id.* at 329, quoting Kerotest Mfg. Co. v. C-O Two Co., 342 U.S. 180, 185 (1952).

[173]*See, e.g.*, Miller Brewing Co. v. Joseph Schlitz Brewing Co., 605 F.2d 990, 995 (7th Cir. 1979); Hallal v. Hopkins, 947 F. Supp. 978, 989-990 (S.D. Miss. 1995).

left open the possibility that a *claimant* ought to be permitted to use nonmutual issue preclusion. That is the next, and most controversial, step in the development of this area of the law.

Rejection of Mutuality for Claimants (Nonmutual Offensive Issue Preclusion)

In the wake of cases embracing nonmutual defensive issue preclusion, some commentators started to consider problems that might arise if *claimants* were permitted to use nonmutual issue preclusion.[174] Such use is usually called *nonmutual offensive issue preclusion.* "Nonmutual," as we know, means the person using issue preclusion was not a party to Case 1. "Offensive" means that the person using issue preclusion in Case 2 is a claimant (usually the plaintiff).[175]

The problems came to light especially in mass tort cases.

○ ***Example #30.*** A commercial airplane operated by Airline crashes, injuring 100 passengers. In Case 1, one of the passengers (*P-1*) sued Airline. The case was litigated, and a valid final judgment on the merits was entered in favor of Airline; the fact-finder expressly found that Airline was not negligent. In Case 2, another passenger (*P-2*) sued Airline regarding her injuries from the crash. Can Airline use issue preclusion on the finding that it was not negligent? The answer is no. Why? Because of due process! Airline is attempting to use issue preclusion *against P-2*, who was not a party to Case 1 (and was not in privity with *P-1* by any of the definitions we saw in §11.4.4). This hypothetical raises no problem of mutuality; issue preclusion is being asserted *by* Airline, which was a party to Case 1.

This hypothetical points out, as we saw in §11.4.4, that due process imposes a huge burden on the defendant. To escape liability, Airline would have to win all 100 cases involving the 100 passengers. Because of due process, it can never use issue preclusion against a successive plaintiff.

○ ***Example #31.*** Assume the same facts about the plane crash and that in Case 1, *P-1* sues Airline. The case is litigated and a valid final judgment on the merits was entered in favor of *P-1*; the fact-finder expressly found that Airline was negligent and that its negligence was the proximate cause of *P-1*'s negligence. In Case 2, *P-2* sues Airline. Can *P-2* use issue preclusion on the finding that Airline was negligent? All the

---

[174]The classic article raising such concerns in the wake is Brainerd Currie, *Mutuality of Collateral Estoppel: Limits on the* Bernhard *Doctrine*, 9 Stan. L. Rev. 281 (1957).

[175]Remember, all plaintiffs are claimants but not all claimants are plaintiffs. See text accompanying note 15 above.

basic requirements are satisfied, and issue preclusion is being asserted against Airline, which was a party to Case 1, so due process is satisfied. The problem here is mutuality—issue preclusion is being asserted *by* someone who was not a party to Case 1.

Notice the policy choices raised by this example. If the court follows the mutuality rule, each of the 100 plaintiffs will be required to prove Airline's negligence. The same issue will be litigated, in theory, 100 separate times. Inconsistent results seem inescapable—that is, some plaintiffs will win and some plaintiffs will lose—which would foster the sense that the judicial system is little more than gambling, as Jeremy Bentham said so long ago (see text accompanying note 162 above). Thus, permitting *P-2* to use issue preclusion will foster efficiency and consistency. But at what cost?

Allowing a claimant to use nonmutual issue preclusion means that Airline can be held negligent in 100 separate cases simply by losing Case 1. If *P-1* proves that Airline was negligent and subsequent plaintiffs can use issue preclusion on that finding, *P-2* through *P-100* will not have to prove negligence in their cases.[176] It is the worst of all worlds for Airline: If it loses in Case 1, 99 other plaintiffs can use the finding of its negligence against it; if it wins, however, none of these 99 plaintiffs is bound. Airline can be hurt by issue preclusion but cannot be helped by it. Should the judicial system force Airline to face potentially massive liability on the strength of one adverse finding? The problem can be refined by changing some facts.

> *__Example #32.__* Suppose the first ten passengers bring individual suits against Airline. Airline wins all ten, with the fact-finder in each case expressly finding that Airline was not negligent. Now *P-11* sues Airline. Because of due process, as we have seen, Airline cannot use issue preclusion against *P-11*, so all issues are litigated. Assume *P-11* wins a valid final judgment on the merits, with an express finding that Airline was negligent. Now, can *P-12* through *P-100* use issue preclusion against Airline in their cases? After all, *P-11* won by establishing an issue that *P-12* through *P-100* must establish.

Allowing nonmutual issue preclusion by these claimants seems especially problematic. Why? Because in 10 of 11 cases, Airline was found not negligent. So the finding that Airline was negligent seems like a fluke—an aberration. Why should the legal system repose great

---

[176]Presumably, at least in a contributory negligence state, the issue of whether the individual plaintiff was negligent would have to be litigated in each case. But issue preclusion on Airline's negligence would be a huge step toward each plaintiff's recovering against Airline.

685

faith in it? On the other hand, if *P-1* won, how can we be sure it was not a fluke?

Courts have had these sorts of issues in mind when they addressed whether to permit nonmutual offensive issue preclusion. The leading opinion is *Parklane Hosiery Co. v. Shore*,[177] in which the Supreme Court adopted nonmutual offensive issue preclusion, with several safeguards, as federal law. *Parklane* involved the violation of federal securities laws by a corporation and some of its managers. In Case 1, the Securities and Exchange Commission (SEC) filed a federal civil action against the various defendants, alleging that the defendants had issued a materially false and misleading proxy statement in connection with a merger. The SEC sought only equitable relief. After trial, the court entered a valid final judgment on the merits, based upon the express finding that the proxy statement was materially false and misleading as alleged. In Case 2, private plaintiffs sued the same defendants on the same claim concerning the same proxy statement. They sought damages. The plaintiffs in Case 2 wanted issue preclusion on the finding that the defendants had issued a materially false and misleading proxy statement. Under the mutuality doctrine, they would not be able to use issue preclusion, because they were not parties to Case 1.

In the course of its opinion, the Court contrasted the potential efficiency of nonmutual *defensive* issue preclusion with the potential inefficiency of nonmutual *offensive* issue preclusion. The defensive use of issue preclusion (as in *Bernhard* and *Blonder-Tongue*) gives the claimant an incentive to join all potential defendants in Case 1. After all, if the claimant fails to do so, and loses Case 1, the defendant in Case 2 can use the adverse finding against the claimant in Case 2. Thus, recognizing nonmutual defensive issue preclusion probably promotes efficient joinder of Case 1 — the claimant will probably join all potential defendants in that case.

But the offensive version creates the opposite effect. It counsels potential claimants *not* to join in as a party to Case 1. Why? Because by staying out of Case 1, a potential claimant risks nothing and may gain something. If *P-1* loses in Case 1, *P-2* is not bound by the judgment in that case (because of due process). But if *P-1* wins in Case 1, and the court recognizes nonmutual offensive issue preclusion, *P-2* can use *P-1*'s victory to her own advantage in Case 2. Thus, this type of preclusion "will likely increase rather than decrease the total amount of litigation, since potential [claimants] will have everything to gain and nothing to lose" by not joining in Case 1.[178] The answer is not to

[177]439 U.S. 322 (1979).
[178]439 U.S. at 330.

prohibit the use of nonmutual offensive issue preclusion, but to apply it only in cases in which it will not "reward a private plaintiff who could have joined in [Case 1]."[179]

Moreover, the Court expressed concern that nonmutual offensive issue preclusion might be unfair to a defendant in various circumstances. It provided three paradigms. First, a defendant who is sued in Case 1 for a small amount of money might have little incentive to defend with vigor, especially if she foresees no other litigation concerning the event. If she lost Case 1, it would be unfair to allow issue preclusion in Case 2 where the claimant seeks a large recovery.[180] Second, if there had been multiple judgments concerning the underlying events, it would be unfair to allow a claimant to get issue preclusion from one in which the defendant was found liable and to ignore another in which the defendant won. And third, preclusion would be unfair if the defendant in Case 1 did not have a full and fair opportunity to litigate in Case 1. This latter point is consistent with a safeguard we saw in nonmutual defensive issue preclusion. (Indeed, no preclusion of any sort ought to be accorded if the person against whom it is sought did not have such an opportunity in Case 1. See §11.4.4.)

In the final analysis, the Court in *Parklane* embraced nonmutual offensive issue preclusion, but only in cases in which these concerns could be allayed. And such was the case in *Parklane* itself. First, it was not a case in which allowing preclusion would promote inefficient litigation. The plaintiffs in Case 2 could not have joined in Case 1 because Case 1 was brought by the SEC and private plaintiffs would not have been permitted. Second, none of the three examples of unfairness was present. One, given the seriousness of the allegations in Case 1, and the clear foreseeability that private plaintiffs would sue if the SEC won Case 1, the defendants had every incentive to litigate vigorously in Case 1. Two, there were no inconsistent judgments on the books; the only judgment was unfavorable to the defendants. And three, there were no procedural opportunities available in Case 2 that were not available to the defendants in Case 1. Thus, the Court concluded, "none of the considerations that would justify a refusal to allow the use of offensive collateral estoppel is present in this case."[181]

Interestingly, the Court saw no unfairness in the fact that the use of issue preclusion in *Parklane* robbed the defendant of a right to jury trial on the issue of whether its proxy statement was misleading. That issue was decided by the court in the case brought by the SEC; because that case sought equitable remedies, however, there was no

---

[179]*Id.* at 331-332.
[180]*See* 18 Moore's Federal Practice 132-144.
[181]*Parklane*, 439 U.S. at 332.

right to jury trial. In the ensuing case in federal court, the defendant would have had a Seventh Amendment right to jury trial on that question. Employing issue preclusion to establish the issue meant that the defendant was never entitled to have a jury determine the facts. The Court did not consider this to be a procedural unfairness that rendered issue preclusion unavailable.

Parklane stands for the proposition that nonmutual offensive issue preclusion is appropriate, but only if the court in Case 2 is convinced (1) that the party using issue preclusion could not "easily have joined in the earlier action" and (2) that use of issue preclusion is not unfair to the defendant. While these are reasonable and sensible safeguards limiting the wholesale use of nonmutual offensive issue preclusion, it is unfortunate that the Supreme Court has not revisited the topic to give further guidance. Suppose, for instance, that the claimant in Case 2 could have intervened into Case 1 but did not do so. Does that failure result in forfeiting the privilege of seeking issue preclusion? The *Parklane* opinion characterized it as a "general rule" that one who could have joined easily in Case 1 should not be able to use issue preclusion in Case 2. But the Court gave no guidance on exceptions to this "general rule."

Moreover, exactly what did the Court mean when it spoke of whether the claimant in Case 2 could have joined easily in Case 1? In the usual private civil litigation context, Case 1 will not be brought by a government agency like the SEC, but by a private plaintiff. Presumably, any other potential plaintiff could intervene into that case if she desired. But what if Case 1 is pending in Baltimore and the other potential plaintiff lives in Indianapolis? She could intervene, but it might not be convenient. Does this matter? Again, the Court did not say.

The judicial acceptance of nonmutual offensive issue preclusion — with the limits laid out in *Parklane* — has led to a litigation strategy that might be called *plaintiff shopping*. The attorneys for numerous potential claimants might agree to have the strongest case go to judgment first, so the subsequent claimants can "ride" the successful judgment through nonmutual offensive issue preclusion.[182]

Though *Parklane* has been on the books since 1979, it does not represent the universal (or maybe not even the majority) view. It reflects federal law and an emerging trend,[183] but several states have rejected

---

[182]Though lawyers adopted this strategy in some of the asbestos litigation in the 1970s and 1980s, courts did not permit preclusion to the extent some had predicted. *See* Michael Green, *The Inability of Offensive Collateral Estoppel to Fulfill Its Promise: An Examination of Estoppel in Asbestos Litigation*, 70 Iowa L. Rev. 141 (1984).

[183]*See, e.g.,* Bowen v. Arnold, 502 S.W.3d 102, 115-116 (Tenn. 2016); Garrity v. Md. State Bd.of Plumbing, 135 A.3d 452, 459 (Md. 2016); Exotics Hawaii-Kona, Inc. v. E.I. du Pont de Nemours & Co., 90 P.3d 250, 259-260 (Haw. 2004); Johnson v. Union P. R.R.,

nonmutual offensive issue preclusion[184] and a substantial number appear not to have not addressed the issue after *Parklane*.

Let's wrap up this section by returning to two fact patterns we raised earlier.

> ○ ***Example #33.*** A commercial airplane operated by Airline crashes, injuring 100 passengers. In Case 1, one passenger (*P-1*) sues Airline. The case is litigated and a valid final judgment on the merits is entered in favor of *P-1*; the fact-finder expressly found that Airline was negligent and that its negligence was the proximate cause of *P-1*'s injuries. In Case 2, a second passenger (*P-2*) sues Airline. Can *P-2* use issue preclusion on the finding that Airline was negligent?

For starters, the basic requirements for issue preclusion (Case 1 ended in a valid final judgment on the merits, the issue of Airline's negligence was litigated and determined, and the finding on that issue was essential to the judgment in Case 1) are all satisfied. Next, there is no problem with due process, because preclusion is being asserted against Airline, which was a party to Case 1. But the assertion of preclusion here is nonmutual—it is being made by someone (*P-2*) who was not a party to Case 1. And it is offensive—it is being asserted by a claimant in Case 2. Should nonmutual offensive issue preclusion be permitted?

The answer depends upon the applicable law. If we are applying the law of a state that adopts only the exceptions to mutuality, this assertion will not be permitted. Why? Because the exceptions apply only in vicarious liability situations (not so here) and, even then, only to assertions of issue preclusion by a defendant. If we are applying the law of a state that adopts only *Bernhard* or *Blonder-Tongue*, the answer is also no. Why? Because those cases permit only nonmutual *defensive* issue

---

104 S.W.3d 745, 751 (Ark. 2003); Briggs v. Newton, 984 P.2d 1113, 1120 (Alaska 1999); Tofany v. NBS Imaging Sys., Inc., 616 N.E.2d 1034, 1048 (Ind. 1993); State Mut. Ins. Co. v. Bragg, 589 A.2d 35, 37 (Me. 1991); Property & Cas. Inc. Guar. Ass'n v. Walmart Stores, Inc., 403 S.E.2d 625, 629 (S.C. 1991); Silva v. State, 745 P.2d 380, 384 (N.M. 1987); Oates v. Safeco Ins. Co., 583 S.W.2d 713, 719 (Mo. 1979); Preferred Am. Ins. v. Dulceak, 706 N.E.2d 529, 532 (Ill. App. Ct. 1999).

[184]*See, e.g.*, Ex parte Flexible Prods. Co., 915 So. 2d 34, 45 (Ala. 2005) ("Although the federal courts have held that mutuality—the requirement that the parties in both actions be the same—is no longer a prerequisite, Alabama continues to require that a party may be barred from relitigating an issue, such as duty or breach, only if that issue has previously been found adversely to that same party"); Goodson v. McDonough Power Equip., Inc., 443 N.E.2d 978, 987 (Ohio 1983) ("[W]e reaffirm our prior general stance that collateral estoppel may generally be applied only when the party seeking to use the prior judgment and the party against whom the judgment is being asserted were parties to the original judgment or in privity with those parties"); Trappell v. Sysco Food Servs., 850 S.W.2d 529, 543 (Tex. App. 1992).

preclusion. So only if we are in a jurisdiction that adopts the *Parklane* approach is there any chance to have preclusion here.

Now, if we are in a *Parklane* jurisdiction, we must assess the factors given in that case. First, if *P-2* could have joined in Case 1, the Court indicated, she should not be permitted to use preclusion. To let her do so would reward a "wait and see" attitude that fosters inefficient litigation. On the other hand, as noted, the Court did not say that failure to join always led to forfeiture of issue preclusion. Moreover, it did not say whether this factor alone would obviate preclusion even if the other factors counseled in favor of preclusion. And here the other factors seem to do just that. One, Case 1 was for a serious claim, and Airline knew that the crash injured 100 people, so it is clear that it had every incentive to litigate vigorously and could foresee future litigation by the other passengers. Two, there are no inconsistent judgments on the books here, so *P-2* is not simply picking a finding she likes and ignoring those that hurt her cause. And three, there is no indication that Airline did not have a full and fair opportunity to litigate in Case 1. So where does that leave us? Again, it depends upon how one weighs the factors.

> ○ ***Example #34.*** Suppose the first ten passengers bring individual suits against Airline. Airline wins all ten, with the fact-finder in each case expressly finding that Airline was not negligent. Now *P-11* sues Airline. Because of due process, as we have seen, Airline cannot use issue preclusion against *P-11*, so all issues are litigated. Assume *P-11* wins a valid final judgment on the merits, with an express finding that Airline was negligent. Now, can *P-12* through *P-100* get issue preclusion against Airline in their cases?

Here, the preliminary analyses are the same as above regarding the basic requirements of issue preclusion, due process, and whether nonmutual offensive issue preclusion would be permitted. Only in a *Parklane* jurisdiction is it even arguable. Under *Parklane*, would such preclusion be allowed? Again, we have the problem of not knowing exactly what the Court meant when it assessed whether a later claimant could have joined in an earlier case. Beyond that, however, here we have inconsistent judgments. Airline has won ten times. It has lost only once. It seems grossly unfair to allow *P-12* through *P-100* to take advantage of this one holding. The second of the three "fairness" factors seems to counsel against use of preclusion here. This case is fairly easy because it seems that the judgment in the eleventh case was an aberration. We should not repose much confidence in it.

That fact leaves unanswered the big question, however. Assume *P-1* wins in Case 1. Because it is first, there are no inconsistent judgments on the books, and the argument in favor of applying preclusion is stronger under *Parklane*. But how do we know that this judgment is not the fluke? Maybe, if all 100 cases were litigated separately, Airline would win the other 99. *Parklane* does not tell us why we should repose such great confidence in a single judgment. Perhaps nervousness over this point explains why some jurisdictions have never embraced nonmutual offensive issue preclusion. One way around the problem would be to have a test case (or group of test cases) go through trial to see which way the wind is blowing, as a means of ultimately settling the overall disputes. (We discussed the test case as part of the consideration of *Taylor v. Sturgell* in §11.4.4.)

§11.5 Exceptions to the Operation of Preclusion

§11.5.1 In General

Courts have recognized exceptions to the application of each doctrine. Most of these exceptions are quite narrow. It is inherent in the operation of both claim and issue preclusion that the party against whom preclusion is to be applied in Case 2 had a full and fair opportunity to present its position in Case 1. Thus, the most obvious exception to the operation of preclusion arises in those relatively rare cases in which a party was not accorded a full and fair opportunity to litigate in Case 1. Examples include failure to give appropriate notice to a party in Case 1, gross misconduct (often referred to as "fraud on the court") by another litigant or participant, and egregious error by the court itself in Case 1.[185] Such things may obviate the operation of claim and issue preclusion.[186]

Suppose the controlling principles of law are changed between the entry of judgment in Case 1 and the resolution of Case 2. Should the change in law weaken the application of preclusion, or should the judgment in Case 1 have preclusive consequences in Case 2? The quick answer, subject to a narrow exception discussed below with regard to issue preclusion, is that the change in law does not excuse the operation of claim or issue preclusion.

Courts occasionally are tempted to recognize some *ad hoc* exception to the operation of preclusion in the general interest of "fairness,"

---

[185]*See, e.g.*, United States v. Pueblo of Taos, 515 F.2d 1404, 1407 (Ct. Cl. 1975) (decision by administrative agency concerning Indian lands "probably was tainted" by failing to give a full and fair opportunity to litigate).

[186]It would also be appropriate to raise these sorts of issues in a motion to set aside the judgment in Case 1. We discussed such motions, made under Federal Rule 60(b), at §9.7.

"simple justice," or some similar amorphous notion. As a general rule (and as emphasized by the Supreme Court), such open-ended exceptions are less appropriate with claim preclusion than with issue preclusion. Why? Because the cost to the judicial system is greater when there is an exception to claim preclusion. Recall that claim preclusion is the broader of the two preclusion doctrines and that invocation of claim preclusion usually results in dismissal of Case 2. Thus, recognizing an exception to claim preclusion results in the filing of a case that otherwise would not have been filed. On the other hand, issue preclusion operates to foreclose the litigation only of an issue in Case 2; it streamlines the scope of litigation of a case that will be filed anyway. So recognizing an exception to issue preclusion will not cause the filing of a case that would otherwise not be filed.[187]

§11.5.2   Exceptions to Claim Preclusion

The principal exceptions to claim preclusion are catalogued in §26(1) of the Restatement (Second) of Judgments. One is when either the defendant or the court in Case 1 agrees to allow the claimant to split her claim. Thus, courts generally allow parties to Case 1 to consent that the claimant will split her claim without claim preclusive effect.[188] This recognition allows parties, for example, to simplify litigation by limiting it to one aspect of a claim, while negotiating settlement to the remainder of the claim pending outcome. Obviously, a defendant who consents to such splitting cannot complain that she has lost the protection from multiple litigation that claim preclusion is designed to give her. Express consent of this sort is usually expressed in a settlement agreement or in a consent decree, and common principles of contract interpretation govern to determine the parties' intent. Consent may be implied as well. Because preclusion is an affirmative defense,[189] the defendant might waive a claim preclusion objection by acquiescing in multiple suits on the same claim.[190] Moreover, though the preclusive effect of a judgment is to be determined by the court in Case 2, the court in Case 1 might expressly reserve a claimant's right to split her claim.[191]

Another exception applies if the claimant in Case 1 could not have sought all rights to relief for her claim because of limitations imposed

---

[187]*See* 18 Wright & Miller 385 ("exceptions to issue preclusion may be justified by correspondingly reduced showing of public interest or private justice").

[188]Restatement (Second) of Judgments §26(1)(a).

[189]Fed. R. Civ. P. 8(c)(1). See notes 5 and 6 above.

[190]18 Moore's Federal Practice §131.24[1].

[191]Restatement (Second) of Judgments §26(1)(b).

on the court in Case 1.[192] For instance, if the applicable joinder rules did not permit the claimant to seek damages and injunctive relief in a single case, it would not be fair to impose claim preclusion when the claimant sought one form of relief in Case 1 and a different form in Case 2. More commonly, such limitations on the court in Case 1 will be subject matter jurisdiction rules in a state court.

- o **_Example #35._** *P*, riding her bicycle, was struck by a car driven by *D*. *P* suffered personal injuries and her bike, worth $300, was ruined. In Case 1, *P* sues *D* for property damage, in a state small claims court, which by state law cannot entertain claims exceeding $1,500. *P* wins a judgment for $300. In Case 2, *P* sues *D* to recover $15,000 damages for her personal injuries from the wreck. She files Case 2 in a different state trial court, this one having jurisdiction of claims exceeding $1,500. *D* asserts that Case 2 should be dismissed under the doctrine of claim preclusion, properly noting that the jurisdiction has adopted a transactional test for claim preclusion. The requirements for claim preclusion are met, but can *P* avoid dismissal by invoking an exception to claim preclusion?

On the face of it, the argument for an exception seems sound. After all, because of limitations on subject matter jurisdiction, the court in Case 1 could not have entertained the assertion for damages for personal injuries; the claim would have exceeded the amount in controversy that could be heard in the small claims court. But suppose *P* could have sought relief for both personal injuries and property damage in a single case in the court having jurisdiction of claims exceeding $1,500. Thus, *P* could have achieved efficient joinder in one case in that court. Instead, she chose an inefficient route, one that would force *D* to defend twice. Some courts faced with such a situation reject the argument for an exception and dismiss Case 2 under claim preclusion.[193] Only if state law would not have allowed *P* to bring both assertions in a single case in some court should the exception be recognized.

Closely related to this notion is an exception that recognizes that claim preclusion would be contrary to the appropriate implementation of a constitutional or statutory scheme.[194] Under the Bankruptcy Code, for instance, only certain matters qualify for expedited hearing. The courts have concluded that a claimant proceeding in an expedited hearing on such a matter is not precluded from bringing a separate

---

[192]Restatement (Second) of Judgments §26(1)(c).

[193]*See, e.g.*, Mells v. Billops, 482 A.2d 759, 761 (Del. Super. 1984) (plaintiff "voluntarily chose a court of limited jurisdiction when he could have presented all of his claims . . . had he brought the original action in this Court").

[194]Restatement (Second) of Judgments, §26(1)(d).

action regarding related matters.[195] The scheme established by the Bankruptcy Code envisioned bifurcation of matters in this way. Courts have reached a similar conclusion concerning cases brought under the Declaratory Judgment Act, which we discussed at §4.6.3. A claimant seeking declaratory judgment is asking the court to declare the relative rights of the parties; she is not asking for "coercive" relief, such as damages or an injunction. Seeking declaratory judgment, as a general rule, will not preclude the claimant's later action for coercive relief.[196] (Remember, though, that even if claim preclusion might not bar a second case, issue preclusion from Case 1 might preclude relitigation of particular issues in Case 2.[197])

Suppose that when the claimant files Case 1 she is unaware of the full extent of her injuries. Suppose further that this ignorance causes her to seek only some of the aspects of her claim in Case 1. Can she bring Case 2 to seek recovery for those harms of which she was ignorant in Case 1, or does claim preclusion bar her from a second proceeding? There is some support for the conclusion that claim preclusion should not apply here. In 1978, the Hawaii Supreme Court opined that the majority of jurisdictions "will not bar claims of which the plaintiff was ignorant . . . unless plaintiff's ignorance was due to her own negligence."[198] The opinion relied upon cases that were several decades old, however, and it is arguable that none of those opinions actually established such a liberal rule.[199] The majority view seems to require more of the claimant who is attempting to avoid claim preclusion; she must show that "fraud, concealment, or misrepresentation . . . cause[d] the [claimant] to fail to include a claim in a former action."[200] This tougher approach reflects the modern concern

[195]In re Hooker Investments, Inc., 131 B.R. 922, 929-930 (Bankr. S.D.N.Y. 1991).

[196]See, e.g., Harborside Refrigerated Servs., Inc. v. Vogel, 959 F.2d 368, 373 (2d Cir. 1992). This rule assumes that the claimant did not seek coercive relief in the same action with the request for declaratory judgment. If she did, any subsequent effort to seek coercive relief would be subject to claim preclusion.

[197]And issue preclusion might prove determinative of Case 2. Suppose, for example, that in Case 1, for declaratory judgment, the parties litigate and the court determines that the defendant did nothing wrong and that the claimant was at fault. Though Case 2 may not be dismissed under claim preclusion, the findings on these issues, established through issue preclusion, will be determinative of Case 2; the defendant will win.

[198]Bolte v. Aits, Inc., 587 P.2d 810, 813-814 (Haw. 1978).

[199]See, e.g., McVay v. Castenara, 152 Miss. 106, 113-114 (1928) (noting lack of pleading of issues on applicability of claim preclusion and exception); Badger v. Badger, 69 Utah 293, 300-301 (1927) (refusing to apply an exception to claim preclusion; appellant).

[200]Harnett v. Billman, 800 F.2d 1308, 1313 (4th Cir. 1986). This helpful opinion was written by Judge Dickson Phillips, who taught Civil Procedure for years at the University of North Carolina School of Law, where he also served as Dean. The position espoused in *Harnett* is reflected in Restatement (Second) of Judgments §26, cmt j.

with the policies underlying claim preclusion in an era of crowded dockets.[201]

Beyond these relatively specific exceptions to the operation of claim preclusion, some courts have attempted to create an exception based upon broad concepts of fairness. The Supreme Court slammed the door on the development of such open-ended exceptions, however, in *Federated Department Stores, Inc. v. Moitie*.[202] In that case, purchasers brought several actions against operators of department stores, alleging that the defendants violated federal antitrust law by agreeing to fix prices to be charged to retail customers. In Case 1,[203] the district court dismissed because the plaintiffs could not demonstrate that they suffered a harm recognized by the antitrust laws. The disappointed plaintiffs reacted in different ways. Some of them (Group 1) appealed the judgment of dismissal to the Ninth Circuit. Others (Group 2), however, brought Case 2, which simply reasserted their original claim in state court; the defendants removed to federal court, and the federal court dismissed under claim preclusion—after all, the Group 2 plaintiffs were asserting the same claim as they did in Case 1. The Group 2 plaintiffs then appealed the dismissal of Case 2 to the Ninth Circuit.

While both sets of cases were on appeal to the Ninth Circuit, the Supreme Court decided a different case that changed the rules about antitrust injury; under the law established in this opinion, the plaintiffs in Groups 1 and 2 would be able to show sufficient injury to invoke the antitrust laws. How should this change in the law affect Groups 1 and 2? The Ninth Circuit reversed the judgment as to Group 1 and remanded to the district court, instructing it to reconsider the case in light of the new Supreme Court opinion. That court also concluded that the Group 2 plaintiffs, even though they did not appeal their loss in Case 1, should not be barred by claim preclusion. The court recognized an exception to claim preclusion for "public policy" and "simple justice," and concluded that the Group 2 plaintiffs should be able to proceed.

The Supreme Court reversed and held that the Group 2 plaintiffs were barred by claim preclusion. In unmistakable terms, it rejected open-ended exceptions to claim preclusion. The Court reasserted

---

[201]In one of the old cases espousing the more liberal view about allowing an exception to claim preclusion for the claimant's ignorance, the court said that "[t]he rule applying to splitting a cause of action is one of practice merely, and is not without exception." McVay v. Castenara, 152 Miss. 106, 113 (1928). That view of claim preclusion is quite different from the less flexible view today. See the discussion of policies in §11.1 and the Supreme Court's view as discussed immediately below.

[202]452 U.S. 394 (1981).

[203]Actually, there were multiple suits. We can treat them in the aggregate, however, and refer to the dismissal as a singular Case 1.

the importance of claim preclusion as a key principle of justice. The Court said:

> [W]e do not see the grave injustice which would be done by the application of accepted principles of *res judicata*. "Simple justice" is achieved when a complex body of law developed over a period of years is even-handedly applied. The doctrine of *res judicata* serves vital public interests beyond any individual judge's ad hoc determination of the equities in a particular case. There is simply "no principle of law or equity which sanctions the rejection by a federal court of the salutary principle of *res judicata*." The Court of Appeals' reliance on "public policy" is similarly misplaced. This Court has long recognized that "[p]ublic policy dictates that there be an end of litigation; that those who have contested an issue shall be bound by the result of the contest, and that matters once tried shall be considered forever settled as between the parties." We have stressed that "[the] doctrine of *res judicata* is not a mere matter of practice or procedure inherited from a more technical time than ours. It is a rule of fundamental and substantial justice . . . ."[204]

Finally, as we saw earlier, there is a strong argument in favor of applying the primary rights definition of claim in motor vehicle crash cases involving subrogation of an insurance company.[205] Even in states that otherwise would apply a transactional test to claim preclusion, there may be an exception in such cases to ensure that the driver's insurance company is not barred in seeking damages from another driver involved in a collision with its insured.

§11.5.3   Exceptions to Issue Preclusion

As discussed in §11.4.4, the invocation of preclusion of either type requires that the party against whom it is applied had a full and fair opportunity to litigate in Case 1. Just as failure to give notice, or fraud on the court, or other violations of this fair hearing requirement may vitiate claim preclusion, so will they vitiate issue preclusion. In addition, several of the basic requirements of imposing issue preclusion act to ensure that its use is fair. Specifically, issue preclusion can be used only for an issue actually litigated and determined in Case 1. Moreover, that issue must have been essential to the judgment in Case 1, which tends to ensure that the fact-finder truly focused on the issue before deciding it. Moreover, the court in Case 2 has a good deal of discretion in defining what issue was actually litigated and

---

[204]*Moitie*, 452 U.S. at 400 (citations omitted).
[205]See note 55 above.

determined in Case 1. This discretion might be shaped in Case 2 to avoid results that seem unfair to the court.

The principal exceptions to issue preclusion are catalogued in §28 of the Restatement (Second) of Judgments. Some provisions of that section mirror those we saw for claim preclusion in §11.5.2. So issue preclusion might be avoided if the party against whom it is asserted could not have obtained review of the judgment in Case 1,[206] or if a new determination of the issue is needed because of "differences in the quality or extensiveness of the procedures followed by the two courts or by factors relating to the allocation of jurisdiction between them."[207]

Sometimes the court in Case 2 will be required to assess whether a difference in burden of persuasion should affect application of issue preclusion.[208] For instance, in a criminal case, the defendant must be proved guilty "beyond a reasonable doubt." In a civil case, in contrast, the claimant must prove the elements of her claim only by "a preponderance of the evidence," which is an easier standard to satisfy. Often, an issue in a criminal case may be raised in a civil case for damages by the victim of the crime. For example, if D breaks into P's house and steals P's stereo, D might be prosecuted by the state for committing a crime and P might sue D in a civil case to recover damages caused by the theft.

- *Example #36.* In Case 1, the state successfully prosecutes D for the theft. In Case 2, P sues for damages from the theft. Can P use issue preclusion on the issue of whether D stole the stereo? Yes, because the state in Case 1 proved that issue and proved it to a higher degree of certainty than P needs to satisfy. Thus, assuming the other requirements for issue preclusion are met,[209] P would not have to prove the theft in Case 2.

- *Example #37.* In Case 1, P sues D for damages from the theft and wins (which includes, of course, a determination that D stole the stereo). In Case 2, the state prosecutes D for the theft. Can the state use issue preclusion on the issue of whether D stole the stuff? No, because P proved the theft to a lesser degree of certainty than the state needs to satisfy in the criminal case.

---

[206]Restatement (Second) of Judgments §28(1) (party against whom issue preclusion is sought "could not, as a matter of law, have obtained review of the judgment in the initial proceeding").

[207]Restatement (Second) of Judgments §28(3).

[208]Restatement (Second) of Judgments §28(4).

[209]This would be nonmutual offensive issue preclusion, because the claimant in Case 2 was not a party to Case 1 and is asserting the claim. *See* Illinois Farmers Ins. Co. v. Reed, 647 N.W.2d 553, 560-563 (Minn. App. 2002) (conviction of day care provider of first-degree assault established by issue preclusion in civil suit by provider's insurer for declaratory judgment that policy does not apply to intentional act of insured).

Suppose the defendant pleads guilty in the criminal case. Then the person whose things were stolen sues that person in a civil case, seeking damages for the theft. Can the plaintiff in the civil case use issue preclusion on the question of whether the defendant stole the stuff? The quick answer must be no, because the issue of theft was not litigated and determined in Case 1. After all, that case ended in a guilty plea, and was not resolved by litigation. On the other hand, allowing the defendant to litigate an issue on which he admitted criminal guilt is more than some courts can accept. They will refuse to let the defendant change his tune. Courts doing so are probably applying *judicial estoppel*. As we discussed in the last paragraph of §11.1, that doctrine does not permit a party to take disparate positions in separate litigation.

Occasionally (but rarely), an intervening change in the controlling law might justify an exception to issue preclusion.[210] A famous case is *Commissioner of Internal Revenue v. Sunnen*,[211] which concerned taxability of income from a royalty agreement. An inventor patented his invention and entered a contract with a manufacturer, under which the latter made the machines and paid a royalty to the inventor's wife. The IRS took the position that the income should be taxed to the inventor, not the wife (which was bad news for the inventor, because he was in a higher tax bracket than his wife). In Case 1, the parties litigated the issue, and the inventor won.

After expiration of the contract, the inventor entered another deal with the manufacturer, again providing that the royalty be paid to the inventor's wife. The IRS sued again (Case 2), in an effort to establish that the royalty income should be taxed to the inventor, not his wife.[212] The inventor tried to assert issue preclusion; after all, this very issue had been litigated and determined in Case 1. The Supreme Court held that issue preclusion should not apply, because of an intervening change in the law, which made it clear that the income should be taxed to the inventor.[213] The Court refused to allow the inventor to use issue

---

[210]Restatement (Second) of Judgments §28(2)(b) (a new determination is warranted on a question of law "to take account of an intervening change in the applicable legal context or otherwise to avoid inequitable administration of the laws").

[211]333 U.S. 591 (1948).

[212]There was no claim preclusion because each taxable year constitutes a different claim.

[213]The Court also opined that even though the contracts between the inventor and the manufacturer were identical, Case 2 did not involve exactly the same facts as Case 1. Instead, the facts in Case 2 were "separable" even though they were the same facts! *Sunnen*, 333 U.S. at 599-600. Thus, the basic requirement that the two cases must involve the same facts was not satisfied. This "separable facts" notion is of uncertain present vitality. *See* 18 Moore's Federal Practice §132.02[5][c]. *Sunnen* may demonstrate the occasional difficulty encountered with issue preclusion on rulings of law. See §11.4.2.

preclusion on this question. Because of the intervening change in the law, it would not be proper to allow the inventor to use issue preclusion to lock in for him advantageous tax treatment not available to fellow citizens.

Finally, the Supreme Court has held that nonmutual offensive issue preclusion cannot be used in litigation against the United States.[214] The federal government may litigate the same issue in many cases throughout the country. As a matter of policy, the Court concluded, it should not be required to appeal every adverse ruling in an effort to avoid imposition of issue preclusion.

§11.6 Interjurisdictional Preclusion: Full Faith and Credit and Related Topics

§11.6.1 In General

In this section we deal with preclusion when Case 1 and Case 2 are decided in different judicial systems; this topic has become known as "interjurisdictional preclusion."[215] For instance, if the judgment in Case 1 is entered by a state court in Arizona and Case 2 is brought in a state court in Florida, which state's law determines the preclusive effect of the judgment? Similarly, if Case 1 were decided in a federal court and Case 2 in a state court (or vice versa), does federal or state law determine the preclusion effect of the judgment? Moreover, does it matter whether Case 1 was in federal court under diversity of citizenship jurisdiction, instead of federal question? Such questions are important because each state is free to determine its own preclusion law, so long as that law does not violate due process,[216] and because there is also federal law on preclusion, which may differ from state law.

Interjurisdictional preclusion problems can arise in four general scenarios. The first is when Case 1 and Case 2 are decided in state courts of different states ("state-to-state preclusion"). Second is when Case 1 is decided in a state court and Case 2 is filed in federal court ("state-to-federal preclusion"). Third is when Case 1 is decided in a federal court and Case 2 is filed in a state court ("federal-to-state

---

[214]United States v. Mendoza, 464 U.S. 154 (1984).

[215]*See, e.g.,* 18 Moore's Federal Practice §133; Howard Erichson, *Interjurisdictional Preclusion,* 96 Mich. L. Rev. 945 (1998). Professor Erichson's article builds on a groundbreaking piece by the late Professor Ronan Degnan, *Federalized Res Judicata,* 85 Yale L.J. 741 (1976).

[216]Richards v. Jefferson County, 517 U.S. 793, 797 (1996).

preclusion"). Finally, we have the situation in which Cases 1 and 2 are in federal courts ("federal-to-federal preclusion").

We first encountered the concept of full faith and credit in our discussion of personal jurisdiction, §2.2, where we saw that a valid judgment was entitled to full faith and credit in states other than the one that entered it. We spoke there of being able to sue in the second state to enforce a judgment from the first state. Here we are concerned with a different issue: In determining whether the judgment from Case 1 is entitled to claim or issue preclusive effect in Case 2, what preclusion law does the court in Case 2 use? Full faith and credit plays a role here. As the Supreme Court said in *Durfee v. Duke*: "Full faith and credit thus generally requires every State to give to a judgment at least the *res judicata* effect which the judgment would be accorded in the State which rendered it."[217] Thus, full faith and credit applies not only to the enforcement of a judgment in a second action but to determining the preclusive effect of a judgment.

There are two sources of full faith and credit law: the Full Faith and Credit Clause of the Constitution (Article IV, §1) and the full faith and credit statute, now codified at 28 U.S.C. §1738. The constitutional provision is quite narrow. It requires that each *state* give full faith and credit to (among other things) "judicial proceedings of every other State" and thus applies only in the state-to-state preclusion scenario. The full faith and credit statute is broader. It applies not only in the state-to-state preclusion scenario, but in the state-to-federal situation as well. It provides that a state or federal court in Case 2 must give "the same full faith and credit" as would be given by the state court that entered judgment in Case 1. Interestingly, then, full faith and credit law applies directly only in the first two of our four scenarios. As we will see, however, courts have fashioned similar principles to cover the other two scenarios, though the precise source of those principles is unclear.

§11.6.2   State-to-State Preclusion

○ ***Example #38.*** Case 1 is litigated in state court in Texas and results in a valid final judgment on the merits. Case 2 is brought by the same claimant against the same defendant in a state court in Louisiana. Louisiana preclusion law would permit the second suit but Texas preclusion law would not. What does the Louisiana court do in Case 2?

The answer seems straightforward: Both the constitutional provision for full faith and credit and §1738 require the courts of a second

---

[217]375 U.S. 106, 109 (1963). We discussed *Durfee* at §6.4, concerning collateral attacks on subject matter jurisdiction.

state to honor the judgments, including the preclusion rules, of the courts of the state that decided Case 1. So the Louisiana court should apply Texas law and dismiss Case 2 under claim preclusion.

Example #38 is similar to *Magnolia Petroleum Co. v. Hunt.*[218] In that case, a Texas worker was injured on the job. In Case 1, he recovered an award for his injuries in an administrative proceeding in Texas. Texas law clearly provided that such a worker was not entitled to bring a second proceeding to recover additional compensation from his employer. So the worker brought Case 2 in Louisiana, seeking additional compensation. The Supreme Court held that the Louisiana court should have dismissed Case 2 because under Texas law, the judgment in Case 1 was the end of the matter. Similarly, in another case, the Oregon Supreme Court concluded that an Ohio judgment precluded a second action on the same claim even though Oregon law might have allowed a second case to proceed.[219]

Thus, we seem to have a clear black-letter principle: The court in Case 2 must apply the preclusion law of the state whose court decided Case 1. After all, §1738 requires the court in Case 2 to give the judgment "the same" effect it would have in the state that decided Case 1. Indeed, the Restatement (Second) of Judgments takes the position that the requirement in §1738 that one state accord another state's judgment "the same" effect that it would have in the judgment-rendering state mandates the court in Case 2 "to give to the state judgment the same effect—*no more and no less*—than the court [deciding Case 1] would give it."[220]

But things are not as clear as they seem here. The famous quote from *Durfee v. Duke* above said that full faith and credit "generally requires every State to give to a judgment *at least* the *res judicata* effect which the judgment would be accorded in the State which rendered it."[221] This language seems to recognize that the court in Case 2 might give a *greater* preclusive effect than the state in Case 1 would, but also seems to rule out the possibility of its giving a *lesser* preclusive effect. Commentators have long debated, however, whether the court deciding Case 2 might be free to accord the judgment from Case 1 a lesser effect than it would have in the judgment-rendering state. Professors Wright and Miller, for example, contend that full faith and credit enshrines only the "central" or "core" principles of claim and issue preclusion—those that "support the core values of finality, repose, and reliance, as well as some of the rules that facilitate

---

[218]320 U.S. 430 (1943).
[219]Benjamin v. S.R. Smith Co., 632 P.2d 13 (Or. 1981).
[220]Restatement (Second) of Judgments §86 cmt. g (emphasis added).
[221]375 U.S. 106, 109 (1963) (emphasis added).

control by the first court over its own procedure"—and not "every minute detail" of preclusion doctrine.[222] Specifically, they assert that the nonmutual employment of issue preclusion "is not so central a component of *res judicata* to be swept into full faith and credit."[223] To them, then, the court in Case 2 should not always be forced to accept every aspect of the preclusion law of the jurisdiction that decided Case 1.

Can "The Same" Mean "Less"? The Supreme Court has never held that the court in Case 2 can accord the judgment from Case 1 a *lesser* preclusive effect than would the state in which Case 1 was decided. Case law from other courts is notably scarce on this point. The issue raised by Professors Wright and Miller can be illustrated in this hypothetical.

> ○ ***Example #39.*** *P* sues Pharmaceutical Co. (*PC*) in California. After full trial, *P* wins a judgment, based upon the finding that *PC*'s product was unfit and caused serious physical harm to persons who used it. Now thousands of persons around the country plan to sue *PC* for the same harm. *P-2* sues in Virginia, on the same theory used by *P*, and asks the court to employ nonmutual offensive issue preclusion on the question of whether the product is unfit and causes the physical harm alleged.

Does §1738 require Virginia to apply nonmutual offensive issue preclusion? If the statutory mandate is absolute—that Virginia is to give the judgment "the same" effect as California—the answer would seem to be yes. But if commentators are correct that full faith and credit only embodies the central aspects of preclusion law—principally those supporting the principles of finality—the determination will be considerably more nuanced. Specifically, full faith and credit should not "demand obeisance to . . . aspects of preclusion doctrine that are incidental to the central role of preclusion and that may intrude on substantial interests of later courts."[224] In our example, then, it would be proper to assess whether Virginia ought to be forced to accept nonmutual offensive issue preclusion. California's interest in allowing such preclusion might not be damaged if Virginia does not follow California law on this point. After all, California is still free to use nonmutual estoppel in its own courts. On the other hand, what if

---

[222] 18B Wright & Miller 33-34 ("[F]ull faith and credit embraces the central doctrines of *res judicata*. No other result could be tolerated in a federalistic society as mobile and litigious as ours . . . . None of these decisions, however, compels the conclusion that full faith and credit incorporates every minute detail of *res judicata* doctrine").

[223] 18B Wright & Miller 44.

[224] Wright & Kane, Federal Courts 733.

Virginia's adherence to mutuality in the mass tort situation was its response to the concern we discussed in §11.4.5? The state could have concluded that no defendant should be subjected to massive liability essentially on the basis of losing one case. Is this interest to be swept away through obedience to every tenet of California's preclusion law? The argument that it is not seems especially strong. But the issue is left mostly to the world of academic surmise.

Can "The Same" Mean "More"? There is some case support for the notion that the court in Case 2 can accord a judgment from Case 1 *greater* preclusive effect than the state deciding Case 1 would. Clearly, the court in Case 2 cannot be *required* to give the judgment greater effect than it would have in the state deciding Case 1.[225] But may it choose to do so? Let's see how this issue might come up.

> ○ ***Example #40.*** *P* is involved in a car wreck and suffers personal injuries and property damage. She brings Case 1 in Georgia, seeking recovery only for personal injuries. In motor vehicle crash cases, Georgia adopts the primary rights definition of claim, meaning that *P* has separate claims for personal injuries and for property damage. The court in Georgia enters a valid final judgment on the merits. Now *P* brings Case 2 against the same defendant, seeking to recover for the property damage from the same crash. Case 2 is filed, however, in Nevada, which employs a transactional test for claim preclusion.

If the Nevada court uses the preclusion law of Georgia, there is no claim preclusion, and *P* can proceed in Case 2. Doing so, however, requires Nevada to entertain litigation that its own rules of preclusion would hold barred. Should Nevada be able to dismiss Case 2 under claim preclusion? In other words, should Nevada be permitted to accord the Georgia judgment greater preclusive effect than it would have in Georgia? If so, *P* is "robbed" of the right given her by Georgia law to proceed in separate actions. Given the clash between upsetting *P*'s legitimate expectation that she can proceed separately and Nevada's interest in docket control, which should prevail? Reasonable people may disagree on this point, but there is a strong argument that Nevada ought to be able to dismiss without prejudice to *P*'s right to bring Case 2 in Georgia (or any other state that would allow the suit to proceed).[226]

---

[225]*See* In re Attorney Discipline Matter, 98 F.3d 1082 (8th Cir. 1996). Illinois entered judgment in Case 1 acquitting a lawyer of perjury. Case 2 was in Missouri, and was a discipline proceeding against the same lawyer for suborning perjury. Illinois law would not give issue-preclusive effect to the finding from Case 1, because a criminal case has a higher burden of persuasion than a disciplinary proceeding. Missouri could not be required to give the finding preclusive effect because it cannot be required to give a judgment greater effect than it would have in the rendering state.

[226]18B Wright & Miller 46-48.

The problem may arise as well in the issue preclusion context.

   ○ ***Example #41.*** In Case 1, *P-1* sues *D* in state court in Virginia. The case goes to trial and the court determines that *D* was negligent and that her negligence proximately caused tortious damage to *P.* In Case 2, *P-2*, who was injured in the same episode but who was not a party in Case 1, sues *D* in state court in California. *P-2* wishes to employ nonmutual offensive issue preclusion to establish *D*'s negligence in Case 2.[227] Virginia does not recognize nonmutual offensive issue preclusion but California does. Assuming the requirements for such preclusion are satisfied, should California apply it?

If the California court in Case 2 applies Virginia law, it will not apply issue preclusion, and the parties will litigate the issues of *D*'s negligence and causation afresh. The California court will bear the burden of that litigation. The justice system runs the risk that this second litigation of the same issue will result in an inconsistent finding, with concomitant erosion in the respect accorded that system.

But should the California court be free to give the Virginia judgment a *greater* preclusive effect than it would have in Virginia?[228] The Supreme Court has never addressed the issue in this context. Other courts have reached different conclusions, but there is considerable support for allowing California to apply nonmutual offensive issue preclusion against *D.*[229] Again, reasonable people may disagree, but allowing California to employ preclusion here can be criticized on at least two bases. First, it is possible that in Case 1, *D* relied upon Virginia's adherence to the mutuality rule to conclude that she would not try to join *P-2* in Case 1. It would seem unfair now to tell *D* that, having lost to *P-1*, she will probably lose to *P-2* by preclusion. Second, the California courts have not previously litigated any issue in the case, so the burden imposed upon them is not as great as it would be if Case 1 had been in California. It seems doubtful that the California interest in avoiding judicial effort outweighs Virginia's interest in its preclusion standards.

§11.6.3 State-to-Federal Preclusion

   ○ ***Example #42.*** Case 1 is litigated in a state court in Kansas and results in a valid final judgment on the merits. Case 2 is brought in federal court

---

[227] Or Case 2 could have been brought *by D* against *X*, who was not a party to Case 1. *X* would want to assert nonmutual defensive issue preclusion on the finding from Case 1 that *D* was negligent.

[228] 18B Wright & Miller 49-50 nn.81-82.

[229] *Id.* at 49-50 ("There is substantial support for the view that a second court should be able to rest nonmutual preclusion on the judgment of a court that would deny it. The contrary view is better.") (footnotes omitted).

in New York. Does that federal court apply the preclusion law of Kansas, or New York, or is it free to apply federal law of preclusion?

The federal court in New York applies Kansas law on preclusion. Why? Because the full faith and credit statute requires the federal court in New York to do what a state court in New York would do.[230] And a New York state court (as we saw above) would apply Kansas preclusion law. As the Supreme Court explains: "Congress has specifically required all federal courts to give preclusive effect to state court judgments whenever the courts of the State from which the judgments emerged would do so."[231]

The concerns discussed in §11.6.2, about whether the court in Case 2 can give greater or lesser preclusive effect to the judgment from Case 1, also arise here. Thus, for instance, if Case 1 is decided in a state that does not embrace nonmutual offensive issue preclusion, the federal court in Case 2, it seems, should not apply such preclusion.[232] But there are two special situations deserving attention.

First is the case of *Baker v. General Motors Corp.*,[233] in which the Supreme Court indicated that the full faith and credit statute does not require the court in Case 2 to apply the same methods of enforcing a judgment that the state court in Case 1 would use. In *Baker*, Case 1 involved an employment claim against General Motors (GM), brought by a GM engineering analyst (Elwell) in a Michigan state court. That court entered an injunction that prohibited Elwell from testifying as an expert witness against the corporation in other cases. Case 2 was brought in a federal court in Missouri by a different plaintiff, claiming that GM was liable on various tort theories for wrongful death. The plaintiff in Case 2 called Elwell as an expert witness. GM insisted that the Michigan injunction was entitled to full faith and credit in Case 2, and that it precluded Elwell from testifying.

The Supreme Court held that the federal court in Case 2 was not required to honor the injunction. It relied on two points. First, full faith and credit does not require the court in Case 2 to "adopt the practices of other states regarding the time, manner, and mechanisms for enforcing judgments."[234] Second, the orders of one court "commanding action or

---

[230]As discussed in §11.6.1, however, the full faith and credit provision of the Constitution does not cover the state-to-federal preclusion situation.

[231]Allen v. McCurry, 449 U.S. 90, 96 (1980). *See also* San Remo Hotel v. County of San Francisco, 545 U.S. 323, 342-343 (2005) (refusing to recognize exception to §1738).

[232]*See, e.g.,* Kuehn v. Garcia, 608 F.2d 1143, 1146-1147 (8th Cir. 1979) (judgment in Case 1 entered by North Dakota state court; federal court in Case 2 rejects use of nonmutual offensive issue preclusion because North Dakota does not recognize that doctrine) (*citing* Strudevant v. SAE Warehouse, 270 N.W.2d 794, 798 (N.D. 1978)).

[233]522 U.S. 222 (1998).

[234]*Id.* at 235.

inaction" cannot be allowed to interfere with litigation before a different judicial system.[235] In other words, a Michigan order will not be allowed to prohibit a federal (or state[236]) court in Missouri to permit someone to testify as an expert witness. The Court in *Baker* emphasized that its holding was narrow and stated that it did not intend to create a "general exception to the full faith and credit command."[237] Surely, said the Court, its holding "does not permit a State court to refuse to honor a sister State judgment based on the forum's choice of law or policy preferences."[238]

Does that mean that GM had no recourse? No. The Court made it clear that GM could have enforced the Michigan order in Michigan (by holding Elwell in contempt if he testified in Missouri) or that GM could have sued Elwell in Missouri to enforce the injunction against him personally.[239] Though *Baker* arose in a state-to-federal scenario, it would apply in the state-to-state situation.

The second special situation can only arise when Case 2 is in a federal court under exclusive federal jurisdiction. In such a case, the rule that the federal court gives full faith and credit to the judgment in Case 1, including preclusion rules, can create some odd inquiries. For instance, in *Marrese v. American Academy of Orthopaedic Surgeons*,[240] a group of physicians sued a professional association in an Illinois state court in Case 1. They claimed that the association excluded the plaintiffs from membership in violation of a variety of state laws. The court entered a valid final judgment on the merits against them. Then the physicians brought Case 2 against the association, this time in federal court and this time alleging violations of federal antitrust law. The antitrust claims are among those rare cases in which federal courts have exclusive federal question jurisdiction, as we discussed at §§4.1 and 4.6.1, so those claims could not have been asserted in state court in Case 1. On the other hand, all claims—federal antitrust and state claims—could have been asserted in Case 1 had Case 1 been filed in federal court.[241]

---

[235]*Id.* A Michigan order should not "interfere[] with litigation over which [it] had no authority." *Id.* at 239.

[236]Though *Baker* arose in a state-to-federal scenario, it would also apply in the state-to-state situation.

[237]*Id.*

[238]*Id.* at 239.

[239]*Id.* at 239-240. GM apparently erred by seeking to force the Missouri federal court to give full faith and credit to the Michigan order in the context of the litigation there rather than simply suing Elwell directly.

[240]470 U.S. 373 (1985).

[241]Why? Because the federal antitrust claims would have invoked federal question jurisdiction. The state claims either would have invoked diversity of citizenship jurisdiction or, failing that, supplemental jurisdiction. Why the latter? Because the claims arose from the same transaction or occurrence as the federal question claim. See §4.7.

Should the federal court in Case 2 dismiss under claim preclusion? All the requirements were satisfied, but the question became whether an exception should be recognized because the state court in Case 1 could not have entertained the federal antitrust claims. The federal district court and court of appeals held that Case 2 should be dismissed and noted that the plaintiffs could have brought federal and state claims together in federal court. The Supreme Court reversed and remanded, instructing the district court to apply the preclusion law of Illinois. In so doing, the Court was instructing the lower court to do something that seems fruitless—to determine what Illinois law would say about whether there should be preclusion of an action that could never have been asserted in Illinois courts. As the district judge recognized on remand, its "task is an exercise in extrapolation because, of course, the Illinois courts never address issues pertaining to exclusively federal lawsuits."[242]

The Supreme Court reached the same conclusion in *Matsushita Electric Industrial Co. v. Epstein,*[243] which involved allegations of fraudulent behavior in a securities transaction. Case 1 was a class action in Delaware state court and asserted only state law claims. It resulted in a valid final judgment on the merits. Case 2 was a class action in a federal court in California and asserted federal securities law claims involving the same transaction. The federal securities claims, like the antitrust claims in *Marrese*, invoke exclusive federal question jurisdiction and thus could not have been asserted in Case 1. The Supreme Court held that Delaware law governed the question of whether Case 2 should be dismissed under claim preclusion. The Court was even more forthright than it had been in *Marrese* in recognizing that the inquiry was difficult—the court had to determine whether Delaware would apply claim preclusion as to assertions that simply cannot be made in state court. There is unlikely to be state law on such a question; nonetheless, full faith and credit commands the court in Case 2 to undertake the inquiry. The Court also rejected the notion that the grant of exclusive federal jurisdiction created an exception to the full faith and credit statute and ultimately concluded that the federal action had to be dismissed under the claim preclusive effect of the Delaware judgment.

Marrese and *Matsushita Electric* indicate that the Supreme Court sees the full faith and credit statute as a strict command to give the judgment from Case 1 truly "the same" full faith and credit it would

---

[242]Marrese v. American Academy of Orthopaedic Surgeons, 628 F. Supp. 918, 919 (N.D. Ill. 1986). The district court refused to apply claim preclusion and allowed Case 2 to proceed.
[243]516 U.S. 367 (1996).

receive in the state courts that decided Case 1.[244] The cases may also constitute persuasive evidence that the Supreme Court does not believe that the court in Case 2 can give a lesser preclusive effect than the courts deciding Case 1, even when exclusive federal jurisdiction is at stake. The interest in preserving a federal forum for those with claims invoking exclusive federal jurisdiction might counsel rejection of claim preclusion in these situations, but the Court permitted the state judgments to preclude the federal claim.[245]

§11.6.4   Federal-to-State Preclusion

- ○ ***Example #43.*** Case 1 is litigated in federal court in Indiana, and that court enters a valid final judgment on the merits. Case 2 is filed in state court in Florida. In determining the preclusive effect of the judgment in Case 1, does the Florida court apply federal law, Indiana law, or Florida law?

The general answer is clear: The Florida court will apply federal preclusion law, which is federal common law.[246] Some courts say that the result is dictated by full faith and credit.[247] In fact, however, neither the constitutional nor statutory provisions for full faith and credit apply when the judgment in Case 1 is entered by a federal court.[248] So what is the source of the rule that compels the court in Case 2 to apply federal preclusion law? Some have argued that the notion of "case or controversy" in Article III of the Constitution carries with it the authority to define the scope of the judgments entered in federal

---

[244]These cases also constitute rejection of the position taken in §26(1)(c) of the Restatement (Second) of Judgments, which provides that a state court judgment in Case 1 should have claim preclusive effect in Case 2, when Case 2 is brought in federal court and invokes exclusive federal jurisdiction.

[245]Again, maybe the result is good from an efficiency viewpoint. The plaintiffs could have had all claims—federal and state—determined in a single case had Case 1 been in federal court. It would have invoked federal question jurisdiction for the federal claims and diversity of citizenship or supplemental jurisdiction for the state claims. Efficient joinder of all claims in one case could have been achieved—but only in federal court. When plaintiffs decided to go to state court first, they ran the risk of losing a federal forum for their federal claims.

[246]Though *Erie* held that there was no *general* federal common law, it left the federal courts able to fashion common law in discrete areas; preclusion is one. See §10.9.

[247]*See, e.g.*, Levy v. Cohen, 561 P.2d 252, 257 (Cal. 1977).

[248]The language of each provision speaks only of giving full faith and credit to *state court* judgments. The Supreme Court recognized this fact expressly in *Semtek Int'l, Inc. v. Lockheed Martin Corp.*, 531 U.S. 497, 506 (2001) ("Neither the Full Faith and Credit Clause . . . nor the full faith and credit statute . . . addresses the question. By their terms they govern the effects to be given only to state-court judgments").

courts. In addition, the Supremacy Clause of the Constitution operates to make the federal judgments binding.[249]

Whatever the precise source of the compulsion to apply federal
preclusion law, the conclusion must be correct. After all, if both state
and federal courts must apply the preclusion law of a state court that
entered judgment in Case 1, how can principles of federalism demand
less when a federal court enters the judgment in Case 1? The idea
seems so obvious "that the rule requiring state courts to honor the
res judicata effects of federal court judgments has been stated in an
unbroken line of cases that do not offer any clear judicial thought or
explanation."[250]

Does it matter, however, whether the federal court in Case 1 determined questions of federal law or questions of state law? The easier
case for concluding that federal preclusion law governs is when Case 1
involved questions of federal law. In such a case, there is no arguable
state interest in determining the scope of preclusion to be accorded the
judgment. If Case 1 involved litigation of state law claims, however
(e.g., under diversity of citizenship or supplemental jurisdiction), do
different considerations govern? Though some commentators argued
that state law ought to govern the question of preclusion in such a
case, most courts disagreed. The Second Circuit once said:

> One of the strongest policies a court can have is that of determining
> the scope of its own judgments . . . . It would be destructive of the basic
> principles of the Federal Rules of Civil Procedure to say that the effect
> of a judgment of a federal court was governed by the law of the state
> where court sits because the source of federal jurisdiction is diversity.[251]

The Supreme Court spoke to the issue in *Semtek International, Inc.
v. Lockheed Martin Corp.*[252] In *Semtek*, the plaintiff filed Case 1 in
a California state court and the defendant removed to federal court
on the basis of diversity of citizenship jurisdiction. The federal court
dismissed the case as barred under California's two-year statute of
limitations. The plaintiff filed Case 2, on the same claim, in state court
in Maryland, a state whose longer statute of limitations (three years)
would not bar the claim.[253]

---

[249]18B Wright & Miller 51-55.

[250]18B Wright & Miller 52.

[251]Kern v. Hettinger, 303 F.2d 333, 340 (2d Cir. 1962). The Restatement (Second) of
Judgments §87 took the same position. The leading academic proponent of the view
was Professor Ronan Degnan, *Federalized Res Judicata*, 85 Yale L.J. 741 (1976).

[252]531 U.S. 497 (2001). We discussed another aspect of *Semtek,* dealing with whether
a judgment is "on the merits," in §11.2.2.

[253]The defendant removed that case to federal court in Maryland, which remanded
to the state court. Though the requirements of diversity of citizenship jurisdiction were

The Supreme Court held unanimously that the Maryland court in Case 2 must apply federal common law to determine whether Case 2 ought to be dismissed under claim preclusion.[254] Thus, federal law governs to determine the preclusive effect of a judgment entered by a federal court but based upon state law. The Court did something very interesting, however, in determining the *content* of federal common law on this point. It held that federal common law would usually adopt the preclusion law of the *state* in which the federal court sat in Case 1.

Indeed, the facts of *Semtek* dictated such adoption of California law as federal law, for several reasons. First, because Case 1 was dismissed on the basis of the California statute of limitations, it makes considerable sense to look to California law to determine the effect of a dismissal on such grounds. Second, this conclusion is especially sound in a case, such as *Semtek*, in which there is no need for a uniform federal rule. Third, the Court invoked *Erie* doctrine principles in finding that use of the state rule would reduce the incentive for litigants to shop for a federal forum, in hopes of gaining access to different preclusion rules.[255] Thus, in the final analysis, the Maryland court in Case 2 should dismiss under claim preclusion only if California law would dictate that result.

Though on the facts of *Semtek* the Court found it appropriate to adopt state law as the content for the federal common law of preclusion, the Court left open the possibility that federal law would ignore state law. According to the Court, it could do so when there is a federal interest justifying the crafting of a federal rule. As an example, the Court stated that a willful violation of the discovery provisions of the Federal Rules might properly result in preclusion under federal law, regardless of state law.[256] Beyond that case, the Court gave little guidance as to when federal law would ignore state law. Thus, the Court ensured maximum flexibility; the court in Case 2 can ignore state law when it concludes that there is a good reason to do so.

---

satisfied, the case could not be removed because the defendant was a citizen of the forum. (We saw this limitation on removal jurisdiction at §4.8.) So Case 2 proceeded in state court in Maryland.

[254]The Court said that no "federal textual provision"—either in the Constitution or any statute—"addresses the claim-preclusive effect of a judgment in a federal diversity action." *Semtek*, 531 U.S. at 507. The statement is interesting in view of the efforts of commentators to root in Article III and the Supremacy Clause of the Constitution the rule that federal law governs. See notes 248-252 and accompanying text above.

[255]*Semtek*, 531 U.S. at 508-509.

[256]*Id.* at 509.

§11.6.5 Federal-to-Federal Preclusion

There is every reason to conclude that preclusion questions in this scenario are handled the same as those in the federal-to-state situation discussed in the preceding subsection. Here, as there, neither the constitutional nor statutory provision for full faith and credit applies; those, as we have seen, apply only when Case 1 is decided in a state court. Here, as there, the general answer is that federal law will govern the preclusive effect of the judgment entered in Case 1. And here, as there, it is not entirely clear whether a particular constitutional provision—such as Article III or the Supremacy Clause—dictates this result.

No one has ever doubted that federal common law governs the preclusive effect if Case 1 were decided in federal court and involved a decision based upon federal law.[257] This result is correct regardless of whether the dispute in Case 2 is governed by federal or state law.[258] But what if Case 1 were decided on the basis of state law (as, for instance, under diversity of citizenship or supplemental jurisdiction)? Though the Supreme Court decision in *Semtek*, discussed in the preceding subsection, technically involved the federal-to-state scenario, its approach should be followed here. Thus, the federal court in Case 2 would apply federal common law to determine the preclusive effect of the judgment from Case 1. Federal common law, however, will often incorporate state law of the state in which the federal court in Case 1 sat. The court in Case 2 has considerable flexibility in determining the content of the governing federal common law.

---

[257]*See, e.g.*, Gunter v. Atlantic Coast Line R.R., 200 U.S. 273, 284-289 (1906).
[258]*See, e.g.*, Seven Elves, Inc. v. Eskenazi, 704 F.2d 241, 243-244 n.2 (5th Cir. 1983).

Chapter 12

Defining the Scope of Litigation: Joinder Rules and Subject Matter Jurisdiction

§12.1 Defining the Issue

In this chapter we define the scope of a civil action. Specifically, we are concerned with how many parties can be joined and how many claims they can assert in a single case. Each jurisdiction addresses these topics through its rules on "joinder." Historically, joinder rules were quite restrictive. At common law, for example, the writ system, which we discussed in §7.2, permitted the plaintiff to assert only a single, narrowly defined claim. The concept of a case was, correspondingly, quite narrow. Equity practice was broader and expressed the goal of resolving an entire overall dispute, rather than narrow parts of the disagreement. Modern joinder rules build on the equity practice to expand the concept of a single civil action. The Federal Rules ushered in the modern era of joinder. Of course, the Federal Rules apply to litigation in federal court. Though each state is free to prescribe its own joinder provisions, the Federal Rules have been quite influential. Many states have adopted the Federal Rules on joinder.

The Federal Rules focus largely on the "transaction or occurrence" giving rise to alleged liability. Many (though not all) joinder rules permit joinder of parties and claims along transactional lines. The drafters' goal was to allow resolution of transactionally related disputes in a single case, thereby avoiding piecemeal litigation from what was a single real-world event. This trend toward "packaging" transactionally related parties and claims into a single case is driven at least in part by a desire to promote efficiency and consistency. One case burdens the justice system less than multiple cases. It also avoids the possibility of inconsistent outcomes, which can erode public confidence in the justice system. Of course, the emphasis on packaging, and avoiding duplicative litigation, is heightened in an era of crowded dockets and litigation delay.[1]

We saw a similar focus on the transactional test in discussing claim preclusion in §11.2.3. There, the modern approach defines one's claim as all rights to relief arising from a transaction or occurrence (or series of related transactions or occurrences). That definition forces claimants to package all transactionally related assertions into a single case (or risk claim preclusion). We saw similar policy justifications concerning claim preclusion: The coercive effect of the transactional test for claim preclusion fostered efficiency and consistency, just as the Federal Rules joinder provisions do.

Most of the joinder provisions are *permissive*, however, which means that litigants may take advantage of their packaging potential but are not required to do so. The Rules thus embody a policy of litigant autonomy — that is, they tend to defer to the plaintiff's structuring of the case. Throughout our discussion of joinder, appreciate the tension between the urge to package the litigation efficiently and this sense that the plaintiff ought to be entitled to structure the case as she sees fit. There is significant debate over whether litigant autonomy should not be sacrificed, at least to a degree, in the interest of packaging disputes more efficiently.[2]

---

[1]The classic discussion of the benefits of packaging is John McCoid, *A Single Package for Multiparty Disputes*, 27 Stan. L. Rev. 707 (1976).

[2]Some commentators conclude that litigant autonomy should give way to greater efficiency. *See, e.g.,* Richard D. Freer, *Avoiding Duplicative Litigation: Rethinking Plaintiff Autonomy and the Court's Role in Defining the Litigative Unit*, 50 U. Pitt. L. Rev. 809, 833 (1989) ("The plaintiff is entitled to due process, to a fair and convenient forum, but has no right to exclusive possession of center stage regardless of the consequences on scarce judicial resources"); Martin H. Redish, *Intersystemic Redundancy and Federal Court Power: Proposing a Zero Tolerance Solution to the Duplicative Litigation Problem*, 75 Notre Dame L. Rev. 1347, 1353 (2000) (the traditional preference given to plaintiff's choice of forum does not justify the burdens and waste of duplicative litigation). On the other hand, others assert the need for plaintiffs, particularly

In this chapter, we survey the joinder provisions of the Federal Rules. But mastery of the various joinder rules is not enough. The joinder rules provide the *procedural* tools for joining parties and asserting claims in a single case. They do not (in fact, under Federal Rule 82, they *cannot*[3]) affect the requirements for personal jurisdiction, subject matter jurisdiction, or venue. Thus, *every time* a joinder provision is used in federal court, it raises the need to assess jurisdiction and venue. We do not spend much time on personal jurisdiction in this chapter, beyond stating that when a party is joined by the court or by a litigant, the court must have personal jurisdiction over her. (If a new party intervenes into the case, however, she has submitted to the personal jurisdiction of the court.) Likewise, we will see that venue may be problematic in only a few joinder situations.

On the other hand, we will have a great deal to say about subject matter jurisdiction. Remember, as we saw in §4.1, *every claim joined in federal court must be supported by federal subject matter jurisdiction*. Thus, for every claim asserted, we must assess whether the claim invokes diversity of citizenship, alienage, or federal question jurisdiction. In the context of each joinder rule, then, we have occasion to review much of what we saw in Chapter 4 concerning subject matter jurisdiction. If a given claim does invoke an "independent basis" of subject matter jurisdiction—meaning it invokes diversity of citizenship, alienage, or federal question jurisdiction—obviously, it can be asserted in the pending case.

But what happens if we have a claim—properly asserted under the joinder rules—that does not invoke diversity of citizenship, alienage, or federal question jurisdiction? It might still be asserted in federal court through *supplemental jurisdiction*. As discussed in §4.7, supplemental jurisdiction permits a federal court to hear a claim over which it does not have one of the three major independent bases of subject matter jurisdiction. It is available, however, only if the claim meets the requirements of the supplemental jurisdiction statute, 28 U.S.C. §1367. Because joinder can so easily raise questions of supplemental jurisdiction, you should be familiar with the materials in §4.7, particularly §4.7.4.

Remember, however, that supplemental jurisdiction is only relevant for claims over which there is *no* diversity of citizenship, alienage, or

---

in tort cases, to control the structure of their cases. *See, e.g.,* Roger Trangsrud, *Joinder Alternatives in Mass Tort Litigation,* 70 Cornell L. Rev. 779, 848 (1985) (aggregation of litigation "adversely affects the traditional right of tort litigants to control the individual prosecution of their liability claims and unpredictably skews the fairness of the trial process").

[3]Rule 82 provides that the Federal Rules "do not extend or limit the jurisdiction of the district courts or the venue in those courts."

federal question jurisdiction. It is wise to be mechanical in approaching issues of joinder and subject matter jurisdiction. Whether a claim can be asserted (or a party can be joined) in federal court requires us to address three steps:

- **First**, is there a joinder provision in the Federal Rules that allows assertion of this claim (or joinder of this party)?
- **Second**, if so, does this claim invoke diversity of citizenship, alienage, or federal question jurisdiction? If so, it may be asserted in the pending case.
- If not, the **third** issue is whether the claim can nonetheless be asserted in federal court because it invokes supplemental jurisdiction. Again, the discussion in this chapter assumes that you understand the basic operation of the supplemental jurisdiction statute, particularly §1367(a) and (b).

§12.2 Real Party in Interest, Capacity, and Related Issues

Our legal system does not permit everyone who happens to be displeased about something to pursue a lawsuit. Various legal doctrines address the question of who may sue. One limitation is the doctrine of *standing*. Detailed discussion of standing is beyond our scope.[4] We should know, however, that standing, which is rooted in Article III of the Constitution, requires that the claimant suffer an "injury in fact" because of the defendant's behavior.[5] Standing often becomes an important consideration in public interest litigation, for example, when a citizen seeks to challenge governmental action.[6] Suppose, for

---

[4]Standing and other topics of "justiciability," such as mootness, ripeness, and the political question doctrine, are considered in detail in courses on Constitutional Law and Federal Courts.

[5]Article III permits federal courts to hear "cases" or "controversies." A dispute in which the plaintiff lacks standing does not qualify as a "case" or "controversy." In addition to the injury-in-fact requirement, there must also be a causal connection between that injury and the defendant's action, and it must be likely that a favorable judicial decision will remedy the harm suffered by the plaintiff. Lujan v. Defenders of Wildlife, 504 U.S. 555, 560-561 (1992).

[6]Serious issues of standing can arise as well in litigation between private parties. *See, e.g.*, TransUnion LLC v. Ramirez, 141 S. Ct. 2190 (2021) (only class members concretely harmed by a defendant's statutory violation have Article III standing); Spokeo, Inc. v. Robins, 136 S. Ct. 1540, 1548-1550 (2016) (remanding to lower court to assess whether plaintiff class, asserting claims against a corporation for alleged violation of Fair Credit Reporting Act had standing under Article III because injury was "concrete and particularized"). *Spokeo* presents an increasingly prevalent issue: whether one

instance, that a group interested in environmental issues seeks to stop the federal government from building a dam that might endanger some species of wildlife. By limiting the right to sue to those who are actually harmed by the government action, standing minimizes friction between the judicial branch and other branches of the government.

Real Parties in Interest

More central to our focus is a concept embodied in Federal Rule 17(a)(1): "An action must be prosecuted in the name of the real party in interest." The real party in interest (RPI) is the person or entity "possessing the right or interest to be enforced through the litigation."[7] It serves a function similar to that served by standing: to ensure that the one who has the legal right being vindicated is the named claimant.

Sometimes the RPI is not one who will receive the benefit if the litigation is successful. As the second sentence of Rule 17(a)(1) makes clear, a fiduciary may be the RPI, suing on behalf of others. For example, a trustee suing on behalf of trust beneficiaries is the RPI. Her success (or failure) will bind the beneficiaries for whom she sues. She is the RPI even though any benefit from a successful judgment would go to the beneficiaries.

Assignment of claims can create RPI problems.

- o ***Example #1.*** Suppose A and Z are parties to a contract, and that A has a right to be paid by Z under the contract (because, for example, he delivered the widgets as required by the contract). A may be able to assign that right to be paid to P.[8] (Why would she want to do this? Maybe A owes money to P and does not have enough cash to pay, so assigning the right to this payment may be a way to pay P.) Suppose she does so. (A is the assignor and P is the assignee.) Now P is the holder of the right to receive payment from Z. P is the RPI, and it is P who would bring suit if Z refused to pay.[9]

---

who is given a *statutory* right to sue (for maintenance of incorrect information on a website, for unwanted texts, and the like) has *constitutional* standing.

[7] 4 Moore's Federal Practice 17-10 to 17-11.

[8] We addressed assignment of claims at §4.5.4. The concern there was that someone might assign a claim to create diversity of citizenship jurisdiction, in violation of 28 U.S.C. §1359.

[9] The common law refused to recognize assignments such as this. After A assigned her claim to P, then, the common law would insist that A bring the suit (because the assignment would not be recognized). This rule makes no sense, because A no longer has any interest in the matter and will be unlikely to sue. Equity avoided the harshness of the common law on this score (as in others, as we discussed at §1.2.3) by recognizing the assignment and adopting the commonsense view that P was now the RPI. Rule 17(a) handles the situation as equity did.

Subrogation is an assignment by operation of law. It usually comes up in insurance cases.

> ○ ***Example #2.*** Suppose *P* has automobile insurance with Insco Corp. *P*'s car is damaged in the amount of $5,000 by the negligence of *D*. Because of the insurance, Insco Corp. will pay *P* the $5,000 (or it might just pay the repair shop directly, on behalf of *P*). Insco Corp. is now said to be "subrogated" to *P*'s right to sue *D*. (*P* is the subrogor and Insco Corp. is the subrogee.) All this means is that *P*'s right to sue *D* for damage to her car has now been assigned—automatically—to Insco Corp. This result makes sense, because *P* has been made whole; her car is repaired and she is out of pocket nothing. Insco Corp., on the other hand, is out of pocket $5,000 and now has the right to vindicate *P*'s claim against *D*, so the ultimate loss ends up on *D*. After the subrogation, Insco Corp. is the RPI of the claim. It works just like assignment.

So far, we have assumed that the assignment or subrogation was total, that the entire claim was transferred to the assignee or subrogee. But assignment and subrogation can be partial.

> ○ ***Example #3.*** Suppose *A* assigns to *P* a portion of the right to receive payment under the contract with *Z*. Let's say that *A* assigns to *P* the right to receive 75 percent of the payment owed by *Z*. Who's the RPI? They both are. *A* is an RPI to the tune of 25 percent of the contract amount; *P* is an RPI to the tune of 75 percent of the contract amount. Subrogation often will be partial because the insurance policy has a "deductible." With a deductible, the insured person agrees to pay a set amount (the deductible amount) of any covered damage to her property. In the example above, in which *P* had automobile insurance with Insco Corp., it is likely that the policy had a deductible—say, of $500. This means that *P* agrees that she will pay $500 of damage done to her property, and Insco Corp. will pay the rest.[10] In that case, who's the RPI? As with the partial assignment, they both are. *P* is an RPI to the tune of $500 and Insco Corp. is an RPI to the tune of $4,500.

Rule 17(a)(3) makes it clear that the court should not dismiss a case that is brought by someone other than the RPI until it has provided a "reasonable time" for the plaintiff to fix (courts often say "cure") the defect (usually by substituting the RPI for the person who brought suit[11]). Thus, if someone who is not an RPI asserts a claim

---

[10]Deductibles can vary. Obviously, the higher the deductible, the lower the cost of the insurance (because the insured has agreed to absorb more of the loss personally). Conversely, the lower the deductible, the more expensive the insurance. When you buy such insurance, you have the option of choosing a particular deductible.

[11]Such substitution is made pursuant to Rule 17(a)(3) and is distinguished from substitution under Federal Rule 25. Substitution of an RPI is mandated by the fact that the original claimant is not a proper RPI. In cases under Rule 25, on the other

(a fact that can be noted by the defendant or by the court on its own motion), the court may not grant dismissal immediately. If the matter is cured within a reasonable time, Rule 17(a)(3) provides that the RPI is treated as though she had been joined from the outset of the case. On the other hand, if the RPI defect is not cured within a reasonable time, the court may dismiss on that ground.[12]

Though a case brought by someone other than an RPI cannot be dismissed immediately on that basis, always be alert to the possibility that substitution of the RPI may make it impossible to invoke federal subject matter jurisdiction.

> o ***Example #4.*** *A* and *Z* are parties to a contract, under which *A* has a right to be paid $100,000 by *Z*. *A* assigns her right to receive that payment to *P*. *A* is a citizen of Florida. *P* and *Z* are citizens of Kentucky. *A* sues *Z* in federal court, seeking recovery of the $100,000 under the contract.

The case appears to invoke diversity of citizenship jurisdiction, because it is brought by a citizen of Florida against a citizen of Kentucky, and the amount in controversy exceeds $75,000. The problem, of course, is that after the assignment, *A* is not an RPI. *Z* cannot seek immediate dismissal on that basis. But notice what happens when the RPI (*P*) is substituted for *A*. At that point, there is no diversity of citizenship jurisdiction, because the case is now by a citizen of Kentucky against a citizen of Kentucky. Thus, *Z* will make a motion to substitute *P* as the RPI and will also move to dismiss for lack of subject matter jurisdiction. She should make the motions simultaneously.

> o ***Example #5.*** Take the same fact pattern and assume that the assignment from *A* to *P* was not total. Rather, it was an assignment to *P* of 25 percent of the value of the contract right. As we saw above, that means that *A* is an RPI in the amount of $75,000 and *P* is an RPI in the amount of $25,000. Can either of them sue *Z* under diversity of citizenship jurisdiction? No. Let's see why.

---

hand, the original parties were properly joined but substitution is required because of a change in capacity (e.g., a litigant died, and her executor must be substituted for her) or because of a transfer of interest during the litigation.

[12]*See, e.g.,* Weissman v. Weener, 12 F.3d 84, 86 (7th Cir. 1993) (case dismissed after plaintiff failed to remedy RPI defect). At some point, it seems that the RPI rule adds little of value. After all, if someone other than the RPI sues, the substantive law should prevent her from recovering. For this and other reasons, including the "loan receipt" problem discussed below in this subsection, commentators have long advocated that Rule 17(a) be repealed because the rule is more trouble than it is worth. *See, e.g.,* Thomas Atkinson, *The Real Party in Interest Rule: A Plea for Its Abolition,* 32 N.Y.U. L. Rev. 926 (1957).

As we just saw, *P* cannot sue *Z* under diversity of citizenship jurisdiction because they are cocitizens (Kentucky). Not only that, but *P*'s
claim is for only $25,000, so it does not meet the amount in controversy
requirement. What about *A*? She (a citizen of Florida) is of diverse citizenship from *Z* (a citizen of Kentucky). But she cannot invoke diversity of citizenship jurisdiction because her claim does not meet the
amount in controversy. Why not? Because it is for exactly $75,000 and
does not *exceed* $75,000. This claim is a penny short. See §4.5.3.

Moreover, *A* and *Z* cannot aggregate their claims for jurisdictional
purposes. They are not joint claims and aggregation is permitted only
when there is one plaintiff suing one defendant. Again, see §4.5.3.
Finally, supplemental jurisdiction is of no help. It applies only when
there is a claim that has invoked federal subject matter jurisdiction
independently. Here, neither *A* nor *P*'s claim has. See §4.7.

The same issues can arise, of course, in the subrogation context.
Insurance companies occasionally try to avoid the operation of subrogation through use of a "loan receipt." Here's how it works.

- ***Example #6.*** *P*, a citizen of New Hampshire, has homeowner's insurance with Insco Corp., a citizen of Delaware and of California. *P*'s
  house is damaged by the negligence of *D*, a citizen of Vermont, to the
  tune of $100,000. *P*'s policy with Insco Corp. has a $1,000 deductible.
  If Insco Corp. pays *P* $99,000 under the policy, it is subrogated to her
  right to sue *D*. Insco Corp. is an RPI in the amount of $99,000 and
  could invoke diversity of citizenship jurisdiction against *D*. *P* is an
  RPI in the amount of only $1,000 and thus cannot invoke diversity
  jurisdiction because her claim does not meet the amount in controversy requirement.

Often, however, an insurance company would prefer not to sue in
its own name. Why? It fears jury prejudice, because many jurors have
had problems with their insurance carriers, and because insurance
companies are seen as deep pockets that can easily absorb a financial loss. Some insurance companies have tried the following inventive
argument.

- ***Example #7.*** Insco Corp. argues that the $99,000 it gave to *P* in Example
  #6 was not a payment, but a "loan." Because it was a loan, Insco Corp.
  argues that it is not subrogated to *P*'s right to sue. Thus, *P* remains the
  RPI for the full $100,000 and the suit should be brought solely by *P*.
  (And on the facts of Example #5, *P* can invoke diversity of citizenship
  jurisdiction because the claim would be for $100,000.)

In these "loan receipt" cases, the insurance company always adds a
stipulation to the "loan": that *P* must repay the money if *P* wins the
litigation. Who is the RPI of $99,000 in such a "loan receipt" situation?

Courts have been inconsistent. Some hold (properly, it seems) that the insurance company is the RPI for the $99,000; other courts see the insured as the RPI for the full policy amount.[13]

Capacity to Sue and Be Sued

Federal Rule 17(b) addresses capacity to sue or be sued, which is a broader concept than RPI. While RPI determines whether one holds the legal right to bring a claim in a particular case, capacity is aimed at whether one has the general ability to function as a litigant at all. Some persons are under a "legal disability," which means that they cannot function legally. For example, minors and persons adjudged insane (or "under a disability") usually lack the legal power or authority to litigate or undertake other legal acts, such as entering into a binding contract. Rule 17(b) seeks to ensure that the interests of such persons are adequately represented in litigation. Thus, litigation by or against such a person should be brought by or against a representative. A person under a disability may have someone who is responsible for her in a day-to-day sense—perhaps a general guardian, conservator, or committee. That person may act as the disabled person's representative in litigation. Or a court may appoint a "guardian *ad litem*," which means guardian for the purposes of this litigation, who will represent the person in the particular suit.

Under Rule 17(b)(1), the federal court assesses a human's capacity to sue or be sued by looking to the law of her domicile. Rule 17(b) also addresses the capacity of a business to litigate in its own behalf. For example, under Rule 17(b)(2), the capacity of a *corporation* is determined by the law of the state where the corporation was formed. Today, it is universal in corporation law that corporations have the power to sue and be sued. As we discussed in §4.5.3, concerning diversity of citizenship jurisdiction, however, not all business is conducted by corporations.

Unincorporated associations, such as partnerships and limited liability companies (LLCs), are also addressed by Rule 17(b)(3), which gives the general rule that the capacity of such associations is determined by the law of the state in which the federal court sits. Though a few states still may not permit a partnership to sue or be sued in its common (partnership) name, most states do.[14] Regardless of state

---

[13]*See* June Entman, *More Reasons for Abolishing Federal Rule of Civil Procedure 17(a): The Problem of the Proper Plaintiff and Insurance Subrogation*, 68 N.C. L. Rev. 893, 912 (1990).

[14]The law has always regarded the corporation as an entity, separate from those who own and run it. Historically, however, the law saw a partnership as an aggregate of its members, rather than as a separate entity. Under this "aggregate" view, the common law (and some states today) require suit by or against every member of the

law on this point, Rule 17(b)(3)(A) permits a partnership or LLC to sue in its own name in federal court if it is asserting a federal question claim.

§12.3 Claim Joinder by a Claimant (Rule 18(a))

Procedural and Policy Issues

Federal Rule 18(a) governs the question of what claims[15] the plaintiff can assert in a single case. The rule has no requirements: It allows the assertion of all claims the plaintiff may have against the defendant. The claims need not be related in any way. They can be completely unrelated transactionally, legally, and in terms of the remedy sought. They can be independent or alternate claims; they can be legal or equitable. There are simply no procedural restrictions. While the provision is simple, it raises several points.

First, why should the Federal Rules allow joinder of unrelated claims? Though many states have adopted the Federal Rules on joinder, some states have rejected the "anything goes" approach of Rule 18(a) and limit joinder to claims that arise from the same transaction or occurrence.[16] Such a limitation makes sense when the case goes to trial, because it means that the jury may focus only on transactionally related issues. The Federal Rule, on the other hand, can result in the assertion of disparate and unrelated claims, which runs the risk of confusing the jury. The drafters of the Federal Rules understood this possibility, and addressed it by permitting the trial judge to order separate trials, among other reasons, to avoid such confusion.[17] As a matter of policy, then, the Federal Rules choose to permit the plaintiff to put the entire dispute between the parties into a single case. It may

---

partnership, rather than in the partnership's name. Allowing it to sue or be sued in its partnership name would be to treat it as an entity, contrary to the historical view. The aggregate view is waning, and, increasingly, the law considers partnerships to be entities for various purposes. LLCs, in contrast, are universally allowed to sue and to be sued.

[15]The word *claims*, as used in Rule 18(a), is not necessarily synonymous with the definition of *claims* for claim preclusion purposes. In discussing the latter, we noted that this word might mean different things in different contexts. See §11.2.3. In Rule 18(a), the word refers to assertions or bases of liability. Multiple assertions of liability might, however, comprise a single claim for claim preclusion purposes.

[16]*See, e.g.,* Va. Code Ann. §8.01-272 ("[A] party may plead as many matters, whether of law or fact, as he shall think necessary. A party may join a claim in tort with one in contract provided that all claims so joined arise out of the same transaction or occurrence").

[17]*See* Fed. R. Civ. P. 20(b) and 42(b), discussed at §12.4.

be that such open claim joinder allows the parties to settle all their overall disputes by allowing packaging of all claims in a single proceeding. If the matter goes to trial, the trial judge is armed with tools to keep things manageable for the trier of fact.

Second, the rule provides that the plaintiff "may" join as many claims as she has against the defendant. The word "may" means this rule is "permissive": It permits, but does not *require* the plaintiff to assert all claims in a single case.[18] The plaintiff thus may choose how many assertions to include in a single case. Do not forget, however, that another doctrine, claim preclusion, might affect the plaintiff's choices.

- *Example #8.* *P* and *D*, each driving her own car, collide; each is injured and each car is damaged. *P* sues *D* and asserts only a claim for personal injuries from the collision; she does not seek recovery for property damage. There is nothing wrong with this course of action under Rule 18(a), because it is permissive and does not require her to pack all claims into a single case. Suppose, however, that this case results in a valid final judgment on the merits and that *P* files a second case against *D*, to recover for property damage from the crash. In a jurisdiction adopting a transactional definition of claim, this second case will be dismissed under claim preclusion. See §11.2.3. As a consequence, although Rule 18(a) is permissive, the majority view on claim preclusion operates to force the plaintiff to join all transactionally related assertions in a single case.

Third, though we speak in this section of "claim joinder by the plaintiff," Rule 18(a) does not apply only to plaintiffs. Instead, it permits any party asserting a claim for relief to join "as many claims as it has against an opposing party." This language recognizes (as we did in discussing claim preclusion in §11.2.1) that plaintiffs are not the only claimants. Defendants can become plaintiffs by asserting counterclaims, crossclaims, or third-party claims. Note, however, that Rule 18(a) does not apply to them *until* they become claimants by asserting one of the listed claims.

- *Example #9.* We see in §12.5.2 that a crossclaim is asserted against a coparty and must arise from the same transaction or occurrence as the underlying dispute. Suppose *P* sues two defendants, *D-1* and *D-2*, concerning a contract dispute. Suppose further that *D-1* has a claim against *D-2* that is completely unrelated to that contract dispute. *D-1* *cannot* use Rule 18(a) to assert that unrelated claim *until* she has asserted a crossclaim against *D-2*. Why? Look again at the Rule: The

---

[18]"May" is to be contrasted with "must," which, of course, states a command. See §12.5.1.

"you-can-assert-any-claim-you-want" part of the Rule applies only to a party who is "asserting a claim" (such as a crossclaim).

Thus, if *D-1* has a claim against *D-2* that *does* arise from the underlying contract dispute, she may assert it as a crossclaim and then use Rule 18(a) to join the unrelated claim. Without the crossclaim, however, *D-1* cannot assert the unrelated claim in the pending case.

Subject Matter Jurisdiction

Rule 18(a), like other joinder provisions of the Federal Rules, merely creates a procedure for asserting a claim. The claims can be asserted in federal court *only* if they invoke federal subject matter jurisdiction.

> ○ ***Example #10.*** P, a citizen of California, sues *D*, a citizen of Nevada, and uses Rule 18(a) to join two claims: (1) that *D* had violated federal employment law in firing *P* and (2) that *D* had breached an unrelated contract between the two, causing damage to *P* of $100,000. Joinder of the claims is procedurally proper under Rule 18(a). Is there subject matter jurisdiction over the claims?

Yes. Claim (1) invokes federal question jurisdiction because it arises under federal employment law. Claim (2) invokes diversity of citizenship jurisdiction because it is asserted by a citizen of California against a citizen of Nevada and the amount in controversy exceeds $75,000.

> ○ ***Example #11.*** P, a citizen of Massachusetts, sues *D*, a citizen of Arizona, and uses Rule 18(a) to join two state law[19] claims: (1) that *D* breached a contract between the two, causing damage of $45,000 to *P*; and (2) that *D* committed an unrelated tort, causing damage of $50,000 to *P*. Joinder of the claims is procedurally proper under Rule 18(a). Is there subject matter jurisdiction over the claims?

Yes. The case invokes diversity of citizenship jurisdiction. It is brought by a citizen of Massachusetts against a citizen of Arizona, and the amount in controversy exceeds $75,000. Why? The concept of *aggregation* permits a single plaintiff to add the value of all claims that she asserts against a single defendant. So here the amount in controversy is $95,000. (We discussed aggregation at §4.5.3.)

---

[19]Throughout this chapter, the reference to claims arising under state law is meant to indicate that they will not invoke federal question jurisdiction. Some state law claims do invoke federal question, as we saw in §4.6.4, but we won't go there in this chapter.

○ ***Example #12.*** *P*, a citizen of Tennessee, sues *D*, a citizen of Tennessee, and uses Rule 18(a) to join two claims: (1) that *D* violated federal labor laws in a labor dispute and (2) that *D* violated state law in the same labor dispute. Joinder of the claims is procedurally proper under Rule 18(a). Is there subject matter jurisdiction over the claims?

Yes. Claim (1) invokes federal question jurisdiction, because it arises under federal labor laws. Claim (2) does not invoke federal question jurisdiction (because it arises under state, not federal, law). Claim (2) also does not invoke diversity of citizenship jurisdiction, because the plaintiff and defendant are cocitizens. But Claim (2) does invoke supplemental jurisdiction. Why?

Section 1367(a) grants supplemental jurisdiction over claims that are part of the same "case or controversy" as a claim that properly invoked federal subject matter jurisdiction. As explicated by the Supreme Court, this requirement is satisfied if the claims share a "common nucleus of operative fact." As we discussed in §4.7, this test is broader than transaction or occurrence. Here, the two claims asserted by *P* do arise from the same factual nexus. Section 1367(b), which removes supplemental jurisdiction over certain claims, applies only in cases that invoked diversity of citizenship jurisdiction. This case invoked federal question jurisdiction, so §1367(b) does not apply. (If any of this material is unclear, review §4.7; this fact pattern is the same as the famous *Gibbs* case, which is codified in §1367(a).)

§12.4 Permissive Party Joinder (Rule 20(a))

Procedural and Policy Issues

Many cases involve a single plaintiff suing a single defendant. On the other hand, many cases involve multiple parties—either coplaintiffs or codefendants (or both). Here, we address the question of "proper parties" to a civil case, meaning those who *may* be joined in a single case. The issue is governed in federal court by Federal Rule 20(a). This Rule is available to the plaintiff when she is structuring the case. She decides whether to have multiple parties either on the plaintiff or defendant side and, if so, who those parties will be. As we see in this section, various considerations, including litigation strategy and jurisdictional limitations, may affect her choice. And as we see in §12.6, though the judicial system allows the plaintiff the first choice in determining who the parties will be, other litigants, third parties, and the court itself may override the plaintiff's party structure, at least in limited circumstances.

Rule 20(a)(1) defines who may be joined as coplaintiffs. Rule 20(a)(2) defines who may be joined as codefendants. In each, the Rule prescribes the same two-part test. Put in simple terms, two or more may join together as coplaintiffs if their claims (1) arise "out of the same transaction, occurrence, or series of transactions or occurrences" and (2) raise at least one common question (of law *or* fact). Similarly, two or more may be joined as codefendants if the claims *against them* (1) arise from the same transaction or occurrence and (2) raise at least one common question (of law *or* fact).[20]

Few cases raise problems with the second requirement. The Rule requires the existence of *only one* common question, and it can be a question of law or fact. That common question need not be of predominant importance in the case; it simply must exist, which will be obvious in most instances.[21]

Most of the difficulties encountered with Rule 20(a) involve the requirement that the claims by or against multiple parties must be transactionally related. Before exploring that issue, it is important to note that Rule 20(a) continues a theme we see throughout modern procedure: the packaging in a single case of claims arising from, and parties involved in, a "transaction or occurrence." This focus on the transaction—on the real-world grouping of facts—underlies the modern definition of claim for claim preclusion purposes, as we saw in §11.2.3. It also underlies several claim joinder devices we see in §12.5. And, as we will continue to see, the concept of trans-

---

[20]We will see that several joinder provisions employ either the "transaction or occurrence" or the "common question" mantra (or, as in Rule 20(a), both mantras). Professor Effron has demonstrated that courts are not consistent in defining these concepts. Their breadth depends upon the context of the proposed joinder. She argues that the courts have developed "shadow rules" that account for differing conceptions of how related various claims must be. Robin Effron, *The Shadow Rules of Joinder*, 100 Geo. L.J. 759 (2012).

[21]In §13.3.4, we will see that a case can proceed as a class action under Federal Rule 23 only if, *inter alia*, there are common questions of law or fact. That requirement, like the one we address here in Rule 20, has generally been thought easy to satisfy. In 2011, however, the Supreme Court rejected class action status in an employment discrimination case for lack of such commonality. Wal-Mart Stores, Inc. v. Dukes, 564 U.S. 338, 347-350 (2011). Plaintiffs' expert in that case testified that some employment decisions by the defendant were based upon stereotypical thinking about gender roles. He admitted, however, that he could not tell what percentage of the decisions was so affected. Thus, the Court concluded, the claims by class plaintiffs did not raise common questions of law or fact. It is not clear that this rigorous view of commonality has been employed in the Rule 20 context.

In the article cited in the preceding footnote, Professor Effron demonstrates that courts addressing the requirement of commonality often employ a "shadow rule" of implied predominance in the Rule 20(a) context. They thus focus on whether common questions predominate, which is not an express requirement of Rule 20(a). Effron, note 20 above, 100 Geo. L.J. at 790-799.

actional relatedness defines the general availability of supplemental jurisdiction.

As elsewhere, the concept of "transaction or occurrence" is somewhat elastic. There are many easy cases, of course, such as when there are persons hurt in a single motor vehicle accident or when there are multiple parties to a contract that has been breached. At the margin, however, some courts have been remarkably inventive in stretching the concept of the transaction to allow joinder of parties. Perhaps these courts have been especially liberal because Rule 20(a) (unlike other transaction-based joinder rules[22]) speaks not only of claims arising from the same transaction or occurrence, but of a "series of transactions or occurrences."[23] On its face, this language seems broader than rules that speak only of a transaction or occurrence. Few opinions, however, justify a broad reading of the Rule on the basis of this additional language. What seems more influential are various theories of liability asserted by the plaintiff, particularly in tort cases. Many of the opinions in this area, though ostensibly interpreting Rule 20(a), read like cases that would appear in a casebook on Torts.

One example is *Poster v. Central Gulf Steamship Corp.*,[24] which involved a seaman, Mr. Poster, who contracted a painful gastrointestinal malady, amebiasis, while working on a ship operated by Sinclair. He claimed that he was stricken because that company hired local workers to help the ship's galley staff prepare food while the ship was in the Suez Canal. These local workers, he alleged, used unsanitary food-handling practices, which resulted in his infection. Months later, the unlucky sailor was working for a different shipping line, Gulf. This ship also went through the Suez Canal and the company also hired local workers to help prepare food. And, again, the plaintiff was stricken with amebiasis.

He sued both shipping companies as codefendants in a single case. Though the court recognized that the two voyages were separate "occurrences," it upheld joinder. Significantly, the plaintiff was careful to allege that his present condition was the result of *both* episodes. In other words, he did not say that he was injured once on the first voyage and a second time on the second voyage. Instead, his present state of health resulted from *both* exposures to unsanitary practices. It was impossible to say what percentage of his condition was attributable to which company. As a matter of tort law, then, the way the plaintiff alleged his claim, both companies could be concurrently liable. Thus,

---

[22]*See, e.g.*, Rule 13(a)(1) (compulsory counterclaim); Rule 13(g) (crossclaim), discussed in §12.5.

[23]This language is also reflected in the Restatement (Second) of Judgments definition of claim for claim preclusion purposes. See §11.2.3.

[24]25 F.R.D. 18 (E.D. Pa. 1960).

the court properly concluded that the two companies could be joined as codefendants in a single case.

Imagine the problems Mr. Poster would have faced had the court not been willing to consider the substantive theory of concurrent liability in assessing whether joinder was proper under Rule 20(a). First, Mr. Poster would have had to pay for and prosecute two separate suits—one against each shipping company. Second, if the cases went to trial separately, he could be "whipsawed."[25] That means that in each case, the defendant could say to the jury, in essence: "We feel terrible that Mr. Poster is hurt, but it's not our fault. He sailed on another vessel for another company, and it is that company that hurt Mr. Poster." By focusing attention on the other shipping company, each defendant might be able to escape liability. Third, if Mr. Poster won in his litigation against one shipping company, he could not use issue preclusion from that case in the case against the other company. (Why?[26]) On the other hand, if Mr. Poster lost in the first case to go to judgment, depending on the issues decided, the other company might be able to assert issue preclusion against him in the other case. (Why?[27])

Some notable cases have involved plaintiffs injured by accidents at different times. Courts have been appropriately liberal in permitting joinder of the defendants in a single case when the plaintiff alleges that her present condition is the result of the combined effects of the wrecks, or that the second wreck exacerbated the injuries from the first, or that the injuries inflicted by each cannot be identified separately. An example is *Schwartz v. Swan*, in which a bad-luck plaintiff was injured in completely separate automobile accidents 10 days apart.[28] The court upheld joinder of the drivers involved in the two collisions in a single case, and emphasized that joinder was appropriate when "it appears that the *cumulative effect* of the acts of which plaintiff complains is a single indivisible injury, or that it is unlikely that it can be ascertained to a reasonable degree of medical certainty which occurrence caused the injuries."[29]

---

[25]*See* Thomas D. Rowe & Kenneth Sibley, *Beyond Diversity: Federal Multiparty, Multiforum Jurisdiction*, 135 U. Pa. L. Rev. 7, 15 (1986).

[26]Because issue preclusion can only be asserted against one who was a party to a case. Gulf was not a party to the case by Poster against Sinclair and thus could not be bound by a judgment from that case. See §11.4.4.

[27]Because most jurisdictions allow nonmutual defensive issue preclusion. For example, if in the first case the court found that Mr. Poster assumed the risk by eating the native-prepared food when he did not have to do so, the defendant in the second case might be able to use that issue against him in the second case.

[28]211 N.E.2d 122 (Ill. App. 1965). Talk about having a bad day: The plaintiff in *Watts v. Smith*, 134 N.W.2d 194 (Mich. 1965), was injured in separate automobile collisions on the same day; he was allowed to join the other drivers in a single case.

[29]*Schwartz*, 211 N.E.2d at 126 (emphasis added).

No case strains the concept of transactional relatedness more than *Hall v. E.I. DuPont de Nemours Co.*,[30] which involved injuries sustained by about a dozen children while playing with blasting caps. At the time, six companies manufactured all of the blasting caps in the United States. The injured children were not related to each other. They were injured in separate explosions in ten states over four years. Because the explosions destroyed the blasting caps, no child (or parent) could be certain which company had manufactured the cap that injured him or her. All of the injured children (actually, their representatives—why?[31]) sued as coplaintiffs against all blasting cap manufacturers and their trade association as codefendants. The theory of the suit was that the defendants failed properly to warn by labeling that blasting caps may be harmful.

Despite the obvious fact that the injuries were inflicted in unrelated events at different times and in different places, the court upheld joinder of all parties under Rule 20(a). The court's opinion focused mainly on theories of tort liability. These theories, such as "enterprise liability," move the attention away from separate transactions and toward the overall culpability of the blasting cap industry. The court concluded, "[t]he allegations in this case suggest that the entire blasting cap industry and its trade association provide the logical locus at which precautions should be taken and liability imposed."[32] Thus, the substantive tort theory adopted by the plaintiffs allowed the court to stretch the concept of transactional relatedness by concluding, in essence, that the case was not about 12 separate explosions but, rather, one culpable industry. Not every court would have been so liberal in upholding joinder on such facts.[33]

These cases demonstrate the tension inherent in addressing the propriety of joinder of multiple parties. On the one hand, courts are mindful of the salutary policy of inclusive joinder—of deciding whole disputes in the context of a single case. On the other hand, however, they must be careful not to create an unmanageable and confusing

---

[30]345 F. Supp. 353 (E.D.N.Y. 1972). The opinion was written by Judge Jack Weinstein, who, before being named to the bench, was a full-time professor at Columbia University School of Law.

[31]Because minors lack legal capacity to sue or be sued, so litigation by or against them should be brought by or against the minors' representative. See §12.2.

[32]*Hall*, 345 F. Supp. at 378.

[33]*See, e.g.*, Saval v. BL Ltd., 710 F.2d 1027, 1031 (4th Cir. 1983) (allegations of similar warranty claims on automobiles did not arise from same transaction or occurrence); Demboski v. CSX Transp. Inc., 157 F.R.D. 28, 29 (S.D. Miss. 1994) (personal injuries incurred in different accidents at different times but alleging safety of railroad crossings did not meet transactional test for joinder).

morass. Imagine the difficulties, for example, of going to trial in the *Hall* case: twelve plaintiffs, putting on evidence of injuries from separate explosions over various states at different times, questions of what state's law will govern which case, several defendants, each trying to prove that it did not manufacture the particular cap involved. The court in *Hall* recognized that it had created a fairly unwieldy case and planned to transfer individual claims to the federal district in which the explosions occurred, after making pretrial rulings.[34] Especially in light of the need for such unusual contortions, the opinion in *Hall* seems less a court's effort to apply the language of Rule 20(a) and more an attempt to pressure settlement of multiple claims. This goal may be laudable, but it's not clear that Rule 20(a) is intended to be a tool for realizing it.[35]

Strategic Issues

As we know, joinder of parties under Rule 20(a) is permissive. Because the Rule gives the plaintiff the option to take or leave the joinder opportunity it provides, it allows the plaintiff to engage in strategic choices.

  ○ ***Example #13.*** *P-1* and *P-2* take a ride in a rideshare vehicle. The driver is negligent and causes a crash that injures both *P-1* and *P-2*. Why may those join together in a suit against the driver under Rule 20(a)(1)?

Because their claims against the driver (1) arise from the same transaction or occurrence (the crash) and (2) raise at least one common question (whether the driver was negligent). They are not required to do so. Each may file a separate action against the driver if she prefers.

  ○ ***Example #14.*** Could *P-1* (or *P-2* or both together) sue two defendants—the driver and the rideshare company for which the driver works—in the same case?

---

[34]Functionally, the court thus attempted to replicate the treatment that would have been accorded by multidistrict litigation treatment under 28 U.S.C. §1407. In such an "MDL" transfer, as we saw at §5.5.1, cases originally filed in different districts are transferred by the Judicial Panel on Multidistrict Litigation to a transferee district for consolidated pretrial proceedings. In *Hall*, in contrast, only one case was filed.

[35]Moreover, although this problem may not have arisen in *Hall*, straining to sustain joinder can sweep into the case some defendants whose involvement in the underlying dispute is marginal. Courts should be mindful that doing so can be extremely expensive to such "bystander" defendants, who now, presumably, have to participate in discovery and other aspects of involved and expensive litigation. Just as pusillanimous use of Rule 20(a) can hurt plaintiffs, so can overzealous use hurt defendants.

Yes, joinder would be proper under Rule 20(a)(2) because the claims against those two (1) arise from the same transaction or occurrence (the crash) and (2) raise at least one common question (whether the driver was negligent). Again, the Rule is permissive, so the plaintiff can choose to sue both defendants in a single case or to sue them in separate actions.

Examples #13 and #14 beg the question: Why would a plaintiff ever fail to join all possible plaintiffs and defendants under Rule 20(a)? Depending on the facts, there may be jurisdictional limitations on doing so. For example, perhaps the court cannot get personal jurisdiction over one of the potential defendants or perhaps joining all the parties will make it impossible to invoke diversity of citizenship jurisdiction. Our focus here, however, is on the sorts of litigation strategies that might animate the plaintiff's selective use of Rule 20(a).

Speaking very generally, plaintiffs prefer to have all potential defendants — everyone who might potentially be liable for her harm — joined in a single case. We touched on the reasons for this in discussing the *Poster* case above. First, it is less expensive and less burdensome to sue once than to file a separate case against each potential defendant. Second, the advent of nonmutual defensive issue preclusion gives the plaintiff an incentive to sue several defendants at once; if she sued separately and lost against one defendant, the defendant in another suit may be able to use issue preclusion against the plaintiff on any negative findings. (If this point is unclear, review §11.4.5.) Third, the plaintiff can often benefit from each codefendant's effort in the litigation to shift the blame from itself to other codefendants. Fourth, and quite important as a practical matter, as we saw in discussing the *Poster* case, suing individual defendants allows them to whipsaw the plaintiff. That is, the defendant in one case might convince the jury that the harm to the plaintiff is not her fault, but the fault of someone who is not a party in this case. The defendant in the other case can do the same, leaving a plaintiff who may have convinced two juries that she is entitled to relief, but who recovers nothing because each jury thinks the fault lies with an absentee.

Similarly, as a general matter, plaintiffs prefer not to have coplaintiffs suing with them. First, suing alone may allow the plaintiff to recover from a defendant first, before other plaintiffs can get at the defendant's assets. Second, she may conclude that her case is more compelling than those of the other potential plaintiffs, and that adding a coplaintiff would tarnish her luster and divert the jury's attention from her. Third, even if the case settles without going to trial, there is a widely held view that a single plaintiff fares better simply because she does not have to share a recovery with others. Thus, as a general strategic matter, we expect to see plaintiffs use Rule 20(a)(2) to join all potential defendants into a single case, but to keep center stage to themselves on their side.[36]

What Are Misjoinder, Severance, Separate Trials, and Consolidation?

What happens if the plaintiff structures the case in violation of Rule 20(a)? Rule 21 provides that such "misjoinder of parties" is *not* a basis for dismissal of the suit. Instead, the court may "sever any claim against a party." Severance results in two or more separate suits. Each will have its own docket number and will result in its own judgment. This concept of severance is different from a court's ordering a separate trial under Rule 20(b) or 42(b). A separate trial is just that—a separate adjudication of a claim (or claims) that are part of one case.

- ○ ***Example #15.*** *P-1* and *P-2*, properly joined as coplaintiffs under Rule 20(a)(1), sue *D* on a claim that *D* breached a contract between the three. In addition, *P-1* asserts an unrelated claim against *D*, concerning an entirely separate event. *P-1* has the right to assert this unrelated claim under Rule 18(a)(1), as we saw in §12.3. Although those claims are part of one case, the court may order a separate trial on the unrelated claim asserted by *P-1* against *D*. After all, it involves different facts from the main claim, and might distract or confuse the jury hearing that main claim. So the two claims will be tried separately. But ultimately, they will be determined in a single judgment, because they are part of a single case.[37]

- ○ ***Example #16.*** *P* sues two defendants, *D-1* and *D-2*, alleging that they caused him tortious harm. The court concludes, however, that joinder of the two defendants violates Rule 20(a)(2), because they caused harm to *P*, if at all, in separate transactions. Here, under Rule 21, the court will order severance. The result of that order is to create two cases: (1) by *P* against *D-1* and (2) by *P* against *D-2*. (Actually, the court will simply drop *D-2* as a defendant, and *P* will have to file the second case (against *D-2*) and pay the filing fee for that case.) But there are now two separate cases, which will result in two separate judgments. This result is dictated by the fact that *D-1* and *D-2* were not properly joined in a single case because the claims against them did not satisfy Rule 20(a)(2).[38]

In Example #16, there is another procedural device that might come into play: consolidation under Federal Rule 42(a).[39] That Rule permits a

---

[36]For more detailed discussion of such litigation strategies in structuring a suit, see the articles cited at note 2 above.

[37]In §14.5.1, we see that the court might ultimately treat the separate claims as separate "cases" for purposes of appeal under Rule 54(c). But that's for later. The point here is that these claims, although tried separately, are properly joined in a single case.

[38]The same thing would happen if two plaintiffs were misjoined under Rule 20(a)(1).

[39]*See generally* 9A Wright & Miller §2283.

court in which two (or more) separate cases are pending to consolidate the cases for any or all purposes. The only requirement (beyond the fact that the cases are pending in the same district)[40] is that the cases involve at least one common question of law or fact.[41] Consolidation means that those separate cases will be treated together for whatever purposes the court deems appropriate. For example, the court might order consolidation for purposes of discovery, or for motions, or for trial, or even for all purposes. Consolidation does not merge the cases; they are still separate cases and will result in separate judgments, even if consolidated for all purposes.[42]

As we noted above, plaintiffs often attempt to join multiple defendants in a single case to ensure that they will be tried before the same jury. That way, as we said above, the plaintiff avoids the risk of having the jury conclude that the real "bad guy" is someone who is not in the court. If such a plaintiff loses the battle of joinder under Rule 20(a) (because the court concludes that the claims against the two do not arise from the same transaction or occurrence) she might still win the war at trial if the court orders consolidation for trial.

That is exactly what happened in *Stanford v. Tennessee Valley Authority*,[43] an older but instructive case. The plaintiff owned property in Tennessee and claimed that it was damaged by chemicals poured into the air by two chemical plants. The plants were operated by different companies. The plaintiff joined both companies as codefendants. The court rejected the joinder, however, because it concluded that what each company did was a separate transaction or occurrence.[44] It ordered severance, after which the plaintiff had two separate cases, one against each chemical company. In the same opinion, however, the court ordered that the now-separate cases be consolidated for trial. Thus, the plaintiff would get the advantage of having the two defendants before the same jury at the same time.

---

[40]Thus, a case pending in the Southern District of New York cannot be consolidated with a case pending in the Eastern District of Pennsylvania. Remember, however, that cases can, in appropriate circumstances, be transferred from one federal district to another. If the case in the Southern District of New York were transferred to the Eastern District of Pennsylvania, the two cases could be consolidated. But transfer and consolidation are separate steps.

[41]*See* Effron, note 20 above, 100 Geo. L.J. at 790-799 (courts often imply a requirement of predominance of common questions in ruling on consolidation). *See also* Robin Effron, *Disaster-Specific Mechanisms for Consolidation,* 82 Tulane L. Rev. 2423 (2008).

[42]Johnson v. Manhattan Ry. Co., 289 U.S. 479, 496 (1933). *See* Hall v. Hall, 138 S. Ct. 1118, 1128-1132 (2018) (final judgment in one of several consolidated cases was to be appealed without awaiting final judgments in the other consolidated cases).

[43]18 F.R.D. 152 (M.D. Tenn. 1955).

[44]This holding seems stingy. Perhaps the plaintiff should have argued that his harm was caused by the combined effect of the acts of the two companies, as was done in cases such as *Poster*, discussed above.

Subject Matter Jurisdiction

The plaintiff uses Rule 20(a) to determine how many plaintiffs and how many defendants will be joined in a single case. Once she does so, she must ensure that the case as structured can be brought in the court she chooses. Thus, she must assess whether the court has personal jurisdiction over the defendants and whether venue is proper. And, of course, she must determine that the case will invoke subject matter jurisdiction. Let's assume plaintiff wants to sue in federal court.

○ ***Example #17.*** *P* sues two defendants, *D-1* and *D-2*, properly joining them under Rule 20(a)(2). All three litigants are citizens of California. *P*'s claim against *D-1* alleges that *D-1* violated *P*'s rights under a federal statute. *P*'s claim against *D-2* alleges that *D-2* breached a state law duty to *P*. The claims against the two obviously (given one of the requirements of Rule 20(a)) arise from the same transaction or occurrence. Is there federal subject matter jurisdiction as the case is structured?
  ○ The claim against *D-1* invokes federal question jurisdiction, because it is for violation of a right created by a federal statute.
  ○ The claim against *D-2* does not invoke federal question jurisdiction, because it arises under state, not federal, law. Further, the claim does not invoke diversity of citizenship jurisdiction, because *P* and *D-2* are cocitizens.
  ○ The claim against *D-2* does, however, invoke supplemental jurisdiction (what *Gibbs* called "pendent" jurisdiction; see §4.7.2). First, §1367(a) grants supplemental jurisdiction because the claim against *D-2* involves the same "case or controversy" as the claim that invoked federal subject matter jurisdiction (the claim asserted by *P* v. *D-1*). Why? Because it meets the *Gibbs* "common nucleus of operative fact" test. As discussed in §4.7.2, §1367(a) codifies *Gibbs* and the *Gibbs* test is actually broader than "transaction or occurrence." So any claim, such as the claim here, that arises from the same transaction or occurrence as a claim that invokes an independent basis of federal subject matter jurisdiction will always meet *Gibbs* and, therefore, invoke jurisdiction under §1367(a). Second, §1367(b) does not remove the grant of supplemental jurisdiction, because that subsection applies only in cases that invoked diversity of citizenship jurisdiction. This case invoked federal question jurisdiction, so §1367(b) does not apply.

The fact pattern we just saw is similar to the *Finley* case, the holding that led to passage of the supplemental jurisdiction statute. (If any of this material does not ring a bell, review §4.7.) Now let's push farther with three important hypotheticals in Examples #18-20.

○ ***Example #18.*** Two plaintiffs, *P-1* and *P-2*, properly joined under Rule 20(a)(1), assert state law claims against a single defendant (*D*). *P-1* is a citizen of California. *P-2* is a citizen of Arizona. *D* is a citizen of Nevada. *P-1*'s claim is for $100,000 but *P-2*'s claim is for $60,000. As structured, is there federal subject matter jurisdiction? Because the claims arise under state law, there is no federal question jurisdiction. What about diversity of citizenship jurisdiction? Certainly, there is no problem with citizenship, because the two plaintiffs are citizens of different states from the defendant. But there is trouble with the amount in controversy. *P-1*'s claim meets that requirement, because it exceeds $75,000 and thus invokes diversity of citizenship jurisdiction. But *P-2*'s claim does not satisfy the amount in controversy requirement, since it does not exceed $75,000. And when there are multiple parties such as this, they may not aggregate their claims to meet the amount in controversy requirement, as we discussed in §4.5.3. It seems, then, that the court should drop the claim asserted by *P-2* from the case. But might the supplemental jurisdiction statute change this result?

The claim asserted by *P-1* against *D* invokes diversity of citizenship jurisdiction. The claim asserted by *P-2* against *D* does not. But because the two claims arise from the same transaction or occurrence, §1367(a) grants supplemental jurisdiction over the claim by *P-2*. Obviously, §1367(b) *should* remove supplemental jurisdiction over this claim, or else the amount in controversy requirement will be eviscerated. But does it? Again, look carefully at its terms. Section 1367(b) applies only in cases that invoke diversity of citizenship jurisdiction (which *P-1* v. *D* does). And it removes jurisdiction over claims brought *"by plaintiffs against persons made parties under Rule . . . 20."* That is not the situation in this hypothetical. Here, the claim is asserted *by persons made parties under Rule 20 against a defendant.* Nowhere does §1367(b) remove the grant of supplemental jurisdiction.

This result (apparently not intended by the drafters of §1367) is inconsistent with *Clark v. Paul Gray, Inc.*,[45] in which the Supreme Court held that each plaintiff's claim must satisfy the amount in controversy requirement to invoke diversity of citizenship jurisdiction. Lower courts generally held that the supplemental jurisdiction statute had overruled *Clark*,[46] and commentators generally conclude that this result makes sense.[47] In *Exxon Mobil Corp. v. Allapattah Services*,[48] the Supreme Court embraced this interpretation, and upheld supplemental jurisdiction over jurisdictionally insufficient

[45]306 U.S. 583 (1939).

[46]*See, e.g.*, Stromberg Metal Works v. Press Mech., Inc., 77 F.3d 928, 932 (7th Cir. 1996).

[47]*See* Thomas D. Rowe, *1367 and All That: Recodifying Federal Supplemental Jurisdiction*, 74 Ind. L.J. 53 (1998). The American Law Institute proposed a revision of §1367 that would expressly embrace this result. American Law Institute, Federal Judicial Code Revision Project 9 (2004).

[48]545 U.S. 546 (2005).

claims by plaintiffs, so long as they arose from a common nucleus of operative fact with the claim of a plaintiff that did satisfy the amount in controversy requirement.

> ○ ***Example #19.*** A single plaintiff, *P*, a citizen of California, sues two defendants, *D-1* and *D-2*, properly joining them under Rule 20(a)(2). *D-1* and *D-2* are citizens of Kansas. *P*'s claims against *D-1* and *D-2* arise under state law. The claim against *D-1* is for $100,000 and the claim against *D-2* is for $60,000. Here, the claim by *P* against *D-1* obviously invokes diversity of citizenship jurisdiction. The claim by *P* against *D-2* does not, however, because even though it is by a citizen of California against a citizen of Kansas, it does not exceed $75,000.

Based upon Example #18, however, we would expect the claim by *P* against *D-2* to invoke supplemental jurisdiction. Indeed, the claim does satisfy §1367(a), as in Example #18. But look carefully at §1367(b). It applies in diversity cases, such as this case. And it removes supplemental jurisdiction over claims by plaintiffs against persons joined under Rule 20. That is exactly what we have here! *D-1* and *D-2* were joined under Rule 20, so §1367(b), on its face, removes supplemental jurisdiction over this claim.

This result makes no sense. Why should supplemental jurisdiction be proper to overcome an amount in controversy problem in a diversity case when there are multiple plaintiffs but not when there are multiple defendants? The Court did not address this "multiple defendants problem" in *Allapattah*. And as yet there is no definitive interpretation in the lower courts. Perhaps they can find a way to avoid what the statute seems to command. The hypothetical simply manifests one of many problems caused by a very poorly drafted statute.

> ○ ***Example #20.*** Two plaintiffs, *P-1* and *P-2*, properly joined under Rule 20(a)(1), assert state law claims against a single defendant (*D*). *P-1* is a citizen of California. *P-2* is a citizen of Arizona. *D* is a citizen of Arizona. *P-1*'s claim is for $100,000, and *P-2*'s claim is for $200,000. As structured, is there federal subject matter jurisdiction? Because the claims arise under state law, there is no federal question jurisdiction. What about diversity of citizenship jurisdiction? On the face of it, no. *P-1* is diverse from *D*, but *P-2* is not diverse from *D*. The structure of the case violates the complete diversity rule. But could §1367 affect this outcome?

Applying the statute literally, it seems the answer should be the same as in Example #18 above. Here, as there, it appears that the claim asserted by *P-1* against *D* invokes diversity of citizenship jurisdiction. The claim asserted by *P-2* against *D* does not. But because the two claims arise from the same transaction or occurrence, §1367(a) grants supplemental jurisdiction over the claim by *P-2*. Obviously,

§1367(b) *should* remove supplemental jurisdiction over this claim, or else the complete diversity rule is rendered meaningless. But does it? Again, look carefully at its terms. Section 1367(b) applies only in cases that invoke diversity of citizenship jurisdiction (which *P-1* v. *D* arguably does). And it removes jurisdiction over claims brought *"by plaintiffs against persons made parties under Rule . . . 20."* That is not the situation in this hypothetical. Here, the claim is asserted *by persons made parties under Rule 20 against a defendant.* Nowhere does §1367(b) remove the grant of supplemental jurisdiction.

Arguably, there is no reason that the outcome here, in Example #20, should be any different from that in Example #18. There, supplemental jurisdiction made up for a lack of amount in controversy in a diversity case. Here, it would make up for a lack of complete diversity in a diversity case. Both the complete diversity rule and the amount in controversy requirement are merely *statutory* (not constitutional) provisions of the grant of diversity of citizenship jurisdiction under §1332. As such, each should be equally amenable to change by §1367. On the other hand, concluding that the parties may use supplemental jurisdiction to overcome the complete diversity rule would threaten to inundate the federal courts with more cases than they could hope to handle.

In *Allapattah*, the Court found a way to avoid such inundation. As discussed in §4.5.3, the Court in that case clarified how jurisdiction attaches in diversity cases. If there is complete diversity, the presence of a single claim in excess of $75,000 invokes diversity of citizenship jurisdiction. In other words, as in Example #18 above, the claim by *P-1* against *D* constituted a diversity of citizenship case in the federal courts, to which the claim by *P-2* could be supplemental. In contrast, the Court said in *dictum*, if there is not complete diversity of citizenship between all plaintiffs and all defendants, there is no diversity case at all, and nothing to which supplemental jurisdiction can attach.[49] In Example #20, then, the claim by *P-1* against *D* failed to invoke diversity of citizenship jurisdiction, so there was no case in which to exercise supplemental jurisdiction. Stated another way, the Court concluded, the amount in controversy requirement is "claim-specific" while the complete diversity requirement is "action-specific." (If this is not clear, see §4.5.3.) Thus, according to the Court in *Allapattah*, the case in Example #20 should be dismissed. (In reality, though, courts in this situation appear to use Rule 20 to drop *P-2* from the case and to then allow the case of *P-1* and *D* to proceed.)

---

[49]*Id.* at 552-553.

§12.5 Claim Joinder by a Defendant

As we discussed in §11.2.1, parties other than the plaintiff can be "claimants," meaning that they can assert claims for relief in the pending case. In this section, we look at claims that may be asserted by defendants. These should not be confused with the defensive responses we discussed at §7.4. There, the defendant's concern was avoiding the imposition of liability on her. Here, the interest is in *suing* somebody—in asserting a claim against another party. As we see in detail below, the *counterclaim* is asserted against an "opposing party" (by the defendant against the plaintiff, for example), and the *crossclaim* is asserted against a "coparty"[50] (by one defendant against another defendant, for example).[51]

Of course, it is never enough simply to satisfy one of the Federal Rules allowing joinder. In addition (assuming the case is in federal court), the claim must invoke federal subject matter jurisdiction. For each claim asserted, then, the parties and court must address whether it invokes diversity, alienage, or federal question jurisdiction; failing those, they must determine whether the claim invokes supplemental jurisdiction. On the other hand, personal jurisdiction and venue will not be a problem. If the court lacked personal jurisdiction over the defendant, she should be attempting to get the case dismissed on that basis rather than asserting a claim. And by filing suit, plaintiff generally has waived any personal jurisdiction objection to being sued on a counterclaim. Moreover, the venue statutes, discussed at §5.4, speak of where an action may be "brought," meaning that they dictate the place where the plaintiff can sue the defendant; they do not require separate assessment of venue for counterclaims and crossclaims.[52]

Rule 13(h) provides that a defendant asserting a counterclaim or crossclaim can join new parties to the claim so long as these newcomers are joined in accordance with the provisions of Rules 19 or 20. We discussed Rule 20 in §12.4 and discuss Rule 19 in §12.6.1. Each is concerned with joinder of parties. Rule 13(h) thus puts a defendant asserting a counterclaim or crossclaim on the same footing for party

---

[50]From 1938 until December 1, 2007, the Federal Rules hyphenated this word as *co-party*.

[51]The defendant can also assert a claim against a third party under certain circumstances by invoking Rule 14(a)(1). Because such "impleader" claims involve joinder of a new party to the pending case, however, we address it in a different part of the chapter. See §12.6.2.

[52]*See, e.g.*, General Elec. Co. v. Marvel Rare Metals Co., 287 U.S. 430, 435 (1932) (venue rules do not apply to counterclaims); Mark E. Mitchell, Inc. v. Charleston Library Soc'y, 114 F. Supp. 2d 259, 263 n.7 (S.D.N.Y. 2000) (same); Scott v. Fancher, 369 F.2d 842 (5th Cir. 1966) (venue rules do not apply to crossclaims).

joinder as the plaintiff in originally structuring the suit. We see an example of the use of Rule 13(h) in §12.6.1.

Because the counterclaim and crossclaim are claims for relief, the party against whom they are asserted must respond just as the defendant had to respond to the original complaint. As discussed in §7.4, the defending party may respond under Rule 12 either by motion or by answer.

§12.5.1 Counterclaims (Rule 13(a) and Rule 13(b))

In General

Federal Rule 13 contains several subsections governing counterclaims in federal court. We see below that there are two types of counterclaims: "compulsory" (under Rule 13(a)) and "permissive" (under Rule 13(b)). Here, we look at general characteristics common to both. For starters, a counterclaim is asserted against an "opposing party." This means somebody who has asserted a claim against the party. Thus, if the defendant has a claim against the plaintiff (who has obviously sued the defendant), it is a counterclaim. Most counterclaims are asserted by the defendant against the plaintiff. But realize that *any* party against whom a claim is made may have a counterclaim back against that party. For example, suppose a defendant (*D-1*) asserts a crossclaim (addressed in §12.5.2) against a codefendant (*D-2*). If *D-2* has a claim back against *D-1*, it will be a counterclaim. Once *D-1* asserted the crossclaim against *D-2*, the two became "opposing parties," making *D-2*'s claim against *D-1* a counterclaim.

It also bears repeating that a counterclaim is a *claim*, not a defense. Thus, it does not attempt to "diminish or defeat the recovery sought by the opposing party."[53] That function is handled by responsive pleadings and motions, as we saw in §7.3.3. Instead, with a counterclaim, the defendant is suing the plaintiff. At common law, a defendant was permitted to raise defenses that would offset the plaintiff's recovery, but could not, as a general rule, win a recovery against the plaintiff. Rule 13(c) changes that practice by providing expressly that the counterclaim may exceed the plaintiff's claim. In addition, the counterclaim can be for a different type of relief than the plaintiff's original claim. For instance, if the plaintiff sues for damages, the defendant may counterclaim for an injunction. Similarly, if the plaintiff sues for $80,000, the defendant can counterclaim for $8 million.

---

[53]Fed. R. Civ. P. 13(c).

Under Rule 13(a) and (b), a counterclaim is to be asserted in "[a] pleading." Because the defendant asserting the counterclaim has already been sued, the pleading will be an answer. So the counterclaim is asserted in the defendant's answer. If the party fails to assert the counterclaim in her answer, she may be able to amend the answer to assert the claim. The matter is treated as an amendment question, which we discussed in §7.6.1.

What happens, however, if the defendant's counterclaim does not mature (i.e., the claim does not accrue) until after the defendant has already answered? That situation is addressed by Rule 13(e), which allows the defendant to assert the claim by "supplemental pleading." This provision is consistent with our discussion of supplemental pleadings at §7.6. As you will recall, a supplemental pleading involves events occurring after a pleading has been filed.

The Compulsory Counterclaim

Procedural and Policy Issues. The compulsory counterclaim is created and governed in federal practice by Federal Rule 13(a)(1)(A).[54] Of course, a counterclaim is always asserted against an "opposing party." The *compulsory* counterclaim is one that arises from the "same transaction or occurrence" as the opposing party's claim.[55] In the usual

---

[54]Though states are free to devise their own procedural systems, most adopt a compulsory counterclaim rule that mirrors Rule 13(a)(1)(A). Some states, however, such as Virginia, do not have such a provision. *See* Va. Rules of Court 3:8 (defendant "may, at his option, plead . . . a counterclaim"). Thus, in Virginia, all counterclaims (even those arising from the same transaction or occurrence as the plaintiff's claim) are "permissive." The party has the option of asserting it in the pending case or of suing on the claim in a separate case.

[55]Many claims obviously arise from the same transaction or occurrence, as when two people are injured in a single automobile collision. At the margin, however, it is not easy to say when two claims are transactionally related. In the compulsory counterclaim context, some courts look only to factual overlap between the claims. Other courts look to legal issues presented by the two claims. *See* Effron, note 20 above, 100 Geo. L.J. at 776-790 (courts emphasize factual or legal issues to justify decision whether a counterclaim is compulsory). For an example of a case that is close to the line, see Example #26 below. A classic case interpreting "transaction or occurrence" for compulsory counterclaims is *Moore v. New York Cotton Exch.*, 270 U.S. 593, 610 (1926). It was decided under the compulsory counterclaim provision of the old Federal Equity Rule 30, which was a precursor of Federal Rule 13(a)(1). The Court explained, "'Transaction' is a word of flexible meaning. It may comprehend a series of many occurrences, depending not so much upon the immediateness of their connection as upon their logical relationship." In *Moore*, the plaintiff sued two defendants (a commodities exchange and a telegraph company hired by the exchange to provide quotations to customers), alleging that their agreement violated federal antitrust laws. The exchange counterclaimed that the plaintiff had been stealing exchange quotations. Though the facts underlying the plaintiff's claim and those underlying the counterclaim were "not precisely identical" (and though the counterclaim "embrace[d] additional allegations"),

context, it is a claim asserted by the defendant against the plaintiff, and it arises from the same transaction or occurrence as the plaintiff's claim against the defendant.

The compulsory counterclaim is so named because Rule 13 says the party "must" assert the claim in the pending case. "Must" is mandatory; it commands that the act be done. Interestingly, the Rule does not expressly state the consequence of violating the command. Nonetheless, that consequence is clear: The party failing to assert a compulsory counterclaim loses the claim and cannot assert it in another proceeding.[56]

> ∘ ***Example #21.*** *A* and *Z*, each driving her own car, collide. Each suffers personal injuries. In Case 1, in federal court, *A* sues *Z* to recover for her personal injuries. *Z* answers and defends that suit, which is litigated to conclusion. In Case 2, *Z* sues *A* to recover for her personal injuries from the collision. Case 2 should be dismissed. *Z*'s claim was a compulsory counterclaim in the original case, because it was against an opposing party and arose from the same transaction or occurrence as *A*'s claim in that case.[57] *Z* failed to assert the claim in the then-pending case, so cannot file it anywhere.

When we say "anywhere," we mean not only that *Z* cannot assert her claim in a separate action in a federal court. The compulsory counterclaim rule should operate to bar a subsequent case in state court as well (even if that state does not have a compulsory counterclaim rule). As we discuss momentarily, the compulsory counterclaim rule, properly understood, should be seen as establishing an estoppel against the defendant from asserting her claim in a second case. There is no reason the estoppel should not follow the defendant and preclude the later litigation in any court. Although there are some older decisions to the contrary, most state courts addressing the issue have reached this conclusion.[58] The converse should also be true: Failure to assert a compulsory counterclaim in Case 1 in state court (in a state that has

---

the defendants' refusal to provide quotations to the plaintiff underlay both the original claim and the counterclaim. Accordingly, the counterclaim was compulsory. Courts continue to find the "logical relationship" test helpful. *See, e.g.*, Smith v. Kansas City Public Employees Retirement Sys., 2019 WL 339542 at *2 (D. Kan. 2019).

[56]"It is entirely accepted that the failure to assert a claim as a compulsory counterclaim precludes the party from later bringing an independent action on the claim." Wright & Kane, Federal Courts 567.

[57]Fed. R. Civ. P. 13(a)(1)(A).

[58]*See, e.g.*, Nottingham v. Weld, 377 S.E.2d 621, 623 (Va. 1989); Jocie Motor Lines, Inc. v. Johnson, 57 S.E.2d 388 (N.C. 1950).

such a rule) should bar the defendant from instituting Case 2 on that claim in federal court.[59]

Some courts inject needless confusion into their discussions of *why* Case 2 should be dismissed. Some have used the language of claim preclusion to say why *D* is barred from bringing suit.[60] But claim preclusion plays no role here.[61] Remember from §11.2.1 that claim preclusion applies only when two actions are brought *by the same claimant against the same defendant*. Here, Case 1 was brought by *A* against *Z*. Case 2 was brought by *Z* against *A*. *Z* had never been a claimant before and is not suing twice on the same claim. Other courts use the language of waiver, which is more accurate.[62] Case 2 is dismissed because *Z*, by failing to assert the claim in Case 1, has waived the claim. Some speak of the compulsory counterclaim rule as working "rule preclusion."[63]

The appropriate way to deal with the issue was espoused by the late Professor Charles Alan Wright decades ago: *D* cannot proceed with a separate case because of "estoppel by rule."[64] Failure to assert the claim in Case 1 estops *D* from asserting the claim elsewhere. Because estoppel is an equitable principle, it can be applied with a heart. For example, let's return to Example #21. Suppose that in Case 1, *Z*'s insurance company took over the defense (as would normally be the case[65]) and failed to inform *Z* of the compulsory counterclaim rule. If, through no fault or lack of diligence of her own, *Z* was not informed of her right (let alone obligation) to assert the claim, perhaps she should not be estopped from bringing the separate action.[66]

---

[59]*See, e.g.*, Carnation Co. v. T.U. Parks Constr. Co., 816 F.2d 1099, 1103 (6th Cir. 1987); Chapman v. Aetna Fin. Co., 615 F.2d 361, 363-364 (5th Cir. 1980) (although the result is not required by the full faith and credit statute (see §11.6.3), as a matter of comity, federal court should bar claim that would be barred by defendant's failure to assert compulsory counterclaim in state court action).

[60]*See, e.g.*, Dragor Shipping Corp. v. Union Tank Car Co., 378 F.2d 241, 244-245 (9th Cir. 1967).

[61]*See* United States Fid. & Guar. Co. v. Maish, 908 P.2d 1329, 1340, 1341 (Kan. 1995) ("We conclude that the doctrine of res judicata is not applicable in this case. We believe these facts are more in tune with the estoppel theory, and we adopt that theory as the philosophical basis for the enforcement of the counterclaim bar in the instant matter. . . . [T]he fact that the previous action was settled rather than litigated on the merits does not avoid the compulsory counterclaim bar in this case").

[62]*See, e.g.*, Martino v. McDonald's Sys., Inc., 598 F.2d 1079, 1083-1084 (7th Cir. 1979); Dindo v. Whitney, 451 F.2d 1, 3 (1st Cir. 1971).

[63]*See, e.g.*, Harris v. Huffco Petroleum Corp., 633 F. Supp. 250, 255 (S.D. Ala. 1986).

[64]The classic discussion is Charles Alan Wright, *Estoppel by Rule: The Compulsory Counterclaim Under Modern Pleading*, 38 Minn. L. Rev. 423, 428-436 (1954).

[65]Usually, a liability insurer is required not only to indemnify its insured for covered events, but to afford its insured a defense as well.

[66]*See* Dindo v. Whitney, 451 F.2d 1, 3 (1st Cir. 1971) ("Other courts have viewed the [compulsory counterclaim] rule . . . as creating an estoppel or waiver. The latter approach seems more appropriate, at least when the case is settled rather than tried. . . .

There are surprisingly few published opinions in which courts discuss the nature of the bar worked by the compulsory counterclaim rule.[67] In all likelihood, the paucity of such cases reflects the fact that very few defendants fail to assert compulsory counterclaims.

Though the operation of the compulsory counterclaim rule is not the same as claim preclusion, it serves the same function as the modern approach to that doctrine. Both serve to force the joinder of transactionally related rights to relief into a single case.[68] Doing so is efficient and relatively convenient for the fact-finder, which may wrap up all claims arising from what the parties will generally consider a single real-world event. Moreover, the focus on the transaction is generally consistent with the exercise of supplemental jurisdiction, as we saw in §4.7. To be sure, the definition of "transaction or occurrence" can be troublesome at the margin (as we saw in §11.2.3), but in most cases the lines will be fairly easy to draw.

At this point, we need to refine our definition of compulsory counterclaim to reflect two situations in which the defendant will *not* be estopped from bringing a separate action. First, if an otherwise compulsory counterclaim would "require adding another party over whom the court cannot acquire jurisdiction," Rule 13(a)(1)(B) provides that the claim is not considered compulsory. In other words, if the counterclaim implicates nonparties who should be joined but cannot be joined (because, for example, there is no personal jurisdiction over them), it is not a compulsory counterclaim. This provision implements the policies of Rule 19, concerning joinder of "required," or "necessary," parties, which we see in §12.6.1.

Second, under Rule 13(a)(2)(A), the defendant need not assert an otherwise compulsory counterclaim if she has already asserted the claim in another case before being sued. So in Example #21, suppose Z had already filed suit against A before A sued Z. Then, Z need not assert the counterclaim against A when A sues her.[69] This exception

---

If a case has been tried, protection both of the court and the parties dictates that there should be no further directly related litigation. But if the case is settled, normally the court has not been greatly burdened, and the parties can protect themselves by demanding cross-releases. In such circumstances, absent a release, better-tailored justice seems obtainable by applying principles of equitable estoppel"); United States Fid. & Guar. Co. v. Maish, 908 P.2d 1329, 1340 (Kan. 1995).

[67]*See, e.g.,* Wright & Kane, Federal Courts 568 ("[I]t is remarkable that there have been so few cases in which a party actually has been held to be barred because of failure to plead the claim as a counterclaim in the prior action").

[68]Recall that the modern approach to claim preclusion defines one's "claim" as all rights to relief arising from a transaction or occurrence. See §11.2.3.

[69]Of course, when Z sued A, A's claim against Z would be a compulsory counterclaim in that case (assuming the jurisdiction has a compulsory counterclaim rule like Rule 13(a)). But in some state courts (Virginia is an example), there is no such thing as a compulsory

makes sense; it tells someone who has already asserted her claim that she does not have to do so again.[70]

Remember (as we discussed above in this subsection) that a counterclaim is to be asserted in a "pleading," which means with the defendant's answer.[71] If the case is resolved without the defendant's having to answer, the compulsory counterclaim rule will not apply.

○ *Example #22.* In Case 1, *A* sues *Z* for injuries sustained in an auto collision between the two. *Z* does not answer, but files a motion to dismiss for improper service of process. The motion is granted; the case is dismissed. In Case 2, *Z* sues *A* to recover for her personal injuries from the collision. Case 2 will not be dismissed, because the compulsory counterclaim rule never attached in Case 1. *Z* never answered in Case 1, so she could not have asserted a counterclaim.[72]

Subject Matter Jurisdiction. Rule 13(a)(1) merely provides a procedural mechanism for asserting a claim. The claim must invoke federal subject matter jurisdiction, however, or else it cannot be asserted in federal court. As always, this jurisdictional inquiry is a separate step, undertaken after determining that the claim is properly asserted under Rule 13(a)(1).

○ *Example #23.* *A*, a citizen of Maryland, sues *Z*, a citizen of Delaware, asserting a state law claim of $500,000. *Z* has a claim against *A* that arises from the same transaction or occurrence as *A*'s claim. It is based upon state law and *Z* claims damages of $100,000. Is there subject matter jurisdiction over *Z*'s compulsory counterclaim?

Yes. Because the facts state that all claims in this case arise under state law, there is no federal question jurisdiction. Obviously, though, *A*'s original claim invokes diversity of citizenship jurisdiction: It is asserted by a citizen of Maryland against a citizen of Delaware, and it exceeds $75,000. *Z*'s claim against *A* is a compulsory counterclaim,

---

counterclaim. Even counterclaims arising from the same transaction or occurrence as the plaintiff's claim need not be asserted in the pending case.

[70]Another exception to the operation of the compulsory counterclaim rule is found in Rule 13(a)(2)(B) but should be quite rare. Under that subsection, if the plaintiff's claim is asserted *in rem* or *quasi-in-rem,* and the court did not acquire *in personam* jurisdiction over the defendant, the defendant's claim is not compulsory. The reason for this rule is to avoid forcing the defendant to do something that might subject her to *in personam* jurisdiction. Given the rarity of *in rem* and *quasi-in-rem* cases, however, this provision has seen little action through the years.

[71]Recall also, as discussed immediately before this subsection on the compulsory counterclaim, that if the defendant's claim matures after the plaintiff sues the defendant, it is not a counterclaim. *See* Rule 13(e).

[72]*See, e.g.,* United States v. Snider, 779 F.2d 1151, 1157 (6th Cir. 1985).

because it arises from the same transaction or occurrence as *A*'s claim. It also invokes diversity of citizenship jurisdiction, because the litigants are of diverse citizenship and the claim exceeds $75,000.

> ○ ***Example #24.*** Same facts as Example #23, except that the compulsory counterclaim by *Z* is for $45,000. As above, the original claim asserted by *A* against *Z* invokes diversity of citizenship jurisdiction.

Again, the compulsory counterclaim arises under state law, and thus will not invoke federal question jurisdiction. Here, the compulsory counterclaim does not invoke diversity of citizenship jurisdiction, because it does not meet the amount in controversy requirement; it is a claim for $45,000 and thus does not exceed $75,000. Nonetheless, the federal court can entertain *Z*'s counterclaim under supplemental jurisdiction. Why? Section 1367(a) grants supplemental jurisdiction over claims that are part of the same "case or controversy" as the claim that invoked federal subject matter jurisdiction (the claim asserted by *A* against *Z*).

As interpreted, that requirement embraces the *Gibbs* standard and is met if the claims share a common nucleus of operative fact. As we saw in §4.7, this test is always met by claims that arise from the same transaction or occurrence as the claim that got the case into federal court initially. Thus, the compulsory counterclaim always meets this test. By definition, it arises from the same transaction or occurrence as the underlying case by *A* against *Z*. Section 1367(b) applies in cases that invoke diversity of citizenship jurisdiction (such as the claim asserted by *A* against *Z*) but removes supplemental jurisdiction only over claims asserted by *plaintiffs*. This is a claim asserted by a defendant, so §1367(b) does not remove the supplemental jurisdiction. (If any of this material is not familiar, see §4.7.)

The Permissive Counterclaim

Procedural and Policy Issues. The second kind of counterclaim is the permissive counterclaim, created and governed in federal practice by Federal Rule 13(b). Any counterclaim, as we know, is asserted against an "opposing party." The *permissive* counterclaim is one that is not compulsory. In other words, it does *not* arise from the same "transaction or occurrence" as the opposing party's claim. In the usual context, then, it is a claim asserted by the defendant against the plaintiff and is transactionally *unrelated* to the plaintiff's claim against the defendant.

The Rule 13(b) claim is called *permissive* precisely because the defendant is not *required* to assert it in the pending case. How do we know? The Rule provides that the claim "may" be asserted (not "must" be asserted) in the pending case. Thus, the defendant may file it in that case if she desires, but she may just as readily sue on the claim in a separate case. Rule 13(b) allows the defendant to join in the pending case any and all claims she may have against the plaintiff, regardless of the fact that they are unrelated to the plaintiff's claim against her. This provision mirrors the plaintiff's unlimited right to join claims under Rule 18(a), which we addressed at §12.3. The same policy applies here as there: The idea is to allow the parties to put their entire dispute(s) before the court in one case. We noted in discussing Rule 18(a) that this unlimited joinder might result in a confusing mix of claims in a single case. The permissive counterclaim rule can multiply the confusion. The antidote, as it was with Rule 18(a), is to equip the court with the discretionary authority to order separate trials of the various claims.[73]

In §12.3, we also noted that Rule 18(a), which allows the assertion in a single case of any and all claims, regardless of transactional or legal relatedness, applies not only to plaintiffs, but to any claimant, including one who asserts a counterclaim. But Rule 18(a) is meaningless in the counterclaim situation. If the defendant has claims against the plaintiff that do arise from the same transaction or occurrence as the plaintiff's claim, she will assert them under Rule 13(a)(1); if she also has unrelated claims, she can assert them under Rule 13(b). Rule 18(a) gives such a defendant nothing that Rule 13(b) does not already give her.

Subject Matter Jurisdiction. Of course, Rule 13(b) simply provides a procedural mechanism for asserting a claim. The claim must invoke federal subject matter jurisdiction, however, or else it cannot be asserted in federal court.

> ○ ***Example #25.*** *A*, a citizen of Wyoming, sues *Z*, a citizen of Colorado, in federal court, asserting a state law claim for $200,000; the case clearly invokes diversity of citizenship jurisdiction. *Z* has a permissive counterclaim against *A*, arising under state law, for $400,000. Is there subject matter jurisdiction? Yes. Because the counterclaim arises under state law, it does not invoke federal question jurisdiction. But *Z*'s claim invokes diversity of citizenship jurisdiction. It is by a citizen of Colorado against a citizen of Wyoming and exceeds $75,000.

In this hypothetical, there was no need for supplemental jurisdiction, because the permissive counterclaim invoked diversity of citizenship. What happens, though, when a permissive counterclaim does not invoke federal question or diversity of citizenship jurisdiction? Suppose, for instance, that the permissive counterclaim in this

---

[73]*See* Fed. R. Civ. P. 20(b) and 42(b).

hypothetical were for $50,000, so it could not invoke diversity juris-diction. We would then inquire whether it could invoke supplemental jurisdiction. And here we may well encounter a problem.

Why? The fact that a permissive counterclaim does not arise from the same transaction or occurrence as the underlying dispute means that it generally will not invoke supplemental jurisdiction. Under §1367(a), supplemental jurisdiction attaches only to those claims that are part of the same "case or controversy" as an underlying claim that did invoke federal subject matter jurisdiction. As interpreted, that requirement incorporates the *Gibbs* standard and means that the claim must share a "common nucleus of operative fact" with the underlying claim. As we discussed in §4.7, some courts equate the "common nucleus" test with "transaction or occurrence." Such courts thus state as boilerplate that permissive counterclaims (which by definition do *not* arise from the same transaction or occurrence as the underlying claim) cannot invoke supplemental jurisdiction under §1367(a).[74]

This mechanical approach is wrong. The test for supplemental juris-diction under §1367(a) is broader than "transaction or occurrence," as we discussed in §4.7. Accordingly, it is possible that a permissive coun-terclaim can satisfy §1367(a). One influential case is *Jones v. Ford Motor Credit Co.*,[75] which is the basis for the following hypothetical.

o ***Example #26.*** Plaintiff borrowed money from Defendant to finance the purchase of an automobile. Plaintiff asserted that Defendant engaged in racial discrimination in making the loan, thereby violating federal law. Plaintiff sued for violation of the federal law, invoking federal question jurisdiction. Defendant asserted a counterclaim for the unpaid balance on the car loan.

The Second Circuit concluded that the counterclaim was permis-sive, and not compulsory, because it did not arise from the same trans-action or occurrence as Plaintiff's claim of racial discrimination.[76]

---

[74]*See, e.g.*, Munroe v. Partsbase, Inc., 2008 U.S. Dist. LEXIS 61213 *3 (S.D. Fla. August 11, 2008) ("Supplemental jurisdiction can only be exercised over a compul-sory counterclaim; for permissive counterclaims, the party bringing the claim must assert an independent basis for federal court jurisdiction"). *See also* Ader v. SimonMed Imaging Inc., 324 F. Supp.3d 1045, 1051 (D. Ariz. 2018) ("Prior to the passage of §1367, courts relied on the distinction between compulsory and permissive counterclaims to determine whether jurisdiction over a counterclaim was proper absent an independent basis for subject matter jurisdiction."). See note 78 and accompanying text below.

[75]358 F.3d 205 (2d Cir. 2004).

[76]This is not an inexorable conclusion. Other courts addressing this fact pattern have held that the counterclaim is compulsory because it does arise from the same transaction or occurrence as the plaintiff's claim. *See, e.g.*, Plant v. Blazer Fin. Servs., Inc., 598 F.2d 1357, 1361 (5th Cir. 1979) (emphasizing "logical relationship" between the claims because of their factual overlap). Courts emphasizing factual issues are

Nonetheless, the court concluded, §1367(a) requires only that there be a "loose factual connection" between the supplemental claim and the underlying suit. Though the permissive counterclaim did not arise from the same transaction or occurrence as Plaintiff's claim, it did share sufficient factual overlap to invoke supplemental jurisdiction under §1367(a).[77]

An increasing number of courts agree and hold that some permissive counterclaims may be so closely related to the underlying dispute as to fall within *Gibbs* and invoke supplemental jurisdiction.[78] Indeed, in this context, it seems pointless to determine whether a given counterclaim is compulsory or permissive. After determining that the claim is properly asserted (that it is a claim against an opposing party) and that there is no independent basis of subject matter jurisdiction, the court should proceed to determine whether the claim satisfies §1367(a).

Obviously, many (probably most) permissive counterclaims will be so factually unrelated from the underlying claim that they will not invoke supplemental jurisdiction. But *Jones* and similar cases teach two important lessons: (1) that §1367(a) is broader than "transaction or occurrence" and (2) that supplemental jurisdiction should be assessed on the facts of each case.

---

more likely to find that the claims arise from the same transaction or occurrence; courts looking at legal issues tend to find that the claims do not arise from the same transaction or occurrence because they raise different legal theories. *See* Effron, note 20 above, 100 Geo. L.J. at 776-790.

[77]*Id.* at 210-225. And §1367(b) did not take away supplemental jurisdiction. Because Plaintiff's claim invoked federal question jurisdiction, §1367(b) did not apply at all. Remember that §1367(b) does not apply in cases that got into federal court initially through federal question jurisdiction. Even if the underlying claim by Plaintiff invoked only diversity of citizenship, on these facts §1367(b) would not remove supplemental jurisdiction. Why? Although that subsection applies in diversity of citizenship cases, it removes supplemental jurisdiction only over claims by plaintiffs. Because the counterclaim was not asserted by the plaintiff, §1367(b) did not remove supplemental jurisdiction. If any of this is not familiar, review §4.7.

[78]*See, e.g.*, Global Naps, Inc. v. Verizon New England Inc., 603 F.3d 71, 76 (1st Cir. 2010) ("In an issue of first impression for this court, we hold that [§1367] gives federal courts supplemental jurisdiction over both compulsory and at least some permissive counterclaims. This alters this circuit's former rule, adopted before the enactment of §1367, that required permissive counterclaims to have an independent basis for jurisdiction"); Channell v. Citicorp National Servs., Inc., 89 F.3d 379, 385-386 (7th Cir. 1996); Clear Connection Corp. v. Comcast Cable Commc'ns, 149 F. Supp. 3d 1188, 1206-1207 (E.D. Cal 2015) (though Ninth Circuit has not ruled, court upheld supplemental jurisdiction over permissive counterclaim); United Road Towing, Inc. v. Incidentclear, LLC, 2015 WL 1598101 at *2 (N.D. Ill. 2015); Graf v. Pinnacle Asset Grp., LLC, 2015 WL 632180 at *6 (D. Minn. 2015) (permissive counterclaim "sufficiently related in a factual sense" to invoke supplemental jurisdiction).

§12.5.2 Crossclaims (Rule 13(g))

Procedural and Policy Issues. The crossclaim[79] in federal practice is found in Federal Rule 13(g). It has two important requirements. First, the crossclaim is a claim against a "coparty." The existence of coparties depends upon the plaintiff's original structuring of the suit using Rule 20(a). As we discussed in §12.4, the plaintiff, when instituting suit, may determine that there should be multiple plaintiffs or multiple defendants. If there are multiple parties on either side of the case, they are coparties with each other. Thus, suppose two plaintiffs, *P-1* and *P-2*, are joined in a case against three defendants, *D-1*, *D-2*, and *D-3*. The two plaintiffs are coparties. The three defendants are coparties. Although a plaintiff may assert a crossclaim against a coplaintiff (assuming the other requirement of Rule 13(g) is satisfied and that there is subject matter jurisdiction over the claim), more typically, crossclaims are asserted on the defendant side.[80]

Second, to be a crossclaim, the claim against the coparty must arise from the same "transaction or occurrence" as the "original action or of a counterclaim therein." Thus, to be a crossclaim, the claim must be transactionally related to the underlying dispute between the plaintiff and the defendant. The "transaction or occurrence" provision is familiar language. It serves the same function as in the compulsory counterclaim—to facilitate the joinder of all transactionally related claims in a single proceeding. Such joinder is also consistent with the modern view on claim preclusion, as we saw in §11.2.3 and with the general transactional packaging facilitated by supplemental jurisdiction, as we saw in §4.7.

Rule 13(g) is permissive. Because it says that the claim "may" be asserted, the party is not required to file the crossclaim in the pending case. She may if she wishes to, or she may choose to assert it in a separate case. In other words, there is no such thing as a compulsory crossclaim. This fact is odd because the goal, like that of the compulsory counterclaim, should be not just to facilitate but to *force* joinder of transactionally related claims into a single case. Why should there be an option to assert transactionally related claims against

---

[79]From 1938 until 2007, this word was hyphenated: *cross-claim*.

[80]There is some authority for the proposition that a plaintiff can assert a crossclaim against a coplaintiff only if the defendant has asserted a counterclaim against the coplaintiffs. *See* Danner v. Anskis, 256 F.2d 123, 124 (3d Cir. 1958). There is nothing in Rule 13(g) to suggest that this reading is right. Nowhere does the Rule suggest that *only* a party in a defensive capacity (like a plaintiff who has been sued in a counterclaim) can assert a crossclaim. So *P-1* should be able to assert a crossclaim against *P-2* (or vice versa), regardless of whether a defendant files a counterclaim against the plaintiffs.

a coparty but a command to assert such claims against an opposing party? Recognizing that there is no good reason to treat the claims differently, some states have made the crossclaim compulsory.[81] Though some commentators have urged that Federal Rule 13(g) be made compulsory, there has been no move in that direction. Probably, few litigants fail to assert crossclaims, so the permissive nature of the Rule does not create much duplicative litigation.

On the other hand, surely some parties burden the judicial system by filing separate cases after eschewing the right to assert a crossclaim.[82] And the burden created might not be remedied by issue preclusion. Remember that issue preclusion (like claim preclusion) flows from entry of a valid *final judgment* on the merits, as we saw at §11.2.2. Suppose a defendant in Case 1 refuses to file a crossclaim, but files Case 2 instead. Case 1 might not go to final judgment for years. Thus, issue preclusion cannot streamline the litigation in Case 2 in the meantime, meaning that both cases may proceed in litigation. We end up with two cases where one would do.[83]

The last sentence of Rule 13(g) provides that a crossclaim may include an assertion that the coparty is or may be liable for all or part of the claim against the party asserting the crossclaim. This sentence means that a crossclaim can include a claim against a coparty that that coparty is liable for indemnity or contribution on the plaintiff's claim.[84] This sentence does no harm but is surplusage; a claim for indemnity or contribution would seem to satisfy the "transaction or occurrence" test of Rule 13(g) anyway.

Remember that Rule 18(a), which we saw at §12.3, allows a litigant who asserts a crossclaim (among others) to assert any claim she may also have against that coparty, regardless of transactional or legal relatedness. Such claims, like any others in federal court, must be supported by federal subject matter jurisdiction.

[81]*See, e.g.,* Kan. Civ. Proc. Code Ann. §60-213(g); Citizens Exch. Bank of Pearson v. Kirkland, 344 S.E.2d 409, 410 (Ga. 1986) (though Georgia's cross-claim provision mirrors Federal Rule 13(g), it is treated as compulsory because of a state statute providing that a judgment is conclusive as to matters that could have been raised in a case).

[82]*See, e.g.,* Davis & Cox v. Summa Corp., 751 F.2d 1507 (9th Cir. 1985) (defendant in earlier case refused to assert crossclaim against codefendant but asserted the claim in separate action; permitted because Rule 13(g) is permissive).

[83]One avenue for avoiding overlapping litigation would be for a court to enjoin parties from litigating the dispute in another proceeding in another court. Such injunctions are difficult to get, especially if one seeks a federal court order enjoining parties from litigating in state court. The anti-injunction statute, 28 U.S.C. §2283, reflects an interest in federalism by prohibiting such injunctions outside of three narrow exceptions. The upshot is that it is difficult to stop overlapping *in personam* litigation in federal and state courts.

[84]We discuss these concepts in detail in §12.6.2.

The following hypothetical is useful for reviewing crossclaims and compulsory counterclaims.

    ○ ***Example #27.*** *P,* driving her own car, is involved with a collision with *D-1,* who is driving a car owned by *D-2.* Under applicable law, *D-2* (as owner of the second car) is vicariously liable for the acts of the person to whom she lent the car (*D-1*).[85] *P* brings a single case against both *D-1* and *D-2.* (That means that *D-1* and *D-2* are coparties; why is their joinder proper?[86]) Assume that you represent *D-2.* You don't know who was at fault in the crash. It could have been *P* or it could have been *D-1.* What claims must/may you file in the pending case?

First, you will have *D-2* answer and file a compulsory counterclaim against *P.* The latter is a claim (for damage to *D-2*'s car) against an opposing party and it arises from the same transaction or occurrence as *P*'s claim against *D-2.* Indeed, as we saw in §12.5.1, *D-2 must* assert this claim in the pending case or else she is estopped from asserting it. Second, you may file a crossclaim against *D-1.* This is a claim against a coparty and it arises from the same transaction or occurrence as the underlying case. Note that there will be two aspects to the crossclaim. First, you will claim that *D-1* owes *D-2* indemnity on *P*'s claim. Thus, if *P* wins against *D-2,* this indemnity claim will shift that liability from *D-2* to *D-1.* That protects *D-2* from liability on *P*'s claim. But, if the wreck was *D-1*'s fault, *D-2* will want to recover from *D-1* for damage to her car. So the second aspect of the crossclaim is to recover for the property damage. Both are part of the crossclaim, because both arise from the same transaction or occurrence as the underlying suit.

In sum, by filing these claims, *D-2* has protected herself either way, whether the wreck was *P*'s fault or *D-1*'s fault. If it was *P*'s fault, *D-2* will recover on the compulsory counterclaim. If it was *D-1*'s fault, *D-2* has done two things: (1) ensured that *D-1* (not *D-2*) is ultimately liable to pay for the judgment to *P* (through indemnity) and (2) asserted a claim against *D-1* to recover for the damage to *D-2*'s car. Again, both of these functions are performed by the crossclaim.

By the way, if *D-2* asserted a crossclaim against *D-1 only* for indemnity on the claim asserted by *P* (and not for property damage to *D-2*'s car), what problem might *D-2* run into down the road? Claim preclusion! If *D-2* did this, and the jurisdiction adopted a transactional definition of claim, *D-2* would be splitting her claim. (If this point is fuzzy, review §11.2.)

---

[85]We saw vicarious liability in a similar context at §11.4.5.

[86]Because Rule 20(a) permits joinder of codefendants if the claim against them arises from the same transaction or occurrence and raises as least one common question. We discussed this in §12.4.

○ ***Example #28.*** Now let's take another step. Suppose *D-2* files both the compulsory counterclaim against *P* and the crossclaim for indemnity and for property damage against *D-1*. In addition, suppose *D-2* has a totally unrelated claim against *D-1* (say, for past-due rent). Can she assert that claim in the pending case too?

Yes. Rule 18(a) provides that, *once D-2 asserted the crossclaim*, she may join to it any claim she has against that party.[87]

○ ***Example #29.*** Again, suppose *D-2* files both the compulsory counterclaim against *P* and the crossclaim for indemnity and for property damage against *D-1*. Suppose also that *D-1* has a claim against *D-2* arising from the same accident (say, that *D-2*'s car had defective brakes, which caused the wreck). Can *D-1* assert that claim in the pending case?

Yes. In fact, arguably she *must* or else lose the claim. Why? Once *D-2* asserts a crossclaim against *D-1*, the two have become "opposing parties." Thus, the claim back against *D-2* is a counterclaim. Because it arises from the same transaction or occurrence as *D-2*'s claim against *D-1*, it is a compulsory counterclaim.

Subject Matter Jurisdiction. Rule 13(g) simply provides a procedural mechanism for asserting a claim. The claim must invoke federal subject matter jurisdiction, however, or else it cannot be asserted in federal court.

○ ***Example #30.*** *A*, *B*, and *C*, each driving her own car, collide, and each is injured. Each suffered damages in excess of $75,000. *A* is a citizen of New York. *B* and *C* are both citizens of New Jersey. *A* sues *B* and *C*, as codefendants, in federal court. There is no basis for federal question jurisdiction, but *A*'s case does invoke diversity of citizenship jurisdiction. (Why?[88]) *B* asserts a compulsory counterclaim against *A* to recover for her injuries from the wreck. (Why is it a compulsory counterclaim?[89]) *B* also asserts a crossclaim against *C* for those injuries. It is a crossclaim because it is against a coparty and arises from the same transaction or occurrence as the underlying suit. Now, is there subject matter jurisdiction over the counterclaim and the crossclaim? (Assume that there is no basis for federal question jurisdiction.)

---

[87]In the absence of the crossclaim, *D-2* could not use Rule 18(a) to assert the rent claim against *D-1*. Remember, Rule 18(a) only applies if a party has already asserted a claim, such as a crossclaim. See §12.3.

[88]Because the plaintiff is not a cocitizen with either defendant and the amount in controversy exceeds $75,000. See §4.5.3.

[89]Because it is against an opposing party and it arises from the same transaction or occurrence as that party's claim against *B*.

B's compulsory counterclaim against *A* invokes diversity of citizenship jurisdiction. It is by a citizen of New Jersey against a citizen of New York and the facts indicate that it exceeds $75,000. (Because it invokes diversity jurisdiction, supplemental jurisdiction is irrelevant.) But the crossclaim does *not* invoke diversity of citizenship jurisdiction. Even though it would satisfy the amount in controversy for diversity (because it exceeds $75,000), there is no diversity between *B* and *C*. The crossclaim is by a citizen of New Jersey against a citizen of New Jersey. The only way the crossclaim can get into federal court is through supplemental jurisdiction. Does that work here?

Section 1367(a) grants supplemental jurisdiction over claims that are part of the same "case or controversy" as the underlying claim that did invoke subject matter jurisdiction (*P*'s original claim). Claims meet that test if they satisfy the *Gibbs* standard of sharing a "common nucleus of operative fact" with the underlying claim. This standard is always met if the claim arises from the same transaction or occurrence as the underlying claim.[90] By definition, a crossclaim does, because Rule 13(g) requires that they arise from the same transaction or occurrence as the underlying dispute.

Section 1367(b) applies in cases that invoked diversity of citizenship jurisdiction (as the claim asserted by *A* against *B* and *C* did). It then operates to remove supplemental jurisdiction over certain claims; but that section only removes supplemental jurisdiction over claims asserted by *plaintiffs*. The claim in this case is asserted by a defendant, so §1367(b) does not remove the grant of supplemental jurisdiction. (If any of this material is unclear, see §4.7.)

○ ***Example #31.*** This one may surprise you. Let's use the same facts as in Example #30, with the three-way car crash between *A*, *B*, and *C*. All claims are based upon state law, and all claims exceed $75,000. But here, *B* and *C*, as *coplaintiffs*, sue *A*. *A* is a citizen of New York. *B* and *C* are citizens of New Jersey. As structured—with the two New Jersey plaintiffs against the one New York defendant and with the claims exceeding $75,000—this case invokes diversity of citizenship jurisdiction. Obviously, *A* will have a compulsory counterclaim against the two plaintiffs. But here's the focus: Suppose *B* asserts a crossclaim for her injuries against *C*. It is a crossclaim because it's against a coparty (a coplaintiff here), and it arises from the same transaction or occurrence as the underlying diversity of citizenship claim. Is there subject matter jurisdiction over this crossclaim?

---

[90]Indeed, as we saw at notes 76-78 and accompanying text above, §1367(a) requires only that the supplemental claim have some "loose factual connection" with the jurisdiction-invoking claim.

The crossclaim arises under state law, so it cannot invoke federal question jurisdiction. It also cannot invoke diversity of citizenship jurisdiction, because the crossclaim is asserted by a New Jersey citizen against a New Jersey citizen. Now, can the claim invoke supplemental jurisdiction? The answer should certainly be yes. But apply the supplemental jurisdiction statute. Clearly, §1367(a) grants supplemental jurisdiction, for the same reason as in the previous hypothetical. But look carefully at §1367(b). It applies in cases that invoke diversity of citizenship jurisdiction (as the claims by B and C against A did). And it removes jurisdiction over claims "by plaintiffs against persons made parties under Rule . . . 20." The claim by B against C is a claim asserted by a plaintiff against someone joined under Rule 20.[91] Thus, under a literal interpretation of the statute, there cannot be supplemental jurisdiction over this claim.

This result is absurd. It means that all other claims (by B and C against A; by A against B and C) will be heard in federal court but this crossclaim by B against C must be asserted in state court. Thus, the parties and the judicial system are robbed of the efficiency promoted by the joinder rules and supplemental jurisdiction. This result—denying supplemental jurisdiction to a crossclaim by a plaintiff—is contrary to practice in federal courts before the enactment of §1367. In passing the statute, Congress indicated (as discussed in §4.7) that it intended to codify that earlier practice. In this area, however, as in others, the plain language of the statute changes prior practice. The result of a literal interpretation of the statute in this context is also contrary to the underlying premise of diversity of citizenship jurisdiction. After all, in our hypothetical here, each plaintiff remains diverse from each defendant, so there is no danger that permitting supplemental jurisdiction over P-1's crossclaim will eviscerate the complete diversity rule. There is no clear case authority on this issue, but in view of the literal interpretations accorded §1367 in other contexts, the unfortunate result suggested above may be difficult to avoid.

§12.6   Overriding Plaintiff's Party Joinder Choices

In §12.4, we discussed "proper" parties under Rule 20(a)—those who *may* be joined in a single civil case in federal court. If everyone who could be joined under Rule 20(a) were joined in a single case, there would be no risk of subsequent duplicative or inconsistent litigation; all interested parties would be joined in a single case, and the

---

[91]As we saw in §12.4, the only way B and C could have sued together as coplaintiffs was to have joined as coparties under Rule 20(a)(1).

judgment in that case would bind them all. But as we also saw in §12.4, Rule 20(a) is permissive, so the plaintiff does not have to employ it to the fullest. For a variety of reasons, including jurisdictional limitations and litigation strategy, a plaintiff may eschew full use of the provision and leave out persons who might have been joined under Rule 20(a). We refer to such nonparties as "absentees."

The question for us is whether anyone can override the plaintiff's structuring of the case by forcing the joinder of absentees. The answer is yes, at least in certain circumstances. Three joinder devices — compulsory party joinder under Rule 19 (discussed in §12.6.1), impleader under Rule 14 (discussed in §12.6.2), and intervention under Rule 24 (discussed in §12.6.3) — can be used to restructure the party joinder of the case. Throughout our discussion of these devices, it is important to appreciate the effort to accommodate competing policies. On the one hand, our justice system accords great deference to the plaintiff's choices on party structuring; we value litigant autonomy. On the other hand, the plaintiff's party joinder choices may lead to inefficiency and inconsistent outcomes by promoting multiple litigation; it may also subject the interest of the absentee or of the defendant to possible harm. The Federal Rules take the position that the plaintiff's autonomy must give way in such circumstances. Thus, they recognize three policy interests that will justify overriding the plaintiff's party structuring: (1) efficiency, (2) avoiding harm to the absentee, and (3) avoiding harm to the defendant.

As we will see, compulsory party joinder under Rule 19 embraces all three of these policies. Impleader is based mostly on the first and third policies, and intervention embodies the first two policies. As we also will see, these devices might be invoked by different persons. Rule 19 is usually raised by a defendant, although the judge has the power to raise it on her own. Impleader is invoked by a defending party. Intervention is invoked by the absentee herself. Thus, these three devices empower different persons to assert that one of three policies justifies overriding the plaintiff's autonomy in structuring the suit.

§12.6.1   Compulsory Party Joinder (Rule 19)

"Proper," "Required" (or "Necessary"), and "Indispensable" Absentees

Remember, the issue here (and throughout §12.6) is whether an absentee (someone the plaintiff did not join in the pending case) should be forced into the suit. Federal Rule 19 is the most comprehensive provision providing for overriding the plaintiff's joinder choices. While it, like all Federal Rules, governs practice in federal court, most states have adopted a "compulsory joinder" rule modeled on Rule 19. Before looking at that Rule, however, we must tackle some traditional terminology and concepts embodied in Rule 19.

Parties and potential parties to a civil case fall into one of three traditional categories, which can be viewed as concentric circles. First, the outer (largest) circle reflects "proper" parties to the case. These are persons who *may* be joined, at the option of the plaintiff, because they have sufficient connection to the dispute. Today, such persons are defined in Rule 20(a), discussed at §12.4. Second, inside that circle, as a subset of proper parties, are "required" (or "necessary") parties. These are persons whom the plaintiff did not join in the case, but whose presence is so desirable that the court will override the plaintiff's choice by requiring them to be joined if joinder is possible. Such persons are defined in Rule 19(a). Third, inside this circle, as a subset both of necessary and of proper parties, are what have for generations been called "indispensable" parties. These are persons whom the plaintiff did not join, and who (because "necessary") should be joined, but who cannot be joined (e.g., because the court cannot get personal jurisdiction over them). And in their absence, the court has decided that it will dismiss the pending case rather than proceed without such absentees.

The Supreme Court set out famous formulations for necessary and indispensable absentees in the classic 1855 case of *Shields v. Barrow*.[92] The Court defined necessary absentees as "persons having an interest in the controversy, and who ought to be made parties, in order that the court may act."[93] It defined indispensable absentees as those "who not only have an interest in the controversy, but an interest of such a nature that a final decree cannot be made without either affecting that interest, or leaving the controversy in such a condition that its final termination may be wholly inconsistent with equity and good conscience."[94]

You see the problem. These phrases are hardly self-defining. In the wake of *Shields* and other cases, courts and lawyers began to seize on labels rather than analysis. They focused on notions of "joint" versus "severable" interests and concluded that the label applied was determinative of whether an absentee was merely necessary or indispensable. As one scholar noted, opinions came to show "a ready reliance on labels for solutions of particular cases [and] a thoughtless

---

[92]58 U.S. 130, 139 (1855).
[93]*Id.* at 139.
[94]*Id.*

reiteration—instead of a critical reexamination—of the basic principles of required joinder."[95]

The original version of Rule 19, promulgated in 1938, continued this focus on labels, and proved inflexible in practice. "There seemed to be a sense that absentees in particular kinds of cases automatically fell into one or another category, without looking at the facts of the case."[96] Scholars criticized that Rule and suggested a more pragmatic and flexible approach to the issues.[97] In 1966, the Rules Advisory Committee, in response to this criticism, rewrote Rule 19. That amendment coincided with amendments to the Rules governing intervention of right[98] and class actions,[99] and emphasized the interplay between those concepts and compulsory joinder of parties. Importantly, the 1966 amendments shifted the focus away from labels toward a step-by-step practical assessment of when and why a court should override the plaintiff's structuring of a case by forcing joinder of a new party and, if that party cannot be joined, when and why the court might either proceed without the absentee or dismiss the pending case. The 2007 restyling of the Federal Rules tinkered with terminology and, more irksomely, with subheadings. So cases predating the restyled Rule 19 (including those likely to be in your casebook) will refer to subsections that no longer exist, and have been superseded by the restyled subsections.

We turn now to the Rule and emphasize at the outset that the Rule 19 inquiry is always case-specific. Avoid the temptation to reach an answer by knee-jerk reaction; apply Rule 19 in a pragmatic way—sensitive to the underlying policies of *why* the court might override the plaintiff's party structure.

Applying Rule 19

Rule 19 is somewhat tough to decipher. As Justice (then-Judge)[100] Clarence Thomas noted, Rule 19 prescribes a three-step process, "although this fact is obscured by its language."[101]

---

[95]John Reed, *Compulsory Joinder of Parties in Civil Actions (Pt. 1)*, 55 Mich. L. Rev. 327, 329 (1957).

[96]4 Moore's Federal Practice 19-13.

[97]*See, e.g.*, Geoffrey Hazard, *Indispensable Party: The Historical Origin of a Procedural Phantom*, 61 Colum. L. Rev. 1254 (1961); John Reed, note 95 above, and *Compulsory Joinder of Parties in Civil Actions (Pt. 2)*, 55 Mich. L. Rev. 483 (1957).

[98]Fed. R. Civ. P. 24(a)(2), which we discuss at §12.6.3.

[99]Fed. R. Civ. P. 23, which we discuss at §13.3.

[100]Before Justice Thomas was appointed to the Supreme Court, he served on the United States Court of Appeals for the District of Columbia Circuit. In the federal system, judicial officers on the Supreme Court are called Justices, and those at the court of appeals and district court level are called judges.

[101]Western Md. R. Co. v. Harbor Ins. Co., 910 F.2d 960, 968 n.5 (D.C. Cir. 1990).

o **Step One.** The court must assess whether the absentee is a "required party" under Rule 19(a). Lawyers and judges have always called such an absentee "necessary." As restyled in 2007, Rule 19 avoids that word, but lawyers and judges commonly use "necessary."[102]

o **Step Two.** If the absentee is required, the court then asks whether she can be joined in the pending case. In the language of Rule 19(b), the court assesses whether joinder is "feasible." This requires the court to determine whether (1) the absentee is subject to personal jurisdiction; (2) whether the absentee can be joined without affecting diversity of citizenship jurisdiction; and (3) whether the absentee, once joined, would have a valid objection to venue (thus Rule 19 is one of the few joinder provisions in which venue may be an issue). If joinder is feasible in light of these three inquiries, the absentee is ordered joined to the case.[103]

o **Step Three.** If joinder of the absentee is *not* feasible, the court must determine whether, in "equity and good conscience," the court should (1) allow the case to proceed without the absentee or, on the other hand, (2) dismiss the case. This assessment is made based upon factors in Rule 19(b). If the court decides to dismiss the pending case rather than to proceed without the absentee, the absentee has always been labeled "indispensable." As noted, though, the 2007 restyling of the Rule deletes this word; lawyers and judges continue to use it routinely.[104]

Recall that Rule 12(b)(7) permits a court to dismiss a case for failure to join a party under Rule 19. That motion will be granted only if the court goes through all of these steps and concludes that the case should be dismissed.

Now we look in detail at each of the steps involved in the application of Rule 19.

Step One: Is the Absentee Required (or Necessary)? The absentee will be required if the present party structure of the case satisfies any of the three situations prescribed in Rule 19(a). It is important to understand the policies underlying them; each gives a reason for overriding the plaintiff's structuring of the case. Of the three bases for forcing joinder of the absentee, one is found in Rule 19(a)(1)(A), and the other two are found in Rule 19(a)(1)(B). The difference between

---

[102]*See, e.g.,* Disabled in Action of Pennsylvania v. Southeastern Pennsylvania Transp. Auth., 635 F.3d 87, 97 (3d Cir. 2011) (Rule 19 describes when absentee is "necessary"); Birmingham v. Experian Info. Solutions, Inc., 633 F.3d 1006, 1009 (10th Cir. 2011) (rejecting assertion that absentee was "necessary under Rule 19(a)").

[103]Normally, the court will permit the plaintiff to amend her complaint to join the absentee as a party in the case.

[104]*See, e.g.,* Crowe & Dunlevy, P.C. v. Stidham, 640 F.3d 1140, 1149 (10th Cir. 2011); Call Center Tech., Inc. v. Grand Adventures Tour & Travel Publ'g Corp., 635 F.3d 48, 51 (2d Cir. 2011); Molinos Valle del Cibao, C. por A. v. Lama, 633 F.3d 1330, 1344 (11th Cir. 2011); In re Lorazepam & Clorazepate Antitrust Litig., 631 F.3d 537, 542 (D.C. Cir. 2011).

the two subdivisions of the Rule is significant, as a careful reading of the Rule will demonstrate.

Rule 19(a)(1)(B) requires that the absentee claim "an interest relating to the subject of the suit." To qualify, the interest must be "legally protected, [and] not merely a financial interest or interest of convenience."[105] The absentee "must have a direct stake in the pending litigation; an interest in related subject matter is not sufficient to be defined as a necessary party."[106] We will see examples below. Beyond this interest, Rule 19(a)(1)(B) requires that the *failure* to join the absentee (in view of the absentee's interest) will harm someone—either the absentee (in Rule 19(a)(1)(B)(i)) or the defendant (in Rule 19(a)(1)(B)(ii)). Thus, Rule 19(a)(1)(B) can be called the *prejudice* prong of the compulsory joinder rule, because joinder is ordered expressly to avoid prejudice to someone—either to the absentee or to the defendant.

Rule 19(a)(1)(A), in contrast, does not require that the absentee have any interest in the pending case. It mandates joinder not to avoid harm to anyone, but to achieve efficiency. It can be called the *complete relief* prong of the compulsory joinder rule.

In theory, if the absentee satisfies any of the three situations defined by Rule 19(a)(1)(A) and 19(a)(1)(B), the court should order her joinder if joinder is feasible. Now we address these three definitions of a necessary absentee in more detail.

Rule 19(a)(1)(A). Under Rule 19(a)(1)(A), the absentee should be joined if, without her, "the court cannot accord complete relief among existing parties." This clause reflects the traditional aim of equity to decide disputes by the whole, rather than bit by bit.[107] Joinder under this provision is said to ensure that a court will not enter a "hollow" or "partial" judgment, one that fails effectively to resolve the overall dispute.[108] Joining the absentee obviates the need for other suits and binds the absentee to the judgment in the pending case; this, in turn,

---

[105]Northrop Corp. v. McDonnell Douglas Corp., 705 F.2d 1030, 1043 (9th Cir.), *cert. denied,* 464 U.S. 840 (1983).

[106]4 Moore's Federal Practice 19-47 to 19-48.

[107]Much of what is reflected today in the joinder provisions of the Federal Rules came from equity practice and from the Federal Equity Rules, which predated the Federal Rules of Civil Procedure. It is a common theme of equity that the court desired to resolve the entire dispute in one suit, rather than permit the litigants to sue serially over one dispute. We discussed the development of equity courts and procedure at §1.2.3. *See* Stephen N. Subrin, *How Equity Conquered Common Law: The Federal Rules of Civil Procedure in Historical Perspective,* 135 U. Pa. L. Rev. 909 (1987).

[108]*See, e.g.,* Northrop Corp. v. McDonnell Douglas Corp., 705 F.2d 1030, 1043 (9th Cir.), *cert. denied,* 464 U.S. 849 (1983) ("This factor is concerned with consummate rather than partial or hollow relief as to those already parties"); Southern Union Co. v. Southwest Gas Corp., 165 F. Supp. 2d 1010, 1036-1037 (D. Ariz. 2001).

avoids the inconsistent results that could arise from multiple litigation.

Though these goals are laudable, Rule 19(a)(1)(A), as a practical matter, is pretty worthless. Why? It is capable of being interpreted in two ways, one of which is always satisfied and the other of which is never satisfied. (A rule that is either always or never met is not much of a rule.)

First, the Rule may mean that the absentee must be joined whenever leaving the absentee out will fail to resolve the overall dispute—will fail to "do justice" in some grand sense among all potentially affected persons. The problem is that this interpretation is satisfied *every time* there is an absentee who will sue (or will be sued) after resolution of the pending case. A few courts have adopted this interpretation of Rule 19(a)(1)(A), which amounts to holding that the absentee must be joined to avoid multiple litigation.[109] The archetypal case is said to involve a case by the plaintiff against an "excess insurer," which is an insurance company that agrees to cover losses *over* a particular amount.

  ○ ***Example #32.*** *P*'s warehouse burns down. *P* had insurance on the warehouse and its contents with two companies: Primary Ins. Co. (Primary) contracted to cover losses through $200,000, and Excess Insurance Co. (Excess) insured losses over $200,000. *P* sues only Excess, asserting that the damage from loss of the warehouse was $350,000 (and thus that Excess owes *P* $150,000[110]). Some courts and commentators argue that Primary is required under Rule 19(a)(1)(A), because if the court in this case (by *P* against Excess) finds that the damage to *P* was only $195,000, its judgment will be "hollow." Why? Two reasons: (1) it could not be enforced against Excess (because Excess is not liable for amounts of $200,000 and less), and (2) it could not be asserted against Primary (because Primary was not a party to the case and thus, under due process, cannot be bound by the judgment (as we discussed in §11.4.4)).

While there is no doubt that such a judgment would be hollow in the ways described, that does not mean that Rule 19(a)(1)(A) should apply to compel joinder of Primary. Such an interpretation of the Rule is contrary to its language. The Rule does not require joinder whenever failure to join the absentee will result in the court's not resolving all disputes among everybody in the world. Instead, it says that joinder is required only when nonjoinder of the absentee means that the court

---

[109]*See, e.g.*, Walsh v. Centeio, 692 F.2d 1239, 1243 (9th Cir. 1982) (failure to join absentees "would subject trustees to multiple litigation"); Whyham v. Piper Aircraft Corp., 96 F.R.D. 557, 560 (M.D. Pa. 1982); Davila Mendez v. Vatican Shrimp Co., 43 F.R.D. 294, 298 (S.D. Tex. 1966).

[110]Because Excess is liable only for the losses of over $200,000.

cannot accord complete relief "among existing parties." The judgment in the above hypothetical *does* resolve the entire dispute between those who are already parties, because it tells Excess that it owes *P* nothing. More basically, such a broad reading of Rule 19(a)(1)(A) would swamp all other joinder devices. Remember that Rule 19(a)(1)(A), unlike Rule 19(a)(1)(B), does not require that the absentee have an interest in the pending case. So if this provision is interpreted to require the joinder of any absentee whose nonjoinder threatens to create multiple litigation down the road, there is no need for impleader or for intervention.

Focusing on the specific language of Rule 19(a)(1)(A) thus leads to the second possible interpretation of Rule 19(a)(1)(A)—that it is invoked only when nonjoinder of the absentee means that the court in the pending case cannot wrap things up completely among those who are presently parties. And, as we just saw, it is hard to conceive of a case in which this test will be met. Either the defendant will owe something to the plaintiff or she won't. No matter what the judgment, it will wrap up the dispute *among existing parties* once and for all. So read, then, the Rule never applies.

In view of these problems with determining the proper scope of Rule 19(a)(1)(A), it is not surprising that courts have shied away from doing much with it. Courts seem never to rely on Rule 19(a)(1)(A) *exclusively* to order the joinder of an absentee. Instead, to the extent that courts pay attention to the subdivision at all, they use it in conjunction with one of the bases for joinder laid out in Rule 19(a)(1)(B).[111] Thus, Rule 19(a)(1)(A) has had little impact on compulsory joinder doctrine. Does that mean that its policy of efficient joinder is meaningless? No. The policy is important but is limited in impact to those cases satisfying one of the prejudice bases for joinder under Rule 19(a)(1)(B). Every time joinder is effected under Rule 19(a)(1)(B), it fosters the efficiency and consistency we desire. It does so, however, in a way that does not simply run roughshod over plaintiff autonomy and render meaningless the other joinder provisions of the Federal Rules.

Rule 19(a)(1)(B)(i). As we saw above, both bases for compelling joinder of the absentee under Rule 19(a)(1)(B)—19(a)(1)(B)(i) and 19(a)(1)(B)(ii)—require that the absentee have some interest in the underlying dispute *and* that somebody (either the absentee or the defendant) stand to be harmed if the litigation proceeds without the absentee. Rule 19(a)(1)(B)(i) focuses on the potential harm to the *absentee's* interest if she is not joined in the pending case. Specifically, the court assesses whether the absentee is so situated that litigating without her "may as a practical matter impair or impede [her] ability

---

[111]*See* 4 Moore's Federal Practice §19.03[2][c].

to protect the interest." The policy basis for joinder here is clear: We should not allow the plaintiff's leaving the absentee out of the case to harm the absentee. We see in §12.6.3 that this same policy underlies intervention of right.

Notice that this provision focuses on *practical* harm to the absentee's ability to protect her interest. This language reflects the fact that the absentee generally could not suffer "legal" harm if the case proceeded as originally structured. As we discussed in §§11.2.1 and 11.4.5, absentees (unless in privity with a party, which is rare) cannot be bound legally by the judgment in a case. In many circumstances, however, an absentee not bound legally might be adversely affected in a practical way by the judgment. Suppose, for example, that *P* sues a Trustee, seeking to recover trust funds held by the Trustee. Absentee (*A*) claims to be the proper beneficiary of the trust. If *P* wins the pending case, *A* is not bound by the judgment. But, as a practical matter, *A*'s ability to protect her interest may be impaired, because the money will be in *P*'s pocket, and may be squandered or removed from the country before *A* can sue *P*.

One interesting question is whether the absentee's ability to protect her interest might be harmed by the *stare decisis* effect of the judgment in the pending case. *Stare decisis* is the doctrine of precedent, which stands for the proposition that an appellate decree on a question of law binds all lower courts within that jurisdiction. As commonly understood, *stare decisis* cannot emanate from a trial court determination of issues of fact. Occasionally, but rarely, *stare decisis* can constitute a relevant harm under Rule 19(a)(1)(B)(i).

A good example of the proper use of *stare decisis* as relevant harm involved disputed ownership of reefs near Florida.[112] Two private parties claimed ownership. If the reefs were part of the outer continental shelf, however, they would be owned by the United States. The case was brought by the United States against one of the private claimants to the reefs. The other private claimant to the reefs was the absentee. The court recognized that the issue was important enough to the parties to ensure that it would be appealed to the court of appeals for a determination of the legal question of government ownership. That ruling would result in precedent that would be very difficult for the absentee to undo in subsequent litigation.[113] In such circumstances, the court properly concluded, the precedential effect of the case could

---

[112]Atlantis Dev. Corp. v. United States, 379 F.2d 818 (5th Cir. 1967).

[113]Specifically, if the United States won the first case, the Fifth Circuit would have decreed as a matter of law that the reefs were part of the outer continental shelf. For the absentee to press its claim of private ownership in a separate case, it would have to get the Fifth Circuit to overrule that holding *en banc* or to get the Supreme Court to overrule it. Either was a long shot. *Atlantis*, 379 F.2d at 828.

constitute a harm justifying joinder of the absentee.[114] Some other opinions have not been nearly as careful and have invoked the "*stare decisis*" label to justify finding a harm to absentees from what seem to be nothing more than findings of fact by a trial court.[115]

Rule 19(a)(1)(B)(ii). Again, with Rule 19(a)(1)(B)(ii), the absentee has an interest in the pending case. But here the absentee must be joined to prevent potential harm to an existing party in that case. Specifically, as in Rule 19(a)(1)(B)(i), the absentee must have "an interest relating to the subject of the action" and must be so situated that not joining her might subject a party "to a substantial risk of incurring double, multiple, or otherwise inconsistent obligations." The policy basis for forcing joinder here is also clear: It is not to avoid harm to the absentee, but to a present party. The litigation is structured in such a way that going forward without the absentee involved puts a party at risk of being hit with double or inconsistent obligations.

We must raise two points here. First, although the Rule focuses on harm to anyone who is already a party in the pending case, in fact it is concerned about harm to a *defending party*; in most cases, of course, this means the defendant.[116] If the plaintiff has so structured the case as to subject herself to harm, it is not clear why the judicial system should try to help her. But if she has so structured the case as to cause harm to a party brought into court in a defensive position, the system should try to ameliorate the situation. Second, note that the Rule is aimed at a specific kind of harm to the defendant: the risk of being put to "double, multiple, or otherwise inconsistent *obligations*" because of the absentee's interest.[117] The Rule does not say the joinder is required to avoid subjecting the defendant to multiple *litigation*. Thus, if the party structure merely threatens the defendant with potential multiple suits, that is not enough. This fact is another factor that counsels a narrow reading of Rule 19(a)(1)(A), as we saw above.

   o **_Example #33._** Busline provides bus transportation. One of its buses is involved in a wreck, injuring six passengers. Passenger #1 sues Busline

---

[114]Actually, the case involved intervention of right under Rule 24(a)(2). As we see in §12.6.3, however, the operative test for harm to the absentee is the same in that Rule as it is in Rule 19(a)(1)(B)(i).

[115]*See, e.g.*, Ranger Ins. Co. v. United Housing of N.M., Inc., 488 F.2d 682, 684 (5th Cir. 1974) (holding in declaratory judgment case brought by insurance company concerning whether its coverage responsibilities under a policy might bind absentees through *stare decisis*).

[116]Remember, though, a plaintiff can be a defending party if the defendant has asserted a counterclaim against her.

[117]Because "double" is a form of "multiple," reference to the former seems unnecessary. The Rule should simply express concern about "multiple or otherwise inconsistent obligations." The word *double* adds nothing to the phrase.

for personal injury damages. Are Passengers #2 through #6 necessary under Rule 19(a)(1)(B)(ii)?

No. Although the litigation as structured certainly threatens Busline with multiple litigation, it does not subject Busline to potential multiple or inconsistent *obligations*.

As envisioned by Rule 19(a)(1)(B)(i), inconsistent obligations are created when two (or more) orders put the defendant in a position in which she cannot satisfy one order without violating the other. Such problems usually arise in claims for equitable relief (like an injunction or declaratory judgment) and not in claims for damages. For example, the Rule would be invoked if one judgment ordered a corporation to issue stock in one person's name while another judgment ordered the corporation to issue stock in a different person's name. There, the corporation cannot honor one judgment without violating the other. This problem is not faced with monetary damages. If Passenger #1 wins, the court will order Busline to pay money to her. Then, if Passenger #2 loses, the court will order that Busline does not have to pay money to her.[118] These are not inconsistent obligations. There is nothing inconsistent in Busline's having to write a check to one passenger and not to another.[119]

Applying Rule 19(a). Let's try some hypotheticals.

○ **Example #34.** *P* has surgery in which a metal "plate and screw device" is implanted in her spine. The device was manufactured by Corporation. The surgery was performed by Doctor at Hospital. The device broke in *P*'s spine, causing serious personal injuries. *P* sues only Corporation and does not join Doctor or Hospital. (Quick review question: Could *P* have joined Doctor and Hospital with Corporation as three codefendants?[120]) Are Doctor or Hospital necessary under Rule 19(a)?

These are the facts of *Temple v. Synthes Corp.*,[121] in which a unanimous Supreme Court answered emphatically: no. According to the Court, joint tortfeasors are not necessary parties. Period. The Court simply says, "It has long been the rule that it is not necessary for

---

[118]In this case, perhaps Passenger #2 could have won if she could have used nonmutual offensive issue preclusion against Busline, on the issue of Busline's negligence (assuming that issue was litigated and determined in the first case). But many jurisdictions do not recognize nonmutual offensive issue preclusion. See §11.4.5.

[119]We revisit this point in discussing class actions under Rule 23(b)(1)(B), at §13.3.5.

[120]Yes. This question is covered by Rule 20(a). Joinder of codefendants is proper when the claims against them arise from the same transaction or occurrence and raise at least one common question of law or fact. Here, the claims against all three arise from implanting the device in *P*'s spine, and all present the common question of who, if anyone, was negligent. (If any of this material is fuzzy, see §12.4.)

[121]498 U.S. 5 (1990).

all joint tortfeasors to be named as defendants in a single lawsuit. Nothing in the 1966 revision to Rule 19 changed that principle."[122] Thus, if a party wants to force the joinder of additional joint tortfeasors, she must find some joinder device other than Rule 19 (we see below that the appropriate action is for the defendant to implead the absentees).

> ○ ***Example #35.*** *D* operates a shopping mall. It leases a space to *P*, who will operate a jewelry store. *D* now plans to lease another store in the same mall to *A*, who will also operate a jewelry store. *P* claims that this deal with *A* violates a clause in her lease that says that *D* would not allow another jewelry store to operate in the mall. *P* sues *D*, seeking an injunction to stop *D* from signing the lease with *A*. Is *A* necessary?

These are the facts of *Helzberg's Diamond Shops, Inc. v. Valley West Des Moines Shopping Center, Inc.*[123] Rather than reacting to the question intuitively, apply Rule 19(a) pragmatically. Because Rule 19(a)(1)(A) has had little independent impact, let's start with Rule 19(a)(1)(B). (Remember that anytime the court orders joinder of an absentee under Rule 19(a)(1)(B), the efficiency and consistency goals of Rule 19(a)(1)(A) are realized.)

First, *A* does have an interest in the pending suit, because *A* has negotiated a lease in the same mall. (Remember, under both parts of Rule 19(a)(1)(B), the absentee must have such an interest.) Second, the present joinder scheme threatens to harm *A*'s interest, because if *P* wins the pending suit, the court will issue an injunction stopping *D* from leasing the store to *A*. Thus, *A* satisfies Rule 19(a)(1)(B)(i) because failure to join *A* may *as a practical matter* impair or impede *A*'s ability to protect her interest.[124] Third, this case also satisfies Rule 19(a)(1)(B)(ii) because the present party structure threatens *D* with inconsistent obligations. If *P* wins the present case, the court will order *D* not to sign the lease with *A*. Then *A* will sue *D* in a separate case, seeking an injunction to force *D* to sign the lease. If *A* wins that

---

[122]*Id.* at 7. The opinion is extraordinary because the Supreme Court granted *certiorari* and issued the opinion (reversing the Fifth Circuit's holding that the absentees were necessary) without oral argument. This procedural background is undoubtedly a sign that the Court considered the issue to be obvious. *See also* Adkins v. Labor Ready, Inc., 205 F.R.D. 460, 463 (S.D. W.Va. 2001) ("The fact that a party may be jointly and severally liable for damages with a non-party does not make the non-party a necessary party").

[123]564 F.2d 816 (8th Cir. 1977).

[124]The judgment in the case by *P* against *D* will not bind *A* as a legal matter. She is not a party, nor in privity with a party to that case, and thus, as a matter of due process, cannot be bound. See §§11.2.1, 11.4.4. Rather, the harm to *A*'s interest is practical—*D* won't sign the lease to her.

case, *D* is put in an untenable situation: One decree tells it not to sign the lease with *A*, and another tells it to sign the lease with *A*. Rule 19(a)(1)(B)(ii) is aimed at avoiding exactly that sort of inconsistent obligation by forcing the joinder of *A* in the present case.

> ○ ***Example #36.*** *A* owns 1,000 shares of stock in Corporation, in her own name. *P* claims that she and *A* had bought the stock together and that the stock was supposed to have issued in both names as joint owners. *P* sues Corporation, seeking to have *A*'s stock canceled and the shares reissued in the joint names of *P* and *A*. Is *A* necessary?

This hypothetical is similar to the preceding one and is similar to the facts in *Haas v. Jefferson National Bank*.[125] First, *A* obviously has an interest in the pending suit, since the fight is about stock she presently owns outright. Second, the present joinder scheme threatens harm to *A*'s interest, because if *P* wins, *A*'s stock is canceled and reissued to her and *P* jointly. *A* goes from being sole owner of the stock to joint owner of the stock. Although *A* would not be bound legally by the judgment (because she was not a party to the case), as a practical matter, her interest would be worth demonstrably less than it is now. Third, the present party structure also satisfies Rule 19(a)(1)(B)(ii) because it threatens Corporation with inconsistent obligations. If *P* wins this case, the court will order Corporation to cancel *A*'s stock and reissue the shares in the joint names of *P* and *A*. Then *A* will sue Corporation. If *A* wins that case, the court will order Corporation to issue the same shares in the name of *A* only. Corporation cannot satisfy one decree without violating the other.

> ○ ***Example #37.*** *P* represents the estate of a decedent who was killed in the crash of a chartered airplane. *P* sues the manufacturer of the airplane. Are any of these absentees necessary: the company that owned and operated the plane, the company that serviced the plane, the estate of the pilot?

The quick answer to this case is no, based upon the Supreme Court decision in *Temple v. Synthes Corp.*, which we saw above.[126] That case held that joint tortfeasors are not necessary parties. The case on which this hypothetical is based—*Whyham v. Piper Aircraft Corp.*[127]—was decided before *Temple* and is a good example of sloppy Rule 19 analysis.

---

[125]442 F.2d 394 (5th Cir. 1971). Throughout our discussion of cases applying Rule 19, keep in mind that the restyling of the Rules in 2007 affected the subheadings of the provision. What is today Rule 19(a)(1)(A) was Rule 19(a)(1). What is today Rule 19(a)(1)(B)(i) was Rule 19(a)(2)(i). What is today Rule 19(a)(1)(B)(ii) was Rule 19(a)(2)(ii).

[126]See notes 121-122 and accompanying text above.

[127]96 F.R.D. 557 (M.D. Pa. 1982).

The court in *Whyham* held that all three bases of Rule 19(a) were satisfied. First, it concluded that Rule 19(a)(1)(A) was met because the failure to join the absentees would result in multiple litigation. We discussed above why this conclusion is an erroneous interpretation of the Rule. Second, it concluded that Rule 19(a)(1)(B)(i) was met because the absentees somehow would be harmed by the judgment in the pending case. It is impossible to see how that can be the case, however. If the court orders the manufacturer to write a check to *P*, how does that harm the absentees? True, the manufacturer may now sue the absentees for contribution or indemnification, but the judgment in this case does nothing to the absentees. Finally, the court concluded that Rule 19(a)(1)(B)(ii) was met because the manufacturer would be subjected to multiple or inconsistent obligations. The argument is this: If the manufacturer loses this case and then sues the absentees for contribution or indemnity and loses, the manufacturer will have to pay the entire loss. Here, finally, the court is on solid ground. Such a scenario does seem to subject the defendant to multiple obligations as envisioned by Rule 19(a)(1)(B)(ii). In most cases, however, the defendant will be able to protect itself by impleading the absentee under Rule 14(a)(1) (see §12.6.2).[128]

To this point, we have determined that the absentees are necessary.

Step Two: Is Joinder of the Absentee Feasible? Assuming the absentee is required, the next focus is whether the absentee can feasibly be joined to the pending case. If the answer is yes, the court will force joinder of the absentee under Rule 19(a)(2).

Three factors are relevant to the feasibility inquiry. First, for joinder to be feasible, the absentee must be "subject to service of process," which means she must be subject to personal jurisdiction in the pending case. As we discussed at §2.5, the federal court in which the case is pending may use any long-arm statute available to state courts in the state in which it sits. In addition, the "bulge rule" allows for service outside the forum state, regardless of state law, within 100 miles of the federal courthouse.[129] In addition, the absentee may waive any personal jurisdiction objection by agreeing to be joined in the pending case.

Second, Rule 19(a)(3) also provides that if the absentee "objects to venue and the joinder [of the absentee] would make venue improper," the court must dismiss the absentee from the case. Such an absentee

---

[128]In *Whyham*, the defendant manufacturer could not use impleader, because the persons it would implead were not subject to personal jurisdiction. Thus, Rule 19 was the only vehicle for raising the potential harm to the defendant in that case.

[129]Fed. R. Civ. P. 4(k)(1)(B). The bulge rule is not available for service upon an original defendant, but may be used to serve process on a necessary absentee. See §3.3.4.

is treated as one whose joinder is not feasible.[130] Again, however, the absentee may simply waive a venue objection and be joined if she prefers.

Third, and most important, Rule 19(a) provides that joinder will be feasible if "joinder [of the absentee] will not deprive the court of subject matter jurisdiction." As we have seen repeatedly, every claim asserted in federal court must be supported by federal subject matter jurisdiction. The subject matter limitations on federal jurisdiction are not waivable and the parties cannot avoid them by stipulation. The Federal Rules *cannot* affect the jurisdiction of the federal courts.[131] It is also important to remember that subject matter jurisdiction attaches to claims, not to parties.[132] Thus, the *claim asserted by or against the necessary party* must be assessed for subject matter jurisdiction. Obviously, if the claim asserted by or against the absentee arises under federal law, it will invoke federal question jurisdiction. Joinder is feasible and the court will order it. Most problems in this area concern state law claims asserted by or against the absentee, and the effect of joinder on diversity of citizenship jurisdiction.

In such cases, a crucial step in assessing subject matter jurisdiction is the *alignment* of the necessary party. Once the court determines that the absentee should be joined, it must then align the absentee in the pending litigation, which means it must determine whether the absentee should be joined as a plaintiff or as a defendant. The parties (and perhaps even the absentee) will brief this issue for the court, but the decision is made by the court itself. The court must determine, on the basis of the facts of the individual case, whether the absentee's interest is more closely aligned with the plaintiff or the defendant. The decision can have important ramifications for subject matter jurisdiction.

> ○ ***Example #38.*** *P*, a citizen of Oregon, sues *D*, a citizen of Colorado, on a state law claim (so there is no federal question jurisdiction) for $200,000. The claim invokes diversity of citizenship jurisdiction and is properly filed in federal court. *A*, the absentee, is a necessary party and is a citizen of Colorado. If *A* is joined as a defendant, against whom *P* will then assert a state law claim of more than $75,000, joinder is feasible. Why?

Because there is diversity of citizenship jurisdiction over the claim asserted by *P* against *A*. In other words, joining *A* does not harm subject matter jurisdiction as between *P* and *D*. Because joinder is feasible, the court would order that *A* be joined.

---

[130]4 Moore's Federal Practice 19-74.

[131]Fed. R. Civ. P. 82 (Federal Rules "shall not be construed to extend or limit the jurisdiction of the United States district courts or the venue of actions therein").

[132]Personal jurisdiction is exercised over parties, not claims.

○ **_Example #39._** But suppose instead that the court aligns *A* as a plaintiff to assert a state law claim of more than $75,000 against *D*. Because *A* and *D* are cocitizens, the claim asserted by *A* against *D* cannot invoke diversity of citizenship jurisdiction. Unless supplemental jurisdiction can be used (which we address momentarily), joinder is not feasible, and the court would then go to Inquiry Number Three (below) to determine whether to proceed in the litigation without *A* or dismiss the case.

The problem encountered in this last hypothetical is not limited to cases in which the absentee is brought in as a plaintiff. The same problem would be encountered if *A* in our hypothetical were a citizen of Oregon aligned as a defendant. In that case, the claim asserted by *P* against *A* would lack diversity of citizenship jurisdiction (because it would be by an Oregon citizen against an Oregon citizen). As another example, even if there were diversity of citizenship between the absentee and the party on the opposite side of the litigation, if the state law claim did not satisfy the amount in controversy requirement for diversity cases, the claim could not invoke diversity of citizenship jurisdiction and joinder would not be feasible.

Can supplemental jurisdiction support the claim asserted by or against a necessary party? Supplemental jurisdiction, as we have seen repeatedly, allows federal courts to entertain claims that by themselves do not invoke an "independent" basis of federal subject matter jurisdiction—in other words, claims that do not invoke diversity of citizenship, alienage, or federal question jurisdiction. If supplemental jurisdiction will support claims by or against necessary parties, it will render joinder feasible because it will allow the claim to be joined in the pending case. (If any of this material is unclear, review §4.7; the remainder of the discussion here builds on that material.)

Historically, before the supplemental jurisdiction statute became law in 1990, courts refused to exercise supplemental jurisdiction over claims by or against necessary parties. Several commentators criticized the lack of supplemental jurisdiction in this context. First, it made inclusive joinder less feasible in federal court. Second, it was completely inconsistent with the view the courts had taken concerning supplemental jurisdiction over claims by and against intervenors of right under Rule 24(a)(2) (which we address in §12.6.3). For now, it is sufficient to observe that the test for a necessary party under Rule 19(a)(1)(B)(i) and the test for intervention of right under Rule 24(a)(2) are functionally identical. Stated another way, an absentee who qualifies for intervention of right under Rule 24(a)(2) will usually also be a necessary party under Rule 19(a)(1)(B)(i). Yet, inconsistently, the courts would exercise supplemental jurisdiction in one situation—regarding intervention of right[133]—but not the other—regarding necessary parties. This inconsistency can be called the *Rule 19/Rule 24 anomaly.*

Every commentator who expressed a view on the Rule 19/Rule 24 anomaly urged that it be fixed by making supplemental jurisdiction available in both situations.[134] Not one commentator suggested that the anomaly should be fixed by removing supplemental jurisdiction over claims by and against an intervenor of right. Yet, that is exactly what Congress did in the supplemental jurisdiction statute. Though it said it intended to codify extant practice,[135] Congress changed it with regard to supplemental jurisdiction involving intervention of right—and changed it in a way not one person had advocated! As to Rule 19, the statute evidently retains the historic rule rejecting supplemental jurisdiction. Because drafters of the statute have argued that it actually expanded supplemental jurisdiction in this area, however, we must review the application of §1367 to claims by and against absentees joined under Rule 19.

Section 1367(a) grants supplemental jurisdiction over claims that comprise part of the same "case or controversy" as a claim that invokes an independent basis of federal subject matter jurisdiction. As we discussed in §4.7, this means supplemental jurisdiction attaches to claims that share from a "common nucleus of operative fact" with the claim that invoked federal question or diversity of citizenship jurisdiction. There has never been serious doubt that claims by and against necessary parties satisfy this test.[136] By definition, such an absentee has an interest in the case and is so closely related to it that either her interest may be impaired or her nonjoinder threatens the defendant with multiple or inconsistent obligations. Thus, §1367(a) clearly grants supplemental jurisdiction over claims by or against a necessary party.

The problems arise with the application of §1367(b), which cuts back on the grant of supplemental jurisdiction. Section 1367(b) applies

---

[133]*See, e.g.,* Curtis v. Sears, Roebuck & Co., 754 F.2d 781, 783 (8th Cir. 1985); Burger King Corp. v. American Nat'l Bank & Trust Co., 119 F.R.D. 672, 678 (N.D. Ill. 1988).

[134]George Fraser, *Ancillary Jurisdiction of Federal Courts of Persons Whose Interest May Be Impaired If Not Joined,* 62 F.R.D. 483, 485-487 (1974); Richard D. Freer, *Rethinking Compulsory Joinder: A Proposal to Restructure Federal Rule 19,* 60 N.Y.U. L. Rev. 1061, 1085-1088 (1985); John Kennedy, *Let's All Join In: Intervention Under Federal Rule 24,* 57 Ky. L.J. 329, 362-363 (1969); Joan Steinman, *Postremoval Changes in the Party Structure of Diversity Cases: The Old Law, the New Law, and Rule 19,* 38 U. Kan. L. Rev. 863, 950 (1990).

[135]The express goals of Congress were (1) to overrule the result of the *Finley* case and (2) in all other respects to "codify pre-*Finley* practice." See §4.7. Pre-*Finley* practice recognized supplemental jurisdiction over claims by and against intervenors of right. As we see in §12.6.3, however, §1367 changed that practice.

[136]*See* 4 Moore's Federal Practice, §19.04[1][b].

only in cases that invoked diversity of citizenship jurisdiction and then removes supplemental jurisdiction over specific listed claims. Those claims fall into three categories, two of which are relevant here. Specifically, there is no supplemental jurisdiction in a diversity of citizenship case "over claims by plaintiffs against persons made parties under Rule . . . 19 . . . of the Federal Rules" or "over claims by persons proposed to be joined as plaintiffs under Rule 19 of such rules." Thus, supplemental jurisdiction is *not* available in a diversity of citizenship case for claims (1) asserted by the plaintiff against a necessary party joined as a defendant or (2) asserted by the necessary party if she is joined as a plaintiff.

- *Example #40.* Assume that all claims are based upon state law and that they exceed $75,000. *P*, a citizen of Texas, sues *D*, a citizen of Missouri. The claim invokes diversity of citizenship jurisdiction and is properly filed in federal court. *A* is a necessary party and is a citizen of Missouri. If *A* is joined as a plaintiff, her claim against *D* does not invoke diversity of citizenship jurisdiction, because *A* and *D* are citizens of the same state. Supplemental jurisdiction is not available (even though the claim asserted by *A* against *D* satisfies §1367(a)) because this is a claim asserted by a person proposed to be joined as a plaintiff under Rule 19; §1367(b) prohibits supplemental jurisdiction.

- *Example #41.* Same facts except here *A* is a citizen of Texas and will be joined as a defendant. Here, there is no diversity of citizenship over the claim asserted by *P* against *A*, because each is a citizen of Texas. Does supplemental jurisdiction help? Again, the claim by *P* against *A* will satisfy §1367(a). But §1367(b) precludes supplemental jurisdiction over the claim by *P* against *A* because it is a claim asserted by a plaintiff against a person joined under Rule 19; section 1367(b) prohibits supplemental jurisdiction over that claim.[137]

On the other hand, the Fifth Circuit has employed supplemental jurisdiction in the Rule 19 context. It did so on a claim asserted by a defendant under Rule 13(h). As we saw in §12.5.1, that Rule permits a

---

[137]Although the statute precludes supplemental jurisdiction over the claims asserted there, some commentators have argued that nothing in §1367 prohibits *joining* the absentee as a defendant. They argue that *A* could be brought into the case as a defendant consistent with §1367(b) and go on to hail the statute for having expanded the availability of supplemental jurisdiction in the necessary-parties context. Thomas D. Rowe, Stephen B. Burbank, & Thomas M. Mengler, *Compounding Confusion and Hampering Diversity? A Reply to Professor Freer*, 40 Emory L.J. 943, 955-959 (1991). The assertion is odd. The reason *A* is aligned as a defendant, presumably, is that *P* has a claim against her; she is joined precisely because *P* has a claim against her. Yet, §1367(b) makes it clear that there is no supplemental jurisdiction over that claim. So it is not at all clear what is gained by joining *A* in this scenario. *A* becomes a party but *P* cannot assert a claim against her. Why bother? The commentators seem to be advocating the exercise of supplemental jurisdiction over a *party*, which is a

defendant to join a new party to its counterclaim or crossclaim, so long as the party joined satisfied either Rule 19 or 20. In *State National Insurance Co. v. Yates*,[138] a diversity of citizenship case, the defendant asserted a compulsory counterclaim against the plaintiff. The counterclaim independently satisfied the requirements of diversity of citizenship jurisdiction. The defendant used Rule 13(h) to assert the counterclaim against an absentee, who was a necessary party under Rule 19. The absentee was a cocitizen of the defendant, however, which meant that counterclaim failed to invoke diversity (neither did it invoke federal question jurisdiction). The court held that the claim invoked supplemental jurisdiction. First, it fell within the grant of §1367(a) because it was sufficiently related to the underlying dispute to satisfy *Gibbs*. Second, though §1367(b) applies in diversity cases, nothing in that subsection removed supplemental jurisdiction. Specifically, the provision removes jurisdiction over claims by plaintiffs under specific Federal Rules. The claim in *Yates* was asserted by a defendant under Rule 13(h), which is not mentioned in §1367(b).[139]

So, ultimately the supplemental jurisdiction statute may help facilitate joinder of absentees under Rule 19, at least if they are brought in as additional parties to a counterclaim or crossclaim. It does not seem to help, however, when the absentee is brought in directly under Rule 19. (And don't forget that §1367(b) only applies in diversity of citizenship cases.)

- o ***Example #42.*** *P*, a citizen of Tennessee, sues *D*, a citizen of Tennessee, for violating her rights under a federal statute. The claim invokes federal question jurisdiction and is properly filed in federal court. *A*, the absentee, is a necessary party and is also a citizen of Tennessee. She is joined as a plaintiff and asserts a state law claim against *D*. This claim is not supported by federal question jurisdiction (because it's based on state law) or by diversity of citizenship jurisdiction (because *A* and *D* are citizens of the same state). Does it invoke supplemental jurisdiction? Yes. First, §1367(a) grants supplemental jurisdiction because the claim derives from a common nucleus of operative fact from the underlying case. Second, §1367(b) does not apply, so it cannot remove this supplemental jurisdiction. Remember, §1367(b) applies only in cases

---

fundamental misconception. Supplemental jurisdiction, like all subject matter jurisdiction, is exercised over *claims*, not parties. The First Circuit rejected the argument made by these commentators in *Picciotto v. Continental Cas. Co.*, 512 F.3d 9, 23 (1st Cir. 2008) ("[W]e fail to see how supplemental jurisdiction, which supports the addition of related claims, could be helpful to the [plaintiffs] in their argument for the joinder of a party against whom no claims would be asserted").

[138]391 F.3d 577, 579-581 (5th Cir. 2004).
[139]*Id.* at 578-581.

that invoke diversity of citizenship jurisdiction. The original claim here invoked federal question jurisdiction.

To this point, then, the court has determined that the absentee is necessary and has assessed whether her joinder is feasible. If joinder is feasible, the court ordinarily gives the plaintiff an opportunity to amend her complaint to add the absentee. Should the plaintiff fail to do so, Rule 19(a)(2) provides that the court "must order that [the absentee] be made a party." The court may order joinder as a defendant or as a plaintiff. If she is joined as a defendant, ordinarily the plaintiff will then amend her complaint to state a claim against the absentee. If she is joined as a plaintiff, she will file an appropriate pleading setting forth her claim.[140]

What happens, though, if the court finds that the absentee cannot feasibly be joined? Then, the court must move to the third step of the analysis.

Step Three: If Joinder Is Not Feasible, Should the Court Proceed Without the Absentee or Dismiss the Pending Case? To this point, the court has concluded that the absentee ought to be joined but that her joinder is not feasible. Now, the court must either (1) proceed with the present litigation, without joining the absentee, or (2) dismiss the present case. Each choice is troublesome. If the court proceeds, it risks subjecting either the absentee or the defendant to the kind of harm Rule 19 is intended to avoid. On the other hand, if the court dismisses the case, it denies the plaintiff the forum she selected. If it chooses this latter course, the absentee has long been called "indispensable," and the case is dismissed under Rule 12(b)(7).

How does the court decide which way to go? The choice is governed by Rule 19(b), which starts by saying that the court should consider whether dismissal is appropriate "in equity and good conscience."[141] Beyond this open-ended phrase, Rule 19(b) lists four nonexclusive factors for guiding the decision. The factors are not listed in hierarchical order. At first blush, the factors do not seem original; they echo the sorts of concerns addressed under Rule 19(a) in determining whether

---

[140]If a necessary absentee should be aligned as a plaintiff but refuses to participate, the court may order her joinder as a defendant and then realign her as a plaintiff. In rare cases, such an absentee can be joined as an "involuntary plaintiff," who will be bound by the judgment even if she refuses to participate in the case. Courts have applied the involuntary plaintiff doctrine only when the absentee and the plaintiff are so closely related that the absentee must allow the use of her name to allow the existing plaintiff to secure relief. These are rare cases and include suits by an exclusive licensee of a patent; the patent holder might be joined as an involuntary plaintiff. *See* 4 Moore's Federal Practice §19.04[4][b].

[141]This phrase comes from the classic case of *Shields v. Barrow*, 58 U.S. 130, 139 (1855), and is adopted verbatim in Rule 19(b).

the absentee was required in the first place. Importantly, however, the thrust of the Rule 19(b) assessment is different. While Rule 19(a) asks the court to determine whether the sorts of harm envisioned by that Rule *might* occur[142] if the absentee is not joined, here the assessment is whether such harm *really will* occur. "There is a difference in degrees. The decision of whether to proceed or dismiss the case requires a closer look at the real probability and severity of prejudice caused by nonjoinder versus prejudice caused by dismissal."[143]

Reflecting this emphasis on *probability* rather than *possibility*, Rule 19(b)(1) instructs the court to consider "the extent to which a judgment rendered in the person's absence might prejudice that person or the existing parties." Here, the court may sneak a peek at the merits and determine whether the plaintiff's claim is likely to result in harm of either type. In addition, the court should consider whether either the absentee or the defendant might be able to avoid harm by taking some action. For instance, the absentee might be able to intervene; her refusing to do so may indicate that the absentee does not consider the potential harm to be great. Likewise, the defendant may be able to avoid multiple or inconsistent obligations by impleading the absentee or, if the dispute concerns ownership of property, by instituting interpleader.

Rule 19(b)(2) calls for the court to be creative and to consider "protective provisions in the judgment," "shaping the relief," and other measures to avoid or lessen potential harm to the absentee or the defendant. Some people refer to this power as the court's "molding the decree" to let the case go forward while protecting the absentee and defendant from potential harm. For example, if the plaintiff sues for rescission of a contract to which the absentee is a party, the court might avoid the harm that rescission would cause by having the successful plaintiff recover damages.[144] Or, as the Supreme Court suggested in *Provident Tradesmens Bank & Trust Co. v. Patterson*,[145] in litigation concerning conflicting claims to a fund, the court might

[142]Rule 19(a)(1)(B) requires only that one of the relevant harms "may" occur; it does not require that such harm must or necessarily will occur.

[143]4 Moore's Federal Practice 19-82. Some courts disagree. For instance, in *Glancy v. Taubman Ctrs., Inc.*, 373 F.3d 656, 670 n.12 (6th Cir. 2004), the court, after quoting the passage that appears in text to this note, said: "However persuasive these commentators' rationales may seem, they are not supported by the text of Rule 19, which uses the word 'may' in Rule 19(a)(2)(i) and the word 'might' in Rule 19(b), belying any argument that the two are substantively different."

[144]*See, e.g.*, Campbell v. Triangle Corp., 56 F.R.D. 480, 482 (E.D. Pa. 1972) ("prejudice to [the absentee's] interests can be avoided by limiting relief to money damages should plaintiff prevail").

[145]390 U.S. 102, 115 (1968).

order that some of the fund remain undistributed, so it is available to satisfy a subsequent claim asserted by the absentee.

Rule 19(b)(3) instructs the court to address whether the judgment can be adequate if the case proceeds without joinder of the absentee. This factor implicates both the goal of avoiding harm to the absentee and defendant and also "the interest of courts and the public in complete, consistent, and efficient settlement of controversies."[146] Again, the court looks to whether the harm that is the center of compulsory joinder doctrine will actually result if the case proceeds and not just that it is a theoretical possibility.

Finally, Rule 19(b)(4) counsels the court to address the flip side of the coin: "whether the plaintiff would have an adequate remedy if the action were dismissed for nonjoinder." In other words, if the court dismisses the pending case, will the plaintiff be able to get justice? In assessing this issue, most courts look to whether the plaintiff would have an adequate alternative forum in the event of dismissal. If there is a forum in which all interested persons (including the absentee) can be joined in a single proceeding, dismissal of the pending case may make great sense: It can result in a single case in another court that binds all interested persons, thus avoiding duplicative litigation and any potential harm either to the absentee or the defendant. As we saw in the second step in applying Rule 19, often the reason the absentee cannot be joined is that her presence in the case would destroy diversity of citizenship jurisdiction. When that is the case, there may well be a state court in which all parties are subject to personal jurisdiction and can be joined in a single proceeding. The result of invoking Rule 19, then, may be that the plaintiff is induced to give up her federal forum for a state court.

○ ***Example #43.*** *P*, a citizen of Louisiana, sues *D*, a citizen of Texas, in a federal court in Texas, properly invoking diversity of citizenship jurisdiction. Absentee (*A*) is a necessary party and is a citizen of Texas. The court concludes that *A* should be joined in the pending case as a plaintiff. Her claim against *D*, however, cannot invoke diversity of citizenship jurisdiction (because *A* and *D* are citizens of the same state), so joinder is not feasible. In determining whether to proceed without *A* or to dismiss the case, the court might consider whether all three parties can be joined in a single case in a state court in Texas (or elsewhere). This inquiry will include an assessment of whether Texas would have personal jurisdiction. If so, dismissing the federal court case can result in the most efficient litigation package possible. If the court dismisses, essentially it

---

[146]*Id.* at 111 ("We read the Rule's third criterion . . . to refer to this public stake in settling disputes by wholes, whenever possible").

will be telling *P* that she must give up her federal forum in the interest of an efficient litigation package that will avoid harm to *D* and to *A*.

The Supreme Court applied Rule 19(b) in an interesting context in *Republic of Philippines v. Pimentel*.[147] Ferdinand Marcos was a corrupt and brutal leader in the Philippines. While in power, he stole billions of dollars from the country and placed them in various places for the rainy day when he would be forced from power. The holder of most of those assets, a corporation founded by Marcos, instituted an interpleader case concerning the assets. In §13.2, we study interpleader, which allows the holder of property to force claimants to the property to litigate ownership in a single proceeding. Thousands of claimants were joined, most of whom sued for human rights violations.

Two claimants, the Republic of the Philippines and the commission it created, could not be joined, because they were immune from suit (because of sovereign immunity). The Court concluded that the interpleader case could not proceed without these two absentees. First, they were necessary under Rule 19(a)(1)(B)(i). Why? If they were not joined, the assets would be distributed to others and lost to these claimants. Second, under Rule 19(b), the case had to be dismissed. The Court confirmed that judges routinely must consider the merits of claims and defenses when they apply Rule 19. The lower courts erred in dismissing as frivolous the claims by the Philippines and its commission. In equity and good conscience (and to allow a sovereign nation to determine in its own courts who owns the assets stolen by its former leader) the Court held that the interpleader in federal court must be dismissed.

Raising Rule 19 Issues

Almost always, the defendant raises Rule 19 concerns, either in a motion to join a necessary party or a motion to dismiss the case under Rule 12(b)(7). The plaintiff will rarely do so, because the structuring of the case was the plaintiff's idea. It would be unusual for the plaintiff to change her mind and call to the court's attention that she failed to join someone who satisfies Rule 19. Why would the defendant do so? Obviously, in cases satisfying Rule 19(a)(1)(B)(ii), the defendant's self-interest dictates that she will raise the issue. In those cases, the present structure threatens the defendant with multiple or inconsistent obligations; she will want to avoid those by forcing joinder of the absentee. Or, if joinder is infeasible, she will want to argue that the case should be dismissed under Rule 12(b)(7).

---

[147]553 U.S. 851 (2008).

What about cases that satisfy only Rule 19(a)(1)(B)(i)? Here, the threatened harm from the present structure is to the *absentee*. Why would the defendant raise this issue to the court? First, she might do so out of altruism. Second, and more likely, she may do so if joinder of the absentee is not feasible and thus the case might be dismissed. In the absence of possible dismissal, it is difficult to see why the defendant would be worried about potential harm to the absentee. She simply has nothing to gain unless she can get the case dismissed. Thus, the absentee may be most threatened in precisely the case in which she could feasibly be joined. In such a case, the defendant cannot get the case dismissed under Rule 12(b)(7), so it is not clear why anyone will be looking out for the absentee's interest.

In theory, there are two protections for the absentee in such a case. One is Rule 19(c), which requires a party asserting a claim to "state the name, if known, of any person who is required to be joined if feasible but is not joined" as well as the "reasons for not joining that person." The idea is to put the court in a position to raise necessary-parties issues. In practice, this Rule provides little protection, because it seems to be ignored more than it is honored. The requirement of Rule 19(c) should be expanded to require all parties (not just claimants) to inform the court of Rule 19 absentees and should be given teeth by being included in the certification made under Rule 11.

The other protection theoretically available to the absentee is intervention. We see in §12.6.3 that intervention of right is available essentially to those absentees who would be found necessary under Rule 19(a)(1)(B)(i). Such an absentee can join the case of her own volition. But the right to intervene is worthless if the absentee is not aware of the pending case. The advisory committee that drafted the 1966 amendments to Rule 19 relied here upon Rule 19(c). The drafters opined that once the court knew of absentees who satisfied Rule 19, it could contact the absentees and inform them of their right to intervene.[148] Again, however, this protection suffers from the lack of respect accorded Rule 19(c).

§12.6.2 Impleader (Third-Party Practice) (Rule 14)

Procedural and Policy Issues

Third-party practice, which is more commonly known as impleader, is an important tool in the panoply of joinder devices. It is governed

---

[148]1966 Advisory Committee Notes to Rule 19(c).

in federal practice by Rule 14(a)[149] and results in overriding the plaintiff's party structure. Importantly, only a "defending party" can join an absentee through impleader. Obviously, a defending party is one against whom a claim has been asserted. Usually, of course, that party will be the defendant. But a plaintiff can be a defending party if, for example, another party has asserted a counterclaim or crossclaim against her. Rule 14(b) makes this point clear, by providing that a plaintiff who has been hit with a claim can implead. The provision is unnecessary, because Rule 14(a) already provides that only a "defending party" can implead. In fact, even someone who is impleaded is a defending party, and may, if she has a proper impleader claim, implead someone else.[150]

The defending party asserting impleader is known as the "third-party plaintiff," and the absentee joined by impleader is the "third-party defendant" (TPD). So, in the usual case, in which the defendant uses impleader, the defendant will be called *defendant and third-party plaintiff.* The pleading seeking relief from the TPD is the "third-party complaint." Rule 14(a)(1) establishes that a defending party has a right to implead within 14 days after she serves her original answer to the plaintiff's complaint. Beyond 14 days, she must make a motion seeking court permission to implead. Such motions are routinely granted unless doing so will unduly delay resolution of the case on the merits. Is a defending party *required* to implead? No. Rule 14(a)(1) is clearly permissive; the first sentence provides that the defending party "may" (not "must") implead.

The fact that only a "defending party" can assert an impleader claim becomes obvious when we see what kind of claim is asserted in impleader. The claim must be against an absentee "who is or may be liable to the [defending party] for all or part of the claim against it." This limitation is extremely important. The defending party is not permitted to join an absentee just because she has a claim against that absentee or because the plaintiff may have a claim against the absentee. Rather, the claim against the absentee reflects that the absentee owes the defending party for all or part of the claim that has been asserted against that defending party. Such claims are almost always for indemnity or contribution. In the usual case, then, the defendant

---

[149]As we see below in this paragraph of text, Rule 14(b) is irrelevant. Rule 14(c) applies only in admiralty or maritime cases, and thus is beyond our scope. Although Rule 14 applies only in federal court, many states have impleader rules patterned on it.

[150]When a third party is impleaded and then impleads another absentee, some courts call the latter claim a "fourth-party claim." *See, e.g.,* Interstate Power Co. v. Kansas City Power & Light Co., 992 F.2d 804, 806 (8th Cir. 1993). In fact, there can be successive impleaders; the record appears to be five. Bevemet Metais, Ltd. v. Gallie Corp., 3 F.R.D. 352 (S.D.N.Y. 1942).

impleads an absentee (TPD) who owes indemnity or contribution to the defendant for all or part of the plaintiff's claim against the defendant.

We discussed indemnification at §11.4.5, concerning issue preclusion. The duty to indemnify is a duty to hold someone harmless—to "pick up the tab" for that person's liability in full. For example, if you lend a classmate (*D*) your car, and *D* runs your car into *P*, you are vicariously liable for *D*'s act. *P* can sue you. If she does, and recovers a judgment against you, however, you can sue your classmate, *D*, because she (as the primarily liable actor) owes *indemnification* to you (the vicariously liable party). Another example is insurance coverage. If you drive your car negligently and injure someone who then sues you and recovers, the insurance company will have to pay that judgment on your behalf.[151]

Contribution is similar, but usually involves a pro-rata payment by another person. A good example is contribution among joint tortfeasors.

> o ***Example #44.*** *X*, *Y*, and *Z* are joint tortfeasors who injure the plaintiff. As a matter of joinder, the plaintiff can sue all three in a single case. (Why?[152]) But the plaintiff does not have to do so. (Why?[153]) Assume the plaintiff sues only *X*. Accordingly, *Y* and *Z* are absentees. They cannot be forced to join the pending case as necessary parties under Rule 19. (Why?[154]) But *X* can implead *Y* and *Z* because they, as joint tortfeasors, owe her a duty of contribution, which means that they each owe their pro-rata share of the liability. If the plaintiff won a judgment against *X* for $150,000, *Y* would owe contribution for $50,000 (one-third of the liability) and *Z* would also owe contribution of $50,000 (one-third of the liability).

Without impleader, *X* would have to litigate the pending case and, if she lost, would have to pay the entire judgment, say $150,000, to *P*. Then, in a separate action, she would sue *Y* and *Z* and hope to win her claims for contribution from them. She might lose that case, because, after all, *Y* and *Z* would not be bound by the judgment in the case by *P* against *X*. (Why?[155]) If she lost that case, she would absorb the entire $150,000 loss. Even if she wins the case against *Y* and *Z*, however, she

---

[151]Assuming, of course, that the event was within the coverage of your insurance policy and was within the policy limits. If your policy limit is $100,000 and the plaintiff recovers a judgment against you of $130,000, the insurance company is only on the hook for $100,000. You pay the rest.

[152]Because under Rule 20(a)(2), the claims against all three arise from the same transaction or occurrence and raise at least one common question. See §12.4.

[153]Because Rule 20(a) is permissive. See §12.4.

[154]Because the Supreme Court held that joint tortfeasors are not necessary parties in *Temple v. Synthes Corp.*, 498 U.S. 5 (1998). See §12.6.1.

[155]Because *Y* and *Z* were not parties to the case by *P* against *X*, and thus, as a matter of due process, cannot be bound by the judgment in that case. See §§11.2.1, 11.4.4.

would have had to pay the entire judgment in the interim and would have to pay for a second litigation to perfect her right to contribution.

Impleader, then, overrides the plaintiff's party structure of the case to avoid potential harm to the defendant. Without impleader, the defendant (*X* in Example #44) runs the risk of losing to *P* and then losing in a separate case against her alleged joint tortfeasors. Avoiding such a loss is akin to the goal of Rule 19(a)(1)(B)(ii), which compels joinder of an absentee to avoid the defendant's being saddled with multiple or inconsistent obligations. (See §12.6.1.) Thus, impleader fosters efficiency, consistency, and fairness to the defendant. These benefits outweigh the interest in plaintiff autonomy and justify allowing the defendant to restructure the case.

In some states, the substantive law provides that one may not sue for indemnity or contribution until she has already paid a judgment in full. In other words, in our hypothetical above, the law may provide that *X* may not sue *Y* and *Z* for contribution until after *X* has lost to *P* and paid the entire judgment. In such states, can *X* use Rule 14(a)(1) in federal court to implead *Y* and *Z* as TPDs in the pending case? Yes. Rule 14(a)(1) merely *accelerates the assertion* of the claim.[156] That is, *X* can file the claim against *Y* and *Z* in the pending case, but the claim does not come to fruition, does not ripen, until *P* wins the underlying case; then the court can go ahead and determine whether *X* is entitled to contribution from *Y* and *Z*. Rule 14(a)(1), then, allows the "early" filing of the claim to ensure that all related issues can be determined in a single case. Obviously, however, Rule 14(a)(1) does not (and could not) create a claim for contribution or indemnity that does not otherwise exist. So if the relevant state law does not allow contribution among joint tortfeasors, Rule 14(a)(1) will not permit impleader.[157]

Thus, for example, *Y* and *Z* could argue that they were not joint tortfeasors with *X*, and thus that they do not owe contribution to her.

[156]*See, e.g.*, Hiatt v. Mazda Motor Corp., 75 F.3d 1252, 1255 (8th Cir. 1996); Markvicka v. Brodhead-Garrett Co., 76 F.R.D. 205, 207 (D. Neb. 1977).

[157]This issue is governed by *Hanna v. Plumer*, which we discussed at §10.6. Under *Hanna*, if there is a federal directive on point (such as Rule 14(a)(1) here), it controls the issue in federal court, so long as it is valid. For a Federal Rule to be valid under the Rules Enabling Act, it must be "arguably procedural" and not "abridge, enlarge, or modify any substantive right." 28 U.S.C. §2072(b). Again, here, Rule 14(a)(1) merely accelerates the filing of a claim that exists under state law. If the claim did not exist under state law, Rule 14(a)(1) could not allow its assertion. To do so would be to enlarge a substantive right and would violate the Rules Enabling Act. *See* Connors v. Suburban Propane Co., 916 F. Supp. 73, 76 (D.N.H. 1996) ("Rule 14 does not operate to create causes of action; it merely prescribes a method for bringing causes of action already recognized under applicable statutory or common law").

Do not confuse impleader with the crossclaim under Rule 13(g), which we discussed at §12.5.2. The crossclaim is asserted by a party against a coparty. The impleader claim is asserted by a party against an absentee. Moreover, the crossclaim arises from the same transaction or occurrence as the underlying case. The impleader claim, as we have seen, is narrower—it is for indemnity or contribution on that underlying claim.

We can review these and other points about Rule 14(a)(1) with a hypothetical. This is a great fact pattern, and it will review a good bit of ground. Before working on it, read Rule 14(a) with great care.

- ○ ***Example #45.*** *T* has permission from *D* to drive *D*'s truck. While doing so, he strikes *P*, a pedestrian. *D* is vicariously liable for *T*'s acts. By the same token, *D* will have a right of indemnity from *T*. *P* sues only *D*. *D* may implead *T* in the pending case, because *T* is or may be liable to *D* for all or part of the underlying claim by *P*. Why? Because, as we said, *T* owes a duty of indemnification to *D*. *This is not a crossclaim. A crossclaim is asserted against a coparty.* D *and* T *are not coparties, because* P *did not sue the two of them as codefendants under Rule 20(a).*[158] Indeed, *T* is an absentee, a nonparty, until *D* joins him through impleader. Let's assume that *D* properly impleads *T*.

- ○ When we think about it, *T* now is hoping that *D* wins the underlying claim. If *D* wins against *P*, *T* cannot be held liable; there would be no judgment for which he would have to indemnify *D*. Suppose *T* notices that *D* failed to raise an important defense to the underlying claim by *P* against *D*. Say, for example, *D* forgot to raise the statute of limitations as an affirmative defense. Can *T* raise this defense, even though it is a defense that *D* should have raised? The answer is yes. Exactly what part of Rule 14(a) makes this clear?[159]

- ○ What if *T* thinks he has a defense against *D*'s impleader claim? What part of Rule 14(a) allows him to raise that defense in the pending case?[160]

- ○ After *D* impleads *T*, suppose *T* has a *claim* against *D* that arises from the same transaction or occurrence as the impleader claim. Suppose, for instance, that *T* feels the accident was caused by faulty brakes in the truck. *T* was injured in the same wreck and wants to recover against *D*. Not only *may T* assert this claim in the pending case, he

---

[158]*P* could have joined them as codefendants under Rule 20(a), but in this hypothetical did not do so.

[159]The answer here is governed by Rule 14(a)(2)(C), which allows *T* to raise against *P* any defenses that *D* could have raised.

[160]It is Rule 14(a)(2)(A). Once *D* impleads *T*, *T* is a defending party, and, like any defending party, must respond within 21 days of service under Rule 12.

probably *must* do so. Why?[161] Do *not* call this claim a crossclaim. Why is it not a crossclaim?[162]

o Go back to the stage in which *D* impleads *T*. Suppose (as is likely) that *D* wants to recover from *T* for two things. First, he wants indemnification, so if *P* wins against *D*, *T* has to pick up the tab on that judgment. Second, if the wreck was really *T*'s fault, *D* wants to recover from *T* for the damage to his truck. We know that he can seek the first of these things through impleader, because this is exactly the kind of claim for which impleader is designed. Why can *D* *not* seek the recovery for property damage through impleader?[163]

o So if *D* impleads *T*, and asserts the indemnification claim there, can he also assert the claim for damage to his truck in the pending case? Yes. How does he do that?[164]

o Indeed, not only *may D* assert the property damage claim against *T* in the pending case, but arguably he *should* do so. Why? What risk does he run if he impleads *T* without also joining the property damage claim?[165]

The foregoing concerned the basic impleader claim under Rule 14(a)(1) as well as some other joinder provisions and a review of some preclusion materials from Chapter 11. Now we take one more step, pursuing other claims for which Rule 14(a) provides.

o ***Example #46.*** Assume the same basic facts as in Example #45: *T* borrows *D*'s truck with *D*'s permission, and runs into *P*, a pedestrian. *D* is vicariously liable for *T*'s acts and *D* has a right of indemnity from *T*. *P* sues only *D*. *D* then impleads *T* for indemnification and joins a Rule 18(a)(1)[166] claim for damage to his truck. *T* files a compulsory counterclaim against

---

[161]The claim by *T* against *D* is a compulsory counterclaim under Rule 13(a)(1), which we saw in §12.5.1. Why? A counterclaim is a claim against an "opposing party." Once *D* impleaded *T*, he became an opposing party. This claim by *T* arises from the same transaction or occurrence as the impleader claim, so it is compulsory under Rule 13(a)(1). If *T* does not assert it here, he will be estopped from suing on the claim anywhere.

[162]A crossclaim is asserted against a coparty. *D* and *T* are not coparties; *P* did not sue the two of them as codefendants under Rule 20(a)(2).

[163]Because Rule 14(a)(1) impleader only allows recovery against the TPD for all or part of the plaintiff's claim against the defending party who institutes impleader. It does *not* allow recovery for all things that arise from the same transaction or occurrence as the underlying dispute, so it is narrower than the crossclaim under Rule 13(g).

[164]By using Rule 18(a)(1), which we discussed in §12.3. Remember, it allows a claimant who has asserted one of the listed claims to join any other claim — regardless of relatedness — against that person. One of the listed claims is an impleader claim under Rule 14(a)(1).

[165]He runs the risk of claim preclusion. Because the indemnity claim and the property damage claim arise from the same transaction or occurrence, they are part of the same "claim" for claim preclusion purposes in most jurisdictions. So if the pending case goes to a valid final judgment on the merits, and *D* does not seek property damage, he may be precluded from asserting the property damage claim in a separate case. See §11.2.

[166]See note 164 above.

D, asserting that D lent him a truck with defective brakes, which caused the wreck and personal injuries to T.[167]

o Now that T has been joined in the case, P wants to assert a claim *against* T, arguing that T is also liable for P's injuries. May P assert such a claim in the pending case? Yes. Why?[168]

 o Does anything *require* P to assert this claim against T in the pending case? No. Why?[169]

 o Assume that P does assert the claim against T. Oddly, this claim under Rule 14(a)(3) does not have a commonly accepted name. It is not a counterclaim, since P and T are not yet opposing parties; it is not a crossclaim, because P and T are certainly not coparties. Based upon the diagram of the case, one good suggestion for a name is an "upsloping 14(a) claim."[170]

 o After P asserts the upsloping 14(a) claim against T, suppose T has a claim against P—say, that P somehow caused the wreck by acting negligently, and that T was injured. T wants to recover from P for these injuries. T may assert that claim in the pending case. In this scenario, however, Rule 14(a)(1) is irrelevant to her doing so. Why?[171]

o Now go back to the stage where P has sued D, D has impleaded T, and T has asserted a compulsory counterclaim against D.

 o Now suppose T wants to assert a claim against P in the pending case. He asserts that the wreck was all P's fault, and that he (T) was injured because of it. May T assert such a claim in the pending case? Yes. Why?[172] *Must* he assert the claim in the pending case? No. Why?[173]

 o This claim by T against P also does not have a commonly accepted name. Based again on the diagram of the case, a good suggestion is that we call this a "downsloping 14(a) claim."

---

[167]See note 161 above.

[168]Rule 14(a)(3) permits the plaintiff to assert a claim against the TPD if it arises from the same transaction or occurrence as the plaintiff's underlying claim. This claim by P against the TPD does arise from the same wreck that forms the basis of the case, so it meets this test and may be asserted.

[169]Rule 14(a)(3) says the plaintiff "may" assert the claim, not that she "must" assert it. Thus, the claim is permissive. Also, there is nothing to fear from claim preclusion, because P has never asserted another claim against T, so cannot be guilty of splitting a claim.

[170]*See* 3 Moore's Federal Practice §14.06.

[171]The claim by T against P here is a compulsory counterclaim. Once P sued T, she became an "opposing party" to T. T's claim arises from the same transaction or occurrence as P's upsloping 14(a)(1) claim, and thus must be asserted in the pending case under Rule 13(a)(1).

[172]Rule 14(a)(2)(D) permits the TPD to assert a claim against P if it arises from the same transaction or occurrence as the underlying dispute.

[173]Rule 14(a)(2)(D) says the TPD "may" (not "must") assert the claim. It is permissive. And there is no risk of claim preclusion against T here, because T has not been a claimant against P in another proceeding.

○ After T asserts this downsloping 14(a) claim against P, assume that P wants to assert a claim against T in the pending case. What is the claim?[174]

Thus, Rule 14(a) creates three claims: (1) the impleader claim under Rule 14(a)(1) asserted by a defending party against an absentee (the TPD) who may owe her indemnity or contribution on the underlying claim against her; (2) the upsloping 14(a) claim asserted by the plaintiff against the TPD, under Rule 14(a)(3); and (3) the downsloping 14(a) claim asserted by the TPD against the plaintiff, under Rule 14(a)(2)(D). The latter two claims must arise from the same transaction or occurrence as the underlying dispute. Having mastered the procedural propriety of these claims, now the fun begins, as we assess jurisdictional and related issues.

Jurisdictional and Related Issues

Impleader joins a new party (the TPD) to the case. The TPD is brought in, moreover, in a defensive capacity, meaning that she faces possible liability. Accordingly, the TPD must be subject to personal jurisdiction in the forum. Indeed, the first sentence of Rule 14(a)(1) assumes as much, since it requires that the TPD be served with summons and the third-party complaint. In most cases, the federal court obtains personal jurisdiction over the TPD just the way it does over an original defendant.

Recall from our discussion at §2.3 that the personal jurisdiction inquiry in federal court usually is the same as it is in the state courts in the state in which the federal court sits. The first step is to consult jurisdictional statutes of that state, such as long-arm statutes, to see whether jurisdiction is possible.[175] There is, however, an additional method of exercising personal jurisdiction in the impleader situation. Under the "bulge rule" of Federal Rule 4(k)(1)(B), the TPD can be served outside the forum state (even in the absence of a state long-arm statute) so long as she is served within 100 miles of the federal courthouse in which the case is pending. Thus, assume the case is pending in the Eastern District of Pennsylvania, in Philadelphia, and that the TPD is in New Jersey. Ordinarily, the federal court would look

---

[174]It is a compulsory counterclaim. Once T asserted the claim against P, he became an "opposing party" to P. So any claim by P against T is a counterclaim, because it arises from the same transaction or occurrence as T's downsloping 14(a) claim, it is a compulsory counterclaim under Rule 13(a)(1) and must be asserted in the pending case.

[175]The second step, of course, is to assess whether the exercise of personal jurisdiction under that statute on the facts of the case comports with due process. See §2.4.

first to Pennsylvania law for a statutory provision allowing the exercise of jurisdiction out of state. If there is no such provision, but the TPD can be served in New Jersey within 100 miles of the Philadelphia federal courthouse, the bulge rule allows exercise of personal jurisdiction over the TPD.[176]

Venue provisions do not create barriers to joining the TPD. For starters, most courts agree that the general venue statutes, §§1404(a) and 1406(a), apply only to the initial claims against the defendant, and not to subsequent claims. Beyond this, the impleader claim is so closely related to the underlying case (after all, it is for indemnity or contribution *on* the underlying claim) that courts routinely recognize "ancillary venue." In other words, as long as venue is proper in the underlying case, the TPD has no right to object that venue is not proper as to her.[177] This practice makes great sense. As we are about to see, the impleader claim is so closely related to the underlying case that it will invoke supplemental jurisdiction, so there is no need for an independent basis of subject matter jurisdiction. That being so with regard to subject matter jurisdiction, which is not waivable, it must also be available for the concept of venue, which is waivable. For the remainder of this discussion, we assume that the court has personal jurisdiction over the TPD and that venue is proper.

The big question usually will be subject matter jurisdiction. Remember, there are three potential claims: the impleader claim, the upsloping 14(a) claim under Rule 14(a)(3), and the downsloping 14(a) claim under Rule 14(a)(2)(D). Of course, there must be subject matter jurisdiction over each that is asserted in federal court. As always, any of these might invoke an "independent" basis of subject matter jurisdiction (diversity of citizenship, alienage, or federal question jurisdiction) or it may invoke supplemental jurisdiction. Failing all of these, the claim must be asserted, if at all, in state court.

We will use the same fact pattern discussed above, in which T drives D's truck, with D's permission, and hits P, a pedestrian. D is vicariously liable for T's acts, and T owes a duty to indemnify D. We worked through the various procedural aspects to this scenario earlier in this subsection. Now we look at subject matter jurisdiction. The discussion gets pretty involved, as we deal with several different claims and address more problems raised by the supplemental jurisdiction statute. We deal with several factual scenarios.

---

[176]Remember that the bulge rule applies only to join TPDs in impleader and necessary parties under Rule 19. It is not available to join original defendants to the case. See §§3.3.4, 12.6.1.

[177]*See* 3 Moore's Federal Practice §14.42.

○ ***Example #47.*** *P* is a citizen of California and *D* is a citizen of Arizona. All claims in this hypothetical are based upon state (not federal) law and all claims exceed $75,000. *P* sues *D*, properly invoking diversity of citizenship jurisdiction. *D* impleads *T*. *T* is a citizen of Utah. Is there subject matter jurisdiction over the impleader claim? Yes. That claim invokes diversity of citizenship jurisdiction, because it is asserted by a citizen of Arizona against a citizen of Utah, and it exceeds $75,000. Accordingly, it invokes diversity of citizenship jurisdiction and can be asserted in the pending case.

○ ***Example #48.*** Same facts as Example #47 except here *T* is a citizen of Arizona. The impleader claim thus cannot invoke diversity of citizenship jurisdiction because it is asserted by an Arizona citizen against an Arizona citizen.[178] And there is no federal question jurisdiction because the claim is based upon state law. Does the claim invoke supplemental jurisdiction?

Yes. There has never been any question that the impleader claim satisfies the *Gibbs* test for supplemental jurisdiction.[179] As discussed in §4.7, *Gibbs* always allows supplemental jurisdiction over claims arising from the same transaction or occurrence as the underlying case. The impleader claim is even *narrower* than that: It is for indemnity or contribution on that underlying claim.

Section 1367(a) grants supplemental jurisdiction, precisely because that section adopts the *Gibbs* test. (See §4.7.) Section 1367(b) applies in cases that invoked diversity of citizenship jurisdiction (as *P* v. *D* does) but removes supplemental jurisdiction only over claims asserted by *plaintiffs*. Here, the impleader claim was asserted by the defendant, so §1367(b) does not remove the grant of supplemental jurisdiction. The impleader claim can be joined in the pending case.[180] (If any of this material is fuzzy, see §12.4.)

○ ***Example #49.*** Same facts as Example #48 except that here *D* impleads *T* and joins a claim under Rule 18(a)(1) for the property damage to his truck. (If this point is unclear, see note 164 above.) As in the preceding example, *T* is a citizen of Arizona, so again there is no diversity of citizenship or federal question jurisdiction. We saw in Example 48 that the impleader claim will invoke supplemental jurisdiction. What about the Rule 18(a) claim for property damage? The answer is yes.

---

[178]Remember we could raise the same issue by having *T* be a citizen of a state other than Arizona and the claim fail to exceed $75,000. Such a claim would fail to invoke diversity of citizenship jurisdiction because it fails to meet the amount in controversy requirement. See §4.5.3.

[179]*See, e.g.*, Alumax Mill Prods., Inc. v. Congress Fin. Corp., 912 F.2d 996, 1005 (8th Cir. 1990) (impleader claim satisfies *Gibbs* constitutional test for supplemental jurisdiction).

[180]*See generally* 3 Moore's Federal Practice §14.41[4][d].

Again, §1367(a) grants supplemental jurisdiction over this claim because it meets *Gibbs*—it shares a common nucleus of operative fact with the underlying claim (the collision with *P*) that did invoke federal subject matter jurisdiction (the claim by *P* against *D*). Just because Rule 18(a) does not *require* that a claim be transactionally related to the underlying case does not mean that a claim asserted under that Rule cannot satisfy the *Gibbs* test. Section 1367(b) applies in cases that invoked diversity of citizenship jurisdiction (as *P* v. *D* does), but removes supplemental jurisdiction only over claims asserted by plaintiffs. This claim is asserted by a defendant, so §1367(b) does not remove the grant of supplemental jurisdiction. The claim can be asserted in the pending action.[181]

- ○ ***Example #50.*** Same facts as in Example #49, except here *T* is a citizen of California. So *D*, a citizen of Arizona, is impleading a citizen of California. And remember, *P* is a citizen of California. Is there subject matter jurisdiction over *D*'s impleader claim (and property damage claim) against *T*? Yes—diversity of citizenship! This is a claim by a citizen of Arizona against a citizen of California, and it exceeds $75,000. The fact that *T* is a cocitizen of *P* is absolutely irrelevant in assessing this claim; *P* is not a party to this claim.
  - ○ Now it gets tough. *P* now asserts an upsloping 14(a) claim against *T*, to recover for the personal injuries she suffered when *T* drove *D*'s truck into her. We know that this claim is procedurally proper under Rule 14(a)(3) because it arises from the same transaction or occurrence as the underlying case. But is there subject matter jurisdiction over *this* claim? There is no diversity of citizenship, because this claim is asserted by a California citizen (*P*) against a California citizen (*T*). There is no federal question jurisdiction because the claim is based upon state law. So what about supplemental jurisdiction?

This question—whether there is supplemental jurisdiction over an upsloping 14(a) claim (under Rule 14(a)(3)[182])—requires us to discuss the lamentable case of *Owen Equipment & Erection Co. v. Kroger*.[183] The Supreme Court decided *Kroger* more than a decade before the supplemental jurisdiction statute was passed; the decision clearly influenced the drafters of that statute. In *Kroger*, a citizen of Iowa sued a citizen of Nebraska, properly invoking diversity of citizenship jurisdiction. The defendant impleaded a TPD, and the plaintiff asserted an upsloping 14(a) claim, based upon state law, against the

---

[181]*See id.* at §14.41[4][c].

[182]When you read *Kroger*, you will find no reference to Rule 14(a)(3). There was no such subsection until the Rules were restyled in 2007. Before that, the upsloping 14(a) claim was found in the seventh sentence of Rule 14(a).

[183]437 U.S. 365 (1978).

TPD. At the time the plaintiff asserted the upsloping 14(a) claim there appeared to be diversity of citizenship between the plaintiff and the TPD. Only during trial did the court and the plaintiff discover that the TPD was a cocitizen of the plaintiff.[184] Thus, there was no diversity of citizenship jurisdiction over the upsloping 14(a) claim. And because that claim arose under state law, it did not invoke federal question jurisdiction either.

Though the district court and the Eighth Circuit concluded that the claim was supported by supplemental (then called *ancillary*) jurisdiction, the Supreme Court reversed and held that supplemental jurisdiction was absolutely precluded. The Court assumed that the upsloping 14(a) claim satisfied the *Gibbs* constitutional test for supplemental jurisdiction.[185] Nonetheless, it was unwilling to permit supplemental jurisdiction over an upsloping 14(a) claim because doing so could open the door for a scheming plaintiff to avoid the complete diversity requirement (which we discussed at §4.5.3). For example, a plaintiff might sue a diverse defendant, invoking diversity of citizenship jurisdiction, knowing that the defendant would implead a TPD who is a cocitizen of the plaintiff. If the plaintiff can then assert an upsloping 14(a) claim against that nondiverse TPD, she would be permitted to sue a nondiverse party in federal court. Stated another way, the plaintiff could not have sued those two (the defendant and the TPD) as codefendants initially, because such joinder would have violated the complete diversity rule. The Court concluded that the plaintiff was trying to do by indirection what she could not do directly and thus slammed the door by rejecting supplemental jurisdiction over the upsloping 14(a) claim.

While there is some appeal to the Court's reasoning, there are significant problems with it. For instance, there was no hint that the plaintiff in *Kroger* had engaged in such scheming. Indeed, given the confusion about the citizenship of the TPD, such gamesmanship would have been impossible. Moreover, a plaintiff who did engage in such a scheme to create diversity of citizenship jurisdiction would violate

---

[184]The TPD was a corporation. A corporation is a citizen of the state in which it is incorporated and of the state in which it has its principal place of business. See §4.5.3. The TPD was incorporated in Nebraska and most folks assumed its principal place of business was there as well, because it was on the "Nebraska side" of the Missouri River. But there had been a change in the course of the Missouri River. As it turns out, the principal place of business was actually in Iowa, even though it was on the "Nebraska side" of the river. This fact did not become generally appreciated until a few days into trial. If the case is in your casebook (it probably is), read footnote 5 of the opinion.

[185]It had to assume this fact. After all, by definition, Rule 14(a) claims (both upsloping and downsloping) must arise from the same transaction or occurrence as the underlying dispute. As such, they satisfy the *Gibbs* test. See §4.7.

§1359, which prohibits collusive joinder to manufacture subject matter jurisdiction. (We discussed §1359 in §4.5.4.)

In the course of its opinion, the Court seized upon two factors to justify its conclusion that Congress, in passing the diversity of citizenship statute, intended not to grant supplemental jurisdiction over upsloping 14(a) claims.[186] First, the claim in *Kroger* was not "logically dependent" to the underlying case.[187] The Court discussed the impleader claim as the archetype of a logically related claim, and indeed it is. If the plaintiff's underlying claim against the defendant fails, the impleader claim becomes irrelevant. On the other hand, if the plaintiff prevails on the underlying claim against the defendant, the court must assess the impleader claim to see whether the loss should be shifted from the defendant to the TPD. In contrast, the upsloping 14(a) claim is not logically dependent—its outcome is not necessarily affected by the resolution of the underlying claim between the plaintiff and the defendant.[188] While this is true, it is not clear why it matters. Supplemental jurisdiction has always been tied to *transactional relatedness* of the claims, not their logical dependence. A strict insistence on logical dependence would mean that only impleader claims may invoke supplemental jurisdiction. And that has never been the rule. Indeed, the *Kroger* opinion undid much of its argument here by recognizing the universal acceptance of supplemental jurisdiction over compulsory counterclaims, crossclaims, and claims by and against intervenors of right,[189] even though none of those is necessarily logically dependent on the underlying claims.[190]

Second, the Court noted that the claim requiring supplemental jurisdiction was asserted by the plaintiff, and not by a party in a defensive posture.[191] Apparently, the Court felt, true supplemental claims must be asserted by parties who are reacting to having been sued. It is difficult, however, to reconcile this statement with *Gibbs* itself, in which the Court upheld supplemental jurisdiction over a claim asserted by a plaintiff. The difference, of course, was that *Gibbs* was a federal question case. So perhaps the Court simply meant to limit the requirement of defensive invocation to diversity of citizenship cases.

---

[186]This holding was quite a stretch. There is no evidence that Congress ever considered supplemental jurisdiction in any way—let alone as to upsloping 14(a) claims—in passing the diversity of citizenship statute, §1332.

[187]*Kroger*, 437 U.S. at 376.

[188]That is, whether the plaintiff wins against the defendant has absolutely no bearing on how the plaintiff's claim against the TPD will come out.

[189]*Kroger*, 437 U.S. at 375 n.18.

[190]*See* 13 Wright & Miller §3523.

[191]*Kroger*, 437 U.S. at 376.

The lower courts interpreted *Kroger* narrowly. Indeed, they limited its effect to the facts of the case. Thus, *Kroger* meant that there was no supplemental jurisdiction over upsloping 14(a) claims, but it meant nothing else. The "logical dependence" language did not lead courts to cut back on the use of supplemental jurisdiction over all manner of transactionally related claims, regardless of logical dependence. After *Kroger*, courts continued to allow supplemental jurisdiction over downsloping 14(a) claims by the TPD against the plaintiff.[192] The narrowness of *Kroger* is best demonstrated by this scenario: After the TPD asserts a downsloping 14(a) claim against the nondiverse plaintiff, the plaintiff files a compulsory counterclaim right back against the TPD. Had the plaintiff filed this claim before the TPD filed her downsloping 14(a) claim, *Kroger* would have defeated supplemental jurisdiction. But by waiting, the plaintiff is now acting in a defensive capacity and supplemental jurisdiction attaches.[193]

We have discussed before that Congress's expressed intent in passing the supplemental jurisdiction statute was (1) to overrule the unfortunate *Finley* decision and (2) to codify the use of supplemental jurisdiction recognized by the federal courts before *Finley*.[194] Obviously, then, it was incumbent upon Congress to codify the result in *Kroger*. Congress did so. Section 1367(a) clearly grants supplemental jurisdiction to all Rule 14(a) claims. As we have seen several times, that section codified *Gibbs*, which permits supplemental jurisdiction over all claims that constitute part of the same "case or controversy" as the claim that invoked federal subject matter jurisdiction. As interpreted, this means the claim must share a nucleus of operative fact as the underlying claim. Upsloping (and downsloping) 14(a) claims always meet this test, because Rule 14(a) permits them to be asserted only if they arise from the same transaction or occurrence as the underlying claim.[195] Section 1367(b) applies only in cases that invoked diversity of citizenship jurisdiction (such as *Kroger* and Scenario Four). It removes supplemental jurisdiction over several claims, including

---

[192]*See, e.g.*, Revere Copper & Brass Inc. v. Aetna Cas. & Sur. Co., 426 F.2d 709 (5th Cir. 1970).

[193]Courts reached this result even though the plaintiff in this scenario might be as devious as the plaintiff so feared by the Court in *Kroger*. That is, the plaintiff might have sued only the diverse defendant, knowing that the defendant would implead the TPD and that the TPD would assert a downsloping 14(a) claim against her. Now she can achieve by indirection—a compulsory counterclaim in response to a downsloping 14(a) claim—what she could not have achieved directly.

[194]See §§4.7, 12.5.2.

[195]*See* Rule 14(a)(2)(D) and Rule 14(a)(3). The common nucleus of operative fact test of *Gibbs* is broader than "same transaction or occurrence." Therefore, claims that arise from the same transaction or occurrence as a jurisdiction-invoking claim will always invoke supplemental jurisdiction under §1367(a).

those by "plaintiffs against persons made parties under Rule 14." The claim asserted by the plaintiff in *Kroger* (and in Scenario Four) was precisely that—a claim against a TPD, brought into the case under Rule 14(a)(1). Clearly, then, the result in this hypothetical is the same under §1367 as it was under *Kroger*.

If Congress truly was attempting to codify pre-*Finley* practice, it was incumbent on the drafters to embrace the courts limiting *Kroger* to its facts. Unfortunately, they failed to do so. Section 1367(b) goes beyond the holding in *Kroger* and removes supplemental jurisdiction in situations in which it had always been used. By doing so, the statute maims efficient joinder in diversity of citizenship cases. The statute embodies an antidiversity bias.

> ○ ***Example #51.*** *P*, a citizen of Missouri sues *D*, a citizen of Kansas. All claims are based on state law and all exceed $75,000. This original claim invokes diversity of citizenship jurisdiction and the case is properly filed in federal court. *D* files a counterclaim against *P*, which also invokes diversity of citizenship jurisdiction. Now *P* impleads *T*, who, *P* asserts, owes her indemnity or contribution for the counterclaim by *D* against *P*. *T* is a citizen of Missouri. Thus, the impleader claim is asserted by a citizen of Missouri against a citizen of Missouri. Obviously, then, this claim cannot invoke diversity of citizenship jurisdiction. And because it arises under state law, the claim also cannot invoke federal question jurisdiction. Is there supplemental jurisdiction over this impleader claim by *P*?

The impleader claim, as we discussed in Example #48 above, certainly meets the *Gibbs* test. Moreover, because the claim is asserted by one acting in a defensive capacity, *Kroger* did not counsel rejection of supplemental jurisdiction. Thus, before adoption of the supplemental jurisdiction statute, the answer was quite clear: Supplemental (then called *ancillary*) jurisdiction applied to impleader claims asserted by the plaintiff.[196]

But what does the supplemental jurisdiction statute do? Section 1367(a) clearly grants supplemental jurisdiction over the impleader claim because, as we just said and as we saw in Scenario Two, it satisfies *Gibbs*. Section 1367(b) applies in cases that invoked diversity of citizenship jurisdiction (as *P* v. *D* does) and removes jurisdiction over certain claims, including claims asserted by "plaintiffs against persons made parties under Rule 14." The claim in this hypothetical is exactly such a claim: It is asserted by a plaintiff against someone impleaded

---

[196]*See, e.g.*, Brown & Caldwell v. Institute for Energy Funding, Ltd., 617 F. Supp. 649, 651 (C.D. Cal. 1985) (exercising "ancillary" jurisdiction over impleader claim by plaintiff filed in response to counterclaim against the plaintiff).

under Rule 14. Thus, on its face, the statute *prohibits* supplemental jurisdiction over this claim.

This result is unfortunate. It changes jurisdictional law that was well established before passage of the statute. Moreover, it means that the underlying claim by P against D and the counterclaim by D against P will proceed in federal court, while the impleader claim by P against TPD must go to state court. This subjects P to precisely the kinds of harm impleader is designed to avoid. It burdens P with the risk of unfair loss and burdens the judicial systems with two cases over what is clearly one transactionally related dispute.

Moreover, the result in Example #51 is apparently unintended by the drafters of the statute. Three professors who were involved in drafting the statute have argued that the statutory interpretation described above is too wooden, that courts will be able to apply the "spirit of *Kroger*" to permit supplemental jurisdiction over claims asserted by a plaintiff in a defensive capacity.[197] They point to the last phrase of §1367(b), which provides that supplemental jurisdiction is removed from various claims "when exercising supplemental jurisdiction . . . would be inconsistent with the jurisdictional requirements of §1332," and argue that it incorporates the flexible "spirit of *Kroger*."[198]

No doubt there *should* be supplemental jurisdiction over these claims. But courts are stuck with the language of the statute, and that language makes no express exception for claims asserted by plaintiffs in a defensive capacity. Predictably, courts have interpreted the statute to *prohibit* supplemental jurisdiction in this fact pattern.[199] Is it possible that other courts will hold the other way? Yes, which simply creates another area in which this statute has created uncertainty.

○ ***Example #52.*** P, a citizen of South Carolina, sues D, a citizen of Kentucky. All claims are based upon state law and exceed $75,000. The case thus invokes diversity of citizenship jurisdiction and is properly filed in federal court. D impleads T, a citizen of South Carolina. As in Example #50 above, this claim invokes diversity of citizenship jurisdiction. Now, T asserts a downsloping 14(a) claim against P. That claim does not invoke diversity of citizenship jurisdiction, because T and P are citizens of the same state. It does not invoke federal question jurisdiction, because the claim arises under state law. Does it invoke supplemental jurisdiction?

---

[197]Rowe, Burbank, & Mengler, note 137 above.

[198]*Id.*

[199]*See, e.g.*, Chase Manhattan Bank v. Aldridge, 906 F. Supp. 866, 868-869 (S.D.N.Y. 1995) (terms of statute dictate this result); Guaranteed Sys., Inc. v. American Nat'l Can Co., 842 F. Supp. 855, 856-858 (M.D.N.C. 1994) (recognizing the unfortunate result but "bound by the plain terms of the statute").

Yes. Section 1367(a) grants supplemental jurisdiction because 14(a) claims, by definition, must arise from the same transaction or occurrence as the underlying case; thus, they satisfy *Gibbs*. Section 1367(b) applies in cases that invoked diversity of citizenship jurisdiction (such as this) but only removes supplemental jurisdiction over claims by plaintiffs. This is a claim asserted by the TPD, so §1367(b) does not remove the grant of supplemental jurisdiction. The claim can be joined in federal court. (This result is consistent with the law before enactment of §1367.)

> ○ ***Example #53.*** Now one more step. Suppose *P* now asserts a compulsory counterclaim against *T*. Once *T* asserted the downsloping 14(a) claim against *P*, *T* became an "opposing party," so *P*'s claim back is a counterclaim. This one arises from the same transaction or occurrence as *T*'s claim, so it is a compulsory counterclaim under Rule 13(a). Is there subject matter jurisdiction over this claim? Obviously, there is no diversity of citizenship or federal question jurisdiction; the two are citizens of the same state and the claim arises under state law. Is there supplemental jurisdiction?

Before Congress enacted §1367 there was.[200] But the statute creates the same problem we saw in Example #50. The compulsory counterclaim would clearly invoke supplemental jurisdiction under §1367(a) because it arises from the same transaction or occurrence as the underlying claim that invoked subject matter jurisdiction. The problem, again, comes from §1367(b), which applies in cases that invoked diversity of citizenship jurisdiction (such as this), and removes supplemental jurisdiction over claims by "plaintiffs against persons made parties under Rule 14." This claim is exactly that. Obviously, there should be supplemental jurisdiction, because *P* is acting in a defensive capacity and, in fact, is filing a *compulsory* counterclaim. But, just as obviously, this statute fails to address this situation, and creates uncertainty as to the viability of supplemental jurisdiction in this scenario.

> ○ ***Example #54.*** *P*, a citizen of Wisconsin, asserts a federal question claim against *D*, a citizen of Delaware, properly invoking federal question jurisdiction. All other claims are based upon state law and exceed $75,000. *D* impleads *T*, a corporation that is incorporated in Delaware with its principal place of business in Wisconsin. (So, as we saw in §4.5.3, the corporation is a citizen of both of those states.) *P* asserts an upsloping

---

[200]*See, e.g.*, Finkle v. Gulf & Western Mfg. Co., 744 F.2d 1015, 1018-1019 (3d Cir. 1984); Berel Co. v. Sencit F/G McKinley Assoc., 125 F.R.D. 100, 102-103 (D.N.J. 1989) (both cases exercising "ancillary" jurisdiction over a compulsory counterclaim by the plaintiff against the third-party defendant).

14(a) claim under Rule 14(a)(3) against *T*. Neither the impleader claim nor the upsloping 14(a) claim invokes diversity of citizenship or federal question jurisdiction. Does either claim invoke supplemental jurisdiction?

Yes—they both do. Why? First, §1367(a) grants supplemental jurisdiction over both, because both satisfy *Gibbs*. Second, §1367(b) does not apply, and thus cannot remove the grant of supplemental jurisdiction over those claims. Remember, §1367(b) applies only in cases that invoked diversity of citizenship jurisdiction. This case did not, so §1367(b) does not apply and does not remove the grant of supplemental jurisdiction.

§12.6.3   Intervention (Rule 24)

Procedural and Policy Issues

Intervention is exactly what it sounds like—an absentee brings herself into a pending case. By doing so, obviously, the absentee overrides the plaintiff's party structure of the case. Intervention is governed in federal practice by Federal Rule 24, which recognizes both intervention of right (under Rule 24(a)) and permissive intervention (under Rule 24(b)).[201] The difference between these two is clear from the names. With the former, the court (at least theoretically) must allow the absentee to join; with the latter, the court has the discretion to permit the absentee to join.

Intervention of Right. An absentee may qualify for intervention of right in one of two ways. First, Rule 24(a)(1) notes that a federal statute might confer such a right. A good example is 28 U.S.C. §2403, which requires that the Attorney General of the United States be notified whenever a case calls into question "the constitutionality of any Act of Congress affecting the public interest."[202] After notification to the Attorney General, the United States has a right to intervene.

Rule 24(a)(2) is more important. It provides for intervention of right in the absence of a statute, if the absentee can establish (1) that she "claims an interest relating to the property or transaction that is the subject of the action" and (2) that she is "so situated that disposing of the action may as a practical matter impair or impede the [intervenor's]

---

[201]An absentee who intervenes to assert a claim must have standing to assert the claim. Town of Chester v. Laroe Estates, Inc., 137 S. Ct. 1645, 1651 (2017). See notes 4-5 and accompanying text above.

[202]Many people have noted that this statute (actually its predecessor) was not followed in *Erie*, in which the Supreme Court questioned the constitutionality of the Rules of Decision Act.

ability to protect its interest." But there is a third requirement. Notice that the Rule makes clear that the absentee will not have a right to intervene if an existing party adequately represents her interest.[203] On its face, then, Rule 24 seems to suggest that the party opposing intervention would have the burden of showing that an existing party adequately represented the would-be intervenor's interest. But the courts have made it clear that the intervenor has the burden on all three requirements, including, then, that the extant parties do not adequately represent her interests.

This test for intervention of right should ring a bell. The two basic requirements are the same as the two requirements for finding an absentee necessary under Rule 19(a)(1)(B)(i). We discussed those factors in detail in §12.6.1 and need not repeat that discussion here. Suffice to say that an absentee who would be found necessary under Rule 19(a)(1)(B)(i) will have a right to intervene under Rule 24(a)(2), provided she can also show that existing parties do not adequately represent her interest. This latter point has no counterpart in Rule 19. The Supreme Court has made clear that the burden of showing that no party adequately represents the intervenor's interest is "minimal," and is satisfied by showing that the existing parties have some interest that differs from that of the absentee.[204] Thus, while it cannot be ignored, observers seem to agree that this factor has not had great independent significance. In the words of some, the absentee "should be treated as the best judge of whether the existing parties adequately represent . . . her interests, and . . . any doubt regarding adequacy of representation should be resolved in favor of the proposed intervenors."[205]

> o ***Example #55.*** *A* owns 1,000 shares of stock in Corporation, in her own name. *P* claims that she and *A* had bought the stock together and that the stock was supposed to have been issued in both names as joint owners. *P* sues Corporation, seeking to have *A*'s stock canceled and the shares reissued in the joint names of *P* and *A*. Does *A* have a right to intervene?

We saw the same fact pattern in Example #36, in which the question was whether *A* was a required party under Rule 19. The answer to that question and to the question asked here is yes. *A* has a right to intervene under Rule 24(a)(2) for essentially the same reasons that she was necessary under Rule 19(a)(1)(B)(i). First, she has an interest in the pending litigation; *A* is currently the sole owner of the

[203]Trbovich v. United Mine Workers of Am., 404 U.S. 528, 538 (1972).
[204]*Id.* at 538 n.10.
[205]6 Moore's Federal Practice 24-42.

stock at issue in the litigation. Second, she is so situated that litigation without her joinder might impair or impede her ability to protect that interest; if *P* wins the pending case, *A*'s stock is canceled and reissued to make her merely a joint owner, instead of outright owner. These two facts meant that *A* was necessary under Rule 19(a)(1)(B)(i). With Rule 24(a)(2) we must also assess the third factor: that *A*'s interest is not adequately represented by any of the present parties. This certainly seems to be the case; *P* wants to take away *A*'s present sole ownership of the stock. *D* is probably ambivalent on the issue; at least, it is not clear why the corporation cares who owns the 1,000 shares. Accordingly, *A* has a right to intervene under Rule 24(a)(2).

We are left, then, with two Rules, 19(a)(1)(B)(i) and 24(a)(2), that overlap significantly. Indeed, they were revised together in 1966 to emphasize their interrelatedness.[206] Both Rules are aimed at overriding the plaintiff's party structure for one reason: to protect an interested absentee from harm to her ability to protect her interest. Why would two Rules do the same thing? The answer is that the two Rules empower different persons to force the joinder of the absentee. Rule 19 is invoked principally by the defendant, although the court may also raise Rule 19 issues on its own (assuming that it knows about interested absentees). In contrast, the absentee herself invokes Rule 24. Thus, she is given a mechanism by which to override the plaintiff's structuring of the case expressly to protect herself.[207]

An absentee who qualifies to intervene of right is not required to do so. Rule 24(a)(2) makes it clear that the absentee "may" intervene but does not require that she do so. Nonetheless, Justice Harlan once suggested that an absentee who eschews the opportunity to assert a claim in intervention under Rule 24(a)(2) should be barred from asserting a claim in another action.[208] The Supreme Court rejected this suggestion and confirmed the voluntary nature of intervention of right in *Martin v. Wilks*.[209] There, Black firefighters sued a city, alleging racial discrimination in promotion. The resulting consent decree gave the plaintiffs relief that moved them ahead of White firefighters on the

---

[206]The Supreme Court emphasized the relationship between Rules 19 and 24 in *Martin v. Wilks*, 490 U.S. 755, 765 (1989). An entertaining discussion of the overlap between the two Rules is *Atlantis Dev. Corp. v. United States*, 379 F.2d 818 (5th Cir. 1967). The case was decided within months of the effective date of the 1966 revisions to the two Rules.

[207]Of course, an absentee can intervene only if she is aware of the pending case. Rule 19(c) is a feeble attempt to put the court in a position to know of absentees who might have a right to intervene under Rule 24(a)(2). The drafters of that Rule foresaw the possibility that the court might then inform absentees of their right to intervene. We discussed this point in detail at §12.6.1.

[208]Provident Tradesmens Bank & Trust Co. v. Patterson, 390 U.S. 102, 114 (1968).

[209]490 U.S. 755 (1989).

promotion list. Those White firefighters then sued the city. Although they were aware of the original case and satisfied the basic test for intervention of right under Rule 24(a)(2),[210] the district court rejected their petition to intervene as untimely.[211] That failure to join the White firefighters created duplicative litigation and put the city in a difficult position.[212] Nonetheless, the Court held, Rule 24(a)(2) is voluntary; the absentees had not been joined in the earlier case and thus could not be bound by the judgment in that case.[213]

Permissive Intervention. The second type of intervention, permissive intervention, is not available of right. Instead, whether to permit the absentee to intervene is addressed to the discretion of the district court. A permissive intervenor generally is not as closely related to the pending case as an intervenor of right. She does not have a statutory right to come into the case and her nonjoinder does not threaten her interest with harm. Accordingly, there is less need for allowing her to join the case, and the trial judge may look at a wide range of factors relating to fairness and convenience in deciding whether to allow permissive intervention. Permissive intervention should be granted only if the court determines that its benefits outweigh the burdens it creates.

Like intervention of right, there are two provisions concerning permissive intervention. First, under Rule 24(b)(1)(A), the absentee may seek to intervene if a federal statute confers "a conditional right to intervene." There is such a statutory provision in the Bankruptcy Code, for example, which allows a party in interest to seek to intervene.[214] Such statutes do not confer a *right* to intervene, and even

---

[210]Remember why: because they had an interest in that case and were so situated that their ability to protect that interest may be impaired or impeded, and their interest was not adequately represented by an existing party. If plaintiffs won the first case, the absentees' relative places on the promotion ladder would have been lowered; the plaintiffs would have been put above them.

[211]As noted, under Rule 24, any application to intervene must be "timely." Contrast this requirement with the timing requirement for Rule 19. Under Rule 12(h)(2), a motion to dismiss for failure to join an indispensable party may be made any time before entry of judgment at trial; in other words, indispensability under Rule 19 could be raised at the trial on the merits.

[212]The city was subject to multiple or inconsistent obligations. The judgment in one case might have told the city to promote certain firefighters and the judgment in a second case might have told the city to promote different firefighters to the same positions. For this reason, the White firefighters were necessary under Rule 19(a)(1)(B)(ii) in the original case.

[213]*Martin*, 490 U.S. at 765 ("Joinder as a party, rather than knowledge of a lawsuit and an opportunity to intervene, is the method by which potential parties are subject to the jurisdiction of the court and bound by a judgment").

[214]*See* 11 U.S.C. §1109(b).

those who fall within them must submit their intervention fate to the discretion of the trial judge.

Rule 24(b)(1)(B) is more significant and allows permissive intervention when the absentee "has a claim or defense that shares with the main action a common question of law or fact." The reference to "claim or defense" recognizes that an intervenor might come in on either side of the case, as a plaintiff or as a defendant. The requirement of a common question is not very demanding. Recall that it would take more than that for persons to be joined together as coparties. Under Rule 20(a)(1), as we discussed in §12.4, persons can join as coplaintiffs, for instance, only if their claims (1) arise from the same transaction or occurrence and (2) raise at least one common question. Here, the showing required for permissive intervention is merely the second of those two tests.

The common-question standard is the same as we saw for consolidation under Rule 42(b), which we also discussed in §12.4. Note that it does not require the absentee to have any interest in the pending case. Further, it does not require that the common question predominate in the litigation; there simply has to be at least one common question presented both by the pending case and the absentee's claim or defense. Demonstrating that there is such a common question is no guaranty that permissive intervention will be granted. Again, permissive intervention (like consolidation) is a discretionary call for the trial judge. The court usually looks to such things as (1) whether the absentee has delayed unduly in seeking to intervene; (2) whether intervention might prejudice any existing parties; and (3) the status of the pending proceedings. For instance, if the pending case is nearing completion, and intervention would introduce collateral issues that would delay resolution, the court should probably deny the application to intervene.[215]

Allowing permissive intervention overrides the plaintiff's structuring of the suit and can be disruptive to the existing parties. Accordingly, many courts will permit it only if they are convinced that the absentee will make some useful contribution to the development of the case or issues in the case. As Professor Brunet has said, "[C]ourts should welcome unique input, . . . especially on subjects within the special expertise of the intervenor."[216] Thus, one court allowed intervention by the NAACP in a redistricting case, noting that the organization could bring a useful perspective to the court's constitutional inquiry.[217] In

---

[215]*See, e.g.,* Southmark Corp. v. Cagan, 950 F.2d 416, 419 (7th Cir. 1991) (intervention denied while dispositive motion pending); Sellers v. United States, 709 F.2d 1469, 1472 (11th Cir. 1983) (intervention would introduce collateral issues).

[216]6 Moore's Federal Practice 24-55.

[217]Johnson v. Mortham, 915 F. Supp. 1529, 1538-1539 (N.D. Fla. 1995).

a case involving a challenge to election procedures under the Voting Rights Act, however, a county was not permitted to intervene; the court concluded that the county's involvement would not contribute to development of the relevant issues.[218] Moreover, intervention can be sought for limited purposes, for example, to litigate only on specific issues. For example, when the court in a civil rights case ordered that the settlement terms be kept confidential, it should have granted the motion of newspapers to intervene to challenge the order of confidentiality.[219]

Procedure and Timing. Under Rule 24(c), the absentee seeking to intervene must serve on all parties (1) a motion to intervene and (2) her pleading in intervention. Even when the case involves intervention of right, she must make the motion to intervene and does not become a party until the motion is granted. Thus, the absentee must choose to participate on one side of the dispute. The plaintiff-intervenor will offer a complaint in intervention, which states her claim against the defendant. The defendant-intervenor will offer an answer in intervention, which responds to the plaintiff's anticipated claim against her once intervention is granted. She makes this decision by determining which side is more consistent with her position. Often, there will not be a perfect match of interests, so she must decide which side offers less conflict with her position. The court has the discretion to look beyond the absentee's characterization and realign her according to what the court sees as the interests of the parties. This realignment may have serious consequences for subject matter jurisdiction, as we will see shortly.

Both Rule 24(a) and (b) begin with the words "on timely application," meaning that any motion to intervene, whether of right or permissive, must be timely. Rule 24 does not define what that means. There is no magic time frame. In one case, intervention was untimely when made four months after a case was filed.[220] In another, intervention was timely although made four years after a case was filed.[221] The question is addressed to the discretion of the district judge, who must assess not simply the passage of time since the case was filed, but all relevant circumstances.[222] While there is no single exhaustive

[218]League of Latin Am. Citizens v. Clements, 884 F.2d 185, 189 (5th Cir. 1989). As an alternative to permissive intervention, a court might permit the absentee to participate as *amicus curiae*, or "friend of the court," to brief issues and even present oral argument and, in some cases, to cross-examine witnesses. *See* 6 Moore's Federal Practice §24.23[2].

[219]Pansy v. Borough of Stroudsburg, 23 F.3d 772, 778 (3d Cir. 1994).

[220]NAACP v. New York, 413 U.S. 345 (1973).

[221]Mountain Top Condominium Ass'n v. Dave Stabbert Master Builder, 72 F.3d 361, 369 (3d Cir. 1995).

[222]NAACP v. New York, 413 U.S. 345, 366 (1973).

list of such factors, many courts look to these: (1) how long the absentee knew of her interest (or, with reasonable diligence, should have known of her interest) before seeking to intervene; (2) the extent of prejudice caused to existing parties by the absentee's delay; (3) the extent to which denial of intervention might prejudice the absentee; and (4) unusual facts that augur for or against a finding of timeliness.[223] Although it is unusual, there are cases in which courts have granted intervention after entry of judgment. For instance, an absentee whose interests are affected by the judgment might wish to intervene to prosecute an appeal when the original parties have refused to appeal.[224]

As a general rule, courts are more likely to find the effort to intervene "timely" with intervention of right under Rule 24(a)(2) than with permissive intervention.[225] The reason is clear: With intervention of right under that Rule, the absentee's ability to protect her interest will be impaired by the pending litigation. Joinder is required to avoid such potential harm to the absentee.

Jurisdictional and Related Issues

Because an intervenor voluntarily enters into a pending case, she has no basis on which to object to a lack of personal jurisdiction; she has waived any personal jurisdiction objection she might have had. Similarly, an intervenor has no basis on which to complain about venue; she has waived any venue objection she might have had as well.

But, as we know, parties cannot waive or stipulate around limits on federal subject matter jurisdiction. Every claim in federal court must be supported by a basis of subject matter jurisdiction. Thus, the court must assess whether intervention can be accomplished consistent with the restrictions on federal subject matter jurisdiction. Some courts and commentators have been sloppy in discussing this issue, by framing the inquiry as whether the court would have subject matter jurisdiction over the *intervenor*. Remember, though, that the intervenor comes into the case either to assert a claim (as a plaintiff) or to have a claim asserted against her (as a defendant). Subject matter jurisdiction is exercised over *claims*, not over *parties*.[226] So the appropriate focus is

---

[223]*See, e.g.*, Edwards v. City of Houston, 37 F.3d 1097, 1105 (5th Cir. 1994); Farmland Dairies v. Commissioner of the N.Y. State Dep't of Agric. & Mkts., 847 F.2d 1038, 1044 (2d Cir. 1988).

[224]*See, e.g.*, NL Industries, Inc. v. Secretary of the Interior, 777 F.2d 433, 436 (9th Cir. 1985).

[225]*See, e.g.*, Fiandaca v. Cunningham, 827 F.2d 825, 832 (1st Cir. 1987).

[226]Personal jurisdiction is exercised over parties, not claims.

whether the *claim asserted by or against the intervenor* invokes federal subject matter jurisdiction.

- ○ ***Example #56.*** P, a citizen of Delaware, asserts a state law claim of $100,000 against D, a citizen of Illinois. The claim invokes diversity of citizenship jurisdiction and is properly filed in federal court. A, an intervenor of right who is a citizen of California, intervenes as a plaintiff to assert a $100,000 state law claim against D. A's claim invokes diversity of citizenship jurisdiction and thus is properly asserted in this case.

- ○ ***Example #57.*** Same facts as in Example #56, except here the intervenor is a citizen of Illinois. Obviously, A's claim against D does not invoke diversity of citizenship, because A and D are citizens of the same state. Also, there is no federal question jurisdiction, because A's claim arises under state law. Can A's claim invoke supplemental jurisdiction?

This is an important question. As with the discussions of supplemental jurisdiction for each of the joinder devices addressed in this chapter, you must be familiar with the operation of §1367, which we covered in §4.7. In addition, because of the functional identity between Rule 24(a)(2) and Rule 19(a)(1)(B)(ii), we addressed the issue of supplemental jurisdiction over claims asserted by or against intervenors of right in §12.6.1. That discussion is summarized briefly here. Before §1367, the federal courts agreed that claims by or against intervenors of right under Rule 24(a)(2) invoked supplemental jurisdiction.[227] An intervenor of right, as we have seen, is an absentee with an interest in the pending case who is so situated that litigation may impair or impede her ability to protect that interest. Everyone agreed then, and seems to agree today, that a claim asserted by or against such a person is so closely related to the underlying claim to constitute part of the same case or controversy as that claim and thus to fall within supplemental jurisdiction recognized by the *Gibbs* case.[228] (If any of this material is uncertain, review §4.7.)

---

[227]*See, e.g.*, Curtis v. Sears, Roebuck & Co., 754 F.2d 781, 784 (8th Cir. 1985).

[228]There is a quick aside to this assertion. Courts recognized supplemental jurisdiction over claims by or against intervenors of right, but some then often added that such jurisdiction would not attach if the absentee would have been held indispensable under Rule 19. Commentators have criticized this latter proviso as part of an antiquated view that failure to join such an absentee is a jurisdictional defect. Moreover, under the 1966 amendments to Rule 19, this proviso makes little sense. Remember that under Rule 19 an "indispensable" absentee is one (1) who is necessary, but (2) cannot feasibly be joined in the pending case, and (3) as to whom the court has decided to dismiss rather than proceed. That third step was determined based upon an assessment of flexible factors under Rule 19(b). One relevant factor was whether the absentee can protect her interest in the absence of dismissal. Because the absentee satisfying Rule 19(a)(1)(B)(i) can intervene under Rule 24(a)(2), she can protect herself and thus the court should not dismiss. In other words, the court should not find the absentee (to use a term no longer found in Rule 19, but widely used) "indispensable."

The recognition of supplemental jurisdiction in the intervention of right context, however, created an anomaly. Why? Because claims by or against necessary parties under Rule 19(a)(1)(b)(ii) did not invoke supplemental jurisdiction. This result is odd, because, as we discussed above, the absentee who satisfies Rule 19(a)(1)(B)(ii) will also satisfy Rule 24(a)(2).[229] Thus, under the law before enactment of the supplemental jurisdiction statute, these absentees, though identically situated, were treated differently when it came to supplemental jurisdiction. If they intervened, there would be supplemental jurisdiction; if they were joined under Rule 19, there would not. Commentators have referred to this as the "Rule 19/Rule 24 anomaly."

We saw in §12.6.1 that every commentator discussing the issue concluded that the anomaly should be removed by extending supplemental jurisdiction to the necessary party situation. Instead, with the supplemental jurisdiction statute, Congress "fixed" the anomaly by removing supplemental jurisdiction in the intervention situation. Not one commentator had ever suggested that this be done, and the move is contrary to Congress's assertion that the supplemental jurisdiction statute was intended to codify practice as it had existed. Predictably, then, a chorus of commentators criticized the statute on this point.[230] In the words of one court, the statute "significantly limited the usefulness of the intervention mechanism."[231]

Let's return to Example #57. Before adoption of the supplemental jurisdiction statute, the claim by *A* against *D* would be permitted in the pending case because it would invoke supplemental jurisdiction. What about today? Under §1367(a), *A*'s claim against *D* would invoke supplemental jurisdiction, because it does satisfy the *Gibbs* test, as we saw above. But §1367(b) applies in cases that invoked diversity of citizenship jurisdiction (such as our hypothetical) and removes supplemental jurisdiction over certain claims. Among them are claims by persons "seeking to intervene as plaintiffs under Rule 24." *A* is such a person, so §1367(b) removes supplemental jurisdiction over

---

[229]The basic tests for the two Rules are the same, with one addition in Rule 24(a)(2) that the absentee show that her interest is not adequately represented by extant litigants. As we discussed above, however, this latter requirement imposes a minimal burden on the absentee.

[230]*See, e.g.*, 7C Wright & Miller §1917; Wright & Kane, Federal Courts 545-546; Christopher Fairman, *Abdication to Academia: The Case of the Supplemental Jurisdiction Statute*, 19 Seton Hall Legis. J. 157, 185-188 (1994); Richard D. Freer, *Compounding Confusion and Hampering Diversity: Life After* Finley *and the Supplemental Jurisdiction Statute*, 40 Emory L.J. 445, 475-487 (1991); Marilyn Ireland, *Supplemental Jurisdiction over Claims in Intervention*, 23 N.M. L. Rev. 57, 72-74 (1993); Denis McLaughlin, *The Federal Supplemental Jurisdiction Statute—A Constitutional and Statutory Analysis*, 24 Ariz. St. L.J. 849, 860 (1992).

[231]Glancy v. Taubman Ctrs., Inc., 373 F.3d 656, 670 (6th Cir. 2004).

that claim. This means, of course, that *P*'s claim against *D*, and any counterclaim by *D* against *P*, will be litigated in federal court, while *A*'s claim against *D* must be litigated in state court. The supplemental jurisdiction statute robs the federal court of the ability to resolve the overall dispute. As noted earlier, because §1367(b) only applies in diversity of citizenship cases, and because it increased the situations in which courts would not have supplemental jurisdiction, the statute reflects an anti-diversity-jurisdiction bias.

The language of §1367(b) is problematic in another way. Because the subsection applies to those "seeking to intervene as plaintiffs," does it include someone who seeks to intervene as a defendant, but who is realigned as a plaintiff? The uncertainty on this point simply creates more confusion. Some courts have been willing to realign an intervening plaintiff as a defendant, expressly to save jurisdiction.[232] Others have not done so, feeling bound by the absentee's choice to intervene on the plaintiff's side.[233] Some litigants have even tried to exploit this language by intervening as defendants when their interests are more closely aligned with the plaintiff.[234]

> ○ ***Example #58.*** *A* holds a stock certificate for 1,000 shares of Corporation, issued in *A*'s name. *P* claims that she and *A* had agreed to buy the stock together, each paying half, and that the stock should have been issued in their joint names. *P*, a citizen of Alabama, sues Corporation, a citizen of Delaware, seeking to have *A*'s stock canceled and then reissued in the joint names of *P* and *A*. The stock is worth $500,000. *P*'s claim against Corporation invokes diversity of citizenship jurisdiction and is properly filed in federal court. *A* is required under Rule 19(a)(1)(B)(i) and has a right to intervene under Rule 24(a)(2).[235] Will there be subject matter jurisdiction if she intervenes?

In all likelihood, *A* will choose to intervene as a defendant. Her interest is antithetical to that of *P*. After all, *P* wants to dilute *A*'s interest in the stock. Corporation is probably ambivalent about who owns the stock and may be satisfied with the status quo. *A* wants to keep the status quo. Let's say, then, that *A* would intervene as a defendant. She is a citizen of Alabama, so *P*'s claim against *A* does not

---

[232]*See, e.g.*, Development Fin. Corp. v. Alpha Hous. & Health Care, Inc., 54 F.3d 156, 159-160 (3d Cir. 1995).

[233]*See, e.g.*, Maryland Cas. Co. v. W.R. Grace & Co., 1996 U.S. Dist. LEXIS 868 (S.D.N.Y. Jan. 29, 1996).

[234]*See, e.g.*, Atherton v. Casey, 1992 U.S. Dist. LEXIS 9976 (E.D. La. June 29, 1992). The court realigned the intervenor as a plaintiff to reject supplemental jurisdiction.

[235]Remember why: *A* has an interest in the pending case; her ability to protect that interest may be impaired or impeded by the pending case, and (for Rule 24(a)(2)) her interest is not adequately protected by those who are presently parties.

803

invoke diversity of citizenship jurisdiction (because they are cocitizens). The claim likewise does not invoke federal question jurisdiction because it arises under state law. Is there supplemental jurisdiction?

As we saw above, §1367(a) will grant supplemental jurisdiction over the claim, because of its close relationship with the pending case. But does §1367(b) remove that grant? It applies only in cases that invoked diversity of citizenship jurisdiction, such as this, and removes jurisdiction over particular claims.

Some commentators argue that joinder is proper in this case because nothing in §1367(b) precludes it.[236] After all, there is no claim here asserted by a person "seeking to intervene as a plaintiff under Rule 24." So that prohibition does not apply. The problem with the argument, as we also saw with regard to Rule 19(a)(1)(B)(i) in §12.6.1, is that it assumes that subject matter jurisdiction is granted over *parties*. Why did *A* intervene as a defendant? Presumably so she could defend against *P*'s claim to her stock. Notice, however, that §1367(b) expressly removes supplemental jurisdiction over claims asserted by a plaintiff against "persons made parties under Rule . . . 24." This provision applies to *A* in this hypothetical. Hence, the claim by *P* against *A*—which was the very reason for *A*'s intervening—cannot be asserted in the pending case.

Finally, claims asserted by or against a permissive intervenor will rarely invoke supplemental jurisdiction. Permissive intervention under Rule 24(b)(2) requires only that the intervenor's claim or defense have at least one question in common with the pending case. There is thus no requirement that the claim or defense be so closely related to the pending case as to arise from a common nucleus of operative fact; thus, satisfying the requirement of Rule 24(b)(2) does not necessarily satisfy the degree of relatedness required for supplemental jurisdiction under §1367(a). There may be cases, however, in which the claims asserted by or against a permissive intervenor will share enough factual overlap with the underlying dispute to invoke supplemental jurisdiction, but they are unusual.[237] In most cases, claims involving permissive intervenors have to invoke diversity of citizenship, alienage, or federal question jurisdiction to be heard in federal court.

---

[236]Rowe, Burbank & Mengler, note 137 above.

[237]*See, e.g.,* Beckham Indus., Inc. v. International Ins. Co., 966 F.2d 470, 473 (9th Cir.), *cert. denied,* 506 U.S. 868 (1992). Recall from §12.5.1 that there is authority that the grant is even broader than this and requires only that the claims have some "loose factual connection." See notes 76-78 and accompanying text above. Such a broad interpretation of the grant of supplemental jurisdiction might encompass claims involving permissive intervenors.

Chapter *13*

Special Multiparty Litigation

§13.1 Defining the Issue

In this chapter we study two specialized kinds of multiparty litigation: interpleader and the class action. With each, we revisit some policy themes we saw in Chapter 12. Specifically, in §12.6, we discussed three policies that justified overriding the plaintiff's structuring of a case: efficiency, avoidance of harm to the absentee, and avoidance of harm to the defendant. Each of these makes appearances in this chapter. Here, though, we are not overriding the plaintiff's party structure of the case. Instead, we are structuring a multiparty case at the outset, employing those policies.

Though interpleader and the class action share some policy underpinnings—particularly a desire for efficient resolution of multiple claims—they are fundamentally different forms of litigation. Interpleader allows resolution of competing claims to property in a single case. It is thus limited to the question of who owns specific property. The class action permits a representative (or multiple representatives) to assert or to defend against claims on behalf of a group whose members are similarly situated. Properly executed, class litigation by the representative(s) will bind all class members.

It is useful to distinguish the litigation we see here from a *shareholder derivative suit*. Though most Civil Procedure courses do not cover this type of litigation, you will encounter it in some of your readings and should know what it is. Indeed, two classic Civil Procedure cases—*Shaffer v. Heitner* (concerning *quasi-in-rem* jurisdiction, discussed at §2.4.4) and *Cohen v. Beneficial Industrial Loan Corp.* (an *Erie* case, discussed at §10.5)—were derivative suits. In federal court, derivative suits are governed by Federal Rule 23.1.

Such a case is filed by a shareholder of a corporation to vindicate a claim that belongs to the corporation.[1] Almost always, the claim is against corporate managers for violating duties that they owe to the corporation. (A good example is when corporate directors steal corporate assets; that breaches their duty of loyalty to the corporation.) Though the corporation has a right to sue the bad managers, often it will not (because the bad managers usually make the decision of whether the corporation should sue). If the corporation does not file suit, a shareholder is permitted to assert the claim *on its behalf*. So while a class action seeks to vindicate the individual claims of numerous class members, the derivative suit asserts a claim that belongs to a corporation.

§13.2 Interpleader

§13.2.1 What Interpleader Is and How It Works

Policy and Terminology

Interpleader is a procedural device that allows someone in possession of property or money to force all adverse claimants to that property to litigate the ownership of that property in a single proceeding. It has existed in some form for seven centuries and is the model of efficient litigation: The question of ownership is litigated once, with all claimants and the present possessor of the property bound by the judgment.

---

[1]*See generally* Richard D. Freer & Douglas K. Moll, Principles of Business Organizations 507-514 (2d ed. 2018).

○ ***Example #1.*** Insurance Co. issued a $250,000 life insurance policy. The insured died, and Insurance Co. must now pay out the benefit. Three people—*A, B,* and *C*—each claim to be the beneficiary of the entire policy amount. Consider how difficult things would be for Insurance Co. if it could not force *A, B,* and *C* to assert their claims to the policy in a single interpleader case.

Suppose *A* sued Insurance Co. and won. The court would enter a judgment requiring the company to pay the policy amount to *A.* Then suppose *B* sued Insurance Co. The judgment in the case by *A* against Insurance Co. would not be binding on *B,* so *B* is free to assert her claim that she should get the money. (By the way, why is the judgment in the case by *A* v. Insurance Co. not binding on *B*?[2]) Suppose *B* wins. The court would enter a judgment requiring the company to pay the policy amount to *B.* Insurance Co. would now be subject to inconsistent obligations: It could not satisfy the judgment from the first case without violating the judgment from the second case. If it has to pay both, it will pay out twice as much in insurance proceeds as it contracted to do. And things might get even more complicated when *C* sues to claim that she should get the insurance money.

Interpleader avoids these problems by allowing Insurance Co. (or anyone in a similar situation) to join in a single case all the persons who claim to own the property. Thus, it is supported by the same policy interest we saw undergirding joinder of necessary parties under Rule 19(a)(1)(B)(ii)[3] and impleader under Rule 14(a)(1).[4] And because interpleader resolves the conflicting claims in a single proceeding, it saves judicial resources and avoids the inconsistent results that can erode confidence in the system of justice. In summary,

> a many-sided dispute can be resolved economically and expeditiously in a proceeding, and the stakeholder can be relieved from the obligation of determining who has the rightful claim to the money or property. In addition, the stakeholder avoids possible multiple liability resulting from inconsistent judgments for different claimants in different suits. Even if multiple liability is unlikely, both the stakeholder

---

[2]Because due process provides that a judgment cannot be binding against one who was not a party in an earlier case. See §11.4.4. *B* was not a party in *A* v. Insurance Co., nor was any party representing *B*'s interest. So *B* is not bound.

[3]That rule permits overriding the plaintiff's structuring of a suit expressly to avoid subjecting a party to double, multiple, or inconsistent obligations such as those seen here. See §12.6.1.

[4]Impleader permits a defending party to join in an absentee who owes her indemnity or contribution. Doing so protects the defendant from the possibility of losing in the pending case and then failing in a separate case to collect indemnity of contributions. Thus, impleader, like joinder of necessary parties under Rule 19(a)(1)(B)(ii) and interpleader, avoids imposition of multiple liability. See §12.6.2.

and the judicial system avoid the expense and delay of multiple litigation. Conflicting claimants to the stake also may benefit from interpleader, since all conflicting claims are resolved in a single action and a limited fund can be distributed equitably. Furthermore, interpleader frequently eliminated the need to find and execute on the debtor's assets. The contested stake generally will be on deposit with the court.[5]

Interpleader involves specialized terminology:

- The property to which the litigants have conflicting claims of ownership is the *stake* or *res*.[6]
- The person in possession of the property is the *stakeholder*.
- The persons who are joined in the interpleader proceeding, whose conflicting claims of ownership will be adjudicated, are the *claimants*.

Historically, interpleader was possible only if the stakeholder did not claim to own the stake — that is, if the stakeholder was *disinterested*. Traditionally, then, the stakeholder was one who found herself in possession of property, did not know to whom it belonged, knew that various people claimed to own it, but who did not claim ownership herself. Interpleader invoked by such a disinterested stakeholder is called *true* (or sometimes *strict*) *interpleader*. Over time, courts relaxed the requirement that the stakeholder not claim to own the stake and permitted an *interested stakeholder* to institute interpleader. Such a proceeding was (and is) known as *in the nature of interpleader*. (As we see in §13.2.2, the question of whether the stakeholder is interested may affect the invocation of subject matter jurisdiction.)

- ***Example #2.*** S finds an expensive wristwatch in the basement of the house she buys. The previous owner of the house (*O*) claims to own it and argues that she left it in the basement by mistake. A contractor (*C*) also claims to own it and argues that she left it in the basement while doing renovation work. *S* is the stakeholder. *O* and *C* are the claimants. If *S* does not claim to own the wristwatch, she is a disinterested stakeholder, and the proceeding will be a true (or strict) interpleader.
  - If, however, *S* claims that she should be able to keep the wristwatch (because, for example, of a finders' statute), she will be an interested stakeholder, and the proceeding will be in the nature of the interpleader.

---

[5] 4 Moore's Federal Practice at 22-9 to 22-11.

[6] *Res* is the Latin word for "thing," as we saw when we studied *in rem* personal jurisdiction in §2.2.

Two Types of Interpleader in Federal Court

Interpleader practice in the federal courts is complicated because there are two types of interpleader. Rule 22 permits interpleader. This is known as *Rule interpleader.* Because no Federal Rule can affect federal subject matter jurisdiction or venue, Rule 22 provides only a procedural mechanism. It can only be used if some basis for federal subject matter jurisdiction (discussed in Chapter 4) and some basis for federal venue (discussed in Chapter 5) apply. Typically, Rule interpleader cases invoke diversity of citizenship jurisdiction under 28 U.S.C. §1332(a)(1).

In addition, however, there is the Federal Interpleader Act, which consists of three statutes—28 U.S.C. §§1335, 1397, and 2361. This Act creates a different right to interplead and a separate basis of federal subject matter jurisdiction, as well as provisions for venue and service of process. These three statutes together create what is known as *statutory interpleader.*

The jurisdictional and venue differences between Rule and statutory interpleader are important and are addressed in detail in §13.2.2. Other differences are discussed in the remainder of this subsection. Throughout your consideration of this topic, keep in mind that there are two completely separate vehicles—Rule interpleader and statutory interpleader—for invoking interpleader in federal court.

Claims That Exceed the Stake and Prospective Claims

In the examples we have seen so far, each adverse claimant claimed to own the entire stake—either the wristwatch in the previous hypothetical or the $250,000 life insurance fund in the first example. But interpleader is also appropriate when the total claimed by the claimants exceeds the value of the stake. Such cases usually involve competing claims to a liability insurance fund.

> *Example #3. D* has automobile insurance that covers her against liability to a total of $300,000 per occurrence. She is involved in an automobile crash that severely injures five people. Each of the five (*P-1* through *P-5*) files a case against *D* for personal injuries from the crash. The total demand in the five separate cases is $1,500,000. Thus, the claims exceed fivefold the amount of insurance coverage. *D's* insurance company may wish to interplead the $300,000 fund and join the five claimants. There are three important points to note here.

First, interpleader litigation deals *only* with who is entitled to recover the *stake*; it involves *only* adverse claims *to* the stake. In this hypothetical, we do not know yet whether the claims by each of the five individual tort plaintiffs will result in judgments that exceed the $300,000 insurance coverage. The five tort claims are "unliquidated," because we do not know whether they will actually become claims against the insurance fund and, if so, for how much. The individual tort cases by *P-1* through *P-5* against *D* are *not* part of the interpleader case. Those claims are asserted against *D* to impose upon *D* personal liability; they are not claims against the stake.[7] As those cases are litigated (or settled), the claim of each plaintiff will become "liquidated," which means that a dollar figure will be attached to it. Then, each plaintiff will have a claim against the stake, because each will want to recover her judgment from the insurance money. (If the stake is exhausted without compensating the claimants fully, the claimants will attempt to recover the shortfall from *D* personally.)

Second, if the claims of the various tort plaintiffs in this case are not yet liquidated (and might not be liquidated for years because they are in litigation in separate cases), how can the insurance company interplead *now*? Some states have "direct action" statutes, which allow claimants to sue insurance companies before winning a judgment against the person insured. In such a state, there is no problem with allowing interpleader at this stage, because *P-1* through *P-5* can sue the insurer in advance of winning a judgment against *D*. But many states do not permit such direct actions, and permit suit against the insurance company only after one has won a judgment against the insured. Is interpleader possible at this stage? Though the answer was debated for some time, it is now clear, at least in federal court, that the answer is yes. Under Rule interpleader by Rule 22, the stakeholder may proceed if separate claims "may expose [the stakeholder] to double or multiple liability. . . ." Under statutory interpleader, the stakeholder may join any who "are claiming or *may* claim to be entitled to the stake."[8] Thus, even if the applicable substantive law does not permit a direct action in the absence of a judgment against the insured, interpleader is proper at the outset.[9]

---

[7]In all likelihood, *D*'s insurance company will have the duty to defend *D* in each of those cases, regardless of what the ultimate recoveries by each plaintiff may be. It usually is part of a liability insurer's contractual obligation not only to provide the policy coverage from which claimants can recover but also to defend the insured in litigation against her.

[8]28 U.S.C. §1335(a)(1) (emphasis added).

[9]State Farm Fire & Cas. Co. v. Tashire, 386 U.S. 523, 533 (1967) ("Were an insurance company required to await reduction of claims to judgment, the first claimant to obtain such a judgment or to negotiate a settlement might appropriate all or a disproportionate slice of the fund before his fellow claimants were able to establish their claims. The difficulties such a race to judgment pose for the insurer, and the unfairness which may result to some claimants, were among the principal evils the interpleader device was intended to remedy"). Though this case involved statutory interpleader, there is no

Third, what happens if the claims of the five plaintiffs, as finally liquidated, exceed the value of the stake? Suppose, for example, that *P-1* wins a judgment of $50,000; *P-2* wins a judgment of $100,000; *P-3* wins a judgment of $150,000; *P-4* wins a judgment of $200,000; and *P-5* wins a judgment of $400,000. That is a total of $900,000 in judgments against *D*. The available insurance fund is $300,000. If interpleader were not available, we would have a race to recover from the insurance fund. The race might leave the tardy claimants with nothing. Thus, in addition to the policy advantages discussed above, allowing interpleader in this situation also serves the same principle addressed by Rule 19(a)(1)(B)(i) (discussed in §12.6)—avoiding harm to an absentee.

> o ***Example #4.*** In this situation, interpleader serves to "slice the pie" equitably among the five claimants. As noted, their liquidated claims total $900,000, which is three times as large as the insurance fund. Accordingly, the interpleader court will allow each claimant to recover one-third of her claim. Thus, *P-1* will recover $16,666.66 from the fund; *P-2* will get $33,333.33; *P-3* will get $50,000; *P-4* will get $66,666.67; and *P-5* will get $133,333.33. None recovers her amount in full, but, more important, none is left out altogether. (Each one is now free to try to enforce her judgment against *D* personally for the two-thirds not covered by insurance.)

Injunctions Against Other Proceedings; Limitations of Interpleader

The efficacy of interpleader would be threatened if the claimants were free to assert their rights to the stake in separate litigation. For instance, assume *S* institutes interpleader and joins *O* and *C* as claimants. If *C* can sue *S* in a separate suit in another court to recover the stake from *S*, the advantages of interpleader will be lost. To avoid such duplicative litigation, it would behoove the interpleader court to issue an injunction against the claimants, prohibiting them from suing for the stake in another case. In the federal system, interpleader courts certainly have the authority to enter such injunctions.

Section 2361, which is part of statutory interpleader, expressly provides that the federal court overseeing an interpleader case may "enter its order restraining [the claimants] from instituting or prosecuting any proceeding in any State or United States court affecting the

---

serious doubt that Rule 22 also permits interpleader of prospective claims, as shown by the language that separate claims "may" expose the stakeholder to harm. *See* 6247 Atlas Corp. v. Marine Ins. Co., 155 F.R.D. 454, 463 (S.D.N.Y. 1994).

[stake]."[10] Note that the language permits the federal court to issue an injunction against claimants from proceeding either in another federal court *or* in any state court.[11] But §2361 does not apply to Rule interpleader cases.[12] As to such cases, then, there is no express grant of injunctive power. Nonetheless, the interpleader court can issue an injunction, though getting to that conclusion is more complicated. For starters, it is well established that the interpleader court may issue an injunction against overlapping litigation in another *federal* court.[13] This result is dictated by the "first-filed rule," which provides, as a general matter, that the court in which a matter is first filed has the power to enjoin litigants from proceeding in another federal court on the same matter.

What if the overlapping litigation is in a state court? Here, things get more complicated because of the Anti-Injunction Act, 28 U.S.C. §2283, which provides that a federal court may not issue an injunction against litigants proceeding in a state court, unless one of three exceptions applies. This statute recognizes an important policy of federalism—that it is generally inappropriate for the courts of the federal government to interfere with the courts of a sovereign state government.[14] Thus, a federal Rule interpleader court can issue an injunction against a pending state action only if one of the exceptions to the Anti-Injunction Act applies.[15] The exceptions are: (1) when Congress provides that the federal court may enjoin litigants from proceeding in state court;[16] (2) when an injunction is "necessary in aid" of the jurisdiction of the court; and (3) when an injunction

---

[10]28 U.S.C. §2361.

[11]Any such injunction is not issued to the other courts. It would be unseemly for one court to order another court not to proceed with a matter; such orders are extremely rare. Instead, the injunction is against the claimants personally, forbidding them from litigating in another court. If a claimant violates the injunction, the federal court issuing it can hold the claimant in contempt, which means that the court can fine that party or even order her jailed until she agrees to abide by the injunction.

[12]United States Indus., Inc. v. Laborde, 794 F. Supp. 454, 459 (D.P.R. 1992).

[13]*See, e.g.*, Pan Am. Fire & Cas. Co. v. Revere, 188 F. Supp. 474, 483 n.46 (E.D. La. 1960).

[14]This federalism concern is not present, of course, when the overlapping cases are both in federal court. In such cases, the first-filed rule can apply, because the different courts involved are in the same judicial system.

[15]If the claimant has not yet instituted a state court action, the Anti-Injunction Act does not apply and the federal court thus may issue the injunction. Why? The Act applies only to injunctions against pending state court proceedings, and not to state court actions that have not yet been filed. Dombrowski v. Pfister, 380 U.S. 479, 484 n.2 (1965) (Act does "not preclude injunctions against the institution of state court proceedings, but only bar stays of suits already instituted").

[16]This exception applies with *statutory* interpleader, because §2361 makes such an express provision.

is necessary to enable the court to effectuate a judgment it has entered.[17] Courts have concluded that the second exception applies in Rule interpleader cases.[18] In other words, the federal court in Rule interpleader can issue an injunction "in aid of its jurisdiction," because simultaneous litigation in state court would interfere with the interpleader court's efforts to distribute the stake.[19]

Any injunction prohibiting a claimant from litigating outside the interpleader proceeding must be properly limited. Specifically, it can only prohibit other claims *to the stake itself.* This fact drives home the limitation of interpleader: It is a device for placing in one proceeding claims to specific property; it is not a device that allows a court to force all potential tort claimants into a single case. *The interpleader case must involve only claims to the stake.*

The leading case on the scope of interpleader is *State Farm Fire & Casualty Co. v. Tashire,*[20] which involved a horrible collision between a Greyhound bus and a truck. The truck was driven by Clark and owned by Glasgow (who was a passenger in the truck at the time of the collision). The Greyhound bus was driven by Nauta. The collision killed two passengers on the bus and injured 33 other passengers, as well as Clark, Glasgow, and Nauta. Clark carried insurance with State Farm. The policy covered Clark (the driver of the truck) for claims up to $10,000 per person for bodily injury, with a maximum of $20,000 per occurrence. It was obvious that the claims against Clark for the collision would exceed the policy limit. State Farm filed an interpleader action. As claimants, it joined Clark, Glasgow, Nauta, Greyhound Lines, and each passenger (or, if deceased, the passenger's estate). The district court permitted the interpleader to proceed and entered an injunction requiring that all claims against State Farm, Clark, Greyhound, and Nauta be prosecuted in the interpleader proceeding. Thus, tort claims against the insurer and insured, as well as those against others involved in the wreck, could be asserted only in the interpleader case.

The Supreme Court drastically modified the injunction to reflect the proper scope of interpleader. Interpleader is limited to claims to

---

[17]28 U.S.C. § 2283.

[18]*See, e.g.,* General Ry. Signal Co. v. Corcoran, 921 F.2d 700, 707 (7th Cir. 1991).

[19]In addition, once the interpleader judgment is entered, the Rule interpleader court can issue an injunction against state court proceedings that would seek to undo the result of the interpleader. Such an injunction satisfied the third exception to the Anti-Injunction Act, that the injunction enable the court to effectuate its judgments. *See, e.g.,* Truck-A-Tune v. Re, 856 F. Supp. 77, 81 n.10 (D. Conn. 1993), *aff'd on other grounds,* 23 F.3d 60 (2d Cir. 1994).

[20]386 U.S. 523 (1967).

the fund. In many cases, the Court noted, such claims will constitute the entire dispute, and there will be no collateral litigation. For example, in our hypothetical above concerning the wristwatch, the interpleader case would resolve the entire dispute between the homeowner, the previous owner, and the contractor; the only controversy was ownership of the watch.

In cases like *Tashire*, however, there are more assertions of liability than the mere claims to the fund of insurance money. In that case, there were tort claims against Greyhound, Nauta, Glasgow, and Clark. None of these tort claims constituted property brought within the interpleader proceeding. The interpleader could determine *only* who gets the $20,000 of State Farm insurance money for claims against Clark. Thus, anyone who had *already recovered* a judgment against Clark could seek to recover it from the State Farm fund. Those claims were properly asserted *only* in the interpleader case. But the underlying tort claims against Clark (and against the others) are not part of the interpleader case; quite simply, they are not claims against the stake until one tries to enforce a judgment against the insurance fund. As the Court summarized:

> State Farm's interest in this case, which is the fulcrum of the interpleader procedure, is confined to its $20,000 fund. That interest receives full vindication when the court restrains claimants from seeking to enforce against the insurance company any judgment obtained against its insured, except in the interpleader proceeding itself. To the extent that the District Court sought to control claimants' lawsuits against the insured and other alleged tortfeasors, it exceeded the powers granted to it by the [interpleader] scheme.[21]

The court recognized that its holding meant that interpleader "cannot be used to solve all the vexing problems of multiparty litigation arising out of a mass tort. But interpleader was never intended to perform such a function, to be an all-purpose 'bill of peace.'"[22] The bill of peace was a tool of equity that permitted a court to join all interested parties in a single case, in an effort to resolve an overall dispute. There is no modern counterpart to the bill of peace. The lack of such a tool is frustrating, but this is part of the price we pay for the value we place on litigant autonomy. As the Court emphasized in *Tashire*, had interpleader been intended as a bill of peace, "careful provision would necessarily have been made to insure that a party with little or no interest in the outcome of a complex controversy [like

---

[21]*Id.* at 535.
[22]*Id.*

State Farm] should not strip truly interested parties of substantial rights—such as the right to choose the forum in which to establish their claims. . . ."[23]

Invocation of Interpleader

Interpleader is odd because it reverses the normal role of plaintiff and defendant. Usually, when a plaintiff sues a defendant, it is to impose liability on the defendant. In interpleader, however, the stakeholder, as plaintiff, sues the claimants not to impose liability on them, but to force them to assert their claims to the property in the interpleader proceeding. In essence, she sues them to force them to sue her! She does so, however, because interpleader allows her to avoid being sued multiple times by the various claimants.

What happens, though, if one of the claimants sues the stakeholder before she institutes interpleader? Can there be *defensive invocation of interpleader*? Yes. Let's return to the fact pattern we saw above in Example #2. Here, though, assume that O has sued S, seeking to recover the wristwatch. S is the defendant, but is also the stakeholder, and wants to invoke interpleader by bringing C into the case as well, so all the claimants can litigate the ownership question in a single proceeding. What does she do? She files a compulsory counterclaim against O, invoking interpleader and naming O as one of the claimants.[24] Rule 13(h) (see §12.5) permits S to join as additional parties to the counterclaim any absentee (such as C) who satisfies Rule 19 or Rule 20.[25] By definition, absentee claimants in interpleader (here, C) satisfy Rule 19 and thus can be joined under Rule 13(h).[26]

---

[23]*Id.* at 536.

[24]The claim against O is a compulsory counterclaim because it is against an opposing party and arises from the same transaction or occurrence as that party's claim. Here, O's claim against S is for ownership of the wristwatch. S's counterclaim is for interpleader as to the same property; thus, it obviously arises from the same transaction or occurrence as O's claim. We discussed the compulsory counterclaim at §12.5.1. *See* Fed. R. Civ. P. 22(a)(2): "A defendant exposed to similar liability may seek interpleader through a crossclaim or counterclaim."

[25]Rule 20 concerns permissive joinder of parties. See §12.4. Rule 19 concerns joinder of necessary parties. See §12.6.1.

[26]An absentee stakeholder satisfied Rule 19(a)(1)(B)(ii) because her nonjoinder subjects a party (the stakeholder) to the possibility of multiple or inconsistent obligations. As we noted above, if the claimants sue individually, in separate litigation, the stakeholder may be subjected to inconsistent obligations, such as one judgment that C is the owner and another that O is the owner. Avoiding such potential harm underlies Rule 19(a)(1)(B)(i) and is the basic underlying reason for interpleader.

Stages of Interpleader Litigation and Deposit of Stake or Bond

Assuming the court has personal jurisdiction over the parties and subject matter jurisdiction over the interpleader claim (which we discuss in §13.2.2), interpleader litigation proceeds in two stages. First, the court determines whether the case is appropriate for interpleader at all—whether the litigation consists of claims to property that meet the various requirements for interpleader. If so, the case proceeds to the second stage, in which the claimants litigate the question of who owns the stake. In true interpleader (where the stakeholder has no claim to the stake), the stakeholder does not participate in the second stage; she is discharged from the case at the close of the first stage.[27] If, on the other hand, the proceeding is in the nature of interpleader (where the stakeholder claims to own the property), the stakeholder will participate in the second stage; she is one of the claimants. The result of the second stage of the litigation is a judgment as to who the rightful owner is. The judgment will bind all claimants who were joined in the case.

What happens to the stake during the litigation? Under the statute, the stakeholder must deposit the stake with the court or post a bond with the clerk of the court.[28] Indeed, this deposit is a *jurisdictional prerequisite*, so failure to abide by the requirement deprives the court of jurisdiction to proceed with statutory interpleader.[29] Rule 22, in contrast, does not require deposit of the stake or of a bond, so such a deposit is not a jurisdictional requirement for Rule interpleader.[30] Nonetheless, the court in a Rule interpleader case can and usually does order the stakeholder to deposit the stake or a bond.[31]

Deposit of the stake with the court is a salutary event. The property cannot be lost, transferred, stolen, or squandered while the litigation is ongoing. It also ensures that the property is present for distribution at the end of the case. In §13.2.2 we will see that the

---

[27]Commercial Nat'l Bank v. Demos, 18 F.3d 485, 487 (7th Cir. 1994).

[28]28 U.S.C. §1335(a)(2).

[29]*See, e.g.*, U.S. Fire Ins. Co. v. Asbestospray, Inc., 182 F.3d 201, 210 (3d Cir. 1999) ("A proper deposit or bond is a jurisdictional prerequisite to bringing [statutory] interpleader"); In re Sinking of the M/V Ukola, 806 F.2d 1, 5 (1st Cir. 1986); A&E TV Networks, LLC v. Pivot Point Entertainment, LLC, 771 F. Supp. 2d 296, 300 (S.D.N.Y. 2011).

[30]Gelfgren v. Republic Nat'l Life Ins. Co., 680 F.2d 79, 82 (9th Cir. 1982); John v. Sotheby's, Inc., 141 F.R.D. 29, 33 (S.D.N.Y. 1992) ("deposit of the asset is not a jurisdictional prerequisite for rule interpleader").

[31]Central Bank v. United States, 838 F. Supp. 564, 566 (M.D. Fla. 1993). Federal Rule 67 authorizes the court to order such a deposit.

court's determination of what is to be deposited affects the amount in controversy of the case for jurisdictional purposes.

As we know from §9.2.2, the Seventh Amendment preserves the right to jury trial in actions at law, but not in suits at equity. What does this mean for interpleader? As we will see in a moment, interpleader developed both at equity and common law. Today, it is clear, however, that the availability of a jury trial in federal court interpleader depends upon the stage involved. The first stage of interpleader—in which the question is whether the case meets the requirements for interpleader—is tried to the judge; there is no right to a jury.[32] The second stage of interpleader—in which the question is who rightfully owns the stake—is tried to a jury under the Seventh Amendment if there would be a right to a jury trial if the same issues were raised in "regular" civil litigation.[33] So we make the jury assessment in the second stage as we would if the case were in federal court without the interpleader mechanism.

Historic Equitable Restrictions on Interpleader

Interpleader originated in the common law courts and then "crossed over" into equity. Much of the interpleader practice therefore developed in the equity courts.[34] Those courts, and subsequently the equity courts in the United States, imposed four restrictions on the right to invoke interpleader. All four unduly limit the availability of interpleader and serve no worthwhile purpose. In federal court—under both Rule interpleader and statutory interpleader—three of the four restrictions are jettisoned expressly, and most courts seem to think that the fourth also ought to be. Of course, states are free to permit interpleader on whatever terms they see fit. While most states have followed the federal lead and removed these historic equitable restrictions on interpleader, no doubt some states still adhere to at least some of them.[35] We review the four restrictions and how they are treated in federal practice.

The first is one we have already mentioned: that the stakeholder must be disinterested and not make a claim of ownership of the disputed property. In other words, classic equitable practice did not permit actions "in the nature of interpleader." This requirement is rejected

---

[32]*See* 4 Moore's Federal Practice §22.03[3].

[33]*See, e.g.,* Hyde Props. v. McCoy, 507 F.2d 301, 305 (6th Cir. 1974).

[34]*See generally* Geoffrey Hazard & Myron Moskovitz, *An Historical and Critical Analysis of Interpleader,* 52 Cal. L. Rev. 706 (1964).

[35]*See, e.g.,* Midland Nat'l Life Ins. Co. v. Emerson, 174 S.E.2d 211, 212 (Ga. Ct. App. 1970) (refusing to allow interested stakeholder to invoke interpleader at equity; led to legislative rejection of the rule).

in Rule interpleader by the provision in Federal Rule 22(a)(1)(B) that no one may object if the stakeholder "denies liability in whole or in part to any or all of the claimants." In statutory interpleader, the rejection of this historical restriction is more direct, with the provision in §1335(a) that the stakeholder may proceed with an action "in the nature of interpleader."

The second and third equitable restrictions on interpleader are closely related. The second is that claimants must be claiming the same thing or debt, and the third is that their adverse claims to the property are dependent on or derived from a common source. Rule 22(a)(1)(A) expressly rejects both of these requirements for Rule interpleader. Similarly, §1335(b) expressly rejects both for statutory interpleader.

The final equitable restriction is that the stakeholder has no independent liability to any claimant. Oddly, neither Rule interpleader nor statutory interpleader expressly addresses this requirement. Nonetheless, most federal courts conclude that the requirement should not be followed.[36] These courts are correct, because this restriction no longer makes sense. It was imposed in an era when claimants had no procedural mechanism for asserting a claim against the stakeholder in an interpleader case; at the time interpleader developed, there was no counterclaim in equity practice. Historically, courts determined that permitting interpleader in such a case would be unfair to the claimant who had a separate claim against the stakeholder. Today, because the claimant in interpleader can assert a counterclaim against the stakeholder, there is simply no need for this restriction. Still, there are occasional opinions in which a court will deny interpleader because the stakeholder has an independent liability to one of the claimants.[37]

> ○ ***Example #5.*** Return to the facts of Example #2, in which *S* claims ownership of a wristwatch she found in the house she just bought. *O*, the previous owner of the house, also claims to own the watch, as does *C*, a contractor who had done work on the house. *S* institutes a proceeding in the nature of interpleader, joining *O* and *C*. Suppose *C* has a claim against *S* arising from the work *C* had done on the house; she claims that *S* did not pay her for various work done. The existence of this independent ground of potential liability of *S* to *C* violates the fourth equitable restriction on interpleader, and, if followed, would render interpleader impossible. Most federal courts recognize, however, that *C* can simply

---

[36]*See* Ohio National Life Assur. Corp. v. Langkau, 353 Fed. Appx. 244, 248 (11th Cir. 2009) ("The law of this circuit has not maintained the independent liability restriction on interpleader explicitly"); Libby, McNeill & Libby v. City Nat'l Bank, 592 F.2d 504 (9th Cir. 1978); Companion Life Ins. Co. v. Schaffer, 442 F. Supp. 826, 829 (S.D.N.Y. 1977).

[37]*See, e.g.*, Nevada Eighty-Eight, Inc. v. Title Ins. Co. of Minn., 753 F. Supp. 1516, 1527 (D. Nev. 1990).

assert a counterclaim against *S* in the pending interpleader case; thus, they ignore the fourth equitable restriction and allow the interpleader to proceed.

§13.2.2 Jurisdiction and Related Issues

The Development of Two Types of Interpleader

We have said that there are two types of interpleader in the federal court system: Rule interpleader under Federal Rule 22 and statutory interpleader under 28 U.S.C. §§1335, 1397, and 2361. Why do we have two separate vehicles for doing the same thing? To a degree, it is a historical fluke. The original Federal Rules of Civil Procedure, promulgated in 1938, adopted as Rule 22 a provision that had been included in the earlier Federal Equity Rules. When the Federal Rules merged what had been separate law and equity practice in the federal courts, it was natural to include the interpleader provision. As we studied in detail in Chapter 12, however, the Federal Rules cannot affect the jurisdiction of the federal courts. Thus, Rule 22 interpleader — then and now — can be invoked only if the case brought under it invokes a basis of federal subject matter jurisdiction. As we know from Chapter 4, the main bases of such jurisdiction are diversity of citizenship and federal question. Very few Rule interpleader cases invoke federal question jurisdiction. Nearly all such cases invoke diversity of citizenship jurisdiction (which we review in detail later in this subsection). Similarly, whether venue is proper is determined for Rule interpleader, just as it is for any basic civil case, under §1391(b). And, finally, personal jurisdiction over the claimants must be asserted as it would in any diversity of citizenship case. In sum, then, Rule interpleader is — for purposes of jurisdiction, venue, and service of process — just a diversity of citizenship case.

But statutory interpleader is a completely different proposition. Congress enacted statutory interpleader — again, today codified at §§1335, 1397, and 2361 — in 1917, in response to a Supreme Court case we will discuss in a moment. The three statutes, respectively, (1) create the claim for interpleader and grant subject matter jurisdiction therefor, (2) create a special venue provision for statutory interpleader claims, and (3) permit nationwide service of process for statutory interpleader cases.

Rule 22 is completely irrelevant to statutory interpleader. And statutory interpleader is completely irrelevant to Rule 22. If a stakeholder proceeds under statutory interpleader, she is invoking subject matter jurisdiction under §1335, and not under the general diversity of citizenship statute, §1332(a)(1). Now we compare Rule interpleader and statutory interpleader in terms of personal jurisdiction, subject matter jurisdiction, and venue. Keep in mind that Rule interpleader is simply a diversity of citizenship case, while statutory interpleader has its own special provisions for personal jurisdiction, subject matter jurisdiction, and venue.

Personal Jurisdiction

In the 1916 case of *New York Life Insurance Co. v. Dunlevy*, the Supreme Court held that an interpleader court must have *in personam* jurisdiction over the claimants.[38] This holding was not a foregone conclusion. Indeed, it seems wrong. An interpleader proceeding appears to be a *quasi-in-rem* action of the first type, because it involves the issue of ownership of a stake placed in the court's possession.[39] Under the established doctrine of the day, judgments in such *quasi-in-rem* cases were valid if the court had jurisdiction over the disputed property and the parties were given notice of the proceeding.[40] Nonetheless, in *Dunlevy* the parties and the Court seemed simply to assume that the proceeding was *in personam*. And it has been so considered ever since.

The facts of *Dunlevy* demonstrate the importance of its holding. An insurance company held $2,500 under an insurance policy, to which there were three claimants. First, the insured, Joseph Gould, claimed that the money was his. Second, his daughter, Effie Dunlevy, claimed that her dad had assigned the proceeds to her. Third, a department store claimed the money because it had a judgment against Effie; if Effie were entitled to the money, then, the store asserted that it (not Effie) should get it. The insurance company interpleaded the three claimants in a state court in Pittsburgh. Joseph and the department store were served with process and thus brought before the jurisdiction of the court. Effie, however, had moved to California, and the court did not have *in personam* jurisdiction over her. The interpleader court held that Joseph was entitled to the money and ordered that it be paid to him. Then Effie brought a separate case against the insurance company in California. The Supreme Court upheld judgment in her favor. Because the interpleader court in Pittsburgh did not have *in personam*

---

[38]241 U.S. 518 (1916).

[39]We discussed *quasi-in-rem* actions of the first type at §2.2. They concern ownership of specific property, and the property itself is the basis of jurisdiction. These cases are contrasted with *quasi-in-rem* of the second type, in which property is used as the basis of jurisdiction, but the claim in litigation is unrelated to ownership thereof.

[40]Indeed, even after *Shaffer v. Heitner*, it is arguable that the court's jurisdiction over the disputed property satisfies due process. See §2.4.4. At any rate, it's difficult to figure out why *Dunlevy* was not treated as a *quasi-in-rem* case. It may be that the lawyers simply did not think of it. There is also some possibility that no one ever gave notice of the interpleader proceeding to one of the claimants, who was in another state.

jurisdiction over Effie, she was not bound by its judgment. Thus, nothing precluded her from suing the insurance company.

The result, of course, was that the insurance company had to pay the policy amount twice. In other words, it suffered exactly the kind of harm (double liability) that interpleader is intended to avoid. In the wake of the holding in *Dunlevy*, every insurance company had cause to worry: Unless it could get *in personam* jurisdiction over all claimants in a single court, it could not bind all claimants to the interpleader judgment.

What could the insurance companies do to avoid this risk? Not much if they were left to litigate in state courts. Though a state court's *in personam* jurisdictional reach is far greater today than it was when *Dunlevy* was decided, absent consent no state court can bind anyone who lacks minimum contacts with the forum.[41] In contrast, though, federal courts can be empowered to exercise *in personam* jurisdiction over anyone with minimum contacts with the United States itself (and not just with a particular state).[42] In other words, federal courts can be given power to serve process nationwide. Insurance companies lobbied Congress to address the problem presented by the holding in *Dunlevy* by providing for interpleader jurisdiction in federal court, and to permit nationwide service of process in such cases. The lobbying led to passage of the Federal Interpleader Act, or what we call *statutory interpleader.* The aspect of statutory interpleader allowing nationwide service of process on claimants is now found in §2361.

In contrast, Rule interpleader does not have its own separate statutory basis for service of process and personal jurisdiction. A Rule interpleader case is treated just as any other case in the federal court. Thus, as we discussed in §3.3.4, personal jurisdiction and service of process outside the state in which the federal court sits are possible only if they would be proper in a state court there.

---

[41]By "minimum contacts," we mean satisfaction of the *International Shoe* test. See §2.4.3.

[42]If this point is fuzzy, see §2.4. Remember, the cases we studied, starting with *Pennoyer*, concern due process limitations on a *state's* power to exercise personal jurisdiction. The federal government can exercise jurisdiction over anyone having minimum contacts with the country, even if she does not have minimum contacts with the state in which the federal court sits. As a matter of comity, the Federal Rules have adopted the general notion that a federal court will exercise personal jurisdiction outside the state in which it sits only if a state court in that state could do so. See §3.3.4. Constitutionally, however, Congress can empower the federal courts to exercise nationwide service of process and thus to have personal jurisdiction over anyone who can be served anywhere within the United States. Statutory interpleader is one of the rare instances in which Congress has done so.

- ◦ ***Example #6.*** Trustee holds a fund of $100,000, to which there are three claimants, *C-1*, *C-2*, and *C-3*. Trustee institutes interpleader in federal court in California. Assume that subject matter jurisdiction and venue are proper. *C-1* is a citizen of California and can be served with process there. *C-2* is a citizen of Arizona but clearly has sufficient minimum contacts with California to be subject to *in personam* jurisdiction there. *C-3* is a citizen of Florida and has absolutely no contact with California.
  - ◦ If the case is brought under Rule interpleader, the federal court in California will have *in personam* jurisdiction (and can serve process outside state lines) to the same extent as a California state court. Thus, *C-1* and *C-2* can be brought before the jurisdiction of the court, because they clearly have sufficient contacts with California. But *C-3* cannot be brought before the jurisdiction of the federal court in California, because she lacks minimum contacts with California. Because a California state court could not exercise *in personam* jurisdiction over *C-3*, neither can a federal court under Rule interpleader.
  - ◦ If the same case were brought under statutory interpleader, however, *C-3* could be brought before the jurisdiction of the federal court in California. Under §2361, *C-3* is subject to nationwide service of process. Anyone found anywhere in the United States can be served with process for a statutory interpleader proceeding in a federal court anywhere in the country.

Subject Matter Jurisdiction

Rule 22, like all Federal Rules on joinder, provides a procedural device. It does not and cannot affect subject matter jurisdiction requirements. Thus, Rule interpleader is proper only if the case invokes one of the independent bases of federal subject matter jurisdiction: diversity of citizenship, alienage, or federal question. On the other hand, statutory interpleader has its own legislative basis of subject matter jurisdiction, separate from the general grants of diversity of citizenship, alienage, and federal question jurisdiction.

Federal Question Jurisdiction. Whether interpleader arises under federal law can be difficult to assess. For one thing, as we have seen, interpleader is an odd kind of "claim"—it is really a device by which the stakeholder demands that others assert their claims *against* her. As a result, it is tough as a conceptual matter to characterize whether interpleader involves a federal right.[43] Moreover, interpleader can present the same problem we encountered with deciding whether declaratory judgment cases arise under federal law. In those cases, discussed at §4.6.3, courts look to whether coercive action by the stakeholder would invoke federal question jurisdiction.[44]

---

[43]*See, e.g.,* Commercial Union Ins. Co. v. United States, 999 F.2d 581, 585 (D.C. Cir. 1993).

[44]Bell & Beckwith v. United States, 766 F.2d 910, 913 (6th Cir. 1985).

Very few Rule interpleader cases invoke federal question jurisdiction. Examples include interpleader concerning an escrow account claimed under the Small Business Act[45] and funds ostensibly subject to federal tax liens.[46]

Subject Matter Jurisdiction Based upon Citizenship and Amount in Controversy. Almost all Rule interpleader cases invoke diversity of citizenship jurisdiction. Because Rule 22 cannot affect jurisdictional requirements, Rule interpleader cases are treated simply as diversity of citizenship cases under §1332(a)(1). So all principles about invoking diversity of citizenship jurisdiction, which we discussed at §4.5, apply in Rule interpleader. Statutory interpleader is a completely different proposition. Though as a constitutional matter, the subject matter basis for statutory interpleader is diversity of citizenship, as a statutory matter, it does not rely on the general diversity statute, §1332(a)(1). Instead, §1335 applies. The requirements for subject matter jurisdiction for Rule and statutory interpleader differ markedly.

To Determine Diversity. Rule and statutory interpleader differ in two fundamental ways: (1) whose citizenships are relevant, and (2) what kind of diversity (complete or minimal) is required. Rule interpleader is just a regular diversity case under §1332(a)(1). Accordingly, the courts look to the citizenship of the stakeholder, on the one hand, and the citizenships of the claimants, on the other. In addition, in keeping with the complete diversity rule of *Strawbridge v. Curtiss*,[47] the stakeholder must be diverse from every claimant.[48]

With statutory interpleader, however, §1335 requires only that one claimant be of diverse citizenship from any other claimant. In general, then, the stakeholder's citizenship is irrelevant in statutory interpleader: We look only to the citizenship of the claimants. Moreover, the statute requires only "minimal" diversity: The statute is satisfied if *any one* claimant is of diverse citizenship *from any other claimant.*

> o ***Example #7.*** Stakeholder is a corporation, incorporated in Delaware with its principal place of business in Illinois. There are four claimants: *C-1* is a citizen of Illinois; *C-2* is a citizen of Ohio; *C-3* is a citizen of Ohio; and *C-4* is a citizen of Minnesota.

---

[45]Kim v. Kang, 154 F.3d 996, 999 (9th Cir. 1998).

[46]Amoco Prod. Co. v. Aspen Group, 8 F. Supp. 2d 1249, 1252 (D. Colo. 1998).

[47]7 U.S. 267 (1806). See §4.5.3.

[48]*But see* Kristen DeWilde, Comment, *Catch Rule 22: When Interpleader Actions Violate Statutory and Constitutional Diversity Jurisdiction Requirements,* 168 U. Pa. L. Rev. 467, 487-504 (2020) (arguing that in true interpleader, in which the stakeholder does not claim the property, there must be diversity among the claimants, rather than between the stakeholder and the claimants).

- o This case cannot invoke Rule interpleader, because the stakeholder is not of diverse citizenship from every claimant. Stakeholder is a citizen of Illinois, and so is *C-1*. Thus, the case does not satisfy the complete diversity rule applicable in Rule interpleader.
- o This case can invoke statutory interpleader. The stakeholder's citizenship is irrelevant. Thus, the fact that Stakeholder and one of the claimants, *C-1*, are citizens of the same state (Illinois) does not matter. In looking at citizenships of the claimants, all that is required is that one be diverse from at least one other. Here, the stakeholders are citizens of Illinois, Ohio, and Minnesota, so the requirement is satisfied. The fact that there are two claimants who are citizens of Ohio is irrelevant. Statutory interpleader is based upon minimal diversity; complete diversity is not required.

There is no doubt that Congress, in enacting statutory interpleader in 1917, intended to permit jurisdiction based upon minimal diversity. The only question was whether the statute was constitutional. The Supreme Court upheld the statute in *State Farm Fire & Casualty v. Tashire*,[49] in which it established that the Article III grant of diversity of citizenship jurisdiction is satisfied so long as any two adverse parties are not cocitizens.

Statutory interpleader offers considerable advantages (such as jurisdiction based upon minimal diversity, lower amount in controversy, and nationwide service of process). So why does Rule interpleader ever get used? There is one fact pattern in which Rule interpleader is possible but statutory interpleader does not appear to be.

- o ***Example #8.*** Stakeholder is a citizen of Texas. All claimants are citizens of Louisiana. Obviously, this arrangement would satisfy the citizenship requirements for Rule interpleader, because Stakeholder is of diverse citizenship from all claimants. But it does not meet the citizenship requirements for statutory interpleader. Why?

Because the statute requires at least one claimant to be diverse from at least one other claimant. Here, they are all cocitizens, so the statute appears not to be available.

- o ***Example #9.*** Suppose, however, on this fact pattern that the amount in controversy requirement for Rule interpleader (in excess of $75,000) is not satisfied, but that the amount requirement for statutory interpleader ($500 or more) is satisfied.

---

[49]386 U.S. 523, 531 (1967) ("Article III poses no obstacle to the legislative extension of federal jurisdiction, founded on diversity, so long as any two adverse parties are not cocitizens").

Stakeholder cannot invoke Rule interpleader here because the jurisdictional amount in controversy requirement is not met. On the face of things, it appears that Stakeholder cannot invoke statutory interpleader either, because there is no minimal diversity among the claimants; all claimants are cocitizens.

> ○ ***Example #10.*** But what if the case involves an *interested stakeholder*? That is, as discussed in §13.2.1, what if Stakeholder in this case claims she is entitled to the stake?[50]

The better view in this situation is that the stakeholder should be considered as one of the claimants, and thus that her citizenship should be relevant.[51] On the facts of this case, that would mean that statutory interpleader is invoked, because now one plaintiff is a citizen of Texas while the others are citizens of Louisiana. This result makes sense, because the stakeholder, after all, truly is a claimant, and will participate in the second stage of the interpleader litigation. Most courts addressing the issue appear to have adopted this view.[52] On the other hand, some courts refuse to consider the stakeholder's citizenship, and deny jurisdiction on these facts.[53] A word to the wise student: If you covered this fact pattern in class, watch for it on the exam and be prepared to argue both ways for application of statutory interpleader.

To Determine the Amount in Controversy. To invoke diversity of citizenship jurisdiction in Rule interpleader, the amount in controversy must exceed $75,000. In statutory interpleader, §1335 requires only $500 or more. The amount in controversy is the value of the stake to be distributed.

As we saw in §13.2.1, statutory interpleader requires the stakeholder to deposit the stake or a bond with the court; it is a jurisdictional requirement. Rule interpleader does not require a deposit, though the court usually orders one. Interpleader cases often involve fights over money, such as trust funds or insurance. The parties may

---

[50]An exam question might simply say that the case was "in the nature of interpleader," which means that the stakeholder makes a claim to the stake. See §13.2.1.

[51]Remember, by "this situation" we are referring to a case in which the stakeholder is making a claim to the stake—in which we have an interested stakeholder. If the stakeholder is disinterested (not making a claim to the stake), her citizenship is absolutely irrelevant in determining whether a statutory interpleader case invokes federal subject matter jurisdiction. Treinies v. Sunshine Mining Co., 308 U.S. 66, 72 (1939).

[52]*See, e.g.*, Lummis v. White, 629 F.2d 397, 403 (5th Cir. 1980), *rev'd on other grounds sub nom.* Cory v. White, 457 U.S. 85 (1982); Mt. Hawley Ins. Co. v. Fed. Sav. & Loan Ins. Corp., 695 F. Supp. 469, 473 (C.D. Cal. 1987).

[53]*See, e.g.*, American Family Mut. Ins. Co. v. Roche, 830 F. Supp. 1241, 1248 (E.D. Wis. 1993).

disagree about the amount actually in dispute. In Rule interpleader, the stakeholder deposits the amount it believes to be in dispute.[54] In statutory interpleader, however, she must deposit the highest amount claimed by any of the claimants. The stakeholder must deposit that amount even if she asserts that a lesser amount is actually in controversy.[55] Depositing the larger amount does not waive that assertion.[56]

Supplemental Jurisdiction. There is some uncertainty concerning the operation of supplemental jurisdiction in interpleader cases. We discussed supplemental jurisdiction in detail at §4.7. Section 1367(a) grants to the federal courts supplemental jurisdiction over claims so closely related to a claim that invokes federal subject matter jurisdiction as to be considered part of the same case or controversy as that claim. An interpleader claim should satisfy §1367(a). After all, the claimants are asserting a right to the same thing.[57]

Section 1367(b) applies to remove supplemental jurisdiction but does so only in cases brought under §1332. Thus, §1367(b) does not apply to statutory interpleader cases, because such cases are brought not under §1332, but under §1335.[58] Section 1367(b) would apply, however, to a Rule interpleader case that invoked diversity of citizenship jurisdiction (under §1332), but would not remove any grant of supplemental jurisdiction. Why? Recall that §1367(b) lists various claims that will not invoke supplemental jurisdiction in diversity cases; Rule 22 is *not* included in the list. In sum, then, if the interpleader claim invokes supplemental jurisdiction under §1367(a), nothing in §1367(b) should remove it. The exercise, however, seems to be more work than it is worth, since any case involving supplemental jurisdiction would seem to invoke statutory interpleader.

o ***Example #11.*** Stakeholder is a citizen of Missouri, and there are three claimants: *C-1* is a citizen of Kansas, *C-2* is a citizen of Colorado, and *C-3* is a citizen of Missouri. On the face of things, Rule interpleader is not possible, because the stakeholder is not of diverse citizenship from every claimant. But it is arguable that Stakeholder could assert interpleader

[54]*See, e.g.*, National Union Fire Ins. Co. v. Ambassador Grp. Inc., 691 F. Supp. 618, 621 (E.D.N.Y. 1988) (while "under rule interpleader a stakeholder may deposit the amount it believes to be in dispute, under statutory interpleader an interpleading plaintiff must deposit with the court the highest amount claimed by defendants"); United Benefit Life Ins. Co. v. Leech, 326 F. Supp. 598, 600 (E.D. Pa. 1971).

[55]*See, e.g.*, A&E TV Networks, LLC v. Pivot Point Entertainment, LLC, 771 F. Supp. 2d 296, 302 (S.D.N.Y. 2011) (in statutory interpleader, "the dispositive inquiry is not whether the stakeholder has deposited what it views to be its maximum possible liability, but whether the stakeholder has deposited the amount the claimants claim").

[56]Nationwide Mut. Ins. Co. v. Eckman, 555 F. Supp. 775, 777 (D. Del. 1983).

[57]There is very little case law concerning supplemental jurisdiction in interpleader, and most of it predates the enactment of §1367.

[58]Statutory interpleader cases are brought under §1335.

against *C-1* and *C-2*, invoking diversity of citizenship, then join *C-3* and argue that the interpleader claim against *C-3* invokes supplemental jurisdiction. As noted immediately above, the claim against *C-3* surely satisfies the relatedness requirement of §1367(a); and nothing in §1367(b) removes that grant. But why bother with this approach? The case as structured satisfies the requirements for statutory interpleader without jumping through these supplemental jurisdiction hoops. (The same would be true with defensive invocation of interpleader through a counterclaim.)

Venue

Rule Interpleader.   Again, a Rule interpleader case is treated simply as a "regular" case—either federal question or diversity of citizenship. Thus, venue is governed by §1391(b). Those statutes provide for venue, basically, in either of two places: (1) any district where all the defendants reside or (2) any district in which a substantial part of the claim arose.[59] As to the second of these choices, there is little meaningful case law guidance on where an interpleader claim (or a substantial part thereof) arises. In practice, then, that statutory choice offers no help. Thus, the stakeholder/plaintiff must lay venue in a district where all defendants (claimants) reside. If they reside in different districts of the forum state, remember, she may lay venue in any of the districts in which one resides, as we saw in §5.4.1. Thus, for Rule interpleader, venue can be a significant (and frustrating) restriction.

> ○ ***Example #12.*** Stakeholder, a citizen of Iowa, wants to interplead two claimants, *C-1*, who is a citizen of Illinois and resides in the Northern District of Illinois, and *C-2*, who is a citizen of Michigan and resides in the Eastern District of Michigan.

There is no district in which venue is proper based upon the residence of the defendants. They do not reside in the same district, nor do they reside in different districts of the same state. So §1391(b)(1) is not met. And because no one seems to know where an interpleader claim arises, §1391(b)(2) gives no help.

But let's take a closer look at §1391(b)(2). It also permits venue in a district where "a substantial part of property that is the subject of the action is situated." This seems perfectly suited to interpleader. Under it, in the preceding hypothetical, Stakeholder could lay venue in the district in which the property is found. If it is movable property, she

---

[59]We discussed these choices, and what happens if there is no district in the United States satisfying either choice, at §5.4.1.

can take it to whatever district she prefers for venue. She might, for instance, lay venue in the district in Iowa in which she resides; certainly, that would be most convenient for her. This means the stakeholder may manipulate venue. The manipulation does not seem unfair to the defendant, however, because the chosen venue must have personal jurisdiction over the claimants.[60]

What if the interpleader is asserted defensively? We discussed this possibility in §13.2.1. The scenario is usually this: A claimant sues the stakeholder to recover the stake, and the stakeholder files a counterclaim against the claimant, to which she joins additional claimants under Rule 13(h). How is the venue handled in such a case? Most courts adopt the idea of "ancillary venue" in such circumstances. As long as venue was proper in the original case by the claimant against the stakeholder, venue is proper even as to additional claims involving joinder of additional parties.[61] Some courts reach this conclusion by noting that the venue statute, §1391, speaks only of the district in which an action is "brought." Thus, the statute only addresses venue as to the original claim by the plaintiff against the defendant, and does not apply to subsequent claims involving additional joinder of parties.[62]

Statutory Interpleader.   Statutory interpleader includes its own section for venue. Section 1397 provides that venue may be laid in any district where *any* claimant resides. The courts have determined that this provision is exclusive in statutory interpleader cases; in other words, §1397 replaces, and does not augment, §1391.[63] They reason that §1391 provides for venue only in cases in which there is no statutory provision to the contrary; §1397 provides the contrary legislation. In most cases, the exclusivity of §1397 will not create a problem, because it is easier to satisfy than §1391(b)(1).

- *__Example #13.__* Stakeholder interpleads three claimants, *C-1*, *C-2*, and *C-3*. Assume that personal jurisdiction and subject matter jurisdiction are proper. *C-1* resides in the Eastern District of Pennsylvania. *C-2* resides in the Western District of Pennsylvania. *C-3* resides in the Northern District of Illinois.
  - If the case invokes Rule interpleader, no district is a proper venue under §1391(b)(1), because there is no district in which all claimants reside.[64]

---

[60]*See* 7 Wright & Miller §1712, at 612.

[61]*See, e.g.*, Bredberg v. Long, 778 F.2d 1285, 1288 (8th Cir. 1985).

[62]*See, e.g.*, Nine Point Mesa of Nashville, Inc. v. Nine Point Mesa of Lexington, Inc., 769 F. Supp. 259, 263 (M.D. Tenn. 1991).

[63]*See* 4 Moore's Federal Practice §22.04[4][b].

[64]The provision in §1391(b)(2) permitting venue in a district where the property subject to litigation is found—which we discussed in the text above—would provide venue in this case.

o If the case invokes statutory interpleader, venue may be laid against all three claimants in any of three districts: the Eastern District of Pennsylvania, the Western District of Pennsylvania, or the Northern District of Illinois. Why? Because §1397 (applicable only in statutory interpleader) permits venue in any district where *any* claimant resides.

Summary. This chart should be helpful in summarizing the major differences between Rule interpleader (invoking diversity of citizenship jurisdiction) and statutory interpleader.

Type	Personal Jurisdiction	Venue	Diversity	Jurisdictional Amount
Statutory	Nationwide service of process	District where any claimant resides	Minimal diversity between any two claimants	$500 or more
Rule	Same as state court in state in which situated; service per Federal Rule 4	Per §1391(b) (where *D*'s residence or property located)	Complete diversity between stakeholder, on one hand, and all claimants, on the other	In excess of $75,000

§13.3 The Class Action

§13.3.1 Overview of the Class Action and Underlying Policy Issues

A class action is brought by or against a representative (or multiple representatives) on behalf of a group (the class members). If it's done correctly, the group is bound by the result of the litigation. This procedure promotes efficiency, because it means that the individual members of the group do not litigate. In addition, the class action can promote the same policies of avoiding harm that underlie Rule 19 (see §12.6.1). Class actions raise significant due process issues, precisely because they do bind persons who are not technically parties. In addition, the class action is subject to abuse, and raises significant ethical issues, as we will see.

Development of Federal Rule 23

Federal Rule 23 governs class action practice in federal court. The Supreme Court amended the original Rule to its present basic form in 1966, along with Rules 19 and 24. Recall from Chapter 12 that Rules 19 and 24 govern, respectively, joinder of necessary (or "required") parties and intervention. Recall further that there was great overlap in the functions of Rules 19 and 24 and in the language used to determine when an absentee ought to be joined in a pending case. The amendments to all three Rules prescribed pragmatic assessments of the circumstances of a case under those two Rules. The focus is on practicality—on fact patterns rather than on legal relationships.

The 1966 drafters made a clean break from the original Rule 23, promulgated in 1938. The original rule was unworkable, mostly because it relied on arcane legal relationships that are difficult to fathom. For instance, it defined the "true" class action as one in which the class right was "joint" or "common." The "hybrid" class action was one in which the class members asserted "several" rights to common property. The "spurious" class action also involved the assertion of "several" rights but involved common questions and common relief. None of these terms is self-defining and none is very helpful.

The 1966 version of the Rule provided a practical, step-by-step method for analyzing when class litigation is appropriate. The Rule was amended substantially in 2003 to change some procedural aspects of administering class actions (but not the prerequisites and definitions of types of class actions). In addition, there was a major amendment to the procedure for settling a class action in 2018, as we discuss in §13.3.7. Though most states have adopted Rule 23 as their model for class actions, some have not kept up with these periodic amendments.

Almost all class actions involve a *plaintiff class*, in which the class is asserting a claim (or claims) against a defendant (or defendants). It is possible under Rule 23 to have a *defendant class*, in which a plaintiff (or plaintiffs) seeks to impose liability upon a group represented by a named defendant. Defendant classes are rare. It is even possible to have a plaintiff class sue a defendant class. Throughout these materials, unless we specifically mention defendant class actions, we assume that the class is on the plaintiff side.

Class Representatives and Class Members

The person (or persons) suing on behalf of a plaintiff class is named as a formal party in the case. She is referred to as the "named representative" or just the "representative." She is a formal party (the plaintiff) in the case. What about the other[65] class *members*: Are they parties to the case? The quick answer is no. Emphasizing this fact, some courts refer to them as "absentee" class members.

One important question arises immediately: If class members are not parties to the litigation, how can they be bound by the judgment? As we discuss in detail in §13.3.2, it is through representation. Recall from our discussion of the preclusion doctrines in Chapter 11 that a valid final judgment on the merits binds only those who were parties to the case *or who were in "privity" with a party*. Though "privity" is sometimes difficult to define, it includes the notion of representation. Accordingly, a valid final judgment on the merits binds parties to the case and those who were represented by parties to the case. One focus of the procedural rule concerning class actions, then, is that the members' interests be adequately represented, precisely so the class members can be bound by the judgment in the case.

Though class members are not parties, they have no license to ignore court orders. In the usual case, however, class members will not be subjected to discovery requests. They are, in almost every case, "along for the ride." They are passive.[66]

Policy Considerations (and the "Negative-Value" Class Action)

In many cases, class members may feel that their interests have taken a back seat to those of the lawyers for the class. This fact underscores significant policy issues related to aggregate litigation, particularly with the "negative-value" class action. A negative-value claim is one that is not worth pursuing in individual litigation; the cost and burden of litigating would outweigh the recovery.

> o ***Example #14.*** Suppose a chain of retail stores overcharges customers on a product in violation of state law. Each customer is overcharged an average of $50. If there were no class action device, there would be no civil litigation about this overcharge. Why? Because no individual

---

[65]We say "other" class members because the representative is a member of the class as well. Here we are speaking of class members other than the representative.

[66]In an important book, in which Professor Redish argues that class actions are unconstitutional, he offers this characterization: "The so-called class itself is all but comatose. Many class members are likely not even aware that they are plaintiffs in a major legal action, and the overwhelming majority will never even benefit directly from a successful prosecution." Martin H. Redish, Wholesale Justice: Constitutional Democracy and the Problem of the Class Action Lawsuit 14 (2009). *See also* Alexandra D. Lahav, *Are Class Actions Unconstitutional?*, 109 Mich. L. Rev. 993, 999-1000 (2011) (book review); Linda S. Mullenix, *Aggregate Litigation and the Death of Democratic Dispute Resolution,* 107 Nw. U. L. Rev. 511, 516 (2013).

customer would sue to recover $50; the effort is greater than the return to be gotten.

This lack of civil litigation does not necessarily mean that the retail store is "getting away" with its bad behavior. If the overcharge violates the criminal law or some regulation, there may be a criminal prosecution or administrative fine. But it is unlikely that there will be any compensatory damages to the injured consumers.

What happens, though, if we do have a class action device? Let's assume that there are 500,000 consumers similarly situated. As a class action, there are 500,000 class members, each harmed by an average of $50. That is an aggregate claim of $25,000,000, which certainly will attract a lawyer to take the case (on a contingent fee basis). This fact leads us to an interesting irony of the class action. The device is praised for its efficiency because it permits one (large) case to take the place of thousands of (smaller) cases. But when the case involves negative-value claims, the class action creates litigation that otherwise would not exist at all.

Is that a good thing? It depends on one's point of view. If we emphasize the fact that the class action empowers a group to sue when individually they would not, we might hail the class action as "one of the most socially useful remedies in history."[67] The Supreme Court has explained: "Where it is not economically feasible to obtain relief within the traditional framework of a multiplicity of small individual suits for damages, aggrieved persons may be without any effective redress unless they may employ the class-action device."[68] Pointedly, Judge Posner said:

> The *realistic* alternative to a class action is not 17 million individual suits, but zero individual suits, as only a lunatic or a fanatic sues for $30. But a class action has to be unwieldy indeed before it can be pronounced an inferior alternative—no matter how massive the fraud or other wrongdoing that will go unpunished if class treatment is denied—to no litigation at all.[69]

On the other hand, the class action is coercive, even if the claim on the underlying merits is weak. Precisely because the class action

---

[67]Abraham Pomerantz, *New Developments in Class Actions—Has Their Death Knell Been Sounded?*, 25 Bus. Law. 1259, 1259 (1970). *See also* Alexandra D. Lahav, *The Political Justification for Group Litigation,* 81 Fordham L. Rev. 3193, 3199 (2013) (class action, properly used, promotes the democratic values of transparency, accountability, equality, and deliberation).

[68]Deposit Guaranty Nat'l Bank v. Roper, 445 U.S. 326, 339 (1980).

[69]Carnegie v. Household Int'l, Inc., 376 F.3d 656, 661 (7th Cir. 2004) (emphasis original).

permits the assertion of huge potential liability in a single case, it creates enormous pressure on the defendant to settle. Rather than proceed to trial and take a chance on losing $25,000,000 in our hypothetical, the defendant would see the wisdom of settling the case. Even a defendant convinced that it has done nothing wrong will be reluctant to roll the dice at trial with its entire financial future at stake. Some empirical studies suggest that class claims (at least in certain substantive areas) are settled regardless of the strength of the class claim on the merits.[70] Based upon such evidence, some decry the class action as "legalized blackmail."[71]

Neither side has a monopoly on virtue. For us, it is well to keep in mind that the class action is both an important device for achieving justice and a powerful weapon subject to abuse. But what drives the class action? One possibility is the representative. What is her interest? Though some courts allow the representative to recover a bonus for vindicating the group's claim, in general there is no financial reason for the representative to take on the responsibility of the job. And in the usual case she does not recover anything other than her personal damages. Thus, in Example #14, the representative will recover $50 (or whatever her damages were). Why would anyone take on the responsibilities of class representation to recover that amount? Rather than economics, sometimes the representative is motivated by principle—by a desire to "get justice" for the class.

It is possible, though, that the real moving force behind the class action is not the representative, but her lawyer. Most plaintiff class actions are taken on a contingent fee basis, which means the lawyer is paid a percentage of what the class recovers. This arrangement is praised because it permits prosecution of actions that otherwise could not be brought if the plaintiff had to pay an attorney by the hour. But the fee structure may create incentives for the lawyer that can conflict with her professional duties to her clients.[72] For example, suppose the

[70]Most of the studies seem to be in the securities fraud area. *See, e.g.,* Janet Cooper Alexander, *Do the Merits Matter? A Study of Settlements in Securities Class Actions,* 43 Stan. L. Rev. 497, 449 (1991); John Coffee, Jr., *The Regulation of Entrepreneurial Litigation: Balancing Fairness and Efficiency in the Large Class Action,* 54 U. Chi. L. Rev. 877, 877 n.1 (1987). *See also* Linda S. Mullenix, *Ending Class Actions as We Know Them: Rethinking the American Class Action,* 64 Emory L.J. 399, 448 (2014) ("[T]here is scant evidence that class action litigation . . . accomplishes the stated goals of compensation, deterrence, and efficiency").

[71]Milton Handler, *The Shift from Substantive to Procedural Innovations in Antitrust Suits,* 71 Colum. L. Rev. 1, 9 (1971). *But see* Alexandra D. Lahav, *Symmetry and Class Action Litigation,* 60 UCLA L. Rev. 1494, 1499 (2013) ("In almost no other area of procedural law does the argument that litigation symmetry will result in ruinous results for one party have the kind of traction it does in the context of class actions.").

[72]By the way, who is the client in a class action? Is it the representative (who hired the attorney) or is it the class? The answer to this question has profound ramifications

defendant offers to settle the case on terms that include a substantial payment of attorney's fees to the class lawyer. Going to trial, however, might lead to a better result for the class. The lawyer must resist the temptation to put her own interest ahead of that of the class.

One common criticism of the class action concerns "sweetheart" deals or "coupon" settlements. Here, the defendant offers to settle the class action by paying large fees to the class lawyer and to compensate class members by providing them with coupons for discounts on future purchases of products or services from the defendant. Class counsel may be tempted by such an offer, because it provides her with a substantial fee without the risk of going to trial. The defendant finds such a deal advantageous, because it avoids both the expense of litigation and the risk of devastating liability at trial. The persons whose interests may be lost in the shuffle are the class members, for whom coupons may provide little actual compensation. Indeed, it's likely that most of the coupons will go unused, which may further reduce the defendant's ultimate outlay to settle the case.[73] Concern with such settlements underlay passage of the Class Action Fairness Act, which we discuss at §13.3.9.

The Role of the Court

In view of the potential for abuse, such as that described in the preceding paragraph, who looks out for the interest of the class members? We are tempted to say that the representative herself is charged with this responsibility. In reality, though, most class representatives are ill-equipped for the task: They are lay people, unfamiliar with the law and with civil procedure. The only person who can protect the class from overreaching by lawyers is the judge who oversees the case. We discuss this role of the court in reviewing settlements and dismissals in §13.3.7. For present purposes, it is sufficient to note that the court is responsible for protecting the class members from an unscrupulous deal.

The notion that the court must protect class members from overreaching by class counsel seems inconsistent with our traditional view of the court's role. Historically, the court has been seen as neutral and

---

for various matters of professional responsibility, including the application of the attorney/client privilege and the question of whether the lawyer is justified in recommending terms of a settlement over the objections of her client. In general, the client is the representative until the court "certifies" the case to proceed as a class action. At that point, the class itself is seen as the client.

[73]*See generally* Bruce Hay & David Rosenberg, *"Sweetheart" and "Blackmail" Settlements in Class Actions: Reality and Remedy,* 75 Notre Dame L. Rev. 1377, 1390-1407 (2000).

essentially passive; it reacts to the arguments and evidence presented by the litigants but does not undertake to help either side do its job. The need for protection of class members, and the emergence of complex forms of litigation generally, has fostered the contemporary view of the judge as a case manager. The job of the judge has become increasingly bureaucratic, focused on getting cases through the long queue, and involved, of necessity, in ensuring that class members do not get left behind. We saw some aspects of this move to "managerial judging" in §§8.5 and 8.6, concerning judicial oversight of litigation and use of adjunct personnel to assist in that task.[74] In §13.3.10, we discuss a contemporary threat to the efficacy of class actions that trial judges may be powerless to avoid: the inclusion in consumer contracts of arbitration provisions coupled with a waiver of the right to pursue class relief.

§13.3.2 Due Process: How Can Class Members (Who Are Not Parties) Be Bound by a Class Judgment?

The most important case on the due process requirements for a class action is *Hansberry v. Lee*,[75] which concerned the enforcement of a racially restrictive covenant in a subdivision in Chicago. The covenant forbade homeowners in the subdivision (who were White) from renting or selling their property to non-Whites. The case was decided eight years before *Shelley v. Kramer*, which declared such restrictions unconstitutional.[76] So when the Court decided *Hansberry*, such covenants were generally enforceable. The covenant in *Hansberry* provided that it would be effective only if the owners of 95 percent of the frontage in the development signed it.

The outcome in *Hansberry* depended upon the validity of a judgment in the earlier case of *Burke v. Kleiman*.[77] In *Burke*, a White homeowner named Kleiman, who did not favor the racially restrictive covenant, rented property in the subdivision to Dr. James Hall, a Black man. Other property owners, led by Burke, sued for an injunction to stop Kleiman's renting to Dr. Hall. At the trial in that case, the

---

[74]Federal judges, concerned with increasing caseloads, have imposed various restrictions on adjudication of mass claims. As a result, parties increasingly turn to settlement. *See* Alexandra D. Lahav, *Fundamental Principles for Class Action Governance,* 37 Ind. L. Rev. 65 (2003); Alexandra D. Lahav, *The Law and Large Numbers: Preserving Adjudication in Complex Litigation,* 59 Fla. L. Rev. 383, 432 (2007) (suggesting bureaucratic scheme as an alternative to private settlement for processing mass claims)

[75]311 U.S. 32 (1940).

[76]334 U.S. 1 (1948).

[77]277 Ill. App. 519 (1934).

parties stipulated that the covenant had been signed by the requisite 95 percent of owners in the subdivision, and thus had become effective. In fact, only 54 percent of the relevant owners had signed the covenant, and thus it never should have gone into effect. Nonetheless, because of the parties' stipulation, the court upheld the covenant and stopped the proposed rental to Dr. Hall. The Illinois Court of Appeals affirmed. *Burke* was a class action, and thus, arguably, bound all owners in the subdivision.

A few years later, a White homeowner in the subdivision entered into a contract to sell his house to a Black family named Hansberry.[78] Lee, another White homeowner in the subdivision, sued in state court to stop the sale. At trial, the Hansberrys proved that only 54 percent of the relevant homeowners had signed the covenant. The court nonetheless concluded that the judgment in *Burke v. Kleiman* bound the people who were trying to sell to the Hansberrys. The people selling to the Hansberrys had been represented by the homeowner in the class action in *Burke* and were bound by the outcome: that the covenant was effective. (By way of review, why — as a matter of preclusion law — should the stipulation from *Burke* (that 95 percent of the homeowners had signed the covenant) not have been entitled to issue preclusion?[79]) The Illinois Supreme Court affirmed.

The United States Supreme Court reversed and held that the people selling to the Hansberrys were *not* bound by the class action judgment in *Burke v. Kleiman*. The Court started by recognizing that, generally, one cannot be bound by a judgment unless she is a party to the case in which the judgment is entered. It further noted, however, that "to an extent not precisely defined by judicial opinion," a judgment in a class action "may bind members of the class or those represented who were not made parties to it."[80] For this proposition, the Court cited *Smith v. Swormstead*[81] and *Supreme Tribe of Ben-Hur*

---

[78]One of the children of the Hansberry family was the playwright Lorraine Hansberry, who wrote *A Raisin in the Sun*, which was a successful play and movie. It was based in part upon the family's experiences in Chicago. Ironically, the homeowner who wanted to sell to the Hansberrys was the husband of the plaintiff who sued to enforce the covenant in *Burke v. Kleiman*. For interesting discussions of the case and the persons involved, *see* Allen Kamp, *The History Behind* Hansberry v. Lee, 20 U.C. Davis L. Rev. 481 (1987); Jay Tidmarsh, *The Story of* Hansberry: *The Foundation for Modern Class Actions,* in Civil Procedure Stories 217 (Kevin Clermont, ed.) (2d ed. 2008).

[79]Because issue preclusion applies only to issues that were actually litigated and determined in the earlier case. Because of the stipulation, the question of how many homeowners had signed the covenant was not litigated in *Burke v. Kleiman*. See §11.4.2.

[80]*Hansberry*, 311 U.S. at 41.

[81]57 U.S. 288 (1853).

v. Cauble.[82] In *Smith*, a class of one group of clergy members of the Methodist Episcopal Church sued another group to recover its share of a book fund established by the church. The clergy members had split into two factions—North and South—over slavery. Though 5,000 preachers were not joined as parties, all were bound by the class litigation, because "the parties interested are numerous, and the suit is for an object common to them all. . . ."[83] In *Ben-Hur*, a class action on behalf of the members of a fraternal benefits organization bound all 70,000 members. As in *Smith*, the class members shared identical and nonseparable interests.

In *Hansberry*, however, the claims of the class members were different, because they were not held jointly. Rather, each person who signed the covenant entered into an agreement with the others who signed the agreement. The claims were not held jointly but were "several" (separate) obligations. The Court recognized that a judgment may bind class members even when those members do not hold joint claims—even "when the only circumstance defining the class is that the determination of the rights of its members turns upon a single issue of fact or law. . . ."[84] To do so, however, those represented must be members of the same class as those purporting to represent them. The plaintiff class in *Burke* sought to *enforce* the restrictive covenant. While the judgment in that case would bind all members of that class, it could not bind those homeowners (like Kleiman) who *opposed* enforcement of the covenant. Put simply, those in favor of the covenant and those opposed to it are not members of the same class. A representative from one camp cannot bind someone in the other. As the Court explained:

> Those who sought to secure [the] benefits [of the covenant] by enforcing it could not be said to be in the same class with or represent those whose interest was in resisting performance, for the agreement by its terms imposes obligations and confers rights on the owner of each plot of land who signs it. If those who thus seek to secure the benefits of the agreement were rightly regarded by the state Supreme Court as a constituting class, it is evident that those signers or their successors who are interested in challenging the validity of the agreement and resisting its performance are not of the same class in the sense that their interests are identical so that any group who had elected to enforce rights conferred by the agreement could be said to be acting in the interest of any others who were free to deny its obligation. . . . [A] selection of representatives for purposes of litigation, whose substantial interests are not

---

[82] 255 U.S. 356 (1921).
[83] *Smith*, 57 U.S. at 302.
[84] *Hansberry*, 311 U.S. at 43. This type of class action is now found in Federal Rule 23(b)(3). See §13.3.4.

necessarily or even probably the same as those whom they are deemed to represent, does not afford that protection to absent parties which due process requires. . . . In seeking to enforce the agreement the plaintiffs in [*Burke*] were not representing the petitioners here whose substantial interest is in resisting performance.[85]

Under *Hansberry*, then, due process permits a class judgment to bind class members *only* if they are members of the same class as the representative. Stated another way, if the representative and the class members disagree on the key issue in the litigation, they are not members of the same class; the representative cannot represent people who disagree with her on that key issue. In *Hansberry*, the disagreement was clear—the representative in *Burke v. Kleiman* wanted to enforce the covenant and thus could not be allowed to bind those homeowners who opposed the covenant.

Importantly, *Hansberry* does *not* stand for the proposition that there can be no disagreement between the representative and class members. There may be disagreements on matters of strategy and remedy. So long as the class members and the representative are united on the core issues in litigation, however, there will be no constitutional problem with the judgment's binding all class members.

Thus, *Hansberry* recognizes that class members can be bound if they are *adequately represented*. They do not need to be joined as parties. But do they need to be given notice of the proceeding? *Hansberry* says nothing about it. The later case of *Mullane v. Central Hanover Bank*[86] (see §3.2) held that nonparties can be bound if given appropriate notice of the proceeding. *Mullane* did not involve a class action but concerned numerous beneficiaries to a pooled trust. The Court concluded that "notice reasonably certain to reach most of those interested in objecting is likely to safeguard the interest of all, since any objection sustained would inure to the benefit of all."[87]

Do *Hansberry* and *Mullane* together require that class members in a class action be adequately represented *and* be given notice of the proceedings? Apparently not. As we see in §13.3.4, Rule 23 requires notice of the pendency of the class action in only one of three types of class action. In all class cases, however, the representation must be adequate. The drafters of the Rule seem to have concluded that, at least in some types of class action, adequate representation (without notice) satisfies due process.[88]

---

[85]*Hansberry*, 311 U.S. at 44, 45-46.

[86]339 U.S. 306 (1950).

[87]*Mullane*, 339 U.S. at 319.

[88]In §13.3.6, we will see that the decision in *Wal-Mart v. Dukes*, 564 U.S. 338 (2011), may support this conclusion.

§13.3.3 Prerequisites for Any Class Action Under Rule 23(a)

In *Hansberry v. Lee*, which we discussed immediately above, the Supreme Court was required to determine the class membership and adequacy of representation of a class action that had already been litigated. This after-the-fact analysis is difficult. The drafters of Rule 23 envisioned that the assessments of class membership and adequacy of representation are best made before the fact. Thus, the Rule prescribes specific factors for determining *at the outset* whether a case should proceed as a class action. Satisfaction of the requirements of Rule 23 will avoid constitutional problems of the type encountered in *Hansberry*.[89]

A class action is commenced like any other case—by filing a complaint. The class representative's complaint contains all the elements of any complaint under Rule 8(a) (see §7.3.2). In addition, she alleges that the case is brought as a class action, and usually states that she is suing "on behalf of a class of persons (or entities) similarly situated." In the complaint, the representative will define the class. As we see below, it is important that the definition strike the court as a manageable group. There is no need to list the individual members of the class. (Indeed, in many cases that would be impossible.)

At this point, the case is a "putative class action" and the group is a "putative class." The case does not become a class action until the court enters an order "certifying" it as such. Thus, at some point after filing the case (and after the defendant has responded to the complaint), the class representative will make a motion to certify the case as a class action. We discuss this process and the court's role in detail in §13.3.5. The focus in the motion to certify will be whether the class (1) satisfies the prerequisites of a class in Rule 23(a), and (2) falls within one of three types of classes recognized in Rule 23(b).[90] We discuss the prerequisites in this section and the types of classes in §13.3.4.

---

[89]As we saw above, in *Hansberry*, the "class" involved in the antecedent litigation of *Burke v. Kleiman* should never have been permitted to proceed. The representative (who wanted to enforce the restrictive covenant) had no business representing a group that sought exactly the opposite result. Under Rule 23, the case would not have proceeded as structured. Under the Illinois rule of that era, however, the court was simply not required to undertake a meaningful before-the-fact analysis.

[90]Professor Lahav argues convincingly that the governance model embodied in Rule 23, which relies on a class representative, is vague and ineffective. In fact, she concludes, classes are actually governed by "attorney dictatorship with limited judicial oversight." She proposes revision of Rule 23 to provide more effective protection of the interests of class members. Alexandra D. Lahav, *Fundamental Principles for Class Action Governance*, 37 Indiana L. Rev. 65 (2003).

Implicit Requirement of a "Class" and (Perhaps) "Ascertainability"

Before listing four express prerequisites, Rule 23(a) refers to the existence of a "class." The wise lawyer will be aware of the need to convince the court, as a practical matter, that a "class" does indeed exist. In her complaint and in the motion to certify the class,[91] then, counsel should avoid defining the group in open-ended terms, such as people "interested in peaceful political discussion"[92] or by subjective intent, such as "those people who were eligible to apply for aid but who were dissuaded because of the relevant agency's treatment of others."[93] If the class prevails, or if the class action is settled, the court needs to determine who will receive what remedy. The prudent lawyer will continually assure the judge that this will be a manageable task. The first opportunity to do this is in the complaint, and counsel will do well to impose reasonable temporal and geographic limitations on the class.

On the other hand, there is no need to name each class member. Defining the group by salient characteristics generally is sufficient. For example, in a securities fraud case, the class might consist of "all persons who (or entities which) purchased common stock of the XYZ Corporation after November 15, 2021, and before February 28, 2022." Depending on the size of that group, the lawyer might consider circumscribing the class to purchasers of the stock who reside in a particular state or region. As a rule of thumb, the more detail and precision the lawyer can provide, the better.

We see in §13.3.4 that there are different types of class actions. One type, under Rule 23(b)(3), requires that the identifiable members of the class be given individual notice of the pendency of the case. That type of class action usually involves claims for monetary relief. In such cases, because the court will need to give individual notice and (if the class wins) to award money to the various class members, the court will expect especial specificity in the class definition. In contrast,

---

[91]Plaintiff must define the class in the complaint and will do so again in the motion for certification. Often, these definitions will differ, because in the interim (perhaps because of discovery) the class lawyer may have learned something that makes the class definition more definite. From the outset, though—starting with the complaint— it behooves the class lawyer to define the class in a way that convinces the judge that the case will be manageable.

[92]*See, e.g.*, Yaffe v. Powers, 454 F.2d 1362, 1364 (1st Cir. 1972); Lopez Tijerina v. Henry, 48 F.R.D. 274, 277 (D.N.M. 1969) ("poor people within the state"). How would a court go about finding members of such classes?

[93]*See, e.g.*, Simer v. Rios, 661 F.2d 655, 669 (7th Cir. 1981) ("individuals certified for Crisis Intervention Program but who were denied such or discouraged from applying for such"). The inclusion of a subjective element in class membership makes it impossible for the court to manage the case.

another type of class action, under Rule 23(b)(2), involves claims for injunctive or declaratory relief. Because there is no requirement of notice to individual members of such a class, or to distribute damages to individuals, courts require relatively less specificity in defining a class in such cases.

In recent years, courts have addressed whether there is an implicit requirement that the class representative demonstrate "ascertainability." Rule 23 contains no mention of such a requirement. And though an increasing number of courts refer to it, there is no single definition of ascertainability.[94] The cases may be reconciled, however, by focusing on the Third Circuit, which has addressed the issue more than most courts.

In *Carrera v. Bayer Corporation*,[95] the Third Circuit established two prongs to ascertainability: (1) the class must be "defined with reference to objective criteria" and (2) the class representative must show that "there is a reliable and administratively feasible mechanism for determining whether putative class members fall within the class definition."[96] The insistence on objective criteria in prong (1) is not controversial; it is consistent with the discussion in the preceding paragraphs that there in fact be a "class"—a group objectively defined and appropriately focused. All courts subscribe to this notion. The disagreement is about prong (2). It is important to note that even in the Third Circuit, prong (2) applies only to Rule 23(b)(3) classes.[97]

The Third Circuit requires the representative in a Rule 23(b)(3) class to demonstrate, in the motion to certify, some administratively feasible way in which to identify individual class members. The First and Fourth Circuits agree with this requirement of administrative ascertainability.[98] But the emerging majority of courts of appeals reject it. Thus, while courts generally require "ascertainability" (as described in prong (1)), the Second, Sixth, Seventh, Eighth, Ninth, and Eleventh

---

[94]*See, e.g.*, Briseno v. ConAgra Foods, Inc., 844 F.3d 1121, 1124 n.3 (9th Cir. 2017) ("we refrain from referring to 'ascertainability' in this opinion because courts ascribe widely varied meanings to that term"). *See* Note, *Class Ascertainability*, 124 Yale L.J. 2354 (2015).

[95]727 F.3d 300, 305 (3d Cir. 2013).

[96]The House of Representatives passed the "Fairness in Class Action Litigation and Furthering Asbestos Claim Transparency Act" in 2017. Among other things, it would require that, in every federal class action seeking monetary recovery, the representative "demonstrate[] a reliable and administratively feasible mechanism for the court to determine whether putative class members fall within the class definition and for the distribution of any monetary relief directly to a substantial majority of class members." The Senate twice referred the matter to committee, but never acted on the bill.

[97]*See* Shelton v. Bledsoe, 775 F.3d 554, 563 (3d Cir. 2015) (not required in Rule 23(b)(2) class action).

[98]In re Nexium Antitrust Litigation, 777 F.3d 9, 19 (1st Cir. 2015); EQT Prod. Co. v. Adair, 764 F.3d 347, 358-359 (4th Cir. 2014).

Circuits expressly reject a requirement of administrative feasibility at the certification stage.[99]

> o *__Example #15.__* Thousands of people purchase a vitamin supplement. Many claim that the supplement did not do what it was advertised to do. Representative brings a class action under Rule 23(b)(3) against the manufacturer, seeking damages. (This is a negative-value class action because each person's damages are so small that no one would sue individually.) Because these were small over-the-counter transactions, there will be no centralized record of who bought the supplement.

It is quite possible that the Third Circuit (and First and Fourth Circuits) would deny certification because the class is not administratively feasible.[100] Other courts, however, might certify the class. On similar facts, for example, the Sixth Circuit upheld class certification because the class was defined by objective criteria: persons who purchased the pharmaceutical in given places at given times.[101]

The real points of departure appear to be twofold. First, the Third Circuit in *Carrera* seemed to expect perfection—"100 percent accuracy"—in identifying every class member.[102] Second, the Third Circuit imposes its administrative feasibility requirement at the class certification stage. Most courts are willing to certify a class if they are convinced that *ultimately*, including when the remedy (if any) will be distributed, they will be able to determine who is in the class. As one

---

[99]Cherry v. Dometic Corp., 986 F.3d 1296, 1303 (11th Cir. 2021) ("Our ascertainability precedents . . . do not mandate proof of administrative feasibility."); In re Petrobras Securities, 862 F.3d 250, 266 (2d Cir. 2017); *Briseno*, 844 F.3d at 1126; Sandusky Wellness Ctr., LLC v. Medtox Sci., Inc., 821 F.3d 992, 995-996 (8th Cir. 2016); Rikos v. Procter & Gamble Co., 799 F.3d 497, 524-525 (6th Cir. 2015); Mullins v. Direct Digital, LLC, 795 F.3d 654, 657-658 (7th Cir. 2015). In an earlier case, the Second Circuit said that it must be "administratively feasible for the court to determine whether a particular individual is a member." Brecher v. Republic of Argentina, 806 F.2d 22, 24 (2d Cir. 2015). In *Petrobras*, however, the court held: "The ascertainability doctrine that governs in this Circuit requires only that a class be defined using objective criteria that establish a membership with definite boundaries." *Id.* at 264.

One Third Circuit judge has urged that court to eliminate the administrative feasibility requirements. Byrd v. Aaron's Inc., 784 F.3d 154, 177 (3d Cir. 2015) (Rendell, J., concurring). Another Third Circuit judge, dissenting from the denial of *en banc* review, worried that *Carrera*, note 95 above, "gives the impression to many that we now carry [the ascertainability requirement] too far." *Carrera*, 2014 WL 3887938 at *1 (Ambro, J.).

[100]Example #15 is based upon *Carrera*, note 95 above.

[101]*Rikos,* 799 F.3d at 524-525.

[102]The court in *Rikos* characterized the Third Circuit's position as requiring "100 percent accuracy" in identifying individual members. *Rikos* rejected such a requirement and noted that membership can be determined "with reasonable accuracy" at the appropriate time. 799 F.3d at 525, *quoting* Young v. Nationwide Mut. Ins. Co., 693 F.3d 532, 538-539 (6th Cir. 2012).

court put it: "If class actions could be defeated because membership was difficult to ascertain at the class certification stage, there would be no such thing as a consumer class action."[103] So the issue in most courts is whether, *when the time comes to distribute money*, individuals will be able to prove that they purchased the drug at a relevant time and place.[104] For example, online purchases would generate a record of buyers, physicians might confirm that they recommended the drug for their patients, or members might be permitted to file affidavits or receipts concerning purchases.[105]

The Four Express Prerequisites and the Need for Evidence

Assuming the existence of a "class" and (if required) a showing of "ascertainability," Rule 23(a) sets forth four prerequisites, usually referred to, respectively, as "numerosity," commonality, typicality, and adequacy of representation. Though all four should be addressed in any case, they are not hermetically sealed from one another. Indeed, there is a good argument that the four can be collapsed into two: numerosity and adequacy of representation.[106] The party seeking certification has the burden of persuading the court that all requirements are satisfied.

The burden is on the representative to show that the requirements of Rule 23(a) and 23(b) are satisfied. Historically, courts were not demanding about the level of evidence required for this purpose; indeed, they often treated the matter as one of pleading, rather than of proof.[107] That changed in 2011 with *Wal-Mart Stores, Inc. v. Dukes*,

---

[103]Astiana v. Kashi Co., 291 F.R.D. 493, 500 (S.D. Cal. 2013) (internal quotations omitted).

[104]In the Rule 23(b)(3) class, as noted, common questions must predominate over individual questions. It may be that individual proof of damages would be so onerous as to overwhelm the common questions underlying liability. This fact would counsel against certification of the class. On the other hand, it might be permissible to certify the class solely on the questions underlying liability, and then to allow individual adjudication of the remedy for each member. See §13.3.5, "Issue Certification and Subclasses."

[105]In *Rikos*, class certification was aided by the fact (not true in *Carrera*) that many purchases were online and therefore could be tracked by credit card records.

[106]The Supreme Court has treated commonality and typicality as essentially collapsing into the requirement of adequate representation. General Tel. Co. of the Southwest v. Falcon, 457 U.S. 147, 157 n.13 (1982).

[107]They did so largely by misinterpreting *Eisen v. Carlisle & Jacquelin*, 417 U.S. 156, 177 (1974). That case contained broad language against conducting "a preliminary inquiry into the merits" of a case and that factual allegations relating to the merits of the case should be considered true for purposes of class certification. As explained in the next sentence in the text, however, the Court subsequently made clear that the broad statements in *Eisen* did not apply to the question of evidence to be considered on class certification.

which held that Rule 23 does not impose "a mere pleading standard."[108] The Court emphasized that the plaintiff must "be prepared to *prove* that . . . in fact" the requirements of Rule 23(a) and 23(b) are satisfied. There must be "rigorous analysis," "significant proof," and "actual, not presumed, conformance with Rule 23."[109]

This requirement of an evidentiary showing raised three issues with which lower courts have struggled. First, can the court assess evidence relevant to class certification even if that evidence will relate to the merits of the underlying dispute? Courts had long been reluctant to do so. *Wal-Mart,* however, makes clear that the court must assess whatever facts are necessary to class certification, even if they also are relevant to the merits of the underlying dispute.[110]

Second, the Court in *Wal-Mart* hinted that expert witness testimony considered on a class certification motion must be assessed for admissibility under the Federal Rule of Evidence, including *Daubert v. Merrell Dow Pharmaceuticals*.[111] Lower courts generally have treated this hint as a command, though there is some debate over whether a full *Daubert* or modified *Daubert* analysis is required at the certification stage.[112]

Third, outside the expert witness area, must the evidence considered at certification be vetted for admissibility under the Federal Rules of Evidence? In a case decided before *Wal-Mart*, the Fifth Circuit rejected the district court's reliance on internet printouts in granting class certification and held that rulings on certification must be based "on admissible evidence."[113] The Ninth Circuit reached the opposite conclusion in 2018 and held that it is an error to reject "evidence

---

[108]564 U.S. 338, *357-361.Wal-Mart* made this clear regarding Rule 23(a). Later, the Court extended the holding to Rule 23(b). Comcast Corp. v. Behrend, 569 U.S. 27, 33 (2013) ("The party must also satisfy through evidentiary proof at least one of the provisions of Rule 23(b).").

[109]All of the quoted phrases came from the earlier case of *General Tel. Co. of Sw. v. Falcon*, 457 U.S. 147, 156 (1982).

[110]*Wal-Mart*, 564 U.S. at 351 n.6. The court should not, however, make preliminary inquiries into factual issues that do not relate to class certification.

[111]509 U.S. 579 (1993). *Daubert* set the standard for judging the reliability and relevance of expert testimony. Today, those standards are part of the analysis for admissibility of expert testimony under Federal Rule of Evidence 702. In *Wal-Mart*, the Ninth Circuit held that expert testimony relevant to class certification need not be analyzed under *Daubert*. After referring to this ruling, the majority opinion of the Supreme Court said "[w]e doubt this is so." 564 U.S. at 354.

[112]*Compare, e.g.,* American Honda Motor Co. v. Allen, 600 F.3d 813, 815-816 (7th Cir. 2010) (pre-*Wal-Mart* decision holding that if an expert's opinion is "critical" to class certification, the court "must perform a full *Daubert* analysis") *with* In re Zurn Pex Plumbing Prods. Liability Litigation, 644 F.3d 604, 612-614 (8th Cir. 2011) (district court did not err in applying a "tailored" *Daubert* approach).

[113]Unger v. Amedisys Inc., 401 F.3d 316, 325 (5th Cir. 2005).

that likely could have been presented in an admissible form at trial" merely because it was not in an admissible form at the certification stage.[114] Formal evidentiary objections, said the court, were relevant only to the weight that should be accorded the evidence in the certification motion.

The Sixth Circuit sided with the Ninth Circuit in 2021 and emphasized that the nature of evidence required may shift through various stages of litigation. In *Lyngaas v. Ag*, that court upheld certification of a class based in part on summary report logs of faxes that had not been formally authenticated.[115] Though such evidence would not be proper, for example, on summary judgment, a court dealing with class certification has greater evidentiary freedom. Because the plaintiff assured the district court that the summary logs could be authenticated for trial, they were properly considered in ruling on certification.[116]

Even with this emerging liberal view on non-expert evidence to be considered, we emphasize that class certification is addressed relatively early in the case. The requirement of evidence (not merely allegations) demonstrating that Rule 23 is satisfied and the likely requirement that expert testimony be qualified under *Daubert* clearly "front-load" the litigation, making the class certification motion more difficult and expensive.

Rule 23(a)(1): Numerosity. This word (if it is one) does not appear in Rule 23; courts made it up to cover the requirement in Rule 23(a)(1) that the class be "so numerous that joinder of all members is impracticable." This requirement ensures that the class action is necessary. If the number of class members involved is low enough that joinder would be practicable, a class action simply is not needed; the affected persons can join as coplaintiffs under Rule 20(a)(1). Whether a proposed class satisfies Rule 23(a)(1) involves a case-by-case analysis.[117]

One factor, of course, is the sheer number of putative class members. Some classes are so large that numerosity is obvious. For example, some classes have hundreds or thousands (or even millions) of members. Though courts should consider other factors besides sheer

---

[114]Sali v. Corona Reg. Med. Ctr., 909 F.3d 996, 1000 (9th Cir. 2018).

[115]992 F.3d 412, 438 (6th Cir. 2021).

[116]The court relied upon the Ninth Circuit decision in *Sali*, note 114 above, as well as the Eighth Circuit in *Zurn Pex*, note 112 above, to make the point that certification is determined before the close of merits discovery. Thus, at the certification stage one expects some evidentiary uncertainty. 992 F.3d at 429. The court also noted that the Supreme Court's decision in *Falcon*, note 109 above, had instructed courts to assess evidence relevant to certification but that sometimes "the issues are plain enough from the pleadings." 457 U.S. at 160.

[117]*See generally* Alexandra D. Lahav, *The Curse of Bigness and the Optimal Size of Class Actions*, 63 Vand. L. Rev. En Banc 117, 123 (2010) (urging focus on variations among class members, as opposed simply to size of class).

numbers, as we discuss in a moment, such large groups generally pose no numerosity problems. When is numerosity not obvious? Most courts agree that there are no automatic rules and there is no magic number. Some, however, have espoused this rule of thumb: Fewer than 21 members is insufficient, more than 40 members is sufficient, and the range in between varies depending upon other factors.[118] Again, however, this is at best a general rule, and there are cases in which courts have certified classes with fewer than 21 members[119] and cases in which courts have denied certification of classes with scores of putative members.[120]

Such cases demonstrate the importance of factors other than the raw numbers. For instance, geographic dispersion of class members is relevant. In one case, the court rejected class status for 350 political subdivisions of a state because the members were not geographically dispersed and could join in a single case in which a state officer could represent them all.[121] On the other hand, a relatively small group might be seen as numerous if the members are geographically widespread, since joinder would be relatively more difficult.[122]

We see in §13.3.6 that, for diversity of citizenship purposes, the court looks only to the citizenship of the class representative, not all the class members. If joinder of the individual members would make it impossible to satisfy the complete diversity rule, joinder might arguably be impracticable.

Another relevant factor is the ability of members to pursue individual litigation. In negative-value classes, when individual claims are so small that members would not pursue them alone, joinder may be seen as impracticable. The Supreme Court recognized this possibility in *Phillips Petroleum Co. v. Shutts*, a case involving a class of claimants whose claim averaged $100; the Court explained "most of the plaintiffs would have no realistic day in court if a class action were not available."[123]

The court may consider other issues that affect an individual's incentive or ability to pursue individual litigation. In one case, for instance, the court concluded that a class of 19 was proper, in part

[118]*See, e.g.*, Cox v. Am. Cast Iron Pipe Co., 784 F.2d 1546, 1553 (11th Cir. 1986).

[119]*See, e.g.*, Allen v. Isaac, 99 F.R.D. 45, 53 (N.D. Ill. 1983) (17 members); Davy v. Sullivan, 354 F. Supp. 1320, 1325 (M.D. Ala. 1973) (10 members).

[120]*See, e.g.*, Liberty Lincoln Mercury, Inc. v. Ford Mktg. Corp., 149 F.R.D. 65, 73 (D.N.J. 1993) (123 purported members).

[121]Utah v. American Pipe & Constr. Co., 49 F.R.D. 17, 19 (C.D. Cal. 1969).

[122]*See, e.g.*, Alvarado Partners, LP v. Mehta, 130 F.R.D. 673, 675 (D. Colo. 1990) (joinder of 33 individuals impracticable in part because they resided in different areas of the United States).

[123]472 U.S. 797, 809 (1985). *Shutts* is an important case concerning personal jurisdiction in the class action. See §13.3.8.

because the individuals would be too intimidated to bring individual discrimination claims.[124] Similarly, factors such as limited financial resources, mental disability, or inability to speak English may render joinder impracticable.[125]

Rule 23(a)(2): Commonality. Rule 23(a)(2) requires that there be "questions of law or fact . . . common to the class." Though the rule uses the plural word "questions," courts have long agreed that a single common question is sufficient. Historically, this was not a difficult requirement. Through the years, the difficult issue about commonality came up not under Rule 23(a)(2), but under Rule 23(b)(3). That provision requires that common questions *predominate* over individual questions (see §13.3.4). But the basic existence of a common question under Rule 23(a)(2) was rarely discussed in detail in any case.

That changed in 2011, with the Supreme Court's decision in *Wal-Mart Stores, Inc. v. Dukes*.[126] There, the Court reversed the Ninth Circuit, which had upheld a class of 1,500,000 members. The class consisted of female employees of Wal-Mart, and alleged gender discrimination in violation of Title VII.[127] Wal-Mart gives managers great discretion in setting pay (within ranges) and awarding promotion. Plaintiffs asserted that this discretion was exercised disproportionately in favor of men, which caused an unlawful disparate impact on women employees. They sought injunctive and declaratory relief, punitive damages, and back pay. The Court held, five-to-four, that the class failed to satisfy the commonality requirement of Rule 23(a)(2). (The Court also held (unanimously) that the class could not be certified under Rule 23(b)(2), which we discuss in §13.3.4.)

The majority in *Wal-Mart* recognized that Rule 23(a)(2) requires only a single question of law or fact in common to the class but held that there was none. Saying that all plaintiffs suffered a violation of federal employment law was insufficient, because that law can be violated in different ways. Rather, the members must have suffered the "same injury," so "their claims can productively be litigated at once."[128]

The substantive law required a showing of a general policy of discrimination. Though the plaintiffs alleged such a policy, the Court

[124]Arkansas Educ. Ass'n v. Board of Educ., 446 F.2d 763, 765-766 (8th Cir. 1971).

[125]*See, e.g.*, Jackson v. Foley, 156 F.R.D. 538, 542 (E.D.N.Y. 1994) (low-income claimants less likely to be able to bring individual suits); Rodriguez v. Berrymore Farms, Inc., 672 F. Supp. 1009, 1013 (W.D. Mich. 1987) (inability to speak English and lack of knowledge of legal system render individual suits unlikely).

[126]564 U.S. 338 (2011).

[127]Title VII is part of the Civil Rights Act, and, *inter alia*, forbids sex-based discrimination in employment.

[128]564 U.S. at 349-351. This requirement was not satisfied by a general assertion that all women employees suffered gender-based discrimination. Rather, they must show class members suffered the same injury to satisfy the commonality requirement.

concluded that they had no proof to justify certification. Plaintiffs presented the "social framework" analysis of a sociologist, who concluded that Wal-Mart's structure and corporate culture made it "vulnerable" to "gender bias." The expert conceded, however, that he could not calculate what percentage of employment decisions might be affected by "stereotyped thinking." Accordingly, the majority concluded, a court "can safely disregard what he has to say."[129]

Plaintiffs likewise failed in their attack on the Wal-Mart policy of allowing local managers to exercise discretion in making pay and promotion decisions. Here, they failed to identify a "common mode of exercising discretion that pervades the entire company." Because they could not show an employment practice that "ties all their 1.5 million claims together," plaintiffs failed to demonstrate the existence of a common question under Rule 23(a)(2). "Without some glue holding the alleged *reasons* for all those decisions together, it will be impossible to say that examination of all the class members' claims will produce a common answer to the crucial question *why was I disfavored*."[130] Anecdotal evidence did not suffice; plaintiffs provided only one affidavit for every 12,500 class members, relating to only 235 of the 3,400 Wal-Mart stores. "[A] few anecdotes selected from literally millions of employment decisions prove nothing at all."[131]

After *Wal-Mart*, Rule 23(a)(2) presents a higher hurdle for plaintiffs than it previously did.[132] But it is not insuperable. The requirement that the class members suffer the "same injury" is satisfied by showing a *common instance of injurious conduct* even though class members' harm may vary greatly.[133] *Wal-Mart* does not require that every question be common; "a single significant question of law or fact" suffices.[134] Though it is difficult to quantify how much more rigorous the new practice is, *Wal-Mart* shifted the focus from common questions

---

[129]*Id.* at 354-356.

[130]*Id.* at 351-352 (emphasis original).

[131]*Id.* at 358 n.9.

[132]*See, e.g.,* Brown v. Nucor Corp., 785 F.3d 895, 903 (4th Cir. 2015) ("heightened requirement of commonality"); M.D. v. Perry, 675 F.3d 832, 839 (5th Cir 2012) ("has heightened the standards for establishing commonality under Rule 23(a)(2)"); Olney v. Job.com, Inc., 2013 WL 5476813 at *12 (E.D. Cal. 2013) ("has made the commonality hurdle somewhat more difficult for plaintiffs to clear"). *See generally* Elizabeth Chamblee Burch, *Constructing Issue Classes*, 101 Va. L. Rev. 1855, 1863-1864 (2015) (after *Wal-Mart*, "defendants have convinced courts to scrutinize the plaintiffs' commonality vis-à-vis one another and have thereby dodged class certification . . ."). *But see* Cunningham v. Multnomah Cnty., 2014 U.S. Dist. LEXIS 180960 at *18 (D. Or. 2014) ("The commonality standard is not strictly construed").

[133]*See, e.g.,* In re Deepwater Horizon, 739 F.3d 790, 810-811 (5th Cir. 2014).

[134]Mazza v. American Honda Motor Co., 666 F.3d 581, 589 (9th Cir. 2012).

to generating common *answers*. This shift has resulted in denials of some certifications for failure to satisfy Rule 23(a)(2).[135]

Rule 23(a)(3): Typicality. Rule 23(a)(3) mandates that the representative's claims be typical of those of the class.[136] This factor is closely related to the next, which is that the representative fairly and adequately represent the class. Both requirements focus on the relationship between the class members and their representative. The function and goal of the class action is to bind the entire class to the judgment obtained by the representative. As discussed in §13.3.2, this cannot be accomplished, as a matter of due process, unless the representative adequately represents the interests of the class members. The requirement that the representative's claim be typical of the claims of class members helps to ensure adequate representation. If the representative has suffered a similar harm—if she can "feel the pain" of the class members—it is more likely that her representation will be adequate. Stated another way, without a typical claim, it is difficult to see what incentive the representative would have to assert the class claims vigorously.

Rule 23(a)(3) does not require that the representative's claims be *exactly* the same in all particulars as those of class members. Instead, courts focus on the "essential characteristics" of the claims and recognize that minor factual differences, even as to damages, will not make class treatment improper.[137] Obviously, though, if the class members' claims will require a high degree of individualized proof, class treatment is not appropriate, and the representative's claim will not be typical of those of the group.[138]

> o ***Example #16.*** Retail Store engages door-to-door salespeople to sell refrigerators. Fifty salespeople go to various neighborhoods and enter into discussions with residents, during which they offer to sell the refrigerator on discount if the person agrees on the spot. About 200 people agree to buy and make the required payment, and Retail Store never delivers the refrigerators.

In a class action for common law fraud, one serious problem will be the substantive requirement of showing a misrepresentation of fact by the defendant. If each representation by a salesperson to a prospective purchaser was unique, a class action would seem impossible, because

---

[135]*See, e.g.,* DL v. District of Columbia, 713 F.3d 120, 126-128 (D.C. Cir. 2013).

[136]Or, in a defendant class, that her defenses are typical of those of the class.

[137]*See* 5 Moore's Federal Practice §23.24[4].

[138]*See, e.g.,* In re American Med. Sys., Inc., 75 F.3d 1069, 1083 (6th Cir. 1996) (various members of putative class used different prosthetic model and experienced different harms).

nobody's claim would be typical of anyone else's claim. But if Retail Store provided its sales force with a standard sales pitch to be memorized and delivered to each person, a class action might be possible. In such a situation, the misrepresentations would have been identical, even though each conversation was slightly different.[139]

Beyond this, it is important that the representative suffer the same general kind of harm suffered by the class.

> o **_Example #17._** The class consists of Mexican American persons who applied for employment with Defendant. They claim that Defendant refused to hire them on the basis of their national origin. Representative is a Mexican American who is employed by Defendant, but who claims that Defendant refused to promote him because of his national origin.

Representative cannot represent the class, because he did not suffer the same harm. While both he and the class assert that they were hurt by Defendant's discriminatory behavior, they were hurt in different ways. The class members were never hired. Representative was hired (but not promoted), and thus his claim could not be typical of those of the class members.[140]

Moreover, the fact that a representative is subject to a defense that class members generally are not may preclude a finding of typicality (or adequacy of representation). The existence of such a defense will require litigation unrelated to the class and may distract the representative from prosecuting the class claim. For example, in one case, the fact that the representative bought certificates of deposit from the defendant after the alleged fraud was uncovered subjected it to a unique defense and defeated typicality.[141] Similarly, the fact that the

---

[139]These facts are similar to those in *Vasquez v. Superior Court*, 484 P.2d 964, 966-967 (Cal. 1971). *See also* Rosario v. Livaditis, 963 F.2d 1013, 1018 (7th Cir. 1992) (claim typical because part of same overall fraudulent course of dealing). In securities fraud claims under Rule 10b-5, a federal court will presume reliance if the alleged misstatement was included in a public press release. In establishing this rule, the Supreme Court expressly noted that a contrary rule would make it impossible to prosecute such cases as class actions, because of the variations from class member to class member. Basic Inc. v. Levinson, 485 U.S. 224, 246-247 (1988). The Court reaffirmed this result in *Halliburton Co. v. Erica P. John Fund, Inc.*, 573 U.S. 258, 268 (2014). In *Goldman Sachs Grp., Inc. v. Arkansas Teacher Retirement Sys.*, 141 S. Ct. 1951, 1967-1969 (2021), the Court held that defendants bear the burden to rebut the *Basic* presumption by showing, by a preponderance of the evidence at certification, that the alleged misrepresentations did not affect the price of the stock.

[140]General Tel. Co. of the Southwest v. Falcon, 457 U.S. 147, 158 (1982). The Court recognized that the question might be seen as one of typicality or of adequacy of representation. *Id.* at 157 n.13. Note also the potential for conflict of interest between Representative and the class members. If the class succeeds, the members will be hired, which will create greater competition for the promotion Representative seeks.

[141]Gary Plastic Pkg. Corp. v. Merrill Lynch, 903 F.2d 176, 178-180 (2d Cir. 1990).

representative of a class was subject to deportation (and other class members were not) defeated typicality.[142]

It is also important that the representative suffered a typical harm at the hands of the same defendants as the class members.

> ○ **_Example #18._** The class consists of persons in a city who did business with pawn shops that allegedly violated federal truth-in-lending laws. There are five defendant pawn shops, joined under Rule 20(a). The representative, however, dealt only with one of the defendants. The fact that she was not harmed by the other four pawn shop defendants means that her claim is not typical of the class members, who dealt with the other four. She did not suffer at the hands of those other four and cannot represent persons who did.[143]

There are three ways around this problem. First, the case may be structured with multiple representatives, one having dealt with each of the defendants. Then the representative who dealt with Defendant 1 has a claim typical of all class members who dealt with Defendant 1, the representative who dealt with Defendant 2 has a claim typical of all class members who dealt with Defendant 2, and so forth. This solution will not work, however, if there are too many defendants for practicable joinder. In such a situation, however, the case might be structured with a defendant class; if certified, the representative defendant will represent all defendants, who will then be bound by the judgment (just as plaintiff class members are bound by the judgment).

Second, if the defendants had engaged in a conspiracy to violate the truth-in-lending laws, the representative need not have had dealings with each defendant. The idea here is that each class member, including the representative, was harmed by the concerted efforts of the defendants; thus, one person so harmed can speak for others so harmed.[144]

Third, it is possible that members of a class have a _juridical relationship_ that enables the court to conclude that one may speak for and bind the others. The term is not well defined and seems limited to

---

[142]Hagan v. City of Winnemucca, 108 F.R.D. 61, 65-66 (D. Nev. 1985). The court noted that the probable deportation proceedings against the representative would be an "outside entanglement" that would also rob her of her ability to be an adequate representative.

[143]These facts are similar to those in _LaMar v. H&B Novelty & Loan Co._, 489 F.2d 461, 466 (9th Cir. 1973). The problem presented here is similar to the notion of standing. One who has not been harmed by a defendant has no standing to raise claims of others against that defendant.

[144]The _LaMar_ case in the preceding footnote has a well-known discussion of this point. _See_ 489 F.2d at 466. _See also_ Thillens, Inc. v. Community Currency Exch. Ass'n, 97 F.R.D. 668, 676 (N.D. Ill. 1983).

persons who occupy coordinate governmental positions. For example, in one case, plaintiffs sued a class of defendant jailers, who allegedly segregated prisoners unconstitutionally. Though the plaintiffs had not dealt with each jailer, all the defendant class members were officers of a single state. Their juridical relationship meant, in essence, that a plaintiff who had dealt with one could assert a claim against all.[145]

Rule 23(a)(4) (and Rule 23(g)): Protecting the Class Interests. Rule 23(a)(4) requires that the representative "fairly and adequately protect the interests of the class." This is the linchpin for assuring that the class members can be bound consistent with due process. This factor overlaps greatly with the Rule 23(a)(3) requirement of typicality. Indeed, some courts treat the two as virtually interchangeable. While recognizing overlap between the two, it is important to see, however, that certain factors must be addressed under Rule 23(a)(4). Though that Rule refers only to adequacy of the *representative*, we will see in §13.3.5 that the court must appoint class counsel (under Rule 23(g)), who is also charged with providing fair and adequate representation for class members' interests.

In contrast to the class lawyer (who, under Rule 23(g)(2), must be the applicant "best able to represent the interests of the class") there is no requirement that the class representative be "the best" available. Rule 23(a)(4) requires "adequate" protection of the class interests. The representative owes a fiduciary duty of loyalty to the class. At a minimum, her interests cannot be antagonistic to those of the class. Mere differences of opinion concerning litigation strategy will not defeat class certification. Rather, a disqualifying conflict is one that relates to the core subject of the case and is immediate, not speculative.

As we saw above in discussing typicality, a representative may *not* be adequate if she is subject to a unique defense, one not available against class members generally. Similarly, if the representative's credibility is subject to legitimate attack, the court may find her inadequate.[146] In addition, some courts have found a representative inadequate if she has a close personal, business, or familial relationship with the class lawyer.[147] In such a case, the representative might be tempted to approve settlement on terms favorable to the lawyer and relatively less favorable to the class members.

The class representative must litigate with vigor. Courts generally recognize, however, that the representative is rarely a lawyer, and cannot be expected to have detailed knowledge of the law. At

---

[145]Washington v. Lee, 263 F. Supp. 327, 330 (M.D. Ala. 1966).

[146]*See, e.g.,* Dubin v. Miller, 132 F.R.D. 269, 272 (D. Colo. 1990).

[147]*See, e.g.,* Kirby v. Cullinet Software, Inc., 116 F.R.D. 303, 309-310 (D. Mass. 1987).

some level, however, the representative must have at least some rudimentary understanding of the nature of the dispute. Otherwise, she cannot serve as a brake on the actions of the class counsel. If the representative is wholly clueless on such things, the class is essentially "headless." This robs members of a measure of representation and essentially permits suit by the lawyer, who lacks standing to bring the claim.[148]

Defendants also often challenge a class representative by pointing to her lack of financial ability to prosecute the litigation. Many lawyers take plaintiff class actions on a contingent fee basis, so the representative need not pay attorney's fees as the litigation proceeds.[149] But the representative must pay various costs of the litigation as they are incurred. For example, there are filing fees, witness fees, and costs of discovery. In a class action under Rule 23(b)(3), as we see in §13.3.4, the representative must pay to give the required notice to class members. If the litigation is successful, the losing side generally will have to pay the prevailing party's costs. In the interim, however, the representative must bear the expenses as they are incurred. The court must be convinced that the representative can finance this aspect of the litigation.

Can the class counsel advance money to the representative to pay these expenses? Historically, the answer was yes, so long as the representative agreed to reimburse the lawyer if the class lost the litigation. More recently, led by Rule 1.8(e) of the American Bar Association Model Rule of Professional Responsibility, some states permit the lawyer to advance expenses on a contingent basis. That means that the client repays the lawyer for these costs only if the class recovers some

[148]Standing is one of several "justiciability" doctrines that you may study in detail in courses on Constitutional Law or Federal Courts. It requires, basically, that the person asserting a claim be one who was actually harmed by the defendant's behavior. This ensures that there is a true dispute—a "case or controversy"—as required by Article III of the Constitution for invocation of federal subject matter jurisdiction.

[149]With a contingent fee arrangement, the lawyer does not charge the plaintiff a fee by the hour or on any other basis. Rather, the lawyer and client agree that the lawyer's fee will be a percentage of the plaintiff's recovery, whether that recovery comes from a judgment or settlement. The lawyer is taking a calculated risk. If the plaintiff loses, the lawyer simply receives no fee. On the other hand, if the recovery is huge—as might be the case in a class action, where the claims of many are asserted in one proceeding—the lawyer's recovery is correspondingly huge. The fact that a lawyer on a contingent fee is, in essence, financing the litigation explains the concern that she might want to settle rather than go to trial. By settling, she is guaranteed some recovery; by going to trial, she invests a tremendous amount of time while potentially recovering no pay. This conflict of interest for the lawyer emphasizes the need for an active class representative—to ensure that the class members' desires, and not those of the lawyer, govern what action is taken. (Of course, defendants cannot get lawyers to work on a contingent fee. They pay their lawyers by the hour.)

remedy. Some have criticized this arrangement as permitting a lawyer essentially to "buy" a class claim.[150]

Recognizing potential abuses of the class action, Congress passed the Private Securities Litigation Reform Act in 1996.[151] With this Act, Congress intended to ensure that sophisticated institutional investors serve as representatives ("lead plaintiffs") in federal court class actions based upon alleged violations of federal securities law. Among other requirements, the Act provides that the court must appoint as lead plaintiff the person having the largest financial interest in the class claim. The Act applies, however, only in litigation arising under the federal securities laws.

§13.3.4   Types of Class Actions Recognized Under Rule 23(b)

Assuming the party seeking certification convinces the court that the prerequisites of Rule 23(a) are satisfied, that party then must demonstrate (again, based upon evidence, not mere pleadings) that the case fits within one of the types of classes recognized by Rule 23(b). Thus, under Rule 23(b), there is a choice; the party seeking certification need satisfy only one of the types of classes recognized. On the other hand, nothing in Rule 23 precludes the representative from seeking certification under more than one type of class action, and some parties do seek certification under more than one type.

Rule 23(b)(1): The "Prejudice" Class Action. Reading Rule 23(b)(1) will remind you of Rule 19(a)(1)(B). The Rules Advisory Committee amended the two (along with Rule 24(a)(2)) together in 1966 expressly to emphasize their similarities. In §12.6.1, we saw that Rule 19(a)(1)(B) mandates the joinder of an absentee in either of two situations: (1) when nonjoinder of an absentee might subject the absentee's interest to practical impairment or (2) when nonjoinder of the absentee might subject the defendant to the risk of incurring multiple or inconsistent

---

[150]Historically, the American legal system has frowned on allowing people to buy a claim by advancing legal expenses to a party in return for a piece of any recovery. Indeed, such "maintenance" or "champerty" was a crime. Today, these restrictions are waning, but still exist in some states. They are being tested by an emerging trend, started in 2007, of publicly traded companies that invest in American commercial litigation. *See* Deborah R. Hensler, *The Future of Mass Litigation: Global Class Actions and Third-Party Litigation Funding,* 79 Geo. Wash. L. Rev. 306 (2011); Jason Lyon, *Revolution in Progress: Third-Party Funding of American Litigation,* 58 UCLA L. Rev. 571, 574 (2010). *See also* Elizabeth Chamblee Burch, *Financiers as Monitors in Aggregate Litigation,* 87 N.Y.U. L. Rev. 1273 (2012).

[151]15 U.S.C. §§77z-1, 78u-4.

obligations.[152] Rule 23(b)(1) addresses the same potential harms, but in the class context, where there are so many absentees that their joinder is not feasible. Just as Rule 19(a)(1)(B) consists of two subparts, so does Rule 23(b)(1). Because the Rule is concerned with avoiding potential prejudice (either to the absentees or to a party), we can refer to the Rule 23(b)(1) classes as "prejudice" class actions. These are "mandatory" classes, because members have no right to request exclusion.

Rule 23(b)(1)(A) permits a class action if individual suits "would create a risk of inconsistent or varying adjudications with respect to individual class members that would establish incompatible standards of conduct for the party opposing the class." This is the class analog to Rule 19(a)(1)(B)(ii); the focus is on the impact of nonclass litigation on the party opposing the class. Assuming a plaintiff class, the focus thus is on the defendant. The court asks this question: If the putative class members sue individually (not in a class), might it subject the defendant to incompatible standards of conduct?

> o **_Example #19._** Stockholders of a corporation claim that the corporation must convert their stock from one class to another. If the stockholders sue individually, some may win and some may lose, which would leave the corporation uncertain as to how to treat this class of stockholders. To avoid that potential uncertainty, a stockholder may sue on behalf of the other stockholders under Rule 23(b)(1)(A).[153]

As we saw with Rule 19, inconsistent outcomes in damages claims will not satisfy Rule 23(b)(1)(A), because such inconsistent claims do not constitute "incompatible standards of conduct."

> o **_Example #20._** A train operated by TrainCo crashes and injures 120 people. If the 120 people sue individually, some may win and some may lose. This possibility does not satisfy Rule 23(b)(1)(A), however, because the individual cases against TrainCo will not subject it to incompatible standards of conduct. There is nothing incompatible in this sense between writing a check to one passenger and not to another.

The focus here—as in Rule 19(a)(1)(B)(ii)—is on the effect of individual litigation on the ways in which the defendant must do something in the real world. In the first hypothetical above, for example, individual litigation might leave the corporation subject to orders

---

[152]In both instances, the absentee must claim an interest in the subject of the litigation.

[153]_See_ Van Gemert v. Boeing Co., 259 F. Supp. 125 (S.D.N.Y. 1966) (similar facts, but concerning holders of debentures, which are securities, but differ from stock in ways not relevant here).

(1) that this class of stock be converted into another class of stock and (2) that this class of stock not be converted into another class of stock. The corporation could not satisfy one without violating the other. In the TrainCo hypothetical, in contrast, there is no comparable inconsistency in having to pay a judgment to one passenger but not to another.

Rule 23(b)(1)(B) provides for a class action if individual suits "would create a risk of adjudications with respect to individual class members that, as a practical matter, would be dispositive of the interests of the other members not parties to the individual adjudications or would substantially impair or impede their ability to protect their interests." This is the class analog to Rule 19(a)(1)(B)(i); the focus is on the would-be class members. The court asks this question: If the putative class members sue individually, might some be harmed as a practical matter? Such harm might be caused by the fact that there is a limited fund from which all class members can recover. Individual actions might deplete the fund, leaving some essentially without a remedy. Everyone seems to accept the theory behind these "limited fund" classes. Courts take different approaches, however, about the degree of proof required to invoke Rule 23(b)(1)(B).

> o ***Example #21.*** A fire raged through a crowded dinner theater and killed more than 100 people. Based upon litigated claims for wrongful death in the area, the judge estimated that the total liability, though not precisely subject to calculation before trial, could exceed $16,000,000. In addition, defendants' lawyers estimated that the defendants had a net worth of approximately $3,000,000. Based upon these estimates, the court certified a Rule 23(b)(1)(B) class, because it found "good reason to believe" from these estimates "that total judgments might substantially exceed the ability of defendants to respond."[154]

Notice the reason for invoking Rule 23(b)(1)(B). If the claimants sued separately, according to the court, they would likely recover judgments totaling $16,000,000. But the pool of assets from which those judgments could be satisfied totaled only $3,000,000. If the litigations proceeded individually, the first few successful plaintiffs would exhaust the $3,000,000.[155] That scenario would prejudice those plaintiffs who were not first in the litigation line. Those whose cases went to trial later might win, but the victory would be hollow, because the defendants at

---

[154]Coburn v. 4-R Corp., 77 F.R.D. 43, 45 (E.D. Ky. 1977).

[155]Not only that, but the net worth of the defendants would be eroded further by the attorney's fees and other litigation expenses from over 100 separate cases. By the way, notice how this fact pattern could raise issue preclusion concerns. If the first plaintiff won, and established at trial that the defendants' negligence caused the fire, could successive plaintiffs take advantage of that finding? The answer might be yes, if the applicable law adopted nonmutual offensive issue preclusion. See §11.4.5.

that point would have no assets from which the judgment could be satisfied. To avoid that harm—to avoid the possibility that "individual actions would as a practical matter be dispositive of the interests of the other[s] not parties . . . or substantially impair their ability to pro-tect their interests"—the group may proceed as a class action. In that way, each member will receive a proportional part of what money there is. Instead of some plaintiffs recovering their full damages and many recovering nothing, this theory would allow all plaintiffs to recover a percentage of their damages.

The problem is that some courts have erected a dauntingly high burden of proof for invoking the limited fund class action under Rule 23(b)(1)(B). An example is the Ninth Circuit opinion in *In re Northern District of California Dalkon Shield IUD Products Litigation*,[156] which concerned claims related to an allegedly defective intrauterine birth control device. Injured women filed thousands of claims throughout the United States. The opinion involved the punitive damages claims[157] of a nationwide class of injured women. The district court added the punitive damages claims asserted by all class members; the total was $2.3 billion. The court then noted the net worth of the defendant, as asserted in discovery documents, which was $280,000,000. Finding an "unconscionable possibility that large numbers of plaintiffs who are not first in line at the courthouse door will be deprived of a practical means of redress," the district court certified a class under Rule 23(b)(1)(B).[158]

The Ninth Circuit reversed and criticized the district court for failing to undertake sufficient factual inquiry into the value of the claims and the net worth of the defendant. According to the Ninth Circuit, a limited fund class action is appropriate only when individual judgments "inescapably will alter the substance of the rights having similar claims." Nothing in Rule 23 even remotely requires such a degree of proof; the phrase "inescapably will alter" is not found in the Rule. Moreover, the Ninth Circuit opinion failed to indicate what kind of evidence would suffice to satisfy the standard it set for invoking Rule 23(b)(1)(B).

The Supreme Court addressed the limited fund class action in *Ortiz v. Fibreboard Corp.*,[159] which involved part of the massive litigation

[156]693 F.2d 847 (9th Cir. 1982).

[157]Punitive damages are intended to punish the defendant. They are sometimes called *exemplary* damages, because they make an example to the defendant that its behavior was so outrageous that it should be hit with liability beyond that for merely compensating the plaintiff for the harm done to her.

[158]In re Northern Dist. of Cal. Dalkon Shield IUD Prods. Liability Litigation, 526 F. Supp. 887, 893 (N.D. Cal. 1981).

[159]527 U.S. 815 (1999).

arising from exposure to asbestos.[160] The parties, including a large manufacturer of asbestos and its insurance companies, entered into a very complicated "Global Settlement Agreement" settling millions of personal injury claims. The agreement set out a complex system for compensating the victims from a fund that was created mostly from insurance money; the manufacturer contributed some money to the fund but ended up with nearly its entire net worth intact.

The Supreme Court rejected use of the Rule 23(b)(1)(B) limited fund class action on the facts of the case. In discussing three problems with such certification, the Court set out three requirements for a limited fund class action. First, the parties must *demonstrate* (not merely assert) that the available funds are insufficient to cover the numerous claims. In *Ortiz*, the parties simply stipulated about how much money was available; there was no proof, for example, of the value of the available insurance funds. Second, the proposed distribution must be equitable. The proposed settlement in *Ortiz* simply did not ensure that all claimants would be treated fairly. Third, the Court was quite concerned that the agreement permitted the manufacturer to retain nearly all its net worth; it contributed relatively little to the settlement fund. In the "historical use" of the limited fund class, the Court noted, the defendant is essentially wiped out by the litigation. In sum, the problem was that the defendants simply stipulated how much they would make available for potential plaintiffs. Individual suits might result in determinations that more insurance money was available and certainly could have recovered greater amounts from the manufacturer. Thus, there was no showing of a true limited fund that was insufficient to cover the prospective claims. While not ruling out the possibility of limited fund class actions under Rule 23(b)(1)(B), *Ortiz* certainly raises significant barriers to their use.[161]

The Court was also concerned that the actions under Rule 23(b)(1) are "mandatory" class actions. This means that the class members have no right to opt out; they are stuck in the class, and they are bound by the judgment in the class litigation.[162] In contrast, as we see

---

[160]We mentioned asbestos litigation in §11.4.4. Asbestos is a fire-resistant building material used routinely throughout much of the twentieth century. In the last third of that century it became clear that exposure to asbestos could cause cancer. Innumerable plaintiffs filed personal injury and wrongful death claims; in addition, there were thousands of claims concerning the financial responsibility for the federally mandated clean-up of asbestos from buildings. Asbestos has created more litigation than any other product in history.

[161]*See, e.g.*, Doe v. Karadzic, 192 F.R.D. 133, 139 (S.D.N.Y. 2000) (noting that though Rule 23(b)(1)(B) requires only "risk of impairment," courts have interpreted the phrase narrowly).

[162]Professor Redish concludes that mandatory classes, such as those permitted by Rule 23(b)(1) and (b)(2) violate due process by subverting an individual's right in favor

below, members of a Rule 23(b)(3) class have a right to opt out and
pursue individual litigation. Traditionally, damages claims have been
pursued under Rule 23(b)(3). Because the limited fund theory robs
individuals of control over their own claim, the Court in *Ortiz* counseled caution. Moreover, in *Wal-Mart* the Court raised the "serious
possibility" that due process requires notice and opt-out anytime class
members seek individualized monetary recovery.[163]

Though it seems strange, sometimes the *defendant* will seek certification of a *plaintiff* class under Rule 23(b)(1)(B). In the classic limited fund class action, the defendant understands that it will be wiped
out financially by the judgments to be rendered against it. The claims
vastly exceed the defendant's net worth. (This is why some courts
refer to limited fund classes as "constructive bankruptcy" classes.)
Rather than litigate each claim individually, the defendant might prefer to have the entire liability decided in a class action under Rule
23(b)(1)(B). Functionally, such a case starts to look a bit like interpleader (discussed in §13.2), in which the net worth of the defendants
is considered as the stake to which the numerous class members have
claims. Ironically, *plaintiffs* might oppose such a class, because they
(or their lawyers) might prefer to litigate alone and recover their individual judgments in full.[164] By doing so, they may be paid in full, while
others run the risk of being left out in the cold.

In addition to the limited fund, there is another theory, called *limited generosity*, on which Rule 23(b)(1)(B) classes might be certified. It
concerns only claims for punitive damages, which, as we said in footnote 157, are intended to punish the defendant for outrageous conduct.
Many observers have argued that it is unfair (perhaps even unconstitutional) to impose multiple punitive damages awards against a
defendant for a single bad act.[165]

○ ***Example #22.*** D engages in a single example of outrageous conduct
    that injures hundreds of plaintiffs. Of course, each plaintiff has a claim
    against *D* for compensatory damages. Suppose the plaintiffs sue for

---

of the collective. Redish, Wholesale Justice, note 66 above, at 159-162 (discussing one's
right to be free from forced association).

[163]*Wal-Mart*, 564 U.S. at 363.

[164]In *Coburn* and *Northern District of California Dalkon Shield IUD Prod. Litigation*,
notes 154 and 156 above, defendants sought certification of a plaintiff class. In addition
to avoiding serial litigation concerning the same events, a class action would probably
reduce the amount paid by the defendant in attorney's fees; this, in turn, would preserve more of defendant's assets for recovery by injured plaintiffs.

[165]*See* Nancy J. King, *Portioning Punishment: Constitutional Limits on Successive
and Excessive Penalties*, 144 U. Pa. L. Rev. 101, 106 (1995); Richard W. Murphy,
Superbifurcation: Making Room for State Prosecution in the Punitive Damages Process,
76 N.C. L. Rev. 463, 501 (1998).

punitive damages as well. Let's say the first several plaintiffs all win punitive damages against *D*. At some point, a court might say to the next plaintiff, in essence: "*D* has been punished enough for the outrageous conduct; nobody else may recover punitive damages against *D* for this act."

This conclusion means that no other plaintiffs may recover punitive damages. The argument is that these later plaintiffs have suffered the kind of harm that triggers Rule 23(b)(1)(B): They lose out because they got to trial later than the ones who recovered punitive damages. That is, the possibility that some court may step in and say "enough is enough" on punitive damages might rob later plaintiffs of the chance to recover them. According to the argument, the court should certify a class action for punitive damages; that way, each plaintiff will recover a proportional share of punitive damages and none will be left out.[166] This theory has met with some success.

Finally, no matter what theory is used under Rule 23(b)(1)(B), it is important that all potential claimants be members of the class. Otherwise, the litigation risks precisely the harm the Rule was intended to avoid. In one case, a class of school districts sued to recover the expenses of having to comply with the federal mandate to remove asbestos from buildings. The court refused to certify a Rule 23(b)(1)(B) class, in part because the class did not include all such claimants. The class would have the incentive to recover first, precisely to leave other claimants out in the cold.[167]

Rule 23(b)(2): Injunctive or Declaratory Relief. The Rule 23(b)(2) class action is appropriate when the party opposing the class (usually the defendant) "has acted or refused to act on grounds that apply generally to the class, so that final injunctive relief or corresponding declaratory relief is appropriate respecting the class as a whole." Thus, there are two requirements: one relating to the action or inaction of the party opposing the class and one relating to the relief sought by the class. It is a "mandatory" class, meaning that members have no right to request exclusion.

The provision was intended to facilitate desegregation suits,[168] though other cases can be brought under it. Typical class actions under

---

[166]*See, e.g.,* In re School Asbestos Litigation, 789 F.2d 996, 1003-1004 (3d Cir. 1986).

[167]*Id.* at 1006 (because thousands of other claimants are not in the class, there is still "a race to the courthouse door").

[168]*See* David Marcus, *Flawed But Noble: Desegregation Litigation and its Implications for the Modern Class Action,* 63 Fla. L. Rev. 657, 661 (2011) ("Rule 23(b)(2) was written for a very specific purpose. Judicial sympathy for racial integration and the 1966 authors' political commitments, rather than some conception of what due process requires, best explain why Rule 23 requires the mandatory class treatment of injunctive relief claims").

Rule 23(b)(2) deal with employment discrimination or with claims to restructure public institutions. Each of the following examples would be appropriate under Rule 23(b)(2).

- *__Example #23.__* A group of workers claims that Employer has denied them promotion because of their national origin, in violation of federal law. They seek an injunction compelling Employer to promote them (or a declaratory judgment that they are entitled to such relief).[169]
- *__Example #24.__* A group of pretrial detainees (persons charged with a crime and in custody while awaiting trial) claims that Sheriff is denying them "contact" visits from family members, in violation of the Constitution. They seek an injunction ordering Sheriff to permit such visits (or a similar declaratory judgment).

At this point, we might ask this: Why go to the trouble of a class action in such cases? Why not just have one person from the affected group sue? If she proves that Employer is discriminating against a group of workers on the basis of national origin and wins an injunction against such discrimination, won't all the affected workers "win"? The answer may be no. Suppose one plaintiff (*P*) brings the suit and wins. The result is an injunction ordering Employer to promote *P*, including, let's say, some broad language about not discriminating against the group on the basis of national origin. Now Employer promotes *P* but continues to discriminate against the other members of that group. Can they sue to enforce the injunction against the Employer? Probably not, because they were not parties to that case, nor were they represented by *P* (because it was not a class action). Accordingly, those people cannot enforce the judgment. A class judgment, in contrast, will permit any member of the class to enforce the injunction against Employer. Thus, if the class sues and wins, and Employer later continues to discriminate against a member of the class, the member can ask the court to hold Employer in contempt for violating an injunction entered in favor of all class members.

Rule 23(b)(2) speaks only of injunctive and declaratory relief. Through the years, however, some courts permitted Rule 23(b)(2) classes to recover money, at least in limited circumstances. Specifically, these courts permitted recovery of damages if they (1) "flowed automatically" from the grant of injunctive or declaratory relief and (2) were readily calculable.[170] The most common example was an award of back pay.

---

[169]As we noted in §4.6.3, a declaratory judgment is a judicial decree of the rights of the parties. It developed in equity.

[170]*See, e.g.*, Moody v. Albemarle Paper Co., 474 F.2d 134, 142 (4th Cir. 1973).

    ○ ***Example #25.*** Suppose a class discriminated against on the basis of national origin wins an injunction requiring Employer to promote them. That order avoids future harm to the class members by ordering Employer to do what the law requires. But what about the past discrimination? After all, the class members were denied their rightful promotions for some time and thus were underpaid over that period. Recovery of damages for the past discrimination will remedy that harm.

Some courts permitted such recovery in the Rule 23(b)(2) class. They did so on one of three theories. One, some courts justified recovery of money that could be characterized as "equitable" relief, such as restitution. Two, some courts held that money could be recovered as long as the demand for equitable relief "predominated" over the claim for money. The Supreme Court unanimously rejected both of these theories in *Wal-Mart*, which we discussed in §13.3.3 regarding the commonality requirement of Rule 23(a)(2).[171] The first theory is wrong because Rule 23(b)(2) speaks of "injunctive" and "declaratory" relief, but not of "equitable" remedies. The second theory is wrong because nothing in Rule 23(b)(2) refers to predominance (that concept arises only in the Rule 23(b)(3) class action).

But the Court in *Wal-Mart* did embrace the third theory by which courts had permitted monetary recovery in a Rule 23(b)(2) class action. This is when the monetary relief is "incidental" to equitable relief; in other words, when the money remedy will "flow directly from liability to the class as a whole on the claims forming the basis of the injunctive or declaratory relief."[172] This is likely the case in Example #25. The damages for past harm flow automatically from the injunction; the injunction puts the class members at the proper pay level, but they were denied that pay level before the injunction. Moreover, the damages are easily calculated; the court can simply apply a formula based upon the difference between the two pay grades and the length of time each was discriminated against.

The facts of *Wal-Mart* did not fall within this model, so the Court rejected certification under Rule 23(b)(2). *Wal-Mart* involved a class of 1,500,000 female employees who alleged gender discrimination. The Court emphasized two points concerning Rule 23(b)(2).

First, the injunctive or declaratory relief sought must be the same for each class member. The Rule "does not authorize class certification

---

[171]The holding that the class did not satisfy Rule 23(a)(2) was a five-to-four decision. The holding that the class should not be certified under Rule 23(b)(2), however, was unanimous.

[172]*Wal-Mart*, 564 U.S. at 366. The Court quotes *Allison v. Citgo Petroleum Corp.*, 151 F.3d 402, 415 (5th Cir. 1998), and discusses it with approval. Example #25 reflects the facts of *Allison*.

when each individual class member would be entitled to a *different* injunction or declaratory judgment against the defendant."[173] In other words, a class action cannot be used to vindicate unique individual equitable claims. Because the circumstances of alleged discrimination in *Wal-Mart* were unique to each class member, this requirement could not be met.

Second, Rule 23(b)(2) does not authorize a class action when "each class member would be entitled to an individualized award of monetary damages."[174] Again, each class member had a unique claim. The Ninth Circuit attempted to avoid the need for individual hearings on back pay by holding that a subset of cases would be tried, with other members' back pay being extrapolated from those results. The Supreme Court rejected this plan, which it called "Trial by Formula," because it would deny Wal-Mart the right under employment law to present defenses to individual claims.[175] The need for individualized proof doomed a class under Rule 23(b)(2). And, as noted earlier, the Court hinted that due process requires that class members seeking individualized monetary relief be given notice and the right to opt out of the class.[176]

Finally, most courts conclude that Rule 23(b)(2) generally cannot be used for a defendant class.[177]

Rule 23(b)(3): Common Questions Predominate. A class action under Rule 23(b)(3) is appropriate when (1) common questions *predominate* over individual questions, *and* (2) the class action is superior

---

[173]*Wal-Mart*, 564 U.S. at 360 (emphasis original).

[174]*Id.*

[175]There is no blanket prohibition against use of representative evidence to support a motion for class certification. The Court upheld representative evidence in a 2016 case discussed at notes 176-177 below. Professor Lahav concludes that the use of representative evidence manifests a clash between the goals of liberty and equality. Alexandra D. Lahav, *The Case For "Trial by Formula,"* 90 Texas L. Rev. 571 (2012). *See also* Alexandra D. Lahav, *Mass Tort Class Actions – Past, Present, and Future,* 92 N.Y.U. L. Rev. 998 (2017).

[176]564 U.S. at 363 ("While we have never held that [due process requires notice and the right to opt out] where the monetary claims do not predominate, the serious possibility that it may be so provides an additional reason not to read rule 23(b)(2) to include the monetary claims here"). Again, the Court left open the possibility of monetary recovery in the *Allison* situation, which is reflected in Example #25. *See generally* Alexandra D. Lahav, *Due Process and the Future of Class Actions,* 44 Loy. U. Chi. L.J. 545 (2013).

[177]They do so based upon language of the Rule, which requires that the party opposing the class to have acted in such a way as to make injunctive or declaratory relief appropriate. With a defendant class, the party opposing the class is the plaintiff, who generally will not have acted in any such way. Courts also rely on advisory committee notes in concluding that 23(b)(2) is intended for plaintiff classes only. *See, e.g.,* Tilley v. TSX Cos., Inc., 345 F.3d 34, 40 (1st Cir. 2003).

to other means of adjudicating the dispute. Though the Rule does not require that the class seek any particular form of relief, Rule 23(b)(3) class actions usually (but not always) involve claims for damages. (In fact, some people use the shorthand "damages class action" for a Rule 23(b)(3) class.)

The Rule 23(b)(3) class action is more controversial than the others. Classes certified under Rule 23(b)(1) and (b)(2) tend to involve fairly cohesive groups, simply because of the nature of the actions. Under Rule 23(b)(1), the class members are so closely related that adjudication of their claims individually will subject someone (either the defendant or the other class members) to some sort of harm. Classes under Rule 23(b)(2), by definition, involve members who have been subjected to the same treatment by the defendant. But the Rule 23(b)(3) class is held together only by common facts. Frequently, the class members just happened to be in the same place at the same time—perhaps travelers on an ill-fated flight or investors in an ill-fated venture. If they sued individually, the fact that some would win and others would lose would create none of the problems that underlie the need for the class action under Rule 23(b)(1) or (b)(2).

Because the Rule 23(b)(3) class tends to be a disparate group, the drafters imposed special procedural protections, which we address in §13.3.6. First, the court must give notice to all class members of the pendency of the class action, including individual notice to those who can be identified with reasonable effort. Second, class members have the right to "opt out"—to leave the class action and proceed on their own (or, perhaps, decide not to sue). These protections are required *only* in the Rule 23(b)(3) class action. In *Wal-Mart v. Dukes* (discussed above regarding the 23(b)(2) class action), the Court hinted that notice and the right to opt out are constitutionally required in classes seeking monetary relief. In this subsection, we focus on the two requirements for certifying a Rule 23(b)(3) class.

The Need for Predominant Common Questions. We know from Rule 23(a)(2) that all class actions have common questions; the existence of common questions among all class members is part of the definition of the class itself. In the Rule 23(b)(3) class, it is not enough simply to have common questions; instead, the "questions of law or fact common to class members" must "predominate over any questions affecting only individual members." This requirement does not mean that the class members must share *every* issue in the case. Indeed, it is hard to imagine a case in which every issue—of causation, harm, and damages, for instance—will be identical to all class members.

The operative language defining the Rule 23(b)(3) class was part of the 1966 amendment to the Rule. Interestingly, the Rules Advisory Committee responsible for the language concluded in its Notes that a "mass accident resulting in injuries to numerous persons [would] ordinarily not [be] appropriate for class action"[178] under Rule 23(b)(3). Why? The Committee pointed out that individual questions, such as damages, and possibly defenses raised against individual class members, would require individual resolution. "In these circumstances," the Committee concluded, "an action conducted as a class action would degenerate in practice into multiple lawsuits separately tried."[179] Reflecting these concerns, courts initially were reluctant to use the Rule 23(b)(3) class in mass tort cases. In the 1980s, however, as courts became increasingly crowded with mass tort litigation, many judges had a change in attitude, and some demonstrated creativity in adapting the Rule 23(b)(3) class action to mass tort situations. Doing so was relatively easier in cases involving a single cataclysmic event.

> ○ ***Example #26.*** An explosion of a gas main in an office building injures
> scores of people. All were hurt at the same time in the same general locale
> by the same thing. Thus, litigation *en masse* of many issues, including
> causation and other questions related to liability, would be economical.
> The individual damages suffered by each class member (which might
> vary radically) can be left to individual proceedings.[180]

Outside the scenario of the single cataclysmic event, it becomes more difficult to show that common questions will predominate over individual questions. For example, consider antitrust cases, in which the class attempts to demonstrate that the defendant's anticompetitive behavior (such as monopolizing a market) harmed them. This might require individual showings by each class member of the damage suffered. Such individual questions may overwhelm the common questions in the case, thus making it impossible to satisfy Rule 23(b)(3) that common questions predominate over individual questions.

An example is *Comcast Corp. v. Behrend*,[181] in which a consumer class alleged that Comcast had unlawfully "clustered" cable television providers in the Philadelphia area, thereby excluding companies that could have provided cheaper alternatives for cable service. The key

---

[178]Fed. R. Civ. P. 23, advisory committee's notes (1966).

[179]*Id.*

[180]*See, e.g.*, Sterling v. Velsicol Chem. Corp., 855 F.2d 1188, 1197 (6th Cir. 1988), in which the court upheld the trial court's certifying a Rule 23(b)(3) class action on its own motion. The court explained: "In mass tort accidents, the factual and legal issues of a defendant's liability do not differ dramatically from one plaintiff to the next. No matter how individualized the issue of damages may be, these issues can be reserved for individual treatment with the question of liability tried as a class action. Consequently, the mere fact that questions peculiar to each individual member of the class remain after the common question of the defendant's liability have been resolved does not dictate the conclusion that a class action is impermissible."

[181]569 U.S. 27 (2013).

question was whether the plaintiffs could show at the certification stage that (1) injury and (2) damages to class members could be demonstrated on a class-wide basis. They were not required to *prove* injury and damages themselves at certification — that would be done at trial. But they had to convince the judge now that when the time came at trial, there would be a way to show both of those on a class-wide basis. If they could not do that, they could not show that common questions predominated and therefore could not satisfy Rule 23(b)(3).

The plaintiffs attempted to meet the challenge by presenting expert testimony that injury and damages could be shown on a classwide basis. But there was a problem. The plaintiffs asserted four theories of antitrust impact on the class. The district judge rejected three of these and permitted the plaintiffs to proceed solely on something called the "overbuilder" theory (we don't need to know what that means — just that the court permitted the plaintiffs to proceed only on one of their four theories). But the expert testimony on damages was based upon all four of the original theories of antitrust impact; it was not limited to the "overbuilder" theory. The Court concluded that this disconnect between the theory of impact and the damages model was fatal.[182] Moreover, the lower court erred by refusing to allow the defendant to present evidence at the certification stage against the plaintiffs' proffered damages model.[183]

More recently, the Court upheld a classwide demonstration of damages in *Tyson Foods, Inc. v. Bouaphakeo*.[184] There, a group of employees at a meat-packing plant sued to recover compensation for time spent putting on and removing (donning and doffing) protective gear. The claims related only to overtime work, which required each employee to show that she had worked more than 40 hours per week, including time spent donning and doffing. Because the defendant had failed to keep records of time spent donning and doffing, the class presented representative evidence based upon an expert's videotaped observations, from which he averaged the times for various groups of employees. The Court distinguished the expert testimony rejected in *Wal-Mart*, discussed above in the penultimate paragraph concerning Rule 23(b)(2). In *Tyson Foods*, individual plaintiffs, suing individually, would be permitted to rely on the expert sample. Why? Because they were similarly situated. The class members in *Wal-Mart*, in contrast,

---

[182]*Id.* at 35 ("[A] model purporting to serve as evidence of damages . . . must measure only those damages attributable to [the 'overbuilder'] theory").

[183]*Id.* at 34. This holding further contributes to "front-loading" by requiring more extensive litigation early in the proceedings.

[184]577 U.S. 442 (2016).

could not have relied upon the representative evidence in that case, because each member's situation was different.[185]

The requirement of predominant common questions can be difficult to satisfy in toxic torts and other cases involving harm suffered at different places and at different times. For instance, consider hundreds of people harmed by an adulterated or defective product. Unlike injuries caused by a single cataclysm, here the harms are caused by hundreds of individual uses of the product. Still, Rule 23(b)(3) certification is not out of the question. One example is *Jenkins v. Raymark Industries, Inc.*,[186] one of thousands of cases concerning personal injuries caused by exposure to asbestos. Class members suffered different levels of harm caused by different levels of exposure to asbestos over different periods in different places. Yet all their claims shared at least one thing: the assertion by the manufacturer-defendants that they could not be held liable under the "state of the art" defense; the argument was that they could not be responsible because the state of scientific knowledge at the time did not alert anyone to the risks of asbestos. Because each defendant had raised this defense in each individual injury case already litigated, the court upheld a Rule 23(b)(3) class simply to litigate *that issue* for all concerned.

Jenkins is a good example of how it is easier to find predominance of common questions if one defines the class relatively narrowly. If one sees the class as all issues relating to the personal injury claims arising from asbestos exposure, there could be hundreds of individual issues. In this context, it is ridiculous to say that the common questions relating to the state-of-the-art defense predominate over individual questions. But if one defines the class as raising only the viability of the state-of-the-art defense, common questions obviously predominate; in fact, the common questions are the only questions.[187] And class determination of the defense can bring great judicial economy. If the defense is upheld, all class members lose. If the defense is not upheld, the individual claims can proceed, and the defendants—having lost on this key defense—cannot raise the defense again.

---

[185]*Id.* at 459 ("While the experiences of the employees in *Wal-Mart* bore little relationship to one another, in this case each employee worked in the same facility, did similar work, and was paid under the same policy"). In addition, the Court noted that, unlike *AT&T Mobility LLC v. Concepcion*, 563 U.S. 333 (2011) (discussed at note 286 below), reliance on representative evidence did not deprive the defendant of the ability to litigate individual defenses. Because the defendant failed to keep records of time spent donning and doffing, the only defense available was to attack the validity of the representative evidence, and this issue was common to every class member. *Id.* at 456-457.

[186]782 F.2d 468 (5th Cir. 1986).

[187]See "Issue Certification and Subclasses" later in this subsection.

Some trial courts have gone too far in forcing mass torts into the class action form. In the 1990s, several appellate opinions sent the message that trial judges had overreached in certifying mass tort class actions under Rule 23(b)(3). For example, in *In re Rhone-Poulenc Rorer, Inc.*,[188] the Seventh Circuit took the extraordinary step of issuing a writ of mandamus[189] to overturn the certification of a nationwide class action in a case concerning allegedly tainted blood products. In *Castano v. American Tobacco Co.*,[190] the Fifth Circuit reversed the certification of a nationwide class of nicotine-dependent persons numbering in the millions. The trial judge had failed to analyze whether or how any common questions predominated. Not only did the complaint purport to rely on nine causes of action, but variations from state to state made the finding of predominant common questions nearly laughable. Such overzealous efforts, while perhaps understandable in an era of crowded dockets, created inappropriate pressure on defendants to settle.

Superiority of the Class Action. The second requirement for certification of a Rule 23(b)(3) class is that the class action be "superior to other available methods for fairly and effectively adjudicating the controversy." The Rule lists four nonexclusive factors to aid in the assessment.[191] As a review of the factors reveals, the drafters clearly intended to force the judge to consider whether any other tools—joinder, multidistrict litigation under §1407,[192] consolidation, etc.—might be more readily managed than the class action. Under Rule 23(b)(3), the class action need not be *easy* to manage and administer; it rarely will be. It just has to be better than the other options. Clearly, the two requirements for a Rule 23(b)(3) class are closely related. If common questions do not predominate, manageability suffers. If the class can be defined with sufficient narrowness so that the common questions predominate, it might be relatively easy to manage.

---

[188]51 F.3d 1293 (7th Cir. 1995).

[189]As discussed in §14.6, mandamus is appropriate only when the lower court has erred so profoundly that it has, in effect, overreached its jurisdiction. Today, interlocutory appellate review of class certification decisions is available through Rule 23(f).

[190]84 F.3d 734 (5th Cir. 1996).

[191]They are: (1) the class members' interest in individual control over their case, (2) the extent and nature of related litigation already begun, (3) the desirability of concentrating litigation of the claims in a particular forum, and (4) the difficulties in managing the class action.

[192]Section 1407 allows the Judicial Panel on Multidistrict Legislation (a panel of federal judges appointed by the Chief Justice) to transfer related cases to a district of its choosing for consolidated pretrial proceedings.

§13.3.5 Filing and Certification of a Class Action (and Possible Appellate Review of the Certification Decision)

Putative and Certified Classes

We noted at §13.3.3 that a class action is started by filing a complaint in which the representative purports to sue on behalf of a class. At this point, though, it is merely a "putative" class. The case generally is not considered a class action until the court "certifies" it. Thus, in the absence of class certification, would-be members of the class are not bound by a judgment of the court or by the representative's actions.[193]

Under Rule 23(c)(1)(A), the court must make the certification determination "[a]t an early practicable time." The parties may have to undertake discovery to determine whether the requirements for class certification have been met. The representative may determine during this interval that the class definition set forth in the complaint can be honed or refined in ways to increase the likelihood that the court will grant certification; it is common for the class definition in the motion to certify to differ from that set forth in the complaint.

When the representative moves for class certification, she and the defendant will brief the certification issues for the court, and the court will entertain oral argument on the motion. The question for the court is whether the plaintiff has demonstrated that the case satisfies the prerequisites of Rule 23(a) and fits one of the types of classes recognized in Rule 23(b).

The certification decision is usually the watershed event in the litigation. If the court certifies the class, the defendant's incentive to settle the case will raise exponentially because the defendant now faces potentially enormous liability. On the other hand, if the court denies

---

[193]*See* Standard Fire Insurance Co. v. Knowles, 568 U.S. 588, 591-593 (2013) (putative members of uncertified class not bound by representative's attempted waiver of damages); Smith v. Bayer Corp., 564 U.S. 299, 307 (2011) (court, having denied certification, lacked authority to enjoin putative class members from pursuing class action in state court). The *Smith* case permits a second representative to seek class certification of the same class after a first representative's motion to certify was denied. Professor Redish criticizes this result. Martin H. Redish & Megan B. Kiernan, *Avoiding Death by a Thousand Cuts: The Relitigation of Class Certification and the Realities of the Modern Class Action,* 99 Iowa L. Rev. 1659 (2014). Professor Clermont argues that putative class members should be estopped from re-litigating the issue of class certification. Kevin M. Clermont, *Class Certification's Preclusive Effects,* 159 U. Pa. L. Rev. 203 (2011). Professor Wasserman has assessed judicial tools available to ameliorate duplicative litigation in the class context. Rhonda Wasserman, *Dueling Class Actions,* 80 B.U. L. Rev. 461 (2000).

certification, all that remains is the representative's individual claim. If that claim is sizeable, that individual litigation will proceed. If, however, the class was to have consisted of numerous persons who suffered relatively small harm (such as in a typical consumer class action), the case will probably be dismissed voluntarily; nobody will litigate over a few dollars. Accordingly, the motion for certification usually is the real battleground in the litigation. The parties throw significant resources into litigating the certification motion.

Possible Appellate Review of the Certification Decision

In Chapter 14, we will see that there is a right to appeal "final judgments" by a federal district court to a federal court of appeals. The court's determination of whether to certify the class is not a "final judgment," however, because it does not conclude the trial court's assessments of the merits of the case. Accordingly, there is no right to appeal that decision. Because the order is of such practical importance, however, courts of appeals long struggled to find some exception to the "final judgment rule" to permit appellate review of the order.[194] Their efforts did not lead to consistent treatment of the issue. The situation was remedied in 1998, with the promulgation of Federal Rule 23(f), which grants courts of appeals the discretion to review orders either granting or denying class certification. We consider that provision in §14.5.1.

Our purpose here is to note the effect this provision has had on the desirability of class litigation in federal court. When Rule 23(f) went into effect, many observers assumed it was a good thing for defendants and a bad thing for plaintiff classes. That is, observers assumed that federal appellate courts might be more willing to grant review under Rule 23(f) to reverse orders certifying classes than to reverse denials of class certification. Preliminary empirical work on the issue supports this assumption, at least based on early cases. A study based upon cases through 2007 found that 52 percent of the cases in which courts of appeals undertook review under Rule 23(f) resulted in reversals of class certification. Only 10 percent resulted in reversals of denials of certification.[195] Thus, in federal court, the

---

[194]One such effort was the "death knell" doctrine, which allowed appeal when denial of class certification effectively ended the litigation. This doctrine was rejected in *Coopers & Lybrand v. Livesay*, 437 U.S. 463, 470 (1978). In *Microsoft Corp. v. Baker*, 137 S. Ct. 1702, 1715 (2017), the Court rejected an effort of the class representative to raise denial of class certification on appeal from voluntary dismissal. See §14.5.1.

[195]Richard D. Freer, *Interlocutory Review of Class Action Certification Decisions: A Preliminary Empirical Study of Federal and State Experience*, 35 W. St. U. L. Rev. 13, 19 (2007). Perhaps these results are not surprising. Judge Posner has indicated that Rule 23(f) reflected "concern with asymmetric discovery burdens and the potential for extortionate litigation." Swanson v. Citibank, N.A., 614 F.3d 400, 411 (7th Cir.

grant of a motion to certify may be a short-lived victory for the plaintiff. Rule 23(f) allows the court of appeals to step in (if the defendant requests and the appellate court agrees to do so) and reverse. Because most states have not adopted Rule 23(f), class plaintiffs may prefer to litigate in state court. We will see in §13.3.9, however, that defendants have been given a powerful new tool to remove state court class actions to federal court.

Definition of the Class and Appointment of Class Counsel

If the district court grants certification, it enters an order that, under Rule 23(c)(1)(B), must "define the class and the class claims, issues, or defenses, and must appoint class counsel under Rule 23(g)." The order certifying a class is not necessarily permanent. Rule 23(c)(1)(C) expressly recognizes that an order regarding certification "may be altered or amended before final judgment." Thus, the court is able to react as the litigation unfolds, perhaps to alter the definition of the class or perhaps to "decertify" and forgo the class action altogether. This fact emphasizes a point made in §13.3.1: The court constantly monitors the class action, both to ensure that the interests of class members are adequately represented and to consider the continuing viability of class action status. For instance, maybe discovery will reveal that there are so few members in the class that a class action is not needed, and that each individual should sue on her own.

Unless a statute provides otherwise, the court certifying a class action must appoint class counsel. One prerequisite of any class action (see §13.3.4) is that the *representative* be able to provide fair and adequate representation of the class interests. For years, courts routinely also required that the *lawyer* for the class be an adequate representative. This requirement is now "codified" in Rule 23(g)(4), which provides that "[c]lass counsel must fairly and adequately represent the interests of the class."

Rule 23(g)(1)(A) lists various factors the court must consider in making the finding, including work undertaken by the lawyer in identifying and investigating the class claims, her experience in handling complex litigation, her knowledge of the applicable law, and the resources she will commit to representing the class. Rule 23(b)(1)(B) counsels the court to look to any other facts pertinent to the lawyer's ability to represent the class interests fairly and adequately. In practice, even before Rule 23 listed factors to be considered, courts had

---

2010) (Posner, J., dissenting). Judge Posner was speaking of pleading rules but made the point that the concern was "similar to that created by class actions, to which Rule 23(f) . . . was a response." *Id.*

long looked to matters such as the lawyer's experience in naming class counsel.[196]

Some observers criticize this focus on the lawyer's experience because it makes it difficult for new lawyers to "break in" to what seems to be a "closed shop." In other words, how is one to get the experience necessary to be a class counsel unless the court allows her to be class counsel? In fact, the same few law firms with great expertise in plaintiff class litigation seem to show up in cases around the country. Still, though the focus on expertise may make it difficult for newcomers to get experience, the focus is appropriate. Remember, the class will be bound by the outcome of the case, and that outcome will be determined more by the actions of the lawyer than those of the representative herself.

Rule 23(g)(2) provides detailed procedures for the appointment of class counsel.[197] Obviously, lawyers will covet this appointment, because class counsel (1) gets to call the shots in the litigation on behalf of the class and (2) will be paid, often a significant amount. If more than one lawyer applies for the appointment as class counsel, Rule 23(g)(2)(B) provides that "the court must appoint the applicant best able to represent the interests of the class." Even if there is only one applicant, the court must ensure that she satisfies the Rule 23(g)(1) and 23(g)(4) standard: fairly and adequately representing the interests of the class. The order of appointment may include any relevant "provisions about the award of attorney's fees or nontaxable costs under Rule 23(h)."[198]

"Issue Certification" and Subclasses

Not every issue in a class case must be litigated on a class basis. Significant economy of scale can be realized if some issues are determined *en masse*. Rule 23(c)(4) permits a case to "be brought or maintained as a class action with respect to particular issues." For instance, it might be possible to have a class determination of the defendant's liability. If the class loses that case on the merits, all class members are bound. If the class wins that case on the merits, all class members may then proceed individually to demonstrate their damages. Indeed,

---

[196]*See, e.g.,* In re Asbestos Litigation, 90 F.3d 963, 977 (5th Cir. 1996).

[197]Rule 23(g)(3) permits the court to appoint interim class counsel before determining whether to certify the class.

[198]Fed. R. Civ. P. 23(g)(1)(D). Rule 23(h) provides procedures for moving for an award of attorney's fees and nontaxable costs. Importantly, it does not create any substantive rights to recover these things. Thus, for example, attorney's fees are recoverable only if there is some exception to the general rule that each side bears her own attorney's fees.

courts may certify a class for litigation of a single issue; for instance, whether a particular defense applied to bar class members' claims.[199]

One important issue concerns how issue certification may be used in Rule 23(b)(3) classes. In those cases, common questions must predominate over individual questions. Can issue certification be used to "manufacture" such predominance? For example, suppose individual class members' claims will vary dramatically (because each person was exposed to different amounts of a toxin at different times and in different places, with different manifestation). Can a court nonetheless certify a Rule 23(b)(3) class on the issue of whether a particular defense bars all claims? If we look only at that issue, the common questions predominate because every class member will either be barred or not barred by the defense. But if we look at the entire litigation, common questions might not predominate because there are so many distinctive features to the damages suffered by each class member.

Initially, courts rejected certification in such circumstances.[200] Over time, however, the clear majority of federal courts of appeals have embraced issue certification to facilitate certification under Rule 23(b)(3).[201]

---

[199]*See, e.g.,* In re Agent Orange Prod. Liability Litigation, 818 F.2d 145, 151 (2d Cir. 1987) (personal injuries class concerning exposure to defoliant certified on "military contractor defense," which, if applicable, would have barred all claims); Jenkins v. Raymark Indus., Inc., 782 F.2d 468, 472-473 (5th Cir. 1986) (personal injuries class concerning exposure to asbestos certified, *inter alia,* on whether particular products were capable of producing dust sufficient to cause harm and whether defendant manufacturers should have been aware of the risk of cancer ("state-of-the-art" defense).

[200]A leading case taking this position was *Castano v. American Tobacco Co.*, 84 F.3d 734, 745 n.21 (5th Cir. 1996) ("A district court cannot manufacture predominance through the nimble use of subdivision (c)(4). The proper interpretation . . . is that a cause of action, as a whole, must satisfy the predominance requirement of (b)(3) and that (c)(4) is a housekeeping rule that allows courts to sever the common issues for a class trial").

[201]The Fifth Circuit overturned its holding in *Castano* on this point (discussed in the preceding footnote) in *In re Deepwater Horizon,* 739 F.3d 790, 806 (5th Cir. 2014). *See also* Valentino v. Carter-Wallace, Inc., 97 F.3d 1227, 1234 (9th Cir. 1996) ("Even if the common questions do not predominate over the individual questions so that class certification of the entire action is warranted, Rule 23 authorizes the district court in appropriate cases to isolate the common issues under Rule 23(c)(4)(A) and proceed with class treatment of these particular issues"). According to one survey, this is the overwhelming majority view, adopted in the First, Second, Third, Fourth, Sixth, Seven, Ninth, and Eleventh Circuits. Elizabeth Chamblee Burch, *Constructing Issue Classes,* 101 Va. L. Rev. 1855, 1892 (2015). Section 2.02(a)(1) of the American Law Institute's Principles of Aggregate Litigation (2010) supports issue certification when resolving a single issue will "materially advance the resolution of multiple civil claims by addressing the core of the dispute in a manner superior to other realistic procedural alternatives. . . ." *See generally* Myriam Gilles & Gary Friedman, *The Issue Class Revolution,* 101 B.U. L. Rev. 133 (2021) (suggesting that issue certification be used to certify

Rule 23(c)(5) provides that "a class may be divided into subclasses that are each treated as a class under this Rule." Subclasses can be used, for example, to avoid typicality and adequacy-of-representation issues.[202] They can help handle differences in law that may apply to different class members, as seen here.

> ○ ***Example #27.*** A class seeks recovery of punitive damages. Each state is free to determine the kinds of behavior that will give rise to a claim for punitive damages. In some, the plaintiff may have to show "willful misconduct." In others, perhaps the standard is "reckless disregard of the consequences of her actions." How can there be a class action if different plaintiffs must satisfy different substantive standards? For starters, the court might have an overall determination of the facts applicable to everyone — for example, whether the defendant in fact did certain things. If the court finds that the defendant did nothing of the sort alleged, the entire class claim would fail on the merits. On the other hand, if the court finds that the defendant did X, Y, and Z, the court might then divide the group into subclasses. For one, the litigation would focus on whether the defendant's actions constituted "willful misconduct." For the other, the question would be whether the acts showed "reckless disregard," and so forth.[203]

Can the Court Consider Evidence Relating to the Merits of the Case?

In ruling on the motion to certify, can the judge consider evidence relating the underlying merits of the case? For example, how can the court know if the representative's claims are "typical" of those of the class without looking at the merits of those claims? How can the court determine whether common questions predominate over individual questions without assessing the underlying facts of the dispute? On the other hand, doing so is troublesome, because assessment of the merits should await the adjudication phase of the litigation.[204]

Rule 23(b)(2) classes to seek declaratory judgment concerning defendant's liability, with separate litigation to determine damages for individual class members).

[202]In Example #17, for instance, there could be a subclass of Mexican American job applicants who were not hired, headed by a representative who suffered that harm and a separate subclass of Mexican American employees who were denied promotion, with a representative who suffered that harm.

[203]The court did something similar to this in *In re School Asbestos Litigation*, 789 F.2d 996, 1003-1004 (3d Cir. 1986). There, the court certified a nationwide class action and determined that state law on the relevant issues fit into a handful of approaches.

[204]Moreover, if there is a right to jury trial, a pretrial determination of the merits by the judge (in the certification motion) could raise a Seventh Amendment problem. Courts may avoid the problem by making clear that their findings made for purposes of the certification decision will not bind the jury if the case goes to trial.

Discovery from Class Members

Because class members are not parties, they are not subject to various Federal Rules directed at parties. For example, because interrogatories and requests to produce can only be served on parties to the case, the adverse party (usually the defendant) has no right to serve such requests on class members. On the other hand, the defendant may have a legitimate interest in obtaining information from class members. Courts have balanced this need against the fact that a class member is not a party, and have, on occasion, allowed limited discovery from class members. Because the class representative is a party, interrogatories and requests to produce may be proper as to them. Even here, though, the court will not hesitate to protect the representative from harassing or overly burdensome discovery requests. Nonparties may be deposed, as a general rule, and occasionally defendants attempt to take depositions of class members. Again, though, a court will protect class members from harassment and burden. As a general rule, depositions are taken only of class members who are expected to testify at trial.

One older but still instructive case about discovery from class members is *Brennan v. Midwestern United Life Ins. Co.*,[205] in which the court approved an order requiring that a cross-section of the class be required to answer questions under oath. Some class members took the position that they could not be required to give any information. They refused to comply with the court's order, despite warnings that the court would dismiss them from the class if they did not answer the questions. Upon further intransigence, the court dismissed them from the class. The Seventh Circuit affirmed their dismissal.

A Note About Class Remedies

A class may seek whatever remedies are permitted by the substantive law, including damages, injunctions, and declaratory judgments. Here we address a special remedy, the *cy pres* distribution. The *cy pres* doctrine developed in the law of trusts and estates. Suppose someone's will provided for distribution of money to a charitable organization. By the time the decedent died, however, that organization no longer existed. Under *cy pres*, which means "as near as possible," the court can designate another recipient for the gift. The substitution ensures

---

[205]450 F.2d 999, 1004-1005 (7th Cir. 1971). *See also* Jean-Louise v. Clear Springs Farming, LLC, 2015 U.S. Dist. LEXIS 109490 (M.D. Fla. 2015) (permitting defendant to serve interrogatories on class members, noting *inter alia* that the interrogatories requested "simple, non-technical" information that would "not require professional assistance to understand.").

that the gift will not fail and must be made to serve the same charitable purpose intended by the decedent.

In class litigation, the concept emerged in cases involving common funds. Here, the class litigation resulted (either by judgment or settlement) in a fund of cash to be distributed to class members. After all of the class members had recovered, suppose there is money left over. What does the court do with that money? Some people argue that it should be returned to the defendant. This may make sense under the compensatory goal of the law, because all class members have been compensated; it makes less sense, however, under the deterrent effect of the law, because the court ordered the defendant to pay the full amount. Other people argue that the money should escheat to the government. Many courts, however, borrowed the concept of *cy pres* and awarded the surplus to a non-profit organization that will advance the causes of the class. For example, in litigation for injuries caused by the use of tobacco, the court might order the surplus awarded to an organization dedicated to awareness of the harms of tobacco.

The controversial aspect of *cy pres* today is the "cy-pres-only" class, in which class members receive no recovery and the entire common fund created by the litigation (less attorney's fees for the class lawyer) goes to a non-profit organization. Though this practice has its defenders,[206] it raises fundamental questions. It is one thing to use *cy pres* to distribute surplus funds after class members have been compensated (which is the traditional use). There, the compensatory goal of the law has been satisfied. When class members receive no remedy whatever, the compensatory goal is not satisfied (though the deterrent goal may be).

Many *cy-pres*-only cases involve violations of statutes, such as those in the Telephone Consumer Protection Act, which create claims with statutory damages about things like unauthorized texts and errors in credit reports. For such claims to invoke federal jurisdiction, the plaintiff must have "standing" under Article III of the Constitution, which requires that she suffer a concrete injury in fact.[207] Even if class members have standing, can a judgment or settlement that awards all relief to an organization (which clearly does not have standing because it suffered no harm) constitute a "case" or "controversy"? Professor

---

[206]*See, e.g.,* Robert G. Bone, *In Defense of the Cy-Pres-Only Class Action,* 24 Lewis & Clark L. Rev. 571 (2020).

[207]*See, e.g.,* Transunion LLC v. Ramirez, 141 S. Ct. 2190 (2021) (only class members concretely harmed by a defendant's statutory violation have Article III standing); Spokeo, Inc. v. Robins, 136 S. Ct. 1540, 1553-1554 (2016) (remanding for consideration of constitutional standing). If the plaintiff lacks Article III standing, the dispute cannot constitute a "case" or "controversy" over which federal courts can exercise jurisdiction. The topic of standing is beyond our scope and is studied in detail in Constitutional Law.

Redish and others have argued that it does not.[208] Add to this the fact that most *cy-pres*-only classes are the results of settlements in which the defendant is given a significant voice in deciding on the organization to which the funds are awarded. Can a case that gives no remedy to class members be certified as a class action? Can a settlement on such terms be approved as fair and reasonable? The Supreme Court has given no meaningful guidance in the area.[209]

Tolling and the Statute of Limitations

We know that a case is not technically a class action until the court certifies it as such. Nonetheless, for some purposes, courts will treat the putative class as a class. The best example is the statute of limitations.

> o **_Example #28._** Representative files a class action on June 1. The relevant statute of limitations would run and bar the assertion of claims on June 15. Thus, the case was filed timely. The court denies class certification, however, in September. Now Connie, a member of the putative class, wants to assert her claim. Is she barred by the statute of limitations?

The answer depends upon whether Representative's filing of the class action on June 1 tolled (stopped) the running of the statute of limitations on June 1. Certainly, it did for Representative's personal claim, so that claim is timely. But what about the claims of class members? On the one hand, we might say the filing should not toll their claims, because the class certification was rejected. On the other hand, if the courts do not recognize tolling, all class members in our hypothetical would have to file individual suits before June 15 simply to protect their claims. Impressed by this latter practical point, the Supreme Court has held that filing of a class action tolls the statute of limitations for all class members, even if class certification is later rejected.[210] Thus, in Example #28, Connie has 14 days after the denial

---

[208]Martin H. Redish et al., *Cy Pres Relief and the Pathologies of the Modern Class Action: A Normative and Empirical Analysis,* 62 Fla. L. Rev. 617, 634-638 (2010).

[209]In *Marek v. Lane* 134 S. Ct. 8, 9 (2013), Chief Justice Roberts published a statement in a denial of *certiorari*, noting questions that the Court would someday need to address about *cy-pres*-only classes. The Court had an opportunity in *Frank v. Goas,* 139 S. Ct. 1041 (2019), but issued a *per curiam* remand with instructions to address the question of standing.

[210]Crown, Cork & Seal Co. v. Parker, 462 U.S. 345 (1983). This rule applies regardless of the basis on which class certification is rejected. For instance, suppose class certification is denied because the representative is inadequate. One might argue that such a representative should have no ability to toll the running of the statute for putative class members. The Court rejected such a notion, however, in favor of a clear, easily applied rule: Filing tolls the statute of limitations for all class members. *See generally*

of class certification in which to file her individual case.[211] On the other hand, pendency of a class action does not toll a statute of repose.[212]

§13.3.6 Notice to Class Members and "Opting Out"

Rule 23 has three provisions about notice. The first, found in Rule 23(c)(2)(B), is notice of the pendency of a class action, which applies *only* to Rule 23(b)(3) classes. The second, found in Rule 23(c)(2)(A), permits the court to give notice of the pendency of class actions under Rule 23(b)(1) and (b)(2). We discuss both of these (the first of which is far more important) in this subsection. The third, found in Rule 23(e)(1), concerns notice of a settlement or dismissal of a class action. It applies to all classes (not just Rule 23(b)(3) classes) and is discussed in §13.3.7.

We saw in the preceding subsection that the Rule 23(b)(3) class is more controversial than the other types because the group usually is bound only by common questions and not by any legal relationship. The claims of these members generally are independent of one another. As a result, the Rule 23(b)(3) class presents great stress between the desire for efficient resolution of numerous claims and the requirements of due process. To address this stress, the drafters imposed a notice requirement in Rule 23(b)(3) classes that simply does not exist

---

Rhonda Wasserman, *Tolling: The* American Pipe *Tolling Rule and Successive Class Actions*, 58 Fla. L. Rev. 803 (2006).

[211]This is because, in our hypothetical, Representative filed the putative class action on June 1, which was 14 days before the statute would have run (on June 15). Tolling means that the running of the statute was arrested on June 1. The statute starts to run again, however, as soon as the class certification is denied. The clock has 14 days left.

[212]California Public Employees' Retirement Sys. v. ANZ Secs., Inc., 137 S. Ct. 2042, 2051-2052 (2017). A statute of limitations is intended to ensure diligent prosecution of claims. A statute of repose serves a different purpose. It is intended to provide a defendant with an absolute bar: a time beyond which it cannot be held to account for an act. Statutes of limitations are ubiquitous. Statutes of repose are fairly rare. For example, suppose a medical malpractice claim has a statute of limitations of two years and a statute of repose of six years. In most instances, a statute of limitations is tolled (stopped) while the plaintiff is a minor. Assume the defendant committed medical malpractice when the plaintiff was ten years old. Under usual statute-of-limitations doctrine, the two-year statute of limitations would not start to run until the plaintiff turned age 18 (and thus was no longer a minor). Thus, under the statute of limitations, she could sue until age 20. But a statute of repose would cut the statute of limitations short by providing that in no event may the suit be filed more than six years after the claim arose. Thus, a statute of repose can cut short but can never extend the time permitted by a statute of limitations. *See generally* Stephen B. Burbank & Tobias Barrington Wolfe, *Class Actions, Statutes of Limitations and Repose, and Federal Common Law,* 167 U. Pa. L. Rev. 1 (2018) (tolling under *American Pipe* is an instance of federal common law and not "equitable tolling").

in the other class actions. Under Rule 23(c)(2)(B), the court is required to direct notice to class members, "including individual notice to all members who can be identified through reasonable effort." In *Wal-Mart v. Dukes*, which we discussed in §13.3.4, the Court hinted that notice and the right to opt out are constitutionally required in classes seeking monetary relief.

The purpose of this notice is to protect the members' individual interests. Rule 23(c)(2)(B) requires the notice to inform class members of these things: (1) the nature of the action; (2) the definition of the class certified; (3) the class claims, issues, or defenses; (4) that a class member may enter an appearance through her own counsel if she desires; (5) that a class member may request exclusion (and when and how members may elect to be excluded); and (6) that the class judgment will bind class members who do not properly request exclusion. Requesting exclusion has traditionally been called "opting out" of the class action, though the Rule does not use that phrase. This notice affirms to each class member that she does not have to depend on the class representative and class counsel to protect her interest. She can either request exclusion from the class and pursue her own remedy in a separate action (either alone or with others) or she can stay in the class but have her own lawyer act to represent her interests. If she fails to request exclusion, she will be bound by the class judgment.

Rule 23(c)(2)(B) requires that this notice be "the best notice that is practicable under the circumstances," including, as we said above, individual notice to those members who are identifiable with reasonable effort. This provision is more stringent than the Constitution would require. We saw in §3.2 that due process, interpreted in *Mullane v. Central Hanover Bank*,[213] requires notice "reasonably calculated, under all the circumstances, to apprise the parties of the pendency of the action. . . ." In addition, the Court spoke of giving "the best notice practicable."[214] In *Mullane* itself, however, the Court did not require individual notice to every person whose interest could be affected by the judgment, even if that person could be identified through reasonable effort. Nonetheless, in an appropriate abundance of caution, the drafters of Rule 23 require individual notice to those who can be identified reasonably. Such notice is usually given by mail, though nothing in the Rule specifies the manner in which it is to be given. It is not unusual to have some members who are reasonably identified and some who are not; in such a case, individual notice is given to those in the former group and publication notice, perhaps on websites, social media, in newspapers, or on television, is sufficient for the latter.

---

[213]339 U.S. 306, 314-315 (1950).
[214]*Id.* at 318.

Mailing individual notice to the reasonably identifiable class members can be an expensive proposition. Before the Supreme Court decision in *Eisen v. Carlisle & Jacquelin*,[215] courts occasionally would require the defendant to pay a percentage of the expense, based upon the court's assessment of the likelihood that the plaintiff class would prevail. *Eisen* rejected that practice, and the Court held that the expense of notice is a cost of litigation to be borne by the class representative. In other words, the court cannot impose any of that expense on the defendant at the outset. As a general rule, the loser is usually required to pay the winner's cost of litigation (as opposed to attorney's fees) once the case is completed. So should the class prevail, this cost will ordinarily be shifted to the defendant. Initially, however, the representative must foot the bill.

Eisen undoubtedly makes it more difficult to bring a class action. Many representatives are reluctant to advance the cost of notice, which may outweigh the value of their claims. In *Eisen* itself, the class asserted a securities claim in which Mr. Eisen personally would stand to recover about $70. The cost of notice was over $225,000. Very few representatives will put up $225,000 for the course of litigation on the hope of recovering that sum as a cost of successful litigation, plus his own claim of $70.[216]

The Rule 23(c)(2)(B) notice emanates from the court. Judges rarely write such notices themselves, however. Ordinarily, the court asks the lawyers for the two sides to suggest notice. Not surprisingly, these efforts can be slanted. The plaintiff class lawyer usually wants the notice to say something like "you are a member of a class that has been ripped off by the greedy defendant, and you are lucky that we will do the litigating for you and will send you a check when it's all done; so don't opt out." The defendant's lawyer wants the notice to say something like "you are a putative member of a putative class that some lawyer is trying to gin up to sue the poor defendant, and none of the allegations has been proved." From these extremes, the court usually requires the lawyers to work together to craft something both sides can live with. Unfortunately, the result is often unintelligible.

Professor Arthur Miller collected some telling responses to class notice from an actual case involving allegations that class members were overcharged for antibiotics.[217] The notice was the product of

---

[215]417 U.S. 156 (1974).

[216]One interesting issue is whether the class lawyer can advance the cost of notice for the representative. After wrestling with the issue, the American Bar Association has concluded that the lawyer can do so on a contingent basis. See §13.3.3 (subsection addressing Rule 23(a)(3) and 23(a)(4)).

[217]Arthur Miller, *Problems of Giving Notice in Class Actions*, 58 F.R.D. 313 (1972). The article is very amusing.

compromise, as described above, and attempted to tell the members the basics of the allegations. Class members were invited to respond with their opt-outs if they wanted to do so. In reading the responses below (which were actually received by the court), imagine how bad the notice must have been.

> Dear Mr. Clerk: I have your notice that I owe you $300 for selling drugs. I have never sold any drugs, especially those you have listed; but I have sold a little whiskey once in a while.

> Dear Sir: I received this paper from you. I guess I really don't understand it, but if I have been given one of those drugs, nobody told me why. If it means what I think it does, I have not been with a man in nine years.

> Dear Sir: I received your pamphlet on drugs, which I think will be great value to me in the future. I am unable to attend your class, however.

In an effort to combat the sort of "legalese" that typifies notice sent to class members, Rule 23(c)(2)(B) requires that the notice "clearly and concisely state [the required contents] in plain, easily understood language."

It is important to remember that the notice we are discussing here (of the pendency of the class action and of one's membership in the class) is *required* only in the Rule 23(b)(3) class action. For Rule 23(b)(1) and 23(b)(2) classes, no such notice is required. But Rule 23(c)(2)(A) does permit the court, in its discretion, to give notice in such cases. In addition, Rule 23(d)(1) gives the court great discretion in handling class litigation.

Can the lack of required notice in Rule 23(b)(1) and (b)(2) classes be constitutional? In §13.3.2, we noted that due process might be satisfied by providing notice or by ensuring adequate representation for the interests of class members. Rule 23 envisions a combination of these protections in the Rule 23(b)(3) class. On the other hand, the drafters apparently concluded, in view of the close relationship of most class members in Rule 23(b)(1) and (b)(2) classes, that adequacy of representation (without notice) satisfies due process. No serious argument to the contrary has been mounted.

As a practical matter, it is unthinkable that the Court would find the present provisions for binding members in mandatory classes unconstitutional. The Court showed its hand in this regard in *Wal-Mart v. Dukes*.[218] In rejecting the recovery of monetary relief in a Rule 23(b)(2) class (discussed at §13.3.4), the Court said:

[218]564 U.S. 338 (2011).

[Rule] 23(b)(2) does not require that class members be given notice and opt-out rights, presumably because it is thought (rightly or wrongly) that notice has no purpose when the class is mandatory, and that depriving people of their right to sue in this manner complies with the Due Process Clause. In the context of a class action predominately for money damages we have held that absence of notice and opt-out violates due process. [Citing *Shutts.*] While we have never held that to be so where the monetary claims do not predominate, the serious possibility that it may be so provides an additional reason not to read rule 23(b)(2) to include the monetary claims here.[219]

Thus, while not holding that due process requires notice and the right to opt out anytime a class seeks monetary recovery, the Court certainly hints in that direction. By implication, Rule 23(b)(1) and (b)(2) classes (which, after *Wal-Mart*, will rarely involve claims for money) can be bound by representation, without notice and opt-out.

§13.3.7　Judgment, Settlement, and Dismissal of a Class Action

A judgment in a class action binds all class members, except those who properly requested exclusion from a Rule 23(b)(3) class. This binding effect is expressly stated in Rule 23(c)(3).[220] Many class actions, however, do not go to judgment on the merits, but are settled or voluntarily dismissed.

In most civil litigation, the parties are free to settle the dispute on whatever terms they consider appropriate. Likewise, any plaintiff is free to dismiss her case voluntarily if she meets the requirements of Rule 41(a). The court generally plays no role in these matters. In the class action, however, things are different. Because of potential conflicts of interest, as we discussed in §13.3.1, Rule 23 does not permit the parties to settle or to enter voluntary dismissal of a certified class action alone. Rule 23(e) requires court approval. We emphasize at the outset that Rule 23(e) applies only if the court has certified the

---

[219]*Id.* at 363.

[220]One increasingly important issue is whether a class action judgment or settlement entered by a court in the United States will be enforced abroad. If the class includes significant numbers of non-U.S. citizens, the defendant may realistically fear that a judgment in its favor will not be honored in another country. Indeed, this lack of transnational binding effect may be a reason to deny certification of such a class action. For an insightful discussion of this topic, see Rhonda Wasserman, *Transnational Class Actions and Interjurisdictional Preclusion*, 86 Notre Dame L. Rev. 313 (2011).

class and only if the settlement, dismissal, or compromise affects class issues.[221]

Rule 23(e) was amended significantly in 2018. One goal, reflected in Rule 23(e)(1)(A), was to ensure that the parties proposing settlement provide to the court sufficient information from which it can assess "whether to give notice of the proposal to the class." This standard requires the parties to show that the court is likely to be able to approve the proposed settlement and to certify the class for purposes of the proposed settlement. If the parties fail to do so, the court rejects the settlement. If, on the other hand, the court gives its preliminary approval to the proposal, it will give notice as provided in Rule 23(e)(1)(B). The notice is given "in a reasonable manner," which can be by electronic means.

Under Rule 23(e)(5)(A), class members are permitted to object to the proposed settlement. The objection must be specific and must indicate the class members on whose behalf it is made. Rule 23(e)(5)(B)(i) forbids payment to an objector for withdrawing her objection (unless the court agrees). This provision recognizes the possibility that a party may try to "buy off" an objector for her silence. Similarly, Rule 23(e)(3) requires the parties seeking approval to identify "any agreement made in connection with the [proposed settlement, voluntary dismissal, or compromise]." This provision helps the court determine whether the representative is being "bought off" in a "side agreement," leaving the class members with less than appropriate relief.

After the time set for objections, the court will hold a "fairness hearing" under Rule 23(e)(2), at which it will determine whether the settlement should receive final approval. The settlement cannot be finally approved without such a hearing and without the court's conclusion that the settlement is "fair, reasonable, and adequate." That subrule provides factors to be considered in making this decision. The court considers not only the arguments of the parties in favor of the settlement but the views of objectors as well.

Under Rule 23(e)(4), the court may refuse to approve settlement of a Rule 23(b)(3) class action unless the settlement "affords a new opportunity to request exclusion to individual class members who had an earlier opportunity to request exclusion but did not do so." In §13.3.4, we saw that members of a Rule 23(b)(3) class have a right to request exclusion from the class (and thus to avoid being bound by class judgment). The right is afforded by Rule 23(c)(2)(B), which gives notice of pendency of the class action only in Rule 23(b)(3) classes. Rule 23(e)(4)

---

[221]Rule 23(e) expressly applies only to a "certified class" and not a putative class. It provides, in Rule 23(e)(1), that "[t]he claims, issues, or defenses in a certified class action may be settled, voluntarily dismissed, or compromised only with the court's approval."

permits such members a second right to opt out, one that comes up when the case is being settled. Thus, members of a Rule 23(b)(3) class who do not like the terms of the settlement are not bound by it and may request exclusion and sue on their own. Note that Rule 23(e)(4) does not permit the court to rewrite the proposed settlement to require this additional opportunity to opt out. Indeed, the court cannot rewrite the parties' proposal in any way. Its job is either to approve the proposal or to reject it.

Sometimes the lawyers will agree to settlement of a Rule 23(b)(3) class action before class members were notified of their inclusion in the class and right to opt out. In such a case, it is possible for the court to give hybrid or unified notice under Rule 23(c)(2)(B) and Rule 23(e): Class members are told that they are members of a Rule 23(b)(3) class and have the right to request exclusion, and that the case is provisionally settled on terms listed in the notice. Thus, each member can decide whether to request exclusion, to object to the terms of the settlement, or to accept the terms of the settlement.[222]

A "settlement class" is one that everyone knows will never go to trial. That is, before the representative even files the putative class action, the parties work out a settlement. In such a case, is it necessary for the court to go through the entire certification inquiry under Rule 23(a) and 23(b)? Or is it enough simply to go through the settlement approval procecdure in Rule 23(e)? In *Amchem Products, Inc. v. Windsor*,[223] the Court held that the court must certify the class before it can approve the settlement. The fact that the case will settle and thus not require a trial is relevant to the manageability of the class but does not justify wholesale ignorance of the requirements of Rule 23(a) and 23(b).

The holding in *Amchem Products* is salutary.[224] Without certification, the parties and the court are free to allow settlement of massive disputes that do not fit within any recognized form of litigation. By requiring certification, *Amchem* at least attempts to limit the court to acting within a properly constructed litigative unit. Because the case will settle, however, the certification decision of a Rule 23(b)(3) class need not assess whether trial would present difficult managerial

---

[222]Professor Wasserman discusses these "back-end" opt-outs and the interesting issue of whether the federal court which approved settlement may enjoin such a party from litigating in state court to an extent not allowed by the terms of the settlement. Rhonda Wasserman, *The Curious Complications with Back-End Opt-Out Rights*, 49 Wm. & Mary L. Rev. 373 (2007).

[223]521 U.S. 591 (1997).

[224]*See* Redish, Wholesale Justice, note 66 above, 206-227 (pre-certification settlement of class action violates the requirement of adverseness inherent in Article III).

problems (as required in Rule 23(b)(3)(D)), for the simple reason that there will be no trial.

§13.3.8 Jurisdiction and Related Issues

Personal Jurisdiction

The Supreme Court has rarely addressed the question of personal jurisdiction in a class action. In most cases, as we saw in our detailed consideration of personal jurisdiction in Chapter 2, the relevant question is whether the court has personal jurisdiction over the defendant. Indeed, the due process protections of cases such as *International Shoe v. Washington*[225] provide that a court may not enter a binding judgment *against* someone unless she has "minimum contacts" with the forum. Generally, there is no issue of personal jurisdiction over the plaintiff, because the plaintiff initiates the litigation and thereby submits herself to the personal jurisdiction of the court.[226] Thus, the plaintiff is bound by the outcome, even if it is negative.

In the class action context, however, the issue regarding plaintiffs may not be so clear. In the plaintiff class, the representative is a party and can be seen as having invoked the jurisdiction of the court. But the class members are not parties and did not choose the forum (or the representative or the class lawyer). Must they be subject to personal jurisdiction in the forum? The issue might not seem important if the class wins and the class members receive some benefit. But what if the class loses? The defendant has a right to expect that the class members are bound by the judgment and cannot sue her separately.

The Supreme Court addressed the topic, at least in one context, in *Phillips Petroleum Co. v. Shutts*,[227] a class action brought in a Kansas state court. The class consisted of 33,000 owners of royalty interests in gas wells. They claimed that the defendant had delayed paying their royalties and that they were entitled to recover interest on the delayed payments. The average claim of each member of the class was about $100. The class was certified under Rule 23(b)(3) (the Kansas class action rule mirrors the Federal Rule), and the court gave notice to the class members. About 3,400 opted out, leaving a class of over 29,000 members. Of these, however, only 1,000 were Kansas citizens. The defendant was concerned that the 28,000 non-Kansas class members

---

[225]We discussed this case in detail in §2.4.3.

[226]This is true even if the plaintiff lacked any contacts with the forum. Remember that personal jurisdiction is a waivable defense, and one who lacks minimum contacts with a forum may nonetheless submit to its authority. See §6.2.1.

[227]472 U.S. 797 (1985).

would not be bound by the judgment because they lacked minimum contacts with Kansas. If that were true, those 28,000 could sue the defendant separately if the defendant won the class action.

The Supreme Court held that all class members (even the 28,000 non-Kansas citizens) were bound by the judgment. Though it recognized that an adverse judgment would extinguish the claims of the class members, the Court emphasized the difference between defendants, who must have minimum contacts with the forum, and the plaintiff class members. A defendant faces significant burdens: She generally must hire an attorney in the forum, must participate in discovery, and faces liability for damages, possibly other relief and litigation costs (and maybe attorney's fees[228]) if she loses. In sum, "[t]hese burdens are substantial, and the minimum contacts requirement of the Due Process Clause prevents the forum State from unfairly imposing them upon the defendant."[229] In contrast, the member of a plaintiff class is not brought into court to face imposition of liability. Indeed, "[a] class-action plaintiff is not required to do anything. He may sit back and allow the litigation to run its course, content in knowing that there are safeguards provided for his protection."[230]

In view of these differences, the Court concluded that the class members' due process rights were protected by the state rule requiring individual notice to known class members and a right to opt out of the class. *Shutts* stands for the proposition that members of a Rule 23(b)(3) plaintiff class need *not* have minimum contacts with the forum state. Rather, their choice, after receiving notice, not to opt out constitutes their submission to the *in personam* jurisdiction of the forum.

This holding raises an interesting question. A class member will be bound by a class judgment unless she takes affirmative steps to opt out. But how does a court have the power to command such an affirmative act unless the person being commanded has minimum contacts with the forum? The Court did not explain how this could be so in *Shutts*.[231]

And *Shutts* leaves other unanswered questions. First, does the holding apply to Rule 23(b)(1) and (b)(2) class actions? The Court was

---

[228]The general rule is that the prevailing litigant recovers her litigation costs from the losing side. Absent an exception, however, each side bears her own attorney's fees. Thus, the losing defendant would routinely be expected to pay the plaintiff's costs but could be required to pay the plaintiff's attorney's fees if some exception to the general rule applied.

[229]*Shutts*, 472 U.S. at 808.

[230]*Id.*

[231]The Court did, however, reject the assertion that due process requires that class members opt in to be bound by the judgment. The provision for notice and a right to opt out satisfies due process. *Id.* at 812.

careful to limit its holding to a Rule 23(b)(3) class.[232] And, as noted, it relied heavily upon the fact that the class members did not opt out of the class in concluding that they had consented to *in personam* jurisdiction. There is no such opportunity to use consent as a basis for personal jurisdiction under Rule 23(b)(1) or (b)(2). Class actions certified under those rules are "mandatory": There is no right to opt out. Perhaps this means that members of mandatory classes should not be bound unless they have minimum contacts with the forum. But such a conclusion is contrary to the Court's emphasis in *Shutts* on the differences between plaintiff class members and defendants. It would, as a practical matter, make Rule 23(b)(1) and (b)(2) class actions much more difficult to bring. Moreover, as discussed in §13.3.2, it is likely that due process is satisfied in Rule 23(b)(1) and (b)(2) cases by adequate representation, without notice or the right to opt out.

Second, must there be minimum contacts over members of a *defendant* class? In *Shutts*, the Court made it clear that its holding did not address defendant classes.[233] Though defendant class members are not parties and may be "along for the ride," just as plaintiff class members are, they may be held liable for a judgment in favor of the plaintiff. Thus, it seems likely that only those defendant class members over whom the forum has *in personam* jurisdiction may be bound. Some courts have permitted judgments involving defendant classes so long as there is *in personam* jurisdiction over the representative, even if the other class members were not subject to jurisdiction.[234] These cases were decided before *Shutts*, however, and seem of doubtful validity today.

Finally, even with regard to a plaintiff class, did the Court in *Shutts* underestimate the possibility that the class might lose the case and class members might be asked to contribute to an award of defendant's costs (or, if justified, attorney's fees)? Suppose, for example, that the case is litigated and the defendant wins. The defendant would have a right, in the ordinary course, to recover her costs from the plaintiff. Should those costs be borne solely by the named plaintiff, or can she "pass the hat" to the class? The defendant raised this issue in *Shutts*, but the Court noted that it could find no case in which such an award has been made. It did not decide the issue.[235]

[232]In a footnote, the Court said it would "intimate no view concerning other types of class actions, such as those seeking equitable relief." *Id.* at 811-812 n.3.

[233]*Id.* at 811-812 n.3.

[234]*See, e.g.*, Dale Electronics, Inc. v. R.C.L. Electronics, Inc., 53 F.R.D. 531 (D. N.H. 1971); Canuel v. Oskoian, 23 F.R.D. 307 (D.R.I. 1959).

[235]*Shutts*, 472 U.S. at 810 n.2. Similarly, in cases in which the prevailing party may recover her attorney's fees from the losing party, there is a question of whether class members in an unsuccessful case could be required to contribute to the defendant's attorney's fees. The Court in *Shutts* did not address this question either.

Choice of Law

We just saw that *Phillips Petroleum Co. v. Shutts* held that members of a plaintiff Rule 23(b)(3) class who did not opt out had, essentially, submitted to the *in personam* jurisdiction of forum and thus were bound by the judgment. In the same case, the Court also addressed the choice of law rules in the plaintiff class. The class in *Shutts* contended that the defendant had delayed making royalty payments on gas leases, and that the class members were entitled to recover interest on the late payments. The legal interest rate for such claims may differ from state to state. Though the class included citizens of several states, the Kansas court applied Kansas law to determine the interest to be recovered by all 28,000 class members. The Supreme Court reversed this decision and held that the law of a state may apply only to parties who have some significant connection with that state. Accordingly, even though Kansas had personal jurisdiction over all class members, Kansas law could not be applied to claims of the non-Kansas class members.

This raises the possibility of subclasses. Indeed, in *Shutts*, the Court remanded with instructions to consider their use. For example, Texas citizens, as to whom Texas law would apply, could constitute one subclass, Oklahoma citizens another, and Kansas citizens another. The court would apply Kansas law only to the Kansas class members, Texas law to the Texas class members, Oklahoma law to the Oklahoma class members, and so forth. Though this procedure is undoubtedly complex, the use of subclasses would enable the Kansas court to achieve the kind of efficiency for which the class action was designed.

Subject Matter Jurisdiction

Like any claim in federal court, the claims asserted by a plaintiff class (or against a defendant class) must invoke federal subject matter jurisdiction. We discussed the principal bases of federal subject matter jurisdiction in Chapter 4. They included federal question jurisdiction and diversity of citizenship (including alienage) jurisdiction.

Federal Question Jurisdiction. A plaintiff class may invoke federal question jurisdiction by asserting a claim that arises under federal law. The jurisdictional rules for such cases (§4.6) apply in the class context. So if the claim itself (not an anticipated defense) arises under federal law, the class action may be heard in federal court, regardless of the citizenship of the parties and regardless of the amount in controversy. Many federal class actions invoke federal question jurisdiction.

○ ***Example #29.*** A class of investors who bought stock in reliance on a misleading corporate press release sues the corporation and appropriate officers, alleging that the press release violated federal securities laws. The class claims invoke federal question jurisdiction.

Diversity of Citizenship Jurisdiction. A class action might invoke diversity of citizenship jurisdiction. Here we discuss "regular" diversity of citizenship jurisdiction under §1332(a)(2). (In §13.3.9, we discuss the expanded subject matter jurisdiction provided by the Class Action Fairness Act.) Recall from §4.5 that in a "regular" diversity case, each plaintiff must be of a different citizenship from each defendant and the amount in controversy must exceed $75,000. In the class context, these requirements present a very straightforward question: In determining citizenship and the amount in controversy, to whom does the court look—to the representative or the class members?

The Class's Citizenship. In *Ben-Hur v. Cauble*,[236] the Supreme Court established that only the representative's citizenship must be diverse from that of the opposing party. In that case, representatives, who were not citizens of Indiana, sued an Indiana defendant. After judgment, the Indiana class members asserted that they were not bound, since they were not of diverse citizenship from the defendant. The Court rejected the argument. So long as the representative was of diverse citizenship from the defendant, diversity was established, and the judgment bound all class members, including those who were Indiana citizens.

The holding in *Ben-Hur* is enormously helpful from a practical standpoint because it makes the class action more readily available in federal court. A requirement that each class member must be of diverse citizenship from the opposing party would make it quite difficult to invoke diversity of citizenship jurisdiction in a class action. Though the Court in *Ben-Hur* did not discuss its holding in these terms, the case may well be seen as an example of supplemental jurisdiction. First, the representative's claim against the diverse opposing party invokes diversity of citizenship jurisdiction. Second, the claims of the class members seem sufficiently related to the representative's claim to invoke supplemental jurisdiction under *United Mine Workers v. Gibbs.*[237] Supplemental jurisdiction, of course, permits a federal court to entertain claims that do not satisfy diversity of citizenship, alienage, or federal question jurisdiction, and therefore would permit

[236]255 U.S. 356 (1921).
[237]We discussed the case at §4.7. The supplemental jurisdiction statute, §1367(a), codifies the *Gibbs* standard in its grant of supplemental jurisdiction.

the assertion of claims by class members who are not of diverse citizenship from the defendant.

The Court has never explained *Ben-Hur* in this way, however. Perhaps it is better simply to see the case as holding that, for purposes of subject matter jurisdiction, the representative is the only party on the class side, and thus the only one who must be diverse from the opposing party. The Court has never questioned its holding in *Ben-Hur*, which remains vital to this day.

> ○ ***Example #30.*** Representative, a citizen of Georgia representing a class consisting of citizens of Georgia and Alabama, sues *D*, who is a citizen of Alabama. Assuming the amount in controversy requirement is satisfied, diversity of citizenship is proper. Representative is diverse from *D*. It is immaterial that members of the class are not of diverse citizenship from *D* because only Representative's citizenship is relevant on the class side.

The Amount in Controversy. How should the court assess whether the amount in controversy requirement is satisfied in a diversity of citizenship class action? Again, here we discuss only a "regular" diversity case under §1332(a)(1), and not the quite different standards under the Class Action Fairness Act, which we see in §13.3.9. For starters, the Supreme Court established in *Snyder v. Harris*[238] that the aggregation rules applicable in diversity of citizenship cases generally also apply in the class action context. Those rules, which we saw at §4.5, provide that multiple plaintiffs generally may not aggregate their claims to satisfy the amount in controversy requirement.[239]

> ○ ***Example #31.*** The class consists of 100 members. Each class member has a claim of $760. The aggregate value of the claims is $76,000. This cannot satisfy the amount-in-controversy requirement, however, because class claims, under *Snyder*, cannot be aggregated. This is still the rule under §1332(a)(1).

Suppose, in contrast, that the representative's claim exceeds $75,000, but the class members' individual claims do not. This fact pattern is different from *Snyder*, because here the claim of the representative alone *does* meet the amount in controversy requirement. It is the same situation as in *Ben-Hur*, in which the representative's citizenship satisfies the jurisdictional rule, but those of the class members do not. Consistency with *Ben-Hur* would counsel that the court

---

[238]394 U.S. 332 (1969).

[239]Some courts say that there is an exception to this rule if the claim asserted is *joint* or *common*. As discussed in §4.5.3, however, these terms do not help much outside the property context.

look only to the representative in determining whether the amount in controversy is satisfied. Inexplicably, in addressing this issue, the Court ignored *Ben-Hur* altogether. In the unfortunate decision of *Zahn v. International Paper Co.*,[240] the Court held that the claim of *each* class member—individually—must meet the amount in controversy requirement.

The holding in *Zahn* cannot be reconciled with *Ben-Hur*: In determining citizenship, the court looks only to the citizenship of the representative, but in determining amount in controversy, the court looks to each class member. The inconsistency is odd, because both the complete diversity rule and the amount in controversy are statutory rules; neither is mandated by the Constitution, so there is no apparent reason for treating them differently. The majority opinion in *Zahn,* amazingly, failed even to address *Ben-Hur* or the possibility of supplemental jurisdiction.[241] The majority was fixated upon the problem of aggregation. But aggregation was not an issue in *Zahn,* because the representative's claim independently met the amount in controversy requirement. The result (and seemingly the intent) of the majority opinion was to make it more difficult to bring diversity of citizenship class actions in federal court. Commentators criticized the Court's effort in *Zahn.*[242]

But the effect of *Zahn* has been tempered by the supplemental jurisdiction statute, §1367. Shortly after the statute went into effect, commentators noticed that by its terms, the statute undermined the result in *Zahn,* at least in some cases.[243] Recall the structure of §1367 (discussed in §4.7). Section 1367(a) grants supplemental jurisdiction to the full extent permitted by the Constitution, which the Supreme Court determined in *United Mine Workers v. Gibbs* to include claims sharing a common nucleus of operative fact with a claim that invokes federal subject matter jurisdiction. So if the representative's claim invokes diversity of citizenship jurisdiction because the representative is of diverse citizenship from the defendant and her claim exceeds $75,000, §1367(a) grants supplemental jurisdiction over all appropriately related claims by class members, even if those claims do not exceed $75,000.

---

[240]414 U.S. 291 (1973).

[241]The dissent took the majority to task for this. *Zahn,* 414 U.S. at 302-312 (Brennan, J., dissenting).

[242]*See, e.g.,* 16 Moore's Federal Practice at 106-61 to 106-64.1; 7A Wright & Miller at 74-76; Thomas D. Rowe, Jr., *Beyond the Class Action Rule: An Inventory of Statutory Possibilities to Improve the Federal Class Action,* 71 N.Y.U. L. Rev. 186, 193-194 (1996).

[243]The first article to make this argument was Richard D. Freer, *Compounding Confusion and Hampering Diversity: Life After* Finley *and the Supplemental Jurisdiction Statute,* 40 Emory L.J. 445, 485-486 (1991).

Section 1367(b) then cuts back on the grant of supplemental jurisdiction, removing it over certain listed claims, but only in diversity of citizenship cases. Nowhere in the catalogue in §1367(b), however, did Congress mention claims asserted pursuant to Rule 23. Thus, by its terms, §1367 does what the Court in *Zahn* would not even address: grant supplemental jurisdiction over claims by class members that do not satisfy the amount in controversy requirement (just so long as the representative's claim does). Evidently, drafters of the statute belatedly saw the problem, and inserted into the legislative history a disclaimer of this result. Specifically, the one-sentence addition to the legislative history says that Congress "did not intend" to affect the result in *Zahn*.[244]

Courts were presented with a bizarre proposition: a statute that by its terms avoids the *Zahn* rejection of supplemental jurisdiction, but whose drafters say, in essence, "We didn't mean it." Commentators criticized the statute for creating what could only result in confusion. Three law professors who participated in drafting the statute, however, concluded that the one-sentence legislative history fixed the problem and saved *Zahn*.[245]

Predictably, confusion reigned. Six Courts of Appeals—the Fourth, Fifth, Sixth, Seventh, Ninth, and Eleventh Circuits—concluded that §1367 avoided *Zahn* and permitted supplemental jurisdiction over jurisdictionally insufficient claims by class members (again, assuming as the representatives did).[246] These courts reached the conclusion by applying fundamental tenets of statutory construction. First, the court consults the language of the statute. Second, only if that language is ambiguous or would lead to an absurd result does the court look to legislative history. Here, as noted above, the language of §1367 unambiguously grants supplemental jurisdiction. And the result of that language—that *Zahn* was avoided—was not absurd. Indeed,

---

[244]H.R. Rep. No. 734, H.R. Rep. No. 101-734, at 29 (1990).

[245]Thomas Rowe, Stephen Burbank & Thomas Mengler, *Compounding or Creating Confusion About Supplemental Jurisdiction? A Reply to Professor Freer*, 40 Emory L.J. 943, 960 n.1 (1991).

[246]*See* Olden v. Lafarge Corp., 383 F.3d 124 (6th Cir. 2004); Allapattah Servs., Inc. v. Exxon Corp., 333 F.3d 1248, 1253-1254 (11th Cir. 2003), *rehearing en banc denied*, 362 F.3d 739 (2004), *cert. granted*, 543 U.S. 927 (2005); Rosmer v. Pfizer, Inc., 263 F.3d 110, 114-119 (4th Cir. 2001); Gibson v. Chrysler Corp., 261 F.3d 927, 933-940 (9th Cir. 2001); In re Brand Name Prescription Drugs Antitrust Litigation, 123 F.3d 599, 607 (7th Cir. 1997); In re Abbott Laboratories, 51 F.3d 524, 527-529 (5th Cir. 1995), *aff'd by an equally divided court*, 529 U.S. 333 (2000). In the latter case, the Court granted *certiorari* to resolve the issue. Justice O'Connor recused herself from the case, and the remaining Justices split four-to-four. Thus, the Court affirmed the lower court opinion without opinion. Such a disposition by the Supreme Court has no precedential value.

given the criticism of *Zahn*, avoiding it made good sense. Accordingly, these six courts refused to address, let alone be bound by, the legislative history.

On the other hand, four other Courts of Appeals—the First, Third, Eighth, and Tenth Circuits—concluded that the supplemental jurisdiction statute did not avoid the *Zahn* holding that each class member's claim must exceed $75,000.[247] The Eighth Circuit opinion on this point was dicta, because in that case the representative's claim did not exceed $75,000 and thus failed to invoke diversity of citizenship jurisdiction as a preliminary manner.[248] The Tenth Circuit reached its conclusion by adopting a theory that a court does not obtain "original jurisdiction" over a diversity of citizenship case unless it has subject matter jurisdiction over *each* claim in the case.[249] Because a court lacks independent subject matter jurisdiction over the claims by class members that do not exceed $75,000, the theory goes, it would have no subject matter jurisdiction over any claim—not even the representative's claim. Thus, no claim is properly in federal court.[250] The Third Circuit justified its holding by resorting to the legislative history.[251]

The Supreme Court resolved this lamentable split of authority in *Exxon Mobil Corp. v. Allapattah Servs., Inc.*,[252] which reversed the First Circuit's handling of the issue and upheld supplemental jurisdiction. The Court adopted the reasoning of the majority of Courts of Appeals—that the result was clear from the face of the statute, and that legislative history is not available to alter that result unless the statutory language compels an absurd result. The Court criticized drafters of the statute for "a *post hoc* attempt"[253] to alter the result compelled by the statutory language. In stinging language, the Court said: "One need not subscribe to the wholesale condemnation

---

[247]*See* Ortega v. Star-Kist Foods, Inc., 370 F.3d 124 (1st Cir. 2004), *reversed,* Exxon Mobil Corp. v. Allapattah Servs., Inc., 545 U.S. 546 (2005); Trimble v. ASARCO, Inc., 232 F.3d 946, 961-962 (8th Cir. 2000); Meritcare, Inc. v. St. Paul Mercury Ins. Co., 166 F.3d 214, 218-222 (3d Cir. 1999); Leonhardt v. Western Sugar Co., 160 F.3d 631, 637-641 (10th Cir. 1998).

[248]*Trimble,* 232 F.3d at 964-965. Accordingly, the court had no occasion to discuss the supplemental jurisdiction issue.

[249]The theory was proposed in James E. Pfander, *Supplemental Jurisdiction and Section 1367: The Case for a Sympathetic Textualism,* 148 U. Pa. L. Rev. 109 (1999).

[250]*Leonhardt,* 160 F.3d at 637-641. This reasoning has not been adopted in any other appellate holding and was criticized by the opinions of the Fourth and Ninth Circuits. It is defended in James Pfander, *The Simmering Debate Over Supplemental Jurisdiction,* 2002 U. Ill. L. Rev. 1209 (2002).

[251]*Meritcare,* 166 F.3d at 21-22.

[252]545 U.S. 546 (2005). In a companion case, the Court addressed the analogous issue in the nonclass context, as we discussed in §12.4.

[253]545 U.S. at 570.

of legislative history to refuse to give any effect to such a deliberate effort to amend a statute through a committee report."[254]

The Court also rejected the theory that the district court does not obtain original jurisdiction over the case unless each and every claim asserted satisfies the amount in controversy.[255] (The Court was unwilling, however, to let supplemental jurisdiction overcome the complete diversity rule. (We discussed this at §12.4.)) It is worth noting that the holding in *Zahn*—that a class can invoke diversity of citizenship jurisdiction only if the claim of each member exceeds $75,000—remains good law. What *Allapattah* and §1367 do is recognize that the representative's jurisdictionally sufficient claim invokes diversity jurisdiction (and gets the case into federal court), *after which* supplemental jurisdiction can be exercised over members' jurisdictionally insufficient claims.[256]

> o ***Example #32.*** Representative sues on behalf of a class of purchasers of a product, alleging violation of state antitrust laws. By statute, each class member's claim is limited to $20,000. Representative, however, is entitled to seek recovery of attorney's fees, so her claim exceeds $75,000. The representative's citizenship is diverse from that of the defendant. Can this class action proceed in federal court?

The answer is clear under *Allapattah*. First, Representative's claim invokes diversity of citizenship jurisdiction; she is of diverse citizenship from the defendant and her claim exceeds $75,000. Second, the claims by class members do not satisfy the requirements of diversity of citizenship jurisdiction because they do not exceed $75,000. Third, the claims by the class members invoke supplemental jurisdiction under §1367(a) because they arise from a common nucleus of operative fact with Representative's claim (if this point is fuzzy, see §4.7). Fourth, though §1367(b) applies in cases that invoke diversity of citizenship jurisdiction, as this one did, it does not remove supplemental jurisdiction over claims asserted under Rule 23.

Though the Supreme Court has resolved a pointed split among the circuits, another problem lurks. Specifically (and oddly), §1367 may only permit supplemental jurisdiction in cases involving a single defendant. Section 1367(b), which applies only in diversity of citizenship cases, removes supplemental jurisdiction over claims joined "by plaintiffs against persons made parties under Rule . . . 20." Rule 20 is the provision allowing joinder of multiple plaintiffs or defendants.

---

[254]*Id.*

[255]*Id.* at 559-567.

[256]The point may be significant because, as seen in §4.7, the exercise of supplemental jurisdiction is discretionary and may be declined in circumstances found in §1367(c).

If a plaintiff class action were asserted against multiple defendants (joined, obviously, under Rule 20), this provision of §1367(b) would deprive the court of supplemental jurisdiction over the claims by class members.[257] There is no definitive interpretation of this Rule 20 issue. So at the end of the day, the wasteful litigation spawned by this poorly drafted statute may not be ended.

Venue

There is no special venue provision for class actions. Thus, unless the case involves a claim for which there is a special venue provision, the general venue statute, 28 U.S.C. §1391, will apply. Recall from Chapter 5 that the general choices for venue are any district where all defendants reside or in which a substantial part of the claim arose.

§13.3.9   The Class Action Fairness Act (CAFA) and Trends in Aggregate Litigation

Background

Concerns about perceived abuses of the class action came to a head in 2005, when Congress passed the Class Action Fairness Act (CAFA). Major corporate interests had long lobbied for such a bill, the purpose of which is to channel large interstate class actions from state to federal courts. CAFA does so by relaxing federal subject matter jurisdiction and by providing defendants with liberal rights to remove class actions from state to federal court.

Speaking generally, there is (or certainly was in the early 2000s) a widespread perception that it was more difficult to pursue class litigation in federal court than in many state courts. Even though most states have adopted the core of Federal Rule 23 as their class rule, various factors may impel a plaintiff class lawyer to file in state court.

First, in decisions such as *Amchem Products, Inc. v. Windsor* (see §13.3.7) and *Ortiz v. Fibreboard Corp.* (see §13.3.5), the Supreme Court imposed the Rule 23 requirements with particular strictness.[258] State courts are not bound to interpret their class rule in the same

---

[257]The Fifth Circuit did not address this point in *Abbott Laboratories*, note 246 above. It should have done so, since the case involved multiple defendants joined under Rule 20. The Supreme Court did not decide the issue in *Allapattah*, note 252 above.

[258]In *Amchem*, 521 U.S. 591 (1997), the Court required full compliance with Rule 23(a) and (b) even in a class formed for settlement purposes. In *Ortiz*, 527 U.S. 815 (1999), the Court rendered it particularly difficult to satisfy the requirements of a particular type of class action. For an excellent discussion of these factors and overview of CAFA, *see* Georgene M. Vairo, *Class Action Fairness Act of 2005* (LexisNexis 2005).

way. Second, in federal court, Rule 23(f) permits immediate appellate review of class certification decisions. As we saw in §13.3.5, this Rule has been used primarily to reverse class certifications; it is thus seen as anti-plaintiff. Few states have adopted Rule 23(f). Third, federal court pleading under *Twombly* and *Iqbal* (see §7.3.2) may be more rigorous than state pleading. Fourth, there is a sense that summary judgment is more readily available in federal court than in state court, based in large measure on cases decided by the Supreme Court in 1986 (see §9.4). Fifth, as a matter of proof at trial, in cases involving expert evidence (which includes many class actions), federal courts appear less hospitable to plaintiffs than some state courts.[259] After *Wal-Mart v. Dukes,*[260] the federal requirements for admission of expert witness testimony at trial apparently apply at the class certification stage in federal court (see §13.3.5).

These hurdles in federal court may make state court more attractive, particularly in those states that developed reputations for being pro-plaintiff and for certifying class cases quite freely (sometimes called "drive-by certification"). Without doubt, some state courts permitted abuse in class actions. Much of the abuse consisted of approving sweetheart deals and coupon settlements, which lined the pockets of plaintiff's counsel while affording little relief for the class members. These courts failed to provide meaningful judicial oversight.

In passing CAFA, Congress made express findings that some state court handling of class suits had "harmed class members with legitimate claims and defendants that have acted responsibly," and had "undermined public respect for our judicial system."[261] In response, it opened the doors to federal court to an unprecedented degree—not only for class actions but for "mass actions," which are nonclass cases joined for trial and involving 100 or more plaintiffs.[262]

Proponents of CAFA praise it as a vehicle to have the federal courts take over large interstate disputes and, *inter alia,* "to assure fairer outcomes for class members and defendants."[263] Critics decry the Act

---

[259]This impression is based upon *Daubert v. Merrell Dow Pharmaceuticals,* 509 U.S. 579 (1993), which imposed strict requirements for the admission of expert scientific testimony in federal court. The holding has since been expanded to cover all expert witnesses, and not just those presenting scientific evidence. Kumho Tire Co. v. Carmichael, 526 U.S. 137 (1999).

[260]564 U.S. 338 (2011).

[261]28 U.S.C. §1711(a)(2).

[262]28 U.S.C. §1332(d)(11). This section treats such mass actions as class actions, and is based upon the practice of some state courts to allow hundreds of plaintiffs to join in a single case. *See generally* Linda S. Mullenix, *Class Actions Shrugged: Mass Actions and the Future of Aggregate Litigation,* 32 Rev. Litig. 591, 599 (2013); Vairo, *Class Action Fairness Act,* note 258 above, at 32-33.

[263]CAFA, Sen. 5, 109th Cong. (2005), *quoted in* Vairo, *Class Action Fairness Act,* note 258 above, at 4.

as inimical to the interests of federalism. It expresses lack of faith in state courts and allows state court defendants to get class actions funneled into federal court, where it is often more difficult for plaintiffs to prevail. Thus, critics assert, CAFA is seen not as providing a mere change of forum for class suits, but as a means of effectively denying access to the class device. If this is right, Congress essentially enacted tort reform in the guise of jurisdictional legislation.[264] Whatever one thinks of CAFA, it clearly works a profound reallocation of judicial authority in large interstate cases and ensures that state courts will play a less important role in such disputes than they have historically.

Statutory Provisions

CAFA is complicated. Our purpose is to sketch the broad outline of the Act, to demonstrate how it facilitates access to federal court. Provisions of CAFA are spread throughout Title 28 of the United States Code. Section 1711 contains definitions for the Act. Section 1712 defines "coupon settlements," and requires that when a proposed settlement of a class action in federal court provides coupons for class members, the attorney's fee attributable to the award of coupons must be based upon the actual value of the coupons to the class members. This provision, at §1712(a), is intended to avoid the award of large counsel fees to lawyers who procure for the class coupons that are essentially worthless. The remainder of §1712 deals with other matters relating to attorney's fee awards and judicial scrutiny of coupon settlements.[265] Section 1713 addresses settlements in which a class member is required to pay class counsel, resulting in a net loss to the class member. Such settlements can be approved "only if the court makes a written finding that nonmonetary benefits to the class member substantially outweigh the monetary loss." Section 1714 prohibits approval of a settlement that discriminates in favor of class members geographically situated closer to the court than others. Section 1715, a very detailed provision, is aimed at requiring notification of a federal officer (usually the attorney general) and a state officer of a proposed settlement of a case. The court cannot approve final settlement of a case under CAFA earlier than 90 days after such notice is given. The

---

[264]*See generally* Stephen B. Burbank, *The Class Action Fairness Act of 2005 in Historical Context: A Preliminary View,* 156 U. Pa. L. Rev. 1439 (2008).

[265]There is a rather abiding perception among some that class action settlements unfairly line the pockets of lawyers at the expense of class members. In one empirical study of federal class settlements, attorney's fee awards averaged about 15 percent of the settlement fund. Brian T. Fitzpatrick, *An Empirical Study of Class Action Settlements and Their Fee Awards,* 7 J. Empirical Legal Stud. 811 (2010).

purpose of §1715 is to allow governmental input on the desirability of the settlement.

The most important aspect of CAFA is its addition of §1332(d).[266] Section 1332(d)(1) defines various terms, including *class action*, which is a case "filed under rule 23 of the Federal Rules of Civil Procedure or similar State statute or rule. . . ." That subsection also defines *class certification order* as one "issued by a court approving the treatment of some or all aspects of a civil action as a class action." Section 1332(d)(5)(B) requires that there be at least 100 members in the class.

The core of CAFA is the grant of subject matter jurisdiction in §1332(d)(2). The amount in controversy is one that "exceeds the sum or value of $5,000,000, exclusive of interest and costs." According to §1332(d)(6), this figure is determined by aggregating the claims of all class members. Thus, CAFA represents a radical departure from the method of determining amount in controversy in a "regular" diversity of citizenship class action, which we discussed in §13.3.8. Recall that in a diversity class action, claims of the members generally cannot be aggregated.

As to citizenship, CAFA requires a class action in which any of three things is true:

1. Under §1332(d)(2)(A), "any member of a class of plaintiffs is a citizen of a State different from any defendant"; or
2. Under §1332(d)(2)(B), "any member of a class of plaintiffs is a foreign state or a citizen or subject of a foreign state and any defendant is a citizen of a State"; or
3. Under §1332(d)(2)(C), "any member of a class of plaintiffs is a citizen of a State and any defendant is a foreign state or a citizen or subject of a foreign state."

As with §1332(a), the capitalized use of "State" refers to a state of the United States; the uncapitalized use of the word refers to a foreign country. The most significant provision is §1332(d)(2)(A). It requires merely that a single member of the class be of diverse citizenship from any defendant. This provision is far broader even than the practice permitted under the *Ben-Hur* case in "regular" diversity cases (see §13.3.8). Under that case, the *representative* of the class must be diverse from *every* defendant. Under CAFA, however, a case invokes subject matter jurisdiction even if the representative and

---

[266]The provision previously found at §1332(d), which provides that the District of Columbia and other federal enclaves are to be considered "States" for purposes of diversity of citizenship jurisdiction, was re-enacted at §1332(e).

the defendant are cocitizens—so long as *some* member of the class is diverse from a defendant. Obviously, and unlike in a "regular" diversity case, the complete diversity rule does not apply. So long as a class member is diverse from *any* defendant, the statute is satisfied.[267]

Is the broad CAFA grant of subject matter jurisdiction constitutional? We know that the Supreme Court upheld the minimal diversity provision of the Federal Interpleader Act in *State Farm Fire & Cas. Co. v. Tashire*, in which the Court held that "Article III poses no obstacle to the legislative extension of federal jurisdiction, founded on diversity, so long as any two adverse parties are not cocitizens."[268] So our immediate reaction may be that CAFA is constitutional. The point might not be clear, however. The rationale underlying diversity jurisdiction is that a federal forum reduces the risk to noncitizen litigants of being sued in a state court. Congress did not rely on this, however, in passing CAFA. Instead, it justified the Act by pointing to efficiency and to an interstate commerce interest in national class actions. Some scholars debate whether these bases fit the purposes of the diversity grant in Article III.[269]

Though plaintiffs can invoke CAFA, the real impact of the Act comes from §1453, which permits removal of cases under §1332(d)(1). Here, too, Congress has reached far beyond what it has done in "regular" diversity cases. In §4.8, when we discussed removal of such a diversity case invoking §1332(a)(1), we saw that (1) removal was not permitted if any defendant was a citizen of the forum, and (2) generally, no diversity case could be removed more than one year after the case was filed in state court. Neither of these restrictions applies, however, in removal of cases invoking CAFA.

○ ***Example #33.*** *P*, a citizen of Alabama, is named the representative of a class action filed in Alabama state court. The aggregate claims of the members exceed $5,000,000. Class members are citizens of Alabama, Mississippi, and Georgia. The complaint names five defendants, one of which is a citizen of Alabama.

---

[267]Congress also has permitted jurisdiction based upon minimal diversity in the Multiparty, Multiforum Trial Jurisdiction Act (MMTJA), the principal jurisdictional provision of which is §1369. MMTJA concerns cases in which at least 75 people are killed in an "accident" at a "discrete location." It has special venue and service of process provisions as well as very broad removal provisions in §1441(e). *See generally* 7 Wright & Miller §1659.

[268]386 U.S. 523, 531 (1967). See §13.2.2.

[269]*See* Burbank, note 264, above, at 156 U. Pa. L. Rev. 1527-1528; C. Douglas Floyd, *The Inadequacy of the Interstate Commerce Justification for the Class Action Fairness Act of 2005,* 55 Emory L.J. 487, 500-507 (2006); James Pfander, *Protective Jurisdiction, Aggregated Litigation, and the Limits of Article III*, 95 Cal. L. Rev. 1423, 1453-1454 (2007).

The defendants cannot remove this case under the regular provisions applicable to diversity of citizenship cases. First, there is no diversity because the representative is not of diverse citizenship from all defendants. Second, one of the defendants is a citizen of the forum, which defeats removal under §1446(b).

Under CAFA, however, diversity is satisfied because at least one class member is of diverse citizenship from at least one defendant. And the restriction of §1446(b)—precluding removal if a defendant is a citizen of the forum—does not apply under CAFA. The case can be removed to federal court in Alabama.

This broad grant is tempered, however, by three exceptions. First, §1332(d)(3) is a "discretionary" provision that permits (but does not require) the court to decline jurisdiction "in the interests of justice and looking at the totality of the circumstances." This provision applies only if (1) more than one-third but fewer than two-thirds of the members of the class and (2) the "primary defendants" are citizens of the state in which the case was filed. The provision lists six factors to be considered in determining whether to decline jurisdiction, including whether the case involves "matters of national or interstate interest." By implication, a class action involving local interests should proceed in state court.

Second, §1332(d)(4) sets forth the "local controversy" exception, which requires the court to decline jurisdiction if (1) more than two-thirds of the class members and (2) at least one defendant from whom "significant relief" is sought, whose "alleged conduct forms a significant basis" for the claims are citizens of the forum.

Third, §1332(d)(4)(B) embodies the "home state" exception, which requires the court to decline jurisdiction if (1) more than two-thirds of the class members and (2) the "primary defendants" are citizens of the forum.

These exceptions are difficult to apply, in part because terms like *"primary defendants"* and *"significant relief"* are not self-defining. Moreover, how is the court to determine whether one-third or two-thirds of the class members are citizens of a particular state?[270] The jurisdictional inquiry is made early in the case, before such details about the class may be known. Some courts have concluded that whether the "significant relief" and "conduct forms a significant basis" requirements of the "local controversy" exception are met is to

---

[270]Some courts conclude that the two-thirds requirement in the "home state" exception refers to two thirds of the members of the present class, and not two thirds of all plaintiffs in related actions. *See, e.g.,* In re Sprint Nextel Corp., 593 F.3d 669, 672 (7th Cir. 2010); In re Hanaford Bros. Co. Customer Data Security Breach Litigation, 564 F.3d 75, 78-79 (1st Cir. 2009).

be determined from the pleadings, without discovery.[271] On the other hand, the citizenship of parties is subject to discovery.[272]

There are also significant questions about which party has the burden of proof in cases removed from state court. In *Preston v. Tenet Healthsystems Memorial Med. Ctr., Inc.*, the court concluded, reasonably it seems, that the defendant has the initial burden of showing that the basic CAFA requirements are satisfied.[273] Thereafter, the party seeking remand on the basis of one of the three exceptions to CAFA jurisdiction bears the burden of demonstrating that the exception is satisfied.[274]

Finally, CAFA recognizes something called a "mass action," which is addressed in §1332(d)(11) and which is a case "in which monetary relief claims of 100 or more persons are proposed to be tried jointly on the ground that the plaintiffs' claims involve common questions of law or fact." This provision is aimed at the practice in some state courts of permitting joinder of hundreds of plaintiffs in a single case, without certification as a class action.[275] Such cases can invoke subject matter jurisdiction on the same bases as class actions under CAFA. They also can be removed on the same bases. CAFA contains a staggering array of other provisions in §1332(d), including exceptions for certain securities claims and for cases involving internal affairs or governance of a corporation, and definitions and rules for determining citizenships of various litigants. It is controversial and seems aimed at permitting defendants to get virtually any large, truly interstate class action or mass action into federal court. There, the critics argue, the relatively high procedural hurdles for such cases will make it difficult and often impossible to proceed with litigation *en masse*. That being the case, they assert, CAFA fosters channeling complex cases into the federal court system, where they will fail. Without doubt, CAFA skews the

---

[271]*See* Coleman v. Estes Express Lines, Inc., 631 F.3d 1010, 1019-1020 (9th Cir. 2011); Coffey v. Freeport McMoran Copper & Gold, 581 F.3d 1240, 1245 (10th Cir. 2009); Kaufman v. Allstate N.J. Ins. Co., 561 F.3d 144, 157 (3d Cir. 2009). The Eleventh Circuit has looked at extrinsic evidence on the "significant basis" element, though it failed to address why or whether the evidence was properly considered. Evans v. Walter Indus., Inc., 449 F.3d 1159, 1167-1168 (11th Cir. 2006).

[272]*See Coleman*, 631 F.3d at 1015-1016. The court noted that the statute speaks of defendants from whom "significant relief is sought" and concluded that this relates to what has been pleaded. In contrast, the statute speaks of the state where the defendant "is a citizen," which implies that it is a fact to be established by proof.

[273]485 F.3d 804, 810 (5th Cir. 2007) (CAFA "requires the removing defendant to prove minimal diversity and an aggregated amount in controversy of $5,000,000 or more").

[274]*Id.* at 812 ("Under CAFA, the moving party on the remand motion, not the defendant seeking federal jurisdiction, bears the burden to establish the domicile of at least one-third of the class members at the time of filing the lawsuit").

[275]*See* Vairo, *Class Action Fairness Act,* note 258 above, at 32-38.

historic allocation of class action litigation between the state and federal courts. Whether this is a good idea, and what effect it will have on litigation and, potentially, on the economy and the administration of justice, remain to be seen.

Trends in Aggregate Litigation

The class action is not the only way to deal with widespread harm. Though detailed discussion is beyond the scope of this book, it is worth noting two alternatives. One is the "victim compensation fund" (VCF), which creates a source for compensating persons harmed by a product, disaster, or attack. In the wake of the terrorist attacks of September 11, 2001, Congress created a VCF that permitted compensation of up to $8,500,000 to some victims. Similar VCFs aided victims of the BP oil spill in the Gulf of Mexico and of mass shootings. The goal of a VCF is to provide relief for victims without their having to demonstrate tort liability. Some programs, such as the one dealing with 9/11, required claimants to waive their right to sue. Others exist alongside the right to sue in tort. There is a robust literature on VCFs,[276] and considerable debate about whether victims prefer VCFs over tort litigation, including the class action.[277]

In §5.5, we discussed "multidistrict litigation" (MDL) under §1407. That statute empowers a panel of seven federal judges, the Judicial Panel for Multidistrict Litigation, to order transfer of related cases to a single district and judge. This transfer facilitates coordinated treatment of the case by a single judge. The transfer is for pretrial purposes only, and does not permit the transferee judge to try the cases. Today, over one-third of the federal civil docket consists of these MDL cases. The overwhelming majority of tort cases in the federal courts are MDL cases.[278]

---

[276]*See, e.g.*, Paul Heaton, Ivan Waggoner & Jamie Morikawa, *Victim Compensation Funds and Tort Litigation Following Incidents of Mass Violence,* 63 Buff. L. Rev. 1264 (2015); Linda S. Mullenix, *Mass Tort Funds and the Election of Remedies: The Need for Informed Consent,* 31 Rev. Litig. 833 (2012); Linda S. Mullenix, *Prometheus Unbound: The BP Gulf Oil Fund as a Means for Resolving Mass Tort Claims,* 71 La. L. Rev. 819 (2011).

[277]Professor Hensler found that victims of the 9/11 attacks preferred the tort system, which focuses on economic loss, to the VCF, which is based more upon need. Deborah R. Hensler, *Money Talks: Searching for Justice Through Compensation for Personal Injury and Death,* 53 DePaul L. Rev. 417, 432-451 (2003). *See also* Stephen Landsman, *A Chance to Be Heard: Thoughts About Schedules, Caps, and Collateral Source Deductions in the September 11th Victim Compensation Fund,* 53 DePaul L. Rev. 393 (2003).

[278]*See* Thomas Metzloff, *The MDL Vortex Revisited,* 99 Judicature 37 (2015).

Increasingly, the transferee judge in MDL endeavors to get the parties to enter into a "global settlement" to resolve as many of the cases as possible. Though the cases retain their status as separate suits, MDL practice looks a great deal like class litigation. Suppose, for example, that 500 related tort cases are transferred to a single judge for MDL proceedings. To streamline proceedings, the judge will appoint lead counsel to speak for the plaintiffs' side (and, if there are enough defendants, for the defendants' side).[279] That lead counsel takes control of the matter much the way the class lawyer does under Rule 23. And the plaintiffs in the other cases start to look a lot like class members: Even though they filed their own cases, they are now "along for the ride," with the lead counsel calling the shots. Some judges have gone so far as to refer to MDL matters as "quasi-class actions"[280] to justify various practices, including cajoling global settlement. See §5.5. Global settlement of MDL cases raises significant questions of fairness, because (unless the MDL cases are certified as class actions) none of the Rule 23 protections (including judicial review of settlements) apply.[281]

As alternatives such as VCF and MDL global settlement gain momentum, there is debate about the future of the class action. Some say the class action is dead,[282] but reports of that demise are vastly overstated.[283] Some types of actions, though, such as the consumer class, are threatened by a development to which we next turn.

---

[279]*See* Elizabeth Chamblee Burch, *Monopolies in Multidistrict Litigation*, 70 Vand. L. Rev. 67 (2017); Elizabeth Chamblee Burch, *Optimal Lead Plaintiffs*, 64 Vand. L. Rev. 1109 (2011).

[280]*See, e.g.*, In re Vioxx, 650 F. Supp. 2d 549, 553-554 (E.D. La. 2009).

[281]There is a substantial literature on these and related issues. *See, e.g.*, Elizabeth Chamblee Burch, *Judging Multidistrict Litigation*, 90 N.Y.U. L. Rev. 71 (2015); Elizabeth Chamblee Burch, *Procedural Justice in Nonclass Aggregation,* 44 Wake Forest L. Rev. 1 (2009); Jaime L. Dodge, *Facilitative Judging: Organizational Design in Mass-Multidistrict Litigation*, 64 Emory L.J. 329 (2014); Jaime L. Dodge, *Privatizing Mass Settlement*, 90 Notre Dame L. Rev. 335 (2014); Myriam Gilles, *Tribal Rituals of the MDL*, 5 J. of Tort Law 173 (2012); Linda S. Mullenix, *Aggregate Litigation and the Death of Democratic Dispute Resolution*, 107 Nw. U. L. Rev. 511 (2013); Linda S. Mullenix, *Dubious Doctrines: The Quasi-Class Action,* 80 U. Cin. L. Rev. 389 (2011); Charles Silver & Geoffrey P. Miller, *The Quasi-Class Action Method of Managing Multi-District Litigation: Problems and a Proposal*, 63 Vand. L. Rev. 107 (2010).

[282]Mullenix, *Aggregate Litigation*, 107 Nw. U. L. Rev. at 511 (*quoting* Ken Feinberg, the special master in the September 11 VCF, as saying "class actions are dead").

[283]Linda S. Mullenix, *Class Actions Shrugged: Mass Actions and the Future of Aggregate Litigation*, 32 Rev. Litig. 591 (2013); Linda S. Mullenix, *Ending Class Actions As We Know Them*, note 70 above, 64 Emory L.J. 399; Georgene Vairo, *Is the Class Action Really Dead? Is That Good or Bad for Class Members?*, 64 Emory L.J. 477 (2014).

§13.3.10   The Arbitration Threat to Class Enforcement of Private Rights

In §1.3, we discussed contractual arbitration, in which the parties agree to hire someone (or a panel of people) to resolve their dispute. Arbitration is adversarial, with the presentation of evidence by both sides, but is less formal than court litigation. As we saw in §1.3, the Federal Arbitration Act (FAA) was passed in 1925 to ensure that courts enforce valid arbitration provisions (historically, courts were reluctant to do so). At that time, the only contractual arbitration provisions were found in contracts between businesses, which presented no issue of whether one party was imposing arbitration upon the other; the businesses are generally of comparable bargaining power. In recent decades, however, arbitration provisions have been included in "adhesion contracts," offered by a party with superior bargaining power on a "take it or leave it" basis. Indeed, these are virtually ubiquitous; we have all signed or clicked on contracts containing arbitration provisions.

The Court has embraced contractual arbitration with zeal. As detailed in §1.3, it has upheld arbitration for a variety of federal statutory claims, thereby depriving plaintiffs of access to the federal courts to enforce such claims. Moreover, the Court has applied the FAA to contracts of adhesion. Accordingly, if your wireless provider, bank, credit card company, etc. violates your rights in some way, an arbitration provision in the contract is probably enforceable.[284] That means you have waived your right to sue and have agreed to submit your claim to arbitration (usually under rules prescribed by the company).

When you waive your right to sue in court, you give up a great deal. Arbitration, as we discussed in §1.3, is private (and so does not take place in a court to which the public has access), is not constrained by the rules of evidence or civil procedure (although arbitration providers do have their own rules), provides no jury trial, and is subject to very little judicial oversight. Even the arbitrator's clear mistake of law does not necessarily require a court to vacate an arbitration decision.[285] So even though you did not negotiate the issue with the company, you have agreed to arbitrate.

---

[284]This assumes, of course, that the contract and the clause are valid under applicable contract law principles.

[285]*See, e.g.,* Stolt-Nielsen S.A. v. Animal-Feeds Int'l Corp., 559 U.S. 662, 671 (2010) ("It is not enough . . . to show that the [arbitrator] committed an error—or even a serious error"). The theory is that the parties agreed to arbitration and must live with the results except in cases in which the provision is not enforceable under contract law—for example, for unconscionability.

In recent years, companies have added another clause to their adhesion contracts: the "class action waiver" or "aggregation waiver." This requires the consumer to arbitrate alone, without other consumers. This provision is not a problem if the claims are sizeable. Then, an individual consumer will be able to find a lawyer who will take the arbitration; the size of the claim makes it worth the lawyer's time. But most consumer claims are not sizeable; they are negative-value claims. Thus, no lawyer will take the case unless there are aggregate claims. Yet the waiver provision of the contract forbids aggregate arbitration.

This fact pattern sets up a fundamental clash between the policy of enforcing contracts and the policy of access to the courts. The Court has sided with the former. In *AT&T Mobility LLC v. Concepcion*,[286] consumers signed up for a cellphone plan that offered a free phone. The provider then charged the customers for the sales tax on the phone ($30.22 per phone). The agreement provided for arbitration of disputes and forbade customers from arbitrating together. Nonetheless, customers filed a class action in federal court, asserting claims under California consumer protection law. The provider moved to compel arbitration, which the lower courts denied. They relied upon a California Supreme Court case which held that waivers of the right to arbitrate collectively are unconscionable and therefore unenforceable.[287]

The Court reversed and held that the FAA preempts the California law. Specifically, §2 of the FAA provides for enforcement of arbitration clauses "save upon such grounds as exist at law or in equity for revocation of any contract." As interpreted, this clause permits invalidation of arbitration clauses on state-law grounds that apply to contracts generally, but not on grounds that apply only to arbitration clauses.[288] Because the California rule singled out arbitration clauses, it stood as "an obstacle to the accomplishment of the FAA's objectives" and was preempted.[289]

In *Concepcion*, the Court concluded that the arbitration provision provided meaningful redress for consumers. The agreement required that the arbitration take place in the customer's home county, that the provider pay all arbitration costs, and, if the award was higher than the provider had offered in settlement, that the customer would recover $7,500 plus double attorney's fees. These provisions meant that individual arbitration would realistically be pursued and provide "effective vindication" of the plaintiffs' claims.

---

[286]563 U.S. 333 (2011).
[287]Discover Bank v. Superior Court, 113 P.3d 1100 (Cal. 2005).
[288]563 U.S. at 339-341.
[289]*Id.* at 343.

But what if the arbitration clause is not so generous,[290] and individual arbitration will not be economically feasible? That issue arose in *Italian Colors Restaurant v. American Express Travel Related Services Co.*[291] There, a class of restaurant owners sued a credit card company, alleging that it had violated federal antitrust laws by using monopoly power to force them to accept higher interest rates than those charged by competitors. The agreement required arbitration and forbade aggregation. The claims were not *de minimis*, since they amounted to tens of thousands of dollars. Nonetheless, they were negative-value claims because retaining expert witnesses on relevant economic issues would likely exceed any recovery. The Second Circuit held that the aggregation waiver could not be enforced. It distinguished *Concepcion* because the plaintiffs in *Italian Colors* showed that individual pursuit of claims was not feasible. It concluded that a court may compel class arbitration when it finds that such aggregate assertion is the "only economically feasible means" for plaintiffs to pursue their federal claim.[292] In other words, because individual arbitration would not be pursued, it could not afford effective vindication of claims.

The Supreme Court reversed. Here, the Court could not say, as it had in *Concepcion*, that the arbitration provisions facilitated individual vindication of claims. Indeed, it was willing to assume that individual litigation would be economically infeasible (because of the expense of expert testimony). *Concepcion* nonetheless governed. Why? Because nothing in the FAA, the antitrust laws, or Rule 23 demonstrates an intention to prohibit parties from foregoing their right to assert class claims. Thus, "the antitrust laws do not guarantee an affordable procedural path to the vindication of every claims" and the fact that it is not economically worth pursuing the claim "does not constitute the elimination of the right to pursue that remedy.[293]

The Court has continued in its FAA decisions to elevate the policy of contract over various substantive policies.[294] There are many critics

---

[290]*See generally* Myriam Gilles, *Killing Them with Kindness: Examining 'Consumer-Friendly' Arbitration Clauses After* AT&T Mobility v. Concepcion, 88 Notre Dame L. Rev. 825 (2012).

[291]570 U.S. 228 (2013).

[292]In re American Express Merchs. Litigation, 667 F.3d 204, 213-214 (2d Cir. 2012).

[293]*Italian Colors*, 570 U.S. at 236-237. To bolster this point, the majority opinion noted that Congress created the antitrust damages claim asserted by the plaintiffs 48 years before Rule 23 was promulgated. Thus, Congress did not require facilitation of the aggregate assertion of the claims. *Id.* at 249.

[294]*See, e.g.*, Kindred Nursing Ctrs. Ltd. v. Clark, 137 S. Ct. 1421, 1426-1429 (2017) (Kentucky rule requiring that power of attorney expressly state that a representative may waive litigation rights is preempted by FAA; wrongful death claims against nursing home must be pursued in arbitration); DirecTV v. Imburgia, 577 U.S. 47, 51-58 (2015) (provision that arbitration clause would be unenforceable if the "law of your

of this trend,[295] but the upshot is clear: If the plaintiffs agreed to arbitrate instead of to litigate in court and to go it alone instead of *en masse*, they will be bound by their contract. Though Congress may provide that aggregate assertion of claims is necessary for vindication of particular claims, it has rarely done so. When it does not, the contract reigns supreme.

The parties are free to provide in the contract for group or class arbitration.[296] Presumably, however, such cases will be rare, and companies will put aggregation waivers into their contracts routinely.[297] Unless Congress intervenes, there is every reason to believe that companies will increasingly couple arbitration clauses with waivers of aggregate litigation and may thereby, in some cases at least, effectively close the door to effective enforcement of some laws. Again, this state of affairs raises significant policy issues. Enforcing contracts as written is undeniably important. But so is meaningful access to relief.

---

state" made class arbitration waivers unenforceable is preempted by FAA; state-law claim regarding early termination fees must be pursued in arbitration).

[295]Professor Gilles has been a particularly effective critic. *See, e.g.*, Myriam Gilles, *After Class: Aggregate Litigation in the Wake of* AT&T v. Concepcion, 79 U. Chi. L. Rev. 623 (2012); Myriam Gilles, *Class Dismissed: Contemporary Judicial Hostility to Small-Claims Consumer Class Actions*, 59 DePaul L. Rev. 305 (2010); Myriam Gilles, *Gutting the Vindication-of-Rights Challenge to Arbitration Agreements*, 82 Geo. Wash. L. Rev. 1683 (2013); Myriam Gilles, *Mandatory Arbitration and the Anti-Lawsuit Movement*, Pound Civil Justice Inst., Forum for State Appellate Court Judges (2014).

[296]*See, e.g.*, Oxford Health Plans LLC v. Sutter, 569 U.S. 564, 569-570 (2013) (upholding arbitrator's decision that parties agreed to class arbitration).

[297]*See* Brian T. Fitzpatrick, *The End of Class Actions?*, 57 Ariz. L. Rev. 161 (2015).

Chapter *14*

Appellate Review

§14.1 Defining the Issue

Almost everything we study in Civil Procedure relates to proceedings in a trial court. In this chapter, we study what happens at the appellate level of judicial systems, a topic we introduced in §1.2.2. A party who is dissatisfied with the outcome of litigation in a trial court might seek review by an appellate court. There is no federal *constitutional* right to appeal in a civil case.[1] Nonetheless, many state systems provide a right of appeal, either by statute or state constitution. The federal system has long granted a *statutory* right to appeal "final decisions" from the trial court (the United States District Court) to the United States Court of Appeals.[2] From those intermediate federal appellate courts, there is the possibility of discretionary review by the Supreme Court of the United States (SCOTUS). Accordingly, in the federal system, there are two appellate courts: the court of

---

[1] *See, e.g.,* Estate of Kanter v. Commissioner of Internal Revenue, 337 F.3d 833, 884 (D.C. Cir. 2003).

[2] 28 U.S.C. §1291. In very rare circumstances (beyond our scope), there is direct review of district court rulings in the Supreme Court of the United States.

appeals and the Supreme Court. They play quite different roles, as we see in §14.2.

Many state court systems, including those in California and New York, also adopt this tripartite model, in which the three levels of courts—trial, intermediate appellate, and supreme court—function similarly to those in the federal system.[3] But states are not required to adopt this model, and some, including Maine and Wyoming, have opted for a two-level system, in which there are trial courts and a supreme court, but no intermediate court of appeals. In still other states, such as Virginia, there is an intermediate court of appeals, but it hears appeals only in specialized types of cases and not in the relatively typical civil suit. In such states, there is simply no right to appeal a civil judgment. The state supreme court has discretion to review trial court results.[4]

§14.2   Purposes of Appellate Review

Appellate courts serve two functions. First, they review the trial court proceedings to determine whether the trial judge committed reversible error.[5] This function ensures that the trial court applied the law properly in resolving the case. In the federal system, this function is performed by the United States Court of Appeals. In many state court systems, it is performed by the intermediate court of appeals to which there is often some right to appeal. In these courts, the party pursuing the appeal is usually called the *appellant*, and the other party is the *appellee*.

Second, appellate courts interpret and exposit the law, thereby providing clarity and guidance for citizens and for the lower courts. This function is performed primarily by the ultimate court of the judicial system, where review is usually discretionary, rather than provided as a matter of right. As to matters of federal law, of course, this ultimate tribunal is SCOTUS. In matters of state law, it will be the state supreme court. Such courts usually decide to hear cases only if they

---

[3]States are free, of course, to call their courts whatever they wish. In New York, for example, the supreme court is the trial court, the intermediate court of appeals is called the appellate division, and the ultimate court is the New York Court of Appeals. In most states, the term *supreme court* applies to the ultimate court. In California, the intermediate appellate court is the court of appeal (singular). In most states in which an intermediate appellate court exists, it is the court of appeals (plural).

[4]In many states, the supreme court has mandatory review of capital criminal cases.

[5]Do not confuse this function with the renewed motion for judgment as a matter of law under Federal Rule 50(b), or the motion for new trial under Federal Rule 59(a), or the motion to set aside a judgment under Federal Rule 60(b) (all of which we discussed in Chapter 9). Those motions are addressed to the trial court, not an appellate court.

present an opportunity to clarify or to resolve splits of authority among the lower courts.[6] The party seeking such review has a heavy burden; she must convince the highest court that the issue presented is of such importance as to require elucidation by the ultimate court. In most court systems, the party whose case the supreme court agrees to hear is called the *petitioner*, because she petitions the court to exercise its discretionary jurisdiction, and the other party is the *respondent*.

Historically, there was an important distinction between whether one sought review at SCOTUS by appeal or by discretionary writ of *certiorari*.[7] By statute, certain rulings could be reviewed by appeal; in theory, the Court had no discretion in such matters and was required to take the case. Other cases, in contrast, could be reviewed only if the Supreme Court granted the writ of *certiorari*, a decision over which it had complete discretion. Through the years, however, the Court came to treat review by appeal as discretionary.[8] Recognizing this, in 1988 Congress largely abolished Supreme Court review by appeal, meaning that today the Court has virtually unfettered discretion in deciding which cases to hear.[9]

In deciding whether to grant the writ of *certiorari* and hear a case, the Court uses an informal "rule of four." This means the Court will take the case if four of the nine Justices agree that it is worthy of review. The criteria for case selection tell us a great deal about the Court's view of its role in the federal judicial system. Supreme Court Rule 10, which lists factors to be considered in ruling on a request for *certiorari*, says that a petition "is rarely granted when the asserted error consists of erroneous factual findings or the misapplication of a properly stated rule of law."[10] Fixing such errors is the role of the court of appeals. The Supreme Court is concerned with clarifying the law and resolving splits among the lower courts.

The Court grants *certiorari* and hears oral argument in very few cases. In a typical Term, the Court disposes of around 8,000 cases, almost all of which are handled by order, usually an order denying *certiorari* and thus refusing to hear the case. Such an order has no precedential value. Of the 8,000 or so cases handled during a Term, the Court typically will hear oral argument in only perhaps 70 or 80.

---

[6]Lower courts are sometimes referred to as *inferior* courts. This term is descriptive of the position of the court in the judicial system and is not pejorative.

[7]There is a surprising lack of consensus on how this word is pronounced—even among Justices of the Supreme Court. James J. Duane, *The Proper Pronunciation of Certiorari*, 17 Green Bag 2d 279 (2014).

[8]*See* Zucht v. King, 260 U.S. 174, 177 (1922) (hearing appeals only if they present "substantial" federal question).

[9]*See* 28 U.S.C. §1254(1) (review by *certiorari*).

[10]Supreme Court Rule 10.

Of those, most are then decided with signed opinions.[11] In a handful of cases, the Court may grant *certiorari* and enter an order without oral argument. For example, it might grant the writ and remand a case to the court of appeals for reconsideration in light of a new Supreme Court opinion.

Of course, there is no further judicial review after the Supreme Court has entered its final decision. As the late Justice Jackson put it, famously: "We are not final because we are infallible, but we are infallible only because we are final."[12] In the words of many others, if you lose at SCOTUS, your only appeal is to God.

§14.3   Appellate Procedure in General

Sections 14.4 and 14.5 address the sorts of trial court orders that can be appealed. Here, we assume that the trial court has entered a final judgment that is subject to appellate review, and the question is how an aggrieved party gets the appropriate appellate court[13] to perform its review function. Practice varies from state to state, and counsel must be careful to research the applicable requirements in her jurisdiction. We can draw some general observations, however, based upon the practice in the federal courts. Throughout this book, we have referred to many provisions of the Federal Rules of Civil Procedure (Federal Rules). Those Rules, some of which are relevant to appeal,

---

[11]Signed opinions are those to which Justices append their names, so we know which Justice adopted what approach. In contrast, a *per curiam* opinion is "by the court," and readers are not told which Justice wrote the opinion. In the 2013 Term, the Court issued two *per curiam* opinions. Statistics are available at www.supremecourt.gov and at www.uscourts.gov. The October 2019 Term resulted in only 53 signed opinions, the lowest total since the Civil War. The year was exceptional because of the COVID-19 pandemic, which required the Court to shut its doors and conduct hearings remotely. It was also exceptional because of the death of Justice Ginsburg and relatively fast confirmation of Justice Barrett. A very interesting blog for all things related to the Supreme Court is scotusblog.com.

[12]Brown v. Allen, 344 U.S. 443, 540 (1953) (concurring opinion).

[13]In the federal system, each district court is located within a particular circuit. The courts of appeals are arranged geographically into these circuits. One appeals from the district court to the circuit in which that district sits. So, for example, all appeals from district courts in New York go to the United States Court of Appeals for the Second Circuit; all appeals from district courts in Texas go to the Fifth Circuit. The one exception to this geographic model is the Federal Circuit, which generally has exclusive jurisdiction over appeals from district courts throughout the nation in cases arising under patent and similar laws.

In some states, the practice is similarly arranged geographically. In others, however, the intermediate appellate court sits only in one city, and all appeals from trial courts throughout the state go there.

govern practice in federal trial courts. Here we must also become aware of the Federal Rules of Appellate Procedure (FRAP), which is a different body of provisions that govern practice in the United States Courts of Appeals.

Under FRAP 3(a)(1), the appellant must file a "notice of appeal." Surprisingly, perhaps, the notice of appeal is *not* filed in the court of appeals, but in the district court.[14] Under FRAP 3(d)(1), the clerk of the district court then serves a copy of the notice on counsel for every other party to the case. The notice of appeal is a relatively simple document, which, under FRAP 3(c)(1), must specify the party or parties taking the appeal, the order from which appeal is taken, and the court to which the appeal is taken. Courts are fairly liberal, however, in accepting documents that fail to satisfy even these minimal requirements. As long as the notice identifies the parties and makes clear the desire of one of them to appeal a judgment of the trial court, it is likely to be found sufficient.[15]

This assumes, however, that the notice of appeal is filed timely. The general rule, contained in FRAP 4(a)(1)(A), requires the appellant to file the notice of appeal within 30 days after entry of the appealable order.[16] We discuss the application of this rule in §14.4.2. Here, we emphasize the Court's holding in *Bowles v. Russell*[17] that this timing

[14]The same seems to be universally true in state court systems: The notice of appeal is filed in the trial court.

[15]*See* Foman v. Davis, 371 U.S. 178, 180-181 (1962). Courts have been very strict, however, with the requirement that the name of the appellant be stated. Torres v. Oakland Scavenger Co., 487 U.S. 312, 315 (1988) (inadvertent omission of one of 17 appellants' names from notice of appeal fatal to the one omitted). In 1993, Fed. R. App. P. 3(c) was amended to allow general terms in naming appellants; an appeal will not be dismissed as to someone for whom the intent to appeal is clear from the notice as a whole. *See* 1993 Advisory Committee Note to Fed. R. App. P. 3(c).

[16]Under FRAP 4(a)(5), the district court may extend the time for filing a notice of appeal if a party makes such a motion no later than 30 days after the time prescribed for filing the notice has expired and shows excusable neglect or good cause.

[17]551 U.S. 205, 208-213 (2007). The result of the holding in *Bowles* was unfortunate. There, a state prisoner brought an unsuccessful federal habeas corpus proceeding. The district court granted his motion to re-open the period during which he could file an appeal, and entered an order giving him 17 days in which to do so. He brought the appeal 16 days later, and thus acted within the period set by the district court. By statute, however, the court was entitled only to extend the period by 14 days. Because the Court concluded that the requirement was jurisdictional, there was no appellate jurisdiction over the case.

For a series of articles discussing *Bowles* and its implications, *see* Elizabeth Burch, *Nonjurisdictionality or Inequity*, 102 Nw. U. L. Rev. Colloquy 64 (2007) (in which the author likens the situation in *Bowles* to an employee whose employer tells her to take a ten-day vacation and then fires her for violating company policy of being absent more than eight days); Perry Dane, *Sad Time: Thoughts on Jurisdictionality, the Legal Imagination, and* Bowles v. Russell, 102 Nw. U. L. Rev. Colloquy 164 (2008); Scott Dodson, *Jurisdictionality and* Bowles v. Russell, 102 Nw. U. L. Rev. Colloquy 42 requirement is *jurisdictional*, which means that failure to file the notice of appeal within 30 days means that the appellate court has no power to hear the appeal. Such jurisdictional rules are to be distinguished from "claims processing" rules, which are not jurisdictional and thus may be extended. For example, the Court held that the time limit for objecting to a discharge in bankruptcy[18] and the time in which to seek new trial in criminal cases[19] are not jurisdictional, but merely procedural. The Court admits that its opinions have not been helpful in determining jurisdictional from claims processing provisions, and that its use of the term "jurisdictional" has been "profligate" and "less than meticulous."[20] There is a very interesting emerging body of scholarship in the area of "jurisdictionality."[21]

(2007); E. King Poor, *The Jurisdictional Time Limit for an Appeal: The Worst Kind of Deadline—Except for All the Others,* 102 Nw. U. L. Rev. Colloquy 151 (2008).

[18]Kontrick v. Ryan, 540 U.S. 443, 454-455 (2004).

[19]Eberhart v. United States, 546 U.S. 12, 20 (2005). The Court has been busy in this area. *See* United States v. Wong, 575 U.S. 402, 408-12 (2015) (requirements of Federal Tort Claims Act that claimant meets temporal deadlines are not jurisdictional); Gonzalez v. Thaler, 565 U.S. 134, 138-45 (2012) (requirement that habeas corpus petitioner's certificate of appealability set forth a specific constitutional issue is non-jurisdictional); Henderson ex rel. Henderson v. Shinseki, 562 U.S. 428, 438-441 (2011) (120-day deadline for filing appeals from the Board of Veterans' Appeals to the United States Court of Appeals for Veterans Claims is not jurisdictional); Morrison v. National Australia Bank, 561 U.S. 247, 253-254 (2010) (extraterritorial application of §10(b) of Securities and Exchange Act is not jurisdictional); United Student Aid Funds, Inc. v. Espinosa, 559 U.S. 260, 271-272 (2010) (requirement of adversary proceeding in particular bankruptcy dispute is not jurisdictional); Reed Elsevier, Inc. v. Muchnick, 559 U.S. 154, 160-163 (2010) (registration requirement regarding copyright claims is not jurisdictional).

[20]Arbaugh v. Y&H Corp., 546 U.S. 500, 510-511 (2006) (provision applying Title VII only to employers with at least 15 employees is not jurisdictional, but relates to merits).

[21]See note 17 above. Professors Dodson and Wasserman and E. King Poor, a distinguished Chicago lawyer who argued the *Kontrick* case at the Supreme Court, are leading figures in this discussion. They emphasize that courts must delineate the boundaries not just between jurisdiction and claims-processing rules, but with determinations on the merits as well. *See* Scott Dodson, *Mandatory Rules,* 61 Stan. L. Rev. 1 (2008); Scott Dodson, *The Complexity of Jurisdictional Clarity,* 97 Va. L. Rev. 1 (2011); E. King Poor, *Jurisdictional Deadlines in the Wake of* Kontrick *and* Eberhart: *Harmonizing 160 Years of Precedent,* 40 Creighton L. Rev. 181 (2007); Howard M. Wasserman, *The Demise of "Drive-By" Jurisdictional Rulings,* 105 Nw. U. L. Rev. Colloquy 184 (2011); Howard M. Wasserman, *Jurisdiction and Merits,* 80 Wash. L. Rev. 643 (2005); Howard M. Wasserman, *Jurisdiction, Merits, and Non-Extant Rights,* 56 U. Kan. L. Rev. 227 (2008); Howard M. Wasserman, *Jurisdiction, Merits, and Procedure: Thoughts on Dodson's Trichotomy,* 102 Nw. U. L. Rev. Colloquy 215, 220 (2008) ("While jurisdictional rules define *whether* a court can exercise power to hear and resolve a case, procedural rules dictate *how* a court will do so. Timing rules might fit logically in either category") (emphasis original). *See also* Erin Morrow Hawley, *The Supreme Court's Quiet Revolution: Redefining the Meaning of Jurisdiction,* 56 Wm. & Mary L. Rev. 2027 (2015).

After filing the notice of appeal (timely), the appellant must take other steps to perfect the appeal. None of these steps is jurisdictional, though failure to satisfy these time requirements gives the appellate court the discretionary authority to dismiss the appeal. The appellant is required to pay certain filing fees and may be required to post a bond to cover costs on appeal. Interestingly, the pendency of an appeal does not stay the trial court's judgment. Indeed, a judgment against a defendant is still enforceable unless the defendant/appellant posts a bond. Such a bond—called *supersedeas* or a *suspending bond*—will "suspend" the operation of the judgment and preclude the plaintiff from executing on the judgment in the meantime. This requirement of a bond means that the defendant is required to deposit money with the court. How much money? It is usually the amount of the judgment plus interest set by law. The bond ensures that if the plaintiff ultimately wins, she will recover not only her judgment, but post-judgment interest on the judgment, which compensates her for the time during which she did not have access to the money.

> ○ ***Example #1.*** The trial court enters a final judgment in favor of Plaintiff, requiring Defendant to pay Plaintiff $250,000. Defendant files a notice of appeal. The appellate process will take months, maybe even years. Plaintiff wants her money now. The fact that Defendant has noticed an appeal does not stop Plaintiff from enforcing the judgment by having property belonging to Defendant seized and sold to raise the judgment amount. To stop Plaintiff from doing that, Defendant will post a suspending bond. The bond amount will be $250,000 plus some percentage thereof, to ensure that Plaintiff (if she wins on appeal) receives the judgment amount plus interest as set by law.[22]

In addition, the appellant is responsible for ensuring that the record of the trial court is transmitted to the appellate court. Under FRAP 10(a), this record consists of the original papers and exhibits filed in the district court, the transcript (if any) of proceedings at the trial court, and a certified copy of the docket entries prepared by the district court clerk.[23] Counsel must work with the office of the clerk at

---

[22]As a general rule, a winning claimant is entitled to recover interest on the judgment, commencing the day the judgment is entered. Stated another way, she is entitled to "post-judgment" interest. She is not entitled to "pre-judgment" (or "aleatory") interest. So, assume a plaintiff sues for $100,000. Generally, she is not entitled to recover interest on that sum for the time spent in litigation in trial court (even if that takes years to complete). Once the judgment is entered, however, she is entitled to recover that amount plus interest (the rate of which is set by law).

[23]Notice that FRAP 10(a)(2) refers to the transcript "if any." There is no requirement that trial proceedings be recorded stenographically, but they almost always are, at least in federal court. Having the stenographic record converted to transcript form is an expensive proposition and is a cost the appellant must bear. She pays the court

the district court to have the record prepared and transmitted to the appellate court.

Then counsel for each side will brief the issues raised on appeal. The appellant's brief is filed first, followed by the appellee's brief, sometimes followed by a "reply brief" by the appellant. The parties also prepare and file an "appendix," which is a collection of important documents from the record. This puts the relevant materials directly in the hands of the appellate judges who will be hearing the case.

The appellant generally can seek reversal only on the basis of an objection she made in the trial court. It is important, therefore, that counsel make objections on the record, so they can be the basis for an appeal. Objections at the trial court must be timely; for example, objections to jury instructions usually are waived if not made before the jury retires to deliberate.[24] The appellee can defend the judgment on any basis that is supported in the record. Thus, without filing a cross-appeal, she may ask the appellate court to affirm the judgment based upon any matter properly in the record, even if it involves an attack on the trial court's reasoning or reliance on a matter the trial court ignored.[25] In general, an appellee must file a cross-appeal if she seeks to have the court of appeals modify or reverse some part of the trial-court judgment.[26]

Appellate courts do not hold trials. They do not hear the presentation of evidence. Rather, the judges of the appellate court read the briefs and, in appropriate cases, hear oral argument by counsel for appellant and appellee. An appellate court's functions, then, are discharged "on the record."[27] The court is there to review what happened at the trial court; it does not augment the record by taking evidence or considering issues not addressed to the trial court. Oral argument, when permitted, is strictly limited (typically 30 minutes per side) and is usually punctuated by active questioning from the judges. Most

---

reporter for this service. In some states, where there is no transcript, counsel may prepare a written summary of the trial, which is presented to the trial judge for correction before being transmitted to the appellate court.

[24]*See, e.g.,* Larson v. Neimi, 9 F.3d 1397, 1399 (9th Cir. 1993) (requirement strictly enforced).

[25]United States v. American Rw. Express Co., 265 U.S. 425, 435 (1924).

[26]The cross-appeal doctrine can get very complicated. *See* 15A Wright & Miller §3904.

[27]In some state court systems, a party may "appeal" the judgment of a trial court to another trial court. Such a procedure usually involves what are essentially small claims courts. For example, in Virginia, the general district court can hold trials in civil cases involving damages of $15,000 or less. An aggrieved litigant may "appeal" to the circuit court, which is the trial court of general subject matter jurisdiction. This "appeal," however, consists of a trial de novo. In other words, the case is treated as if it had been filed originally in the circuit court. Because this is not a true appellate review on the record, the general district courts are known as courts "not of record."

intermediate appellate courts, including the federal courts of appeals, hear cases in panels of three judges.[28] In contrast, all justices[29] of supreme courts, including SCOTUS, usually sit at oral argument.

After oral argument, the judges retire to "conference," where they decide the case. This conference is attended only by the judges, and the discussions are confidential and closely guarded. The senior judge of the panel, if she is in the majority, assigns to herself or one of the other judges in the majority the task of writing the opinion. If she is in the minority, she may issue a dissenting opinion. Drafting the opinion, even in a case in which the judges are unanimous, may take several months. The judge then circulates her draft opinion to the other judges on the panel. There may be some give-and-take on language and reasoning. Eventually, however, the majority signs the opinion and it is entered along with the judgment resolving the appeal. The court will then decide whether the opinion should be published. Opinions of the United States Courts of Appeals are published in the Federal Reporter.[30]

---

[28]In extraordinary cases, as when panels of the same circuit have rendered inconsistent opinions, a United States Court of Appeals might hear a case "en banc," which means that all active judges of that circuit would participate in the oral argument and decision. *See* FRAP 35(a).

[29]In the federal system, "justice" refers only to a member of the Supreme Court. Members of the United States Courts of Appeals and the federal district court judges are referred to as "judge." State practice varies. In New York, the term "justice" refers to the trial judge. (Remember, New York calls its trial court the supreme court; see note 3 above.) Judicial officers on the other courts in New York are called *judges*.

[30]The overwhelming majority of federal court of appeals decisions are not "published." That means they are sent to the parties but are not formally printed in the Federal Reporter. Historically, "unpublished" decisions were not seen, except by people who took the trouble to go to the clerk's office and look for them. The world has changed with online access to opinions. Now, even unpublished opinions are accessible on Lexis and Westlaw, as well as on websites maintained by the various courts and by others. Local rules of most circuits provided that such opinions could not be cited as precedent. The Eighth Circuit shocked everyone by holding that its local rule on this point was unconstitutional, because, the court concluded, Article III did not permit it to render non-precedential rulings. Anastasoff v. United States, 223 F.3d 898, 899-900 (8th Cir. 2000), *vacated as moot on reh'g en banc*, 235 F.3d 1054 (8th Cir. 2000). Other circuits rejected the reasoning and upheld their local rules on this point. *See, e.g.*, Hart v. Massanari, 266 F.3d 1155, 1162 (9th Cir. 2001) ("few, if any, appellate courts have the resources to write precedential opinions in every case that comes before them"). *See generally* Polly Price, *Precedent and Judicial Power After the Founding*, 42 B.C. L. Rev. 81 (2000). Federal Rule of Appellate Procedure 32.1, promulgated in 2006, permits the citation of "unpublished" opinions (issued in or after 2007) but does not address the weight to be accorded such decisions. Some courts treat unpublished opinions as "persuasive" but not binding. *See, e.g.*, Gibbs v. United States, 865 F. Supp. 2d 1127, 1133 n.3 (M.D. Fla. 2012).

Unpublished opinions can be accessed through a government website titled Public Access to Court Electronic Records (PACER). PACER allows the public access to federal

The court of appeals may dispose of the appeal in one of several ways. It might affirm what the trial court did. Or it may reverse and command the trial court to enter a particular order. It might reverse and remand for further proceedings. It may vacate the trial court order, which essentially expunges it from the record. One bit of terminology should be emphasized (one we mentioned in §1.2.2). When an appellate court disagrees with the result reached by a lower court in the same case, it may "reverse" that order. When an appellate court decides that an earlier case should no longer be considered precedent for its jurisdiction, it "overrules" that opinion. Thus, for example, in the famous *Erie* case (which is the focus of Chapter 10), the Supreme Court overruled *Swift v. Tyson.*

§14.4 The Final Judgment Rule

§14.4.1 Section 1291

In the federal system, 28 U.S.C. §1291 provides that the courts of appeals "shall have jurisdiction of appeals from all final decisions of the district courts of the United States...."[31] Thus, the statutory right to appeal in federal court is limited to "final decisions." For present purposes, it is helpful to consider that every order and decision by a trial court is either "final" or "interlocutory." The two are mutually exclusive. What constitutes a "final" judgment, however, can be difficult to determine. In the words of one judge, "'final' is not a clear one-purpose word; it is slithery, tricky."[32] For present purposes, it is enough to say that a final judgment is one that finally determines all issues as to all litigants in the case, leaving the trial court with only such ministerial acts as determining the award of costs and, possibly, attorney's fees. In other words, a final judgment wraps up the entire dispute.[33] Such rulings are appealable under §1291. All other trial court rulings are interlocutory and are not appealable under §1291.[34]

---

court records with a login and password. *Public Access to Court Electronic Records,* https://pacer.uscourts.gov/ (last visited May 20, 2021).

[31]The provision makes an exception for the United States Court of Appeals for the Federal Circuit, which has specialized subject matter jurisdiction, including appeals in patent cases. *See* 28 U.S.C. §§1292(c) and 1295(d) regarding the Federal Circuit.

[32]United States v. 243.22 Acres of Land in Town of Babylon, 129 F.2d 678, 680 (2d Cir. 1942). The judge concluded, "There is, still, too little finality about 'finality.'" *Id.*

[33]*See generally* 15A Wright & Miller §3909. For discussion of how pending motions for costs or attorney's fees do not rob an otherwise final judgment of its finality, see notes 42 and 43 below and accompanying text.

[34]An order remanding a case from federal court to state court (after the case was removed—see §4.8) ends the jurisdiction of the federal court. Nonetheless, by statute,

The Final Judgment Rule §14.4

Obviously, most decisions made during a case are interlocutory. Indeed, there may be hundreds of interlocutory decisions during a case. For example, orders permitting an amended pleading, allowing permissive intervention, compelling answers to discovery, setting a trial date, limiting cross-examination, and overruling or granting objections to evidence at trial are all interlocutory. These issues may be important, even pivotal, to the outcome of the case, and they might be decided once and for all, but they do not resolve the *case* finally, and thus cannot be appealed as "final decisions" under §1291. In addition, *denials* of motions that would resolve the case—such as denials of motions to dismiss or for summary judgment or for judgment as a matter of law—are interlocutory. Again, they may be important, but such decisions do not resolve the case. They leave the case in status quo and thus cannot be appealed as "final decisions" under §1291.

Does the final judgment rule mean that the litigant who lost the ruling on an interlocutory order is without appellate remedy? No. Such a litigant has two possible routes to the appellate court: Either the issue qualifies for an exception to the final judgment rule (see §14.5 below) or she must await entry of the final judgment. Under the final judgment rule, review is delayed until the entire case is resolved. The final judgment rule does not *preclude* appellate review of interlocutory rulings; it simply *delays* such review.

The final judgment rule is based upon the policy of avoiding piecemeal review of issues as they arise in the trial court. If the system permitted a disgruntled party to appeal each issue as it came up, the trial court proceedings could be delayed markedly. Piecemeal appellate review would interrupt the flow of the trial court proceedings. In addition, the final judgment rule ultimately avoids appellate review of many issues altogether. That is, a litigant who feels that the trial judge made various errors, but who ultimately wins the case, will not appeal. If the issues had been appealable as they arose in the case, the appellate court would have made determinations that, in the long run, were unnecessary. Further, the final judgment rule permits the appellate court to have the entire case before it at once. This allows

the order generally cannot be reviewed by appeal or otherwise. 28 U.S.C. §1447(d). Section 1453(c)(1) permits a party to seek discretionary review by the court of appeals of an order granting or denying a motion to remand a case to state court. The Supreme Court can review the court of appeals' decision to deny appellate review for abuse of discretion. Dart Cherokee Basin Operating Co. v. Owens, 574 U.S. 81, 90-95 (2014). *See generally* Bryan Lammon, *Finality, Appealability, and the Scope of Interlocutory Review,* 93 Wash. L. Rev. 1809 (2018).

919

it to view the various alleged errors in context, which may inform its ultimate resolution.[35]

Despite these benefits, some jurisdictions reject the final judgment rule and permit *ad hoc* appeals throughout the course of litigation.[36] On the positive side, such review does permit the appellate court to remedy an error before it can compound problems at the trial court. But this benefit can be realized in a jurisdiction adopting the final judgment rule by recognizing exceptions to permit interlocutory review when it would be ameliorative.

§14.4.2   The Single Litigative Unit Approach to "Final Decision"

Jurisdictions might adopt different definitions of what constitutes a final decision that can be appealed under the final judgment rule. For example, one might consider that once the trial court has definitively resolved *a particular issue* in the case, that decision is "final" and can be appealed. Such a reading might be especially appropriate in federal court under §1291 because that statute permits appeals from final "decisions," and does not mention final "judgments." But the federal courts have not adopted this interpretation. Instead, federal courts embrace the notion that the *entire case* before the trial court constitutes a single litigative unit for which there can be but a single final judgment and a single appeal.[37] This idea made sense under older joinder rules, when the entire case consisted only of closely related parties and claims. Then, awaiting the final judgment, while occasionally frustrating, worked no particular hardship.

Under modern joinder principles such as those applicable in federal court, however, the single litigative unit theory can make far less sense. As we saw in Chapter 12, a single civil case in federal court can involve many completely unrelated claims and parties. For example, under Federal Rule 18, which we discussed in §12.3, a plaintiff may assert any claims she has against a defendant, regardless of factual or legal relatedness. Similarly, a defendant may inject into the case claims wholly unrelated to the underlying dispute by filing a permissive counterclaim, which we saw at §12.5.1. As interpreted in federal court under the single litigative unit theory, however, an order

---

[35]Cohen v. Beneficial Industrial Loan Corp., 337 U.S. 541, 546 (1949) (final judgment rule "combine[s] in one review all stages of the proceeding that effectively may be reviewed and corrected if and when final judgment results").

[36]For instance, New York permits appeal of any order, including an interlocutory order, that "involves some part of the merits" of the case. N.Y. CPLR §5701(a)(2)(iv).

[37]*See, e.g.*, Collins v. Miller, 252 U.S. 364, 370 (1920).

completely resolving one claim—but leaving unrelated claims to be determined—is not a "final decision" under §1291. And because it does not resolve the *entire case*, it is not appealable.

- ○ ***Example #2.*** *P* sues *D* for injuries from a tort and asserts a completely unrelated claim for breach of contract in a business deal between the two. The court dismisses the tort claim as barred by the statute of limitations. Under the single litigative unit theory, *P* cannot appeal that dismissal now, because the contract claim is still pending.
- ○ ***Example #3.*** *P* sues *D* on a tort claim; *D* asserts a permissive counterclaim under Federal Rule 13(b) for a completely unrelated contract claim. The court grants summary judgment in favor of *D* on *P*'s claim. Again, under the single litigative unit theory, *P* cannot appeal now, because the contract claim is still pending.
- ○ ***Example #4.*** Mother and Daughter, as coplaintiffs, sue a pharmaceutical company. They allege that a drug it manufactured, which Mother took while pregnant with Daughter, caused harm to both. The court dismisses Mother's claim as barred by the statute of limitations. Under the single litigative unit theory, Mother cannot appeal now, because the claim by Daughter remains pending.[38]

In such instances, application of the single litigative unit theory can be wasteful and even unfair. Suppose, for example, that in each of these three examples, the parties spend a year litigating the remaining claim before final judgment is entered. Then the appellate court reverses the dismissal of the first claim and remands that claim for trial. In the meantime, the parties have lost more than a year in prosecuting a wholly unrelated claim at the trial court. During the delay, witnesses might have died or forgotten key facts or evidence might have disappeared. Clearly, a more flexible approach would be appropriate in cases involving final disposition of separate and unrelated claims. Federal Rule 54(b) provides such a flexible approach, as we see in §14.4.3.

In §12.4, we saw that separate cases pending in a single district may be consolidated under Rule 42(a). There, we noted, among other things, that consolidation of cases, even for all purposes, does not merge the cases; they retain their character as separate cases. The Supreme Court confirmed this understanding in *Hall v. Hall*,[39] in which it held that a final judgment in one of several consolidated cases was to be

---

[38]*See* Robinson v. Parke-Davis & Co., 685 F.2d 912, 913 (4th Cir. 1982).

[39]138 S. Ct. 1118, 1128-32 (2018). The same is true for cases consolidated for multidistrict litigation (MDL) under 28 U.S.C. §1407, which we discussed in §5.5. That statute permits transfer of multiple civil cases to a single district for consolidated pretrial proceedings. The cases retain their separate character for purposes of appeal under §1291. A final judgment as to one of the MDL cases is appealable and must be pursued on its own, without awaiting the outcome of the other cases. Gelboim v. Bank of America Corp., 574 U.S. 405, 415-16 (2015).

appealed then, without awaiting final judgments in the other consolidated actions.

We saw in §14.3 that FRAP 4(a)(1)(A) requires the appellant to file her notice of appeal in the district court within 30 days after entry of the appealable order, and that this requirement is jurisdictional. In most cases, the date on which the 30 days starts to run will be clear.[40] As we saw in §9.3, Federal Rule 58 provides that a judgment of the district court is effective only after it is entered as a separate document in accordance with Federal Rule 54 and noted on the docket sheet in the district court. One reason for such mechanical requirements is to set a precise date from which to measure the time for filing a notice of appeal. The situation becomes more complicated, however, when a party makes a post-judgment motion in the district court.

Suppose the district court enters final judgment on June 1. As we saw in §§9.5 and 9.6, the losing party might, within 28 days after entry of that judgment, move for a new trial or make a renewed motion for judgment as a matter of law (assuming she had met the requirements for doing so). Suppose a party makes such a motion on June 20, and the district court rules on the motion on June 30. When did the 30-day period under FRAP 4(a)(1)(A) start to run—on June 1 or on June 30? Fortunately, the answer is made clear by FRAP 4(a)(4)(A), which provides the 30-day period starts to run on the date on which the court rules on the motion (assuming, of course, the motion was timely). Hence, the party taking an appeal would have 30 days from the court's ruling on the motion (June 30) in which to file her notice of appeal.[41]

The court's ruling on a post-trial motion might render non-final a judgment that was final. Consider a motion for new trial under Rule 59(a), which we discussed in §9.6.

> ○ ***Example #5.*** The district court enters a final judgment. The losing party could appeal, because there is a final judgment. Instead, however, the losing party moves for a new trial. The district court *grants* the new

---

Things are different, however, in bankruptcy proceedings. Those cases aggregate multiple disputes that would be individual cases if the debtor were not bankrupt. Appeal in bankruptcy implicates different statutes, which permit appeal from bankruptcy orders that finally determine specific disputes, even though the bankruptcy proceeding as a whole is not concluded. Bullard v. Blue Hills Bank, 575 U.S. 496, 501-502 (2015).

[40]We discussed timing in general in §7.3.3. The day on which the judgment is entered does not count toward the 30 days. The following day is Day 1 of the 30. The notice of appeal must be filed no later than Day 30. If that day falls on a Saturday, Sunday, or holiday, the notice of appeal may be filed on the next business day.

[41]The same would be true under FRAP 4(a)(4)(A) if a party had moved to alter or amend the judgment under Federal Rule 59, or to amend or make additional factual findings under Federal Rule 52(b), or to set aside the judgment under Federal Rule 60(b) (if such motion was filed within 14 days after entry of judgment).

trial. There is now no appealable final judgment. The grant of new trial does not wrap up the litigative unit. Indeed, it requires that the litigation continue at the district court with a new trial.

o ***Example #6.*** The district court enters a final judgment. The losing party could appeal, because there is a final judgment. Instead, however, the losing party moves for a new trial. This time, the district court *denies* the new trial. This denial is a final judgment: It ends the litigation on the merits in the district court (by refusing to order the parties to a new trial). Under FRAP 4(A)(4)(a), the losing party must file her notice of appeals no later than 30 days after the denial of the motion for new trial.

Let's compare these examples with a party's renewed motion for judgment as a matter of law under Rule 50(b), which we discussed in §9.5. This motion, if granted, does not result in the parties going through a new trial. Instead, the court grants the motion and enters final judgment in favor of the party that had lost. Notice, then, that however a district court rules on a renewed motion for judgment as a matter of law—whether it grants the motion or denies the motion—the ruling constitutes an appealable final judgment. Why? Because either the court leaves the judgment exactly where it is or it enters judgment for the other side; either way, the trial court case is over. The losing party must file her notice of appeal within 30 days of that ruling.

One post-trial motion that has gotten litigants into trouble is the motion for an award of attorney's fees under Federal Rule 54. Under the American Rule, discussed at §§1.1 and 9.3, each side bears her own attorney's fees, but exceptions to that rule permit a prevailing party in some circumstances to recover her attorney's fees from the losing side. In *Budinich v. Becton Dickinson & Co.*,[42] the trial court entered final judgment. The prevailing party then moved for an award of attorney's fees under an exception to the American Rule. The court entered its order awarding fees. Only then did the losing party file a notice of appeal. It filed the notice within 30 days after entry of the order awarding fees. Unfortunately, however, this was more than 30 days after entry of the final judgment. The Supreme Court held that the appeal was late; the appellate court had no jurisdiction. In other words, as a general rule, the motion for attorney's fees (or for taxation of costs) does *not* extend the time for filing the notice of appeal.[43]

---

[42] 486 U.S. 196, 198-199 (1988).

[43] In *Budinich*, the claim for attorney's fees was based upon a state statute (applicable because the case was brought under diversity of citizenship jurisdiction). In *Ray Haluch Gravel v. Central Pension Fund*, 571 U.S. 177, 184-90 (2014), the claim for fees was based upon a contractual provision. Other than that, the facts of *Ray Haluch Gravel* were indistinguishable from those in *Budinich*. In *Ray Haluch Gravel*, the Court held that the source of the claim for attorney's fees was irrelevant, and that the appeal was not timely.

This matter is expressly addressed in FRAP 4(a)(4)(A)(iii), which provides that the 30-day period will run from the district court's ruling on a motion for attorney's fees *only* if the district court extended the time to appeal under Federal Rule 58. The latter Rule provides, *inter alia*, that the time for appeal is not extended "to tax costs or award fees, except that, when a timely motion for attorney's fees is made under Rule 54(d)(2), the court, before a notice of appeal has been filed ... may order that the motion have the same effect under [FRAP] 4(a)(4) as a motion [for new trial]." Thus, ordinarily, a motion for attorney's fees does not extend the time for appeal. Only if the district court expressly orders that the motion has the effect of a new trial motion will the motion extend the time in which to appeal.

In any case, the prevailing party generally is permitted to recover her costs from the losing party (see §9.3). She will make a motion to recover such costs after entry of the judgment. A motion for the award of costs does not extend the time for filing the notice of appeal. As the Court in *Budinich* made clear, assessment of fees and costs is merely a "housekeeping" matter that has no bearing on the outcome of the case on the merits, and therefore should not delay the time for filing the notice of appeal.

§14.4.3   Federal Rule 54(b) and Multiclaim or Multiparty Cases

Federal Rule 54(b) is not an exception to the final judgment rule. Rather, it shifts the focus away from the single litigative unit theory and allows appeal of final judgments of discrete parts of a case—parts that involve final determination of one or more (but fewer than all) claims or one or more (but fewer than all)[44] parties. The Rule has three requirements. In discussing them, we refer back to Examples #2, 3, and 4 above.

First, the case must involve "more than one claim for relief" or "multiple parties." In most instances, it will be obvious whether this requirement is met. Examples #2 and #3 involve multiple claims for relief, because the assertions of liability involved unrelated factual circumstances.[45] Similarly, Example #4 falls within Rule 54(b) because it involves disposition of the entire claim involving one of multiple parties; after the ruling, Mother has no role in the litigation.

---

[44]Obviously, if a judgment concluded all claims as to all parties, it would be appealable as a final judgment under §1291.

[45]*See, e.g.*, Hudson River Sloop Clearwater, Inc. v. Department of the Navy, 891 F.2d 414, 418 (2d Cir. 1989) (factually distinct claims are separate under Federal Rule 54(b)).

Unfortunately, not all cases are this clear. The definition of "more than one claim for relief" has proved difficult in some contexts. For starters, the fact that a claimant seeks to recover under different legal theories does not necessarily mean that the case involves multiple claims. In one case, for example, the plaintiff alleged separate counts for negligence and strict liability concerning the same event. The court concluded there was only one "claim" and thus that Rule 54(b) did not apply.[46]

In making the assessment of whether there are multiple claims, some courts have drawn an analogy to claim preclusion. They conclude that Rule 54(b) will not apply if the claims would be considered a single claim under principles of claim preclusion.[47] Though this proxy may be useful, it cannot always be determinative.[48] In §11.2.3 we saw that most courts define "claim" for claim preclusion purposes as all rights to relief arising from a transaction or occurrence. The Supreme Court has held, however, that the fact that claims arise from the same transaction or occurrence does not automatically mean that they are not separate for purposes of Rule 54(b).[49]

A more useful proxy may be to ask whether the different "claims" would support only a single recovery.[50] If so, they cannot be separate claims under Rule 54(b). As we have seen in other areas, however, the search for a single test is futile. Matters of this sort are best decided pragmatically, with sensitivity to the underlying purpose of Rule 54(b). The ultimate question is whether, on the facts of each case, assertions for relief are so different as to justify immediate appeal when they are resolved.[51]

Second, the trial court's order must be a final judgment as to at least one claim or as to at least one party. As noted above, Rule 54(b) does not obviate the final judgment rule. Rather, it changes the focus. Instead of requiring a final judgment as to the *overall case*, there must

[46]*See, e.g.,* Indiana Harbor Belt R.R. v. American Cyanamid Co., 860 F.2d 1441, 1444-1445 (7th Cir. 1988).

[47]*See, e.g.,* Automatic Liquid Packaging, Inc. v. Dominik, 852 F.2d 1036, 1038 (7th Cir. 1988).

[48]*See* Olympia Hotels Corp. v. Johnson Wax Dev. Corp., 908 F.2d 1363, 1368 (7th Cir. 1990) (suggesting limits of claim preclusion analogy).

[49]Cold Metal Process Co. v. United Engineering & Foundry Co., 351 U.S. 445, 451-452 (1956) (fact that unadjudicated claim was a compulsory counterclaim, arising from the same transaction or occurrence as the adjudicated claim did not preclude appeal under Rule 54(b)).

[50]In re Southeast Banking Corp., 69 F.3d 1539, 1549-1550 (11th Cir. 1995).

[51]Curtiss-Wright Corp. v. General Electric Co., 446 U.S. 1, 8 (1980) (court should "consider such factors as whether the claims under review were separable from the others remaining to be adjudicated and whether the nature of the claims already determined was such that no appellate court would have to decide the same issues more than once even if there were subsequent appeals").

be a final judgment as to at least one claim or party.[52] One helpful way to assess this factor is to ask whether the order would be a final judgment if the claim adjudicated had been a separate case.[53] In each of the three Examples above, the answer would be yes. If *P*'s tort claim in Examples #2 and #3 were a separate case, the order dismissing it under the statute of limitations would be a final judgment under §1291. Likewise, if Mother's claim in Example #4 had been a separate suit, the dismissal would have been a final judgment as to it.

- o **_Example #7._** Suppose in Example #4 that the trial court orders that Mother answer particular questions at her deposition, over her objection. Can Mother use Federal Rule 54(b) to gain appellate review of that issue now? No, because the order does not constitute a final judgment on the claim involving Mother. If Mother's case were seen as a separate suit, this order would not be appealable under §1291.

Third, Rule 54(b) requires that the trial court "may direct entry of a final judgment as to one or more" claims or parties, but only if it "expressly determines that there is no just reason for delay." Not only must the judge refer to the order as a final judgment as to the claim or party involved; she must also make the express determination on the record that there is no just reason to delay appeal on that claim or as to that party. These express requirements are salutary, because they ensure that there is no doubt about when the time for appeal starts to run.

- o **_Example #8._** Assume the district court enters an order disposing of one of multiple claims or of all matters regarding one of multiple parties. But the trial court does not make the express certification required by Rule 54(b). Can the appropriate party take an appeal now? No. Rule 54(b) only applies if the court makes the express determination required on the record.[54] If it fails to do so, Rule 54(b) does not apply. In that case, the single litigative unit theory applies. Because this order did not resolve the overall litigation, it is not appealable under §1291.

The trial court's certification that the requirements of Rule 54(b) have been met is not binding on the appellate court. That court must determine whether the requirements are met and thus whether the

---

[52]The Supreme Court has upheld the validity of the Rule under 28 U.S.C. §2072(c), which is part of the Rules Enabling Act (discussed in §10.6). Sears, Roebuck & Co. v. Mackey, 351 U.S. 427, 437 (1956).

[53]*See* Horn v. Transcon Lines, 898 F.2d 589, 593 (7th Cir. 1990) ("ask whether [the order adjudicating the claim] would count as a final decision in a hypothetical independent case").

[54]Reiter v. Cooper, 507 U.S. 258, 270 (1993) (no appeal of final determination of claim in multiclaim case absent Rule 54(b) determination and direction).

appeal is properly before it.[55] Again, Rule 54(b) is not an exception to the final judgment rule. Rather, it simply changes the focus of what constitutes a final decision. We turn now to actual exceptions to the basic rule requiring entry of a final judgment.

§14.5 Exceptions to the Final Judgment Rule

The final judgment rule imposes a significant restriction on appellate jurisdiction. Systems adopting the final judgment rule approach, including the federal system, recognize the need for exceptions to permit occasional appeal of interlocutory orders. In the federal system, authority for interlocutory review can be found in statutes and Federal Rules, as well as in judge-made doctrine. In each, it is important to note the policy interests that permit the appellate court to override the usually controlling principal of avoiding piecemeal appeals.

§14.5.1 Statutory and Rules-Based Exceptions

Section 1292(a)

The three subsections of 28 U.S.C. §1292(a) expressly permit appeal from specific, narrow types of interlocutory orders:

1. Those "granting, continuing, modifying, refusing or dissolving injunctions, or refusing to dissolve or modify injunctions";
2. Those "appointing receivers, or refusing orders to wind up receiverships or to take steps to accomplish the purposes thereof"; and
3. Those "determining the rights and liabilities of the parties to admiralty cases in which appeals from final decrees are allowed."

Congress has determined that these orders are so important that appellate review should not await final judgment. As to such orders, the policy against piecemeal appeals, reflected in the final judgment rule, is overborne by the importance of immediate appellate review.

○ ***Example #9.*** *P* sues *D* for a permanent injunction to stop *D*'s operation of a business that allegedly violates zoning restrictions and damages *P*. The trial court enters a preliminary injunction shutting down *D*'s business pending final disposition of the case (or refuses so to order). That order (or the refusal so to order) is appealable immediately under §1292(a). Clearly, the order has such immediate and important

---

[55]Liberty Mutual Ins. Co. v. Wetzel, 424 U.S. 737, 742, 743 (1976) (trial court incorrectly concluded that it had finally adjudicated one of multiple claims).

consequences that permitting interlocutory review outweighs the usual policy of avoiding piecemeal appeals.

○ ***Example #10.*** Would that order for (or refusing) a preliminary injunction be appealable under Rule 54(b) (which we saw in §14.4.3)? No. The trial court could not have certified the issue for immediate appeal under Rule 54(b) because it is not a final judgment. Remember that Rule 54(b) requires a final judgment (not an interlocutory order) as to one or more claims or parties in a case.

Because it permits appeal without final judgment, courts conclude that §1292(a) must be strictly construed.[56] On the other hand, courts have taken a pragmatic approach to whether an order falls within the statute. Thus, an order that has the *effect* of an injunction will trigger §1292(a) even if the court did not refer to it as an injunction.[57] Conversely, the fact that relief is referred to as injunctive does not ensure that §1292(a) applies. Again, it is the practical effect of the order that controls.[58]

In addition to considering the actual effect of the order (whether it is injunctive in nature) the courts impose requirements that do not appear on the face of the statute: (1) that the order create the risk of serious consequences for the appealing party, and (2) that the order effectively be unreviewable if the parties must await final judgment. In *Carson v. American Brands, Inc.*,[59] the trial court refused to approve a class action settlement. The refusal created a serious possibility of harm to the erstwhile class members because it denied them the terms of the settlement (including injunctive relief). The Supreme Court characterized the order as having the practical effect of the denial of an injunction. For this reason, and because serious harm could result, which would not effectively be subject to review if the parties awaited final judgment, the order was appealable under §1292(a). Similarly, in another case, grant of partial summary judgment invoked §1292(a) because it had the injunctive effect of terminating employee contributions to a union's pension fund and thus threatened serious consequences for the fund's beneficiaries.[60]

[56]*See, e.g.*, In re Ingram Towing Co., 59 F.3d 513, 515 (5th Cir. 1995).

[57]*See, e.g.*, Aetna Cas. & Ins. Co. v. Markanian, 114 F.3d 346, 348-349 (1st Cir. 1997) (order preventing party from leaving jurisdiction, although called writ of *ne exeat*, operates as an injunction and invokes §1292(a)).

[58]*See, e.g.*, Metex Corp. v. ACS Industries, Inc., 748 F.2d 150, 155-156 (3d Cir. 1984) (although styled as a motion for injunction, in effect the order sought discovery; not appealable under §1292(a)).

[59]450 U.S. 79, 80-81 (1981).

[60]Manchester Knitted Fashions, Inc. v. Amalgamated Cotton Garment & Allied Industries Fund, 967 F.2d 688, 690 (1st Cir. 1992).

One area of uncertainty is whether §1292(a) applies to orders concerning temporary restraining orders (TROs), which we discussed in §3.5. The general rule is that TROs are not subject to interlocutory review as injunctive orders under §1292(a).[61] This rule makes sense, because TROs are usually of very limited duration; the issue will almost always be moot by the time the appellate court could entertain the appeal.[62] As with other topics, however, the courts look to the substance of the matter, and not the terminology. Thus, if what the trial court called a TRO has in effect become a preliminary injunction, §1292(a) will apply.[63] Similarly, although denial of a TRO is not generally appealable, a party may invoke §1292(a) if she can show that the denial effectively removes the possibility of receiving any injunctive relief and causes serious harm that could not be reviewed meaningfully on final judgment.[64]

Section 1292(b)

Section 1292(b) of the Judicial Code (28 U.S.C. §1292(b)) permits appeal of interlocutory orders if both the trial and appellate courts agree that three things are true. When they do so, the two levels of the judiciary are in accord that the situation warrants a departure from the final judgment rule. First, the order must "involve[] a controlling question of law." Second, that controlling question must be one "as to which there is substantial ground for difference of opinion." And third, "an immediate appeal from the order may materially advance the ultimate termination of the litigation." The district judge must first conclude that these requirements are met, after which the appellate court must agree that the interlocutory review should be permitted.[65]

---

[61]*See* Board of Governors v. DLG Financial Corp., 29 F.3d 993, 1000 (5th Cir. 1994).

[62]A TRO cannot exceed ten days unless the trial court extends it up to an additional ten days on showing of good cause. It may be extended further on agreement of the parties. Fed. R. Civ. P. 65(b).

[63]*See, e.g.,* Baker Elec. Cooperative v. Chaske, 28 F.3d 1466, 1472 (8th Cir. 1994) (TRO in effect 30 months had become a preliminary injunction).

[64]*See, e.g.,* Religious Tech. Center v. Scott, 869 F.2d 1306, 1308-1309 (9th Cir. 1989) (denial of TRO effectively constituted the denial of a preliminary injunction and thus was appealable).

[65]The party taking the appeal must apply to the court of appeals within ten days of the district court's certification as to the first two requirements. 28 U.S.C. §1292(b). Note the contrast between §1292(b) and Federal Rule 54(b). In the former, both the trial and appellate courts must independently agree that the three requirements are satisfied. In the latter, the appellate court may only review whether the trial court properly assessed the requirements. Of course, the major difference between the two provisions is that the former applies to interlocutory rulings while the latter addresses final rulings disposing of fewer than all claims or parties in the case.

The procedure is usually referred to as "certification" of the issue by the district court to the court of appeals.

This statute strikes a salutary balance between the general policy of avoiding piecemeal appeals and the need to permit some interlocutory review. Unlike §1292(a), it is not subject-specific. The interlocutory order might involve any legal issue, just so the three requirements are met. When they are, the final judgment rule is appropriately obviated to permit decision of an important and difficult question, the resolution of which may speed the ultimate disposition of the dispute. Whether the statute is satisfied is a fact-specific, *ad hoc* determination.

The issue subject to appeal might be wholly unrelated to the substance of the underlying controversy. Indeed, one use of this device has been to assess subject matter jurisdiction.

> ○ ***Example #11.*** *P* sued two defendants, *D-1* and *D-2*. As to *D-1*, *P*'s claim invoked diversity of citizenship jurisdiction. As to the claim against *D-2*, however, *P* sought to invoke supplemental jurisdiction. The case arose before the passage of the supplemental jurisdiction statute, and the supplemental jurisdiction issue was a difficult one, on which the courts of appeals had disagreed. The trial court concluded that it had supplemental jurisdiction but certified the question under §1292(b). The court of appeals agreed to hear the issue, as did the Supreme Court, which ultimately held there was no supplemental jurisdiction.[66]

This case demonstrates the utility of the statute. Had the issue not been certified and reviewed on an interlocutory basis, the parties would have been required to litigate the case on the merits fully before obtaining appellate review of the jurisdictional issue. In view of the ultimate holding that there was no subject matter jurisdiction over the claim by *P* against *D-2*, such litigation would have been a complete waste of time, effort, money, and judicial resources.

But judicial savings alone does not justify use of §1292(b). The matter must involve a question of law on which there is ground for disagreement and, thus, a reasonable chance of reversal. Accordingly, topics addressed to the discretion of the trial judge, on which there is little likelihood of reversal, are less appropriate for treatment under §1292(b). Moreover, the issue may be so collateral to disposition of the case that its expeditious resolution will not advance the ultimate disposition of the case.[67]

---

[66]These are the facts in *Finley v. United States*, 490 U.S. 545 (1989), which led to the passage of the supplemental jurisdiction statute. See §4.7.

[67]*See, e.g.*, People Who Care v. Rockford Bd. of Education, 921 F.2d 132, 134 (7th Cir. 1991) (appellate review of attorneys' fee award will not advance ultimate disposition of dispute).

○ ***Example #12.*** Suppose in Example #11 that the district court had held there was no supplemental jurisdiction over the claim against *D-2* and had entered dismissal of *P*'s claim as to that defendant. Could *P* have sought appellate review under §1292(b)? No. Such an order would have been a final judgment in a multiparty case, and thus would have been eligible for treatment under Rule 54(b). Because it thus was not an interlocutory order, §1292(b) would not apply.

Federal Rule 23(f)

This provision gives the federal courts of appeals discretion to review a trial court order either granting or denying certification as a class action. Before its promulgation in 1998, appellate review of class certification orders was problematic. Obviously, a decision either to certify a class or to deny such certification is not a final judgment, because it leaves the merits of the underlying dispute unresolved (indeed, unaddressed). On the other hand, the decision has enormous practical impact. The parties usually consider the class certification issue the watershed event in the litigation; its resolution often determines whether the case will proceed to trial or settle, and on what terms. Thus, some appellate courts decided to review denials of class certification, on the theory that such denial of class status sounded the "death knell" of the case.[68]

But the Supreme Court rejected the death knell doctrine in 1978, in a case that also rejected use of the collateral order doctrine,[69] which we see at §14.5.2 below. After that, courts wrestled unsatisfactorily with whether orders about class certification could be reviewed by extraordinary writ, which we see in §14.6.[70] The addition of Rule 23(f) brings some clarity by giving the appellate court discretion to review class

---

[68]The leading case was *Eisen v. Carlisle & Jacqueline*, 370 F.2d 119, 120-121 (2d Cir. 1966) (accepting appellate jurisdiction when denial of class certification would end the litigation because the plaintiff would abandon his individual claim).

[69]Coopers & Lybrand v. Livesay, 437 U.S. 463, 468 (1978) (the fact that an interlocutory order denying class certification "may lead a party to dismiss his claim before final judgment is not a sufficient reason for considering it a 'final judgment' within . . . §1291"). In 2017, the Court again rejected the "death knell" doctrine. In *Microsoft Corp. v. Baker,* 137 S. Ct. 1702, 1705 (2017), the district court granted a motion to strike class action allegations from the case. Rather than proceed, the plaintiffs stipulated to voluntary dismissal of the case with prejudice, which meant the case could not be refiled. The plaintiffs then appealed their voluntary dismissal and sought to raise the issue of class certification. The effort failed; the Court concluded: "Plaintiffs in putative class actions cannot transform a tentative interlocutory order into a final judgment within the meaning of §1291 simply by dismissing their claims with prejudice."

[70]*See, e.g.*, In re Rhone-Poulenc Rorer, Inc., 51 F.3d 1293, 1294 (7th Cir. 1995) (issuing mandamus to decertify class).

certification orders. As discussed in §13.3.5, there is some evidence
that Rule 23(f) has been employed mostly to reverse orders granting
class certification.

Under Rule 23(f), the party seeking review—either of a grant or
denial of class certification—must petition the court of appeals within
14 days of the order. That timing provision is mandatory and is not
subject to "equitable tolling." In *Nutraceutical Corp. v. Lambert*,[71]
the district court entered an order that decertified a class that the
court had earlier certified. Instead of seeking Rule 23(f) review of the
decertification order within 14 days, the plaintiff asked the district
court to reconsider its decertification order. The district court denied
reconsideration, after which the plaintiff sought Rule 23(f) review. The
problem was that this was more than 14 days after the decertification
order. The Court held that failure to seek review within 14 days of the
decertification order waived the right to proceed under Rule 23(f). It
did not matter that the court of appeals held that the plaintiff had
acted diligently; the time limit is mandatory.

The decision whether to engage in appellate review is entirely
in the appellate court;[72] the trial court plays no role. Each court of
appeals is free to determine for itself the standards by which to decide
whether to hear the appeal. Though there is some variation, each court
appears to embrace a multifactored balancing approach.[73] Whatever
the approach, we should emphasize that appeal under Rule 23(f) is
exceptional; the Eleventh Circuit says that permitting such an appeal
"should be an avenue of last resort."[74]

The pendency of a petition for appellate review does not stay proceedings at the trial court. Indeed, even if the court of appeals decides
to hear the appeal, proceedings at the trial court are not stayed unless
either the trial court or the court of appeals so orders.

---

[71]139 S. Ct. 710, 714-717 (2019).

[72]Rule 23(f) offers no guidance on when an appellate court should take an appeal,
and the courts have struggled to lay out relevant factors. One instructive case is
Carnegie v. Household International, Inc., 376 F.3d 656, 658 (7th Cir. 2004), in which
Judge Posner said: "The rule does not state criteria for the exercise of this discretionary authority. But the case law teaches that the more novel the issue presented by
the appeal and so the less likely that the district court's resolution of it will stand, the
more important the resolution of the issue is either to the particular litigation or to the
general development of class action law, and the more likely the prompt resolution of
the issue is to expedite the litigation and prevent a coercive settlement, the stronger
the case for allowing the appeal."

[73]*See* Bryan Lammon, *Dizzying* Gillespie: *The Exaggerated Death of the Balancing
Approach and the Inescapable Allure of Flexibility in Appellate Jurisdiction*, 51 U. Rich.
L. Rev. 371, 382, 385-410 (2017).

[74]Shin v. Cobb Cty. Bd. of Educ., 248 F.3d 1061, 1064 (11th Cir. 2001). *See also* In re
Sumitomo Copper Litigation, 262 F.3d 134, 140 (2d Cir. 2001) ("the standards of Rule
23(f) will rarely be met.").

Should the existence of Rule 23(f) affect the potential availability of other forms of interlocutory review? Many believe the answer should be yes, that Rule 23(f) should be seen as the exclusive method for seeking appellate review of an order regarding class certification. The Seventh Circuit has concluded that "district judges should not, and we shall not, authorize appeal under 28 U.S.C. §1292(b) when appeal might lie under Rule 23(f)."[75] Similarly, the existence of Rule 23(f) should obviate the availability of an extraordinary writ to review class certification orders. Such writs, which we discuss in §14.6 below, are not proper if an avenue for appeal exists. Rule 23(f) provides such an avenue, even when the appellate court refuses to take the appeal.

§14.5.2   Judicial "Exceptions"

The federal courts have occasionally interpreted some interlocutory orders as "final" for purposes of appeal under §1291. The Supreme Court insists that such interpretations do not eviscerate the final judgment rule. Rather, they give that rule a "practical rather than a technical construction."[76] Thus these case-law rules are not so much "exceptions" to the final judgment rule as they are doctrines manipulating the interpretation of the word "final" in §1291. The effect is the same, however: These doctrines permit immediate appeal of rulings that do not satisfy the general understanding of the final judgment rule.

Collateral Order Doctrine

The Supreme Court established the collateral order doctrine in *Cohen v. Beneficial Industrial Loan Corp.*[77] *Cohen* was a shareholder derivative suit (see §13.1) in federal court. The defendant argued that a state statute required the plaintiff to post a bond as security for costs and made a motion for an order requiring such a bond.[78] The trial court denied the motion. The defendant sought to appeal that decision to the Second Circuit. Though that court held the order nonappealable, the

---

[75]Richardson Electronics, Ltd. v. Panache Broadcasting of Pennsylvania, Inc., 202 F.3d 957, 959 (7th Cir. 2000). Federal Rule 23(f), unlike §1292(b), does not require that the appeal raise a controlling issue of law on which there is substantial ground for difference of opinion. The court recognized that some cases might present an issue satisfying §1292(b) and not involving the merits of class certification. *Id.*

[76]Firestone Tire & Rubber Co. v. Risjord, 449 U.S. 368, 375 (1981) (*quoting* Cohen v. Beneficial Indus. Loan Corp., 337 U.S. 541, 546 (1949)).

[77]337 U.S. 541, 546-547 (1949).

[78]The Court determined that Federal Rule 23.1, and not state law, governed. We saw this case in discussing the *Erie* doctrine, at §10.5.

Supreme Court disagreed. It upheld appealability under §1291 and established the three requirements of what has become known as the collateral order doctrine.

First, the issue appealed must be both legally significant[79] and "not an ingredient of the cause of action and does not require consideration with it."[80] It is, as more commonly stated, an important issue "collateral" to the merits of the underlying dispute. Because of this, immediate appellate review will not violate the policy against piecemeal appeals; the issue presented here is unrelated to the merits, so review of this issue will not interfere with consideration of the merits by the trial court. Second, the issue appealed must have been decided finally by the trial court. It was "concluded and closed,"[81] and not subject to amendment during the pendency of the case. Third, waiting for final judgment would effectively deny appellate review of the issue.

On the facts of *Cohen*, all requirements were met. The question of whether the plaintiff had to post a bond was important and could affect other derivative litigation. It was also collateral to the merits of the underlying dispute, which had to do with alleged breaches of duties by corporate management. The issue had been resolved completely by the district court; there was little chance that the court would revisit it. And, finally, the issue could not be reviewed effectively if the parties awaited final judgment, because in the meantime the appellant would have to suffer through litigation that would be obviated if the plaintiff had been required to post a bond.

The Supreme Court has interpreted *Cohen* sparingly. In *Firestone Tire & Rubber Co. v. Risjord*,[82] it held that an order denying a motion to disqualify attorneys from representing a party in the case was not appealable under the collateral order doctrine. Although the order was collateral to the merits and had been determined conclusively, there was no reason the ruling could not be effectively reviewed after final judgment. In *Cunningham v. Hamilton County*,[83] the Court refused to apply *Cohen* to an order imposing a monetary discovery sanction against an attorney, even though she no longer represented a party in the case. First, the order was not collateral to the merits of the

---

[79]This goes without saying. It is hard to imagine that anyone would argue for an exception to a well-established rule to permit immediate appeal on a legally insignificant issue. The whole idea is to get something that matters before the court of appeals more quickly than would otherwise be the case.

[80]*Cohen*, 337 U.S. at 546-547.

[81]*Id.* at 546.

[82]449 U.S. 368, 375 (1981).

[83]527 U.S. 198, 207-210 (1999).

case; whether the sanction was justified would require a review of the underlying facts.[84]

This is not to say that the *Cohen* doctrine is never successfully invoked. In *Puerto Rico Aqueduct & Sewer Authority v. Metcalf & Eddy, Inc.*,[85] the defendant, an agency of the Puerto Rican government, claimed immunity from being sued in federal court under the Eleventh Amendment.[86] The trial court's denial of the motion to dismiss satisfied the collateral order doctrine. It raised an important legal issue that was collateral to the merits of the underlying claim against the agency. The issue had been determined finally by the district court. And the issue could not effectively be reviewed on appeal from a final judgment. Without immediate appeal, the very protection claimed under the Eleventh Amendment (immunity from suit itself, not just from immunity from liability) would be lost.

Closely related are cases in which individuals claim "qualified immunity" from suit. Such cases usually involve claims under 42 U.S.C. §1983, which permits suit for deprivation of federal rights under color of state law. These are frequently asserted against state officers who allegedly violated a constitutional right of the plaintiff. Defendant officers are immune from suit altogether, however, if they acted in good faith and did not violate clearly established rights.[87] It is common in §1983 cases to have defendants move for summary judgment on the basis of this immunity. Denial of such a motion is not a final judgment, because it leaves the case intact. Nonetheless, because immunity is aimed at sparing the defendant not just from liability, but from suit itself, courts have permitted immediate appeal, at least if the motion for summary judgment presented only a question of law, and not a dispute of fact.[88]

In *Ortiz v. Jordan*,[89] defendant officers' motion for summary judgment was denied, and they did not seek immediate appellate review.

---

[84]In *Coopers & Lybrand v. Livesay*, 437 U.S. 463, 473-474 (1978), the Court rejected use of the collateral order doctrine concerning an order certifying a class action. Such orders are continually subject to reconsideration by the trial court in light of factual development and thus intimately connected with the merits. *Coopers & Lybrand* is most notable for its rejection of the "death knell" doctrine, discussed in §14.5.1 above with regard to Federal Rule 23(f).

[85]506 U.S. 139, 142-143 (1993).

[86]The Eleventh Amendment shields states from being sued for damages in state court. It provides not just immunity from *liability*, but from being *sued in federal court at all*. Thus, making a defendant wait until final judgment to raise the issue on appeal robs it of this protection from being sued. *See* 13 Wright & Miller §§3524-3524.6. Though Puerto Rico is not a state, it may be entitled to Eleventh Amendment immunity. *See* McLeod-Lopez v. Algarin, 603 F. Supp. 2d 330, 342 (D.P.R. 2009) ("enjoys the protection of the Eleventh Amendment").

[87]Harlow v. Fitzgerald, 457 U.S. 800, 818 (1982).

[88]Johnson v. Jones, 515 U.S. 304, 313 (1995).

[89]562 U.S. 180, 181 (2011).

After trial on the merits and entry of final judgment against them, they attempted to appeal the denial of their motion for summary judgment. Resolving an issue that had split the courts of appeals, the Supreme Court held that once a case proceeds to trial, a party cannot appeal denial of her motion for summary judgment. The proper course would be to preserve the issue by moving for judgment as a matter of law and renewing it after judgment (see §9.5).[90]

In the past decade, the Court has been reluctant to permit invocation of the collateral order rule. In *Will v. Hallock*,[91] federal officers seized plaintiff's computer as part of a criminal investigation; they damaged the computer, resulting in loss of data and ultimately causing plaintiff's business to fail. Plaintiff sued the United States under the Federal Tort Claims Act, which waives the federal government's sovereign immunity in some circumstances. The government won that case, however, because the court found that the officers had acted in good faith, which was an exception to the government's waiver of immunity. Plaintiff then sued the individual officers, alleging that they had violated her constitutional right to due process. The officers raised as a defense the ruling in the previous case in favor of the government. By statute, a judgment in favor of the government constitutes a bar to suit against individual officers. The district court rejected the defense, however, because it held that the judgment in favor of the government was based upon a procedural ground and did not bar the suit against the officers.

The question was whether that order denying the officers' motion to dismiss was appealable under *Cohen*. The Court held that it was not. It emphasized that something more than merely avoiding trial had to be at stake—"some particular value of high order."[92] In *Puerto Rico Aqueduct*, for example, forcing the defendant to endure trial would have imposed the burden of litigation *and* have constituted a denigration of Puerto Rico's dignitary interest as a government entitled to protection by the Eleventh Amendment. On the facts in *Will*, the Court found no such important interest beyond the ordinary desire to avoid the rigors of trial. Avoidance of litigation "for its own sake"

---

[90]*Id.* at 184, 189 ("Once the case proceeds to trial, the full record developed in court supersedes the record existing at the time of the summary judgment motion.... Absent a [motion for judgment as a matter of law], we have repeatedly held, an appellate court is 'powerless' to review the sufficiency of the evidence after trial"). For this point, the Court cited *Unitherm Food Systems, Inc. v. Swift-Eckrich, Inc.*, 546 U.S. 394, 405 (2006). In that case, the Court held that a party's failure to make a renewed motion for judgment as a matter of law or for new trial on the basis of insufficient evidence precluded it from seeking a new trial on appeal on that basis. See §9.6.

[91]546 U.S. 345, 347-348 (2006).

[92]546 U.S. at 352.

is not sufficient; if it were, "collateral order appeal would be a matter of right whenever the government lost a motion to dismiss under the Tort Claims Act. . . ."[93]

In *Mohawk Industries, Inc v. Carpenter*,[94] the Court held that an order requiring a party to disclose material that it considers protected under the attorney-client privilege was not appealable under the collateral order doctrine. The appealing party made an argument reminiscent of that made in *Puerto Rico Aqueduct* by asserting that disclosure of privileged material could not be reviewed effectively on appeal from final judgment; specifically, the privilege protects against not only the use of privileged material at trial but the disclosure of material in the first place. The Court rejected this argument, concluding that: "Appellate courts can remedy the improper disclosure of privileged material in the same way they remedy a host of other erroneous evidentiary rulings: by vacating an adverse judgment and remanding for a new trial in which the protected material and its fruits are excluded from evidence."[95]

It also rebuffed the argument that delayed review might undermine the core purposes of the attorney-client privilege, saying: "Mohawk is undoubtedly correct that an order to disclose privileged information intrudes on the confidentiality of attorney-client communications. But deferring review until final judgment does not meaningfully reduce the *ex ante* incentives for full and frank consultations between clients and counsel."[96] The Court instructed that one faced with a "particularly injurious or novel privilege ruling" had other options for immediate appellate review. The party could seek review under §1292 or mandamus (see §14.6), or it could defy the court order, be punished for criminal contempt of court, and appeal that ruling.[97]

The trend of the cases is clear: The collateral order doctrine is of limited utility except in cases involving immunity from suit, such as that provided by the Eleventh Amendment.[98]

---

[93]*Id.* at 353-354.

[94]558 U.S. 100, 109 (2009).

[95]*Id.*

[96]*Id.*

[97]*Id.* at 111. *See generally* Cassandra Burke Robertson, *Appellate Review of Discovery Orders in Federal Court: A Suggested Approach for Handling Privilege Claims*, 81 Wash. L. Rev. 733 (2006).

[98]Bryan Lammon, *Assumed Facts and Blatant Contradictions in Qualified-Immunity Appeals*, 55 Ga. L. Rev. 959, 975, 995 (2021); Michael E. Solimine, *Are Interlocutory Qualified Immunity Appeals Lawful?*, 94 Notre Dame L. Rev. Online 169, 173 (2019); Adam N. Steinman, *Reinventing Appellate Jurisdiction*, 48 B.C. L. Rev. 1237, 1250 (2007).

Other Case-Law Relaxation of the Final Judgment Rule

In the old case of *Forgay v. Conrad*,[99] the Court permitted an interlocutory appeal basically to avoid hardship on one of the parties. There, the trial court made a partial adjudication of the claim but directed the defendant to deliver property to the plaintiff. It seemed to treat the order as a final judgment. Although no final accounting had been made, and the order thus was interlocutory, the Court permitted the appeal. The holding was born of necessity; the defendant simply needed immediate access to the appellate court, and the Supreme Court permitted it.[100] *Forgay* has not been invoked frequently.[101] Though they are not final judgments, federal courts traditionally have allowed immediate appeal of a denial of an absentee's motion to intervene of right.[102] Such immediate appeal can delay resolution of the underlying case.

Finally, as noted above in discussion of the *Mohawk* case, the federal courts will allow immediate appeal of a criminal contempt citation. Criminal contempt is a separate proceeding from the underlying civil case, so an order of contempt is appealable as a final judgment. Obviously, this is a risky route, but is often the only option in discovery cases. A famous example is *Hickman v. Taylor*,[103] in which lawyers and a party asserting work product protection refused to comply with an order compelling production. After conviction for criminal contempt, they prevailed on appeal.[104]

---

[99]47 U.S. 201, 203-204 (1848).

[100]In *Gillespie v. United States Steel Corp.*, 379 U.S. 148, 152-153 (1964), the Court seemed to say that it would allow interlocutory review whenever it would be salutary. The broad language has not generated support. Indeed, the Court later criticized it. *Coopers & Lybrand*, above, 437 U.S. at 477 n.30. *But see* Bryan Lammon, *Dizzying* Gillespie*: The Exaggerated Death of the Balancing Approach and the Inescapable Allure of Flexibility in Appellate Jurisdiction,* 51 U. Rich. L. Rev. 371 (2017) (balancing approach to appellate jurisdiction persists in some substantive areas).

[101]*See, e.g.*, Richard A. Matasar & Gregory S. Bruch, *Procedural Common Law, Federal Jurisdictional Policy, and Abandonment of the Adequate and Independent State Grounds Doctrine*, 86 Colum. L. Rev. 1291, 1354 n.314 (1986). *See also* In re Chateaugay Corp., 922 F.2d 86, 91 (2d Cir. 1990).

[102]*See, e.g.*, Cascade Natural Gas Corp. v. El Paso Natural Gas Co., 386 U.S. 129, 131 (1967). *See generally* Wright & Kane 547.

[103]329 U.S. 495, 497-499 (1947), discussed at §8.3.2.

[104]The situation may be different if the privileged material is in possession of a third party. For example, suppose documents pertaining to a business deal are held by a party's attorney. In litigation concerning that business deal, the court issues a subpoena to the attorney to produce the documents and rejects the argument that the documents are privileged. In *Perlman v. United States*, 247 U.S. 7, 15 (1918), the Court held that the discovery order should be immediately appealable, without requiring the third party to defy it and be held in contempt (after all, few third parties will be willing to do this). The Ninth Circuit has held that *Perlman* survives *Mohawk*. United States v. Krane, 625 F.3d 568, 572-573 (9th Cir. 2010).

§14.6   Review by Extraordinary (or "Prerogative") Writ

What we have seen above are circumstances in which one party may appeal an order of a trial court to an appellate court. In addition, an aggrieved litigant may, in rare circumstances, ask an appellate court to issue a writ—an order—to the trial court. A party seeking such a writ actually commences a new proceeding by filing a petition for the appropriate writ *in the appellate court*. That party is the "petitioner" and the other parties in the case at the trial court are "respondents" in the writ proceeding.[105] Technically, in some judicial systems, the trial judge or court is actually named as a respondent in the petition for the writ,[106] although only the litigants brief and argue the issue. This was true in federal practice until 1996, when the applicable rule was amended to provide that only litigants are to be named as respondents. Accordingly, in the federal system, writ proceedings no longer bear the name of the district judge or the district court. Writ proceedings are entitled "In re [name of petitioner]."[107]

The main extraordinary writs are those of *mandamus* (or "mandate") and *prohibition*. Technically, mandamus lies to order the trial court to do something it has a mandatory duty to do. Prohibition lies to stop the trial court from doing something it has no jurisdiction to do. The distinctions between these two have eroded, however, and the label used is not terribly important in federal practice;[108] most litigants seem to use "mandamus" as the label of choice. The main point is that whatever label is used, issuance of such writs is extraordinary; it is limited to exceptional and rare circumstances.

---

[105]FRAP 21(a)(1).

[106]Sometimes the trial judge is named personally. An example is *World-Wide Volkswagen v. Woodson*, which we studied in §2.4.4. Woodson was the state court trial judge who held that there was personal jurisdiction over the two New York defendants. When those two defendants sought an extraordinary writ from the state appellate court, Woodson was named as respondent. In some systems, the court (rather than the specific trial judge) is named in the application for a writ. An example is *Asahi v. Superior Court*, another personal jurisdiction case discussed in §2.4.4. There, the state trial court had upheld jurisdiction over Asahi, which then sought a writ from the state appellate court. In the federal system, before 1996 amendments to FRAP 22, the district court was named as a respondent. Now, however, only the other parties to the case are respondents. The appellate court may invite the trial judge to participate in the writ proceeding, although this is rarely done.

[107]FRAP 21(a)(2)(A).

[108]Indeed, federal courts have long been forgiving about the technical misnaming of a writ. *See In re Simons*, 246 U.S. 231 (1918) (form or label of writ not important to ultimate disposition).

In the federal judicial system, the All Writs Act[109] permits the courts of appeals to issue appropriate writs to district courts.[110] The writ must be "in aid of" the court of appeals' jurisdiction, which basically means it is necessary to confine a lower court to the lawful exercise of its jurisdiction or to compel that court to exercise its power when there is a duty to do so.[111] So an extraordinary writ is *not* a vehicle simply for correcting legal error. Rather, it is a device to confine the lower court to its proper jurisdiction. Issuance of a writ is never automatic but is vested in the discretion of the court of appeals. It is limited to cases in which the district court has done something it has no power to do or has so abused its discretion as to have usurped power.[112] The error must be clear and indisputable, and not just a matter on which the court of appeals has a difference of opinion with the district court. Thus, writ practice is not a substitute for appeal.[113] As a general matter, a petition for a writ will be denied if the aggrieved party has any other remedy, including appeal.[114]

A trial court that has improperly exercised personal or subject matter jurisdiction may be reined in by an extraordinary writ from the appellate court.[115] In addition, a transfer of venue to a different circuit might be corrected by writ to protect the jurisdiction of the appellate court.[116] Mandamus has been invoked to review a judge's refusal to disqualify herself from presiding over a case.[117] Likewise, mandamus is appropriate to correct the lower court's refusal to permit jury trial under the Seventh Amendment.[118] Mandamus will lie when a trial

---

[109]28 U.S.C. §1651(a) ("The Supreme Court and all courts established by Act of Congress may issue all writs necessary or appropriate in aid of their respective jurisdictions and agreeable to the usages and principles of law").

[110]The Act applies to any court created by Congress, and thus applies to the Supreme Court of the United States and federal district courts as well. It permits a court to issue a writ to a lower court within its jurisdiction. The most common use—the one on which we focus—is by a court of appeals to make an order to a district court.

[111]*See* United States v. Victoria-21, 3 F.3d 571, 575 (2d Cir. 1993).

[112]*See* Mallard v. United States District Court, 490 U.S. 296, 309 (1989). *See also* 20 Moore's Federal Practice §321.15 (3d ed. 2005) (discussing different showings required for issuance of mandamus in different circuits).

[113]*See, e.g.*, In re Chesson, 897 F.2d 156, 159 (5th Cir. 1990).

[114]*See* In re Ivy, 901 F.2d 7, 10 (2d Cir. 1990).

[115]See note 106 above (personal jurisdiction cases involving appellate review by writ).

[116]*See, e.g.*, Roofing & Sheet Metal Servs., Inc. v. La Quinta Motor Inns, Inc., 689 F.2d 982, 988 (11th Cir. 1982) (intercircuit transfer more appropriately reviewed by writ than intracircuit transfer).

[117]By statute, federal judges may be required to "recuse" (disqualify) themselves from sitting on a case. For example, a judge who owns stock in a corporate litigant must recuse. 28 U.S.C. §455(b)(4).

[118]*Beacon Theatres, Inc. v. Westover*, 359 U.S. 500, 511 (1959), discussed in §9.2.2, was such a case.

court abdicates its responsibility by referring all aspects of a case to a judicial surrogate.[119] These examples show the use of an extraordinary writ to compel the lower court to act within its power.

Moreover, however, such use of the "heavy artillery"[120] of mandamus serves a didactic function. It sends a message to the lower courts as a whole about proper exercise of their authority. This use of the writ has been called *supervisory mandamus*. Indeed, the Supreme Court has said that use of the writ to exercise "supervisory control of the district courts by the Courts of Appeals is necessary to proper judicial administration."[121] A judge's improper refusal to disqualify herself, for example, casts a cloud not only on the individual case, but on the judicial process itself.[122]

There was some thought in the 1990s that the courts of appeals were expanding the use of the extraordinary writ beyond the traditional use of confining a lower court to its proper jurisdiction. Most of the high-profile cases, however, involved issuance of mandamus to overturn district courts' certification of class actions.[123] The cases predated the promulgation of Rule 23(f), which, as we saw in §14.5.1, expressly permits the court of appeals to review orders granting or denying class certification. Today, then, the availability of Rule 23(f) should preclude requests for an extraordinary writ regarding class certification.

Outside the class-certification context, there have been occasional broad invocations of mandamus. In one case, for instance, a trial court rejected a party's assertion of privilege and compelled it to disclose a document in discovery. Although interlocutory discovery orders have never been readily reviewed by appellate courts, the Second Circuit issued a writ to overturn the order compelling production.[124] The order was surprising given the fairly clear precedent that appellate review in such instances is available through appeal of a contempt citation, as we noted in §14.5.2. Still, despite the occasional arguably expansive

[119]LaBuy v. Howes Leather Co., 352 U.S. 249, 256 (1957) (involving wholesale abdication of case to a special master, who should be used as an adjunct, with ultimate authority resting in the district judge).

[120]In re Bituminous Coal Operators' Ass'n, 949 F.2d 1165, 1168 (D.C. Cir. 1991).

[121]*LaBuy*, 352 U.S. at 259-260.

[122]*See* Union Carbide Corp. v. U.S. Cutting Serv., Inc., 782 F.2d 710, 712 (7th Cir. 1986).

[123]*See, e.g.*, Jackson v. Motel 6 Multipurpose, Inc., 130 F.3d 999, 1006-1007 (11th Cir. 1997) (decertifying nationwide class allegedly suffering discrimination); In re American Medical Syst., Inc., 75 F.3d 1069, 1089 (6th Cir. 1996); In re Rhone-Poulenc Rorer, Inc., 51 F.3d 1293, 1304 (7th Cir. 1995) (decertifying nationwide class regarding allegedly tainted blood products). *See, e.g.*, Amy Schmidt Jones, *The Use of Mandamus to Vacate Mass Exposure Tort Class Certification Orders*, 72 N.Y.U. L. Rev. 232 (1997).

[124]In re Steinhardt Partners, LP, 9 F.3d 230 (2d Cir. 1993).

use of mandamus in such cases, it seems unlikely that the extraordinary writ will become a free-wheeling substitute for appeal in the federal system.[125]

§14.7 Standards of Review

Here, we assume that a case is properly before the appellate court. The issue here is the standard by which that court will review what the trial court did. Different issues are reviewed by different standards. It is useful to think of the varying standards employed by the appellate court as being relatively more or less deferential to the trial court. On some issues, the appellate court may give no deference at all, and may be free to substitute its own conclusion. On other issues, the court of appeals may give enormous deference, concluding that it will affirm the trial court unless its result is simply bizarre. On still other issues, there may be some intermediate position.

The determination of how much deference is due the trial court is based upon a variety of factors. First, of course, is the concern that the judicial system "get it right," that it apply the law correctly and reach the appropriate decision. Second, there is a concern with the relative expertise of the two judicial levels. For example, the appellate court should defer to the trial judge on matters such as credibility of witnesses, since only the trial judge saw the witnesses testify. Third, we are concerned with finality—that cases not be reversed for silly, insubstantial reasons.

Matters of Law

On issues of law, the appellate court gives no deference to the trial court ruling. There is no presumption that the trial court "got it right." The court of appeals is required to assess the issue *de novo*. This intrusive review is appropriate because the determination of what the law is, is not something on which the trial court would have especial expertise. It is not dependent upon anything that goes on in the trial. It is a dry question of research, which the appellate court may actually be better equipped than the trial court to perform. After all, part of its very function is to explicate the law for the benefit of the parties, the lower courts, and the community at large.[126]

---

[125]Some states, notably California, permit more liberal use of mandamus than the federal system.

[126]In fact, the appellate court may decide that the law was properly applied but ought to be changed. Its holding on this point would create precedent and, under the doctrine of *stare decisis*, be binding on all lower courts in the jurisdiction. We discussed precedent at §1.2.2.

There are many pure questions of law that may arise in any case, such as whether the trial judge properly instructed the jury on the elements of the claim or a defense, whether the trial judge properly allocated the burden of proof at trial, or whether she applied the correct standard for summary judgment or a motion to dismiss for failure to state a claim or a motion for judgment as a matter of law. On all such questions, the appellate court may substitute its judgment for that of the trial court.

Questions of Fact

By questions of fact, we mean what the Supreme Court has called *historical facts*;[127] that is, what happened in the real world. Was the traffic light red or green? Did the defendant drink alcohol before driving? If so, how much and when? Did the plaintiff sign the letter? What, if anything, did the defendant say to the plaintiff? Did the plaintiff pay for the goods? Is that witness lying? Such questions are important to the immediate parties, to be sure, but do not have the community-wide impact of a ruling on a question of law. Moreover, because only the fact-finder saw the witnesses and heard the testimony, an appellate court should defer at least in some measure to the determination of the fact-finder at trial. And indeed, that is the case.

The fact-finder at trial, of course, might be the judge or a jury. In §9.2, we discussed the right to a jury trial in civil cases in federal court. If there is no right to a jury trial, or if the parties waive the right to jury trial, the judge will act as the finder of fact in what is called a *bench trial*. Federal Rule 52(a)(6) provides that the trial judge's determination of the facts in a bench trial must be affirmed on appeal unless they are "clearly erroneous." Further, the Rule expressly requires that "due regard shall be given to the opportunity of the trial court to judge the credibility of the witnesses." Thus, such findings are presumptively correct; the appellate court defers to the trial judge's findings unless, "on the entire evidence [it] is left with the definite and firm conviction that a mistake has been committed."[128] The appellate court does not have to conclude that the trial judge necessarily got it "wrong." Instead, it must find that there is not enough evidence in the record to support the finding. Deference reflects the institutional judgment that the trial judge was in a position to see and study the witnesses, and to put testimony and other evidence into an overall context before making her decision. The appellate court is able to do none

---

[127]Pullman-Standard v. Swint, 456 U.S. 273, 289 n.19 (1982).

[128]United States v. United States Gypsum Co., 333 U.S. 364, 395 (1948) (the leading definition of "clearly erroneous").

of these things. Not surprisingly, because of this deferential standard, few cases are reversed because of erroneous fact-finding by the judge.

But what if the trial consisted mostly of deposition testimony in the record, without live witnesses? In such a case, some courts concluded that the trial court's findings of fact were entitled to less, or even no, deference.[129] They reasoned that an appellate court could review deposition testimony as readily as the trial judge.[130] The Supreme Court rejected this notion, however, in *Anderson v. City of Bessemer City*.[131] *Anderson* holds that all bench findings are entitled to review under the clearly erroneous standard, "even when the district court's findings do not rest on credibility determination, but are based instead on physical or documentary evidence or inferences from other facts."[132] The Court further noted that when the judge bases findings on her assessment of credibility of witnesses, "Rule 52(a) demands even greater deference to the trial court's findings. . . ."[133]

Rule 52(a)(1) does not apply to cases involving jury trial. Jury findings of fact are entitled to even greater deference than judge findings, because of the reexamination clause of the Seventh Amendment. That clause provides that "no fact tried by a jury, shall be otherwise re-examined in any Court of the United States, than according to the rules of common law." The appropriate standard of review on appeal of a jury verdict is similar to that used by a trial judge in determining whether to grant a motion of judgment as a matter of law under Federal Rule 50(a)(1).[134] Specifically, then, the appellate court views all evidence—including credibility determinations and inferences—in the light most favorable to the verdict and must affirm so long as a reasonable fact-finder could have reached that conclusion.[135]

---

[129]*See, e.g.*, Orvis v. Higgins, 180 F.2d 537, 539 (2d Cir. 1950).

[130]While this is true, the courts adopting this approach overlooked (1) that Rule 52(a) did not make such a distinction and (2) that even if the appellate court was in as good a position to judge the facts as the trial court, disregarding the trial court's findings "impairs confidence in the trial courts and multiplies appeals with attendant expense and delay." Wright & Kane, Federal Courts 690.

[131]470 U.S. 564, 573-575 (1985).

[132]*Id.* at 574. Federal Rule 52(a) was amended within months of the *Anderson* decision to apply the clearly erroneous standard to all bench findings of fact, "whether based on oral or documentary evidence." This requirement is now set forth at Rule 52(a)(6).

[133]*Id.* at 575.

[134]Most states refer to this motion as one for a directed verdict. We discussed this motion at §9.5.

[135]*See, e.g.*, Dresser-Rand Co. v. Virtual Automation Inc., 361 F.3d 831, 838 (5th Cir. 2004); Abvan v. Level 3 Communications, Inc., 353 F.3d 1158, 1164 (10th Cir. 2003).

Mixed Questions of Law and Fact

The preceding discussion treated questions of law and questions of fact as clearly identifiable, separate things. In some cases, the exercise of drawing the line between law and fact proves difficult, and "varies according to the nature of the substantive law at issue."[136] Moreover, the two—law and fact—are not hermetically sealed from one another. Sometimes, trial courts will be called upon to decide "mixed questions of law and fact." There are two sources of great confusion concerning such mixed questions. First, what are they? Second, what is the standard of review of a mixed question? The issue is important because a great many cases state that mixed questions are reviewed *de novo*.[137] Under this view, mixed questions are treated as questions of law, with the appellate court free to substitute its own conclusion, based upon the entire record.

The Supreme Court has defined mixed questions as:

> questions in which the historical facts are admitted or established, the rule of law is undisputed, and the issue is whether the facts satisfy the statutory standard, or to put it another way, whether the rule of law as applied to the established facts is or is not violated.[138]

This definition does not always yield a clear answer. Perhaps it is best to see what courts have done with this definition in different cases, to get a feel for what constitutes a mixed question. The words and actions of the defendant are pure facts, but whether they constitute intentional discrimination on the basis of race or national origin has been considered a mixed question of law and fact.[139] The representation the defendant made is a pure question of fact, but whether it is material for purposes of securities fraud has been seen as a mixed question of law and fact.[140] The *interpretation* of a contract is considered a mixed question of law and fact,[141] as is the question of whether use of

[136]Bose Corp. v. Consumers Union of the United States, Inc., 466 U.S. 485, 501 n.17 (1984).

[137]*See, e.g.*, Cooper Tire & Rubber Co. v. St. Paul Fire & Marine, 48 F.3d 365, 369 (8th Cir. 1995); Banker v. Nightswander, Martin & Mitchell, 37 F.3d 866, 870 (2d Cir. 1994) (whether efforts to mitigate damages were reasonable). The Supreme Court has hinted that this is the appropriate general rule in *Strickland v. Washington*, 466 U.S. 668, 698 (1984), but has not ruled definitively. Pullman-Standard v. Swint, 456 U.S. 273, 289 n.19 (1982).

[138]Pullman-Standard v. Swint, 456 U.S. 273, 289 n.19 (1982).

[139]Woods v. Graphic Contractors, 925 F.2d 1195, 1199 (9th Cir. 1991). On the other hand, the Supreme Court has held that the question of discriminatory intent is one of fact. Pullman-Standard v. Swint, 456 U.S. 273, 274 (1982).

[140]TSC Indus., Inc. v. Northway, Inc., 426 U.S. 438, 450 (1976); ABC Arbitrage Plaintiffs Group v. Tchuruk, 291 F.3d 336, 359 (5th Cir. 2002).

[141]Tyler v. Cuomo, 236 F.3d 1124, 1134 (9th Cir. 2000).

copyrighted material constituted a permitted "fair use."[142] Whether a worker is a "seaman" covered by the Jones Act is also seen as a mixed question of law and fact.[143] Whether parties agreed to arbitrate a dispute apparently presents a mixed question of law and fact.[144]

The characterization of an issue as a mixed question affects the standard of appellate review. It is worth asking, however, why a mixed question of law or fact ought to be reviewed *de novo*. The most famous example of such a case is *Bose Corp. v. Consumers Union of United States, Inc.*,[145] in which Bose sued for product disparagement. It alleged that the defendant had made a false statement about Bose's product, and that the false statement was made with actual malice.[146] Bose won at trial, and the issue was whether the appellate court was limited to reviewing the actual malice question under the "clearly erroneous" standard of Federal Rule 52(a)(6). While the trial judge's assessment of witness credibility was subject to deference under Rule 52(a), the existence of actual malice presented a mixed question of law and fact. As such, the Court held, it was subject to *de novo* review on appeal. Why? To protect First Amendment rights. The appellate court had to be free to search the entire record to be sure the result in the case did not impinge on the defendant's constitutional right of free speech.[147] In other words, whether the defendant had actual malice—an issue that seems at first blush purely factual—will have a direct impact on an important constitutional right. Thus, the appellate court cannot be hampered in its review.

As the cases cited in the paragraph preceding the discussion of *Bose* make clear, courts have not limited the finding of "mixed questions of law and fact" to cases involving constitutional rights. Thus, the rationale of *Bose*—that searching appellate inquiry is necessary to protect a constitutional right—is not the only justification for characterizing an issue as a mixed question. It is impossible to rationalize or explain the variety of approaches on this issue seen in the case law. There is enough elasticity in these concepts to allow an appellate court to characterize close issues as mixed questions, thereby justifying *de novo* review.

---

[142]Harper & Row, Publishers, Inc. v. The Nation Enterprises, 471 U.S. 539, 560 (1985).

[143]Endeavor Marine v. Crane Operators, Inc., 234 F.3d 287, 290 (5th Cir. 2000).

[144]Bailey v. Fannie Mae, 209 F.3d 740, 744 (D.C. Cir. 2000).

[145]466 U.S. 485 (1984).

[146]*New York Times, Inc. v. Sullivan*, 376 U.S. 254, 279-280 (1964), requires plaintiffs to show actual malice in some (not all) defamation cases.

[147]The case of *New York Times v. Sullivan*, discussed in the preceding footnote, stands for the proposition that the First Amendment freedom of speech protects erroneous statements unless they are uttered with actual malice.

Discretionary Matters

During the course of a case, the trial judge may be called upon to decide any number of matters vested in her "sound discretion." Issues such as whether to permit amendment of pleadings, permissive intervention, to compel discovery, to consolidate cases, to order separate trials, and a hundred similar issues relating to the management of the case are examples. The determination of whether there is no just reason for delaying appeal under Rule 54(b), which we saw at §14.4 above, is also an example.

Such issues present fact-specific circumstances, and appellate courts are very deferential to whatever the trial court orders. The court of appeals can reverse on such matters only if the trial judge "abused her discretion." This means the appellate court must affirm even if the appeals judges would have decided the matter differently. As long as the trial judge's decision was not plainly wrong or without basis, the appellate court will affirm. This high degree of deference is appropriate because the trial judge is in the best position to place the issue at hand in the context of the entire case and weigh all competing factors. Moreover, the decisions on many of these issues simply cannot be "right" or "wrong." Different reasonable people might disagree. About all the appellate court can do here is ensure that the trial judge exercised her discretion and made a decision that is "in the ballpark"—within the realm of reasonable decisions on the facts.

Table of Cases

Table of Cases

Table of Cases

Table of Cases

Table of Authorities

Table of Authorities

Table of Authorities

Table of Authorities

Table of Authorities

Table of Authorities

Table of Authorities

Table of Authorities

977

Table of Authorities

Table of Authorities

Table of Authorities

Table of Authorities

Table of Federal Rules of Civil Procedure

Table of Federal Rules of Civil Procedure

Table of Federal Rules of Civil Procedure

Table of Federal Rules of Civil Procedure

Table of Federal Rules of Civil Procedure

Index

Index

Index

Index

Index

Index

Judgment as matter of law (JMOL), 495-496, 539-548
  alternative of RJMOL to motion for new trial, 554-555
  compared to summary judgment, 531, 539-540
  renewed motion (RJMOL), 540-544, 551-552, 910n5
  Seventh Amendment, 543n133
  sufficiency of evidence to avoid, 544-548
  timing of motion, 541-544
Judgment notwithstanding the verdict. *See* Judgment as matter of law
Judicial adjuncts, use of, 487-489
Judicial estoppel, 630, 698
Judicial Panel for Multidistrict Litigation, 902-903
Judiciary Act (1789), 208, 210, 241
Jurisdiction. *See also* Personal jurisdiction; Subject matter jurisdiction
  of federal courts, 12, 13
  by necessity, 53-54, 54n20
Jurisdiction and Venue Clarification Act (2011), 245n138, 296n12
Jury and jury trials
  Batson challenges, 513-516
  burden of persuasion, 518-519
  challenges for cause, 513, 516
  class actions, 874n204
  deadlock, 520
  deliberations, 518-519
  excused jurors, 516-517
  gender bias in, 514-515
  instructions (jury charge), 494, 496, 517-519
  misconduct of juror giving rise to new trial, 549-551
  mistrials, 520
  motion to strike jury demand, 389
  number of jurors, 517
  panel, 516
  peremptory challenges, 513-516
  petit jury vs. grand jury, 494n4
  racial bias present in, 514-516
  requirement of written demand, 511
  right to in federal civil cases, 496-511
  role of, 493-496
  selection process (*voir dire*), 512-517, 550-551
  straw poll, 518
  strikes, 513
  venire, 512
  verdicts, 496, 512n52, 520-521, 551-552
  waiver of right to, 511
"Justiciability," 716n4

L

Labor unions, citizenship of, 226
Land patents, 57n24
Law and equity, bifurcation of, 22-27
Law of the case, 629
Letters of request, 189
Letters rogatory, 189
Limited appearance, 337
Limited generosity theory, 859
Limited liability companies (LLCs)
  capacity to sue or be sued, 721-722
  citizenship determination for, 225-228
Litigation, 2-4
  adversarial nature, 4-6
  alternatives to, 27-35
  civil procedure, overview of, 35-39
  civil vs. criminal, 3-4
  defined, 42
  English influence, 22-27
  expenses of, 8-11
  length of process, 7-8
  parties, roles of, 4-6
  state and federal courts, interaction between, 14-22
Litigation hold, 480
Local action doctrine, 295-298, 297n18
Local rules, 406, 448, 452, 485n122, 486
"Lone Pine" orders, 486
Long-arm statutes, 55, 140-145, 183
Low-numbering, 357n6

M

Magistrate judges, 438, 487-489
Malpractice by attorney, motion to set aside judgment due to, 559-560
"Managerial judges," 6, 482-486
Mandamus, writ of, 939-942
Masters, 438, 489, 506
MDL. *See* Multidistrict litigation

Index

Index

Index

U

Unincorporated associations
  capacity to sue or be sued, 721-722
  citizenship determination for,
    225-228
  principal place of business for,
    122n207
  service of process on, 181-182
Unions, citizenship of, 226
United States Marshal's Service, 173
United States Supreme Court. *See*
  Supreme Court, U.S.

V

Validity of judgment, 593-595,
  633-634
  earlier judgment (on which
    judgment is based) vacated or
    reversed, 556-558
Variance during and after trial,
  420-423
Venue, 36, 293-328
  business associations, residence of,
    302-304
  class actions, 895
  corporations, residence of,
    302-304
  counterclaims and crossclaims, 738
  defined, 36, 293-295
  events as basis for, 304-305
  fall-back provision, 305-306
  in federal court, 299-306
  forum non conveniens
    contrasted, 295
  forum selection issues, review of,
    295, 311-317
  impleader, 785
  interpleader, 827-829
  local action doctrine, 295-298
  natural persons, residence of,
    301-302

originally filed in federal court,
  299-306
personal jurisdiction distinguished
  from, 121n203
removal cases, 306-307
residence as basis for personal
  jurisdiction, 65-66
residence, defined, 301-302
"residential venue," 300-304
selection issues, 322-323
in state court, 298-299
"transactional venue," 304-305
transfer. *See* Transfer of venue
transitory actions, 295, 298-307
Verdicts, 496, 512n52, 520-521,
  551-552
Verified pleadings, 528
Vicarious liability, 678, 680-681
Victim compensation fund (VCF), 858,
  902-903
Void judgment, motion to set aside,
  556, 560
Voir dire, 512-517, 550-551
Voluntary dismissal, 399-404

W

Well-pleaded complaint rule, 250-256
  declaratory judgment cases,
    254-255
Witnesses
  consulting experts distinguished
    from, 467-469
  credibility of, jury to assess, 547
  examination and cross-examination
    of, 495
  expert witnesses, 440-442, 467-469
  lay witnesses, 441
Workers' compensation, 28
Work product, 455n49, 462-467
Writs of *certiorari*, 20-21, 911
Writs of execution, 173n42, 522n81
Writs of mandamus, 939-942